AF535163

Distributed Computing: Concepts and Implementations

OTHER IEEE PRESS BOOKS

Engineers & Electrons, *By J. D. Ryder and D. G. Fink*
Land-Mobile Communications Engineering, *Edited by D. Bodson, G. F. McClure, and S. R. McConoughey*
Frequency Stability: Fundamentals and Measurement, *Edited by V. F. Kroupa*
Electronic Displays, *Edited by H. I. Refioglu*
Spread-Spectrum Communications, *Edited by C. E. Cook, F. W. Ellersick, L. B. Milstein, and D. L. Schilling*
Color Television, *Edited by T. Rzeszewski*
Advanced Microprocessors, *Edited by A. Gupta and H. D. Toong*
Biological Effects of Electromagnetic Radiation, *Edited by J. M. Osepchuk*
Engineering Contributions to Biophysical Electrocardiography, *Edited by T. C. Pilkington and R. Plonsey*
The World of Large Scale Systems, *Edited by J. D. Palmer and R. Saeks*
Electronic Switching: Digital Central Systems of the World, *Edited by A. E. Joel, Jr.*
A Guide for Writing Better Technical Papers, *Edited by C. Harkins and D. L. Plung*
Low-Noise Microwave Transistors and Amplifiers, *Edited by H. Fukui*
Digital MOS Integrated Circuits, *Edited by M. I. Elmasry*
Geometric Theory of Diffraction, *Edited by R. C. Hansen*
Modern Active Filter Design, *Edited by R. Schaumann, M. A. Soderstrand, and K. R. Laker*
Adjustable Speed AC Drive Systems, *Edited by B. K. Bose*
Optical Fiber Technology, II, *Edited by C. K. Kao*
Protective Relaying for Power Systems, *Edited by S. H. Horowitz*
Analog MOS Integrated Circuits, *Edited by P. R. Gray, D. A. Hodges, and R. W. Brodersen*
Interference Analysis of Communication Systems, *Edited by P. Stavroulakis*
Integrated Injection Logic, *Edited by J. E. Smith*
Sensory Aids for the Hearing Impaired, *Edited by H. Levitt, J. M. Pickett, and R. A. Houde*
Data Conversion Integrated Circuits, *Edited by D. J. Dooley*
Semiconductor Injection Lasers, *Edited by J. K. Butler*
Satellite Communications, *Edited by H. J. Van Trees*
Frequency-Response Methods in Control Systems, *Edited by A. G. J. MacFarlane*
Programs for Digital Signal Processing, *Edited by the Digital Signal Processing Committee, IEEE*
Automatic Speech & Speaker Recognition, *Edited by N. R. Dixon and T. B. Martin*
Speech Analysis, *Edited by R. W. Schafer and J. D. Markel*
The Engineer in Transition to Management, *I. Gray*
Multidimensional Systems: Theory & Applications, *Edited by N. K. Bose*
Analog Integrated Circuits, *Edited by A. B. Grebene*
Integrated-Circuit Operational Amplifiers, *Edited by R. G. Meyer*
Modern Spectrum Analysis, *Edited by D. G. Childers*
Digital Image Processing for Remote Sensing, *Edited by R. Bernstein*
Reflector Antennas, *Edited by A. W. Love*
Phase-Locked Loops & Their Application, *Edited by W. C. Lindsey and M. K. Simon*
Digital Signal Computers and Processors, *Edited by A. C. Salazar*
Systems Engineering: Methodology and Applications, *Edited by A. P. Sage*
Modern Crystal and Mechanical Filters, *Edited by D. F. Sheahan and R. A. Johnson*
Electrical Noise: Fundamentals and Sources, *Edited by M. S. Gupta*
Computer Methods in Image Analysis, *Edited by J. K. Aggarwal, R. O. Duda, and A. Rosenfeld*
Microprocessors: Fundamentals and Applications, *Edited by W. C. Lin*
Machine Recognition of Patterns, *Edited by A. K. Agrawala*
Turning Points in American Electrical History, *Edited by J. E. Brittain*
Charge-Coupled Devices: Technology and Applications, *Edited by R. Melen and D. Buss*
Spread Spectrum Techniques, *Edited by R. C. Dixon*
Electronic Switching: Central Office Systems of the World, *Edited by A. E. Joel, Jr.*
Electromagnetic Horn Antennas, *Edited by A. W. Love*
Waveform Quantization and Coding, *Edited by N. S. Jayant*
Communication Satellite Systems: An Overview of the Technology, *Edited by R. G. Gould and Y. F. Lum*
Literature Survey of Communication Satellite Systems and Technology, *Edited by J. H. W. Unger*
Solar Cells, *Edited by C. E. Backus*
Computer Networking, *Edited by R. P. Blanc and I. W. Cotton*
Communications Channels: Characterization and Behavior, *Edited by B. Goldberg*
Large-Scale Networks: Theory and Design, *Edited by F. T. Boesch*
Optical Fiber Technology, *Edited by D. Gloge*

Distributed Computing: Concepts and Implementations

Edited by

Paul L. McEntire

Vice President for Research and Development
Optimization Technology, Inc.

John G. O'Reilly

President
Network Design Associates

Robert E. Larson

Chairman and Chief Executive Officer
Optimization Technology, Inc.

A volume in the IEEE PRESS Selected Reprint Series, prepared under the sponsorship of the IEEE Computer Society.

The Institute of Electrical and Electronics Engineers, Inc., New York

PRINTED IN THE UNITED STATES OF AMERICA

IEEE Order Number: PC01693

Library of Congress Catalog Card No.: 84-6648

ISBN 0-87942-175-4

Contents

Preface

THE efficient allocation and control of resources in a distributed computing system pose many new challenges to computer system users and designers. This volume of reprints contains outstanding articles covering almost all aspects of such systems. Many of the articles are introductory in nature and should allow the reader to quickly understand the terminology and issues of a given area. Also included are technical papers that provide depth in selected topics.

In particular, we discuss the problems of interprocess communication and synchronization, processor management and task scheduling, distributed database management, data security, languages, and experience with actual implementations. A perusal of the table of contents should provide a reasonable guide to the papers.

The reprints focus on computing systems with several processors. In some cases the processors are identical (homogeneous), and in some they are different (heterogeneous). However, we concentrate on tightly coupled systems and local area networks, and have mostly excluded long-haul networks. Furthermore, we have only peripherally touched upon the topics of architectural design and network software layering; these topics are complex enough to deserve separate treatment.

Operating Systems

Some of the articles contained in this book discuss higher level issues associated with operating systems. An operating system is the program or programs that act as an interface between the users of a computer system and the physical hardware. A principal function of an operating system is to allow the user to share efficiently the total resources of a computer system. In the case of tightly coupled systems, the term "user" may be interpreted broadly enough to include tasks associated with various processors in the system.

Most of the literature on operating systems was written in the last 20 years and most of the literature on *distributed* operating systems in the last 10 years. This is due to the dramatic decreases in communication and processor costs. The interconnection of the ubiquitous computers has significant economic benefits. Yet the single machine operating systems cannot be readily extended to handle a distributed system. Many of the problems and solutions associated with this extension are discussed here, particularly in Parts III and IV.

Altogether, the articles in this book should give the reader a good foundation in the current state of knowledge in this rapidly expanding area. By using the bibliographies in the individual papers as well as the one provided at the end of this volume, the reader should be able to embark on journeys to almost any important area of distributed computing.

Part I
Distributed Computing Concepts

THE papers in this part discuss broad issues of distributed computing systems. The first paper, by D. A. Anderson, gives an excellent overview of operating systems, traces many historical developments, and introduces much of the terminology. The chapter continues with an enjoyable article by P. H. Enslow, Jr., entitled "What is a 'Distributed' Processing System?"

Next, the problem of concurrency in operating systems is discussed by J. W. Atwood. Concurrency is a key problem for distributed computing systems since several CPU's may be simultaneously working on data that would affect or be affected by a given data file.

The problem of software design for distributed computing systems is then studied in an article entitled "An Approach to Distributed Software Systems" by J. Bacon. A conceptual framework is given for a distributed software system, and alternative implementations are discussed.

Although network operating systems are not emphasized in this volume, the following two articles have been included to introduce the subject: "Operating Systems for Computer Networks" by H. C. Forsdick *et al.*, and "Resource-Sharing Computer Communication Networks" by R. E. Kahn. Together, they provide an adequate overview of recent and past work in this area.

Finally, since many distributed systems have a structure that is principally determined by the database structure, this part concludes with an article on distributed database management systems. F. J. Maryanski surveys the field and includes a good bibliography. More articles on this topic are contained in Part V.

Research during the last decade has revealed techniques by which future operating systems can avoid the problems associated with previous and present systems.

Operating Systems

D. A. Anderson
Bell Telephone Laboratories

An operating system is a program that resides on a computer and acts as an interface between the user or application programmer and the bare machine. It is a layer of software that surrounds and hides the physical hardware—a relationship depicted in Figure 1. The chief purpose of an operating system is to allow several users or applications to share the computer in an efficient and noninterfering manner.

Although all computers have some form of operating system, exactly which program modules are part of the operating system can be a matter of opinion. Generally, those modules controlling machine resources such as processors, primary and secondary memory, and peripheral devices are considered the operating system. Compilers, loaders, debuggers, and other application-oriented modules are usually not considered part of the operating system.

While operating systems have existed since the first stored program computers over 30 years ago, the common features and problems of operating systems have been studied extensively only in the last 10 to 15 years. Concepts and techniques resulting from this research are applicable to all operating systems and help us to avoid many of the pitfalls of the past. Highlights from this research include the notion of processes and monitors for the synchronization of parallel tasks,memory management techniques, and improvements in system performance, protection, and reliability.

Purpose. The earliest operating systems did little more than initialize the hardware, bringing the machine up into a state to run the first job. Initialization remains an important function of all operating systems. However, in most modern operating systems, this function now includes not only total initialization for initial system bring up but also partial initialization to flush an insane job or recover from a transient hardware error without losing all active jobs.

Total initialization is also called "bootstrapping" or "initial program loading." Typically, the bootstrap mechanism consists of either hardware or firmware reading in a small bootstrap program which in turn reads in the operating system. In addition, the processor, memory, and peripherals are initialized to the extent necessary before accepting the first external inputs or jobs.

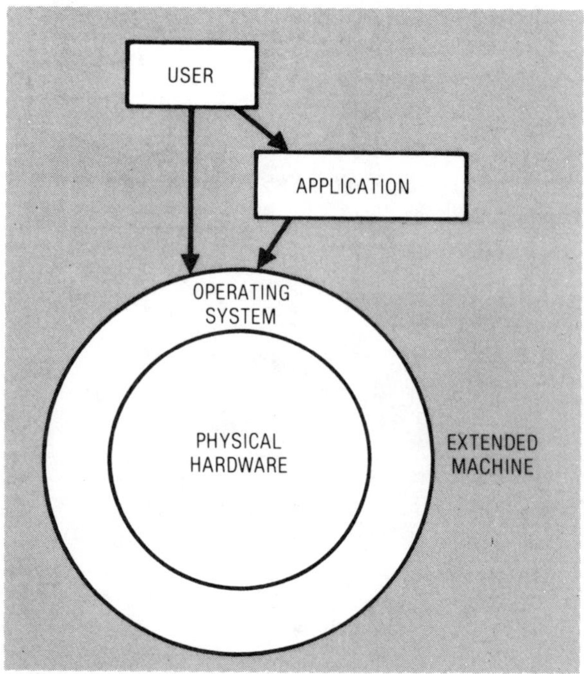

Figure 1. Operating system relationship.

Reprinted from *Computer*, vol. 14, pp. 69–82, June 1981.

Partial initialization can be much more difficult than total initialization since it involves being selective about what is initialized to preserve as many active jobs as possible. Partial initialization can also involve complex schemes for recovery and rollback to save all active jobs. Triggers for partial initializations include hardware errors, sanity timer timeouts, or protection violations. Schemes for partial initialization are especially important in fault-tolerant, real-time, or large multiuser systems.

Another important function of an operating system is acting as an "extended machine" to hide the complexities of the bare machine from the user. To do this, an operating system must provide both an internal and an external interface. For example, an internal user such as an application programmer may perform I/O via system calls to the operating system. The complexities of controlling the physical I/O device are hidden by an I/O device driver in the operating system. Such system calls are the internal view of the operating system. The external view of the operating system, on the other hand, is the command or job control language or other method of presenting external inputs or jobs to the system. Such an input language attempts to provide a simple method for entering new work into the computer.

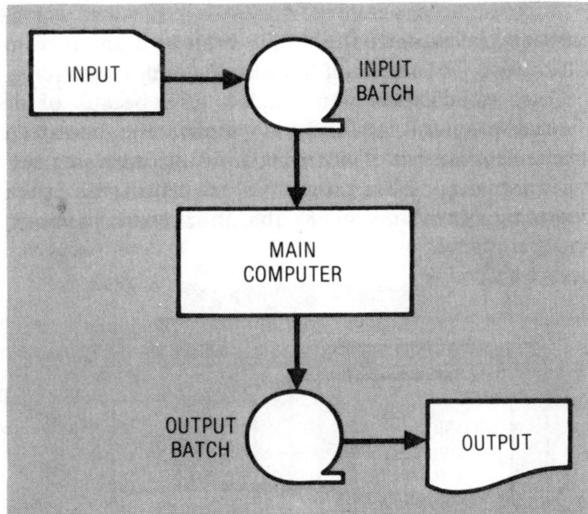

Figure 2. Batch system flow.

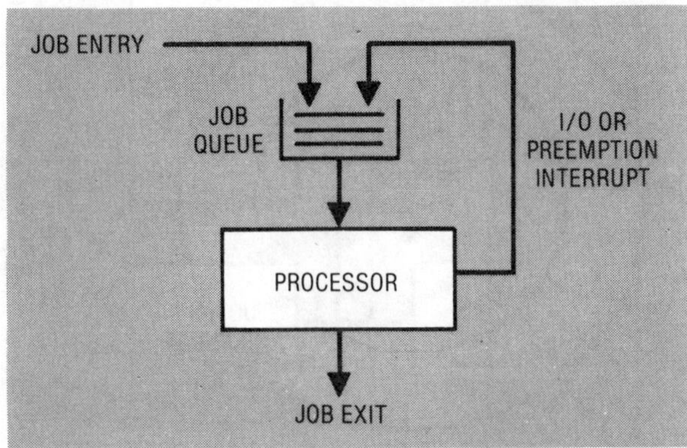

Figure 3. Multiprogramming in a uniprocessor.

The third function of an operating system is providing a resource management facility so that many users or processes can share the machine. By far the most important function of an operating system, this is also the most difficult to implement reliably. It is important primarily for economic reasons, since the throughput of a computer system is maximized when each resource—processor, memory, or peripheral device—is managed well. Resource management is the means by which these resources are shared among several concurrent processes in a manner that is both fair and guaranteed to prevent unwanted interference. The purpose of sharing is to maximize the percent utilization of each resource.

Evolution of systems and techniques

General-purpose operating systems—the ones with which most users have contact—run a wide variety of jobs in a short period of time and are designed to handle such a job mix well. The evolution of these general-purpose operating systems can be traced from the first simple single-job-at-a-time systems to the current complex, multiprogrammed distributed processing systems.

Single job. The earliest general-purpose operating systems were very primitive, executing only a single job at a time. The typical input device was a card reader and the typical output device was a line printer—both very slow in comparison with a computer processor. The chief drawbacks of executing only one job at a time were that the processor and I/O devices were idle a large percentage of the time and job execution was strictly sequential. Early systems also had problems with erroneous user programs bringing the machine down.

Batch. Improvements in system performance occurred when secondary memory devices, such as magnetic tape and disks, were used. These I/O devices operate at speeds closer to that of the processor and primary memory. Throughput on the main computer increased when it got all of its input from and put all of its output on secondary memory. Several small inexpensive computers would copy input jobs from the card readers to the input batch tapes and then copy the output batch tapes to the line printers. These were known as the first batch systems, since several jobs were batched together on tape. Figure 2 shows the flow of a job through a batch system.

While the first batch systems were improvements over the earlier single-job systems, they still ran jobs sequentially. Consequently, short jobs could have lengthy turnaround time if they ended up behind long jobs. Further delays resulted since the printed output of the first job on a batch tape was not available until the entire batch had executed. Manual delays for mounting tapes were also a drawback of these early batch systems.

Multiprogramming. These problems associated with the early batch systems were solved by introducing the interrupt. When an interrupt occurs, a processor suspends the execution of the current program and starts another program. The execution of the interrupted program is resumed later, when it has finished handling the interrupt. Interrupts are ways of breaking up the strictly sequential nature of a computer as well as mechanisms by which several jobs can be made to execute concurrently. The technique supporting this concurrent operation is called "multiprogramming."

Multiprogramming was introduced to keep the processor and I/O devices busy as much as possible. The basic technique is to have several jobs in memory at any one time. One job executes on the processor until it needs to do some peripheral I/O. The I/O device, being much slower than the processor, needs attention from the processor only at infrequent times which can be signaled by means of an interrupt. The one executing job starting an I/O operation is suspended, and a second job ready to execute is given control and begins execution on the processor. The I/O of the first job is done in small pieces at each interrupt during the execution of the second job. In this way, several jobs can execute concurrently, with one job actually executing on the processor and the rest performing some I/O operation. This technique utilizes the system well as long as the jobs have a nice mix of computation and I/O.

Soon it was realized that a timed interrupt could be used to force multiprogramming. A job could be allowed to execute for a certain period of time, say one second, at which time the job is interrupted by a timer. Then, the operating system selects another job which runs until stopped by I/O or the timed interrupt, and so forth. Thus, a long job with little I/O is forced to execute concurrently with other jobs. This is called "preemptive" scheduling. Since job execution is no longer strictly sequential, a short job can have good turnaround time—even if it starts behind a long job. Figure 3 shows a multiprogramming block diagram.

Spooling. Multiprogramming introduced the possibility of interleaving the output of several jobs on the line printer, a problem solved by a technique called "spooling,"—that is, simultaneous peripheral operations online. When a job tries to write to the line printer, a spooling program intercepts the request and converts it to a write to secondary memory, such as a disk, converting one line printer into many "logical" line printers on the disk. The output from a job is printed correctly on a physical line printer after it is done executing. This technique is also applied to any slow output or input device, such as a card reader, which would otherwise have to be dedicated to a job throughout its execution. Figure 4 shows how a spooling system is organized.

Protection. Although multiprogramming greatly improved the performance of general-purpose systems, it also increased system complexity. It was important to keep concurrently running users from interfering with one another or with the operating system. Protection was provided by building computers that executed in two different states—a "privileged" state for the operating system and a "restricted" state for the user. In the restricted state, an interrupt to the operating system occurred if the user tried to use privileged commands or to access certain areas of memory. Furthermore, program synchronization techniques, described more fully below, were developed to eliminate unwanted interaction.

Multiprocessing. With multiprogramming, one processor could control all of the I/O devices and keep them and itself busy. However, the overhead of handling many interrupts tended to slow a single processor. This situation led to the use of several processors—or "multiprocessing"—to improve throughput. Multiprocessing is characterized by two or more processors sharing the same memory. The techniques developed to support multiprogramming on a single processor, where two or more jobs share the same memory, are equally applicable to multiprocessing. Figure 5 provides an example of a multiprocessor system.

The most successful multiprocessing configurations have been master/slave arrangements where one main processor controls several specialized I/O processors or channels. In turn, the I/O processors each control one or more I/O devices and, with direct memory access, require little help from the main processor. In this way, the interrupt overhead of the main processor is significantly reduced.

Multiprocessing configurations with several main processors in a loadsharing arrangement have been less successful because each processor tends to perform worse in a multiprocessor configuration than as a uniprocessor. The main advantages of loadsharing multiprocessor systems are that they are more fault tolerant because of their inherent redundancy and they are more expandable or shrinkable as workloads change. Multiprocessing is becoming even more attractive as processors become cheaper, since maximizing the utilization of each pro-

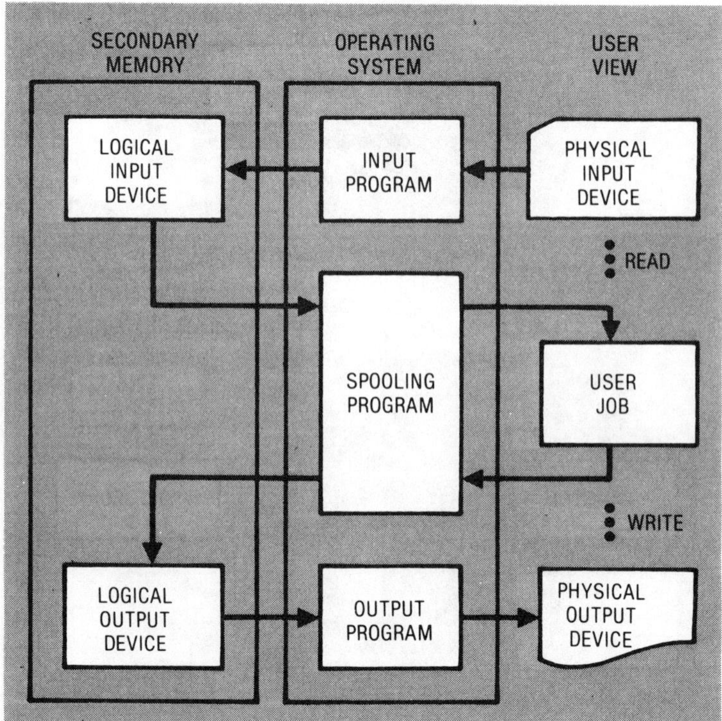

Figure 4. Spooling organization.

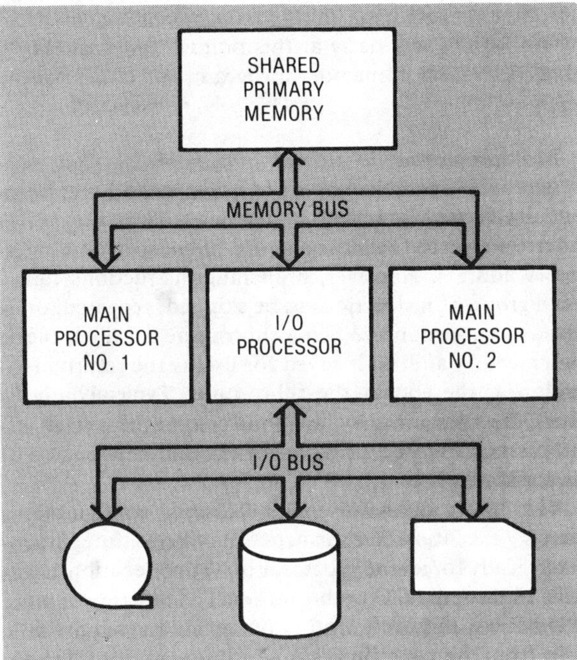

Figure 5. Example multiprocessor system.

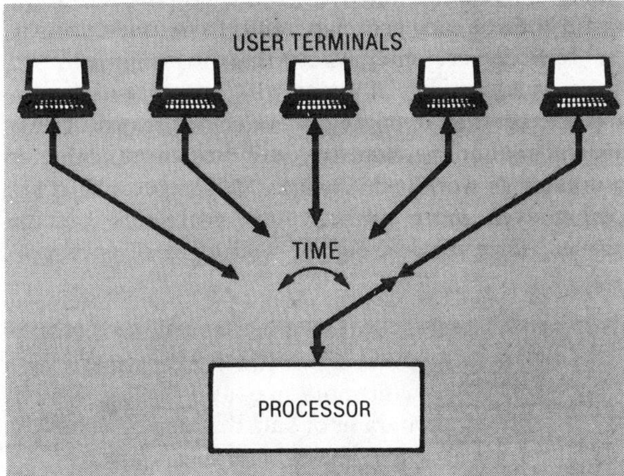

Figure 6. Timesharing system.

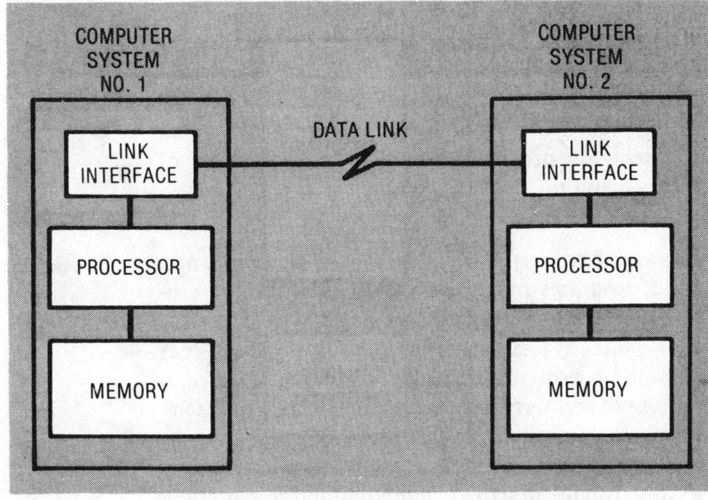

Figure 7. Distributed processing system.

cessor becomes less important. This trend is especially apparent in microprocessor systems.

Timesharing. The job-oriented operating systems described above are still referred to as batch systems. The next major improvement was to get rid of the card reader and minimize the use of the line printer. This was accomplished by introducing timesharing operating systems that interact with users via terminals. All input and much output goes directly to and from the individual user at a terminal. Instead of submitting multistatement jobs, the user types simple single-statement commands on the terminal. This mode of interaction is also called "interactive" or "conversational" since, for most commands, the computer responds quickly with a simple answer. A multiterminal timesharing system is shown in Figure 6.

To minimize response time to terminal-originated commands—an important requirement for timesharing operating systems—these operating systems rely heavily on multiprogramming techniques and preemptive scheduling. Responding to terminal commands is referred to as "foreground" work in a timesharing system. Most timesharing systems also allow input to be submitted in a batch mode as "background" work, which is given a lower priority for use of the processor.

Distributed processing. Distributed processing, also called "computer networking," is the latest research area regarding operating systems. A computer network is a multicomputer arrangement where the computers communicate via special processor-to-processor data links. This is a looser coupling than the shared memory communication of multiprocessing systems. A network can link computers hundreds of miles or just a few feet apart. Short-distance networks, perhaps contained in one building, are referred to as "local" networks. Figure 7 shows a simple distributed processing arrangement with just two computers. Most networks, however, contain many computers.

Computer networks have the same advantages of fault tolerance and growth that multiprocessing systems have. In addition, computer networks can greatly extend the accessibility and, hence, utilization of an expensive localized subsystem such as a high-speed processor or large data base. These advantages have been enhanced by the availability of low-cost microprocessors and data link interfaces produced by LSI circuit techniques.

Special-purpose systems

Although general-purpose operating systems are the most well-known, many special-purpose operating systems do exist and it would be an oversight not to mention some of their features. Special-purpose operating systems are custom-built either for a unique computer architecture, such as an array processor, or for an application with unique requirements, such as industrial process control. While most operating system research has been directed toward improving general-purpose operating systems, many of the ideas that have emerged can also be applied to special-purpose systems.

Real-time. An important example of special-purpose systems, real-time operating systems have requirements that are similar to timesharing systems. However, there are also some significant differences. Real-time inputs do not wait indefinitely to be accepted by the computer. If not accepted quickly, they may disappear or become erroneously out-of-date. Real-time systems typically are dedicated and run the same programs over and over again. Many of these programs may be tied down in primary memory to ensure a good response to the inputs they handle.

Examples of real-time systems are computer systems that control rapid-transit vehicles, collect data from nuclear physics experiments, interpret radar data on an aircraft, or control a telephone switching system. All of these systems have as a common feature that they monitor and/or control external ongoing activities with input data rates that cannot be forced to adhere to a particular pace. Sometimes real-time systems in business applications are also referred to as "on-line" systems.

Fault tolerance. Fault-tolerant computer systems are used in applications where providing continuous service or preventing data mutilation is worth the additional expense of the redundancy necessary for fault tolerance. Operating systems in such computer systems must provide the means for detecting errors and possibly recovering from them. Recovery may mean either switching to a standby unit when a fault occurs in an active unit or stopping certain actions to prevent loss of data.

While fault-tolerant systems can be used in applications and environments where repair is possible, they can also be used in environments where repair is not possible, such as with space-borne applications. Different strategies are used in each case. In addition, real-time systems are often designed to be fault tolerant.

Virtual. Virtual operating systems are designed to run several other operating systems concurrently on one machine, creating the illusion of several machines. To do this, an operating system running under a virtual operating system physically executes in restricted state but behaves as if it were in the privileged state. When a privileged instruction is executed, an interrupt occurs. The virtual operating system handles the interrupt in a way that corresponds to the privileged instruction actually being executed. In this way, several different operating systems—or several different versions of one operating system—may operate concurrently on one machine. This technique can be used to check out new operating system releases or to defer or eliminate user conversions to a different operating system.

Review of computer structures

All operating systems must provide certain common services. Furthermore, they execute on machines with common features and deal with similar program and data structures. Since the discussion that follows concentrates on these aspects common to operating systems, it would be useful to review briefly at this point a few basic attributes of processor, memory, program, and data structures.

Processor. A processor or CPU executes program instructions fetched from primary memory. These instructions are normally executed sequentially by increasing memory address. However, branching instructions can cause a group of instructions to be skipped, repeated, or called as a subroutine. When a subroutine is called, the return memory address is saved for use by the return instruction at the end of the subroutine. Typically, the return address is saved by being pushed on the top of a stack in memory. The top of the stack is identified by a stack-pointer register in the processor.

Interrupts are another way of breaking up the strict sequential execution of instructions. An interrupt automatically forces the processor to begin execution at a fixed address and, like a subroutine call, saves the return address and usually a few other processor state registers on the top of the stack. Such saving is necessary so that the interrupt handler can return and resume proper execution of the interrupted program.

Processors also have a number of general registers for doing arithmetic, logical, and addressing operations. These registers are directly referred to in assembly language programs, but the compiler keeps track of them in high-level language programs. In some microprocessors, these general registers are actually in memory, rather than in the processor device, at a position identified by a register-pointer register in the processor.

Memory. Used to store programs and data for immediate access by the processor, primary memory is most often read/write RAM with access times compatible with the processor. Primary memory may also contain some ROM for tied down programs or data that do not change. While ROM information is available after power up, many types of RAM must be reloaded following power up.

For economic reasons, computer systems generally have secondary memory devices which are slower but much less costly per bit of storage. These devices may be further classified as direct access, such as disk, or sequential access, such as tape. Secondary memory is always accessed through I/O drivers in the operating system. In many cases, user programs do not have to be aware of secondary memory.

Program. For portability and ease of maintenance, most user programs and operating systems today are written in a high-level language. Some parts of an operating system—generally less than 10 percent of the code—may still have to be written in assembly language. In the past, operating systems were usually written entirely in assembly language to minimize overhead.

Large programs written today, including operating systems, are usually designed in a modular hierarchical fashion consisting of one or more structures of nested subroutine calls as shown in Figure 8.* Such a nested structure makes considerable use of the subroutine stacking capability of the processor.

Data. Program languages also provide the means for defining and allocating data structures and referencing them symbolically in a program. There are primitive data types, such as "character" and "integer," and structured data types which are a prescribed collection of primitive types. For example, an array—a structured type—may be used to allocate a stack.

Most high-level languages provide the means for localizing data structure references to a single function or set of functions. Such hiding of data structures is important for enforcing at compile time any unwanted program interactions. Hiding of data structures can be provided in a compiler by limiting the scope of variable names—that is, the portion of the code over which the name is defined. For example, the symbolic name of a variable declared local to a single function would stand only for that variable within the body of the function. Use of the name external to the function would either reference a different variable or be flagged as an error by the compiler.

Processes

The concept of a process, or task, is crucial to understanding an operating system. The basic multiprogramming unit in a computer, a process is defined as the set of states of a program in execution.

*In this article, the terms "module," "subroutine," "function," and "procedure" all mean the same thing: a body of code with one entry point that can be called and that returns upon completion of execution. It may receive input parameters and return a result.

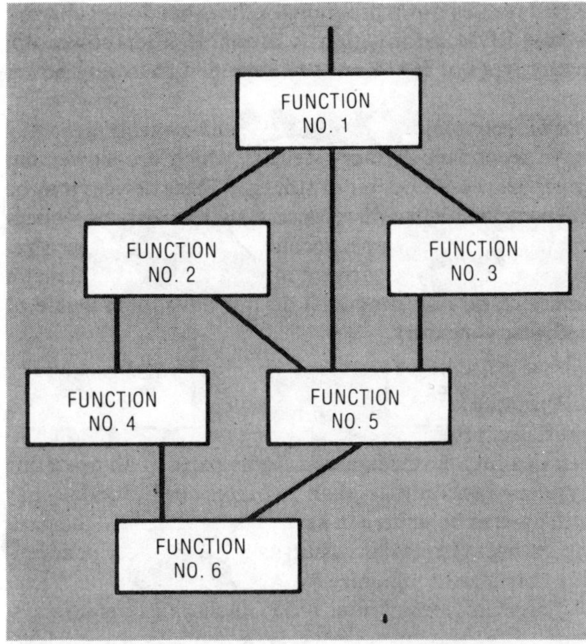

Figure 8. Modular hierarchical program structure.

When a new job enters the system, a process is created by allocating memory to that job for program and data. This block of memory can be thought of as the process since it defines the current state of the process. As the program executes and writes data, the state of the process changes. When the program is interrupted, the state of the process is temporarily fixed. When the program completes, the process is destroyed.

One's first impression may be that there is little difference between a job and a process. However, they are not the same since a job may result in the creation of several processes. For example, the initial job process may spawn a second I/O process to write a file. This I/O process may execute on the same processor or on another I/O processor. Another example of a job creating several processes would be a job consisting of several parts that can be run in parallel. Each of these parts could be assigned to separate concurrent processes.

Concurrency. Processes can be run concurrently with no effect on each other—unless they interact by mistake or by design. A single process is sequential and deterministic. That is, its operations are executed in sequence one at a time, and its outputs and ending state are always predicable from its inputs and initial state.

Process images. The process image is that portion of writable memory belonging to a process and defining its state. The process image changes with the execution of a program associated with the process. Process images, or the head cells for them, are also called "process descriptors" or "process control blocks." For all practical purposes, the terms "process" and "process image" are interchangeable.

A process image contains items such as process identifier, current state, active work area, local save area, and system save area. It contains the local variables written as the process executes as well as the variables that must be saved intact when the process is interrupted or asks to be interrupted by calling an operating system function. The program associated with the process may be a single function, but more likely it is a nested structure of functions. In the latter case, the process image must contain the string of return addresses and local variables of each partially executed function. In stack machines, these save areas are on a stack which must be contained within the process image. In any case, a process image can be quite large.

Reentrant programs. If the program associated with a process is reentrant, it need not be a part of the process image. A reentrant program does not modify itself or write global variables outside of the process image. Thus, a single copy of a reentrant program in memory may support several identical processes, each in a different state of execution. In fact, this program can be stored in ROM since it does not change. Many operating system I/O processes are implemented in this manner—that is, they are supported by a single reentrant program copy.

Some of the problems of associating a nonreentrant program with a process are worth mentioning. For example, a program that modifies itself must be contained in its associated process image, and a program that writes global variables can be associated with only one process at a time.

Process states. The contents of the process image define the precise state of the process at any time. Furthermore, a few high-level states common to all processes can be defined. For example, a "running" process is one that is actually executing on the processor. In a uniprocessor system, only one process can be in the "running" state. A "waiting" process is one that is waiting for an event such as the completion of an I/O process or the expiration of a certain period of time. A "ready" process is one that is ready to be selected by the operating system to enter the "running" state. A process is "dormant" before it is created and after it is destroyed. Figure 9 shows these four possible process states and the transitions between them.

Such states can be implemented in an operating system in numerous ways. One way would be to define a linked-list head cell for each state defined and then to link the process image to the appropriate list for each process in that particular state.

Process communication

As mentioned above, processes can execute concurrently until they need to interact. Planned and controlled interaction is referred to as "process communication" or "process synchronization." Process communication must take place through shared or global variables external to each process image.

Readers/writers. Improper reading and writing of shared variables is the classic cause of difficult-to-find operating system bugs. The basic problem is that two processes, executing concurrently, may interleave read and write operations in such a way that improper decisions are made and the shared variables are left in an improper state. This kind of bug is insidious, for it may only show up infrequently—and then with symptoms that rarely or never repeat since they depend on a particular concurrency relationship.

Since processes that are only readers of shared variables cannot cause this problem by themselves, several read-only processes may execute concurrently with no problems at all. However, to write correctly, a writing process must have a clever rule worked out with other processes or else ensure that the shared variables are not being accessed by any other process while the variables are being examined and modified.

Cooperation. Cooperating processes must communicate to synchronize or limit their concurrency. The relationship between two cooperating processes regarding a resource falls into one of two fundamental categories. They are either competitors or producers/consumers. Since process communication takes place through shared memory, competitors access this memory to seize and release permanent, or reusable, resources. Producers/consumers access this memory to pass temporary, or consumable, resources such as messages and signals. Figure 10 illustrates the competing and noncompeting relationships between two processes.

Deadlock. Known more descriptively as a "deadly embrace," deadlock is a situation in which two or more processes wait indefinitely for resources that are held by each other and, thus, never available. Such a situation is pictorially represented in Figure 11. Deadlocks are a possibility in any system where processes wait for resources. However, they can and should be prevented from existing indefinitely in any reliable system.

A number of deadlock avoidance schemes have been proposed, and some have been implemented. First, let us consider schemes pertaining to permanent resources that are seized and released by competitive processes. Dead-

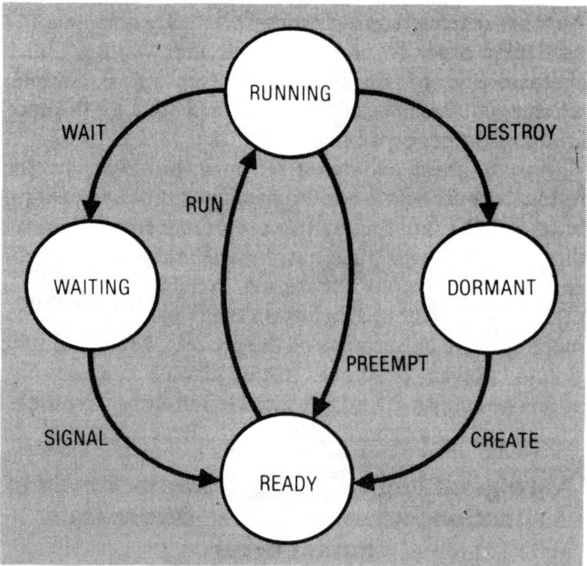

Figure 9. Possible process states and transitions.

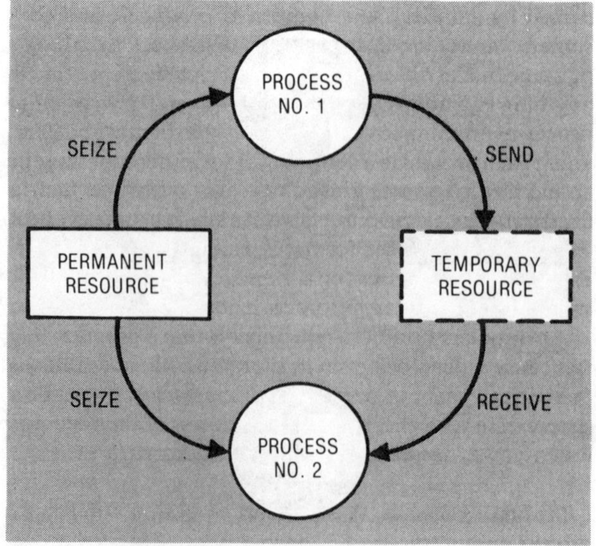

Figure 10. Competing and noncompeting relationships.

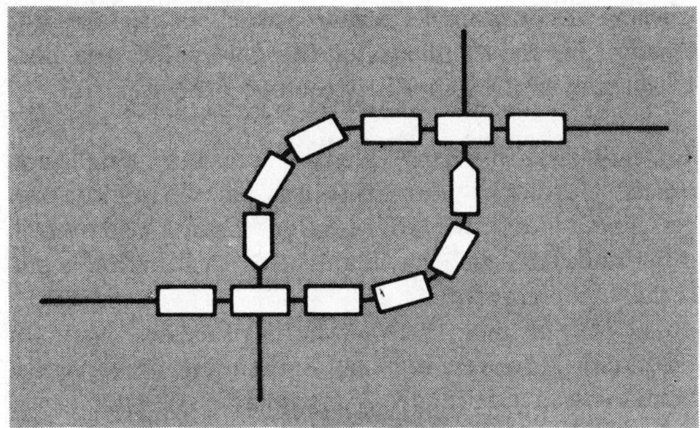

Figure 11. Deadlock situation.

locks can be avoided by having processes seize all resources at one time—that is, by not allowing processes to wait for a resource while holding other resources. Another scheme requires processes to seize resources in a particular order to prevent the circular waiting that is characteristic of deadlock. An even more complex scheme requires processes to declare in advance the maximum resources possibly needed.

Most of these avoidance schemes, however, are too restrictive or too time-consuming. The simplest technique is not to wait indefinitely for a resource. But this means that when a process times out, it must be aborted from the system and its resources released. Whether or not this is perfectly acceptable depends on the frequency of occurrence and the importance of the process. Most real-time systems prevent deadlocks in this manner because their processes cannot afford to wait indefinitely for resources.

A program bug can cause a deadlock even in situations where deadlocks theoretically cannot occur.

Finally, let us consider temporary resources, such as messages, that are produced by one process and consumed by another. Any number of producers and consumers cannot be deadlocked with respect to a single message buffer as long as a consumer is willing to remove anything in a nonempty buffer. However, if two or more processes are connected in a circle by two or more buffers, and if each process is willing to wait for either a message or an acknowledgment, a deadlock may occur. In fact, a deadlock may even occur between a single producer and a single consumer if the former is waiting for an acknowledgment and the latter for a message. A simple deadlock solution for temporary resources is not to wait indefinitely.

An important point to remember is that a program bug can cause a deadlock even in situations where deadlocks theoretically cannot occur. An ultimate timeout can be a simple defensive check on the correctness of the system as well as a way to prevent indefinite deadlocks.

Mutual exclusion. A sufficient condition for proper process communication is the exclusion of mutual accessing of shared variables in time. The sections of a program that access shared variables are referred to as "critical regions." If means are introduced to keep processes from executing concurrently within their associated critical regions, the requirement for mutual exclusion will be met and time-dependent errors will not occur. Standard techniques for providing such synchronization are becoming well-known and essential to modern operating systems.

Synchronization. The simplest synchronization technique in a uniprocessor system is for a program to block interrupts before entering a critical region and restore them after exiting. This ensures that the critical region is executed as an indivisible block. In more complex systems, the following techniques are used.

Test and set. A solution suitable for a multiprocessor system is to use processors with the ability to test and set a flag in a single instruction. This technique also works in a uniprocessor system since it reduces the critical region associated with the shared flag variable to a single indivisible instruction.

Using these machine-level techniques, higher-level sychronization primitives can be built as operating system functions to be called by cooperating processes. These higher-level primitives must be indivisible. Generally, they include a process waiting queue that saves processor time by preventing looping—called "busy waiting" or "spin lock"—when a process tries to enter a critical region.

Semaphore. A standard synchronization primitive, the semaphore consists of a counter, a process waiting queue, and two functions, P and V. Initially, the counter equals the number of resources, and the waiting queue is empty. The P function decrements the counter by one. If the result is less than zero, the process is placed on the waiting queue (effectively interrupted); otherwise, the process continues. The V function increments the counter by one. If the result is greater than zero, the process continues; otherwise, one of the waiting processes is placed on the ready queue and the process continues. When negative, the counter identifies the number of waiting processes. When nonnegative, the counter identifies the number of resources left. Semaphores with an initial value of one are sometimes called "binary semaphores" since they act as lock bits, allowing only one process at a time within an associated critical region.

Although simple, semaphores are known to be sufficient solutions to synchronization problems for permanent resource competitors and temporary resource producers/consumers. However, semaphores are often very inconvenient because they are too primitive. For this reason, most operating systems provide other process communication mechanisms. Two examples are events and messages.

Events. Event primitives are typically provided by two functions, "wait" and "signal." A process can wait on an event or a combination of events to be true. When another process signals an event, all processes waiting on that event are placed on the ready queue. Other variations are also possible. One potential problem with events is that a process has the possibility of waiting on an event that either never becomes true or was signaled earlier. A slight variation of waiting on an event, used especially in real-time systems, is waiting on a timing queue administered by the operating system for a specified time period to elapse.

Messages. Messages provide an even more flexible and direct method of process-to-process communication, especially for producer/consumer relationships. Typical primitives are the functions "send" and "receive" which allow a string of characters to be passed between processes. Implementation variations are numerous. For example, send may or may not wait for an acknowledgment. Receive usually waits if no message has been sent.

Some systems also provide other very efficient ways of communicating with certain operating system processes. These are sometimes called "demons" or "phantoms" since they interact frequently—and often mysteriously—with many user processes.

Monitors

If the evolution of synchronization techniques has an acme, the concept of a monitor may very well be it. A monitor is a shared data structure and a set of functions that access the data structure to control the synchronization of concurrent processes. This very unspecific definition includes semaphores, events, and messages as specific implementations. The notion of a monitor is not more powerful than these other techniques—just more general. While a process is a useful abstraction for multiprogramming, a monitor is a useful abstraction for process communication.

To assure the correctness of a program, it is useful to associate data structures with the operations performed on them. A monitor provides a body in which to associate shared data structures with their critical regions. By so doing, the data structures are no longer shared or global, but local or hidden within the body of a monitor. In addition, process functions no longer contain critical regions. Instead, the critical regions are centralized and protected within the monitor functions. The restricted access to shared data structures provided by a monitor is even more attractive if it can be checked by a compiler. Many high-level languages today provide the means for controlling the scope of variable names.

Monitors provide support for processes to form a multiprogramming system. While a process is active in the sense that it performs a job, a monitor is passive in the sense that it only executes when called by a process. A monitor is necessary only when two or more processes communicate to ensure that they communicate properly. Figure 12 is a representation of two processes communicating through shared data hidden by a monitor.

Pushing the monitor concept to its logical limit suggests that systems should be designed as collections of processes and monitors only. In this case, every data structure would be local to either a process or monitor. This decomposition would be valuable in large systems since it would simplify the problems of program validation and maintenance. If a data structure changed, it would be clear which functions were affected, and the addition of a new process or monitor would not require the revalidation of unchanged components.

Monitor images. A monitor image is the portion of writable memory associated with the monitor program and defining the current state of the monitor. A monitor image represents either permanent or temporary resources which are the elements of process interaction. In the absence of process activity, process images and monitor images differ significantly. In this idle state, process images are of no importance and may vanish. However, monitor images—at least those representing permanent resources—must remain and resume a nonassigned state.

Monitor functions are reentrant but contain nonreentrant sections—i.e., critical regions—that must not be executed concurrently by more than one process. Indeed, monitor functions must be designed to protect against this. Monitor functions need not be considered as part of the monitor image. In fact, if two different monitor variables are accessed in the same way, a single copy of a program may be shared between the two monitors.

When a monitor function is called but is blocked from handling the request immediately, it may take several actions. It may immediately return a blocked indication, it may loop or busy wait until the request can be handled, or it may place the process on a waiting queue for the resource requested. In the latter case, the waiting queue must be a part of the monitor data structure. In real-time systems, it is sometimes best to return a blocked indication and let the process decide whether to try again later or give up.

Kernel. The kernel, or nucleus, of an operating system contains a few special processes to handle initialization and interrupts and a basic monitor to support the concept

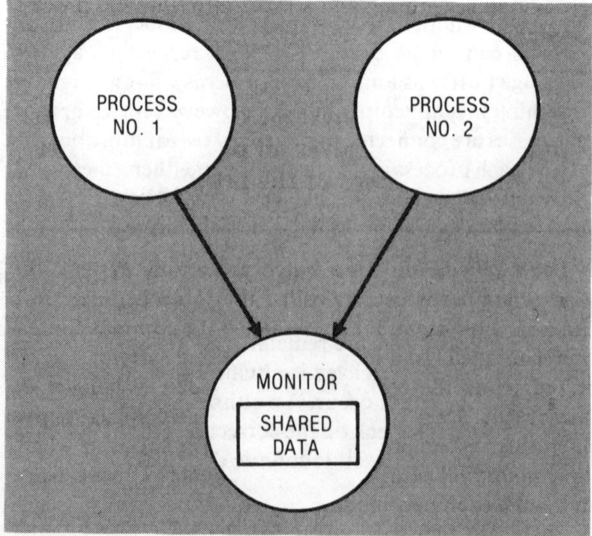

Figure 12. Monitor representation.

of a process. The basic monitor includes functions to switch environments between processes and to "create"—sometimes called "spawn" or fork"—new processes. The kernel is also one part of an operating system that executes in the privileged state.

Besides the kernel, an operating system consists of many monitors and a few processes. The processes include several kinds of I/O processes that are activated as needed and at least one active process to look for new jobs and create user processes for them. All monitors are part of the operating system and form the bulk of the system. They are used to manage the resources of the system. For example, monitors transmit messages between processes, control competing processes, enforce access rights, and communicate with I/O processes.

Process creation. In some systems when processes are created, they exist as unrelated units, independent of each other. In other systems, the order of creation is remembered and a parent/child relationship is maintained between one process and the new process it creates. Both approaches have advantages and disadvantages. Typically, a "child" process is limited to using only those resources owned by its "parent" and is destroyed if its "parent" is destroyed.

In most general-purpose systems, when a process is destroyed, its process image is returned to a pool of unallocated memory. However, in many dedicated or real-time systems, processes are never destroyed. Instead, they are created at compile time or initialization time and run forever, even at times when there is no work to do.

Management

Processor management. Processor management is concerned with scheduling work to be done on a physical processor. It is a term describing the managing of the processor as a shared resource among both external users and internal processes. As a result, processor management consists of two basic kinds of scheduling: a long-term external load scheduling and a short-term internal process scheduling.

Preemption can increase operating system overhead, but it gives all processes a more equal share of the processor.

Load scheduling. In a batch processing system, the load scheduler is usually called the job scheduler. In a timesharing system, it may be called the command interpreter or shell. In a telephone switching system, it is referred to as the telephone line scanner. Whatever its name, the load scheduler is a continuously active operating system process responsible for choosing which new inputs will enter the system. It creates a user process to handle each new input accepted.

There are two basic ways for the load scheduler to discover new inputs—interrupt or polling. Systems that allow new inputs to cause interrupts are said to be interrupt-driven. The interrupt-driven method provides immediate attention for important inputs at the expense of delaying current work. However, most systems poll or scan for new inputs because it is less expensive and allows better control of excessive inputs.

If there are more inputs available than the system can handle, the load scheduler must perform the important function of limiting the inputs accepted to the maximum number that can be handled concurrently. This overload control is important because system throughput can actually decrease if too many inputs enter the system at once. Nevertheless, many operating systems—including ones widely used today—behave poorly when given too many jobs because they lack adequate overload controls. When inputs are limited by the load scheduler, the policy for deciding which inputs are accepted is an important design consideration that depends on the system application and other factors.

Process scheduling. The process scheduler, or dispatcher, performs its function each time the running process is blocked or preempted. Its purpose is to select the next running process from the ready queue. The process scheduler resides in the kernel and can be considered a monitor for the ready queue. Probably the most frequently executed program in the system, it should be fairly efficient to minimize operating system overhead.

Process scheduling can be either preemptive or nonpreemptive. In nonpreemptive systems, processes execute until they are blocked voluntarily by a monitor call. Obviously, some jobs can monopolize the processor in such a system. In preemptive systems, each ready process is given, in turn, a time slice for execution. At the end of a time slice, the running process is interrupted, placed at the end of the ready queue, and the next process is given control. This cycle is repeated endlessly. Preemption can increase the operating system overhead, but it gives all processes a more equal share of the processor. Therefore, short jobs are not penalized by big jobs monopolizing the processor.

Scheduling policies. Scheduling policies are used in both load scheduling and process scheduling. A load scheduling policy is a rule for selecting the next input; a process scheduling policy is a rule for selecting the next process to run. In a particular operating system, these two policies may not be the same.

A good policy should be fair—giving preference to high priority jobs, yet preventing "starvation" of low priority jobs—and maximize system throughput. Since "fair" and "priority" are subjective terms, many different scheduling policies are used in systems today. Only a few of the more common policies will be mentioned here.

"First-come-first-served" is a simple policy for load scheduling. However, in real-time systems, "last-come-first-served" is sometimes used to obtain the least stale input and maximize the probability of it being processed correctly. Other policies are based on externally assigned priorities or give I/O intensive jobs preference to keep the peripherals busy.

"Round robin" is a typical process scheduling policy. Multilevel round robin is used to give higher priority processes more frequent control without starving lower priority ones. Policies based on priority can be static, whereby priority remains fixed, or dynamic, whereby priority is allowed to change.

A quickly evaluated policy is important for preemptive process scheduing in order to minimize the interrupt level overhead of each time slice. For this reason, round robin is often used in preemptive systems. Long time slices also reduce the overhead, but this tends to approach a first-come-first-served nonpreemptive scheduling policy as the time slice interval increases. Other policies that favor short jobs are shortest-job-first or smallest-remaining-time, both of which require jobs to declare run-time estimates.

Environment switching. There are several forms of environment, or context, switching in a computer system. When one function calls another, a return address and possibly other state variables must be saved to permit return to the environment of the calling function. This is a very simple form of environment switching supported by subroutine calling instructions, compiler conventions, or other methods.

A more significant form of environment switching occurs when a process is interrupted by hardware or is placed on a monitor waiting queue. In these cases, a process switch must occur. The entire process image must be saved intact so that the process may resume execution later. This also requires saving various important processor register contents before passing control of the processor to another process.

Since process switching generally occurs quite often in an operating system, it should be implemented as efficiently as possible. This means that as little data as possible should be moved in memory. In stack-oriented machines, this may be accomplished by changing the stack-pointer register instead of moving the stacks themselves.

The user should be unaware of process switches to preserve the illusion that he has sole use of the processor, albeit a slower one. Voluntary process switches should appear to the user as a monitor function call that returns at a later time. This is important, since it allows application programs to be structured in a modular hierarchical fashion.

Memory management. Memory management is concerned with administering the use of primary memory, which is where program instructions and associated data must be stored for direct access by the processor. Memory management by the operating system is needed for one or both of the following reasons.

- The size of primary memory exceeds the addressing range of the processor.
- The primary memory is not large enough to store all programs and data needed.

In both cases, the processor is not able to directly address all of the existing programs and data without help from the operating system. In the first case, techniques such as bank switching are used to identify which parts of the primary memory are currently accessible by the processor. In the second case, secondary memory is used to store the information, parts of which are physically transferred to and from primary memory as required. Numerous methods exist for controlling this information transfer between secondary and primary memory. The relationship among the processor and primary and secondary memory is depicted in Figure 13.

Operating systems differ in their needs for memory management. In some small dedicated systems, especially those using microprocessors, there is no memory management. All programs are resident in primary memory. There is no secondary memory containing "nonresident" programs, and the primary memory is directly accessible by the processor as a linear contiguous address space.

Bank switching. If the size of primary memory exceeds the addressing range of the processor, the physical memory can be divided into blocks—called "banks" or "pages"—and a bank select register or page map is used to identify which blocks are immediately accessible by the basic processor addressing capability. In variations of this basic idea, instruction fetches are mapped differently than data fetches. An example of a bank switching scheme is shown in Figure 14.

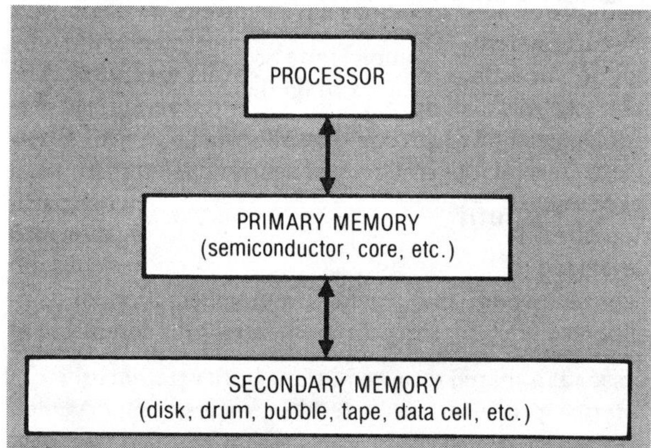

Figure 13. Primary/secondary memory relationship.

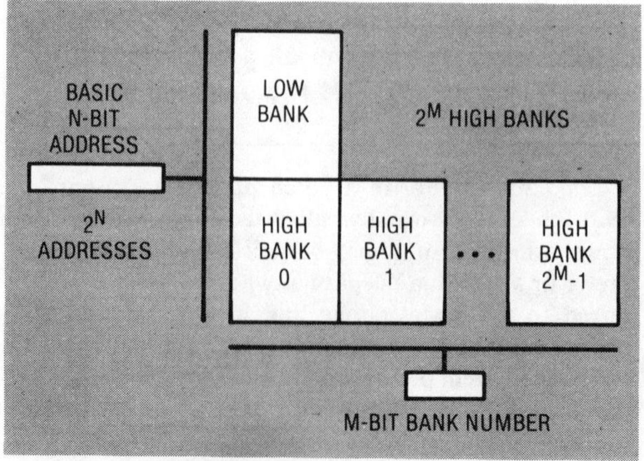

Figure 14. Example bank switching scheme.

The combination of the basic address and the bank number (or page map state) forms an enhanced addressing capability. Note that the entire enhanced address must be saved in many environment switching situations to permit the proper restoration of the old environment.

Bank switching is very similar to using secondary memory, except that it is much faster since no physical transfer of information from a slow peripheral device has to take place. Many of the strategies are the same. For example, in both cases, it is important to hide memory management mechanisms from users so that they do not have to be concerned about the details of the machine. This can be done by having the operating system receive control each time an unaccessible block is addressed by the user. This is sometimes called a "page fault." The operating system reconfigures the memory before returning control to the user.

Allocation. The use of secondary memory to store programs and data is required largely for economic reasons. The cost per bit of secondary memory can be several orders of magnitude less than primary memory. Not many systems need to or can afford to store all information in primary memory. Therefore, most operating systems—from the earliest to the most modern ones—use secondary memory.

Memory "allocation" refers to the rules for assigning primary memory to jobs for execution. To review the methods of allocation that have evolved, we begin with the early systems. They allocated primary memory to only one job at a time for the duration of its execution. The next step was to divide the memory into several fixed partitions, each of which could be allocated to a job. Afterwards, several jobs could run concurrently, but there was a lot of wasted memory because job sizes did not match partition sizes. As a result, dynamic memory allocation was developed to produce variable partitions that matched job sizes. However, this resulted in fragmentation of unallocated memory since different sized jobs completed at different times. The solution was to make programs relocatable during execution. This required that address sensitive instructions in a program be based relative to a relocation register. Unallocated memory fragments could then be combined into a large usable area by relocating executing programs.

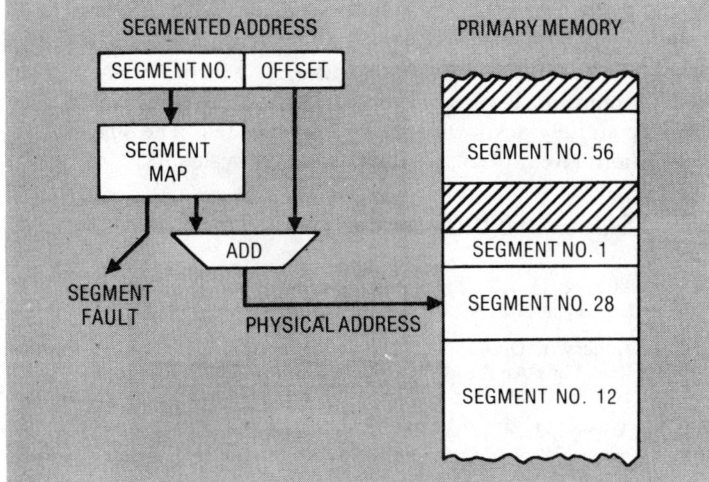

Figure 15. Segmented addressing.

Swapping. Jobs do not have to remain continuously in primary memory until they complete. A low priority job can be "rolled out" to secondary memory to accommodate a high priority job and later be "rolled in" to complete. Many small-scale timesharing systems use this technique. Swapping is greatly aided by a relocatable environment since jobs do not have to be rolled in to exactly the same memory space from which they were rolled out.

Overlays. All parts of a job do not have to be simultaneously in primary memory for the job to execute. Large programs can be accommodated by allowing program sections to overlay other sections that do not have to be in memory at the same time. The disadvantage of overlays is that the user generally has to specify the overlay structure in advance. However, the notion of swapping combined with automatic overlays led to two important developments—segmentation and paging.

Segmentation. All programs consist of a number of logical segments, such as data areas and program functions. All segments do not have to be in primary memory at one time and all do not have to be stored in contiguous address locations for proper execution. Any word in a program can be identified by a two-part segmented address consisting of a segment number and a segment offset. A segment map converts the segmented address to a physical address. If a program tries to access a segment which is not in primary memory—an occurrence called a "segment fault"—the operating system intervenes and brings the segment in from secondary memory. The segment map is also updated. Figure 15 shows the conversion from segmented address to physical address.

Segmentation has many advantages. Swapping and overlaying are done automatically since only actively used segments are kept in primary memory. Memory is not wasted since variably sized segments accommodate program divisions of any size. However, there is difficulty in managing variably sized segments in secondary memory. Furthermore, primary memory allocation is more complicated with variably sized segments.

Paging. Paging is identical to segmentation except that all segments are the same size. While this eliminates the major disadvantages of segmentation, it is also slightly more wasteful of memory since programs seldom break up into an integral number of pages. One way to gain the benefits of both segmentation and paging is to subdivide each segment into pages and use a three-part address consisting of a segment number, a page number, and an offset.

Virtual memory. The major advantage of paging or segmentation is that it supports the notion of virtual memory. With virtual memory, each process "thinks" that it has all of its information in a very large primary memory. The memory management required by the operating system to provide this view is invisible to the user and need not be considered when programs are written.

However, virtual memory or paging requires significant memory management overhead. Each time a new page is brought in, an old page must leave primary memory. If the old page was modified, it must first be written back into secondary memory. The page replacement policy is very important to the performance of the system. Some policies used are "first-in-first-out" and "least-recently-used."

Furthermore, when primary memory becomes overcommitted, system performance can be seriously degraded by a phenomenon called "thrashing." This occurs when every page fault forces the replacement of a useful page, perhaps belonging to another job. As a result, operating system overhead increases severely since most processor time is spent servicing page faults. To prevent thrashing, each job requires some minimum number of pages, sometimes referred to as the "working set," to efficiently utilize the processor. The number of pages in a working set depends on the pattern of execution over a period of time.

It is important to remember that virtual memory—as well as any other memory management technique—has a certain overhead associated with it and that problems can occur if it is not implemented carefully. Furthermore, memory management does not necessarily eliminate the need for a large primary memory. In large systems, performance may be unacceptable due to thrashing if the primary memory is too small.

Future trends

Operating system techniques are becoming more acceptable today, even in small microprocessor systems with dedicated applications. It is recognized now that all computer systems perform certain common operating system functions and that most systems must support some form of concurrent process execution. As a result, process communication is inevitable. Techniques that ensure proper synchronization can eliminate many of the time-dependent program bugs that have occurred in many operating systems.

Operating systems will continue to have a major effect on processor designs. Single-chip microprocessors and larger processors will become less clumsy for operating systems to use. System performance will improve dramatically as more operating system primitives are provided in hardware or microcode. This will include support for process synchronization, queue manipulation, environment switching, process scheduling, and memory management. The frequently executed sections of today's operating system programs will be implemented in the future by large microprograms. In addition, these features will decrease the development cost and increase the security and correctness of future operating systems.

Improved operating systems will, in turn, improve the quality of application programs by requiring certain structures and interfaces. With these restrictions and proper operating system support, the quality of application programs will be less tied to the skill of programmers.

While the distributed processing capabilities provided by computer networks are presently generating a lot of interest, they are also creating a number of new operating system problems. With no shared memory, processes in two different computers must communicate via messages over a data link. Reliable communication is provided by several layers of protocol to handle various kinds of errors.

The frequently executed sections of today's operating system programs will be implemented in the future by large microprograms.

Local networks favor simple protocols and possible error-handling by the application (rather than by the operating system) due to the high reliability of the local network. Geographically dispersed networks are less reliable and require more complex protocols to preserve message order and to prevent message loss, duplication, or mutilation. Long distances also introduce problems associated with significant time delays and limited transfer rates. All of these problems have yet to be solved completely.

Computer networks usually imply distributed data bases. This means that there are multiple copies of portions of a data base, each copy at a different site. Although this is necessary to increase the availability of important information, it introduces some new synchronization problems. With multiple copies of shared memory, traditional synchronization techniques will have to be augmented or replaced by new techniques to maintain data integrity.

One proposal is to attach network-wide sequence numbers to data-base transactions to ensure that updates are applied in the same order to multiple copies of a data base. Limiting transactions to those that are repeatable—that is, that have the same effect if accidentally run twice—has also been proposed. Attaching a version number to each copy of distributed data has also been proposed for resolving conflicts. ■

Acknowledgments

The careful review of this tutorial by Professors A. V. Pohm and T. A. Smay, both of Iowa State University, is gratefully acknowledged and appreciated. The suggestions given for improvement were very valuable.

Selected bibliography

Alsberg, P. A., et al., *Synchronization and Deadlock,* CAC Document No. 185, University of Illinois, Mar. 1976.

Anderson, D. A., "A Microprocessor Operating System for Real-Time Applications," *Proc. Compsac 78,* Chicago, Nov. 1978, pp. 104-109.*

Atwood, J. W., "Concurrency in Operating Systems," *Computer,* Vol. 9, No. 10, Oct. 1976, pp. 18-26.

Bierman, E., "Changing Technology in Switching System Software," *Proc. IEEE,* Vol. 65, No. 9, Sept. 1977, pp. 1329-1335.

Brinch Hansen, P., *Operating System Principles,* Prentice-Hall, Englewood Cliffs, N.J., 1973.

Dijkstra, E. W., "Hierarchical Ordering of Sequential Processes," in *Operating System Techniques,* ed. by C. A. R. Hoare and R. H. Perrott, Academic Press, New York, 1972.

Habermann, A. N., *Introduction to Operating System Design,* Science Research Assoc., Chicago, 1976.

Hoare, C. A. R., "Monitors: An Operating System Structuring Concept," *Comm. ACM,* Vol. 17, No. 10, Oct. 1974, pp. 549-557.

Hoare, C. A. R., and R. M. McKeag, "Store Management Techniques," in *Operating System Techniques,* ed. by C. A. R. Hoare and R. H. Perrott, Academic Press, New York, 1972.

Holt, R. C. "Some Deadlock Properties of Computer Systems," *Computing Surveys,* Vol. 4, No. 3, Sept. 1972, pp. 179-196.

Katzan, H., Jr., *Operating Systems,* Van Nostrand Reinhold, New York, 1973.

Madnick, S. E., and J. J. Donovan, *Operating Systems,* McGraw-Hill, New York, 1974.

Patterson, D. A., and C. H. Séquin, "Design Considerations for Single-Chip Computers of the Future," *IEEE Trans. Computers,* Vol. C-29, No. 2, Feb. 1980, pp. 108-116.

Rauscher, T. G., and P. M. Adams, "Microprogramming: A Tutorial and Survey of Recent Developments," *IEEE Trans. Computers,* Vol. C-29, No. 1, Jan. 1978, pp. 2-20.

Ritchie, D. M., and K. Thompson, "The Unix Time-Sharing System," *Bell System Technical J.,* Vol. 57, No. 6, Part 2, July 1978, pp. 1905-1929.

Satyanarayanan, M., "Commercial Multiprocessing Systems," *Computer,* Vol. 13, No. 5, May 1980, pp. 75-96.

Thompson, K., "Unix Implementation," *Bell System Technical J.,* Vol. 57, No. 6, Part 2, July 1978, pp. 1931-1946.

Tsichritzis, D. C., and P. A. Bernstein, *Operating Systems,* Academic Press, New York, 1974.

*These proceedings are available from the Order Desk, IEEE Computer Society, 10662 Los Vaqueros Circle, Los Alamitos, CA 90720.

What is a "Distributed" Data Processing System?

Philip H. Enslow, Jr.
Georgia Institute of Technology

Introduction

Words have only one purpose in a technical context—the transmission of information. When they fail to do that, they lead to confusion and misunderstanding. "Distributed data processing" and "distributed processing" are two phrases which illustrate that axiom. Like many other words in the lexicon of the computer professional, these have become cliches through over-use, losing much of their original meaning in the process. This paper is an attempt to reverse that trend.

A great many claims of improved performance (the table below presents only a partial list) are being made for "distributed data processing" systems by vendors as well as authors.[1-4] Hardly anyone reasonably knowledgeable about the current state of the art in multiple-processor data processing systems would claim that major advances toward any significant number of these goals are possible with present technology. To fulfill such a claim, distributed data processing must be something *new* and must represent a large research area. However, what is usually presented today as distributed data processing is just a warmed-over version of an old concept with a new sales word attached.

Claims made for "distributed" data processing systems.

HIGH SYSTEM PERFORMANCE, FAST RESPONSE, HIGH THROUGHPUT
HIGH AVAILABILITY
HIGH RELIABILITY
REDUCED NETWORK COSTS
GRACEFUL DEGRADATION (FAIL-SOFT CAPABILITY)
EASE OF MODULAR, INCREMENTAL GROWTH AND CONFIGURATION FLEXIBILITY
RESOURCE SHARING
AUTOMATIC LOAD SHARING
HIGH ADAPTABILITY TO CHANGES IN WORD LOAD
INCREMENTAL REPLACEMENT AND/OR UPGRADING OF COMPONENTS (BOTH HARDWARE AND SOFTWARE)
EASY EXPANSION IN BOTH CAPACITY AND FUNCTION
EASY ADAPTATION TO NEW FUNCTIONS
GOOD RESPONSE TO TEMPORARY OVERLOADS

This paper discusses some of the essential characteristics for a new class of systems, still in the research stage, that will provide some of the benefits given in the table. We do not deprecate present work in improving systems for increased performance or reliability, even if it has been labeled "distributed data processing." Rather, we hope to introduce some precision of terminology and evaluation for this new area.

What is distributed?

At least four physical components of a system might be distributed: hardware or processing logic, data, the processing itself, and the control (such as the operating system). Some speak of a system that has any *one* of these components distributed as being a "distributed data processing system."

However, a definition that is based solely on the physical distribution of some components of the system is doomed to failure. A proper definition must also cover the concepts under which the distributed components interact. Trivial examples abound of system organizations that exhibit physical distribution but are not considered distributed data processing systems—for example, physical distribution of input/output processing hardware and function. Similarly, there is certainly no distribution of processing functions if there is no distribution of processing hardware, and, conversely, a system that distributes hardware without distributing processing is difficult to imagine.

Reprinted from *Computer*, vol. 11, pp. 13-21, Jan. 1978.

A working definition of a distributed data processing system adheres to the claim that "new" system designs will be required to achieve a major portion of the benefits cited in the table. Therefore what is presented might be considered the "research and development" definition of distributed data processing systems. This definition has five components:

- A *multiplicity* of general-purpose resource components, including both physical and logical resources, that can be assigned to specific tasks on a dynamic basis. Homogeneity of physical resources is not essential.

- A *physical distribution* of these physical and logical components of the system interacting through a communication network. (A network uses a two-party cooperative protocol to control the transfers of information.)

- A *high-level operating system* that unifies and integrates the control of the distributed components. Individual processors each have their own local operating system, and these may be unique.

- *System transparency,* permitting services to be requested by name only. The server does not have to be identified.

- *Cooperative autonomy,* characterizing the operation and interaction of both physical and logical resources.

These properties and operating characteristics are present in a number of systems to varying degrees, providing *some* of the benefits listed in the table. However, only the combination of *all* of the criteria uniquely defines distributed data processing systems.

The first essential ingredient

If there were not a multiplicity of assignable resources to provide services within the system, there could be no distribution of processing throughout the system. The modifier "general-purpose" has often been used to describe these "assignable" resources, such as general-purpose computer systems or general-purpose processors. However, it is not clear that this modifier is either necessary or sufficient. What is necessary is that the system have the ability to be dynamically reconfigured on a short-term basis with respect to those resources that provide specific services at any given time. This reconfiguration or reassignment of resources must be possible without affecting the operation of those resources not directly involved. If the purpose of the system is to provide service that requires a general-purpose processor, the system must have a multiplicity of general-purpose processors. If the purpose is to fulfill some other function, such as transaction processing or on-line control, the system could meet all of the five criteria while the assignable hardware resources might be considered special-purpose in the larger sense. However, they are general-purpose and reassignable within *that* system. A system typically has both general-purpose and special-purpose (fixed function) components, perhaps with some of the latter being dedicated (nonreassignable).

Many variations are possible, from the situation in which there is only one resource of each type, which does not meet the first criterion of the definition, to the other extreme in which every resource is replicated. Between these extremes are configurations having some single and some replicated resources. Since the management of freely assignable, multiple, duplicate resources within a system that is not totally replicated is amost as difficult as the situation with total replication, and may provide almost the same benefits, the general discussion that follows covers both types of systems.

The availability of multiple resources and the capability to utilize them effectively are essential to attaining the objectives of high availability, overall system reliability, and graceful degradation. These characteristics also directly contribute to flexibility, adaptability, and incremental expansion.

Physical distribution and intercommunication

Although there are many ways to define a network and many different aspects of it to consider, the most important one here is the transfer of messages. The physical transfer of messages through a network is an excellent example of cooperation between two physical resources. Such transfers follow a two-party protocol, in which the two parties *must cooperate* to successfully complete the transfer. This transfer mechanism is in contrast to that of a gated transfer, where the master has full authority to force a slave to physically accept a message. Under a two-party protocol, the destination can physically refuse the message by returning an indication such as NOT READY, BUSY, or NOT ACKNOWLEDGE. The unit of transfer in the system then is a message, not a signal. Gated or master-slave control of information transfer would preclude autonomous operation, discussed later, whereas a high degree of autonomy among all resources is essential to attain a high availability for the system.

To support the concept of autonomous operation of processes, the concept of "network" interconnection must be extended to logical as well as physical resources, with respect to the transfer of information such as status, requests for service, synchronization between logical resources, and so on.

The most important characteristics of a two-party cooperative protocol is that it allows any resource, either physical or logical, to refuse the transfer or acceptance of a message based on its *own* knowledge of its *own* status. This definition of a network establishes no criteria for the length of the interconnection paths of the network. They may be as short as a connection between two resources on a single integrated circuit chip. The essential defining characteristic is the utilization of a two-party protocol.

Unity of system operation

To integrate the physical and logical components of a distributed data processing system into a functioning whole, the concept of a high-level operating system must be implemented. The various processors may have individual operating systems, but a well-defined set of policies must govern the integrated operation of the total system. The mechanisms implementing these policies may be uniquely identifiable within each individual operating system, or they may be merely logical extensions of the local policies. There must be no *strong* hierarchy existing between the high-level operating system and the local operating system for an individual physical resource, since that would violate the criterion of autonomous operation. Also, local operating systems need not be homogeneous, although the existence of a variety of interfaces certainly complicates the system design problem.

As emphasized by another author, "[System] software makes the difference between a cluster of computers that act independently and that same cluster integrated into a smooth-working, cost-effective distributed data processing operation."[5]

A distributed system has multiple loci of control as well as processing activity. These multiplicities, as well as dynamic changes in the loci of control, must both exist to meet all of the five criteria of our definition. Additionally, the physical binding of the loci of control or processing activities must be minimized. The nucleus of the operating system essential for each processor must be minimized, and the loci of overall system control must be dynamic during runtime. The degree of permanent binding must be minimized, and the system must have no "critical paths" or "critical components," such as permanent binding of any single copy of a resource, to include global state information. The performance of the system must not be catastrophically affected or even seriously degraded by the failure or overload of a resource that has a permanently assigned system control function. A similar comment applies to processing activities, although there will be instances in which the requirement for a specialized resource might require permanent binding of a processing function—for example, a special transfer or data base or a unique I/O device.

Other properties that must characterize the high-level operating system are the support of an effective transfer bandwidth between processors larger than that found in simple communicating computers, the ability of a processor to continue to operate and effectively utilize its local resources when disconnected from the network and to be easily reconnected and reintegrated into the system without affecting other operations in progress, and the support of process and processor interactions at a "fine-grain" level when appropriate. In particular, the effective transfer bandwidth between processors must be wider than that found in simple communicating computers. Likewise, a processor must continue to operate and effectively utilize its local resources when disconnected from the network, and it must be easily reconnected and reintegrated into the network without affecting other operations.

The high-level operating system, whether it exists as distinct and identifiable blocks of code or only as a design philosophy, converts the available resources from a mere collection of hardware into a functioning, coherent system. The design of the high-level operating system is obviously the key factor in overall system design, and it presents a number of problems that will require extensive further research to solve. Several of these aspects of the high-level operating system are discussed later in this article.

System transparency

If any system is to provide the capabilities listed above, the interface presented to the user must be one of services and not servers. The user must be able to request an action by specifying what is to be done and not be required to specify which physical or logical component is to provide that service.

An important characteristic of the distributed system is that its existence is totally transparent to the user, unless he wishes to take cognizance of it for specific reasons of efficiency. He should be able to develop routines and programs and handle data bases just as if he were communicating with a single, centralized system. In fact, the user interface to a distributed system must be even simpler than those of present centralized systems. This results from the fact that the user communicates with the high-level operating system; one function of a portion of the control software is to deal with all varieties of command languages and data definitions present in the system. Initial work on nonhomogeneous network systems has provided some of the strongest motivations for better (even standardized) operating system command languages. Because the organization of the system can be totally transparent to the user, system status information can be hidden from him, so that it would be impossible for him to know what resources are currently available or which would be the best to execute his task. Therefore, he must be able to request services by the name of the service and not by the designation of the server. If he wants a virtual uniprocessor, he should be able to get it. If another application would be better served by designated resources, that user should also be able to request that form of service.

The nature of the user's interface with a distributed system dictates one of its most important characteristics: the services provided by a distributed processing system could be provided by a single-processor system if the necessary hardware existed and could be so configured. However, such a single system would not provide the other benefits of a distributed data processing system, such as reliability, adaptability, and modularity.

Cooperative autonomy

This is the final, and perhaps most important, essential ingredient. A distributed data processing system must be designated so that the operations of all components or resources, both physical and logical, are very highly autonomous. At the physical level, this may be accomplished by the use of network transmission protocol in which the transmission of a message requires cooperative actions by both the sender and the receiver. At the logical level, between processes, the same degree of cooperation must exist. Further, any resource must be able to refuse a request for service, even after it has accepted the physical message. This is a result of the fact that there is no hierarchy of control within the system.

This is *not* anarchy. All components follow a "master plan," which is reflected in the philosophy of the high-level operating system. This mode of operation should be described as cooperative autonomy rather than simply autonomy. A high degree of autonomy between all components is essential to attaining many of the benefits listed in the table, and this characteristic of system operation and component interaction will result only from meeting all of the five criteria of the definition.

Some excluded systems

Considerable work has been done on new system designs to achieve subsets of these benefits, but very few systems have made substantial progress toward meeting all of the criteria. Perhaps the most widely known of these is Arpanet; however, only the communication subsystem of that network qualifies in this respect. Many other systems, some of which are discussed elsewhere in this magazine, have made substantial improvements in subsets of the areas of system performance; examples are the Honeywell Experimental Distributed Processor, the Cm* system at Carnegie-Mellon University, Mininet at the University of Waterloo and ICOPS at Brown University. However, the number of systems mislabeled as distributed data processing systems far exceeds these.

Most of the criteria contained within the definition are met by crossing a threshold on a particular dimension. The definition is not a set of binary criteria, and better understanding of these criteria and their thresholds can be obtained by considering some systems that are excluded by the definition.

It excludes, for example, distribution within a single mainframe. One writer has characterized the architecture of several of the modern processor systems that include independent I/O channels as "incorporating distributed processors since [it] contains separate I/O processors, arithmetic logic processors and possibly diagnostic processors."[6] Such a categorization has little utility and has not found very wide acceptance. Obviously, there is a permanent binding of tasks to the various components in this type of system organization.

A front-end processor that controls communication with a mainframe definitely does not constitute the type of distributed system defined here.[7] Although it may meet some of our criteria, it also is dedicated to one function and is not freely assignable.

Many instances of a master/slave relationship occur in both hardware and software control. The key point is that the recipient of the information transferred, be it data or a control signal, cannot decide whether or not to accept the transfer and act upon it. When this concept is implemented in hardware, it is often referred to as gated transfer. In software control systems the master/slave relationship is quite commonly encountered in multiple computer and basic multiprocessor operating systems.

The continued decline in the price of hardware has made more and more attractive new multiple-processor system organizations incorporating specialized functional units, such as vector multiplier, a floating-point arithmetic unit, or a fast Fourier transform unit. In the general concept of operation, such dedicated function processing is only slightly different from a master/slave relationship. The major difference is that the master/slave control relationship also excludes many hardware systems containing multiple general-purpose processing units from our definition. What causes some of the terminology confusion with these configurations is that these specialized services are often provided by a general-purpose unit, such as a programmable microprocessor. The functional unit may be "specialized" by a microprogram, or it may be completely general but utilized in a dedicated functional role, such as a minicomputer to control input/output in a larger system. The distinguishing characteristic of this class of excluded systems is the *dedication of the resource to a single or a fixed set of functions.* It operates in a master/slave mode, as far as the control over its own activities is concerned. The criteria of both free assignment and autonomy are violated.

There is wide agreement (except perhaps among marketing and advertising people) that a single host processor with a collection of remote terminals that simply collect and transmit data does not qualify as a distributed data processing system, even if the terminals are intelligent and do some editing and formatting.

Even the presence of multiple hosts in a complex network interconnection structure does not necessarily make the system distributed. It may be distributed from the point of view of switching; but from the point of view of overall operations and control, it usually is centralized. Systems such as these do not have the capability for dynamic reallocation or reassignment of tasks in the event of hardware failure.

Intelligent terminals systems are most often presented as distributed processing systems in advertising copy. However, the operation of a system with intelligent terminals or local processors has to be studied carefully to determine to what extent the processing is actually distributed. Such a system (several are commercially available) consists of several terminals connected to a local processor that has secondary storage capabilitites, such as disks or cassettes. It offers intelligent data entry—field editing and similar functions executed in the local processor through the execution of a program stored there. It has shared file access, but only to local files. It communicates with a main processor, but to do so, the local processor must emulate a "dumb" terminal in order to use normal protocols. Finally, it is capable of remote job entry. There is no indication of any distribution of the control function, for the distribution of work is fixed and a local terminal cannot affect it.

A terminal with a resident text editor, whether it is provided by hardware or software, is not an example of a distributed data processing system. In order to meet the definition, the terminal must be "smart" enough, first, to do some real work, and second, to recognize when it cannot accomplish its assigned work and to pass it on to another appropriate service unit. The simple off-loading of work to a higher level when this level is fully utilized is just the beginning of the transition to fully distributed processing. If the terminal coordinates several concurrent and simultaneous remote jobs, giving each a different type of service at a different location, without human intervention, then it more closely resembles a distributed system. The threshold is reached when the local control system can decide whether work should be done locally or passed on to the rest of the system, basing its decision on an analysis of local workloads and capabilities. Distributed processing is definitely not equated with merely "moving equipment to the periphery of a business system to capture and process data at the source."[4]

Perhaps the intelligent terminal does have a role to play in the development of distributed processing systems. It may facilitate a painless transition to more decentralized organizations for hardware and data storage as well as control. This is accomplished by adding features to the local system and making other modifications that increase the local functions, prior to establishing higher-level system connections and a complete build-up of global functions.

Dimensions that characterize distribution

From the point of view of system implementation, three "dimensions" can be used to characterize the degree of decentralization of a system, as well as to define distributed systems. These three dimensions represent decentralization in hardware organization, control point organization, and data base organization.

Several points can be identified along the dimension of hardware organization. In order of increasing decentralization, they are as follows:

- A single central processor unit with one control unit, one arithmetic/logic unit, and one central memory.
- Multiple execution units; systems containing one control unit, multiple identical ALU's (for example, the processing elements in the Illiac IV), and, perhaps, multiple independent central memories.
- Separate specialized functional units; systems consisting of one general-purpose control unit and multiple ALU's or processing units. Of the latter, some may be specialized units, such as channels or input/output processor, fast Fourier transforms, processors, vector units, or floating-point arithmetic units. Additional control units may be associated with the specialized functional unit, but these are fixed- or limited-capability control units. Meanwhile, some of the additional ALU's may be identical general-purpose units.
- Multiple processors; systems consisting of multiple control units, multiple ALU's (general-purpose units), and, perhaps, multiple independent central memories, but only one single coordinated input/output system.
- Multiple computers—each a general-purpose CPU with control unit, ALU, central memory, and input/output system.

The five general criteria exclude all but the last two of these organizations from the class designated as distributed systems.

Similarly, control organization is a dimension, delineated by the following points, also in order of increasing decentralization:

- Single fixed control point, either physically or conceptually.
- A fixed master/slave relationship. There may be multiple levels of master-slave relationships, and the relationships between the slaves may be nonsymmetric. The important point is that the master/slave relationship is fixed until modified by totally outside actions.
- A dynamic master/slave relationship, modifiable by software.
- Multiple (perhaps replicated) loci of system control operating *totally* autonomously. An example is two separate computers interacting only at the I/O level through the transfer of complete files.
- Multiple control points cooperating on the execution of a task that has been fragmented into subtasks.
- Replicated, identical control points cooperating on the execution of a task.
- Multiple control points, not necessarily homogeneous, fully cooperating on the execution of a task.

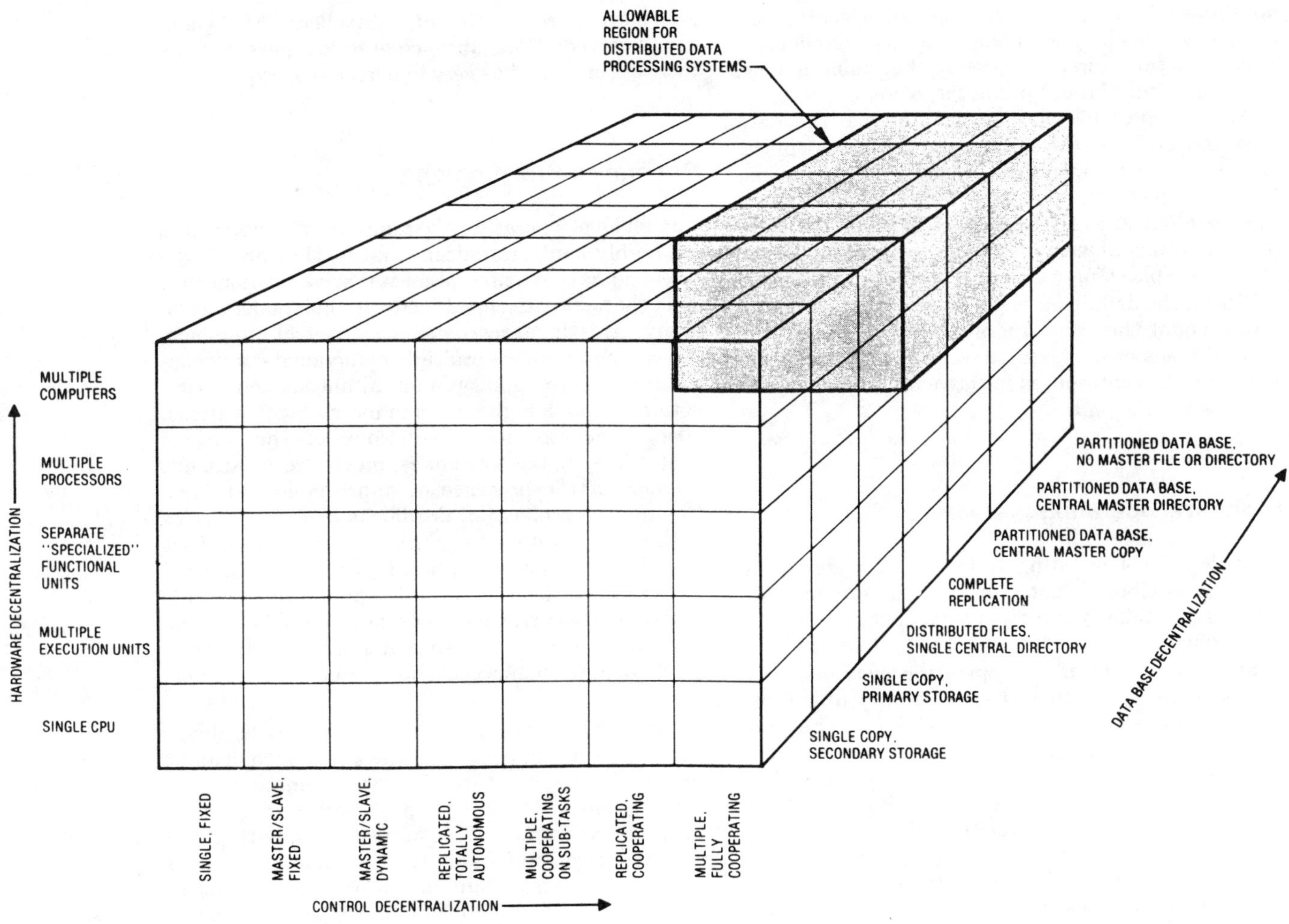

Dimensions characterizing distribution

The region excluded from distributed processing along this dimension consists of the first four entries.

The characterization or ordering of points along the axis of the data base dimension is not so simple. The proper ordering of points along this axis is not apparent. We have attempted an ordering here; however, the use and maintenance of various organizations of distributed data bases are not yet fully understood.

The data base itself has two components that may be distributed—the files and the directory cataloging those files. Either one of these can be distributed without regard to the other, although some combinations are obviously meaningless or impractical. In addition to the issue of distribution, there is also the aspect of replication of the files and/or directory. The points in our list, given in order of increasing "distribution," refer to concepts that have actually been implemented or have been seriously considered for implementation:

- Centralized data bases, including a single copy of both files and directory, held in secondary storage.
- The same, held in primary memory.
- Distributed files with a single centralized directory, and no local directory. All accesses have to be processed through the single central directory.
- Replicated data base, with a complete copy of all files and a directory of the system at each processing node.
- Partitioned data base, consisting of the data most directly required at each node kept at that node, with copies as required at other nodes, plus a complete duplicate copy of all files at the master node. Under this arrangement any transaction causing an exception at a local node is processed by the master.
- Partitioned data base, with local data (files and directory) being retained at the processing nodes, but not duplicated at the master node. However, the master node maintains a complete directory for the routing of transactions that cause local exceptions.
- Partitioned data base with no master file or directory—no single source of information as to the location of a specific file.

The first three of these data base organizations exhibit one common characteristic. They all have a single entry point, a single copy of a centralized directory, for any use of the data base. Obviously, this situation directly affects the vulnerability, reliability, and throughput of the system.

Another possible way to characterize the data base is to consider the naming and the storing of the data as distinct dimensions. Again, several combinations are possible, such as a common name space (file catalog) and distributed storage of the data itself, contrasted with maintenance of totally separate name spaces on a single shared storage device.

Within the definition given previously, and taking into account the exclusion of various regions in the three dimensions, a class of systems that are distributed can be represented in three-dimensional space as shown in the figure.[8]

High-level operating systems

The high-level operating system is a key ingredient in the distributed data processing system. Its design must take into account several characteristics and problems.

The classical design for operating systems, as it has developed, assumes the availability of a large amount of system information. Although the completeness and validity of information about the work being presented by the user is questionable, the operating system is usually assumed to have access to complete and accurate information about the environment in which it is functioning. This is not the case in a distributed data processing system; complete information about the system will never be available. The resources provide a service, but they may, either intentionally or unintentionally, shield information from outside inspection.

In distributed systems, there will always be a time delay in the collection of information about the status of the system components. The ramifications of these time delays are extremely important. In a conventional centralized processor, the operating system can request status information, being assured that the interrogated component will not change state while awaiting a decision based on that status information, since only the single operating system asking the question may give commands. In a distributed data processing system, the time lags that occur can become significant; as a result, inaccurate (badly out-of-date) information can be transmitted because the autonomous component proceeds along its own path. If you have ever worked with input/output device handlers, you surely have often wondered whether or not the information that has been obtained is accurate. For distributed data processing systems, it will be essential to raise the degree of paranoia of the system designer to a much higher level than for centralized systems. The system must be designed to work even with erroneous or inaccurate status information.

A further complication with regard to system information available is the possibility of variations in the information presented to different system controllers. These variations may be a result both of time delays and of differences in the shielding of information from different controllers. As Lelann has observed, "This absence of uniqueness, both in time and in space, has very important consequences."[9]

General control problems

High-level operating systems as described here are highly nonhierarchical—that is, they are single-level and have no internal master/slave relationships. This characteristic, combined with component autonomy, greatly exacerbates the control problems. Even if autonomous multiple components are cooperating, the probability of simultaneous conflicting actions is much higher than in hierarchical systems. Also, synchronizing the actions of the various controllers in the system is much more difficult, because of the presence of appreciable time-lags. Finally, the problem of deadlocks or infinite cycles within the system is quite different from that associated with other systems. Some proposals call for an umpire (an outside third party) to solve this problem; however, such an umpire would have to be transient, since the presence of a permanent umpire would denote an unacceptable degree of hierarchical control.

From the operating characteristics of the distributed processing system, some conclusions can be drawn about the nature of system communication. The second criterion of our definition requires a message-type protocol for all transfers, both physical and logical, both in interprocess communications and interprocess*or* communications. There must be no global variables and there must be no tunneling across system components. All parameters must be passed across well-defined and rigidly enforced interfaces.

Much of the work done on communication in uniprocessor and multiprocessor environments is applicable, but extensions to the solutions found there are definitely required to cope with the autonomous nature of the system components in the distributed system.[10]

The user must communicate with the system by directives containing service names only. Our criterion of system transparency makes unnecessary and perhaps impossible the user designation of the system component offering a desired service. However, this requirement introduces new problems of system failure and user error detection, since no one processor can establish whether the service requested can be provided anywhere in the system, or even whether it is legal.

Resource management in a distributed processing system is a multidimensional job. Thus far, very little work has been done on the aspects of resource management that apply specifically to distributed processing systems. However, low-level functions are quite similar to those performed on uniprocessors; they include physical resource allocation, and management of those facilities required by a process after it has been scheduled on a particular system component. Before that can be done, however, the required resources may have to be assembled at one location, or linkage mechanisms established so that they can be used remotely. The problems that have to be addressed in that process are locating the resources, determining which components are suitable, and determining the best way to move the resources to the selected location. At an even higher level is the scheduling problem, determining when a function should be initiated or terminated.

Any system exhibiting monolithic, autonomous control presents completely new problems in system scheduling. A request for service in a nonhierarchical system might well result in an initial denial of that service by all physical resources. In that instance, the requesting entity might initiate an evaluation of relative priorities between the new request and currently executing tasks, followed perhaps by bidding (priority adjustments) and preemption. The efficient execution of this procedure is one of the most important functions of the high-level operating system.

When all of these problems and their possible solutions are compared to similar problems and solutions encountered in uniprocessor systems, the major factor exacerbating the distributed system control problem is seen as communication within the distributed data processing system, which is asynchronous with respect to the detailed execution of the functions, and which exhibit time-lags in addition to the communication processing time itself. Uniprocessors cope with many of the problems with semaphores, flags, lockout gates, or timeouts. To attempt to do this in a reasonably complex distributed system requires too much time, in the sense that such practices greatly reduce the throughput rate of the system. Bear in mind that transit time for signals transmitting the semaphores is on the order of 100 milliseconds. In addition to the lowering of performance, the reliability and the robustness of most of the uniprocessor solutions are in doubt, since a system operation such as TEST and SET cannot be replicated as a single indivisible machine-level instruction that can be executed immediately on the next machine cycle.

The problem of time is further complicated by the fact that most of the procedures, such as voting and software synchronization, which have been presented as solutions to the difficulties introduced by transit time, require even more processing by every component in the system.[11-13]

Conclusions

Distributed data processing systems are a new class of organizations and operations that exhibit a high degree of distribution in all dimensions, as well as a high degree of cooperative autonomy in their overall operation and interaction. Numerous systems have been designed that meet one or another of the criteria in the definition for distributed data processing; however, a large number of research issues must still be solved before we can implement a true and complete distributed data processing system. ■

Acknowledgments

I cannot accept the credit for many of the ideas and finer points of discussion in this article; however, I do accept the responsibility for the manner in which they have been combined and presented as a somewhat controversial definition of a new class of systems. Space does not permit me to acknowledge individually all of those that have contributed, but I would like to take special note of the participants in the Workshops on Distributed Data Processing, as well as other individuals who have taken the time to discuss with me at length these definitional issues.

References

1. G. A. Champine, "Six Approaches to Distributed Data Bases," *Datamation*, May 1977, pp. 69-72.
2. Dixon R. Doll, "Relating Networks to Three Kinds of Distributed Function," *Data Communications*, March 1977, pp. 37-42.
3. General Automation, "Distributed Processing Networks," Advertising Brochure, March 1977.
4. Arthur Lynch, "Distributed Processing Solves Mainframe Problems," *Data Communications*, December 1976, pp. 17-22.
5. Stephen A. Kallis, Jr., "Networks and Distributed Processing," *Mini-Micro Systems*, March 1977, pp. 32-40.
6. Jules H. Gilder, "Distributed Processing: Keyword for Tomorrow's Supercomputers," *Computer Decisions*, April 1976, p. 14.
7. Foster Brown, "There Ain't No Free Lunch," *Computer Decisions*, April 1977, pp. 46 and 48.
8. P. H. Enslow, Jr., "What Does 'Distributed Processing' Mean?" *Distributed Systems*, Infotech State of the Art Report, Maidenhead, England, 1976, pp. 257-272.
9. Gerard Le Lann, "Distributed Systems—Towards a Formal Approach," *1977 IFIP Congress Proc.*, pp. 155-160.
10. E. Douglas Jensen, "Distributed Processing in a Real-Time Environment," Infotech State of the Art Report on Distributed Systems, pp. 303-318.
11. Peter A. Alsberg, and John D. Day, "A Principle for Resilient Sharing of Distributed Resources," Center for Advanced Computation, University of Illinois, Urbana, Illinois. Prepared for the Brown University Workshop on Distributed Processing, August 1976.
12. Enrique Grana and Geneva G. Belford, "Techniques for Update Synchronization in Distributed Data Bases," Center for Advanced Computation, University of Illinois, Urbana, Illinois.
13. Robert H. Thomas, "A Solution to the Update Problem for Multiple Copy Data Bases Which Uses Distributed Control," Bolt Beranek and Newman, Cambridge, Mass. Prepared for the Brown University Workshop on Distributed Processing, August 1976.

Concurrency in Operating Systems

J. William Atwood
Concordia University

Introduction

As general-purpose computing systems become larger and more complex, it has become uneconomical to restrict their use to a single user or program. This has introduced the necessity of finding ways to safely share them.

Sharing may be cooperative or competitive. It implies that mechanisms are present to permit the objects (e.g., programs) which are sharing the computer to communicate with each other, in order to coordinate their sharing. Sharing also requires adherence to certain rules of behavior which guarantee that correct interaction occurs.

In this paper we will examine the idea of concurrency as a mechanism for sharing a computing system and discuss two operating systems which implement concurrency through the use of *ad hoc* mechanisms. We will then introduce some more formal mechanisms for implementing and controlling interaction—mechanisms leading to proposals for language constructs which simplify the management of concurrency. These constructs also permit the formalization of the rules of behavior, and thus the introduction of mechanisms for enforcing correct interaction.

The need for concurrency

Early computing systems exhibited no concurrency of operation between computations and input/output operations. Typically a single program ran on the central processor, and computation was suppressed while interaction with the environment (I/O) was being effected. This represented a substantial inefficiency in the use of the processor's computing capability, since useful computation was not being performed during I/O, even though the processor was actively testing for completion of the interaction.

Subsequent introduction of the asynchronous data channel allowed the activities of computation and I/O to proceed in parallel. However, it was the responsibility of the (single) program to make use of this available concurrency by, for example, requesting input prior to the time when it was actually required. It was difficult or unnatural to write a program in which more than one or two I/O operations would proceed concurrently with the computation. Since the number of possible *sequences* of interaction was small, the problem of coordination of environmental interaction with internal computation was reducible to an enumeration of the possible cases, and *ad hoc* solutions could be formulated.

Keeping the level of concurrency down to two or three parallel operations represents an under-utilization of available resources. The variety of programs processed by a general-purpose computing system is such that if one program requires a certain set of resources, especially peripherals, other programs will require different sets. A computing system configured to meet or exceed the union of resource demands over all programs is likely to exhibit low average resource utilization.

If mechanisms can be found to increase the average utilization of the system resources, then a more cost-effective system will result, as long as the overhead in managing the mechanism does not exceed the gain in productivity. One such mechanism is to perform more than one computation at a time, providing that two programs (computations) can be found whose total resource requirements are not greater than the total available on the system. If this can be achieved for even part of the time, average utilization will rise. A side benefit is that greater throughput is achieved—i.e., more programs can be processed per unit time.

To do this, it is necessary to introduce sharing of the central processor among several programs: each program will be permitted to utilize the central processor for a period of time (for example, until it requires I/O), at which point the central processor will be allocated to another program. Thus we may say that the central processor is *time-multiplexed* among several programs. This will introduce *apparent* concurrency of programs on the processor,

Reprinted from *Computer,* vol. 9, pp. 18–26, Oct. 1976.

and may raise the level of *actual* concurrency present in the I/O hardware.

When several programs are simultaneously active, they can no longer be permitted to access I/O equipment such as card readers directly, since the ordering of their requests for individual input records is, in general, unknown. A new "program" must be introduced (and allowed to access the central processor) whose function is to copy card images to a disk unit for subsequent (random) access. This program is, in effect, a "card reader manager."

A second reason for time-multiplexing of a processor is to allow for interactive use of the computing system. Interactive computation is characterized by relatively long periods of time (programmer think time) wherein neither the processor nor the peripherals (with the possible exception of the interactive terminal itself) are being used, followed by short periods of computation. Introduction of this mode of operation (which is very convenient for the individual user) implies sharing of the central processor among the several programs associated with the interactive users.

The process concept

The programs that participate in the sharing of the central processor are, in general, independent units, which could all proceed in parallel if enough separate central processors were available. (In fact, the single central processor is time-multiplexed among these independent units according to some strategy.) These independent units are called *sequential processes.* *

Dijkstra[2,3] has suggested that concurrent activity on one (or more) processors can be modeled by a set of processes which alternate between independent activity and periods of communication.

The concept of a community of n processes sharing a single processor may be immediately generalized to a community sharing multiple processors. The strategy for time-multiplexing must then select m processes to be executed rather than only one.

Process interaction

The restrictions on the number of available resources (e.g., tape drives, card readers) in a computing system mean that one process must necessarily influence the action of others, as it competes for resources. The need for specialization of function (e.g., card reader manager vs. "user" process consuming data) also implies that processes must, at times, cooperate to achieve the desired performance of the computing system.

Process cooperation. As mentioned in the Introduction, process cooperation implies that communication is taking place between the processes. If two processes are going to cooperate by communicating with each other, it is clear that their address spaces must overlap in some way—i.e., provision must be made for both processes to access the "message." It is apparent that confusion may result if both processes attempt to access (and especially to update) the shared address space at the "same" time. (On a single processor this means in an interleaved fashion. On a multiple processor system, access may in fact be simultaneous.) This problem is typical of the timing-dependent errors which may occur in the interaction between concurrent processes. Later we will examine rules and language constructs which permit the prevention of these classes of errors.

Typical examples of process cooperation involve two processes which bear a producer/consumer relationship to each other. This often occurs in the context of I/O—e.g., a card reader manager process and a user process.

Process competition. In systems with multiple concurrent processes, the presence of resources such as unit record peripherals and tape drives, which must not be used simultaneously by several processes (if program operation is to be correct), introduces the requirement for exclusive access to these devices. This requirement may also be imposed on shared objects such as disk files during periods of updating.[7] Processes desiring exclusive access to a resource must compete for it.

The same competition arises concerning access to what may be called *virtual* resources—e.g., tables recording the system state, communications buffers between two cooperating processes. Since it must be guaranteed that both processes do not access the buffer simultaneously, exclusive access to the buffer must be ensured. This exclusiveness of access is called *mutual exclusion* between processes.

It is important to note that resource allocation (request for mutual exclusion on the use of a resource) implies communication of the desire to reserve or release the resource. Similarly, process cooperation (e.g., communication) requires mutual exclusion at a lower level (e.g., accessing the shared message buffer). Cooperation and competition may both be implemented if a mechanism is provided for process coordination or synchronization.

Process Scheduling. The above requirements for process cooperation and competition have obvious implications on short- and medium-term scheduling of the central processor.[8] If a desired resource or object is not available, the process expressing the desire to use it must be prohibited from further activity until it becomes available. For example, a process which requires a tape drive must suspend operation (temporarily) if none is available.

There are two extreme levels of exclusiveness here—requirements for deferral of access to a data structure (virtual resource), which may often be of short duration; and requirements for a (perhaps substantial) delay until a real resource becomes available. If the delay is short, it is not worthwhile to shift the attention of the processor from the process which is running on it to another process. If the delay exceeds the time required to switch the processor, the ability to shift attention may be vital to efficient utilization of the processor.

Processor sharing. The sharing of the central processor is achieved by placing the several processes together in central memory and providing a mechanism for rapidly switching the attention of the processor from one process to another.

In the case of interactive computing, an additional level of complexity is introduced, since the processes which are currently not making use of the processor may have been placed in memory image form on secondary storage and must therefore be loaded into central memory when computation resumes. As long as this loading time is negligible with respect to the cycle time of the think-compute cycle, the system will operate effectively—i.e., the phrase "rapidly switching" still applies.

*A complete discussion of the concept of a process may be found in Horning and Randell.[1] Early use of the process concept appears in Dijkstra,[2,3] Morris and Detlefsen,[4] and Brinch Hansen.[5] A more recent discussion is presented in Presser.[6]

Responsibility for managing process scheduling, processor multiplexing, and other related functions is normally assigned to a separate *control program.*[8] The control program may be co-resident in central memory with the several processes, or it may reside on separate processor(s) dedicated to the control program function. It may itself be a process, a community of processes, or a collection of control program functions which are invoked by user processes.

The state of a processor (and thereby the state of the active process) is defined by the set of processor registers. *Context switching* is the swapping of the contents of these registers for another register image. If this register image represents the (previously saved) state of another process, then the attention of the processor is switched from one process to another when a context switch takes place.

Context switching between processes is typically invoked when the active process is unable to proceed further without requesting a service provided by the control program, such as I/O, or when a process requires cooperation from another process. In addition, a context switch may occur when the user and control programs coexist on the same processor, and a control program function is invoked by the environment.

Sharing of the central processor introduces three subordinate problems: (1) protection of the resources of one program from willful or accidental damage by other programs; (2) provision for communication among programs, and between user programs and the control program; and (3) allocation of resources among processes so that resource demands can always be fulfilled.

Protection. One process can be protected from another through a variety of mechanisms. Essentially the goal of protection is the achievement of inviolate firewalls between any two processes. The requirement is absolute —i.e., it must be highly reliable. Efficiency considerations therefore imply a hardware solution, although purely software schemes are possible in special cases.[9] Typical hardware solutions involve some sort of key and lock mechanism, coupled with a privileged state for the control program.

We will not explore the protection problem any further here. An excellent discussion may be found in Saltzer and Schroeder.[10]

Communication. Communication among processes implies provision of (controlled) mechanisms for circumventing the protection features of a computing system. For example, although the address spaces of two processes are normally separate, they must share access to the buffer in which the message will be placed. It is the role of the communications mechanism to verify that objects desiring to communicate with each other have the right to do so, and that they do it in permitted ways.

Resource allocation. If two or more processes wish to access a resource (or a pool of identical resources) within a computing system, it is necessary to allocate the resources in such a way that the total resources of the system are not exceeded. In addition, if it is possible for a process to acquire a portion of the resources that it requires, and then subsequently make a request for more, it is necessary to ensure that future demands can always be satisfied. As an example, suppose that a computing system has one card reader and one printer. Process 1 requests the card reader and process 2 requests the printer. If processes 1 and 2 subsequently request the printer and card reader, respectively, then the system is in a state where two processes are blocked indefinitely. This situation is called *deadlock* or *deadly embrace,* and methods for detecting and preventing it are thoroughly discussed in Holt.[11] The point here is that although communication is necessary to achieve resource allocation, correct communication is not sufficient to guarantee correct (deadlock-free) resource allocation.

Two example systems

In this section we will examine the architecture of two large-scale computing systems, and the basic facilities provided by their control programs to support concurrency. The examples are chosen to illustrate the impact that hardware architecture can have on the design of the control program software.

CDC 6000 and CYBER Series: Kronos

System architecture. The CDC 6000, CYBER 70, and CYBER 170 series architecture[12,13] consists of one (in some cases two) large central processors assisted by up to 20 peripheral processors. The central processor is well equipped for arithmetic calculation, but it is not capable of explicitly communicating with its environment (e.g., it has no I/O instructions in its instruction set). The peripheral processors, on the other hand, are designed to handle interaction with the environment through a number of I/O channels which may all be accessed by any peripheral processor. The central memory is accessible to both the central and peripheral processors. Each peripheral processor has a small local memory which is inaccessible to any other processor.

Control program structure. The control program (Kronos[14]) may be viewed as a collection of cooperating processes, augmented by a number of "monitor" functions which are shared by these processes. The control program processes run on the peripheral processors. Certain monitor functions (e.g., scheduling, accounting, disk track allocation) which require substantial arithmetic or logical calculation are run on the central processor, at the request of a peripheral processor. These functions, plus certain functions provided for user processes (see below), are known collectively as CPUMTR. The remaining shared functions, which usually involve coordination of potentially conflicting control program process activity, are provided by a process called MTR, which runs on a dedicated peripheral processor.

One other peripheral processor is dedicated to a specific function (process): control of the master console (DSD). The remaining peripheral processors form a pool for the execution of other control program processes. Scheduling of the activity of these peripheral processors is the responsibility of a peripheral processor allocator function (part of CPUMTR), which executes on the central processor.

Context switching. The central processor of all CYBER processors has two operating states: *monitor* mode and *program* mode.

Peripheral processors request execution of central processor functions by issuing a MONITOR EXCHANGE JUMP (MXN) instruction. This forces the central processor to being execution in monitor mode, in response to the function request. When the service has been completed, the requesting peripheral processor is informed (see the section on communication, below). The issuing peripheral processor will normally wait while the function is in progress.

If a peripheral processor completes its current activity, it will use MXN to invoke the allocator function on the central processor, so that the peripheral processor may be reassigned.

While the central processor is in monitor mode, other requests for entry into monitor mode will not be honored—i.e., monitor mode activation may be viewed as a resource to which mutual exclusion of access is applied.

User programs. User programs run as processes on the central processor(s). These processes compete for access to a *control point,* which represents the right to be in central memory. Scheduling of processes to control points is the responsibility of the job scheduler (1SJ), which runs on a pool peripheral processor.

A user program requests control program services by issuing a CENTRAL EXCHANGE JUMP (XJ) instruction. This causes the central processor to begin execution in monitor mode—i.e., CPUMTR is activated. If the request is for a central processor (CPUMTR) function, it is serviced. If the request is for activation of a peripheral processor process, a pool processor is assigned, if available; otherwise the request is queued. Note that user programs may not initiate peripheral processor activity directly, but must ask CPUMTR to do it for them.

Certain CPUMTR functions are quite lengthy. They are executed in program mode by a special system control point—i.e., the monitor mode exclusion is released. This system control point has highest priority, so these program mode routines are guaranteed first access to the central processor when the monitor mode is exited.

Return from monitor mode to program mode occurs when a CPUMTR routine running in monitor mode issues an XJ instruction. Return is always to the highest priority waiting control point. Multiprogramming of user programs is achieved when a control point explicitly vacates the central processor by requesting a control program function, when the real time clock manager (part of MTR) forces the central processor into monitor mode on completion of a prescribed time interval, or on completion of a peripheral processor function, as described above.

Process communication. Communication between a central process running at a control point and CPUMTR is achieved through a message buffer (word one of the central memory segment assigned to the control point). Requests for control program services are made by placing a three-character name in the message buffer, and then issuing XJ. Additional parameters or addresses of parameters may be in the rest of the message buffer.

Communication between CPUMTR and a peripheral processor occurs through two message buffers in the low addresses of central memory—an "input register" and an "output register."

When a pool processor is to be assigned (e.g., as a result of a user program request for a control program service), CPUMTR will place the three-character name of the required process in the input register of the assigned peripheral processor. The pool processor, which has been periodically examining its input register, will locate and load the named process, and begin execution of it.

If a peripheral processor requires CPUMTR services, it will place the function code of this service in its output register and issue MXN to activate CPUMTR. Additional parameters may be placed in a 6-word central memory area adjacent to the output register. Completion of the service is indicated when CPUMTR clears the leading 12 bits of the output register to zero. (Results may be returned in the remaining 48 bits or in the 6-word area.)

Completion of peripheral processor activity is indicated by requesting the CPUMTR function DROP PERIPHERAL PROCESSOR, in which case both the input and output registers are cleared by CPUMTR, and the peripheral processor enters its idle loop, waiting for reallocation.

If a peripheral processor requires MTR services, it will use the output register as for CPUMTR services, except that it will not issue the MXN. Since there is no mechanism for a peripheral processor to force a context switch in another peripheral processor, requests for MTR services must be "noticed" by MTR as the result of a periodic scan of all the output registers. If MTR notices a nonzero output register requesting a service which it does not provide (e.g., a CPUMTR function), it will ignore the request. Completion of the service is again indicated by clearing of the leading 12 bits of the output register.

On some 6000 series processors, the MXN/XJ instructions are not implemented, and the monitor/program mode distinction is not made. In this case, MTR must react to *all* output register requests and pass CPUMTR function requests to CPUMTR using the EXCHANGE JUMP (EXN) instruction. This forces an unconditional context switch on the central processor and activates CPUMTR. (The mutual exclusion on the activation of CPUMTR is thus implemented by funneling the requests for activation through a single peripheral processor.)

A primary function of MTR is thus to periodically examine the message buffers that it shares with other processes, to see if a request has been made or a service has been completed. Since MTR can only examine (and respond to) one request at a time, the problems of timing-dependent errors due to "simultaneous" requests disappear. In effect, correct interaction is ensured by requiring all potentially conflicting communication to take place through MTR and defining a protocol to be followed for accessing the message buffers.

Event notification. Two types of control program services are available to a user process: those which can or must be completed before the user process can proceed (e.g., inquiry as to time of day), and those which may admit parallelism (e.g., buffered-ahead request for I/O). In the first case, completion of the service is indicated by zeroing of the leading 48 bits of the message buffer. In the second case, completion of the *initiation* of the service is indicated by the above mechanism, and notification of completion of the function is achieved by setting the rightmost bit of a central memory word designated by the requesting process, which can be periodically checked by that process. Alternatively, the process can request the CPUMTR function RECALL, or it can ask for recall along with the function request. This will cause it to be quiesced until CPUMTR detects that the designated bit has been set. Safety is ensured by the fact that the central process must clear the bit prior to invocation of the function and will do nothing but examine it until it is subsequently changed. (This is another example of a protocol to be followed to achieve correct interaction.) Protection against the case where the central process does not clear the bit first must be provided by the control program routines at the time the function is invoked.

Subordinate control points. Recent versions of Kronos permit the creation of a subordinate control point within a control point. A program running at a subordinate control point has some of the characteristics of a child process. However, it operates in an extremely limited environment. Activation of a subordinate control point causes the father process (running at the control point) to quiesce. All subordinate control point requests to CPUMTR (the subordinate control point makes requests using the same message buffer mechanism as a control point) are trapped by CPUMTR, and cause reactivation of the control point, rather than provision of the requested service. The father process must then interpret the request, and reissue it to CPUMTR if a control program function is actually required.

An example of the use of subordinate control points is the Tranex (Transaction Executive) subsystem of Kronos.[15] Each subordinate control point represents a transaction being performed for a (probably interactive) user. The Tranex system, running at a control point, is responsible for I/O to terminals and files, memory management within the control point memory allocation, and time slice allocation among the subordinate control points. It regains control from the subordinate control point each time I/O is required, or when an allocated time slice has been depleted. The subordinate control point is an example of a set of restrictions on process activity which ensure that timing-dependent interactive errors do not occur but which still permit a program to be run in a supervised environment.

Resource allocation. Allocation of certain system resources is achieved by funneling requests through MTR. For example, if two peripheral processors attempt to activate a single I/O channel at the same time, both will deadlock. The right to access I/O channels is granted only by MTR. In other cases, exclusive access will be granted by MTR to the table (shared variable) in which resource allocations are recorded. This implementation of mutual exclusion thereby guarantees that in no case do two (or more) peripheral processes simultaneously allocate a resource requiring exclusive access. Note, however, that there is no enforcement of these mechanisms at the system level of programming. The programs are all written in assembler language and the mechanisms are just software conventions that are adhered to by the system designers. Any enforcement of the mechanisms must be through run-time checking.

IBM 360/370 Series: OS

System architecture. The IBM 360/370 Series architecture[16,17] normally consists of a single central processor assisted by a number of extremely specialized processors called I/O channels, which are capable of executing programs of I/O commands (channel command words). These channels are activated when an I/O instruction is performed on the central processor. IBM channels do not have the general-purpose calculation capability of a CDC peripheral processor. As a result, many of the computations related to I/O, which are done in the peripheral processor of a CDC system, must be done on the central processor of an IBM system prior to the issuing of the I/O instruction. Central processor and channel programs are both stored in the commonly accessible central memory.

Context switching. All 360/370 central processors have two operating states: a *supervisor* state, in which all instructions are available, and a *program* state, in which instructions that communicate with the environment and those that alter the state of the processor are forbidden. [One exception is the instruction SUPERVISOR CALL (SVC) which invokes the control program.]

Context switching begins as the result of SVC, as the result of a programming error or machine error being detected by the hardware, or as the result of action being completed in the environment causing an I/O or external interruption. In each case the processor is switched to supervisor state, the external and I/O interrupts are disabled, and a portion of the control program is activated. The activated routine must complete the context switch by storing the central processor registers in central memory. The control program may thus be said to be interrupt-driven: each service is implemented as an effective procedure call on a function provided by the control program. Completion of a function is normally indicated by execution of the LOAD PROGRAM STATUS WORD instruction, which forces a context switch (and typically returns the processor to program state).

The context switching (interrupt) mechanism on the IBM 360/370 Series is similar to the central exchange jump/monitor exchange jump feature on the CDC CYBER, except that certain classes of interrupt source can be suppressed while allowing others to proceed.

Control program structure. The control program (OS[18]) is a collection of monitor functions which run in supervisor state on the central processor. The functions are divided into four classes. Class I functions are resident in central memory. They may not invoke other control program functions using the SVC mechanism, although other functions may be invoked as procedures. Class II functions are also resident in central memory, but may invoke Class I functions through SVC. Classes III and IV are nonresident. They are loaded into *transient areas* in central memory on demand. They may request Class I and II functions through the SVC mechanism. All SVC functions begin execution in supervisor state, with I/O and external interrupts disabled, but they may choose to release any of these exclusions. Control program functions are always invoked by explicit request (interrupt). This interrupt may come from a central process; a Class II, III, or IV control program function; or from the environment (e.g., completion of I/O activity).

The presence of the single (general purpose) processor means that all process concurrency is only apparent. Concurrency is little used within the control program itself, the preferred method of operation being to disable all possibility of externally-forced context switching while the control program is running.

User programs. The user programs run as processes, in the program state, on the central processor. These processes are called *tasks* by IBM. A *region* is a contiguous area of central memory allocated to a task.

Process communication. Communication between a user task and the control program is achieved by placing parameters in the processor registers and requesting context switching by issuing the SUPERVISOR CALL instruction. (This same mechanism is, of course, used by Class II, III, and IV functions when invoking SVC.)

Substantial use is made of the fact that actual concurrency is not present. Therefore, the problems of simultaneous updating of shared variables are reduced. In effect, correct interaction is ensured by requiring all control program activity to take place strictly in sequence.

Event notification. As with Kronos, two types of control program services are available to a user task: those which can be completed quickly (i.e., before the next instruction after SVC is executed) and those which admit or require parallelism. In the first case, completion of the operation is assumed when the user task resumes. In the second case, notification of the completion of actions performed by the control program is signalled by the use of a control program function called POST, which sets the leftmost bit of a central memory word (EVENT CONTROL BLOCK) designated by the requesting task and checks to see if any task is waiting on the event. Waiting for an action to complete is achieved by invoking the function WAIT. The ECB is also used to contain an address identifying the waiting task when there is one. Use of the ECB as a signalling mechanism is subject to the same criticism as that mentioned earlier in the context of process communication for the CDC 6000: protection against inadvertent error must be provided by the system functions when invoked. For example, setting an ECB to zero immediately *after* requesting a service that uses an ECB to report completion, and then invoking WAIT, may result in task deadlock if the service was in fact completed before the task regained control after issuing the SVC.

Subtasks. OS permits a task to create a subtask within the central memory region allocated to the task. This subtask may proceed independently of the originating task, is permitted to issue its own SVC requests, and competes with all other tasks for system resources, such as central processor time, in accordance with its allocated priority.

Communication between a task and its subtask is implemented using the POST/WAIT functions mentioned above, either explicitly, or implicitly at subtask termination (the control program can be requested to issue POST to a designated ECB, when the subtask terminates).

Resource allocation. Physical resources are allocated by control program procedures which rely for their correct operation on the fact that externally-forced context switching is inhibited. Where mutual exclusion is required on shared resources such as disk files, which are being updated by various tasks, two control program functions called ENQUEUE and DEQUEUE are provided. Normally, if a task requests an ENQUEUE function on a certain resource, and it is not available, the task is delayed until the resource becomes available. However, it is possible to request control only if it will be immediately granted. Requested control may be exclusive (no other task permitted to access the resource while control is held), or shared (always granted unless another task currently has, or is waiting to establish, exclusive control). The resource is represented by a pair of identifiers supplied as parameters to the ENQUEUE or DEQUEUE function, and no protection is provided against inadvertent use, at the system-wide level, of the same pair of identifiers by two different tasks. For example, if a user program uses the identifiers, which are used by control program functions to indicate enqueuing on the volume table of contents of a disk volume, then it will cause deadlock if it attempts to open any file on that volume.

Process coordination

In previous sections we have examined some concepts related to process coordination and resource management, and two implementations which have formulated rules to guarantee correct interaction between processes. These rules are extremely dependent on the architecture of the system for which they were formulated, and they rely on the careful following of conventions.

There is a need for formalisms to describe these concepts, in ways which are amenable to *a priori* demonstration of the correctness of the implementation. Use of these formalisms leads to proposals for language constructs which aid in their correct use.

In this section we will present a formalism for process coordination, and examine its utility in the control of concurrency in operating systems. In the following section we will examine two concepts that are more useful for resource management, and the language constructs that may be derived from them.

Critical sections. In the CDC 6000 and CYBER series, any peripheral processor can access any physical I/O channel. In order to ensure that no two peripheral processors access a channel at the same time, it is necessary for a process running on a pool peripheral processor to request access rights to the channel (from MTR) prior to use, and then release it immediately after use.

This is a typical pattern for use of a resource which must be allocated to only one process at a time:

establish exclusive access;
use the resource;
release exclusion.

The section of program text during which the necessary exclusive access holds is called a *critical section.*

Establishment of exclusive access. When establishment of exclusive access is being attempted, the requesting process must be delayed if the required resource is not currently available. Similarly, releasing the exclusion may result in the resumption of a waiting process.

In Kronos, the process running on the pool processor, which has requested exclusive access to a resource, delays itself by periodically testing for an answer to its request until the request is satisfied. On a shared processor, however, this "busy waiting" is extremely undesirable, since it represents a consumption of processor resource that might otherwise be avoided. It may also prevent the process which will respond to the request from ever executing, thus causing indefinite blocking (deadlock) of the waiting process. It is preferable to have a basic operation which will establish the exclusive access if the resource is available, and place the process in a blocked state otherwise.[8]

In Kronos, requests for access to channels take the form of function requests (messages) to MTR, containing the request number and the desired channel number. In this approach there is one communication path (the output register), and several possible messages, such as REQUEST CHANNEL, ASSIGN EQUIPMENT, REQUEST JOB SEQUENCE NUMBER, etc.

An alternative approach is to provide a toggle (reserved/not reserved) associated with each channel. This toggle would then be accessed directly by any processor. If the toggle were already set to "reserve," then the accessing processor would be delayed until the toggle was reset. This corresponds to having a number of communication paths (toggles) and a single message (reserve the channel).

Access to the toggle associated with each channel is access to a shared "variable," and the mutual exclusion on this access is required in order to guarantee correct operation—i.e., it must not be possible for a second process to access the toggle between the time the toggle is tested by the first process and the time it is set to "reserved."

Exclusive access for "testing and updating" of a memory location is provided on the IBM 360/370 Series by the TEST AND SET instruction. This instruction tests the leftmost bit of the addressed memory location and sets the addressed memory location to all ones. No other access to the addressed location is permitted between the moment of fetching and the moment of storing all ones. In this way there is no possibility of another process intervening and testing the shared variable. This mechanism does not provide for any automatic action; if the resource is not available, the process must suspend itself. The TEST AND SET instruction is used to effect coordination between two central processors in a multiprocessor system.* The waiting processor cycles in a "spin loop," repeatedly issuing TEST AND SET, until the tested memory location is cleared by the other processor.

On the CDC CYBER, an *interlock register* is available as an option. Bits or words in this register can be tested and updated by any peripheral processor, with guaranteed exclusion of access. Operation of this interlock register is similar to TEST AND SET, except that several optional actions are available (e.g., READ, TEST, TEST AND SET, TEST AND CLEAR, etc).

Semaphores. Dijkstra, in a now classic paper,[2] has offered a formal mechanism for the solution of the problem of establishing exclusion with the introduction of two primitive operations, called P and V, and a specialized integer data type called a *semaphore.*

When a process executes a P-operation on a semaphore S and the value of S is greater than zero. S is decremented by one and the process continues. If the value of S is not greater than zero the process is blocked from further execution. The value of S is also decremented by one either (1) as soon as the resulting value would be non-negative[2] or (2) immediately: the magnitude of the (negative) value of the semaphore indicates the number of processes waiting.[3] If the process is allowed to continue, then the P-operation is indivisible. If the process is to be blocked, then the test and the blocking of the process constitute an indivisible operation and the "deciding to release" and the actual release of a waiting process also constitute an indivisible operation.

When a process executes a V-operation on a semaphore S, then S is incremented by one, and the process continues. In addition, if any process is waiting on that semaphore, exactly one is removed from the waiting queue and permitted to continue execution. The V-operation is also indivisible.

The indivisibility of these two primitive operations is the required guarantee of mutually exclusive access to the shared variable (the semaphore).

A semaphore (initialized to 1) can be used to establish and release exclusive access to a resource. If RES is a semaphore representing a resource (compare with the toggle discussed above) then the use of the resource is preceded by a P-operation to reserve the resource and followed by a V-operation to release it:

P(Res);
use the resource;
V(Res).

If the first definition of the P-operation is used, then the semaphore will have value 0 while the resource is in use; an attempt by a second process to access it will result in a delay of the second process until a V-operation is performed by the first process. At this point the semaphore becomes greater than zero and is immediately decremented again, granting access to the second process and completing its P-operation. This form of the semaphore is called a *binary* semaphore, because the only values it can have are 0 and 1.

Process cooperation. Two cooperating processes can coordinate their access to a shared address space by only accessing that space while they are within a critical section delimited by P and V. Producer/consumer relationships can also be controlled with semaphores—if a portion has not yet been produced, the consumer will be delayed. The initial value for a producer/consumer semaphore, representing available portions, is zero. Since the producer may produce several portions before the consumer can consume them, the semaphore may take on arbitrarily large values. This form of semaphore is called a *general* semaphore.

Process Competition. The mutual exclusion required for resource allocation can also be implemented using semaphores. If there is only a single instance of a nonsharable resource, the associated semaphore will be binary. If there is a pool of identical resources, the semaphore will be general. In both cases the initial value of the semaphore is equal to the number of resources.

Note that the ENQUEUE/DEQUEUE functions of OS can be used in very similar ways for resource allocation. They are more complex to analyze in that the enforced waiting is conditional.

Process Scheduling. Semaphores have obvious implications on the scheduling of processes—a V-operation on a specific resource semaphore will result in the release of a process, if any is waiting for that resource (so that it can then complete its delayed P-operation). A P-operation by a process may result in the delay of that process until the resource which it desires becomes available. Semaphores are defined in such a way that if several processes are waiting to complete a P-operation, only one of them will be selected to proceed when a V-operation is performed. The only requirement is that the selection of a candidate by "fair"—i.e., that no one process be indefinitely overtaken by others.[19]

Semaphore implementation. On a uniprocessor system, semaphores can be implemented by the control program using the global masking of interrupts to guarantee the indivisibility of the P- and V-operations. On a multiprocessor system, special hardware is needed to guarantee mutual exclusion of access to the semaphore (i.e., "cycle stealing" by another I/O or central processor must be prohibited while the semaphore is being updated). Both the 360/370 TEST AND SET instruction and the CYBER interlock register satisfy this constraint.

Recent extensions and adaptations. The semaphore as proposed by Dijkstra may be viewed as a signaling mechanism, but one which only signals that the desired event has occurred. Associated with a semaphore is always a queue (empty if $S > 0$) of processes waiting on that semaphore. It is customary to associate the pointer to that queue with the semaphore itself. (This may be compared with the address of the task descriptor recorded in the OS EVENT CONTROL BLOCK.) This association is used in the Venus system,[20,21] in which semaphores are known to the microprogram of a small computer—i.e., P and V are instructions on the machine.

A further extension is used in the Honeywell Series 60/Level 64.[22] Here a firmware convention is adopted concerning the availability of a short (16-byte) message area (from a pool) associated with each V-operation. This is useful, for example, for making a status report on completion of an I/O operation available directly to the process which initiates the request for I/O, without the need for either a shared, dedicated status area in central memory or a separate buffer management semaphore. Various other extensions are discussed by Presser.[6]

It may also be noted that the availability of semaphores makes the I/O interrupt superfluous. Completion of an I/O operation can be indicated by a hardware- or firmware-generated V-operation, which is "noticed" by a software process as the result of a P-operation on that same semaphore. Thus the equivalence of external (real) concurrency and internal (apparent) concurrency is established.

*Note that multiprocessing is not supported by regular versions of OS.

Resource management

Semaphores may be viewed as powerful but relatively low-level constructs. When they are used for resource management, they are typically used in certain "standard formats." Failure to use them in precisely the right way can lead to errors which are particularly difficult to detect and diagnose. In addition, it can be argued that the variables which represent a resource, and which must be manipulated within critical sections distributed among all of the competing processes, are not properly part of the state space of *any* of these processes.[23] In this section we will introduce two mechanisms for resource management (and, therefore, the control of concurrency) which attempt to make the design of operating systems safer. Both do this by isolating the resource management from the users of the resources: the first, by creating a separate process to manage the resource; the second, by defining precise properties of a control program function to manage the resource, and removing the variables that represent the resource from the address space of the requesting processes.

Secretaries. The actions of reserving and releasing a resource may be viewed as procedures *reserve* and *release* acting on a variable (or a data structure) which represents the resource. A possible move in the direction of increased safety is to associate the procedures with the data structure on which they operate, in a separate process. In this way it can be guaranteed that the data structure is *only* operated on by the defined procedures, because the variable(s) representing the resource are no longer part of the address space of the requesting processes.

Resource allocation can then be likened to the actions of a group of directors (competing processes) being scheduled by a secretary, which is a special, high-priority process which implements the procedures acting on the data structure.[19] A secretary is in fact a "semi-sequential" process,[19] in that her procedures represent the allowed operators on the data structure, and the order in which her actions are performed is undefined—i.e., it depends on the order in which the directors ask for her services.

This concept may also be used recursively: a process which is a secretary to one group of processes may act as a director to another. This allows the construction of hierarchical systems.[24,25]

Monitors. Another approach to the idea of combining shared variables with their operators (procedures) is provided by the "class" concept of SIMULA 67.[26] To this concept we may add the requirement that access to the procedures of the class be restricted to strictly one-at-a-time—i.e., the mutual exclusion, which we have previously associated with the distributed critical sections, is now associated with a centralized object.

The combination of the shared variables, the set of meaningful operations on them, and the mutual exclusion, is called a *monitor.*[27] The shared variables become a data structure which is syntactically local in the scope of the monitor itself. The mutual exclusion of procedure execution is implied and need not be explicitly coded. The procedures thus appear to be critical sections within a process, but they are different in that the shared variables are no longer in the address space of the invoking processes.

A monitor may be viewed as an *abstract data type*—i.e., a language notation which associates the procedures with the data structure on which they operate.

Monitors are used primarily to construct resource schedulers. If the desired resource is not available when the monitor is entered (this is reflected in the state of the local variables), then the calling process is delayed until the resource is released by another process. The mutual exclusion on the access to the monitor procedures is also released, for otherwise no other process would be able to enter the monitor and release the desired resource.

The concept of a monitor is similar to the implementation of control program functions in OS—the explicit disabling of the possibility of externally-forced context switching provides the mutual exclusion aspects of a monitor. However, in OS there are only four structural levels (the four classes of SVC). Monitors have greater potential for the construction of hierarchical systems.

Monitors have been illustrated and examined extensively in the recent literature.[28-30] There appears to be agreement that the basic idea of a class-like structure is sound, but there are various proposals concerning the detailed syntax of the abstract data type, and on the syntax and semantics of the delaying operator. For the present, insufficient experience has been gained to evaluate the relative merits of these proposals.

Language proposals. Control of concurrent activity is, in general, more difficult to achieve than control of sequential activity. It is therefore desirable that a higher-level language be used in the development of control programs. The programming language Pascal[31,32] provides a base with elegant data structuring capability, in which the addition of abstract data types is quite natural. Recent proposals[30,33] to extend Pascal with processes (which could be secretaries), monitors, and queues of waiting processes are now being used in pilot projects to test the usefulness of these constructs.

The advantage of monitors and secretaries over other mechanisms is that they package the operations and the data structures so that they must be used correctly. Specifically, it is possible to check for correct usage at compile time, and thereby avoid the need for extensive execution-time verification of parameters, etc. Also, the operations on the data structure are defined in only one place, and are therefore less prone to errors in coding.

Summary

As computing systems have become increasingly complex, real and apparent concurrency have been introduced in order to increase utilization. This has necessitated the development of mechanisms for controlling concurrency and preventing errors due to arbitrary interleaving of sequences of instructions from separate processes.

In this paper we have examined the structure of two control programs and the ways in which they have solved the problem of the management of concurrency. These solutions have been based on rules which must be explicitly followed in the coding of the control program.

These rules form the basis for proposals for coordination primitives and language constructs. Semaphores are ideally suited to the establishment of short-term mutual exclusion for process coordination. Secretaries and monitors represent attempts to derive a superior mechanism when the problem is one of scheduling of resources. Neither semaphores nor monitors are inherently more powerful, since each can be implemented in terms of the other, but the semaphore is the more primitive concept. For this reason it is more likely that semaphores, or some similar construct, will be implemented within the basic instruction set of new computers. Monitors are more likely to be a feature of systems programming languages, because of the way in which they package data structures and operations (procedures) into an abstract data type. ■

Acknowledgements

The assistance of J. Vaucher, M. Collins, J. Woodrow, S. Bush, T. Davidson, and the reviewers is most gratefully acknowledged.

The writing of this paper was supported in part by the National Research Council of Canada.

References

1. J. J. Horning and B. Randell, "Process Structuring," *Computing Surveys,* Vol. 5, No. 1 (March 1973), pp. 5-30.

2. E. W. Dijkstra, *Cooperating Sequential Processes,* Technological University, Eindhoven, The Netherlands, 1965. Reprinted in *Programming Languages* (F. Genuys, ed.), Academic Press, New York, 1968.

3. E. W. Dijkstra, "The Structure of the 'THE'—Multiprogramming System," *CACM,* Vol. 11, No. 5 (May 1968), pp. 341-346.

4. D. Morris and G. D. Detlefsen, "A Virtual Processor for Real Time Operation," *Proc. COINS Symposium,* 1969. (Also published as a report from the Department of Computer Science, University of Manchester, U.K.).

5. P. Brinch Hansen, "The Nucleus of a Multiprogramming System," *CACM,* Vol. 13, No. 4 (April 1970), pp. 238-250.

6. L. Presser, "Multiprogramming Coordination," *Computing Surveys,* Vol. 7, No. 1 (March 1975), pp. 21-44.

7. P. J. Courtois, et al., "Concurrent Control with 'Readers' and 'Writers'," *CACM,* Vol. 14, No. 10 (October 1971), pp. 667-668. See also C. A. R. Hoare, *CACM,* Vol. 17, No. 10 (October 1974), Section 6, pp. 209-215.

8. Bunt, R. B., "Scheduling Techniques for Operating Systems," *Computer,* Vol. 9, No. 10 (October 1976), pp. 10-17.

9. C. G. Bell and A. Newell, *Computer Structures: Readings and Examples,* McGraw Hill, New York, 1971, p. 76.

10. J. H. Saltzer and M. D. Schroeder, "The Protection of Information in Computer Systems," *Proc. IEEE,* Vol. 63, No. 9 (September 1975), pp. 1278-1308.

11. R. C. Holt, "Some Deadlock Properties of Computer Systems," *Computing Surveys,* Vol. 7, No. 3 (September 1972), pp. 179-196.

12. *Control Data CYBER 70/Model 73 Computer System Reference Manual,* Publication No. 60347200, Control Data Corp., Arden Hills, Minnesota, 1971.

13. *Control Data 6000 Series Computer Systems Reference Manual,* Publication No. 60100000, Control Data Corp., Arden Hills, Minnesota, 1971.

14. *Kronos 2.1 Reference Manual,* Publication Nos. 60407000 (Vol. 1) and 60448200 (Vol. 2), Control Data Corp., Arden Hills, Minnesota, 1975.

15. *Transaction Subsystem Reference Manual,* Publication No. 60407900, Control Data Corp., Arden Hills, Minnesota, 1973.

16. *IBM System/360 Principles of Operation,* Form GA22-6821, IBM, Poughkeepsie, New York, 1970.

17. *IBM System/370 Principles of Operation,* Form GA22-7000, IBM, Poughkeepsie, New York, 1970.

18. *IBM System/360 Operating System MVT Supervisor PLM,* Form GY28-6659, IBM, Poughkeepsie, New York, 1970.

19. E. W. Dijkstra, "Hierarchical Ordering of Sequential Processes," *Acta Informatica,* Vol. 1, No. 2, 1971, pp. 115-138. Reprinted in *Operating System Techniques,* (C. A. R. Hoare and R. H. Perrott, eds.) Academic Press, New York, 1972.

20. D. C. Tsichritzis and P. A. Bernstein, *Operating Systems,* Academic Press, New York, 1974.

21. B. H. Liskov, "The Design of the Venus Operating System," *CACM,* Vol. 15, No. 3 (March 1973), pp. 144-149.

22. T. Atkinson, "Architecture of Series 60/Level 64," *Honeywell Computer Journal,* Vol. 8, No. 2 (1974), pp. 94-106.

23. C. Bron, "Trends in the Synchronization of Parallel Processes." Paper presented at Annual Symposium of the Dutch Computer Society, Technological University, Eindhoven, The Netherlands, February 6-7, 1974.

24. K. C. Sevick, et al., "Project SUE as a Learning Experience," *AFIPS Conference Proceedings, 1972 FJCC,* Vol. 41, pp. 331-338.

25. R. C. Holt and M. S. Gruschow, "A Short Discussion of Interprocess Communication in the SUE/360/370 Operating System," *Proc., SIGPLAN/SIGOPS Workshop on Programming Languages and Operating Systems,* Savannah, Georgia, April 1973.

26. O. J. Dahl, B. Myhrhaug, and K. Nygaard, *Simula 67—Common Base Language,* Norsk Regnesentral, Oslo, Norway, May 1968.

27. P. Brinch Hansen, *Operating System Principles,* Prentice Hall, Englewood Cliffs, New Jersey, 1973, p. 121.

28. C. A. R. Hoare, "A Structured Paging System," *Computer Journal,* Vol. 16, No. 3 (1973), pp. 209-215.

29. C. A. R. Hoare, "Monitors: An Operating System Structuring Concept," *CACM,* Vol. 17, No. 10 (October 1974), pp. 549-557.

30. P. Brinch Hansen, "The Programming Language Concurrent Pascal," *IEEE Transactions on Software Engineering,* Vol. SE-1, No. 2 (June 1975), pp. 199-207.

31. N. Wirth, "The Programming Language Pascal," *Acta Informatica,* Vol. 1, No. 1 (1971), pp. 35-36.

32. K. Jensen and N. Wirth, "Pascal—User Manual and Report," Springer Study Edition, Springer-Verlag, Berlin and New York, 1975.

33. D. W. Bustard, "Progress towards a Structured Operating System," Technical Report, Department of Computer Science, The Queen's University of Belfast, May 1975.

An Approach to Distributed Software Systems

by
Jean Bacon
The Hatfield Polytechnic, UK

Abstract

A conceptual framework is given for software designed as an integrated whole for a distributed system or local area network. The ISO reference model for open systems interconnection is incorporated into the design approach. A summary of mechanisms provided in systems and languages for inter-process communication is given and each mechanism is evaluated in the context of support for distributed software. A classification of typical inter-process interactions is given as a further basis for comparison.

1.0 INTRODUCTION

This paper is concerned with software designed as an integrated whole for a distributed system or local area network. In the area of languages supporting concurrency a variety of design proposals have been made and attention is being directed towards distribution issues. In the area of network design the ISO reference model for open systems interconnection is being evaluated and refined. It is felt that a summary of developments in languages and an integrated approach to distributed software incorporating networking principles is timely.

A multicomputer topology is assumed based on processors with local store only. A conceptual framework is given for a distributed software system and alternative implementations are discussed.

2.0 THE SINGLE SITE MODEL

A general model of a software system, the "process model", is of a kernel supporting concurrent processes. The kernel may be implemented in hardware, microprogram or software. The model is equally applicable to a single language system for a language supporting concurrent processes where the run time support routines of the language augment or replace the kernel.

As emphasised in [19], the kernel should provide mechanisms. Policy decisions should be implemented at the process level.

In outline, the functions of the kernel are:-

1. To provide facilities for process management via primitives to create, kill, start and stop processes.

2. To "field" interrupts on behalf of processes.

Reprinted with permission from *Oper. Syst. Rev.*, vol. 15, pp. 62–74, Oct. 1981.

3. To provide facilities for processes to communicate via primitives which implement signalling and exchange of data between processes.

4. To maintain information on processes, for example a "descriptor" for each process which holds its state information and also queues of processes which are waiting for various events.

5. To implement mechanisms for scheduling, protection and memory management.

A generalisation of the above is the "object model" in which the kernel mechanisms support objects. In this model a process is one type of object. For the purposes of this paper the more conventional process model is preferable although some aspects of section 4.3 could be handled more elegantly in the context of the object model.

3.0 THE DISTRIBUTED MODEL

The process model for a distributed software system consists of a kernel at each site supporting concurrent processes. Inter-process communication may be between processes at the same site or at different sites. In the latter case, communication software and hardware must provide the inter-site inter-process communication.

The ISO reference model for open systems interconnection [16], proposes a hierarchy of software and hardware to implement inter-site inter-process communication. All processes in the single site model are at the highest level, level 7, of the ISO model, named the application layer.

For each level of the ISO model a virtual connection is made with the corresponding level at other sites. This virtual communication is implemented by real communication through the layers. Each layer provides a transparent, error-free service to the layer above, through the implementation of communication protocols.

In a given implementation the division of ISO levels between software and hardware will depend on the sophistication of the communication hardware. A serial interface connection would provide only level 1 (that is, only the physical connection) in hardware whereas a Cambridge Ring or an Ethernet would provide levels 1 to 4 (that is, the entire transport service). Communication handling software is divided between kernel and process levels. Software concerned with communication interrupt handling will reside in the kernel whereas higher level protocols will be implemented at the process level.

4.0 SYSTEM PRIMITIVES

Fig 1 gives a classification of inter-process communication primitives. Message primitives (Fig 1a) were introduced as a higher level of kernel provision than that in semaphore based systems such as THE [9]. An alternative approach to improving the kernel primitives is to hide them. The run-time support package of a high level language supporting concurrent processes may provide higher level primitives than those of the system kernel. In practice such languages have tended to provide the procedural primitives of Fig 1c. Within each basic type of primitive a number of variations have been implemented in systems and languages and these will now be summarised and their interdependence with process management primitives will be shown.

4.1 The Conventional Message System

Messages are buffered in the kernel. There is therefore, in general, no delay on SEND and a potential delay on WAIT if the required message is not available (Fig 1a).

Buffer overflow is a problem since the kernel is unable to request more store being at a level below that at which virtual memory is provided. The method of managing the buffer space may also imply that the space available to one process is affected by the behaviour of other processes.

A message may be sent to a named process or to some named attribute of a process such as a port, channel, link or pipe which must be bound to a process or processes before run-time.

A process may have one or many ports. Also, a port may be associated with a set of processes. Ports may be created dynamically for the duration of a transaction such as file access.

Messages may be fixed or variable length, the latter being comparable with a list of arguments on a procedure call. A typed message may be associated with a port that will only accept messages of that type. In some systems, data may only be passed explicitly; in others, references may be passed.

The WAIT primitive may specify a single port, a fixed set of ports or a selected set of ports. A conditional WAIT or a timeout facility on WAIT may be provided so that an unwanted delay on WAIT may be avoided. Alternatively, a dedicated process may have the specific task of waiting for a message. In this case a request from a client process will involve the creation of a new process to service it. Alternatively, a process may be created dynamically for the purpose of waiting.

In some systems event signalling is available in addition to message handling. In one implementation [25] an interrupt type message is used to force transfer of control to an interrupt procedure within a process.

Examples of system kernels providing message style primitives are RC4000 [5], GEC 4000 series, MUSS (Manchester University Software System) [23], DCS (Distributed Computing System) [10], SODS/OS (IBM Series One Distributed System) [25], Roscoe (links) [26], Medusa (pipes) [24] and RIG (Rochester Intelligent Gateway) [2]. Examples of existing and proposed languages containing message style primitives are Babbage for the GEC 4000 series, *MOD [8], Plits [11] and Pascal M [1].

4.2 Messages With No Hidden Buffering

In this case a delay on SEND is involved until the intended destination process WAITs, since messages are not buffered (Fig 1b). Buffering may be introduced explicitly by means of an intermediate process which manages a message buffer. The problem of buffer overflow in the kernel is therefore avoided at the expense of introducing an additional process.

Comments on message design and the implementation of WAIT are as for the previous section. An unwanted delay on SEND may be avoided if a conditional SEND or a timeout on SEND is provided. Alternatively, a new process might be created dynamically to SEND a message and perhaps synchronise with the reply.

The language Real Time BASIC uses message primitives of this type. The language CSP [14] proposed by Hoare also uses this style of primitive, syntactically in the form of input and output statements.

4.3 Passive Procedural Primitives

In systems based on this style of primitive, system facilities are often provided as passive procedures which may be called by relevant processes. If the procedures access shared, writeable data they are encapsulated together with the data in monitors and serial use of monitors is enforced and managed by the system. Dedicated system processes are only used in such systems when synchronisation with external, asynchronous events such as interrupts is necessary. Inter-process communication is implemented through shared data encapsulated in monitors. Monitors are passive structures.

The CALL primitive therefore involves a potential delay, through waiting to enter a monitor, unless a new process is created to execute the CALL. There may also be a potential delay within the procedures of a monitor for synchronisation purposes, when the exclusion on the monitor is temporarily released. Early proposals [3,13] involved explicit event signalling within monitor procedures. More recent proposals [12] have been for synchronisation at the procedure or operation level through path expressions.

Message passing may be constructed as required by encapsulating a message buffer in a monitor, together with procedures to append and remove a message.

Most languages supporting concurrent processes are designed for single-site architectures and use primitives of this type, for example Modula 1 [28], Concurrent Pascal [4], Mesa [18], Alphard [29], CLU [21] and Path Pascal [7]. Object or domain oriented architectures or Operating Systems such as CAL TSS, Plessey S250, Hydra, StarOS, CAP 1 and Intel 432 are also based on this design philosophy.

4.4 Active Procedural Primitives

In this model all domains are managed by active processes; there are no passive structures available to many processes. Inter-process communication is implemented as the CALL by one process of a procedure owned by another process. A rendezvous must be made between two processes, by the equivalent of a WAIT by the called process, before the procedure is executed.

There is a potential delay on CALL until the rendezvous is achieved. This delay may be avoided as discussed in the previous section. Synchronisation is at the operation level since the called process will only rendezvous with processes calling procedures that can be executed.

Third party or intermediate processes may be used as mailbox managers to implement message buffering between two processes through exported procedures to append and remove a message.

This mechanism was proposed by Brinch-Hansen in the language Distributed Processes [6] and has been implemented in Ada [15].

5.0 PRIMITIVES FOR DISTRIBUTED SYSTEMS

Since message passing (Fig 1a), does not require shared memory for inter-process communication it is suitable for a distributed software system and has been used in several implementations [10,24]. However, continuation after SEND implies that a message has reached the input buffer of its intended destination. In a distributed system such a condition would introduce a delay on SEND while the communication software and hardware passed a message to the input buffer of a process at another site. A decision must therefore be made on the meaning of continuation after SEND. Also, if process migration between sites is allowed, possibly for load balancing reasons, the movement of message buffers would also have to be managed. A decision must also be made over whether data is always passed explicitly or whether references are allowed at least at some levels.

The message system with no hidden buffering is also suitable for communication between distributed processes and involves explicit synchronisation between processes at different sites.

Passive procedural primitives (Fig 1c), although widely used for single-site languages, do not naturally distribute because of their use of shared memory. A distributed software system based entirely on the use of this type of primitive would have to solve the problem of frequent inter-site procedure call and subsequent return by processes. Proposals have been made to add message passing primitives for inter-site communication to procedural primitives for intra-site communication, for example *MOD [8] and extended CLU [21]. This scheme implies a static software allocation.

Active procedural primitives (Fig 1d) allow procedural primitives to be retained for a distributed system. The problem of inter-site procedure call is solved since a process is available to execute the called procedure at the called site.

It is feasible to use any of these primitives as the basis of a distributed software system; although the passive procedural style, perhaps most widely used in single site implementations, seems least suitable. In addition to the mere practicality of implementation, three further issues should be considered, namely,

1. Is it preferable to base a system design exclusively on a single style of primitive ?

2. Is the implementation efficient enough for communication between distributed processes ?

3. Are practically occurring problems solved equally elegantly by each style of primitive ?

6.0 REAL TIME PROGRAMMING PROBLEMS

To evaluate the primitives as concurrent programming tools it is useful to categorise typical inter-process interactions and to consider whether the primitives provide natural and elegant implementations.

6.1 Communication Between Groups Of Processes

It should be established early in the design process which of the following are required so that undesirable constraints are not introduced.

1. One to one communication.

   The most restrictive form of one to one communication is when the names of both parties to a conversation must be known to both in advance as, for example, in CSP. A more common form is that the initiator knows the name of the recipient but not vice-versa. Indirection via a named buffer object is often used.

2. Many to one communication.

   The communication between a single server and multiple clients may be managed in a variety of ways as described in Section 2 above. If indirect naming is used, the server may be replaced without the knowledge of the client, for example, if a faulty device is removed from service.

3. One to many communication or broadcasting.

   This type of communication may be needed for notifying an exceptional condition to many interested parties. Also, rather than requesting service from one specific resource manager a client may wish to request service from any manager of a given type of resource. For example, if a local printer is busy any similar one in the system might suffice. A solution at the inter-process communication level, in which processes able to provide a service send a bid to the potential client is given in [10]. Solutions at command level using centralised [27] or distributed [22] resource management have also been implemented.

4. Many to many communication.

In practice, simultaneous communication between multiple clients of replicated servers is resolved into many to one communication, via a shared port or a dedicated interface process, followed by one to one [24,26].

6.2 Shared Data

In addition to the data that passes between processes in a message or on a procedure call, access to certain data structures may be required by several processes. An example of data of this type is file directory information required by each process executing file management code.

In a passive procedural system shared data may be encapsulated in a monitor together with access procedures.

In a pure message system shared data does not exist. A data segment must pass from one process to another in a message, the sender relinquishing access. In some implementations, for example [24], data may be in the address space of several processes simultaneously and access is synchronised by means of a semaphore. This approach is not suitable for a distributed system based on local memory.

In message and active procedural systems, shared data should be encapsulated with access procedures and managed by a process.

6.3 Exceptional Events

A very common requirement for a process is that it responds in a cyclic fashion to some outside stimulus. There is often an additional requirement that it must also respond quickly to an exceptional, asynchronous event. A variety of solutions have been proposed:-

1. In each cycle the process WAITs for the exception with a timeout.

2. A flag in shared memory is tested by the process on each cycle to see whether the exceptional event has occurred.

3. When the exception occurs an interrupt type mechanism is used to transfer control to an exception routine in the process.

4. A dedicated process which is the parent of the cyclic process has the sole function of synchronising with occurrence of the exception. If the exception occurs, this process, being the parent of the cyclic process, uses process management primitives to stop the child, handle the exception on its behalf and restart the child.

6.4 Concurrency During Nested Communication

Suppose that a server process itself needs to request service from some other process while carrying out a service request. A file manager, for example, may call on a memory manager for more store or a disc manager for disc access. It is essential in the latter case that concurrency with disc access is achieved in the file management module. It should be considered in general to what extent concurrency is desirable with nested requests and how this should be achieved.

File management software will typically reside in a dedicated server computer. This implies the need for multiple activations of the file management software supported by segmentation hardware and suitable inter-process communication primitives. In addition, process management primitives might be used to create a new process to service each new request. A detailed example is given in [24].

7.0 CONCLUSIONS

A classification of inter-process communication primitives has been given and it has been noted that a distributed software system could be contrived based on any of these types, although the passive procedural style, which is most widely used in single site languages, seems least suitable. It should also be noted that process management primitives, the dynamic creation of a new process for example, might provide a more elegant solution to a given problem than increased sophistication in the inter-process communication primitives.

An attempt has been made to classify basic types of inter-process interactions and it is felt that more work in this area is required.

Since the sophistication and potential of hardware is constantly increasing a consensus from software designers on a set of natural, powerful and elegant tools which can be incorporated into language and system design is of great importance.

8.0 ACKNOWLEDGEMENT

I wish to thank Adrian Stokes for his help in the development of this material.

9.0 REFERENCES

1. Abramsky, S. and Bornat, R.,
PASCAL M: A Language for Distributed Systems.
QMC Research Report CSL 245 1980

2. Ball, J. E. et al,
Perspectives on Message Based Distributed Computing
Proc NBS/IEEE Networking Symposium 1979

3. Brinch-Hansen, P.,
Operating Systems Principles
Prentice Hall 1973

4. Brinch-Hansen, P.,
The Architecture of Concurrent Programs
Prentice Hall 1977

5. Brinch-Hansen, P.,
The Nucleus of a Multiprogramming Operating System
Comm ACM 13, 4, 238-250 April 70

6. Brinch-Hansen, P.,
Distributed Processes: A Concurrent
Programming Concept
Comm. ACM., 21(11), 934-941, Nov 78.

7. Campbell, R.H. and Kolstad, R.B.,
Path Expressions in Pascal
Proc. 4th Int. Conf. Software Eng.
212-219, Munich 1979

8. Cook, R.P.
*MOD- A Language for Distributed Programming
IEEE Trans SE SE6(6), 563-571, Nov 80

9. Dijkstra E.W.
The Structure of THE Multiprogramming System
Comm. ACM 11(5), 341-346, May 68

10. Farber, D.J.
The Distributed Computing System
Proc. COMPCON 73, 31-34, 1973

11. Feldman, J.H.,
High Level Programming for Distributed Computing
Comm. ACM 22(6), 353-368, Jun 79

12. Flon, L. and Haberman, A. N.,
Towards the Construction of Verifiable
Software Systems
ACM Sigplan notices, 8(2), 141-148, 1976

13. Hoare, C.A.R.,
Monitors: An Operating System Structuring Concept
Comm. ACM, 17(10), 549-557, Oct 74

14. Hoare, C.A.R.,
Communicating Sequential Processes,
Comm. ACM, 21(8), 666-677, Aug 78.

15. Ichbiah, J.D. et al,
Rationale for the Design of the ADA Programming
Language and Preliminary ADA Reference Manual,
ACM SIGPLAN Notices, 14(6), Jun 79.

16. ISO TC 97 SC16
Open Systems Interconnection
N227 Aug 79

17. Jones, A.K. et al,
StarOS, A Multiprocessor Operating System for the Support of Task Forces
Proc ACM SOSP7, 117-127, Dec 79

18. Lauer, H. C. and Satterthwaite, E. H.,
The Impact of Mesa on System Design
Proc. 4th Int. Conf. on Software Eng. 174-182, Munich 1979

19. Levin, R. et al,
Policy/Mechanism Separation in Hydra
Proc. ACM SOSP6, 132-140, Nov 77

20. Liskov, B.
Primitives for Distributed Computing
Proc. ACM SOSP7, 33-42, Dec. 79

21. Liskov, B. et al,
Abstraction Mechanisms in CLU
Comm. ACM, 20(8), 564-576, Aug 77

22. Lunn, K. and Bennett, K. H.,
An Algorithm for Resource Location in a Loosely Linked Distributed Computer System
ACM SIGOPS, 15(2), 16-20, April 81

23. Morris, D. and Detlefsen, G.D.,
A Virtual Processor for Real Time Operation
Comm. ACM, 11(5), 17-28, May 68

24. Ousterhout, J. et al,
Medusa: An Experiment in Distributed Operating System Structure
Comm. ACM, 23(2), 92-104, Feb 80

25. Sincoskie, W. D. and Farber, D. J.,
SODS/OS: A Distributed Operating System for the IBM Series/1
ACM SIGOPS, 14(3), 46-54, July 80

26. Solomon, M.H. and Finkel, R.A.
The Roscoe Distributed Operating System
Proc. ACM SOSP7, 108-114, Dec 79

27. Wilkes, M.V. and Needham, R.M.
The Cambridge Model Distributed System
ACM SIGOPS 14(1), 21-29, Jan 80

28. Wirth, N.,
Modula: a Language for Modular Multiprogramming
Software Practice and Experience, 7, 3-35, 1977

29. Wulf, W. et al,
An Introduction to the Construction and Verification
of Alphard Programs
IEEE TransSE SE2(4), 253-264, Dec 76

Fig 1 Inter-Process Communication Primitives

(● = potential delay)

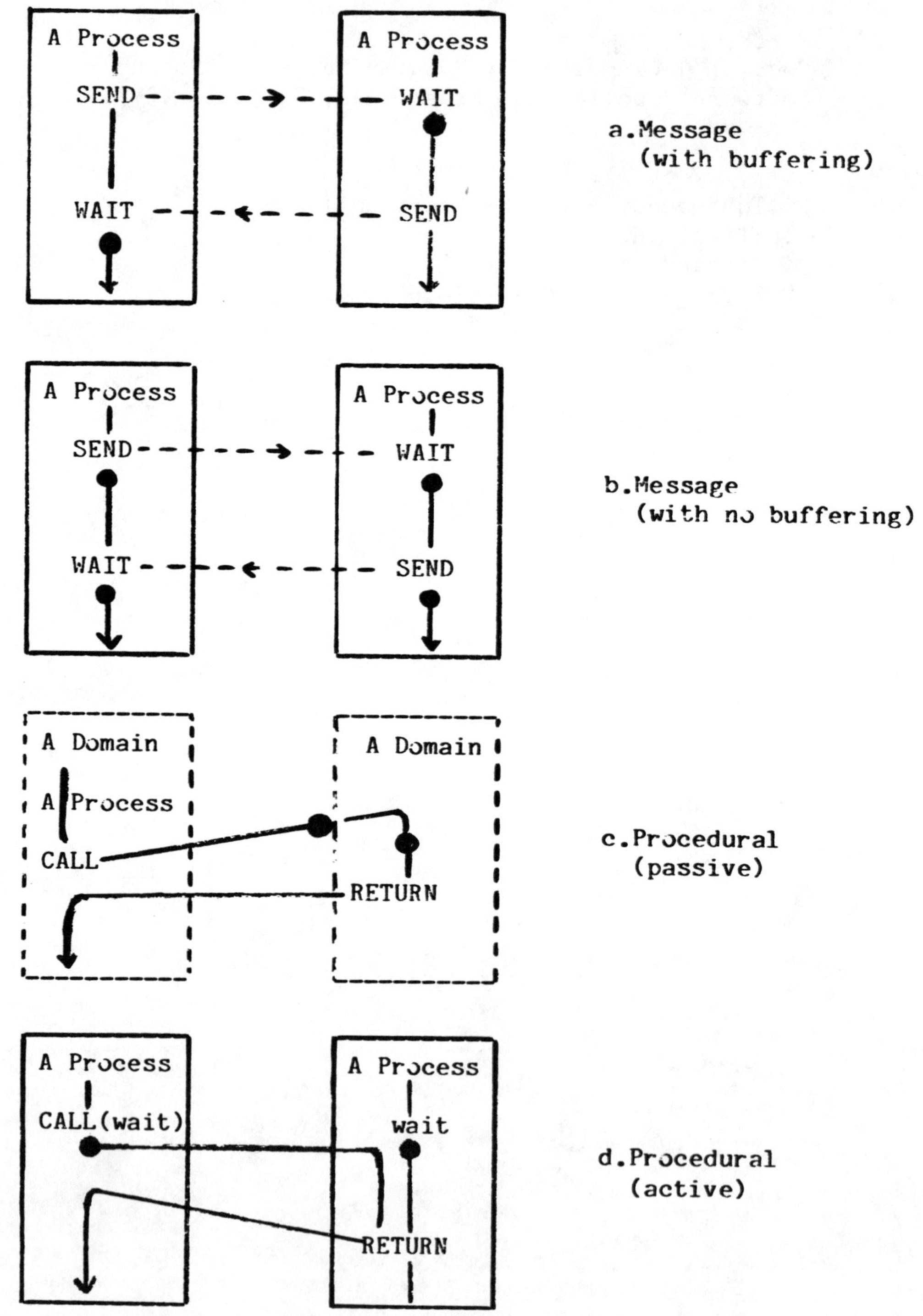

Operating Systems for Computer Networks

Harry C. Forsdick, Richard E. Schantz, and Robert H. Thomas
Bolt Beranek and Newman, Inc.

Introduction

The last decade has seen the rapid evolution of computer communication networks from research curiosities to operational utilities. The Arpanet,[1] for example, currently supports communication among more than 100 computer systems and is used daily by hundreds of users. Commercial networks, such as Telenet[2] in the United States and Datapac[3] in Canada, have very bright futures. One attraction of these networks is their ability to provide access to a wide variety of resources distributed among the connected computers.

A typical network (Figure 1) includes a communication subsystem, to which a collection of computers, called *hosts*, are connected. This subsystem usually consists of communication processors interconnected by communication links, such as coaxial cable, telephone lines, or satellite channels. Communication processors have two functions: they cooperate to support communication between the hosts, and they provide the interface through which the host computers are connected to the communication facility. Each host includes an operating system that supports one or more application processes. The principle purpose of the communication network is to permit access by a user, or by a process acting on his behalf, to resources of the other machines.

Networks such as the Arpanet have stimulated the development of protocols that support terminal access to remote hosts[4] and file transfer between hosts.[5] However, at present the amount of resource sharing that occurs on computer networks falls far short of that which is possible—for several reasons:

- To use the network resources effectively, the user must know not only the access mechanisms of the network, but also the operating systems of the hosts whose resources he wishes to use.
- Resources of the various hosts are generally not compatible with each other.
- Information about the available resources and how to use them is difficult to obtain.
- Accounting and billing for resource utilization are generally maintained by each host, so that a user must establish a separate account with each organization whose host he plans to use.

The fact is that a network, even with terminal access and file transfer protocol implementations, is not an integrated operating system.

The concept of a network operating system represents a promising approach for overcoming these difficulties and thus realizing the full potential of computer communication networks. A network operating system (NOS) is a collection of software and associated protocols that allow a set of autonomous computers, which are interconnected by a computer network, to be used together in a convenient and cost-effective manner. An NOS would help users and their programs exploit the resources distributed among network hosts in much the same way that a single-host operating system provides its users with controlled access to local resources. It would tend to make the underlying network and the boundaries between host systems transparent to users. It would remove many of the logical distinctions between resources that are local and those that are remote. Such a system would provide an environment within which uniform accounting throughout the network would be feasible. In addition, an NOS environment could support a wide range of easily accessible information services, which might range from current information on the

Reprinted from *Computer*, vol. 11, pp. 48–57, Jan. 1978.

status of constituent systems to information about the hardware and software resources available. Because of the potential for redundancy and the inherent autonomy of the constituent host systems, an NOS can, in principle, provide service of far higher availability than can a single-host operating system. However, the potential for decreased availability also exists, if the NOS depends on system components that are subject to failure. Thus, an NOS must be carefully designed to produce a system with increased, rather than decreased, availability.

Several projects have been undertaken to study, design, and build such systems. The technical problems uncovered in these efforts are illustrated in two projects with which we have been involved: the Resource Sharing Executive Project, supported by the Defense Advanced Research Projects Agency (DARPA), and the National Software Works Project, supported jointly by DARPA and the Air Force Rome Air Development Center.

In these projects, intensive study was devoted to the first two of the four previously mentioned factors: facilitating access to network resources and resolving incompatibilities among different host systems. Although the other two factors are equally important, a thorough discussion of them is beyond the scope of this article. Although both systems provide an environment capable of supporting effective information services, these services have not been extensively developed. With regard to the fourth factor, the accounting problem, we feel that the unresolved issues are largely political and administrative rather than technical.

The RSEXEC System

The Resource Sharing Executive System[6] was developed as an experimental vehicle to explore a wide variety of NOS issues, ranging from the types of features that would be useful to network users, to system structures and mechanisms for implementing those features, to strategies for ensuring reliable, fail-soft performance.

The initial emphasis of the RSEXEC System was to couple the operation of the many PDP-10 hosts connected to the Arpanet which use the Tenex operating system.[7] The goal was to provide access to the combined resources of these hosts much as the Tenex operating system and command language interpreter provide access to a single Tenex host (Figure 2). The RSEXEC includes both a command language interpreter for users and an execution environment for user programs.

The system has three principal components: (a) the RSEXEC program, which is an interface between each active user and the system resources; (b) the RSEXEC server (RSSER) program, which runs on each of the hosts and makes the resources of that host accessible to remote users; and (c) the RSEXEC/RSSER protocol, the set of conventions governing the interactions between the RSEXEC and RSSER programs that is necessary to support the various system features.

Although RSEXEC was designed primarily for a homogeneous system composed of similar Tenex hosts, dissimilar host systems (Multics, IBM 360/TSO, PDP-10/ITS, Arpanet TIPs) have been partially

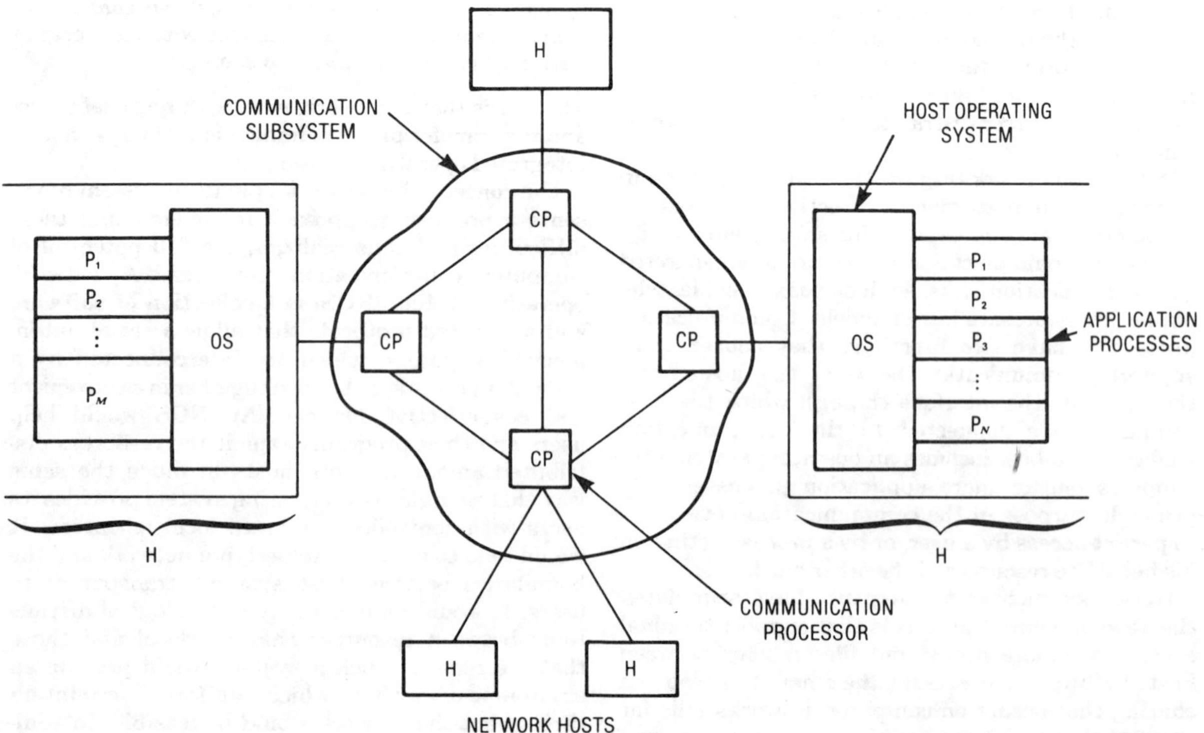

Figure 1. In a network, a communication subsystem interconnects host computers, host operating systems, and application processes with one another.

integrated into it. Currently over 40 hosts are part of the system. To integrate a new type of host into the system, RSEXEC and RSSER programs are prepared for it. The protocol, which is independent of host type, specifies the functional requirements of the RSSER program. For a given host type the RSEXEC program is intended to provide access for local users and programs to the combined resources of the RSEXEC hosts in the same style that the local operating system provides access to local resources. Although the form that user interactions take could be expected to vary from one host type to another, the functionality supported by RSEXEC programs for different host types is similar.

RSEXEC features. RSEXEC has a distributed file system that supports access to files that reside with the constituent hosts. The file system satisfies two principal goals: to make all files regardless of location uniformly accessible, and to provide convenient access to frequently used files. Uniform file access is achieved through a file-naming syntax applied to all hosts that extends the syntax within each single host by adding a field for network location. From the operating system viewpoint, a file name implies a series of steps through the file system hierarchy to reach the file, and is therefore called a pathname. Convenient file access is achieved through the use of partially qualified pathnames (which need not include network host location) to specify frequently used files. RSEXEC interprets these partial pathnames with the help of a private working directory, which it maintains for the user. The working directory, in general, spans host boundaries in the sense that it catalogs files from several hosts. Thus, knowledge of a file's location is not essential to make use of it. The host and its local operating system, acting alone, would normally reject such a partial pathname as an error; RSEXEC translates it into the full pathname for the host storing the file.

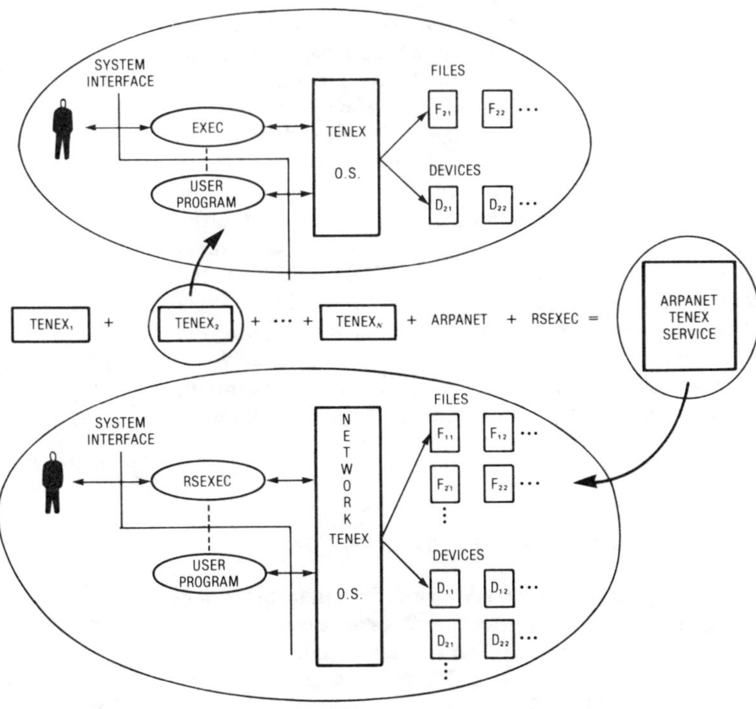

Figure 2. The RSEXEC couples the operation of Tenex hosts on the Arpanet. One Tenex system includes the components in the upper part of the diagram; when combined with other systems, the network, and RSEXEC, it becomes effectively a much larger system, shown beneath.

A third goal of the RSEXEC file system was to support multiple copies of critical files, so as to ensure that they would be accessible even when one or more of the hosts storing them had failed. The RSEXEC does help a user maintain multiple file copies by, for example, attempting to update all copies of the file when the user updates one copy. However, if a host in which a copy is stored is inaccessible when the attempt is made, the RSEXEC simply informs the user and takes no further responsibility for updating that particular file copy. To that extent it falls short of the third design goal.

Implementation of the file system features are largely the responsibility of the RSEXEC program. When a file is requested, the RSEXEC program's first step is to determine where the file resides, by interpreting the file name. File location is explicit in a full pathname. Partial pathnames are interpreted in the context of the current RSEXEC working directory, which is maintained locally for each user. A local copy ensures faster response by allowing partial pathnames to be interpreted without incurring the delay and other overhead of querying one or more remote hosts. Since the working directory spans several hosts, it is, in effect, a composite directory whose components are individual directories at these several hosts.

RSEXEC maintains a profile of each user that ordinarily has access to RSEXEC resources. Each profile includes a list of the component directories the user customarily accesses together with securely encrypted passwords to gain access to these directories. When the user begins an RSEXEC session, the RSEXEC program builds his working directory for that session from the profile. As he continues, the working directory expands and contracts, acquiring and discarding catalog information as necessary, and going out of existence at the end of the session, to be reconstituted when needed at the beginning of the next session. For component directories maintained by remote hosts, this catalog information is obtained from RSSER programs; for local component directories, it is obtained directly from the local operating system. For each file, the composite working directory includes the site at which the file is stored, along with other file descriptor information. After the RSEXEC program determines the location of a requested file, it initiates file operations at the appropriate host.

The features of the RSEXEC file system are supported at both the command language level and the executing program level. The RSEXEC program interprets commands typed by the user for manipulating files, while operations initiated by programs are performed in the context of the distributed file system.

An example of the former is a "RUN" command, with which a user executes a program within the RSEXEC environment. The program is retrieved from the RSEXEC file system and thus may reside on any participating host. The current implementation of RUN requires that the program execute on the local (RSEXEC program) host, where the user is working. (The underlying system structure will support remote program execution—that is, the RSEXEC/RSSER protocol includes commands for placing programs into execution under the control of an RSSER program at a remote host. However, the RUN command currently does not use that protocol feature.) When a remote file is the parameter of the RUN command, the RSEXEC program retrieves a copy of the file for its own direct control.

File operations initiated by executing programs use a technique called "encapsulation."[8] An application program executing on a stand-alone computer system issues many calls to its operating system to have tasks such as file operations performed for it. For the program to execute successfully in a multi-host system, these systems calls must be interpreted in the context of the larger set of multi-host resources. A section of the RSEXEC program acts to encapsulate application programs so that calls are interpreted from the RSEXEC viewpoint of distributed resources. RSEXEC intercepts certain file operations and interprets them in the context of the network file system as previously described. Operations referring to local files are then passed directly to the local operating system. Remote operations are forwarded to the appropriate remote RSSER server program. An important benefit of this encapsulation technique is that programs written for a single host environment need not be rewritten to operate within the network environment. Thus the value of existing software, such as text editors and language processors, is significantly enhanced by being able to work with remote as well as local data files.

RSEXEC includes commands with which users can obtain status information, such as current loads of constituent host systems—for example, the number of active users, load factors, etc. In addition, a user can link his terminal directly to that of another user, who may be logged into either the local system or a remote system, in order to engage in an on-line dialog. Users initiate and terminate remote links and local links in the same way. However, remote linking requires cooperation with a remote RSSER program, whereas local linking is directly supported by the local operating system.

Augmenting small host capabilities. One of the ideas investigated in the context of the RSEXEC system was to expand the usefulness of small machines by letting them obtain services from larger ones.[9] This has been particularly beneficial to some users who access the Arpanet and its hosts via TIPs[10] The TIP is a small host system designed to provide terminal access to the network for users who are remote from the hosts they normally use. There are currently more than 20 TIPs in the Arpanet. The TIP itself offers no computational services and no user services beyond the ability to connect a terminal to a remote host through the network. Thus, the TIP does not directly provide status information or interact with the user.

However, the TIP does have a command that obtains access to an RSEXEC, which can provide these services. Several hosts on the network offer this service; they form a pool, to which the TIP broadcasts requests, selecting the one that responds first. This simple selection mechanism tends to distribute the service load among the hosts in the pool, and ensures that the service is available as long as at least one of the hosts is accessible.

An important application of this approach of using large-host resources to support small-host functions was the implementation of access control and accounting for Arpanet TIPs. Because TIPs have no long-term storage, they are incapable of authenticating their users or maintaining long-term usage information. Therefore, when an Arpanet user activated a TIP terminal port, perhaps by dialing it over a telephone line, the TIP would automatically connect to an RSEXEC, which would attempt to authenticate the user's identity. If the user failed to log in successfully, further use of the TIP would be denied—that is, the TIP would break its connection to the user. After logging in, the user would be permitted to use the TIP in the normal way. As part of the log-in procedure, the RSEXEC would pass the user's unique network identification to the TIP for accounting purposes, and the TIP would account for the user's connect time and network message traffic. Periodically, the TIP would send the usage data and the user's identification to an RSEXEC host for storage and subsequent processing and billing. (This access control and accounting procedure, though it was operational at one time, has been disabled for a number of non-technical reasons. Its mechanism, however, illustrates the potential of the approach.)

The National Software Works

The National Software Works[11] is a network operating system to support software development. Designed and implemented by personnel from Bolt Beranek and Newman, Inc., Massachusetts Computer Associates, MIT, SRI International, and UCLA, NSW provides managers of programing projects access to a collection of management tools for monitoring and controlling project activities and gives programmers uniform access to a wide variety of software production aids. These include conventional tools such as text editors, simulators, compilers, interactive debuggers, emulators, and test data generators, as well as experimental aids being developed as part of various research projects, such as program verification systems and systems to support program development methods.

Although tools such as these, which span the software development process from design through implementation and checkout, have been available on a variety of computers for many years, they are seldom applied together in an effective way to support software implementation projects. One reason is that existing tools have been implemented for different computer systems, and programmers typically do not have access to the range of machines that house them. Furthermore, even if they did, programmers would have to master a variety of different host operating systems and command languages, and deal individually with basic interhost incompatibilities to use the tools. The NSW system addresses both of these problems. It supports access to a wide variety of tool-bearing hosts and provides a simple, uniform means to invoke a tool regardless of the host that provides the tool.

Scenario of NSW application. The initial release of the NSW system included as tool-bearing hosts several PDP-10's operating under Tenex, some Honeywell 6000 computers operating under Multics,[12] and one IBM 360/91 operating under OS. Part of the user community is a group developing software for the AN/UYK-20 computer, a small machine that does not itself support a wide range of software development aids and is generally configured for production use rather than program development. This group's use of the NSW in the edit-compile-debug cycle illustrates the system capabilities.

Programmers prepare and modify their routines with interactive text editors that run on Tenex and Multics. Then they compile their source programs using language processors that run on the 360/91, and form executable AN/UYK-20 object modules from the compiled output with loaders that can run either on the 360/91 or on Tenex. Finally they debug the AN/UYK-20 programs interactively within NSW using a debugger tool that runs on Tenex. This interactive debugger is, in fact, a multicomputer tool. Part of it runs on Tenex and part of it runs on a microprogrammable computer, the MLP-900, which is connected as a peripheral device to one of the Tenex hosts and is programmed to emulate the AN/UYK-20. After making several edit-compile-debug cycles and producing a debugged AN/UYK-20 program, the user can "export" his modules from the NSW for final checkout and operation on a real AN/UYK-20 machine.

To apply any tool, a user simply specifies its name—such as CMS2M, an AN/UYK-20 compiler—and the NSW system starts the tool and connects the user to it. The user need not know which tool-bearing host supports the tool nor the command language of that particular host. He need only learn the NSW command language. To support tool execution the NSW implements a distributed file system. All NSW tools utilize this single system for their file references. When a tool calls for a data file (for example, a source program for a compiler), the NSW system ensures that the access refers to the correct file, independent of its actual location. If the addressed file is stored on another host, the file is automatically transported to the requesting host. In addition, NSW may transform certain aspects of the file to compensate for incompatibilities between the hosts or their file systems. Thus, the user and the tools he employs need not concern themselves with the location of data files, the details of the file systems on the various constituent hosts, the movement of files between hosts, or the data translations that may be required to make a file created on one host usable on another host. However, the file translations currently included in NSW are limited to those that support the existing set of NSW tools; NSW does not address the general problem of data translation, which is a difficult one.

It should be emphasized that the primary objective of the NSW project is not to develop tools, but rather to develop a system framework for tools—a framework to support uniform access to and integrated use of a diverse collection of tools, some already existing and some to be developed, all of them programs that run on one or more of a wide range of host processors under a variety of different operating systems.

NSW system structure. A useful view of the principal components of the NSW system is as processes that cooperate to provide NSW services. These components include front end (FE), works manager (WM), tool-bearing host foreman (FM), and file package (FLPKG) processes (Figure 3).

Each active user has a dedicated front-end process which is his interface to the NSW system. The principal function of the FE is to interpret the NSW command language and make requests of other components as necessary to satisfy user commands.

The works manager is the resource allocation and access control module for the NSW system. All requests for NSW resources, such as tools for files, must be authorized by the WM. To perform its task, the WM maintains data bases such as an NSW file system catalog, tool descriptor information, and user password and account information. These data bases and the WM software reside in one of the hosts included in the NSW system—possibly but not necessarily one of the tool-bearing hosts.

Interactions between WM processes and other system components occur as required, for each transaction involved. That is, the system dynamically allocates and deallocates WM processes as necessary to support a user session, rather than dedicating a single WM process to each active user for the duration of his session. For example, when a user initiates a command that requires access to an NSW resource, a WM process is allocated to handle requests related to that command. Upon completion of the command, the WM process is deallocated—that is, either returned to a pool of free WM processes or effectively destroyed. In the latter case, it is unavailable for reuse except by repeating the start-up procedure. Continuity across such instances of WM service is achieved by sharing a dynamic data base.

The tool-bearing host foreman[13] is the tool's interface to the NSW. When a user requests the start of a tool, an FM process on the appropriate TBH is allocated for the duration of the tool session. The FM process provides an execution environment for the tool and controls its operation. This execution environment differs somewhat from the standard environment of the local operating system. For example, a "file open" operation must be carried out in the context of the entire NSW, taking into account all of the network resources, not just those at the tool's host. The FM process responds to the file opening by calling on a WM process to complete the file reference. The WM process consults the NSW file catalog to verify the existence of the file specified by the FM, and to verify that the user and tool are authorized to use the file.

Next, the WM acts to ensure that the file can be physically accessed by the FM/tool. This may require movement of the file to the FM host and possible translation of the file data to a form usable by the tool. The WM process arranges for FLPKG[14] processes at the file source and destination hosts to cooperate to accomplish this movement and translation. Like WM processes, FLPKG processes are allocated on a transaction-oriented basis. When the file movement is completed, the WM process is notified by one of the FLPKG processes and then both FLPKG processes are deallocated. The WM process then informs the FM process that the file reference can be completed and is itself deallocated. Finally, the FM uses information provided by the WM—for example, the name of a local temporary copy of the file, accessible to the tool—to complete the tool file reference.

Communication between the various FM system processes, as well as the allocation and deallocation of those processes, is the responsibility of a component called MSG.[15] Two addressing modes, generic and specific, are supported by MSG. Generic addressing is the means by which a process initiates a transaction with another previously unrelated process. It is used when any process of a given type is acceptable. For example, to initiate the file operation in the AN/UYK-20 scenario, the FM process sends a generically addressed message to a WM process. Similarly, the FLPKG processes on the file source and destination hosts are activated by generically addressed messages. MSG allocates a process of the appropriate class, such as WM or FLPKG, to receive such messages.

Specific addressing, the second mode, is used when the sending process must communicate with a particular process. In the preceding example, the replies by the FLPKG process to the initiating WM and by that WM to the initiating FM are specifically addressed messages. When a process executes a receive operation, it declares whether a generically or specifically addressed message is requested.

The FM component provides two different tool interfaces to NSW. One of these is an encapsulation interface, which permits software packages that were developed to run under a particular TBH operating system to be installed as NSW tools. As in the encapsulation used in the RSEXEC system, the FM intercepts certain requests made by the tool of the local tool-bearing host operating system and transforms them into equivalent NSW operations. Ideally, the encapsulation interface would allow existing software to be installed into NSW without modification. In practice, the success of encapsulation for a given TBH depends upon the functional commonality between the TBH operating system and NSW, and the degree to which various tools exercise TBH functions not naturally mapped into NSW functions. Encapsulation has been fairly successful for the Tenex hosts; however, the integration of a new Tenex tool sometimes requires minor enhancements to the FM encapsulation interface.

The second tool interface provided by the FM is for tools developed specifically for operation within the NSW environment. This direct interface permits tools to explicitly call NSW functions. Generally the FM must interact with other NSW processes to satisfy these tool calls. The design intent is for the direct tool interface provided at different tool bearing hosts to be functionally equivalent. The manner in which tools invoke NSW system operations, of course, may vary from one host to another.

The NSW supports a wide variety of tool-bearing host types. As mentioned previously, the system

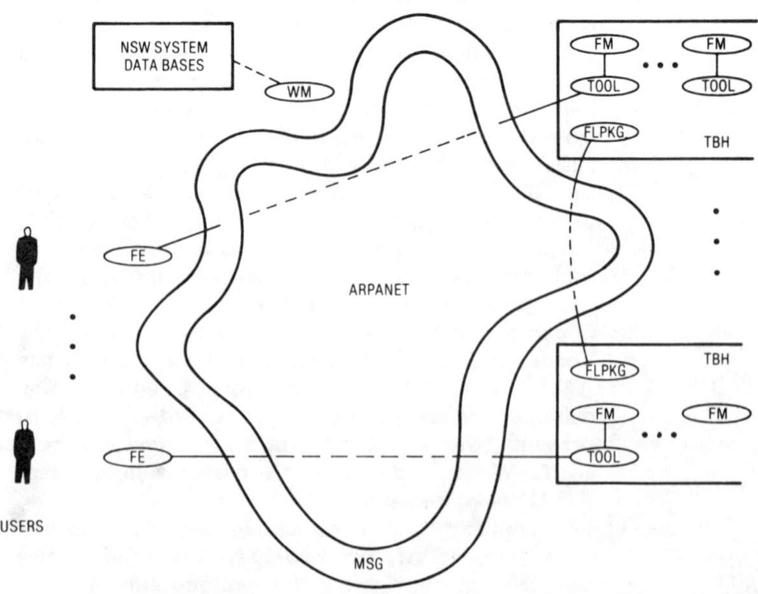

Figure 3. NSW components include front end (FE), works manager (WM), foreman (FM), and file package (FLPKG) processes. NSW tools run on tool-bearing host (TBH) computers under control of FM. The MSG interprocess communication facility supports communication among the distributed system components.

includes three different types at present. For a host to be integrated into the NSW, it must have its own MSG, FM, and FLPKG components.

NSW file system. The NSW file system is built upon the file systems of the constituent hosts, which are used simply as a storage pool for NSW files. For each NSW file, the file catalog maintained by the WM contains an entry that includes the NSW name for the file, the location of the file in a constituent host file system, and various other file attributes. Like RSEXEC, the NSW file system supports the use of both partial and complete pathnames; but unlike RSEXEC, complete NSW file pathnames do not include a host name component.

NSW file operations are logically centralized in that the central WM file catalog is almost always used to resolve file references. (Exceptions occur with some tool-bearing host FM processes that maintain a "cache" of information about previous references to NSW files. This cache eliminates the need to interact with the WM when a tool refers to a file previously used by a tool during a particular session.) This approach is somewhat different from that of the RSEXEC file system, which makes more direct use of the constituent host file systems in the sense that it does not maintain a central file catalog independent of those of the constituent host operating systems. In RSEXEC, file operations are decentralized. The RSEXEC program acquires file catalog information with which it maintains the user's composite working directory, by interacting as necessary with various RSSER server programs. This direct use of the constituent host file systems is more feasible in the RSEXEC system because it is homogeneous, designed primarily to work with a network of similar systems—whereas NSW was intended to work with a heterogeneous network of dissimilar systems. On the other hand, the NSW design goal to isolate itself entirely from syntax specific to any host precludes direct use of the constituent file systems.

When a tool opens a file, a copy of the file is moved from its storage space into a workspace maintained by the tool's FM. The file manipulated by the tool is truly a copy, in that any modifications the tool makes to it will not be reflected in the NSW file maintained by the WM unless the FM or the tool explicitly returns the copy into the NSW file system. This "copy on open" mechanism prevents tools from sharing the same file dynamically in the way permitted by many modern single-host operating systems, such as Multics and Tenex. However, it does ensure that the NSW always contains an internally consistent version of each file.

Because of its modular structure, the NSW system architecture is potentially resilient to individual host failures. Indeed, the intercomponent protocols make continued system operation possible in the presence of failures in the front end or tool host processors. In addition, mechanisms have been developed to recover files trapped in a tool workspace by a tool-bearing host crash. When the crashed host is restarted, tool workspaces that were in use when the crash occurred are preserved in a way that allows a user to retrieve selected files, either upon restart or later.

At present the WM is the principal weakness of the system from a realiability point of view. Because the WM and its central data bases reside in a single host, the NSW system is vulnerable to failure of that host. A multi-host implementation of the WM function is being designed that would mitigate this weakness. In addition, it would also allow the system to expand gracefully as the number of users grows, by permitting the WM load to be distributed among several hosts.

The principal technical problem in the multi-host WM results from the fact that the WM data base is logically centeralized. To distribute the WM, its data base must be distributed. This distribution requires a synchronization mechanism that ensures that the distributed parts are consistenly maintained. Several synchronization mechanisms of this sort have been developed recently.[16]

Points of comparison

As of October 1977, an RSEXEC implementation supporting the features previously described had been operational for over two years. An initial NSW operating capability is just emerging, and implementation efforts are continuing. Some consequences of the different design techniques represented by the two systems give insight into alternative designs for network operating systems. By focusing on the differences between the systems we hope to illustrate the great flexibility open to the designer of an NOS.

Degree of host coupling. One point of comparison is the degree to which the constituent host computers are operationally and administratively coupled. How autonomous are the host computers in the larger context of the network operating system? RSEXEC is completely distributed in concept and implementation. Each constituent host maintains its own descriptive and state information about its own resources. Thus, any RSEXEC host can operate autonomously, although obviously with diminished scope, compared with cooperative operation with other RSEXEC hosts. Because no attempt is made to maintain a long-term system-wide data base of network resources, such autonomous operation may lead to conflicting interpretations of global file names. For example, the existence of multiple copies of a file is evident with RSEXEC only when reestablished dynamically each time an environment is configured for a user.

The RSEXEC hosts permit non-NOS computer activity on NOS resources. In particular, since RSEXEC uses local host file systems directly for maintaining its own file system status information, "network files" may be manipulated from outside the context of the network operating system. This provides more flexible access to these resources, but may also lead to occasional inconsistencies in network operation. These inconsistencies can occur because, as just mentioned, no attempt is made to keep long-term data bases of network resources, nor is file activity that occurs outside of RSEXEC synchronized with the short-term dynamically acquired RSEXEC data bases. The impact of such inconsistencies usually is not severe. Typically, an inconsistency results in the failure of an attempt to obtain a file because the RSEXEC file catalog entry for it is no longer valid. The RSEXEC itself is resilient to such failures; it merely returns an appropriate error indication to the user or his program.

The user can recover from the failure by instructing RSEXEC to rebuild the portion of his file catalog that is no longer valid. In principle, this reconstruction of the file catalog could be automatic. When a file operation fails after having been expected to succeed, on the basis of RSEXEC file catalog information, RSEXEC could automatically reacquire the appropriate file catalog information and reinitiate the operation. The current RSEXEC system does not behave in this way; instead it requires the user to initiate recovery action.

The total autonomy of the RSEXEC hosts has the further administrative implication that a user must register individually with each host whose resources he plans to use. This involves establishing valid accounts, acquiring sufficient resource guarantees, and setting up appropriate access controls for each constituent host. Once this has been done, RSEXEC facilitates the use of the resources on these hosts. When looking at RSEXEC in this context, one should keep in mind the initial concept of RSEXEC as a tool for helping users cope with the administratively autonomous, distributed environment brought about by the advent of the Arpanet.

In contrast to the distributed nature of RSEXEC, the initial concept of the NSW is a centrally administered service facility. The NSW has a logically centralized system structure supporting a collection of distributed system resources. The responsibility for managing the distributed resources lies with the WM. Since the WM maintains state information concerning all the distributed resources, a WM host must be part of every NSW configuration and takes part in every operation that utilizes a resource. Thus, autonomous tool-bearing host operation within NSW is not feasible, except in the special case where a WM host is also a tool-bearing host. However, since the state information is maintained apart from the tool-bearing hosts, NSW operation in the absence of a tool-bearing host cannot lead to data base and system inconsistencies. Maintenance of this information external to the tool-bearing hosts is also the basis for achieving uniform NSW file naming.

An individual computer system can be a tool-bearing host within NSW and at the same time directly service non-NSW users. However, the resources supporting the computer as a tool-bearing host are dedicated exclusively for this purpose, and cannot ordinarily be manipulated from outside the NSW environment. This too helps maintain the integrity of the globally maintained system resource data base.

The administrative centralization of network resources in NSW means that procedures for establishing access rights to these distributed resources are quite simple. One merely negotiates with a single NSW administrative organization to arrange potential access to all NSW resources. The logical centralization of authentication, resource allocation, and access control functions within a single component simplifies the software implementation of these functions. It also means that a convenient framework is available for preparing a single accounting of NSW resources utilized by an individual user.

Visibility of distribution. An important issue to resolve in the design of a network operating system is the nature of the interface to the network resources as seen by a user or a program. Part of this issue is the degree to which the distributed nature of the underlying system is visible. At one extreme is complete invisibility, where a user is not necessarily aware of the network operations being peformed on his behalf, nor is he able to exercise direct control over the use of distributed resources. At the other extreme is complete network visibility, where the user is aware of the network and its constituent hosts, and must directly assert control over the selection of resources to service his requests.

The NSW attempts to mask almost all details of network operation for the user, and thus tends toward the invisible end of the design spectrum. This position is based on the belief that dealing with the network or the constituent host systems at any level would impair a user's ability to easily utilize combinations of software development tools. The NSW system itself currently assumes all responsibility for selection and placement of system resources, without notifying or consulting the user. Neither the syntax nor the semantics associated with the NSW user interface includes any provision to specify actions directly relating to the distributed nature of the system. (However, the network aspects of the system intrude somewhat into the user's conceptual model in such areas as the movement of files between NSW file space and secondary storage not under NSW control, and also with the use of tool workspaces. The visibility in these areas represents dealing with the operational realities rather than a change in philosophy.) As a result, all network resources are uniformly and easily accessible within a simple user framework.

A number of factors suggest that a more visible approach to network systems is sometimes more appropriate. In currently available systems, performance frequently decreases appreciably with access to remote resources. Similar resources may have slightly different characteristics on different host types. Additionally, certain operations may be supported only for co-located entities—that is, resources in the same host. For these and other reasons, some system designers have opted for user interfaces that acknowledge the distributed nature of the system and allow users to influence, if not specify, resource selection patterns. Usually coupled with this is a set of judiciously selected system defaults, which specify certain "standard" resources if the user's command omits them. These are chosen to involve the user as little as possible in resource selection decisions. RSEXEC is visibly distributed; users deal with the distribution in terms of physical host names. It also provides mechanisms for operating in an NSW-like fashion where the user is not compelled to specify details relating to distribution.

Extendable program set. Although the designs for both RSEXEC and NSW permit users to execute programs on the network hosts, there are somewhat subtle design differences between them. For RSEXEC, the object program that is to be executed is obtained from the distributed file system. To add to his collection of executable programs, a user need do nothing more than create a new network file. In NSW, however, the object program that a user can execute can be selected only from a tool list, separately maintained by the WM for the entire system. New programs can be added to the available tool set only by the NSW administrative staff. Although at first this might seem arbitrary, it is a result of the NSW philosophy of providing access only to "well debugged, documented programs," and of extending the concept of managing software projects to include the ability to control the use of certain programming tools.

The somewhat closed tool set supported by NSW exemplifies another distinguishing characteristic. NSW is not designed to be the execution facility for completed software, nor to be a general purpose computer utility. As mentioned earlier, its purpose is to support software development. The software created within NSW is meant to be exported to machines outside of the NSW domain for production runs. RSEXEC was conceived in more general terms, and can be viewed as an attempt at a self-contained system which would ultimately lead to a general-purpose computer utility.

Implementation strategies. There are several alternative NOS implementation strategies. One approach is to determine the operations basic to the NOS and implement them directly on the hardware base. Another strategy is to use the basic functions provided by the constituent host operating systems as the building blocks for the NOS; any operations required for the NOS not provided by the base operating system must be included in the software that implements the NOS. This approach was chosen for both RSEXEC and NSW implementations in order to take advantage of the large investment in proven base operating system and application-level software. Furthermore, for these systems the first approach was viewed as infeasible, particularly for NSW, which utilizes several different base hardware systems. However, building upon the hardware base might have resulted in a set of basic functions somewhat better matched to the needs of the NOS.

An example of such a system is Mininet,[17] a special purpose system designed for transaction processing on distributed data bases. This implementation approach is feasible, in part, because the hardware on which it runs is homogeneous, and because there is no large investment in existing application software.

Because they are built upon existing operating systems, neither RSEXEC nor NSW directly performs certain traditional operating system functions, such as processor scheduling or memory management. Rather they rely upon the underlying operating systems to provide these functions. The emphasis of both implementations is to provide the expanded functionality, such as distributed file systems and interhost interprocess communication, required to support users in a network environment.

Another aspect common to both systems is the use of processes to structure the implementations. For example, the RSSER program runs as a service process on each site that participates in RSEXEC. Processes are used to an even greater extent in NSW, where, for example, WM, FE, and FM are all separate processes. The use of processes is attractive for several reasons. First, it isolates one function from the effects of another. Second, the resulting logical separation forces a more explicit definition of the interactions between NOS components.

An NOS for personal computers?

Despite their different and sometimes very specific design goals, RSEXEC and NSW do exhibit general approaches to many of the common problems inherent in building a network operating system. They also have in common the use of large, general-purpose, shared computer systems as basic building blocks. But just as a technological base for such systems is becoming established, other factors are causing reappraisal. For example, system economics are apparently changing, in a way which reduces the need for large, costly system hardware shared by many users, and which leads to the feasibility of dedicated, general-purpose personal computers.

Although hardware economics were the prime motivation for developing large shared facilities, users soon discovered that the systems could also support other forms of sharing. The ease with which users could share programs and data of all forms within these systems has left an indelible impression and set an irreversible trend. Because of this need to share, the widespread use of personal machines is likely to stimulate even more demand for systems that couple the operation of such machines. Thus, a whole new set of NOS design issues providing new challenges for system designers can be expected. ■

Acknowledgment

This work was supported by the Rome Air Development Center under contract number F30602-76-C-0425, and by the Advanced Research Projects Agency of DOD under contract No. N00014-75-C-0773.

References

1. L. G. Roberts and B. D. Wessler, "Computer Network Development to Achieve Resource Sharing," *AFIPS Conf. Proc., Vol. 36, 1970 SJCC,* pp. 543-549.
2. R. B. Hovey, "The User's Role in Connecting to Value Added Networks," *Data Communications,* May/June 1974.
3. W. W. Clipsham, F. E. Glave, and M. L. Narraway, "Datapac Network Overview," *Proc. Third International Conf. on Computer Communications,* Toronto, Canada, August 1976, pp. 131-136.
4. J. Davidson, N. Mimno, R. Thomas, D. Walden, W. Hathaway, and J. Postel, "The Arpanet Telenet Protocol: Its Purpose, Principles, Implementation and Impact on Host Operating System Design," *Proc. Fifth Data Communications Symposium,* Snowbird, Utah, September 1977, pp. 4-10—4-18.
5. E. Feinler and J. Postel, "File Transfer Protocol for the Arpanet," Arpanet Protocol Handbook, 1976 Edition, pp. 117-235, National Technical Information Service, Accession No. ADA027964.
6. R. H. Thomas, "A Resource Sharing Executive for the Arpanet," *AFIPS Conf. Proc., Vol. 42, 1973 SJCC,* pp. 155-163.
7. D. G. Bobrow, J. D. Burchfiel, D. L. Murphy, and R. S. Tomlinson, "Tenex, a Paged Time Sharing System for the PDP-10," *CACM,* Vol. 15, No. 3, March 1972, pp. 135-143.
8. R. H. Thomas, "JSYS Traps—A Tenex Mechanism for Encapsulation of User Processes," *AFIPS Conf. Proc., Vol. 44, 1975 NCC,* pp. 351-360.
9. B. P. Cosell, P. R. Johnson, J. H. Malman, R. E. Schantz, J. Sussman, R. H. Thomas, and D. C. Walden, "An Operational System for Computer Resource Sharing," *Proc. Fifth ACM Symposium on Operating System Principles,* published as *ACM Operating Systems Review,* Vol. 9, No. 5, November 1975, pp. 75-81.
10. S. M. Ornstein, F. E. Heart, W. R. Crowther, S. B. Russell, H. K. Rising, and A. Michel, "The Terminal IMP for the ARPA Computer Network," *AFIPS Conf. Proc., Vol. 40, 1972 SJCC,* pp. 243-254.
11. S. D. Crocker, "The National Software Works: A New Method for Providing Software Development Tools Using the Arpanet," presented at Consiglio Nazionale delle Richerche Instituto Di Elaborazione Della Informazione Meeting on 20 Years of Computer Science, Pisa, Italy, June 1975.
12. F. J. Corbató, J. H. Saltzer, and C. T. Clingen, "Multics—The First Seven Years," *AFIPS Conf. Proc., Vol. 40, 1972 SJCC,* pp. 571-583.
13. R. E. Schantz and R. E. Millstein, "The Foreman: Providing the Program Execution Environment for the National Software Works System," BBN Report No. 3442; also available as Massachusetts Computer Associates Document No. CADD-7701-011, January 1977.
14. P. M. Cashman, R. A. Faneuf, and C. A. Muntz, "File Package: The File Handling Facility for the National Software Works," Massachusetts Computer Associates Document No. CADD-7612-2711, December 1976.
15. NSW Protocol Committee, "MSG: The Interprocess Communication Facility for the National Software Works," BBN Report No. 3483; also available as Massachusetts Computer Associates Document No. CADD-7612-2411, December 1976.
16. R. Peebles and E. Manning, "System Architecture for Distributed Data Management," *Computer,* this issue, pp. 40-47.
17. J. Labetoulle, E. Manning, and R. Peebles, "A Homogeneous Network for Data Sharing—Modelling and Analysis," *Computer Networks,* Vol. 1, No. 4, 1977.

Resource-Sharing Computer Communications Networks

ROBERT E. KAHN, MEMBER, IEEE

Invited Paper

Abstract—**The development of resource-sharing networks can facilitate the provision of a wide range of economic and reliable computer services. Computer-communication networks allow the sharing of specialized computer resources such as data bases, programs, and hardware. Such a network consists of both the computer resources and a communications system interconnecting them and allowing their full utilization to be achieved. In addition, a resource-sharing network provides the means whereby increased cooperation and interaction can be achieved between individuals. An introduction to computer-to-computer networks and resource sharing is provided and some aspects of distributed computation are discussed.**

I. Introduction

THE INTERACTION between computers and communications has steadily developed over the last two decades. While many universities, government agencies, and business firms prefer to make use of thier own computers, an increasing number of people are using communication facilities to access commercial computer services [1]. Time-sharing and batch processing services are offered in most major United States cities or are accessible via telephone circuits, and communication charges for local telephone access to these services are, in general, substantially lower than the computer charges. As the use of computer services increases, the demand for reliable and low-cost means of communicating over wide geographic areas also increases.

For many years, networks of interconnected computers have been planned or under study, and more recently several have been under development [16], [18], [24]. A common objective underlying the interest in these networks has been to demonstrate that economic savings or increased capabilities are possible by sharing computer or communication resources. Program access to specialized data bases is an important example of resource sharing in a computer-to-computer network.

The growing usage of these data-processing services and the objective of sharing resources raise communication issues far more extensive than those of achieving increased capability and lower costs in the telephone network, or developing improved communication services [2]. They involve a num-

Manuscript received June 7, 1972; revised August 1, 1972. This work was supported by the Advanced Research Projects Agency of the Department of Defense under Contract DAHC-71-C-0088.

The author is with Bolt Beranek and Newman Inc., Cambridge, Mass. 02138.

Reprinted from *Proc. IEEE,* vol. 60, pp. 1397–1407, Nov. 1972.

ber of complex regulatory issues, the need for common methods of access to and interchange between data-processing systems, the pooling of computer resources for increased utilization and reliability, the provision of specialized services, data conferencing, and so forth. A set of associated regulatory issues involving telecommunications policy has been raised and is under intensive study. Are separate common-carrier data networks desireable or not? What is the most effective way to plan for interconnection of data networks and how should their usage be tariffed? (Some of these questions are discussed in the paper by S. L. Mathison and P. M. Walker, this issue.)

It is too early to accurately predict in what way this interaction of computers and communications is likely to evolve. The technology is changing rapidly, and regulatory policies are in flux. If communication costs are not to dominate the overall cost of using remote data-processing services, technological advances must allow communications at substantially lower per bit costs than are possible with the current switched telephone plant.

In this paper, we present one view of computer communications network development and explore a number of the important issues in distributed computation which have arisen. This paper is neither a completely general treatment of computer networks, nor a full case study, but rather it contains selected aspects of the two. The reader will no doubt be able to identify where general considerations give way to specific ones derived primarily from the author's experience with the development of the Advanced Research Projects Agency Computer Network (ARPANET) [7], [8]. It is impossible for this to be an exhaustive treatise, or even a comprehensive one, and no such attempt is made.

II. Distributed or Concentrated Resources

Many economic factors support the conclusion that geographic "clustering" of computers is a desirable strategy for computer service organizations [9]. One possible advantage is better equipment utilization due to the pooling of resources. Clustering implies that a single maintenance staff (which is often underutilized) and scarce system personnel can support more equipment, more reliably, and that space, auxiliary equipment, and overhead can be consolidated. In fact, several commercial time-sharing firms have already chosen to concentrate their computer resources in a small number of geographic areas. In contrast, however, many individual research or development machines under private or government ownership are distributed throughout the United States. The valuable resources on many of these machines provide a strong incentive for them to be made available to users and computers at many other locations [10], [11], [33].

The location of computers at a few geographic locations requires that both local and remote users be provided with an economic and reliable way to access the service. The switched telephone network currently appears to be a poor candidate to provide the long-distance communications service. In addition to being considerably more costly than local service, the error performance of long-distance circuits is degraded from shorter circuits and is insufficient for many computer applications. In addition, frequent disconnections, busy signals, etc., during peak traffic hours often make its usage inconvenient. These factors, coupled with user desires for increased bandwidth, lower setup times, and more suitable tariffs, have encouraged several vendors to competitively enter the common-carrier market [28].

The tariffs and the technical characteristics of the circuit-switched telephone network reflect the nature of voice communication requirements that are quite different from those of computer communications. Due to the "bursty" nature of computer traffic and the extremely low utilization of a typical voice-grade circuit by a terminal, a substantial portion of the data-communications capacity in a circuit-switched system is simply not used. This results in inefficient utilization of telephone company resources from the users' point of view. Frequency- or time-division multiplexing techniques have been usefully applied for deriving individual channels, but the statistical nature of computer traffic makes fixed allocation strategies such as these inefficient or unacceptable.

On the other hand, statistical multiplexing techniques allow these circuit resources to be more widely shared, at the possible expense of occasional delays in transmission. Message switching employs a generalized form of multiplexing for a network environment that allows all circuits to be shared among all users in a statistical fashion without being allocated in advance. (Multiplexing is the subject of a separate paper in this issue by D. R. Doll.)

This has been the motivation for the development of new communication systems as well as combined computer communication networks. The construction of both common-carrier data-communication systems and "private" networks (using leased common-carrier facilities) is a natural outcome of the need for economic and reliable communication between users and geographically distributed computers. In addition to potential cost savings, many of these networks provide error control, as well as asynchronous operation, local echoing, speed, and code conversion, which are better suited to data communication with computers than use of the telephone network alone. A reevaluation of the tariff structures for data communication has recently been undertaken by the FCC, and efforts are being made to provide the public with data-communications service having lower error rates, smaller service charging intervals, and faster setup times than the switched voice network currently provides.

III. Computer-to-Computer Communications

A computer network is a complex collection of many types of resources, including data bases, programs, operating systems, and special-purpose hardware, all of which are capable of being accessed from any other resource in the net. Computer-to-computer communication is necessary to achieve effective resource sharing, but the ability to transfer information between machines does not automatically result in useful machine-to-machine interactions. Aroused by the exciting possibilities in using multiple machines, system designers have recently begun to provide the major technical effort required to achieve effective computer-to-computer communication. The existence of the ARPANET is having precisely this effect, and as a result the extent of computer-to-computer interactions is certain to grow substantially in the next few years [6].

The ARPANET is one of the most advanced examples of a computer communication network [8], [16], [18]. It consists of a geographically distributed set of different computers, interconnected by a communication system based upon very fast response (interactive) message switching. This network was developed to ultimately allow economic and reliable sharing of specialized computer resources. The ARPANET has demonstrated the feasibility of message-switching technology, illustrated its advantages, and fostered the development of techniques for computer-to-computer communication. It is interesting to note that the ARPANET was originally designed with the notion of computer-to-computer communication in mind. It has subsequently been extended in capability to allow users with terminal equipment but no computer to connect to the net and communicate with computers and other users. In this sense, the ARPANET has taken the opposite approach from every other network designed with user access originally in mind.

For many years, the National Physical Laboratory (NPL) in England has experimented with the use of "single packet" messages for switching in the "local area of a data communication network" [31]. A number of terminal devices were successfully interconnected into a local network at NPL, and recently they have been concerned with extending the local network into a distributed network [30]. A computer-to-computer network is also under development in France to allow data sharing without costly duplication of files and its attendant problems of control, updating, security, etc. Central files, each accessible via a local computer, will be made accessible to other computers and hence to an extended user community. This network is expected to use a message-switching technique similar to that used by the ARPANET in the United States. In addition, networks are under design or development in other countries (e.g., Canada and Japan). Some of the European networks are described in other papers in this issue.

In general, the properties and structure of a computer communications network must reflect the overall requirements for which it was designed. This may consist of high-speed (megabit/second) circuits for rapid computer-to-computer communication, or low-speed (voice and telegraph grade) circuits for terminal access or slow-speed communications; it may be circuit switched or message switched, etc. Whatever its detailed structure, the network contains a communication system (private or common carrier) and a set of computer-system resources and users that interact via the communications system. This system is also called a communication subnet or simply a subnet for short. This organization not only characterizes the organization of geographically distributed networks, but can also serve as a model for the local structure of a single computer complex [3]. Its structure is therefore quite fundamental.

In operating a computer communications network as a "marketplace" for computer-related services, a number of important issues arise [34]. We allude to a few of them here. What criteria are appropriate to determine whether a service may be removed from the system? When and where should additional services be incorporated and what procedures are needed to maintain effective competition? What subnet changes are appropriate for changes in the distribution of resources? The total operational procedure should also include a strategy for utilization of the resources consistent with its intended functions (e.g., load sharing, data sharing, etc.).

An overriding concern of the network design is the overall reliability of the communications and computer resources. For a user to entrust his computing to a network, he must develop confidence in its availability when he needs it. It must be convenient to use and it must provide a believable guarantee to maintain standard and expected grades of service. An investment in time and energy to use a network resource can be negated by the failure to maintain a consistent service offering. Insuring that proper concern exists for the remote user of a computer resource is an important administrative problem that affects almost every phase of computer network development.

IV. Message-Switched Communications

Since the message-switching technology is not as well established as the circuit-switched technology, the fundamentals of its operation are reviewed in this section. Considerable discussion on the nature of these two switching doctrines is taking place. Are they merely different ends of a common spectrum (with a key variable such as packet size), or are they fundamentally different communication techniques? An argument in favor of their similarity is that both types rely on store and forwarding of data, whether a single bit is transiently stored, a byte-sized envelope, or a larger sized packet. The most significant external characteristics that "appear" to distinguish the two systems are that 1) circuit-switching systems are better equipped to maintain a time frame for users that require continuity in transmission, as in speech, while 2) message-switching systems allow speed and code conversion, thus permitting direct connection of and communication between devices of widely varying type. But it is possible to mask even these "seemingly" essential differences by the provision of a small amount of buffering and "byte manipulation" capability at the periphery of either system. It is actually the manner in which internal system resources are managed and utilized that provides a useful measure of comparison between them.

Briefly, in a circuit-switched network, the source and destination are connected by a dedicated communication path that is established at the beginning of the connection and broken at the end. This type of connection was specifically selected for use in switched telephony, where subscribers require a continuity in voice transmission and reception. Since the communication path remains fixed for the duration of a conversation, the output speech signal appears to be a time translate of the input speech signal as far as the ear can tell. In addition, for most voice conversations, the allocated analog voice channel is used in a fashion that seems reasonably efficient to the average user.

To establish a connection, the subscriber provides the local central office with an address which is used in setting up a path. Central office equipment detects off-hook, provides a dial tone, retains dialed digits, generates ringing, busy signals, etc. In the current telephone plant, long-haul circuits are primarily multiplexed analog channels. Routing selection is performed using a set of prespecified paths and usually based on the first few dialed digits. Call setup times generally take between 5 and 25 s, depending upon the number and type of central offices in the link and the amount of traffic. Recent experience has also indicated that reliability and overload problems are becoming increasingly prevalent in certain high-density population areas.

A message-switching system accepts, transmits, and delivers discrete entities called messages. In such a system, no physical path is set up between the source and the destination and no resources (e.g., capacity, buffer storage, etc.) are allocated to its transmission in advance. Rather, the source includes a destination address at the beginning of each message. The message-switching system then uses this address to guide the message through the network to its destination, provides error control, and notifies the sender of its receipt [17], [18].

A simple form of message-switching system employing a single central switching computer is commonly referred to as a "star" configuration and has all its lines connected to the central message switch. For many local applications this configuration can be quite practical. Three of its main disadvantages are 1) the central switch may be an unreliable link which will disrupt all communications if it fails, 2) the total circuit mileage for geographically distributed users to connect to the switch may be substantially larger than necessary, resulting in excessive communications cost, and 3) every circuit failure can result in some loss of user communications.

A distributed message-switching system is one in which many distributed switching computers are employed and the network control is decentralized in such a way that the failure of any switching computer disrupts communications only for its local customer. The distributed system is usually more economic and reliable than a star configuration for handling geographically distributed users.

The components of a message-switching system are dedicated point-to-point communication circuits and switching nodes which interconnect the circuits in such a way that a message arriving on one circuit may be transmitted out another. Communication over a message-switched system occurs via a sequence of transmitted messages, each consisting of its address followed by text. The address is inspected by each node in routing the message to the next node on the way to its destination. In the ARPANET, one or more computers may be directly connected to a node and are known as Host Computers, or Hosts for short. The nodes are called Interface Message Processors or IMP's for short.

A distributed message-switched network, such as the ARPANET, contains no mass storage, and as little buffering in the nodes as necessary to utilize the full capacity of the communication circuits.[1] The network design allows a message to remain in the net only as long as necessary to transport it from source to destination; no long-term storage is provided in the communication system. Messages that cannot be delivered to the destination are simply not accepted into the net and must be retransmitted at a later time. Clearly, one or more Hosts on the net with low cost per bit bulk storage could provide or even be dedicated to providing long-term storage of messages with subsequent automatic retransmission.

The combinatorial aspect of the interconnection of large numbers of computers is an important consideration in network design. Each computer in a message-switching system is connected to the net via a single full-duplex channel to its IMP over which messages are multiplexed. This single connection to the network makes the computing service accessible to all computers and all users on the net. Furthermore, all users and all computers on other digital networks can access this computer by the simple expedient of a single interconnection between nets. Thus not only is complete digital access possible, it is achieved in a strikingly economic way for each installation. This technique solves a massive combinatorial access problem with a single economic stroke.

In Fig. 1, we show the communications portion of the ARPANET as of April 1972 when it consisted of twenty-four nodes and 28 circuits. Since that time it has grown to over thirty nodes. Each node is a possible source and destination of

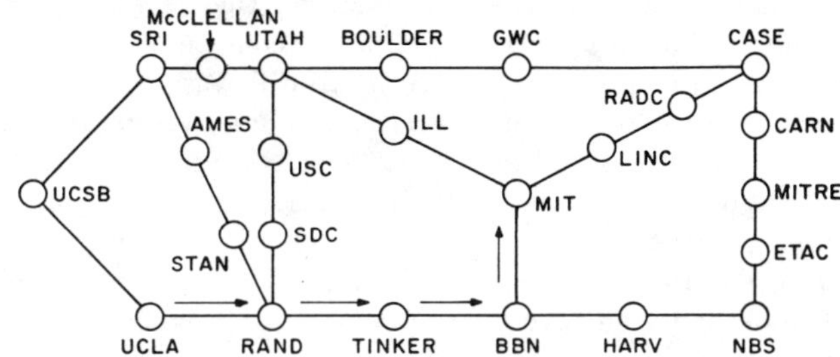

Fig. 1. Routing a message through the ARPANET.

messages. We assume (for the moment) that messages may be of variable length up to a maximum of 1000 bits,[2] and are known as packets while in the network. The path taken by a packet traversing the net from node 1 (UCLA) to node 6 (M.I.T.) is indicated by arrows in the figure. The circles indicate the nodal processors and the lines indicate synchronous point-to-point circuits. The message enters the net at node 1, which examines its address and decides to transmit it out its circuit to node 7 (RAND). Upon receipt, node 7 examines the address and decides to send it to node 21 (TINKER), which in turn sends it to node 5 (BBN) which sends it to node 6 (M.I.T.). Node 6, discovering the message is for itself, replaces the destination address by the source address (which is carried along by the message-switching system) and "delivers" the message. The text of the message thus appears at the destination exactly as it was transmitted and the address portion identifies the sender. After delivery, the sender is notified of its receipt by a small message that goes back across the network.

An important part of a computer network design is the specification of the location and capacity of all circuits in the net. Fifty kilobit/second circuits are currently used in the ARPANET to achieve an average delay of 0.2 s or less. Programs have been developed that iteratively analyze various possible network configurations and select reliable high-throughput low-cost designs through the use of circuit-exchange heuristics [20], [22]. Analytical techniques have been developed for estimating the average transit-time delay under assumed traffic loads. These techniques show that the delay remains almost that of an unloaded net until the capacity of one or more "cutsets" begins to saturate [7]. (Network optimization is the topic of a paper by H. Frank and W. Chou in this issue.)

An important design consideration is the method for dynamically selecting routes. (We assume that routes are not allocated in advance.) A central controller could provide the routing information and distribute it to all the processors, or the processors could collaborate in computing the routing information directly. This is but one of many instances of a design choice between distributed and centralized control. In the initial ARPANET design, the route selection is performed independently by each IMP according to a distributed routing algorithm. Routing information is stored in a table and individually maintained by each IMP for rapid look-up. It identifies the output line to select for each destination and is updated according to a rule evaluated periodically (e.g., every half second). It could also be evaluated asynchronously (whenever status changes occur) or a combination of both. In the

[1] The Defense Departments Autodin network, however, employs mass storage in the communication network for deferred retrieval and delivery of messages.

[2] In the ARPANET, messages may actually vary up to 8095 bits in length.

simple algorithm used in Fig. 1, each IMP sends the message on its choice of a path with the fewest intermediate IMP's and, using the update procedure, each IMP adapts its routing to other IMP and circuit failures.

A simple method for implementing this algorithm is for each IMP to keep a table with the count of the number of IMP's on the shortest path to each destination, which it frequently transmits to its immediate neighbors. Each IMP also announces to its neighbors that it is 0 IMP's away from itself. Upon receipt of the routing information from its neighbors, the IMP increments the neighbors' counts and keeps the lowest value for each destination.

Each IMP buffers a packet until receipt is acknowledged by the adjacent IMP. A cyclic checksum, generated in hardware by each IMP, is appended to the transmitted packet for error control. If an error is detected by the hardware at the adjacent IMP, or no buffer space exists, the packet is simply discarded and will shortly be retransmitted by the neighboring IMP when a condition (such as a time-out) occurs and no acknowledgement is received.

The design of an efficient network without mass storage requires that the number of buffers be kept to a minimum, and that they be used so that each IMP is able to use its circuits efficiently and to their maximum capacity. This means that the minimum number of buffers must be at least as large as the number of full-sized packets which must be stored from the time one full-size packet is transmitted until its acknowledgment returns. This number is determined by the circuit propagation delay, the packet size, and the circuit data rates, as well as the total number of circuits. To utilize these buffers efficiently, stored packets must be quickly released upon receipt of their acknowledgement or activated for retransmission, as appropriate, in a timely way.

Each IMP contains only a small amount of buffering for messages in transit and no mass storage, and a flow control strategy is needed to insure that the IMP's do not become "congested" thus preventing useful data from being communicated. This situation is particularly apparent if the network design allows the source or the destination to temporarily stop the transmission or reception of data and then continue without a loss of messages. This is appropriate to time-sharing computers, and is used in the ARPANET, because it allows occasional delays to occur, for example, while a word is stored in memory or a procedure is activated by the processor. In practice, a Host can neither guarantee to accept all messages at their instantaneous arrival rate, guarantee not to crash while receiving heavy traffic, or expect the transmitting Host to buffer messages should he prefer to discard them upon receipt. In particular, flow control is necessary to protect the network against the sudden dispatch of a larger number of messages to a single destination than it is prepared to accept [13].

An often overlooked but important consideration in the network design is whether or not to keep the circuits fully loaded even in the absence of maximum traffic. For instance, should "test messages" be continuously transmitted or only periodically transmitted to check circuits? Under light traffic loads, is it desireable to transmit duplicate packets and accept the first one with a valid checksum, in order to reduce occasional retransmission delays or to improve the response time on a very noisy circuit? For land-based circuits, the extra traffic during otherwise light loads appears to be acceptable and desireable to reduce delays on noisy circuits. The extra processor capacity is ordinarily available for heavy traffic in any event. For multiaccess satellite circuits, however, the extra traffic during light loads may interfere with other processors sharing the same channel.

In an unloaded net, the transit time is determined primarily by the number of IMP's encountered in the routing and the time for the packet to pass from one IMP to the next. This, in turn, is determined directly from the packet length, the circuit data rate, and the speed of light propagation delay. Under increasing traffic loads, the transit time also begins to increase due to occasional delays in the IMP's. However, if the network is designed to begin rejecting the further input of traffic as the capacity limitation of the network is approached, these delays can be kept to a few times that of an unloaded net. Traffic is thus queued outside the net (rather than allowed to enter and be queued inside the net) so the nominal transit time during peak traffic is not very different from that experienced in an unloaded net. In these cases, an attempt must be made to insure that the effective bandwidth is shared "fairly" among all the competing sites.

Network usage generally requires a combination of short transit times for interactive usage and high bandwidth for file transmission. These two objectives may be attained with single-packet messages. To achieve interactive transit times, no setup delay must be incurred. A simple way to achieve this is for the source IMP to retain a copy of each packet which is nominally discarded after the delivery is made, but retransmitted when, for lack of buffer space, the original is discarded at the destination IMP. To achieve high bandwidth, enough messages must be allowed to enter the net between source and destination so as to fill the "pipeline," but this flow must be able to be readily quenched at the source when the buffer space at the destination IMP begins to fill.

The current ARPANET design actually allows variable length messages with a maximum size just over 8000 bits. The message is partitioned by the source IMP into separate 1000-bit packets to speed its transmission through the network. Each packet makes its way to the destination independently where it may conceivably arrive out of order. These packets could be reassembled into the proper order by the destination Host (using sequence numbers), but when the assumption is made that the communications net should preserve sequencing at least at the level of a single process-to-process conversation, the IMP's are obliged to reassemble the packets. The destination Host thus receives the text of each message exactly as it was transmitted in a single-block transfer.

When these larger messages are used and the IMP's undertake the responsibility for reassembly, yet another type of congestion phenomenon called reassembly lockup is introduced [13]. The flow-control mechanism, which is used to prevent the backup of messages in the net, is also powerful enough to prevent the lockup problem. But in its application, it can subject long messages to setup delays and thus delay succeeding short messages from its Host.

If "sufficient" buffer space were available for reassembly at the destination IMP, there would be no *a priori* compelling reason for the subnet to preclude a Host from sending full 8000-bit messages (or even somewhat larger ones). However, the presence of 8000-bit messages may noticeably delay shorter messages from other Hosts 1) while it is being delivered to the destination, and 2) by tying up 8 buffers rather than 1 during reassembly. This provides one valid reason to restrict the Hosts to single-packet messages, if these delays become significant. However, as we indicate in Section V, there may be other factors which favor retention of the larger size.

If there is a fundamental distinction between circuit switching and message switching, it is undoubtedly in the way internal resources are managed. For example, circuit switching requires that network bandwidth as well as local control equipment and storage be allocated to a given transmission circuit in advance, whereas a message-switching system does not. Secondly, the presence of circuit-switched routes means that user messages are identified by their circuit and no user control signalling need accompany the transfer of information. In message switching, however, all record of activity (except accounting) associated with a message is contained in the message, which vanishes when the message leaves the system. This signaling information, in the form of an address, must accompany each message and the message must be examined and processed at each stage of the transmission process.

Two practical consequences of the difference are that the circuit-switched system usually requires a nontrivial setup time to allocate resources. Message-switched systems can avoid setup delays, but may introduce occasional variations in transit time. These delays can generally be maintained to within a few times the delay of an unloaded net, but wider variations may result from queueing delays outside the net, particularly under heavy traffic load. Under similar conditions, though, a circuit-switched user might fail to obtain a circuit and would incur this probabilistic situation on subsequent tries. Any allocated but idle channels are simply unavailable at this time to handle these overload conditions.

V. Network Use of Individual Computer Systems

The term network has been used and misused in a variety of ways. Some people have referred to the use of dial-up facilities to access a single computer as a network. Others have referred to any interaction between computers and a communication system as a network capability. Several distributed networks were developed to allow simple forms of communication between identical machines using standard dial-up or leased voice circuits, thus providing a convenient way to transfer jobs and files and to maintain and update the systems in the net. This latter application exemplifies a true networking activity, even though it only concentrates on selected aspects of computer resource sharing [19], [21].

In general, only a subset of the network sites possess computing power, and certain of them will offer regular service to users via the network. Other sites may choose to offer service only on a limited basis, or to cooperatively interact via the net with selected co-workers, but not offer general service. This latter situation is more likely to occur for many specialized research facilities. In addition, large private computer centers as well as commercial firms may welcome the opportunity to connect their systems, since it offers a large potential market for usage of unused capacity.

Host service on the network ought to be as reliable as the communications, although this objective is often difficult to achieve. For example, in the ARPANET, total uptime of the IMP at any site is currently on the order of 98 or 99 percent, while Host availability is generally no higher than 90 percent. It is certainly possible to improve on this score; some commercial firms claim to provide over 99-percent availability of service, and certain private and government systems must obviously be operated with near-perfect reliability. The airline systems and the computers in the space program provide two key examples.

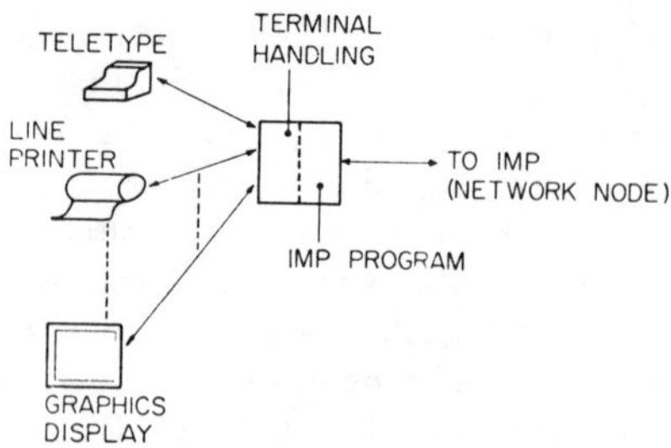

Fig. 2. Terminal IMP.

A. Network Access

In a network that supports computer-to-computer communication, user groups with a local computer can access another computer in the net by first logging into their home computer and then into the other computer, using the home computer in a transparent mode as a switch. However, this is an expensive way to access another computer since it incurs charges in two computers and ties up jobs in both. Furthermore, since Hosts may be unreliable, the connection is more vulnerable than a direct connection into the other machine.

Sites with expensive computer installations might deem it economic to depart from their machine if "equivalent" service can be economically obtained via the net. In general, such a site requires the ability to service local users with a full complement of terminals and peripheral devices, such as Teletypes, graphics displays, line printers, magnetic tapes, and possibly other mass storage. In addition, many sites with no computer will derive maximum benefit in connecting to a net if the full range of peripherals can be provided locally. Other users, however, may be satisfied with a simpler approach that provides terminal access to remote computers but does not handle peripheral devices other than line printers.

For this latter class of users, an addition may be made to the IMP which allows a set of terminals to be directly connected. This addition consists of multiplexing equipment that collects characters from the terminals and packages them in the form suitable for delivery to the IMP. Likewise, it receives messages from the IMP and sorts the characters out to the various terminals. This addition requires hardware and software designed to make the set of terminals interface to the network as a "mini-Host," and this IMP is referred to as a Terminal IMP. (See Fig. 2.)

A more elaborate approach is appropriate for user sites that wish to support many different types of peripheral equipment. Since their characteristics and operation can vary widely, device-dependent programming is mandatory, and substantial buffering may be required for the higher speed devices. Furthermore, sites with mass storage will generally wish it to be accessible from other computers in the net, which generally requires the implementation of a full set of standard and specialized network protocols. These considerations make it appropriate to provide a separate processor devoted to the handling of peripherals.

This latter approach is particularly desirable for a site which is both a user site and a server site. The architecture of such a site should be organized so that if the serving site central processing unit (CPU) is down, local users can access other network computers and local mass storage can be accessed by them over the net. Similarly, if the local storage should fail, others across the net can temporarily replace them. If the net fails, local users can still obtain full access to the local system. Only if both the local CPU and the network fail will the users be unable to obtain computation.

Modularity and logical reconfiguration are conveniently achievable in this way. Substantial progress in the design of modular communication-oriented architectures can be expected from innovative usage of interconnection ideas [3]–[5].

B. User Requirements

Let us now turn our attention to the use of these facilities by the user. We note three potential locations where user computation can be performed—in the terminal itself, in the peripheral processor (or Terminal IMP), or in the Host computer(s). Although the bulk of the "pure computation" will undoubtedly take place in the Host computers, some aspects of the processing must, in general, be distributed. For example, local echoing is required to obviate the otherwise noticeable effects of speed of light propagation delay, as on satellite links. This raises the important question of location of functions in a distributed network. In other words, what intelligence is needed to allow distributed system usage and where should it be placed?

Let us concentrate on the echoing problem for the moment. As a general rule, a remote user should see the same output and otherwise obtain service from a remote Host as if he were a local user. To achieve this objective, the user's local system (programmable terminal, "mini-Host," etc.) must have considerable information available to it about each subsystem in use at the remote Host. For example, a simple local echo/remote echo strategy is generally insufficient to handle echoing for users on half-duplex terminals, or users on full-duplex terminals that prefer to type ahead. A remote user editing the character string ABCDEFG can delete the last three characters by typing successive delete characters (echoed as\) and he sees the output ABCDEFG\G\F\E. Using the system from a remote site with local echoing and typeahead he would see ABCDEFG\\\GFE.

More striking, perhaps, is the remote use of a debugging program DDT. To examine successive registers 120–123, a local user would first type 120/ to print the contents of the first register and then strike successive line feed characters to examine the successive registers. The system would respond with (say the contents are all zeroes):

120/ 0
121/ 0
122/ 0
123/ 0

and leave the cursor following the last 0. A remote user with typeahead and local echo would see one of several possible responses (depending on the remote systems response to a received line feed). Assuming the remote system echoes only the formatted data and the local system echoes linefeed as linefeed (no carriage return), the output would look as follows:

120/

0121/ 0122/ 0123/ 0.

In general, the local echoing system should have full knowledge of the time-varying syntactical operation of the subsystem in use. This requires feedback of information about subsystem break and separator characters, control signalling, special conventions, etc.

Each terminal has characteristics peculiar to it and a convention is required for a computer system to initially recognize a terminal. Although the remote computer could then convert to the characteristics of the terminal, it is far more manageable if each terminal could appear to the network as a standard terminal employing an agreed upon set of characters and signalling conventions. One such standard (developed for the ARPANET) is 7-bit United States of America Standard Code for Information Interchange (USASCII) with the eighth bit set to 0. In that scheme, the other 128 possible characters are reserved for special control characters. In addition, most terminals need attention to details, such as carriage return, keyboard locking and unlocking, interrupt signalling, and other peripherals indicate out of paper, buffer full, and may require complete two-way channel control, etc.

Local computation is therefore needed for the user's terminal to interact properly with other remote systems and their subsystems. At a minimum, his local computation must allow the user to 1) identify his terminal to the network, 2) select a destination Host, 3) select a transmission mode, 4) perform echoing and code conversion, and 5) allow the remote Host to be interrupted.

It seems probable that, in the long run, many terminals will contain mini-processors and thus user programming in a separate "mini-Host" will be unnecessary. (This is amplified in the paper on terminals by L. C. Hobbs in this issue.) However, until this possibility is a widespread reality rather than an expectation, users may be hindered if they are unable to provide local user code in one place or the other.

C. Message Processing

Before considering various examples of usage of a computer network, let us briefly indicate how messages are processed within the Host computers [15], [32]. Messages travel through several layers of protocol in the Host system. The first layer of protocol handles the IMP, activating I/O buffers, fielding control messages, etc. The second layer interacts with the local processes and remote Hosts monitor, allocating buffer storage, providing process identification, formatting control information, etc. Subsequent layers correspond to specific user-oriented functions, such as the standard network terminal, file transmission, etc.

The ARPANET Host protocol utilizes the notion of connections over which messages are transmitted. A connection must first be established before communication over it may occur. The Hosts at either end of the connection must keep full information about the use of the connection (which is obtained during its establishment) to handle flow control. This strategy appears to be close in spirit to telephone circuit switching.

A few limitations to this strategy are apparent [14]. An important concern is that it requires each Host to maintain resources in the form of connection tables that can become filled, thus preventing any further communication with that Host. In particular, a single process can attempt to establish its maximum limit of connections, although it cannot, in general, make full use of them at one time. Entries in this connection table are permanently allocated, and thus only a fixed number of connections can be established at any time.

A second limitation with the use of a connection table is that it can be vulnerable to error conditions and Host status, particularly since both Hosts must generally agree on its contents for flow control. Finally, the strategy requires the connection information to be used for termination, which means that information which otherwise would be nominally discarded by Hosts with limited space, must be retained merely to close the connection. These limitations, as well as others, may be obviated with a message-switched Host protocol [14].

The desired size of Host messages may have an important impact on the operating system as well as on the communication system. The original ARPANET design specification allowed individual messages to be as large as 8192 bits, a design choice based largely on intuition.

As the design specification originally stated [29]:

> . . . a packet is defined as the inter-IMP unit and Message as the inter-Host unit. A packet will not exceed 1024 bits in length. The IMPs must break all longer messages into multiple packets. Messages will be limited to 8192 bits so as not to require excessive buffer space.

Undoubtedly, this latter reference is interpretted as referring to buffer space in the IMP's, but it could equally well apply to buffer space in the Hosts. In particular, the argument defends why the size is not larger, but does not entertain the possibility that it ought to be kept smaller for any specific reason.

If there is a convenient maximum Host message size, it is probably a maximum-sized page, which corresponds to 1 K of 36-bit (or possibly 48-bit) words. However, transmission of such large messages (say 50 000 bits) to the IMP and from the IMP to the Host produces excessive delays for short messages queued up behind them, and provides a prime reason for Hosts to prefer that these long messages be subdivided into shorter messages. Since no experience with network software was available during the initial design, it was intuitively concluded that a shorter 8192-bit message was short enough. Interestingly, we note that two hardware paths between each Host and its IMP, one for short messages and one for long messages, could remedy this problem at some extra cost in hardware and buffer storage.

Since efficient transmission is possible with 1024-bit packets, it appears in retrospect that the selection of the larger message size may be unnecessary. The Host overhead in network communication increases with the number of messages, so there is some incentive for making all Host messages sufficiently large that a typical short transaction can occur in a single message. No evidence yet obtained by us indicates that 1024-bit Host messages would impose a limitation that is significant, but an increased demand for page transfers or the presence of higher bandwidth circuits could tip the balance more strongly in favor of a larger size. The jury seems to be still out on this issue.

VI. Applications of Multicomputer Interaction

Network utilization involving the combined use of two or more computers in a productive way began during the initial experimentation with the ARPANET. It has provided experience in the development of techniques for performing distributed computation and allowed some simple application areas to be identified. Some applications involving multiple computers have been discussed for many years, partly as a result of their inherent interest and ease of conceptualization. One important example is the access to specialized data bases that are only available from a remote source. Several information banks have already been developed or are under development, and their expected usage is being projected upward. Another example is in the use of "future" computer communication networks for handling the distribution and delivery of mail and other transient information. However, these applications are only beginning to develop in any significant way. Much effort has already been devoted to the study of topics such as concurrency and parallel processing, which may result in faster program execution and otherwise make efficient usage of available resources. We expect that computer networking will enhance these efforts. For other applications, the sensation of dealing with one system rather than two (or more) is overwhelmingly evident to the user and this pleasant feeling often generalizes to other multicomputer interactions as well.

Three areas in which applications have already occurred are briefly identified below.

A. File Transfer

The first application for combining two computer systems in the ARPANET in a nontrivial way involved the use of an XDS-940 computer at Stanford Research Institute (SRI) and a PDP-10 computer at Utah. SRI, anticipating the delivery of a PDP-10, began to use the Utah machine in the development of PDP-10 software.

At first a higher level language was developed. Source code was generated on the 940, converted to object code, and executed on the 10. Patches were made on the Utah machine during debugging and, periodically, an updated source and binary version would be generated at SRI and sent over the net. Subsequently, other higher level languages were similarly developed.

A simple protocol to handle file transfers was developed for the TENEX operating system [10] and has proven useful for transferring new subsystems and system revisions between TENEX sites. In addition, it has been a useful initial step to allow cooperating processes in two TENEX systems to share a single file.

In this protocol, the network appears as a device to which a file may be output or from which a file may be input. The two ends of the transfer must coordinate by having one end execute the input and the other end execute the output. This simple file transfer protocol requires the intervention of the user to log into both ends, assign a file name for the destination, invoke the proper format, etc. Other experience in the transfer of files has been recorded by the University of California at Santa Barbara, as well as by IBM, by Control Data and others [19], [21].

B. Remote Job Service

A simple example of a computer-to-computer interaction is provided by users who write, debug, edit, and store programs on an interactive time-sharing facility and run them on a separate batch processing system. While time sharing has created an interactive environment for programming and the development of programming techniques, batch processing systems, and small dedicated computers have maintained a predominance for performing extensive computations. The availability of both kinds of service in a computer-communications network provides a single user with convenient access to the best features of both. (See Fig. 3.)

While a user can become accustomed to using both services independently, he need not be required to physically collect

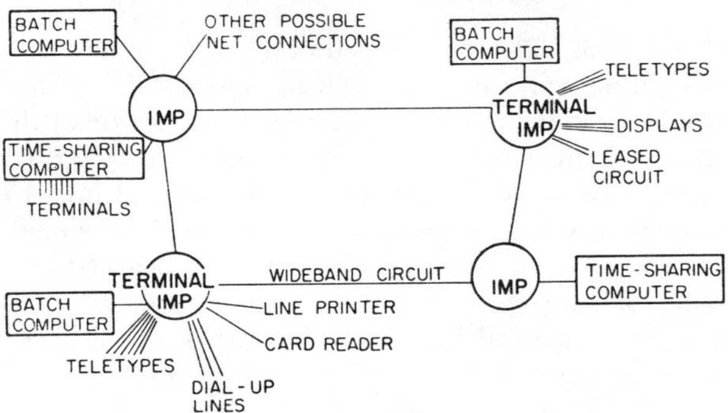

Fig. 3. A simple IMP network.

time-sharing output on tape or punched cards for submission to the batch system. The most convenient user option is for the interactive machine to submit his job to the batch processing machine under user initiated control. He can then specify the location for output to be stored or printed, revise the program in the time-sharing system, and resubmit it under fully interactive procedures from a single location, with no need to keep physical copies of files, program, etc.

For over a year the RAND Corporation had been using the ARPANET for remote job service from an IBM 360/65 at RAND to a 360/91 at UCLA [26], [27]. This facility was only accessible to internal RAND users until recently when it was replaced by a PDP-10, which allowed network users to create and submit jobs for remote service elsewhere.

Both the program and its relevant files must be transferred to the 360/91 before a job can be run. They are typically shipped together as successive "card images." The remote job service program will allow the users to start or stop the execution of his program, cause the system output to be stored on a designated file, or be output on a device such as a local printer. The user is also provided with options to check the status of the execution, receive confirmation and error messages that indicate its progress, and allow certain actions to be taken.

These facilities are used by RAND researchers in the generation and processing of simulated weather data. Weather modeling programs can be activated from a remote site, output from these programs can be temporarily stored, or shipped to a remote site for preparation and display. This separation of the computation into components is particularly appropriate when one part may be devoted almost exclusively to extensive numerical or symbolic computation and another part to user-related manipulation or preparation of the output data.

A "complex" weather simulation program requires many hours of computation on the 360/91, and thus is not well suited to rapid on-line activities such as the updating of a display. Rather, precomputed weather data (from the models) are retrieved from 360/91 disk packs (with operator assistance) and used by the PDP-10 for further processing and display. The availability of a high-speed parallel processing system such as the Illiac IV [33] may eventually allow real-time weather experimentation without operator intervention.

C. *Multiprocess Operation in Many Machines*

The combined use of two or more computers allows additional processing capability over the use of a single system. One such example is provided by the McRoss system [12] that coordinates the operation of two or more cooperating air-traffic-control simulation programs running in one or more TENEX systems. Each simulation program, called Route Oriented Simulation System (ROSS) [23], models the airspace of one air-traffic-control center in detail. To simulate the airspace of a Boston to New York flight, four simulation programs would be activated; one for the Boston terminal area, one for the Boston enroute area, one for the New York enroute area, and one for the New York terminal area. The four ROSS programs may be run simultaneously in as many as four TENEX systems in the ARPANET.

When a single machine is used to house all the components of a programming system, it has the disadvantage that computing will stop if that machine crashes. When one piece of a multicomputer programming system becomes unavailable, the other parts can learn to adjust to the change in configuration. A desirable objective is to provide enough backup information to enable the multicomputer programming system to be restarted in the event of a single Host failure and to proceed from a recent point in simulated time as if nothing had happened.

Other applications involving multiple computers are certain to arise for which simple examples are more difficult to construct. For example, as special areas of expertise develop, it is natural to expect that individual efforts by specialists also trained in the use of computers will produce new and useful resources on different machines. These resources may represent state of the art or proprietary developments that cannot be conveniently transferred to other machines, and must therefore be used at the site of their creation or where they currently exist. An important application for distributed computation is thus likely to involve the coordination of separate research projects into combined efforts that utilize these specialized or proprietary and hence nontransferable resources.

A second major application of distributed computation is likely to be the facilitation of interactive cooperation between people at different locations. Interactive cooperation may be regarded as an extension of normal voice communication to include the ability for several persons at different locations to "simultaneously" observe, communicate about, and manipulate both common data structures and programs. Since the people are assumed not to be colocated, the programs which support the interactive cooperation (such as display protocol routines) must also be distributed.

A third major application for distributed computation is in providing for conveniently feasible demonstrations of prototype systems to be performed from different locations. This technique can allow new capabilities to be readily conveyed without the inconvenience of moving the observer to a home site for the demonstration.

VII. A Distributed Operating System

A network in which basic differences exist between the computers at each installation is said to be inhomogeneous. It is possible to develop a standard network protocol for an inhomogeneous system that allows usage of various pieces of the system to be coordinated in a uniform manner. However, this task is one of substantial complexity that will probably require changes in system architecture and program design techniques before it can be fully realized. Even if it were a straightforward matter, it would not be generally useful to transfer portions of any one system to another, and standard operations that involve systems at a remote site must typically be performed at that remote site.

A collection of similar operating systems may also be organized into a virtual subnetwork of homogeneous computers that interact with each other in a uniform way. These systems are more easily organized into a single distributed operating system with common file systems, address space, naming conventions, etc. In general, every type of interaction between two systems in a homogeneous network must be evaluated to determine what is to be transmitted and what is to be remotely evaluated. No single answer will suffice for all applications. As we noted above, it is not generally possible to apply both alternatives in an inhomogeneous network. We consider some of the properties a system like this ought to possess.

The user accesses the distributed homogeneous network by logging into a distributed system rather than into a specific computer in the net. An appropriate machine is selected for him and he logs in with the standard log-in sequence for his home computer, including password, account number, and other information as required. Upon completion of the log-in sequence, the computer initiates a brief exchange with the users home computer to notify it of the impending job which it then proceeds to service. The home computer may then request that the job be transferred, alter credit or accounting information, or merely note the event.

Under conventional design constraints, the combined operation of several Host computers will require a separate job to be established in each machine. In a distributed system, though, it is important to allow access to each system without the user logging into each system individually. Furthermore, it is also desireable to permit certain transient activities to occur which do not tie up valuable resources or otherwise interfere with users on the system. The system merely performs the transient activity and logs the transaction into a suitable file for accounting purposes. Once logged into one of the Hosts, the user is able to access and utilize any programs, files, and most other facilities on other computers in the system as if they were all on one virtual machine.

The availability of many resources in this system makes it possible to achieve reliable operation when one or more resources are disabled. The user can be affected by failure in several ways. For example, his program or a piece of it may be aborted by machine failure or he may lose part or all of his files. The user may also find the local file storage to be unusable while running his job. If local storage is not initially available, he can specifically designate another system to store his files. Alternatively, he can allow the local system to store files in other Hosts and expect them to be returned without his knowing the identity of the temporary storage location. Obviously, a small amount of local storage is needed for this application. The distributed system thus not only makes resources more widely available; it can use them to provide increased reliability to a user.

A system designed to operate stand-alone may not be as efficient in serving its network users as in serving its local users. Certain performance improvements are obtainable by streamlining critical portions of the system code, attention to organizational details and to carefully engineered improvements to scheduling, the file system, etc. However, a major improvement in speed and efficiency may require structural overhaul of the system organization to allow for efficient process-to-process communication at high bandwidths and for efficient overall utilization of resources. In particular, the portion of the system devoted to protocol and message handling (byte manipulation) can consume a considerable amount of CPU time at high bandwidth. In a time-sharing system, particularly, these functions, which appear to be communication functions, can be usefully separated from the "computation" functions. This decomposition also allows more human engineered network interfacing, since a local CPU failure can usually be reported by the communications portion of the system if it remains up. The delegation of all protocol functions to a separate processor that can directly deposit into and retrieve from process buffers makes it possible for the operating system to communicate over the network at speeds at least an order of magnitude faster than before. This increase in capability is achieved by performing the protocol operations on the fly in a separate processor and by avoiding the unnecessary overhead in moving real-time data around in memory.

Techniques for computer-to-computer communication are still in their infancy and a great deal of exploration and experimentation is occurring in this area. How should programs be written to run in a network environment and what debugging and control techniques are suitable for distributed computation? What operating system architectures are appropriate to computer communication? The efficient utilization of a distributed operating system involves the sensible decomposition of a task into components. This requires timely access to status information and the ability to use this information wisely in the allocation of tasks to resources and in their scheduling. Just as the management of communication resources was central to the operation of a communication subnet, so will the management of computer resources be to the overall utilization of a computer network.

VIII. Conclusions

A principal motive underlying computer network development is to provide a convenient and economic method for a wide variety of resources to be made available and to be shared. Such a network provides more than an increased collection of hardware and software resources; it affords the capability for computers as well as individuals to interact in the exchange and processing of information.

It is not usually the case that a program written for one computer can be shipped to another computer and run there to completion, correctly. It may be possible in a number of cases where the machines are nominally identical, but it is usually the case that a program must be run on the machine for which it was written. It is thus desireable to strive for compatibility between at least a subset of the system resources, including the use of machine-independent higher level languages, the use of network wide standard protocols, or the use of nominally identical systems.

The development of communication subnets has been strongly influenced by the regulatory climate and the need for reliable and economic ways to achieve both remote terminal access and high bandwidth switched computer-to-computer communication. Message switching has emerged as a strong contender for computer-to-computer communications. It has been demonstrated to provide a highly reliable, error-free method of achieving interactive switched communications. Although its technical feasibility has been firmly established, its practical utility is under evaluation, and under close scrutiny it may prove to be a viable economic alternative to conventional circuit switching.

It is important that a communication system not preclude the possibility that separate or private data networks may be accessed through it in a standard and convenient way. A digital message-switched network has this property, while an analog frequency-based system may not. Incompatible data networks are clearly undesirable if all resources are to be mutually accessible. If separate data networks are jointly planned before development, at least at the interconnection level, they may be connected at a later date and viewed together as a single network that evolved by way of separate networks.

The great diversity of resources in a computer network may initially hinder its growth. Users must familiarize themselves with many different systems often without the aid of substantive interaction with systems personnel or clear and complete documentation. But the potential benefits of computer networks are sufficiently great that, over time, this obstacle will surely be surmounted, and in the process may lead to superior standards for system operation and documentation.

Computer networks provide a unique mechanism for increased participation between individuals. Participation in research and development using the distributed resources of a computer network can lead to the close cooperation between individuals who might otherwise have little incentive to work together. This interaction can further cross-fertilize the network community and encourage even higher levels of achievement through technical cooperation.

References

[1] "Pinched budgets promote growth of university computer networks," *Commun. Ass. Comput. Mach.*, vol. 15, no. 3, pp. 206–207.

[2] P. M. Walker and S. L. Mathison, "Regulatory policy and future data transmission services," *Computer Communication Networks*. Abramson and Kuo Eds. Englewood Cliffs, N. J.: Prentice-Hall, 1973, ch. 9.

[3] D. Farber and K. Larson, "The architecture of a distributed computer system—An informal description," Dept. Informat. Comput. Sci., Univ. of California, Irvine, Tech. Rep. 11. 1970.

[4] H. Baskin, B. Borgerson, and R. Roberts, "PRIME—An architecture for terminal oriented systems," presented at the AFIPS Spring Joint Comput. Conf., pp. 431–437, 1972.

[5] R. Davis, S. Zucker, and C. Campbell, "A building block approach to multiprocessing," presented at the AFIPS Spring Joint Comput. Conf., pp. 685–703, 1972.

[6] S. Crocker *et al.*, "Function oriented protocols for the ARPA network," presented at the AFIPS, Spring Joint Comput. Conf. pp. 271–279, 1972.

[7] H. Frank, R. E. Kahn, and L. Kleinrock, "Computer communication network design—experience with theory and practice," presented at the AFIPS Spring Joint Comput. Conf., pp. 255–270, 1972.

[8] L. G. Roberts and B. Wessler, "The ARPA network," in *Computer Communication Networks*, Abramson and Kuo, Eds. Englewood Cliffs, N. J.: Prentice-Hall, 1973.

[9] M. Beere and N. Sullivan, "Tymnet—A serendipitous evolution," presented at the 2nd Ass. Comput. Mach. IEEE Conf. Problems in the optimization of Data Communication Systems, Palo Alto, Calif., 1971.

[10] D. G. Bobrow, J. Burchfiel, D. Murphy, and R. Tomlinson, "TENEX—A paged time-sharing system for the PDP-10," *Commun. Ass. Comput. Mach.*, vol. 15, no. 3, pp. 135–143, Mar. 1972.

[11] F. J. Corbato *et al.*, "An introduction and overview of the multics system," presented at the AFIPS Fall Joint Comput. Conf., pp. 185–196, 1965.

[12] R. Thomas and D. Henderson, "McRoss—A multi-computer programming system," presented at the AFIPS Spring Joint Comput. Conf., pp. 281–293, May 1972.

[13] R. E. Kahn, and W. R. Crowther, "Flow control in a resource-sharing computer network," *IEEE Trans. Commun. Technol.* (*Special Issue on Computer Communications*, pt. II), vol. COM-20, pp. 539–546, June 1972.

[14] D. C. Walden, "A system for interprocess communication in a resource sharing computer network," *Commun. Ass. Comput. Mach.*, vol. 15, no. 4, pp. 221–230, Apr. 1972.

[15] *The Host/Host Protocol for the ARPA Network*, Network Informat. Center, Stanford Research Institute, Menlo Park, Calif., Document No. 7147.

[16] L. G. Roberts and B. Wessler, "Computer network development to achieve resource sharing," presented at the AFIPS Spring Joint Comput. Conf., pp. 543–549, 1970.

[17] P. Baran, S. Boehm, and P. Smith, "On distributed communications," RAND Corporation, Santa Monica, Calif., Series of RAND Reps., 1964.

[18] F. Heart, R. E. Kahn, S. Ornstein, W. Crowther, and D. Waldenk. "The interface message processor for the ARPA computer network," presented at the AFIPS Spring Joint Comput. Conf., pp. 551–567, 1970.

[19] A. H. Weis, "Distributed network activity at IBM," IBM Res. Rep. RC3392, June 1971.

[20] H. Frank, I. Frisch, and W. Chou, "Topological considerations in the design of the ARPA computer network," presented at the AFIPS Spring Joint Comput. Conf., pp. 581–587, 1970.

[21] W. J. Luther, "Conceptual bases of CYBERNET," Courant Symp. 3, 1970, in *Computer Networks*. Englewood Cliffs N. J.: Prentice Hall, pp. 111–116.

[22] R. Van Slyke and H. Frank, "Reliability of computer communication networks," in *Proc. 5th Conf. Applications of Simulation*, New York, Dec. 1971.

[23] W. Sutherland, T. Myer, D. Henderson, and E. Thomas, "Ross, A route oriented simulation system," in *Proc. 5th Conf. Applications of Simulation*, New York, Dec. 1971.

[24] T. Marill and L. G. Roberts, "Toward a cooperative network of time-shared computers," presented at the Fall Joint Computer Conf., 1966.

[25] Project MAC Conf. on Concurrent Systems and Parallel Computation, Woods Hole, Mass., June 1970.

[26] E. Harslem. RAND Corporation, Unpublished Memo, 1972.

[27] R. Braden, Univ. of California at Los Angeles, Unpublished Memo, 1972.

[28] C. R. Fisher, "Introduction to the DATRAN switched digital network," in *Proc. Int. Conf. Communication*, pp, 23-1–23-3, June 1971.

[29] Request for Quotation (Interface Message Processors for the ARPA Computer Network), Defense Supply Service, Washington, D. C., July 1968.

[30] R. A. Scantlebury and P. T. Wilkinson, "The design of a switching system to allow remote access to computer services by other computers," presented at the 2nd Ass. Comput. Mach. IEEE Symp. Problems in the Optimization of Data Communication Systems, Palo Alto, Calif., Oct. 1971.

[31] D. W. Davies, K. A. Bartlett, R. A. Scantlebury, and P. T. Wilkinson, "A digital communication network for computers giving rapid response at remote terminals," presented at the Ass. Comput. Mach. Symp. Operating System Principles, Gatlinburg, 1967.

[32] "Specifications for the interconnection of a Host and an IMP," Bolt Beranek and Newman Inc., Cambridge, Mass. 02138, Rep. 1822, Oct. 1971.

[33] W. J. Bouknight *et al.*, "The Illiac IV system," *Proc. IEEE*, vol. 60, pp. 369–388, Apr. 1972.

[34] *Datamation*, pp. 36–46, Apr. 1972.

A SURVEY OF DEVELOPMENTS IN DISTRIBUTED DATA BASE MANAGEMENT SYSTEMS

Fred J. Maryanski
Kansas State University

Introduction

Distributed data base management systems extend the capacities of computing systems to give many people access to a wide range of information. These systems, which arise from the combination of recent important advances in computer networks with general-purpose data base management systems, should shortly represent another significant step in commercial system development. So it is not surprising that they have been the focus of much research and development activity in both the academic and industrial environments.

Distributed data base systems share many design problems with both single machine data base systems and computing networks; in addition, they introduce several new dilemmas.[1] For example, a completely generalized distributed DBMS would reside on a heterogeneous computer network with different data base systems available at various processors. Communications and data transfer would be possible among any nodes in the network. The realization of this goal is still several years in the future. However, considerable progress in both academic and industrial environments has been made.

Distributed data base classification

Development of a completely general distributed data base management system must evolve through several less complex forms (see table). It begins with data base management systems for single, general-purpose computers, the development of which is among the most significant events in computer science. Many such systems are commercially available. The next class is data base machines, which are special-purpose processors whose function is data management.[2] These two classes are combined, in a sense, in a network of two or more machines, one of which is dedicated to the data base management function. The dedicated data base processor, known as the *back-end machine*, may contain specialized hardware for firmware, or it may be a general-purpose computer.

Next in this classification is a special-purpose distributed DBMS. Several such systems have been implemented on computer networks, including medical information systems,[3,4] airline reservation systems,[5] and others. All the computers in such a system are essentially identical, with hardware and software designed specifically for the DBMS.

The next step in distributed DBMS development is a single software system running on a homogeneous network. This stage utilizes conventional facilities for communication between machines, which many hardware manufacturers provide, but requires the data base software to be enhanced for communication between tasks residing in different processors. This is different from the previous step in that the various processors in an airline reservation system, for example, are all performing the same task—maintaining an inventory of available seats. The problems of file allocation, privacy, and deadlock become quite complex at this level.

By introducing different brands of processors, the network becomes heterogeneous, and compatibility problems appear. Communication protocols and data conversion schemes are necessary for this extension.

Finally, the most general distributed DBMS has hardware obtained from multiple vendors, and accommodate users with different data base software systems. In addition to containing all the problems of the previously mentioned systems,

Reprinted from *Computer,* vol. 11, pp. 28–38, Feb. 1978.

these systems impose the difficult task of data base translation, which entails both structural and code conversion.

Today research is ongoing in all of the problem areas mentioned in this classification. Although some simpler systems are in development, only the first two or three can be said to be in production. Even the medical and airline systems cited have been built only on a one-shot basis, no two of them—even from the same manufacturer—being alike.

CLASSIFICATION OF DISTRIBUTED DBMS	
SINGLE GENERAL-PURPOSE COMPUTER	↑
SINGLE SPECIAL-PURPOSE DATA BASE COMPUTER	LEAST COMPLEXITY
ONE SPECIAL-PURPOSE COMPUTER COMBINED WITH ONE OR MORE GENERAL-PURPOSE COMPUTERS	
TWO OR MORE SPECIAL-PURPOSE COMPUTERS	
SINGLE SOFTWARE SYSTEM, HOMOGENEOUS NETWORK (IDENTICAL COMPUTERS)	
SINGLE SOFTWARE SYSTEM, HETEROGENEOUS NETWORK (NONIDENTICAL COMPUTERS)	GREATEST COMPLEXITY
MULTIPLE SOFTWARE, HETEROGENEOUS NETWORK	↓

Data base machines and back-end processors

The terms "data base machine" and "back-end processor" have recently been added to the computer lexicon. Since they have evolved independently, their accepted definitions overlap somewhat. A data base machine is a special-purpose computer dedicated to data base management; a back-end processor is a computer that performs the data management function for one or more different computers. Clearly, a data base machine can be used as a back-end processor.

One of the most common operations performed in a DBMS is using a key to locate data. Optimizing this operation naturally tends to make the DBMS more efficient. One approach to optimization is an associative processor; its parallel search capabilities outperform an inverted list structure,[6,7] which is generally regarded as the most efficient data base organization for searching on a conventional processor. A data management system using associative memory has been developed at Rome Air Development Center. The system uses the associative processor as a small, fast memory buffer. The data base is stored on conventional secondary storage devices and paged into the associative memory, thus permitting searches in the order of microseconds, although the page transfer rate is in the order of milliseconds. The CASSM project at the University of Florida[8] developed the concept of a context-addressable disk system capable of performing data manipulation in secondary memory without intervention by the CPU. Since the data base is stored on the associative machine, the excessive loading delay is eliminated. Similarly, at the University of Toronto, an associative processor called RAP has been designed;[9] its instruction set is a high-level relational data base language. By processing data operations at the machine level, RAP has the potential of overcoming the execution time problems that have hampered relational data base systems. RAP is designed to operate a data base of up to 100 megabits. This capacity can be extended with conventional mass storage devices.

The concept of a processor with data base primitives is also under investigation; one proposal, developed by Donald Anderson of Sperry Univac, places the data base functions in firmware, in a back-end machine.[10] This processor could either connect directly to a single general-purpose processor or act as a specialized data base processing node in a network.

The Datacomputer is a special-purpose data base processor developed at Computer Corporation of America for use in heterogeneous networks.[11] Its current version, which employs a DEC PDP-10 that provides data base service for the Arpanet, features an inverted file structure implemented in software. All requests for data base operations by the Datacomputer are specified in a high-level data base language. Since the Arpanet contains a variety of machine types, the Datacomputer must translate between various physical data representations and logical data structures. The Datacomputer relies upon the standard Arpanet communication facilities to exchange information with its host processors. Its high-level data base language can be viewed in this context as a standardized message facility.

Because of its ability to communicate with heterogeneous machines, the Datacomputer as implemented in the Arpanet is the closest existing approximation to a completely distributed data base system. The principle could be extended to geographically distributed data by placing Datacomputers at several points in the network and incorporating different software data base systems into the network. Communication between such different data base systems remains a major barrier to a completely generalized distributed DBMS.

Thus far, the discussion has centered upon a single data base processor or back-end machine. However, data bases could be managed with a complex of microprocessors.[12] One such system, called Infoplex, is presently under design at MIT. Intended as a highly parallel information management system, Infoplex functionally decomposes each high-level data base request into segments that are executed in parallel by the microprocessor complex. This concept of decomposition of data base requests could be applied at a higher level to a network of minicomputer data base machines which share the management of a data base.

The single host, single back-end approach has been implemented as a prototype called XDMS at Bell Laboratories,[13] with a Univac 1108 host to execute the application programs and a Digital

Scientific Corp. Meta-4 back-end for the data base functions. The software system was DMS-1100, which is derived from the specifications of the Committee on Data System Language (Codasyl). XDMS was the first working back-end system, and has provided impetus for considerable future work in this area.

that additional computing power becomes available at a relatively low price.

The simple front-end-plus-back-end configuration forms a module, or well-structured compact unit, to which new machines can be added easily, either sharing the power of the back end or in a stand-alone mode.

Benefits of a back-end DBMS

A back-end processor is the basic building block of a distributed data base system. Work presently under way suggests that back-end computers will appear as important commercial products in the near future.

The first versions of the back-end computers will be general-purpose minicomputers with software data base systems. The back-end machines will interface with IBM 360's, 370's, or similar machines, through conventional linkages. One the basis of the recent research advances outlined in the previous section and discussions with individuals in the data base industry, it would appear that later versions will include special-purpose data base machines and faster, more general interconnections.

The feasibility of a back-end DBMS in a data processing environment has been the subject of several reports, which indicate that a back-end DBMS can provide benefits in a wide range of areas, including higher performance, better reliability, more security, lower cost, and modularity.

Performance is the critical measure of a system. A back-end computer can ovelap its execution with the host machine, so that more computation can take place.[14]

The overall reliability of a DBMS is enhanced with a back-end processor, because the host and back-end can verify each other's operation. Therefore, machine errors can be detected either before or immediately after they affect the data base. However, a back-end DBMS also tends to reduce reliability somewhat, since the failure rate of a two-machine system is higher than that of a single computer.

If the back-end computer executes only data base functions, but no application programs of any kind, the data base is more secure[15]—primarily because software that spies on the data base cannot be constructed. However, such a back-end configuration does not solve all security problems. The privilege of executing an application program must be carefully guarded, and the security of the communication link must be maintained.

A back-end computer is economical in that it extends the life of a host processor. Its acquisition cost is an order of magnitude less than the upgrade cost of a large mainframe. Since it takes over a large amount of processing from the host, resources of the latter become available for additional processing. Furthermore, if the back-end machine is a general-purpose minicomputer, data base management is unlikely to occupy all of its resources, so

Organization of distributed data base systems

The function of the distributed data base system, the geographic distribution of the data, and the philosophy of the designers all influence the organization of the distributed system. Similarly, organizations can be classified in several different ways.

One classification is according to the geographical distribution of data bases and directories.[16] Either of these may be centralized or distributed under this scheme (Figures 1 and 2). Another classification is by the amount of redundancy—the data base is either partitioned or replicated.[17] A partitioned data base is spread across several computers, perhaps with one large central portion and several remote subsidiaries (Figure 3). When a large, active file is divided among several back-end processors in a distributed system, data accessibility increases—

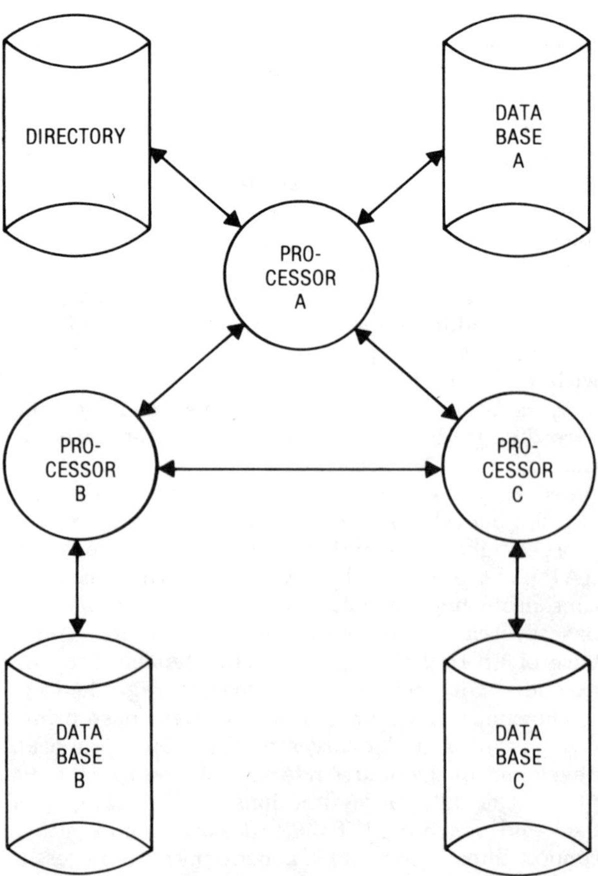

Figure 1. Distributed data bases, central directory.

at the cost of more control and communications overhead than is seen in a single data file in one computer. Efficient network software minimizes this overhead.

A replicated data base stores some portions of the base redundantly at different nodes in the network. Redundancy should probably be based upon accessibility, locating files at the machines where they are most likely to be heavily used. This technique reduces the amount of intermachine communication, which is often the limiting factor in distributed data base performance. In addition, redundancy offers increased access to the multiple copies of the data, readily available backup, and—since a copy can be located close to its point of use—decreased communication time.[18] On the other hand, redundancy imposes additional cost and complexity in updating a data file, and it requires additional storage.

Communication in a distributed data base network

A distributed DBMS is usually built upon a computer network. (Certain cases when a network is not involved are discussed later in this article.) Since communication time is a critical factor in the performance of a network-oriented distributed data base, an efficient communication mechanism is essential. Furthermore, the complexity of the network control software is related to the homogeneity of the machines in the network; if the software data base systems on conversing machines are different, then the network software must translate between the two.

In a message switching environment, certain information is essential for both the host and back-end processors.[16] The host communication task must have the identification of the back-end task; the data base name of the requested data; translation requirements; the interprocess protocol; and the mechanism for interpreting the response.

Similarly, the back-end communication task must have the type of message received; translation requirements; the mechanism to satisfy the data base request; identification of sending process; conditions for sending a response; and interprocess protocol.

A separation of the network communication and data base control functions has been proposed by Peebles at the Moore School of Electrical Engineering.[19] The proposal calls for a network control language for generalized intermachine communication,

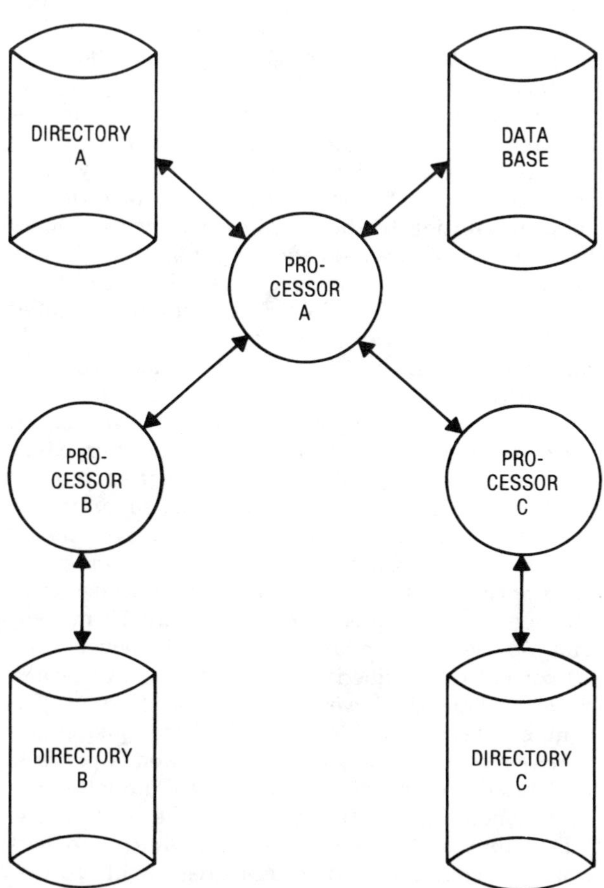

Figure 2. Centralized data base, distributed directories.

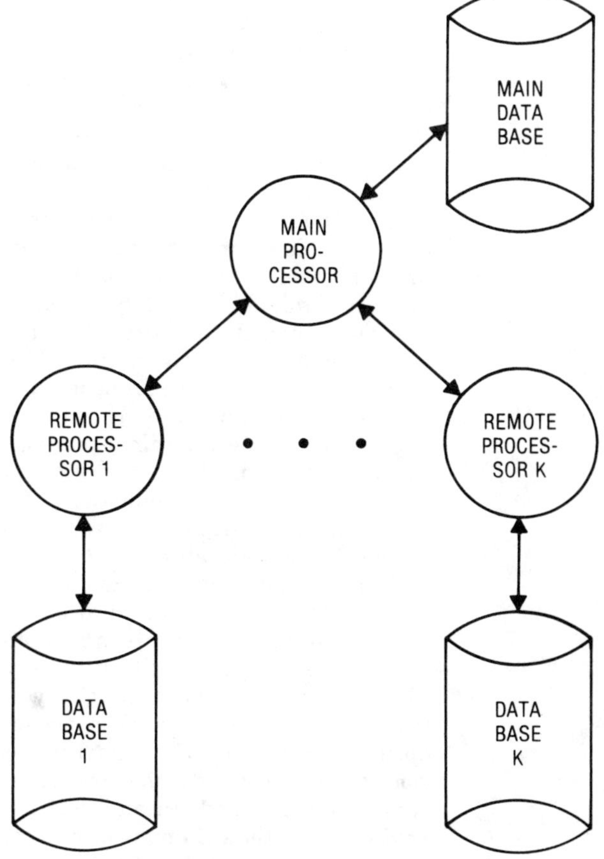

Figure 3. Vertically partitioned data base.

containing a translation mechanism and supporting a distributed DBMS.

A proposed interface between a data base management system and a network communication system would provide standard methods for intertask communication and a protocol for the transmission of information among processors.[20,21] In this system, the translation mechanism is considered a part of the data base software, not that of the network.

The Datacomputer[11] relies upon the standard Arpanet communication facilities to exchange information with its host processors. All communication occurs in Datalanguage, which can be viewed in this context as a standardized message facility. The Datacomputer performs all translations internally. However, the form of stored data is determined by the host machine.

File allocation in distributed DBMS

One of the key decisions to be made by a data base administrator is the allocation of data files among physical devices, so that all the devices are utilized equally. Therefore his file allocation policy requires information, actual or hypothesized, concerning file utilization. In many environments, data base behavior is dynamic, so that utilization patterns must be constantly monitored to ensure an acceptable file distribution.

When a data base is distributed over several machines, the file allocation problem is more complex than in a one-machine data base. In a centralized DBMS, poor file allocation results in heavy traffic and long waiting times on certain channels. Data must be allocated first among back-end processors and then among the devices attached to the back-end processors.

Three parameters have been proposed for file allocation algorithms in a distributed DBMS.[22] The first of these is the level of data sharing, which indicates whether the DBMS is partitioned or replicated, and if the latter, to what extent. The second parameter is the nature of the access patterns, which may range from inquiry-only to total update, and in some systems can vary significantly from time to time. The final parameter is whether the information on the nature of the access patterns is deterministic or probabilistic.

The usual approach in file allocation problems is to develop a generalized cost equation and then seek a file assignment to minimize that equation. At the highest level, the total cost is the sum of the costs of inquiry, update, and storage. Naturally both monitoring file utilization and reallocating files also cost money and occupy some machine resources; a balance between the cost of a non-optimal file organization and the cost of reallocation is necessary, with the cost added to the basic sum just mentioned. In addition, in a distributed environment, the communication cost of obtaining data from a file residing at another network node is an important factor. In some models, the cost is measured by linear programming techniques with some or all of the preceding factors as variables.

Allocation for deterministic patterns

At the present time, the results obtained for file allocation in distributed data base networks are for cases of static, deterministic access patterns, while research is under way on the properties of networks in which access patterns vary dynamically or are described by probability distributions.

The multiple file allocation problem for the static, deterministic case can be solved by determining the optimal allocation for the individual files.[23]

In a tree network, internode paths form no loops; therefore trees have no routing problems and are the optimal organization in a distributed data base when a single back-end processor is used with multiple hosts.[24] They also have less complex cost functions than more general network organizations.

A different computational approach to the optimal file allocation is a linear cost model that is similar to models used to determine the most economical location for plants and warehouses.[25] Developed by R. G. Casey at IBM this approach uses a search procedure that produces an optimal allocation. The report of this research includes some empirical steps that are intended to improve performance of the algorithm. This work, in effect, applied goal-oriented searching techniques commonly used in artificial intelligence work to the file allocation problem.

The relationship between access pattern and distributed data base organization yields cost equations for partitioned, partially replicated, and fully replicated data bases.[26] The network is assumed to contain, in addition to the usual communication links between processors, several very high speed links (memory-to-memory connections). Processors so interconnected form a cluster. A partially replicated configuration contains one copy of every data file for each cluster in the network, while the fully replicated case has a copy of a file at each node that accesses the file. With a cost equation based upon communication, storage, and translation costs, the intuitively appealing result is that in inquiry mode a replicated data base provides superior performance, while under heavy update, a partitioned data base organization is more efficient. Under the assumption that transmission cost is higher than storage cost, the breakeven points are 10 percent and 50 percent update. That is, if fewer than 10 percent of the queries are updates, the replicated data base has the lowest cost; if more than 10 percent but fewer than 50 percent of the queries are updates, the least expensive organization is partially replicated. For more than 50 percent updates, the partitioned organization would be the best choice.

Distributed data bases are not limited to networks of computers. It is quite reasonable to distribute a data base over the storage hierarchy of a single processor.[27] However, the storage devices, ordered in terms of access speed, must have direct access between each level and the next higher and lower levels (Figure 4). The most significant performance feature of this proposed storage arrangement is the buffering of data: If data is found at any particular level, it is also present at all higher levels (more remote from the processor). Probabilistic models indicate that buffering provides performance benefits for sequential, random, and linked-list file organizations.

File organization has been studied more thoroughly than other subjects related to distributed data bases. Although many linear programming methods have been proposed for the determination of optimal file placement, their practicality in data processing environments is a matter of conjecture. The main problems are that the algorithms require precise usage statistics and do not consider constraints imposed by security or company policy.

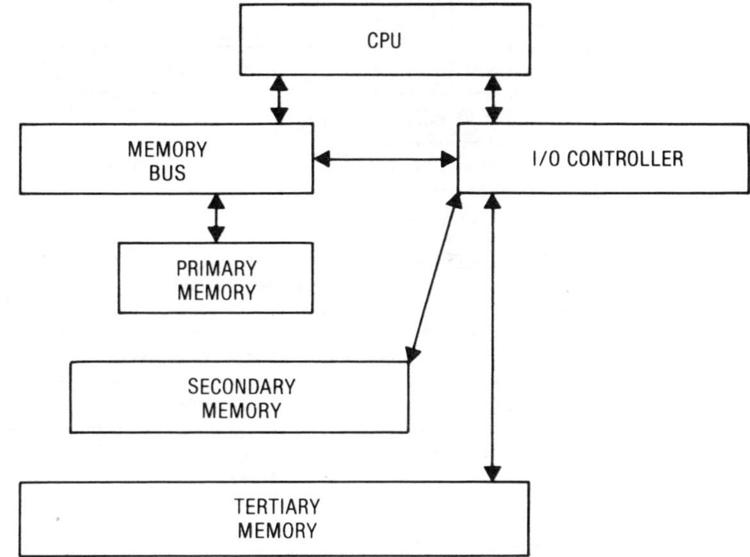

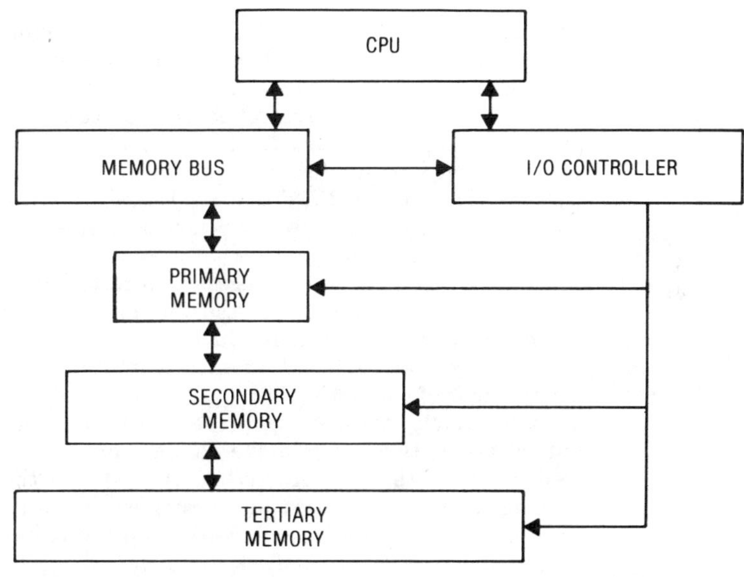

Figure 4. Conventional (a) and hierarchical (b) storage organization.

Deadlocks

A good file allocation scheme results in efficient utilization of a distributed data base management system. However, if a distributed DBMS designer ignores file allocation, the system will probably still operate, although perhaps very inefficiently. This will not be the case if the designer fails to consider the possibility of deadlocks, which occur when two or more tasks have blocked each other from execution by locking shared portions of the data base.

Deadlock in a DBMS is an unfortunate side effect of the need for a task to establish temporary exclusive control over a portion of the data base. For example, if a record is to be updated by a task, no other task can be allowed access to the record during the updating. Failure to provide a blocking mechanism can permit incorrect information to appear in the data base. If portions of the data base may be addressed simultaneously by several tasks, then a deadlock condition may occur.

For example, two tasks that ordinarily are executed independently may both require the same two records at one time, but in reverse order (Figure 5). If Task B requests Record 1 while Task A has it locked, pending A's update of Record 2, B at that moment also has Record 2 locked and therefore inaccessible to A.

The underlying cause of deadlock in data base systems is the organization of conventional secondary storage media. In order to optimize the utilization of secondary storage, several requests must be processed simultaneously. This organization tends to reduce disk head movement and latency, which is often the limiting factor in the performance of a data base system. The deadlock problem can be avoided in systems which do not use conventional secondary storage. Associative machines[6-9] batch all data base requests and provide the task issuing the request exclusive control of the database, thus avoiding deadlock.

The deadlock problem is primarily one of operating systems, but the general principles for its detection or prevention also apply to data base management. However, the DBMS deadlock problem is compounded by the need to ensure that uniformly correct data is maintained throughout the system.

For example, the deadlock just described could be resolved by returning Task A to a point before it requested Record 1 and releasing its recources (this procedure is called "rollback"). If this is done, then Record 1 must be restored to its condition

TASK A STEP	TASK A ACTION	TASK B STEP	TASK B ACTION
a_0	REQUEST RECORD 1	b_0	REQUEST RECORD 2
a_1	RECEIVE RECORD 1	b_1	RECEIVE RECORD 2
a_2	LOCK RECORD 1	b_2	LOCK RECORD 2
a_3	MODIFY RECORD 1	b_3	MODIFY RECORD 2
a_4	REQUEST RECORD 2	b_4	REQUEST RECORD 1
a_5	RECEIVE RECORD 2	b_5	RECEIVE RECORD 1
a_6	LOCK RECORD 2	b_6	LOCK RECORD 1
a_7	MODIFY RECORD 2	b_7	MODIFY RECORD 1
a_8	RELEASE RECORD 1	b_8	RELEASE RECORD 2
a_9	RELEASE RECORD 2	b_9	RELEASE RECORD 1

Sequence of steps leading to deadlock:
$a_0\, b_0\, a_1\, a_2\, b_1\, b_2\, a_3\, b_3\, a_4\, b_4$

Figure 5. DBMS deadlock.

prior to its modification by Task A. If the locking procedure permits retrieval while preventing updates by other tasks, then a third task C, not shown in the diagram, may have retrieved and operated upon the modified Record 1. The operating system may not have been notified of C's access to Record 1; or it may have been notified that the locked Record 1 received an inquiry, but not by which task; in either case C is off and runing with what may turn out to be incorrect data. Or if C's access was recorded, it too must now be rolled back, and this may require rolling back still other tasks in the system, thus causing a substantial performance degradation at the moment of contention.

Alternatively, the locking procedure may freeze out all tasks, those that make simple inquiries as well as those that update. While this avoids the "falling-dominoes" scenario just described, it blocks Task C unnecessarily from Record 1 if Task A has just updated it, even if Task B is *not* about to request it—perhaps even when Task B is not running at all. Over the long run, this could produce a nibbling degradation in performance even worse than the rare catastrophic combination when A, B, and C all want the record at nearly the same time.

Although simple DBMS deadlock has been extensively investigated (see bibliography), relatively little work has concentrated on deadlock in distributed DBMS, where the problem is complicated when the interacting tasks reside upon different machines. In this case, the communication overhead in rollback is substantial. Consequently, in a distributed DBMS, deadlock prevention may yield better system performance than deadlock detection.

Two approaches to deadlock prevention have been proposed.[28] The first method requires each data base task to indicate its file requirements before initiation. Execution of a task begins only if all requested files can be assigned to it. This approach is very straightforward. However, in a given execution, a task may not use all files to which it normally has access, so that its initiation could be needlessly delayed.

The second technique for deadlock prevention permits tasks to be initiated, but may suspend them before completion. It is based upon the notion of the *task sets*—a collection of tasks with access to common files. Since the DBMS is usually in a network, the tasks in a task set may be in different machines. Whenever a task requires access to a file, the system looks at all files that are accessible to the requesting task and other members of its task set, and determines whether or not all of them are available. If all such files are free, the task is permitted to proceed; otherwise, the task must wait until its files are available. The task sets change as tasks are initiated and terminated. The technique includes an algorithm for assigning a processor node in the network to the chore of checking availability of files for task sets. All requests for files by tasks in the set must be directed to the controlling processor.

The dynamic nature of the second technique has both benefits and drawbacks. It has the advantage of allowing tasks to proceed until an actual file request occurs. However, the maintenance of the task sets may require considerable communication overhead in a network.

An important factor for any proposed deadlock-handling algorithm is operational efficiency. The complexity of distributed data systems makes an analytical determination of efficiency difficult. Therefore, the algorithm has to be tested in practice, and such operational tests obviously require more distributed data bases than presently exist.

Data translation

Data incompatibility is a major problem that faces the designer of a distributed DBMS composed of multiple software systems on a heterogeneous network. It is complicated by different logical structures in the data base systems. Since these differences are a fact of life in data processing, a method of data base translation is necessary for the most general distributed network.

The art of generalized data translation is currently at the prototype stage. Progress (or lack of it) in data translation is one of the limiting factors in the development of heterogeneous distributed data base systems. The two major problems facing workers in the data translation area are structural translation and query translation. The latter has been addressed to a limited extent in the Datacomputer project, described above, which is a special case of the general data translation problem. The fact that it is at work in one node of the Arpanet illustrates the feasibility of that approach. Structural translation can range from a "brute force" machine-by-machine approach to fairly sophisticated techniques involving intermediate languages. The development and wide acceptance of standardized data base systems would of course reduce the need for structural translation. This is the intent of the Codasyl proposals; it would also be a benefit of relational data base systems.

The "brute force" technique constructs a unique translator for each pair of data base systems. For one pair, the construction of such a translator is a well-defined but nontrivial task; but a network of K systems would require $K(K-1)$ translators to map from each node to every other node—a project of nearly impossible magnitude.

However, there are several alternatives to the "brute force" technique. One such is the University of Michigan Data Translation Project.[29-31] (Figure 6). In this approach, a universal Stored Data Definition Language (SDDL) describes all data bases in the network. The correlation for each pair of systems is stored in a table; another table expresses the relationship between the source and target data bases in a Translation Definition Language (TDL). Compilers for the two languages produce the tables. This translation method requires only one translation program at each DBMS node, instead of $(K-1)$ programs, but the translator must be supplemented with an SDDL table and $(K-1)$ TDL tables.

Another alternative to "brute force" translation is a Data Specification and Conversion Language (DSCL),[32] a high-level language for data translation. One machine in the distributed DBMS can be the network translator (Figure 7). DSCL is used for all communication with the translation machine, which effectively contains $(K-1)^2$ different translation programs. The main advantage of this technique is that the only additional software required on the DBMS nodes are utility routines that map to and from DSCL.

Not all approaches to data translation are totally automatic. For example, in one interactive translation system, the user participates in composing the logical structure of the target data base.[33] The system requires a separate translator for each distinct target machine. This approach has considerable flexibility in restructuring the target data base, but it requires user intervention for any inter-machine data base communication. Therefore, the interactive approach is best suited for infrequent large scale data transfers.

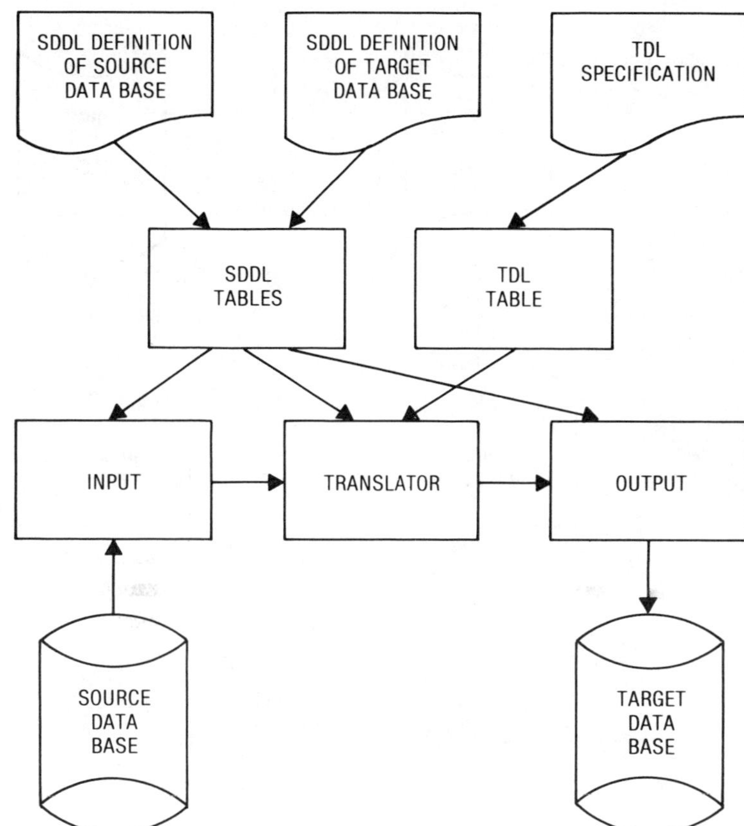

Figure 6. University of Michigan translation approach.

Security

A distributed DBMS with information and control spread over a number of computers poses many interesting security problems. Since many data bases contain classified or private information, its security must be assured before determining what benefits are to be gained by multicomputer access. The principal security question in a distributed data base is whether it is inherently more or less secure than a single machine system. An analysis indicates that distribution has both advantages and drawbacks with respect to security.

The security benefits appear with dedicated back-end machines, because the dedicated computer can screen every data base request.[15] Furthermore, no application programs execute on the dedicated back-end machine, eliminating the threat of a malevolent program monitoring data base activity.

The most outstanding security liability of a distributed data base system is the use of public communication lines in geographically dispersed networks. An intruder using current technology can easily monitor the transmissions between remote installations. Therefore, a designer of a secure geographically distributed DBMS must rely upon encryption techniques to preserve security.

State of the industry

Distributed data bases are on the verge of becoming a commercial reality. Back-end data base systems are presently in the development stage by several hardware and software vendors. Industrial progress is difficult to report thoroughly without revealing proprietary information. However, some light can be shed on the subject by describing the work under way in the commercial sector.

The back-end machine has been a focal point of the industry's thrust into distributed systems.

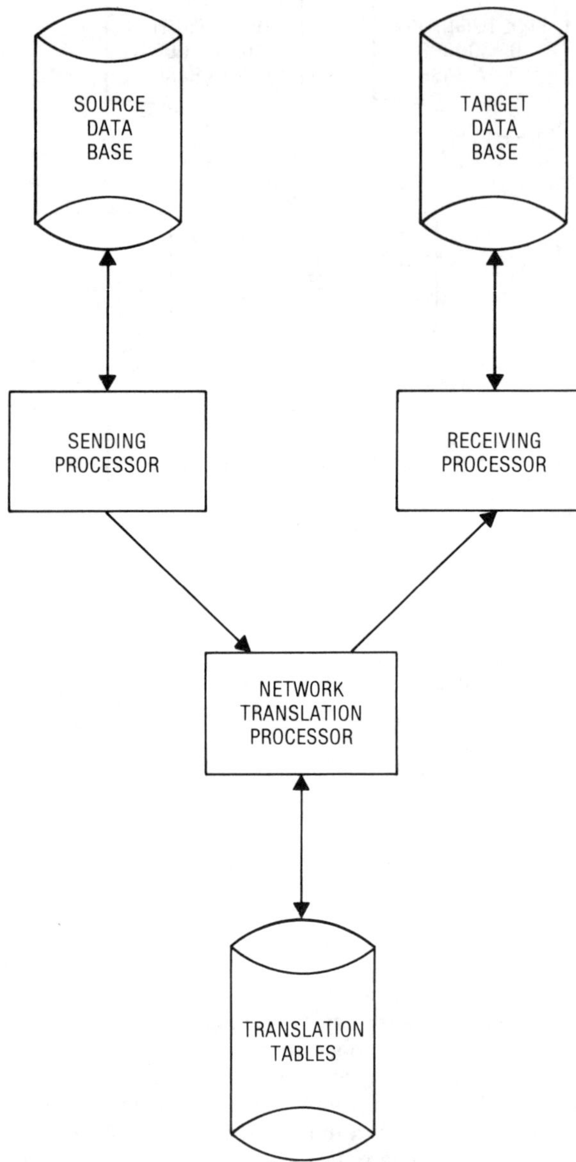

Figure 7. DSCL network organization.

Virtually all vendors have followed the Bell Laboratories XDMS prototype by using a minicomputer as the back-end machine. One software vendor, the Cullinane Corporation, is presently developing a back-end version of IDMS for use with a specific large host, IBM 370, and minicomputer back-end, PDP 11. IDMS presently operates in a stand-alone mode on either machine, while developmental effort continues on a communication system between the two machines. When complete, the back-end version of IDMS will be suitable for use with both locally and remotely connected machines.

Another software vendor, MRI, is studying the data base machine approach to distributed data base systems. This company is exploring the possibility of developing a back-end DBMS version of its software—System 2000—on a minicomputer, along with a generalized communication system written in an easily portable system implementation language. The minicomputer could be marketed, along with the company's communication software, as a "black box" for use with any of several large mainframe computers.

Hardware vendors are also actively pursuing the idea of distributed data bases. One manufacturer (name withheld by request) is studying the feasibility of constructing a back-end machine from a cluster of microcomputers, in a manner similar to MIT's Infoplex. In the system being studied, a data base request would be decomposed into primitives and processed in parallel by the microcomputers. This approach is very well suited for a relational DBMS.[34]

Another hardware manufacturer (who also prefers to remain anonymous) is investigating the concept of a microprogrammable back-end machine. This back-end processor would be a minicomputer that could be connected through a high speed interface to the vendor's large mainframe CPU's. Through the use of special-purpose data base instructions in firmware, a high-performance back-end machine can be developed. The vendor is also considering configurations of multiple back-end processors.

Clearly, this small sample of the activity in the data base industry shows that distributed data base systems—in particular, back-end machines—will soon appear in the marketplace. It would seem that advances in hardware and software technology have intersected a genuine need for greater access to and sharing of information.

Conclusion

As is typical of computer advances, the hardware technology of distributed data bases has advanced further than the software, but rapid development of the latter continues. Nevertheless, many obstacles remain before a truly general distributed DBMS will appear. However, back-end data base systems, data base machines, and distributed information systems are available now, or will become available within the next year. In the next several years, advances in distributed DBMS should be among the most significant in the computer field. ■

Acknowledgment

This work was supported in part by US Army Computer Systems Command Grant No. DAAG 29-76-G-0108.

References

1. J. P. Fry and E. H. Sibley, "Evolution of Data-Base Management Systems," *Computing Surveys,* Vol. 8, No. 1, March 1976, pp. 7-42.

2. R. I. Baum and D. K. Hsiao, "Database Computers—A Step Toward Data Utilities," *IEEE Trans. on Computers*, Vol. C-25, No. 12, Dec. 1976, pp. 1254-1259.

3. E. Chang, "A Distributed Medical Data Base," *Computer Networks*, Vol. 1, No. 1, June, 1976, pp. 33-38.

4. G. Wiederhold, J. F. Fries, and S. Weyl, "Structured Organization of Clinical Data Bases," Proceedings, *AFIPS Conf. Proc., 1975 NCC* Vol. 44, May 1975, pp. 479-485.

5. J. Knight, "A Case Study—Airline Reservation Systems," *Proc. IEEE*, Vol. 60, No. 11, Nov. 1972, pp. 1423-1431.

6. P. B. Berra, "Some Problems in Associative Processor Applications to Data Base Management," *AFIPS Conf. Proc., 1974 NCC*, Vol. 43, June 1974, pp. 1-5.

7. C. R. deFiore and P. B. Berra, "A Data Management System Utilizing an Associative Memory," *AFIPS Conf. Proc., 1973 NCC*, Vol. 42, June 1973, pp. 181-185.

8. S. Y. H. Su, G. P. Copeland, Jr., and G. J. Lipovski, "Retrieval Operations and Data Representations in a Context-Addressable Disk System," *Proc. ACM-SIGPLAN, SIGIR Interface Meeting*, November 1973, pp. 144-160.

9. E. A. Ozkarahan, S. A. Schuster, and K. C. Smith, "RAP—an Associative Processor for Data Base Management," *AFIPS Conf. Proc., 1975 NCC*, Vol. 44, May 1975, pp. 379-387.

10. D. R. Anderson, "Data Base Processor Technology," *AFIPS Conf. Proc., 1976 NCC*, Vol. 45, June 1976, pp. 811-818.

11. T. Marill and D. Stern, "The Datacomputer—A Network Data Utility," *AFIPS Conf. Proc., 1975 NCC*, Vol. 44, May 1975, pp. 389-395.

12. S. E. Madnick, "INFOPLEX—Hierarchical Decomposition of a Large Information Management System Using a Microprocessor Complex," *AFIPS Conf. Proc., 1975 NCC*, Vol. 44, May 1975, pp. 581-586.

13. R. E. Canaday et al., "A Back-end Computer for Data Base Management," *CACM*, Vol. 17, No. 10, Oct. 1974, pp. 575-582.

14. F. J. Maryanski and V. E. Wallentine, "A Simulation Model of a Back-end Data Base Management System," *Proc., Pittsburgh Conf. on Modeling and Simulation*, April 1976, pp. 252-257.

15. E. I. Lowenthal, "The Backend Computer," MRI Systems Corp., P.O. Box 9968, Austin, Texas, 78766, April 1976.

16. F. Aschim, "Data Base Networks—An Overview," *Management Informatics*, Vol. 3.1, Feb. 1974, pp. 12-28.

17. G. M. Booth, "Distributed Information Systems," *AFIPS Conf. Proc., 1976 NCC*, Vol. 45, June 1976, pp. 789-794.

18. G. M. Booth, "The Use of Distributed Data Bases in Information Networks," *Proc., First International Conf. on Computer Communication: Impacts and Implications*, Oct. 1972, pp. 371-376.

19. R. Peebles, "Design Considerations for a Distributed Data Access System," Ph.D. dissertation, Moore School of Electrical Engineering, University of Pennsylvania, May 1973.

20. F. J. Maryanski et al., "A Minicomputer-Based Distributed Data Base Management System," *Proc., NBS-IEEE Trends and Applications Symposium: Micro and Mini Systems*, May 1976, pp. 113-117.

Part II
Processor Management and Task Scheduling

THE potential computational power of distributed computer systems, vis-à-vis centralized systems, has been much heralded. Ideally, this power can be translated into decreases in software execution times from those that are achievable with a centralized computer. Such decreases are feasible since some parts of the software may be executed, in parallel, on the distributed system's different processors.

However, tremendous problems arise when one tries to exploit this computational potential. One of the main problem areas centers about the development of methods to schedule the software tasks on the different processors. In this section we will explore the development of different types of scheduling algorithms and discuss their practical application to distributed systems.

The least sophisticated mathematical technique for scheduling problems is enumeration. Here, all the possible assignment combinations are tried and a performance measure for each is calculated. Although the method has the distinct advantage of guaranteeing a globally optimum solution, the time required for it to do so is outrageously large. As an example, consider the assignment of n modules with deterministic execution times to be executed on a system of m processors. If the modules are not constrained by precedence relationships then there are

$$\frac{(n+m-1)!}{(m-1)!}$$

possible module arrangements which must be considered. For a relatively small system consisting of 25 modules and 5 processors, there are 3.7×10^{29} possibilities.

Estimating that each assignment requires 10^3 machine instructions to be evaluated (a low estimate), then a post-1990 Josephson junction computer capable of 2.5×10^8 instructions per second would require 4.7×10^{16} years to examine all combinations. For comparison, the age of the earth is approximately 5.0×10^9 years.

Restricting the possible module assignment order by imposing precedence relationships on the modules reduces the number of combinations to a minimum of m^n. Of course, the actual number of combinations depends on the severity of the precedence constraints. Again, for $n=25$ and $m=5$ there are at least 3.0×10^{17} possibilities to be tested. Although this number is smaller than that of the unconstrained case, it is still not a workable situation. Clearly, enumeration is not a feasible method of solution for scheduling problems consisting of more than a few modules and processors.

The first paper reprinted in this section is "On the Computational Complexity of a Generalized Scheduling Problem." In the paper the authors shed further light on the complexity of the problem and develop several theorems regarding multiprocessor scheduling algorithms.

The next paper reprinted, "Scheduling Techniques for Operating Systems," has been included to set several of the "ground rules" for process management and scheduling. This paper does not discuss multiprocessor systems, but nonetheless it serves as an excellent reference for the general scheduling problem. Following is an early paper by Lampson entitled "A Scheduling Philosophy for Multiprocessing Systems." The paper contains "A collection of basic ideas . . . which have been evolved by various workers over the past four years to provide a suitable framework for the design and analysis of multiprocessing systems."

The first three papers reprinted in this part provide the user with an excellent introduction to the problems of multiprocessor scheduling and with some of the early attempts to solve those problems. The remaining papers deal with more recent and powerful methods.

Various mathematical programming methods have been used to solve large constrained optimization problems, a category into which the processor scheduling problem falls. Integer programming is, for example, particularly appropriate for such problems since the assignment of a software module to a hardware unit can be represented by a binary decision variable. The objective function (or performance index) chosen for allocation evaluation may be either linear or nonlinear. In either case, the performance index is a function of a set of binary decision variables representing the state of the system. Solution of the equations is generally done in the presence of linear and/or nonlinear constraints and results in a determination of the values of the decision variables. Hence, the optimal state of the system is determined.

As an example, consider a set of software modules (without precedence relationships) which is to be mapped onto a set of connected memories and processors. However, the modules are allowed to communicate with each other. For simplicity, assume that associated with each processor is one and only one memory, i.e., the memories are dedicated. Furthermore, constrain the memories to have finite storage capacities. A possible architecture for this system is shown in Fig. 1.

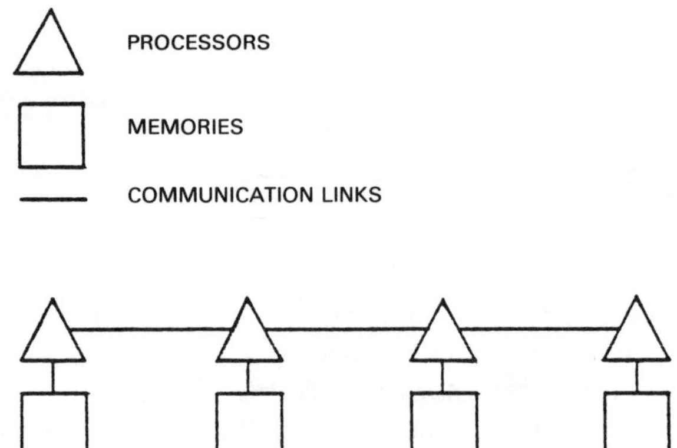

Fig. 1. A system of processors and dedicated memories.

Define the decision variable x_{ik} as follows:

$$x_{ik} = \begin{cases} 1 & \text{if module } i \text{ is assigned to processor } k \\ 0 & \text{otherwise.} \end{cases}$$

Also, define

t_{ik} = execution time of module i on processor k.

C_{ijkl} = communication time for modules i and j when i is assigned to processor k and j is assigned to processor l.

m_i = memory requirement of module i.

M_k = capacity of the memory associated with processor k.

There are several choices for an objective function, but we choose to define T as the time required for all modules to complete. Thus, it is desired to

$$\text{Min } \{T\} \tag{1}$$

subject to

$$\sum_i [x_{ik}t_{ik} + \sum_{j \neq i} \sum_{l \neq k} C_{ijkl}x_{ik}x_{jl}] \leq T \text{ for all } k \quad \text{(time constraint)}$$

$$\sum_i m_i x_{ik} \leq M_k \text{ for all } k \quad \text{(memory constraint)}$$

$$\sum_k x_{ik} = 1 \text{ for all } i \quad \text{(all modules must must be assigned once)}$$

$$x_{ik} = 0,1 \quad \text{(binary assignment variable).}$$

This is an integer programming problem (T will assume integer values if all the parameters are integers), with quadratic constraints and a linear objective function. The intermodule communication transforms what would have otherwise been a linear objective function into a quadratic one containing the term $x_{ik}x_{jl}$. Such objective functions are representative of the so-called "quadratic assignment problem" first discussed by Koopmans and Beckman [1]. Since then the problem has been treated by many authors (see [2]–[6]).

Quadratic assignment problems can be linearized by the inclusion of additional constraints. Once this has been done, standard integer programming methods such as "branch-and-bound" can be applied. E.L. Lawler [7] provides a review of the linearization and solution procedure.

The main advantage in applying the integer programming methodology to real-time scheduling problems is that module precedence relationships cannot be modeled efficiently. Indeed, if there are such constraints, then other scheduling algorithms must be used. Such methods also rely on integer programming methods by redefining the decision variable x as

$$x_{ik} \rightarrow x_{ikt}$$

where

$$x_{ikt} = \begin{cases} 1 & \text{if module } i \text{ runs on processor } k \text{ at time } t \\ 0 & \text{otherwise.} \end{cases}$$

Here, the object is to minimize a function similar or identical to (1) subject to linear and/or nonlinear constraints.

To illustrate such a mathematical programming technique, the paper "Task Allocation in Distributed Data Processing" by Chu *et al.* has been included. Also, covered in the paper is a summary of a potentially useful heuristic scheduling methodology.

Along quite different lines, an interesting graph theoretic approach to the module allocation program was taken by H.S. Stone and S.H. Bokhari in "Control of Distributed Processes," and was later expanded in "Assignment of Tasks in a Distributed Processor System with Limited Memory," by Rao *et al.*, both of which are reprinted here.

The components of this system consist of several connected processors ($N \leq 3$) and a set of software modules with deterministic execution times. The modules communicate with each other, but are not subject to precedence relationships. System performance is defined to be the total time taken for all of the modules to complete. The time taken for a single module i to complete consists of two components: the time for the actual execution of the module code (t_i) and the time required for the module to communicate (c_{ij}) with all other modules j. The objective is to find the module to processor mapping which minimizes

$$\sum_i t_i + \sum_i \sum_{\substack{j \\ j \neq i}} C_{ij}.$$

Although this model is quite simplified, the solution technique guarantees a globally optimal solution for the two-processor case and allows bounds to be set on the optimality of the three-processor system solution.

Finally, this part concludes with a set of three papers summarizing a variety of other task scheduling methodologies. The papers are "Optimal Preemptive Scheduling on Two-Processor Systems," "Optimal Scheduling Strategies in a Multiprocessor System," and "A Task Allocation Model for Distributed Computing Systems."

References

[1] T. C. Koopmans and M. J. Beckman, "Assignment problems and the location of economic activities," *Econometrica,* vol. 25, pp. 52–76, 1957.

[2] P. C. Gilmore, "Optimal and suboptimal algorithms for the quadratic assignment problem," *J. Soc. Ind. Appl. Math.,* vol. 10, pp. 305–313, 1962.

[3] G. W. Graves and A. B. Whinston, "A new approach to discrete mathematical programming," *Management Sci.,* vol. 15, pp. 177–190, 1968.

[4] A. H. Land and A. G. Doig, "A problem of assignment with interrelated costs," *Oper. Res. Quart.,* vol. 14, pp. 185–199, 1965.

[5] R. S. Lashkari and S. C. Jaisingh, "A heuristic approach to the quadratic assignment problem," *J. Oper. Res. Soc.,* vol. 31, pp. 845–850, 1980.

[6] R. F. Love and J. Y. Wong, "Solving quadratic assignment problems with rectangular distances and integer programming," *Management Sci.,* vol. 13, pp. 42–57, 1978.

[7] E. L. Lawler, "The quadratic assignment problem," *Management Sci.,* vol. 9, pp. 586–599, 1963.

On the Computational Complexity of a Generalized Scheduling Problem

K. VAIRAVAN, MEMBER, IEEE, AND RICHARD A. DEMILLO

***Abstract*—The parallel scheduling of a partially ordered set of tasks has received great attention. The partially ordered tasks can be viewed as components of a straight-line program. In this note, we discuss some aspects of the nonpreemptive parallel scheduling of a program with more general control structures. We examine the existence of optimal k-processor schedules, and in line with recent interest in the complexity of computer computations and algorithms, we study the complexity of constructing optimal k-processor schedules. In particular we show that, for every $k > 1$, any algorithm that would yield an optimal k-processor schedule of a loop-free program, when such a schedule exists, will be of exponential-time complexity.**

***Index Terms*—Complexity of scheduling, generalized scheduling, parallel computation, task systems with control structures.**

Manuscript received January 7, 1975; revised January 26, 1976. This work was partially supported by the National Science Foundation under Grant DCR75-01773.

The authors are with the Department of Electrical Engineering, University of Wisconsin-Milwaukee, Milwaukee, WI 53201.

I. INTRODUCTION

PARALLEL computation has received much attention recently because of the possibilities of significant increases in speed in contrast to strictly sequential computation. One aspect that has been investigated extensively is the parallel scheduling of a partially ordered task system [1]. A task system $\tau = \langle T, < \rangle$, where $T = \{T_1, \cdots T_n\}$ is a set of tasks to be executed on k identical processors and $<$ is a partial order (precedence relation) on T so that if $T_i < T_j$, then the task T_i must be executed before T_j can be initiated. Associated with each task T_i there is a nonnegative real number α_i which represents the time required to execute T_i on a single processor. In this paper we will be interested in equal-time tasks, i.e., in the case $\alpha_i = t$, $1 \leq i \leq n$. A schedule is an assignment of the tasks to k processors as a function of time so that the precedence relation between tasks is not violated. A common

Reprinted from *IEEE Trans. Comput.*, vol. C-25, pp. 1067–1073, Nov. 1976.

objective of task scheduling is to construct a schedule which is optimal in the sense that the total time for the execution of the set of tasks T is minimized. An underlying assumption in traditional scheduling theory is that all the tasks must be executed and that the task system does not admit predefined control structures such as branches and cycles. Although a reference to the problem of scheduling a program with branches and cycles is made in [2], the main thrust of the results reported in [2] and other related works is directed at task systems without control structures. In this paper, we consider the problem of scheduling task systems which admit predefined control structures, in addition to data dependencies. Thus, one may view the results reported here as pertaining to the scheduling of operations in a flow chart. The discussion is based on a framework developed by the authors to study generalized scheduling where the number of processors available is assumed to be unbounded [3], [4]. The resulting model of schedule turns out to be a model of synchronous parallel computation and is related to the Karp–Miller model of parallel program schemata [5]. In this paper, we consider k-processor schedules of a flow chart and present results concerning the existence and the construction of optimal k processor schedules when k is fixed at some value. In particular, we show that the problem of constructing optimal k-processor schedules, k fixed, is of exponential time complexity for task systems that have branches.

II. Representing Automata and Schedules

Formal studies of computer programs for sequential as well as for parallel execution have been made, the most well known among these being [5], [6]. Karp and Miller, whose work motivated the authors, discuss unbounded asynchronous parallel computations. In this section we briefly discuss our model of synchronous sequential computation, called *representing automata* (RA's), and the associated model of parallel computation called *schedules*. Intuitively, the state diagram of representing automaton M may be thought of as denoting the flow chart of a program where the states of M denote the operations of the program. More precisely an RA is a finite automaton $M = \langle K,\Sigma,\delta,q_0,F\rangle$, where 1) the state set $K = \{a,b,c, \cdots\}$ denotes a finite set of synchronous operations for which there is a fixed $t > 0$ such that each operation in K is completed in time t; 2) for each $a \in K$, there is a finite set of outcomes denoted by $\Sigma(a) = \{a_1,a_2, \cdots\}$ and the alphabet $\Sigma = \bigcup_{a\in K} \Sigma(a)$; 3) δ is a next-state map δ: $K \times \Sigma \rightarrow K$ such that for $a \in K, x \in \Sigma, \delta(a,x)$ is defined iff $x \in \Sigma(a)$, and 4) $q_0 \in K$ is the starting state and $F \in K$ is the terminal state. $\Sigma(F) = \phi$, by convention.

The operation of M may be explained as follows. If M is in state a, then the operation with name a is performed and a test is made to determine the outcome. If the outcome is a_i, then the next operation performed is $\delta(a,a_i)$ and so on. If the size of $\Sigma(a)$ is one, then $\Sigma(a)$ is written for simplicity as $\{a\}$. Let $|x|$ denote the operation in K whose outcome is x. For any RA M, the set of sequences over Σ accepted by $M = \{J | \hat{\delta}(q_0,J) = F\}$ will be denoted by $T(M)$ and referred to as the set of *executions* of M. Note that $\hat{\delta}$ is the usual extension of δ to $K \times \Sigma^*$. An RA is *acyclic* if its state-transition diagram does not contain a cycle.

The example 1 of Fig. 1(a) shows the state diagram of an RA M whose state set $K = \{a,b,c,d,e,f\}$. Note that $q_0 = a$ and $F = f$. There is only one operation, namely, b with multiple outcomes b_1 and b_2. For simplicity only transitions corresponding to multiple outcome operations are labeled. Note that the regular set $T(M)$ corresponds to different possible executions of M and is denoted by the regular expression $a(b_1cd)^*b_2e$. We emphasize here that the state diagram represents the control structure of the task system rather than the precedence relation which is considered next.

A *precedence relation* ρ on the operation set K of an RA is a binary reflexive relation on K. Precedence represents an *a priori* decision concerning the potential parallelism in a program. Hence, $(a,b) \in \rho$ can be interpreted as an assertion of the data dependency of b on a. An intuitive rendering of $(a,b) \in \rho$ is that if a_i is ever followed by b_j in some $\alpha \in T(M)$, then b depends upon a in such a way that the computation specified by a must be completed before b can be initiated, in any schedule. Reflexivity of ρ will ensure that no operation can be executed simultaneously with itself.

Consider an execution $\alpha = x_1x_2 \cdots x_l \in T(M)$. The string $x_{i_1}x_{i_2} \cdots x_{i_j}$ is called a *ρ-chain* in α iff 1) $i_m < i_{m+1}$, $1 \leq m < j$; 2) for $1 \leq m < j$, $(|x_{i_m}|, |x_{i_{m+1}}|) \in \rho$ and for all k, $i_m < k < i_{m+1}$, either $(|x_{i_m}|, |x_k|) \notin \rho$ or $(|x_k|, |x_{i_{m+1}}|) \notin \rho$. A ρ-chain Ω in the string α is said to be preserved in another string β iff Ω is also a ρ-chain in β.

A schedule $\bar{M} = \langle \bar{K},\bar{\Sigma},\bar{\delta},\bar{q}_0,\bar{F}\rangle$ of an RA $M = \langle K,\Sigma,\delta,q_0,F\rangle$ and ρ is an automaton with a unique starting state $\bar{q}_0$ and a terminal state $\bar{F}$ together with a function g: $\bar{K} \rightarrow 2^K$, which assigns to each state q in $\bar{K}$ a subset of the operations in K so that 1) for $q \in \bar{K}, g(q) = (P^1,P^2, \cdots ,P^n)$ implies $(P^i,P^j) \notin \rho$, $1 \leq i,j \leq n, i \neq j$; 2) $\bar{\Sigma} \subseteq \{\Sigma^n | n \geq 1\}$ such that $(x_1, \cdots ,x_m) \in \bar{\Sigma}$ iff for some state $q \in \bar{K}, g(q) = (P^1, \cdots ,P^m)$ and $x_i \in \Sigma(P^i)$, $1 \leq i \leq m$; 3) $\bar{\delta}$: $\bar{K} \times \bar{\Sigma} \rightarrow \bar{K}$ is a partial map where $\bar{\delta}(q,\bar{x})$ is defined iff $x_i \in \Sigma(g(q)_i)$ for $\bar{x} = x_1 \cdots x_i \cdots x_n$; 4) let $T(\bar{M})$ denote the sequences over $\bar{\Sigma}$ accepted[1] by $\bar{M}$. Then for each $\alpha \in T(M)$ there is a unique $\beta \in T(\bar{M})$ called $\tau_{\bar{M}}(\alpha)$ which preserves all ρ-chains in α; and 5) $\beta \in T(\bar{M})$ only if for some $\alpha \in T(M)$, β preserves all ρ-chains in α. For simplicity, in a state transition diagram of $\bar{M}$, we will label a state q with $g(q)$. Hence, it is possible to have different states with the same labels.

We now return to example 1 shown in Fig. 1(a). Although ρ is reflexive, for compactness of notation we do not explicitly show elements of the form (x,x) in subsequent discussion. A schedule $\bar{M}$ of the RA, M and ρ of Fig. 1(a)

[1] Strictly speaking, $\bar{M}$ accepts strings and not sequences. However, since $\bar{\Sigma}$ contains strings we will avoid ambiguity problems by conceiving acceptors which receive input *sequences*. Alternatively, we may assume a uniform convention for adding parentheses to punctuate strings of strings.

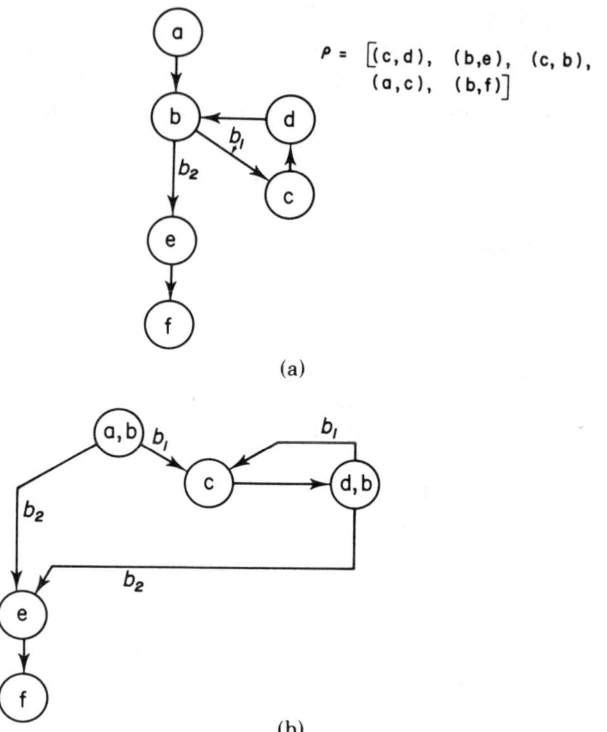

Fig. 1. (a) An RA M and a precedence relation ρ. (b) A schedule of the RA M shown in Fig. 1(a).

is shown in Fig. 1(b). Consider the execution $\alpha = ab_1cbd_2e$ in M. The length of the string α over the alphabet Σ, $L_\Sigma(\alpha)$, is 6. The corresponding execution $\tau_{\bar{M}}(\alpha)$ in $\bar{M}$ is $\beta = (ab_1)(c)(db_2)(e)$. It can be verified by inspection that β preserves all ρ-chains in α. For example, the ρ-chain acb_2 in α is also a ρ-chain in β. Also, $L_{\bar{\Sigma}}(\beta) = 4$, where $\bar{\Sigma} = \{(ab_1), (c), (db_1), (db_2), (e)\}$. The execution β in $\bar{M}$ can be explained as follows: at time unit one, the operations a and b are scheduled. When the outcome is b_1, the operation c is scheduled at the next unit of time, and so on. Thus, in asequential computational environment, α takes six units of time for completion, whereas in the parallel schedule $\bar{M}$ the corresponding execution β is completed in four units of time.

A schedule $\bar{M}$ is a k-bounded (or k-processor) schedule if the maximum number of operations in any node q is not greater than k.

A schedule $\bar{M}$ for an RA (M,ρ) is a *(k-bounded) optimal schedule*[2] iff for any $\alpha \in T(M)$ and for any (k-bounded) schedule $\bar{M}'$ of (M,ρ), $L_{\bar{\Sigma}}(\tau_{\bar{M}}(\alpha)) \leq L_{\bar{\Sigma}'}(\tau_{\bar{M}'}(\alpha))$. Intuitively, a schedule $\bar{M}$ of (M,ρ) is a (k-bounded) optimal schedule if there does not exist another (k-bounded) schedule of (M,ρ) which would result in a shorter execution time than $\bar{M}$ for *any* execution in the RA (M,ρ). It is important to note that this notion of optimality reduces to the property of optimality commonly used in connection with the scheduling of a partially ordered task system.

It has been shown that when there are no restrictions on the number of processors, an optimal schedule always exists [3], [4]. In the next section, we discuss the existence and complexity of the construction of k-bounded optimal schedules of RA's.

III. Existence and Complexity of Optimal Schedules

Theorem 1: An RA may not always possess a k-bounded optimal schedule for every k.

Proof: For justification we present an (M,ρ) shown in Fig. 2, and show that for $k = 2$, there does not exist an optimal schedule with two processors.

There are only a finite number of schedules, and in particular two-processor schedules of (M,ρ). By exhaustive enumeration we can verify that there does not exist an optimal two-processor schedule for (M,ρ). We also present the following argument to show that (M,ρ) does not possess an optimal two-processor schedule. There are two executions of M, namely, $\alpha = abc_1df$ and $\beta = abc_2ef$. A maximal length ρ-chain in α is $\theta = adf$ of length three. *Any* schedule $\bar{M}$ of (M,ρ) will be such that $L_{\bar{\Sigma}}(\tau_{\bar{M}}(\alpha)) \geq 3$; otherwise θ will not be preserved by $\tau_{\bar{M}}(\alpha)$. Fig. 2(b) shows the *only* schedule $\bar{M}'$ with the property that $L_{\bar{\Sigma}'}(\tau_{\bar{M}'}(\alpha)) = 3$. Note that $L_{\bar{\Sigma}'}(\tau_{\bar{M}'}(\beta)) = 4$. But in Fig. 2(c), we demonstrate the existence of the only schedule $\bar{M}''$ of (M,ρ) such that $L_{\bar{\Sigma}''}(\tau_{\bar{M}''}(\beta)) = 3$. Hence, the only schedule $\bar{M}'$ ($\bar{M}''$) which optimizes the execution of α (β) does not optimize the execution of β (α). It follows that (M,ρ) does not possess a two-processor optimal schedule. Q.E.D.

The choice of $k = 2$ in the proof of Theorem 1 is critical, for if the number of available processors $k \geq 3$, then the (M,ρ) of Fig. 2(a) possesses an optimal k-processor schedule as shown in Fig. 3.

In the remainder of this section, we present some results concerning the computational complexity of the construction of optimal schedules of RA's when such optimal schedules exist. We begin by reviewing some relevant concepts and results in the theory of complexity of algorithms. For details, the reader is referred to the classic treatment of the subject by Karp [7], or to a recent book [8]. The complexity of an algorithm can be given by a function $F: N \rightarrow N$ (where N is the set of natural numbers), which characterizes the execution time of the algorithm in terms of the size of its input. Algebraic characterizations of $F(\cdot)$ (i.e., constant, logarithmic, linear, polynomial, exponential, etc.) are used to identify the complexity of the associated algorithm. Let P be the set of all problems π for which there exists a deterministic polynomial-time algorithm to solve the problem π. Likewise, let NP be the set of all problems which have nondeterministic polynomial-time algorithmic solutions. A problem π is said to be NP-complete if 1) $\pi \in NP$, and furthermore, 2) $\pi \in P$ implies $P = NP$. Since it is widely believed that $P \neq NP$, a demonstration that a problem π is NP-complete is likely equivalent to showing that π cannot be solved efficiently and that *probably* the best deterministic algorithm to solve π is at least of exponential-time complexity.

[2] Note that (M,ρ) denotes an RA M together with a precedence relation ρ.

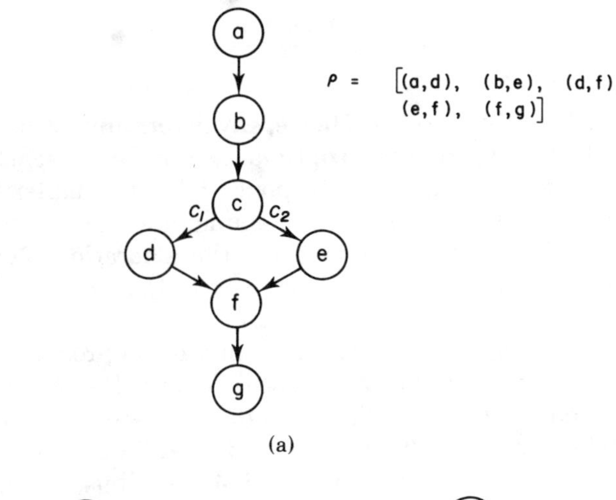

(a)

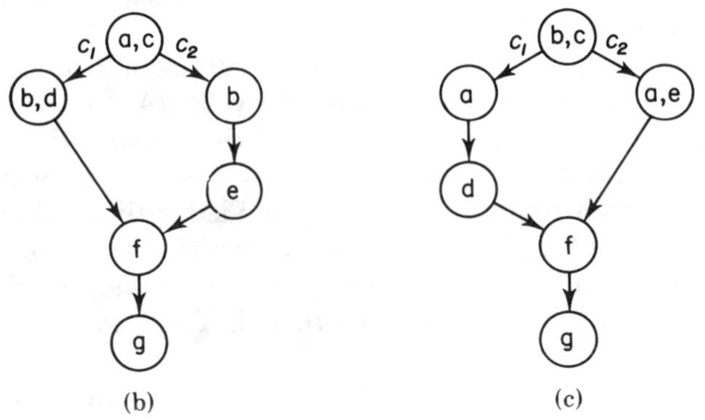

(b) (c)

Fig. 2. (a) An RA M which does not possess an optimal two-processor schedule. (b) and (c) Two nonoptimal schedules of the RA shown in Fig. 2(a).

Karp has shown that the problem of constructing a schedule for a set of partially ordered, possibly unequal-time, tasks among k-processors (where k is a variable) is NP-complete [7]. More recently, Ullman has shown that the restriction of the above problem to equal-time tasks is also NP-complete [9]. However, for the case in which the number of processors k is fixed at two, Coffman and Graham [1], and independently Fuju *et al.* [10], have developed efficient (polynomial-time) algorithms to construct an optimal schedule for a set of partially ordered equal-time tasks (or equivalently a straight-line RA). We show that any algorithm, which would yield two-processor optimal schedules of acyclic RA's when they exist, is of exponential-time complexity. Later in this section we consider some generalizations of this result.

It is important to observe here that in all of the above problems, the time complexity of interest is that which pertains to the construction of a schedule, rather than its execution. Also it is assumed that the complete schedule is to be constructed before parallel execution begins. For a discussion of the significance of this last assumption see Section IV.

Theorem 2: Any algorithm designed to construct optimal two-processor schedules of acyclic RA's, when such schedules exist, is of exponential-time complexity.

Proof: First, we will show that the stated problem is at least of exponential-time complexity by demonstrating the existence of an acyclic RA M and a precedence ρ such that the number of distinct states in any two-processor optimal schedule $\bar{M}$ of (M,ρ) is an exponential function of the number of states of M. Thus, *any* deterministic algorithm to generate an optimal schedule of (M,ρ) would be of exponential-time complexity.

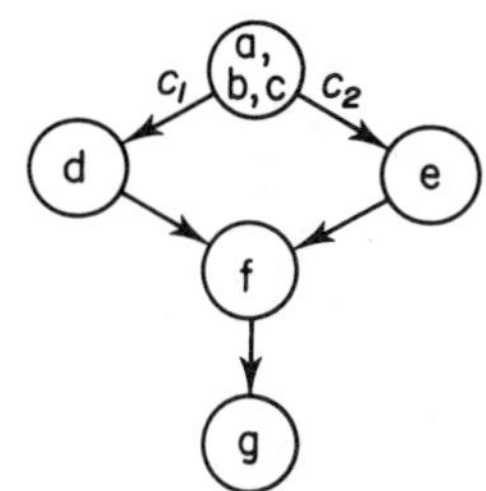

Fig. 3. An optimal schedule of the RA shown in Fig. 2(a).

Consider the RA M whose state diagram is shown in Fig. 4. Let n be an even integer and let $\rho = \{(a^j,b^1), (b^t,b^{t+1}) \mid j = 1,2,\cdots,n; t = 1,2,\cdots,n-1\}$. For simplicity of the subsequent discussion, we introduce the following notation. When an operation such as a^1 has two outcomes we indicate the outcomes by + and −. Thus, the transitions in M corresponding to the two outcomes of a^1 are labeled + and −. Also note that when an operation such as A^1 has a single outcome, the corresponding transitions are not labeled. Let the initial state be a and the final state be F.

Note that in any execution $\gamma \in T(M)$, the number of operations is not less than $2n$. Since the tasks $a^j(1 \leq j \leq n)$ will have to be completed before b^1, and the task b^t must be completed before $b^{t+1}(1 \leq t \leq n-1)$, the length of any execution γ in *any* two-processor schedule $\bar{M}$ of (M,ρ), $L_{\bar{\Sigma}}(\tau_{\bar{M}}(\gamma)) \geq n + n/2$. The schedule $\bar{M}'$ partially shown in Fig. 5 has the property that $\forall\ \gamma \in T(M)$, $L_{\bar{\Sigma}'}(\tau_{\bar{M}'}(\gamma)) = (n/2) + n$. Hence, $\bar{M}'$ is an optimal two-processor schedule of (M,ρ) (see Fig. 6).[3] Now we will show that in any two-processor optimal schedule of (M,ρ), all decision (i.e., multiple outcome) operations will have to be scheduled before any of the A^j operations can be scheduled, as in $\bar{M}'$. The proof is by contradiction. Assume there exists an optimal two-processor schedule $\bar{M}''$ of (M,ρ) with the property that in some execution $\Gamma \in T(\bar{M}'')$, the set $\{A^{j_1},\cdots,A^{j_L}\}$ is scheduled before *all* the multiple-outcome operations are scheduled. Now clearly,

$$L_{\bar{\Sigma}''}(\Gamma) \geq n + \left\lceil \frac{n + j_L}{2} \right\rceil,$$

where $\lceil x \rceil$ is the ceiling of x, and hence $\bar{M}''$ is not optimal. Thus, the portion of any optimal two-processor schedule $\bar{M}$ of (M,ρ) in which the multiple outcome operations are scheduled, will have a tree structure similar to $\bar{M}'$. Now, the question that may arise is that since many nodes in the tree portion of $\bar{M}$ can have identical labels, can they not be merged? We will show that this cannot be done. Consider two nodes X,Y with identical label (a^{t-1},a^t). Let t be even without loss of generality. Let the distinct paths

[3] An optimal schedule $\bar{M}'$ is shown in Fig. 6 for the case $n = 4$.

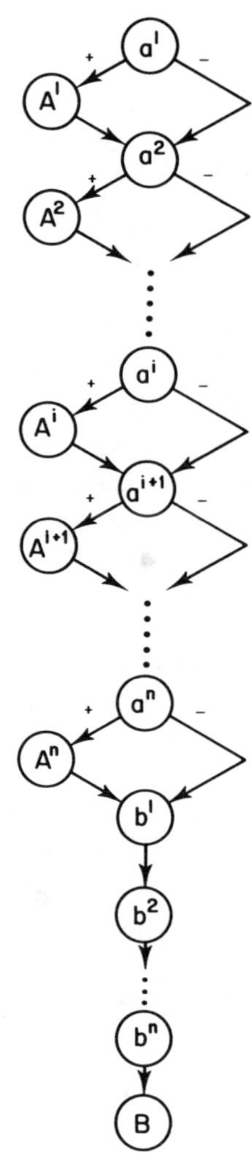

Fig. 4. The RA M of Theorem 2.

that terminate in X and Y in $\bar{M}$ be characterized by + decisions associated with the distinct sets of operations $T = \{a^{j_1}, \cdots, a^{j_u}\}$ and $V = \{a^{i_1}, \cdots, a^{i_v}\}$, respectively. The set of A operations that must be scheduled after state y is reached is $\{A^{i_1}, \cdots, A^{i_u}\} \neq \{A^{j_1}, \cdots, A^{j_u}\}$, the set of A operations that must be scheduled after X is reached. Hence, X and Y cannot be merged into a single node. Thus, the state diagram of every two-processor optimal schedule of (M,ρ) contains a tree, the depth of which is $n/2$. It follows that the number of distinct nodes N that must be set up in an optimal two-processor schedule of (M,ρ) (no matter what deterministic algorithm is used to generate it) is greater than

$$\sum_{i=0}^{n/2} 4^i = N_T,$$

the number of nodes in the tree part of $\bar{M}$. It can be verified that

$$N_T = \frac{4^{n/2+1} - 1}{3}$$

and since the number of nodes in M is $m = 3n + 1$,

$$N > \frac{(4^{m/3})(16)^{1/3} - 1}{3}$$

or $N = 0(p^m)$, $p > 1$. Hence, any deterministic algorithm which will generate an optimal two-processor schedule of acyclic RA's is at least of exponential-time complexity. But in the acyclic case, one can enumerate all two-processor schedules in time $0(4^m)$. Thus, the generation of optimal two-processor schedules for acyclic RA's is of exponential-time complexity. Q.E.D.

Although we considered the number of processors to be fixed at two in the above discussion, the RA (M,ρ) of Fig. 4 and an argument similar to the one used in the proof of Theorem 2 can be used to show that Theorem 2 can be extended to cases where $k = 3, 4$, etc. Thus, we have the following corollary.

Corollary: The problem of constructing a k-processor (for a fixed k) optimal schedule of acyclic RA's, where such a schedule exists, is of exponential-time complexity.

Also, when the number of processors is arbitrarily large, then the starting state of any unbounded optimal schedule of (M,ρ) of Fig. 4 would contain *all* multiple-outcome operations $a^1, a^2, \cdots, a^n$. Hence, 2^n distinct successors of this state would have to be constructed. Thus, we have the following.

Corollary: Any algorithm which will generate an unbounded optimal schedule of acyclic RA's is of exponential-time complexity.

Finally, we point out that it has been proved [3], [4] that when an RA contains cycles, it may not always possess a finite optimal schedule, but may possess an infinite optimal schedule.

IV. Conclusions

We have discussed some results related to the parallel scheduling of a program made up of equal-time operations. Specifically we showed that, unlike the optimal scheduling of a partially ordered set of tasks (which can be viewed as components of a straight-line program), a program with branches may not always possess an optimal schedule when the number of processors is fixed at some value k. Also we showed that any algorithm designed to generate an optimal k-processor (k fixed) schedule of a loop-free program, when such a schedule exists, would be of exponential-time complexity. We conclude this paper by stating some problems that appear worthy of study.

1) Since a program may not always possess an optimal k-processor schedule, alternate characterizations such as "suboptimal" schedules can be formulated and efficient algorithms to generate such schedules can be studied.

2) Although the general complexity of algorithms to construct an entire optimal k-processor schedule appears formidable, one may be still interested in the study of algorithms which will dynamically generate pertinent portions of schedules during execution time so that large numbers of nodes of an entire schedule may not have to be constructed initially. Of course, such an "on-line-sched-

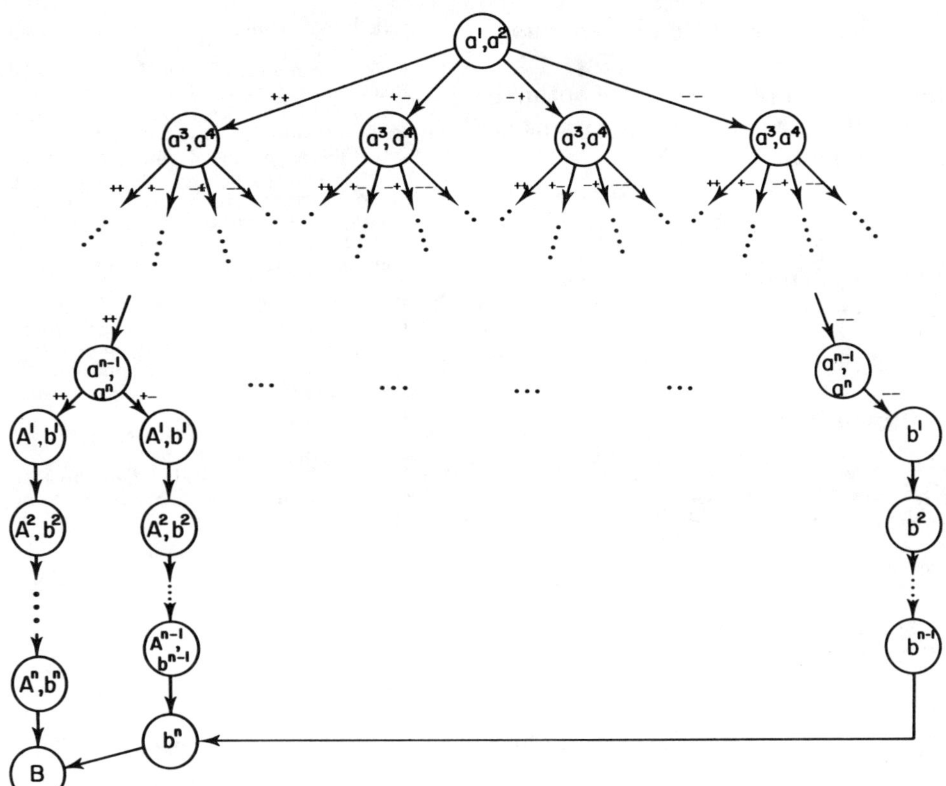

Fig. 5. The optimal schedule $\bar{M}'$ of Theorem 2 (partially shown).

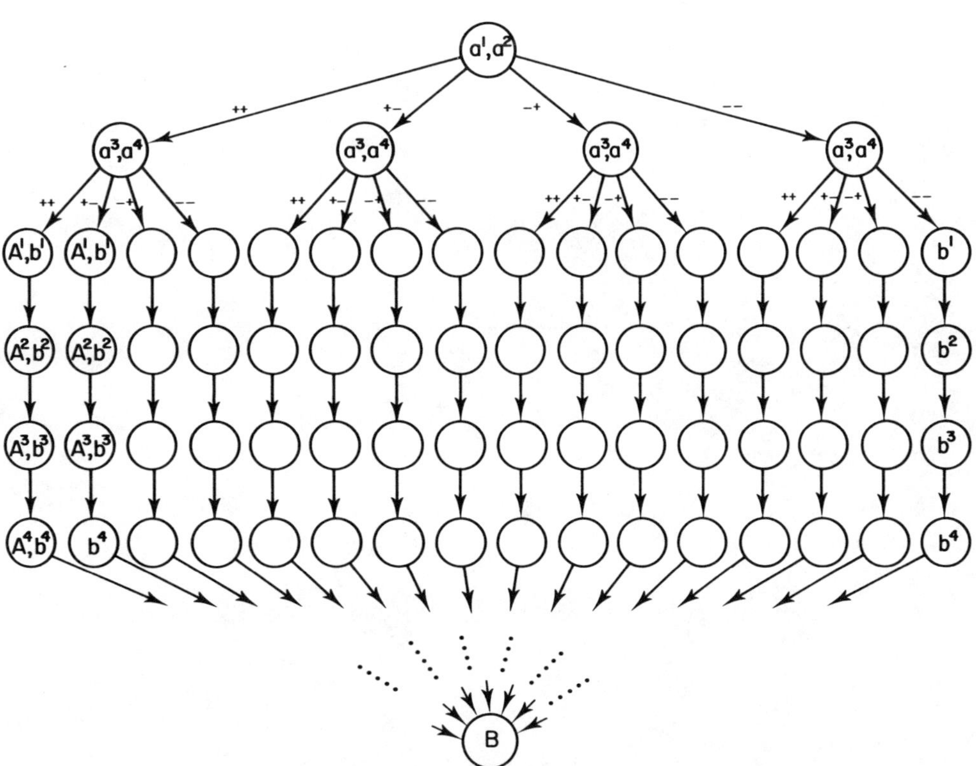

Fig. 6. An optimal schedule $\bar{M}'$ for the case $n = 4$.

uling" scheme can cause significant overhead every time the program is to be run as compared to the one-time overhead that will be incurred in the complete generation of the schedule before execution begins. Furthermore, if the schedule is dynamically generated when a program is to be run, the total time for the parallel execution of the program would be greater with a consequent reduction speed gain. Clearly, there are tradeoffs that appear worthy of study.

3) The identification of control structures of programs

for which optimal schedules can be efficiently generated appears worthwhile.

4) Finally, although a study of the problems of optimal scheduling of programs with unequal-time operations is more difficult it is quite important.

ACKNOWLEDGMENT

The authors would like to thank R. E. Miller and R. J. Lipton for helpful discussions and the referees for several useful suggestions.

REFERENCES

[1] E. A. Coffman and P. J. Denning, *Operating Systems Theory.* Englewood Cliffs, NJ: Prentice-Hall, 1973, ch. 3.

[2] C. V. Ramamoorthy, M. J. Gonzales, and K. M. Chandy, "Optimal scheduling strategies in a multiprocessor system," *IEEE Trans. Comput.*, vol. C-21, Feb. 1972.

[3] K. Vairavan and R. A. DeMillo, "Parallel scheduling of programs in a restricted model of computation," in *Proc. 6th ACM Symp. on Theory of Computing*, pp. 248–255, May 1974.

[4] R. A. DeMillo, K. Vairavan, and E. Sycara-Cyranski, "A study of schedules as models of synchronous parallel computation," Univ. of Wisconsin-Milwaukee, Dep. Elec. Eng., Tech. Rep., Jan. 1975.

[5] R. M. Karp and R. E. Miller, "Parallel program schemata," *J. Comput. Syst. and Sci.*, vol. 3, no. 3, May 1969.

[6] D. C. Luckham, M. R. Park, and M. S. Paterson, "On formalized computer programs," *J. Comput. Syst. and Sci.*, vol. 4, no. 2, May 1970.

[7] R. M. Karp, "Reducibility among combinatorial problems," in *Complexity of Computer Computations*, R. E. Miller, Ed. New York: Plenum Press, 1972.

[8] A. V. Aho, J. E. Hopcroft, and J. D. Ullman, *The Design and Analysis of Computer Algorithms.* Reading, MA: Addison-Wesley, 1974.

[9] J. D. Ullman, "NP-complete scheduling problems," *J. Comput. Syst. and Sci.*, no. 3, June 1975.

[10] M. Fuju, T. Kasami, and N. Ninomiya, "Optimal sequences of two equivalent processors," *SIAM J. Appl. Math.*, vol. 17, no. 3, 1969.

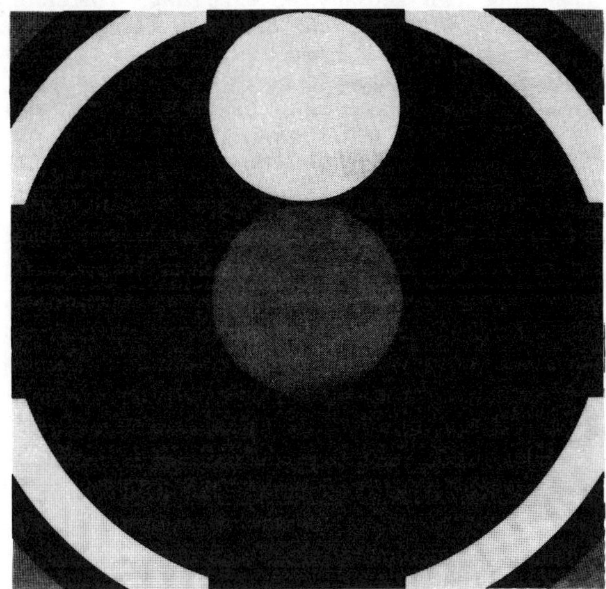

Scheduling Techniques for Operating Systems

R. B. Bunt
University of Saskatchewan

Introduction

One of the primary functions of an operating system is to distribute the resources under its control among the users of the system in such a way as to achieve installation standards of performance (including service).

One of the most important resources in a computer system is, undeniably, the processor. For example, all system activities require time on at least one processor. So it is hardly surprising that processor scheduling has received considerable attention since the very early days of computing, and that many techniques for accomplishing this essential task have been developed. These have been variously simulated, analyzed mathematically, and occasionally, implemented in actual systems. This paper looks at some techniques for scheduling processors and compares their implementations in a number of familiar operating systems.

A general model of processor scheduling

According to one definition, given by Hellerman and Conroy,[1] an operating system scheduler "is an algorithm that uniquely specifies which job is to receive next service by a resource."

Schedulers are usually described in isolation (if at all), and consequently it is sometimes difficult to see how they are related to one another. In this section, to provide a common framework for the description of actual implementations, a general model will be presented. For simplicity, this discussion is based on a single-processor system; extensions to multiprocessor systems are straightforward.

For the sake of convenience, the overall scheduling function is often divided into distinct levels, as shown in Figure 1. Both the operating constraints and the performance objectives change with the levels. Although the terminology may differ from author to author, the basic division remains much the same. At the lowest level, decisions are made concerning the allocation of physical resources such as CPU cycles to processes* in the system. This level of scheduling will be referred to as *process management.* Since actual physical resources of the system are being managed at this level, the performance objectives should be given in terms of measures of resource utilization and efficiency. In effect, the process manager takes a *real* processor and through its scheduling presents the illusion of (or simulates) a number of independent *virtual* processors. Higher-level decisions, concerning the allocation of these virtual processors, are made at the level of *job management.* At this level it is assumed that a certain number of these virtual processors exists (the maximum allowed level of multiprogramming).

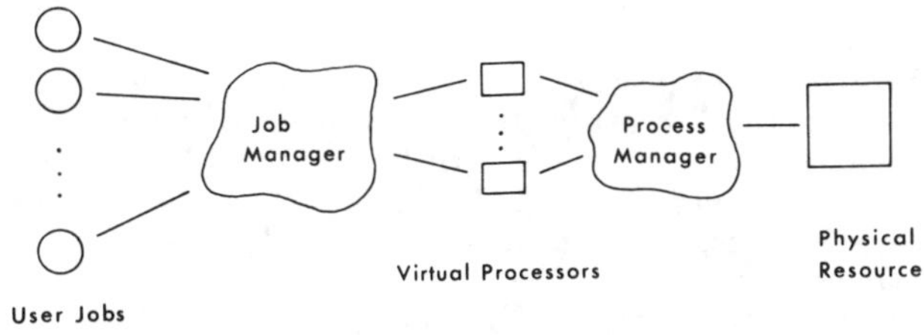

Figure 1. The division of the scheduling function.

*It is assumed that the reader is familiar with the concept of process or task. The literature abounds with definitions (see, for example, Dijkstra[2] and Horning and Randell[3]). For the purpose of this paper it suffices to view a process simply as a program in execution.

Reprinted from *Computer,* vol. 9, pp. 10–17, Oct. 1976.

The job manager sees a set of user-submitted jobs competing for these virtual processors and allocates them according to some predetermined policy. The process manager sees a community of sequential processes, each executing on its own virtual processor, requesting actual physical resources such as CPU cycles. Whereas the process manager is primarily concerned with measures of resource utilization, the job manager, since it deals directly with users of the system, ought to have its performance assessed in terms of measures of service to the users (such as turnaround time).

It is possible now to chart the history of a user request under this model. A user requests some action of the system by submitting a job to the system. The job manager allocates a virtual processor to this job if one is free, and a corresponding process (or possibly more than one) is created to perform the requested action. If there are no free virtual processors, the job is queued until one becomes available. At this level it is assumed that the virtual processor will actually execute the process. The process manager, however, must allocate to the process whatever resources it may need (including CPU time) for the action to be performed. Allocation strategies are required for each level. Again, it is important to keep in mind both the operating constraints and the performance objectives at each level. Decisions by the process manager must be made very quickly and generally last for only a brief period. Strategies involving complicated queuing methods, complex data structures, or a lengthy analysis of process characteristics may consume unwarranted quantities of the very resource being scheduled. At the job level more effort can be (and ought to be) expended on making decisions resulting in the best service to the users of the system. In terms of performance objectives, evaluation of the job manager should focus on job-oriented measures such as turnaround or throughput. Hellerman and Conroy[1] refer to these as "job performance measures," normal indicators of the level of service afforded users of the system. On the other hand, the process manager is most appropriately evaluated in terms of system-oriented measures such as CPU utilization. Hellerman and Conroy refer to these as "resource performance measures." In the remaining portions of this section some classical allocation strategies used at both the process and job levels will be described. (A very good presentation along the same lines is given by Muntz.[4])

Strategies for process management. Process managers appear in the literature under a number of aliases. The process manager is known variously as the "dispatcher,"[5] the "traffic controller,"[6] the "CPU scheduler,"[7] the "short-term scheduler,"[8] the "process scheduler,"[9] or simply "the scheduler."[10]

Most strategies operate by moving processes through a series of well-defined states. For the model of the paper, a process having instructions executed by its virtual processor is said to be in the *running* state; it is *blocked* if it is waiting for some *wakeup* signal (from another process or an external agent) to resume execution. For example, if a running process wants to perform an input operation, it issues the appropriate input command and blocks, remaining blocked until a signal that the requested input operation has been completed permits it to resume. The process manager handles the block and wakeup instructions.

Although all the virtual processors are logically operating in parallel, the real processor (here, the CPU) can in fact be executing only one instruction at a time. Thus, while several processes may be running, only one process at a time can actually be *executing*. Therefore, from the point of view of the actual processor, three states are possible for each process. Processes that are neither executing nor blocked are said to be *ready*. If the executing process becomes blocked, the process manager decides which of the ready processes is to run next. The movement through states is summarized in Figure 2.

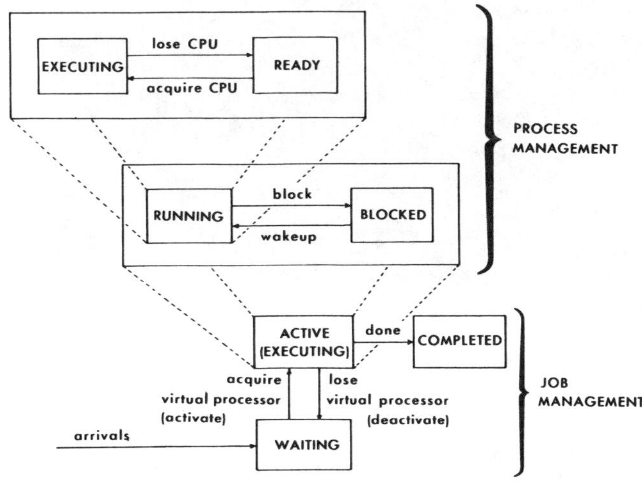

Figure 2. A two-level scheduling model.

The running processes are often ordered in priority according to some criterion, and each time the executing process blocks, the process manager passes control to the highest-priority ready process. Priority may be purchased by the user, deserved by his status or rank, or earned by way of the executing process displaying certain desirable characteristics.[11] For example, in some systems the I/O activity of the running processes is monitored dynamically and higher priority is given to those processes that seem to be doing a lot of I/O. An I/O-bound process will frequently release control of the CPU for its I/O operations. The time necessary to complete the requested operation can then be overlapped with processing of a lower-priority process. This technique improves system throughput and at the same time alleviates a possible system bottleneck by keeping I/O devices busy. This scheme can be elaborated to include other characteristics of running processes as well.

A second method of distributing the CPU is through *time slicing*. Rather than allow processes to run until they block themselves, each ready process receives in turn some small amount of CPU time known as a *time slice* (or quantum), at the end of which it is interrupted by a signal from an interval timer (or clocking process). The time slice may be fixed or varied, and the sequence in which ready processes are allocated time slices (as well as the time slice duration) may be determined in a variety of ways. For example, the ready processes may be allocated fixed-length time slices in a cyclical or round robin fashion.

In theoretical or simulation studies, true parallel execution is often assumed. A method known as *processor sharing* serves all the ready processes simultaneously at a rate inversely proportional to their current number. Thus a process that would run at a rate r if it were the only one being processed, runs at a rate *r/n* if there are *n* ready processes. This assumption makes possible the parallel advancement of jobs without requiring the complication introduced by the mechanics of process switching. Although this strategy cannot be implemented in conventional computers (and therefore will be considered no further in this paper), it is often useful as a yardstick against which other strategies can be compared in theoretical or simulation studies. A good discussion of processor sharing is given by Coffman and Kleinrock.[12]

Strategies for job management. At the level of job management, the real processor has been replaced logically by some number of virtual processors (as determined by the level of multiprogramming). In a standard batch processing environment, users submit jobs to the computer system in the form of programs. The number of virtual processors is usually considerably smaller than the number of jobs competing for them. If there are no available virtual processors, the jobs are queued by the job manager according to some priority. When a virtual processor becomes available, the job manager allocates it to the waiting job with the highest priority.

The decision algorithm used by the job manager, commonly referred to as the "scheduling algorithm," enforces a sequencing discipline on the jobs waiting for virtual processors and determines the order in which they will be allowed access to the virtual processors. Although in large part a political decision, the choice of scheduling discipline is a significant factor in the performance of the system and should be made according to the needs of the particular system. For example, in a system devoted to interactive use, emphasis may be placed on minimizing worst-case response to short terminal requests. In other systems average turnaround might be considered most important. These two systems would require different scheduling strategies at the job level.

The simplest scheduling discipline is "first-come-first-served" (FCFS), also known as "first-in-first-out" (FIFO).* All jobs are assumed to be equally preferred, and thus are serviced to completion in the order that they arrive. Although it has been said[13] that "an inherent sense of fair play has elevated [the FCFS rule] to an eminence out of all proportion to its basic virtue," it can be quite adequate in certain situations, and is often used as a basis of comparison for other disciplines. Little is required in the way of system overhead for queue management, but the system performance can be very erratic, particularly under heavy loading.

An important class of rules selects certain users as preferred and gives them better service (possibly at increased cost). A valuable principle to be borne in mind is known as Kleinrock's conservation law[14] which states, informally, that for given arrival and service patterns, a particular weighted sum of average waiting times for all jobs is invariant to the scheduling discipline used. This says that scheduling can only improve the service afforded some jobs at the expense of that given others. Preferential scheduling algorithms differ in their choice of users to be given preferential treatment.

A common preferential discipline is "shortest first." This rule requires *a priori* knowledge of each job's running time and bases the job's priority on this information. Each time a job is completed, its virtual processor is allocated to the waiting job having the smallest processing requirement. A distinction may be made[13] between the case in which the processing requirements are known exactly [called "shortest processing time" (SPT) or "shortest job first" (SJF)] and the case wherein they are estimated in some fashion [such as "shortest expected processing time" (SEPT)]. This is not a difficult rule to implement but requires more overhead for queue management than is required by FCFS. It gives much better service to jobs with small processing requirements, but does so by giving poorer service to the longer jobs. Since users with short jobs would be quite unhappy with delays that might be tolerated by users with much longer jobs, this seems a reasonable approach. In job mixes distributed in such a way that there are many more short jobs than long jobs (which is often the case in the normal operating environment**), this rule makes many people happy at the expense of relatively few. Of all the rules not using preemption, this rule yields the smallest mean turnaround time[13] provided that accurate *a priori* knowledge is available.

In both FCFS and SPT, a job once scheduled (or allocated a virtual processor) is served until it is completed. The introduction of a preemption mechanism leads to interesting variations of nonpreemptive rules. Preemption involves interrupting the job currently executing on a particular virtual processor, recording the current state of its execution, perhaps rolling the job out to secondary storage, and allocating the virtual processor to a new job. A certain amount of processor time (called "preemption overhead" or cost) is consumed by this operation.*** Normally, preempted jobs are returned to the same queues in which the arriving jobs are held. When a preempted job again comes up for service, execution resumes at the point of interruption; consequently, this technique is known as *resume preemption.*

The incorporation of preemption in the SPT rule, yielding "shortest remaining processing time" (SRPT) or "preemptive shortest job first" (PSJF), results in still sharper service discrimination between short jobs and long jobs with the added cost of some preemption overhead. SRPT is simply the natural extension to SPT, applying the "shortest first" rule at every arrival as well as every completion. If the new arrival has a smaller processing requirement than that remaining for the job currently in service, the job being serviced is preempted and replaced by the new arrival. It can be shown[17] that SRPT scheduling yields the smallest average turnaround time (but with the highest variance) when arrivals occur intermittently. However, the cost of preemption in some systems may negate the advantage of SRPT over SPT.

Both SPT and SRPT require the scheduler to have exact *a priori* knowledge of each job's processing requirements. Such information is not generally available in most systems. In some systems, estimates provided by the users themselves form the basis of the scheduling decisions. Although experienced users can, with some practice, learn to estimate fairly closely, in many cases for a variety of reasons (such as rapidly changing environments, novice users, weak penalties for bad estimates) the overall accuracy of estimates may be questionable.

*In a multiprogramming system, jobs may not complete in the order they arrive because of the interleaved execution enforced by the process manager. Thus "first-in" does not necessarily imply "first-out."

**In one study of a CP-67 system[15] it was observed that 85% of the jobs comprised only 7% of the demand for CPU. Similar findings have been reported elsewhere.

***The cost of preemption varies from system to system depending on the amount of work involved, the number of programs in the system, and the proportion of time that can be overlapped.[16]

A final class of rules requires no *a priori* knowledge of processing requirements for scheduling decisions. In the round robin discipline shown in Figure 3, each job, in turn, is allocated a quantum of uninterrupted service. If it does not complete within the quantum, it is preempted and returned to the waiting queues, and a new job is started. The strategy is basically one of sampling the jobs in turn to see which of them can complete with a small amount of additional time.

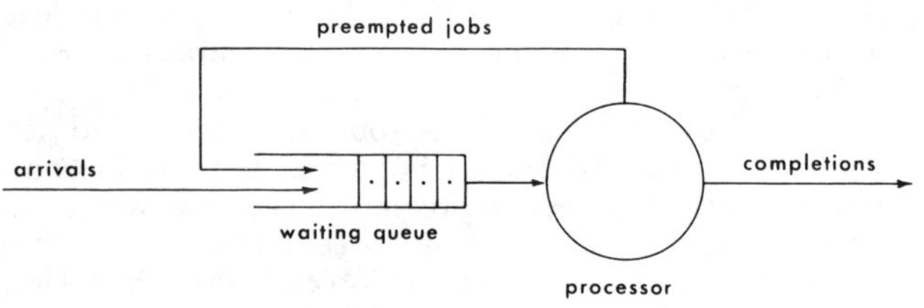

Figure 3. The round robin scheduling strategy.

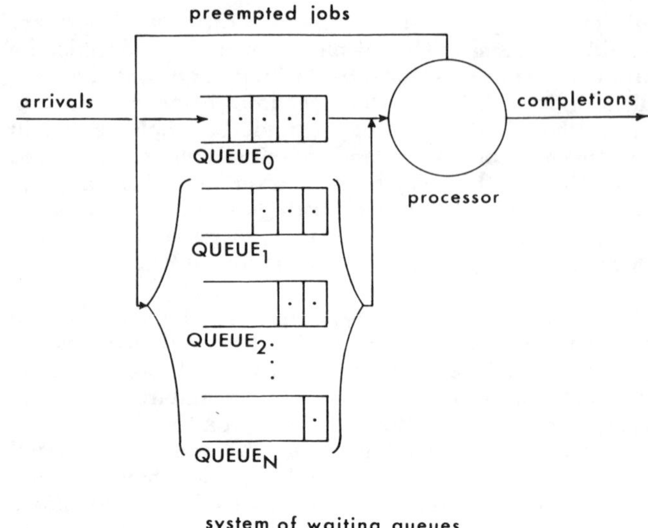

Figure 4. The FB_N scheduling strategy.

Some form of round robin scheduling is used in many interactive systems, and is appropriate since most of the jobs (or requests for service) are short (perhaps requiring only a single quantum) and fast response is essential. The size of the quantum is a design parameter and a critical factor in the performance of the algorithm. The expected time any given job might wait to receive its next quantum of service is proportional to the number of active jobs n, the quantum size q, and the overhead due to switching jobs s (assume $s << q$). This overhead comprises the cost required for preempting the job currently running and starting a new one, and is clearly associated with the sampling operation. As n increases, the expected response time must also increase if q and s remain constant. A variable quantum size can allow the algorithm to be more responsive to the current load. For example, under light loads n is small and adequate response can be achieved with a large quantum; therefore, the amount of switching done (and thus the total sampling overhead) can be reduced by choosing a fairly large quantum size. As the load increases, response degrades; once it becomes unacceptable the quantum size should be reduced. If q becomes too small, however, the s term will become significant and the cost of repeated switching will limit the achievable response.

An important variation of the round robin rule is the multilevel feedback rule (FB, sometimes called "multilevel foreground/background") shown in Figure 4. An ordering is imposed on the system of waiting queues corresponding to the number of service periods that the jobs in the queue have already had. Thus $QUEUE_0$ contains new arrivals, $QUEUE_1$ contains jobs that have been preempted once, and so on. Each of the queues is ordered FCFS. After the quantum of a job being serviced is exhausted, the first job in the lowest-numbered nonempty queue is selected for service, and the preempted job is returned to a queue one level higher than the queue from which it was chosen. If there are at most N waiting queues, the rule is sometimes known as FB_N. The FB rule results in sharper short-job discrimination than the round robin rule by ensuring that long jobs do not interfere. The result of the movement to lower-priority queues is an implicit ordering of the jobs by length of running time (within the limits of accuracy of the quantum size). Thus the effect is similar to that of a "shortest first" rule, but is achieved without any advance knowledge of running times. Like round robin, however, there is associated sampling overhead.

In this section, a number of classical scheduling methods have been described. These can be classified in a variety of ways. First, we have non-preemptive rules, such as FCFS and SPT, versus preemptive rules, such as SRPT, round robin, and FB. The preemption mechanism enhances the discriminatory capability of the scheduling rule, at a cost of a certain amount of system overhead required for the preemption. If the cost of preemption can be kept reasonably small, preemptive rules should outperform non-preemptive rules.[7]

Scheduling rules could also be classified according to the information they require about the jobs *a priori*. Rules such as FCFS, round robin, and FB require no information, whereas rules such as SPT and SRPT require exact information. As expected, schedulers perform better if they can take advantage of information about the nature of the jobs they are scheduling, but in many systems exact knowledge is not available. Rules such as SEPT ("shortest expected processing time") rely on estimates.

Most operating system schedulers resemble one (or may combine several) of the classical rules. These are normally altered to meet certain special requirements of the particular system. In the remainder of this paper, several important operating systems will be described. In the descriptions, an attempt will be made to separate the scheduling component from other aspects of resource allocation, an approach that is neither easy to do nor advisable in practice. This approach has been taken in the interests of space, and hopefully, clarity of description. Apologies are extended in advance to those who might rightfully object to this simplification.

IBM System/360 and System/370 Operating Systems

IBM provides a family of operating systems for its System/360 and System/370 lines of computers. More complete descriptions of these systems, the services they provide, and details of their design are found in the literature.[1,9] In this section the techniques for both job management and process management in some of the more common systems will be described.

The terminology used by IBM differs in some respects from both that used elsewhere and that used earlier in this paper. Here we will be as uniform as possible—and that means some liberties will have to be taken with actual system terminology. In IBM systems, a job is actually submitted by a user as a collection of job steps. For purposes of simplification each job step will be referred to simply as a job in this discussion. Similarly, the terms "process" will be used in place of "task," and "virtual processor" in place of "initiator," "main storage," or "region."

The IBM operating systems operate essentially on a job classification basis. The user is allowed considerable opportunity to make input to the classification decision. In some of the more sophisticated systems, scheduling parameters are modified dynamically, with the user information giving starting values.

OS/MFT. The operating system OS/MFT (multiprogramming with a fixed number of tasks) is the simplest of the systems offering a multiprogramming capability. Essentially, a fixed number of virtual processors (no more than 15, typically less) are made available for users of the system. Associated with each is a fixed amount of main memory. The virtual processors are numbered P_0, P_1, . . . , P_N with the index used to determine the dispatching (or process management) priority. The user classifies his job according to the nature of its resource demands according to the class definitions established by the installation. For example, class A might indicate a job that is I/O-bound, class B a job that is CPU-bound, class C a short express run, class D a job requiring tape and/or disk mounts, and so forth. A system queue is established for each class. Since several jobs will often belong to the same class, a scheme is needed to break ties. First, the user is allowed to specify a priority for his job. If this fails to produce a unique candidate, the jobs are selected in the order they entered the queue (i.e., FCFS within priority and class).

The system operator assigns up to three of the possible job classes to each virtual processor. The order the classes are assigned indicates the job scheduling priority for that particular virtual processor. That is, the first class assigned to a virtual processor has highest priority for the use of that processor, the second class (if there is one) has second priority, and so on. A job may not be scheduled on a virtual processor unless it is from a class assigned to that virtual processor.

In the example illustrated in Figure 5, virtual processor P_0 has been assigned, in order of decreasing priority, classes C, A, and B. This means that first call on this virtual processor goes to class C jobs, second call goes to class A jobs, and in the event that both class C and A queues are empty, a class B job is scheduled. Class D jobs are not eligible to be scheduled on P_0. Classes have been assigned to the remaining virtual processors in a similar manner.

The process management technique used in OS/MFT is known as "highest static priority first" (with preemption). Associated with each virtual processor is a fixed priority with processes running on P_0 having the highest priority and processes running on P_N, the lowest. The highest-priority-ready process is scheduled and executes until one of two events occurs:

(1) the process blocks, for example, on a request for an I/O operation, or

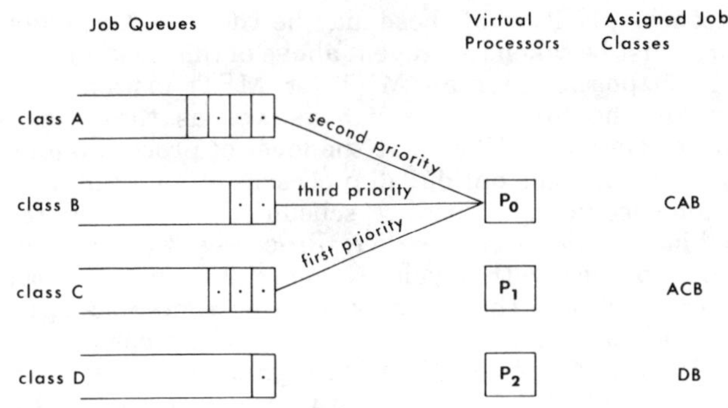

Figure 5. Scheduling from classes in OS/MFT.

(2) a process with a higher priority (i.e., running on a higher-priority virtual processor) becomes ready, for example, by completing an I/O operation (signaled by an interrupt).

The assignment of classes to virtual processors has a significant effect on performance as a result of the actions of the process manager, illustrating the effect of interactions between the two levels of scheduling. For example, if CPU-bound processes are assigned to high-priority virtual processors they will seldom relinquish control of the real CPU, and I/O-bound processes with lower priority will have little chance to execute. As a result, system throughput will be low. Note also that the user has only indirect control over the attention his job receives at the process management (or dispatching) level. The definition of the classes and the assignment of priorities to these classes (through their assignment to certain virtual processors) is out of his hands. He is allowed to specify a job management priority that affects the service he receives *relative to other jobs of the same class.* It is important for the performance of the entire system for the installation to ensure the users do not attempt to misrepresent their jobs.

OS/MVT. OS/MVT (multiprogramming with a variable number of tasks) is similar in many ways to OS/MFT. The job class and priority within class are once again determined at the time of job submission. The assignment of classes to virtual processors and the selection of jobs are done as in MFT. Because the amount of main memory associated with a virtual processor in MVT can vary, further processing of a scheduled job may have to be postponed until the requested amount of memory can be made available. The additional complication is described by Hellerman and Conroy[1] and will not be dealt with here.

Process management techniques in MVT differ from those of MFT. Once again the "highest-static-priority-first" rule is used, but in MVT the virtual processors have no inherent priority; the process management priority is taken from the priority specified by the user on submission of his job (explicitly or by default), which now serves two purposes:

(1) for breaking ties within classes at the level of job management, and
(2) as the process priority at the level of process management.

This now allows the user to assign high process management priority to I/O-bound jobs and low priority to CPU-bound jobs to achieve the high resource usage and improved throughput described earlier. Of course, this presumes that the user knows his job characteristics, and further, that they remain constant throughout the job's execution. Neither of these may be the case. Once again, care must be taken to prevent abuse of this system.

It is possible for an MVT (or MFT) installation to employ the *time slice option* as well as the "highest-static-priority-first" rule at the level of process management. Under this option, all processes at a certain installation-specified priority are scheduled in a round robin fashion as described earlier. Processes with priorities above or below this value are handled in the normal manner. When the priority of the time slice group becomes the highest among all the ready processes, each ready process of the time slice group receives a fixed quantum of CPU time in turn until interrupted by a higher-priority process or until all processes in the time slice group enter the blocked state. Conventional scheduling then takes over.

Among the features offered by HASP is an option called *heuristic dispatching,* which tries to improve resource utilization and increase system throughput by giving high priority to I/O-bound processes. This is done by monitoring process characteristics as the processes execute. Each executing process is given a quantum of CPU time. If the process uses the entire quantum, it is assumed to be CPU-bound and placed in the CPU subgroup. If the process blocks for an I/O operation during its quantum, it is assumed to be I/O-bound and placed in the I/O subgroup. The heuristic dispatcher gives higher priority to processes in the I/O subgroup and schedules the CPU subgroup only if all processes in the I/O subgroup are blocked. Processes in the I/O subgroup are allowed to preempt processes in the CPU subgroup. As processes change their characteristics during execution, HASP will change their subgroup. The effectiveness of the current quantum size in making the distinction between I/O-bound processes and CPU-bound processes is also monitored at specified long intervals (of many quanta). If the proportion of processes identified as I/O-bound is more than a proportion specified as desired by the installation, the quantum size is shortened so as to increase the number of processes identified as CPU-bound and bring the ratio down. If the observed ratio is less than desired, the quantum size is lengthened. The adjustments are made within specified upper and lower bounds. The technique of heuristic dispatching has been found to be very effective, with throughput improvements of almost 19 percent reported by Marshall.[19]

As mentioned, it is often difficult for users to make judgments on the execution characteristics of jobs, particularly when these characteristics change as the job executes (for example, jobs may alternate between periods of CPU-boundedness and I/O-boundedness) or when inferences on the characteristics of jobs other than the user's own are required. The HASP (Houston Automatic Spooling Priority) system offers an enhancement that attempts to meet these difficulties.[5]

HASP was originally developed as part of an enhancement to OS/360 for real-time spaceflight control for NASA's Apollo spaceflights (see the work of Johnstone[18] for a description of the extensions made to OS/360 for this purpose), but it soon became a popular addition to many OS/360 installations. HASP is primarily concerned with peripheral functions, such as the collecting of the job stream and its output (following execution) on direct access devices, and the scheduling of printing and punching of this output from the direct access devices. Many of the HASP functions have been designed directly into the more recent IBM operating systems.

IBM also offers a number of operating systems capable of supporting virtual storage on the System/370 (The reader not familiar with the concept of virtual storage is referred to treatments by Doran,[20] Shaw,[21] or Hellerman and Conroy.[1]). Basically they are enhanced versions of OS/MFT and OS/MVT, originally developed for the System/360. The major differences are in the area of memory management; the scheduling techniques are similar to those already described for MFT and MVT.

OS/VS2 is the enhanced version of OS/MVT (OS/VS1 is the enhanced MFT). The major differences in job management between VS2 and MVT are the support of more virtual processors (up to 63 as compared to 15), and the inclusion of techniques to reduce contention of I/O devices (see IBM guide[22] for details). The process manager incorporates a facility called "automatic priority grouping," based on HASP's heuristic dispatching. A particular priority level can be specified as an automatic priority group to which the techniques described earlier are applied. A restriction imposed is that this priority level cannot also be specified as a time-slicing group. Job management in VS2 is closely tied to memory management. For example, a "load leveler" can interrupt and temporarily halt an active job if the paging rate is assessed to be too high. Thus the number of running virtual processors is dynamically varied. A good description of the facility is given by Hellerman and Conroy.[1]

MULTICS

The IBM operating systems described in the previous section are primarily oriented to a batch environment, although options such as TSO (timesharing option) are available. An example of an operating system design to meet a somewhat different need is MULTICS (*Multi*plexed *I*nformation and *C*omputing *S*ervice), developed jointly by MIT and General Electric. MULTICS offers both interactive and batch service with considerable emphasis placed on the concept of information sharing. Performance objectives vary in such a system, and as a result the scheduling function is handled in a different fashion. A very complete discussion of all aspects of the MULTICS system is given by Organick.[23] The MULTICS virtual storage structure is discussed by Doran.[20]

In a system oriented toward interactive timesharing, the distinction between jobs and processes is somewhat fuzzy. "Jobs" are normally very short requests entered from some type of terminal. The request might be for an edit of some line of text, or it might be for the execution of some previously saved job, such as a compiler. Once a request is received, a "process" is created to perform the requested action. For the sake of uniformity in the presentation, the distinction between job management and process management will be retained in this description. In general, the processor time required to service a request is not known in advance. Consequently, the scheduler is usually one that assumes no knowledge.

The MULTICS job manager is a modified FB_N scheduler. To provide for different service requirements, each job (or request) is assigned, on submission, a range of priority levels (l_1, l_2) and given the initial priority l_1. The range of priorities indicates roughly the type of service the job will receive. Highly interactive jobs (such as line edits) will require very fast response and therefore will be given high priority. Longer-running interactive jobs (such as compilations) or "absentee user" jobs (such as batch jobs) are given a lower-priority range. The levels may, in fact, overlap. Corresponding to the priority levels is a set of N queues from which jobs are scheduled according to the FB_N rule, with the additional complication that each job begins at the queue corresponding to its assigned l_1 value, and is not allowed to drop to queues lower than its assigned l_2 value. As described earlier, the FB_N rule implicitly determines the amount of service required by a job and relegates longer jobs to lower-priority queues. The quantum allocated in MULTICS varies with the level, doubling at each successive lower-priority level. This policy tends to reduce total sampling overhead. The number of jobs permitted to be active at any time (or the multiprogramming level) is determined dynamically from an assessment of the current memory demands of all the active jobs. This is similar to the load leveler embodied in OS/VS2.

At the process management level, control is given to the highest-priority process that is ready to run. If the process blocks, control passes to the next highest-priority process. If the quantum allocated to the job by the job manager expires, the job is deactivated and returned to the system of FB queues. The policy is designed to increase the amount of "effective work" done, or minimize resource wastage. Service considerations, such as fast response, are the province of the job manager.

UNIX

UNIX is a general-purpose multiuser, interactive operating system developed by a group at Bell Laboratories for the Digital Equipment Corporation's PDP-11/40 and PDP-11/45 computers.[24] Unlike the systems described previously, it is quite feasible to run UNIX on relatively small and inexpensive machines, yet the system still offers very effective interactive service. It was primarily designed with objectives such as simplicity, elegance, and ease of use in mind.

Because it is devoted entirely to interactive use, scheduling decisions are somewhat simpler than those made by the MULTICS system. The UNIX job manager examines the jobs in the waiting queue and selects the one that has been waiting the longest. If there is sufficient main memory available to accommodate the needs of this job, it is immediately transferred to the running state. If this is not the case, the job manager tries to find enough "easy core," that is, memory occupied by processes currently in the blocked state. If this additional search fails to meet the specified needs, then a decision is made to acquire the needed memory by deactivating the job that has been active for the longest uninterrupted period, provided it has been active for more than 2 seconds. If all efforts to acquire memory fail, the job manager itself is put to sleep until either a period of 1 second elapses, or until one of the executing jobs blocks, at which time the job manager is reinvoked and the above operation is repeated.

The objective of this job manager is to attempt to give each user a "fair crack" at the processor; that is, no user will wait excessively long for a virtual processor, and once given a virtual processor, each user has a chance to do a reasonable amount of work before deactivation. This objective is consistent with the overall response needs of an interactive system.

The UNIX process manager is very simple. The CPU is given to the highest-priority ready process which retains control for up to 1 second. If the process should block before 1 second has elapsed, control will pass to the next process in the ready queue. This is much the same strategy as that employed in the MULTICS system.

Concluding remarks

In an attempt to provide a common framework for the description of diverse schedulers, a general model was proposed. A number of classical scheduling techniques were described using this model and their characteristics were assessed. Actual implementations of these techniques often compromise the classical definitions to accommodate some special requirements or constraints of the particular system. A common problem is that of balancing the total resource demand of the jobs in the system against the resources available. For example, a scheduling decision resulting from the application of one of the classical rules may have to be overridden because of insufficient available memory. Clearly, any discussion that attempts to concentrate solely on processor scheduling will be deficient in some of these areas. A scheduler must be an integral part of the resource allocation component of an operating system.

In this paper the scheduling methods of a number of popular operating systems have been described. The IBM systems described (OS/MFT, OS/MVT, OS/VS2) are all primarily oriented to an environment of batch submissions. The MULTICS system and the UNIX system, offering different types of service, have different performance objectives and hence employ a different scheduling approach to meet these objectives. ■

Acknowledgments

The preparation of this paper was supported in part by the Defence Research Board of Canada, Grant No. 9931-40. The author is grateful for the help of Chris Thomson for gathering material and of Dianne Good for typing the manuscript.

References

1. H. Hellerman and T. F. Conroy, *Computer System Performance*, McGraw-Hill, New York, 1975.
2. E. W. Dijkstra, "Cooperating Sequential Processes," *Programming Languages* (F. Genuys ed.), Academic Press, New York, 1968, pp. 43-112.
3. J. J. Horning and B. Randell, "Process Structuring," *ACM Computing Surveys*, Vol. 5, No. 1 (March 1973), pp. 5-30.
4. R. R. Muntz, *Software Systems Principles: A Survey* (P. Freeman, ed), Chapter 7, Science Research Associates, 1975.
5. K. D. Ryder, "A Heuristic Approach to Task Dispatching," *IBM Systems Journal*, Vol. 9, No. 3 (1970), pp. 189-198.
6. J. H. Saltzer, "Traffic Control in a Multiplexed Computer System," Sc.D. thesis, Dept. of EE, MIT, Cambridge, Massachusetts, 1966.
7. S. Sherman, F. Baskett, and J. C. Browne, "Trace-Driven Modeling and Analysis of CPU Scheduling in a Multiprogramming System," *CACM*, Vol. 15, No. 12 (December 1972), pp. 1063-1069.
8. P. Brinch Hansen, *Operating Systems Principles*, Prentice-Hall, Englewood Cliffs, New Jersey, 1973.

9. S. E. Madnick and J. J. Donovan, *Operating Systems,* McGraw-Hill, New York, 1974.

10. B. W. Lampson, "A Scheduling Philosophy for Multiprocessing Systems," *CACM,* Vol. 11, No. 5 (May 1968), pp. 347-360.

11. E. G. Coffman, Jr., and L. Kleinrock, "Computer Scheduling Methods and Their Countermeasures," *Proc. AFIPS, SJCC,* Vol. 32 (1968), pp. 11-21.

12. E. G. Coffman, Jr., and L. Kleinrock, "Feedback Queueing Models for Time-Shared Systems," *JACM,* Vol. 15, No. 4 (October 1968), pp. 549-576.

13. R. W. Conway, W. L. Maxwell, and L. W. Miller, *Theory of Scheduling,* Addison-Wesley, Reading, Massachusetts, 1967.

14. L. Kleinrock, "A Conservation Law for a Wide Class of Queueing Disciplines," *Naval Research Logistics Quarterly,* Vol. 12, No. 2 (June 1965), pp. 181-192.

15. J. Rodriguez-Rosell and J. Dupuy, "The Design, Implementation and Evaluation of a Working Set Dispatcher," *CACM,* Vol. 16, No. 4 (April 1973), pp. 247-253.

16. U. N. Bhat and R. E. Nance, "Dynamic Quantum Allocation and Swap Time Variability in Time-Sharing Operating Systems," Tech. Report No. CP-73009, Department of Computer Science and Operations Research, Southern Methodist University, Dallas, Texas, April 1973.

17. L. Schrage, "A Proof of the Optimality of the Shortest Remaining Processing Time Discipline," *Operations Research,* Vol. 16, No. 3 (May-June 1968), pp. 687-690.

18. J. L. Johnstone, *Software Systems Principles: A Survey* (P. Freeman, ed.), Chapter 17, Science Research Associates, 1975.

19. B. S. Marshall, "Dynamic Calculation of Dispatching Priorities Under OS/360 MVT," *Datamation* (August 1969), pp. 93-97.

20. R. W. Doran, "Virtual Memory," *Computer,* Vol. 9, No. 10 (October 1976), pp. 27-37.

21. A. C. Shaw, *The Logical Design of Operating Systems,* Prentice-Hall, Englewood Cliffs, New Jersey, 1974.

22. IBM Corporation, *OS/VS2 Planning and Use Guide,* Form No. GC28-0600-2, September 1972.

23. E. I. Organick, *The MULTICS System: An Examination of Its Structure,* MIT Press, Cambridge, Massachusetts, 1972.

24. D. M. Ritchie and K. Thompson, "The UNIX Time-Sharing System," *CACM,* Vol. 17, No. 7 (July 1974), pp. 365-375.

A Scheduling Philosophy for Multiprocessing Systems

Butler W. Lampson

University of California, Berkeley, California

A collection of basic ideas is presented, which have been evolved by various workers over the past four years to provide a suitable framework for the design and analysis of multiprocessing systems. The notions of *process* and *state vector* are discussed, and the nature of basic operations on processes is considered. Some of the connections between processes and protection are analyzed. A very general approach to priority-oriented scheduling is described, and its relationship to conventional interrupt systems is explained. Some aspects of time-oriented scheduling are considered. The implementation of the scheduling mechanism is analyzed in detail and the feasibility of embodying it in hardware established. Finally, several methods for interlocking the execution of independent processes are presented and compared.

KEY WORDS AND PHRASES: time-sharing, multiprocessing, process, scheduling, interlocks, protection, priority, interrupt systems

CR CATEGORIES: 4.31, 4.32, 6.21

Introduction

One of the essential parts of any computer system is a mechanism for allocating the processors of the system among the various competitors for their services. These allocations must be performed in even the simplest system, for example, by the action of an operator at the console of the machine. In larger systems more automatic techniques are usually adopted: batching of jobs, interrupts, and interval timers are the most common ones. As the use of such techniques becomes more frequent, it becomes increasingly difficult to maintain the conventional view of a computer as a system which does only one job at a time; even though it may at any given instant be executing a particular sequence of instructions, its attention is switched from one such sequence to another with such rapidity that it appears desirable to describe the system in a manner which accommodates this multiplexing more naturally. It is worth while to observe that these remarks apply to any large modern computer system and not just to one which attempts to service a number of online users simultaneously.

We consider first, therefore, the basic ideas of *process* and *state vector* and the properties of processes which are, so to speak, independent of the hardware on which they may happen to be executing. The interactions between processes are dealt with and the necessary machinery is constructed to permit these interactions to proceed smoothly. Many of these ideas were first expounded by Saltzer [5], from whose treatment we have borrowed most of our terminology. We then go on to analyze the mechanisms by which processes increase their capabilities.

In the next few sections we consider mechanisms for sharing processors among processes. Our attention centers first on priority-driven scheduling systems, which have obvious analogies with interrupt systems. After detailed treatment of a reasonably efficient implementation of a priority scheduler, we turn to some of the problems of time-driven scheduling, in which the objective is to get work done at certain fixed times. A scheme for embedding time-driven processes in the priority system is discussed, and the generally neglected problem of guaraneted service is analyzed at some length; unfortunately, its surface is only scratched.

There follows a detailed analysis of how an interrupt system might be replaced with a quite general scheduling system which permits any user process to run in response to any external signal and which removes all constraints on the relative priorities of different processes and the order in which their execution may be started and stopped. In conclusion we consider the very important problem of interlocking processes which access a common data base and analyze its relation to the scheduling system in use.

Presented at an ACM Symposium on Operating System Principles, Gatlinburg, Tennessee, October 1–4, 1967; revised January, 1968.

The work reported in this paper was supported in part by the Advanced Research Projects Agency of the Department of Defense under Contract SD-185.

Preliminaries

We begin by defining some terms which will permit a precise discussion of what happens in a complex computer system. The most important of these terms is *process*. The intuitive basis for the idea represented by this word is the observation that certain sequences of actions follow naturally, one upon the other, and are more or less independent of other sequences. For example, a disk-to-printer routine and a matrix inversion program running on the same processor are two quite distinct programs, which can normally execute entirely independently of each other. The independence is not complete, however, since information may be written into the disk file by the inversion program while earlier information is read by the printer driver. Furthermore, the fact that clearly different programs are being executed is not essential; two inversions operating on different data would have just as much right to be considered distinct. Indeed, it might well be that a single inversion program could be coded in such a way that several parts of it could be in execution simultaneously.

To summarize, the essential characteristic of a process is that it has, at least conceptually, a processor of its own to run on, and that the state of its processor is more or less independent of all the other processors on which all the other processes are running. Since there are usually not as many physical processors as three are processes, it becomes necessary to create enough logical processors by multiplexing the physical ones. Techniques for doing this are one of the subjects of this paper.

We now consider more carefully what is involved in switching a physical processor from one process to another. When a processor is executing instructions, there exists a collection of information (called the *full-state vector*) which is sufficient to completely define its state at any given moment, in the sense that placing the processor in some arbitrary state and then resetting it from the full state vector will cause execution of instructions to proceed as though nothing had happened. For a central processor of conventional organization the full-state vector includes:

(a) The contents of the program counter.

(b) The contents of the central registers of the processor. For convenience, we will confine our attention to points in time between the execution of instructions at which registers directly accessible to the programmer are the only ones of interest. The use of address mapping schemes involving segmentation may make it necessary to consider also certain nonaccessible registers involved in indirect addressing. This complication will be ignored.

(c) The address space of the processor and the contents of every address in it. By this we mean a list of all the legal memory addresses which may be generated by the program and the contents of each one.

(d) The state of all input-output devices attached to the processor.

The information just specified consists of a rather large number of bits. Furthermore, it contains considerably more detail than is usually desired. In a time-sharing system, for example, the physical state of the input/output devices is not normally of interest to the program, and even the address of the next word to be read from a file may not be information which we wish to associate with a process, since such an association makes it difficult for two processes to share the file.

Similar considerations apply to the contents of the words in the address space; these might be changed by another process. The address space itself, however, has a better claim to be regarded as an integral part of the process. To clarify this point, we pause to consider (or define) exactly what the address space is. We may think of all the words which can possibly be addressed by any process as being numbered in some arbitrary fashion. Each word is then identified by its number, which we will call its absolute address. Note that we are not saying anything about the physical location of the words, and that the absolute address we have just defined has nothing to do with this location, but is simply a conceptual tool. Then the *address space* of a process (also called the *map*) is a function from the integers into the set consisting of the absolute addresses of all the words in the system and two symbols U and N; i.e. it associates with every address generated by the program an absolute address, or specifies that the address is undefined or not available. The address space may also carry information about the accessibility of a word for which it supplies an absolute address, specifying, for example, that the word may not be written into.

Observe now that what the address space really does is to define the memory of the process. Any of the words of this memory may also be part of the memory of some other process, which may refer to them with the same or different addresses. The words, however, are considered to have an existence independent of their addresses in any particular address space.

We recognize, then, that the definition we want for the state vector of a process is not a direct analog of the one used in system theory. In fact, it leaves unspecified a number of things which can affect the future execution of a process, namely just those things which we wish to think of as being shared between processes. With this point in mind, we define the *state vector* (or *stateword*) of a process to consist of the program counter, central registers, and address space of the processor on which it is running. From the above discussion we conclude that the process can still exist even if it is not running on the processor, since the state vector carries sufficient information to allow it to be restarted. A process should be sharply distinguished from a program, which is a sequence of instructions in memory. We can speak of either a process or a processor executing a program. The process is the logical, the processor the physical environment for this execution. It seems reasonable to say that the process is executing even if it is not running on any processor.

To give practical substance to the distinction between process and program, it is required that execution of the program should not cause it to be modified. If this restriction is observed, it is clear that more than one process can be executing the same program at the same time. Note that it is not necessary to have more than one processor for this to be possible, since we do not insist that a process be running in order to be executing. To return to the matrix inversion example: in a particular problem it may be necessary to invert six independent matrices, and to this end six processes may be established, one to work on each matrix but all executing the same program. On the other hand, one of these processes may, after inverting a matrix, go on to execute a different program which calculates its eigenvalues.

Operations on Processes

In this section we take up some points which are independent of processor multiplexing. A number of these points center around the observation that a process does not always want to execute instructions even if there is a physical processor available. A typical example of such a process is a compiler which has exhausted its available input and is waiting for more cards to be read. This is a special case of a very general situation, in which a process is waiting for some external condition to be satisfied and has nothing useful to do in the meantime. There are basically two ways in which this situation can be handled. The simplest is for the process to loop, testing a flag which records the state of the external condition. The objection to this scheme is that it is wasteful if there is any other process which could use the processor. Alternatively, the process can record somewhere the fact that it is waiting for, say, 14 cards to be read, and *block* itself. It will then execute no more instructions until the 14th card has been read and it has received a *wakeup* signal. The part of the system responsible for handling block and wakeup instructions will be called the *scheduler*. When a processor is executing instructions for a process, the process is said to be *running*.

From the point of view of the scheduler, then, the life history of a process is an alternation of running periods and blocked ones. Each running period is terminated by a request to the scheduler that the process should be blocked; this request may be made by the process itself or by some other process. Each blocked period is terminated by a wake up signal whose characteristics are described above. Since the process can do nothing to help itself while it is blocked, it must make arrangements to be awakened before blocking itself. Let us consider what the nature of these arrangements might be.

The simplest situation is one in which the process has requested some service to be performed and wishes to wait until it is completed. Typical services have to do with input-output: a process might block itself until an input buffer is filled. In this case the process performing the service is expected to provide the wakeup signal. This idea is so simple as to require only one further comment. A reciprocal situation is that of the input-output process: it expects to be awakened by a demand for service and blocks itself when it has done its job. The situation is sketched in Figure 1. Readers familiar with the concept of coroutines will find this picture familiar.

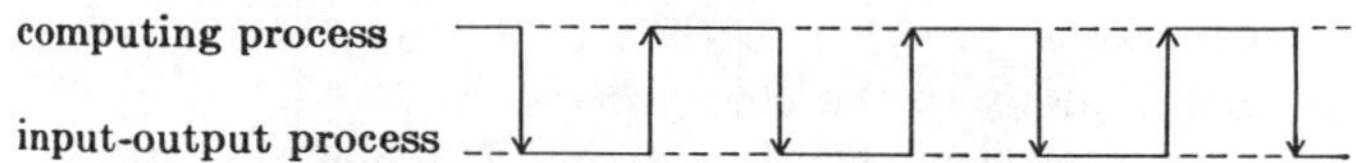

FIG. 1 Reciprocally blocked processes. Solid horizontal lines indicate running periods, dashed ones blocked periods. The arrows are wakeup signals.

A slightly more involved situation is shown in Figure 2. Here the input is assumed to be buffered, so that the computing process, after making a request for input, is able to continue running for a while. In the figure it continues to run on buffered input data until after the input-output process has completed its work and sent it a wakeup, which has no effect on an already running process. Finally, it blocks itself, but by this time the wakeup has passed and will never come again.

This situation can of course be alleviated by having the input process set a flag indicating that it has filled the next buffer. The computing process could then test this flag and not block itself if the operation is complete. This approach, however, will only serve to make the bad situation shown in Figure 2a less common; it will not eliminate it entirely, since it is still possible for the input process to send its wakeup in the interval between an unsuccessful test and the subsequent block. What is necessary is to reduce this interval to zero, which can be done with a simple device called a *wakeup-waiting* switch. There is one of these for each process. Whenever a wakeup signal arrives at a running process, the switch is turned on. Whenever the process is blocked, it is turned off, and the process can also turn it off explicitly. If a process tries to block itself and the wakeup-waiting switch is on, the switch is turned off and the process is simply allowed to continue running without interruption. This sequence of events is illustrated in Figure 2b.

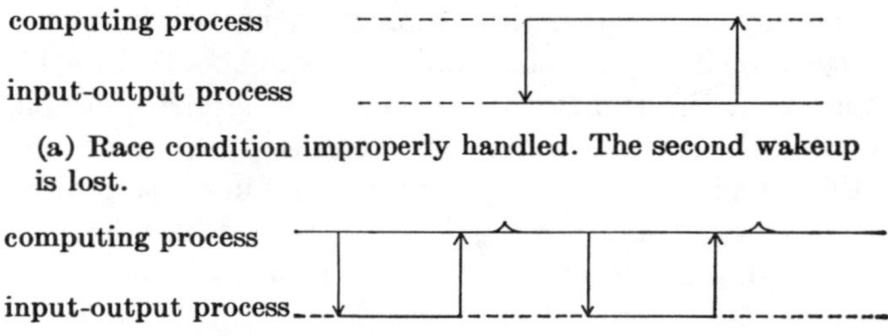

(a) Race condition improperly handled. The second wakeup is lost.

(b) Race conditions handled correctly. The cusps are attempts to block thwarted by the wakeup-waiting switch.

FIG. 2. Race conditions in the scheduler

Note that a single switch for each process is quite sufficient. Any function which might be accomplished with a stack of wakeup signals handled by the scheduler can be equally well accomplished by communication through shared memory.

The proper way to program a process which blocks itself periodically, like the ones in Figure 2, is to check explicitly after a wakeup signal is received that there is in fact work to be done, and to block again if there is not. This procedure will circumvent the problems which would otherwise arise if the work for which a wakeup is received gets done before the process tries to block. Often the simplest way to make this check is with a loop back to the code which made the decision to block, as, for example, in the following routine to read data from an input buffer being filled by another process:

a. Is input buffer empty?
b. If not, read data and exit.
c. Otherwise, block.
d. When wakeup arrives, go to (a).

An additional complication is introduced by the fact that it is not unusual for several processes to be blocked waiting for the same condition to occur. If this situation can arise, the process generating the wakeup must be prepared to send it not just to one process, but to an entire *wakeup list* of processes. Alternatively, it may be preferable to leave this process unaware of the problem and to make one of the processes receiving a wakeup signal responsible for sending wakeups to the others (if such action is appropriate; in the case of several processes competing for a single device it may not be). The possible existence of wakeup lists is not important to the basic scheme and has been mentioned only to illustrate a complication which can be handled without difficulty.

We now have two states for a process: blocked and running; and two basic operations on processes: block and wakeup. Let us consider what else is required. Two things are obvious: it is necessary to be able to create and destroy processes, and to establish restrictions on the kind of access allowed to one process by another. These problems, however, have to do with the general mechanism in the system for granting capabilities, with which we are not concerned here. The precise operations required to create a process are considered in a later section.

It is, however, very convenient for a process to have one other property in addition to being blocked or running. Suppose, for example, that a program involving several processes is being debugged online. A valuable tool in this situation is the ability to stop execution of the program, examine the state of things, and then continue as though nothing had happened. During the pause in execution, all the processes being debugged are *suspended*; i.e. they are prevented from executing. If a wakeup signal is directed at a suspended process, it is recorded and will be acted upon when the process is released. In other words, being suspended is a quality unrelated to being blocked; a suspended process can be either blocked or running, but it will execute no instructions until it is released.

Approximately the same effect can be obtained by reading the state words of all the processes, destroying them, and then recreating them later and putting back the statewords. This approach, however, requires a potentially large amount of information to be recorded and then restored. It is also likely to be quite time-consuming, especially since it is usually not possible to destroy a process at any arbitrary point in its execution, e.g. when it is operating on system tables. Furthermore, if any wakeup signals for a process arrive after it has been destroyed, they will be lost, which is not very satisfactory.

Acquistion of Capabilities. We conclude this section with a brief discussion of the relationship between processes and protection. It has been taken for granted so far, as in almost all of the published literature, that a process (or a group of processes) is the basic entity to which capabilities should be attached [2, 3]. Since this doctrine cannot easily be made to cover all situations, it is usually modified in running systems by more or less inelegant devices for allowing a process to have different capabilities depending on what it is doing.

To make this point clearer, let us consider an ordinary unprivileged process which wishes to obtain permission to use a tape unit, for example. It will make some kind of "call on the system." That is, it will transfer to a system routine which will determine whether the process is authorized to use tape units and whether the specified unit is free. If everything is in order, the system will grant the desired permission. To avoid unnecessary digression, let us assume that permission is granted by turning on a bit in the stateword, and that the hardware allows execution of instructions for this tape unit only when the bit is on. The point is that the process running the system program must have much greater capabilities than the user process; it has at least the capability to set the hypothetical bit just introduced, and the user process does not have that capability or it would have set the bit itself. In fact, we can dispense with the bit if anyone can set it, since it would serve no useful purpose.

This discussion suggests that the "call on the system" mentioned above is really a wakeup directed to a process with great capabilities, which we call a system process. There must also be some mechanism for communicating data between user and system processes, so that the latter can find out what is wanted and the former obtain information about the fate of its request. We may assume that the two processes share some memory, and neglect a host of questions about how such an arrangement can actually be implemented with reasonable efficiency. The situation is then quite clear: the user process puts information about its request into this shared memory, wakes up the system process, and blocks. The system process examines the request, modifies the user process stateword appropriately, records what it has done in the shared memory, wakes up the user process, and blocks. The entire interaction depends on cooperation between the two processes, which is precisely why it is a suitable mechanism for its purpose: the user process cannot force the system process to do anything, but can only call attention to its desires.

It is worth noticing, however, that the use of two processes in the manner just discussed is completely different from the usual applications of multiprocessing, where two processes are running (more or less) in parallel. Here no parallel execution takes place at all; the system process runs when, and only when, the user process is blocked. The entire transaction in fact looks exactly like a subroutine call and return implemented in a very clumsy way. The only reason that the system process is a *process* rather than a *program* is that it has capabilities which we wish to deny to the user process.

If we approach the discussion of capabilities from a different viewpoint, it will become clear why very few systems use the multiple process scheme described above. The first point to observe is that instead of thinking of a process as starting out with no power and acquiring *capabilities*, one may think of it as starting out with absolute power and then being restricted by the system's *protection* mechanisms. This is of course the customary way of looking at things; the word "absolute" is especially appropriate on a mapped machine, since protection is usually enforced primarily by the map and the ability to use absolute addresses allows a process to do anything. Let us consider briefly the fundamental characteristics of protection systems.

The simplest way of describing what is required is to say that certain processes must be prevented from executing certain words as instructions, namely those which violate the constraints of the protection they operate under. For purposes of implementation, however, it has proved convenient to make a further distinction and say that a process must be prevented from (1) accessing, changing, or transferring control to certain words in the physical memory of the machine (*memory* protection), and from (2) executing instructions with certain operation codes, which are often called privileged (*control* protection).

To accommodate the first requirement a variety of arrangements has been tried, which fall into two general classes, namely the protection of particular physical regions of core and the provision of an address mapping function which transforms every address generated by the program before sending it to the physical memory. The relative merits of various schemes in both classes have been debated at some length and need not concern us here. We turn our attention to the problems of control protection.

Protection Systems. What might be called the minimal solution to these problems, and one which has been implemented on many machines, is the provision of two modes called "monitor" and "user," or "master" and "slave" modes. In the first, or monitor, mode all the instructions of the machine can be executed, including those which change the address space of the process. In user mode, on the other hand, all the opcodes which might interfere with the operation of the system or of another user are prohibited. This prohibition is usually enforced by causing a switch into monitor mode and a transfer to a standard system routine whenever attempted execution of a privileged opcode is detected. These include any opcode which is undefined or which halts the machine, all input-output opcodes, and all opcodes which invoke the scheduling or address mapping hardware.

One of the implications of this kind of organization is that calls on the system, say in the form of a switch to monitor mode and a transfer to one of a small number of standard entry points, must be provided for any operation which a user program may be authorized to perform and which requires execution of privileged instructions. Because the ability to execute such instructions attaches to a *process*, and because there are only two possible states which a process can be in as far as its authority to execute such instructions is concerned, there is no way of avoiding a call to a system routine every time the need for a privileged instruction arises. Furthermore, this routine will in general have to check the validity of the call every time it is entered. Some improvement can be obtained by providing a number of different modes in which various classes of instructions are prohibited, but the number of input-output devices attached to a system is likely to be large enough to prevent this approach from effecting much improvement, since in general every device must be protected independently of every other one. Matters are still worse when it comes to mass storage devices and it is desired to allow access only to certain *areas* of the device.

An alternative approach to the whole problem of control protection—one which is capable of eliminating the problems we have been considering—is to attach the authority to execute privileged instructions not to the process executing them but to the memory locations from which they are executed. Almost any memory protection scheme for a time-sharing system will allow an area of memory to be made read-only to a process. A system routine which controls the memory protection hardware can obtain read/write access to this area and therefore can put into it anything it likes. What we envision now is an extension of the memory protection mechanism which allows this area to be made not merely read-only, but also privileged. If a memory location is part of a privileged area, then the control protection hardware will allow a privileged instruction fetched from this location to execute. Otherwise, execution of such an instruction will be suppressed.

The system then simply arranges that the memory available to any process which is authorized to execute privileged instructions contains those instructions which the system wants to allow the process to execute, and no others; the process executes them by addressing them with an execute instruction. The result of such an arrangement is that from the point of view of the system control protection is absorbed into memory protection: the ultimate authority which a process can exercise is determined by the memory it can write, since not only the ability to execute privileged instructions but also the state of the memory protection system itself is determined by the contents of certain areas of memory. A process can do anything if it can write into privileged memory and can set up the memory protection for itself or for another process.

It therefore follows that to change the capabilities of a process it suffices to change the map. The operation of waking up a system process can be replaced by a subroutine call which makes some memory accessible which was formerly forbidden. One popular implementation falls back temporarily on the monitor mode concept—a transfer of control which changes the protection (called a *leap*) must go through a standard routine which, running in monitor mode, is not subject to the usual restrictions of the system. This scheme is completely general and quite elegant; its only drawback is that leaps are likely to be slow.

At least two proposals have been made for making most or all of the map-changing operation automatic. The MULTICS group has suggested a hardware implementation of their "ring" structure, which divides the address space of a process into concentric rings and allows access to ring n from ring m only if $m < n$. Evans and LeClerc [4] have put forward a mapping and protection system which permits individual control of the access every segment has to every other segment. Neither of these proposals has yet been implemented.

In many cases, of course, the entire problem is evaded by performing the desired privileged operation entirely in monitor mode, i.e. outside the confines of the protection system. This approach makes it unnecessary to worry about how to increase the capabilities of a process, but has obvious disadvantages in flexibility and security and is gradually becoming unpopular.

Scheduling

In this section we consider some algorithms which may be used to implement a scheduler, and complete the discussion of basic principles with an analysis of processor multiplexing. The scheduler consists of two sets of procedures which are logically quite independent of each other, and a data base which connects them.

The first set of procedures may be called the *user interface*. Its function is to implement the basic operations which may be called for by a user process:

block
wakeup
suspend
release
test and reset wakeup waiting switch
change priority (see below).

If processor multiplexing is not required this is a very straightforward matter. We define four arrays indexed by process or processor number (these are equivalent if there is no multiplexing):

run[*i*] is 1 if processor **i** is executing instructions, 0 if it is not. This value controls the processor.

suspend[*i*] is 1 if process **i** is suspended, 0 if it is not.

runstate[*i*] is 0 if the process was blocked more recently than it was awakened, 1 otherwise.

wws[*i*] is 1 if the wakeup waiting switch for process **i** is on, 0 if it is off.

These arrays, together with some other data to be introduced shortly, constitute the *scheduler data base*. Pseudo ALGOL procedures for the basic operations are:

```
procedure block (i);
begin
  if wws[i] = 0 then run[i] := runstate[i] := 0 else wws[i] := 0
end;
procedure wakeup(i);
begin
  if runstate[i] = 1 then   wws[i] :=1;  runstate[i] := 1;
  if suspend[i] = 0 then run[i] := 1
end;
procedure suspend(i);
begin
  run[i] := 0;  suspend[i] := 1
end;
procedure release(i);
begin
  suspend[i] := 0;  run[i] := runstate[i]
end;
integer procedure trwws(i);
begin
  trwws := wws[i];  wws[i] := 0
end
```

In the absence of multiplexing this is the entire implementation of the scheduler. It is assumed that the action specified by one of these procedures is taken instantaneously as far as the rest of the system is concerned. We defer a consideration of how this can be done and of the general problems of interlocking parallel processes to a later section. Note that we have not said anything about how these procedures are executed; it will be sufficient for the moment to imagine a special processor whose sole function is to do this.

Multiplexing. As soon as we begin to consider processor multiplexing, life becomes much more complicated and more interesting. In order to introduce the complications one at a time, let us assume that the user interface procedures continue to function as before, but that the array *run* no longer directly controls the operation of a processor. In fact, since there are no longer enough processors to allow one to be assigned to each program, the data base arrays are not directly related to processors at all. To specify the indirect relationship, we define two more arrays:

processor[*i*] specifies the processor assigned to process *i*. It is 0 if no processor is assigned.

process[*j*] specifies the process running on processor *j*. It is 0 if no process is running.

A process *i* is called *ready* if *run*[*i*] = 1 but *processor*[*i*] = 0.

The procedures which establish connections between processes and processors constitute the second half of the scheduler, which is called the *enforcer*. The algorithm used by the enforcer to assign processors is called the *scheduling algorithm*. A very simple and very unsatisfactory scheduling algorithm might be the following:

```
        i := 0
ploop:  for j := 1 step 1 until np do
          if process[j] = 0 then
          begin
qloop:      i := if i = nq then 1 else i + 1;  if run[i] = 0
            ∨ processor[i] ≠ 0 then goto qloop;
            processor[i] := j;  process[j] := 1
          end
          else if run[process[j]] = 0 then
          begin
            process[j] := processor[process[j]]:= 0; goto qloop
          end;
        goto ploop;
```

Here *np* is the number of processors, *nq* the number of processes. This procedure simply cycles around the processes in fixed sequence, assigning free processors to processes which wish to run as it finds them. Again we assume that where there is any possibility of confusion the enforcer's actions are performed instantaneously.

Priorities. In order to improve on this algorithm it is necessary for the scheduler to have some idea about the relative importance of different processes. For purposes of discussion we consider that two measures of importance exist:

An integer assigned to each process called its *priority*. The enforcer regards process *i* as more important than process *j* if *priority*[*i*] > *priority*[*j*]. The array *priority* is added to the scheduler data base.

The amount of time which has elapsed since a process was ready and assigned a particular priority. For processes of equal priority the enforcer operates on a first-come, first-served basis.

Two modifications to the user interface are required to accommodate this new idea. One is a change in wakeup which allows a priority to be supplied along with the wakeup signal:

```
procedure wakeup(i,p);
begin
  if runstate[i] = 1 then wws[i] := 1;
  runstate[i] := 1;  priority[i] := p;
  if suspend[i] = 0 then run[i] := 1
end;
```

The other is a new operation:

```
procedure chpri(i,p);  begin priority[i] := p end;
```

These two operations make it possible to establish priorities for the various processes. The way in which this is done will determine which processes get to run, and will therefore have an important influence on the behavior of the system. It should be clear, however, that priority assignment is not an integral part of the scheduler, and it will therefore receive only passing consideration.

We expect the enforcer to select from the processes with *run*[*i*]=1 those *np* which have the highest priority at each instant. The precise length of an instant will be considered later; obviously we want it to be as short as possible provided the overhead stays low. A typical situation which the scheduling algorithm might encounter in a two-processor system might involve four processes computing with various priorities, another four processes blocked for ordinary input-output operations, and two processes awaiting real-time interrupts. At one moment the system should be running two of the computing processes, at the next one of these and then a process activated because of the receipt of teletype input, and at the next two top priority real-time processes. See Figure 3.

We now proceed to consider a possible implementation of the multiplexing philosophy just described. The idea is that the scheduler should not be aware of a process at all until it receives the wakeup signal, i.e. it should look only at processes on a list called the *ready list*. This list should be organized so as to make the selection of highest priority processes as natural as possible and to facilitate

C, 6 **C, 6** *C, 7* *C, 8* Computing processes
I/O, 4 I/O, 3 I/O, 6 I/O, 8 Processes blocked for I/O
I, 1 I, 2

(a) A possible state of the system. The running processes are in boldface, the ready ones in italics. Numbers indicate priorities; the highest priority is 1.

C, 6 **C, 6** *C, 7* *C, 9*
I/O, 4 I/O, 3 *I/O, 6* *I/O, 8*
I, 1 I, 2

(b) Another possible state

C, 6 *C, 6* *C, 7* *C, 8*
I/O, 4 I/O, 3 *I/O, 6* *I/O, 8*
I, 1 I, 2

(c) A higher priority process becomes ready

C, 6 (1) *C, 6* (2) *C, 7* (3) *C, 8* (4)
I/O, 4 (5) I/O, 3 (6) *I/O, 6* (7) *I/O, 8* (8)
I, 1 (9) **I, 2** (10)

(d) Two urgent real-time processes are running. Process numbers in parentheses.

Fig. 3. Running, ready, and blocked processes in a two-processor system

the introduction of new processes. The former requirement can be very simply satisfied by keeping the process numbers of the ready processes in a table of consecutive registers in order of their priority. This arrangement is extremely inconvenient, however, when it comes to adding processes, since on the average half of the list will need to be moved for each addition.

A slight improvement can be effected by replacing the table with a linked list, so that insertion requires only a splicing of pointers. It still requires a search through the list, however, to find the appropriate point at which to make the insertion. In order to eliminate this search it will be necessary to introduce more structure into the ready list. One way to do this is the following: restrict priorities to be integers in the range from 1 to n, and equip the scheduler with an n-word table called the priority list. Each entry of this table contains either 0 or a pair of process numbers, *plfp* and *plrp*. Associated with each process there are also two process numbers, *fqp*[*i*] and *bqp*[*i*], which serve the purpose of forward and backward queue pointers.

The significance of these arrangements is as follows: every nonzero priority list entry contains pointers to the head and tail of a queue of ready processes which have the priority given by the index of the entry in the priority list. When a new process arrives, it is added to the tail of the queue; processes are run beginning at the head. The queue is kept as a symmetric list to facilitate deletions.

To clarify the ready list pointer structure, the situation in Figure 3 is displayed in full in Figures 4 and 5.

Management of the Ready List. To take advantage of this data structure it is desirable to integrate the enforcer with the user interface procedures, since the enforcer needs to act only in response to a block, wakeup, or change priority operation (suspend and release, if they involve the enforcer at all, are equivalent to block and wakeup). Constant scanning of the scheduler data base is therefore not necessary. The pointer manipulations now become sufficiently complex, however, that a description in words seems more satisfactory than explicit procedures.

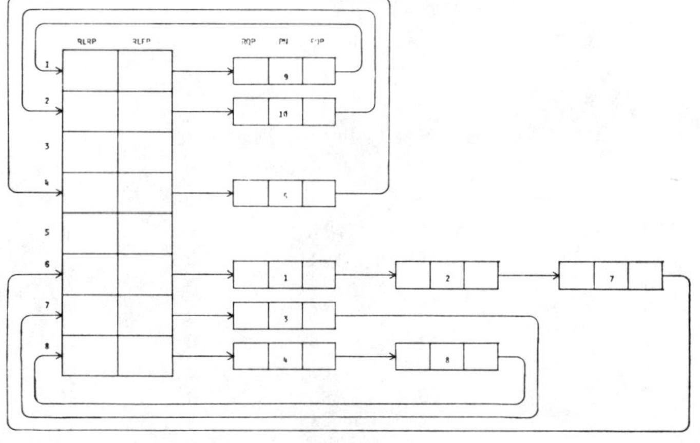

ready list processes

Fig. 4. Ready list and queues for Figure 3d

There are two basic cases in which the enforcer is activated.

The first case is when a process is awakened. It is necessary to

(W1) Enter this process in the ready list at the appropriate priority on the tail of the queue (unless it is already on the ready list at a higher priority).

(W2) Check to see whether this priority is higher than that of some running process. If not, there is nothing to do.

(W3) If so, switch the processor running the lowest priority process so that it will run the newly introduced process instead. The abandoned process remains on the ready list and will run in due course. It has been *preempted.*

The second case is when a running process blocks and its wakeup-waiting switch is not set.

(B1) Remove its queue cell from the ready list.

(B2) Find the lowest priority running process. Examine its forward pointer.

(B3) If it is a pointer to another queue cell, run the process in that queue cell, which is now the lowest priority process.

(B4) Otherwise, scan down the priority list from the entry at the priority level of the lowest priority running process. When a nonzero entry is found, run the process in the queue cell pointed to by its head pointer.

A change priority operation, the only other one which affects the enforcer, can be implemented with the sequence

block; *priority*[*i*] := *new priority*; *wakeup*;

In practice, of course, this can be improved upon, since there are many cases in which no changes in processor assignment are called for.

Priority	*rlfp*	*rlrp*
1	9	9
2	10	10
3	0	0
4	5	5
5	0	0
6	1	7
7	3	3
8	4	8

Fig. 5a. Ready list for Figure 3d

Process	*Priority*	*fqp*	*rqp*	*Processor*	*Run*
1	6	2	*6	0	1
2	6	7	1	0	1
3	7	*7	*7	0	1
4	8	8	*8	0	1
5	4	*4	*4	0	1
6	—	—	—	0	0
7	6	*6	2	0	1
8	8	*8	4	0	1
9	1	*1	*1	2	1
10	2	*2	*2	1	1

Fig. 5b. Ready list queues for Figure 3d.

If it is assumed that the priority list and the queue cells are kept in memory, then the cost of block and wakeup operations in memory references (assuming that queue pointers are packed two per word) is

(W1) Three references to enter a new cell in a queue (one if level was empty). Two of these (to splice pointers) can be made in parallel. One more reference is needed to record the new state of the process; it can be made in parallel with all of the first three.

(W2, 3) One reference to switch processes on a processor (not counting loading and storing of the state vector), followed by another reference to record the new state of the preempted process. This assumes that the priority and queue cell address of every running process are kept in registers associated with the processor running it.

(B1) Three references to delete a process (two if it is the only one on its priority level). Two of these (to splice pointers) can be made in parallel.

(B3) Two references to get the process number of the new lowest priority process if it is on the same level as the current one. Only one is required if the process blocked is the lowest one, since the pointer to the next one is obtained in the splicing operation.

(B4) Two references also if it has lower priority, plus references wasted in the scan.

The cost of the scan can be reduced to one reference by providing a bit word with one bit for each priority level and turning this bit on if the level is occupied. This scheme requires an extra reference every time a level becomes empty or ceases to be empty. Its value therefore depends on the density of empty levels.

If the actual lowest priority process (the one farthest down the queue at the lowest priority level) is not known, step B3 is complicated by the possibility that we may have to pass over queue cells for already running processes. If there are many priority levels containing only one process, the cost of entering or deleting a process can be reduced by one cycle if we treat this as a special case and put the single process number directly in the ready list.

Observe that the algorithms described above can be implemented in a mechanism, independent of any processor, which is able to read and write memory, accept block and wakeup requests, and send to a processor the information that it should dump the process it is now running and start executing another one. If the process number of the new process is held in a fixed memory location unique to the processor, then only one control line is required from the scheduler to each processor. The line simply says: switch processes.

If we neglect the possibility of wakeup signals which come from the outside world, however, it is also clearly possible for everything to be done by one of the processors being scheduled. Since every scheduling operation is initiated by an ordinary user process, there is no problem in finding a processor to do the work. The only other difficulty is in getting a processor to switch processes. This may be done with a signal which any processor can send to any other, including itself, provided this signal is not sent until all the other manipulations connected with the scheduling operation have been completed. See Saltzer [5] for a more detailed discussion of this point.

Timers. So far we have seen two mechanisms which can cause a process to lose its processor:

It may be blocked, by itself or by some other process.

It may be preempted by a higher priority process.

If every process could be counted on to run for only a short period before blocking, these mechanisms would be entirely sufficient. Unfortunately, in the real world processes run for sufficiently long periods of time that it is necessary to have some method for stopping their execution, or at least reducing their priority, after a certain amount of time has elapsed.

The period for which a process is allowed to run before such disagreeable things begin to happen to it is usually called a quantum. It may vary with the priority, the process, the time of day, or anything else, and how its value is established is a policy decision with which we are not concerned. Some attention must be paid, however, to the methods by which the policy decision, once arrived at, is to be enforced. It is desirable that these methods should allow as much flexibility as possible in the choice of quantum and should not add significantly to the cost of scheduling.

What we wish to do is to attach to each process, as part of its stateword, an integer which we call a *timer*. When the process is running, the time is held in a hardware register and decremented at fixed intervals. When it reaches zero, the process is forced to transfer to a standard location where the system leaves a transfer to a routine which decides what to do. Two alternatives seem plausible: (1) Assign a lower priority to the process, an action which may cause it to be deprived of its processor. (2) Leave the process at the same priority, but give preference to all the other processes at the same priority level. Neither one, however, need be built into the scheduling mechanism.

The choice of an initial setting for the timer is another policy decision, which can be made when the process is blocked or when it is awakened. The latter alternative is somewhat more appealing, since it allows for the possibility that different wakeup signals may arrive for the process, with different priorities and requiring different amounts of time. The drawback is that a wakeup signal must carry an additional piece of information. In either case we may observe that the choice of quantum and the action to be taken when it is exhausted can, like the assignment of priority, be left within limits to the discretion of the user.

One other point ought to be brought out in regard to the kind of priority multiplexing scheme we have been discussing: it does not guarantee that a ready process will ever be run; if enough processes of higher priority exist, it will in fact not be run. This may be exactly what is intended, but if it is not, the design of the priority and quantum assignment algorithms must take the unpleasant possibility into account. This might be done by restricting the frequency with which a process may enter the ready list with high priority. Another alternative is to restrict the length of time it may run at high priority, although this one may be subverted by the fixed overhead imposed by the need to swap in the memory for the process. Still a third approach is to increase the priority of processes which have been waiting for a long time at low levels.

Fixed Time Scheduling

Everything we have said so far about wakeup signals has implied that they originate in some definite action on the part of some unblocked process, whether this process be within the system or entirely external to it. A signal originated by an external process might be the result of a circuit breaker opening. There is one particular class of wakeup signals, however, which demand special consideration, and that consists of the signals arising from the elapse of specified intervals of time. It is extremely common for a process to wish to block itself until, say, noon arrives, or for 5 seconds to give a user opportunity to respond to some stimulus, or for that fraction of 100 msec remaining since it was last awakened if it wishes to give attention to some input signal at that interval.

Another important case arises from the following observation: there is a large class of applications for which a user sitting at a teletype prefers a uniform 2-second response time to one which has, say, a uniform distribution between .5 and 2 seconds, or even one which is .5 seconds with probability .75 and 2 seconds the rest of the time. This is a fortunate circumstance from the point of view of the system, since it is only required to provide service sometime within a 2-second period chosen at its convenience. It does, however, require reasonably flexible timing facilities, both to give warning of the close approach of the deadline and to delay the generation of output until 2 seconds have elapsed.

Such requirements can of course be satisfied by the provision of an interval timer for each one; when a process blocks itself for n μsec, one of these timers is set for that interval and the signal which it will emit on its expiration is routed to the process. This solution is, however, obviously wasteful in the extreme.

To improve on it we create a list called the *fixed-time list*, each entry of which contains:

1. A process number and priority.
2. A time.
3. A pointer to the next entry on the list.

The contents of the first entry on this list is kept in a fast register and the time constantly compared with a real-time clock. As soon as the latter becomes greater, the specified process is awakened, the entry put on a free storage list, and the contents of the new first entry loaded into the registers. Any process desiring service at a fixed time simply puts the proper entry on this list and blocks itself. Note that it is possible for the contents of the registers to be changed by the appearance of a request with time earlier than that now in them.

This arrangement ensures that the scheduler will at

all times be aware of the requirements of processes which wish to run while it remains ignorant of those whose wakeup time has not yet arrived. In case there are not enough processors to run all the processes demanding service, the priority mechanisms of the scheduler can be relied upon to allocate processors to the most important ones. This means that, given information about the distribution of processes at various priorities, it is possible to compute beforehand what kind of service a process can obtain at a given priority level or, alternatively, what priority it must have to obtain a given level of service. For those processes on the fixed-time list precise information is available. For those being awakened in other ways only probabilities can be known beforehand. This uncertainty can be eliminated by assigning higher priorities to the fixed-time processes than to any others, or, if the cost of this scheme is unacceptable, it is still possible to work out expected average and maximum delays. Since the system can enforce its decisions about priority and running time, it can guarantee the correctness of its estimate for these delays (barring hardware failure or bugs in the system programs). The important point is that no computations need to be made when it is time to wake up a process; everything can be worked at when the process makes a request for service, and it can be informed exactly what kind of response can be obtained at what price.

Some elementary observations about this response may be in order here. These are intended to suggest the scope of the problem; very little attention has been given to it, and much work needs to be done. Let us ignore the existence of nonfixed-time processes for simplicity, and let us also assume that no time elapses between the arrival of a wakeup signal and the execution of the first useful instruction of a process. Then if there are n processors we can guarantee to n processes any kind of service they may require, simply by giving them all the highest priority. After that, the situation becomes a little more complex, and some information must be required of the processes about the frequency, quality, and duration of service which they require. This information might include any of the following items:

1. With what frequency will the process wake up? Must it run at fixed *times*, or only at fixed *intervals* with an arbitrary origin? For most sampling processes the latter will suffice. What times and intervals does it wish to run at?

2. What errors in the satisfaction of the above requirements can be tolerated, and with what probability? Is it acceptable, for instance, to miss 1 percent of the samples entirely? This might frequently be the case. What is the desired distribution of error versus frequency of occurrence? Perhaps a 2-msec error is completely acceptable, one of 5 msec tolerable 10 percent of the time, and one of 10 msec intolerable. Or perhaps 40-μsec accuracy is required with 0 tolerance for greater error. Presumably a real system will have a minimum error, determined by the response time of the scheduler, which is independent of priority.

3. How long will the process run each time? Perhaps no more than 200 μsec. Perhaps 1 msec usually, 2 msec 10 percent of the time. To what extent can it tolerate interruptions? Must it perform 5 msec of computation in 5 msec of real time, or is it acceptable for 7 msec of real time to elapse?

Needless to say, not all users will be able or willing to supply accurate information about all of these items. For those who do not, the system can make worst case assumptions and charge accordingly; an incentive is thus provided for the user to state his requirements as precisely as possible.

When all this information has been collected for all the fixed-time processes and suitable statistics and worst case information supplied for the others, a routine can be run to figure out what service can be provided with what probability. This routine will certainly be complex and slow if it is to do a good job, but this is not particularly objectionable, since it runs only when a user requests a different grade of service, not whenever he is served. Too frequent running of the routine can be discouraged by charging for it. As each new request for service comes in, it is thus possible to determine whether it can be satisfied (together with all the other requests already accepted) and at what cost; and if not, what service can be provided. The user can thus obtain precise information about what to expect. If the system is overloaded, of course, some users will not be able to get what they want. The proper response to this situation is to expand the system (if the user requests are justified; this is of course a policy decision which cannot be made by the system); if the service allocation routine is good, there can be reasonable assurance that the system is doing as well as it can.

Hardware Implementation

The concepts and techniques described in the last three sections have been developed to provide the sole scheduling mechanism for a reasonably large time-shared system. Nearly all such systems in existence or under development are based on a dichotomy between two different schedulers: one implemented in hardware and usually called the interrupt system, the other implemented in software and used to schedule user programs. Such an organization has a number of drawbacks. First, it leads to a sharp distinction between interrupt routines, which are regarded as part of the basic system, usually run in some unprotected mode, and cannot call on the system services available to ordinary programs; and user processes, which cannot respond directly to external signals and cannot run for short periods of time without incurring overhead considerably greater than their running time.

Second, the software scheduling system is usually quite slow and cumbersome. It requires a considerable amount of time to convince both the processor hardware and the system software that a different process is being run, and the computation required to properly handle the highly nonuniform load of user processes is substantial. As a result the time required to schedule a process is on the order of milliseconds, except possibly for a very small class of processes which can be given special treatment. On the other hand, a process scheduled in this way can call on all the services which the system provides without taking any special precautions (can, for example, open a disk file, which is a highly nontrivial operation), and it runs within the elaborate framework of protection normal for a user process which prevents it from damaging other users or degrading the service too much and insulates it from many of the consequences of its own folly.

Third, it is nearly impossible to establish any kind of communication between the priority system established by the interrupt hardware and the one defined by the software. The usual rule is simply that all interrupt routines take precedence over any "normal" processes. It is, of course, possible to persuade the software scheduler to, in effect, turn an interrupt routine into an ordinary process, but this is a messy and time-consuming procedure. Related to this problem is the fact that the interrupt system's priority scheme is not likely to be satisfactory in demanding situations; many routines need much more flexibility to establish their priorities than the hardware can conveniently allow, especially where the set of interrupts which are expected during any given five-minute period is a small and varying subset of all those which might be handled in a week.

A fourth point which is somewhat unrelated to the first three is that interrupt systems do not switch enough of the state of a processor automatically. The most obvious omission is the interval timer and elapsed time clock.

These considerations suggest that it might be worthwhile to develop a system which would eliminate interrupts and drastically speed up the software scheduler by centralizing all responsibility for assigning processors to processes into one mechanism. A basic objection to any such proposal might well be the following: once something has been built into hardware it is very difficult to change. Scheduling algorithms are not well understood, and it is not likely that we can lay down rules today for deciding what processes to run which will satisfy us next year. Therefore, we should not freeze our present inadequate ideas into the system forever.

To see why this argument is weak, observe that a broad distinction can be made between a *policy-making* and an *administrative* module in a system. The latter performs some function in a manner controlled by parameters supplied to it by the former. Of course, it is true that the organization of an administrative module affects the kinds of parameters that can be fed to it, and consequently determines the system's policy within certain limits. These limits are very wide, however, in many cases of practical interest. Consider, for example, an input/output buffering system. By adjusting the number of buffers, the blocking factor, the organization of buffers into pools, and the priorities of files competing for buffers, the behavior of the system can be varied over a wide range.

Similarly with a scheduler: its behavior is determined by the priority assignment algorithms, the choice of quanta for running processes, and the action taken on quantum overflow, as well as by decisions of the swapper and the input-output system. The scheduler itself simply provides a framework for enforcing the decisions taken by policy modules.

Furthermore, the scheduler is such a basic part of the system that it is difficult to see how it could be drastically altered without a complete revision of the rest of the system. The effort required for such a change is probably greater than that required to rebuild any reasonable piece of hardware, so that the flexibility offered by software is likely to be illusory.

With these preliminaries out of the way, let us consider how an interrupt system might be replaced by a more powerful mechanism. The functions of an interrupt system are three: to continually monitor a fairly large number of external signals and take appropriate action when one of them changes state; to start a processor executing instructions for a new process within a fairly small number of microseconds after an interrupt arrives, regardless of what it is doing at the time; to recognize a sequence of priorities among interrupt signals and keep the processors executing the highest priority ones.

To replace it we clearly need a piece of equipment which functions independently of the processors being scheduled, and which is capable of examining say 50 external lines, recognizing that one of them is high, putting a process on the ready list, and giving it a processor, all within a period of perhaps 10 μsec. Present-day hardware technology allows such a device, which we henceforth call the scheduler, to be built with a read-only microprogram memory and some small number of internal registers, say 5 or 10, and to operate with a cycle time of 100 to 200 nsec. The major delays it encounters are due to the main memory of the system. This, however, is likely to be organized in numerous modules, so that the scheduler can make several references to main memory in parallel if this is convenient.

All the external interrupt lines are directed into the scheduler, which in its normal state loops constantly, examining them and the request lines from the processors for activity. Associated with each line is a fixed core location (possibly relative to a programmable base register). When the scheduler finds an active line it goes to this location to find out what to do. In most cases the line will carry a wakeup signal, and the core location will containing either 0, which causes the signal to be ignored, or the arguments for a wakeup operation, which are a process number and a priority. The process number is actually a pointer to a block of words which contain:

- the state word for the process (or its core or drum address).
- bits which specify whether it is blocked, ready, or running, what processor it is running on, whether it is suspended or not, and the wakeup waiting switch.
- forward and backward pointers for the ready list queue it is on, if any.

If the process is ready or running at a higher priority than its current one, there is nothing to do. Otherwise, it must be added to the ready list or moved to the appropriate level; the steps required to accomplish this have already been presented. If its priority is high enough it must be given a processor, which is done by storing its stateword address into a standard place and sending the selected processor a *switch* signal. The scheduler then sets the status bits for the newly running process and for the one which has been preempted and goes on its way.

Processor Switching. The processor which receives the switch signal must store the stateword of the process it is currently running in the proper place, which it is responsible for remembering, and pick up the address of its new stateword from the cell where the scheduler left it. Note that the stateword of a process is always associated with the process itself and never with the one which preempts it. This means that it is not necessary to exit from "interrupt routines" in the order in which they are entered. In fact, the whole idea of an interrupt routine does not have much meaning. The time required to store a stateword and pick up a new one will depend on memory speed and the number of central registers, but with a memory of reasonable bandwidth and 1 μsec cycle time it should not be more than 4 or 5 μsec.

The stateword, of course, defines the process. The information it contains, together with a minimal amount of other status information and temporary storage for essential system routines, is all that is needed to allow a process to run (although to do anything useful it will have to have some user program and data storage as well). All these data can be held in a block of memory locations which we may call the *context block*. The address of this block is then sufficient information to give to a processor when it starts to run the process, and the operation of creating a process consists precisely in creating a new context block. The layout of a context block is shown in Figure 6.

In a paged swapping system it will probably be convenient to assign a page to the context block, which may then be identified by its drum address if it is not in core. Of course, it is not possible for a processor to run the process if its context block is out of core, but the scheduler can detect this situation and wake up a system process instead. This process, which might be called the context block swapper, can then take responsibility for bringing the context block into core and waking up its process again.

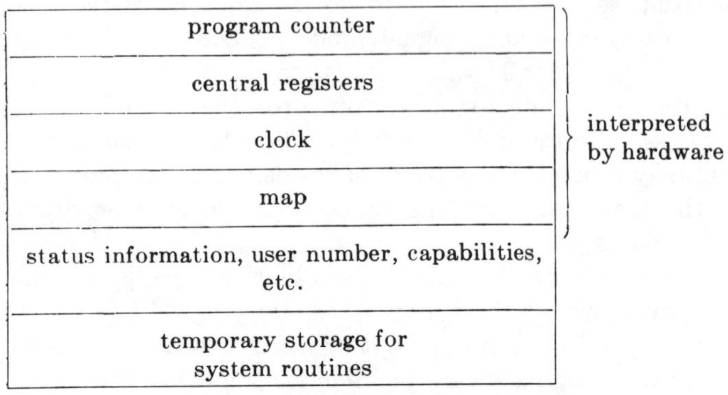

Context block	
program counter	interpreted by hardware
central registers	interpreted by hardware
clock	interpreted by hardware
map	interpreted by hardware
status information, user number, capabilities, etc.	
temporary storage for system routines	

FIG. 6. Contents of a context block

The algorithms for block and change priority have already been considered and present no new problems. The treatment of the timer has also been considered. Recall that it does not involve the scheduler at all; decisions about what to do when a timer trap occurs are matters of policy and must be left as flexible as possible.

It should be pointed out that there is a distinction between interrupts, which are wakeup signals, and traps, which are forced transfers of control within a single process. This distinction is made very sharp by a hardware scheduler, which has complete jurisdiction over wakeups but knows nothing about traps. In addition to the timer trap, there are also likely to be traps for various conditions having to do with memory addressing, for protection violations, for floating-point overflow, and possibly for a variety of other conditions. A call on the system by a user process is also a kind of trap, and indeed in some systems it takes the same form as an illegal instruction execution. This observation should illuminate the relationship of a trap to a wakeup signal, especially in the light of our earlier discussion of system calls.

Interlocking of Processes

It is very often the case in a large system, whether it be an entire time-sharing complex or simply an applications program, that independent processes work on the same data base. When the data base is being modified, it is generally not in a fit state to be looked at. It is therefore necessary for a process which intends to modify the data base to lock out any other process which might want to modify or look at it. The sequence of events required is

1. Test the lock to see if it is set. If so, loop in this step. If not, go on.
2. Set the lock. There must not be any opportunity between steps one and two for another process to set the lock. If this event should occur, both processes would proceed to access the data base simultaneously, exactly the condition we are trying to avoid.
3. Examine or modify the data base.
4. Clear the lock.

In some cases these precautions are required only when data are being changed. At other times, especially when pointers are involved, it is dangerous even to look at the data if another process might be modifying them. The details will vary with the specific application, but the nature of the problem remains the same.

Several techniques exist for implementing locks. The first is to provide a machine instruction of the following general form: test the contents of the memory word addressed. If it is negative, skip. Otherwise make it negative and take the next instruction. If we call this instruction TSL for test and set lock, then the sequence

```
TSL  LOCK
BRU  OK        branch unconditionally
BRU  * - 2
```

will not allow control to reach OK unless the lock has been found not to be set, and when control does reach OK the lock will be set again. Probably two memory references to LOCK will be required by TSL. If this is the case, access to that cell by any other process must be inhibited between the two references of the TSL.

This mechanism allows an arbitrary number of locks to exist. A lock is cleared by storing some positive number in the lock cell. A minimum of two instructions must be executed, and a minimum of four memory cycles is required. The biggest drawback is that a process hung up waiting for a lock to be cleared expends memory cycles without doing any useful work. These memory references degrade the performance of the rest of the system.

An alternative method is to supply each process with a lock register consisting of n bits. The equivalent of TSL hangs the process until a specified bit is off, then turns it on and proceeds. Two instructions are still required, but only two memory references. The cost of waiting for a lock to clear is simply the cost associated with the processor which is delayed; there is no drain on the rest of the system. There are two drawbacks: the number of different locks which may be set is limited by the length of the lock register, and a physical connection between processors other than the memory is required, even though it is a simple one. Furthermore, it is not clear what to do with the lock register if a process is blocked and the processor given to another process.

If processors are being shared, either method has the following further drawback. Suppose there is only one processor, and that process A is running, sets a lock, and is deprived temporarily of its processor in favor of process B, which attempts to set the same lock. Process B will hang, but the lock will never be cleared, since A will never be able to continue (unless B is preempted by a timer runout). This is rather serious. The difficulty can be avoided by increasing the priority of process A so much that it cannot be preempted, but this scheme has obvious disadvantages.

The problem is handled in most existing systems by precisely this means, however. "Increasing the priority of process A" is accomplished by disabling the interrupt system, so that any interrupt signals which come in are stacked until an enable instruction is executed. The process which executes the disable instruction will run without interference, since on most systems all the mechanisms for taking the processor away from it are dependent on interrupts.

The fact that this method stops the entire scheduling system from functioning is not particularly objectionable if it does so only for a few microseconds. A much more serious problem is that it requires explicit action to re-enable the interrupts; if this action is omitted, the entire system ceases to function. This method can therefore be used only by highly privileged processes and with the greatest of care.

With the TSL instruction a completely general solution to the entire interlocking problem is possible along the following lines. When a process tests a lock and finds it set, it blocks itself. Before doing so, however, it adds itself to a list of processes waiting for the lock to be cleared, which we call a *wakeup list*. The process which clears the lock does so through a standard routine which checks for the existence of this list and wakes up one or all of the processes on it, depending on the nature of the lock. The cost of this operation is very low if there is nobody to wake up, probably just one conditional branch. The generality is, however, necessary since most locks used by the basic system programs can be tested by a large number of processes at once, not just by two. Obvious examples are locks on storage allocation tables or input/output devices.

Short-Term Interlock. The arrangement described above is a complete solution to the problem we are considering. Its only drawback is that it requires a good deal of machinery to be brought to bear even if only a few instructions are to be interlocked. This point becomes painfully clear when the details of constructing a wakeup list are considered: since a process can in general be interrupted or preempted between the execution of any two instructions, there is no guarantee that the list will not disappear while a process is in the middle of adding itself to it. We would therefore like to have a very cheap mechanism for ensuring that a short sequence of instructtions can be completed without interference from the scheduler.

We therefore introduce a new instruction called PROtect, whose function is to ensure that during some short period after the execution of PRO:

a. The process which executes the PRO cannot lose its processor or be preempted by the timer.

b. No other PRO can be executed. If another processor attempts to do a PRO, it is forced to wait until the current one is complete. Simple hardware synchronization techniques can ensure this.

The "short period" mentioned above is probably best measured in memory references by the processor and about 15 is probably the right number. Time is not satisfactory since the amount of time required to execute an instruction is unlikely to be predictable in advance, and instruction execution is even worse, since an indirect addressing loop can cause the processor to hang without executing any instructions. Since a PRO cannot hang up a processor for more than a small number of memory cycles it does not need to be a privileged instruction, and can therefore be used by ordinary programs, which occasionally have as much need for locks as system programs.

The PRO mechanism has one serious weakness which limits its usefulness: if a memory fault occurs while the PRO is in force, its effect on the following instructions is lost. It is therefore necessary to ensure that all addresses generated during the PRO fall either in the page containing the program, or in pages guaranteed to be in core, or in one other page which is first referenced before anything critical is done. If the return from a memory fault re-enables PRO, all will then be well.

With this much machinery (PRO is the only new instruction which is really essential) we have a very satisfactory system for interlocking independent processes. Short sequences of instructions can be protected by PRO; if every other sequence of instructions which is executed by another process and references the sensitive data is also covered by a PRO, it is not possible for two such sequences to be executed simultaneously. Larger operations on shared data bases can be interlocked with locks in memory. The cost of setting and clearing such a lock is only a few instructions.

The methods discussed in this paper depend on cooperation among the processes referencing a shared data base and on correct programming of each reference to the data. As Van Horn and others have pointed out, the bugs introduced by incorrect handling of this problem occur in a random and generally irreproducible manner and are very difficult to remove. Van Horn [6] has proposed a scheme which enforces proper handling of shared data; it does however require more substantial hardware modifications than the methods suggested here.

REFERENCES

1. Dennis, J. et al. Machine Structures Group Memos 19, 40, 41. M.I.T., Cambridge, Mass., 1966.
2. Dennis, J. B. Segmentation and the design of multiprogrammed computer systems. *J. ACM 12*, 4 (Oct. 1965), 589–602.
3. ——, and Van Horn, E. Programming semantics for multiprogrammed computations. *Comm. ACM 9*, 3 (Mar. 1966), 143–155.
4. LeClerc, Jean-Yves. Memory structures for interactive computers. Project Genie Document 40.10.110, U. of California, Berkeley, Calif., May 1966.
5. Saltzer, J. H. Traffic control in a multiplexed computer system. MAC-TR-30 (thesis), M.I.T., Cambridge, Mass., July 1966.
6. Van Horn, E. C. Computer design for asynchronously reproducible multiprocessing. MAC-TR-34 (thesis), M.I.T., Cambridge, Mass., Nov. 1966.

Load balancing increases throughput but creates interprocessor overhead. This research suggests that a programming approach is the task allocation strategy most likely to balance these conflicting factors.

Task Allocation in Distributed Data Processing

Wesley W. Chu, Leslie J. Holloway, Min-Tsung Lan, and Kemal Efe
University of California at Los Angeles

The advent of LSI technology and low-cost microprocessors has made distributed computing an economic reality in today's computing environment. The modularity, flexibility, and reliability of distributed processing makes it attractive to many types of users, and several distributed processing systems have been designed and implemented in recent years. Distributed processing applications range from large data base installations where processing load is distributed for organizational efficiency to high-speed signal processing systems where extremely fast processing must be performed in a real-time environment. But, like any new concept, distributed processing has problems which must be solved before it can become part of the accepted processing repertoire of system designers.

A serious problem is the degradation in throughput caused by the saturation effect. In an ideal multiple processor environment, we would expect throughput to increase linearly as the number of processors increases. That is, we expect to double throughput by doubling the number of processors available to perform a task, if the modules being processed are independent of each other (excluding the effects of control overhead, which we would expect to decrease performance). This expected performance is shown by the "ideal" curve in Figure 1. Early experience in multiple processor systems, however, has demonstrated behavior in operational systems is more like the "actual" curve. In practice, the throughput in a multiple processor system increases significantly only for the first few additional processors. At some point the throughput actually begins to decrease with each additional processor—this can be as few as three or four if the system is improperly designed. Examples of this phenomenon are documented by Chu[1] and Jenny.[2] This decrease in throughput is due to excessive interprocessor communication. Like the thrashing behavior observed in early memory paging systems, the decrease in performance due to interprocessor communication—IPC—is caused by processing overhead. This overhead is incurred when software modules resident on different processors must communicate with each other. Software overhead is incurred for communication protocols and for the management of the distributed storage and external resources. There are also delays in processing due to waiting time in queues at both the sending and the receiving ends of the communication path. The extra processing and waiting time due to IPC grows rapidly and system

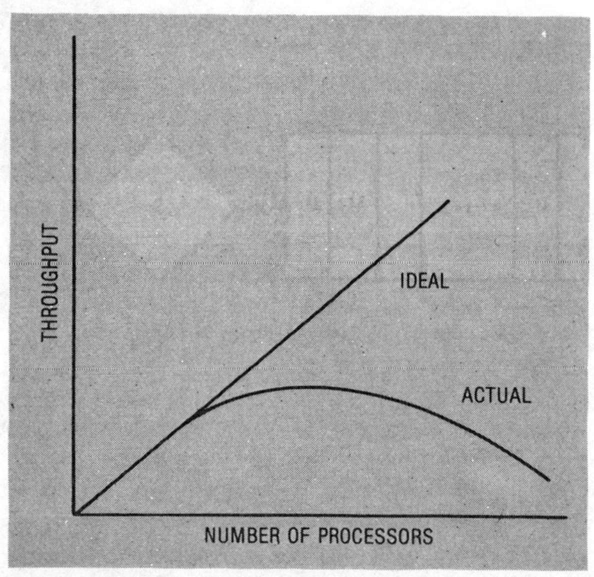

Figure 1. The saturation effect.

Reprinted from *Computer,* vol. 13, pp. 57–62 and 64–69, Nov. 1980.

performance quickly begins to degrade. This degradation in throughput for incremental increase in computing resources is the saturation effect.

In order to avoid the saturation effect, we must investigate the nature of IPC. IPC cost is incurred when data is transferred from one module to a module residing in a different processor. IPC is, therefore, a function of intermodule communication—IMC—and the module allocation. IMC is the amount of data to be transferred between each pair of modules. This is independent of the allocation. Clearly, IPC = IMC if the two modules are not coresident. When modules are coresident on a processor, no IPC cost is incurred. (We have assumed here that overhead due to communiction between coresident modules is negligible.)

Task partitioning and task allocation are the two steps necessary to minimize IPC. Task partitioning refers to the breakdown of a processing task into several individual modules with minimum IMC. This can be considered a software design issue.[3,2] Task allocation is the process of allocating modules to processors with minimum overhead due to IPC.

We will assume that the task partitioning process has been performed by the software designer and that each task arrives in the distributed processing system already partitioned into a set of modules along its own natural boundaries, a concept discussed in some detail by Jenny.[2] In this article, we emphasize how to optimally allocate modules to processors. Since the number of modules is usually much larger than the number of processors, several modules may be assigned to the same processor. This assignment of clusters of modules to processors is often referred to as task partitioning. We find this terminology confusing, and differentiate between task partitioning and task allocation as defined above.

In the next section we define a generic distributed processing system and discuss the basic issues involved in developing a task allocation strategy. The subsequent section discusses model formulation and solution strategies for the task allocation problem by introducing two major approaches researchers are currently pursuing: a graph theoretic approach and a programming approach.

Because of the computational complexity of optimum solution strategies, a need has arisen for a simplified, suboptimum approach to the task allocation problem. Results from some current research efforts are presented in the section on heuristic approaches. A fundamental need in task allocation is the development of a strategy for assigning costs to intermodule communication. This issue is addressed in the subsequent section. We conclude with a brief summary of the state of the task allocation problem, and suggestions for future research.

Task allocation strategy

The task allocation environment. Distributed processing enhances system performance by employing several processors to handle the processing load. A representation of a generic distributed processing system is shown in Figure 2. The key elements in this system are a set of modules to be processed, $\{M_1, M_2, \ldots M_m\}$, and a module allocation mechanism, S, which assigns each of the m modules to one of the n processors, $\{P_1, P_2, \ldots P_n\}$. It is convenient to consider a module an indivisible entity, the smallest viable computational unit. In

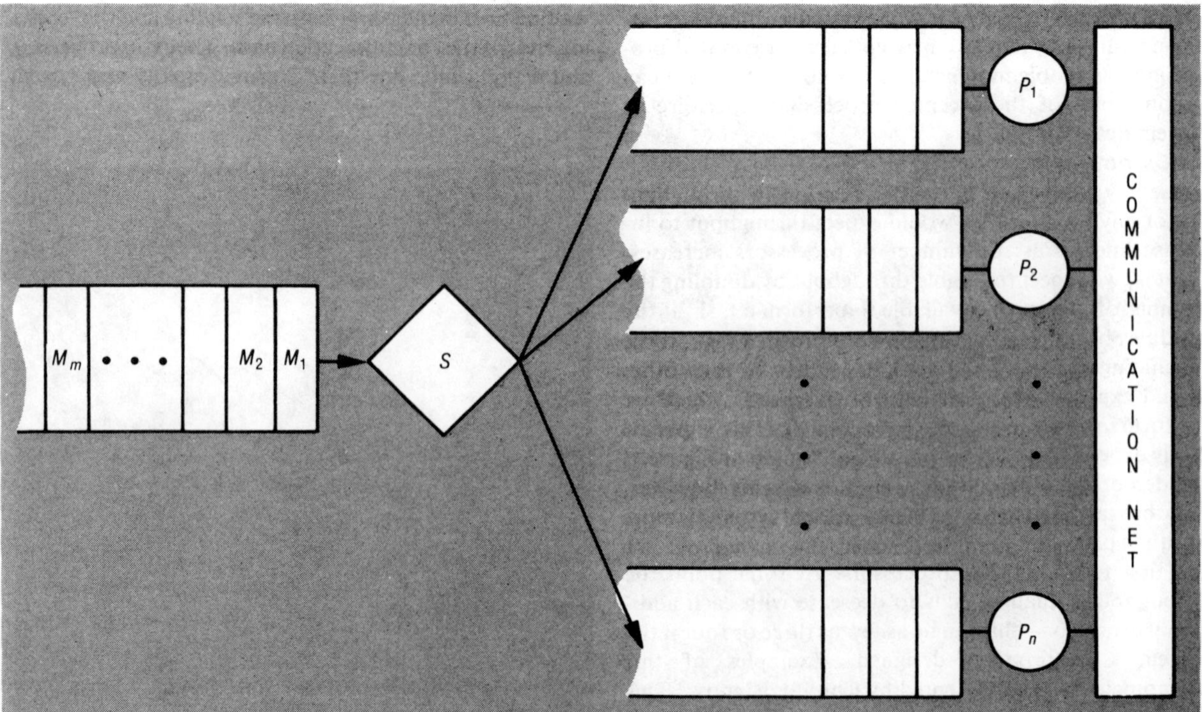

Figure 2. A distributed processing system.

general, the number of modules is much larger than the number of processors. The set of m modules makes up a task; a task is a single processing entity. The processors in this environment communicate among themselves via an interconnection mechanism. Modules may be assigned to different processors. When modules have data to communicate to one another, the processors to which they are assigned must then communicate with each other. Therefore, processors share resources, and communication among processors is essential.

The IMC between any pair of modules is determined by the software design and is a fixed attribute of the modules at the time of module allocation. Since the amount of IMC may vary considerably from one pair of modules to another, the way in which modules are allocated to processors can change the overall processing cost dramatically. For example, if two modules, M_i and M_j, have high mutual IMC and they are assigned to different processors, the IPC load will be high. Total processing costs could be decreased by assigning M_i and M_j to the same processor. On the other hand, if two modules have little IMC and no precedence relations, assigning them to different processors may well speed up overall processing time.

Factors affecting system performance. Assuming independent processing modules, intuition suggests the maximum throughput allocation strategy is one which assigns modules to processors so that all processors in the system are approximately evenly loaded. This balanced-load allocation strategy is shown in Figure 3 for an example system. The incoming task has been partitioned into a set of six noncommunicating modules, $\{M_1, M_2, \ldots, M_6\}$, which are to be allocated among the three available processors, $\{P_1, P_2, P_3\}$. We assume each module has identical processing requirements and each processor has identical processing abilities. For simplicity, let us also assume the processing speed of each processor is one module per unit of time. For the illustrated case, the system is able to process the task in two time units.

Let us study the behavior of IPC for the same set of modules and processors. We now assume the incoming task consists of six modules with a known IMC profile. If we attempt to maximize system performance by minimizing IPC without considering load balancing, all modules will be assigned to the same processor as shown in Figure 4. This allocation strategy produces a minimum IPC allocation, but processing time for the task increases by a factor of three.

It is clear that two conflicting factors, load balancing and IPC, influence the allocation strategy for optimal system performance. Maximum throughput is achieved by load balancing (in the absence of IPC), which tries to distribute modules as much as possible, but overhead due to IPC drives the allocation strategy to cluster modules to as few processors as possible. The task allocation problem is to assign modules to processors for maximum system performance (as measured by throughput) by balancing these two competing factors.

Applications of task allocation. The task allocation problem is important in the initial design phase of a distributed processing system, in the normal operational mode, and in the reconfiguration phase of a dynamic reallocation environment.

During the design phase, it is necessary to evaluate competing design configurations including network topology, channel bandwidth, number of processors, etc. Task allocation allows determination of the value of these parameters to achieve a desired level of performance.

In the normal operational mode of certain real-time distributed systems, such as on-board signal processing, it is important to assign incoming modules to processors to meet critical timing constraints. An additional complication arises in this mode due to the presence of unfinished modules still resident in processor queues, and in the processors themselves, at the time of a new task allocation. It cannot be assumed that all processors are ready and available at task allocation time. An additional feature must be introduced into the strategy to allow for the effect

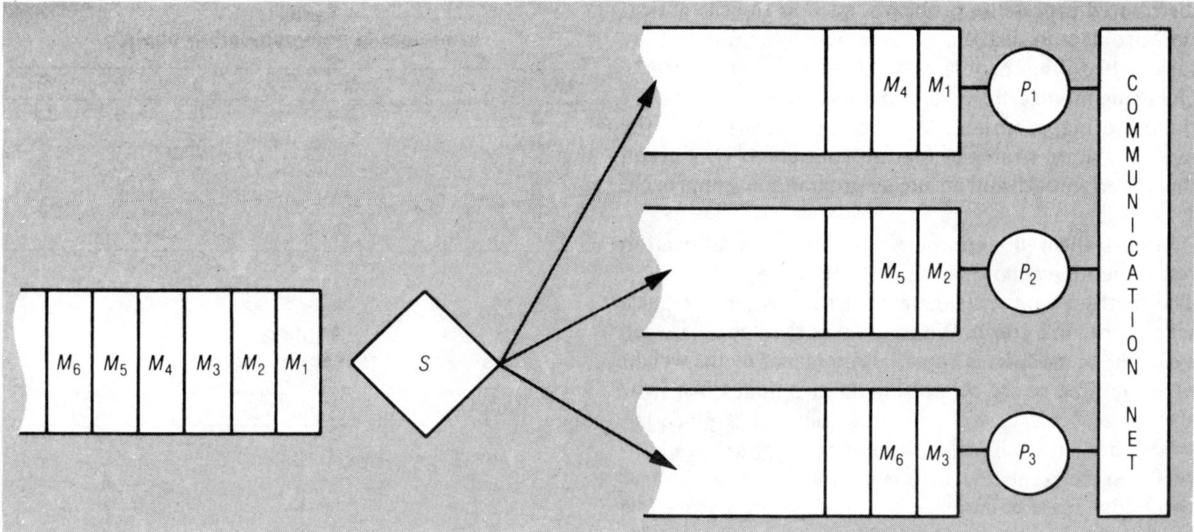

Figure 3. Balanced load allocation strategy.

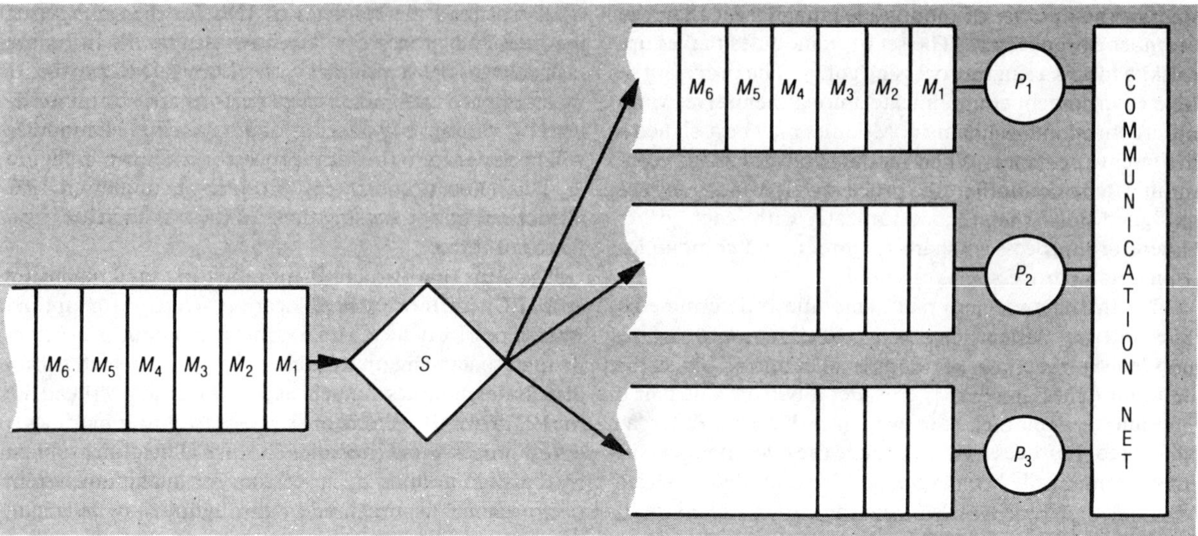

Figure 4. Minimum IPC allocation strategy.

of current system state on the task allocation.

Task allocation is also important during reconfiguration due to changing operating environment. These changes may be a result of changes in task input rate, in processing, channel capacity, etc. Task allocation should provide a strategy to reallocate modules dynamically, and the process should be transparant to the user.

Further, we must assume that system resources are limited. That is, the number of available processors, processor speed, memory capacity, and number and types of peripheral devices are fixed and limited by available system resources. In real-time applications, allowed elapsed time is also a limited resource. In this case, the module allocation methodology should be simple and fast enough to meet system performance requirements.

Model formulation and solution strategy

The task allocation problem is related to other distributed processing problems, such as the file allocation problem in distributed data base systems[4] and the task scheduling problem in queueing networks.[5,6,7] Queueing models, however, do not consider IPC and are therefore inappropriate. We will introduce two of the task allocation strategies that *do* consider IPC: a graph theoretic approach and an integer programming approach.

Graph theoretic approach. Several task allocation researchers have chosen a graph theoretic approach.[2,8,9,10] This method represents the modules to be allocated as a set of nodes in a graph. We assume the IMC cost between each pair of modules is known, represented by the weight of a nondirected arc connecting the two nodes. An IMC cost of zero means no communication takes place between the two modules, and therefore they are not connected in the graph. An IMC cost of infinity means these two nodes *must* be assigned to the same processor. The arc weights then represent the cost of communication between a pair of modules not coresident on a processor. Any pair of coresident modules is assumed to have zero IPC cost.

The task allocation strategy in this model is to minimize total cost, defined as the sum of processing cost and IPC cost. These costs are functions of the module-to-processor allocation. In order to represent the allocation of modules to processors we define an assignment matrix X such that

$$x_{i,k} = \begin{cases} 1 \text{ if module } M_i \text{ is assigned to processor } P_k \\ 0 \text{ otherwise} \end{cases}$$

Processing cost is given by the Q matrix,

$$Q = \{q_{i,k}\}, i=1, \ldots m, k=1, \ldots n$$

where $q_{i,k}$ represents the processing cost for module M_i on processor P_k. We assume this cost is available. It is a

Table 1.
Intermodule communication costs.

MODULE	A	B	C	D	E	F
A		6	4	0	0	12
B			8	12	3	0
C				0	11	0
D					5	0
E						0
F						

Table 2.
Processing costs.

MODULE	P_1 COST	P_2 COST
A	5	10
B	2	∞
C	4	4
D	6	3
E	5	2
F	∞	4

measure of the processing requirements of the module. A value of infinity, $q_{i,k} = \infty$, implies that module M_i cannot be executed at processor P_k.

Let $c_{i,j}$ represent the IMC cost between modules M_i and M_j. The total cost for processing a given task can then be expressed as a function of the allocation, X.

$$\text{Cost}(X) = \sum_k \sum_i \{ q_{i,k} x_{i,k} + \sum_{l<k} \sum_{j<i} c_{i,j} x_{i,k} x_{j,l} \} \quad (1)$$

The first summation term of (1) represents the processing cost for each module on its assigned processor. The second term represents the IPC cost between non-coresident modules. The minimum cost allocation is obtained by performing a min-cut algorithm on the graph.[11]

To illustrate, consider an example from Stone.[9] The task consists of six modules, {A,B,C,D,E,F}, which have IMC costs as given in Table 1 and processing costs as given in Table 2, on two processors, P_1 and P_2. The graph in Figure 5 can then be constructed with nodes for each of the modules and IMC costs on the arcs joining the nodes. In order to represent processing costs, as desired in the cost equation, two additional nodes are added to the graph to represent the two available processors, P_1 and P_2. The cost of running each module on processor P_1 is denoted on the arc joining that module node to node P_2. Similarly, the cost of running each module on processor P_2 is denoted on the arc joining that module node to node P_1. If we perform a min-cut algorithm on the graph in Figure 6, we obtain the cut shown by the heavy dark line. This provides the minimum cost allocation of the given modules between two processors. As we can see from the unbalanced allocation in this example, this strategy provides no mechanism for load balancing.

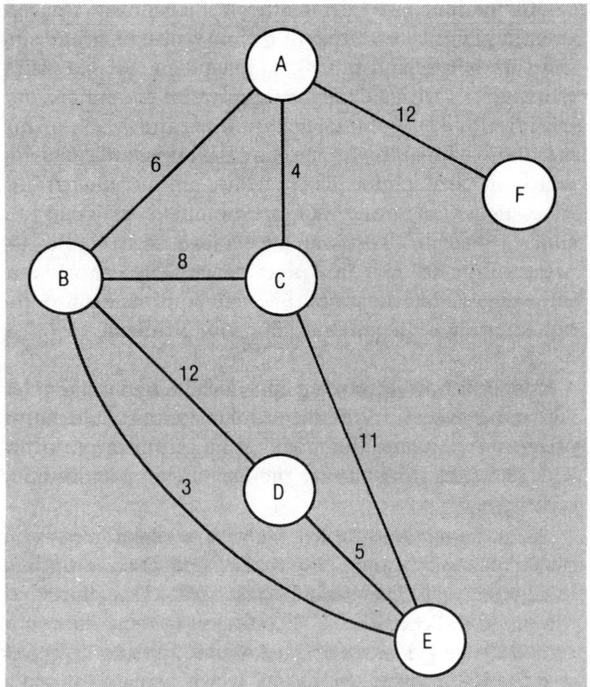

Figure 5. Communication graph.

While this method is attractive in its simplicity, it has several serious limitations. First, the basic min-cut solution provides for a minimum cost allocation between two to three processors. In general, an extension of this method to an arbitrary number of processors requires an n-dimensional min-cut algorithm which quickly becomes computationally intractable.[11] This limits the usefulness of the method in many applications. An extension of this method to allow allocation among four or more processors has been proposed for cases where the IMC pattern can be constrained to be a tree.[10]

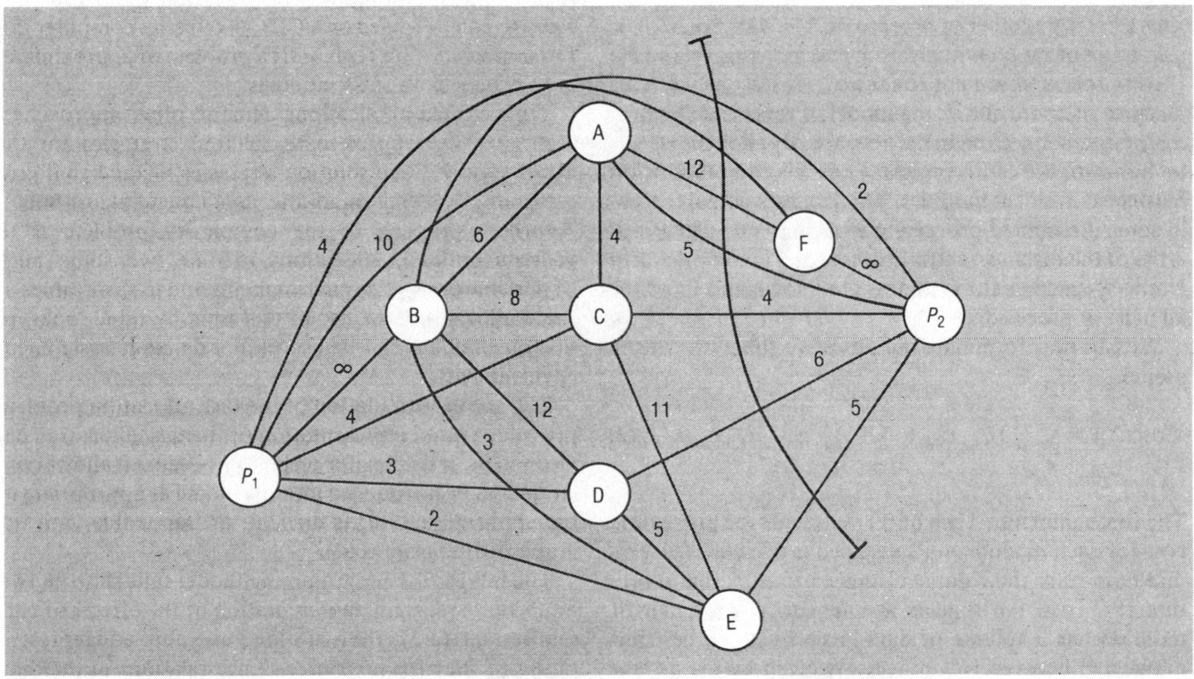

Figure 6. Complete graph.

This method provides neither a mechanism for representing limited resources in memory size or processing time, nor a mechanism for load balancing. An extension to include a restricted memory constraint is complex, and the solution is NP-complete.[8] Another drawback of this method is its inability to measure the impact of queueing delays on throughput. These delays are introduced into the system when more than one module is assigned to a single processor. Also, no mechanism is available for preservation of data flow precedence. These shortcomings suggest that the graph theoretic approach is not the best solution to the module allocation problem.

Integer 0-1 programming approach. A method applied with some success to the file problem and task allocation problem formulates the model as an optimization problem, and then solves it via a mathematical programming technique.[4,12]

As in the previous model, we wish to maximize system performance by minimizing total system cost, as defined in Equation (1). The minimization again takes place over the module allocation, X. Processing cost can be represented by the Q matrix defined above. In order to represent the IPC costs in this model we will replace the single cost matrix C with the product of a volume matrix and a distance matrix. We define IMC by a volume matrix,

$$V = \{v_{i,j}\}, i=1, \ldots m, j=1, \ldots m$$

where $v_{i,j}$ represents the volume of data sent from module M_i to module M_j. If $v_{i,j} = 0$, then module M_i does not communicate with module M_j.

Consider the distributed processing environment portrayed in Figure 2. We define a distance matrix on the set of processors

$$D = \{d_{k,l}\}, k=1, \ldots n, l=1, \ldots n$$

where n is the number of processors. The distance, $d_{k,l}$, is a measure of the communication cost between P_k and P_l. If two processors are not connected, then $d_{k,l} = \infty$. This distance measure allows the model to represent the processor interconnection in the network. By allowing $d_{k,k}$ to be nonzero, we can represent a cost of communication between coresident modules. This can be a useful feature in some distributed processing environments. The properties of the distance matrix are discussed in some detail in Lee.[13] We assume the distances are known and fixed for all pairs of processors.

We can now formulate the objective function for the model.

$$\text{Cost}(X) = \sum_k \sum_i \{q_{i,k}x_{i,k} + \sum_{l<k} \sum_{j<i} wv_{i,j}d_{k,l}x_{i,k}x_{j,l}\} \quad (2)$$

The first summation term of (2) represents the processing cost for each module on its assigned processor. The second term sums the volume-distance products that represent IPC cost. For a given assignment X, each pair of modules has a volume of data given by V, to be communicated between two processors given by the assignment at a distance given by D. The normalization constant w is used to scale processing cost and IPC cost to account for any differences in measuring units.

Load balancing will be achieved through imposition of constraints. The constraints we have identified as significant in our environment are memory size, processor speed, and real-time constraints on processing time. Processor speed is reflected in the processing cost matrix Q, so we need only discuss the memory size constraint and the real-time constraint.

A limited memory environment is represented by the constraint

$$\sum s_i x_{i,k} \le R_k, k=1, \ldots n \quad (3)$$

where s_i represents the amount of memory storage required by module M_i and R_k represents the memory capacity at processor P_k. Equation (3) states that the amount of memory consumed by all modules assigned to a processor must not exceed its memory capacity.

The real-time constraint is given by

$$\sum u_i x_{i,k} \le T_k, k=1, \ldots n \quad (4)$$

where u_i represents processing time required by module M_i, and T_k represents the required time limit for processing the modules that reside in processor P_k for a given task. Equation (4) states that the length of time required to process all the modules assigned to a single processor must not exceed the required real-time limit.

We may now perform the task allocation for any given system by minimizing Equation (2) subject to the constraints of Equations (3) and (4). This can be solved as a nonlinear 0-1 integer programming problem. Further, the nonlinear 0-1 equation can be linearized by adding further constraints, which greatly simplifies the solution process. A problem consisting of 8000 constraints and 2500 unknowns can be solved on a CDC 6000 series computer in a few minutes.[14] This represents a problem of approximately 15 processors and 25 modules.

Time-critical applications demand other approaches. One is to use approximate solution strategies for the above model. Such solution strategies include goal programming[15,16] and quadratic assignment algorithms.[17] Another approach to the complexity problem is to generate optimum allocations, off-line, over some range of possible processing environments and to store tables of these allocations for use in real time by table look-up. Such techniques can be useful in a dynamic assignment environment.

The above formulation of the task allocation problem provides a good representation of the task allocation environment. It is a flexible technique because it allows constraints to be introduced into the model as appropriate to the application. This is difficult or impossible with the graph theoretic approach.

The integer 0-1 programming model falls short in two important areas: the representation of the effects of current system state in the real-time constraint, and representation of the effects of precedence relations in the data flow among the modules. Further study is required here because both factors introduce queueing delays into the system in a complex manner. Under these considerations, the real-time constraint becomes

$$\sum_i f_i(u_i x_{i,k}, p_{i,j}) \leq T_k, k=1, \ldots n, i, j=1, \ldots m \quad (5)$$

where $p_{i,j}$ represents the precedence relation between modules M_i and M_j. The function f_i then represents the processing time, including queueing delay, for processing module M_i at processor P_k.

Heuristic methods

Some simplifying assumptions reduce the amount of computing time for module allocation: processors in the network are homogeneous; they are fully connected; and the effect of precedence relationships among modules can be ignored. Under these assumptions, a heuristic module clustering algorithm (grouping modules with high intermodule communication cost) can be used for module allocation subject to the real-time and memory constraints. Such an algorithm has been proposed by Gylys.[12]

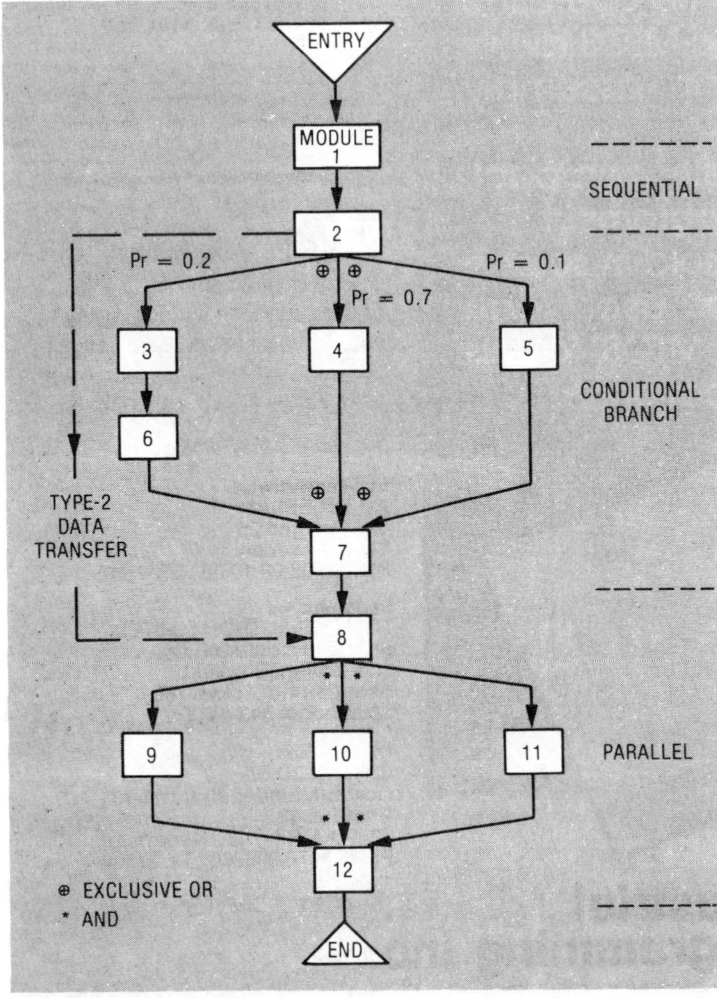

Figure 7. A control flow graph.

The process of assigning two modules to the same processor is called fusion. In this algorithm, after finding a pair of modules—fusion of which will eliminate the greatest amount of IPC cost—we check to see whether this fusion satisfies the real-time and memory constraints. If it does, that module pair is fused. Otherwise, the eligible pair with the next highest IMC cost is chosen as a possible candidate. We repeat this process until a fusion is made. That module pair is then represented by a module cluster for the next iteration. This fusing process continues until all eligible pairs are allocated.

In the above algorithm, the real-time constraint does not consider the queueing delays and precedence relationships among modules, since both are difficult to estimate or model. Since we know balancing the load among the set of processors yields high throughput and faster response time, we propose replacing the real-time constraint with a load-balancing constraint. This should yield a faster computational solution, since it is a simpler constraint.

We propose that the module allocation for minimizing IPC costs and satisfying the load-balancing and memory constraints be treated in two stages. The modules are first fused among a set of processors with a clustering algorithm. We then check to see whether or not the system satisfies the load-balancing requirements and memory constraints. Since it is difficult—if not impossible—to achieve perfect load balancing, we consider the system balanced if the loading of the processors is within a certain tolerance of the ideal level; we reassign some modules from processors exceeding the tolerance level to processors that are below this level.

Although heuristic algorithms achieve only a suboptimum solution, they are useful in applications where an optimum solution is not required, not obtainable, or cannot be obtained within the critical time limit.

Estimation of intermodule communication

The task allocation strategies discussed above depend on the availability of IMC measurements. In this section, we develop a methodology to estimate IMC. This methodology will be particularly useful in the early design phase of a distributed processing system, before the programs are actually coded. It will also enhance the performance of a partitioning compiler to compile and then partition the compiled code.[18] The concept of this methodology is based on the program specifications and the module interreference patterns.

In this section, we represent the task and the intermodule data transfers by a flow graph, then develop equations to estimate the intermodule communication using branching probabilities and loop frequencies. To facilitate discussion, we classify the IMC into three categories for (1) shared or intermediate data transfer, (2) distributed database management, and (3) system control. IMC due to system control refers to scheduling of distributed system resources and their management, including task scheduling, synchronization, processor status and/or peripheral device status broadcasting, maintenance of data base consistency, system reconfiguration information, etc. Since these are fixed overhead costs, we will consider only the first two categories of IMC.

IMC for shared or intermediate data transfer. The module partitioning of a task in a control and data flow graph is represented in Figure 7. A control and data flow graph has an entry point and a termination point. A distributed task can have multiple entry points and multiple termination points, as shown within the dotted square boundary in Figure 8. These multiple entry points and termination points can be combined into a single entry point and a single termination point, as shown. Therefore, we need only consider single-entry single-termination control flow graphs.

The rectangular block in Figure 7 represents a computational module, and the directed arc represents the precedence relationship between the two connected modules. When there is an arc from M_i to M_j, it implies data transfer from M_i to M_j. If M_i and M_j are not allocated to the same processor, there is a transfer of data from one processor to another, referred to as the type-1 data transfer.

Data may have to be transferred from one module to another even when there is no direct connecting arc between the two modules. Consider the example in Figure 7. M_2 may generate data to be used by M_8 but not by M_3 through M_7. In this case, it is desirable to have M_2 transfer these data directly to M_8 instead of routing them through M_3, M_6, and M_7 (assuming that M_2, M_3, M_6, M_7, and M_8 are not coresident in the same processor). This type of data transfer, the type-2 data transfer, is represented by dotted lines in the figure.

There are three basic types of control flow: sequential, conditional branching (Exclusive OR), and parallel (AND). As will become clear, all control flow can be represented as a combination of these three basic types.

The loop control flow as shown in Figure 9 is a variant of conditional branching because the control is conditionally branched back to some previous point in the program. There are two categories of loops in a sequential program. For example, let us consider the DO loops in the following Fortran program.

```
      DO 10 I = 1, 15
      SUMA = SUMA + A(I)
   10 SUMB = SUMB + B(I)
      DO 12 I = 1, 15
      C(I) = A(I) + B(I)
   12 D(I) = C(I) ** 2
```

There are two loops in this program. The first one must be executed in a sequential manner; that is, the loop for index $I = k+1$ should not be executed before the loop for $I = k$ is completed. If we examine the second loop, we find it is actually a set of 15 parallel-executable sequences, with two statements in each sequence. Therefore, it should be represented with the AND-type control flow in the graph.

The control flow at the conditional branching points and the number of times a loop will be repeated may be constant (given in the system or program design specifications) or data dependent. When these parameters are data dependent, their values must be obtained through experience or simulations. In the following discussion, let us assume: (1) the probability that each arc will be chosen is known at each conditional branching point; (2) the average number of times each loop is executed is known.

With these assumptions, we can proceed to calculate the number of times an arc i-j is traversed, $N^a_{i,j}$, and the number of times a module M_i is executed, N^m_i. If we can obtain these values, we are able to calculate the IMC for common data, $v_{i,j}$, as follows:

$$v_{i,j} = \begin{cases} v'_{i,j} * N^a_{i,j} & \text{for type-1 data transfer} \\ v''_{i,j} * N^m_i & \text{for type-2 data transfer} \\ 0 & \text{otherwise;} \end{cases} \quad (6)$$

where $v'_{i,j}$ = the volume of data transfer required each time the connecting arc i-j is traversed, and $v''_{i,j}$ = the volume of data transfer required along the dotted line i-j each time M_i is executed.

The $N^a_{i,j}$ is easily obtained from N^m_i as follows: (1) if there is a sequential control flow from M_i to M_j and there is no other arc leaving M_i, then

$$N^a_{i,j} = N^m_i \quad (7)$$

(2) If more than one Exclusive-OR arcs leaves M_i, then the $N^a_{i,j}$ for each such arc i-j is

$$N^a_{i,j} = N^m_i \times \Pr(i,j) \quad (8)$$

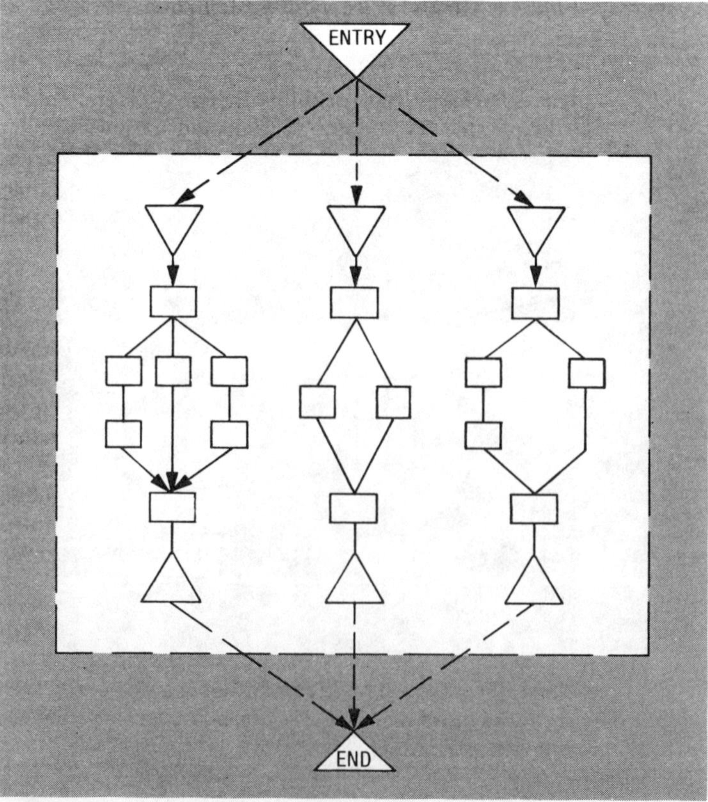

Figure 8. Combining several control flow graphs into one.

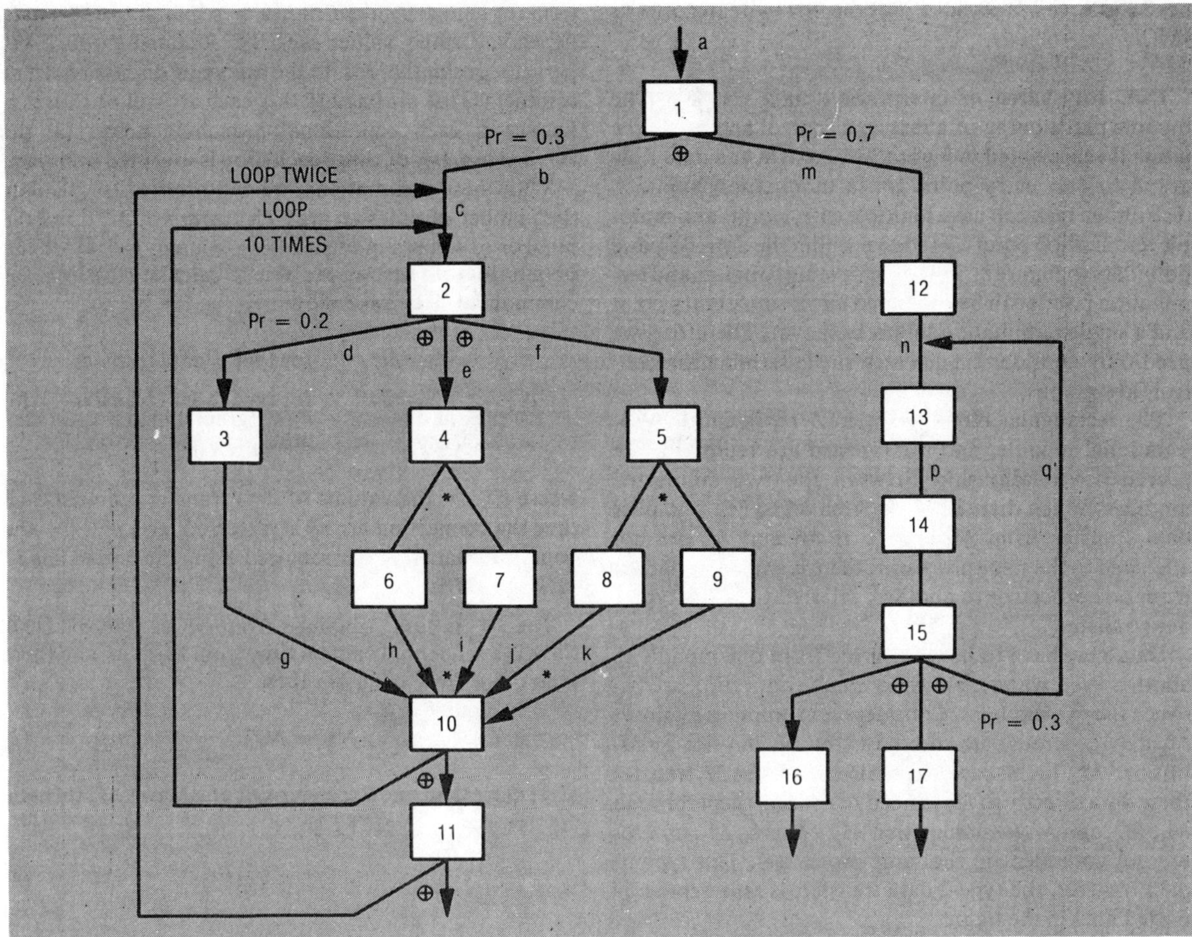

Figure 9. Graph for N^a and N^m calculation.

where Pr(i, j) is the probability that arc i-j is chosen. For example, if M_2 in Figure 7 is executed 10 times within a certain period (e.g., a job cycle or a certain mission) and Pr(2,3) = 0.2, then $N^a_{2,3} = 10 \times 0.2 = 2$ times. (3) If there are more than one AND arcs leaving M_i, then every such arc i-j has an $N^a_{i,j}$ as

$$N^a_{i,j} = N^m_i \tag{9}$$

Having shown the calculation of the $N^a_{i,j}$'s in terms of the N^m_i's, we can now show the calculation of the N^m_j's in terms of the $N^a_{i,j}$'s. That is, we want to show that the number of times a module M_j is executed can be obtained from the number of times all its incoming arcs are traversed. The following is a set of three rules corresponding to the three basic types of control flow: (1) If the control passes through a sequential flow arc, from M_i into M_j, then

$$N^m_j = N^a_{i,j} \tag{10}$$

This is illustrated at M_2 in Figure 7 where $N^m_2 = N^a_{1,2}$. (2) If there are more than one Exclusive-OR arcs meeting at a single module M_j, then

$$N^m_j = \sum_i N^a_{i,j} \tag{11}$$

where the summation takes place over all the modules M_i which have an outgoing arc connected to module M_j, since only one of these arcs may be traversed at a time. This is illustrated at module M_7 where

$$N^m_7 = N^a_{6,7} + N^a_{4,7} + N^a_{5,7}$$

(3) If more than one AND arcs $(i$-$j)$'s merge into a single module M_j, then

$$N^m_j = \text{any}\,(N^a_{i,j}) \tag{12}$$

since all these arcs are invoked at the same time. This is illustrated at M_{12} in Figure 7 where

$$N^m_{12} = N^a_{9,12} = N^a_{10,12} = N^a_{11,12}$$

All other cases can be decomposed into one or more of the above three basic cases. For example, the number of times M_{10} in Figure 9 is executed can be obtained as

$$N^m_{10} = N^a_{3,10} + N^a_{6,10} + N^a_{8,10}$$

because arcs 6-10 and 7-10 can be merged into a single arc with the number of traversals equal to $N^a_{6,10}$ $(= N^a_{7,10})$.

Likewise, arcs 8-10 and 9-10 can be merged into a single arc.

If M_j is the first module within a specific loop with loop index range I, and if $N^a_{i,j}$ for the arc i-j which leads into module M_j has been calculated, then

$$N^m_j = N^a_{i,j} \times I \tag{13}$$

For example, N^m_2 in Figure 9 is equal to $N^a_{1,2} \times 2 \times 10$. If arc a is traversed 10 times, then arc d is traversed $10 \times 0.3 \times 2 \times 10 \times 0.2$ times.

Let us examine another situation. Assume a conditional branching point exists, emanating from a module M_l, and the control might branch back to a previous module with a given probability, Pr. Note that this is not a fixed-index-range loop. Then, the first module M_j encountered after the branching back has

$$N^m_j = N^a_{i,j} \times \sum_{k=0}^{\infty} \tag{14}$$

If $N^m_{12} = 100$ in Figure 9 and $\Pr = 0.3$, then

$$\begin{aligned} N^m_{13,} &= 100 \sum_{k=0}^{\infty} (0.3)^k \\ &= 100 * 1/(1-0.3) \\ &= 143. \end{aligned}$$

To compute the N^m's and N^a's, we always start from the top of the control flow graph and deal with the outermost loop first. Once we obtain all N^a's and N^m's, we can use Equation (6) to compute all desired IMC, the $v_{i,j}$'s. Since the estimation of $v'_{i,j}$ and $v''_{i,j}$ are identical, it is sufficient to consider only one of them, the $v'_{i,j}$. It is simply

$$v'_{i,j} = O(i) \cap I(j) \tag{15}$$

where $O(i)$ = output from M_i, i.e., the set of new data generated by M_i; $I(j)$ = input to M_j, i.e., the set of data generated from other modules and used by M_j for its computation.

IMC for distributed data base management. The data base-related activities of a module can be grouped into three classes: (1) Read (Get) data from the data base, (2) Write (Insert) data into the data base, and (3) Modify (Rewrite) data in the data base (see Figure 10). The files of a distributed data base are placed at various processor locations. Interprocessor communication is involved when a program module at a processor needs to access a file at another processor.

With the aid of a control flow graph, we can estimate the frequency—$f_{i,k}$—with which the kth I/O statement in module M_i accesses file j. Then the communication volume $v_{i,j}$ is

$$v_{i,j} = \sum_k f_{i,k} d_{i,k,j} \tag{15}$$

where $d_{i,k,j}$ is the volume of communication invoked by executing the kth I/O statement in M_i under the condition that module M_i and file j are not allocated at the same processor. The actual value of $d_{i,k,j}$ depends on such parameters as record length, communication protocol used, and query complexity.

Conclusions and future directions

The object of task allocation is to counterbalance the related but opposite factors of interprocessor communication cost and load balancing, to achieve maximum throughput and to satisfy real-time constraints. Assuming a task is partitioned into modules, models are

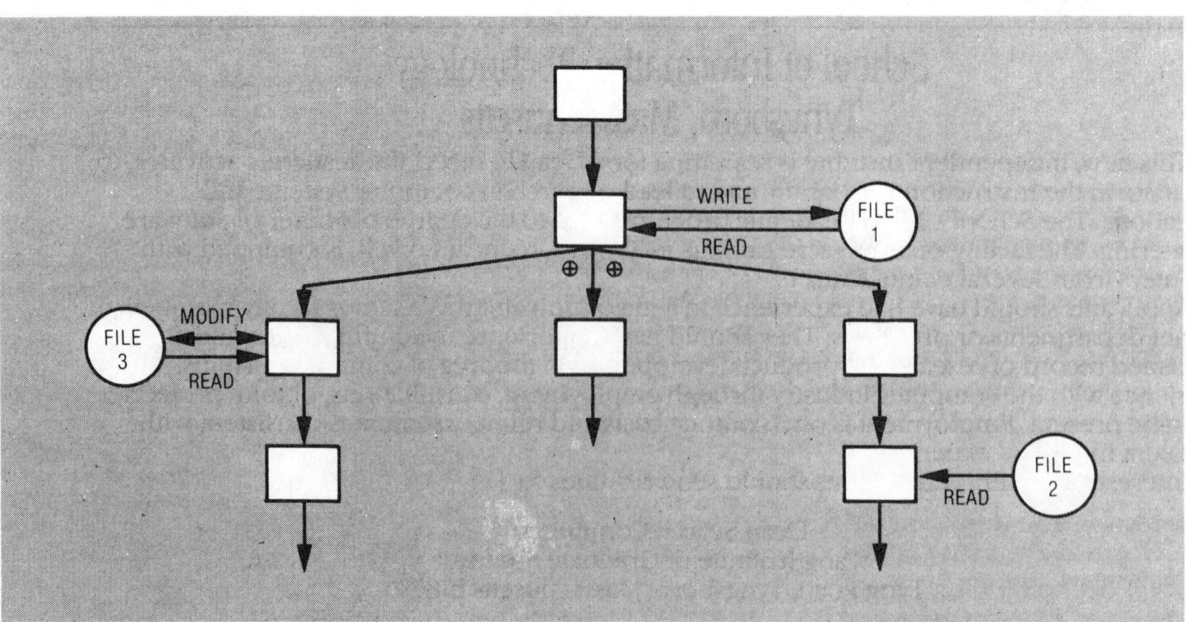

Figure 10. Distributed data base activities.

developed to accomplish task allocation to minimize total processing cost.

A graph model represents modules as nodes in a graph and the intermodule communication cost as weights on the nondirected arcs connecting the nodes of the graph. The task allocation methodology is to allocate modules to processors so that total processing cost is minimized. Total processing cost is the sum of module processing cost and interprocessor communication cost. Standard min-cut algorithms can obtain the optimum task allocation. However, the computation costs become intractable for n-dimensional (n-processor assignment) min-cut algorithms. Moreover, this model does not consider load balancing and resource limitation issues.

The integer 0-1 programming model minimizes total processing cost subject to such resource limitation constraints as memory capacity and real-time requirements. The real-time constraint is rather complex; it must include the queueing delay at various processor queues and the precedence relations between the modules. However, the integer programming model does consider the system resource limitations and real-time requirements, necessary attributes for any methodology to be useful under real system requirements. Although there are problems in accurate representation of real-time constraints and computation problems in solving large-scale problems, there have been some promising results with this methodology.

Heuristic models provide approximate solutions to the task allocation problem. The basic idea of heuristic methods is to find an allocation to balance the costs between IPC and load balancing. This technique requires much less computation time than integer programming methods. As a result, it can solve time-critical cases and also larger dimensional problems.

Control flow graphs can be constructed to represent module interrelationships. The intermodule communication cost can then be estimated from the control and data flow graph, based on the frequency of module references as well as the module I/O characteristics. The module interrelationships are important both for estimating interprocessor communication and for representing queueing delays in interprocessor communication.

Task partitioning is an important problem in distributed processing systems, a problem far from being solved. How will the relationships among response time, precedence relations, and queueing delay be expressed? How will we express the dynamics of IPC, particularly in light of data dependency in system operation time? How will tradeoffs of replicated programs and data files for response time and reconfiguration considerations, etc., be included? Much more work will be required to resolve these and other questions. ■

Acknowledgments

This research is in part supported by the US Office of Naval Research, Contract No. N00014-75-C-0650, and in part by the US Army, Contract No. DASG60-79-C-0087.

References

1. W.W. Chu, D. Lee and B. Iffla, "A Distributed Processing System for Naval Data Communication Networks," *AFIPS Conf. Proc.*, Vol. 47, NCC 1978, pp. 783-793.
2. C.J. Jenny, "Process Partitioning in Distributed Systems," *Digest of Papers NTC '77,* 1977, pp. 31:1-1—10.
3. M.P. Mariani and D.F. Palmer, *Tutorial: Distributed System Design,* IEEE Computer Society, 1979.*
4. W.W. Chu, "Optimal File Allocation in a Multiple Computing System," *IEEE Trans. Computers,* Vol. C-18, No. 10, Oct. 1969, pp. 885-889.
5. V. Balachandran, J.W. McCredie and V.I. Mikhail, "Models of the Job Allocation Problem in Computer Networks," *Digest of Papers COMPCON Fall 76,* Sept. 1976, pp. 211-214.*
6. F. Baskett, K.M. Chandy, R.R. Muntz and F.G. Palacios, "Open, Closed and Mixed Networks of Queues with Different Classes of Customers," *J. ACM,* Vol. 22, No. 2, Apr. 1975, pp. 248-260.
7. Y. Chow and W.H. Kohler, "Models for Dynamic Load Balancing in a Heterogeneous Multiple Processor System," *IEEE Trans. Computers,* Vol. C-28, No. 5, May 1979, pp. 354-361.
8. G.S. Rao, H.S. Stone and T.C. Hu, "Assignment of Tasks in a Distributed Processor System with Limited Memory," *IEEE Trans. Computers,* Vol. C-28, No. 4, Apr. 1979, pp. 291-299.
9. H.S. Stone, "Multiprocessor Scheduling with the Aid of Network Flow Algorithms," *IEEE Trans. Software Eng.,* Vol. SE-3, No. 1, Jan. 1977, pp. 85-93.
10. H.S. Stone and S.H. Bokhari, "Control of Distributed Processes," *Computer,* July 1978, pp. 97-106.
11. F. Harary, *Graph Theory,* Addison-Wesley, New York, N.Y., 1969.
12. V.B. Gylys and J.A. Edwards, "Optimal Partitioning of Workload for Distributed Systems," *Digest of Papers, COMPCON Fall 76,* Sept. 1976, pp. 353-357.*
13. R.P. Lee, *Optimal Task and File Assignment in a Distributed Computing Network,* Doctoral Dissertation, UCLA, 1977.
14. P.L. Price and D.W. Smith, "Analysis and Use of an Integer Programming Model for Optimally Allocating Files in a Multiple Computer System," DTNSRDC-78/102, David W. Taylor Naval Ship and Research and Development Center, Bethesda. Md., Nov. 1978.
15. J.P. Ignizio, *Goal Programming and Extensions,* D. C. Heath and Co., Indianapolis, Ind., 1976.
16. S.M. Lee, *Goal Programming for Decision Analysis,* Auerbach Publishers, Pennsauken, N.J., 1972.
17. G.W. Graves and A.B. Whinston, "An Algorithm for the Quadratic Assignment Problem," *Management Sci.,* Vol. 17, 1970, pp. 453-471.
18. O. El-Dessouk, W. Huen and M. Evans, "Towards a Partitioning Compiler for a Distributed Computing System," *Proc. Int'l Conf. Distributed Computing Systems,* 1979, pp. 296-304.

* These tutorials and digests are available from the IEEE Computer Society Publications Office, 5855 Naples Plaza, Suite 301, Long Beach, CA 90803.

Cost-effective control of distributed computing systems requires practical models for reassigning program modules among the processors in real time.

Control of Distributed Processes

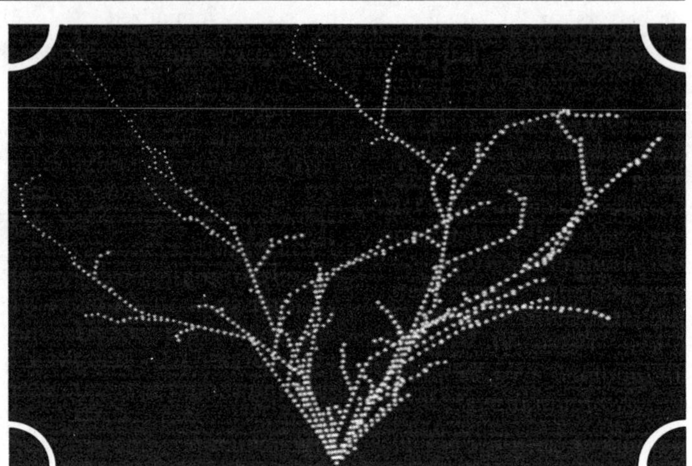

Harold S. Stone
Shahid H. Bokhari
University of Massachusetts

The introduction of the microprocessor has made distributed processing an increasingly popular notion in the computer industry. Economies of fabrication have substantially reduced the cost of replicating processors in a system, making multiple-processor systems economically attractive. Concurrent with the hardware developments in microprocessors has been the development of data base management systems with sophisticated techniques for sharing data. These two major trends in the computer industry—microprocessors and large shared data bases—have created an environment that is fostering the growth of distributed computation. The idea, of course, is that each user has the local processing power that he requires in the form of a private dedicated computer. He can access a central bank of data when necessary for either current information or peak computational power, when these needs cannot be met by his private computer.

While the idea behind distributed computation is tantalizing, there are serious practical and theoretical problems that must be solved to realize the potential of the idea. In a practical sense, the communication links in a distributed network are inherent bottlenecks. Typical bandwidths available on high-speed communication links are still a factor of 10 to 100 lower than memory bandwidths. Protocol and error protection further reduce the bandwidth available to the user. In the face of high penalties for communication, the practical solution for using a distributed system is to do as little communication between processors as possible, relegating such communication to file transfers before and after major blocks of computation are run. Future data links, using fiber optics and broadband communications satellites, may remove the bottlenecks we see now. At that time the communication bottleneck will all but disappear, so that distributed processing can take on a new character, with interprocessor accesses becoming frequent and beneficial.

On the theoretical side of the issue is the fact that the behavior of programs in a distributed environment is not well understood. We are today in a situation analogous to the development of virtual memory systems in the middle 1960's. At that time the promise of virtual memory systems was quite clear, but the early implementations, in looking back, can now be termed disastrous. Experience and research have shown that programs exhibit local behavior and that, when all of the programs and data for a locality reside in physical memory simultaneously, computation is relatively unimpaired by page faults. If, on the other hand, a significant fraction of the items in a locality does not reside in physical memory, the computation will incur excessive page faults due to requests for absent items. Moreover, when two or more programs are run concurrently in this condition, they can compete for precious memory resources so that over a long duration there is continual "thrashing" with net computational output plunging to near zero.

If in drawing the analogy to distributed computation we leap into the area without understanding how distributed programs behave, we may well recreate a thrashing monster, but this one enveloping multiple computers. There is every reason to believe that distributed programs exhibit strong local behavior like programs in virtual memory systems. Consequently, the algorithms that dis-

Reprinted from *Computer,* vol. 11, pp. 97–106, July 1978.

tribute and redistribute modules in a distributed system must do so to enhance the effects of locality (if it exists). If they do not, distributed system performance might well be much worse than if no interconnections existed at all.

In this article we summarize a number of theoretical results that point the way toward the control of distributed computer systems. We present a very simple initial model that serves to set the framework for the more comprehensive results that follow. The model shows that a network flow algorithm is an efficient tool for optimum distribution of program modules across two processors. Also, real-time load balancing is possible on two-processor systems because there is a very simple algorithm for calculating optimum assignments under varying load conditions. Next we generalize the basic algorithm to three-processor systems. We show that the basic algorithm for finding optimal *static* assignments extends easily to finding optimal *dynamic* assignments. We return to many-processor systems in the final section, which discusses a situation in which the program structure of the distributed program is tree-like (hierarchical).

Definitions and assumptions

By a *distributed computer system* we mean a computer system in which there exist several programmable processors, and in which typical computations visit two or more processors during an execution.

This definition is purposely given in vague terms so that it encompasses many types of existing and proposed systems. For example, Arpanet fits the definition and, indeed, one may view Arpanet as an early implementation of a distributed system. The low communication bandwidth between nodes in the Arpanet severely increases the cost of inter-computer transfers so that typical computations rarely shift from node to node during the course of execution. The principal use of Arpanet is as a communication link between a user and a single remote site. More representative examples of a distributed system are C.mmp (a multi-miniprocessor).[1] Cm* (an innovative distributed microprocessor-based system),[2] Pluribus (a communications-switching multiprocessor),[3] and recent releases of computer systems with microprocessor-driven "intelligent" peripherals. The dual-processor system at Brown University[4,5] has served as a model for some of the research presented in this article.

The distributed programs that we consider in our analyses are assumed to be made up of modules that are, in general, free to reside on any processor in the distributed system. There are two costs we must consider in finding a good assignment:

1. Each module has a running cost that depends on the processor to which it is assigned. Let $\mathrm{RUN}_x(i)$ be the cost for running module i in assignment x.

2. Each pair of modules that communicate during a program suffer a penalty if they have to communicate over a link, because they are assigned to different computers. Let the communication cost be $\mathrm{COMM}_x(i,j)$ for the module pair i,j in assignment x, and this cost is zero if modules i and j are placed on the same processor by assignment x.

The minimum cost is simply the minimum sum of the RUN and COMM costs taken over all assignments. Thus, we want to find an assignment x such that x minimizes

$$\sum_i \mathrm{RUN}_x(i) + \sum_i \sum_{j \neq i} \mathrm{COMM}_x(i,j)$$

RUN and COMM have to be measured in the same units. When they are measured in dollars, we minimize the true out-of-pocket expenditures. When they are measured in time, we minimize the true time utilization of resources. This also happens to be the minimal completion time if the distributed program is executed in a purely serial fashion so that all RUN and COMM costs are incurred at disjoint points in time. (This is an accurate model of program behavior at Brown.[5])

Basic results for two-processor systems

In this section we describe a network flow algorithm that may be used to find the optimal assignment of modules to processors in a dual-processor system.

Figure 1 shows a program graph and a table of execution times for program modules in a two-processor distributed system. The nodes on the program graph represent modules, and the links represent intermodule communication patterns. The numbers on the edges, also called *edge weights*, represent the cost of communication between modules when the modules are not coresident on the same computer. Intermodule communication costs are assumed to be zero when the pair of modules are coresident. Both costs are usually given in units of time or dollars, and the units used to represent both kinds of costs must be the same.

The table in Figure 1 shows the execution costs of the program modules when run on computer P_1 or computer P_2. An infinite cost indicates that a module cannot be executed on that computer.

For any given module assignment, the cost of the assignment is the sum of the execution costs from the table plus the sum of the intermodule communication costs for those modules that are not coresident. The latter can be determined from the graph in Figure 1 by noting which edges connect non-coresident modules, and summing the weights of these edges.

To find the optimal allocation, the researcher must create a modified graph as shown in Figure 2.

This graph has two additional nodes, one for computer P_1 and one for computer P_2. Each original module has an edge to each of the computer nodes. The weights of the new edges are such that the edge to the P_1 node carries the P_2 execution cost and the edge to the P_2 node carries the P_1 execution cost. A cutset in this new graph is a collection of edges such that

1. when removed from the graph, node P_1 is disconnected from node P_2, and
2. no proper subset of a cutset is also a cutset.

The dark line in the figure indicates a cutset. Note that each cutset corresponds to a module assignment, and that every assignment corresponds to a cutset.

The *weight* of a cutset is the sum of the weights of the branches in a cutset. In the graph in Figure 2, the weight of the cutset is equal to the cost of the corresponding module assignment since the weight of a cutset sums up the execution and communication costs for that assignment. Note that if module A is assigned to P_1 then the edge to P_2 is cut, but this edge carries the cost of executing on P_1. Similarly, other edges cut between module A and other nodes of the graph represent actual communication costs incurred by this assignment for communication between module A and other corresponding nodes. A full exposition of the graph model appears in Stone.[6] The main point of this discussion is the following:

> Each cutset in the graph in Figure 2 corresponds in a one-to-one fashion with a module assignment. The optimal assignment corresponds to a minimum weight cutset.

The optimum module assignment can then be solved by use of network flow algorithms, which are among the class of algorithms with relatively low computational complexity.[7,8,9,10] The algorithm

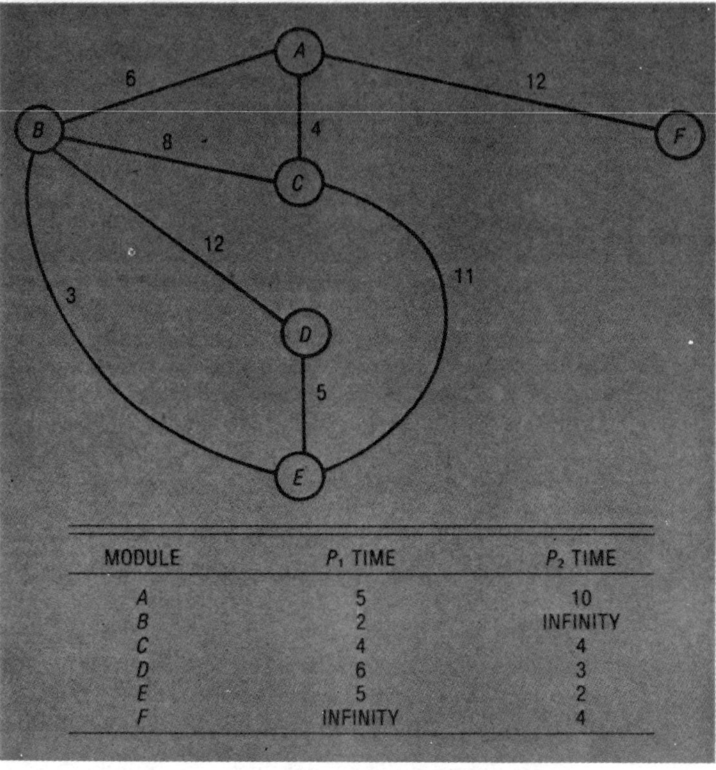

MODULE	P_1 TIME	P_2 TIME
A	5	10
B	2	INFINITY
C	4	4
D	6	3
E	5	2
F	INFINITY	4

Figure 1. Execution and communication costs for a distributed program.

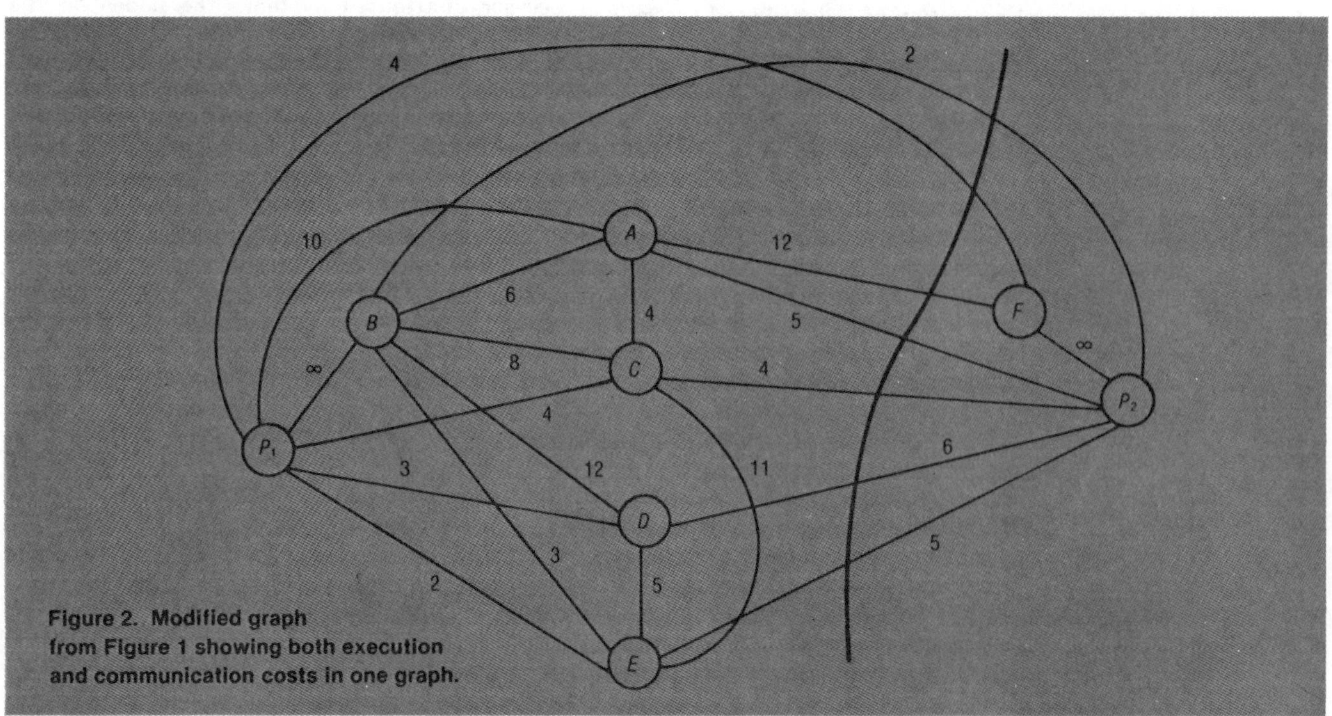

Figure 2. Modified graph from Figure 1 showing both execution and communication costs in one graph.

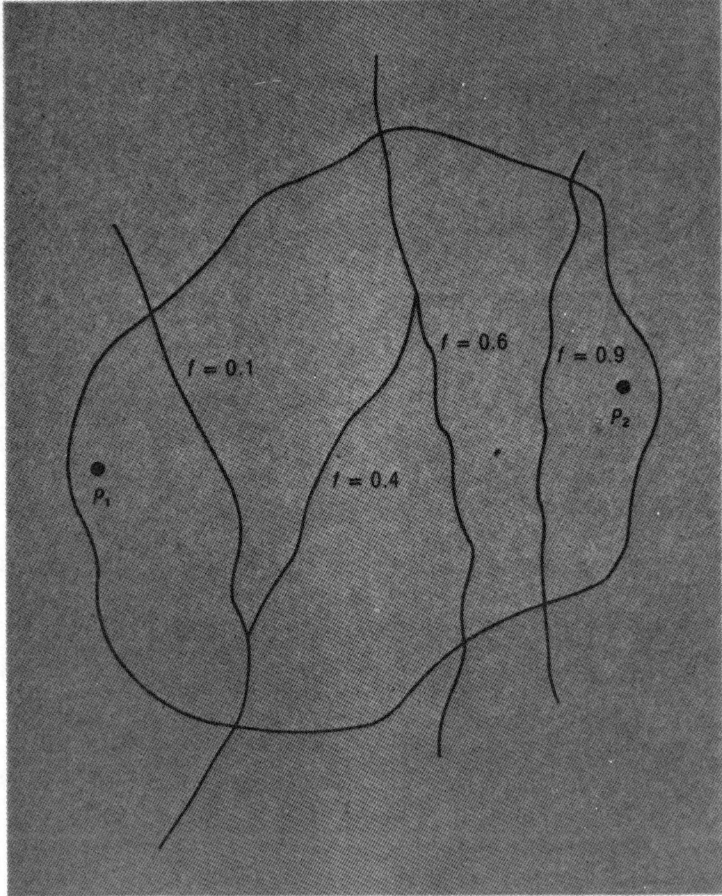

Figure 3. As load on P_1 increases, the successive optimal assignments correspond to nonintersecting cuts.

with least complexity that is known at present is the one described by Karzanov,[10] which has complexity not in excess of $N \cdot E$ where N is the number of nodes and E is the number of edges in a graph.

Thus, with network flow algorithms as a basic tool, optimum module assignments can be found for programs distributed across two processors. That this idea works on real data has been separately verified by Michel and van Dam.[4]

We now consider what happens when we are able to gather all requisite data about program behavior ahead of time, leaving only the system load as an unknown realtime variable. We show that, under this assumption, there exists a very simple algorithm based on critical load factors that can be used to do module assignments in real time.

Suppose we hold all system parameters fixed except the load on one computer, processor P_1. By hypothesis, processor P_1 delivers only a fraction of its useful cycles, say a fraction f of its cycles, to a specific program because the remaining cycles are delivered to other programs that are simultaneously competing for system resources. The fraction f is known as the *load factor*, and f is a time-varying function dependent on the load on the system at any given time.

The load factor varies between 0 and 1 with a program running at maximum speed, when $f = 1$, and running at essentially zero speed, when $f = 0$. In a distributed system we intuitively expect that as f varies from 1 to 0 for processor P_1, program modules will tend to shift from processor P_1 to processor P_2 to take advantage of the computational power of P_2, as processor P_1 becomes less and less available for computation. In fact, it has been shown in Stone[11] that the flow of modules as f decreases is unidirectional from P_1 to P_2. The major result here is that for each module M there exists a critical load factor f_M such that for load factors $f > f_M$, M is assigned to P_1, and for all load factors $f < f_M$, M is assigned to P_2 by optimum module assignments.

The unidirectional movement of modules is illustrated by the nonintersecting cuts in Figure 3.

It follows that for systems in which a single processor load factor is the only variable parameter, optimum assignments can be made by calculating all critical load factors ahead of time and comparing the computed load factors against the actual load factors experienced at run time. An efficient algorithm to compute the critical load factors for all modules appears in Eisner and Severance.[12]

We have assumed in the above discussion that each of the two processors has enough memory to hold all of the modules in the program. The problem of finding the optimal assignment when either or both processors have memory of limited size is very difficult. However, Rao, Stone, and Hu[13] show that there exist some techniques that solve some instances of the problem or, in most cases, reduce the size of the problem substantially.

Extension to three processors

In this section we show how the module assignments to three processors can be accomplished by using an extension of the network flow approach described in the previous section.

Let us take as a running example the three-processor program shown in Figure 4. Since we have to assign the nodes to three rather than to two processors, we need to extend the notion of the cutset. Let us designate the source and sink nodes of a commodity network to be distinguished nodes, and that they are of type *source* or type *sink*. For the three-processor problem we shall have three types of distinguished nodes. This leads naturally to the following definition:

> A *tricutset* in a graph with three source/sink nodes is a subset of arcs of that graph whose removal partitions the graph into three distinct subgraphs, such that each source/sink node lies in a distinct subgraph. No proper subset of a tricutset is also a tricutset.

A tricutset for the network of Figure 4 appears in Figure 5.

Proceeding as before we modify the program graph to incorporate the relative running-time costs of each module on each processor. Again we add an edge from each interior node to each distinguished node as in the two-processor case. The weight on each such branch is computed by a formula explained below and exemplified in Figure 6. The weights are selected so that, as in the two-processor case, the value of a cutset is equal to total running time.

For simplicity Figure 6 does not show the edges from nodes A, B, and C to nodes to which they are not assigned. Suppose that module D runs in time T_i on processor P_i, $i = 1,2,3$. Then the edge from node D to distinguished node S_1 carries the weight $(T_2 + T_3 - T_1)/2$, and likewise the edges to nodes S_2 and S_3 carry the weights $(T_1 + T_3 - T_2)/2$, and $(T_1 + T_2 - T_3)/2$, respectively. Under this weight assignment, if D is assigned to processor P_1, the edges to S_2 and S_3 are cut, and their weights sum to T_1, the running time of D on P_1.

Stone[6] treats this in more detail and shows how to resolve problems due to negative weights.

At this point we come to the question of finding the minimum tricutset in a three-processor graph. The solution can be found using an algorithm given in Stone.[14] The basic idea behind that algorithm is to run a network flow algorithm between nodes S_1 and S_2, then between S_1 and S_3 and finally between S_2 and S_3. While the actual details of the algorithm are too complex to describe here, it suffices to say that it finds the minimum tricutset very efficiently for almost all graphs (requiring on the order of three network flow solutions). There are graphs, however, for which the algorithm fails to find the absolute minimum-cost three-processor assignment, but it does indicate that the solution found is not optimal and bounds the amount of the suboptimality. On a large collection of random graphs, the algorithm never failed to find the best assignment.

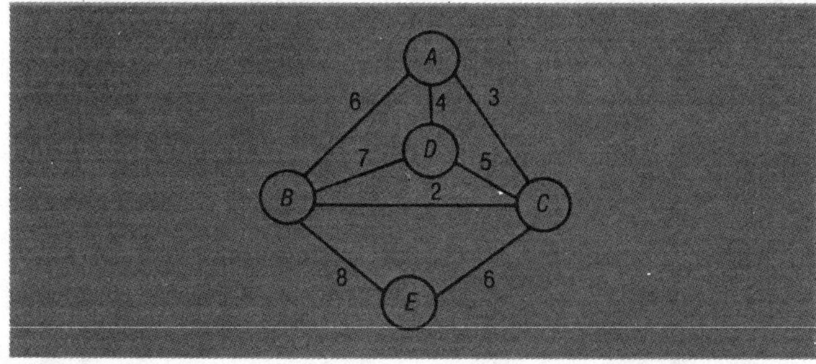

MODULE	P_1 TIME	P_2 TIME	P_3 TIME
A	4	INFINITY	INFINITY
B	INFINITY	6	INFINITY
C	INFINITY	INFINITY	7
D	10	7	5
E	4	7	3

Figure 4. Execution and communication costs for a program to be assigned to three processors.

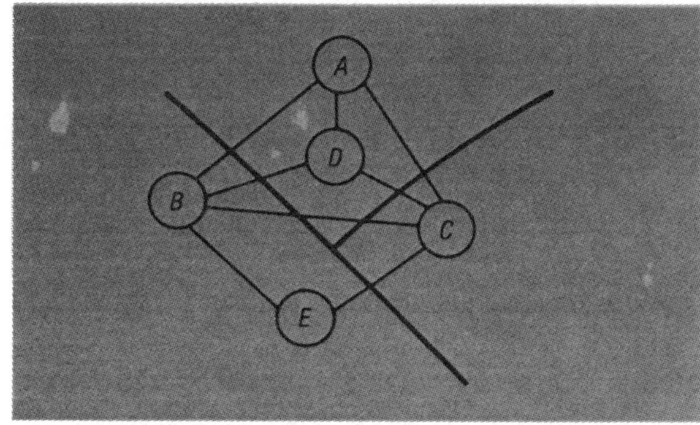

Figure 5. A tricutset representing a module assignment to three processors.

The dynamic assignment problem

The cost figures used in the network flow models discussed so far represent the net execution and communication costs for the entire lifetime of the program. These models yield the optimal static assignment—a module assigned to a particular processor is assumed to stay on that processor for the lifetime of that assignment.

In this section we examine the case where the cost of reassignment cannot be ignored and we treat exclusively the two-processor problem. The objective here is to relocate modules during the execution of the program to take advantage of changes in the locality of the program.

The basis for our mathematical model of the dynamic assignment problem is the concept of the *phase* of a modular program. This is defined as follows:

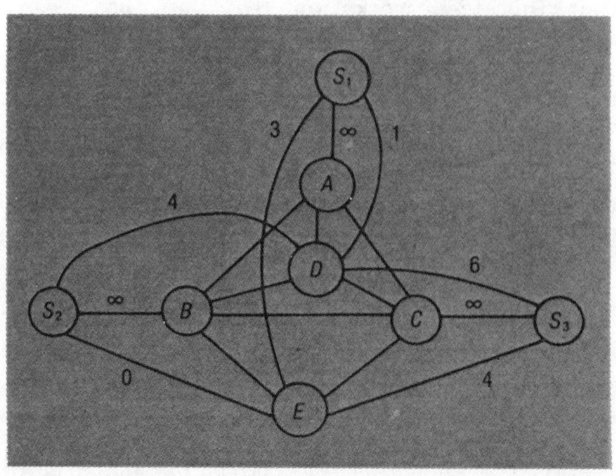

Figure 6. Modified module interconnection graph for a three-processor assignment.

The *phase* of a modular program is a contiguous period of time during which only one module executes. During this period the executing module may communicate with any number of the remaining modules. A module *may not* be moved from one processor to another during a phase—it may be moved only *between* phases.

With each phase is associated the following information:

1. Which module executes during this phase.

2. Run costs of this module for either of the two processors.

3. Costs of residence of the remaining modules for each of the two processors.

4. Intermodule communication costs between the executing module and all other modules assigned to different processors.

5. Relocation cost for each module—the cost of relocating each module from one processor to the other *if relocation were to be carried out at the end of this phase.*

As an example we consider a program made up of three modules (*A*, *B*, and *C*) and five phases. Complete information about this program is given in Table 1.

Consider phase 3—the entries corresponding to this phase in Table 1 indicate that during this phase module *A* executes. The cost of running this module on processor 1 is 4, on processor 2 it is 17.

Table 1. Tabulation of costs for a dynamic assignment problem with three modules.

PHASE	MODULE	EXECUTION COST		RESIDENCE COST	
		P_1	P_2	P_1	P_2
1	A	4	10	–	–
	B	–	–	1	3
	C	–	–	3	1
2	A	–	–	1	2
	B	INFINITY	12	–	–
	C	–	–	3	1
3	A	4	17	–	–
	B	–	–	1	2
	C	–	–	4	2
4	A	–	–	1	1
	B	–	–	4	2
	C	6	4	–	–
5	A	–	–	3	1
	B	–	–	3	2
	C	9	3	–	–

PHASE	COST OF COMMUNICATION BETWEEN EXECUTING MODULE AND			RELOCATION COSTS OF		
	A	B	C	A	B	C
1	–	3	2	2	1	3
2	4	–	3	2	3	2
3	–	7	0	3	2	3
4	0	4	–	2	1	4
5	4	3	–	–	–	–

The residence costs of the nonexecuting modules (*B* and *C*) are also listed. During this phase there is no communication between the executing module and module *C*. The cost of communication between modules *A* and *B* is 7. Costs for relocating modules *A*, *B*, and *C* at the end of this phase are 3, 2, and 3, respectively.

Figure 7 shows how this information may be represented by a graph. The number of nodes in this graph equals the number of program modules multiplied by the number of phases. The nodes are arranged in a grid with the vertical "columns" of nodes representing the modules and the horizontal "rows" representing the phases. Each individual node represents the *residence* of a module during a specific phase, as will become clear in what follows. Each node is labeled with an upper-case letter which identifies the module it represents and an integer which identifies the phase. The single module that executes during each phase is marked with an asterisk.

The "vertical" edges in this graph connect successive residences of the same module and the weight of these edges represents the cost of relocating the module. The "horizontal" edges connect

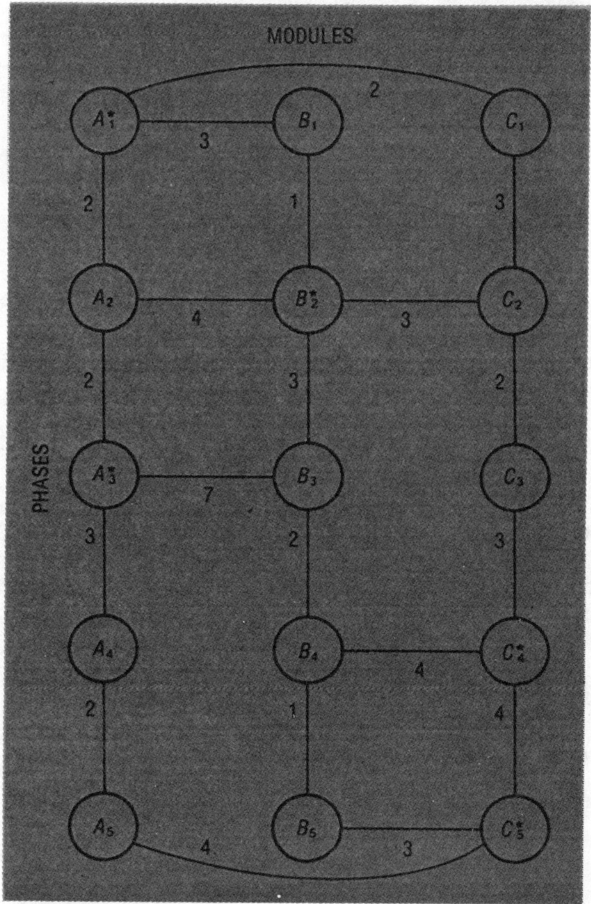

Figure 7. Incomplete dynamic assignment graph. The horizontal edges represent communication costs, and the vertical edges represent relocation costs. Asterisk denotes executing module.

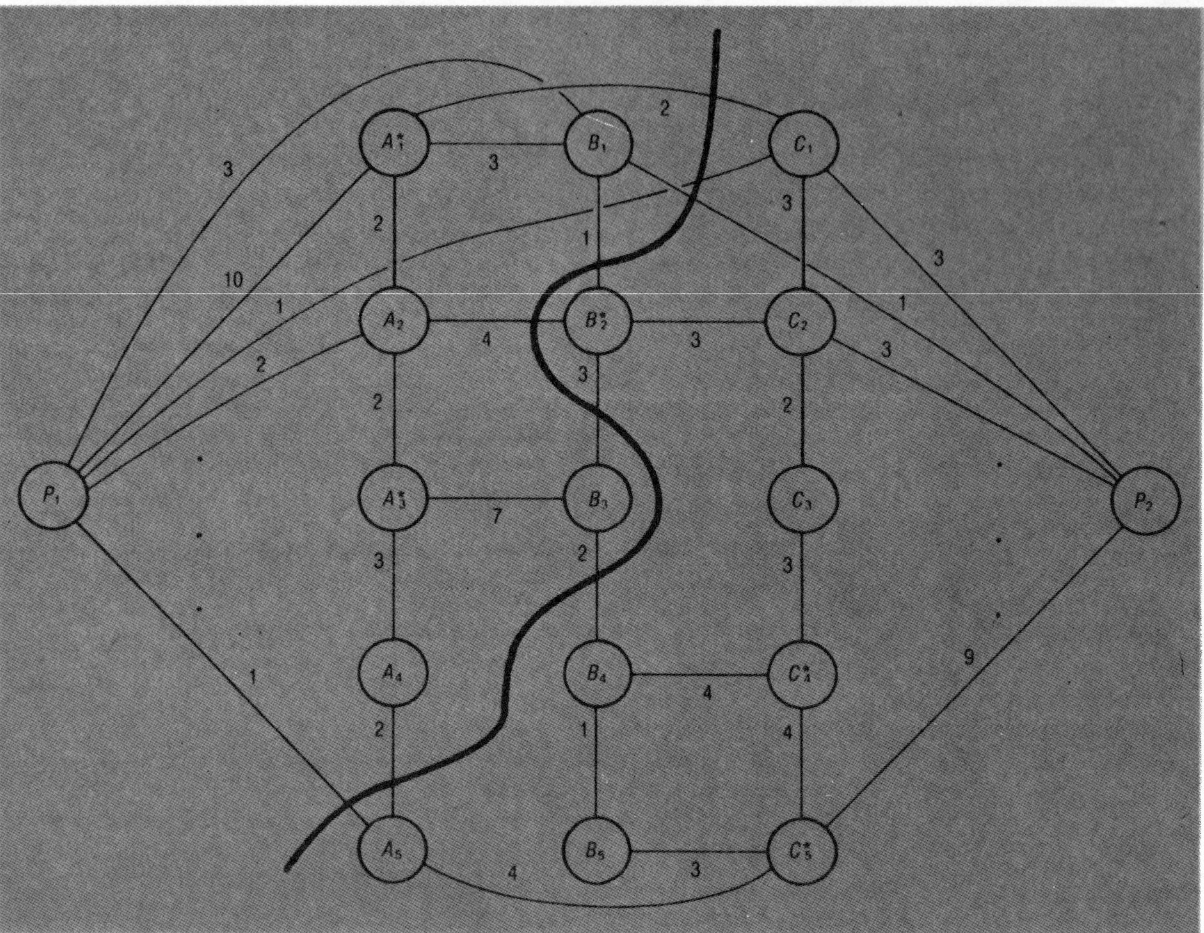

Figure 8. A minimum weight cut in the dynamic assignment graph.

the executing module with other modules during the same phase and represent intermodule communication costs between the executing module and the other modules.

In Figure 8 we have added two nodes, marked P_1 and P_2, which represent the two processors. Edges representing the run costs are drawn from P_1 and P_2 to each of the nodes representing executing modules (those marked with an asterisk). As in the simple assignment problem of Figure 1, the edge between a node and P_1 represents its run cost on P_2 and vice-versa. In a similar fashion, edges representing residence costs are drawn from P_1 and P_2 to the remaining nodes. For clarity, only a few of these edges are shown in Figure 8.

The resulting graph is called a *dynamic assignment graph*. It has been shown in Bokhari[15] that a cutset in this graph gives a dynamic assignment of modules, i.e., it specifies which modules are to reside on which processor during each phase. The weight of a cutset gives the total cost of the corresponding dynamic assignment. It follows that the minimum weight cut gives the optimal dynamic assignment. This mincut may be found by running a network flow algorithm between nodes P_1 and P_2 in the dynamic assignment graph. A mincut in our running example is shown by the dark line in Figure 8.

Extensions to four or more processors

The assignment problem for four or more processors, as described in earlier sections of this paper, is known to be in the class of "hard" problems for which an efficient solution may not even exist.

However, should the intermodule communication pattern be constrained to be a tree, the problem may be solved efficiently for any arbitrary number of processors, as is demonstrated in this section. We mention that the tree-like structure assumed here is a structure common to programs when they are written as a hierarchy of subroutines.

Figure 9 illustrates one such program graph made up of eight modules. In this directed tree (which we call an *invocation tree*) program activity starts in module 1. At one or more points during the execution of the program, module 1 invokes module 2, which in turn invokes module 3. Module 3 invokes two modules, 4 and 6. This "branching" of program activity corresponds to two or more

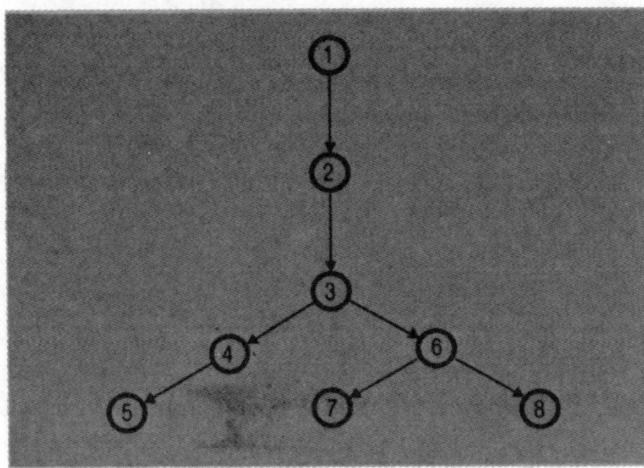

Figure 9. An invocation tree.

sets of calls in the body of module 3, some to module 4, and some to 6.

Thus, the edge joining two nodes in the tree indicates, in general, that the module represented by the ancestor node calls the descendent *many times* during the lifetime of the program. (A precedence ordering on module executions is *not* implied.)

With each module in the tree are associated the costs of executing that module on the various processors in the system. Thus e_{ij} represents the cost of executing module i on processor j. With each edge that joins nodes p and q is associated the intermodule communication cost c_{pq}, the cost of communicating between modules p and q, should they not be coresident.

To find the minimum cost assignment for this tree we first draw up an *assignment graph* as shown in Figure 10. The node $[ij]$ in this graph represents the assignment of module i to processor j. The edge joining node $[ij]$ to node $[kj]$ is labeled with the weight e_{kj}. The edge joining $[ij]$ to node $[pg]$ is labeled with the weight $e_{pq} + c_{ip}$. For clarity, edge weights have been omitted from Figure 10.

For example, node [63] represents the assignment of module 6 to processor 3. The weight on the edge joining nodes [32] and [42] is e_{42}, representing the run cost of module 4 on processor 2. The weight on the edge joining nodes [32] and [61] is $e_{61} + c_{36}$.

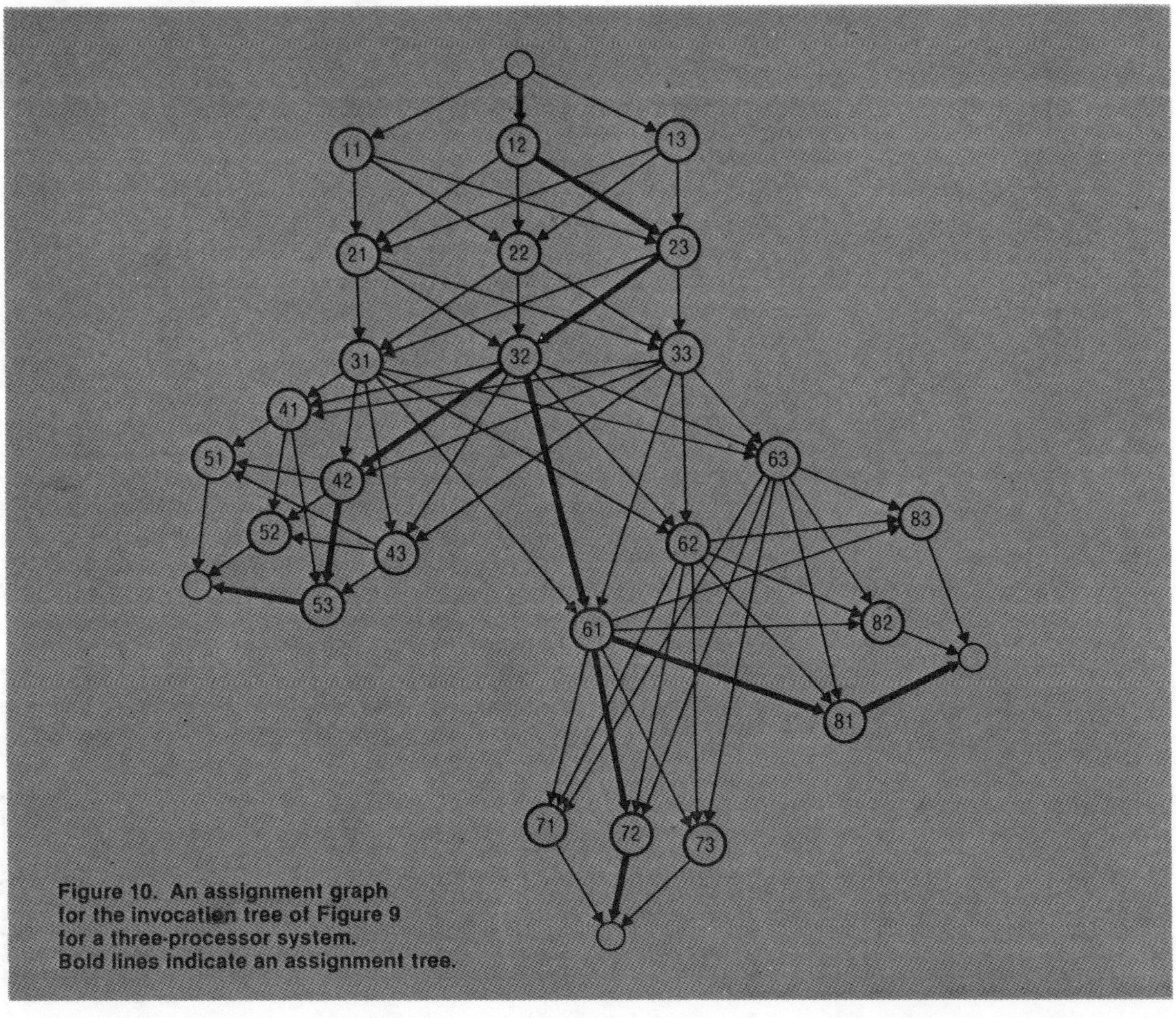

Figure 10. An assignment graph for the invocatien tree of Figure 9 for a three-processor system. Bold lines indicate an assignment tree.

The assignment graph has a source node s and three terminal nodes t_1, t_2, and t_3. There is one terminal node in the assignment graph for each of the three leaf nodes in the corresponding invocation tree.

An *assignment tree* is a tree in the assignment graph such that it (1) contains a directed path from s to all terminal nodes t_1, t_2, t_3, ... and (2) contains one and only one node from each layer of the graph.

Each assignment tree represents an assignment of modules to processors. A little reflection reveals that the weight or length of the tree gives the cost of the corresponding assignment.

The edges drawn with thick lines in Figure 10 form one such tree. This tree is shown in isolation in Figure 11, with the edges labeled appropriately.

The assignment tree corresponds to an assignment of modules to processors. The weight of the tree gives the cost of that assignment. Therefore, the minimum weight or shortest tree gives a minimum cost assignment.

The shortest assignment tree may be found using an efficient dynamic programming approach given in Bokhari.[16]

Conclusions and projections

The work presented in this article consists largely of efficient solutions to simple mathematical models of distributed systems. There are several open questions concerning the applicability of these results to the real world. In this section we ponder how these results might be applied to achieve our end goal of controlling a distributed computer system in real time.

1. Is it realistic to assume that the control algorithm has available complete future knowledge of the behavior of a program? The system at Brown University suggests that this assumption might be valid. For that system it is possible to develop the requisite statistics on program behavior by monitoring the program in real time. Of course, there is an overhead incurred in monitoring. Wherther or not this burden can be reduced to a negligible burden on practical systems is still unknown.

2. Do we need to solve four-processor and n-processor systems in real time? If programs exhibit strong locality in distributed systems, then they

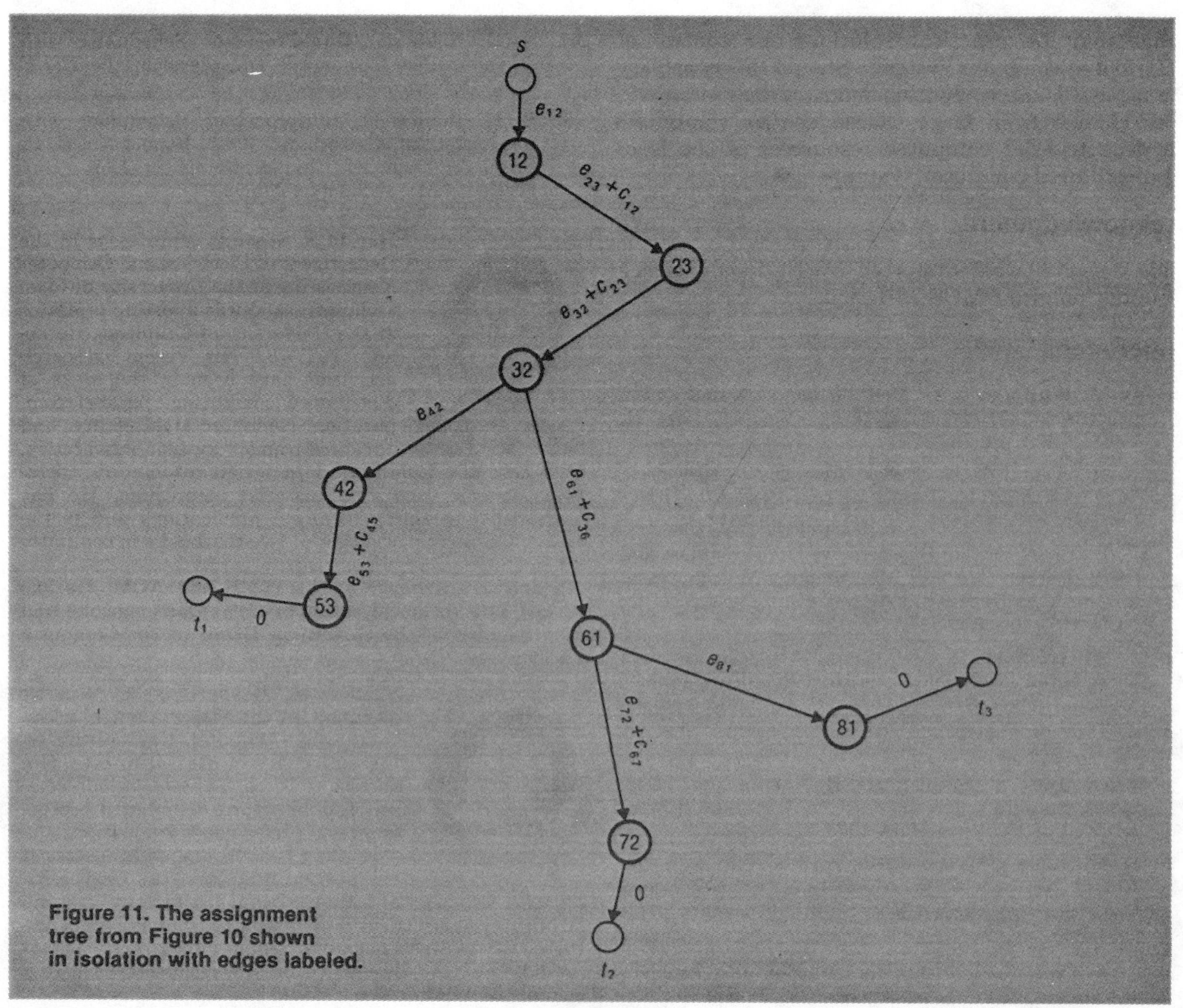

Figure 11. The assignment tree from Figure 10 shown in isolation with edges labeled.

will tend to have their modules cluster on one or two processors. If this is the case, then algorithms for two-processor sytems (possibly three-processor systems) will be the computational core of an n-processor control algorithm.

3. What about the "stability" of an assignment algorithm that is optimal for each program in a multiprogrammed system but possibly very bad for the system as a whole? It is quite possible that a control algorithm that optimizes each individual program can create a disastrous situation. For example, it can decide individually that each program should move to a lightly loaded processor P. At this point P becomes overloaded. Then the control program individually decides that each program should move its modules from P. Then P becomes lightly loaded, and the scenario repeats. It is unknown at this time how to create a globally stable control algorithm.

These three open problems are merely the tip of the iceberg, and are indicative of the work that remains to be done. We hope that these obstacles and others like them can be eliminated so as to open the way for the potential benefits of distributed computer systems.

The results cited here have pointed the way to what may be practical solutions for control of distributed computer systems. Should this capability be achieved, the computing industry may dramatically change from large shared central computers to decentralized computer resources, in the form of distributed computer systems. ■

Acknowledgment

This research was supported by National Science Foundation grant MCS-76-11650.

References

1. W. A. Wulf and C. G. Bell, "C.mmp—A multi-mini-processor," *AFIPS Conf. Proc.*, Vol. 41, Part II, FJCC, 1972, pp. 765-777.
2. R. J. Swan, S. H. Fuller, and D. P. Siewiorek, "Cm*—A Modular, Multi-Microprocessor," *AFIPS Conf. Proc.*, Vol. 46, NCC, 1977, pp. 637-644.
3. F. E. Heart; S. M. Ornstein, W. R. Crowther, and W. B. Barker, "A New Minicomputer/Multiprocessor for the Arpa Network," *AFIPS Conf. Proc.*, Vol. 42, NCC, 1973, pp. 529-537.
4. J. Michel and A. van Dam, "Experience with Distributed Processing on a Host/Satellite Graphics System," *Proc. SIGGRAPH '76*, available as *Computer Graphics* (SIGGRAPH newsletter), Vol. 10, No. 2, 1976.
5. A. van Dam, G. Stabler, and R. Harrington, "Intelligent Satellites for Interactive Graphics," *Proc. IEEE*, Vol. 62, No. 4, Apr. 1974, pp. 83-92.
6. H. S. Stone, "Multiprocessor Scheduling with the Aid of Network Flow Algorithms," *IEEE Trans. Software Engineering*, Vol. SE-3, No. 2, Jan. 1977, pp. 85-93.
7. E. A. Dinic, "Algorithm for Solution of a Problem of Maximum Flow in a Network with Power Estimation," *Soviet Math. Doklady*, Vol. 11, No. 5, 1970, pp. 1277-1280.
8. J. Edmonds and R. M. Karp, "Theoretical Improvements in Algorithmic Efficiency for Network Flow Problems," *JACM*, Vol. 19, Apr. 1972, pp. 248-264.
9. L. R. Ford, Jr., and D. R. Fulkerson, *Flows in Networks*, Princeton University Press, Princeton, N.J., 1962.
10. A. V. Karzanov, "Determining the Maximal Flow in a Network by the Method of Preflows," *Soviet Math. Doklady*, Vol. 15, No. 2, 1974, pp. 434-437.
11. H. S. Stone, "Critical Load Factors in Distributed Computer Systems," to appear in the *IEEE Trans. Software Engineering*.
12. M. J. Eisner and D. G. Severance, "Mathematical Techniques for Efficient Record Segmentation in Large Shared Data Bases," *JACM*, Vol. 23, Oct. 1976, pp. 619-635.
13. G. S. Rao, H. S. Stone, and T. C. Hu, "Scheduling in a Distributed Processor System with Limited Memory," submitted for publication to the *IEEE Trans. Computers*.
14. H. S. Stone, "Program Assignment in Three-Processor Systems and Tricutset Partitioning of Graphs," Tech. Report No. ECE-CS-77-7, Dept. of Elec. & Computer Eng., University of Massachusetts, Amherst.
15. S. H. Bokhari, "Dual-Processor Scheduling with Dynamic Reassignment," To appear in the *IEEE Trans. Software Engineering*.
16. S. H. Bokhari, "Multiprocessor Scheduling with Shortest Path Algorithms," Tech. Report No. ECE-CS-77-11, Dept. of Elec. & Computer Eng., University of Massachusets, Amherst.

Assignment of Tasks in a Distributed Processor System with Limited Memory

GURURAJ S. RAO, HAROLD S. STONE, MEMBER, IEEE, AND T. C. HU

***Abstract*—A recently published algorithm shows how to assign modules to a two-processor computer system with distributed execution so as to minimize the total of execution costs and interprocessor communication costs. In this paper we consider the same problem except that one processor has limited memory capacity. Although this problem is *NP*-complete, techniques based on the Gomory–Hu tree from network flow theory can be applied to instances of the problem to obtain a reduction in complexity. A new technique based on a graph called the inclusive cut graph is shown to be an even more powerful tool. These two techniques can solve some instances of the problem completely; still others are reduced sufficiently to be susceptible to enumerative techniques. In the worst case, the techniques yield no reduction in problem size.**

***Index Terms*—Computer networks, cutsets, distributed computers, Ford–Fulkerson algorithm, Gomory–Hu cut trees, load balancing, multiterminal maximal flows, *NP*-complete problems.**

I. Introduction

DISTRIBUTED computing has received increased attention in the recent literature (see [18], [5], [16], [9], [15], and [13]). The term "distributed computing" is used here to mean computer systems with intermediate coupling in the terminology of Fuller and Siewiorek [6]. In such computer systems, control passes from one processor to another as the program progresses. Stone [15] has shown how the program modules of a program may be assigned to the processors of a distributed computer system so as to minimize the overall cost, including two types of costs: the cost of running an individual module on a processor and the cost of interprocessor communication that arises in the event of transfer of control of execution from one processor to another.

In this paper we consider the problem of minimum cost assignment of program modules to two processors when one processor has limited memory. We assume that the other processor has unlimited memory. This assumption is justified in many host-satellite systems [17] due to the large memory or virtual memory on the host system. We shall first solve the problem by constructing the Gomory–Hu tree, and then develop the inclusive cut graph to solve the same problem.

Section II describes network flow algorithms and reviews briefly the Gomory–Hu cut tree construction for finding the maximum flow between all pairs of nodes in a network. Section III discusses the properties of the G–H cut that are used to simplify the problem. Section IV presents an efficient reduction technique based on a graph called the inclusive cut graph.

II. Module Assignment Using Network Flow Algorithms

In the assignment of modules to processors, there are two types of costs: the cost of execution of a module on a processor and the cost of interprocessor communication.

The graph model of a program represents modules as nodes of a graph, with an arc between two nodes if and only if the modules communicate with each other. The total interprocessor communication cost between two modules is the weight on the arc between those two nodes.

In addition to this, the cost of execution of each of the modules on each of the processors is given. If a module cannot be assigned to a particular processor, the model represents this by assigning infinite cost of execution for the module on this processor.

Given this module interconnection graph, Stone [15] shows how to obtain the minimum cost assignment for two processors P_1 and P_2.

1) Add two nodes S and T, which represent the processors P_1 and P_2, respectively.

2) For every node other than S and T, add an arc from that node to each of S and T. The weight of the arc to S is the cost of execution of the module by P_2, and the weight of the arc to T is the cost of executing the module on P_1. The resulting graph is called the network.

3) We can regard the modified graph as a network with S as the source and T as the sink. Using the max-flow min-cut theorem [4], we can partition the nodes representing the modules into two disjoint sets, one associated with each processor. This association determines the minimum cost assignment. Thus, the module assignment problem can be solved efficiently (in a time upper bounded by N^3 for a network with N nodes) (see [12]; cf. [2] and [1]; even 1976 contains an exposition of the Dinic–Karzanov algorithm).

An example of the assignment produced by the max-flow, min-cut theorem for the module interconnection graph in

Manuscript received April 3, 1978; revised September 27, 1978. This research was supported by the National Science Foundation under Grants DCR74-20025, MCS76-11650, and DCR75-06270, and by the U.S. Army Research Office under Grant DAAG 29-76-G-0031.

G. S. Rao was with the Laboratory for Computer Science and Engineering, Department of Electrical Engineering Rice University, Houston, TX 77001. He is now with IBM T. J. Watson Research Center, Yorktown Heights, NY 10598.

H. S. Stone is with the Department of Electrical and Computer Engineering, University of Massachusetts, Amherst, MA 01002.

T. C. Hu is with the Department of Applied Physics and Information Science, University of California, La Jolla, CA 92037.

Reprinted from *IEEE Trans. Comput.*, vol. C-28, pp. 291–298, Apr. 1979.

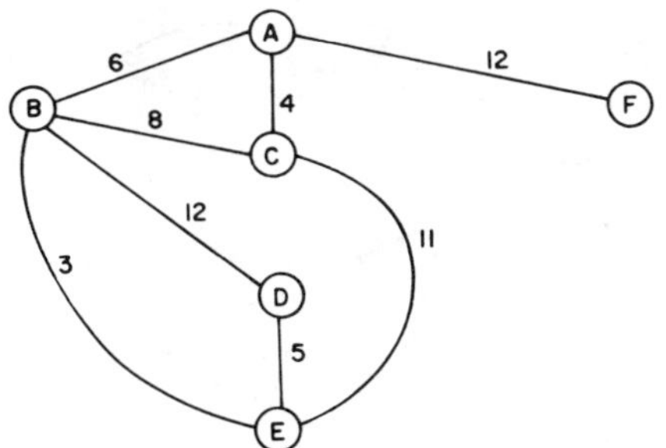

Fig. 1. A module interconnection graph.

TABLE I

Module	P_1 Run Time	P_2 Run Time
A	5	10
B	2	Infinity
C	4	4
D	6	3
E	5	2
F	Infinity	4

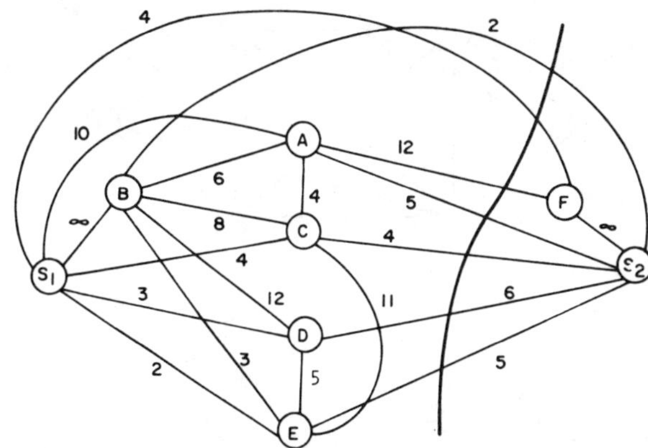

Fig. 2. Minimum cost assignment for the module interconnection graph in Fig. 1 with execution times in Table I.

Fig. 1 and the cost of execution on the processors in Table I, is shown in Fig. 2.

Maximal Flows, Cutsets and Multiterminal Maximal Flows

Now we give the relevant terminology and a few results pertaining to maximal flows in networks (for details, see Hu [8]).

In a network the source can generate an infinite amount of flow while the sink can absorb an infinite amount of flow. The *weight* or *capacity* of an arc represents the maximum amount of flow that can go through the arc.

A *feasible flow* is a set of arc flows assigned to the arcs such that 1) the capacity of every arc is not exceeded and 2) the flow is conserved at every node except the source and the sink.

The *value* of a flow is the net flow out of the source node.

A *maximal flow* is a feasible flow whose value is maximum among all feasible flows.

A *cut* of a network is a minimal set of arcs, the removal of which separates the source node from the sink node. The *weight* or *capacity* of a cut is the sum of the capacities of the arc in the cut.

The Max-Flow, Min-Cut Theorem [4]

The value of the maximum flow in a network is equal to the minimum capacity of a cut of the network.

Multiterminal Maximum Flows

We shall consider maximal flows between several pairs of nodes. Gomory and Hu [7] show that for a network with p nodes, maximal flows between all the $p(p-1)/2$ pairs of nodes can be obtained by using the max-flow, min-cut Theorem only $p-1$ times. They describe a procedure for constructing a tree corresponding to the given network with values on the links of the tree and with the following property:

1) The maximum flow value between any pair of nodes N_p and N_q is equal to

$$\min\,(v_{pi}, v_{ij}, v_{jk}, \cdots, v_{tq})$$

where v_{ij} are values associated with the links of the Gomory–Hu cut tree (abbreviated as G–H tree).

2) Any link L_{ij} of the G–H tree corresponds to a minimum cut $(X, \bar{X})$ separating N_i and N_j in the original network. The set X is the set of nodes connected to N_i in the G–H tree when the link L_{ij} is removed.

Fig. 3(b) is the G–H tree for the network in Fig. 3(a). For example, the maximal flow between nodes 1 and 5 is 13, that between 3 and 4 is 14.

In addition, the minimum cut separating nodes 1 and 5 is ((1, 2, 6), (3, 4, 5)), that separating 3 and 4 is ((1, 2, 6, 5, 3), (4)).

III. Cost Assignments with a Memory-Size Constraint

Every node has a weight that is the memory requirement of that node. The sum of weights of nodes assigned to a processor should not exceed the memory of the processor.

Let T denote the processor with limited memory and S the other processor. A feasible assignment is an assignment that does not exceed the memory of T.

First, we show that the minimum cost feasible assignment does not reassign to T any of the modules assigned to S by the minimum cost assignment. Then we show that certain sets of nodes in the network can be condensed into single nodes for the purpose of searching for a minimum cost feasible assignment.

Theorem 1: The modules assigned to T by the minimum cost feasible assignment form a subset of the modules assigned to T by the minimum cost assignment.

Proof: Let I denote the cut producing a minimum cost assignment and II the cut producing a minimum cost feasible assignment (see Fig. 4).

First we observe that II cannot be as shown by dotted lines in Fig. 4, because this cut assigns modules to T in

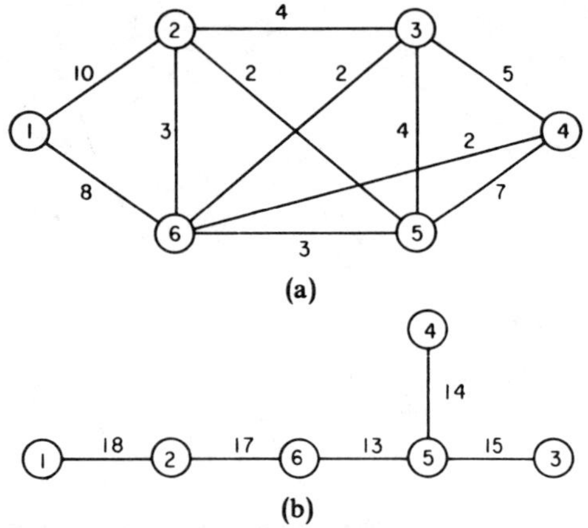

Fig. 3. (a) A network. (b) The corresponding G–H tree.

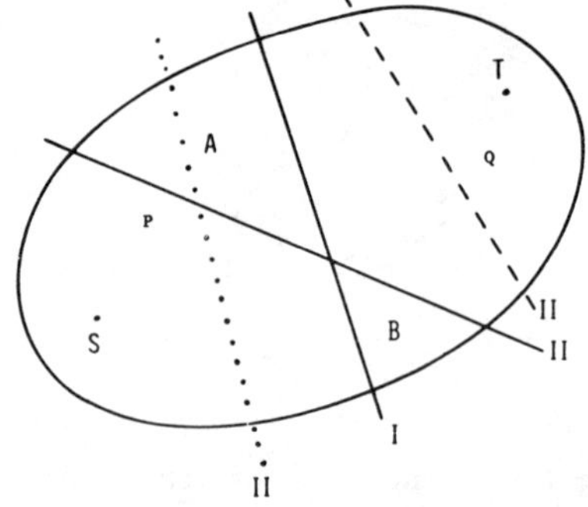

Fig. 4. Illustration for the Proof of Theorem 1.

addition to all the modules assigned by I. If cut II is the dashed line in the figure, then the theorem is trivially proved. Thus, we consider the case where cut II is shown as a solid line.

Since I and II cross, the nodes are partitioned into four disjoint regions marked A, B, P, and Q. (Two cuts cross if none of the four regions is empty.)

Let $c(U, V)$ be the sum of weights of all the arcs between the regions U and V.

Since I is the minimum cut separating S and T, its capacity is no bigger than that of any other cut separating S and T, in particular the cut produced by rerouting I to include region A with Q. Thus,

$$c(A, Q) + c(P, Q) + c(A, B) + c(B, P) \leq c(A, P) + c(P, Q) + c(B, P) \quad (1)$$

or

$$c(A, Q) + c(A, B) \leq c(A, P) \quad (2)$$

or

$$c(A, Q) \leq c(A, P) + c(A, B) \qquad (\text{since } c(A, B) \geq 0).$$

Adding $c(P, Q) + c(B, Q)$ to both sides of (2), we have

$$c(A, Q) + c(P, Q) + c(B, Q) \leq c(A, P) + c(A, B) + c(P, Q) + c(B, Q). \quad (3)$$

Thus, the cut $(A \cup P \cup B, Q)$ has less or the same capacity as II; the cut $(A \cup P \cup B, Q)$ also separates S and T and represents a partition of nodes which demands less memory of T, since Q is a subset of $Q \cup B$ which is the partition implied by I. This proves the theorem. Q.E.D.

Thus in searching for a minimum cost, feasible assignment, we need only to produce the minimum cut, and then reassign some subset of modules from T to S.

Let min (T) be the set of nodes assigned to T by the minimum cost assignment. We now study the effect of assigning a node N belonging to min (T) to S.

Assigning $N \in$ min (T) to S

Let us increase the arc capacity between S and N to ∞ and then find the minimum cut separating S and T in the new network. This minimum cut is denoted by $N(S)$. Because of the infinite arc capacity, S and N will be on the same side of the cut $N(S)$. We shall use $N[S]$ to denote the set of nodes on the same side as S and N. For every node $N \in$ min (T), we could do this and locate a minimum cut. We call this process the assignment of N to S.

Lemma 1: If N is assigned to S by a minimum feasible flow, then all of $N[S]$ is assigned to S by a minimum feasible flow.

Proof: The proof is identical to the proof of Theorem 1. In Fig. 4, let cut I be $N(S)$, and cut II be a minimum feasible cut. Since N is assigned to S by both cuts, N is in region P. Using the method of proof of the theorem, we find that the cut separating region Q from regions A, B, and P has a weight not exceeding that of cut II, and is feasible if cut II is feasible. This cut assigns all of $N[S]$ to S. Q.E.D.

Lemma 2: If $N_i \in N_j[S]$ and $N_j \in N_i[S]$, then N_i and N_j are not separated by a minimum feasible cut.

Proof: From Lemma 1 it follows that if $N_i \in N_j[S]$, and a minimum feasible cut assigns N_j to S, then a minimum feasible cut assigns both N_i and N_j to S. Similarly, if a minimum feasible cut assigns N_j to S, then a minimum feasible cut assigns both N_i and N_j to S. Then N_i and N_j are not separated by a minimum feasible cut. Q.E.D.

Node Condensation in the G–H Tree

We now show how the G–H tree indicates some subsets of nodes that are not separated by a minimum feasible cut. Such nodes can be condensed together and treated as a single node in the process of seeking a minimum feasible cut.

Theorem 2: Let N_i, N_j, and N_k be three nodes in a network, and let each be members of min (T) such that the following properties hold in the G–H tree for that network:

a) N_j is on the unique path in the G–H tree between N_i and T,

b) N_k is a node adjacent to N_j and N_k lies on the path between N_j and T, and

c) the edge $y = (N_j, N_k)$ has smaller weight than any other link weight on the path between N_i and T.

Then all nodes N_r on the path between N_i and N_j (including N_i and N_j) lie on the same side of a minimum feasible cut.

Proof: We consider two cases depending on whether or not N_j lies on the path between S and T in the G–H tree.

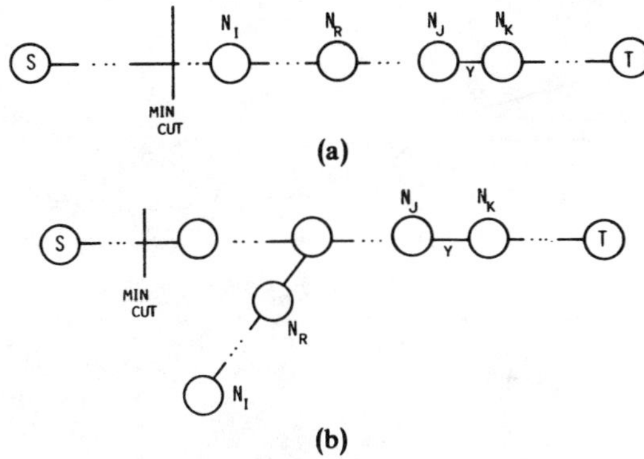

Fig. 5. (a) and (b) Case i) of Theorem 2.

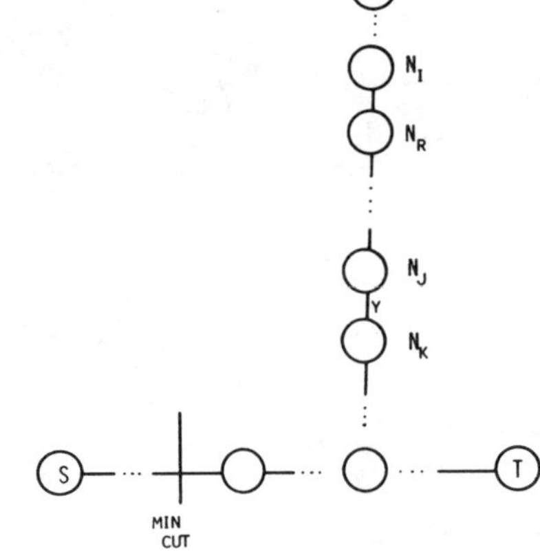

Fig. 6. Case ii) of Theorem 2.

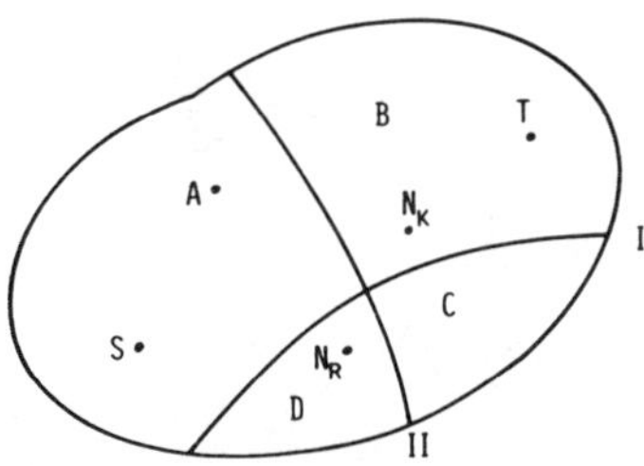

Fig. 7. Intersecting cuts for Case ii) of Theorem 2.

Case 1: N_j lies on the path between S and T in the G–H tree.

Fig. 5(a) and (b) show two ways this case arises. In either event, y is the min cut between N_i and T because of condition c) and the properties of the G–H tree. Similarly, y is the min cut between T and each node N_r. Since y assigns N_i to S, and y is a minimal cut between N_i and T, y must be the cut $N_i(S)$, and by similar reasoning y is the cut $N_r(S)$ for each node N_r between N_i and N_j. Thus, for each r we have $N_i \in N_r[S]$ and $N_r \in N_i[S]$. From Lemma 2, these nodes are not separated by a minimum feasible cut, which proves the theorem for this case.

Case 2: N_j (and hence N_i) is not on the path between S and T.

Fig. 6 shows this case. To prove the theorem for this case, it is sufficient to show that for each r, $N_r \in N_i[S]$ and $N_i \in N_r[S]$, at which point Lemma 2 applies as in the previous case. We proceed by first showing that $N_r(S)$ does not cross the min cut between N_r and N_k.

Fig. 7 shows the min cut separating N_r and N_k (cut I) and the cut $N_r(S)$ (cut II). Since cut I is a min cut, its capacity does not exceed the capacity of any other cut separating N_r and N_k. Thus

$$c(A, C) + c(A, D) + c(B, C) + c(B, D) \leq c(A, D) + c(B, D) + c(C, D)$$

or

$$c(A, C) + c(B, C) \leq c(C, D)$$

or

$$c(B, D) \leq c(C, D) + c(A, C) \qquad (\text{since } c(A, C) \geq 0).$$

Adding $c(B, A) + c(B, D)$ to both sides yields

$$c(B, A) + c(B, C) + c(B, D) \leq c(A, B) + c(A, C) + c(B, D) + c(C, D).$$

The left-hand cut is a cut assigning N_r to S that does not cross the min cut between N_r and N_k, and the right-hand cut is $N_r(S)$. Thus $N_r(S)$ can be rerouted to include region C with N_r without increasing its cost. Note that this argument holds if N_k is in region A or B.

From Fig. 6, condition c), and the basic properties of the G–H tree, we see that the min cut between N_r and N_k is simply the edge y, and this is true for each N_r between N_i and N_j. From above, $N_r(S)$ does not cross the cut y, yet $N_r(S)$ assigns N_r to S. This is satisfiable only if $N_r(S)$ assigns the entire path between N_i and N_j to S for each r. Then we have $N_i \in N_r[S]$ and $N_r \in N_i[S]$, which is what we seek to complete the proof of the theorem. Q.E.D.

We conclude from Theorem 2 that for the purposes of discovering a minimum feasible cut, we may condense the nodes on the path between N_i and N_j into a single node, since these nodes are not split by a minimum feasible cut. All subtrees from the original G–H tree that are rooted to nodes on this path become rooted to the new node into which the nodes N_r condense.

By successive applications of Theorem 2 to the subtrees of the G–H tree, the network can be reduced so that the path from each node N to T has nondecreasing arc weights along the path.

Using the results obtained so far, we can condense certain sets of nodes in the G–H tree. We can do these condensations using only the G–H tree, and need not refer to the original network. When the G–H tree is reduced by Theorem 2, we call it the reduced G–H tree. Even further reductions are possible to determine from the reduced G–H tree as indicated in the following two corollaries.

Lemma 3: Let N_i be any node in the G–H tree. Then $N_i(S)$ assigns to S, not only N_i, but all nodes in the G–H tree whose paths to T pass through N_i.

Proof: If N_i lies on the path between S and T, then $N_i(S)$ consists of a single edge on that path, and Theorem 2 holds

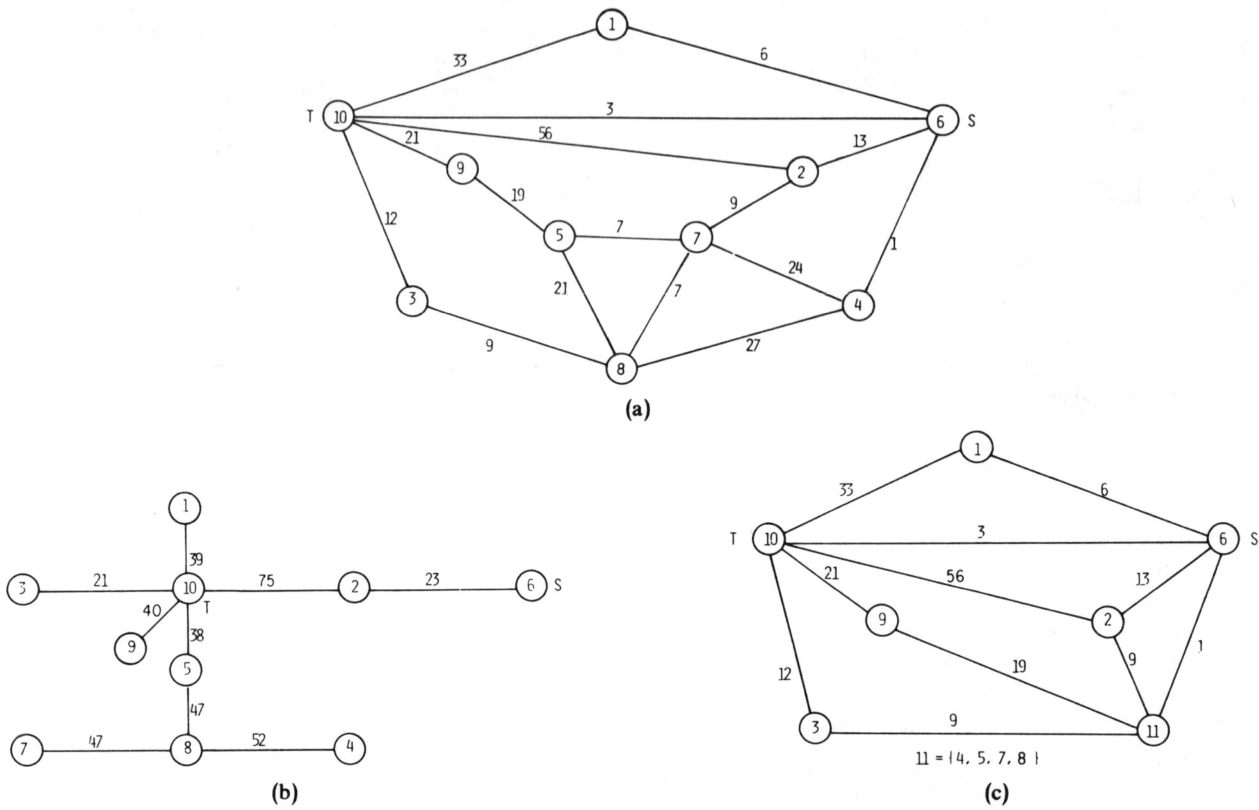

Fig. 8. (a) A commodity network. (b) The G–H tree for the commodity network. (c) The reduced commodity graph.

for this case. If N_i is not on the path between S and T, let N_k be the node adjacent to N_i on the path between N_i and T. In the proof of Theorem 2, we showed that $N_i(S)$ does not cross the min cut between N_i and N_k. Then $N_i(S)$ assigns to S not only N_i, but all of the nodes in subtrees rooted at N_i on the far side of N_i from T for otherwise $N_i(S)$ would cross the min cut between N_i and N_k. The nodes in the subtrees assigned to S are the nodes whose paths to T pass through N_i. Q.E.D.

Lemma 4: Let $N_i \in \min(T)$ be a node in a network, and in the G–H tree for that network let N_j be a node on the path between N_i and T. If $N_j \in N_i[S]$, then N_i and N_j can be condensed.

Proof: From Lemma 3 and the hypothesis, we conclude that $N_i \in N_j[S]$. This and the fact that $N_j \in N_i[S]$ together with Lemma 2 yield that N_i and N_j are not split by a minimum feasible cut. Q.E.D.

A network is shown in Fig. 8(a), and its G–H tree appears in Fig. 8(b). Note that the link between nodes 10 and 5 has the weight 38, which is smaller than all the other link weights in the subtree rooted at node 5. Thus nodes 4, 5, 7, and 8 can be condensed into a single node 11 by Theorem 2. When this reduction is made, all paths in the G–H tree leading to T have increasing arc weights. No further reduction by Theorem 2 is possible at this point. The network after node condensation appears in Fig. 8(c).

Note that the condensation property is an equivalence relation so that if nodes N_i and N_j can be condensed, and N_i and N_k can be condensed, then N_j and N_k can be condensed as well. Then all three nodes N_i, N_j, and N_k can be condensed into a single node.

Node condensation in a G–H tree may be sufficiently powerful to reduce some problems to trivial graphs that can be solved by enumeration. However, for some networks, little or no condensation occurs. The next section presents a node condensation method that is at least as powerful as the G–H tree method described in this section.

IV. Efficient Reduction Techniques

In searching for a minimum feasible assignment, we can condense certain subsets of nodes in the network into a single node, since these subsets move as a block. All the reductions obtained so far are based on the G–H tree (except Lemma 1). The reduction techniques described in this present section can be applied to the reduced G–H tree, or can be applied to the original network without first calculating the G–H tree to perform reductions.

Note that the problem of finding a minimum feasible assignment in some cases is equivalent to a knapsack problem, and hence is an *NP*-complete problem. Consider the n-node network in which every node is of degree two and the source and the sink both have degrees $(n-2)$. The weight w_i of the node N_i corresponds to the weight of the ith item in the knapsack problem. A feasible cut corresponds to a subset of items whose weights do not exceed the knapsack constraint weight w. A minimum feasible cut corresponds to a knapsack packing of maximum value.

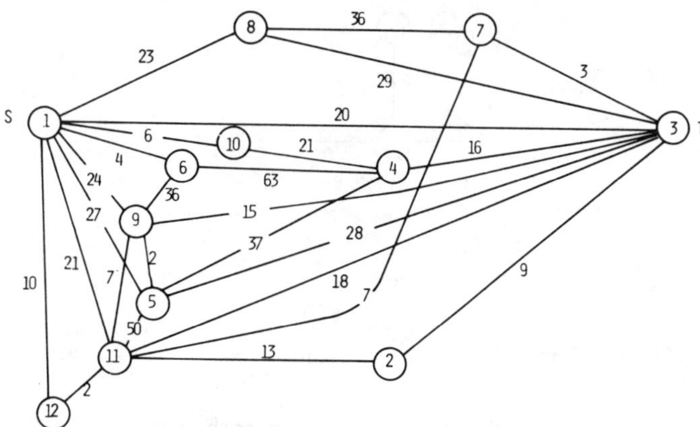

Fig. 9. A commodity network.

TABLE II

$N \in$ Min(T)	N[S]	N(S)
2	1,2,4,5,6,9,10,11,12	136
4	1,2,4,5,6,9,10,11,12	136
5	1,2,4,5,6,9,10,11,12	136
6	1,2,4,5,6,9,10,11,12	136
7	1,2,4,5,6,7,8,9,10,11,12	138
8	1,2,4,5,6,7,8,9,10,11,12	138
9	1,2,4,5,6,9,10,11,12	136
10	1,2,4,5,6,9,10,11,12	136
11	1,2,4,5,6,9,10,11,12	136

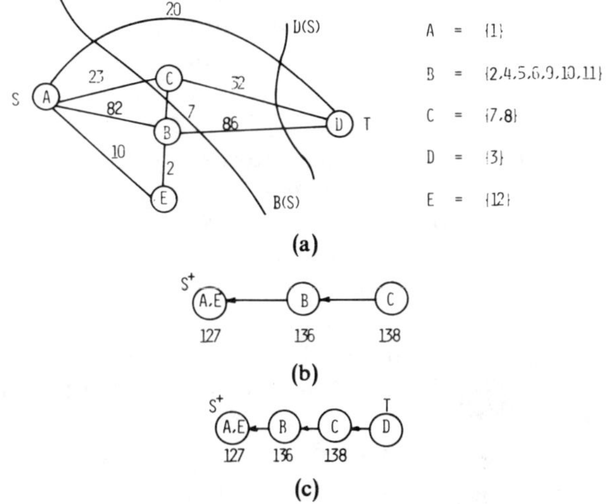

Fig. 10. (a)–(c) Steps in the construction of the inclusive cut graph.

In spite of the *NP*-complete nature of the problem, we seek an algorithm that can solve the problem efficiently for most of the input data although the algorithm could be inefficient for the worst case. We shall construct a graph called the *inclusive cut graph* whose cuts are possible minimum feasible cuts of the network. We solve the original problem by examining the cuts of the inclusive cut graph. In some cases the resulting computation is very small, and in no case are there more cuts to consider in the inclusive cut graph than in the original network.

The inclusive cut graph is constructed in the following manner (using Fig. 9 as a running example):

1) For each node $N \in \min(T)$ in the network, find $N(S)$, the min cut assigning N to S. The subsets $N[S]$ of nodes assigned to S by $N(S)$ are shown in Table II.

2) If $N_i[S] = N_j[S]$ for nodes N_i and N_j, condense N_i and N_j. Repeat this as many times as possible until no further condensations can be done. Condense all nodes in min (S) with S into the node S^+. Fig. 10(a) shows the network after node condensation of the nodes in min (T). min (T) now has only three nodes, B, C, and T, and the cuts $B(S)$ and $C(S)$ are shown in the figure.

3) Let the nodes of the condensed graph be labeled M_1, $M_2, \cdots, S^+$, and T. Each node M_i in the condensed graph is associated with a subset of nodes of the original graph consisting of the nodes condensed into M_i. Let N_i be one such node condensed into M_i for each M_i. Note that the sets $N_i[S]$ are each distinct after node condensation, and they are partially ordered by the set inclusion relation. Draw the graph of the partial ordering of these sets, labeling each node in the graph with the name of a condensed node, and placing an arc from M_i to M_j if $N_i[S] \supset N_j[S]$, and there is no intermediate node M_k such that $N_i[S] \supset N_k[S] \supset N_j[S]$. The least node in this graph is the node S^+. With each node M_i, associate a weight equal to the cut $N_i(S)$. This graph is shown in Fig. 10(b).

4) Add a node labeled T, and direct an arc from T to each maximal node in the partial ordering. These arcs connect T to all nodes that have no arc directed into them. Fig. 10(c) shows the graph with T added. At the conclusion of this step the construction is complete.

The purpose of this construction is to combine as many nodes as possible and to have as few arcs as possible in a graph such that one of the cuts in the reduced graph is a minimum feasible cut of the original graph. The reduced graph may be sufficiently simple to permit us to enumerate its cuts, and thus solve the original problem. Fig. 10 is an example of such a reduction.

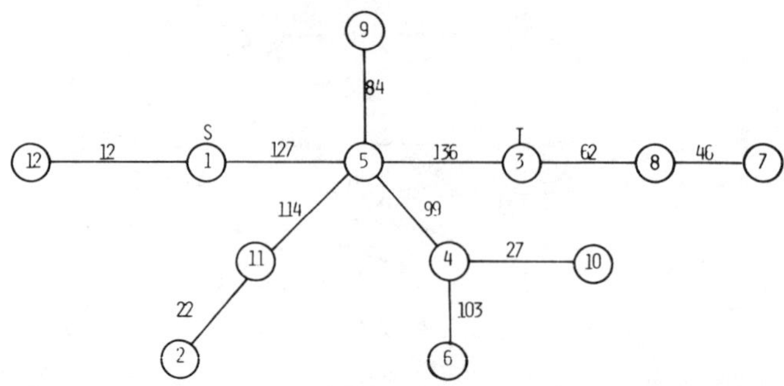

Fig. 11. The G–H tree for the commodity network of Fig. 9.

Note that the node condensation operation of Step 2 makes use of Lemma 2 in that $N_i[S] = N_j[S]$ implies that $N_i \in N_j[S]$ and $N_j \in N_i[S]$, so that N_i and N_j are not separated by a minimum feasible cut. Since all reductions performed on the G–H tree have this property, the construction given here is at least as powerful as the G–H tree method in terms of node condensation. Fig. 11 shows the G–H tree for the network of Fig. 9, and we note that the condensations obtained in Fig. 10 by the present method are not obtainable from the G–H tree in Fig. 11, so the present method is more powerful than the G–H tree method.

The purpose of incorporating arcs in the inclusive cut graph that exhibit the partial ordering on the subsets $N_i[S]$ is to be sure that if a cut assigns node M_i to S, then the corresponding cut in the original graph assigns N_i and the entire subset $N_i[S]$ to S. This is proved in the following theorem.

Theorem 3: If $N_j \in N_i[S]$, then $N_j[S] \subset N_i[S]$.

Proof: This proof is similar to the proof of Theorem 1. In Fig. 4, let cut I be the $N_i(S)$ and cut II be $N_j(S)$. Observe that cut II cannot be as shown in the dashed line for the value of $N_i(S)$ (which assigns both N_i and N_j to S) is not less than the value of $N_j(S)$. If cut II were the dashed line, then we could select it to be cut I as well.

If cut II were the dotted line in the figure, the theorem holds. There remains then to show that cut II cannot be as shown by the solid line labeled II. Note that N_j is in region P, and N_i in region A or P.

Using methods given in the proof of Theorem 1, we find that the value of the solid cut II does not exceed the value of cut I, and consequently, the cut separating the regions A, B, and P from region Q does not exceed the value of cut I. The latter cut can be taken to be $N_i[S]$ in place of cut I, and for this cut $N_j[S] \subset N_i[S]$. Q.E.D.

From Theorem 3, we observe that a cut in the condensed graph that assigns N_i to S assigns all of $N_i[S]$ to S.

We now show that it is sufficient to treat the inclusive cut graph in the search for a minimum feasible cut.

Theorem 4: The minimum feasible cut of the original graph corresponds to some cut in the inclusive cut graph.

Proof: If the theorem were false, then either

a) (node condensation) in condensing nodes to create the inclusive cut graph some pair of nodes are joined that lie on different sides of a minimum feasible cut, or

b) (partial ordering) in placing arcs between condensed nodes in the inclusive cut graph some pair of nodes lie on a path in the order $S^+ - M_i - M_j - T$, and there is a minimum feasible cut that groups M_i with T and M_j with S^+, which is not a cut in the inclusive cut graph.

We show that neither case occurs.

Case 1: By Lemma 2, if $N_i \in N_j[S]$, and $N_j \in N_i[S]$, then N_i and N_j are not separated by a minimum feasible cut. This is satisfied when $N_i[S] = N_j[S]$, which is the rule used for node condensation. Thus nodes condensed together are not separated by a minimum feasible cut.

Case 2: Suppose there exists a path in the inclusive cut graph of the form $S^+ - M_i - M_j - T$, and there is a minimum feasible cut of the original graph joining N_i with T and N_j with S. The path in the inclusive cut graph indicates that $M_j[S] \supset M_i[S]$, so that $N_j[S] \supset N_i[S]$, and $N_i \in N_j[S]$. Then by Lemma 1, N_i is assigned to S by the minimum feasible cut that assigns N_j to S, which is a contradiction. Q.E.D.

It is very simple to enumerate the cuts in inclusive cut graph when the graph is a simple chain as in Fig. 10(c). In this case, to find the minimum feasible cut for the original graph, perform the following algorithm:

1) Number the nodes from S^+ to T in the chain as $M_1, M_2, \cdots, M_p$.

2) Set $i = 1$, and place a cut between S^+ and M_1.

3) Move the cut just to the right of node M_i. Check to see if this cut is feasible, that is, if the nodes condensed into M_j for $j > 1$ can be accommodated together on T. If feasible, terminate. If not, increment i and repeat.

Since the cut placing all nodes in S^+ is feasible, the algorithm is guaranteed to find a feasible cut, and will terminate. The value of the minimum feasible cut is the weight of the node M_{i+1} if the cut passes between M_i and M_{i+1}. Note that the node weight values for a chain graph are strictly increasing on the path between S^+ and T, for if not, we could find a cut $N_i(S)$ whose value could be made smaller by assigning more nodes to S.

Let us consider a larger example as shown in Figs. 12 and 13. Fig. 12 shows a network and Fig. 13 shows its corresponding inclusive cut graph. The cuts in Table III show all possible ways of cutting the inclusive cut graph in Fig. 13. This is much smaller than the number of ways of cutting the original graph.

In closing this section we mention that the complexity of the construction of the inclusive cut graph does not exceed the complexity of the construction of the G–H tree in the worst case since both require no more than one maximum flow computation for each node in min (T).

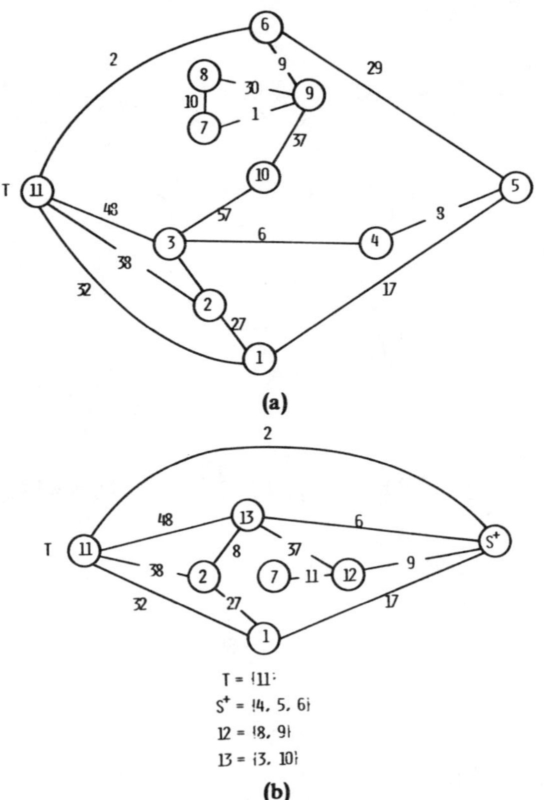

Fig. 12. (a) A commodity network. (b) The commodity network after node condensation.

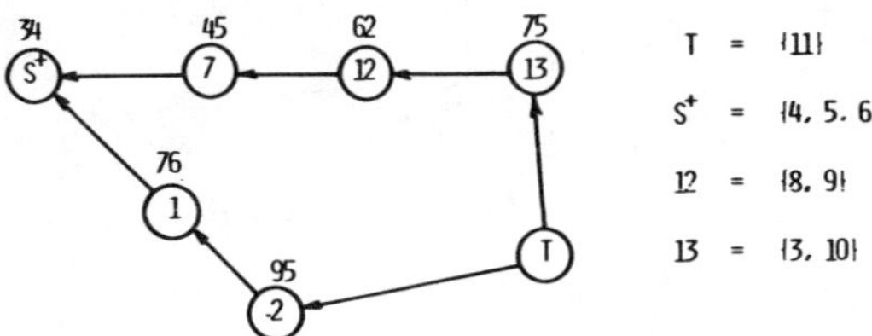

Fig. 13. The inclusive cut graph for the commodity network of Fig. 12.

TABLE III

Nodes Assigned to S^+	Weight of Cut
7	45
7,12	62
7,12,13	75
1	76
1,7	87
1,2	95
1,7,12	104
1,2,7	106
1,7,12,13	117
1,2,7,12,13	120
1,2,7,12	123

Once we have computed the inclusive cut graph, we need an efficient procedure for enumerating its cuts, prefereably in order by increasing or decreasing amount of memory assigned to T. This problem is an open research problem.

V. Summary and Conclusions

We have considered the problem of finding a minimum feasible assignment of the modules to two processors, one with limited memory. We have shown that the modules that are assigned to the processor with limited memory by the minimum cost feasible assignment form a subset of the modules assigned to the same processor by a minimum cost assignment. We have not been able to construct an algorithm of guaranteed polynomial efficiency in the general case, and the general problem is known to be NP-complete.

We have shown that substantial reductions in the size of the problem can be made by condensing certain sets of modules into single modules. These reductions can be made by inspection of the G–H tree or by the construction of the inclusive cut graph, with the latter being a more powerful method than the former in terms of discovering node condensations. We finally show that the solution to the original problem can be done by enumerating the cuts of the inclusive cut graph, which can be very efficient for some problems. An efficient way of enumerating the cuts of the inclusive cut graph in order of increasing or decreasing value is still an open problem.

References

[1] E. A. Dinic, "Algorithm for solution of a problem of maximum flow in a network with power estimation," *Soviet Math. Doklady*, vol. 11, no. 5, pp. 1277–1280, 1970.

[2] J. Edmonds and R. M. Karp, "Theoretical improvements in algorithm efficiency for network flow problems," *J. Assoc. Comput. Mach.*, vol. 19, no. 2, pp. 248–264, Apr. 1972.

[3] S. Even, "The max flow algorithm of Dinic and Karzanov: An exposition," Lab. Comput. Sci., MIT, Cambridge, MA, MIT/LCS/TM-80, Dec. 1976.

[4] L. R. Ford, Jr., and D. R. Fulkerson, *Flows in Networks*. Princeton, NJ: Princeton Univ., 1962.

[5] J. D. Foley *et al.*, "Graphics system modeling," Rome Air Develop. Ctr., Final Rep., Contr. F30602-73-C-0249, and Rep. RADC-TR-211, Aug. 1974.

[6] S. H. Fuller and D. P. Siewiork, "Some observations on semiconductor technology and the architecture of large digital modules," *Computer*, vol. 6, pp. 14–21, Oct. 1973.

[7] R. E. Gomury and T. C. Hu, "Multi-terminal network flows," *J. SIAM*, vol. 9, pp. 551–570, Dec. 1961.

[8] T. C. Hu, *Integer Programming and Network Flows*. Reading, MA: Addison-Wesley, 1970.

[9] R. E. Kahn, "Resource-sharing computer communications networks," *Proc. IEEE*, vol. 60, pp. 1397–1407, Nov. 1972.

[10] R. M. Karp, "On the computational complexity of combinatorial problems," *Networks*, vol. 5, pp. 45–68, 1975.

[11] ——, "The probabilistic analysis of some combinatorial search problems," in *Algorithms and Complexity*, J. F. Traub, Ed. New York: Academic Press, pp. 1–19, 1976.

[12] A. V. Karzanov, "Determining the maximal flow in a network by the method of preflows," *Soviet Math. Doklady*, vol. 15, no. 2, pp. 434–437, 1974.

[13] J. Michel and A. van Dam, "Experience with distributed processing on a host/satellite graphics system," Tech. Rep., Department of Electrical Engineering, Brown University, 1976.

[14] G. M. Stabler, "A system for interconnected processing," Ph.D. dissertation, Brown University, Oct. 1974.

[15] H. S. Stone, "Multiprocessor scheduling with the aid of network flow algorithms," *IEEE Trans. Software Eng.*, vol. SE-3, pp. 85–94, Jan. 1977.

[16] R. H. Thomas and D. Henderson, "McRoss—A multi-computer programming system," in *AFIPS Proc., 1972 SJCC*. Montvale, NJ: AFIPS Press, 1973.

[17] A. van Dam and G. Stabler, "Intelligent satellites for interactive graphics," *NCCE*, June 4, 1972.

[18] A. van Dam, G. Stabler, and R. Harrington, "Intelligent satellites for interactive graphics," *Proc. IEEE*, vol. 62, pp. 83–92, Apr. 1974.

Optimal Preemptive Scheduling on Two-Processor Systems

RICHARD R. MUNTZ, MEMBER, IEEE, AND EDWARD G. COFFMAN, JR., MEMBER, IEEE

Abstract—**One of the important potentials of multiprocessor systems is the ability to speed the completion of a computation by concurrently processing independent portions of the job. In this paper we consider the static scheduling of computations for a system containing two indentical processors. The object is to complete the computation in the minimum amount of time. A computation is assumed to be specified as a partially ordered set of tasks and the execution time for each task. A solution for the two-machine case with preemptive scheduling is presented.**

Index Terms—**Computation graphs, multiprocessing, parallel processing, preemptive scheduling, static scheduling.**

INTRODUCTION

MULTIPROCESSOR computer systems have been shown to have several advantages [1] over conventional systems. One of great importance to a large class of users is the potential increase in computing speed beyond that achievable with the more conventional single-processor organization. On the other hand, how to best exploit the multiple, independent processor organization in order to obtain maximum performance remains a little-understood problem. It is this problem which has motivated the research reported in this paper.

Informally, the specific question we seek to answer is the following. Given a set of tasks or computations along with a set of operational precedence relationships that exist between certain of these tasks, and given a set of k identical processors, how does one sequence (or schedule) these tasks on the k processors so that they execute in minimum time? In order to describe the extent to which this question has been answered by the present study and by earlier work on this problem, we shall require a number of definitions.

First, a *multiprocessor system* consists quite simply of a set of identical processors capable of independent operation on independent tasks. *Jobs* submitted to the system consist of a set of tasks and a partial ordering of these tasks. The interpretation of the partial ordering is that if n_i and n_j are tasks, and $n_i > n_j$ (to be read n_i precedes n_j or n_j follows n_i), then n_i must be completed before n_j is started. It is natural to associate a graph with each job such that the nodes correspond to tasks and the arcs correspond to the precedence relations defining the partial ordering. More formally, there is a directed arc from the node representing task n_i to the node representing the task n_j if and only if $n_i > n_j$ and there is no task n_l such that $n_i > n_l > n_j$. We shall use the terms "job," "graph," and "computation graph" interchangeably. Task execution times are represented by node weights.

Informally, a *schedule* or *assignment* for k processors and a given computation graph is a description of the work done by each machine as a function of time. Of course, the schedule must not violate the given precedence relations and we are not permitted to assign more than one machine to a task at any time. The

Manuscript received September 16, 1968; revised June 2, 1969. This work was supported in part by Bell Telephone Laboratories, Inc., Murray Hill, N. J. This paper was presented at the 1969 IEEE Computer Group Conference, Minneapolis, Minn., June 17–19, 1969.

R. R. Muntz is with the School of Engineering and Applied Science, University of California, Los Angeles.

E. G. Coffman, Jr., was with the Department of Electrical Engineering, Princeton University, Princeton, N. J. Until July, 1970, he will be at the Computing Laboratory, University of Newcastle-upon-Tyne, England.

Reprinted from *IEEE Trans. Comput.*, vol. C-18, pp. 1014–1020, Nov. 1969.

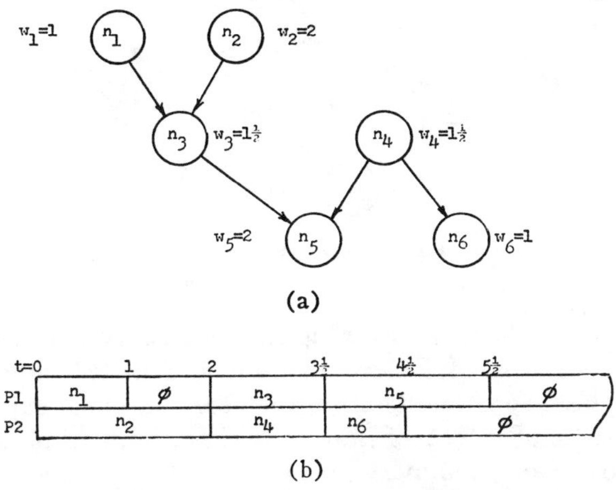

Fig. 1. An example graph and schedule for two processors: P1 and P2.

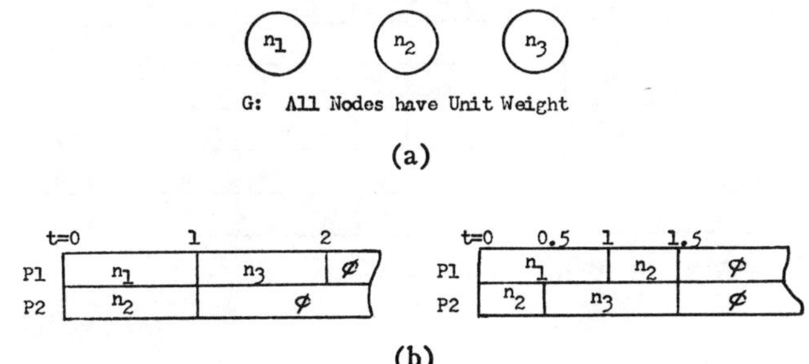

Fig. 2. Illustration of the advantage of preemptive scheduling.

simplest way of specifying a schedule is to use a Gantt chart which consists of a time axis for each processor with intervals marked off and labeled with the name of the task being processed. We use the symbol ϕ to represent an idle period. In Fig. 1(a) we have shown a graph G, and in Fig. 1(b) a schedule for G with two processors. The computation times are shown next to the node representing the task.

In the next section we shall define the principal types of scheduling disciplines of interest to us, after which a preview of the remainder of the paper will be given.

From a more general point of view, it is clear that the static scheduling models we have introduced are most applicable to those cases in which a program or computation is to be executed many times, particularly in real-time situations. In these cases it is worth some effort to investigate the program structure and execution times.

With respect to the task execution times, assumed known in the static model, there are two interpretations which increase the usefulness of the results when these times are not known exactly. First, the execution times may be interpreted as maximum processing times. In this case the schedule length is the maximum time to complete the graph [8]. Second, the execution times may be regarded as expected values of the run times considered as random variables. With this interpretation the length of the schedule produced is an (optimistic) estimate of the mean length of the computation over many runs [9].

The constraint to partial orderings of tasks as a model of computations obviously means that loops and conditional branching cannot be represented. If the tasks are large functional blocks, this may not be a serious problem. Note also that a particular execution of a graph containing a conditional branch will be representable as the execution of a partially ordered set of tasks, since one branch or the other must be taken. This clearly extends to any number of branches and to loops as well. An efficient solution to the problem of optimally scheduling partially ordered tasks can be used as a tool in studying the more general problem. For example, it gives a standard for comparing scheduling heuristics for these graphs rather than having only relative measures of performance.

Preemptive Scheduling Disciplines

In most investigations of the problem of constructing minimum length schedules for computation graphs, it is assumed that once a processor is assigned to a task it must work continuously on this task until it has been completed. (As in Fig. 1(b), for example.) This procedure for assigning processors to nodes will be termed the *basic scheduling* (BS) discipline. Clearly, the problem of finding an optimal BS for any given graph is effectively solvable by exhaustion. However, practical solutions for large problems have consisted only of a result for rooted trees with equally weighted nodes [2], and more recently, an unpublished result for the two-machine case and an arbitrary partial ordering of equally weighted tasks [3].

A more recent study on multiprocessor scheduling [4], which forms the point of departure for the results presented in this paper, has focused on scheduling disciplines in which this run-to-completion constraint has been relaxed. In particular, with the *preemptive scheduling* (PS) discipline it is permitted to interrupt any processor at any time and reassign it to a different task. A solution of the scheduling problem for rooted computation trees has also been found [4] for the PS discipline. Fig. 2 shows how effective use can be made of the preemption capability. Fig. 2(b) shows a minimum length assignment for G with $k=2$ machines and using the BS discipline. The length of this schedule is two time units. By comparison, we see in Fig. 2(c) a PS requiring only 1.5 time units and one preemption. In constructing the PS in Fig. 2, we have assumed that the preemption itself did not require any time. Notice, however, that as long as the total cost of the preemption is less than one unit of time, an optimal PS for G will be less than two units in length. So we see that even with relatively large costs for preemptions, there are jobs which can be completed in less time when preemptions are permitted. Furthermore, from existing and proposed multiprogramming/multiprocessing systems, there is reason to believe that the costs of preemptions may be

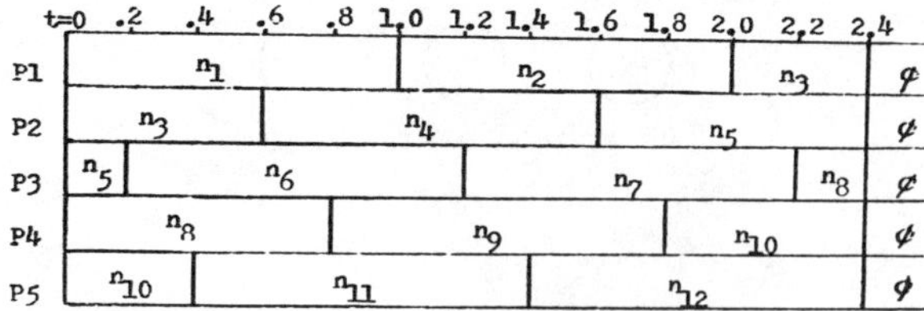

Fig. 3. A PS for twelve independent unit weight nodes with five machines.

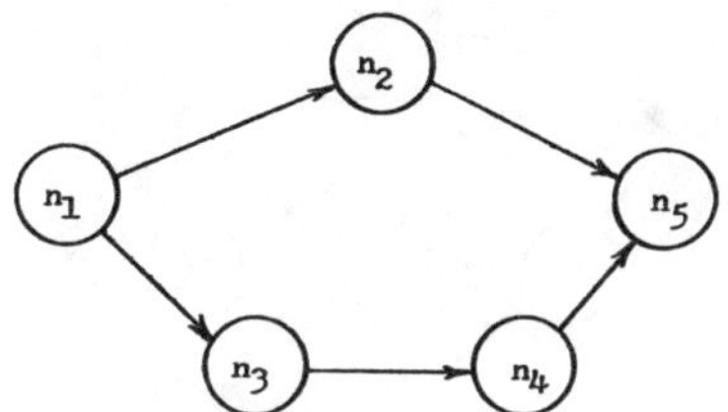

Fig. 4. G: all nodes have unit weight.

quite nominal in some applications. Contributing factors are: 1) the existence of large main memories out of which programs are executed, and 2) the overlapping of transfers between main and auxiliary storage and program execution. In any case, we shall continue to make the assumption that preemption delays are negligible.

Static preemptive scheduling to minimize maximum flow-time has received only slight attention in the literature. A solution for a special case of the problem we have posed has been given by McNaughton [5]. This result is stated in the following lemma.

Lemma 1: For a set of independent tasks with weights $\{w_1, w_2, \cdots, w_n\}$ and k available processors, the optimal PS has length

$$\max\left\{\max_{1\leq i\leq n}\{w_i\}, \frac{\sum_{i=1}^{n} w_i}{k}\right\}.$$

To illustrate the lemma, suppose we have a graph G consisting of twelve independent nodes all of unit weight and $k=5$ available processors. A minimal length PS for this case is shown in Fig. 3. The tasks are assigned, in order, to the first processor until a task (in this case n_3) extends beyond the computed optimal schedule length. When this occurs, the remaining time on the task is assigned to the next machine starting at $t=0$.

McNaughton [5] and Rothkopf [6] have considered preemptive scheduling problems with various objective functions but for independent tasks only.

Subset Schedules

The development of the algorithm for optimal preemptive scheduling with two processors proceeds by first defining a subclass of preemptive schedules which is shown to contain at least one minimal length schedule. We then show how to construct an optimal schedule for this subclass which from the above statement is also an optimal PS. To describe this subclass of preemptive schedules we must first introduce the notion of a *subset sequence*. A subset sequence for a graph G, with equally weighted nodes, is a sequence of disjoint subsets of nodes of G, $S_1, S_2, \cdots, S_m$ such that: 1) if n is a node of G, then $n \in S_i$ for some i, and 2) if n, m are nodes of G, with $n \in S_i$, $m \in S_j$ and $n > m$, then $i < j$. In other words, a subset sequence for G is any partition of the nodes of G satisfying constraint 2) above.

Since G has equally weighted nodes, we may assume without loss of generality that the nodes have unit weight. From the definition we see that each subset S_i consists of a set of mutually independent nodes. It follows from Lemma 1 that if $|S_i| \leq k$[1] we can construct a schedule to execute all nodes in S_i in one unit of time, and if $|S_i| > k$ we can construct a schedule to execute all nodes in S_i in $|S_i|/k$ units of time. From the definition of a subset sequence we know that if we schedule each subset independently we can form a PS for G by using the schedule for S_1 followed immediately by the schedule for S_2, etc. For our purposes we need only consider the schedules formed by this method in which each S_i is scheduled in an optimal way (i.e., achieves the minimum computation times mentioned above). A PS constructed from a subset sequence in the above manner will be called a *subset schedule*.

As an example consider the graph of Fig. 4. One possible subset sequence for G would be $S_1=\{n_1\}$, $S_2=\{n_2, n_3\}$, $S_3=\{n_4\}$, $S_4=\{n_5\}$. Another subset sequence could be formed by making $S_2=\{n_3\}$, $S_3=\{n_2, n_4\}$.

In terms of these definitions, the two major results of this paper are: 1) a proof that an optimal subset schedule for two machines is an optimal PS, and 2) a description of an algorithm for finding the optimal subset schedule for two machines. The corresponding problems for an arbitrary number (k) of machines are as yet unsolved.

Optimal Subset Schedules

In this section we outline the proof that optimal subset schedules for two machines are optimal PSs. The proof is by induction on the number of nodes in a graph. In order to establish the induction step in the proof, we shall need the result of the following lemma. Basically, the lemma states a "normal form" property of PSs for two machines and graphs of equally weighted nodes. The proof is not given here since it is rather long; it can be found in [10].

Lemma 2: Let G be an arbitrary graph all of whose nodes have unit weight. Then any PS for G using two machines can be transformed into a new schedule which is no longer than the first and has one of the two forms shown in Fig. 5 where n, p, and q are nodes of G or ϕ (i.e., an idle period). With this result we can prove the first basic theorem on subset schedules for two machines.

[1] $|S_i|$ = cardinality of S_i.

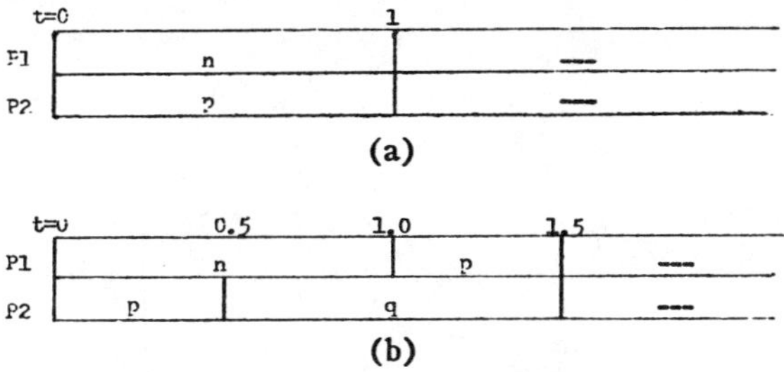

Fig. 5. Schedule forms.

Theorem 1: For $k=2$ machines, an optimal subset schedule for any graph G, with equally weighted nodes, is an optimal PS for G.

Proof: Without loss of generality, assume all nodes of G have weight 1. The proof is by induction on the number of nodes in G. For the graph of one node, the theorem is obvious. Assume the theorem is true for all graphs of less than n nodes, and let G be a graph with n nodes.

First, suppose G has only one or two initial nodes. In a PS it is never advantageous to leave a machine idle when a node is available, and therefore we need only consider schedules which work on these one or two initial nodes from $t=0$ to $t=1$. The remainder of G has less than n nodes, and by the induction hypothesis can be completed in a minimum amount of time by a subset schedule. Putting these two schedules together, we have a subset schedule for G which is clearly optimal.

Now assume G has more than two initial nodes. By Lemma 2 we may assume further that any given PS for G (call this assignment A) has been transformed into a new assignment which is no longer than A and has one of the two forms shown in Fig. 5. Suppose, for instance, that A has been transformed into the second form and n, p, and q are nodes of G. The remainder of the schedule from $t=1.5$ on is a PS for the graph formed by removing n, p, and q from G. Call this graph G'. From the induction hypothesis we know there exists a subset schedule for G' which is an optimal PS for G'. Let the corresponding subset sequence be $S_1, S_2, \cdots, S_m$. It follows that $\{n, p, q\}, S_1, S_2, \cdots, S_m$ is a subset sequence for G whose corresponding subset schedule is no longer than A. Since this is true for any PS for G, it is true for any optimal PS for G. Therefore, there exists a subset schedule for G which is an optimal PS for G. A similar argument holds if we get A into the first form. This completes the induction step and the proof of the theorem. Q.E.D.

It is now desirable to extend the previous result to the case of graphs with arbitrary node weights. Specifically, we shall now consider graphs having *mutually commensurable* node weights, i.e., there exists a real number w such that each node weight is an integer multiple of w. Such graphs are not very restrictive since more general graphs may be approximated arbitrarily closely by ones with mutually commensurable node weights. Before extending Theorem 1 so that it applies to these latter graphs, we must introduce the following definitions.

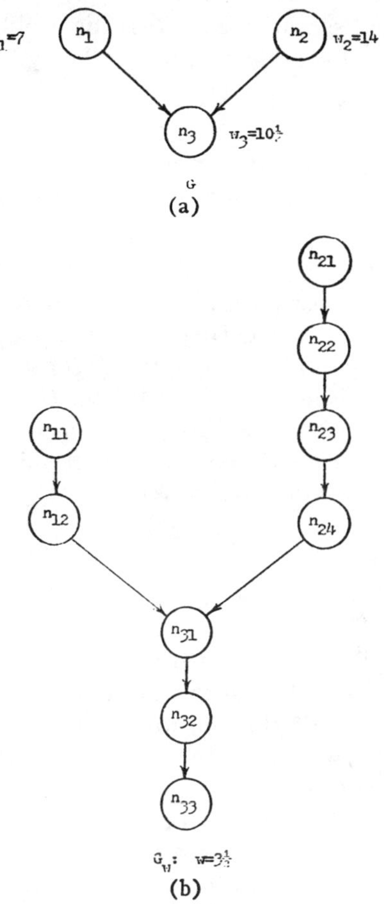

Fig. 6. Transformation of G to G_w.

Let G be a graph with the mutually commensurable node weights $w_1, w_2, \cdots, w_n$, and let w be the largest real number such that w_i/w is an integer for all i. We now define a graph G_w derived from G as follows. We take each node n_i of G with weight w_i and replace it by a series connection of nodes of weight w so that the total weight of these nodes is w_i. We require that all edges that were incident into n_i are incident into the first node in the series connection. Similarly, all edges that were incident out of n_i now leave the last node of the connection. Observe that G and G_w are related by a simple homomorphism. As an example, consider the graph of Fig. 6 for which $w=3\frac{1}{2}$. As shown, a node n_i of G is expanded into nodes $n_{i1}, n_{i2}, \cdots, n_{ij_i}$ of G_w where $j_i = w_i/w$.

From the above definition it follows that a PS for G defines a PS for G_w, and vice versa. Furthermore, an optimal PS for G_w defines an optimal PS for G. Now if we define a subset schedule for G (with unequally weighted nodes) to be a subset schedule of G_w, then we have the following corollary to Theorem 1.

Corollary 1: Let G be any graph with mutually commensurable node weights. Then an optimal subset schedule for G_w is an optimal PS for G with $k=2$ machines.

In the next section we address the problem of finding an optimal subset schedule for a given graph with $k=2$ machines.

An Algorithm for Finding an Optimal Subset Schedule for Two Processors

Let G be a graph with mutually commensurable node weights and let G_w be as defined above. Let L be the length of a longest path in G. We propose the following algorithm for constructing a subset sequence for G_w which corresponds to an optimal subset schedule for G_w (and therefore an optimal PS for G) with $k=2$ machines. The *level* of a node is defined as the length of the longest path from that node to a terminal node. The level of node n is denoted by $l(n)$.

Algorithm:

Step 1) Set index $j=1$.

Step 2) Let Λ_j be the set of all nodes which have not yet been assigned to subsets and are at level $L-j+1$. Assign all nodes in Λ_j to S_j. If $|\Lambda_j|=1$ then go to step 4).

Step 3) If $j=L$ then stop, otherwise, set $j=j+1$ and go to step 2).

Step 4) Let $\Omega=\{q_i\}$ be the set of all nodes which have not been assigned to subsets, but all of whose predecessors are contained in $S_1 \cup S_2 \cup \cdots \cup S_{j-1}$. If $\Omega=\phi$ then go to Step 3). If $\Omega=\phi$ then assign q_u to S_j where q_u is such that $l(q_u)=\max_{q_i \in \Omega}\{l(q_i)\}$, and go to Step 3).

An informal statement of the algorithm is worthwhile at this point. It is proposed that the nodes be assigned to subsets level by level with higher level nodes assigned to subsets first. The only exception to this rule is when it would result in a subset containing only one node while there is at least one other node at a lower level which can be assigned to this subset without violating any precedence relations. In this case a second node is selected which is at the highest possible level.

As an example we have shown in Fig. 7 a graph G and a subset sequence for G constructed by the algorithm. Note that in constructing S_2, the only task at level 5 was n_3. Both n_2 and n_4 are executable but the algorithm states that n_2 is to be assigned to S_2. If n_4 were chosen we could not achieve an optimal subset sequence.

It is an easy matter to show that the construction specified by the algorithm does result in a valid subset sequence. We now prove that the algorithm produces a subset sequence which corresponds to an optimal subset schedule. By Theorem 1 this will also be an optimal PS.

Theorem 2: The subset schedule corresponding to the subset sequence constructed by the algorithm is optimal.

Proof: Let G be any graph with equally weighted nodes, and $A=S_1, S_2, \cdots, S_m$ be a subset sequence for G with $k=2$ machines. Without loss of generality, assume the nodes of G have unit weight. Suppose subset S_j contains $x_j \geq 2$ nodes. Then by Lemma 1 we can schedule these nodes in $x_j/2$ units of time. If S_j contains only one node, then S_j requires one unit of time. Let W be the total weight of G, let N be the number of subsets containing only one node, and let ϕ be the set of all j such that S_j contains more than one node. Then the schedule for G using this subset sequence requires

$$\left(\sum_{j\in\phi} \frac{x_j}{2}\right)+N=\frac{W-N}{2}+N=\frac{W+N}{2} \text{ units of time.}$$

It follows that a subset schedule for two machines is optimal if its corresponding subset sequence has the least number of subsets with only one element. This is what we shall prove is true of any subset sequence constructed by the algorithm. The proof of the theorem is easier if we prove a somewhat stronger statement. Before giving this latter statement, we need the following notation.

Let G be any graph with equally weighted nodes. Let L be the length of a longest path in G, and $n_1, n_2, \cdots, n_L$ be the nodes, in order, in a maximum length path. Let $A_1=S_1, S_2, \cdots, S_m$ be any subset sequence for G. We know that each of the n_i must appear in one of these subsets and they must be in distinct subsets. Let us consider just those subsets of A_1 that contain an n_i. If S_j contains n_i we shall rename the subset and call it S_{n_i}. Let $S_{n_1}, S_{n_2}, \cdots, S_{nL}$ be this family of subsets. Clearly, the number of subsets in A_1 that have only one element is no less than the number of subsets with one

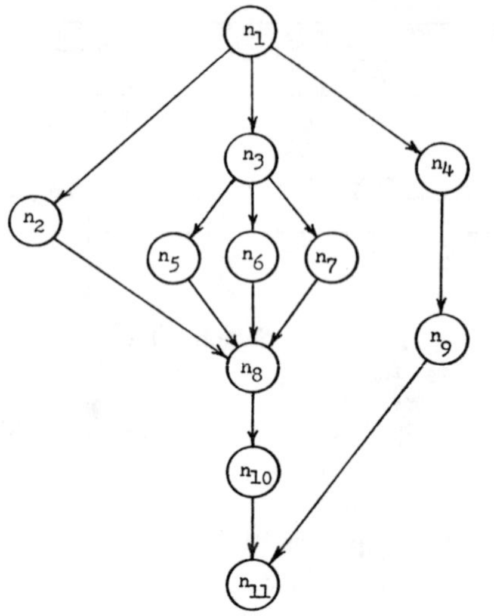

G: All Nodes have Unit Weight

(a)

$\{n_1\}, \{n_3,n_2\}, \{n_5,n_6,n_7\}, \{n_8,n_4\}, \{n_{10},n_9\}, \{n_{11}\}$

Optimal Subset Sequence for G

(b)

Fig. 7. Illustration of the algorithm.

element in $\{S_{n_1}, S_{n_2}, \cdots, S_{nL}\}$. Let $N_{A_1}(i)$ denote the number of subsets with one element in $\{S_{n_1}, S_{n_2}, \cdots, S_{n_i}\}$. Let $A_2 = S_1', S_2', \cdots, S_L'$ be a subset sequence as constructed by the algorithm. It is clear from the statement of the algorithm that for $1 \leq i \leq L$, $n_i \in S_i$.

We now seek to prove (the stronger statement) that if A_1 is any subset sequence for G, and A_2 is any subset sequence for G constructed in accordance with the algorithm, then $N_{A_1}(i) \geq N_{A_2}(i)$ for $1 \leq i \leq L$. Clearly, $N_{A_1}(L) \geq N_{A_2}(L)$ is all we need in order to prove that A_1 is at least as long as A_2.

The proof is by induction on the number of nodes in G. The statement is obvious for the case of one node, so assume that the theorem is true for all graphs with less than m nodes, and assume that G has m nodes. With G, A_1, and A_2 as above, let $n_L, p_1, p_2, \cdots, p_n$ be the terminal nodes of G, and let G' be the graph remaining when these terminal nodes are removed from G. Clearly, if we delete $n_L, p_1, p_2, \cdots, p_n$ from the subsets in A_1, we are left (after removing any empty subsets) with a valid subset sequence A_1' for G'. Furthermore, it is a straightforward matter to verify that when $n_L, p_1, p_2, \cdots, p_n$ are removed from A_2, we are left with a subset sequence A_2' for G' that can be constructed by the algorithm (the statement must be made this way since the algorithm does not generate a unique subset sequence). Therefore, since G' contains less than m nodes, we have from the induction hypothesis

$$N_{A_1'}(i) \geq N_{A_2'}(i); \qquad 1 \leq i \leq L - 1.$$

The two properties below follow easily from the statement of the algorithm and will be used in the induction step of the proof.

Property 1) Any p_i that is assigned to a subset S_j', $j<L$, must be the only node other than n_j assigned to that subset.

Property 2) If S_j' contains only one node, i.e., n_j, then any p_i which is independent of n_j is assigned to a subset of lower index.

Suppose $N_{A_1}(j) < N_{A_2}(j)$ for some j, $1 \leq j < L$. In fact, let j be the first time this happens so that $N_{A_1}(j-1) = N_{A_2}(i-1)$ and S_j' contains one element while S_{n_j} contains at least two nodes. From $N_{A_1}(j) < N_{A_2}(j)$ and $N_{A_1'}(j) \geq N_{A_2'}(j)$ it follows that when $n_L, p_1, p_2, \cdots, p_m$ are removed from A_1 and A_2, the number of subsets in $S_{n_1}, S_{n_2}, \cdots, S_{n_j}$ that become subsets with less than two elements is at least one greater than the number of such subsets in $S_1', S_2', \cdots, S_j'$. This implies that there exists a p_r belonging to one of the $S_{n_1}, S_{n_2}, \cdots, S_{n_j}$ that is either assigned to one of the subsets $S_1', S_2', \cdots, S_j'$ which also contains another node of G(in addition to an n_i), or is not assigned to any of the subsets S_1', $S_2', \cdots, S_j'$. The former contradicts Property 1) above and the latter contradicts Property 2).

For the special case $j=L$ we know that S_L' contains only n_L and it follows from Properties 1) and 2) that in A_2 each p_i is assigned to a subset of cardinality 2 and index less than L. Therefore, $N_{A_2'}(L-1) = N_{A_2}(L-1) + n$. From the fact that at least one of the p_i is an element of S_{n_L} it follows that $N_{A_1'}(L-1) < N_{A_1}(L-1) + n$. Since $N_{A_2}(L-1) = N_{A_1}(L-1)$, we have $N_{A_1'}(L-1) < N_{A_2'}(L-1)$ which is a contradiction. Q.E.D.

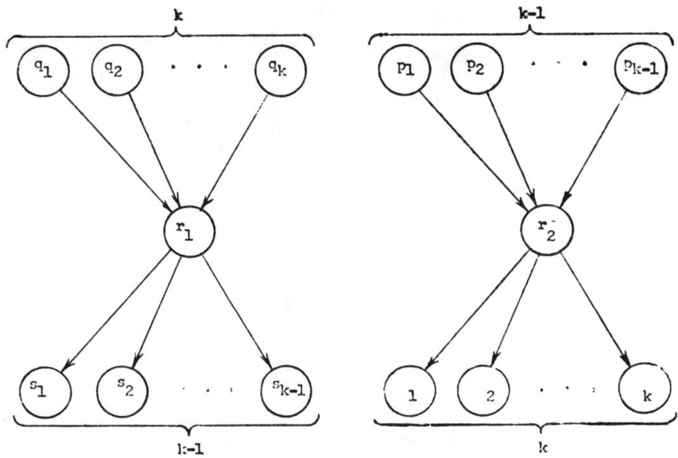

Fig. 8. A counterexample to the algorithm for $k>2$.

There is an obvious generalization of this algorithm to three or more machines. Nodes are again assigned to subsets level by level except when there are $u<k$ nodes at the highest level. In the latter case, as many as possible of the $k-u$ nodes necessary to "fill" the subset are chosen from the executable nodes at lower levels. Of course, if there are more than $k-u$ nodes to choose from, those at the higher levels are selected first.

There is a simple counterexample to show that this algorithm does not produce an optimal subset schedule (and therefore certainly not an optimal PS) for arbitrary graphs when $k>2$.

If we have a graph of the form shown in Fig. 8 and $k \geq 3$ machines, then the subset sequence constructed by the above algorithm would be $\{q_1, q_2, \cdots, q_k, p_1, p_2, \cdots, p_{k-1}\}$, $\{r_1, r_2\}$, $\{s_1, s_2, \cdots s_{k-1}, u_1, u_2, \cdots, u_k\}$. The computation time for the corresponding subset schedule is $2k-1/k+1+2k-1/k=5-2/k$. However, the subset schedule corresponding to $\{q_1, q_2, \cdots, q_k\}$, $\{p_1, p_2, \cdots, p_{k-1}r_1\}$, $\{s_1, s_2, \cdots, s_{k-1}, r_2\}$, $\{u_1, u_2, \cdots, u_k\}$ has computation time equal to four units which for $k>2$ is less than $5-2/k$.

Unfortunately, Theorem 1 is not true for $k>2$ processors. Consider the graph shown in Fig. 9 when there are k available processors.

We claim that the optimal PS for any value of k has length 3 and that this computation time can be achieved by a subset schedule for $G_{1/(k-1)^2}$ but not for $G_{1/m}$ when

[2] For n an integer, $G_{w/n}$ is formed from G by replacing each node by a series connection of nodes of weight w/n. A node of weight w_i is replaced by $n(w_i/w)$ nodes.

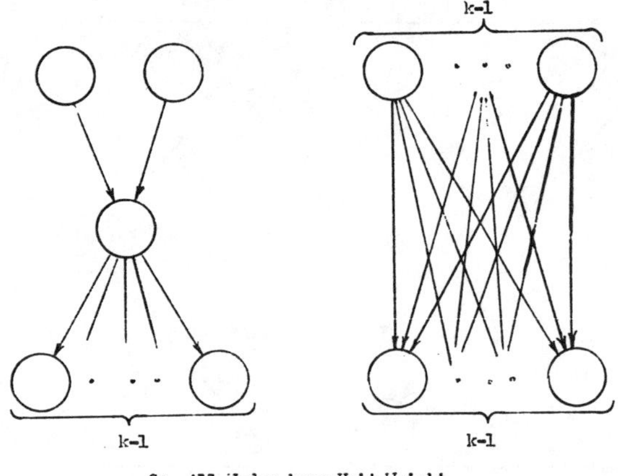

Fig. 9. A counterexample to Theorem 1 when $k>2$.

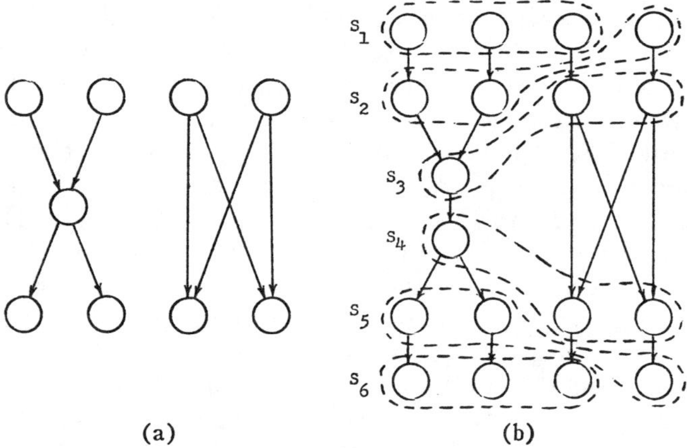

Fig. 10. The counterexample to Theorem 1 when $k=3$. (a) G when $k=3$. (b) $G_{\frac{1}{2}}$ when $k=3$.

$m<k-1$. For example, when $k=3$ we have the graph shown in Fig. 10(a). It is left to the reader to verify that no subset schedule for this graph will achieve a computation time of three units of time. On the other hand, a subset schedule for $G_{\frac{1}{2}}$ does give this result as illustrated in Fig. 10(b). It is conjectured that, in general, an optimal subset schedule for $G_{1/(k-1)!}$ is an optimal PS for G. Incidentally, this is equivalent to the conjecture that an optimal BS for $G_{1/k!}$ with k machines is an optimal PS for G with k machines. This follows from the fact that each task in a subset will be preempted only at integral multiples of $1/k$ times its execution time.

Conclusions

The problems of finding algorithms for determining optimal basic assignments or optimal preemptive assignments for arbitrary computation graphs and using an arbitrary number of processors are as yet unsolved. The present paper represents a positive step towards the preemptive assignment scheduling problem by giving a solution for the two-processor case.

The basic notions leading to the results of the present study are that of the subset sequence and the corresponding subset schedule. The present study is part of a larger research effort in which this relationship between subset assignments and optimal PSs is being explored in depth.

References

[1] A. J. Critchlow, "Generalized multiprocessing and multiprogramming systems," 1963 *Fall Joint Computer Conf., AFIPS Proc.*, vol. 24. Baltimore, Md.: Spartan, 1963, pp. 107–126.
[2] T. C. Hu, "Parallel sequencing and assembly line problems," *Operations Res.*, vol. 9, pp. 841–848. November 1961.
[3] R. L. Graham, private communications.
[4] R. R. Muntz and E. G. Coffman, Jr., "Multiprocessor scheduling of computation graphs," Computer Science Laboratory, Department of Electrical Engineering, Princeton University, Princeton, N. J., Rept. 63, June 1968.
[5] R. McNaughton, "Scheduling with deadline and loss functions," *Management Science*, vol. 6, pp. 1–12, October 1959.
[6] M. H. Rothkopf, "Scheduling independent tasks on parallel processors," *Management Science*, vol. 12. pp. 437–447. January 1966.
[7] R. R. Muntz, "Scheduling of computations on multiprocessor systems: the preemptive assignemnt discipline," Ph.D. dissertation, Princeton University, Princeton, N. J., April 1969.
[8] G. K. Manacher, "Production and stabilization of real-time task schedules," *J. ACM*, vol. 14, pp. 429–465, July 1967.
[9] D. F. Martin, "The automatic assignment and sequencing of computations on parallel processor systems," Ph.D. dissertation University of California, Los Angeles, 1966.
[10] R. R. Muntz and E. G. Coffman, Jr., "The optimization sequencing of computation graphs on two processor systems," Computer Science Laboratory, Department of Electrical Engineering, Princeton University, Princeton, N. J., Rept. 68, July 1968.

Optimal Scheduling Strategies in a Multiprocessor System

C. V. RAMAMOORTHY, MEMBER, IEEE, K. M. CHANDY, AND MARIO J. GONZALEZ, JR., MEMBER, IEEE

Abstract—This paper describes a set of techniques that can be used to optimally schedule a sequence of interrelated computational tasks on a multiprocessor computer system. Using a directed graph model to represent a computational process, two basic problems are solved here. First, given a set of computational tasks and the relationships between them, the tasks are scheduled such that the total execution time is minimized, and the minimum number of processors required to realize this schedule is obtained. The second problem is of a more general nature. Given k processors, the tasks are scheduled such that execution time is again minimized.

Consideration is given to tasks of equal and unequal duration, and task preemption is not allowed.

Index Terms—Directed graphs, multiprocessing, optimal scheduling, parallel processing.

I. Introduction

THE problem of decomposing a large program into many small concurrently executable (parallel processable) segments has attracted both theoretical and practical interest and effort. Parallel processability permits faster execution times of programs on multiprocessing computing systems beyond the speeds imposed by technological limitations, as well as other advantages, such as better utilization of resources. In a previous paper [1], a general technique was developed that recognized the various parallel processable segments in a sequentially coded program (task) and defined an orderly way of parallel processing these various segments in a multiprocessor. The object of this paper is to develop processor assignment and scheduling techniques that use a minimum number of processors to execute the program in the least time. In addition, given k processors, we develop algorithms for processor assignment to minimize the execution time of the program.

In the following discussion, we shall assume the usual definition of a multiprocessor as being a set of identical processors capable of independent operation on independent tasks. A job or a compound task submitted to the system consists of a set of tasks and a partial ordering of these tasks. This partial ordering can be associated with a dependency graph, such that, if there is a directed path from node i to node j, it implies that task i precedes task j or $n_i < n_j$. The dependency graph clearly gives the precedence relationships indicated by the partial ordering. Given a computation graph and a multiprocessor with k processors, a task assignment or a schedule must be developed such that it gives a description of the tasks to be done by each processor as a function of time. The schedule must not violate any of the precedence relationships or the requirement that no more than one processor can be assigned to a task at any time. It will be assumed that the execution time for each task is known *a priori*. The execution times of each task can either be interpreted as maximum processing time or as the expected processing time. In the former case, the time to complete the schedule would be considered the maximum time to complete the job, and in the latter case the length of the schedule represents a rough estimate of the mean length of the computation.

In this paper, we assume that once a processor is assigned a task (program) it must work continuously on this task until it is completed.

This study has two objectives: 1) to develop theorems on

Manuscript received January 31, 1971; revised August 24, 1971. This work was supported in part by NSF Grant GJ-28452 and in part by the Joint Services Electronics Program under Contract F44620-71-C-0091.

C. V. Ramamoorthy and M. J. Gonzalez are with the Department of Electrical Engineering, University of Texas at Austin, Austin, Tex. 78712.

K. M. Chandy is with the Department of Computer Sciences, University of Texas at Austin, Austin, Tex. 78712.

Reprinted from *IEEE Trans. Comput.*, vol. C-21, pp. 137–146, Feb. 1972.

optimal parallel scheduling and to write on the basis of these theorems a program that determines the optimal schedule; 2) to evaluate a near-optimal heuristic using the results of the optimal parallel schedule as a yardstick. It must be emphasized that the optimal scheduling algorithm is not intended for real-time application. It is useful as a means of evaluating heuristics and as a design aid in dedicated systems that process a few basic programs that can be pre-analyzed.

The theoretical portion of this study is in Sections IV, V, and VI; Sections IV and V deal with bounds on optimal schedules and Section VI is concerned with the actual algorithms. Experiments and computational results are presented in Section VII.

II. Previous Work

The work in the area of parallel processing of single jobs can be classified into: 1) modeling and representation of parallelism [12]; 2) languages and facilities that permit explicit indication of parallelism [Tranquil, APL]; 3) recognition techniques that automatically detect implicit parallelism in a sequentially represented algorithm or program [1]; and 4) scheduling and allocation of tasks to processors in such a way that some objective (e.g., minimum execution time) is realized [2], [3]. It is with the latter efforts that we are most concerned in this paper. Muntz and Coffman [2] considered the problem of static scheduling of computations for a system containing identical processors and developed an optimal preemptive scheduling technique. Manacher [3] and Graham [13] considered parallel processing in a real time environment. They developed simple but effective control schemes using task lists and proved a number of useful results.

III. Representation of a Computation Task Graph

Given the permissible transition graph of a computer program, the maximal strongly connected (MSC) subgraphs in the given graph can be uniquely determined. A final program graph, called the reduced graph of the system, can be derived by replacing each MSC subgraph with a single vertex. In this graph a vertex that initiates a branching operation will be called a decision or branch vertex. The next step is to derive the parallel task graph and its connectivity matrix T. The elements of T are determined by analyzing the inputs of each vertex in the reduced graph. An element T_{ij} is a "1" if and only if the jth task of the reduced graph has as one of its inputs the output of task i; otherwise T_{ij} is "0."

From the necessary and sufficiency conditions for task parallelism [1], [4], two tasks can be executed in parallel if the input set of one task does not depend on the output set of the other and vice versa. Whether the graph represents task dependencies in computer programs or other situations, these functions can be given the appropriate interpretation.

So far we have considered task graphs in which the process starts out as a single stream, subsequently spawns a number of parallel tasks, and culminates as a single completed task in the end. These graphs represent typical computer programs and are characterized by single-entry (starting) and single-exit (ending) nodes. These single-entry single-exit connected (SEC) graphs do not have any strongly connected components in them. The distinguishability and decomposition properties of these graphs have been studied extensively in [5]–[7]. There also exist task graphs that represent the evaluation of a compound arithmetic expression from parallel computation of a number of its component subexpressions [14]. Such graphs generally have many entry nodes representing several autonomous concurrently executable subexpressions, but with all computations converging at a single-output exit node.

These and other variations can be taken care of without loss of any generality by single-entry and single-exit graphs as follows. If there are multiple input nodes (multiple entry points), add a new node to the graph such that branches from it reach the nodes that are entry points. Such a node would correspond to a computation requiring zero computation time and cost. Similarly, where there is more than one exit node, a new node is added such that branches would enter into it from every exit node. In the following discussion we shall confine our attention to SEC graphs only.

IV. Bounds

Given a program P represented by a task graph G, we can construct a program P' represented by task graph G' in which all tasks have equal weight, as follows. Let t_i be the time required to process task T_i. We shall assume without loss of generality that t_i is an integer.

If task T_i in problem P requires t_i units of processing time ($t_i > 1$), we replace task T_i by t_i tasks, all of which require one unit of processing time, as shown in Fig. 1. Note the following points.

1) The minimum number of processors required to process program P' in the smallest possible time is a lower bound on the minimum number of processors required to process P in the smallest possible time.

2) Given k processors, the minimum time taken to process program P' is a lower bound on the minimum time taken to process P. We shall use the phrases "process the task graph G" and "process the program P" interchangeably.

In this section we determine lower bounds for the minimum number of processors required to process a task graph G in the smallest possible amount of time and the minimum time required to process a task graph G given a fixed number k of processors, where all tasks in G require one unit of processing time. It follows that these bounds are also lower bounds for the case where some tasks require more than one unit of processing time.

Given a task graph G' in which all tasks require one unit of processing time, consider the generation of E and L partitions [1], [5]. The tasks T_i can be partitioned into l subsets $(E_1, E_2, \cdots, E_l)$ called the earliest (or E or column) precedence partitions such that

$$E = \bigcup_{i=1}^{l} E_i = \bigcup_{j=1}^{m} T_j, \qquad \text{where } T = \{T_1, T_2, \cdots, T_m\}$$

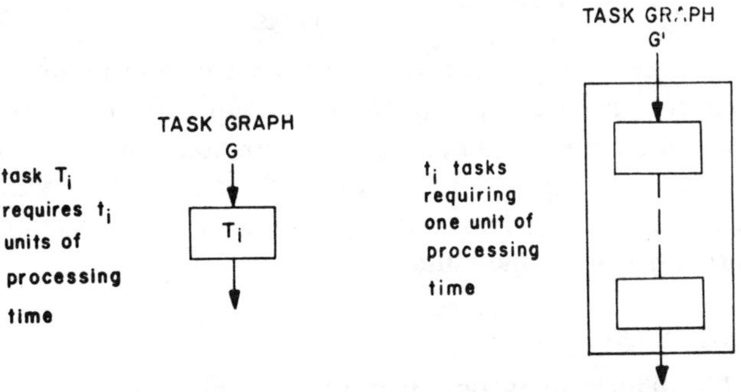

Fig. 1. A task graph G and its equivalent G'.

is the set of tasks and $E_i \cap E_j = \phi$ when $i \neq j$. The meaning of the E-precedence partitions is as follows: E_1 is the subset of tasks that can be initiated and executed in parallel at the very start. E_2 is the subset of tasks that can be initiated and executed in parallel after the tasks E_1 are done and so on. Thus the elements of E_i represent those tasks that can be processed at the *earliest* time corresponding to *level i*, even though some of these can be possibly postponed to a later time (level).

The E-precedence partitions can be determined very simply from the connectivity matrix of the task graph as follows. Using the connectivity matrix T, a column (or columns) containing only zeros is located. The tasks corresponding to these all-zero columns form partition E_1. Next delete from T both the column and row corresponding to the tasks in E_1. The first E-precedence partition is E_1. Using the remaining portion of T, locate tasks that correspond to columns containing only zeros. The second E-precedence partition E_2 thus contains the tasks corresponding to these columns. We next delete from T the columns and rows corresponding to the vertices E_2. This procedure is repeated to obtain the other E-precedence partitions until no more columns or rows remain in the T matrix. It can be shown that this partitioning procedure is valid for all graphs which have no strongly connected components, such as SEC graphs and trees.

The tasks $\{T\}$ can also be partitioned into l subsets called the latest (or L or row) precedence partitions $(L_1, L_2, \cdots, L_l)$ such that

$$\bigcup_{i=1}^{l} L_i = \bigcup_{j=1}^{m} T_j$$

and $L_i \cap L_j = \phi$ when $i \neq j$. L_i represents the subset of tasks that must be executed at least by the end of level or job step i. Otherwise the total number of levels (or time) to complete the job would exceed the minimum number of levels l in which all the tasks could be completed. The L partitions are obtained by performing precedence partitioning on the transpose of the T matrix. This process is also called row partitioning.

We use the letter l to represent the smallest possible time required to process a task graph G'. If all the tasks in the task graph require one unit of processing time, then l is also the number of subsets in the E or L partition. If some tasks require more than one unit of processing time, l is the path with the greatest length from the entry vertex to the exit vertex of the task graph. The length of the path, $T_{i(1)}, T_{i(2)}, \cdots T_{i(m)}$ is defined as $t_{i(1)} + t_{i(2)} + \cdots + t_{i(m)}$ where t_i is the time required to process task T_i.

V. Properties of E and L Partitions of a Task Graph

Given a process with n tasks $(T_1, T_2 \cdots T_n)$ whose relationships (dependencies) are indicated by an SEC graph, note the following.

Lemma 1: The number of partitions (levels, job steps) in the E-type and L-type partitions are the same for any specific task graph.

Lemma 2: Let $E = (E_1, E_2 \cdots E_l)$ and $L = (L_1, L_2 \cdots L_l)$ be the E and L partitions of a task graph. Then $E_i \cap L_i \neq \phi$ for all $1 \leq i \leq \ell$. In particular, in any SEC graph $E_1 = L_1 = \{1\}$.

Lemma 3: $E_p \cap L_q = \phi$ for all $p < q$.

G^T is defined as the *reverse graph* of G if its connectivity matrix $C(G^T)$ is the transpose of $C(G)$. The following properties are evident between G and G^T: $E(G) = L(G^T)$, and $L(G) = E(G^T)$, where $E(G)$ and $L(G)$ represent the E and L partitions, respectively, for task graph G.

For the sake of exposition, let us assume that all the tasks are of *equal duration.* This restriction will be removed later when we consider the general problem of task scheduling.

An essential task at level i is defined as an element in the set $(E_i \cap L_i)$. This implies that all essential tasks at level i must be performed during the time sequence corresponding to level i and at *no other time* if the task has to be completed in the least time. The essential tasks are those vertices that lie on the longest paths between the entry and exit vertices.

Theorem 1: Given the dependency graph of a task T, the number of processors needed to compute the job in the least possible time ℓ is bounded below by

$$\max_{\forall j} \{ | L_j \cap E_j | \}$$

and above by

$$\min \{ \max_{\forall j} \{ | L_j | \}, \max_{\forall j} \{ | E_j | \} \}.$$

Proof: The task can be completed in the minimum number of levels with at most

$$\max_{\forall i} \{ L_i \}$$

processors or

$$\max_{\forall i} \{ E_i \},$$

whichever is smaller. Since $|L_j \cap E_j|$ is the number of essential tasks at level j,

$$\max_{\forall j} \{ | E_j \cap L_j | \}$$

specifies the absolute minimum of processors required. Note that

$$\max_{\forall j} \{ | E_j \cap L_j | \} \geq | L_1 |;$$

note also that the upper bound is also valid for the case where tasks have unequal processing times.

Lemma 4: If ℓ is the number of levels in a task (SEC) graph and if n is the number of tasks (vertices) in it, then the minimum number of processors required to process the job in the least time will be equal to or greater than $\lceil (n-2)/(l-2)$.

If ℓ is the number of levels in a task graph with *several* entry vertices and one exit vertex and if n is the number of tasks in it, the minimum number of processors required to process the job in the least time will be greater than or equal to $\lceil (n-1)/(\ell-1)$.

Hu [8] proposed the following bound for the minimum number of processors required to process a task graph in a given amount of time. Let $|L_j|$ be the cardinality of the set L_j. Let $1 \leq x \leq \ell$ be an integer. We define the function $\lceil$ as follows. $\lceil y$ is the smallest integer such that $\lceil y \geq y$. Let c be a nonnegative integer.

Lemma 5: Let k be the minimum number of processors required to process a given task graph G in $\ell+c$ units.

Let

$$\max_{\forall x} \left\{ \frac{1}{x+c} \sum_{j=1}^{j=x} |L_j| \right\} = m. \tag{1}$$

Let

$$M = \lceil m. \tag{2}$$

Then $k \geq M$.

Corollary 1: Given k processors, let t be the minimum time required to process a given task graph G.

Let

$$\max_{\forall x} \left\{ -x + \frac{1}{k} \sum_{j=1}^{j=x} |L_j| \right\} = q. \tag{3}$$

Let

$$\text{LBT} = l + \lceil q. \tag{4}$$

Then $t \geq \text{LBT}$. Hence LBT is a lower bound on time required to process G with k processors.

Corollary 2: Let

$$\text{LBP} = \max \left[\max_{\forall j} \{ | L_j \cap E_j | \}, \max_{\forall x} \left\{ \frac{1}{x} \sum_{j=1}^{j=x} |L_j| \right\} \right],$$

$$\text{UBP} = \min \left[(\max_{\forall j} \{ |L_j| \}), (\max_{\forall j} \{ |E_j| \}) \right].$$

Then LBP and UBP are lower and upper bounds, respectively, on the minimum number of processors required to process a task graph G with one exit vertex in the smallest possible time (i.e., in ℓ time units).

Hu [8] has shown that if G is a graph that is a *tree*, with possibly more than one entry vertex and only one exit vertex, and all tasks require equal processing time, then: 1) the minimum number of processors required to process G in $\ell+c$ time units is M, where M is given by (1) and (2); 2) the minimum time required to process G given k processors is LBT, where LBT is given by (3) and (4).

VI. Algorithms

We shall now present an algorithm for determining the minimum number of processors required to process G in ℓ time units (i.e., in the smallest possible time). We shall make use of Algorithm C (presented later in this section) which determines whether it is possible, given k processors, to process G in ℓ time units.

A. Algorithm A

This algorithm is designed to determine the minimum number of processors to process a graph in the smallest possible time.

Initialization: Determine LBP and UBP from Corollary 2.

ith Step: $i = 1, 2, 3, \cdots,$.

If LBP=UBP, stop; the minimum number of processors required is LBP. If LBP<UBP, use Algorithm C to determine if it is possible to process G in ℓ time units with LBP processors. If it is possible, stop—the minimum number of processors required is LBP. If it is not possible, put LBP=LBP+1 and go to the $i+1$th step.

The efficiency of the algorithm clearly depends on the "tightness" of the bounds LBP and UBP. Examples worked out by the authors seem to indicate that these bounds are quite tight.

We shall next develop an optimal procedure (called Algorithm B) for assigning processors to tasks in a task graph so that they are completed in the least time. We assume that once a processor is assigned a task (program subset), it must work continuously on this task until it is completed. This procedure for assigning processors to tasks is called basic scheduling [2]. We feel that the large overhead associated with keeping track of incomplete tasks predicates a model with no preemption or preemption at some cost. In this section we shall consider the problem of optimally scheduling processors on tasks when only basic scheduling is permitted. A dynamic programming approach [9], [10] is adopted in this section to develop the optimal schedules.

The Problem: We shall say that task i precedes task j (written as task $i<$task j) if there is a directed path from vertex i to vertex j of the task graph. In other words, task $i<$task j if and only if task i must be completed before processing on task j can be started.

The set of predecessor tasks of task i written as $P(i)$ is defined as $P(i) = \{j \mid j < i\}$. In other words, task i can be started if and only if *all tasks* in $P(i)$ have been completed.

The set of successor tasks of task i written as $S(i)$ is defined as $S(i) = \{j \mid i < j\}$. No task in the set $S(i)$ can be started until task i is completed.

An Algorithm for Determining P(i) and S(i): We define a reachability matrix R for a task graph with n vertices as an $n \times n$ matrix whose $i-j$th element R_{ij} is 1 if $i<j$ and is 0 otherwise. The reachability matrix can be readily obtained from the task graph [11].

Lemma 6: $P(i) = \{j \mid R_{ji} = 1\}$; $S(i) = \{j \mid R_{ij} = 1\}$.

Definition: Let t_i be the processing time required by task i. A set of tasks $i_1, \cdots, i_k$ are said to be *equivalent* if $P(i_1) = P(i_2) = \cdots = P(i_k)$, $S(i_1) = S(i_2) = \cdots = S(i_k)$ and $t_{i_1} = t_{i_2} = \cdots = t_{i_k}$. We shall say that a task i *dominates* task j if and only if $P(i) \subseteq P(j)$, $S(i) \supseteq S(j)$, and $t_i = t_j$.

Theorem 2: If task i dominates task j, then there exists an optimal solution in which task i is started before or at the same time as task j.

Proof: Consider any schedule S_1 of tasks on k processors ($k = 1, 2, 3, \cdots$) described by a Gantt chart [see Fig. 2(a)], in which j is processed before i. Let the length of this schedule be t. Let j be processed on processor P_j and let j be started at τ_j. Similarly, let i be processed on processor P_i and let i be started at τ_i. Suppose $\tau_j < \tau_i$. If this schedule is feasible, then

a) if $q \in P(j)$ and q is processed at τ_q,

$$\tau_q + t_q \leq \tau_j; \tag{5}$$

b) if $r \in S(j)$ and r is started at τ_r,

$$\tau_r \geq \tau_i + t_i. \tag{6}$$

Consider another schedule S_2 of tasks that is identical to S_1 except that j is processed on P_i at τ_i and i is processed on P_j at τ_j. [Clearly, the length of S_2 is the same as the length of S_1 since $t_i = t_j$. See Fig. 2(b)]. If S_1 is feasible, then S_2 will be feasible if and only if

a) $v \in P(i)$ and v is processed at τ_v, and

$$\tau_v + t_v \leq \tau_j; \tag{7}$$

b) $v \in S(i)$ and v is processed at τ_v, and

$$\tau_v \geq \tau_i + t_j = \tau_i + t_i. \tag{8}$$

Since i dominates j, $P(i) \subseteq P(j)$; hence if $v \in P(i)$, then $v \in P(j)$ and thus (7) follows from (5). Similarly, since $S(i) \supseteq S(j)$, if $v \in S(j)$, then $v \in S(i)$ and hence (8) follows from (6). Therefore, for every feasible schedule S_1 in which task j is started before task i, there exists another schedule S_2 with length equal to the length of S_1 in which task i is started before task j. Thus, if there exists an optimal solution in which j is started before i then there exists an optimal solution in which i is started before j. This proves the theorem.

Fig. 3 shows an example of a program graph. For this graph we may construct a dominance graph, shown in Fig. 4, that states that there exists an optimal schedule in which 1 dominates 3, 3 dominates 2 and 4, 2 and 4 are equivalent, 2 and 4 dominate 5, and 5 dominates 6.

Definition: Two sets of tasks $I = (i_1, i_2, \cdots, i_k)$ and $J = (j_1, j_2, \cdots, j_k)$ are said to have *similar structure* if there exists a permutation π on $1, 2, \cdots, k$ such that: 1) $t_{j[\pi(q)]} = t_{i[q]}$, for $q = 1, 2, \cdots, k$; and 2) in the subgraph I there exists an edge (i_u, i_v) if and only if there exists and edge $(j_{\pi(u)}, j_{\pi(v)})$ in the subgraph J.

π is referred to as the *similarity permutation.* If such a permutation exists, $j_{\pi(u)}$ and i_u are said to be *similar*, for $u = 1, 2, \cdots, k$.

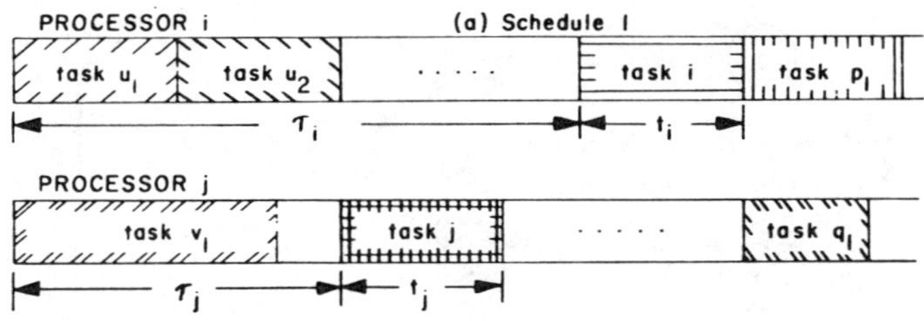

INTERCHANGE POSITIONS OF TASKS i AND j

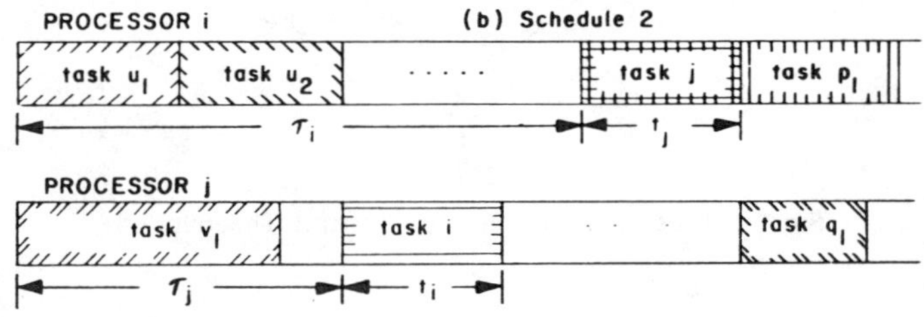

Fig. 2. Examples of schedules used to prove Theorem 2.

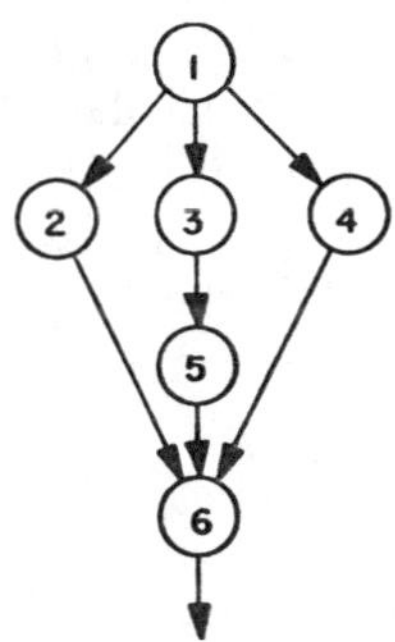

Fig. 3. Example of a program graph.

Fig. 4. Dominance graph for the graph of Fig. 3.

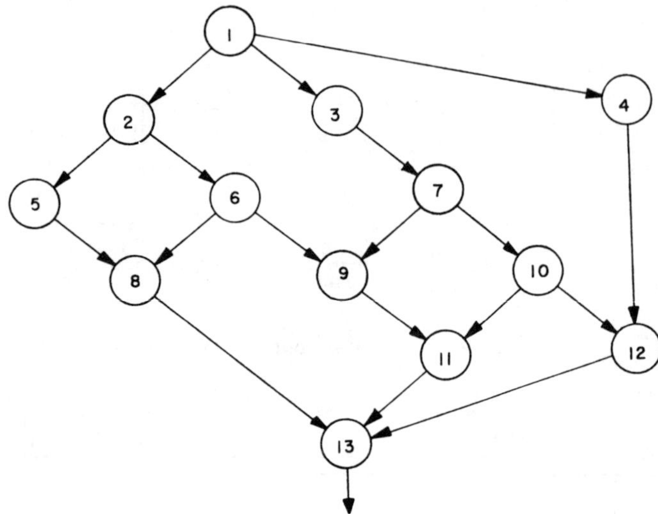

Fig. 5. Program graph used to illustrate Theorem 3.

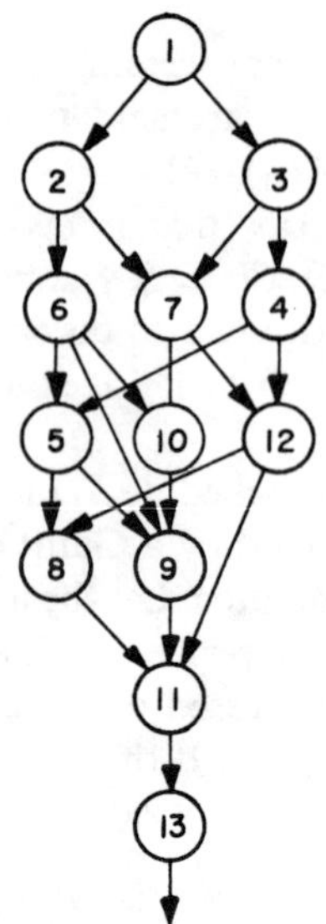

Fig. 6. Dominance graph for the graph of Fig. 5.

We extend the notion of dominance to sets of tasks as follows. The set of tasks $I=\{i_1, i_2, \cdots, i_k\}$ is said to dominate the set of tasks $J=\{j_1, j_2, \cdots, j_k\}$ under the following conditions. 1) I and J have similar structure. 2) If there exists some task u such that $[u \in P(i_q)]$ and $(u \notin I)$, then $[u \in P(j_{\pi(q)})]$ and $(u \notin J)$. 3) If there exists some task u such that $[u \in S(j_{\pi(q)})]$ and $(u \notin J)$, then $[u \in S(i_q)]$ and $(u \notin I)$. The set of tasks I and J are said to be equivalent if I dominates J and J dominates I.

Theorem 3: Let $I=\{i_1, \cdots, i_k\}$ and $J=\{j_1, \cdots, j_k\}$ have similar structure and let i_r be similar to j_r, $r=1, 2, \cdots, k$. If the set of tasks $I=\{i_1, \cdots, i_k\}$ dominates the set of tasks $J=\{j_1, \cdots, j_k\}$, then there exists an optimal solution in which task i_q is started before or at the same time as j_q, $q=1, 2, \cdots, k$.

Proof: Consider any feasible schedule S_1. Let the task j_q be started at time τ_q on processor P_q in this schedule. Let i_q be started at time U_q on processor R_q in this schedule. We shall construct a new schedule S_2 as follows. Start i_q at τ_q on processor P_q and start j_q at U_q on processor R_q in S_2. In other words, if j_q is started before i_q in S_1, interchange the positions of i_q and j_q in S_2. Do this for all such q. Do not alter the starting times or the processors for all other tasks.

Clearly, the length of S_2 is the same as the length of S_1. Furthermore, by the arguments used in Theorem 2, S_2 is also feasible. Hence, given any schedule in which j_q is started before i_q, we can construct a new schedule of the same length in which j_q is not started before i_q. This proves the theorem.

The results of this theorem are illustrated by means of the program graph of Fig. 5. In this graph $\{2\ 5\ 6\ 8\}$ dominates $\{7\ 9\ 10\ 11\}$, where the similarity permutation π is $2 \xrightarrow{\pi} 7$, $5 \xrightarrow{\pi} 9$, $6 \xrightarrow{\pi} 10$, $8 \xrightarrow{\pi} 11$. Similarly, $\{4\ 12\}$ dominates $\{5\ 8\}$, where the similarity permutation π is $4 \xrightarrow{\pi} 5$, $12 \xrightarrow{\pi} 8$. $\{4\ 12\}$ also dominates $\{10\ 11\}$, where the similarity permutation π is $4 \xrightarrow{\pi} 10$, $12 \xrightarrow{\pi} 11$. Also $\{3\ 7\}$ dominates $\{4\ 12\}$. Hence we may construct a dominance graph as shown in Fig. 6. This dominance graph is used merely to illustrate similarity permutations. The entire dominance graph is never needed in the algorithms to be described.

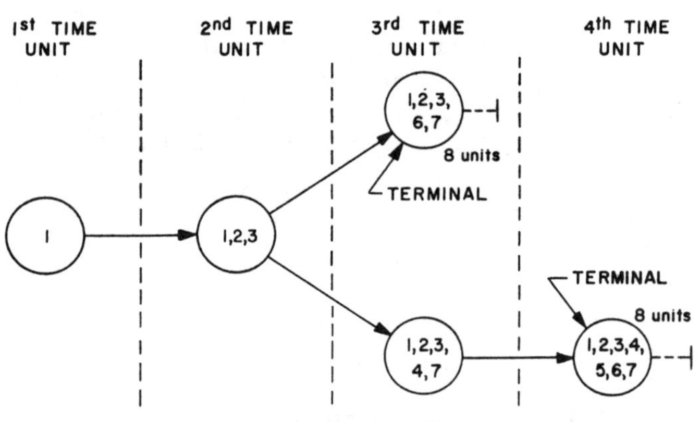

Fig. 7. Solution to the example graph of Fig. 5.

B. Algorithm B

This algorithm is designed to determine the minimum time required to process a task graph, given k processors. We shall first describe the algorithm informally by using it to solve a problem. Consider the task graph of Fig. 5. Assume that two processors are available.

In the first unit of time, the only task that can be processed is task 1. Hence one of the processors must remain idle. This is depicted in Fig. 7. In the second unit of time the only tasks that can be processed are 2, 3, and 4. By Theorem 3, there exists an optimal solution in which tasks 2 and 3 are processed in the second unit of time. Now that tasks 1, 2, and 3 are complete, the graph of the remaining tasks has the form shown in Fig. 8.

Clearly, $\{7\ 10\}$ dominates $\{4\ 12\}$, $\{4\ 12\}$ dominates $\{5\ 8\}$, and $\{7\ 10\}$ dominates $\{6\ 8\}$. The tasks that are candidates for processing in the next unit of time are 4, 5, 6, and 7. The dominance task graph for these

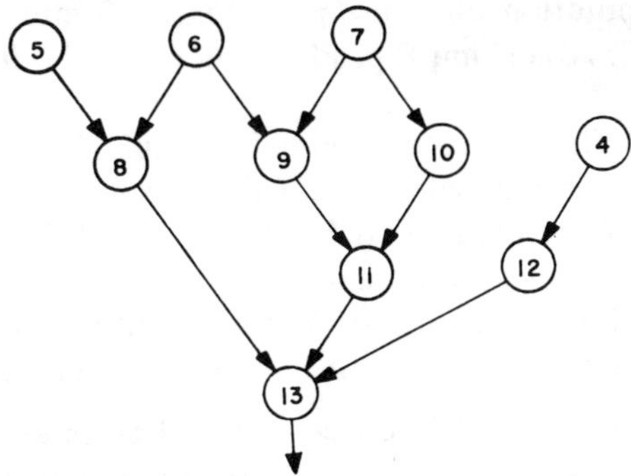

Fig. 8. Example graph after the second time unit.

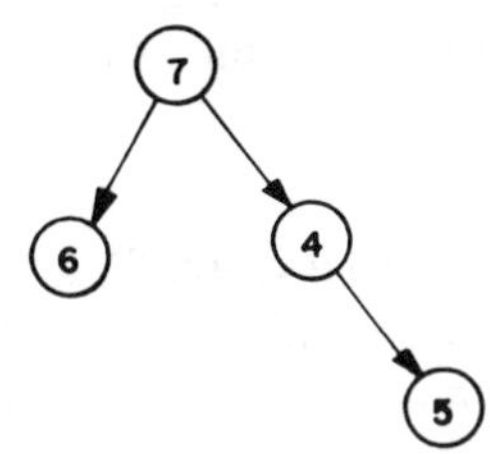

Fig. 9. Candidates for execution in the third time unit.

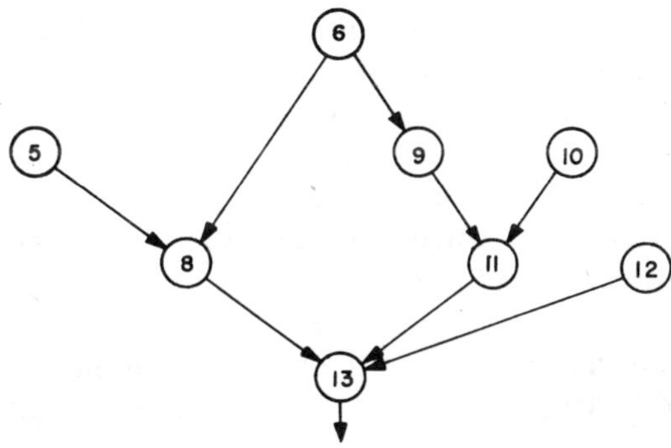

Fig. 10. Remaining graph after execution of tasks 1, 2, 3, 4, 7.

four tasks is shown in Fig. 9. Hence if we pick two tasks by the dominance criterion, we must pick (7 6) or (7 4). These two options are depicted in Fig. 7.

Thus there exists an optimal solution in which either tasks (1, 2, 3, 4, 7) or tasks (1, 2, 3, 6,7) are completed in the first three units. If tasks (1, 2, 3, 4, 7) are completed, the remaining task graph is of the form shown in Fig. 10. The candidates for processing in the next interval are (5, 6, 10, 12). $\{6\}$ dominates (5, 10, 12), $\{5\}$ dominates $\{12\}$, and $\{5\ 8\}$ dominates $\{10\ 11\}$. Hence in the next iteration we process tasks 5 and 6 (see Fig. 7).

If tasks (1, 2, 3, 6, 7) are completed, the remaining task graph is that shown in Fig. 11. The remaining task graph is a tree in which all tasks require equal processing time. Hence the optimal schedule can be readily determined from Hu's algorithm (see the Appendix). The minimum time taken to process the remaining task graph is five units. Since we know the optimal schedule for the remaining task graph, we "terminate" this state of the dynamic program with a total cost of eight units (since it is in the third interval and five additional units of time are required to process the remaining task graph).

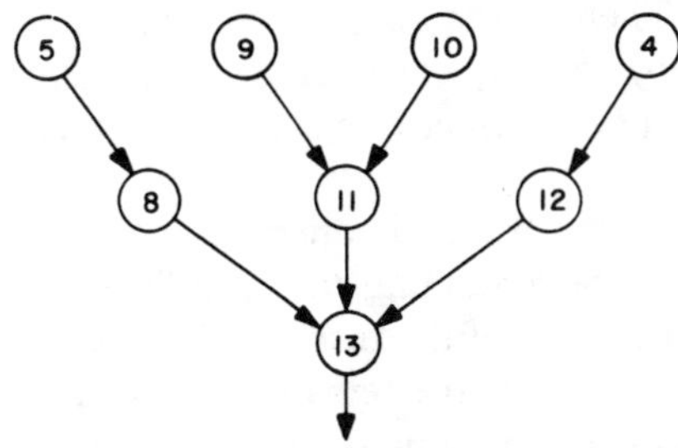

Fig. 11. Remaining graph after execution of tasks 1, 2, 3, 6, 7.

We similarly terminate state (1, 2, 3, 4, 5, 6, 7) with a cost of eight (see Fig. 7). Hence the minimum time required to process this task graph with two processors is eight units.

Note: The theorems developed in this section are valid for the cases where tasks require unequal or equal processing time.

Definitions: The states of the dynamic program are classified in *levels* 1, 2, 3, $\cdots$, where the ith level corresponds to the ith unit of time; zero time is the instant at which the task graph starts getting processed.

Let there be n tasks in the task graph, indexed 1, $\cdots$, n. Let t_i be the processing time required for the ith task. A state in the dynamic program will be described by two sets (J, P) where $J=\{j_1, \cdots, j_q\}$; $j_v \in \{1, 2, \cdots, n\}$ for all v; $P=\{p_1(r_1), p_2(r_2), \cdots, p_u(r_u)\}$; and $p_v \in \{1, 2, \cdots, n\}$ for all v. The r_v are integers for $0<r_v<t_{p_v}$.

State (J, P) at the ith level represents a set of tasks that are completely or partially processed in the first i units of time. If $J=\{j_1, j_2, \cdots, j_q\}$ and $P=\{p_1(r_1), p_2(r_2), \cdots, p_u(r_u)\}$, then tasks $j_1, j_2, \cdots, j_q$ have been completed at the end of the ith unit of time; tasks $p_1, p_2, \cdots, p_u$ have started being processed but are not completely processed at the end of the ith unit of time, and task p_v requires r_v additional units of processing time to be completely processed, $v=1, 2, \cdots, u$. Since no preemption is allowed, the number of partially processed tasks cannot exceed the number of processors. In general, there must be one state of the ith level for each distinct (J, P). We show in the next lemma that several of these states may be ignored.

A state (J_1, P_1) at the ith level is said to be *dominated* if either condition 1) or condition 2) (or both) of the following hold.

1) There exist tasks a and b such that a dominates b and either $b \in J_1$, and $a \notin J_1$, or $b \in P_1$ and $a \notin (J_1 \cup P_1)$.

2) There exists a state (J_2, P_2) at the vth level such that: a) $v \leq i$; b) $J_2 \supseteq J_1$; c) $(J_2 \cup P_2) \supseteq (J_1 \cup P_1)$; and d) if $b \in P_2$, where there are r_2 additional units of processing time required to complete processing b in state (J_2, P_2), then $b \in P_1$, where there are r_1 additional units of processing time required to complete processing b in state (J_1, P_1), and $r_2 \leq r_1$.

A state (J, P) is said to be *infeasible* if there exists tasks a and b such that: a) $a<b$; b) $a \notin J$; and c) $b \in (J \cup P)$.

A schedule of processor assignments can be represented by a sequence of feasible states (J_1, P_1), (J_2, P_2), $\cdots$, (J_f, P_f), where (J_i, P_i) is the set of partially or completely processed jobs at the end of the ith unit of time.

Lemma 6: There exists an optimal schedule of processors represented by a sequence of feasible states (J_1, P_1), $(J_2, P_2), \cdots, (J_f, P_f)$ where no state (J_i, P_i), $i=1, 2, \cdots, f$ is dominated.

Proof: Follows from Theorems 2 and 3.

Definitions: The remaining task graph $R(J, P)$ of a state (J, P) is the subgraph of the task graph obtained by deleting all vertices in $(J \cup P)$. If the remaining task graph is a tree in which all tasks require equal processing time, the optimal schedule for the remaining task graph can be readily obtained by Hu's algorithm (see the Appendix). A state (J, P) is said to be *terminal* if the optimal schedule for processing the remaining task graph $R(J, P)$ has been determined.

A nonterminal state (J, P) is said to be *extended* if the successor states of state (J, P) have been constructed.

In cases where all tasks require equal processing time, we may assume without loss of generality that each task requires one unit of time. In this case, for every state (J, P) the set P will be empty. Hence, if all tasks require equal processing time, we will represent a state by just $J=\{j_1, j_2, \cdots, j_q\}$, the set of tasks that have been *completely processed* at the end of the ith unit of time, and omit P, the set of partially processed tasks.

All Tasks Require Equal Processing Times: We shall first consider a version of Algorithm B in which all tasks require equal processing times. This condition also applies to Algorithm C which follows. The case in which tasks require unequal processing times will be discussed later.

Initialization: Construct one state at the first level. This is the state $\{1\}$ consisting of just task 1. (Note: There is no task a such that $a<1$.)

ith Step: $i=2, 3, \cdots$.

1) If all states at the $(i-1)$th level have been terminated, go to step 2. If not, go to step 3.

2) Pick the terminal state with the minimum cost. The schedule corresponding to the minimum cost terminal state is the optimal schedule; STOP.

3) If all the states in the $(i-1)$th level have been either terminated or extended, go to the $(i+1)$th step. Otherwise, go to step 4.

4) Pick any state S at the $(i-1)$th level that has not been terminated or extended. Determine the remaining task graph $R(S)$ for S. If $R(S)$ is a tree, go to step 5. Otherwise, go to step 6.

5) Determine $T(S)$, the minimum time required to process $R(S)$ using Hu's algorithm. Terminate S with a cost of $T(S)+i-1$. Go to step 1.

6) Extend S to the ith level. Let $D(S)=\{j_1, \cdots, j_q\}$ be the candidates for processing at the next unit of time. Construct a successor state to S for each distinct subset $\{i_1, i_2, \cdots, i_k\}$ of $D(S)$. There are, therefore, $\binom{q}{k}$ such successor states (where we define $\binom{q}{k}=1$ if $q<k$). Eliminate all dominated states from further consideration. Go to step 1.

Note: Algorithm B has been coded in Fortran on a CDC 6600 for the case where k, the number of processors, equals two. Computation times are presented in Section VII.

Lemma 7: Algorithm B produces an optimal schedule in a finite time.

Proof: There exists an optimal schedule that only passes through nondominated states. All sequences of nondominated states are considered by Algorithm B. Hence Algorithm B determines an optimal schedule.

The maximum number of levels constructed cannot exceed $\sum_{\forall i} t_i$, where t_i is the time required to process task i. Hence the number of levels constructed is finite. Since the number of states per level is finite, the total number of states is finite. Since the time taken to construct a state or to compare all states is finite, the algorithm determines an optimal schedule in a finite amount of time.

C. Algorithm C

We shall next discuss Algorithm C, an algorithm designed to determine if a task graph G can be processed in the minimum possible time with k processors.

Corollary 3: Let S be a state of the ith level, and let $R(S)$ be its remaining state graph. Let LBT(S) be a lower bound on the time taken to process $R(S)$. If LBT$(S)>\ell-i$, then there is no feasible schedule that passes through state S and that processes the task graph in ℓ time units.

Definition: If a state S at the ith level is marked "*limit exceeded*," then the minimum time taken to process the remaining task graph $R(S)$ exceeds $(\ell-i)$.

Initialization: Construct a state $\{1\}$ at the first level. This state consists of just task 1.

ith Step: $i=2, 3, 4, \cdots$.

1) If all the states at the $(i-1)$th level are marked "limit exceeded," STOP. It is not possible to process the task graph in ℓ units of time.

2) If all the states at the $(i-1)$th level are either extended or marked "limit exceeded," go to the $(i+1)$th step. Otherwise, go to step 3.

3) Pick any state S at the $(i-1)$th level that has not been extended or marked "limit exceeded." Use Corollary 1 to determine LBT(S), a lower bound on the time required to completely process the remaining task graph $R(S)$. If LBT$(S)>\ell-(i-1)$, mark state S with "limit exceeded." Go to step 1. If LBT$(S)\leq\ell(i-1)$, go to step 4.

4) If $R(S)$ is a tree in which all tasks have equal time, go to step 5. Otherwise, go to step 6.

5) Determine $t(s)$, the minimum time required to process $R(S)$. For the special case that $R(S)$ is a tree with all tasks of equal processing time, it can be shown that $t(s)=$ LBT(S). Hence $t(s)\leq\ell-(i-1)$; STOP. There does exist a schedule for processing the task graph G in l units of time.

6) Extend S to the ith level. Let $D(S)=\{j_1, \cdots, j_q\}$ be the candidates for processing at the next unit of time. Construct a successor state to S for each distinct subset $\{i_1, i_2, \cdots, i_k\}$ of $D(S)$. Eliminate all dominated and infeasible states from further consideration. Go to step 1.

Lemma 8: Algorithm C determines whether or not it is possible to process task graph G in ℓ units. Algorithm C is completed in a finite amount of time.

Tasks Require Unequal Processing Times: We shall now consider the case where tasks have unequal processing times.

We note that the bounds, LBP, LBT, and UBP are also valid for the case of tasks with unequal processing times. We also note that Theorems 2 and 3 are valid for task graphs with unequal task processing times.

Unequal processing times for tasks creates one important complicating factor: it is sometimes optimal to keep a processor idle even when there are tasks that can be processed immediately. It is clear that if all tasks require exactly one unit of time for processing, then there is no time gained by keeping a processor idle when there are candidates for processing. The example of Fig. 12 illustrates this point.

The optimal schedule with two processors is illustrated on the Gantt chart of Fig. 13. However, if we choose to keep a processor busy whenever there is a task available for processing, the Gantt chart will appear as shown in Fig. 14. Therefore, to determine the optimal policy it is necessary to consider the possibility that some (but not all) processors should be kept idle even if there are tasks ready for processing.

With the following modification, Algorithm B will determine the optimal schedule for the case where tasks have unequal processing times. Algorithm C is similarly modified.

Extending a state (J, P) at the ith level if tasks have unequal processing times is accomplished as follows.

Let (J', P') be a state in the $(i+1)$th level and a successor of (J, P). Let $P=\{p_1(r_1), p_2(r_2), \cdots, p_u(r_u)\}$.

1) If $p_v(r_v)\in P$ where $r_v=1$, then $p_v\in J'$.
2) If $p_v(r_v)\in P$ where $r_v>1$, then $p_v(r_v-1)\in P'$.
3) If $j\in J$ then $j\in J'$.

Let there be y tasks $p_v\in P$, where $r_v>1$. Then in all successor states of (J, P) which are in the $(i+1)$th level, y processors will be occupied processing these partially processed tasks. However, it may be optimal to keep some of the $k-y$ processors idle through the $(i+1)$th interval. Let D be the set of tasks (other than the tasks in P) that are candidates for processing in the next interval. Then in the $(i+1)$th interval we may choose to process any subset of D with cardinality not exceeding $k-y$ (the number of free processors). Let the cardinality of D be q.

If there are x processors working on tasks in D in the $(i+1)$th interval $(0\leq x\leq k-y)$ and $k-y-x$ processors idle, then there are $\binom{q}{x}$ different alternatives for choosing tasks in D. Hence there are a total of $\sum_{k=0}^{x=k'} \binom{q}{x}$ alternatives to be considered where $k'=\min\{q, k-y\}$. As in the case of equal-time tasks, several states will be dominated.

For a state (J, P) at the ith level, let F be the complement of $J\cup P$), i.e., $F=\{\text{tasks } f \mid f\notin (J\cup P)\}$. Let the set of tasks (other than tasks in P) that are candidates for processing in the next interval be D (i.e., if $d\in D$, then $d\in F$, and the set of predecessor tasks of d is contained in J).

The number of states that have to be considered can be substantially reduced by using the results of the following lemma.

Lemma 9: If for every $f\in F, f\notin D$ and $d\in D$, it is true that $d<f$, then there exists an optimal solution in which no processor is kept idle during the $(i+1)$th interval unless processors have been assigned to all tasks in D.

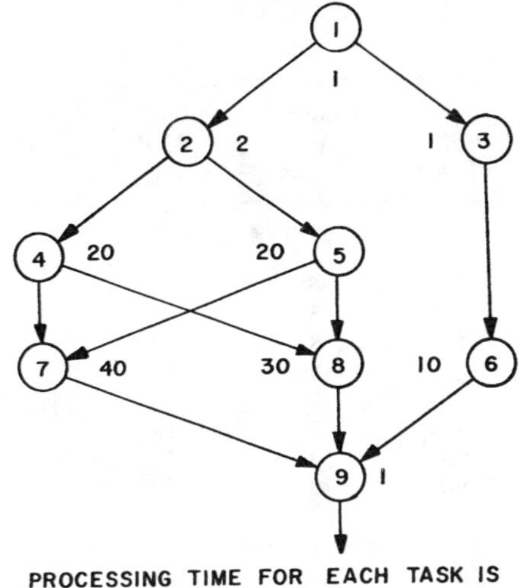

Fig. 12. Program graph used to illustrate unequal task times.

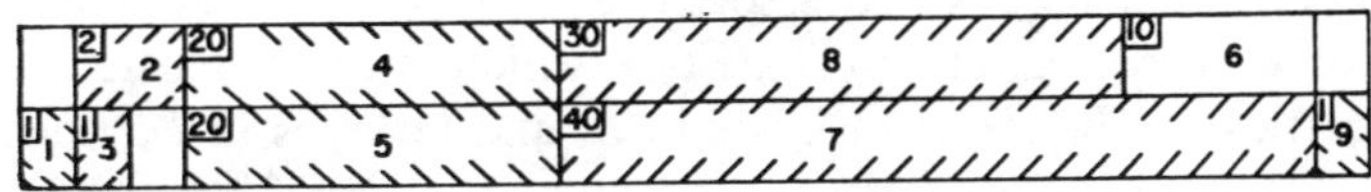

Fig. 13. Optimal schedule for graph of Fig. 12.

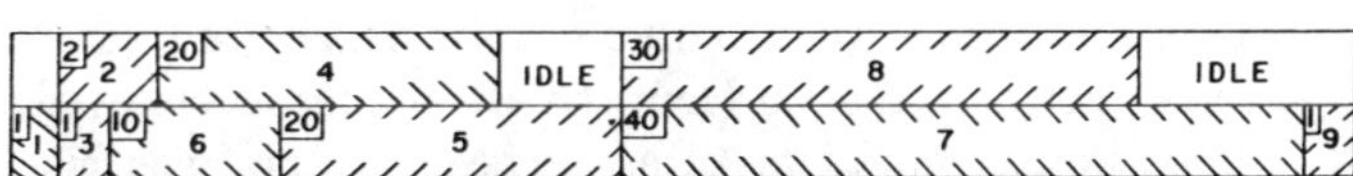

Fig. 14. Schedule that results when processors are activated as soon as possible.

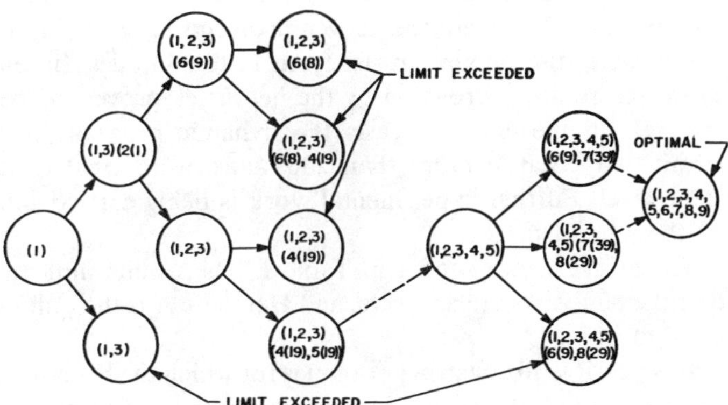

Fig. 15. Dynamic program schedule for graph of Fig. 12.

Example: Determine the minimum number of processors required to process the task graph shown in Fig. 12. We use Algorithm A. LBP=2 and UBP=3. The shortest possible time in which task graph can be processed is $\ell=64$. Hence we determine if it is possible to process the task graph in 64 units with two processors.

Fig. 15 shows the states of the dynamic program. The infeasible and dominated states have not been shown. The minimum number of processors required to process the task graph shown in Fig. 12 in the least possible time is *two.*

TABLE I

COMPUTATIONAL RESULTS

Problem Numbers	Number of Nodes	Number of Levels	Processing Time D.P. Alg.	Processing Time Heuristic A	Processing Time Heuristic B	Random Sequencing	Execution Time (seconds) D.P. Alg.	Execution Time (seconds) Heuristic A	Execution Time (seconds) Heuristic B
1	11	6	7	7	7	8	0.064	0.013	0.027
2	11	6	7	7	7	7	0.077	0.017	0.030
3	11	6	7	7	7	7	0.072	0.009	0.020
4	13	6	8	8	8	8	0.157	0.017	0.037
5	17	8	10	10	10	10	0.407	0.027	0.050
6	20	8	11	11	11	11	3.739	0.040	0.068
7	22	9	12	12	12	12	0.655	0.044	0.071
8	24	9	13	13	13	13	1.896	0.051	0.088
9	29	15	18	18	18	18	0.457	0.100	0.167
10	40	17	22	22	22	23	3.305	0.229	0.331
11	54	27	—	31	31	35	—	0.502	0.772

VII. EXPERIMENTS AND COMPUTATIONAL RESULTS

The following heuristic (called Heuristic A) was evaluated: 1) do not keep any processors idle; 2) if two tasks compete for a processor, choose that task which is in the earlier L partition. That is, if task i is in L_a and task j is in L_b, and tasks i and j are competing for a processor, and if $a<b$, then task j is begun if and only if task i is also begun. This heuristic is the same as the algorithm used by Hu [8] to determine the optimal schedule for program graphs which are trees.

Another heuristic (called Heuristic B), similar to Heuristic A, except that essential tasks are processed first, was also evaluated.

The dynamic programming algorithm and the two heuristics were programmed in Fortran on the CDC 6600 (at the University of Texas at Austin), for the case where two processors had to be scheduled. Eleven problems generated randomly were run, ranging in size from 11 to 54 nodes. In ten cases, the solution provided by the heuristics proved to be optimal. In the eleventh case, the dynamic program was terminated because more than 200 states were created at some level. Further experimental work is being carried out on these heuristics.

These results are shown in Table I. The results indicate that the heuristics are accurate, and Heuristic A is the quickest algorithm.

It is possible to construct examples for which the heuristics are not optimal. However, in most cases the heuristics seem to be optimal.

Additional theorems and quicker *optimal* algorithms can be developed for the case where only two processors are to be scheduled. These theorems and algorithms are the subject of a forthcoming paper.

It is interesting to note that a random sequencing algorithm (in which random selection was made between competing tasks) was near optimal. Of course, the results of a random scheduling algorithm may vary widely, from near optimal to very bad.

VIII. CONCLUSION

An optimal algorithm for basic scheduling of a set of tasks has been presented. Two heuristics and a random sequencing algorithm were experimentally evaluated. The results seem to indicate that the heuristics are accurate and fast enough for real time application.

APPENDIX

HU'S ALGORITHM

Given k processors and a task graph that is a tree in which all tasks require one unit of time. The task graph has one exit vertex (and possibly several entry vertices).

At any instant let D be the set of candidates for processing. Let $|D|$ be the cardinality of D. If $|D| \leq k$, process all tasks in D. If $|D| > k$, process a set $B \subset D$, where if $i \in B$, $j \notin B$, $j \in D$, then if $i \in L_a$, $j \in L_b$, then $a \leq b$ where L_a, L_b are L partitions.

REFERENCES

[1] C. V. Ramamoorthy and M. J. Gonzalez, "A survey of techniques for recognizing parallel processable streams in computer programs," in *1969 Fall Joint Comput. Conf., AFIPS Conf. Proc.*, vol. 35. Montvale, N. J.: AFIPS Press, 1969, pp. 1–15.

[2] R. R. Muntz and E. G. Coffman, "Optimal preemptive scheduling on two-processor systems," *IEEE Trans. Comput.*, vol. C-18, pp. 1014–1020, Nov. 1969.

[3] G. K. Manacher, "Production and stabilization of real-time schedules," *J. Ass. Comput. Mach.*, vol. 14, pp. 429–465, July 1967.

[4] A. J. Bernstein, "Analysis of programs for parallel processing," *IEEE Trans. Electron. Comput.*, vol. EC-15, pp. 757–763, Oct. 1966.

[5] C. V. Ramamoorthy, "A structural theory of machine diagnosis," in *1967 Spring Joint Comput. Conf. AFIPS Conf. Proc.*, vol. 30. Washington, D.C.: Thompson, 1967, pp. 743–756.

[6] W. Mayeda and C. V. Ramamoorthy, "Distinguishability criteria in oriented graphs and their application to computer diagnosis–I," *IEEE Trans. Circuit Theory*, vol. CT-16, pp. 448–454, Nov. 1969.

[7] C. V. Ramamoorthy and L. C. Chang, "System segmentation for the parallel diagnosis of computers," *IEEE Trans. Comput.*, vol. C-20, pp. 261–270, Mar. 1971.

[8] T. C. Hu, "Parallel sequencing and assembly line problems," *Oper. Res.* vol. 9, pp. 841–848, Nov. 1961.

[9] R. M. Karp and M. Held, "Finite state processes and dynamic programming," *SIAM J. Appl. Math.*, vol. 15, May 1967.

[10] R. E. Bellman and S. Dreyfus, *Applied Dynamic Programming.* Princeton, N. J.: Princeton Univ. Press, 1962

[11] C. V. Ramamoorthy, "Analysis of graphs by connectivity considerations," *J. Ass. Comput. Mach.*, vol. 13, pp. 211–222, Apr. 1966.

[12] R. M. Karp and R. E. Miller, "Parallel program schemata," *J. Comput. Syst. Sci.*, vol. 3, pp. 147–195, May 1969.

[13] R. L. Graham, "Bounds on multiprocessing and timing anomalies," *SIAM J. Appl. Math.*, vol. 17, Mar. 1969.

[14] C. V. Ramamoorthy and M. J. Gonzalez, "Subexpression ordering in the execution of arithmetic expressions," *Commun. Ass. Comput. Mach.*, vol. 14, July 1971.

A Task Allocation Model for Distributed Computing Systems

PERNG-YI RICHARD MA, EDWARD Y. S. LEE, MEMBER, IEEE, AND MASAHIRO TSUCHIYA, MEMBER, IEEE

Abstract—**This paper presents a task allocation model that allocates application tasks among processors in distributed computing systems satisfying: 1) minimum interprocessor communication cost, 2) balanced utilization of each processor, and 3) all engineering application requirements.**

A cost function is formulated to measure the interprocessor communication and processing costs. By employing various constraints, the model efficiently generates minimum-cost allocation using a branch and bound technique. With suitable modification of these constraints, both application requirements and load balance can be achieved.

For evaluation, this allocation model was applied to an Air Defense (AD) case study which involves the allocation of 23 real-time software tasks into a network of processors. Simulation was used to validate the resultant allocations against the three goals. The result indicates that the allocation model is applicable to large practical problems. It satisfies all application requirements and generates an allocation that counterbalances interprocessor communication cost and load balancing.

Index Terms—**Branch and bound, distributed processing, interprocessor communication, load balance, NP problem, task allocation.**

I. Introduction

THE RAPID progress of microprocessor technology has made the distributed computing systems economically attractive for many computer applications. However, many problem areas in the distributed computing systems are still in their primitive development stage [1], [2]. Some major problems that prevent the widespread use of distributed systems are as follows.

1) The degradation in system throughput caused by the "saturation effect" [3]: A saturation effect is caused by heavy communication traffic induced by data transfers from one task to another residing in separate processors. The interprocessor traffic is always the most costly and the least reliable factor in the loosely coupled distributed system [1], [4]. As a result of this saturation effect, the incremental increase in computing resources could actually degrade system throughput.

2) The difficulty in evenly utilizing each processor in the distributed system: The saturation effect can be alleviated by loading the tasks with high communication demands into the same processor. However, this often creates load imbalance and thus lowers system throughput. It is very important to balance these two competing forces to achieve a greater system throughput [3], [5].

3) A large gap between the engineering application requirements and the existing distributed network architecture [6]: Application tasks defined by the process designers to meet the engineering requirements do not often map optimally into the existing distributed architecture [6]. Conversely, a gap exists in the design of the distributed architecture to meet the software and system requirements. Hence, a software tool is badly needed for the practical allocation of engineering application tasks in the distributed systems.

4) The difficulty in verifying allocations resulted from any allocation model: Due to the scarcity of real-life data, most research results are limited to theoretical and mathematical models [1], [4], [7], [8] and their merits are difficult to compare [9].

Several approaches to the allocation model have been identified. They are basically graph theoretical, integer programming, and heuristic methods. The graph theoretical approach uses a graph to represent application tasks [4]. It minimizes the total interprocessor communication cost by performing a min-cut algorithm on the graph. The limitation on its generalization is the high computing time complexity when more than two processors are used in the allocation model. Furthermore, it is difficult to incorporate various constraints into such a model.

The integer programming method [10], [11] is based on the implicit enumeration algorithm subject to the additional constraints. It allows constraints to be easily incorporated into the allocation model to meet various application requirements. This approach is limited by the amounts of time and memory needed to obtain an optimal solution since they grow as exponential functions of the problem order.

The heuristic method is to provide fast and effective algorithms for a suboptimum solution [1]. This technique requires less computation time than integer programming methods. They are useful in applications where an optimum solution is not obtainable within a critical time limit. They are also applicable to larger dimensional problems.

This paper presents a task allocation model for distributed computing systems based on a zero-one programming technique, the branch-and-bound method. For a given distributed system configuration and a set of constraints, it generates an optimal solution for medium-size problems satisfying all application requirements. For a large-size problem, the allocation

Manuscript received April 3, 1981; revised July 17, 1981. This work was supported in part by the Ballistic Missile Defense Advanced Technology Center under Contract DASG60-79-C-0039 and the independent research and development project of the TRW Systems Engineering and Integration Division under Project 8100692.

The authors are with TRW, Redondo Beach, CA 90278.

Reprinted from *IEEE Trans. Comput.*, vol. C-31, pp. 41–47, Jan. 1982.

model is judged by the practical engineering application requirements. In order to verify its validity, the allocation model was tested on an Air Defense (AD) case study which involves the allocation of 23 real-time software tasks into three processors. The results show that the model is applicable to large practical problems and that it generates very effective allocation.

II. Problem Statement

The problem involves the development of task allocation model for the distributed computing system. The model must allocate tasks among distributed processors to achieve the following goals:

1) allow specification of a large number of constraints to facilitate a variety of engineering application requirements,

2) balance the utilization of individual processors in the distributed computing system, and

3) minimize interprocessor communication cost.

In order for the task allocation model to effectively satisfy these goals, it should have a structure with supporting functions as shown in Fig. 1. The task preprocessor analyzes the application tasks to acquire relevant information such as coupling factors among tasks and task attribute sizes. The coupling factor between tasks is measured by the number of data units transferred from one task to another. The unit of data is dependent on the application task; it may be word, byte, or bit. The attributes are the inherent characteristics of tasks, e.g., the number of executable statements, or the maximum allowable execution time.

The network preprocessor examines the distributed network and provides information on the network architecture which includes the interprocessor distance and processor constraints. The interprocessor distance is conceptually the physical distance between two processors. However, it may represent any type of cost that can be measured in time or in dollars [4]. Every processor has its hardware constraints which are called processor attributes. For example, the attributes may be the MIPS (million instructions per second) rate, storage space, etc.

Based on the assumption that all necessary information on the tasks and processors is provided by the two preprocessors, this paper presents the development and application of a task allocation model and verification of its results using a simulator.

III. Functional Design of the Allocation Model

The design of a mathematical model for task allocation for a distributed computing system involves the following steps: 1) formulate the cost function to measure the interprocessor communication (IPC) cost and processing cost, 2) formulate a set of constraints to meet the diverse requirements, and 3) derive an iterative algorithm to obtain a minimum total cost solution.

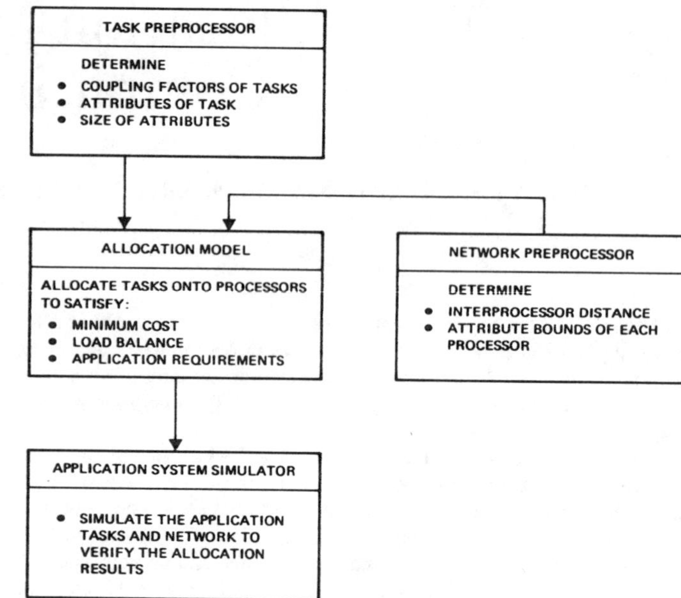

Fig. 1. General structure of the allocation model and its supporting functions.

A. Cost Function

The cost function is formulated as the sum of the IPC cost and the processing cost. IPC cost is a function of both task coupling factors and interprocessor distances. Coupling factor C_{ij} is the number of data units transferred from task i to task j. Interprocessor distance d_{kl} is certain distance-related communication costs associated with one unit of data transferred from processor k to processor l. If tasks i and j are assigned to processors k and l, respectively, the interprocessor cost is $(C_{ij} * d_{kl})$. If $k = l$ then $d_{kl} = 0$. The unit of IPC cost is application dependent. For example, if the unit of C_{ij} is word and d_{kl} is \$/word, the IPC unit is in dollars.

Processing cost q_{ik} represents the cost to process task i on processor k. It can be used to control the processor assignment. For example, if task i must not be executed on processor k, a very large value can be assigned to q_{ik} to inhibit the assignment.

The assignment variable is defined as follows:

$$X_{ik} = \begin{cases} 1, & \text{if task } i \text{ is assigned to processor } k. \\ 0, & \text{otherwise.} \end{cases}$$

The total cost for processing the tasks is stated as [3]

$$\sum_i \sum_k \left(w q_{ik} X_{ik} + \sum_l \sum_j (c_{ij} * d_{kl}) X_{ik} X_{jl} \right).$$

The normalization constant w is used to scale processing cost and IPC cost to account for any difference in measuring units.

B. Constraints

Several constraints are incorporated in the allocation model to achieve the load balance and meet the application requirements (Table I). Attributes are a collection of constraints from

TABLE I
ALLOCATION CONSTRAINTS

Bounded Attributes	Representation of the constraints associated with the tasks and/or processor, e.g., task size is bounded by available memory storage
Task Preference	A task is preferred to be allocated to a certain processor
Task Exclusion	Certain pairs of tasks must not be assigned to the same processor
Task Redundancy	Certain tasks must be assigned to two or more processors

the application tasks and given network topology. For example, the memory attribute is represented by

$$\sum_i M_i X_{ik} \leq S_k$$

where M_i is the amount of memory required by task i, and S_k represents the memory capacity at processor k. This attribute states that the amount of memory required for all tasks assigned to a processor must not exceed the processor memory capacity.

The task preference matrix, task exclusive matrix, and task redundancy are implemented to increase the model capability. The *task preference matrix* indicates that certain tasks can only be executed in the specified processor. It is represented by an $m \times n$ matrix P(m is the number of tasks and n is the number of processors), where $P_{ik} = 0$ implies that task i cannot be assigned to processor k; and $P_{ik} = 1$, otherwise.

The *task exclusive* matrix defines mutually exclusive tasks. It is represented by an $m \times m$ matrix E, where $E_{ij} = 1$ implies that tasks i and j cannot be assigned to the same processor; otherwise, $E_{ij} = 0$.

The *task redundancy* may be provided for system reliability. This permits multiple copies of a task. For example, if task i has a redundancy of three, new tasks $i + 1$ and $i + 2$ are added to the original set of tasks. They have identical constraints to task i. In addition, an additional constraint is added such that tasks i, $i + 1$, and $i + 2$ cannot be assigned to the same processor.

C. Algorithm Derivation

The algorithm was derived from a branch and bound (BB) method. To employ the BB technique, the allocation problem is represented by a search tree. The allocation decision represents a branching at the node corresponding to the given task. Consider a problem of allocating m tasks among n processors. Starting with task 1, each task is allocated to one of the n processors subject to the constraints imposed on the relations on tasks and processors. The number of tree levels m corresponds to m tasks. A feasible sequence of successive branches is called a path. A path from the root node to the last node corresponds to a *complete allocation;* otherwise, it is a *partial allocation.* The cost of a path is computed according to the cost equation. An example of a three-level search tree with three processors is shown in Fig. 2.

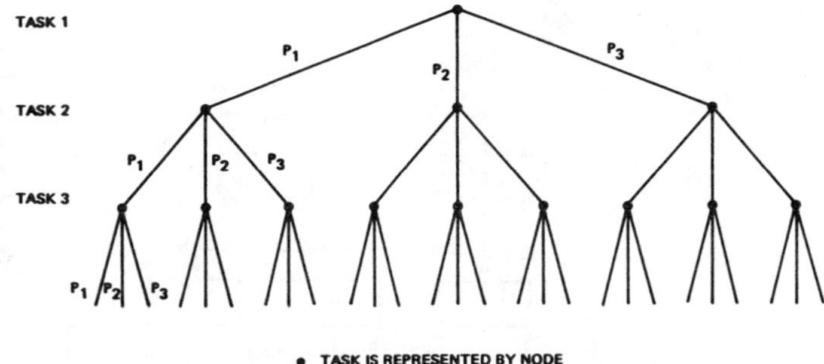

Fig. 2. Decision tree with three tasks and three processors.

The BB method defined by Kohler and Steiglitz [12] consists of nine rules: (B, S, F, D, L, U, E, BR, RB). *Branching rule B* defines the scheme for generating sons of each node. *Selection rule S* selects the next branching node from the currently active nodes. *Characteristic function F* eliminates nodes known to have no completion from the set of feasible solutions. *Dominance relation D* defined on the set of partial solutions is used by rule E to eliminate nodes from the search tree before extending them. *Lower bound function L* assigns a cost lower bound to each partial solution. *Cost upper bound U* of a complete solution is known at the beginning of the algorithm. *Elimination rules E* use D, L, and U to eliminate newly generated and currently active nodes. *Termination rule BR* shows the desired derivation of the optimal cost from an acceptable solution. *Resource bound vector RB* has components that are upper bounds of the resources used in the allocation model. This Kohler and Steiglitz BB method has been modified for our task allocation algorithm.

The following rules determine whether the selected branch i for a given node k should be eliminated.

1) Rule F checks the preference matrix P for task k and processor i. If $P_{ik} = 0$, the branch is eliminated.

2) Rule E checks the exclusive matrix for task k. If task l which is mutually exclusive to task k has already been allocated to processor i, branch i for node k is eliminated.

3) Rule RB checks the cumulative memory requirement of tasks against the processor memory capacity. As task k is assigned to processor i, its size is added to all tasks which are already in processor i. If the cumulative size of all tasks exceeds the processor's memory capacity, branch i for node k is eliminated.

4) Rule D compares the partial cost L with the complete cost U. If L is greater than U, the solution cannot be improved. Hence, branch i for node k is eliminated.

If branch i of node k satisfies all these four rules, the allocation is made. The *iteration count* is incremented indicating that one branch has been investigated for a node.

These rules constitute a depth-first search method. In addition to the elimination rules, the following rules are applied to select the next node and to terminate the algorithm.

5) Selection rules S select the next node to be expanded. It may be the current node, say, node k, the precedent node ($k - 1$), or the descendant node ($k + 1$). Branching rule B selects the branch (processor allocation) for a given node.

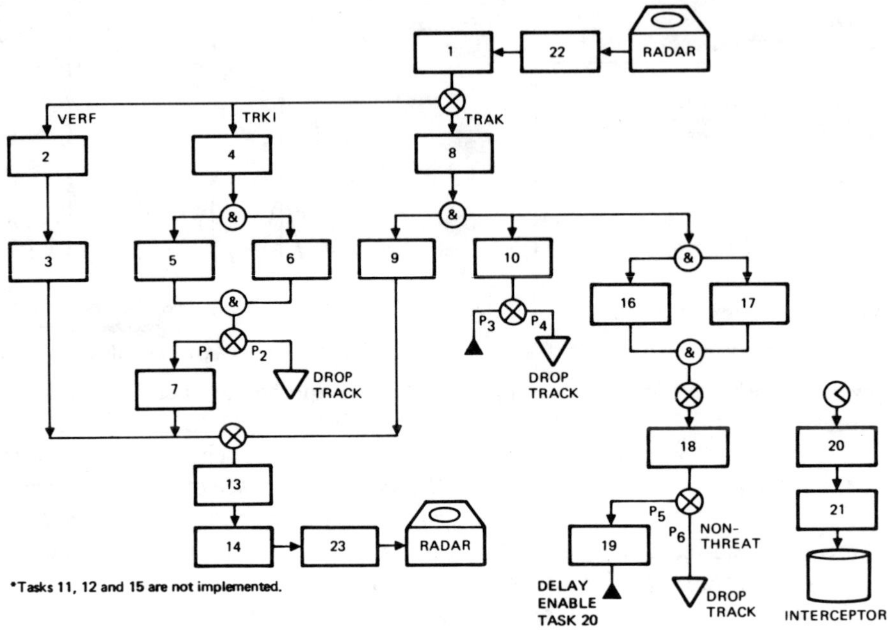

Fig. 3. Task flow diagram for a model AD application.

6) Termination rule *BR* terminates the algorithm when all possible paths have been investigated or the prespecified number of iterations has been reached. This number limits the time allowed for the algorithm to enable trading an optimal solution for a fast algorithmic result.

IV. Application

The Air Defense (AD) application is shown in Fig. 3. This depicts the data processing system interfacing with the radar and the interceptor of a model AD system. Sensor data from the radar are input to the system which tracks and keeps under constant surveillance all possible attacking reentry vehicles (RV) and commands the radar and the interceptor to prevent any RV from penetrating the defended areas. This scenario will have definite influence on the design of the data processing tasks. Twenty three tasks are identified in Fig. 3 (only 20 are shown here; the other three are not implemented yet). These tasks are arranged into seven major processing threads, each consisting of a number of tasks as shown in Fig. 4. These threads can be executed in parallel to a certain extent. Because of the real-time critical nature of this application, they must meet the shown port-to-port (PTP) processing times which confines the total execution time of the specified thread within a certain prescribed limit. Therefore, any allocation of the tasks to the processors must first satisfy these PTP time requirements in order to be qualified as a valid allocation. Since the processing load is scenario dependent, the allocation can be optimized only for a given scenario.

To justify the allocation result, a simulator [13] was designed to simulate the AD data processing system which includes twenty tasks and three processors. The three processors were simulated as homogeneous, fully connected computers with 1.5 million instruction per second (MIPS) rate each. The task attributes and task coupling factors used as inputs to the allocation model were also built into the simulator. The attribute includes the task sizes in machine language instructions. Task coupling factors are in words. Some examples are shown in Table II(A) and (B). The interprocessor distance between any two processors is assumed to be unity.

THREADS	PTP DELAY LIMIT (MSEC)
(22, 1, 2, 3, 13)	100
(22, 1, 4, 13)	50
(22, 1, 4, 5, 6, 7, 13)	40
(22, 1, 8, 9, 13)	40
(22, 1, 8, 10)	40
(22, 1, 8, 16, 17, 18)	40
(22, 1, 8, 17, 18, 19)	50

Fig. 4. Major processing threads and port-to-port time requirements.

The rest of this section reports two applications of the allocation model. In Section IV-A the allocation model is applied to the AD data processing system and its results are compared with those obtained from engineering experience. Section IV-B discusses improvement in allocation results by making suitable modifications to the model inputs.

A. Allocation

Two allocation policies were studied. Twenty tasks were allocated into three processors in the AD data processing system. Allocation *A*-1 [Fig. 5(a)], based on the engineering experience, was designed to satisfy the PTP time by evenly loading the tasks on the processors with an equal MIPS rate.

Allocation *A*-2 [Fig. 5(b)] was based on the allocation algorithm derived in this paper. In the current allocation model, only IPC cost is used in the cost function. The IPC cost is a function of interprocessor distances and coupling factors among tasks. In this model, the units for coupling factor and distance are word and \$/word, respectively, and the distance is assumed to be unity.

TABLE II
(A) SIZE OF TASKS (MACHINE LANGUAGE INSTRUCTIONS). (B) COUPLING FACTOR AMONG TASKS (WORDS)

Task	TASK SIZE (MLI)
1	200
13	1200
14	350
22	150
23	350

(A)

Task \ Task	13	14	20	21	23
13		1000			
14	1000				100
20				200	
21			200		
23		100			

(B)

A - 1	P_1	P_2	P_3
Tasks	1 4 7 10 17 20 22	2 5 8 13 14 18 21	3 6 9 16 19 23

(a)

A - 2	P_1	P_2	P_3
Tasks	13 14 17-19	2 3 6 8 9 23	1 4 5 7 10 16 20-22

(b)

Fig. 5. (a) Engineering experience allocation to achieve load balance. (b) Allocation from the allocation model.

A critical engineering requirement in this AD application is the PTP time. If the execution time of any thread exceeds the specified PTP time, the allocation fails. The simulator can explicitly display the thread PTP time. The second goal, load balance, is expressed by the simulator as the CPU utilization of each processor during every 10 ms interval. The third goal, minimizing IPC cost, is measured by the simulator as the number of words that are transmitted among the three processors within every one ms interval. Note that the unit of IPC cost of simulator is different from that of the allocation model.

Two allocations, *A*-1 and *A*-2, were tested on the simulator. The result is shown in Table III. *A*-1 satisfies the PTP time requirement and achieves good load balancing at the expense of high IPC cost. *A*-2 shows a similar load balancing effects, but at a lower IPC cost. Note that these results are based on the assumption that homogeneous computers are employed in the experiment.

TABLE III
PERFORMANCE OF ALLOCATION *A*-1 AND *A*-2 AS MEASURED BY THE SIMULATOR

	A-1	A-2
PTP	PASS	PASS
CPU_1	39%	40%
CPU_2	55%	52%
CPU_3	42%	40%
IPC	222	184

B. Using the Algorithm

If the distributed system is varied, the user can modify the allocation constraints (algorithm input) to meet the network requirements. Two allocations are designed to trade off IPC cost and load balance. If load balancing is more critical for the system application, two tasks which are heavy CPU users should not be allocated to the same processor. This can be controlled through the exclusive matrix. On the other hand, if minimization of IPC cost is important, tasks with large coupling factor should be allocated together. This is controlled by assigning their coupling factor a large dummy value.

With suitable modifications to algorithmic constraints [5], allocations *A*-3 [Fig. 6(a)] and *A*-4 [Fig. 6(b)] are obtained. *A*-3 is designed mainly for load balance, and *A*-4 is designed mainly for lower IPC cost. The result is shown in Table IV. If the network requires high throughput and is tightly coupled, then *A*-3 is a good candidate. Conversely, if the network is loosely coupled, and IPC cost is extremely high, then *A*-4 is better.

V. EVALUATION

The task allocation algorithm was implemented in Fortran IV on a CDC 6600. Several sets of input data [5] were applied to test the optimality and time complexity of the algorithm.

A. Algorithmic Time Complexity

Using a BB method to find an optimum solution in the search tree is known to be an NP problem [10]. As m tasks are allocated into n processors, total number of enumerations (complete allocations) in the search tree is n^m. However, imposing a large number of constraints on the BB technique greatly reduces the feasible solution space. All enumerations are not necessary because the elimination rules eliminate infeasible solutions before the subtree expansion. As mentioned earlier, the preference matrix limits the candidate processors for each task. Let n_i be the number of 1's appeared in row i of the preference matrix, i.e., task i has n_i choices of possible allocation. The upper bound for algorithmic time is $\Pi_{i=1}^{m}(n_i)$ due to the elimination rule F. This upper bound can be further reduced by other elimination rules. If a branch from a node on level k is eliminated by any of these rules, $n^{(m-k)}$ complete allocations are pruned. For example, in Fig. 2 if branch P_2 from node 1 is eliminated, then $3^{3-1} = 9$ paths are eliminated.

Tasks	A-3		
	P_1	P_2	P_3
	2	8	1
	3	9	4
	13	20	5
	14	21	6
	17	23	7
	18		10
	19		16
			22

(a)

Tasks	A-4		
	P_1	P_2	P_3
	4	6	1
	5	8	2
	7	10	3
	9	16	22
	13	18	
	14	19	
	17	20	
	23	21	

(b)

Fig. 6. (a) Allocation to achieve load balance. (b) Allocation to achieve lower IPC cost.

TABLE IV
PERFORMANCE OF ALLOCATION *A*-3 AND *A*-4 AS MEASURED BY THE SIMULATOR

	A-3	A-4
PTP	PASS	PASS
CPU_1	45%	63%
CPU_2	53%	25%
CPU_3	42%	33%
IPC	236	114

Since pruning is heavily dependent on the input constraints, the lowest upper bound for the algorithm's run time has not been determined.

In the AD case study, the upper bound is $0(10^{10})$ iterations. Each iteration is equivalent to the checking of a branch for a node. Three different allocations *A*-2, *A*-3, and *A*-4 are made. The numbers of iterations required for *A*-2 and *A*-3 are each $0(10^3)$, and for *A*-4 is $0(10^4)$. The CDC 6600 computing power is $0(10^3)$ iterations/s.

B. Algorithm Optimality

Theoretically, the algorithm generates an optimum solution with respect to IPC cost. Several sets of input constraints with small upper bound for algorithm computation time were used to test the algorithm optimality [5]. This upper bound was less than 10^4 iterations for the selected inputs. The final solutions from these tests did provide the minimum IPC cost.

For practical applications with larger upper bound values the optimality is judged by the engineering requirements. Compare allocations *A*-3 and *A*-4, for instance. *A*-3 utilizes processors evenly and would be more suitable for a system which requires a high throughput. Allocation *A*-4 incurrs a smaller IPC cost, suggesting that it is a better solution for loosely-coupled distributed system whose IPC cost is high.

VI. CONCLUSION

The task allocation model presented was derived by using the BB technique. This model can accommodate a large number of constraints and hence is able to incorporate various engineering requirements. Load balance can be achieved by suitable control of model input parameters such as the preference matrix and exclusive matrix. The minimum cost solution is obtained by the model automatically within the constraints.

This model was applied to a large scale practical problem, the AD distributed processing system, and the resultant allocations were tested on the simulator. Results from the simulation indicate that the allocation generated by the model can achieve the multiple goals. Most allocation algorithms [1], [4], [7], [8] are limited to finding the minimum cost solution and/or seldom consider the complexities of constraints and multiple objectives of the practical system design problem.

Obviously, there is still a considerable gap between the engineering problem and the mathematical model. To fully exploit this allocation model, the following are being explored further.

1) Unit Value for Cost Function: Cost unit must be uniform. Cost function must represent both IPC and processing costs that are inherently different in their measurement units. One approach would be to assign weights that reflect the criticality of the costs to particular applications. This would enable the allocation model to incorporate tradeoffs between IPC cost and load balance.

2) Time Complexity: In general, to obtain an optimum solution by the BB technique is an NP problem. However, the constraints placed on the problem greatly reduce the time complexity. A better estimate of the lowest upper bound on time complexity needs to be determined from both the model inputs and the elimination rules.

3) Allocation Model Verification: The allocation results from the model must be validated by testing them either with actual implementation or with simulation. For obvious reasons the latter approach is preferred [14]. More flexible and powerful simulators are needed for this purpose. Currently, the simulator for the AD data processing system is being modified to increase the number of processors that can be simulated.

4) Application Dependence: The allocation model was designed to be a general purpose model. When a specific requirement exists in the application, it takes an engineering experience to tailor the inputs to the model. For example, in order to meet PTP time requirement, a designer must realize that any task should not wait too long in the waiting queue. Hence, the user of the model must translate this requirement into model inputs to achieve the effect of allocating large tasks to separate processors. How to properly identify all application requirements is thus an important research topic.

In order to provide more representative task attributes to the allocation model, some form of requirement engineering methodologies is needed. Currently, there are some research activities in the requirements engineering for distributed systems [15], but further work is necessary. With further progress in this area, the allocation model should prove to be a valuable tool for the design of distributed systems.

ACKNOWLEDGMENT

The authors wish to thank E. Swartzlander for his support as Project Manager of the Distributed Process Design Technology Development Program, and also the following people who worked on various segments of this project: M. L. Green, D. S. Shannon, and R. H. Hoffman developed and implemented the simulator; Y. Fukuda encoded the first version of the allocation algorithm; and H. Wang patiently typed the many versions of this paper.

REFERENCES

[1] V. B. Gylys and J. A. Edwards, "Optimal partitioning of workload for distributed systems," in *Dig. COMPCON Fall 1976*, 1976, pp. 353–357.

[2] W. W. Chu, "Introduction in the Special Issue on distributed processing systems," *IEEE Trans. Comput.*, vol. C-29, pp. 1037–1038, Dec. 1980.

[3] W. W. Chu, L. J. Holloway, M. Lan, and K. Efe, "Task allocation in distributed data processing," *Computer*, vol. 13, pp. 57–69, Nov. 1980.

[4] H. S. Stone, "Multiprocessor scheduling with the aid of network flow algorithm," *IEEE Trans. Software Eng.*, vol. SE-3, pp. 85–93, Jan. 1977.

[5] E. Y. S. Lee and P. Ma, "Final report of the distributed processing design technology development (DPDTD) program—Vol. II research results," TRW Defense Space Syst. Group, Mar. 1981.

[6] C. R. Vick, "A next generation of supercomputers: From mainframes to micros," presented at Euromicro 1980, London, England, Sept. 1980.

[7] B. W. Wah, "An efficient heuristic for file placement on distributed database," in *Proc. COMPSAC 1980*, Oct. 1980, pp. 462–468.

[8] C. C. Price, "The assignment of computational tasks among processors in a distributed system," in *Proc. Nat. Comput. Conf.*, May 1981, pp. 291–296.

[9] P. Chen and J. Akoka, "Optimal design of distributed information system," *IEEE Trans. Comput.*, vol. C-29, pp. 1068–1079, Dec. 1980.

[10] O. I. El-Dessouki and W. H. Huan, "Distributed enumeration on network computers," *IEEE Trans. Comput.*, vol. C-29, pp. 818–825, Sept. 1980.

[11] W. W. Chu, "Optimal file allocation in a multiple computing system," *IEEE Trans. Comput.*, vol. C-18, pp. 885–889, Oct. 1969.

[12] E. G. Coffman, Jr., Ed., *Computer and Job-Shop Scheduling Theory*. New York: Wiley, 1976.

[13] M. L. Green *et al.*, "The DDP underlay simulation experiment: Tactical applications and d-RTOS models," TRW Defense Space Syst. Group, May 1980.

[14] R. H. Hoffman, R. W. Smith, and J. T. Ellis, "Simulation software development for the BMDATC DDP underlay experiment," in *Proc. COMPSAC 1980*, Chicago, Oct. 1980, pp. 569–577.

[15] M. W. Alford, "A requirements engineering methodology for real-time processing requirements," *IEEE Trans. Software Eng.*, vol. SE-3, pp. 60–68, Jan. 1977.

Part III
Communication and Synchronization

AS is indicated by the title, this part will cover the separate but related topics of communication and synchronization for a distributed computer system.

K. J. Thurber's article "Computer Communication Techniques" provides an excellent introduction and analysis of intercomputer communication from an architectural point of view. This article was selected because it contains an excellent overview of the general communications concept and, moreover, because it defines many terms whose meanings are often assumed by other authors.

Following Thurber's introductory article are two articles which, despite the fact that they were both published in 1978, are near-classics in the field. They are "Time, Clocks, and the Ordering of Events in a Distributed System" and "Communicating Sequential Processes." These articles both stand by themselves and are two of the most important articles in this book.

Next is a set of five articles forming a solid foundation in the area of process synchronization and system deadlock. The articles are "System Deadlocks," "Prevention of System Deadlocks," "Avoiding Deadlock in Distributed Data Bases," "Locking and Deadlock Detection in Distributed Data Bases," and "The Exclusive-Writer Protocol: A Low Cost Approach for Updating Replicated Files in Distributed Real Time Systems."

Finally, this section is concluded with an article relevant to the maintenance of database integrity: "Analytic Models for Rollback and Recovery Strategies in Data Base Systems." Although this article does not specifically address distributed systems, it does act as a starting point for such research.

COMPUTER COMMUNICATION TECHNIQUES

Kenneth J. Thurber
Sperry Univac – St. Paul, Minnesota

INTRODUCTION

This paper will take a systems-oriented view of computer communication systems. It will begin with the examination of the concept and relationships of distributed systems and networks.

There are many and varied definitions of distributed systems. For purposes of this discussion we will use a simple definition with which a large number of researchers(1) tend to agree. A distributed system is defined to be a system in which a processing load is distributed across a number of processing elements (PES) which are physically interconnected, but allow varying amounts of software intercommunication. Research in the area of distributed processors is proceeding mainly in three areas: network systems(2), special-purpose systems(3), and high-performance, general-purpose systems(4).

There are three main architectural issues in the design of distributed processing systems:

1) Interprocess communication design,
2) Intercomputer communication system design, and
3) Application and system process partitioning and assignment(5).

Issue 1 (interprocess communication design) is a fairly well understood function since it has a strong background in the operating system works of Dijsktra, et al(6). Intercomputer communication design (Issue 2) is also a fairly well understood subject. In fact, some design techniques are amenable to categorization and the construction of classification schemes(7). The last issue (Issue 3, process partitioning) for general distributed processors has only recently begun to be developed and, as such, researchers are only beginning to be able to construct the vocabulary and terminology of identified design issues(5). The purpose of this paper is to explore the design issues involved with intercomputer communication design techniques as applied to distributed processing systems and networks (Issue 2).

Figure 1 gives a rudimentary description of our view of a distributed system. Since a distributed system has multiple processes allowed to run in it, the system may be viewed as a set of cooperating processes communicating over a communication network via a hierarchy of hardware and software protocols. Figure 1 indicates a simple view of the concept of distributed processing in which there are processing elements (hosts: host processing elements) which are communicating via a communication subnetwork. Both actual and virtual communication occurs in the system. A particular system may have more or less levels than shown in Figure 1.

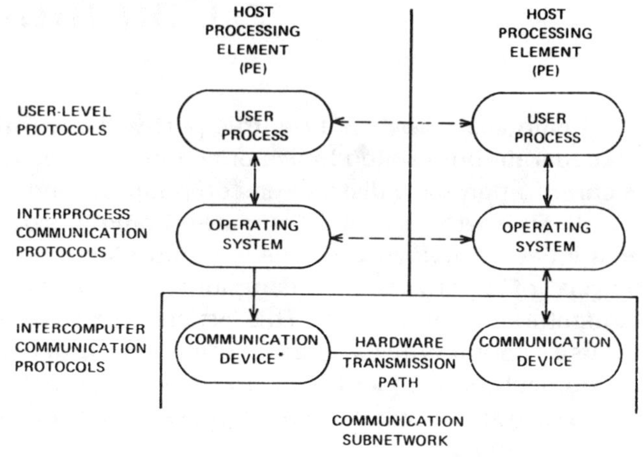

* DEPENDING ON THE SYSTEM THE COMMUNICATION DEVICE COULD BE A MESSAGE (PACKET) SWITCH, A CIRCUIT (CROSSBAR) SWITCH, OR A BUS STRUCTURE (I/O CHANNEL).

FIGURE 1. COMMUNICATION PROCESS MODEL

The Anderson(10) model is based upon three simple concepts:

Message	–	a unit of information transferred between processes executing on processors;
Path	–	The media over which information is transferred; e.g., bus, data link, etc.;
Switch	–	An intervening intelligent device which routes a message between a sender and a receiver.

Considering the consequences of the definitions, it can be seen that the communication of a message between process A and process B may be characterized as being either a direct communication over a path or an indirect communication through a switch in which some intervention occurs such as message routing or address transformation. Further, the switch could be either centralized or decentralized. These two design decisions represent system strategies. No distinction between message, packet, or circuit switching is necessary at this level as long as the reader understands that the communications level of protocol can be further broken down and that switches at the next lower level will actually switch some type of line and that level of detail is not necessary to understand the fundamental distributed system concepts. Anderson next suggests that two tactical decisions must be made: whether the transfer structure is to be dedicated or shared and the system topology. The resultant taxonomy is shown in Figure 2 with important extant system concepts indicated for the system architectures.

SYSTEM LEVEL ISSUES

A number of researchers have attempted to classify distributed systems(8, 9, 10). In the protocol hierarchy in Figure 1, the lowest level was the communications protocol. This section discusses a number of distributed system concepts based upon the Anderson/Jensen model for a taxonomy of distributed systems.

MESSAGES AND PACKET SWITCHING

In the previous section we discussed a number of system configurations useful for distributed processing which were derived based upon a communications view of system architecture. A number of the previous configurations fall into the category of system usually known as network(11, 12, 13, 14); i.e., loop (ring), star, and irregular network.

Reprinted from *Proc. 2nd IEEE COMPSAC,* 1978, pp. 589–594.

TRANSFER STRATEGY: DIRECT
PATH: DEDICATED
TOPOLOGY: DISTRIBUTED CONTROL LOOP
TOPOLOGY: COMPLETE INTERCONNECTION
PATH: SHARED
TOPOLOGY: COMMON MEMORY
TOPOLOGY: COMMON DISTRIBUTED CONTROL BUS
TRANSFER STRATEGY: INDIRECT
ROUTING: CENTRALIZED
PATH: DEDICATED
TOPOLOGY: STAR
TOPOLOGY: CENTRALLY CONTROLLED LOOP
PATH: SHARED
TOPOLOGY: COMMON CENTRALLY CONTROLLED BUS
ROUTING: DECENTRALIZED
PATH: DEDICATED
TOPOLOGY: REGULAR NETWORK
TOPOLOGY: IRREGULAR NETWORK
PATH: SHARED
TOPOLOGY: BUS WINDOW

FIGURE 2. TOPOLOGY TAXONOMY OF ANDERSON/JENSEN

A computer communications network (Figure 3) is a collection of host computers (that provide services to either another host or an end user) and a communications subnetwork that provides communication links between hosts, users, or both. One of the major justifications for networking is resource sharing (i.e., sharing of programs, data, and/or hardware resources). Other important justifications are the ability to provide capabilities for distributed processing and remote communications facilities. Sharing is very important particularly when unique resources are involved (i.e., ILLIAC IV on the ARPANET). Information in a network must be transmitted on some physical medium. A circuit is the physical path over which information is transmitted. A channel is the logical path over which connections are made between users, hosts, or hosts and users[A]. Circuits may be multiplexed to support several channels[15]. Also, a channel may be constructed using several circuits. Circuits represent physical interconnections of hardware. Channels represent logical or virtual interconnections which are constructed using circuits, but which interconnect functional entities (nodes, users, or nodes and users). Figure 3 shows a particular type of switch used to connect circuits known as a packet switch. Connections in distributed networks can be of two major types: broadcast and point-to-point. Broadcast communication subnetworks permit simultaneous transmission or reception to or from a variety of sources. Colliding information must be retransmitted. Broadcast techniques have been implemented in several systems (e.g., radio, coax and satellite). Point-to-point and multi-point communication techniques allow transmission and reception only between clearly defined host nodes. Multi-port techniques tend to be associated with "centralized networks" and thus we will ignore them. Example systems are copper wire, telephone network, and coaxial cables. There are three main switching techniques in use in communication subnetworks:[14]

1) Circuit Switching (CS)
2) Message Switching (MS)
3) Packet Switching (PS)

Further, variations on these three techniques are possible. TYMNET uses a virtual circuit switching scheme[16] and combined packet/circuit switch concepts have been proposed.

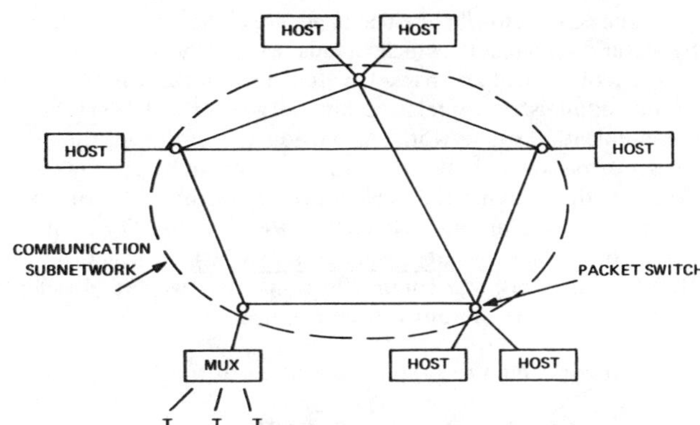

FIGURE 3. MODEL OF A RESOURCE SHARING COMPUTER NETWORK

A message may be defined as a logical unit of information; e.g., telegram or data record from a data file. In message switching techniques, a message is placed into the communications subnetwork. The subnetwork establishes a channel, the message is transmitted, and the channel is released. The main advantage of MS over circuit switching is increased circuit utilization. The main disadvantage of MS in comparison to CS is the facilities required to set up the MS environment. The MS subnetwork may be viewed as a collection of physical circuits interconnected via switches (stored program computers) which are used to store and forward individual messages. A message is routed between the source and destination via any available circuits. The MS system routes the message. Since a circuit may be involved in carrying traffic for any source destination pairs, MS may provide increased circuit utilization. Analysis of MS subnetworks is difficult because messages can vary in size. Kleinrock[17] has utilized queuing theory to model such systems.

Packet switching concepts attempt to solve the problems of variable-length messages in MS concepts by dividing a "message" into "packets." A packet is a subdivision of a message prefaced with an identifier containing suitable address information and information which will allow the message to be reconstructed. Importantly, packets are independent messages subdivisions which can make their own way through the network; i.e., packets can travel independently over different channels. Packet switching is important because it promises a way to provide effective support to many different types of message traffic simultaneously.

ARPANET is an example of an irregular distributed packet switched network. Within a resource-sharing computer network, it is most typical for the individual HOSTs to contain none of the software or hardware facilities required for managing the networks communication responsibility. All communication control resides within a unit typically termed the packet switch. This unit has been variously titled an IMP in the ARPANET, the Communications Computer in MERIT, the TAC in TELENET, or the Ring Interface in DCS. Regardless of its title, the packet switch is typically a dedicated minicomputer (or its functional equivalent) performing its operations independent of the associated HOSTs as indicated previously in Figure 3.

There are three major functional forms of a computer network:

1) RAN – Remote Access Networks
2) VAN – Value Added Networks
3) MON – Mission Oriented Networks[14]

The Kimbleton/Schneider paper raises an issue not discussed by earlier researchers which stands to greatly affect the future design requirements of packet switched networks. This is the issue of the administrative relationship between the HOSTs and the communication subnetwork. As previously mentioned, the original design of packet switches has proceeded on an independence relationship, thus forcing the packet switch design to conform to the existing HOST structure. There is, however, current interest in the design of mission oriented networks (MONs), in which both the HOST subnetwork and communication subnetwork are under the control of a single administrative organization.

Networks tend to support four levels of traffic:

1) **High Throughput Traffic (HTT),**
2) **Low Delay Traffic (LDT),**
3) **Real-Time Traffic (RTT), and**
4) **Guaranteed Bandwidth Traffic (GBT).**

These traffic types differ in their requirements for host-to-host delay, transmission rate, and reliability. The traffic types requirements are:

1) HTT (e.g., transmission of large data files) – transmission delay is relatively unimportant, throughput must be maximized, high reliability is required;

2) LDT (e.g., interactive computing transactions) – transmission delay must be minimized; throughput is relatively unimportant, high reliability is required;

3) RTT (e.g., digital speech transmission) – low delay; constant throughput should be a goal; reliability does not have to be high since redundant data can be sent, and;

4) GBT (e.g., digital speech transmission) – low delay, constant throughput must be guaranteed; reliability does not have to be high since redundant data is sent (late arriving data can thus be discarded).

Numerous good surveys relating to the responsibilities and trade-offs inherent in packet switch design have appeared in the literature, among them, Newport[18], Feinroth[19] and the recent Kimbleton/Schneider survey[14]. They all describe a set of communication responsibilities which lead to an organization similar to the structure of most current packet switches. The communication subsystems of the packet switch which have the specific responsibility of handling the above problems are usually termed the communications protocols. For reasons very similar to those raised within the context of structured programming, communication protocols are almost always multi-layered with each lower layer being entirely transparent to all higher level layers. Figure 4 gives a general organizational diagram of the relationship between these multiple levels of protocol. The lowest level protocols are related to supporting direct switch-to-switch communication along a physical circuit. These protocols are usually termed data link controls (DLC). The DLC addresses itself to the problems of handshaking, message and field synchronization, character vs binary transmission, error detection, and error correction. There have been numerous attempts to standardize the data link controls, but there is no single industry-wide standard in use. Currently popular DLCs include IBM's BISYNC and SDLC, ANSI DLC, and Digitals Equipment's DDCMP. Two excellent overviews of the entire area of data link controls can be found in references[20, 21]. This level

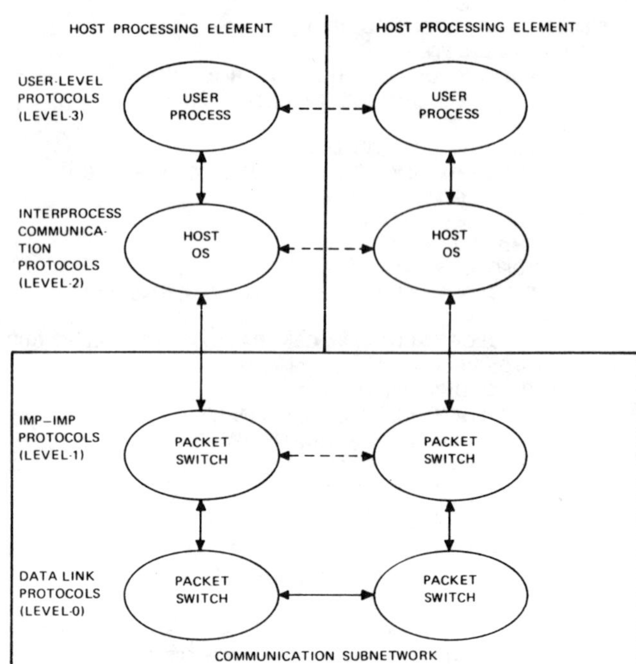

FIGURE 4. RELATIONSHIP BETWEEN MULTIPLE LEVELS OF PROTOCOL

of protocol is analogous to communication on a path and the system hardware exists between two packet switches.

The next level of protocol is concerned with establishing a logical (i.e., virtual) channel between the source and destination packet switches. This now involves us in the areas of routing, message assembly/disassembly, end-to-end acknowledgments and deadlock recovery procedures. These protocols have been termed the transmission protocols or IMP-IMP protocols, and are described in reference[22]. These protocols, along with the necessary conventions for handling the HOST-packet switch link, allow us to create a virtual channel between any pair of HOSTs. The level of protocol results due to the complexity of routing functions in a network of switches. This level of protocol is the highest level usually associated entirely with the communication problem.

The Interprocess Communication (IPC) Protocols are "the entire set of conventions whereby HOSTs operating systems establish, maintain, and terminate connections between user processes running on remote computers". The IPC protocol originally used by the ARPA network is described in reference[22].

Finally, the highest level protocols, or user-level protocols are concerned with such job-oriented directives as file transfers, remote job initiation, or the requesting of a network service. These last two levels of protocol are essentially independent of physical interconnect issues and are really the "logical" interconnect levels of the system. The remainder of this paper will concentrate on the design issues primarily associated with level 1 protocols for PS, CS and Bus-oriented systems. Level 0 design issues and concepts are briefly listed in the last section of this paper.

CIRCUIT SWITCHES

An interconnection switch is an arrangement of circuit switches. This section will deal with the functional aspects of interconnection switch design. Figure 5 indicates the application of interconnection networks into networks[14] and into a general distributed processor as previously defined. We will only deal with Level 1 issues in this section.

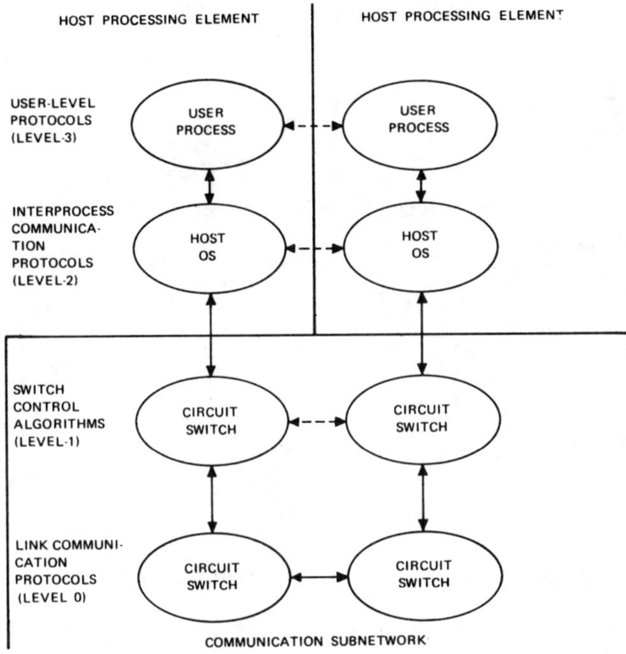

FIGURE 5. CIRCUIT SWITCH PROTOCOL LEVELS

The higher level protocols could be developed as described previously. The Level 0 issues are summarized in the last section of this paper.

First, we will describe how to build elementary circuit switches using TDM techniques. Secondly, we will describe how to build large interconnection networks which are composed of stages of cascaded elementary circuit switches. These elementary circuit switches could be conventional crossbar switches or TDM circuit switches. The reason that one eventually cascades such elementary circuit switches to form an interconnection networks is that a single circuit switch would eventually possess insufficient transmission bandwidth to adequately serve a channel as more and more channels are connected to a fixed bandwidth switch. The reason that one eventually cascades crossbar switches to former interconnection network is that crossbar switches grow as n^2, where n is the number of input lines. In some cases where speed is a major factor, designers have utilized multilevel, crossbar switch-based interconnection networks for small systems such as AN/USQ-67[23]. The AN/USQ-67 system is a 640 device by 640 device interconnection network designed to interconnect high-speed digital computers. The Bell Telephone System uses multistage interconnection networks that contain both crossbar switches and TDM-based circuit switches as elemental switches.[26]

The three main components of an interconnection network are: (1) circuits over which communication can take place; (2) input and output terminals to which devices are attached; (3) crossbar switches or time-division multiplexer circuit switches which can be "programmed" to interconnect the input and output terminals (in various specific connection conditions).

TDM circuit switches and crossbar switches of equal size are functionally equivalent. TDM circuit switches differ from crossbar circuit switches in that they sample inputs, store the samples in memory, and transmit the sample to the output terminals rather than providing a continuous connection between input and output terminals. Each TDM switch is time-shared among several channels.

The primary disadvantages of TDM circuit switches are:

1) Complex control
2) Large, high-speed memories may be required as buffers, and
3) High-speed switching logic may be required.

One of the major advantages of TDM circuit switches is the flexibility that results from the ability to reconfigure the switch every bit period. This eliminates the need for a great deal of redundant hardware to prevent blocking as in the crossbar switch case. Further, if the logic is fast enough and the memories are of sufficient size and speed, then a TDM circuit switch of very large size can be built quite simply.

A simple 4 input/4 output (4 x 4) TDM switch is illustrated in Figure 6. It is functionally equivalent to a unidirectional 4 input/4 output crossbar switch. A slightly different approach is to use a fixed, sequential multiplexer (serializer), route the data stream through a time slot interchanger, then into a sequential demultiplexer[24].

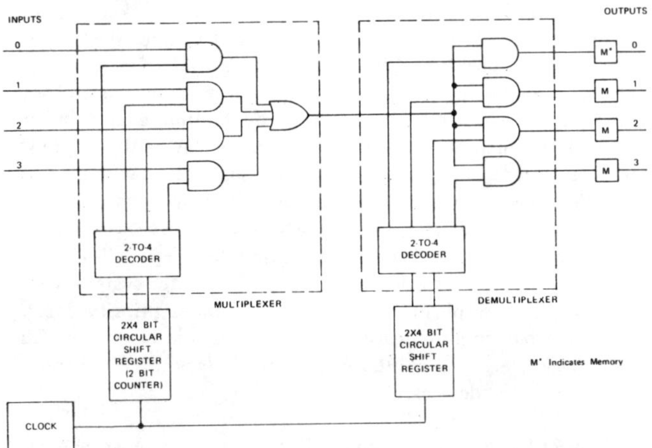

FIGURE 6. 4 X 4 TDM SWITCH

Successive decomposition of crossbar switches using a 3-stage switch model is the technique used to reduce the crosspoint count from n^2 to n log n. Thus to develop a theory of staged interconnection networks, we would use crossbar switch theory techniques; however, since functionally TDM and crossbar systems are identical, the designer could use either TDM or crossbar-based basic building blocks.

Figure 7 shows an asymmetrical 3-stage interconnection network. This network consists of two outside stages of rectangular networks called input switches and output switches, and an inner stage of rectangular networks called middle switches. If $n_1 = n_2$ and $r_1 = r_2$, the network is called a symmetrical 3-stage interconnection network.

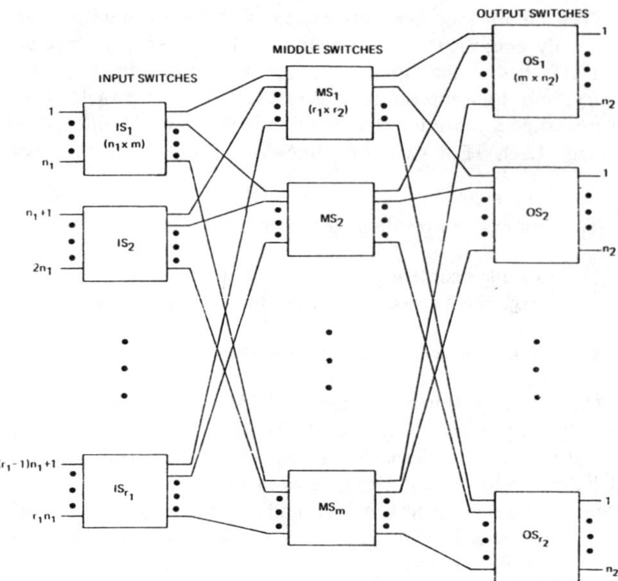

FIGURE 7. AN ASYMMETRICAL 3-STAGE CONNECTION NETWORK

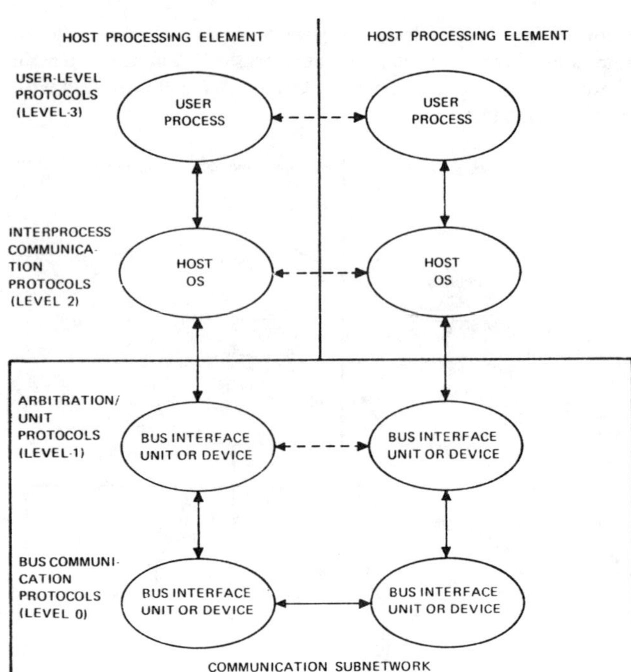

FIGURE 8. BUS SYSTEM PROTOCOL LEVELS

BUS STRUCTURES

One of the major issues involved with path-oriented systems is that of allocation of the path[25]. With systems of dedicated links, the control of the link may be worked out in advance and there is no dynamic control problem since there is no link contention problem. When the path is that of a memory, synchronization techniques such as semaphores, and test and set instructions are available to provide for mutual exclusion or control of the memory location. However, if the path is a bus, there is an interesting control problem. This section will address the problem of bus control and information transfer techniques on the bus. Figure 8 indicates a hierarchial model of the bus-oriented communication system. The bus allocation techniques described herein could be used in other areas of the computer system; e.g., they could be useful in the design of channel priority logic. Further, the bus communication techniques would also be useful in I/O design; e.g., fully interlocked request/acknowledge interfaces to peripheral devices.

When a bus is shared by multiple devices, there must be some method whereby bus usage is assigned and a particular unit is allowed to transmit data over the bus. The major problem in this area is resolution of bus usage conflicts so that only one unit obtains the bus at a given time. The different control schemes can be roughly classified as being either centralized or decentralized. If the hardware used for passing bus control from one device to another is largely concentrated in one location, it is referred to as centralized control. The location of the hardware could be within one of the devices which is connected to the bus, or it could be a separate hardware unit. On the other hand, if the bus control logic is largely distributed throughout the different devices connected to the bus, it is called decentralized control.

The basic concept of a bus is that there exists a set of shared lines over which communication takes place. Some of the lines are used for control and some of the lines are used for information transfer. Essentially, the bus operates in a 3-step cycle as follows:

1) Devices compete for allocation of the bus,
2) The selection device is connected to the bus, and
3) Information is transferred on the bus from one device to another[25].

LEVEL 0 ISSUES

This section will list a large number of these Level 0 considerations. The major Level 0 design issues include:

1) transmission direction and overlap.
2) transmission rate measurements,
3) modulation techniques,
4) multiplexing,
5) modems,
6) character assembly,
7) message assembly,
8) code standards,
9) DLC (Data Link Control) protocols, and
10) synchronous and asynchronous transmission circuitry requirements.

CONCLUSION

This paper has provided a brief summary introduction of computer communications from the architecture point of view. It describes a hierarchial, software system-oriented model of a distributed processor, discusses how that hierarchial model relates to Anderson's distributed system model and discusses the main forms of computer communication subnetwork design techniques.

REFERENCES

1. Computer, Special Issue on Computer Networks, November 1977.

2. Heart, F.E.; Kahn, R.E.; Ornstein, S.M. Crowther, W.R.; and Walden, D.C. "The interface message processor for the ARPA computer network." Proceedings of the SJCC, 1970

3. Thurber, K.J., Large Scale Computer Architecture: Parallel and Associative Processors Hayden, Rochelle Park, New Jersey, 1976.

4. Wulf, W.A. and C.G. Ball, "C.mmp: A multi-Mini-Processor," 1972 FJCC, pp. 765–777.

5. E.D. Jensen and W.E. Bobert, "Partitioning and Assignment of Distributed Processing Software," COMPCON '76 EAST.

6. Lorin, H., Parallelism in Hardware and Software: Real and Apparent Concurrency, Prentice Hall, Englewood Cliffs, New Jersey, 1972.

7. E.D. Jensen, K.J. Thurber, and G.M. Schneider, "A Review of Systematic Methods in Distributed Processor Interconnection," ICC 76.

8. Chen, R.C., Bus Communication Systems, University Microfilms Dissertation 74-20493, 1974.

9. Siewiorek, D.P. "Modularity and multi-microprocessor structures" Proceedings of the Seventh Annual Workshop on Microprogramming, October 1974.

10. Anderson, G.A.; and Jensen, E.D. "Computer interconnection: taxonomy; characteristics, and examples" ACM Computer Surveys, December 1975.

11. IEEE Transactions on Communications, Special Issue on Computer Communications, January 1977.

12. Computer, Special Issue on Computer Networks, November 1977.

13. W. Greene and U.W. Pooch, "A Review of Classification Schemes for Computer Communication Networks," Computer, November 1977.

14. Kimbleton, S.R.; and G.M. Schneider, "Computer Communication Networks: Approach, Objectives, and Performance Considerations" ACM Computing Surveys, September 1975.

15. Chu, W.W. "Asynchronous Time-Division Multiplexing Systems, in Computer-Communication Networks, (Norman Abramson and Franklin Kuo, Eds), Prentice-Hall, Englewood Cliffs, N.J., 1973, pp. 237-268.

16. Tymes, LaRoy. "Tymnet – A Terminal-Oriented Communication Network," 1971 SJCC.

17. Kleinrock, L. Queuing Systems, Volume I: Theory; and Queuing Systems, Volume II: Computer Applications, John Wiley & Sons, New York, 1975.

18. Frank, H.; Kahn, R.E.; and Kleinrock, L. "Computer Communication Network Design – Experiment with Theory and Practice," 1972 SJCC.

19. Newport, C.D.; and Ryzlak, J. "Communication Processor," Proceedings of the IEEE, November 1972.

20. Donnan, R.A.; and Kersey, J.R., "Synchronous Data Link Control: A perspective," IBM Syst Journal 13, 2 (1974).

21. Gray, J.P., "Line Control Procedures," Proceedings of the IEEE, November 1972.

22. Stutzman, B.W. "Data Communication Control Procedures," ACM Computing Surveys, December 1972.

23. Sperry Univac, AN/USQ-67 Converter-Switching System, Signal Data, PX 12233, June 1977.

24. M. Marcus, "Design for Time Slot Interchangers," NEC, 1970.

25. K.J. Thurber, E.D. Jensen, L.A. Jack, L.L. Kinney, P.C. Patton, and L.C. Anderson, "A Systematic Approach to the Design of Digital Busing Structures." Proceedings of the FJCC, 1972.

26. Masson, G.M., "O_μ Rearrangeable and Nonblocking Switching Networks," ICC '76.

Operating Systems

R. Stockton Gaines Editor

Time, Clocks, and the Ordering of Events in a Distributed System

Leslie Lamport
Massachusetts Computer Associates, Inc.

The concept of one event happening before another in a distributed system is examined, and is shown to define a partial ordering of the events. A distributed algorithm is given for synchronizing a system of logical clocks which can be used to totally order the events. The use of the total ordering is illustrated with a method for solving synchronization problems. The algorithm is then specialized for synchronizing physical clocks, and a bound is derived on how far out of synchrony the clocks can become.

Key Words and Phrases: distributed systems, computer networks, clock synchronization, multiprocess systems

CR Categories: 4.32, 5.29

Introduction

The concept of time is fundamental to our way of thinking. It is derived from the more basic concept of the order in which events occur. We say that something happened at 3:15 if it occurred *after* our clock read 3:15 and *before* it read 3:16. The concept of the temporal ordering of events pervades our thinking about systems. For example, in an airline reservation system we specify that a request for a reservation should be granted if it is made *before* the flight is filled. However, we will see that this concept must be carefully reexamined when considering events in a distributed system.

A distributed system consists of a collection of distinct processes which are spatially separated, and which communicate with one another by exchanging messages. A network of interconnected computers, such as the ARPA net, is a distributed system. A single computer can also be viewed as a distributed system in which the central control unit, the memory units, and the input-output channels are separate processes. A system is distributed if the message transmission delay is not negligible compared to the time between events in a single process.

We will concern ourselves primarily with systems of spatially separated computers. However, many of our remarks will apply more generally. In particular, a multiprocessing system on a single computer involves problems similar to those of a distributed system because of the unpredictable order in which certain events can occur.

In a distributed system, it is sometimes impossible to say that one of two events occurred first. The relation "happened before" is therefore only a partial ordering of the events in the system. We have found that problems often arise because people are not fully aware of this fact and its implications.

In this paper, we discuss the partial ordering defined by the "happened before" relation, and give a distributed algorithm for extending it to a consistent total ordering of all the events. This algorithm can provide a useful mechanism for implementing a distributed system. We illustrate its use with a simple method for solving synchronization problems. Unexpected, anomalous behavior can occur if the ordering obtained by this algorithm differs from that perceived by the user. This can be avoided by introducing real, physical clocks. We describe a simple method for synchronizing these clocks, and derive an upper bound on how far out of synchrony they can drift.

The Partial Ordering

Most people would probably say that an event a happened before an event b if a happened at an earlier time than b. They might justify this definition in terms of physical theories of time. However, if a system is to meet a specification correctly, then that specification must be given in terms of events observable within the system. If the specification is in terms of physical time, then the system must contain real clocks. Even if it does contain real clocks, there is still the problem that such clocks are not perfectly accurate and do not keep precise physical time. We will therefore define the "happened before" relation without using physical clocks.

We begin by defining our system more precisely. We assume that the system is composed of a collection of processes. Each process consists of a sequence of events. Depending upon the application, the execution of a subprogram on a computer could be one event, or the execution of a single machine instruction could be one

This work was supported by the Advanced Research Projects Agency of the Department of Defense and Rome Air Development Center. It was monitored by Rome Air Development Center under contract number F 30602-76-C-0094.

Author's address: Computer Science Laboratory, SRI International, 333 Ravenswood Ave., Menlo Park CA 94025.

Reprinted with permission from *Commun. Ass. Comput. Mach.*, vol. 21, pp. 558–565, July 1978.

Fig. 1.

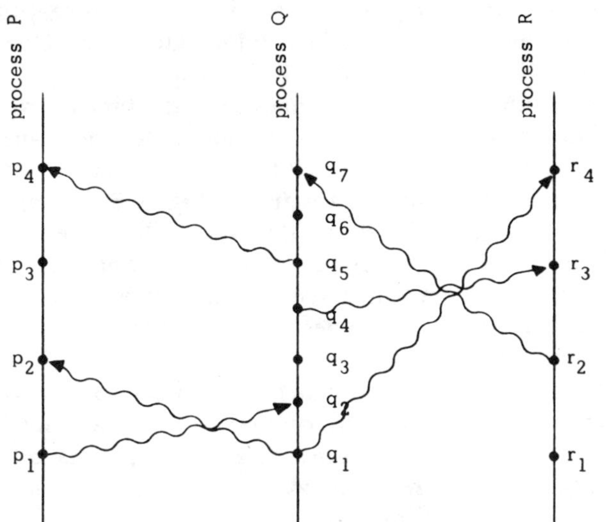

Fig. 2.

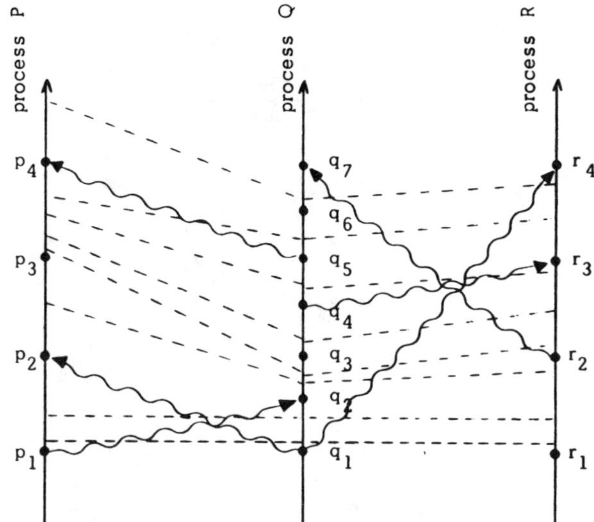

event. We are assuming that the events of a process form a sequence, where a occurs before b in this sequence if a happens before b. In other words, a single process is defined to be a set of events with an a priori total ordering. This seems to be what is generally meant by a process.[1] It would be trivial to extend our definition to allow a process to split into distinct subprocesses, but we will not bother to do so.

We assume that sending or receiving a message is an event in a process. We can then define the "happened before" relation, denoted by "$\rightarrow$", as follows.

Definition. The relation "$\rightarrow$" on the set of events of a system is the smallest relation satisfying the following three conditions: (1) If a and b are events in the same process, and a comes before b, then $a \rightarrow b$. (2) If a is the sending of a message by one process and b is the receipt of the same message by another process, then $a \rightarrow b$. (3) If $a \rightarrow b$ and $b \rightarrow c$ then $a \rightarrow c$. Two distinct events a and b are said to be *concurrent* if $a \not\rightarrow b$ and $b \not\rightarrow a$.

We assume that $a \not\rightarrow a$ for any event a. (Systems in which an event can happen before itself do not seem to be physically meaningful.) This implies that $\rightarrow$ is an irreflexive partial ordering on the set of all events in the system.

It is helpful to view this definition in terms of a "space-time diagram" such as Figure 1. The horizontal direction represents space, and the vertical direction represents time—later times being higher than earlier ones. The dots denote events, the vertical lines denote processes, and the wavy lines denote messages.[2] It is easy to see that $a \rightarrow b$ means that one can go from a to b in the diagram by moving forward in time along process and message lines. For example, we have $p_1 \rightarrow r_4$ in Figure 1.

Another way of viewing the definition is to say that $a \rightarrow b$ means that it is possible for event a to causally affect event b. Two events are concurrent if neither can causally affect the other. For example, events p_3 and q_3 of Figure 1 are concurrent. Even though we have drawn the diagram to imply that q_3 occurs at an earlier physical time than p_3, process P cannot know what process Q did at q_3 until it receives the message at p_4. (Before event p_4, P could at most know what Q was *planning* to do at q_3.)

This definition will appear quite natural to the reader familiar with the invariant space-time formulation of special relativity, as described for example in [1] or the first chapter of [2]. In relativity, the ordering of events is defined in terms of messages that *could* be sent. However, we have taken the more pragmatic approach of only considering messages that actually *are* sent. We should be able to determine if a system performed correctly by knowing only those events which *did* occur, without knowing which events *could* have occurred.

Logical Clocks

We now introduce clocks into the system. We begin with an abstract point of view in which a clock is just a way of assigning a number to an event, where the number is thought of as the time at which the event occurred. More precisely, we define a clock C_i for each process P_i to be a function which assigns a number $C_i\langle a \rangle$ to any event a in that process. The entire system of clocks is represented by the function C which assigns to any event b the number $C\langle b \rangle$, where $C\langle b \rangle = C_j\langle b \rangle$ if b is an event in process P_j. For now, we make no assumption about the relation of the numbers $C_i\langle a \rangle$ to physical time, so we can think of the clocks C_i as logical rather than physical clocks. They may be implemented by counters with no actual timing mechanism.

[1] The choice of what constitutes an event affects the ordering of events in a process. For example, the receipt of a message might denote the setting of an interrupt bit in a computer, or the execution of a subprogram to handle that interrupt. Since interrupts need not be handled in the order that they occur, this choice will affect the ordering of a process' message-receiving events.

[2] Observe that messages may be received out of order. We allow the sending of several messages to be a single event, but for convenience we will assume that the receipt of a single message does not coincide with the sending or receipt of any other message.

Fig. 3.

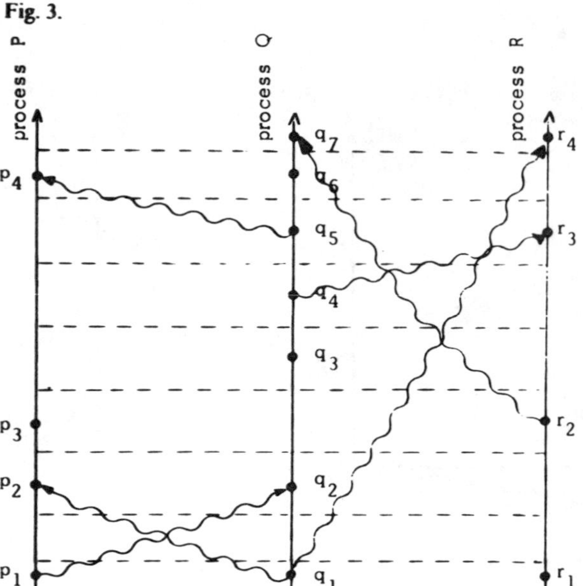

We now consider what it means for such a system of clocks to be correct. We cannot base our definition of correctness on physical time, since that would require introducing clocks which keep physical time. Our definition must be based on the order in which events occur. The strongest reasonable condition is that if an event a occurs before another event b, then a should happen at an earlier time than b. We state this condition more formally as follows.

Clock Condition. For any events a, b:

$$\text{if } a \rightarrow b \text{ then } C\langle a\rangle < C\langle b\rangle.$$

Note that we cannot expect the converse condition to hold as well, since that would imply that any two concurrent events must occur at the same time. In Figure 1, p_2 and p_3 are both concurrent with q_3, so this would mean that they both must occur at the same time as q_3, which would contradict the Clock Condition because $p_2 \rightarrow p_3$.

It is easy to see from our definition of the relation "$\rightarrow$" that the Clock Condition is satisfied if the following two conditions hold.

C1. If a and b are events in process P_i, and a comes before b, then $C_i\langle a\rangle < C_i\langle b\rangle$.

C2. If a is the sending of a message by process P_i and b is the receipt of that message by process P_j, then $C_i\langle a\rangle < C_j\langle b\rangle$.

Let us consider the clocks in terms of a space-time diagram. We imagine that a process' clock "ticks" through every number, with the ticks occurring between the process' events. For example, if a and b are consecutive events in process P_i with $C_i\langle a\rangle = 4$ and $C_i\langle b\rangle = 7$, then clock ticks 5, 6, and 7 occur between the two events. We draw a dashed "tick line" through all the like-numbered ticks of the different processes. The space-time diagram of Figure 1 might then yield the picture in Figure 2. Condition C1 means that there must be a tick line between any two events on a process line, and condition C2 means that every message line must cross a tick line. From the pictorial meaning of $\rightarrow$, it is easy to see why these two conditions imply the Clock Condition.

We can consider the tick lines to be the time coordinate lines of some Cartesian coordinate system on space-time. We can redraw Figure 2 to straighten these coordinate lines, thus obtaining Figure 3. Figure 3 is a valid alternate way of representing the same system of events as Figure 2. Without introducing the concept of physical time into the system (which requires introducing physical clocks), there is no way to decide which of these pictures is a better representation.

The reader may find it helpful to visualize a two-dimensional spatial network of processes, which yields a three-dimensional space-time diagram. Processes and messages are still represented by lines, but tick lines become two-dimensional surfaces.

Let us now assume that the processes are algorithms, and the events represent certain actions during their execution. We will show how to introduce clocks into the processes which satisfy the Clock Condition. Process P_i's clock is represented by a register C_i, so that $C_i\langle a\rangle$ is the value contained by C_i during the event a. The value of C_i will change between events, so changing C_i does not itself constitute an event.

To guarantee that the system of clocks satisfies the Clock Condition, we will insure that it satisfies conditions C1 and C2. Condition C1 is simple; the processes need only obey the following implementation rule:

IR1. Each process P_i increments C_i between any two successive events.

To meet condition C2, we require that each message m contain a *timestamp* T_m which equals the time at which the message was sent. Upon receiving a message timestamped T_m, a process must advance its clock to be later than T_m. More precisely, we have the following rule.

IR2. (a) If event a is the sending of a message m by process P_i, then the message m contains a timestamp $T_m = C_i\langle a\rangle$. (b) Upon receiving a message m, process P_j sets C_j greater than or equal to its present value and greater than T_m.

In IR2(b) we consider the event which represents the receipt of the message m to occur after the setting of C_j. (This is just a notational nuisance, and is irrelevant in any actual implementation.) Obviously, IR2 insures that C2 is satisfied. Hence, the simple implementation rules IR1 and IR2 imply that the Clock Condition is satisfied, so they guarantee a correct system of logical clocks.

Ordering the Events Totally

We can use a system of clocks satisfying the Clock Condition to place a total ordering on the set of all system events. We simply order the events by the times at which they occur. To break ties, we use any arbitrary total ordering $\prec$ of the processes. More precisely, we define a relation $\Rightarrow$ as follows: if a is an event in process P_i and b is an event in process P_j, then $a \Rightarrow b$ if and only if either (i) $C_i\langle a\rangle < C_j\langle b\rangle$ or (ii) $C_i\langle a\rangle = C_j\langle b\rangle$ and $P_i \prec P_j$. It is easy to see that this defines a total ordering, and that the Clock Condition implies that if $a \rightarrow b$ then $a \Rightarrow b$. In other words, the relation $\Rightarrow$ is a way of completing the "happened before" partial ordering to a total ordering.[3]

The ordering $\Rightarrow$ depends upon the system of clocks C_i, and is not unique. Different choices of clocks which satisfy the Clock Condition yield different relations $\Rightarrow$. Given any total ordering relation $\Rightarrow$ which extends $\rightarrow$, there is a system of clocks satisfying the Clock Condition which yields that relation. It is only the partial ordering $\rightarrow$ which is uniquely determined by the system of events.

Being able to totally order the events can be very useful in implementing a distributed system. In fact, the reason for implementing a correct system of logical clocks is to obtain such a total ordering. We will illustrate the use of this total ordering of events by solving the following version of the mutual exclusion problem. Consider a system composed of a fixed collection of processes which share a single resource. Only one process can use the resource at a time, so the processes must synchronize themselves to avoid conflict. We wish to find an algorithm for granting the resource to a process which satisfies the following three conditions: (I) A process which has been granted the resource must release it before it can be granted to another process. (II) Different requests for the resource must be granted in the order in which they are made. (III) If every process which is granted the resource eventually releases it, then every request is eventually granted.

We assume that the resource is initially granted to exactly one process.

These are perfectly natural requirements. They precisely specify what it means for a solution to be correct.[4] Observe how the conditions involve the ordering of events. Condition II says nothing about which of two concurrently issued requests should be granted first.

It is important to realize that this is a nontrivial problem. Using a central scheduling process which grants requests in the order they are received will not work, unless additional assumptions are made. To see this, let P_0 be the scheduling process. Suppose P_1 sends a request to P_0 and then sends a message to P_2. Upon receiving the latter message, P_2 sends a request to P_0. It is possible for P_2's request to reach P_0 before P_1's request does. Condition II is then violated if P_2's request is granted first.

To solve the problem, we implement a system of clocks with rules IR1 and IR2, and use them to define a total ordering $\Rightarrow$ of all events. This provides a total ordering of all request and release operations. With this ordering, finding a solution becomes a straightforward exercise. It just involves making sure that each process learns about all other processes' operations.

To simplify the problem, we make some assumptions. They are not essential, but they are introduced to avoid distracting implementation details. We assume first of all that for any two processes P_i and P_j, the messages sent from P_i to P_j are received in the same order as they are sent. Moreover, we assume that every message is eventually received. (These assumptions can be avoided by introducing message numbers and message acknowledgment protocols.) We also assume that a process can send messages directly to every other process.

Each process maintains its own *request queue* which is never seen by any other process. We assume that the request queues initially contain the single message T_0:P_0 *requests resource*, where P_0 is the process initially granted the resource and T_0 is less than the initial value of any clock.

The algorithm is then defined by the following five rules. For convenience, the actions defined by each rule are assumed to form a single event.

1. To request the resource, process P_i sends the message T_m:P_i *requests resource* to every other process, and puts that message on its request queue, where T_m is the timestamp of the message.
2. When process P_j receives the message T_m:P_i *requests resource*, it places it on its request queue and sends a (timestamped) acknowledgment message to P_i.[5]
3. To release the resource, process P_i removes any T_m:P_i *requests resource* message from its request queue and sends a (timestamped) P_i *releases resource* message to every other process.
4. When process P_j receives a P_i *releases resource* message, it removes any T_m:P_i *requests resource* message from its request queue.
5. Process P_i is granted the resource when the following two conditions are satisfied: (i) There is a T_m:P_i *requests resource* message in its request queue which is ordered before any other request in its queue by the relation $\Rightarrow$. (To define the relation "$\Rightarrow$" for messages, we identify a message with the event of sending it.) (ii) P_i has received a message from every other process timestamped later than T_m.[6]

Note that conditions (i) and (ii) of rule 5 are tested locally by P_i.

It is easy to verify that the algorithm defined by these rules satisfies conditions I–III. First of all, observe that condition (ii) of rule 5, together with the assumption that messages are received in order, guarantees that P_i has learned about all requests which preceded its current

[3] The ordering $\prec$ establishes a priority among the processes. If a "fairer" method is desired, then $\prec$ can be made a function of the clock value. For example, if $C_i\langle a\rangle = C_j\langle b\rangle$ and $j < i$, then we can let $a \Rightarrow b$ if $j < C_i\langle a\rangle \bmod N \leq i$, and $b \Rightarrow a$ otherwise; where N is the total number of processes.

[4] The term "eventually" should be made precise, but that would require too long a diversion from our main topic.

[5] This acknowledgment message need not be sent if P_j has already sent a message to P_i timestamped later than T_m.

[6] If $P_i \prec P_j$, then P_i need only have received a message timestamped $\geq T_m$ from P_j.

request. Since rules 3 and 4 are the only ones which delete messages from the request queue, it is then easy to see that condition I holds. Condition II follows from the fact that the total ordering $\Rightarrow$ extends the partial ordering $\rightarrow$. Rule 2 guarantees that after P_i requests the resource, condition (ii) of rule 5 will eventually hold. Rules 3 and 4 imply that if each process which is granted the resource eventually releases it, then condition (i) of rule 5 will eventually hold, thus proving condition III.

This is a distributed algorithm. Each process independently follows these rules, and there is no central synchronizing process or central storage. This approach can be generalized to implement any desired synchronization for such a distributed multiprocess system. The synchronization is specified in terms of a *State Machine*, consisting of a set C of possible commands, a set S of possible states, and a function $e: C \times S \rightarrow S$. The relation $e(C, S) = S'$ means that executing the command C with the machine in state S causes the machine state to change to S'. In our example, the set C consists of all the commands P_i *requests resource* and P_i *releases resource*, and the state consists of a queue of waiting *request* commands, where the request at the head of the queue is the currently granted one. Executing a *request* command adds the request to the tail of the queue, and executing a *release* command removes a command from the queue.[7]

Each process independently simulates the execution of the State Machine, using the commands issued by all the processes. Synchronization is achieved because all processes order the commands according to their timestamps (using the relation $\Rightarrow$), so each process uses the same sequence of commands. A process can execute a command timestamped T when it has learned of all commands issued by all other processes with timestamps less than or equal to T. The precise algorithm is straightforward, and we will not bother to describe it.

This method allows one to implement any desired form of multiprocess synchronization in a distributed system. However, the resulting algorithm requires the active participation of all the processes. A process must know all the commands issued by other processes, so that the failure of a single process will make it impossible for any other process to execute State Machine commands, thereby halting the system.

The problem of failure is a difficult one, and it is beyond the scope of this paper to discuss it in any detail. We will just observe that the entire concept of failure is only meaningful in the context of physical time. Without physical time, there is no way to distinguish a failed process from one which is just pausing between events. A user can tell that a system has "crashed" only because he has been waiting too long for a response. A method which works despite the failure of individual processes or communication lines is described in [3].

[7] If each process does not strictly alternate *request* and *release* commands, then executing a *release* command could delete zero, one, or more than one request from the queue.

Anomalous Behavior

Our resource scheduling algorithm ordered the requests according to the total ordering $\Rightarrow$. This permits the following type of "anomalous behavior." Consider a nationwide system of interconnected computers. Suppose a person issues a request A on a computer A, and then telephones a friend in another city to have him issue a request B on a different computer B. It is quite possible for request B to receive a lower timestamp and be ordered before request A. This can happen because the system has no way of knowing that A actually preceded B, since that precedence information is based on messages external to the system.

Let us examine the source of the problem more closely. Let $\mathscr{S}$ be the set of all system events. Let us introduce a set of events which contains the events in $\mathscr{S}$ together with all other relevant external events, such as the phone calls in our example. Let $\boldsymbol{\rightarrow}$ denote the "happened before" relation for $\underline{\mathscr{S}}$. In our example, we had A $\boldsymbol{\rightarrow}$ B, but A $\not\rightarrow$ B. It is obvious that no algorithm based entirely upon events in $\mathscr{S}$, and which does not relate those events in any way with the other events in $\underline{\mathscr{S}}$, can guarantee that request A is ordered before request B.

There are two possible ways to avoid such anomalous behavior. The first way is to explicitly introduce into the system the necessary information about the ordering $\boldsymbol{\rightarrow}$. In our example, the person issuing request A could receive the timestamp T_A of that request from the system. When issuing request B, his friend could specify that B be given a timestamp later than T_A. This gives the user the responsibility for avoiding anomalous behavior.

The second approach is to construct a system of clocks which satisfies the following condition.

Strong Clock Condition. For any events a, b in $\underline{\mathscr{S}}$: if $a \boldsymbol{\rightarrow} b$ then $C\langle a\rangle < C\langle b\rangle$.

This is stronger than the ordinary Clock Condition because $\boldsymbol{\rightarrow}$ is a stronger relation than $\rightarrow$. It is not in general satisfied by our logical clocks.

Let us identify $\underline{\mathscr{S}}$ with some set of "real" events in physical space-time, and let $\boldsymbol{\rightarrow}$ be the partial ordering of events defined by special relativity. One of the mysteries of the universe is that it is possible to construct a system of physical clocks which, running quite independently of one another, will satisfy the Strong Clock Condition. We can therefore use physical clocks to eliminate anomalous behavior. We now turn our attention to such clocks.

Physical Clocks

Let us introduce a physical time coordinate into our space-time picture, and let $C_i(t)$ denote the reading of the clock C_i at physical time t.[8] For mathematical con-

[8] We will assume a Newtonian space-time. If the relative motion of the clocks or gravitational effects are not negligible, then $C_i(t)$ must be deduced from the actual clock reading by transforming from proper time to the arbitrarily chosen time coordinate.

venience, we assume that the clocks run continuously rather than in discrete "ticks." (A discrete clock can be thought of as a continuous one in which there is an error of up to $\frac{1}{2}$ "tick" in reading it.) More precisely, we assume that $C_i(t)$ is a continuous, differentiable function of t except for isolated jump discontinuities where the clock is reset. Then $dC_i(t)/dt$ represents the rate at which the clock is running at time t.

In order for the clock C_i to be a true physical clock, it must run at approximately the correct rate. That is, we must have $dC_i(t)/dt \approx 1$ for all t. More precisely, we will assume that the following condition is satisfied:

PC1. There exists a constant $\kappa \ll 1$ such that for all i: $|dC_i(t)/dt - 1| < \kappa$.

For typical crystal controlled clocks, $\kappa \leq 10^{-6}$.

It is not enough for the clocks individually to run at approximately the correct rate. They must be synchronized so that $C_i(t) \approx C_j(t)$ for all i, j, and t. More precisely, there must be a sufficiently small constant ϵ so that the following condition holds:

PC2. For all i, j: $|C_i(t) - C_j(t)| < \epsilon$.

If we consider vertical distance in Figure 2 to represent physical time, then PC2 states that the variation in height of a single tick line is less than ϵ.

Since two different clocks will never run at exactly the same rate, they will tend to drift further and further apart. We must therefore devise an algorithm to insure that PC2 always holds. First, however, let us examine how small κ and ϵ must be to prevent anomalous behavior. We must insure that the system $\mathcal{S}$ of relevant physical events satisfies the Strong Clock Condition. We assume that our clocks satisfy the ordinary Clock Condition, so we need only require that the Strong Clock Condition holds when a and b are events in $\mathcal{S}$ with $a \not\rightarrow b$. Hence, we need only consider events occurring in different processes.

Let μ be a number such that if event a occurs at physical time t and event b in another process satisfies $a \rightarrow b$, then b occurs later than physical time $t + \mu$. In other words, μ is less than the shortest transmission time for interprocess messages. We can always choose μ equal to the shortest distance between processes divided by the speed of light. However, depending upon how messages in $\mathcal{S}$ are transmitted, μ could be significantly larger.

To avoid anomalous behavior, we must make sure that for any i, j, and t: $C_i(t + \mu) - C_j(t) > 0$. Combining this with PC1 and 2 allows us to relate the required smallness of κ and ϵ to the value of μ as follows. We assume that when a clock is reset, it is always set forward and never back. (Setting it back could cause C1 to be violated.) PC1 then implies that $C_i(t + \mu) - C_i(t) > (1 - \kappa)\mu$. Using PC2, it is then easy to deduce that $C_i(t + \mu) - C_j(t) > 0$ if the following inequality holds:

$$\epsilon/(1 - \kappa) \leq \mu.$$

This inequality together with PC1 and PC2 implies that anomalous behavior is impossible.

We now describe our algorithm for insuring that PC2 holds. Let m be a message which is sent at physical time t and received at time t'. We define $\nu_m = t' - t$ to be the *total delay* of the message m. This delay will, of course, not be known to the process which receives m. However, we assume that the receiving process knows some *minimum delay* $\mu_m \geq 0$ such that $\mu_m \leq \nu_m$. We call $\xi_m = \nu_m - \mu_m$ the *unpredictable delay* of the message.

We now specialize rules IR1 and 2 for our physical clocks as follows:

IR1′. For each i, if P_i does not receive a message at physical time t, then C_i is differentiable at t and $dC_i(t)/dt > 0$.

IR2′. (a) If P_i sends a message m at physical time t, then m contains a timestamp $T_m = C_i(t)$. (b) Upon receiving a message m at time t', process P_j sets $C_j(t')$ equal to maximum $(C_j(t' - 0), T_m + \mu_m)$.[9]

Although the rules are formally specified in terms of the physical time parameter, a process only needs to know its own clock reading and the timestamps of messages it receives. For mathematical convenience, we are assuming that each event occurs at a precise instant of physical time, and different events in the same process occur at different times. These rules are then specializations of rules IR1 and IR2, so our system of clocks satisfies the Clock Condition. The fact that real events have a finite duration causes no difficulty in implementing the algorithm. The only real concern in the implementation is making sure that the discrete clock ticks are frequent enough so C1 is maintained.

We now show that this clock synchronizing algorithm can be used to satisfy condition PC2. We assume that the system of processes is described by a directed graph in which an arc from process P_i to process P_j represents a communication line over which messages are sent directly from P_i to P_j. We say that a message is sent over this arc every τ seconds if for any t, P_i sends at least one message to P_j between physical times t and $t + \tau$. The *diameter* of the directed graph is the smallest number d such that for any pair of distinct processes P_j, P_k, there is a path from P_j to P_k having at most d arcs.

In addition to establishing PC2, the following theorem bounds the length of time it can take the clocks to become synchronized when the system is first started.

THEOREM. Assume a strongly connected graph of processes with diameter d which always obeys rules IR1′ and IR2′. Assume that for any message m, $\mu_m \leq \mu$ for some constant μ, and that for all $t \geq t_0$: (a) PC1 holds. (b) There are constants τ and ξ such that every τ seconds a message with an unpredictable delay less than ξ is sent over every arc. Then PC2 is satisfied with $\epsilon \approx d(2\kappa\tau + \xi)$ for all $t \gtrsim t_0 + \tau d$, where the approximations assume $\mu + \xi \ll \tau$.

The proof of this theorem is surprisingly difficult, and is given in the Appendix. There has been a great deal of work done on the problem of synchronizing physical clocks. We refer the reader to [4] for an intro-

[9] $C_j(t' - 0) = \lim_{\delta \to 0} C_j(t' - |\delta|)$.

duction to the subject. The methods described in the literature are useful for estimating the message delays μ_m and for adjusting the clock frequencies dC_i/dt (for clocks which permit such an adjustment). However, the requirement that clocks are never set backwards seems to distinguish our situation from ones previously studied, and we believe this theorem to be a new result.

Conclusion

We have seen that the concept of "happening before" defines an invariant partial ordering of the events in a distributed multiprocess system. We described an algorithm for extending that partial ordering to a somewhat arbitrary total ordering, and showed how this total ordering can be used to solve a simple synchronization problem. A future paper will show how this approach can be extended to solve any synchronization problem.

The total ordering defined by the algorithm is somewhat arbitrary. It can produce anomalous behavior if it disagrees with the ordering perceived by the system's users. This can be prevented by the use of properly synchronized physical clocks. Our theorem showed how closely the clocks can be synchronized.

In a distributed system, it is important to realize that the order in which events occur is only a partial ordering. We believe that this idea is useful in understanding any multiprocess system. It should help one to understand the basic problems of multiprocessing independently of the mechanisms used to solve them.

Appendix

Proof of the Theorem

For any i and t, let us define C_i^t to be a clock which is set equal to C_i at time t and runs at the same rate as C_i, but is never reset. In other words,

$$C_i^t(t') = C_i(t) + \int_t^{t'} [dC_i(t)/dt]dt \tag{1}$$

for all $t' \geq t$. Note that

$$C_i(t') \geq C_i^t(t') \text{ for all } t' \geq t. \tag{2}$$

Suppose process P_1 at time t_1 sends a message to process P_2 which is received at time t_2 with an unpredictable delay $\leq \xi$, where $t_0 \leq t_1 \leq t_2$. Then for all $t \geq t_2$ we have:

$$\begin{aligned} C_2^{t_2}(t) &\geq C_2^{t_2}(t_2) + (1-\kappa)(t-t_2) && \text{[by (1) and PC1]} \\ &\geq C_1(t_1) + \mu_m + (1-\kappa)(t-t_2) && \text{[by IR2' (b)]} \\ &= C_1(t_1) + (1-\kappa)(t-t_1) - [(t_2-t_1)-\mu_m] + \kappa(t_2-t_1) \\ &\geq C_1(t_1) + (1-\kappa)(t-t_1) - \xi. \end{aligned}$$

Hence, with these assumptions, for all $t \geq t_2$ we have:

$$C_2^{t_2}(t) \geq C_1(t_1) + (1-\kappa)(t-t_1) - \xi. \tag{3}$$

Now suppose that for $i = 1, \ldots, n$ we have $t_i \leq t_i' < t_{i+1}$, $t_0 \leq t_1$, and that at time t_i' process P_i sends a message to process P_{i+1} which is received at time t_{i+1} with an unpredictable delay less than ξ. Then repeated application of the inequality (3) yields the following result for $t \geq t_{n+1}$.

$$C_{n+1}^{t_{n+1}}(t) \geq C_1(t_1') + (1-\kappa)(t-t_1') - n\xi. \tag{4}$$

From PC1, IR1' and 2' we deduce that

$$C_1(t_1') \geq C_1(t_1) + (1-\kappa)(t_1'-t_1).$$

Combining this with (4) and using (2), we get

$$C_{n+1}(t) \geq C_1(t_1) + (1-\kappa)(t-t_1) - n\xi \tag{5}$$

for $t \geq t_{n+1}$.

For any two processes P and P', we can find a sequence of processes $P = P_0, P_1, \ldots, P_{n+1} = P'$, $n \leq d$, with communication arcs from each P_i to P_{i+1}. By hypothesis (b) we can find times t_i, t_i' with $t_i' - t_i \leq \tau$ and $t_{i+1} - t_i' \leq \nu$, where $\nu = \mu + \xi$. Hence, an inequality of the form (5) holds with $n \leq d$ whenever $t \geq t_1 + d(\tau + \nu)$. For any i, j and any t, t_1 with $t_1 \geq t_0$ and $t \geq t_1 + d(\tau + \nu)$ we therefore have:

$$C_i(t) \geq C_j(t_1) + (1-\kappa)(t-t_1) - d\xi. \tag{6}$$

Now let m be any message timestamped T_m, and suppose it is sent at time t and received at time t'. We pretend that m has a clock C_m which runs at a constant rate such that $C_m(t) = t_m$ and $C_m(t') = t_m + \mu_m$. Then $\mu_m \leq t' - t$ implies that $dC_m/dt \leq 1$. Rule IR2' (b) simply sets $C_j(t')$ to *maximum* $(C_j(t'-0), C_m(t'))$. Hence, clocks are reset only by setting them equal to other clocks.

For any time $t_x \geq t_0 + \mu/(1-\kappa)$, let C_x be the clock having the largest value at time t_x. Since all clocks run at a rate less than $1 + \kappa$, we have for all i and all $t \geq t_x$:

$$C_i(t) \leq C_x(t_x) + (1+\kappa)(t-t_x). \tag{7}$$

We now consider the following two cases: (i) C_x is the clock C_q of process P_q. (ii) C_x is the clock C_m of a message sent at time t_1 by process P_q. In case (i), (7) simply becomes

$$C_i(t) \leq C_q(t_x) + (1+\kappa)(t-t_x). \tag{8i}$$

In case (ii), since $C_m(t_1) = C_q(t_1)$ and $dC_m/dt \leq 1$, we have

$$C_x(t_x) \leq C_q(t_1) + (t_x - t_1).$$

Hence, (7) yields

$$C_i(t) \leq C_q(t_1) + (1+\kappa)(t-t_1). \tag{8ii}$$

Since $t_x \geq t_0 + \mu/(1-\kappa)$, we get

$$\begin{aligned} C_q(t_x - \mu/(1-\kappa)) &\leq C_q(t_x) - \mu && \text{[by PC1]} \\ &\leq C_m(t_x) - \mu && \text{[by choice of } m\text{]} \\ &\leq C_m(t_x) - (t_x - t_1)\mu_m/\nu_m && [\mu_m \leq \mu,\ t_x - t_1 \leq \nu_m] \\ &= T_m && \text{[by definition of } C_m\text{]} \\ &= C_q(t_1) && \text{[by IR2'(a)].} \end{aligned}$$

Hence, $C_q(t_x - \mu/(1-\kappa)) \leq C_q(t_1)$, so $t_x - t_1 \leq \mu/(1-\kappa)$ and thus $t_1 \geq t_0$.

Letting $t_1 = t_x$ in case (i), we can combine (8i) and (8ii) to deduce that for any t, t_x with $t \geq t_x \geq t_0 + \mu/(1 - \kappa)$ there is a process P_q and a time t_1 with $t_x - \mu/(1 - \kappa) \leq t_1 \leq t_x$ such that for all i:

$$C_i(t) \leq C_q(t_1) + (1 + \kappa)(t - t_1). \tag{9}$$

Choosing t and t_x with $t \geq t_x + d(\tau + \nu)$, we can combine (6) and (9) to conclude that there exists a t_1 and a process P_q such that for all i:

$$\begin{aligned} C_q(t_1) + (1 - \kappa)(t - t_1) - d\xi \leq C_i(t) \\ \leq C_q(t_1) + (1 + \kappa)(t - t_1) \end{aligned} \tag{10}$$

Letting $t = t_x + d(\tau + \nu)$, we get

$$d(\tau + \nu) \leq t - t_1 \leq d(\tau + \nu) + \mu/(1 - \kappa).$$

Combining this with (10), we get

$$\begin{aligned} C_q(t_1) + (t - t_1) - \kappa d(\tau + \nu) - d\xi \leq C_i(t) \leq C_q(t_1) \\ + (t - t_1) + \kappa[d(\tau + \nu) + \mu/(1 - \kappa)] \end{aligned} \tag{11}$$

Using the hypotheses that $\kappa \ll 1$ and $\mu \leq \nu \ll \tau$, we can rewrite (11) as the following approximate inequality.

$$\begin{aligned} C_q(t_1) + (t - t_1) - d(\kappa\tau + \xi) \lesssim C_i(t) \\ \lesssim C_q(t_1) + (t - t_1) + d\kappa\tau. \end{aligned} \tag{12}$$

Since this holds for all i, we get

$$|C_i(t) - C_j(t)| \lesssim d(2\kappa\tau + \xi),$$

and this holds for all $t \gtrsim t_0 + d\tau$. □

Note that relation (11) of the proof yields an exact upper bound for $|C_i(t) - C_j(t)|$ in case the assumption $\mu + \xi \ll \tau$ is invalid. An examination of the proof suggests a simple method for rapidly initializing the clocks, or resynchronizing them if they should go out of synchrony for any reason. Each process sends a message which is relayed to every other process. The procedure can be initiated by any process, and requires less than $2d(\mu + \xi)$ seconds to effect the synchronization, assuming each of the messages has an unpredictable delay less than ξ.

Acknowledgment. The use of timestamps to order operations, and the concept of anomalous behavior are due to Paul Johnson and Robert Thomas.

Received March 1976; revised October 1977

References

1. Schwartz, J.T. *Relativity in Illustrations.* New York U. Press, New York, 1962.
2. Taylor, E.F., and Wheeler, J.A. *Space-Time Physics,* W.H. Freeman, San Francisco, 1966.
3. Lamport, L. The implementation of reliable distributed multiprocess systems. To appear in *Computer Networks.*
4. Ellingson, C., and Kulpinski, R.J. Dissemination of system-time. *IEEE Trans. Comm. Com-23,* 5 (May 1973), 605–624.

Programming Techniques

S. L. Graham, R. L. Rivest Editors

Communicating Sequential Processes

C.A.R. Hoare
The Queen's University
Belfast, Northern Ireland

This paper suggests that input and output are basic primitives of programming and that parallel composition of communicating sequential processes is a fundamental program structuring method. When combined with a development of Dijkstra's guarded command, these concepts are surprisingly versatile. Their use is illustrated by sample solutions of a variety of familiar programming exercises.

Key Words and Phrases: programming, programming languages, programming primitives, program structures, parallel programming, concurrency, input, output, guarded commands, nondeterminacy, coroutines, procedures, multiple entries, multiple exits, classes, data representations, recursion, conditional critical regions, monitors, iterative arrays

CR Categories: 4.20, 4.22, 4.32

1. Introduction

Among the primitive concepts of computer programming, and of the high level languages in which programs are expressed, the action of assignment is familiar and well understood. In fact, any change of the internal state of a machine executing a program can be modeled as an assignment of a new value to some variable part of that machine. However, the operations of input and output, which affect the external environment of a machine, are not nearly so well understood. They are often added to a programming language only as an afterthought.

Among the structuring methods for computer programs, three basic constructs have received widespread recognition and use: A repetitive construct (e.g. the **while** loop), an alternative construct (e.g. the conditional **if..then..else**), and normal sequential program composition (often denoted by a semicolon). Less agreement has been reached about the design of other important program structures, and many suggestions have been made: Subroutines (Fortran), procedures (Algol 60 [15]), entries (PL/I), coroutines (UNIX [17]), classes (SIMULA 67 [5]), processes and monitors (Concurrent Pascal [2]), clusters (CLU [13]), forms (ALPHARD [19]), actors (Hewitt [1]).

The traditional stored program digital computer has been designed primarily for deterministic execution of a single sequential program. Where the desire for greater speed has led to the introduction of parallelism, every attempt has been made to disguise this fact from the programmer, either by hardware itself (as in the multiple function units of the CDC 6600) or by the software (as in an I/O control package, or a multiprogrammed operating system). However, developments of processor technology suggest that a multiprocessor machine, constructed from a number of similar self-contained processors (each with its own store), may become more powerful, capacious, reliable, and economical than a machine which is disguised as a monoprocessor.

In order to use such a machine effectively on a single task, the component processors must be able to communicate and to synchronize with each other. Many methods of achieving this have been proposed. A widely adopted method of communication is by inspection and updating of a common store (as in Algol 68 [18], PL/I, and many machine codes). However, this can create severe problems in the construction of correct programs and it may lead to expense (e.g. crossbar switches) and unreliability (e.g. glitches) in some technologies of hardware implementation. A greater variety of methods has been proposed for synchronization: semaphores [6], events (PL/I), conditional critical regions [10], monitors and queues (Concurrent Pascal [2]), and path expressions [3]. Most of these are demonstrably adequate for their purpose, but there is no widely recognized criterion for choosing between them.

This paper makes an ambitious attempt to find a single simple solution to all these problems. The essential proposals are:

(1) Dijkstra's guarded commands [8] are adopted (with a slight change of notation) as sequential control structures, and as the sole means of introducing and controlling nondeterminism.

(2) A parallel command, based on Dijkstra's *parbegin* [6], specifies concurrent execution of its constituent sequential commands (processes). All the processes start simultaneously, and the parallel command ends only when they are all finished. They may not communicate with each other by updating global variables.

(3) Simple forms of input and output command are introduced. They are used for communication between concurrent processes.

This research was supported by a Senior Fellowship of the Science Research Council.

Author's present address: Programming Research Group, 45, Banbury Road, Oxford, England.

Reprinted with permission from *Commun. Ass. Comput. Mach.*, vol. 21, pp. 666–677, Aug. 1978.

(4) Such communication occurs when one process names another as destination for output *and* the second process names the first as source for input. In this case, the value to be output is copied from the first process to the second. There is *no* automatic buffering: In general, an input or output command is delayed until the other process is ready with the corresponding output or input. Such delay is invisible to the delayed process.
(5) Input commands may appear in guards. A guarded command with an input guard is selected for execution only if and when the source named in the input command is ready to execute the corresponding output command. If several input guards of a set of alternatives have ready destinations, only one is selected and the others have *no* effect; but the choice between them is arbitrary. In an efficient implementation, an output command which has been ready for a long time should be favored; but the definition of a language cannot specify this since the relative speed of execution of the processes is undefined.
(6) A repetitive command may have input guards. If all the sources named by them have terminated, then the repetitive command also terminates.
(7) A simple pattern-matching feature, similar to that of [16], is used to discriminate the structure of an input message, and to access its components in a secure fashion. This feature is used to inhibit input of messages that do not match the specified pattern.

The programs expressed in the proposed language are intended to be implementable both by a conventional machine with a single main store, and by a fixed network of processors connected by input/output channels (although very different optimizations are appropriate in the different cases). It is consequently a rather static language: The text of a program determines a fixed upper bound on the number of processes operating concurrently; there is no recursion and no facility for process-valued variables. In other respects also, the language has been stripped to the barest minimum necessary for explanation of its more novel features.

The concept of a communicating sequential process is shown in Sections 3–5 to provide a method of expressing solutions to many simple programming exercises which have previously been employed to illustrate the use of various proposed programming language features. This suggests that the process may constitute a synthesis of a number of familiar and new programming ideas. The reader is invited to skip the examples which do not interest him.

However, this paper also ignores many serious problems. The most serious is that it fails to suggest any proof method to assist in the development and verification of correct programs. Secondly, it pays no attention to the problems of efficient implementation, which may be particularly serious on a traditional sequential computer. It is probable that a solution to these problems will require (1) imposition of restrictions in the use of the proposed features; (2) reintroduction of distinctive notations for the most common and useful special cases; (3) development of automatic optimization techniques; and (4) the design of appropriate hardware.

Thus the concepts and notations introduced in this paper (although described in the next section in the form of a programming language fragment) should not be regarded as suitable for use as a programming language, either for abstract or for concrete programming. They are at best only a partial solution to the problems tackled. Further discussion of these and other points will be found in Section 7.

2. Concepts and Notations

The style of the following description is borrowed from Algol 60 [15]. Types, declarations, and expressions have not been treated; in the examples, a Pascal-like notation [20] has usually been adopted. The curly braces { } have been introduced into BNF to denote none or more repetitions of the enclosed material. (Sentences in parentheses refer to an implementation: they are not strictly part of a language definition.)

<command> ::= <simple command>|<structured command>
<simple command> ::= <null command>|<assignment command>
|<input command>|<output command>
<structured command> ::= <alternative command>
|<repetitive command>|<parallel command>
<null command> ::= skip
<command list> ::= {<declaration>; |<command>;} <command>

A command specifies the behavior of a device executing the command. It may succeed or fail. Execution of a simple command, if successful, may have an effect on the internal state of the executing device (in the case of assignment), or on its external environment (in the case of output), or on both (in the case of input). Execution of a structured command involves execution of some or all of its constituent commands, and if any of these fail, so does the structured command. (In this case, whenever possible, an implementation should provide some kind of comprehensible error diagnostic message.)

A null command has no effect and never fails.

A command list specifies sequential execution of its constituent commands in the order written. Each declaration introduces a fresh variable with a scope which extends from its declaration to the end of the command list.

2.1 Parallel Commands

<parallel command> ::= [<process>{||<process>}]
<process> ::= <process label> <command list>
<process label> ::= <empty>|<identifier> ::
|<identifier>(<label subscript>{,<label subscript>}) ::
<label subscript> ::= <integer constant>|<range>
<integer constant> ::= <numeral>|<bound variable>
<bound variable> ::= <identifier>
<range> ::= <bound variable>:<lower bound>..<upper bound>
<lower bound> ::= <integer constant>
<upper bound> ::= <integer constant>

Each process of a parallel command must be *disjoint* from every other process of the command, in the sense that it does not mention any variable which occurs as a target variable (see Sections 2.2 and 2.3) in any other process.

A process label without subscripts, or one whose label subscripts are all integer constants, serves as a name for the command list to which it is prefixed; its scope extends over the whole of the parallel command. A process whose label subscripts include one or more ranges stands for a series of processes, each with the same label and command list, except that each has a different combination of values substituted for the bound variables. These values range between the lower bound and the upper bound inclusive. For example, *X(i:1..n)* :: CL stands for

$X(1)$ :: CL_1||$X(2)$ :: CL_2||...||$X(n)$ :: CL_n

where each CL_j is formed from CL by replacing every occurrence of the bound variable *i* by the numeral *j*. After all such expansions, each process label in a parallel command must occur only once and the processes must be well formed and disjoint.

A parallel command specifies concurrent execution of its constituent processes. They all start simultaneously and the parallel command terminates successfully only if and when they have all successfully terminated. The relative speed with which they are executed is arbitrary.

Examples:

(1) [cardreader?cardimage||lineprinter!lineimage]

Performs the two constituent commands in parallel, and terminates only when both operations are complete. The time taken may be as low as the longer of the times taken by each constituent process, i.e. the sum of its computing, waiting, and transfer times.

(2) [west :: DISASSEMBLE||*X* :: SQUASH||east :: ASSEMBLE]

The three processes have the names "west," "*X*," and "east." The capitalized words stand for command lists which will be defined in later examples.

(3) [room :: ROOM||fork(*i*:0..4) :: FORK||phil(*i*:0..4) :: PHIL]

There are eleven processes. The behavior of "room" is specified by the command list ROOM. The behavior of the five processes fork(0), fork(1), fork(2), fork(3), fork(4), is specified by the command list FORK, within which the bound variable *i* indicates the identity of the particular fork. Similar remarks apply to the five processes PHIL.

2.2 Assignment Commands

<assignment command> ::= <target variable> := <expression>
<expression> ::= <simple expression>|<structured expression>
<structured expression> ::= <constructor>(<expression list>)
<constructor> ::= <identifier>|<empty>
<expression list> ::= <empty>|<expression>{,<expression>}
<target variable> ::= <simple variable>|<structured target>
<structured target> ::= <constructor>(<target variable list>)
<target variable list> ::= <empty>|<target variable>
{,<target variable>}

An expression denotes a value which is computed by an executing device by application of its constituent operators to the specified operands. The value of an expression is undefined if any of these operations are undefined. The value denoted by a simple expression may be simple or structured. The value denoted by a structured expression is structured; its constructor is that of the expression, and its components are the list of values denoted by the constituent expressions of the expression list.

An assignment command specifies evaluation of its expression, and assignment of the denoted value to the target variable. A simple target variable may have assigned to it a simple or a structured value. A structured target variable may have assigned to it a structured value, with the same constructor. The effect of such assignment is to assign to each constituent simpler variable of the structured target the value of the corresponding component of the structured value. Consequently, the value denoted by the target variable, if evaluated *after* a successful assignment, is the same as the value denoted by the expression, as evaluated *before* the assignment.

An assignment fails if the value of its expression is undefined, or if that value does not *match* the target variable, in the following sense: A *simple* target variable matches any value of its type. A *structured* target variable matches a structured value, provided that: (1) they have the same constructor, (2) the target variable list is the same length as the list of components of the value, (3) each target variable of the list matches the corresponding component of the value list. A structured value with no components is known as a "signal."

Examples:

(1) $x := x + 1$	the value of x after the assignment is the same as the value of $x + 1$ before.
(2) $(x, y) := (y, x)$	exchanges the values of x and y.
(3) $x :=$ cons(left, right)	constructs a structured value and assigns it to x.
(4) cons(left, right) $:= x$	fails if x does not have the form cons(y, z); but if it does, then y is assigned to left, and z is assigned to right.
(5) insert(n) := insert($2*x + 1$)	equivalent to $n := 2*x + 1$.
(6) $c :=$ P()	assigns to c a "signal" with constructor P, and no components.
(7) P() $:= c$	fails if the value of c is not P(); otherwise has no effect.
(8) insert(n) := has(n)	fails, due to mismatch.

Note: Successful execution of both (3) and (4) ensures the truth of the postcondition $x =$ cons(left, right); but (3) does so by changing x and (4) does so by changing left and right. Example (4) will fail if there is *no* value of left and right which satisfies the postcondition.

2.3 Input and Output Commands

<input command> ::= <source>?<target variable>
<output command> ::= <destination>!<expression>
<source> ::= <process name>

<destination> ::= <process name>

<process name> ::= <identifier>|<identifier>(<subscripts>)

<subscripts> ::= <integer expression>{,<integer expression>}

Input and output commands specify communication between two concurrently operating sequential processes. Such a process may be implemented in hardware as a special-purpose device (e.g. cardreader or lineprinter), or its behavior may be specified by one of the constituent processes of a parallel command. Communication occurs between two processes of a parallel command whenever (1) an input command in one process specifies as its source the process name of the other process; (2) an output command in the other process specifies as its destination the process name of the first process; and (3) the target variable of the input command matches the value denoted by the expression of the output command. On these conditions, the input and output commands are said to *correspond*. Commands which correspond are executed simultaneously, and their combined effect is to assign the value of the expression of the output command to the target variable of the input command.

An input command fails if its source is terminated. An output command fails if its destination is terminated or if its expression is undefined.

(The requirement of synchronization of input and output commands means that an implementation will have to delay whichever of the two commands happens to be ready first. The delay is ended when the corresponding command in the other process is also ready, or when the other process terminates. In the latter case the first command fails. It is also possible that the delay will never be ended, for example, if a group of processes are attempting communication but none of their input and output commands correspond with each other. This form of failure is known as a deadlock.)

Examples:

(1) cardreader?cardimage	from cardreader, read a card and assign its value (an array of characters) to the variable cardimage
(2) lineprinter!lineimage	to lineprinter, send the value of lineimage for printing
(3) $X?(x, y)$	from process named X, input a pair of values and assign them to x and y
(4) DIV!(3*a + b, 13)	to process DIV, output the two specified values.

Note: If a process named DIV issues command (3), and a process named X issues command (4), these are executed simultaneously, and have the same effect as the assignment: $(x, y) := (3*a + b, 13)$ ($\equiv x := 3*a + b; y := 13$).

(5) console(i)?c	from the ith element of an array of consoles, input a value and assign it to c
(6) console(j − 1)!"A"	to the (j − 1)th console, output character "A"
(7) X(i)?V( )	from the ith of an array of processes X, input a signal V( ); refuse to input any other signal
(8) sem!P( )	to sem output a signal P( )

2.4 Alternative and Repetitive Commands

<repetitive command> ::=*<alternative command>

<alternative command> ::= [<guarded command>
{□<guarded command>}]

<guarded command> ::= <guard> → <command list>
|(<range>{,<range>})<guard> → <command list>

<guard> ::= <guard list>|<guard list>;<input command>
|<input command>

<guard list> ::= <guard element>{;<guard element>}

<guard element> ::= <boolean expression>|<declaration>

A guarded command with one or more ranges stands for a series of guarded commands, each with the same guard and command list, except that each has a different combination of values substituted for the bound variables. The values range between the lower bound and upper bound inclusive. For example, $(i{:}1..n)G \rightarrow CL$ stands for

$$G_1 \rightarrow CL_1 \,\square\, G_2 \rightarrow CL_2 \,\square \ldots \square\, G_n \rightarrow CL_n$$

where each $G_j \rightarrow CL_j$ is formed from $G \rightarrow CL$ by replacing every occurrence of the bound variable i by the numeral j.

A guarded command is executed only if and when the execution of its guard does not fail. First its guard is executed and then its command list. A guard is executed by execution of its constituent elements from left to right. A Boolean expression is evaluated: If it denotes false, the guard fails; but an expression that denotes true has no effect. A declaration introduces a fresh variable with a scope that extends from the declaration to the end of the guarded command. An input command at the end of a guard is executed only if and when a corresponding output command is executed. (An implementation may test whether a guard fails simply by trying to execute it, and discontinuing execution if and when it fails. This is valid because such a discontinued execution has no effect on the state of the executing device.)

An alternative command specifies execution of exactly one of its constituent guarded commands. Consequently, if all guards fail, the alternative command fails. Otherwise an arbitrary one with successfully executable guard is selected and executed. (An implementation should take advantage of its freedom of selection to ensure efficient execution and good response. For example, when input commands appear as guards, the command which corresponds to the earliest ready and matching output command should in general be preferred; and certainly, no executable and ready output command should be passed over unreasonably often.)

A repetitive command specifies as many iterations as possible of its constituent alternative command. Consequently, when all guards fail, the repetitive command terminates with no effect. Otherwise, the alternative command is executed once and then the whole repetitive command is executed again. (Consider a repetitive command when all its true guard lists end in an input guard. Such a command may have to be delayed until either (1) an output command corresponding to one of the input guards becomes ready, or (2) all the sources named by the input guards have terminated. In case (2), the repetitive command terminates. If neither event ever occurs, the process fails (in deadlock.)

Examples:

(1) $[x \geq y \rightarrow m := x \,\square\, y \geq x \rightarrow m := y]$

If $x \geq y$, assign x to m; if $y \geq x$ assign y to m; if both $x \geq y$ and $y \geq x$, either assignment can be executed.

(2) $i := 0; *[i < \text{size}; \text{content}(i) \neq n \rightarrow i := i + 1]$

The repetitive command scans the elements content(i), for i = 0, 1, ... , until either $i \geq$ size, or a value equal to n is found.

```
(3) *[c:character; west?c → east!c]
```

This reads all the characters output by west, and outputs them one by one to east. The repetition terminates when the process west terminates.

```
(4) *[(i:1..10)continue(i); console(i)?c → X!(i, c); console(i)!ack();
    continue(i) := (c ≠ sign off)]
```

This command inputs repeatedly from any of ten consoles, provided that the corresponding element of the Boolean array continue is true. The bound variable i identifies the originating console. Its value, together with the character just input, is output to X, and an acknowledgment signal is sent back to the originating console. If the character indicated "sign off," continue(i) is set false, to prevent further input from that console. The repetitive command terminates when all ten elements of continue are false. (An implementation should ensure that no console which is ready to provide input will be ignored unreasonably often.)

```
(5) *[n:integer; X?insert(n) → INSERT
    □n:integer; X?has(n) → SEARCH; X!(i < size)
    ]
```

(Here, and elsewhere, capitalized words INSERT and SEARCH stand as abbreviations for program text defined separately.)

On each iteration this command accepts from X *either* (a) a request to "insert(n)," (followed by INSERT) *or* (b) a question "has(n)," to which it outputs an answer back to X. The choice between (a) and (b) is made by the next output command in X. The repetitive command terminates when X does. If X sends a nonmatching message, deadlock will result.

```
(6) *[X?V() → val := val + 1
    □val > 0; Y?P() → val := val − 1
    ]
```

On each iteration, accept *either* a V() signal from X and increment val, *or* a P() signal from Y, and decrement val. But the second alternative cannot be selected unless val is positive (after which val will remain invariantly nonnegative). (When val > 0, the choice depends on the relative speeds of X and Y, and is not determined.) The repetitive command will terminate when both X and Y are terminated, or when X is terminated and val $\leq$ 0.

3. Coroutines

In parallel programming coroutines appear as a more fundamental program structure than subroutines, which can be regarded as a special case (treated in the next section).

3.1 COPY

Problem: Write a process X to copy characters output by process west to process east.

Solution:

```
X :: *[c:character; west?c → east!c]
```

Notes: (1) When west terminates, the input "west?c" will fail, causing termination of the repetitive command, and of process X. Any subsequent input command from east will fail. (2) Process X acts as a single-character buffer between west and east. It permits west to work on production of the next character, before east is ready to input the previous one.

3.2 SQUASH

Problem: Adapt the previous program to replace every pair of consecutive asterisks "**" by an upward arrow "↑". Assume that the final character input is not an asterisk.

Solution:

```
X :: *[c:character; west?c →
   [c ≠ asterisk → east!c
   □c = asterisk → west?c;
        [c ≠ asterisk → east!asterisk; east!c
        □c = asterisk → east!upward arrow
   ]] ]
```

Notes: (1) Since west does not end with asterisk, the second "west?c" will not fail. (2) As an exercise, adapt this process to deal sensibly with input which ends with an odd number of asterisks.

3.3 DISASSEMBLE

Problem: to read cards from a cardfile and output to process X the stream of characters they contain. An extra space should be inserted at the end of each card.

Solution:

```
*[cardimage:(1..80)character; cardfile?cardimage →
      i:integer; i := 1;
      *[i ≤ 80 → X!cardimage(i); i := i + 1]
      X!space
]
```

Notes: (1) "(1..80)character" declares an array of 80 characters, with subscripts ranging between 1 and 80. (2) The repetitive command terminates when the cardfile process terminates.

3.4 ASSEMBLE

Problem: To read a stream of characters from process X and print them in lines of 125 characters on a lineprinter. The last line should be completed with spaces if necessary.

Solution:

```
lineimage:(1..125)character;
i:integer; i := 1;
*[c:character; X?c →
    lineimage(i) := c;
    [i ≤ 124 → i := i + 1
    []i = 125 → lineprinter!lineimage; i := 1
]   ];
[i = 1 → skip
[]i > 1 → *[i ≤ 125 → lineimage(i) := space; i := i + 1];
    lineprinter!lineimage
]
```

Note: (1) When X terminates, so will the first repetitive command of this process. The last line will then be printed, if it has any characters.

3.5 Reformat

Problem: Read a sequence of cards of 80 characters each, and print the characters on a lineprinter at 125 characters per line. Every card should be followed by an extra space, and the last line should be completed with spaces if necessary.
Solution:

```
[west::DISASSEMBLE||X::COPY||east::ASSEMBLE]
```

Notes: (1) The capitalized names stand for program text defined in previous sections. (2) The parallel command is designed to terminate after the cardfile has terminated. (3) This elementary problem is difficult to solve elegantly without coroutines.

3.6 Conway's Problem [4]

Problem: Adapt the above program to replace every pair of consecutive asterisks by an upward arrow.
Solution:

```
[west::DISASSEMBLE||X::SQUASH||east::ASSEMBLE]
```

4. Subroutines and Data Representations

A conventional nonrecursive subroutine can be readily implemented as a coroutine, provided that (1) its parameters are called "by value" and "by result," and (2) it is disjoint from its calling program. Like a Fortran subroutine, a coroutine may retain the values of local variables (*own* variables, in Algol terms) and it may use input commands to achieve the effect of "multiple entry points" in a safer way than PL/I. Thus a coroutine can be used like a SIMULA class instance as a concrete representation for abstract data.

A coroutine acting as a subroutine is a process operating concurrently with its user process in a parallel command: [subr::SUBROUTINE||X::USER]. The SUBROUTINE will contain (or consist of) a repetitive command: *[X?(value params) → ... ; X!(result params)], where ... computes the results from the values input. The subroutine will terminate when its user does. The USER will call the subroutine by a pair of commands: subr!(arguments); ... ; subr?(results). Any commands between these two will be executed concurrently with the subroutine.

A multiple-entry subroutine, acting as a representation for data [11], will also contain a repetitive command which represents each entry by an alternative input to a structured target with the entry name as constructor. For example,

```
*[X?entry1(value params) → ...
[]X?entry2(value params) → ...
]
```

The calling process X will determine which of the alternatives is activated on each repetition. When X terminates, so does this repetitive command. A similar technique in the user program can achieve the effect of multiple exits.

A recursive subroutine can be simulated by an array of processes, one for each level of recursion. The user process is level zero. Each activation communicates its parameters and results with its predecessor and calls its successor if necessary:

```
[recsub(0)::USER||recsub(i:1..reclimit)::RECSUB].
```

The user will call the first element of

```
recsub: recsub(1)!(arguments); ... ; recsub(1)?(results);.
```

The imposition of a fixed upper bound on recursion depth is necessitated by the "static" design of the language.

This clumsy simulation of recursion would be even more clumsy for a mutually recursive algorithm. It would not be recommended for conventional programming; it may be more suitable for an array of microprocessors for which the fixed upper bound is also realistic.

In this section, we assume each subroutine is used only by a *single* user process (which may, of course, itself contain parallel commands).

4.1 Function: Division With Remainder

Problem: Construct a process to represent a function-type subroutine, which accepts a positive dividend and divisor, and returns their integer quotient and remainder. Efficiency is of no concern.
Solution:

```
[DIV::*[x,y:integer; X?(x,y) →
        quot,rem:integer;quot := 0; rem := x;
        *[rem ≥ y → rem := rem − y; quot := quot + 1];
        X!(quot,rem)
        ]
||X::USER
]
```

4.2 Recursion: Factorial

Problem: Compute a factorial by the recursive method, to a given limit.
Solution:

```
[fac(i:1..limit)::
*[n:integer;fac(i − 1)?n →
  [n = 0 → fac(i − 1)!1
```

```
    []n > 0 → fac(i + 1)!n − 1;
      r:integer;fac(i + 1)?r;fac(i − 1)!(n * r)
    ]]
||fac(0)::USER
]
```

Note: This unrealistic example introduces the technique of the "iterative array" which will be used to a better effect in later examples.

4.3 Data Representation: Small Set of Integers [11]

Problem: To represent a set of not more than 100 integers as a process, S, which accepts two kinds of instruction from its calling process *X*: (1) S!insert(*n*), insert the integer *n* in the set, and (2) S!has(*n*); ... ; S?*b*, *b* is set true if *n* is in the set, and false otherwise. The initial value of the set is empty.

Solution:

```
S::
content:(0..99)integer; size:integer; size := 0;
*[n:integer;X?has(n) → SEARCH;X!(i < size)
[]n:integer; X?insert(n) → SEARCH;
    [i < size → skip
    []i = size; size < 100 →
        content (size) := n; size := size + 1
]  ]
```

where SEARCH is an abbreviation for:

```
i:integer; i := 0;
*[i < size; content(i) ≠ n → i := i + 1]
```

Notes: (1) The alternative command with guard "size < 100" will fail if an attempt is made to insert more than 100 elements. (2) The activity of insertion will in general take place concurrently with the calling process. However, any subsequent instruction to S will be delayed until the previous insertion is complete.

4.4 Scanning a Set

Problem: Extend the solution to 4.3 by providing a fast method for scanning all members of the set without changing the value of the set. The user program will contain a repetitive command of the form:

```
  S!scan( ); more:boolean; more := true;
*[more;x:integer; S?next(x) → ... deal with x ....
[]more; S?noneleft( ) → more := false
]
```

where S!scan( ) sets the representation into a scanning mode. The repetitive command serves as a **for** statement, inputting the successive members of *x* from the set and inspecting them until finally the representation sends a signal that there are no members left. The body of the repetitive command is *not* permitted to communicate with S in any way.

Solution: Add a third guarded command to the outer repetitive command of S:

```
... []X?scan( ) → i:integer; i := 0;
                  *[i < size → X!next(content(i)); i := i + 1];
                  X!noneleft( )
```

4.5 Recursive Data Representation: Small Set of Integers

Problem: Same as above, but an array of processes is to be used to achieve a high degree of parallelism. Each process should contain at most one number. When it contains no number, it should answer "false" to all inquiries about membership. On the first insertion, it changes to a second phase of behavior, in which it deals with instructions from its predecessor, passing some of them on to its successor. The calling process will be named S(0). For efficiency, the set should be sorted, i.e. the *i*th process should contain the *i*th largest number.

Solution:

```
S(i:1..100)::
*[n:integer; S(i − 1)?has(n) → S(0)!false
[]n:integer; S(i − 1)?insert(n) →
   *[m:integer; S(i − 1)?has(m) →
      [m ≤ n → S(0)!(m = n)
      []m > n → S(i + 1)!has(m)
      ]
   []m:integer; S(i − 1)?insert(m) →
      [m < n → S(i + 1)!insert(n); n := m
      []m = n → skip
      []m > n → S(i + 1)!insert(m)
]]]
```

Notes: (1) The user process S(0) inquires whether *n* is a member by the commands S(1)!has(*n*); ... ; [(*i*:1..100)S(*i*)?*b* → skip]. The appropriate process will respond to the input command by the output command in line 2 or line 5. This trick avoids passing the answer back "up the chain." (2) Many insertion operations can proceed in parallel, yet any subsequent "has" operation will be performed correctly. (3) All repetitive commands and all processes of the array will terminate after the user process S(0) terminates.

4.6 Multiple Exits: Remove the Least Member

Exercise: Extend the above solution to respond to a command to yield the least member of the set and to remove it from the set. The user program will invoke the facility by a pair of commands:

```
S(1)!least( ); [x:integer;S(1)?x → ... deal with x ...
               []S(1)?noneleft( ) → ...
               ]
```

or, if he wishes to scan and empty the set, he may write:

```
S(1)!least( );more:boolean; more := true;
      *[more; x:integer; S(1)?x → ... deal with x ... ; S(1)!least( )
      []more; S(1)?noneleft( ) → more := false
      ]
```

Hint: Introduce a Boolean variable, *b*, initialized to true, and prefix this to all the guards of the inner loop. After responding to a !least( ) command from its predecessor, each process returns its contained value *n*, asks its successor for its least, and stores the response in *n*. But if the successor returns "noneleft( )," *b* is set false and the inner loop terminates. The process therefore returns to its initial state (solution due to David Gries).

5. Monitors and Scheduling

This section shows how a monitor can be regarded as a single process which communicates with more than one user process. However, each user process must have a different name (e.g. producer, consumer) or a different subscript (e.g. *X*(*i*)) and each communication with a user must identify its source or destination uniquely.

Consequently, when a monitor is prepared to communicate with *any* of its user processes (i.e. whichever of them calls first) it will use a guarded command with a range. For example: $*[(i{:}1..100)X(i)?(\text{value parameters}) \rightarrow ... ; X(i)!(\text{results})]$. Here, the bound variable *i* is used to send the results back to the calling process. If the monitor is not prepared to accept input from some particular user (e.g. *X*(*j*)) on a given occasion, the input command may be preceded by a Boolean guard. For example, two successive inputs from the same process are inhibited by $j = 0; *[(i{:}1..100)i \neq j; X(i)?(\text{values}) \rightarrow ... ; j := i]$. Any attempted output from *X*(*j*) will be delayed until a subsequent iteration, after the output of some other process *X*(*i*) has been accepted and dealt with.

Similarly, conditions can be used to delay acceptance of inputs which would violate scheduling constraints—postponing them until some later occasion when some other process has brought the monitor into a state in which the input can validly be accepted. This technique is similar to a conditional critical region [10] and it obviates the need for special synchronizing variables such as events, queues, or conditions. However, the absence of these special facilities certainly makes it more difficult or less efficient to solve problems involving priorities—for example, the scheduling of head movement on a disk.

5.1 Bounded Buffer

Problem: Construct a buffering process *X* to smooth variations in the speed of output of portions by a producer process and input by a consumer process. The consumer contains pairs of commands *X*!more( ); *X*?*p*, and the producer contains commands of the form *X*!*p*. The buffer should contain up to ten portions.

Solution:

```
X::
buffer:(0..9) portion;
in,out:integer; in := 0; out := 0;
comment 0 ≤ out ≤ in ≤ out + 10;
  *[in < out + 10; producer?buffer(in mod 10) → in := in + 1
  []out < in; consumer?more( ) → consumer!buffer(out mod 10);
     out := out + 1
  ]
```

Notes: (1) When out < in < out + 10, the selection of the alternative in the repetitive command will depend on whether the producer produces before the consumer consumes, or vice versa. (2) When out = in, the buffer is empty and the second alternative cannot be selected even if the consumer is ready with its command *X*!more( ). However, after the producer has produced its next portion, the consumer's request can be granted on the next iteration. (3) Similar remarks apply to the producer, when in = out + 10. (4) *X* is designed to terminate when out = in and the producer has terminated.

5.2 Integer Semaphore

Problem: To implement an integer semaphore, S, shared among an array *X*(*i*:1..100) of client processes. Each process may increment the semaphore by S!V( ) or decrement it by S!P( ), but the latter command must be delayed if the value of the semaphore is not positive.

Solution:

```
S::val:integer; val := 0;
  *[(i:1..100)X(i)?V( ) → val := val + 1
  [](i:1..100)val > 0; X(i)?P( ) → val := val − 1
  ]
```

Notes: (1) In this process, no use is made of knowledge of the subscript *i* of the calling process. (2) The semaphore terminates only when all hundred processes of the process array *X* have terminated.

5.3 Dining Philosophers (Problem due to E.W. Dijkstra)

Problem: Five philosophers spend their lives thinking and eating. The philosophers share a common dining room where there is a circular table surrounded by five chairs, each belonging to one philosopher. In the center of the table there is a large bowl of spaghetti, and the table is laid with five forks (see Figure 1). On feeling hungry, a philosopher enters the dining room, sits in his own chair, and picks up the fork on the left of his place. Unfortunately, the spaghetti is so tangled that he needs to pick up and use the fork on his right as well. When he has finished, he puts down both forks, and leaves the room. The room should keep a count of the number of philosophers in it.

Fig. 1.

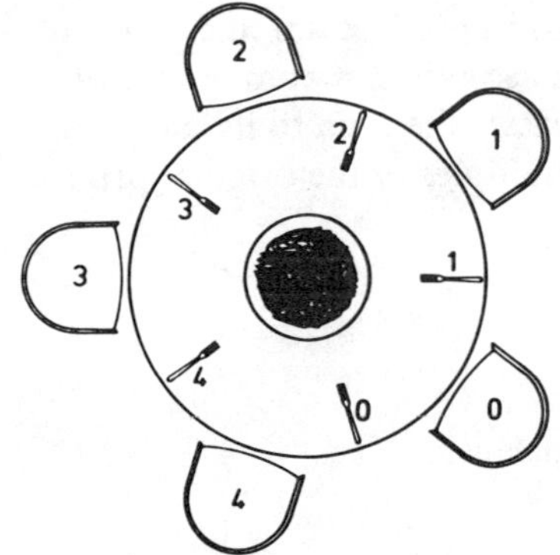

Solution: The behavior of the *i*th philosopher may be described as follows:

```
PHIL = *[... during ith lifetime ... →
          THINK;
          room!enter( );
          fork(i)!pickup( ); fork((i + 1) mod 5)!pickup( );
          EAT;
          fork(i)!putdown( ); fork((i + 1) mod 5)!putdown( );
          room!exit( )
          ]
```

The fate of the *i*th fork is to be picked up and put down by a philosopher sitting on either side of it

```
FORK =
  *[phil(i)?pickup( ) → phil(i)?putdown( )
  []phil((i − 1)mod 5)?pickup( ) → phil((i − 1) mod 5)?putdown( )
  ]
```

The story of the room may be simply told:

```
ROOM = occupancy:integer; occupancy := 0;
  *[(i:0..4)phil(i)?enter( ) → occupancy := occupancy + 1
  [](i:0..4)phil(i)?exit( ) → occupancy := occupancy − 1
  ]
```

All these components operate in parallel:

```
[room::ROOM||fork(i:0..4)::FORK||phil(i:0..4)::PHIL].
```

Notes: (1) The solution given above does not prevent all five philosophers from entering the room, each picking up his left fork, and starving to death because he cannot pick up his right fork. (2) Exercise: Adapt the above program to avert this sad possibility. Hint: Prevent more than four philosophers from entering the room. (Solution due to E. W. Dijkstra).

6. Miscellaneous

This section contains further examples of the use of communicating sequential processes for the solution of some less familiar problems; a parallel version of the sieve of Eratosthenes, and the design of an iterative array. The proposed solutions are even more speculative than those of the previous sections, and in the second example, even the question of termination is ignored.

6.1 Prime Numbers: The Sieve of Eratosthenes [14]

Problem: To print in ascending order all primes less than 10000. Use an array of processes, SIEVE, in which each process inputs a prime from its predecessor and prints it. The process then inputs an ascending stream of numbers from its predecessor and passes them on to its successor, suppressing any that are multiples of the original prime.
Solution:

```
[SIEVE(i:1..100)::
  p,mp:integer;
  SIEVE(i − 1)?p;
  print!p;
  mp := p; comment mp is a multiple of p;
*[m:integer; SIEVE(i − 1)?m →
    *[m > mp → mp := mp + p];
    [m = mp → skip
    []m < mp → SIEVE(i + 1)!m
]  ]
||SIEVE(0)::print!2; n:integer; n := 3;
    *[n < 10000 → SIEVE(1)!n; n := n + 2]
||SIEVE(101)::*[n:integer;SIEVE(100)?n → print!n]
||print::*[(i:0..101) n:integer; SIEVE(i)?n → ...]
]
```

Note: (1) This beautiful solution was contributed by David Gries. (2) It is algorithmically similar to the program developed in [7, pp. 27–32].

6.2 An Iterative Array: Matrix Multiplication

Problem: A square matrix A of order 3 is given. Three streams are to be input, each stream representing a column of an array IN. Three streams are to be output, each representing a column of the product matrix IN × A. After an initial delay, the results are to be produced at the same rate as the input is consumed. Consequently, a high degree of parallelism is required. The solution should take the form shown in Figure 2. Each of the nine nonborder nodes inputs a vector component from the west and a partial sum from the north. Each node outputs the vector component to its east, and an updated partial sum to the south. The input data is produced by the west border nodes, and the desired results are consumed by south border nodes. The north border is a constant source of zeros and the east border is just a sink. No provision need be made for termination nor for changing the values of the array A.

Fig. 2.

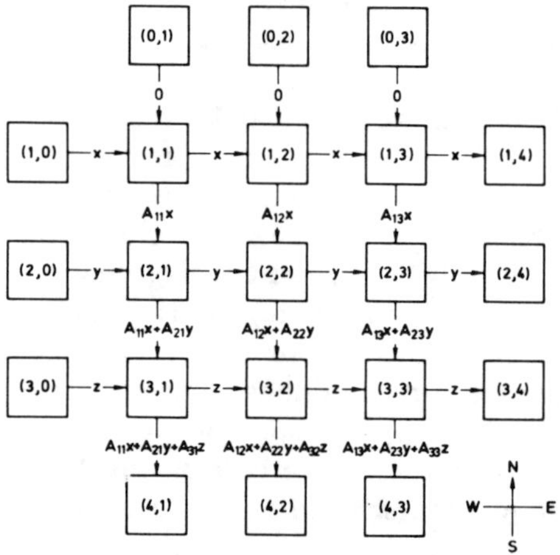

Solution: There are twenty-one nodes, in five groups, comprising the central square and the four borders:

```
[M(i:1..3,0)::WEST
||M(0,j:1..3)::NORTH
||M(i:1..3,4)::EAST
||M(4,j:1..3)::SOUTH
||M(i:1..3,j:1..3)::CENTER
]
```

The WEST and SOUTH borders are processes of the user program; the remaining processes are:

```
NORTH = *[true → M(1,j)!0]
EAST = *[x:real; M(i,3)?x → skip]
CENTER = *[x:real; M(i,j − 1)?x →
    M(i, j + 1)!x; sum:real;
    M(i − 1, j)?sum; M(i + 1,j)!(A(i, j)*x + sum)
  ]
```

7. Discussion

A design for a programming language must necessarily involve a number of decisions which seem to be fairly arbitrary. The discussion of this section is intended to explain some of the underlying motivation and to mention some unresolved questions.

7.1 Notations

I have chosen single-character notations (e.g. !,?) to express the primitive concepts, rather than the more traditional boldface or underlined English words. As a result, the examples have an APL-like brevity, which some readers find distasteful. My excuse is that (in contrast to APL) there are only a very few primitive concepts and that it is standard practice of mathematics (and also good coding practice) to denote common primitive concepts by brief notations (e.g. +,×). When read aloud, these are replaced by words (e.g. plus, times).

Some readers have suggested the use of assignment notation for input and output:

<target variable> := <source>
<destination> := <expression>

I find this suggestion misleading: it is better to regard input and output as distinct primitives, justifying distinct notations.

I have used the same pair of brackets ([...]) to bracket all program structures, instead of the more familiar variety of brackets (**if**..**fi**, **begin**..**end**, **case**...**esac**, etc.). In this I follow normal mathematical practice, but I must also confess to a distaste for the pronunciation of words like **fi**, **od**, or **esac**.

I am dissatisfied with the fact that my notation gives the same syntax for a structured expression and a subscripted variable. Perhaps tags should be distinguished from other identifiers by a special symbol (say #).

I was tempted to introduce an abbreviation for combined declaration and input, e.g. *X*?(*n*:integer) for *n*:integer; *X*?*n*.

7.2 Explicit Naming

My design insists that every input or output command must name its source or destination explicitly. This makes it inconvenient to write a library of processes which can be included in subsequent programs, independent of the process names used in that program. A partial solution to this problem is to allow one process (the *main* process) of a parallel command to have an empty label, and to allow the other processes in the command to use the empty process name as source or destination of input or output.

For construction of large programs, some more general technique will also be necessary. This should at least permit substitution of program text for names defined elsewhere—a technique which has been used informally throughout this paper. The Cobol COPY verb also permits a substitution for formal parameters within the copied text. But whatever facility is introduced, I would recommend the following principle: Every program, after assembly with its library routines, should be printable as a text expressed wholly in the language, and it is this printed text which should describe the execution of the program, independent of which parts were drawn from a library.

Since I did not intend to design a complete language, I have ignored the problem of libraries in order to concentrate on the essential semantic concepts of the program which is actually executed.

7.3 Port Names

An alternative to explicit naming of source and destination would be to name a *port* through which communication is to take place. The port names would be local to the processes, and the manner in which pairs of ports are to be connected by channels could be declared in the head of a parallel command.

This is an attractive alternative which could be designed to introduce a useful degree of syntactically checkable redundancy. But it is semantically equivalent to the present proposal, provided that each port is connected to exactly one other port in another process. In this case each channel can be identified with a tag, together with the name of the process at the other end. Since I wish to concentrate on semantics, I preferred in this paper to use the simplest and most direct notation, and to avoid raising questions about the possibility of connecting more than two ports by a single channel.

7.4 Automatic Buffering

As an alternative to synchronization of input and output, it is often proposed that an outputting process should be allowed to proceed even when the inputting process is not yet ready to accept the output. An implementation would be expected automatically to interpose a chain of buffers to hold output messages that have not yet been input.

I have deliberately rejected this alternative, for two reasons: (1) It is less realistic to implement in multiple disjoint processors, and (2) when buffering is required on a particular channel, it can readily be specified using the given primitives. Of course, it could be argued equally well that synchronization can be specified when required by using a pair of buffered input and output commands.

7.5 Unbounded Process Activation

The notation for an array of processes permits the same program text (like an Algol recursive procedure) to have many simultaneous "activations"; however, the exact number must be specified in advance. In a conventional single-processor implementation, this can lead to inconvenience and wastefulness, similar to the fixed-length array of Fortran. It would therefore be attractive to allow a process array with no a priori bound on the number of elements; and to specify that the exact number of elements required for a particular execution of the program should be determined dynamically, like the maximum depth of recursion of an Algol procedure or the number of iterations of a repetitive command.

However, it is a good principle that every actual run of a program with unbounded arrays should be identical to the run of some program with all its arrays bounded in advance. Thus the unbounded program should be defined as the "limit" (in some sense) of a series of bounded programs with increasing bounds. I have chosen to concentrate on the semantics of the bounded case—which is necessary anyway and which is more realistic for implementation on multiple microprocessors.

7.6 Fairness

Consider the parallel command:

```
[X::Y!stop( )||Y::continue:boolean; continue := true;
    *[continue; X?stop( )→ continue := false
      ▯continue → n := n + 1
      ]
].
```

If the implementation always prefers the second alternative in the repetitive command of Y, it is said to be *unfair*, because although the output command in X could have been executed on an infinite number of occasions, it is in fact always passed over.

The question arises: Should a programming language definition specify that an implementation must be *fair*? Here, I am fairly sure that the answer is NO. Otherwise, the implementation would be obliged to successfully complete the example program shown above, in spite of the fact that its nondeterminism is unbounded. I would therefore suggest that it is the programmer's responsibility to prove that his program terminates correctly—without relying on the assumption of fairness in the implementation. Thus the program shown above is incorrect, since its termination cannot be proved.

Nevertheless, I suggest that an efficient implementation should try to be reasonably fair and should ensure that an output command is not delayed unreasonably often after it first becomes executable. But a proof of correctness must not rely on this property of an efficient implementation. Consider the following analogy with a sequential program: An efficient implementation of an alternative command will tend to favor the alternative which can be most efficiently executed, but the programmer must ensure that the logical correctness of his program does not depend on this property of his implementation.

This method of avoiding the problem of fairness does not apply to programs such as operating systems which are intended to run forever because in this case termination proofs are not relevant. But I wonder whether it is ever advisable to write or to execute such programs. Even an operating system should be designed to bring itself to an orderly conclusion reasonably soon after it inputs a message instructing it to do so. Otherwise, the *only* way to stop it is to "crash" it.

7.7 Functional Coroutines

It is interesting to compare the processes described here with those proposed in [12]; the differences are most striking. There, coroutines are strictly deterministic: No choice is given between alternative sources of input. The output commands are automatically buffered to any required degree. The output of one process can be automatically fanned out to any number of processes (including itself!) which can consume it at differing rates. Finally, the processes there are designed to run forever, whereas my proposed parallel command is normally intended to terminate. The design in [12] is based on an elegant theory which permits proof of the properties of programs. These differences are not accidental—they seem to be natural consequences of the difference between the more abstract applicative (or functional) approach to programming and the more machine-oriented imperative (or procedural) approach, which is taken by communicating sequential processes.

7.8 Output Guards

Since input commands may appear in guards, it seems more symmetric to permit output commands as well. This would allow an obvious and useful simplification in some of the example programs, for example, in the bounded buffer (5.1). Perhaps a more convincing reason would be to ensure that the externally visible effect and behavior of every parallel command can be modeled by some sequential command. In order to model the parallel command

```
Z :: [X!2||Y!3]
```

we need to be able to write the sequential alternative command:

```
Z :: [X!2 → Y!3▯Y!3 → X!2]
```

Note that this *cannot* be done by the command

```
Z :: [true → X!2; Y!3▯true → Y!3; X!2]
```

which can fail if the process Z happens to choose the first alternative, but the processes Y and X are synchronized with each other in such a way that Y must input from Z before X does, e.g.

```
  Y :: Z?y; X!go()
||X :: Y?go(); Z?x
```

7.9 Restriction: Repetitive Command With Input Guard

In proposing an unfamiliar programming language feature, it seems wiser at first to specify a highly restrictive version rather than to propose extensions—especially when the language feature claims to be primitive. For example, it is clear that the multidimensional process array is not primitive, since it can readily be constructed in a language which permits only single-dimensional arrays. But I have a rather more serious misgiving about the repetitive command with input guards.

The automatic termination of a repetitive command on termination of the sources of all its input guards is an extremely powerful and convenient feature but it also involves some subtlety of specification to ensure that it is implementable; and it is certainly not primitive, since the required effect can be achieved (with considerable inconvenience) by explicit exchange of "end()" signals. For example, the subroutine DIV(4.1) could be rewritten:

```
 [DIV :: continue:boolean; continue := true;
 *[continue; X?end() → continue := false
 []continue; x,y:integer; X?(x,y) → ... ; X!(quot,rem)
||X :: USER PROG; DIV!end()
 ]
```

Other examples would be even more inconvenient.

But the dangers of convenient facilities are notorious. For example, the repetitive commands with input guards may tempt the programmer to write them without making adequate plans for their termination; and if it turns out that the automatic termination is unsatisfactory, reprogramming for explicit termination will involve severe changes, affecting even the interfaces between the processes.

8. Conclusion

This paper has suggested that input, output, and concurrency should be regarded as primitives of programming, which underlie many familiar and less familiar programming concepts. However, it would be unjustified to conclude that these primitives can wholly replace the other concepts in a programming language. Where a more elaborate construction (such as a procedure or a monitor) is frequently useful, has properties which are more simply provable, and can also be implemented more efficiently than the general case, there is a strong reason for including in a programming language a special notation for that construction. The fact that the construction can be defined in terms of simpler underlying primitives is a useful guarantee that its inclusion is logically consistent with the remainder of the language.

Acknowledgments. The research reported in this paper has been encouraged and supported by a Senior Fellowship of the Science Research Council of Great Britain. The technical inspiration was due to Edsger W. Dijkstra [9], and the paper has been improved in presentation and content by valuable and painstaking advice from D. Gries, D. Q. M. Fay, Edsger W. Dijkstra, N. Wirth, Robert Milne, M. K. Harper, and its referees. The role of IFIP W.G.2.3 as a forum for presentation and discussion is acknowledged with pleasure and gratitude.

Received March 1977; revised August 1977

References

1. Atkinson, R., and Hewitt, C. Synchronisation in actor systems. Working Paper 83, M.I.T., Cambridge, Mass., Nov. 1976.
2. Brinch Hansen, P. The programming language Concurrent Pascal. *IEEE Trans. Software Eng. 1,* 2 (June 1975), 199–207.
3. Campbell, R.H., and Habermann, A.N. The specification of process synchronisation by path expressions. *Lecture Notes in Computer Science 16,* Springer, 1974, pp. 89–102.
4. Conway, M.E. Design of a separable transition-diagram compiler. *Comm. ACM 6,* 7 (July 1963), 396–408.
5. Dahl, O-J., et al. SIMULA 67, common base language. Norwegian Computing Centre, Forskningveien, Oslo, 1967.
6. Dijkstra, E.W. Co-operating sequential processes. In *Programming Languages,* F. Genuys, Ed., Academic Press, New York, 1968, pp. 43–112.
7. Dijkstra, E.W. Notes on structured programming. In *Structured Programming,* Academic Press, New York 1972, pp. 1–82.
8. Dijkstra, E.W. Guarded commands, nondeterminacy, and formal derivation of programs. *Comm. ACM 18,* 8 (Aug. 1975), 453–457.
9. Dijkstra, E.W. Verbal communication, Marktoberdorf, Aug. 1975.
10. Hoare, C.A.R. Towards a theory of parallel programming. In *Operating Systems Techniques,* Academic Press, New York, 1972, pp. 61–71.
11. Hoare, C.A.R. Proof of correctness of data representations. *Acta Informatica 1,* 4 (1972), 271–281.
12. Kahn, G. The semantics of a simple language for parallel programming. In *Proc. IFIP Congress 74,* North Holland, 1974.
13. Liskov, B.H. A note on CLU. Computation Structures Group Memo. 112, M.I.T., Cambridge, Mass, 1974.
14. McIlroy, M.D. Coroutines. Bell Laboratories, Murray Hill, N.J., 1968.
15. Naur, P., Ed. Report on the algorithmic language ALGOL 60. *Comm. ACM 3,* 5 (May 1960), 299–314.
16. Reynolds, J.C. COGENT. ANL-7022, Argonne Nat. Lab., Argonne, Ill., 1965.
17. Thompson, K. The UNIX command language. In *Structured Programming,* Infotech, Nicholson House, Maidenhead, England, 1976, pp. 375–384.
18. van Wijngaarden, A. Ed. Report on the algorithmic language ALGOL 68. *Numer. Math. 14* (1969), 79–218.
19. Wulf, W.A., London, R.L., and Shaw, M. Abstraction and verification in ALPHARD. Dept. of Comptr. Sci., Carnegie-Mellon U., Pittsburgh, Pa., June 1976.
20. Wirth, N. The programming language PASCAL. *Acta Informatica 1,* 1 (1971), 35–63.

System Deadlocks

E. G. COFFMAN, JR.

Pennsylvania State University, University Park, Pennsylvania

M. J. ELPHICK

University of Newcastle upon Tyne, Newcastle upon Tyne, England

A. SHOSHANI

System Development Corporation, Santa Monica, California

A problem of increasing importance in the design of large multiprogramming systems is the, so-called, deadlock or deadly-embrace problem. In this article we survey the work that has been done on the treatment of deadlocks from both the theoretical and practical points of view.

Key words and phrases: deadlocks, deadly embraces, system deadlocks, multiprogramming, interlock problems

CR categories: 4.10, 4.32

1 INTRODUCTION

One of the objectives of recent developments in operating systems—incorporating multiprogramming, multiprocessing, etc.—has been to improve the utilization of system resources (and hence reduce the cost to users) by distributing them among many concurrently executing *tasks*. In any operating system of this type the problem of deadlock must be considered. Requests by separate tasks for resources may possibly be granted in such a sequence that a group of two or more tasks is unable to proceed—each task monopolizing resources and waiting for the release of resources currently held by others in that group. As a somewhat simplified example, suppose we have a task T_1 that has just produced a request for a file on disk, and that T_1 must suspend operation until the disk becomes available. Suppose another task T_2 has control of the (single) disk channel but that it is still waiting for T_1 to complete the updating of a (shared) file that contains information required by T_2. In order for work to proceed, the disk channel must be given over to T_1. But if we assume that T_2 is in the middle of some file on disk, then, because of hardware or software limitations, a preemption of the disk from T_2 can be effectively tantamount to a sacrifice in the processing already accomplished by T_2. Under these circumstances, if T_1 and T_2 have no (temporary) alternative to waiting, they will be deadlocked and never able to proceed.

As shown by this example, deadlocks, or "deadly embraces" as E. W. Dijkstra has called them, can arise even though no single task requires more than the total resources available in the system. Moreover, deadlocks can arise whether the allocation of resources is the responsibility of the operating system (as is normally the case) or of the programs themselves.

The example also illustrates that the term "resource," in the context of deadlocks, can apply not only to devices (tape and disk drives, channels, card readers, etc.), and processors and storage media (core store, drums, disks, tapes), but to programs, subroutines, and data (tables, files, etc.). Many of these permit only *exclusive* use by one

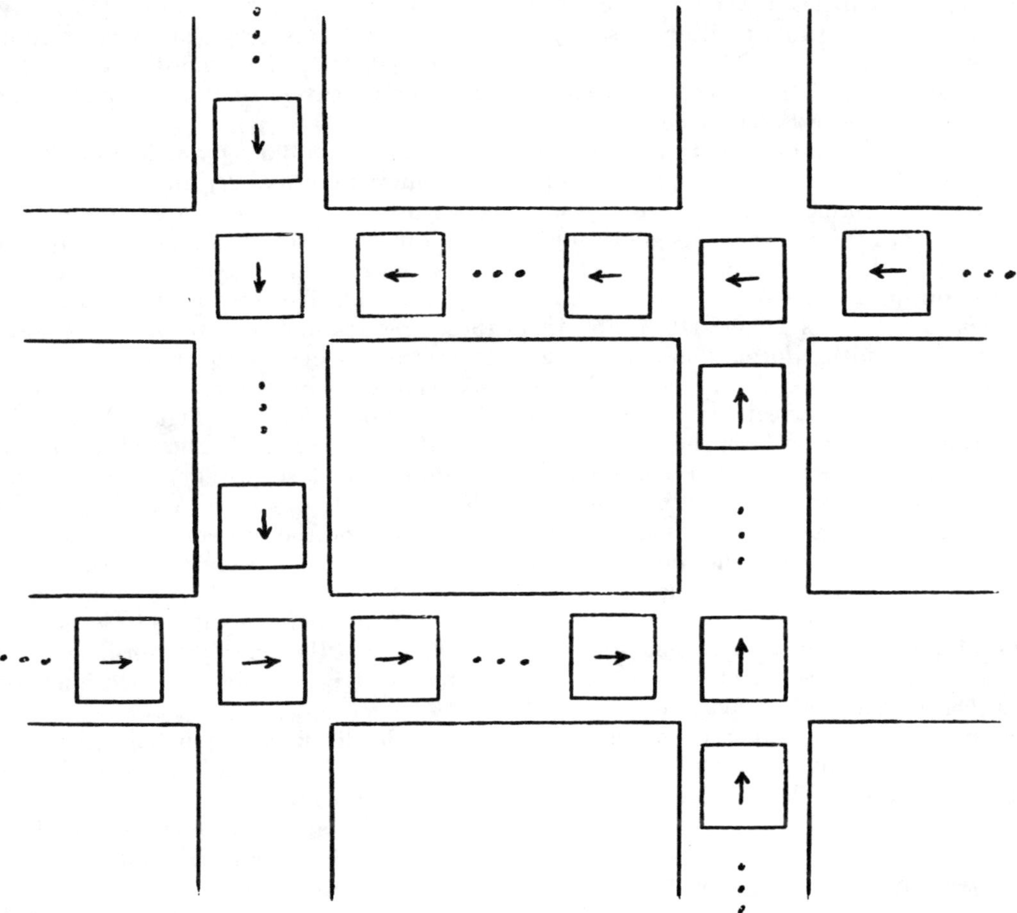

FIG. 1. Traffic deadlock.

Since the deadlock problem is a logical one it can arise in different contexts, provided that tasks and resources are interpreted properly. For example, consider the situation of traffic flow along the edges of a square as shown in Figure 1. The small boxes represent cars, and the arrows the direction in which they want to move. Since there are four cars blocking the traffic at each corner we have a traffic deadlock. In this case we can think of the space occupied by a car as a resource for which other cars are competing. Cars represent tasks that request the next resource (space) before they can release the current resource (space they currently occupy). This is a simple example of deadlock problems that can appear in traffic control. Many other examples arise in production management and control, where machines, tools, people, input information, etc., can be considered as resources needed for the execution of some task.

The deadlock problem becomes more complex when a system has different resource *types* and, in general, more than one resource of the same type. In this case resources of the same type are not labeled differently. When a request is made for a number of resources of a particular type, any resources of that type will do. Thus, the case of only one resource of each type is a special case of the above. Examples of many resources of the same type are memory pages (i.e., units of storage allocation), disk drives (if there is more than one in a system), processors in a multiprocessor system, etc.

The remainder of this paper is organized as follows. In the next section we summarize the conditions necessary for the existence of deadlocks and present two graphical methods for representing deadlocks. In sections 3–5 the treatment of deadlocks is classified according to the assumption of whether advance information about future resource requirements of tasks is available. For the case when no such information is available, we consider in section 3 the design of systems in which the possibility of deadlocks occurring is *prevented* from the start by removing one or more of the necessary conditions. We then discuss in section 4 how a state of deadlock may be *detected,* and how *recovery* can be carried out, preferably at the least cost to the users of the system. If advance estimates of the resources required by each job can be obtained, techniques are available for *avoiding* deadlock, and we discuss their cost and effectiveness in section 5. Finally, we attempt some conclusions about the relative merits of these various approaches to the problem of deadlock.

2 CHARACTERIZATIONS OF DEADLOCKS

In order to illustrate the conditions under which deadlocks can occur, we abstract the previous example and consider two tasks T_1 and T_2, each requiring the exclusive use of two different resources R_1 and R_2 (not necessarily together). We can represent the combined progress of these tasks in the following way (due to Dijkstra). For each task the number of instructions executed subsequent to some selected initial time is used as a measure of its progress, and a pair of such values defines a point in a two-dimensional "progress space," as shown in Figure 2. The joint progress of T_1 and T_2 is then represented by a sequence of discrete points in this space; sub-sequences in which only one coordinate increases correspond to time intervals in which one task is in sole control of the CPU, while simultaneous increases in both coordinates can only occur in a multiple processor system. It is clear that such a "trajectory" can never result in a decrease in either coordinate—progress (i.e., the execution of instructions) is irreversible.

The intervals during which tasks T_1 and T_2 require resources R_1 and R_2 are shown in Figure 2, as are those areas representing simultaneous use of a resource by both tasks. Since we have assumed that each task requires exclusive control of any resources, these areas cannot be entered by the trajectory representing their progress.

Given the sequence of resource usage by the two tasks shown in Figure 2, it is clear that if the trajectory is allowed to enter the region D, then a state of deadlock is inevitable—T_1 holds resource R_1, T_2 holds resource R_2, and the subsequent requests from each task for its second resource must be denied. Other tasks in the system may be able to continue if they do not require these resources, but the overall performance of the system will be degraded by the unavailability of R_1 and R_2.

This deadlock situation has arisen only because all of the following general conditions were operative:

1) Tasks claim exclusive control of the resources they require ("mutual exclusion" condition).
2) Tasks hold resources already allocated to them while waiting for additional resources ("wait for" condition).
3) Resources cannot be forcibly removed from the tasks holding them until the resources are used to completion ("no preemption" condition).
4) A circular chain of tasks exists, such that each task holds one or more resources that are being requested by the next task in the chain ("circular wait" condition).

The existence of these conditions effectively defines a state of deadlock.

In the previous example these conditions were indeed in effect, and a circular wait existed, since T_1 was waiting for T_2 to release R_2, while T_2 was waiting for T_1 to release R_1.

In terms of these necessary conditions it is

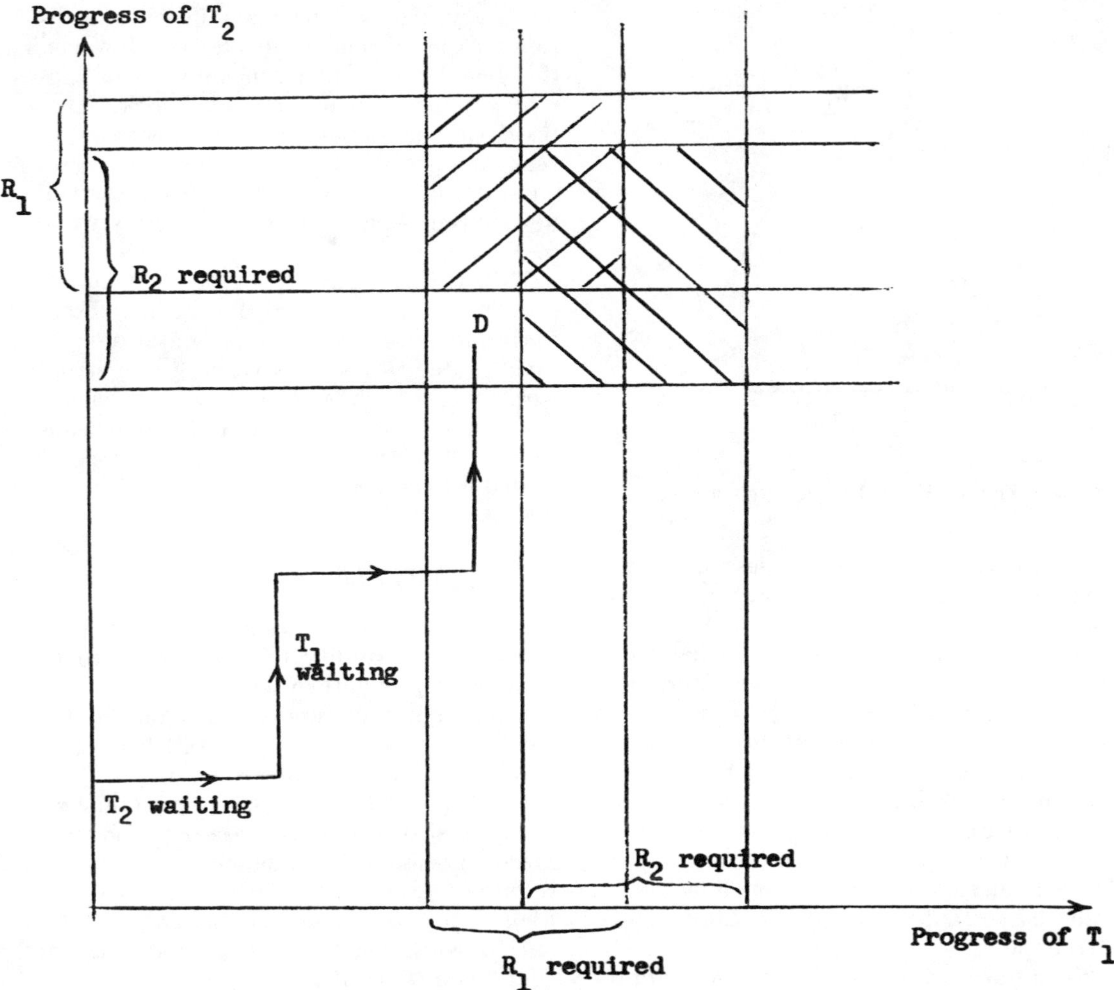

FIG. 2. Joint progress of tasks T_1, T_2.

interesting to examine again the example of traffic deadlocks in Figure 1. In this case there is only one resource of each type, since spaces occupied by cars are all distinguishable from each other. The "mutual exclusion" condition obviously holds since a space cannot be shared by two or more cars. The "wait for" condition exists, since a car cannot release the current space until it gets the next space. The "no preemption" condition clearly holds, assuming that cars are not removable by an outside agent. Finally, circuits in the state graph are possible because of the direction of flow around the square.

Deadlocks can be expressed more precisely in terms of graphs. Suppose we have a set of tasks $\{T_1, T_2, \cdots, T_n\}$ in some arbitrary state of execution; let $\{R_1, R_2, \cdots, R_m\}$ be a set of distinct resources in use by these tasks (i.e., there is only one resource of each type). We define a directed graph (to be called a state graph) whose nodes correspond to the resources $\{R_j\}$ and whose arcs are defined as follows. If, at the time instant to which the graph applies, some task T is allocated (i.e., possesses) resource R_j while requesting R_k, then the graph contains an arc from node R_j to node R_k. An example is shown in Figure 3 for $m = 3$. As can be

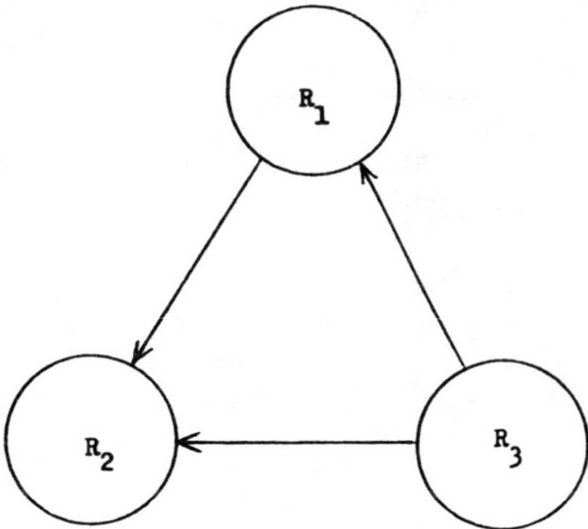

FIG. 3. Example of a state graph.

seen, there exists a task possessing R_1 and requesting R_2, a task possessing R_3 and requesting R_1 and R_2.

It has been shown [4, 6, 8, 14] that a circuit (directed loop) in the request graph is a necessary and sufficient condition for a deadlock, assuming the first three conditions given above are operative. As an example, suppose an arc from R_2 to R_3 is added to the graph in Figure 3. Clearly, there must exist at least three deadlocked tasks; each of the R_i is requested by one task but allocated to another so that none of the R_i can be effectively used.

The state graph described above is appropriate only for systems in which there is only one resource of a type. For the general case of more than one resource of the same type, a state graph was defined [14] as follows: resources are partitioned into types $r_1, r_2, \cdots, r_s$ with the number of resources of each type given by $w_1, w_2, \cdots, w_s$, respectively. The resources of a given type are identical and indistinguishable, and it is assumed that requests for a given resource type r_i can be for any number less than or equal to w_i. State graphs are defined in a way similar to that given earlier. The nodes now become the resource types $\{r_i\}$. There will be an arc from r_i to r_j if and only if there exists at least one task requesting one or more resources of type r_j and possessing one or more resources of type r_i. With this definition a circuit in the state graph is a necessary, but no longer a sufficient, condition for the existence of deadlocks. However, this result may still be meaningful in considering the prevention of deadlocks. If a restriction is imposed on the behavior of tasks in such a way that circuits in the request graph cannot arise, then deadlocks will never occur (such a restriction is discussed in section 3).

Two recent studies [16, 18] of deadlock problems have appeared in which different variations of graphical representations are investigated. Results based on graph structure that are similar to but more extensive than those discussed here under the headings of detection and avoidance are presented for these graphs.

3 PREVENTION OF DEADLOCK

If we undertake the design of a system in which the possibility of deadlock is to be excluded a priori, then we must ensure that at every point in time at least one of the necessary conditions is not satisfied. This implies certain constraints on the way in which requests for resources may be made.

The first of the four necessary conditions given in section 2 cannot be denied for all resources. For example, the sharing of a file by more than one task can only be permitted when neither task is updating the contents of that file.

The following approaches, suggested by Havender [4], in effect deny each of the three remaining conditions in turn.

a) Each task must request all its required resources at once and cannot proceed until all have been granted ("wait-for" condition denied).
b) If a task holding certain resources is denied a further request, that task must release its original resources and, if necessary, request them again together with the additional resources ("no preemption" condition denied).
c) The imposition of a linear ordering of resource types on all tasks; i.e., if a task has been allocated resources of type r_i it may subsequently request only those resources of types following r_i in the ordering. In the case of only one resource

of a type, the linear ordering is of resources. (It can be shown that under this condition the state graph cannot have circuits, and therefore circular wait conditions are prevented.)

When each of these strategies is only partially applicable it is clearly possible to use a combination of them in a given system, and also to implement them either by embodying the constraints in the design of the system (so that no task *can* violate the constraints), or by insisting that all application programs as well as system components follow certain conventions in requesting resources.

Approach (a) may be costly since some of the resources allocated to a task may remain unused for long periods. Approach (b) is convenient only when applied to preemptible resources whose state can be easily saved and restored later, as is the case with a processor. Approach (c) may be feasible and is used in the case discussed by Havender [4], where he describes the way in which the deadlock problem was tackled in the design of that component of the OS/360 (MVT) system responsible for initiating job-steps. Here certain possibilities of deadlock (between separate job-steps, at least) have been prevented by acquiring storage, devices, and data sets for each job-step in a fixed order. However, the possibility of deadlock between several tasks initiated by one or more job-steps has not been prevented completely, since the ENQ and DEQ facilities can be used (or misused) to create a "circular wait."

Other approaches to this problem are discussed in the report by Collier [5], and in the papers by Reiter [6], Murphy [7], and Merikallio and Holland [8].

4 DEADLOCK DETECTION AND RECOVERY

It was discussed in section 2 that in the case of one resource of a type, a deadlock exists at time t if and only if there exists a circuit in the state graph at time t. Thus, a deadlock detection mechanism in this case consists of a routine for maintaining a state graph each time resources are requested, acquired, or released by tasks, and a routine that examines the state graph to determine whether a circuit exists.

For the case of more than one resource of a type, a detection algorithm cannot be similarly based on the state graph since, in this case, a circuit in the state graph is only a necessary condition for a deadlock; a more elaborate state description mechanism is required.

Let $r_1, r_2, \cdots, r_s$ represent resource types and $w_1, w_2, \cdots w_s$ represent the number of resources of each type as in section 2. At an arbitrary time instant t let p_{ij} denote the number of resources of type r_j allocated to (possessed by) T_i and let q_{ij} denote the number of resources of type r_j requested by T_i in excess of those already allocated to T_i. Define the *allocation* and *request* matrices $P = ((p_{ij}))$ and $Q = ((q_{ij}))$ and let P_i and Q_i denote the row vectors giving the resources allocated to T_i and requested by T_i, respectively. Let $V = (v_1, v_2, \cdots, v_s)$ be an *available resources* vector whose ith element $(v_i \leqslant w_i)$ indicates the number of resources of type r_i that are currently available. Note that

$$v_j = w_j - \sum_{i=1}^{n} p_{ij}.$$

That is, the sum of the resources allocated and those available of type r_j must be equal to the total number of that type in the system. In the following, $\underline{0}$ will indicate a (row) vector each of whose s elements is 0. Also, $x \leqslant y$, where x and y are vectors, is defined to hold if and only if it holds for each pair of corresponding elements from x and y.

The algorithm below, which is presented in [14], is designed to reveal a deadlock by simply accounting for all possibilities of sequencing the tasks that remain to be completed. Suppose at time t the state of the system is available in the matrices P and Q, and suppose V is also given. We have the following algorithm for determining the existence of a deadlock at time t.

Algorithm A

1) Initialize $W \leftarrow V(t)$. Mark all rows for which $P_i(t) = \underline{0}$. (All rows are assumed to be "unmarked" at the outset.)
2) Search for an unmarked row, say the ith,

such that $Q_i(t) \leqslant W$. If one is found, go to Step 3; otherwise terminate the algorithm.

3) Set $W \leftarrow W + P_i(t)$, mark the ith row, and return to Step 2.

It is not difficult to verify that a deadlock exists if and only if there are unmarked rows at the termination of the algorithm. Moreover, the set of unmarked rows corresponds precisely to the set of deadlocked tasks.

The running time of this algorithm is proportional to the square of the number of tasks. It is shown in [16] (see also [17]) that by ordering the resource requests by size and associating with each task a count of the number of types of resources being requested, a detection algorithm can be devised which has a running time that varies linearly with the number of tasks. Moreover, the additional cost of ordering requests and maintaining counts is offset by the fact that this method also facilitates finding blocked tasks to activate when other tasks release resources. A number of simplifications are possible in important special cases (e.g., a single resource of each type), and these are also discussed in [16].

Given a detection mechanism, perhaps the simplest approach to recovery from a deadlock situation would involve aborting each of the deadlocked tasks, or, less drastically, aborting them in some sequence until sufficient resources become released to remove deadlocks in the set of remaining tasks. Obviously, we could also design an algorithm that searches for a minimum-sized set of tasks which, if aborted, would remove the deadlocks.

A more general technique [14] has been devised that assigns a fixed cost c_i to the removal (forced preemption) of a resource of type r_i from a deadlocked task that is being aborted. Thus, the cost of removing resources from a deadlocked task T_i is:

$$\sum_{j=1}^{s} c_i \cdot g(q_{ij} - v_j) \quad \text{where } g(x) = \begin{matrix} x; x > 0 \\ 0; x \leqslant 0 \end{matrix}$$

An algorithm has been designed that finds a subset of resources that would incur the minimum cost if preempted. The algorithm finds a minimum cost solution by an efficient tree-search procedure that can be characterized as a branch-and-bound technique. (Algorithm A is used to isolate new sets of deadlocked tasks in the sequence of trial-removals made by the algorithm.)

Note that by using this detection-recovery mechanism the notion of deadlock can be extended to include resource types which are actually preemptible but which have varying preemption costs. In other words, with this extension, deadlocks do not necessarily involve tasks that must be aborted; rather, it may only be necessary to remove certain resources from tasks that incur such costs as supervisor overhead, swapping, etc., but not a loss of input, output, or the progress that has been made in a computation. Clearly, forced resource preemptions involving the latter losses will be assigned high costs so that the recovery algorithm will avoid them.

5 AVOIDING DEADLOCKS USING INFORMATION ON RESOURCE REQUIREMENTS

To avoid deadlocks in a multiprogramming system in which the necessary conditions for deadlocks can exist, it is usually necessary to have some advance information on the resource usage of tasks. A number of interesting models can be envisioned, each differing in the amount of information assumed available. A comprehensive theoretical study of a number of task models can be found in [10]. In this section we shall briefly examine two such models: the first will be the most basic model (full information assumed) and the second will be the more practically oriented model of Habermann [11].

In the basic model a task is assumed to consist of a sequence of *task-steps* during each of which the resource usage of the task remains constant. The execution of a task-step first involves the acquisition of those resources needed by the given task-step but not passed on by the previous task-step. Next follows a period of execution during which the resource requirements do not change. Finally, at the completion of execution, all those resources not needed by the subsequent task-step are released and returned to a pool of available resources.

Before describing how deadlocks are avoided with the task-step model we shall find it convenient to introduce the notion of *safe* states. As indicated in the previous section, the state of the system as it relates to the requesting and allocation of resources at time t is reflected in the two matrices $Q(t)$ and $P(t)$, respectively. For simplicity let us denote this resource-state by $S(t)$. We shall say that $S(t)$ is *safe* when, using the currently available resources and those which will be returned by currently executing task-steps, it is possible to find a valid sequence of the uninitiated task-steps in the currently initiated but incomplete tasks such that all tasks in the system can be run to completion. A sequence of this kind will be valid if the implied sequence of resource requests is such that at the time each request is made there are sufficient available resources to satisfy it.

As an illustration of this definition, consider Figure 2 in which the region D corresponds to points in the joint progress of T_1 and T_2 from which a deadlock is inevitable: As we can see, all points in the region D correspond to unsafe states and all points outside this region (and the shaded region) correspond to safe states.

The following remarks should be made about the definition of a safe state. First, we note that the initial state in which no resources are yet allocated and all are available is always a safe state. Hence, there always exists an initial sequence of all task-steps according to which all tasks are completed. In particular, we can always execute the tasks in strict serial sequence if necessary. In part it follows from this observation that if there is a way to complete the currently executing tasks without getting into a deadlock, we can clearly complete the remaining uninitiated tasks (again, executing them in serial order if necessary). Finally, with an appropriate formalization of the ideas in this and the previous section, it has been shown that the ability to avoid deadlocks subsequent to time t can be guaranteed if and only if $S(t)$ is a safe state [10].

We are now in a position to state precisely the problem confronted by a supervisor designed to avoid deadlocks. Suppose the system is in a safe state $S(t)$ and there exists a set of outstanding resource requests given by the contents of $Q(t)$. The supervisor must be able to determine whether any given one of these requests (if any) is safe in the sense that it is less than or equal to the currently available resources and would leave the system in a safe state if granted. Since, in general, there can be more than one safe request, some other scheduling criterion has to be invoked to determine which safe request is to be granted. Common criteria include first-in-first-out, shortest (or smallest) job first, etc. It is worth emphasizing perhaps that these other scheduling criteria must be applied to the set consisting only of safe requests. Otherwise, if they are applied to all requests, a request that is not safe may be selected, thus artificially creating a deadlock arising from conflicting scheduling policies.

The problem of determining whether a state $S(t)$ is safe following the granting of a request generally requires a procedure to search for an appropriate sequence of task-steps. As implied earlier, the procedure begins by assuming that the currently available resources are augmented by those allocated to currently executing task-steps. This is equivalent to assuming that the first task-step in the sequence sought is not begun until all currently executing task-steps have been allowed to complete. The search time can be improved by the following result [10].

At some stage in the search procedure let $x = p_1p_2 \cdots p_r$ be an initial (trial) subsequence of task-steps. Assuming that this sub-sequence were realized, suppose that the number of resources available following any given task-step is, for each type, greater than or equal to the number of resources available just following the previous task-step. Under this condition it has been shown that if the state $S(t)$ being tested is in fact safe, then there must exist a valid sequence of all uninitiated task-steps in the executing tasks that has x as a prefix (i.e., $p_1p_2 \cdots p_r$ will be the initial task-steps in the sequence). Thus, in organizing a conventional tree-search for appropriate sequences it is never necessary to back-up beyond the last element of an initial sub-sequence having a corresponding sequence of available resource vectors with the above property.

From practical considerations it is likely to be necessary to assume that less is known about the resource usage of tasks than is assumed in the task-step model. We shall now briefly discuss Habermann's model [11] in which we deal with entire tasks rather than task-steps, and in which it is assumed that only the maximum number of resources required by each task is known. In particular, for each task T_i we have a resource vector that gives the maximum number of resources of each type that will be required at any time during execution of T_i.

A state $S(t)$ will be safe in this model if and only if there exists some sequence according to which the currently executing (i.e., initiated but incomplete) tasks can complete, *assuming they will still need their maximum resource requirements* at some time, and assuming that we have only the currently available resources at the beginning of the sequence. The search for sequences of the executing tasks can be significantly more efficient than the search described with the task-step model, even after the fact that there are generally fewer tasks than task-steps is taken into account. The reason for this is as follows. Since each task will return as many resources as it requests, the sequence of available resource vectors corresponding to a sequence of the executing tasks will always have the monotonically non-decreasing property mentioned earlier. Thus, we can show that in the search procedure it is never necessary to back-up to try new initial sub-sequences; and it follows that the search time is proportional to the square of the number of executing tasks.

A further technique mentioned by Habermann for shortening the search time is described as follows. Suppose a request has just been made by task T_i, the system is in a safe state, and we wish to determine if the request is safe. If at *any* point in developing a trial sequence we find that the corresponding available resources are sufficient to complete T_i, we may terminate the search with the decision that the request is safe. The reason is that if T_i, the source of the request, can complete and release all the resources it controls, all other tasks can certainly be completed, since the state previous to the request was safe and they could therefore have been completed before the request was made.*

In summary, the applicability of the basic task-step model means that we can determine precisely when deadlocks are unavoidable on granting a request. Although with Habermann's model false threats of deadlocks may degrade resource utilization, it has the significant advantages of requiring less information about task behavior and a more efficient algorithm for testing whether states are safe. For models that moderate the disadvantages (and the advantages) of both the above models see [10].

Hebalkar [18] uses a graph model to represent processes of more general structure than the sequence of task-steps. In his model, nodes represent transitions of a computation and arcs represent demand vectors of resources. Thus, a computation can split into parallel subcomputations, and subcomputations can merge. A cut-set of a graph represents a state of the system. This model has been shown to facilitate the representation of safe states as well as deadlock states. Algorithms designed to preclude deadlocks are presented, and are based on the advance information in the graph model.

6 CONCLUSIONS

We have described the various strategies that can be used to deal with the problem of deadlock, under the headings of *prevention, detection* (and recovery), and *avoidance*. Algorithms for implementing the last two policies have been outlined briefly.

Where possible, prevention of the possibility of deadlock is better than cure, since in most current systems deadlock is an ex-

* For techniques leading to search times that vary linearly with the number of tasks and for applications to important special cases, see [16]. Such techniques arise from the more efficient detection algorithms mentioned in section 4.

ceptional occurrence, and in many cases it involves only a limited set of resources. Once a deadlock situation has been recognized as such, the problem can often be removed by suitable changes to that part of the system (for example, permitting preemption of a resource where this was not thought necessary before).

If this approach is not feasible—perhaps because the constraints it would impose on jobs are unacceptable—then detection or avoidance may be considered. However, it is not possible at present to predict accurately either the costs or the benefits that can be obtained by use of the techniques described. Good measures of the running time of the various search algorithms and of the resource utilization achieved by systems using them are not available.

Some refinements of the models presented here for the detection, recovery, and avoidance algorithms would be desirable in practice. The recovery model, for example, should use costs (for the preemption of resources from a task) that are functions of the time for which that task has been in progress, and perhaps of its priority. The selection of an appropriate avoidance model involves a balance between the efficiency of the algorithm (for determining whether granting a request is safe), the level of resource utilization possible, and the cost to the user in providing estimates of potential resource requirements.

In avoiding deadlock, an alternative to the search algorithms presented may be feasible when the number of safe sequences is relatively small (and the system may be operating inefficiently, having to deny most requests). This alternative approach is to store the current set of safe sequences, updating them as necessary, and to inspect the first element of each sequence to decide whether a request can be granted. However, as the number of safe sequences increases, the storage and updating problems will make this approach less efficient, and some scheme for switching from one method to the other might be necessary.

In practice, even though complete deadlock is avoided, it may be more important, for the sake of efficiency, to prevent the system from entering a state of "near deadlock," in which progress can be made only by granting requests from one task at a time. Again, when jobs with heavy resource requirements are discriminated against, the situation in which such a job is allowed to acquire control of several valuable resources, but is subjected to long waits as a result of further requests, must be avoided. The models described above might be adapted for this purpose by defining a cost for a given sequence of resource allocations (which would be high when a valuable resource is unavailable for a long sequence of task-steps); a search for a safe sequence having a low cost might be feasible.

On the other hand, one could focus on reducing supervisor overhead rather than improving resource utilization by adopting the following approach. Assuming advance resource-usage information, as in Habermann's model, for example, an operating system could be designed that never multiprograms two or more tasks whose resource requirements are such that circular wait conditions can arise. That is, deadlocks are avoided by inspection of resource requirements only at the beginning of task executions rather than each time a resource request is made. This approach clearly sacrifices potential losses in resource utilization for savings in supervisor execution times.

Needham and Hartley [12] have examined system designs partially involving this approach but have not attempted a complete removal of the possibility of deadlock (or "knotting," as the authors refer to it). In the interest of system operating efficiency, deadlocks (and the resulting "disasters") are allowed to occur, but measures are described that ensure that such events are kept at an acceptably low frequency.

In conclusion, it must be agreed that the problem of deadlock has not been of major (or at least continuing) importance in most current systems, mainly because it has amounted to little more than an isolated debugging problem. However, for future systems sharing an increasingly costly set of services and resources among an increasing number of individual users, these problems are likely to become more pressing.

They will be even more important for those systems that provide a common set of large files (or data bases) available to the many users of the system for both read-only access and updating. The typical resource usage here will be to obtain access to a small subset of records, from which other tasks must be excluded until the task at hand releases the subset. Some techniques for organizing this type of system to avoid deadlock are discussed by Shoshani and Bernstein [13].

REFERENCES

1. Dijkstra, E. W. "Co-operating sequential processes." In *Programming languages: NATO advanced study institute.* F. Genuys (Ed.). Academic Press, London, 1968.
2. *IBM System/360 operating system, supervisor and data management services.* Form C28-6646-2, IBM, White Plains, N. Y., 1968.
3. Dennis, J. B.; and Van Horn, E. C. "Programming semantics for multiprogrammed computations." *Comm. ACM* **9,** 3 (March 1966), 143–155.
4. Havender, J. W. "Avoiding deadlock in multi-tasking systems." *IBM Systems Journal* **2** (1968), 74–84.
5. Braude, E. J. "An algorithm for the detection of system deadlocks." IBM Technical Report: TROO. 791, IBM Data Systems Division, Poughkeepsie, N. Y., 1961.
6. Collier, W. W. "System deadlocks." IBM Technical Report TR-00. 1756, IBM Systems Development Division, Poughkeepsie, N.Y., 1968.
7. Reiter, A. "A resource-allocation scheme for multi-user on-line operation of a small computer." *Proc. AFIPS SJCC,* Vol. 30, pp. 1–7. AFIPS Press, Montvale, N. J., 1967.
8. Murphy, J. E. "Resource allocation with interlock detection in a multi-task system." *Proc. AFIPS FJCC,* Vol. 33, Pt. 2, pp. 1169–1176. AFIPS Press, Montvale, N. J., 1968.
9. Merikallio, R. A.; and Holland, F. C. "Simulation design of a multi-processing system." *Proc. AFIPS FJCC,* Vol. 33, Pt. 2, pp. 1399–1410. AFIPS Press, Montvale, N. J., 1968.
10. Shoshani, A.; and Coffman, E. G. "Sequencing tasks in multi-process, multiple resource systems to avoid deadlocks." In *Proc. 11th Annual Symposium on Switching and Automata Theory,* Oct. 1970, pp. 225–233.
11. Habermann, A. N. "Prevention of system deadlocks." *Comm. ACM* **12,** 7 (July 1969), 373–377, 385.
12. Needham, R. M.; and Hartley, D. F. "Theory and practice in operating system design." *Proc. 2nd ACM Symposium on Operating Systems Principles,* pp. 8–12. Brandon/Systems Press, Princeton, N.J., 1969.
13. Shoshani, A.; and Bernstein, A. J. "Synchronization in a parallel-accessed data base." *Comm. ACM* **12,** 11 (Nov. 1969), 604–607 [Also GE Report No. 69-C-138].
14. Shoshani, A.; and Coffman, E. G. "Prevention, detection, and recovery from system deadlocks." In *Proc. 4th Annual Princeton Conf. on Information Sciences and Systems,* March 1970. (See also Computer Science Lab. Technical Report No. 80, Department of Electrical Engineering, Princeton University, 1969.)
15. Dijkstra, E. W. "The structure of the THE-multiprogramming system." *Comm. ACM* **11,** 5 (May 1968), 341–346.
16. Holt, Richard C. "On deadlock in computer systems." (PhD Dissertation) Department of Computer Science, Cornell University, Ithaca, N.Y., Jan. 1971.
17. Russell, R. D. "A model of deadlock-free resource allocation—preliminary version." Memo CGTM #93, Department of Computer Science, Stanford University, Stanford, Calif., June 1970.
18. Hebalkar, Prakash. "Deadlock-free resource sharing in asynchronous systems." (PhD Dissertation) Electrical Engineering Department, MIT, Cambridge, Mass., Sept. 1970.

B. RANDELL, Editor

Prevention of System Deadlocks

A. N. Habermann
Carnegie-Mellon University, Pittsburgh, Pennsylvania*

A well-known problem in the design of operating systems is the selection of a resource allocation policy that will prevent deadlock. Deadlock is the situation in which resources have been allocated to various tasks in such a way that none of the tasks can continue. The various published solutions have been somewhat restrictive: either they do not handle the problem in sufficient generality or they suggest policies which will on occasion refuse a request which could have been safely granted. Algorithms are presented which examine a request in the light of the current allocation of resources and determine whether or not the granting of the request will introduce the possibility of a deadlock. Proofs given in the appendixes show that the conditions imposed by the algorithms are both necessary and sufficient to prevent deadlock. The algorithms have been successfully used in the THE system.

KEY WORDS AND PHRASES: multiprogramming, time-sharing, scheduling, resource allocation
CR CATEGORIES: 3.72, 4.32, 6.20

Introduction

Consider a set of sequential processes which share system resources in such a way that (1) while a resource A is allocated to a process P_i no other process P_j can seize A, and (2) an allocated resource is not released until it has fulfilled its task.

Dijkstra shows in [2] and [6] how the use of system resources can be made exclusive by means of the primitives P-operation and V-operation. Dennis and Van Horn [3] use the macro instructions *LOCK* and *UNLK*, specially designed for this purpose. These techniques have in common that a process P_i performing a P-operation (e.g. *LOCK* instruction) will get the resource requested if it is free and, if not, process P_i is held up until a matching V-operation (e.g. *UNLK* instruction) is performed. The techniques also have in common the fact that they do not imply any rules for resource allocation. This is still a matter of system design.

If the total request for resources of a certain type can exceed the amount available, some strategy is needed to order the assignment of resources in time. Care must be taken that the strategy applied cannot cause a deadlock: i.e. the situation that cooperating processes prevent their mutual progress even though no single one requests more resources than are available.

* Computation Center

Suppose, for instance, each of two processes P_1 and P_2 needs the resources A and B at the same time, i.e. when either A or B has been allocated to it. P_1 will certainly not release the allocated resource before the other one has also been allocated to it (likewise P_2). Suppose the strategy is such that allocation will follow on request if the resource is free. Then the situation may arise that P_1 has seized resource A and P_2 resource B. From then on, P_1 and P_2 will wait for each other indefinitely, since P_1 certainly does not release A until it has seized B, i.e. not until P_2 has released B, while P_2 will not release B until it has seized A.

One way out of the difficulty is to permit a set of processes to run concurrently only if together they do not claim more resources than are available [4]. However, we will see that such a strategy is unnecessarily restrictive.

In this paper algorithms are described by means of which a deadlock can be prevented, and yet as many resource requests are granted as can be allowed, while neither are resources reserved on account of a claim, nor is resource request restricted to a few processes. The algorithms decide only whether or not granting a request can produce a deadlock, so that assignment rules (according to priority rules, for instance) can be implemented freely.

In the author's thesis [5] different sorts of resource requests are discussed, in particular, the case of temporary lease, i.e. when a process asks for a resource and can promise its release unconditionally, as well as the case of a single directed request, i.e. when a process can continue independently of resource activity. Though [5] also contains the theorems and proofs, albeit in a slightly different form, the aim of the present paper is to show the usefulness and applicability of the algorithms which prevent a deadlock.

Another Form of Deadlock

When resource activity itself may imply resource request, another form of deadlock can occur. Let, for instance, a disk device be controlled by a sequential process D that runs synchronously with the device interrupts. D is to be considered a resource, to which tasks can be ordered by other processes. Before it is going to page in data, process D will ask for free space in main storage S. If a process P is able to seize S and order a task to D, a deadlock results, since D cannot find free space in main storage, while P does not release S until D has completed the ordered task. Here the deadlock is caused by the fact that a request for resource D itself implies another resource request.

Preliminaries

The kind of system considered here consists of sequential processes $P_1, \ldots, P_n$ and resources of m different types

Reprinted with permission from *Commun. Ass. Comput. Mach.*, vol. 12, pp. 373–377, 385, July 1969.

($n \geq 1$, $m \geq 1$). ([7] and [8] treat the case when $m>1$ and each type contains one resource.[1]) Though n can vary, as we see below, n will be considered as fixed now; m is a fixed number. Resources of one type are equal in the sense that they can perform the same tasks; their number is fixed. The reason the processes $P_1, \cdots, P_n$ are distinguished from resources is that a resource works by order of a process P_k or another resource, while a process P_k does not.

As made clear by the deadlock examples, a process P_k must state, before any request is made, its maximum need for each type of resource. We will not go as far as to assume that a process P_k will specify exactly which various combinations of resources it is going to require; so that a process P_k is free to seize and release, in any order, the resources claimed. Consequently, the allocation strategy takes into account the fact that P_k might need all its claimed resources concurrently.

The Allocation State

The allocation state is determined by one vector and two matrices.

$$\mathbf{a} = \begin{pmatrix} a_1 \\ a_2 \\ \vdots \\ a_m \end{pmatrix}$$ describes the resources available in the system;

a_i = number of resources of type i ($i = 1, 2, \cdots, m$).

$$B = (\mathbf{b}_1, \mathbf{b}_2, \cdots, \mathbf{b}_n) = \begin{pmatrix} b_{11}b_{12} & \cdots & b_{1n} \\ b_{21} & & \vdots \\ \vdots & & \\ b_{m1} & \cdots & b_{mn} \end{pmatrix}$$ describes the claim on the system resources; b_{ik} = maximum number of resources of type i that will be needed at one time by process P_k and the resources allocated to it.

$$C = (\mathbf{c}_1, \mathbf{c}_2, \cdots, \mathbf{c}_n) = \begin{pmatrix} c_{11}c_{12} & \cdots & c_{1n} \\ c_{21} & & \vdots \\ \vdots & & \\ c_{m1} & \cdots & c_{mn} \end{pmatrix}$$ describes the allocation; c_{ik} = number of resources of type i allocated to P_k or to the resources allocated to P_k.

A pair $(\mathbf{b}_k, \mathbf{c}_k)$ describes the allocation state of P_k.

A weak ordering between vectors, and also between matrices, is used:

Let $\mathbf{u} \in R_m$, $\mathbf{v} \in R_m$; $\mathbf{u} \leq \mathbf{v}$ means $\forall_i u_i \leq v_i$, and $\mathbf{u} < \mathbf{v}$ means $(\mathbf{u} \leq \mathbf{v}) \wedge (\exists_i u_i < v_i)$.

Let $F = (\mathbf{f}_1, \mathbf{f}_2, \cdots, \mathbf{f}_n)$ and $G = (\mathbf{g}_1, \mathbf{g}_2, \cdots, \mathbf{g}_n)$ be $m \times n$ matrices; $F \leq G$ means $\forall_k \mathbf{f}_k \leq \mathbf{g}_k$, and $F < G$ means $(F \leq G) \wedge (\exists_k \mathbf{f}_k < \mathbf{g}_k)$.

The relational operators $\geq$ and $>$ are defined similarly.

Allocation states, for which the following three relations are true, are called *realizable* states:

R1: $\forall_k \mathbf{b}_k \leq \mathbf{a}$ (no process claims more resources than are available)

R2: $C \leq B$ (no process will try to seize more resources than it has claimed)

R3: $\sum_{k=1}^{n} \mathbf{c}_k \leq \mathbf{a}$ (at most all resources are allocated)

For convenience we use $\mathbf{r}(t) := \mathbf{a} - \sum_{k=1}^{n} \mathbf{c}_k$ and replace relation R3 by R3′, $\mathbf{r}(t) \geq \mathbf{0}$; $\mathbf{r}(t)$ describes how many resources of each type remain free at moment t.

Vector $\mathbf{a}$ is constant in time; matrix C changes when resources are seized or released; elements in matrix B might be decreased at release. (Adding or deleting a process P means extension or shrinking of B and C; this subject is treated separately below.)

The indexing of the processes $P_1, \cdots, P_n$ is arbitrary. It can easily be seen that R1, R2, and R3 are invariant for a permutation of the columns in B and C, so that any indexing according to system numbers or priority rules is allowed. A realizable state does not guarantee that a deadlock cannot occur, as is seen in the next example.

Example of Deadlocks

$$\mathbf{a} = \begin{pmatrix} 4 \\ 5 \end{pmatrix}, B = \begin{pmatrix} 4 & 3 \\ 3 & 4 \end{pmatrix}, C(t') = \begin{pmatrix} 1 & 1 \\ 1 & 2 \end{pmatrix}, C(t'') = \begin{pmatrix} 2 & 1 \\ 1 & 2 \end{pmatrix},$$

$$C(t''') = \begin{pmatrix} 1 & 1 \\ 2 & 2 \end{pmatrix}, \mathbf{r}(t') = \begin{pmatrix} 2 \\ 2 \end{pmatrix}, \mathbf{r}(t'') = \begin{pmatrix} 1 \\ 2 \end{pmatrix}, \mathbf{r}(t''') = \begin{pmatrix} 2 \\ 1 \end{pmatrix},$$

$C(t'')$ and $C(t''')$ are possible successors of state $C(t')$; all three states are realizable states.

There is no deadlock danger at moment t', since a request by P_1 can be held up until P_2 has used the resources it claimed. But at t'' or t''' the deadlock danger occurs: if either P_1 or P_2 asks for what it claimed, $\mathbf{r}(t'')$ and $\mathbf{r}(t''')$ are insufficient, and if P_1 and P_2 do not release any resources until they have been allocated all they claimed, they prevent their mutual progress.

Safe States

When a realizable state does not contain the deadlock danger, it is called a *safe* state; otherwise, it is called an *unsafe* state. Let us try to give a closer definition of a safe state.

$\mathbf{r}(t)$ in the example above apparently must be sufficient to serve at least one process according to its claim. When this one has used and released the resources allocated to it, the new value of $\mathbf{r}$ must likewise be sufficient to serve another process, and so on. So we find that there must be a process P_{k_1} for which $\mathbf{b}_{k_1} - \mathbf{c}_{k_1}(t) \leq \mathbf{r}(t)$, a process P_{k_2} for which $\mathbf{b}_{k_2} - \mathbf{c}_{k_2}(t) \leq \mathbf{r}(t) + \mathbf{c}_{k_1}(t)$, and so on.

Let S be an ordered set of processes, and let $s(k)$ represent the ordinal number of $P_k \in S$; S is called a "full sequence" if it contains all the n processes that claimed resources.

Definition. A realizable state $(\mathbf{a}, B, C(t))$ is called a safe state if there is a full sequence S such that

R4: $\forall_{P_k \in S} \mathbf{b}_k \leq \mathbf{r}(t) + \sum_{s(l) \leq s(k)} \mathbf{c}_l(t)$.

A full sequence fulfilling condition R4 is called a safe sequence for short.

Condition R4 says that the claim by process P_k must not exceed the sum of the free resources and those resources which will become free "in due time," when the processes preceding in S have released theirs.

The significance of the concept "safe" lies in the fact that starting from a safe state there is at least one way to allocate the claimed resources to each process P_k, even

[1] Recently, a deadlock detection policy has been published [10], which, however, does not claim to prevent a deadlock. In that paper a deadlock is resolved by preempting resources.

in the "worst case," i.e. when each process P_k asks for all the resources it has claimed and does not release any resources until it has been allocated all its claimed resources. The worst case can be dealt with if, starting from a realizable state $C(t_0)$, the allocation state can be transformed successively such that it passes through a sequence $C(t_0), C(t_1), \cdots, C(t_n)$ with the following properties:

(1) each $(\mathbf{a}, B, C(t_i))$ is a realizable state;

(2) for each process P_k there is a moment t_k so that $\mathbf{c}_k(t_k) = \mathbf{b}_k$;

(3) $\mathbf{c}_k$ is a nondecreasing function of t until t_k.

"The allocation state is safe" means that the worst case can be dealt with, which fact is expressed in

THEOREM 1. *When no process will release its resources until it has been allocated all its claimed resources, the processes will not get into a deadlock if and only if the allocation state is safe.*

The proof of Theorem 1 is given in Appendix A.

Note. When the allocation state is safe, it is by no means always necessary to serve the processes in the order of a sequence S; condition R4 only guarantees that in case resources become scarce the processes *can* be served in that succession. When a process P_k requires resources, *allocation can be effectuated if the transformed state is also a safe one*, avoiding in this way the introduction of the deadlock danger.

The state at $t = t'$ in the last example is a safe state. At $t = t''$ or $t = t'''$ the state is not safe.

An algorithm to check whether a given state $(\mathbf{a}, B, C(t))$ is safe will try to put the processes in some order, so that condition R4 is fulfilled. This seems a big task, since the processes can be ordered in $n!$ ways. Fortunately, the following strong theorem can be proved.

THEOREM 2. *If the allocation state is safe and a subsequence S fulfills condition R4, S can be extended into a safe sequence.*

This theorem considerably reduces the task of finding a full sequence. It says that, for a safe state, any sequence fulfilling R4 can be extended into a safe sequence, so that we can never be so unfortunate as to pick out an unusable sequence. The theorem also implies that when a subsequence S cannot be extended it is unnecessary to look for another safe sequence under the $n!$ possible sequences, because there will be no safe sequence at all, and so no backtracking is required. Theorem 2 is proved in Appendix B.

An algorithm that decides whether a given realizable state is safe can now be designed quite simply:

1. An empty sequence S fulfills R4;

2. Try to extend a sequence S fulfilling R4, with a $P_k \notin S$, so that the extended sequence also fulfills R4. This attempt can fail for one of the following reasons:

2.1. All the processes are in the sequence; then the state is safe;

2.2. No extension fulfills R4; according to Theorem 2 the state is not safe.

A first description runs as follows [9]:

```
sequence empty;
define set of potential candidates;
while set of potential candidates is not empty do
  begin subtract member from set of potential candidates and let
    candidate point to that member;
    if sequence extensible with candidate then
      begin extend sequence with candidate;
        define set of potential candidates
      end
  end;
safe := sequence full
```

The meaning of the instructions is described concisely in the following version, in which S represents the subset of processes that are part of the sequence, S^* the complementary set of S, and T the set of potential candidates.

```
S := ∅;
T := S*;
while T ≠ ∅ do
  begin candidate := index of member of T; T := T − {P_candidate};
    if b[candidate] − c[candidate] ≤ r + Σ_{P_l∈S} c[l] then
    begin S := S ∪ {P_candidate}; T := S* end
  end;
safe := (S* = ∅)
```

Remark. The algorithm does not say in which order "candidate" will point to the potential candidates successively. It may be that a previously successful sequence has been preserved so that this one can be tried again as likely to be successful.

State Transition

In practice it is even more important to know whether a transition from one state to another can be permitted without introducing the deadlock danger.

Suppose the state $(\mathbf{a}, B, C(t))$ is safe and process P_k asks for one of its claimed resources. P_k may seize that resource if the transformed state is also a safe one. The above algorithm for finding a full sequence fulfilling condition R4 can be applied, of course, to decide whether the transformed state is safe.

However, the following theorem simplifies the inspection.

THEOREM 3. *If a safe state is transformed by allocating resources to process P_k and if any sequence S—not necessarily a full sequence!—can be found containing P_k and fulfilling condition R4, then the transformed state is also a safe one.*

The proof of Theorem 3 is given in Appendix C. Intuitively it is clear that when the allocation state is safe, and thus a safe sequence exists, it will be possible to allow P_k to finish, regardless of the processes after P_k.

Theorem 3 allows a further reduction of the state inspection task, especially when resources are not scarce, because then probably many safe sequences exist, so that there is a good chance there is a safe sequence in which P_k is one of the first elements. According to this theorem it is not necessary to construct such a safe sequence completely, and the inspection can be terminated, fortunately, as soon as P_k appears to be an element of the sequence.

An algorithm that inspects whether a state transition is safe can use Theorem 3 by trying to extend the sequence first with P_k. If the extension is successful, the future state is safe; if not, extension with another process can be tried. So the algorithm differs from the latter algorithm on two points:

1. Every scan for a new extension begins with P_k.

2. As soon as P_k is found to be an element of the sequence, the repetition is stopped.

The algorithm that inspects whether it is safe to allocate resources to a process P_k now runs as follows:

```
sequence empty;
define set of potential candidates;
while not (P_k in sequence or set of potential candidates empty) do
  begin if P_k in set of potential candidates
    then candidate := P_k
    else candidate := a member of set of potential candidates;
    subtract candidate from set of potential candidates;
    if sequence extensible with candidate then
      begin extend sequence with candidate;
        define set of potential candidates
      end
  end;
safe := (P_k in sequence)
```

Remark. If several processes have asked for resources, the choice as to which of these becomes "P_k" (i.e. the process for which allocation, and consequently state transition, will be tried) is made before and independent of the algorithm described here; this algorithm checks only whether a particular request can be granted without introduction of the deadlock danger and does not itself impose any priority order on the processes.

Introduction and Deletion of Processes

Condition R4 can also be used to determine whether other events may be permitted safely. Release does not affect B; it decreases C by the same amount as it increases $\mathbf{r}$. According to condition R4 this kind of transition is safe. (Deallocation can have the effect of allowing several other processes to proceed, and so it implies a potential awakening of other processes [2, 3, 5, 6].) Releasing a resource might also imply a decrease in claim, which implies a decrease in B. In this case condition R4 says that a safe state also transforms into a safe state (note that this case also implies a potential awakening obligation). A decrease in the number of resources might be disastrous, since in that case $\mathbf{a}$ decreases, and $\mathbf{r}$ with it, so that a safe state might transform into an unsafe one. Thus failing devices, for instance, might lead to disaster (and naturally so). An increase in the amount of resources improves the situation of course (and might also imply the awakening obligation). A process P_k is deleted when it has decreased its claim $\mathbf{b}_k$ to $\mathbf{0}$. Deletion is to be considered as a side effect of claim decrease, and it implies decrease of n and shrinking of B and C.

An increase in B might not be permitted according to condition R4, i.e. a claim increased by a process that has already allocated several resources to it might be rejected. However, a new process P_{n+1} claiming resources may be introduced by expanding B with a $(n+1)$-th column $\mathbf{b}_{n+1}$ equal to the claim (if $\mathbf{b}_{n+1} \leq \mathbf{a}$), and by expanding C with a $(n+1)$-th column $\mathbf{c}_{n+1} = \mathbf{0}$. This can be done safely, since $\mathbf{b}_{n+1} \leq \mathbf{r} + \sum_{l \leq n} \mathbf{c}_l$; this means that any safe sequence extended with $\mathbf{b}_{n+1}$ transforms into a sequence which also fulfills condition R4. Thus a safe state transforms into a safe state. Consequently, new claims of processes that have no resources allocated can be accepted at any time.

Applications

It is easy to prove that any request for a resource category for which the sum claim does not exceed the amount available can be granted safely. Therefore, an implemented version of the algorithms has to single out only those resource categories for which the sum claim does exceed the amount available. Moreover, a process that has been allocated none of its claimed resources does not contribute to $\sum \mathbf{c}_l$ and can therefore be left out of consideration when the allocation state is checked for safety.

This means that for the simple cases, when the sum claim does not exceed the available resources, the second algorithm will find immediately that the future state is safe. So the overhead will be very small in these simple cases.

In other cases, the overhead of this deadlock-prevention policy will depend mainly on the scarcity of the resources. Fortunately, Theorem 2 says that there is no need for backtracking, thus reducing the upper bound from $n!$ to $n(n+1)/2$ trials. Recent investigations (which are still in progress) as to how much will be gained by applying the second algorithm show that the number of trials actually needed is considerably less than this upper bound. Suppose, for instance, a subsequence of length $2n/3$ is needed to terminate the second algorithm, and suppose the sequence under construction can be extended each turn with one of the processes in the first two-thirds of the previously safe sequence; even in the extreme case, when there is only one safe sequence, the number of trials will then not be more than about $n(n+6)/12$ for $n \geq 6$. The conjecture is that the coefficient of n^2 is a decreasing function of n.

The insistence that each process state in advance which subset of resources it will need simultaneously appears to be essential for the solution of the problem presented here. When it is assumed that nothing is known in advance about the need for resources, a deadlock situation could be detected, but it would be impossible to prevent it.

Mere detection may be sufficient if the appropriate resources can be released; otherwise, the detection of a deadlock comes too late to prevent it. On the other hand, the proposed solution can be too restrictive when more information can be gathered about the different subsets of resources a process is going to use. If these subsets have an empty intersection, the process asking for these sets can be introduced each time it is going to use the next subset; but if the intersection is not empty, a process must claim, in this policy, the union of the subsets, since a process that has allocated resources to it may not be allowed to change and increase its claim.

The allocation policy could be extended to relieve this constraint in the following way: before a process is introduced in the claim matrix it can try to seize the resources of such an intersection and subtract these from the free resources (thus decreasing $\mathbf{r}$); if successful, it claims the other resources it needs simultaneously; if not, it claims the union or it waits.

It is not necessary that a process claims every resource before asking for it. The claim must contain the smallest set of resources a process will actually need to be able to continue. A process can ask for more resources than it claimed in advance (thus trying to decrease $\mathbf{r}$), but if it has not claimed such a resource, it must also be able to continue lest the requested resource cannot be allocated to it.

Conclusions

The occurrence of a deadlock can be prevented. It seems to be unnecessary to reserve resources in advance. Adding a new one to—or subtracting one from—the set of competing processes is no problem.

The algorithms by means of which a deadlock is prevented are quite simple and can be implemented in such a way that they do a minimal amount of work. The claim a process has to state in advance has to describe only the smallest union of resources that will be needed concurrently, i.e. without which that process is unable to continue. If the need for resources is not known exactly, an upper bound will do, since a resource will not be allocated until it is actually required. The deadlock-prevention algorithms are only a part of a resource allocation policy; they do not decide in which order the resource requests are granted, nor do they decide what to do when a request cannot be granted safely. Denying the request or resource release must help in such a case. However, the answer to such questions is found in the design of an allocation scheme and will, therefore, be solved quite differently in various systems.

Acknowledgment. The deadlock problem occurred to me for the first time when E. W. Dijkstra gave a practical solution of the problem for a special purpose [1]. Later on, I had the pleasure of discussing a general solution of the problem with him when I wrote my thesis. I am grateful to D. L. Parnas, W. A. Wulf, and D. B. Russell for their support and discussion of the matter.

APPENDIX A. Proof of Theorem 1

(a) Let the allocation state be safe at moment t_0 and let S be a safe sequence. Rearrange the columns of B and C according to S; the conditions R1, R2, and R3 are invariant for a permutation of the columns, while condition R4 assumes the form:

$$\mathbf{b}_k \le \mathbf{r}(t_0) + \sum_{l<k} \mathbf{c}_l(t_0) \qquad (k=1, 2, \cdots, n),$$

or, equivalent to this,

$$\mathbf{b}_k \le \mathbf{a} - \sum_{l>k} \mathbf{c}_l(t_0).$$

Define matrix $C(t_k)$: $\mathbf{c}_l(t_k) = 0$ for $l < k$,

$$\mathbf{c}_k(t_k) = \mathbf{b}_k,$$

$$\mathbf{c}_l(t_k) = \mathbf{c}_l(t_0) \quad \text{for} \quad l > k,$$

$C(t_k)$ fulfills condition R3, since

$$\sum_{l=1}^{n} \mathbf{c}_l(t_k) = \mathbf{b}_k + \sum_{l>k} \mathbf{c}_l(t_0) \le \mathbf{a}.$$

Evidently, $(\mathbf{a}, \mathbf{B}, C(t_k))$ is a realizable state, and the sequence $C(t_0)$, $C(t_1)$, $\cdots$, $C(t_n)$ allows the worst case to be treated.

(b) Suppose the allocation state $C(t_0)$ can be transformed along a sequence of realizable states $C(t_0)$, $C(t_1)$, $\cdots$, $C(t_n)$ such that (after rearranging the columns in B and C) $\mathbf{c}_k(t_k) = \mathbf{b}_k$, and $\mathbf{c}_k(t)$ is nondecreasing for $t_0 \le t \le t_k$. The latter implies $\mathbf{c}_l(t_k) \ge \mathbf{c}_l(t_0)$ for $l \ge k$. Since $C(t_k)$ is realizable, we have

$$\mathbf{b}_k \le \mathbf{a} - \sum_{l\ne k} \mathbf{c}_k(t_k) \le \mathbf{a} - \sum_{l>k} \mathbf{c}_k(t_k) \le \mathbf{a} - \sum_{l>k} \mathbf{c}_l(t_0).$$

Consequently, condition R4 is fulfilled at $t = t_0$.

APPENDIX B. Proof of Theorem 2

Let Q be a safe sequence, i.e.

$$\forall_{P_k \in Q} \mathbf{b}_k \le \mathbf{r} + \sum_{q(l)\le q(k)} \mathbf{c}_l. \tag{1}$$

Let S be a subsequence, which fulfills

$$\forall_{P_k \in S} \mathbf{b}_k \le \mathbf{r} + \sum_{s(l)\le s(k)} \mathbf{c}_l. \tag{2}$$

Define S' as follows:

(a) $s'(k) = s(k)$ for $P_k \in S$;

(b) $q(l) \le q(k) \to s'(l) \le s'(k)$ for P_k, $P_l \in Q - S$.

This ordering implies for $P_k \in Q - S$,

$$\sum_{q(l)\le q(k)} \mathbf{c}_l \le \sum_{s'(l)\le s'(k)} \mathbf{c}_l, \tag{3}$$

since every P_l that precedes P_k in Q precedes also P_k in S'.

From (1) and (3) it follows that

$$\forall_{P_k \in Q-S} \mathbf{b}_k \le \mathbf{r} + \sum_{s'(l)\le s'(k)} \mathbf{c}_l. \tag{4}$$

From (2) and (4) it follows that S' is a safe sequence.

APPENDIX C. Proof of Theorem 3

Let $(\mathbf{a}, B, C(t_0))$ be a safe state, and let $C(t_1)$ be the allocation matrix if a certain request of process P_k will be granted. Let S be a subsequence which fulfills condition R4 at $t = t_1$ and contains P_k. S fulfills R4 at $t = t_0$ also, since $\forall_l \mathbf{c}_l(t_0) \le \mathbf{c}_l(t_1)$. According to Theorem 2, S can be extended into a safe sequence S' at $t = t_0$. But S' is also a safe sequence at $t = t_1$, because

(a) S fulfills condition R4,

(b) $P_l \in S' - S$ is preceded by P_k (since $P_k \in S$), and

(c) $\sum \mathbf{c}_l$ has been increased by as much as $\mathbf{r}$ has been decreased for every process preceded by P_k.

Received November, 1968; revised January 1969

REFERENCES

1. Dijkstra, E. W. De Bankiers Algorithme. EWD116, Math. Dep., Technological U., Eindhoven, The Netherlands, 1965.
2. —— Cooperating sequential processes. EWD123, Math. Dept., Technological U., Eindhoven, The Netherlands, 1965.
3. Dennis, J. B., and Van Horn, E. C. Programming semantics for multiprogrammed computations. *Comm. ACM 4*, 3 (Mar. 1966), 143–155.
4. Reiter, A. A resource-allocation scheme for multi-user online operation of a small computer. Proc. AFIPS 1967 Spring Joint Comput. Conf., Vol. 30, Thompson Book Co., Washington, D.C.
5. Habermann, A. N. On the harmonious cooperation of abstract machines. Thesis, Math. Dept., Technological U., Eindhoven, The Netherlands, 1967.
6. Dijkstra, E. W. The structure of the "THE"-multiprogramming system. *Comm. ACM 11*, 5 (May 1968), 341–346.
7. Havender, J. W. Avoiding deadlock in multi-tasking systems. *IBM Syst. J. 2*, 7 (1968).
8. Collier, W. W. System deadlocks. IBM Tech. Rep. TR-001756 (1968).
9. Dijkstra, E. W. Towards correct programming. EWD241, Math. Dep., Technological U., Eindhoven, The Netherlands, 1968.
10. Murphy, J. E. Resource allocation with interlock detection in a multi-task system. Proc. AFIPS 1968 Fall Joint Comput. Conf., Vol. 33, Pt. 2, Thompson Book Co., Washington, D.C., pp. 1169–1176.

AVOIDING DEADLOCK IN DISTRIBUTED DATA BASES*

W. W. Chu[+] and G. Ohlmacher
University of California, Los Angeles

Key Words and Phrases: computer networks, deadlock, distributed data base, file, process sets

ABSTRACT

Deadlock prevention mechanisms and a deadlock protection mechanism for distributed data base systems are presented. The notion of process sets used in preventing deadlock is introduced. Examples are given to illustrate these methods for avoiding file deadlock in computer networks.

I. INTRODUCTION

When a deadlock occurs, if a job is aborted, the resulting partially completed process often represents a serious inconvenience to the user, who in many cases, must reconstruct partially altered files. For this reason, deadlock is an important consideration in the design of operating systems, even though in practice it seldom occurs. As a result, many studies of deadlock protection schemes have been reported [1-9], but the emphasis in these studies has been on centralized data base systems. In order to increase the capabilities of computer systems, remotely located computers are connected via communication links. Such a multiple computer system, or a computer network, enables the sharing of resources, such as hardware, software, and data bases. However, the efficient sharing of data bases creates many problems, such as file allocation [10], deadlock, etc. In these distributed data bases, the deadlock problem is complicated by the necessity of coordinating several computers without impeding their progress.

A deadlock exists whenever two or more processes, which are vying for the same resources, reach an impasse. When the resources required by any process can be obtained prior to starting it, deadlocks can be prevented. A deadlock prevention mechanism examines the resource requirements of all processes and allows a process to proceed only when a deadlock cannot occur. If not prevented, deadlocks can be detected and resolved by eliminating an offending process from contention. When dynamic resource allocation is implemented, deadlock detection mechanisms (which eliminate and automatically restart offending processes) are required. It is possible to combine these mechanisms so that certain resources are serviced by a detection mechanism while other resources are serviced by a prevention mechanism.

This paper examines a means of implementing two deadlock prevention mechanisms and a deadlock detection mechanism on a computer network. In addition, the notion of using process sets is introduced to improve the efficiency of one of the deadlock prevention mechanisms.

II. ACCESS CONTROL METHODS

In many cases, such as program libraries, it is necessary for two or more processes to have simultaneous access to the same file. However, a process which modifies a file cannot share access to that file with any other process at the same time. In order to provide users with this flexibility, a system must provide two methods of access to every file, either <u>shared</u> or <u>exclusive</u>. The user specifies the desired method of access when the file is requested. Using this procedure if no process has been granted exclusive access to a file, then a request for shared access to that file by any process can be granted. In the same manner, if no process has been granted either shared or exclusive access to a file, then a request for exclusive access to that file by any process can be granted. This procedure provides multiple readers <u>or</u> one writer with access to a specific file.

If it is possible for the system to conveniently generate a copy of a file when a process requires exclusive access to a file, the copy may be used for modifications while the original is maintained as a back up until the process terminates. In addition, access to the original can be granted to any process requesting shared access to that file. Consequently, shared access to a file can always be granted and requests for such access need no longer be considered by the deadlock protection mechanism. This procedure allows the system to provide multiple readers <u>and</u> one writer, with simultaneous access to a specific file.

Since most systems allocate files to a single continuous area of mass storage, it is usually inconvenient for a system to generate a copy of a file. However, for systems whose files reside on paged memory, it is possible for the system to create a copy of the file simply by making a copy of

*This research was supported in part by the U.S. Office of Naval Research, Mathematical and Information Sciences Division, Contract No. N00014-69-A-0200-4027, NR 048-129 and in part by the National Science Foundation, Grant No. GJ33007X.

+ Consultant to Advanced Development Laboratory, Xerox Palo Alto Research Center.

Reprinted with permission from *Proc. Ass. Comput. Mach. Symp.*, Nov. 1974, pp. 156–160.

the page table [9] as shown in Figure 1.

When a data base has multiple copies of a file, for shared access of a file, access to any one of its copies can be granted to the requesting process; for exclusive access of a file, all of its copies must be granted to the requesting process. With such a "lock" scheme for the exclusive access, the deadlock mechanisms are not affected by the number of copies of a file.

PAGE TABLE (DUPLICATE COPY) | MASS MEMORY | PAGE TABLE (ORIGINAL)

AVAILABLE PAGE FRAMES

a) Page tables after access has been granted.

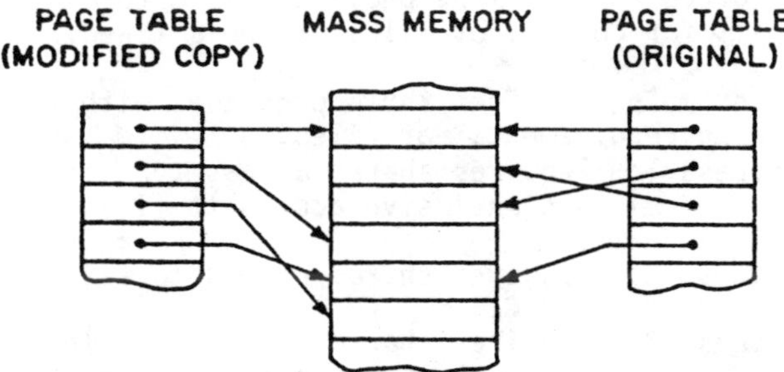

b) Page table after modifications.

Figure 1

Access Control Method for Deadlock Protection in a Paging Memory System

III. DEADLOCK PREVENTION MECHANISMS

One way to implement deadlock prevention on a computer network is to assign a node (computer) as a monitoring node, which examines the file requirements of all processes and allows a process to proceed when a deadlock cannot occur. This is rather inefficient since the monitoring node has to communicate with each node to examine the file requirements before the process can be allowed to start, and the entire network can consider only one process at a time. A more efficient way to implement deadlock prevention is to assign a fixed examining path in the network by assigning every node in the network a number. Then the examining path is determined uniquely by the node numbers as shown in Figure 2. When requests for files are passed around the network according to this path, since the path is unique, each node can consider the requests for files independent of the other nodes. This improves the efficiency of the deadlock prevention mechanism.

Since the lower numbered nodes have better access to the deadlock prevention mechanism than higher numbered nodes, one way to assign the node numbers is to examine the file utilization; that is, the usage rate and the length of each file transaction for the processes at that node, and the file storage size of the node. The nodes that have higher utilization and higher file storage capability should be granted a lower numbered node.

3.1 A Simple Prevention Mechanism

Deadlock prevention mechanisms require the user to specify the files that a process requires prior to the initiation of that process. These requests are usually made through the job control language of the system. The information is used by the system to prevent a deadlock from occurring.

One means of preventing deadlock is for the system to obtain control of all the files requested by a process before initiating the process. One process at a time, the system collects the request for files and examines each one to determine if access to the file can be granted as outlined in the previous section. If all requests can be granted, the process is given access to the files and is initiated. Otherwise, the process is delayed until all processes which have access to requested files terminate. While the process is delayed, the requested files are available to other processes [1].

In a distributed data base, the system examines the requests for files to determine if all the requests are for local files. If they are, the requests are processed as outlined above. Otherwise, the requests for files are passed from node to node in the preassigned order starting with the first node. Each node examines the requests for files located at that node as outlined above. As soon as all the requests for files have been granted, the node at which the requesting process resides is so informed and the process is allowed to proceed.

The simplicity of this mechanism enables easy implementation and requires low system overhead. In addition, interactive users can avoid waiting by simply terminating a delayed process, since such a process has not been initiated. Clearly, using this simple deadlock prevention mechanism intercomputer communication is required only when remote files are requested.

3.2 Process Set Prevention Mechanism

An alternative means of preventing deadlock is to allow the process to proceed unless granting access to a file it requires may lead to a deadlock. The system collects the requests for files and initiates the process without giving it access to the requested files. The process proceeds until access to a file is required; for example, an attempt to reference a file would imply that a process required access to that file. When access to a file is required, the process is allowed to proceed if all of the processes can be completed (a process can be completed if access to all the files that it has requested can be granted, as outlined in the previous section). If a process can be completed, then the files it has access to are considered available with respect to the remaining processes. If access to the file cannot be granted, the process is delayed until some other process either terminates or releases that file [3].

In order to more efficiently determine if access to a file can be granted, processes having requests for the same file(s) can be grouped into process sets. A system may have any number of process sets, the criteria being, if a process requests exclusive access to a file, then that process and all other processes which have requested access (exclusive or shared) to that file are members of the same process set. Further, each process belongs to one and only one process set.

Let us denote F, P, and {P} as file, process and process set respectively. We then have the following properties:

1) If $eF_i \in \{P\}_I$, then $eF_i \notin \{P\}_J$ & $sF_i \notin \{P\}_J$, for $I \neq J$.
2) If $P_i \in \{P\}_I$, then $P_i \notin \{P\}_J$, for $I \neq J$

where F_i = i^{th} file, i = 1, 2, ..., m,
P_i = i^{th} process, i = 1, 2, ..., n,
$\{P\}_I$ = I^{th} process set, I = 1, 2, ..., N, $N \leq n$
e = exclusive access
s = shared access

Such a group of process sets can be formed as follows: Whenever a new process arrives all the process sets that have possession of file(s) that are requested by the new process are combined and the new process is added to the resulting process set. (Of course, if no process sets possess a file that is requested by the new process, then the new process forms a process set by itself). The rules for combining process sets are: If shared access to a file is requested by the new process, the process set containing one or more processes which have requested exclusive access to that file is combined with the new process. If exclusive access to a file is requested by the new process, all the process sets containing one or more processes which have requested access (exclusive or shared) to that file are combined, and the new process is added to the resulting process set. When a process terminates, the remaining members of the process set may be reexamined with respect to each other by the same mechanism to reform their process set or sets.

The advantage of establishing process sets is that once a process has been allocated to a set, the progress of that process is independent of all processes in other process sets. Further, in contrast with the simple deadlock prevention mechanism, a process in a process set does not require complete control of all its files. The use of process sets for deadlock prevention considerably reduces the amount of computation required to determine whether or not all the processes can be completed.

In order to simplify control of the processes, when implementing this mechanism on a distributed data base, the process sets are allocated to certain nodes. For convenience, the process set is allocated to the highest node at which a file requested in the process set is located.

Since a process set may contain processes and files from several nodes, the process set which contains a certain process may not reside at the same node as that process. Consequently, when a process requires access to a file, a request for that file must be transmitted to the node having the corresponding process set. The request is then examined according to the process set deadlock prevention mechanism.

When a system receives a process, it forms the new process set and examines the requests for files to determine if any of the requests are from remote files. If any are, the process set is passed from node to node starting with the first node and forms a process set at each node when necessary until all the files requested by the new process have been found. If all the requests are for local files, the same procedure is followed except that the new process set is started at the node that receives the process instead of the first node.

When this mechanism is used, processes are allowed to proceed until access to a file is required, subsequently files are used more efficiently, especially when they are frequently referenced. In addition, several processes could request control of, modify, and release control of a file concurrently without terminating. On the other hand, this mechanism is not easily implemented and requires considerable system overhead when continually forced to reexamine processes to determine if requests for control of files can be allowed.

As an example, consider three processes with the following requirements for files:

Process 1: Requires shared access to file A and exclusive access to files B and C.
Process 2: Requires shared access to files B and C.
Process 3: Requires shared access to file A, and exclusive access to file D.

Further, let the processes and files be distributed on the network in Figure 2 as follows:

Process 1:	Node 4	File A:	Node 1
Process 2:	Node 3	File B:	Node 2
Process 3:	Node 1	File C:	Node 3
		File D:	Node 5

When using simple deadlock prevention mechanism as described in section 3.1 the request for files of each process are passed around the network according to the preassigned order and yield the following list of processes and file requirements. Then according to the prevention mechanism we grant process 1 access to files A, B, and C, (which are underlined) and process 3 access to files A and D (which are underlined), but would delay process 2 by holding its request for file B at Node 2 until process 1 terminates.

$$\left(\begin{array}{l} \text{Process 1.}\ \ \underline{sA},\ \underline{eB},\ \underline{eC} \\ \text{d Process 2.}\ \ \underline{sB},\ \underline{sC} \\ \text{Process 3.}\ \ \underline{sA},\ \underline{eD} \end{array}\right) \qquad \begin{array}{l} s = \text{shared} \\ e = \text{exclusive} \\ d = \text{delayed} \end{array}$$

The process set deadlock prevention mechanism, as described in this section will form the following two process sets:

$$\text{Process set 1: } \left\{\begin{array}{l} \text{Process 1.}\ \ sA,\ eB,\ eC \\ \text{Process 2.}\ \ sB,\ sC \end{array}\right\}$$

$$\text{Process set 2: } \{\text{Process 3.}\ \ sA,\ eD\}$$

Process set 1 is located at node 3, since file C is located at node 3 and node 3 is the highest node at which a file requested in process set 1 is located. Similarly, process set 2 is located at node 5 because of file D.

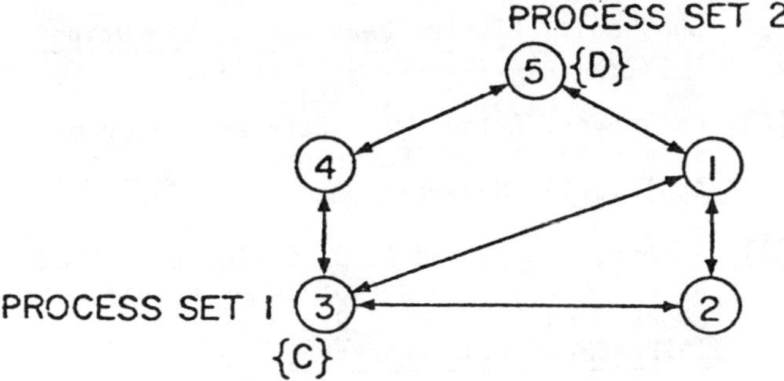

Figure 2. Deadlock Prevention in a Distributed Data Base

If process 1 requests control of files A and B and process 2 requests control of file C, then process set 1 becomes

{ Process 1. $\underline{sA}$, $\underline{eB}$, eC }
{d Process 2. $\overline{sB}$, $\overline{sC}$ }

where process 2 is delayed because if process 2 were granted control of file C and then requested file B and process 1 requested file C, a deadlock would result.

Finally, if process 1 later releases control of file B, process set 1 becomes

{Process 1. $\underline{sA}$, eB, eC}
{Process 2. $\overline{sB}$, $\underline{sC}$ }

Process 2 is no longer delayed since process 2 can be granted access to file B. Since process sets are independent of each other process set 2 which consists of process 3 was not involved in the preceding deadlock determinations. This greatly simplifies and improves the efficiency of the deadlock prevention mechanism.

IV. DEADLOCK DETECTION MECHANISM

A deadlock detection mechanism allows the user to request access to files at any time. The system monitors these requests by maintaining two lists, a list of processes and a list of requested files as in Figure 3. Each element of the lists has a pointer which is used by the system to determine if a deadlock has occurred. When the system receives a request for access to a file, if the request can be granted, the pointer of the corresponding file is set to point to that process and the process is allowed to proceed. Otherwise, the pointer of the process is set to point to the requested file and the file and process lists are traversed until either an open process pointer is found in which case the requesting process is delayed, or the lists return to the requesting process in which case a deadlock exists [8]. When a deadlock is detected, the system returns one of the processes involved in its initial state, releasing and restoring the files it controls. Since the files must be restored, a copy of each file or its original page table as outlined earlier must be available. The removed process is restarted at a later time [9].

The implementation of the deadlock detection mechanism in a distributed data base is accomplished by appointing one node of the network to monitor requests for files and detect deadlocks. The appointed node maintains the process and file lists, and every node is required to transmit to the appointed node information concerning the iniation and termination of each process and all requests for and releases of files. If a request for a file can be granted, the process is allowed to proceed without waiting for the deadlock detection mechanism. For the purpose of improving reliability, a second node may be appointed to monitor requests for files.

This mechanism can be easily implemented and has an advantage in that the user is not required to know in advance which files a process requires. On the other hand, even though actual deadlocks are infrequent, when they do occur, considerable system overhead must be accounted for. For example, an interactive user who is restarted must resupply all the information he had given the process, since the original information has lost its integrity. Finally, while this mechanism requires considerable inter-computer communication, even when local files are being used, processes are never delayed by this communication, since a process whose request for a file can be granted may proceed without waiting for the detection mechanism.

As an example, consider two processes which make the following series of requests for files:

Request 1. Process 1: A   Λ: null pointer
Request 2. Process 1: B
Request 3. Process 2: C
Request 4. Process 2: B
Request 5: Process 1: C

Then the process and file lists whould be formed as follows:

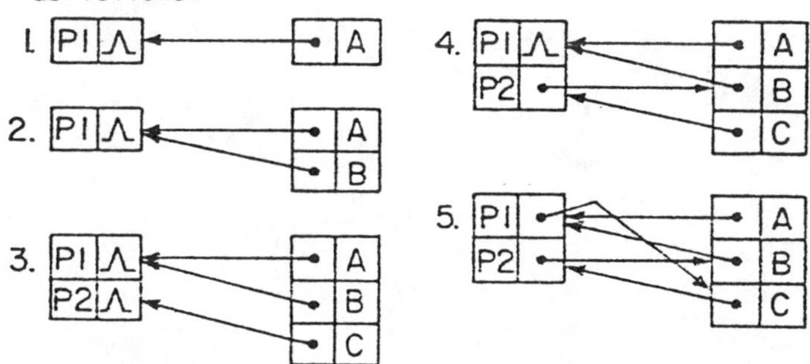

Figure 3. Deadlock Detection in a Distributed Data Base

The deadlock in request 5 is found when the loop P1-C-P2-B-P1 is detected by the mechanism. One of the processes is then returned to its initial state.

V. CONCLUSION

Three methods of protecting the user from deadlocks in a distributed data base have been presented: a simple deadlock prevention mechanism, a prevention mechanism using process sets, and a detection mechanism.

The operation of the simple prevention mechanism is straightforward and uncomplicated, and it does not require the keeping of lists or groups: thus this mechanism is easily implemented and requires less system overhead than the other mechanisms. In addition, since messages are sent to the other nodes of the network only to establish the location and availability of files, such communications are never required to handle processes using only local files. Since the simple prevention mechanism is the only deadlock protection mechanism to exhibit both of these characteristics, it is clearly superior for most applications. However, since the process set prevention mechanism provides more efficient utilization of files, and the detection mechanism provides the user with greater flexibility in that the user may request access to files at any time, in certain instances these mechanisms are preferable.

REFERENCES

[1] Havender, J. W. "Avoiding Deadlock in Multitasking Systems," IBM Systems Journal, 7(2)74-84, 1968.

[2] Murphy, J. E. "Resource Allocation with Interlock Detection in a Multi-Task System," Proceedings of the 1968 Fall Joint Computer Conference, pp. 1169-1176.

[3] Habermann, A. N. "Prevention of System Deadlocks," Communications of the ACM, 12(7): 373-377, 385, July 1969.

[4] Berstein, A. J. and A. Shoshani. "Synchronization in a Parallel Access Data Base," Communications of the ACM, 12(11):604-607, November 1969.

[5] Coffman, E. G., Jr., M. J. Elphick, and A. Shoshani. "System Deadlocks," Computing Surveys, 3(2):67-78, June 1971.

[6] Collmeyer, Arthur J. "Database Management in a Multi-Access Environment," Computer, 4(6):36-46, November/December 1971.

[7] Shemer, J. E., and A. J. Collmeyer. "Database Sharing: A Study of Interference, Roadblock, and Deadlock," Proceedings of the 1972 ACM-SIGFIDET Workshop, 1972.

[8] Holt, Richard C. "Some Deadlock Properties of Computer Systems," Computing Surveys, 4(3):179-196, September 1972.

[9] King, P. F. and A. J. Collmeyer. "Database Sharing - An Efficient Mechanism for Supporting Concurrent Processes," Proceedings of the 1973 National Computer Conference and Exposition, June 1973, Vol. 42, pp. 271-275.

[10] Chu. W. W. "Optimal File Allocation in a Multiple Computer System," IEEE Transactions on Computers, C-18(10):885-889, October 1969.

ACKNOWLEDGMENT

The authors wish to thank Drs. J. E. Shemer and A. J. Collmeyer of Xerox Corporation for their helpful discussions during the writing of this paper.

Locking and Deadlock Detection in Distributed Data Bases

DANIEL A. MENASCE AND RICHARD R. MUNTZ, MEMBER, IEEE

Abstract—This paper describes two protocols for the detection of deadlocks in distributed data bases—a hierarchically organized one and a distributed one. A graph model which depicts the state of execution of all transactions in the system is used by both protocols. A cycle in this graph is a necessary and sufficient condition for a deadlock to exist. Nevertheless, neither protocol requires that the global graph be built and maintained in order for deadlocks to be detected. In the case of the hierarchical protocol, the communications cost can be optimized if the topology of the hierarachy is appropriately chosen.

Index Terms—Data bases, deadlock detection, distributed data bases, graph theory.

I. Introduction

THIS WORK is concerned with issues of locking and deadlock detection mechanisms in distributed data bases. The problem of system deadlocks in multiprogramming and multiprocessing systems has received considerable attention in the literature and is well understood [1]-[3]. There are three approaches to the treatment of deadlocks: deadlock prevention, deadlock avoidance, and deadlock detection and resolution.

Deadlock prevention requires that all the resources be acquired at once by a transaction. This requirement cannot always be satisfied in a data base environment since the resource needs of a transaction may be data dependent and not precisely known at the start of the transaction. Therefore, it would be necessary for a transaction to acquire all possible resources required, thereby decreasing system concurrency.

Deadlock avoidance requires some advance knowledge of the resource usage of transactions in order to determine at each point in time whether there is a valid sequence of actions of the already initiated but not yet completed transactions such that all of them can be run to completion. Again, this approach is not practical in distributed data bases since the necessary advance information to avoid deadlocks is either absent or is distributed enough to render inefficient any attempt to avoid deadlocks.

Deadlock detection can be done by searching for cycles in a "state graph" [3]. A method for the detection and resolution of deadlocks in a centralized data-base system was presented in [4]. In distributed data bases, however, it is not efficient to maintain a global state graph for the whole system. Two methods for detecting deadlocks in distributed data bases, which do not require that a global graph be built and maintained, are presented in this paper—one hierarchical and one distributed. An outline of the proof that both protocols will detect all existing deadlocks is given here. For the case of the hierarchical protocol, the problem of establishing the hierarchy in a way such that the cost of using the protocol is minimized is introduced.

Manuscript received February 6, 1978; revised November 1, 1978. This research was supported in part by the Advanced Research Projects Agency of the Department of Defense under Contract MDA 903-77-C-0211. The work of D. A. Menasce was supported in part by the Conselho Nacional de Desenvolvimento Cientifico e Technologico, CNPq, Brazil. This is an expanded version of a paper presented at the Third Berkeley Workshop on Distributed Data Bases.

The authors are with the Department of Computer Science, University of California, Los Angeles, CA 90024.

II. Formal Model of Transaction Processing

This section introduces the necessary notation and formalism upon which we base the locking protocols and deadlock detection mechanisms presented in this paper. The data base is considered to be distributed among n sites, S1, S2, $\cdots$, Sn, of a computer network. Users interact with the data base via transactions. A *transaction* is a sequence of actions which can be either read, write, lock, or unlock operations. Transactions are assumed to be two phase, i.e., once an unlock operation is issued no other lock can be requested by the transaction. As shown in [6], this is necessary to preserve the data-base consistency. If the actions of a transaction involve data at a single site, the transaction is called *local*, as opposed to a *distributed* transaction which involves resources at several sites. We assume that distributed transactions are implemented as a collection of processes which act on behalf of the transaction. Those processes are called *transaction incarnations.* There may be one or more incarnations of the same transaction at each participating site. A transaction incarnation is responsible among other things for 1) acquiring, using, and releasing resources local to the site at which it is executing, as needed by the transaction, and 2) exchanging messages with remote incarnations of the same transaction for purposes of cooperating with incarnations located at foreign sites. Note that this model of a transaction execution is general enough to accommodate other models.

A transaction can be in two different states, namely, *active* and *blocked.* A transaction is blocked if its execution cannot proceed because a needed resource is being held by another transaction, and the transaction is active otherwise. We now introduce a graphic model which depicts the state of execution of all transactions in the system. This model is in the form of a graph called the *transaction_wait_for* (TWF) graph. The nodes of this graph are associated with transaction in-

Reprinted from *IEEE Trans. Software Eng.*, vol. SE-5, pp. 195–202, May 1979.

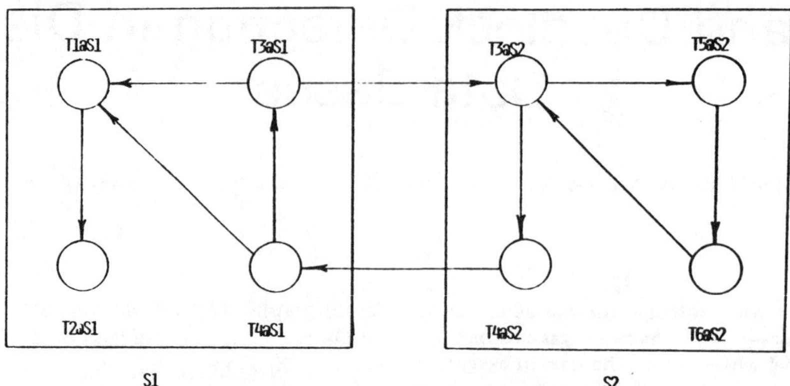

Fig. 1. A transaction_wait_for graph for a network with two sites S1 and S2.

carnations and are labeled by the pair (transaction_name, site_name). Note that labeling transaction incarnations with the pair (transaction name, site name) provides unique global names for these nodes if there is at most one transaction incarnation per site per transaction. If more than one incarnation is to be allowed, then distinct local names should be assigned for them. Since this distinction is irrelevant for the forthcoming discussion, we will assume that there is only one incarnation of any transaction per site.

1) There is a directed arc from node (Ti, S) to node (Tj, S) if the incarnation of transaction Ti at site S is blocked and waiting for the incarnation of transaction Tj to release a resource needed by Ti. (Ti, S) is said to be in "resource wait" for (Tj, S).

2) There is a directed arc from node (T, Si) to node (T, Sj) if the incarnation of transaction T at site Si is blocked and waiting for a message from the incarnation of T at site Sj. (T, Si) is said to be in "message wait" for (T, Sj).

It can be easily seen that the existence of a cycle in the transaction_wait_for graph is a necessary and sufficient condition for a deadlock to occur.

Fig. 1 shows an example of a transaction_wait_for graph for a network with two sites S1 and S2. This graph shows two deadlock cycles. One of them is a local deadlock since it involves only incarnations of transactions at site S2 and, therefore, only resources local to S2. The other deadlock cycle spans both sites and is an example of what we call a global deadlock.

III. Deadlock Detection Approaches

Deadlock detection involves building and maintaining the transaction_wait_for graph and searching for the existence of cycles in the graph. The graph has to be updated every time that a transaction changes state, either from active to blocked or vice versa. It should be noted, however, that new cycles can only potentially arise when a transaction is blocked. Deadlock resolution involves the selection of one or more transactions to be preempted in order for the cycle to be broken. The criteria used in this selection should try to minimize the penalty of preemption by any suitable metric. Examples of deadlock resolution methods are: preempt the transaction which owns less resources, preempt the transaction with the smallest rollback cost, preempt the transaction with the longest expected time to complete, and preempt any transaction in the cycle. The examination of such criteria is beyond the scope of this paper.

A centralized approach for deadlock detection in distributed data bases was suggested by Gray in [5]. In this approach there is a centralized deadlock detector which is responsible for constructing a global graph equivalent to the transaction_wait_for graph considered here. The central deadlock detector builds the graph out of information received from all the participating sites in the network.

While the centralized method may be practical and efficient for local networks, it may impose fairly large communications cost in geographically distributed systems. This observation stems from the fact that the central deadlock detector may be located very "far" from some of the sites in the network. As an example, we certainly do not want deadlocks which only involve resources located at some host computers located in Southern California to be detected at the East Coast. The hierarchical approach to deadlock detection presented in the next section lends itself to an optimization by which deadlocks can be detected by a site which is located as "close" as possible to the sites involved in the cycle.

IV. A Hierarchically Organized Locking and Deadlock Detection

Let the data base (DB) be partitioned into a set of subdata bases BDi's such that DB is the union of all the DBi's, and DBi and DBj are disjoint for $i \neq j$. The locking and deadlock detection mechanism presented here has as its core a hierarchy of lock controllers which interact in a way to be explained in this section. First, we are going to distinguish between the controllers which are at the bottommost level of the hierarchy, called *leaf controllers* or *Lk's*, and the *nonleaf controllers* or *NLK's*.

A leaf controller Lki is assigned to each subdata base DBi. In the example shown in Fig. 2, we have three leaf controllers LK1, LK2, and LK3 and two nonleaf controllers NLK0 and NLK1.

Each leaf controller Lki maintains a transaction_wait_for

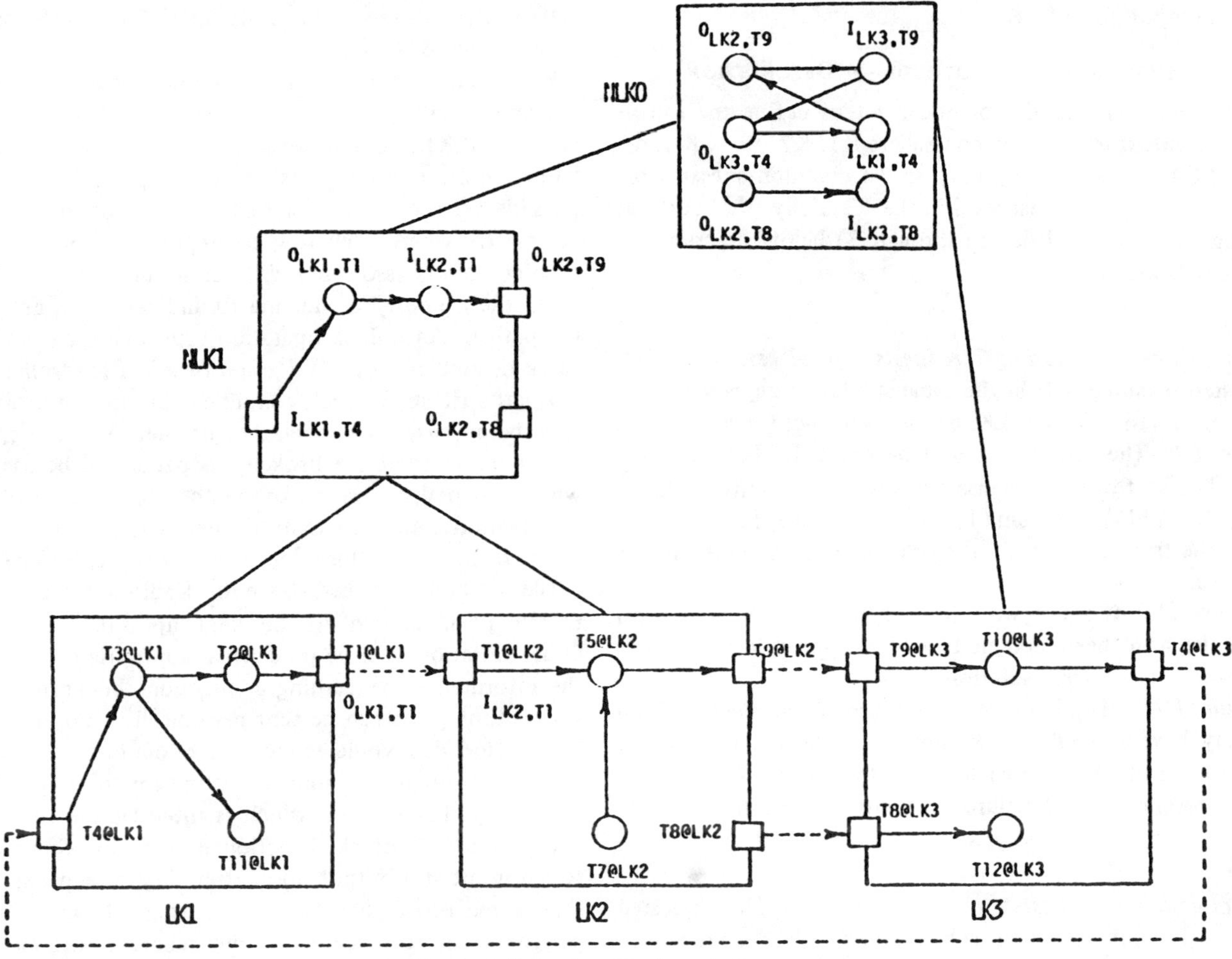

Fig. 2. A hierarchy of lock controllers.

graph, TWF(LKi). This graph contains all the nodes of the global TWF associated with transaction incarnations local to LKi. In addition, two special types of nodes called *output-port nodes* and *input-port nodes* are introduced in the TWF of a leaf controller. These nodes are associated with the arcs of the global TWF which join incarnations in two distinct controllers and are defined as follows.

1) A node in the TWF graph of LKi is called an *output port* and denoted O(LKi, T) if the global TWF contains an outgoing arc from an incarnation of transaction T local to LKi into a nonlocal incarnation of T.

2) A node in the transaction_wait_for graph of LKi is called an *input port* and denoted I(LKi, T) in TWF(LKi) if in the global TWF there is an incoming arc into an incarnation of transaction T local to LKi from a nonlocal incarnation of T.

Note that labels assigned to input and output ports are unique since there is only one transaction incarnation per transaction per site. In the example of Fig. 2, the output port O(LK1, T1) and the input port I(LK2, T1) correspond to an arc in the global TWF from T1@LK1 (the incarnation of Tw at LK1) to T1@LK2. The dashed lines indicate arcs in the global TWF. These arcs are represented explicitly at the upper levels of the hierarchy as will be explained below.

Nonleaf controllers maintain a graph called *input-output-ports* (*IOP*) graph. Nodes of an IOP are associated with input and output ports of leaf controllers. We will refer to them as *i-nodes* and *o-nodes*, respectively. Some of the i-nodes may be themselves input ports for the IOP, and some of the o-nodes may be output ports for the IOP. The IOP for controller NLKi, denoted IOP(NLKi), is defined by the following rules.

1) Arcs from i-nodes can go only to o-nodes and vice versa.

2) There is an arc from o-node Oa to i-node Ib if Oa is an output port of a leaf controller in the subtree rooted at NLKi and Ib is a corresponding input port of another leaf controller in the same subtree. In the example of Fig. 2, there is an arc from O(LK1, T1) to I(LK2, T1) in the IOP of NLK1 since O(LK1, T1) is an output port of LK1 and I(LK2, T1) is its corresponding input port in LK2. LK1 and LK2 are in the subtree rooted by NLK1.

3) There is an arc from the i-node Ia to o-node Ob in IOP(NLKi) if there is a path from an input port Ia to an output port Ob of a son of NLKi. In the example of Fig. 2 there is an arc from I(LK1, T4) to O(LK2, T9) in NLK0 since in NLK1 there is a path between I(LK1, T4) and O(LK2, T9).

4) An input (output) port of IOP(NLKi) is also an input (output) port of a leaf controller in the subtree rooted by

NLKi. In the example of Fig. 2 the input port of IOP(NLK1) is also an input port of LK1.

V. Hierarchical Protocol—A Description

Before we describe the protocol, let us define the *lowest common ancestor* between controllers K1, K2, · · · , K*n*, denoted LCA(K1, K2, · · · , K*n*), as the common ancestor between them at the lowest level in the hierarchy (the root is at the highest level). Rules 1) through 3) below describe the hierarchical protocol.

Rule 1

(*Transaction incarnation T requests a local resource*): The requested resource R is in the same subdata base as the transaction incarnation T. Let LKi be the controller for resource R.

Rule 1.1: The resource cannot be granted. Let {T1, T2, · · · , Tk} be the set of transactions which currently hold resource R. Add an arc from (T, LKi) to (Tj, LKi) for j = 1 to k. Check the transaction_wait_for graph at LKi for the existence of cycles.

Rule 1.1a: If cycles were formed, then one or more local deadlocks have been detected and an appropriate action is required for deadlock resolution.

Rule 1.1b: The addition of the arcs mentioned in Rule 1.1 may have created one or more paths between input and output ports of LKi. For each such path, send the (input port, output port) pair which delimits the path to the father of LKi.

Rule 2

(*Transaction T requests a nonlocal resource*): The requested resource R is in a different subdata base from the previously requested resource. Therefore, it has to be acquired by an incarnation of T local to R. Let LKi be the controller for the previously requested resource and let LKi be the controller for resource R. The incarnation of T at LKi becomes blocked and waiting for a message from the incarnation of T at LKj. The node (T, LKi) is now an output port of the transaction_wait_for graph at LKi, and the node (T, LKj) is an input port of the transaction_wait_for graph at LKj.

Rule 2.1: An arc from O(LKi, T) to I(LKj, T) is created in the IOP graph of the lowest common ancestor between LKi and LKj.

Rule 2.2: An o-node labeled O(LKi, T) is added to the IOP graph of each controller in the path between LKi and LOA(LKi, LKj). Each such o-node is also an output port of the corresponding IOP graph.

Rule 2.3: An i-node labeled I(LKj, T) is added to the IOP graph of each controller in the path between LKj and LOA(LKi, LKj). Each such i-node is also an input port of the corresponding IOP graph.

The protocol followed by a nonleaf controller NLKi is described by Rule 3 below.

Rule 3

An arc is added to IOP(NLKi).

Rule 3.1: If a cycle is generated by the addition of the new arc, then a global deadlock has been detected and an appropriate action is required to resolve it.

Rule 3.2: If no cycle was generated, check whether any input–output port connection has been generated in IOP(NLKi) and report the endpoints of any such connections to the father of NLKi.

We have not yet mentioned how lock releases are reflected in the appropriate graphs in the hierarchy. Let each controller (LK or NLK) maintain a list of the i–o paths (i.e., the paths which connect input ports to output ports) in its graph. A possible representation for this list could be in the form of a bit matrix where each row corresponds to an i–o path, and each column is associated with an arc in the graph. The value '1' in the i, j entry of this matrix indicates that arc j is in the i–o path i. An unlock operation causes an arc (maybe more) to be deleted from a TWF graph of a leaf controller. All the i–o paths (if any) which contained this arc are broken. This may be reported to the father of the LK. There, the arcs which represented the broken i–o paths will be used to find which i–o paths were broken in the nonleaf controller. This propagation continues up in the hierarchy until the deletion of an arc from a graph does not cause any i–o path to be broken.

The method described above for deadlock detection requires that nonleaf controllers be kept up-to-date continuously. Other variations can be used when appropriate. For example, the information concerning connections between input ports and output ports can be sent periodically. For a sufficiently long period this would reduce the amount of traffic generated but may result in a deadlock existing for too long a period of time. Another method which is intermediate to continuous and periodic deadlock detection is to report connections between input and output ports after they have persisted longer than some threshold. Since, if a deadlock occurs the cycle persists until it is detected and relieved, this method will detect a deadlock after some delay. It appears that a judicious choice for the threshold can result in less traffic being generated than with continuous checking and less delay in detecting a deadlock than with periodic checking.

VI. Hierarchical Protocol—Plausibility Argument

The hierarchical protocol has the following properties:

1) deadlocks which involve resources of a single subdata base DBi are detected by the formation of a cycle in the TWF of the leaf controller associated to DBi;
2) deadlocks which involve resources controlled by the leaf controllers LK1, LK2, · · · , LKi are detected by the formation of a cycle in the IOP graph of the nonleaf controller which is the lowest common ancestor between the LKi's.

Property *a* follows directly from Rule 1 of the protocol. The validity of property *b* is not so straightforward and will be shown to hold by the following theorems.

Let us introduce some notation first. Let the arcs which connect an i-node to an o-node in an input-output-ports graph be called i → o arcs and let o → i arcs be the ones which connect o-nodes to i-nodes. Let *tree*(K) be the subtree of the hierarchy rooted at controller K. Let us now extend the notation TWF(K) to indicate the subgraph of the global TWF obtained by considering only the resources controlled by all the LK's in tree(K).

Let us show that if a cycle is detected in the IOP graph of a nonleaf controller, there is a deadlock.

Theorem 1: If there is a cycle in the input-output-ports graph of a nonleaf controller NLKi then there is a deadlock.

Proof: We need to prove that if there is a cycle C in the IOP graph of a nonleaf controller NLKi, there is an associated cycle C′ in TWF(NLKi). Let us show how to construct the cycle C′. Let C be a cycle in IOP(NLKi). For the purpose of this construction, let us label each i → o arc (Ij, Oj) in C with the label Kj if Kj is an immediate son of NLKi such that the creation of an input-output-port connection in Kj caused the arc (Ij, Oj) to be created in IOP(NLKi)—see Rules 1.1b and 3.2 of the protocol. Arcs of the type o → i in IOP(NLKi) will not be labeled. Using the notation (a, b, c) to indicate an arc labeled *c* from node *a* to node *b* let the cycle C be C = (I1, O1, K1), (O1, I2, -), (I2, O2, K2), · · · , (In, On, Kn), (On, I1, -).

The repeated application of Operation 1 below will transform the cycle C into a cycle in which all the labels indicate leaf controllers.

Operation 1: If Kj in (Ij, Oj, Kj) is a nonleaf controller, replace (Ij, Oj, Kj) by a path connecting Ij to Oj in IOP(Kj).

After this transformation, there is a path in the TWF of an LK in tree(NLKi) associated with each i → o arc in C. There is also an arc between incarnations of transactions in the TWF's of distinct LK's associated with each o → i arc in C. More precisely, for each i → o arc (Ii, Oi, Ki) in C there is a path in TWF(Ki) between the input port Ii and the output port Oi of TWF(Ki). Now, by Rule 2.1 of the protocol each o → i arc (Oi, Ii + 1, -) in C connects two incarnations of the same transaction. These incarnations are local to leaf controllers in tree(NLKi). Finally, the sum of all the paths and arcs thus obtained defines the cycle C′ in TWF(NLKi).

In order to conclude the proof we must show that the arcs in the cycle C′ defined above exist simultaneously, and, therefore, C′ is a deadlock cycle. Assume not. Then there is at least a pair of arcs Ti → Tj and Tm → Tn which did not appear simultaneously in C′ and such that there is a path from Tj to Tm in TWF(NLKi). Consider first the case in which Ti → Tj existed (i.e., appeared and disappeared) before Tm → Tn. Then, transaction Tj released the resource it was holding (which was needed by Ti). This implies that all the transactions in the path from Tj to Tm in TWF(NLKi) must have had released at least one resource also. Since transactions are assumed to be two phase, then none of them (including Tm) can issue any further lock requests. Therefore, the arc Tm → Tn cannot exist. This contradicts our assumption and shows that it is not possible for Ti → Tj to have existed before Tm → Tn. Consider now the case in which Tm → Tn existed before Ti → Tj. This case is perfectly possible as long as these two arcs are not part of the same cycle; otherwise, one would have to conclude that every arc in the cycle existed before itself. Therefore, all the arcs in C′ coexist in TWF(NLKi), and C′ represents a deadlock cycle, and the theorem is proved.

We want to show now that given a cycle in the global TWF there is a corresponding cycle in one of the controllers in the hierarchy. In order to state this property more precisely, some definitions are in order. Let the graph G′ be called an *arc condensation* or simply *condensation* of the graph G if the node set of G′ is a subset of the node set of G, and if (v1, v*n*) is an arc in G′ then there is a path from node v1 to node v*n* in the graph G.

Theorem 2: Given a cycle G in the global TWF there is an arc condensation of C in one and only one controller in the hierarchy. This controller is the lowest common ancestor of all the controllers which manage the resources in the cycle C.

Proof: Let C be a cycle in the global TWF which involves resources controlled by leaf controllers LK1, LK2, · · · , LK*n*. Each of the *n* leaf controllers only knows the portion of the cycle which contains resources local to the controller. Let us consider an initial condensation of the cycle C obtained by substituting every path in the TWF from an input port to an output port of a leaf controller by a single arc connecting these ports. For the purpose of this proof, let us introduce a representation for a cycle which clearly illustrates how the knowledge about portions of the cycle is distributed throughout several controllers in the hierarchy. So, let a cycle be represented by a sequence of labeled arcs (IO, OO, KO), (I1, O1, K1), · · · , (Ij, Oj, Kj), · · · , (In - 1, On - 1, Kn - 1) where (Ij, Oj, Kj) indicates that there is a connection between the input port Ij and the output port Oj in the graph of the controller Kj. Also, the output port Oj is connected to the input port Ij + 1(mod *n*). Let *father*(*K*) be the father of controller K in the hierarchy. The repeated application of operations 1 and 2 below gives us the desired condensed cycle C.

Operation 1: If all the labels in C are the same, then stop. Substitute every maximal path P in C composed solely of arcs labeled with sons of a common controller K by a single arc having as endpoints the endpoints of P and having as label the common father controller K. This operation is illustrated in Fig. 3 and can be thought of as a short circuit between consecutive brothers. Repeat Operation 1 until all the labels in C are different and then do Operation 2.

Operation 2: Find all the arcs in C which have as label a controller whose level in the hierarchy is the lowest of all the controllers which appear as labels in C. Substitute the label Ki in each of these arcs by father(Ki). Do Operation 1. Operation 2 is illustrated in Fig. 4.

In order to show the validity of Operation 1, let us refer to Fig. 3 and consider the following observations.

1) There is an arc from Oi to Ii + 1 for i = 1 to (l - 1) in IOP(K), since the controller K is the lowest common ancestor between K1, K2, · · · , Kl. See Rule 2.1 of the protocol.

2) There is an arc from Ii to Oi, for i = 1 to l in IOP(K), since every time a connection between an input and an output port is created it is propagated to its father. See Rules 1.1a and 3.2 of the protocol.

3) Since the controller K0 is not a son of controller K, the input port I1 is also an input port of K which is in the path between K0 and LCA(K1, K0). See Rule 2.3 of the protocol. The same observation applied to controller Kl + 1 and the output port O1 (see Rule 2.2 of the protocol).

The reader should notice that Operation 1 preserves the lowest common ancestor between all the controllers involved in the cycle.

The validity of Operation 2 follows from observations 2) and 3) above. Notice that the choice of a controller at the lowest possible level to substitute during operation 2 preserves the

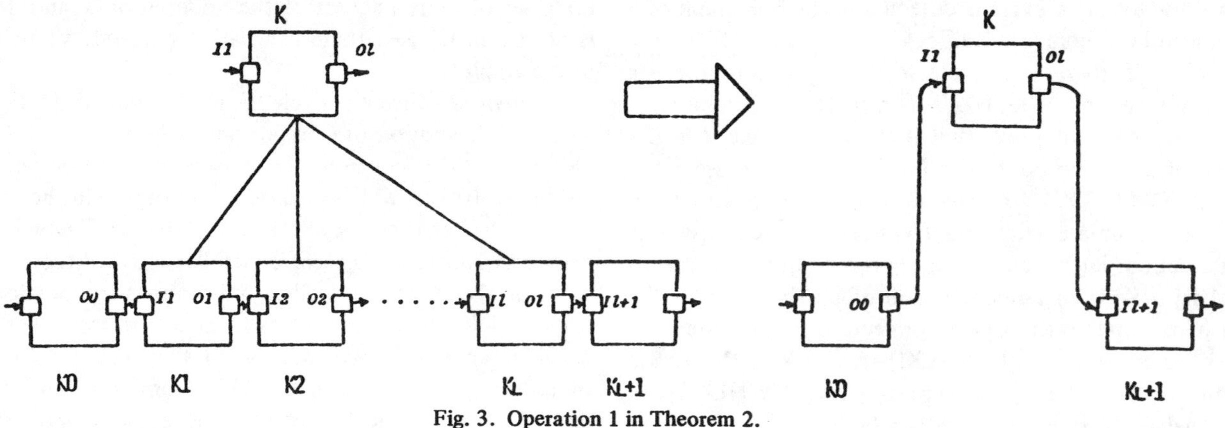
Fig. 3. Operation 1 in Theorem 2.

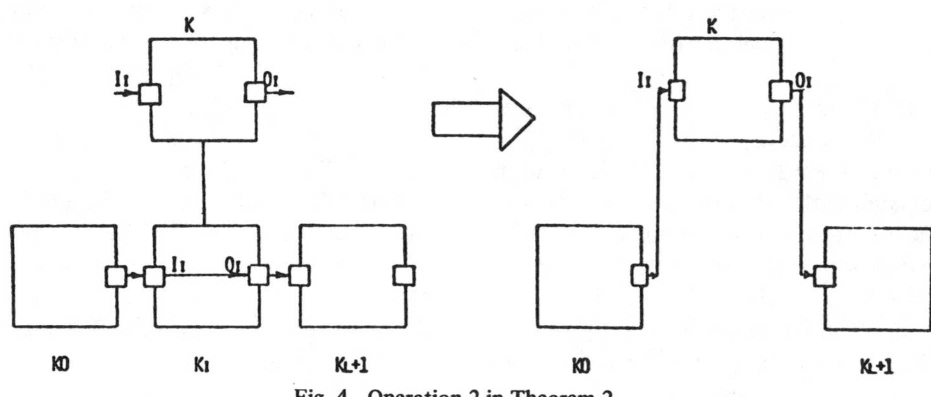
Fig. 4. Operation 2 in Theorem 2.

lowest common ancestor between the controllers involved in the cycle. The reader can easily convince himself that this must be the case.

Therefore, when all the labels are the same we have a representation of a condensed version of the original cycle. The common label is the name of the controller where the cycle is completely represented. Since operations 1 and 2 preserve the lowest common ancestor between the controllers involved in the cycle, the original cycle will be represented in a condensed way in LCA(LK1, LK2, $\cdots$, LKn).

Theorems 1 and 2 together give us a necessary and sufficient condition for a deadlock to be detected in a distributed data base involving resource at different sites. This result will be stated as the following theorem.

Theorem 3: A necessary and sufficient condition for a deadlock involving resources in controllers LK1, LK2, $\cdots$, LKn to exist is that there is a cycle in the IOP graph of ICA(LK1, LK2, $\cdots$, LKn). This cycle is a condensation of the corresponding cycle in the global TWF.

VII. Deadlock Resolution

As pointed out in an earlier section, we are not going to examine in this paper the criteria involved in optimal deadlock resolution since this is mainly a policy issue. This section discusses, however, the mechanisms which are necessary to allow the implementation of any such policy. The reader may have noticed that the condensed cycle in the IOP graph contains less information than the corresponding cycle in the TWF graph. In particular, not all the transactions which participate in the cycle in the TWF graph appear in the IOP graph.

One way to compensate for this loss of information is to require that, whenever an i-o arc is received by an NLK, the name of the controller which generated the arc be stored with the arc. Then, when an NLK detects a deadlock cycle, it can send down the tree to its appropriate sons a message which will continue to propagate down (through the appropriate sons) until it reaches the leaves of the tree. At this point the LK's can report directly to the NLK which detected the deadlock all the necessary information to implement the desired policy for deadlock resolution.

Notice that the additional messages necessary to support the above described mechanism do not substantially increase the total communications cost of the protocol since they must only be sent when deadlocks are detected and not during normal operation.

Another, less flexible alternative is to select the transaction to be preempted from those which appear in the IOP graph only. While no additional messages are required here it is likely that a nonoptimal choice will be taken in resolving the deadlock.

VIII. Hierarachy Establishment

So far we have assumed the existence of the hierarchy without considering how it is established in the first place. The performance of the hierarchical protocol, in terms of the overhead message traffic incurred by it, can be minimized if the hierarchy is appropriately chosen. This choice should consider the pattern of the DB traffic with respect to the locality of access to a controller or group of controllers. For instance, assume that one is able to identify groups or clusters of leaf controllers such that a high percentage of the DB traffic involves controllers in the same cluster while very little traffic is of the intercluster type. One possibility here would be to assign nonleaf controllers to each cluster and try to further cluster the non-leaf controllers or put all of them together under the same root.

The problem in general can be stated as follows. Given a set of leaf controllers assigned to the nodes of a computer network, given the DB traffic pattern, and given the cost of sending messages between every pair of nodes in the network, find a hierarchy which minimizes the total cost incurred in using the protocol.

There are clearly some heuristic rules which, if applied to a given hierarchy, result in another hierarchy of less cost. The general optimization problem, however, is the subject of current research effort.

IX. A Distributed Locking and Deadlock Detection Protocol

A locking protocol which uses distributed control and a distributed deadlock detection mechanism is presented here. Before we describe the protocol, some definitions are in order. Each data-base site controls a set of resources. Transactions request resources by sending their requests to the controller of the resource. Each controller is responsible for

1) processing lock and lock release requests for local resources. Requests may originate from any node in the network.
2) building a simplified version of the transaction_wait_for graph and detecting deadlocks. The TWF maintained by a controller is a subgraph of the global TWF.

For the purpose of stating this algorithm, we will use a simplified version of the transaction_wait_for graph. The reader should be aware that this version is a redefinition of the graph used in the section on the hierarchical protocol although the same name for the graph is retained. In this version, there is no notion of transaction incarnations. Nodes are associated with transactions, and there is a directed arc from transaction T′ to transaction T″ if T′ is blocked and must wait for T″ to release a resource (not necessarily a resource needed by T′) before T′ is able to proceed.

Some definitions are in order. A *nonblocked* transaction is a node in the transaction_wait_for graph with no outgoing arcs or a *sink* node. Let us now define *blocking set*(T) as the set of all nonblocked transactions which can be reached by following a directed path in the TWF graph starting at the node associated with transaction T. This is the set of transactions which are ultimately blocking transaction T. The pair (T, T′) is said to be a blocking pair of T if T′ is in blocking_set(T).

The execution of a transaction can be described as follows. A transaction has a site of origin which is the site where the transaction entered the system. The transaction starts running at this site, performing local operations until operations on nonlocal data are necessary. Then, a lock request in the appropriate mode is built and sent to the controller for the requested resource. This controller will either accept or reject the lock, sending the reply to the site of origin of the transaction. If there are multiple copies of data, lock requests have to be sent to all controllers which keep a copy of the data.

X. Distributed Protocol—A Description

Let *Sorig*(T) be the site of origin of transaction T, and let TWF(K) be the TWF graph at site Sk. The protocol is described by Rules 1 and 2 given below as carried out by controller Sk. Let T be a transaction requesting resource R.

Rule 1

The resource R cannot be granted to T because it is being held by transactions T1, T2, · · · , Tk. Add an arc from transaction T to each of the transactions in the set {T1, T2, · · · , Tk}. If the addition of these arcs caused a cycle to be formed in TWF(K), then a deadlock was detected, and an appropriate action is required for its resolution. For each transaction T′ in blocking_set(T), send the blocking pair (T, T′) to Sorig(T) if Sorig(T) ≠ Sk and to Sorig(T′) if Sorig(T′) ≠ Sk.

Rule 2

A blocking pair (T, T′) is received. Add an arc from T to T′ in TWF(K). If a cycle was formed, then a deadlock exists, and it must be resolved by an appropriate action. If T′ is blocked and Sorig(T) ≠ Sk, then for each transaction T″ in the blocking_set(T), send the blocking pair (T, T″) to Sorig(T″) if Sorig(T″) ≠ Sk.

Some comments are in order.

1) The arcs of the transaction_wait_for graph considered here may represent one of two types of relationships between transactions, namely, a *direct* wait and an *indirect* wait. Transaction T1 is said to be waiting directly on T2 if the resource needed by T1 for its continued execution is being held by T2. A transaction T1 is said to be waiting indirectly on Tk if there is a set of transactions T2, T3, · · · , Tk - 1 such that Ti is waiting directly on Ti + 1 for i = 1 to k - 1.

2) From the previous observation it can be seen that cycles in a TWF graph may be a condensation (in the sense defined in the section on the hierarchical protocol) of the cycle that would exist in the global transaction_wait_for graph for the whole system.

XI. Distributed Protocol—Plausibility Argument

That the protocol described in the previous section is able to detect all deadlocks is shown in the following theorem.

Theorem 4: The above described protocol detects all possible deadlocks.

Proof: In order to show this result we will consider a global deadlock cycle, as shown in Fig. 5, and we will show

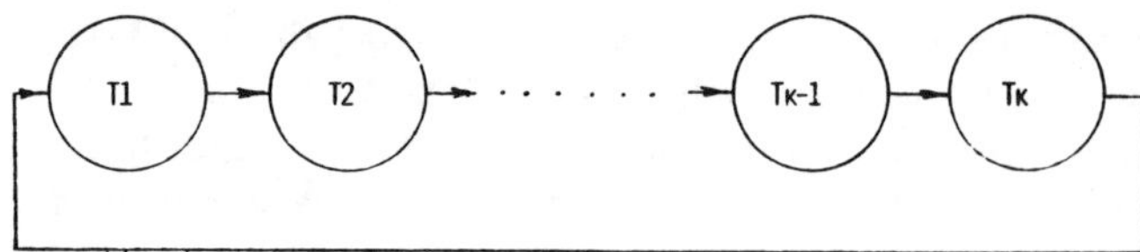

Fig. 5. Deadlock cycle involving transactions T1, T2, · · · , Tk.

that this cycle will appear in the TWF of the site of origin of at least one of the transaction in the cycle.

There are many orderings of resource requests that can lead to the same deadlock cycle. Each time a request is rejected, the newly formed blocking pairs will increase the knowledge that some controllers have about the global graph. Therefore, the more advance knowledge obtained when a request is rejected the more rapidly the deadlock will be detected. The ordering of resource requests used in this proof is such that controllers will get the minimum possible knowledge of the rest of the graph when a request is rejected. The reader should not have any problem in convincing himself that if the theorem holds for this ordering, then it holds for any other. The chosen ordering is the following. Initially, transactions T1 through Tk - 1 are blocked and each of the controllers at the site of origin of these transactions have the knowledge of a single transaction ahead in the cycle. At this point the transaction_wait_for graph at the site of origin of each transaction is shown as follows.

Sorig(T1): T1 → T2
Sorig(T2): T2 → T3
⋮
Sorig(Tk - 1): Tk - 1 → Tk.

Now, when Tk makes a request and is blocked by T1, the blocking pair (Tk, T2) will be sent to Sorig(T2) where a new blocking pair (Tk, T3) is formed and sent to Sorig(T3). There the blocking pair (Tk, T4) is formed and sent to Sorig(T4) and so on until the blocking pair (Tk, Tk - 1) reaches Sorig(Tk - 1). This causes the arc from Tk to Tk - 1 to be added to the TWF graph at that site. Since this graph already contained an arc from Tk - 1 to Tk, a cycle is formed and the deadlock is detected.

XII. Conclusion

This paper presents two solutions to the problem of deadlock detection in distributed data bases. The first solution consists of a hierarchy of lock controllers and is intended to achieve better performance, in terms of communications cost, than a centralized approach. For this purpose, the hierarchy should be established in a way such that deadlocks can be detected by a site which is located as "close" as possible to the sites involved in the deadlock. The problem of finding a hierarchy of lock controllers which minimizes the total cost incurred in using this protocol is the subject of current research. The design of a distributed protocol for deadlock detection was motivated by the desire to support reliable operation in environments subject to failures.

Both protocols use a graph model to depict the current state of execution of all transactions in the system. A cycle in this graph is a necessary and sufficient condition for a deadlock to exist. The protocols presented here do not require that a global graph be built and maintained in order for deadlocks to be detected. An outline of the proof of the correct operation of the proposed protocols is included in the paper.

The communications cost involved in using the solutions presented here depends on several factors such as data-base traffic pattern, distance between participating sites, hierarchy topology (for the hierarchical protocol only), and others. A detailed analysis of the performance characteristics of these protocols is the subject of further work.

References

[1] A. N. Haberman, "Prevention of system deadlocks," *Commun. Ass. Comput. Mach.*, vol. 12, no. 7, pp. 373-377, July 1969.

[2] A. Shoshani and E. G. Coffman, "Sequencing tasks in multiprocess, multiple resource systems to avoid deadlocks," in *Proc. 11th Annual Symp. on Switching and Automata Theory*, Oct. 1970, pp. 225-233.

[3] E. G. Coffman, Jr., M. J. Elphick, and A. Shoshani, "System deadlocks," *ACM Comput. Surveys*, vol. 3, no. 2, pp. 67-78, June 1971.

[4] P. F. King and A. J. Collmeyer, "Database sharing–An efficient mechanism for supporting concurrent processes," in *Proc. AFIPS Nat. Comput. Conf.*, 1973.

[5] J. N. Gray, "Notes on database operating systems," in *Operating Systems and Advanced Course.* Berlin, Heidelberg: Springer-Verlag, 1978, ch. 3.F, pp. 394-481.

[6] K. P. Eswaran, J. N. Gray, R. A. Lorie, and I. L. Traiger, "The motions of consistency and predicate locks in a database system," *Commun. Ass. Comput. Mach.*, vol. 19, no. 11, Nov. 1976.

THE EXCLUSIVE-WRITER PROTOCOL: A LOW COST APPROACH FOR UPDATING REPLICATED FILES IN DISTRIBUTED REAL TIME SYSTEMS*

Wesley W. Chu, Joseph Hellerstein, and Min-Tsung Lan

Computer Science Department
University of California
Los Angeles, California 90024

Abstract — **A new low overhead protocol, the Exclusive-Writer Protocol (EWP), which maintains the consistency of replicated files is proposed in this paper. In the EWP, neither a locking nor a timestamp protocol is used. Mutual consistency is ensured by permitting a file to be written by only a single exclusive writing task, and internal consistency is guaranteed by using the interdependent data set (IDS) update rule. The EWP avoids deadlocks due to shared data access and also eliminates synchronization delays. The design characteristics and performance of the EWP as well as its implications on task assignment are presented. The study concludes that the EWP is simple to implement and has a very low overhead. Therefore, it is appealing for distributed real time systems.**

1. Introduction

In distributed systems, shared files are replicated to improve reliability and reduce read access time. Determining the degree of file replication requires weighing these benefits against the cost (e.g., delay) of updates. Commonly used techniques for updating replicated files include locking and timestamp protocols [BERN81]. While the processing costs and message volume of these techniques can be substantial, this overhead may not be significant for database management systems in which shared files reside on secondary storage. However, for real time systems in which files consist of data in RAM and which use no high level data model, the overhead of locking or timestamp protocols may be prohibitive. This has motivated us to investigate a new low cost protocol for updating replicated files, the *exclusive-writer protocol (EWP)*. In the EWP, mutual consistency is ensured by having only one predetermined task write a shared data item, and internal consistency is guaranteed by using the interdependent data set (IDS) update rule. This approach ensures mutual and internal consistency in a manner suitable for distributed real time systems.

In this paper, we first describe the characteristics of the EWP. Next, we show how the IDS update rule preserves internal consistency without using locking or timestamp protocols. Then, the EWP's performance is compared to that of the primary site locking (PSL) and the read-optimized primary site locking (ROL) protocols. Finally, we discuss EWP performance characteristics and task assignment considerations.

2. Characteristics of the EWP

In the EWP, no inter-site message exchange is required to read a shared data item. On the other hand, *a shared data item is written by only one predetermined task which does not change during system operation.* To handle situations in which multiple tasks must update the same data (hereafter referred to as *multiwriter situations)*, the following approach is used: (1) an *exclusive-writer (EW)* is designated for each shared data item, and (2) to update a shared data item, a non-EW task sends an update-request message to the data item's EW (see figures 1 and 2). Such an approach has been used by the Distributed Processing Architecture Design (DPAD) [GREE80]. Here, we assume that exclusive-writers are dedicated to receiving update-request messages, distributing updates, and performing operations to ensure data consistency.

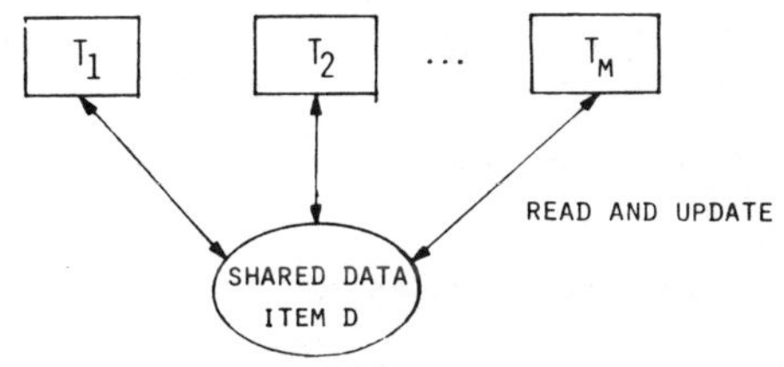

(A) TASKS $T_1, \ldots, T_M$ BOTH READ AND UPDATE D

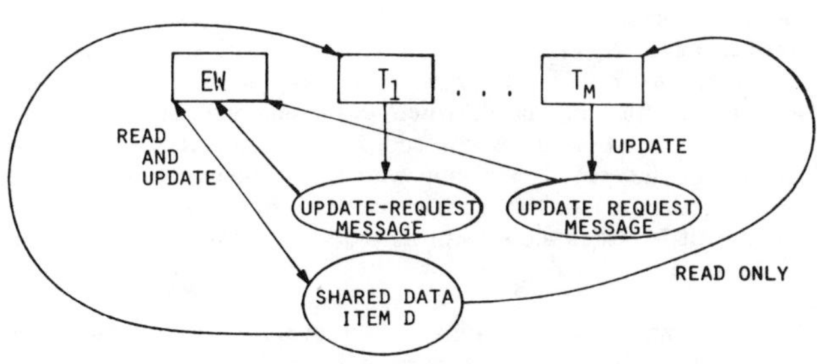

(B) EW IS THE EXCLUSIVE-WRITER OF D. $T_1, \ldots, T_M$ SEND THEIR UPDATE REQUESTS TO EW

FIGURE 1. MULTIPLE WRITERS AND EXCLUSIVE-WRITER FOR A SINGLE SHARED DATA ITEM.

*This research is supported by the U.S. Army Contract No. DASG60-79-C-0087

Reprinted from *Proc. 3rd Int. Conf. Distrib. Comput. Syst.*, Oct. 1982, pp. 269–277.

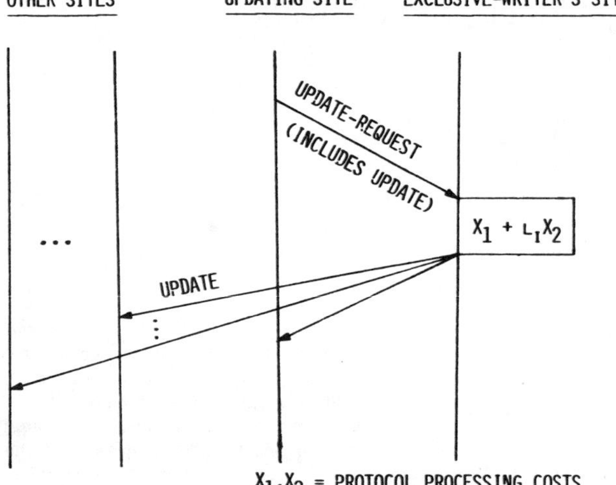

FIGURE 2. PROTOCOL DIAGRAM FOR THE EXCLUSIVE-WRITER PROTOCOL

Let us first discuss how the EWP ensures mutual consistency with low cost. This can be accomplished in two ways. In the first, the following assumptions are made:

1. The sites and interconnection network ensure correct message transmission.

2. Transmissions and updates are processed in a FIFO manner.

3. Tasks are not dynamically reassigned to other sites.

Under these circumstances, updates will be posted at all sites in the order in which they were applied at the EW's site; and no update will be lost.

If the above assumptions are too stringent, then a second approach can be used which only assumes that the network which interconnects the sites ensures correct message transmission (although messages may arrive out of order). To guarantee mutual consistency, a sequence number is associated with each shared data item. When an EW performs an update on a data item, the sequence number of that data item is incremented and is included in the update message. A site compares the sequence number on its copy of the shared data item with the sequence number in the update message. If the update message has a larger sequence number, it is posted along with its sequence number; otherwise, it is discarded.

Using the EWP results in two advantages over employing non-EW techniques such as locking and timestamp protocols. First, the EWP avoids delays due to locking-protocol synchronization and timestamp-protocol rollback. A second advantage relates to deadlocks. Recall that the EWP does not require any locking to ensure data consistency. Thus, *the EWP can eliminate deadlocks due to shared data access.*

The reliability of an EWP design appears to be comparable to that of primary site locking in that the failure of a single site need only affect those files whose EW resides at the failed site. In primary site locking, reliability can be improved by special recovery techniques [STON79]. Similar schemes can be used for the EWP. In any case, the EWP is more reliable than centralized locking, since in the latter the failure of the central site is catastrophic.

Finally, the EWP has some special design considerations. First, to use the EWP, an application must be designed so that there is an EW for each shared data item. A second consideration relates to preserving internal consistency without locking, which will be discussed in the next section.

3. Internal Consistency and the IDS Update Rule

While having an exclusive writer for each shared data item can ensure mutual consistency, it does not necessarily ensure internal consistency. For example, consider a distributed system in which there are two sites: A and B. Let task T_A be at site A and T_B be at site B. T_A and T_B read and update a file which is replicated at both sites. The file has three fields labeled x, y, and z. Suppose that T_A is the exclusive-writer for this file and that we have the internal consistency constraint $x+y+z = 3$, and initially $x = y = z = 1$. Now, if T_A updates the file so that x is -1 and y is 3, internal consistency is preserved. Alternatively, if T_B initiates an update in which y is set to -1 and z to 3, internal consistency is preserved. However, from figure 3 it is apparent that when T_A and T_B execute concurrently, internal consistency may be violated.

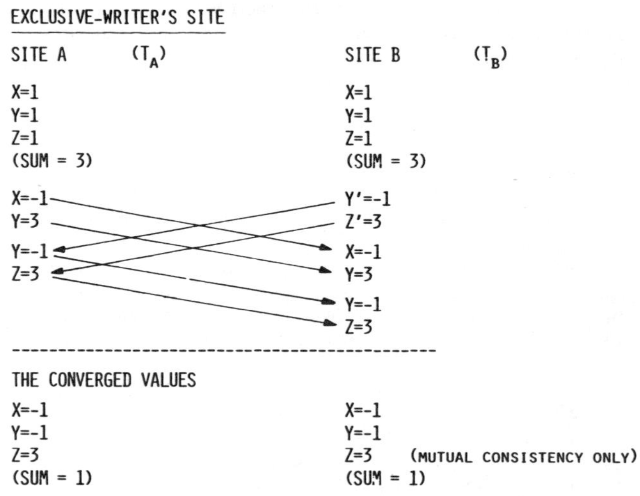

X, Y, Z - UPDATE MESSAGES

X',Y',Z'- UPDATE-REQUEST MESSAGES

FIGURE 3. LOSS OF INTERNAL CONSISTENCY WITH THE EWP

In distributed real time systems, the logical interdependencies among shared data are often known (e.g., the DPAD [GREE80], the logic simulation machine in [ABRA82], the video graphics architecture in [FUCH79], and the signal processing architecture in [ARMS79]). This motivates us to propose a new technique for ensuring internal consistency which does not use locking or timestamp protocols but makes use of this knowledge. Called the *interdependent data set (IDS) update rule*, it operates as follows:

1. When a data item is modified, the resulting update must include the values of all data for which the modified data

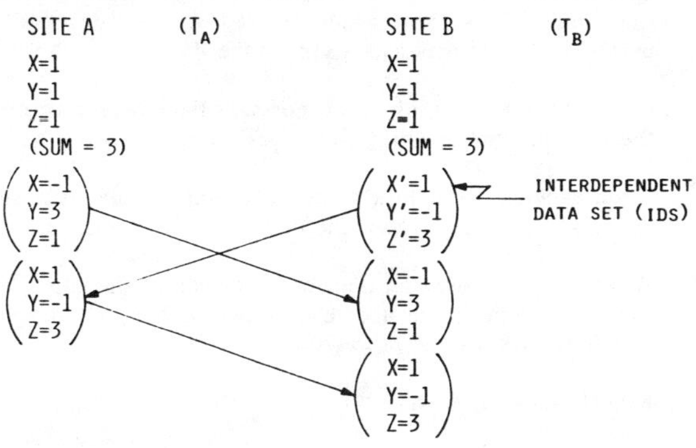

THE CONVERGED VALUES

X=1	X=1	
Y=-1	Y=-1	MUTUAL AND INTERNAL
Z=3	Z=3	CONSISTENCY
(SUM = 3)	(SUM = 3)	

X, Y, Z - UPDATE MESSAGES

X',Y',Z'- UPDATE-REQUEST MESSAGES

FIGURE 4. PRESERVING INTERNAL CONSISTENCY IN THE EWP WITH THE INTERDEPENDENT DATA SET UPDATE RULE.

item has an interdependency. (Applying the IDS update rule to the previous example, T_A must include z in its update, and T_B must include x.) In fact, the transitive closure of this dependency relationship must be used. For example, if x and z are interdependent as well as z and w, then w must be included in an update to x. Thus, *EWP update messages may be larger than those for locking and timestamp protocols.*

2. When a site posts an update, it must guarantee that:

    a. The entire update is processed atomically (i.e., without interruption).

    b. No task is in the process of reading the data to be modified.

Under these conditions internal consistency will be preserved, since the only time during which it can be violated is when an update is in progress; but updates are atomic. Application of the IDS update rule to the example in figure 3 is illustrated in figure 4.

One final aspect of the IDS update rule deserves attention: *the IDS update rule ensures internal consistency but not serializability.* This can be shown from figure 4 in which the following sequence occurs at site B:

1. T_B reads x, y, and z and requests that A (the EW's site) update x, y, and z.

2. T_A's updates are posted at site B (i.e., $x = -1$, $y = 3$, $z = 1$).

3. T_B's updates are posted at site B.

A serial schedule requires that after T_B has read x, y, and z, these data can not be modified until T_B has posted its updates. The above schedule violates this requirement, so it is not serializable.

In distributed real time systems, internal consistency rather than the stronger condition of serializability is often sufficient. For example, in radar tracking applications, each object being tracked has a record in the track file which is periodically updated based on new radar returns for the object and its existing track record. Since this is a computationally intensive task which is done frequently, it can become a system bottleneck. Using distributed processing to resolve this bottleneck requires that track-update tasks be executed in parallel. However, data conflicts can arise if track updates are performed concurrently on the same record (i.e., object). Because the most recently updated track record is not needed to perform a new update, only internal consistency is required.

4. Performance Analysis

In this section, we compare the performance of the EWP to that of two other consistency control techniques: primary site locking (PSL) and read-optimized primary site locking (ROL). Four performance measures are considered: (1) protocol processing cost, (2) number of protocol messages, (3) message volume, and (4) transaction response time. We consider a distributed system in which: k tasks share m files; a copy of a file exists at the file's primary site and at all sites where the file is accessed; inter-file internal consistency requirements are preserved after updates have been completed; and the interconnection network ensures correct message transmission.

We now describe the three consistency control techniques to be compared, beginning with the operation of EWP for multiwriter situations. Let EW_i be the exclusive-writer for file F_i. To update F_i, a task sends an update-request message (which contains the update) to EW_i. Then EW_i distributes the update to the other sites (see figure 2). A distributed system that uses the EWP is shown in figure 5. Note that when F_i is updated by a task assigned to the same site as EW_i, no update-request message is required. Let the probability of such an update be g_i.

Garcia-Molina describes a centralized locking scheme in which all files are controlled by a single site [GARC78]. The *primary site locking (PSL)* protocol described here is similar to his scheme, but each file has a designated *primary site (PS)* that controls access to the file. (A distributed processing system using PSL would be identical to figure 5 except that the EW tasks would be replaced by PS tasks.) Figure 6 shows the message exchanges required for a task at a non-PS to obtain read access. First, a lock-request message for read-only access is sent to the PS. The reading task then waits until the PS replies with a lock-grant message, which indicates that all updates to the requested file are completed. Contained in the lock-grant message is the sequence number of the last update made to the file. If the requesting site has not posted this update, then it waits until all outstanding updates have been posted before the reader is permitted to commence processing. Once the reader completes its processing, a lock-release message is sent to the PS. If there is no other task using the file for read-only access, then update access could be permitted at this time.

Figure 7 shows the file update protocol for PSL. If the requesting task does not reside at the PS of the file, a lock-request message (for update access) is sent, and the PS must reply with a lock-grant message before the requesting task can proceed. The requesting task may incur additional waiting if the sequence number in the lock-grant message indicates that there is an outstanding update message. Once the task completes its processing, its updates are distributed. The sequence number of the update is equal to the sequence number in the lock-grant message plus one. A site receiving the update will post it if the update is in sequence. Otherwise, the new update is queued until outstanding updates arrive. At the PS, an update message has the additional interpretation of an implicit lock-release.

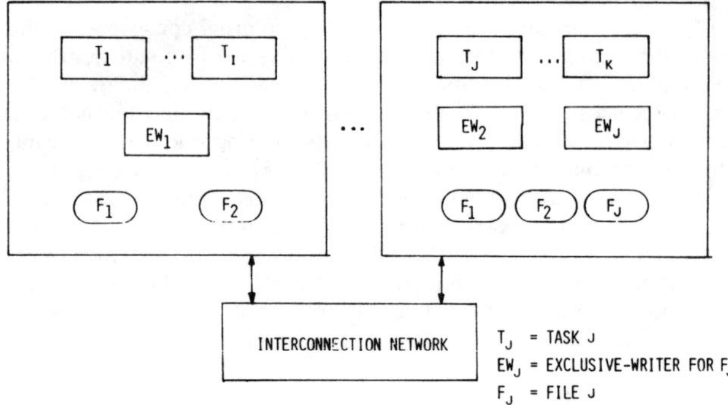

FIGURE 5 A DISTRIBUTED PROCESSING SYSTEM WHICH USES THE EWP

In PSL (as with the EWP), the number of messages required for file access varies with task assignment. In particular, if F_i is updated by a task assigned to F_i's primary site, then no lock-request, lock-grant, or lock-release message is required. We let h_i be the probability of such an update.

The final consistency control technique we consider is *read-optimized primary site locking (ROL)*. ROL is a modification of PSL in which no processing cost or message exchange occurs for read-only access. An update requires the following sequence of interactions (see figure 8):

1. The updating site sends a lock-request message to the PS of F_i.

2. The PS sends a permission-request message to all sites (except the updating site).

3. When a site receives a permission-request message for F_i, it waits until there is no task performing a read on F_i at that site. F_i is then locally locked for update, and a permission-grant message is sent to the PS.

4. Once all the permission-grant messages have been received, the PS sends the updating site a lock-grant message.

5. Upon receiving the lock-grant message, the updating site can modify F_i and forward the update to the other sites.

6. When a site receives an update, it unlocks its file copy. At the PS, receipt of the update message implies that another update request can be processed.

4.1 Protocol Processing Costs

For the EWP, protocol processing costs reflect instructions executed by exclusive-writers to process update-request messages. In PSL and ROL, these costs represent the processing required to determine what actions to take upon receipt of a control message as well as the execution of these actions (other than I/O).

If a task execution instance accesses file F_i, that access may be either read-only or update. Let R_i be the ratio of read-only to update accesses to file F_i, and p_i be the probability that a task execution instance accesses file F_i for update. Thus

$$R_i = \frac{1-p_i}{p_i}$$

After rearranging terms in the above equation, we have

$$p_i = \frac{1}{1+R_i} \qquad (1)$$

$$1-p_i = \frac{R_i}{1+R_i} \qquad (2)$$

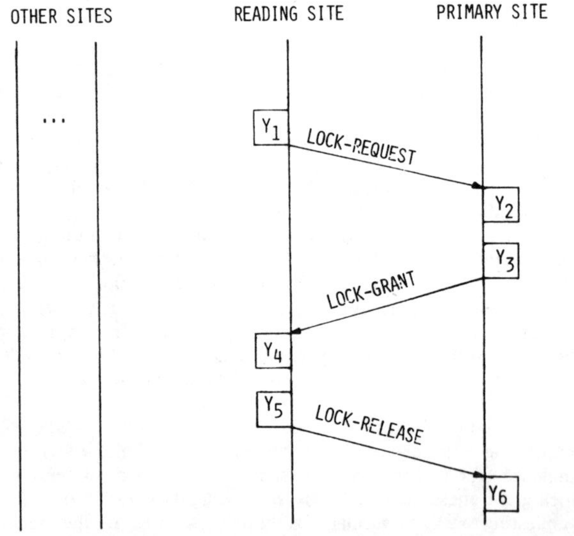

FIGURE 6. PROTOCOL DIAGRAM FOR PRIMARY SITE LOCKING (PSL) READS

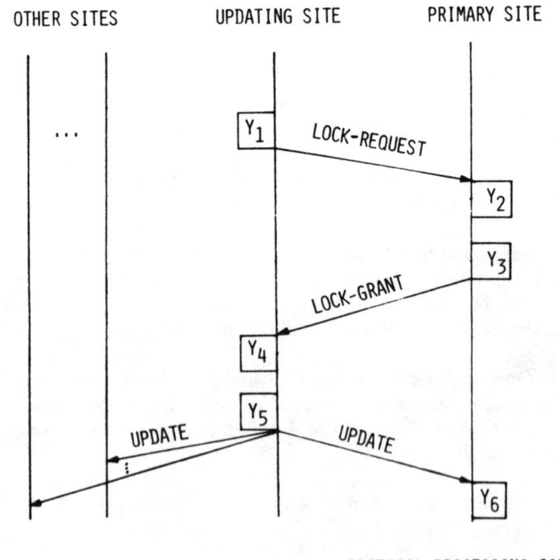

FIGURE 7. PROTOCOL DIAGRAM FOR PRIMARY SITE LOCKING (PSL) UPDATES

For the EWP, the protocol processing cost for accessing file F_i is

$$f_i p_i (x_1 + l_i x_2)$$

where:

f_i = probability of accessing file F_i

l_i = average size (e.g., number of words) of an EWP update to F_i

x_1 = fixed protocol processing cost per update (see figure 2)

x_2 = variable protocol processing cost (e.g., cost per word updated)

The product of the first two terms is the probability that F_i is accessed for update since we assume that p_i and f_i are independent. The last term is the fixed and variable cost of processing an update. Summing over all files in the system and applying equation (1), we have

$$C_{EWP} = \sum_{i=1}^{m} \frac{f_i}{1+R_i}(x_1 + l_i x_2) \qquad (3)$$

For the PSL protocol, the protocol processing cost is

$$C_{PSL} = \sum_{i=1}^{m} f_i (y_1 + y_2 + y_3 + y_4 + y_5 + y_6) \qquad (4)$$

where:

y_1 = protocol processing cost for a lock-request at the requesting site (see figures 6 and 7)

y_2 = protocol processing cost for a lock-request at the PS

y_3 = protocol processing cost for a lock-grant at the PS

y_4 = protocol processing cost for a lock-grant at the requesting site

y_5 = protocol processing cost for a lock-release at the requesting site

y_6 = protocol processing cost for a lock-release at the PS

Note that PSL has the same protocol processing cost regardless of whether the file access is read-only or update.

For the ROL protocol, we must determine which sites are neither the file's primary site nor the requesting site for the update, since a permission-request message will not be sent to these sites and thus they do not send a permission-grant message. If the update originates from the primary site of file F_i, then there will be $n_i - 1$ *non-primary and non-requesting* (NPNR) sites. If the updating task does not reside at the PS of F_i, then there will be $n_i - 2$ NPNR sites. Since h_i is the probability that a task updating F_i resides at the PS of F_i, the average number of NPNR sites is

$$n_i - 2 + h_i$$

Thus, from the definition of the ROL protocol and assuming that f_i and h_i are independent, the protocol processing cost is

$$C_{ROL} = \sum_{i=1}^{m} \frac{f_i}{1+R_i}(z_1 + z_2 + z_3 + (z_4 + z_5 + z_6)(n_i - 2 + h_i) + z_7 + z_8 + z_9 + z_{10}) \qquad (5)$$

where:

n_i = number of sites which have a copy of file F_i

h_i = probability that a task updating F_i resides at F_i's primary site

z_1 = protocol processing cost at the requesting site for a lock-request (see figure 8)

z_2 = protocol processing cost at the PS for a lock-request

z_3 = protocol processing cost at the PS for a permission-request

z_4 = protocol cost for a non-PS and non-requesting (NPNR) site to process a permission-request

z_5 = protocol processing cost at a NPNR site for a permission-grant message

z_6 = protocol cost for the PS to process a permission-grant message

z_7 = protocol processing cost for a lock-grant at the PS

z_8 = protocol processing cost for a lock-grant at the requesting site

z_9 = protocol processing cost for a lock-release at the requesting site

z_{10} = protocol processing cost for a lock-release at the PS

Based on equations (3), (4), and (5), we study the relative cost of the three consistency control techniques using parameter

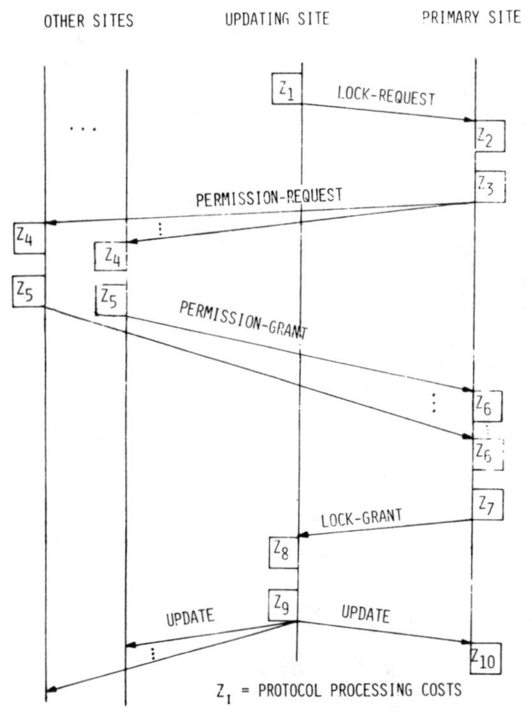

FIGURE 8. PROTOCOL DIAGRAM FOR READ-OPTIMIZED PRIMARY SITE LOCKING (ROL)

values appropriate for distributed real time systems: $x_1 = 50$ machine language instructions (MLI), $x_2 = 6$ MLI, $y_1 + y_2 + y_3 + y_4 + y_5 + y_6 = 50$ MLI, $z_1 + z_2 + z_3 + z_7 + z_8 + z_9 + z_{10} = 65$ MLI, $z_4 + z_5 + z_6 = 10$ MLI, $n_i = n$ file copies, $h_i = h = 1/n$, $R_i = R$, $l_i = l$ words, and $f_i = 1/m$ (each file is referenced with equal probability). Cost values for the EWP were obtained from the DPAD and those for PSL and ROL were estimated from the designs of these protocols. Figure 9 presents protocol processing cost versus read-rate/update-rate, R, for the three consistency control techniques. We note that R significantly impacts which consistency control technique provides minimal cost. For a low R value, PSL produces the lowest cost. However, as R increases, the read overhead of PSL becomes significant, so the EWP as well as ROL yield lower cost. Further, l significantly affects C_{EWP}. For example, the EWP has minimal cost for $l = 10$ and $R \geqslant 1$. But with $l = 30$, this is no longer the case. (In the DPAD, the size of file updates varies from 3 to 100 words.) In ROL, increasing the number of file copies from 12 to 24 increases inter-site communication, and thus C_{ROL} increases dramatically.

4.2 Number and Volume of Messages

Since the number of messages exchanged, M, is directly related to the time spent doing I/O processing (e.g., operating system calls and interrupts) and message volume (i.e., number of words transmitted), V, affects the time to transfer messages between sites, we analyze these quantities for the three consistency control techniques. In all cases, we consider the average number of units (messages or words) exchanged for a task execution instance to perform consistency control.

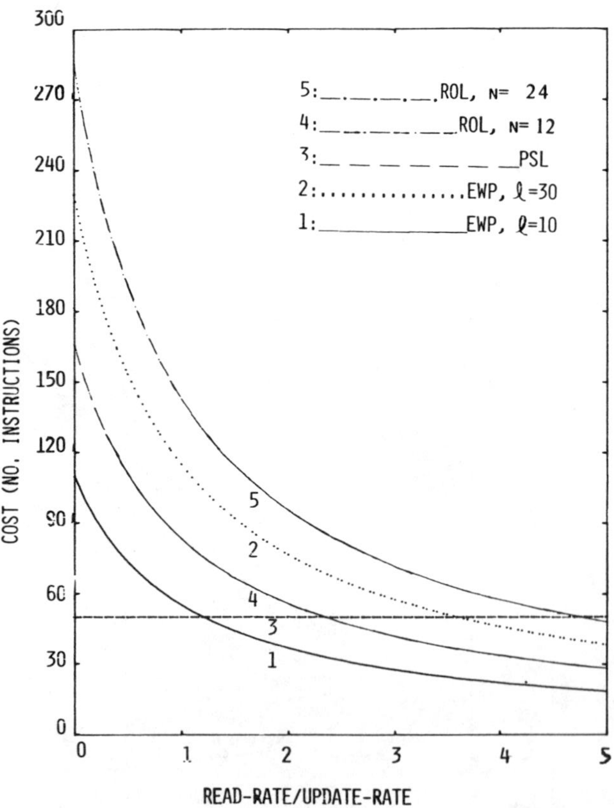

FIGURE 9. COMPARISON OF PROTOCOL PROCESSING COSTS

For the EWP operating in a distributed system with a bus network, the message volume for accesses to file F_i is

$$f_i p_i[(1-g_i)L'_i+L_i]$$

where:

g_i = probability that a task accessing file F_i is assigned to the same site as EW_i

L'_i = size of an update-request message for file F_i

L_i = size of an update message for file F_i

Applying equation (1) and summing over all files, the total bus network message volume is

$$V^B_{EWP} = \sum_{i=1}^{m} \frac{f_i}{1+R_i}[(1-g_i)L'_i+L_i] \tag{6}$$

To obtain the number of messages exchanged, we let $L'_i = L_i = 1$ (i.e., an L'_i, L_i unit is now a message instead of a word).

$$M^B_{EWP} = \sum_{i=1}^{m} \frac{f_i}{1+R_i}(2-g_i) \tag{7}$$

For a totally connected point-to-point network, update messages are transmitted on n_i-1 links. Thus, the message volume is

$$V^P_{EWP} = \sum_{i=1}^{m} \frac{f_i}{1+R_i}[(1-g_i)L'_i+(n_i-1)L_i] \tag{8}$$

Finally,

$$M^P_{EWP} = \sum_{i=1}^{m} \frac{f_i}{1+R_i}(n_i-g_i) \tag{9}$$

For PSL in a bus network, the message volume to update F_i is

$$f_i[(1-h_i)(2S_c+(1-p_i)S_c)+p_iS_i]$$

where:

S_c = size of a control message

S_i = size of an update to file F_i

This equation was derived as follows. When a task that does not reside at the PS of F_i requests access to that file, a lock-request and a lock-grant message, $2S_c$, are required; for read-only access, a lock-release message, $(1-p_i)S_c$, is also necessary. Update access results in an additional message volume of S_i regardless of where the updating task resides. Summing over all files and using equations (1) and (2), we have

$$V^B_{PSL} = \sum_{i=1}^{m} f_i[(1-h_i)(2S_c+\frac{R_i}{1+R_i}S_c)+\frac{S_i}{1+R_i}] \tag{10}$$

To obtain the number of messages exchanged, we set S_i and S_c to 1.

$$M^B_{PSL} = \sum_{i=1}^{m} f_i[(1-h_i)(2+\frac{R_i}{1+R_i})+\frac{1}{1+R_i}] \tag{11}$$

For a totally connected point-to-point network, n_i-1 update messages must be considered.

$$V^P_{PSL} = \sum_{i=1}^{m} f_i[(1-h_i)(2S_c+\frac{R_i}{1+R_i}S_c)+\frac{(n_i-1)S_i}{1+R_i}] \tag{12}$$

As before, we obtain the number of messages by letting $S_i = S_c = 1$.

$$M^P_{PSL} = \sum_{i=1}^{m} f_i[(1-h_i)(2+\frac{R_i}{1+R_i})+\frac{n_i-1}{1+R_i}] \tag{13}$$

Finally, we consider the message volume of ROL in a bus network. For file F_i, this is

$$f_i p_i [2(1-h_i)S_c+S_c+(n_i-2+h_i)S_c+S_i]$$

ROL requires message exchanges only for file updates. Under these circumstances, a lock-request and a lock-grant message are needed only if the updating task is not at the PS for the file, $2(1-h_i)S_c$. A permission-request message will always be generated, S_c, but the number of permission-grant messages sent in reply depends on the number of file copies and the location of the updating task, $(n_i-2+h_i)S_c$. Finally, there is the update message itself, S_i. Summing over all files and applying equation (1), we have

$$V_{ROL}^{B} = \sum_{i=1}^{m} \frac{f_i}{1+R_i}[2(1-h_i)S_c+S_c+(n_i-2+h_i)S_c+S_i] \quad (14)$$

In the same manner as previously, the number of messages exchanged is

$$M_{ROL}^{B} = \sum_{i=1}^{m} \frac{f_i}{1+R_i}[n_i+2-h_i] \quad (15)$$

For a totally connected point-to-point network, the volume of permission-request and update messages is

$$V_{ROL}^{P} = \sum_{i=1}^{m} \frac{f_i}{1+R_i}[2(1-h_i)S_c+2(n_i-2+h_i)S_c+(n_i-1)S_i] \quad (16)$$

The number of messages transferred is

$$M_{ROL}^{P} = \sum_{i=1}^{m} \frac{f_i}{1+R_i}[3(n_i-1)] \quad (17)$$

To compare the number of messages required for PSL and ROL with that for the EWP, we set g_i equal to h_i (since the exclusive-writer acts like a primary site).

$$M_{PSL}^{B}-M_{EWP}^{B} = \sum_{i=1}^{m} f_i(1-h_i)\left(\frac{3R_i}{1+R_i}+\frac{1}{1+R_i}\right) \quad (18)$$

$$M_{PSL}^{P}-M_{EWP}^{P} = \sum_{i=1}^{m} f_i(1-h_i)\left(\frac{3R_i}{1+R_i}+\frac{1}{1+R_i}\right) \quad (19)$$

$$M_{ROL}^{B}-M_{EWP}^{B} = \sum_{i=1}^{m} f_i \frac{n_i}{1+R_i} \quad (20)$$

$$M_{ROL}^{P}-M_{EWP}^{P} = \sum_{i=1}^{m} f_i \frac{2n_i-3+h_i}{1+R_i} \quad (21)$$

Since equations (18) through (21) are always non-negative, *the number of messages required by the EWP will never exceed the number needed by either PSL or ROL.*

To provide insight about V as a function of R, we perform computations for several cases. In all of these cases, we assume a five word header consisting of: source site, bit list of destination sites, file identifier, sequence number, and the number of words in the update. Further, we assume that $S_c = 5$, $S_i = S$, $L'_i = L_i = L$, $R_i = R$, $n_i = 6$, $f_i = 1/m$, and $g_i = h_i = 1/6$. Figure 10 portrays V for the bus network as a function of read-rate/update-rate, R. We note that for small values of R, PSL produces the minimal V value. But as R increases, the EWP (with $L = 15$) and ROL yield a lower V. However, had the IDS update rule required that the size of an EWP update, L, be 45 words instead of 15 words, V for the EWP would have been larger than V for the PSL. For a totally connected point-to-point network, the dominant factor affecting V is the size of an update (see figure 11). A larger update size greatly increases the number of words transmitted, since an update must be transmitted through $n_i-1 = 5$ links.

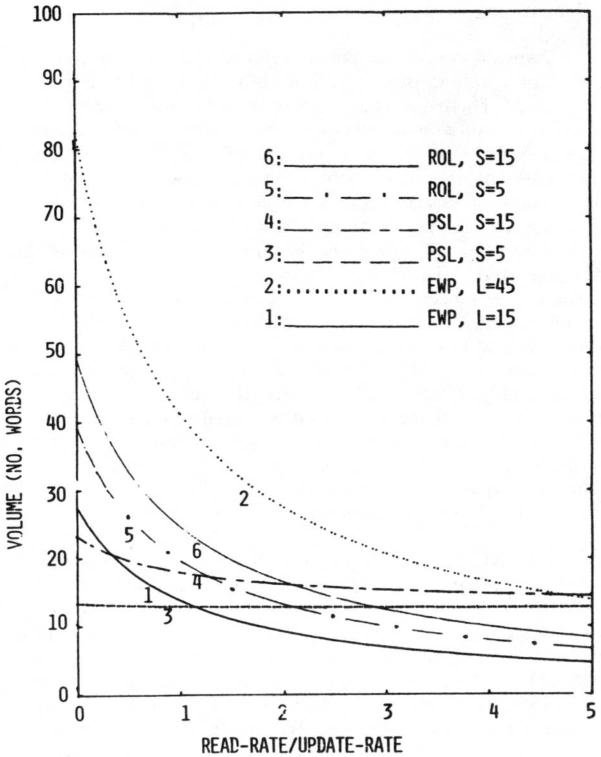

FIGURE 10. COMPARISON OF MESSAGE VOLUME FOR BUS NETWORK

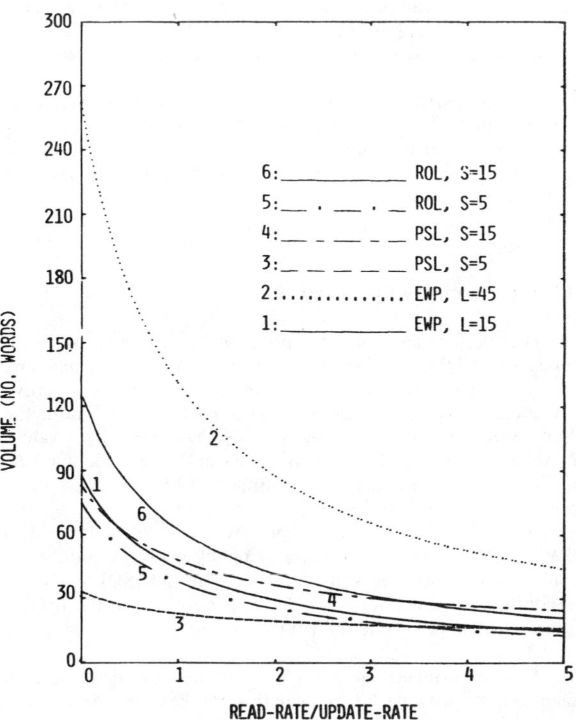

FIGURE 11. COMPARISON OF MESSAGE VOLUME FOR POINT-TO-POINT NETWORK

4.3 Transaction Response Time

Transaction response time is defined as the period from the initiation of a transaction until the resulting updates (if any) have been posted. There are four sources of delay for a transaction: protocol processing time, I/O processing time, message transfer time, and synchronization time. For the EWP, protocol processing delays represent the time spent by exclusive-writers to process update-request messages; for PSL and ROL, it consists of instructions used to determine what actions to take upon receipt of a control message as well as performing the actions themselves (excluding I/O). These costs were analyzed in the protocol processing cost model. I/O processing delays (e.g., system calls, interrupts, and I/O buffer management) reflect the operating system overhead to transfer a message between sites. These delays are proportional to the number of messages exchanged, M. Message transfer time reflects network queueing delay and transmission time for messages, so it is related to message volume, V. Finally, synchronization delay represents the waiting time imposed on transactions so that the consistency control protocol can coordinate activities between sites (e.g., in PSL and ROL, a read request for file F_i must wait until there is no task updating F_i).

We consider each source of delay in turn. For protocol processing, the EWP has a lower delay than PSL for larger read-rate/update-rate ratios and is superior to ROL since ROL is extremely sensitive to number of file copies in the system. Also, since the EWP requires the fewest number of messages, it has the lowest I/O processing delay. In regard to message transfer time, there is a tradeoff between the larger size of EWP update messages (due to the IDS update rule) and the volume of control messages required by PSL and ROL. Since message transfer time includes queueing delays at the interconnection network, this tradeoff depends on the network traffic level. Regarding synchronization delays, *both PSL and ROL impose synchronization delays.* Indeed, these delays may be substantial since messages must be exchanged before a transaction can proceed (e.g., a lock-request message must be sent and a lock-grant must be received before file access is permitted). In contrast, *the EWP imposes no synchronization delay.*

To summarize, the EWP has the lowest I/O processing delay and imposes no synchronization delay. Therefore, as long as EWP updates are not too much larger than those for PSL and ROL or the read-rate/update-rate is not too small, the EWP will have the lowest transaction response time.

5. Discussion

5.1 EWP Performance Characteristics

The performance of the protocols is affected by read-rate/update-rate (R), number of file copies, and size of update and control messages. In order for file replication to improve performance, a large value for R is required [CHU76]. Both the EWP and ROL protocol processing costs decrease with larger values of R while PSL protocol processing costs are independent of R. On the other hand, increasing the number of file copies degrades performance due to overhead increases in protocol processing, I/O processing, and message transfer time. We note that overhead in the EWP and PSL does not increase as rapidly with the number of file copies as does that for ROL. Further, PSL and ROL exchange more control messages than the EWP, and the former impose synchronization delays while the EWP does not.

The performance of the EWP can be degraded since its message volume may be larger than that for PSL and ROL. The size of EWP update messages can be reduced by only including those data values which have changed since the last update. Such a design is possible since only EW_i sends file F_i update messages (other tasks send an update-request message to EW_i) and updates are received in sequence. Using this approach, the size of EWP update messages becomes comparable to that of PSL and ROL update messages, thereby reducing EWP message volume.

Alternatively, the EWP's performance can be improved by eliminating the update-request message. For example, a timestamp could be included in each update message. This permits sites to construct an unique global sequencing of updates to a shared file; hence, mutual consistency is ensured without the use of update-request messages. This approach eliminates the overhead due to update-request messages but increases the size of update messages due to the presence of timestamps. Further investigation is needed to quantify this tradeoff.

5.2 Task Assignment Issues in the EWP

Task assignment has a significant effect on the number, M, and volume, V, of messages exchanged to update a file. By assigning those tasks that update F_i to the site at which EW_i resides, larger g_i values are obtained. As shown in equations (6), (7), (8), and (9), both the M and V decrease as g_i increases. Such a task assignment reduces I/O processing delay and message transfer time. However, it may also increase processor utilization which can increase transaction response time. Further study of these tradeoffs are needed.

Task assignment can be used to resolve internal consistency problems (section 3) by co-locating all tasks that update the same file. This constraint on task assignment is reasonable when the set of files that each task updates is known and small. For example, in the DPAD such an approach has permitted approximately fifty files to be shared by twenty-three tasks and does not significantly limit the degree of distributed processing.

6. Conclusions

The EWP is a new approach for updating replicated files in distributed real time systems. It ensures mutual consistency by having an exclusive-writer for each shared file and guarantees internal consistency by using the IDS update rule. The EWP avoids deadlocks due to shared data access, eliminates synchronization delays, and requires fewer control messages for shared file access than either primary site locking or read-optimized primary site locking. As a result, the EWP can provide a lower transaction response time than locking or timestamp protocols. Thus, the EWP has great appeal for use in distributed real time systems.

ACKNOWLEDGEMENTS

The authors are grateful to Salpy Manjikian for her secretarial assistance in preparing this paper.

REFERENCES

ABRA82 Abramovici, M. et al., "A Logic Simulation Machine," *Proceedings of the 9th Annual Symposium on Computer Architecture,* Austin, Texas, April 26-29, 1982, pp. 148-157.

ARMS79 Armstrong, C.V.W., et al., "An Adaptive Multimicroprocessor Array Computing Structure for Radar Signal Processing Applications," *Proceedings of the 6th Annual Symposium on*

Computer Architecture, Philadelphia, Pennsylvania, April 23-25, 1979, pp. 68-74.

BERN81 Bernstein, Philip A. and Nathan Goodman, "Concurrency Control in Distributed Database Systems," *Computing Surveys*, Vol. 13, No. 2, June 1981, pp. 185-221.

CHU76 Chu, Wesley W., "Performance of File Directory Systems for Distributed Data Bases," *Proceedings of the National Computer Conference*, Vol. 45, 1976, pp. 577-587.

FUCH79 Fuchs, Henry and Brian W. Johnson, "An Expandable Multiprocessor Architecture for Video Graphics," *Proceedings of the 6th Annual Symposium on Computer Architecture*, Philadelphia, Pennsylvania, April 23-25, 1979, pp. 58-67.

GARC78 Garcia-Molina, Hector, "Performance Comparison of Two Update Algorithms for Distributed Databases," *Proceedings of the Third Berkeley Workshop on Distributed Data Management and Computer Networks*, August 29-31, 1978, pp. 108-119.

GREE80 Green, Michael L. et al., "A Distributed Real Time Operating System," *Proceedings of the Symposium on Distributed Data Acquisition, Computing, and Control*, December 1980.

STON79 Stonebraker, Michael, "Concurrency Control and Consistency of Multiple Copies of Data In Distributed INGRES," *IEEE Transactions on Software Engineering*, Vol. SE-5, No. 3, May 1979, pp. 188-194.

Analytic Models for Rollback and Recovery Strategies in Data Base Systems

K. MANI CHANDY, JAMES C. BROWNE, CHARLES W. DISSLY, AND WERNER R. UHRIG

***Abstract*—Rollback and recovery (RR) is a method of enhancing the reliability of file or data base systems. At certain points in time, called checkpoints, a copy of the data or files is made on tape (or other storage devices). A chronological record is kept of all transactions which modify the data stored by the system; this record is called the audit trail. When an error is detected, the copy of the files or data made at the most recent checkpoint is loaded, and all transactions on the audit trail since this check point are reprocessed in chronological sequence, thus recovering from the error. This paper presents models and techniques which aid in determining optimal times for checkpoints.**

***Index Terms*—Data base systems, graph theory, probabilistic models, rollback and recovery strategies, software reliability, systems modeling.**

I. INTRODUCTION

A. Reliability Through Software Redundancy

COMPUTER-based information management systems are becoming increasingly prevalent in business and government. Decisions rendered on the basis of use of these systems thus becomes a significant factor in human affairs. Therefore, the reliability of these systems and their ability to constantly yield accurate responses is a significant problem area. Much effort has gone into the study of *privacy* of computer-based *information* and *protection* of information systems from unauthorized access. Much less attention has yet been paid to increasing their reliability. This paper is an effort to determine cost-effective means of increasing reliability. The reliability *of a computer system* may be increased by enhancing the elemental stability of the elements of a system, both hardware or software, or by building into the systems elements of redundancy which can be used to detect and correct errors which occur in primary processing. This paper attempts to define cost-effective means of introducing redundancy [making periodic copies (checkpoints) of the data whose validity is desired] in an information management or data base system. The use of checkpoints of files and data bases has been a standard technique of system designers. There has, however, been little or no previous attention paid to the effectiveness or cost effectiveness of checkpoint procedures. This paper establishes and analyzes model systems for optimal use of checkpointing. The factors included in the models are: 1) the cost of recovery; 2) cyclic variation in demand for system services; 3) the rate of error detection, and in particular error detection during recovery or reprocessing; 4) the reduction of reprocessing time with respect to normal processing. The optimized variable is the time interval between checkpoints and the metric used for evaluation is system availability measured in terms of fractional availability or in terms of the number of transactions which must wait for processing because of checkpointing or recovery reprocessing. This choice of metric is a reasonable measure for most transaction-oriented data base systems. Total throughput might be more appropriate for batch-oriented systems. The choice of metric was dictated by the characteristics of the data base system which motivated this study, the Nuclear Ordinance Logistics Systems (NOLS) of the Air Force Logistics Command. The entire process of creating checkpoints, reestablishment of the data base as it was at an earlier time, and reprocessing from an audit trail will be characterized as a rollback and recovery (RR) system or process.

B. Error Detection

Error detection may proceed continuously or intermittently. Parity checking is an example of continuous error detection since parity checking can be carried out all the time a system is available. Some systems have multiple copies of key files, all of which are updated continuously, but which are compared against each other only at specified intervals. This is an example of intermittent detection since an error may be detected only when the copies are compared against one another. An error which is not detected as soon as it occurs might propagate. For instance, if an erroneous data value is used to update an item, the updated item may also be in error. When an error is detected, it is not possible to predict precisely when the error occurred or the amount of error propagation.

C. The RR Process

We shall consider a transaction-oriented data base. A transaction might merely query the data base (without

Manuscript received October 1, 1974; revised February 3, 1975. This work was supported in part by the Air Force Logistics Command under Contract F33600-74-C-0314 with the University of Texas, Austin, and in part under Contract F33600-74-C-0251 with Information Research Associates, Inc., Austin, Tex.

The authors are with the Department of Computer Sciences, University of Texas at Austin, Austin, Tex. 78712.

Reprinted from *IEEE Trans. Software Eng.*, vol. SE-1, pp. 100–110, Mar. 1975.

modifying it) or a transaction might change a value or data structure. The total processing time required per transaction is assumed to be small with respect to the mean time between failures (MTBF).

In many systems a permanent record is made of all transactions which modify the system. This record is generally required for auditing. We shall refer to a chronological record of all transactions (or transactions which modify the data base) as an *audit trail*. An audit trail is required to support automated recovery and restart.

At certain points in time called *checkpoints*, a copy of the entire data base is made and stored on magnetic tape (or other archival storage). Special checks may be carried out to ensure that the copy is error free. This process (checkpointing) may take a long time, possibly hours, if a large volume of data is involved. Note that checkpointing is carried out primarily for RR whereas the audit trail may be required for reasons other than RR. Transactions are not allowed to access the data base during checkpointing; they are stored and processed later when checkpointing is complete.

When an error is detected, the following steps are taken.

1) Transactions are not allowed to query the data base. All incoming transactions are stored for future use.

2) The system fault causing the error is repaired if necessary.

3) The copy of the data base made at the most recent checkpoint is loaded on to the physical devices on which the data base is stored. This process of *loading* the data base may also require a substantial amount of time. After the loading is complete, the entire data or file system is exactly as it was immediately after the last checkpoint.

4) All transactions on the audit trail are reprocessed in chronological order; the system will have recovered when this reprocessing is complete. All transactions on the audit trail are notified of corrections in the data base, if necessary.

5) Incoming transactions which were stored during recovery are processed.

The recovery process will function only if the data base was error free at the most recent checkpoint. An error may be detected during recovery for two reasons:

1) an error may have occurred during the process of loading the data base or reprocessing the audit trail;

2) there may be a previously undetected error at the most recent checkpoint.

If an error is detected during recovery, the system could rollback once more to the most recent checkpoint and then if the error persists, to earlier checkpoints. If an error remains undetected through more checkpoints than are stored, the RR process will fail.

D. The Costs of RR

A significant amount of time is required for the checkpointing and recovery processes and for maintaining the audit trail. There are also hardware costs for storage of copies of the data base at different checkpoints. There are also unquantifiable costs deriving from the use of invalid data and from the efforts expended by the individual user processes in protecting their files against error and manually recreating them after detection of errors. Some level of automated reliability management is normally provided in all files and data base systems. The level of automated- or system-level support is usually determined informally on the basis of user complaints.

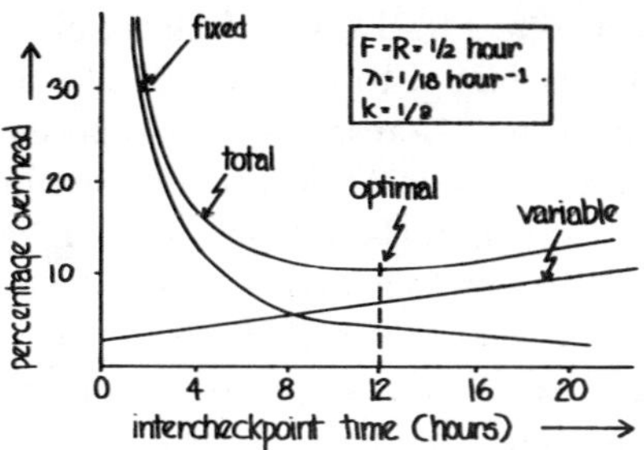

Fig. 1. Overhead versus intercheckpoint time in model *A*.

Hardware costs will be ignored, since once a decision to use RR has been made, hardware costs are largely independent of key parameters in RR. In analogy with inventory control theory, time costs are classified as *fixed* and *variable* costs. Fixed costs are independent of the number of errors detected. Variable costs are incurred only if an error is detected. The fixed cost is the time required to make a copy of the entire data base at each checkpoint. The variable cost is the time associated with recovery, i.e., with repair loading the data base made at a checkpoint and reprocessing the audit trail. The problem is to choose times for checkpointing which maximize system availability or which minimize costs associated with RR.

The recovery time increases with the number of transactions to be reprocessed on the audit trail. Hence, the recovery time increases with the time between the most recent checkpoint and the detection of an error. The greater the intercheckpoint time, the larger will be the average time between a checkpoint and detection of an error. Thus, average recovery time increases with intercheckpoint time. If the intercheckpoint time is too small, too much time is spent in checkpointing, and if the intercheckpoint time is too large, too much time is spent in recovery. A graphical representation of the tradeoff is presented in Fig. 1.

II. MODELS FOR RR

A. Earlier Analytic Models for RR

Chandy and Ramamoorthy [1] presented models for RR in computer programs. They assume that a program is partitioned into tasks and that a program is represented as a directed graph. They assume implicitly that the processing time for each task is comparable to the MTBF. They determine the optimum location of checkpoints *within a single program* such that maximum recovery time never exceeds a given design parameter so as to minimize time spent in checkpointing. The problem analyzed here is different from that studied by Chandy and Ramamoorthy in two respects. Firstly, the time required to process a transaction is assumed to be very small compared with the MTBF. A transaction is not decomposed into tasks, and no attempt is made to locate checkpoints within a transaction. Graph models are not used in our analysis. We are concerned with checkpointing a system handling a stream of transactions rather than checkpointing a single program. Secondly, we place no constraints on the intercheckpoint time. Though the problem discussed here is basically different from that in [1], this work draws upon many of the concepts discussed in [1].

Chandy, Ramamoorthy, and Cowan [2] present models for evaluating hardware-software tradeoffs in reliable systems. This paper restricts attention to RR and presents very detailed models whereas their paper [2] attempts to develop a general framework for the analysis of all schemes for enhancing reliability, including RR.

B. Overview of Three Models

1) Assumptions, Limitations, and Objectives of the Models: In this section we present three models, A, B, and C, for RR in increasing order of complexity. Model A makes two assumptions: the first is relaxed in model B, and the second is relaxed in model C. Cases for which each model is appropriate are discussed. All three models make four common assumptions.

1) The detection of faults occur at random times. Thus, fault detections occur in a (possibly time-varying) Poisson manner.

2) The time required to reprocess the audit trail from a checkpoint is assumed to be directly proportional to the number of transactions recorded on the audit trail since that checkpoint.

3) Transactions which arrive when the system is either checkpointing or recovering from an error are stored until the checkpointing or recovery is complete. The time required to process stored transactions is assumed to be small compared to the MTBF.

4) System availability given optimal checkpointing strategies is assumed to be high.

Model A makes two additional assumptions.

1) No errors occur during recovery, i.e., during the loading of the data base at a checkpoint and during reprocessing of transactions on the audit trail. (This assumption is reasonable if recovery time and checkpointing time are small compared to the MTBF.)

2) The transaction arrival rate is constant at all times.

Model B takes into account the possibility that errors may be detected during checkpointing or recovery. Model C is the most comprehensive model. It considers transaction rates which vary widely over time in a cyclic fashion (Fig. 7). The duration of a cycle is typically a day or a week. A checkpoint instituted during a peak demand period will degrade service for a relatively large number of transactions, since transactions which arrive when a checkpoint is in progress will have to wait for the checkpointing to complete before they can gain access to the data base. A checkpoint instituted during a light demand period will degrade service for relatively fewer transactions. The problem now is not merely to maximize system availability but to keep the system available for the maximum number of transactions.

Several "costs" or objective functions can be developed for this model. In the simplest case the cost of a checkpoint (or recovery) is the number of transactions denied immediate access to the data base due to the checkpoint (or recovery); in other words, it is the number of transactions which arrive during a checkpoint (or recovery). A more realistic cost of checkpoints and recovery is the average time that a transaction is delayed due to checkpoints and recovery. Either cost is allowed in model C. A cost which is not considered here is the number of transactions which may have been given incorrect information due to the presence of undetected error. This cost is difficult to quantify. An upper bound on this cost can be obtained by assuming that all errors occur immediately after a checkpoint though the error may be detected at arbitrary times. Model C can also handle more complex failure mechanisms than A or B. Model C considers the possibility that the probability of an error in any interval $(t, t + \Delta t)$ may be an arbitrary function of time t and the load of the system. Thus, systems which tend to fail more often during heavy load conditions can be handled.

2) Definitions: Let F be the expected time required to perform a checkpoint, i.e., the expected time required to save a copy of the system. *Reestablishing* the checkpointed data base after an error is detected consists of repairing any system malfunctions and then loading a copy of the system saved at the most recent checkpoint. Let R be the expected time required to reestablish the checkpointed data base. *Recovering* from an error consists of first reestablishing the most recently checkpointed data base and then processing the audit trail from the checkpoint to the point of error detection. Let $h(t)$ be the expected recovery time given that an error was detected t time units after the last checkpoint. Clearly, $h(t)$ will be a monotone nondecreasing function of t. Let T be the time between checkpoints. Let $V(T)$ be the total expected time spent in recovery between two successive checkpoints given that the time between checkpoints is T. Clearly, $V(T)$ is monotone increasing with T. Let $0(T)$ be the total overhead time associated with checkpointing and recovery given intercheckpoint time T.

$$0(T) = F + V(T).$$

Let $r(T)$ be the expected unit overhead given an intercheckpoint time T. Thus,

$$r(T) = \frac{0(T)}{T}.$$

We will show that $r(T)$ is a convex function for models A and B. The availability of the system given intercheck-

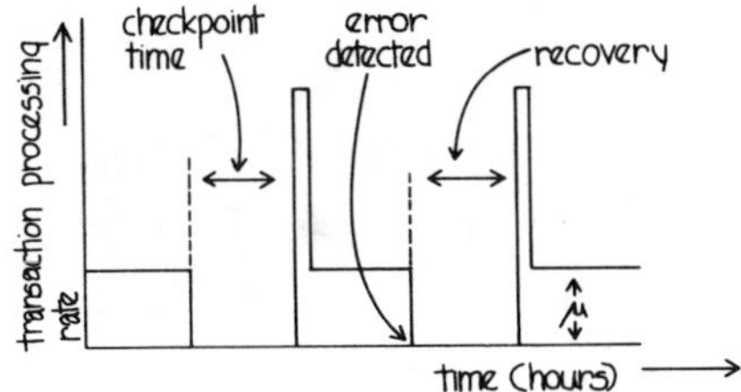

Fig. 2. Actual load on the system.

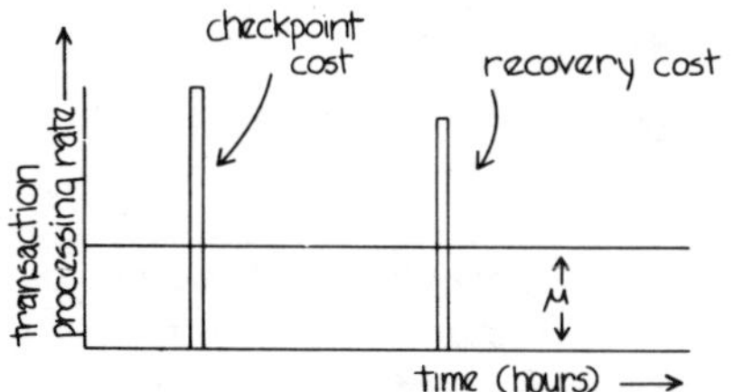

Fig. 3. Approximated load on the system.

point time T is

$$a(T) = 1 - r(T).$$

Let λ be the failure rate: λ is the reciprocal of the MTBF. Let t be the time since the initiation of the last checkpoint. Thus, the last checkpoint is initiated at $t = 0$ and the next checkpoint at $t = T$. The time taken to reprocess the audit trail, given that an error is detected at time t is proportional to t; let the constant of proportionality be k. We refer to k as the *compression* factor. Let the transaction arrival rate be μ transactions per unit time. Let the average transaction processing rate when the audit trail is being reprocessed be "b" transactions per unit time. The expected number of transactions which arrive in t time units is μt, and hence the time required to reprocess these transactions is $\mu t/b$. Hence,

$$k = \mu/b.$$

Let μ' be the arrival rate of transactions which modify the system. Assume that only transactions which modify the system are stored on the audit trail, and let b' be the corresponding reprocessing rate; in this case $k = \mu'/b'$. The fraction of all transactions which modify the data base is small. Furthermore, μ is generally much smaller than b. Hence, values of k of order 1/10 or less are to be expected. For model A we have

$$h(t) = R + kt.$$

Let $C(x)$ be the expected cost of recovery in the interval $t = x$ to $t = T$, i.e., from x to the next checkpoint. Note that $C(T) = 0$ and $V(T) = C(0)$ is the total expected cost of recovery between checkpoints.

Fig. 2 shows the expected load on the system as a function of time, where the load is the number of transactions processed per unit time. There is a surge of requests immediately after a checkpoint or recovery due to the backlog of transactions. This surge is assumed to be of short duration. Furthermore, checkpoints and recoveries are assumed to take a short time compared to the intercheckpoint time. In models A and B we approximate the load on the system as in Fig. 3 where checkpoints and recoveries are assumed to take instantaneous time, but with a cost F associated with each checkpoint, and a cost $h(t)$ associated with a recovery from an error detected t time units after a checkpoint. Clearly, this approximation is reasonable only if availability is very high.

The elasticity $E(f, x)$ of a function with respect to parameter x is the percentage change in f caused by a percentage change in x. More formally,

$$E(f, x) = \frac{\partial f}{\partial x} \cdot \frac{x}{f}.$$

We will show that the elasticity of overhead with respect to most system parameters is small. This is a useful result because it suggests that small errors in estimating system parameters will not greatly influence overhead, availability, or intercheckpoint time.

C. Model A

We present the following theorems with proofs in this section.

Lemma 1: The variable cost function $C(t)$ satisfies the following differential equation:

$$(d/dt)C(t) = -\lambda \cdot h(t) \qquad \text{for } 0 \leq t \leq T. \qquad (1)$$

Proof: Consider the interval $(t - \Delta t, t)$. Let us compute $C(t - \Delta t)$. An error is diagnosed during the interval with probability $\lambda \cdot \Delta t$. If an error occurs during that interval than a variable overhead of $h(t)$ is incurred immediately, and the expected cost incurred after the end of the interval is $C(t)$. If no error occurs during this interval, then the expected cost after the interval to the next checkpoint is $C(t)$. Hence,

$$C(t - \Delta t) = \lambda \cdot \Delta t[h(t) + C(t)] + (1 - \lambda \cdot \Delta t) \cdot C(t). \qquad (2)$$

Taking the limit of (2) as Δt tends to zero gives (1).

Theorem 1: The optimal value of intercheckpoint time T_{opt} which minimizes unit overhead r (and maximizes availability) is

$$T_{\text{opt}} = [(2F)/(\lambda k)]^{1/2}. \qquad (3)$$

The corresponding value of unit overhead is

$$r_{\text{opt}} = \lambda R + (2\lambda k F)^{1/2}. \qquad (4)$$

Proof: Recollect

$$h(t) = R + kt \qquad (5)$$

for model A. Solving (1) and using the boundary condition $C(T) = 0$, we get

$$V(T) = C(0) = \lambda \cdot R \cdot T + \frac{\lambda \cdot k \cdot T^2}{2}. \qquad (6)$$

Hence,

$$r(T) = \lambda \cdot R + \frac{\lambda \cdot k \cdot T}{2} + \frac{F}{T} \qquad (7)$$

and

$$\frac{\partial^2 r}{\partial T^2} = \frac{2F}{T^3} > 0. \tag{8}$$

From (8), r is a strictly convex function of T. Hence, r has a unique local minimum. Differentiating r with respect to T and equating to zero gives (3) and (4).

Corollary 1: At optimality, the maximum recovery time is

$$h(T_{\text{opt}}) = r_{\text{opt}}/\lambda. \tag{9}$$

Substituting (3) and (4) in (5) gives (9).

Corollary 2: The elasticities of unit overhead r with respect to failure rate λ, reestablishment time R, compression factor k, and checkpoint time F are bounded by 1, 1, 1/2, and 1/2, respectively, at optimality.

Proof:

$$\frac{\partial r}{\partial \lambda}\cdot\frac{\lambda}{r} = \left[R + \left(\frac{kF}{2\lambda}\right)^{1/2}\right]\frac{\lambda}{r}$$

$$= \frac{R + (\lambda kF/2)^{1/2}}{R + (\lambda kF)^{1/2}} \leq 1. \tag{10}$$

The other bounds also follow by direct differentiation.

Discussion: Fig. 1 shows a graph of unit fixed overhead F/T, unit variable overhead V/T, and unit total overhead $0/T$ as a function of intercheckpoint time. The unit total overhead drops rapidly, stays relatively flat at optimality, and increases gradually. In real systems it is not possible to determine parameters such as failure rates and compression factors precisely. Therefore, it is important that the unit overhead is relatively insensitive to these parameters in the region of optimality. Corollary 2 provides bounds on the percentage change in unit cost due to percentage changes in key parameters. Note that all elasticities are less than unity. Corollary 2 implies that a 1 percent change in the compression factor will produce a change in unit cost which cannot exceed 0.5 percent. The bounds are weak; most real systems will have elasticities smaller than the bounds.

Fig. 4 shows optimal intercheckpoint times as a function of other parameters. Note that compression factor k plays an important part in determining optimal intercheckpoint time. Fig. 5(a) and 5(b) show optimal unit overhead as a function of key parameters. Note that optimal intercheckpoint times are independent of the reestablishment times R, whereas unit overhead is clearly a function of R. Model A assumes that no errors occur during recovery. This assumption is reasonable if the expected number of errors which occur during a recovery is very small. Corollary 1 states that the maximum recovery time is r_{opt}/λ; hence the maximum value of the expected number of errors in any single recovery is r_{opt}. This suggests that the assumption of no errors during recovery is reasonable provided the unit overhead is under 10 percent (or equivalently if availability is over 90 percent). Model A also assumes that the time required to process incoming transactions

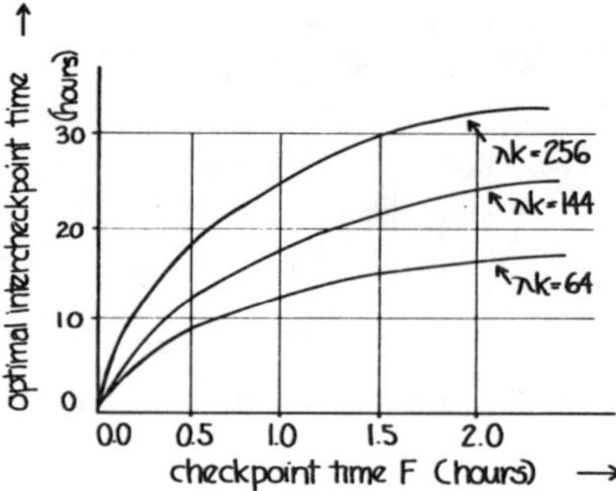

Fig. 4. Optimal intercheckpoint time as a function of checkpoint time.

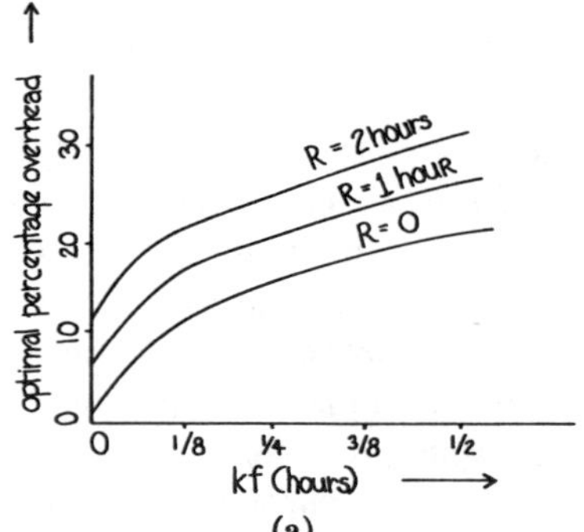

(a)

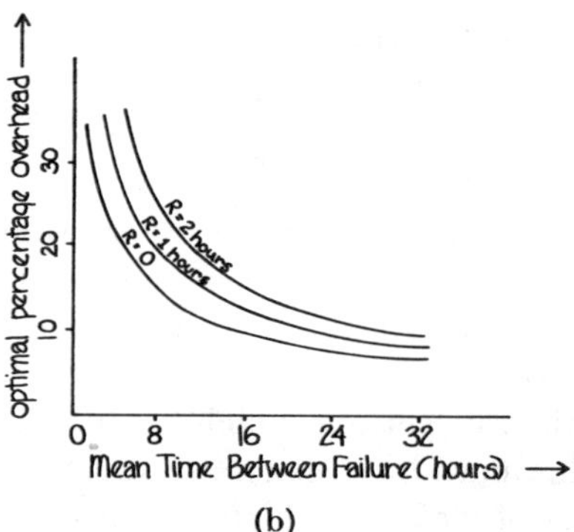

(b)

Fig. 5. (a) Optimal percentage overhead as a function of key parameters in model A. (b) Optimal percentage overhead as a function of key parameters in model A.

which are stored during a recovery is small compared to the MTBF. The maximum value of the expected time required to process buffered transactions is μ/b multiplied by the maximum recovery time. The ratio of the maximum expected time required to process buffered transactions to the MTBF is $(\mu/b)r_{\text{opt}}$; this ratio should be very small if model A is to be valid. Since μ/b is generally much smaller than unity we may conclude that model A is valid provided the transaction arrival rate does not vary significantly with time and the calculated availability exceeds 90 percent. If the calculated availability is less than 90 percent, the intercheckpoint time computed from model A will be larger than optimal and the availability computed will be optimistic.

Example: If the MTBF is 16 h, the compression factor is 1/8, and the checkpoint and reestablishment times are both 1 h, we have an optimal intercheckpoint time of 16 h. A checkpoint time of hours is typical for creating tape copies of large data bases. If the checkpointing time is reduced to minutes (say 3.75 min) by copying to faster mediums such as disk, the intercheckpoint time would be reduced to 4 h. The availability would increase from 81.5 percent to 93.75 percent by going from tape to disk copies assuming a reestablishment time of one hour in the former case and one-half hour in the latter case (note that reestablishment time includes time for repairs). Further reductions in checkpoint time will not increase availability significantly.

D. Model B

Model B takes into consideration possible errors during checkpointing and recovery. Model B should be used if the availability computed from model A is under 90 percent. Clearly, Lemma 1 also holds for model B. In model A, the recovery time $h(t)$, t time units after a checkpoint is given by

$$h(t) = R + kt.$$

In model B, a recovery will be complete only after receiving $R + kt$ time units of *continuous error-free processing*. If an error is detected during a recovery, then the recovery is reinitiated; thus, several abortive attempts at recovery may be made before a recovery is completed.

Theorem 2: If there are no errors during checkpointing, the optimal value T_{opt} of the intercheckpoint time satisfies the equation

$$\exp(\lambda k T_{\text{opt}})(1 - \lambda k T_{\text{opt}}) = 1 - \lambda k F \exp(-\lambda R).$$

If there may be errors during checkpointing, and if the checkpointing process is reinitiated each time an error is detected, T_{opt} satisfies the equation

$$\exp(\lambda k T_{\text{opt}})(1 - \lambda k T_{\text{opt}}) = 1 - (\exp(\lambda F) - 1) \cdot k \cdot \exp(-\lambda R).$$

The proof for this theorem is found in the Appendix.

Discussion: The optimum intercheckpoint time for model B tends to that of model A as the failure rate tends towards zero. Fig. 6 shows the effect of failures during recovery on the variable cost. The variable cost increases nonlinearly with intercheckpoint time, faster than in model A. If there are no errors during checkpointing, the effect of possible errors during recovery is to make the optimal intercheckpoint time for model B smaller than that of model A. Note also that in model B, the optimal intercheckpoint time increases with R. Recollect that the optimal intercheckpoint time in model A is independent of R. The reason for the differences between the two models is interesting. The larger the reprocessing time in model B the greater the probability of detecting an error during reprocessing, and the greater the number of abortive attempts at recovery. Thus, the number of times that the system is reestablished following the detection of a single error increases with reprocessing time in model B, whereas in model A the system will be reestablished exactly once following the detection of a single error independent of reprocessing time.

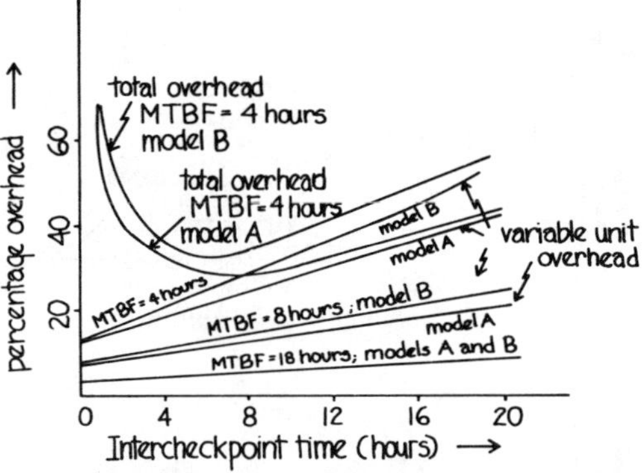

Fig. 6. Percentage overhead as a function of intercheckpoint time in models A and B.

Model B is more comprehensive than A. However, model B does not have a closed-form solution for optimal intercheckpoint time and a numerical solution is used.

E. Model C

1) Introduction to Model C: In this model we assume that the transaction arrival rate varies with time in a cyclic fashion. The duration of a cycle is typically a day or a week. We assume that there is always a checkpoint at the end of a cycle. This assumption is not very restrictive since most systems have a period of light load, and the cycle can be defined so that the load at the end of the cycle is relatively light, in which case a checkpoint can be instituted at relatively small cost. Fig. 7 shows a cyclically time varying load. We assume that the load on the system is known *a priori.*

The cost of a checkpoint or a recovery varies with time in a nonlinear fashion, and the likelihood of error may be a function of the load and may also vary with time in an arbitrary fashion. However, we assume that the probability of error during any interval is independent of events in nonoverlapping intervals. Thus, errors occur in a time varying Poisson manner. Optimally, checkpoints will be instituted during relatively light load periods. However, a checkpoint may be instituted at a relatively busy time if the load on the system will rise even further (Fig. 8), or if this period is long compared to the MTBF. Let us assume that failure rate increases with load. If there is no checkpoint at point α, the recovery time for errors detected in region β will be very large since there will be a large number of transactions on the audit trail. Large recovery times in region β will be costly due to the large number of transactions delayed. Furthermore, the failure rate in region β will be higher than elsewhere. A checkpoint at point α will reduce the number of transactions on the audit trail and the recovery time for errors in region β. Thus, a checkpoint at α may be optimal even though the transaction rate at α is not small. It is impossible to make generalizations about location of checkpoints with time varying loads and failure rates due to the complexity of the model. In the analysis presented in this paper we assume that no errors occur during checkpointing or recovery. The analysis can be extended to consider possible errors during checkpointing or recovery.

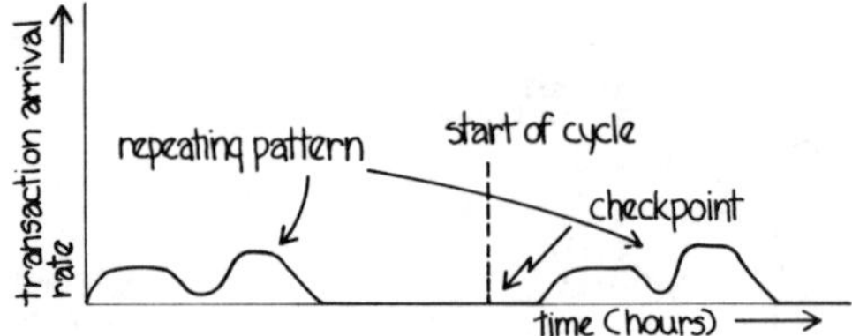

Fig. 7. Cyclic load: an example.

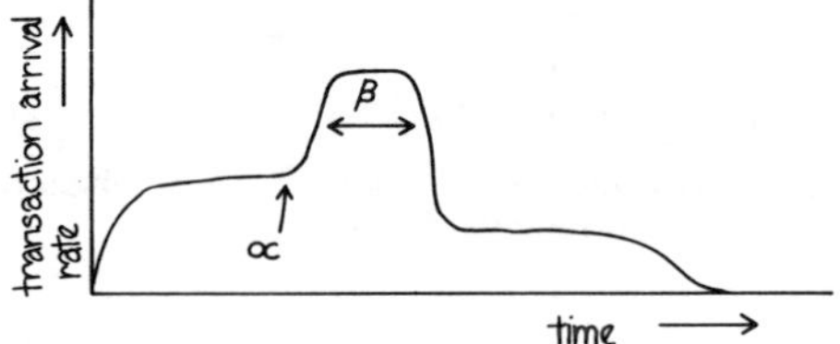

Fig. 8. Time varying load.

2) Analysis: Let t be the time since the start of the cycle. Let the cycle be of duration τ. Let $z(t_0, t_1)$ be the recovery time from an error detected at time t_1 given that the last checkpoint was instituted at time t_0. Let $f(t)$ and $\lambda(t)$ be the transaction arrival rate and failure rate as a function of t. Then,

$$z(t_0, t_1) = R + b \int_{t_0}^{t_1} f(t) \cdot dt$$

if errors do not occur during recovery where R is the reestablishment time, $\int_{t_0}^{t_1} f(t) \cdot dt$ is the number of transactions on the audit trail at $t = t_1$ since the last checkpoint, and b is the average processing time per transaction. Let $h(t_0, t_1)$ be the cost of recovery from an error detected at time t_1 given that the last checkpoint was instituted at time t_0. Recollect that the cost is the number of transactions which arrive while the system is recovering. If a fault is detected at t_1, the system will be recovering in the interval $[t_1, t_1 + z(t_0, t_1)]$. Thus,

$$h(t_0, t_1) = \int_{t_1}^{t_1+z(t_0,t_1)} f(t) \cdot dt.$$

Let $C(t_0, t_1)$ be the total cost (fixed and variable) incurred in the interval $t_0 \leq t \leq t_1$ given that a checkpoint is initiated at $t = t_0$ and that there are no other checkpoints in that interval. We assume that $F \leq t_1 - t_0$ where F is the checkpoint time. Define $C(t_0, t_1) = \infty$ if $t_1 < t_0 + F$. (We assume in this analysis that the cost is the number of transactions delayed by checkpoints or recovery; the analysis for other cost functions is similar. We do not use availability as a metric in model C since we do not wish to maximize availability but rather to maximize the number of transactions which encounter an available system.) The following equation holds for $C(t_0, t_1)$

$$C(t_0, t_1) = \int_{t_0}^{t_0+F} f(t) \cdot dt + \int_{t_0+F}^{t_1} h(t_0, t_1) \cdot \lambda(t) \cdot dt.$$

The first term is the number of transactions which arrive in the interval $t_0 \leq t \leq t_0 + F$. The first term represents the fixed cost. $\lambda(t) \cdot dt$ is the probability of an error in the interval $(t, t + dt)$ and $h(t_0, t)$ is the recovery cost. Hence, the second term represents the variable cost.

Let $g_l(t_0)$ be the *minimum* (optimum) cost incurred in the interval $t_0 \leq t < \tau$ given that a checkpoint was instituted at $t = t_0$, and there are l or fewer checkpoints in the interval $t_0 \leq t < \tau$. (Note that l includes the checkpoint at $t = t_0$.)

The following theorem is presented without proof. The proof is found in the Appendix.

Theorem 3: The following recursive relations hold for $g_l(t)$:

$$g_1(t_0) = C(t_0, \tau) \qquad \text{for } 0 \leq t < \tau$$

and

$$g_l(t_0) = \text{minimum } \{g_{l-1}(t_0), g_l'(t_0)\} \qquad \text{for } l = 2, 3, \cdots \text{ and } 0 \leq t_0 < \tau$$

where

$$g_l'(t_0) = \text{minimum value of } \{C(t_0, t) + g_{l-1}(t)\} \text{ in the interval } t_0 < t < \tau, \qquad \text{for all } 0 \leq t_0 < \tau.$$

Corollary 3: If

$$g_{l+1}(t) = g_l(t) \qquad \text{for all } t,\ 0 \leq t < \tau$$

then

$$g_{l+i}(t) = g_l(t) \qquad \text{for all } t,\ 0 \leq t < \tau \text{ and } i = 1, 2, 3, \cdots.$$

The proof follows immediately from the recursive relations.

Theorem 4: Let j be the minimum value of k such that

$$g_{j+1}(t) = g_j(t) \qquad \text{for all } t,\ 0 \leq t \leq \tau.$$

Let

$$g_j(0) = C(0, t_1) + g_{j-1}(t_1)$$

and

$$g_{j-i+1}(t_{i-1}) = C(t_{i-1}, t_i) + g_{j-1}(t_i) \qquad \text{for } i = 2, 3, \cdots, j - 1.$$

Then optimal checkpoints should be initiated at times t_i, $i = 1, 2, \cdots, j - 1$.

Proof: see Appendix.

Discussion: We use Theorems 3 and 4 to determine the location of optimum checkpoints. Generally, the load function $f(t)$ does not have a simple analytic description. Therefore, it is generally not possible to solve the recursive relations algebraically, and we shall have to discretize the problem. A cycle is divided into M intervals (x_u, x_{u+1}), where $x_0 = 0$ and $x_M = T$, and $x_u < x_{u+1}$ for all u. The load function $f(t)$ and the failure rate $\lambda(t)$ are assumed to be constant in each interval. We first compute $h(x_u, x_v)$ for all $u < v$, then compute $C(x_u, x_v)$ for all $u < v$, and finally use theorems 3 and 4 to compute $g_j(u)$ for all u and thus determine optimal checkpoints.

The discrete problem is analogous to the shortest route

problem. Consider a graph with vertices $\{x_u\}$, $u = 0, 1, \cdots, M$ where the cost of edge $(x_u, x_v)(x_u, x_v)$ is $C(x_u, x_v)$ for $v > u$ and the edge does not exist for $u \geq v$ (Fig. 9). The problem of finding the shortest route from x_0 to x_M is identical with the problem of determining optimal checkpoints. The number of arithmetic operations required to compute optimal checkpoints increases only with the square of M. Therefore, this complex problem has a computationally efficient solution.

A program to analyze model C was programmed in PASCAL and run at the University of Texas Computation Center, Austin, on a CDC 6400.

III. SUMMARY: EXTENSION AND APPLICATIONS

We have analyzed RR strategies for data base systems in some depth, and we have presented computationally efficient techniques for determining the optimal location of checkpoints. Our analysis can be extended in some areas and is deficient in others as outlined below.

A. Multiple Data Bases

We have assumed that the system consists of a single data base and that all transactions query or update this data base. Therefore, we assumed that all incoming transactions were denied immediate access to the system while the system was checkpointing or recovering. However, some systems have multiple, mutually independent data bases; a transaction is assumed to query or update one and only one data base. In such systems it is possible to checkpoint data bases independently. Furthermore, if an error is detected in one data base, it is possible to carry out the recovery process for that data base alone. While a given data base is checkpointing or recovering, incoming transactions for other data bases may continue to be processed on the system. Let us assume that two data bases never share a physical storage device (such as a disk). Also assume that there are separate (and parallel) audit trails for each data base. We wish to determine optimum times for checkpointing each of the data bases. As a first approximation we may carry out the analysis presented in this paper for each data base separately assuming that all data bases are completely independent. However, the response time for transactions on one data base at any given instant of time is clearly dependent on whether another data base is being checkpointed at that time since the different data bases share some common resources (such as the central processing unit). A more detailed model is required to capture this interdependency. However, models presented here are sufficient as a first approximation.

B. Limiting Capability Analysis

It is often important to know the maximum rate at which transactions can be processed; this rate is referred to as the limiting capability. Clearly, the limiting capability is a function of the RR strategies employed. As a first approximation we can compute limiting capability

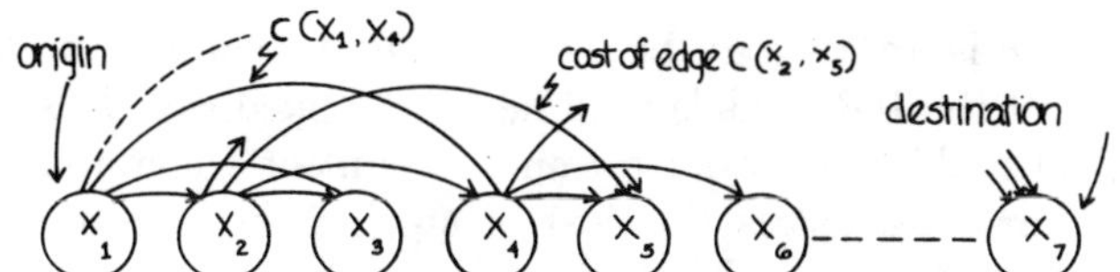

Fig. 9. The graph model corresponding to model C.

in two phases in the following way. In the first phase compute the limiting capability assuming that the system is available *all* the time [3]. In the second phase determine the availability of the system using the methods described in this paper. The true limiting capability is approximately equal to the limiting capability determined in the first phase multiplied by the availability computed in the second. This approximation assumes that the buffer for incoming transactions is arbitrarily large; in reality it is possible that a recovery will take such a long time that incoming transactions might overflow the buffer.

C. Multiple Checkpoints

The copy of a system made at a checkpoint may contain an undetected error. We may detect this error at a later time. If we attempt to recover from the faulty checkpoint we will detect the error again. In such cases we may wish to rollback to earlier checkpoints. How many checkpoints should be stored and what should the intercheckpoint times be in this case? This decision depends on several variables including the cost of storing several copies of the system and the distribution for the length of time between the occurrence and detection of an error. If an error can persist for a very long time without being detected then checkpoints should be far apart or else a large number of checkpoint records must be stored so as to minimize the probability of an error being undetected for all stored checkpoints. This problem is worthy of further study.

D. Differing Load and Checkpoint Cycles

In model C we assumed that there was always a checkpoint at the end of a cycle. It is possible that the transaction arrival rate pattern repeats itself every 24 h (i.e., the load cycle time is 24 h), whereas the optimal intercheckpoint time may be every 16 h. In other words it may be inappropriate to assume that there is a checkpoint at the end of every load cycle. We can determine optimal checkpoints for systems with cyclic loads even without assuming a checkpoint at the end of every load cycle, in a manner similar to that of Section III-C. As in Section III-C the problem can be reduced to a shortest route problem in a graph. The difference in approach is that in Section III-C we wished to make a sequence of optimal decisions to minimize total cost over a *finite* horizon (which was the duration of the cycle), whereas now we wish to minimize average cost per unit time over an *unbounded* horizon [4]. Wagner [4] has a lucid description of solution techniques for unbounded horizon problems.

E. Inventory Control Models

There is an analogy between inventory control models [4] and the RR models used here. The fixed cost F is the cost of making an order for any amount of a commodity. The variable cost is the cost of storing the commodity, and clearly the variable cost increases with the amount of the commodity to be stored. Let T be the time between orders. If T is too small, the fixed cost is incurred often. If T is too large, the amount of commodity to be ordered each time is too large, and therefore the variable (storage) costs are too large. The resolution of the fixed versus variable cost tradeoff in RR models is very similar to that of inventory control models. However, there are some important differences. The variable cost increases with time in RR models whereas it decreases with time in inventory control models. There is no obvious analogy to abortive recoveries and time varying failure rates in inventory control models. Nevertheless it may prove profitable to borrow other ideas from the inventory control area to analyze data base systems.

F. Case Studies

The techniques presented in this paper are being used to study two Air Force data base systems:

1) NOLS Nuclear Ordinance Logistics System;
2) ALS Air Force Logistics System.

NOLS has a relatively small data base, and the assumptions made in model C apply. ALS is a large system with multiple data bases. As a first approximation, the method suggested in Section III-B may be used to determine staggered checkpoints for the different data bases.

NOLS runs one 8-h shift each day. There is a lull in the load during the lunch hour. Because the load on the system is very time dependent, models A and C give different results. Two cases will be considered for the NOLS system. When the NOLS system was being made operational, it did not have its full complement of files. The checkpoint time was $\frac{1}{2}$ h. Later, after more files were added, the checkpoint time increased to $2\frac{1}{2}$ h. We consider both cases.

Assuming a MTBF of 18 h, a checkpoint time and reestablishment time of $\frac{1}{2}$ h and a compression factor of 1/8, we get an optimal intercheckpoint time of 12 h and an availability of 8/9 for model A. However, it is obvious that: 1) checkpointing should be carried out at the end of the 8-h shift rather than every 12 h, and 2) there is no cost associated with checkpointing since there is no load during checkpointing. Therefore, there is only variable overhead cost and no fixed overhead cost. The computed availability is 17/18, assuming no fixed overhead.

Model C suggests that there should be checkpoints at noon (during the lunch hour) and again at the end of the shift since these checkpoints are essentially cost free. The availability computed from model C is 23/24.

If the reestablishment time doubles (due to an increase in repair time for instance), there is no change in the checkpoints suggested by models A, B, and C. However, the availability drops to 11/12 for model A and 67/72 for model C. The checkpoint times suggested by models A and C are very insensitive to changes in system parameters.

When the checkpoint and load times were increased to $2\frac{1}{2}$ h, the optimum intercheckpoint time increased to over 18 h. However, the 8-h shift once again suggests a checkpoint at the end of every workday. The availability in this case is 7/8. Model C also suggests checkpoints at the end of every workday. The NOLS system was and is being checkpointed at times determined by model C.

The analysis of RR strategies on ALS is not complete at this time.

APPENDIX

Theorem 2: If there are no errors detected during checkpointing:

$$\exp(\lambda k T_{\text{opt}})(1 - \lambda k T_{\text{opt}}) = 1 - \lambda k F \exp(-\lambda R). \quad (11)$$

If there may be errors detected during checkpointing:

$$\exp(\lambda k T_{\text{opt}})(1 - \lambda k T_{\text{opt}}) = 1 - [\exp(\lambda F) - 1] \cdot k \cdot \exp(-\lambda R). \quad (12)$$

Proof: We first compute the expected time $e(y)$ for a recovery in model B given that y units of continuous error-free processing are required. Then

$$h(t) = e(R + kt). \quad (13)$$

The conditional expected time to the next error detection given that an error is detected within y time units is

$$E(t/y) = \int_{t=0}^{y} \frac{\lambda \exp(-\lambda t)}{1 - \exp(-\lambda y)} \cdot t \cdot dt$$

$$= \lambda^{-1} - \frac{y \cdot \exp(-\lambda y)}{1 - \exp(-\lambda y)}. \quad (14)$$

Let P be the probability of no error detection in time y. Then

$$P = \exp(-\lambda y). \quad (15)$$

Since the probability of error in nonoverlapping times are independent, the number of attempted recoveries (including the final successful recovery) is a geometric random variable. Therefore the expected number of aborted recoveries is

$$E(n) = \frac{1 - P}{P}. \quad (16)$$

From (14)–(16), the total time spent in aborted recoveries is

$$E(t/y) \cdot E(n) = \lambda^{-1}[\exp(\lambda y) - 1] - y. \quad (17)$$

Hence, the expected total time spent in recovery, including

the final successful recovery is

$$\lambda^{-1}[\exp(\lambda y) - 1].$$

Therefore,

$$h(t) = \lambda^{-1}[\exp(\lambda R + \lambda kT) - 1]. \quad (18)$$

$C(x)$ for model B satisfies Theorem 1; the proof is identical for models A and B.

Solving the differential equation with $h(t)$ given by (18) and boundary condition $C(T) = 0$ we get

$$C(t) = \frac{\exp(\lambda R)}{\lambda k}[\exp(\lambda kT) - \exp(\lambda kt)] - (T - t). \quad (19)$$

Hence

$$V(T) = C(0) = \exp(\lambda R)\cdot\left(\frac{\exp(\lambda kT) - 1}{\lambda k}\right) - T \quad (20)$$

and

$$r(T) = \frac{V(T) + F(T)}{T} = \exp(\lambda R)\left(\frac{\exp(\lambda kT) - 1}{\lambda kT}\right) - 1 + F/T \quad (21)$$

$$dr/dT = \exp(\lambda R)\left(\frac{\lambda kT\exp(\lambda kT) - \exp(\lambda kT) + 1}{\lambda kT^2}\right) - F/T^2 \quad (22)$$

$$d^2r/dT^2 = \frac{\exp(\lambda R)}{\lambda kT^3}\{(\lambda kT - 1)^2\exp(\lambda kT) + [\exp(\lambda kT) - 1]\} + 2F/T^3 > 0. \quad (23)$$

From (23), r is a strictly convex function of T. Therefore r has a unique minimum. This minimum is obtained by solving

$$dr(T)/dT = 0. \quad (24)$$

Substituting (21) in (24) and simplifying gives (11).

Theorem 3: The following recursive relations hold for $g_l(t)$:

$$g_1(t_0) = C(t_0, \tau) \qquad \text{for } 0 \le t_0 < \tau \quad (25)$$

and

$$g_l(t_0) = \text{minimum}\,\{g_{l-1}(t_0), g_l'(t_0)\}$$
$$\text{for } l = 2, 3, \cdots \text{ and } 0 \le t_0 < \tau \quad (26)$$

where

$$g_l'(t_0) = \text{minimum value of } \{C(t_0, t) + g_{l-1}(t)\}$$
$$\text{in the interval } t_0 < t < \tau, \qquad \text{for all } 0 \le t_0 < \tau.$$

Proof: $g_1(t_0)$ is the total cost from time t_0 to τ given that there is one checkpoint at t_0 and no other checkpoint between t_0 and τ. But this is exactly $C(t_0, \tau)$ and hence (25) follows. The total cost incurred from t_0 to τ given a total of k or fewer checkpoints with one at t_0, another at t, and $k - 1$ or fewer between t and τ is

$$C(t_0, t) + g_{k-1}(t).$$

Therefore,

$$g_k(t_0) \le C(T_0, t) + g_{k-1}(t) \qquad \text{for all } t_0 < t < \tau. \quad (27)$$

If there are $k > 1$ checkpoints in the interval $t_0 \le t < \tau$, then there must be at least one in the interval $t_0 < t < \tau$. Let t^* be the time of the very next checkpoint after t. Then there must be $k - 1$ or fewer checkpoints after t^*. Hence, there exists some t^*, where $t_0 < t^* < \tau$ such that

$$g_k(t_0) = C(t_0, t^*) + g_{k-1}(t^*). \quad (28)$$

By definition

$$g_k(t_0) \le g_{k-1}(t_0) \qquad \text{for all } 0 \le t_0 \le \tau. \quad (29)$$

If there is exactly one checkpoint in the interval $t_0 \le t < \tau$ and that checkpoint is at t_0, then there are no checkpoints in the interval $t_0 < t < \tau$.

Hence, in this case

$$g_k(t_0) = g_{k-1}(t_0) = \cdots = g_1(t_0). \quad (30)$$

Hence, either there exists a t^* where $t_0 < t^* < \tau$ and which satisfies (28) or $g_k(t_0) = g_{k-1}(t_0)$.

This fact coupled with (27) and (29) results in (26).

Theorem 4: Let

$$g_{j-i+1}(t_{i-1}) = C(t_{i-1}, t_i) + g_{j-i}(t_i)$$
$$\text{for } i = 1, 2, \cdots, j - 1, \text{ and with } t_0 = 0. \quad (31)$$

Optimal checkpoint times are t_i, $i = 1, 2, \cdots, j - 1$.

Proof: From Theorem 3, $g_k(0)$ is the minimum cost for the entire cycle given k or fewer checkpoints during the cycle. Recollect that we must have a checkpoint at the beginning of each cycle by assumption.

From Corollary 3 there is an optimal solution with j or fewer checkpoints during the cycle. Therefore $g_j(0)$ is the minimum cost for the entire cycle.

Using (31) for $i = 1, 2, \cdots, j - 1$ and (25) we get

$$g_j(0) = \sum_{i=1}^{j} C(t_{i-1}, t_i)$$

with $t_j = \tau$.

But $\sum_{i=1}^{j} C(t_{i-1}, t_i)$ is the total cost in a cycle given checkpoints at times t_i, $i = 0, 1, 2, \cdots, j - 1$ and no other checkpoints. Hence, the theorem follows.

ACKNOWLEDGMENT

The authors would like to thank G. Lasseter of Information Research Associates for his help.

REFERENCES

[1] K. M. Chandy and C. V. Ramamoorthy, "Rollback and recovery strategies for computer programs," *IEEE Trans. Comput.*, vol. C-21, pp. 546–556, June 1972.

[2] K. M. Chandy, C. V. Ramamoorthy, and A. E. Cowan, "A framework for hardware-software tradeoffs in the design of fault-tolerant computers," in *1972 Fall Joint Comput. Conf., AFIPS Conf. Proc.*, vol. 41, part I. Montvale, N. J.: AFIPS Press, 1972, pp. 55–64.

[3] J. C. Browne, K. M. Chandy, R. M. Brown, T. W. Keller, D. Towsley, and C. W. Dissly, "Hierarchical techniques for development of realistic models of complex computer systems," *IEEE Trans. Comput.*, to be published.

[4] H. M. Wagner, *Principles of Operations Research.* Englewood Cliffs, N. J.: Prentice-Hall, 1969.

Note Added in Proof: After the paper was written, the authors discovered that model A was analyzed earlier by J. W. Young [5]. The authors are sorry they did not reference his paper in the body of this text.

[5] J. W. Young, "A first order approximation to the optimum checkpoint interval," *Commun. Ass. Comput. Mach.*, vol. 17, pp. 530–531, Sept. 1974.

Part IV
Application Support Functions

IN previous parts we have examined the scheduling, communication, and synchronization of tasks; these are processes which constitute major operations performed by distributed computer systems. In this part we expand upon these basic processes and discuss application support functions characterizing distributed computing systems. Namely, we discuss 1) allocation of the database to the nodes of the distributed system; 2) processing of database queries; 3) features intended to maximize the system's security; and 4) languages which exploit the inherent processing capabilities of the distributed system.

References for Sections IV-A, IV-B

[1] A. Segall, "Dynamic file assignment in a computer network," *IEEE Trans. Automat. Contr.*, vol. AC-21, pp. 101–173, 1976.

[2] E. Feldman *et al.*, "Warehouse location under continuous economics of scale," *Management Sci.*, vol. 12, pp. 670–684, 1966.

[3] K. Spielberg, "Algorithm for the simple plant-location problem with some side conditions," *Oper. Res.*, vol. 17, pp. 85–111, 1969.

[4] R.D. Spinetto, "A facility location problem," *SIAM Rev.*, vol. 18, pp. 294–295, 1976.

[5] E.F. Codd, "A relational model of data for large shared data banks," *Commun. Ass. Comput. Mach.*, vol. 13, pp. 377–387, 1970.

[6] S.B. Yao, "Optimization of query evaluation algorithms," *Ass. Comput. Mach., Trans. Database Syst.*, vol. 4, 1979.

Section IV-A
Database Allocation

WE start this section by presenting four papers describing the basic problem of allocating the database to the nodes of a distributed computer system. Here, there are two parts of the problem. First, the database must be allocated upon the initial design of the distributed system. That is, the database distribution is initially a "given" upon which operating system decisions are later made.

Second, the operating system must be flexible enough to accommodate hardware failures. Indeed, a static allocation of the database does not accommodate node failures or node isolation due to link failures. Hence, distributed computing systems designed to allow for such occurrences must have the capability to dynamically allocate, or reallocate, the database. As shown in [1], such dynamic allocations decisions are often made in the presence of imprecisely known parameters such as database request rates and data transmission costs.

The first paper included in this section is "Optimal File Allocation in a Multiple Computer System" by W. W. Chu. Although pertinent to the problem of allocating files to the nodes in a network and not to the elements of a distributed computer system, Chu's paper is a good starting point for any study of database allocation. He summarizes the general allocation problem succinctly:

> "Given a number of computers that process common information files, how can one allocate the files so that the allocation yields minimum overall operating costs subject to the following constraints: 1) the expected time to access each file is less than a given bound, 2) the amount of storage needed at each computer does not exceed the available storage capacity."

Chu's problem encompasses memories of finite capacity, costs for storage and transmission, and queuing delays. He formulates the problem as a nonlinear zero-one programming problem, but later provides a method for linearizing it.

Chu's research appears to be the first in which file allocation is analyzed in detail. His work, along with that of many subsequent researchers, is based upon mathematical techniques developed for the "plant-location" problem. Here, the problem is to locate plants (or warehouses) in a given geographical area in a manner that minimizes a particular parameter such as shipment costs. Appropriate papers include [2]–[4].

Among researchers following Chu's initial steps was R.G. Casey. His article, "Allocation of Copies of a File in an Information Network" is also presented in this chapter. As was the case with Chu, Casey's model is more appropriate for networks of computers than for tightly coupled distributed systems. Nonetheless, his formulation and solution of the model allows several basic insights to be made into the general allocation problem.

Casey's model includes the following two types of transactions: "(1) query traffic between a node and the file, and (2) update traffic. An update message is assumed to be transmitted to every copy of the file, whereas a query is communicated only to a single copy."

Casey develops a linear (cost) model and solves it to obtain bounds on the number of copies of a given file to be maintained in the network.

The next paper included is "Some Theorems to Aid in Solving the File Allocation Problem" by E. Grapa and G.G. Belford. The main technical content of this paper consists of three theorems which can be applied to limit the number of possible file allocation combinations for a network. However, in addition to their technical material, the authors present an excellent summary of both the general file allocation problem and previous work done on the problem. Readers are heartily recommended to refer to this work.

The fourth and final paper included to summarize the file allocation problem is "Dynamic File Assignment in a Computer Network" by A. Segall. This paper is the first to consider temporal variations in such system parameters as storage and transmission costs and demand rates. However, an unfortunate limitation to this work was the fact that only one copy of a given file is allowed to exist in the network at any time.

Optimal File Allocation in a Multiple Computer System

WESLEY W. CHU, MEMBER, IEEE

***Abstract*—A model is developed for allocating information files required in common by several computers. The model considers storage cost, transmission cost, file lengths, and request rates, as well as updating rates of files, the maximum allowable expected access times to files at each computer, and the storage capacity of each computer. The criterion of optimality is minimal overall operating costs (storage and transmission). The model is formulated into a nonlinear integer zero-one programming problem, which may be reduced to a linear zero-one programming problem. A simple example is given to illustrate the model.**

***Index Terms*—Computer communication, linear integer programming, multicomputer information system, multiprocessor, nonlinear integer programming, optimal file allocation.**

Introduction

In the automation of large information systems, a major portion of the planning is concerned with storing large quantities of information in a computer system. This requires study of information storage, modification, and transmission. Examples of such efforts are found in business, medical, library, and management information systems. These systems, which may consist of several geographically separated divisions (subsystems), need to process information files in common.

It is apparent that when a given information file is required in common by several computers, it may be stored in at least one of them and accessed by the others when needed. The overall operating cost related to the files is considered to consist of transmission and storage costs. The problem is the following. Given a number of computers that process common information files, how can one allocate the files so that the allocation yields minimum overall operating costs subject to the following constraints: 1) the expected time to access each file is less than a given bound, 2) the amount of storage needed at each computer does not exceed the available storage capacity.

The Model

The file allocation problem can be formulated as an integer (0 or 1) programming model.

Let X_{ij} indicate that the jth file is stored in the ith computer:

$$X_{ij} = \begin{cases} 1 & j\text{th file stored in the } i\text{th computer} \\ 0 & \text{otherwise} \end{cases} \tag{1}$$

where

$i=1, 2, \cdots, n$
$j=1, 2, \cdots, m$
n = total number of computers in the multicomputer system
m = total number of distinct files in the multicomputer system.

For storing r_j redundant copies of the jth in the information system, we have

$$\sum_i X_{ij} = r_j \qquad \text{for } 1 \le j \le m. \tag{2}$$

To assure that the storage capacity of each computer is not exceeded, we have

$$\sum_j X_{ij}L_j \le b_i \qquad \text{for } 1 \le i \le n \tag{3}$$

where

L_j = length of the jth file,
b_i = available memory size of the ith computer.

The expected time for the ith computer to retrieve the jth file from the kth computer (from initiation of request till start of reception) is denoted as a_{ijk}. The maximum allowable retrieval time of the jth file to the ith computer is T_{ij}. We required that a_{ijk} be less than T_{ij}, i.e.,

$$(1 - X_{ij})X_{kj}a_{ijk} \le T_{ij} \qquad \text{for } i \ne k, \quad 1 \le j \le m. \tag{4}$$

When $r_j = 1$ for all j, then from (2) we know that $X_{ij}X_{kj} = 0$ for $i \ne k$. Thus (4) reduces to

$$X_{kj}a_{ijk} \le T_{ij} \qquad \text{for } i \ne k, \quad 1 \le j \le m. \tag{5}$$

Now, a_{ijk} is equal to the sum of the expected queuing delay at the ith computer for the channel to the kth computer[1] $w_{ik}^{(1)}$, the expected queuing delay at the kth computer for the channel to the ith computer $w_{ki}^{(2)}$, and the expected computer access time to the jth file t_{kj}. In most cases, the quantity t_{kj} is much smaller than $w_{ik} = w_{ik}^{(1)} + w_{ki}^{(2)}$ and can be neglected. Hence,

$$a_{ijk} \doteq w_{ik}. \tag{6}$$

[1] The number in the superscripts of $w_{ik}^{(\cdot)}$ and $w_{ki}^{(\cdot)}$ denotes the priority class of the messages that are transmitted between the ith and kth computers, which will be discussed shortly.

Manuscript received July 12, 1968; revised May 29, 1969. This is a generalized version of the paper entitled "Optimal file allocation in a multicomputer information system," presented at the IFIP Congress 68, Edinburgh, Scotland, August 5–10, 1968.

The author was with Bell Telephone Laboratories, Inc., Holmdel N. J. He is now with the Computer Science Department, University of the City of Los Angeles, Los Angeles, Calif.

Reprinted from *IEEE Trans. Comput.*, vol. C-18, pp. 885–889, Oct. 1969.

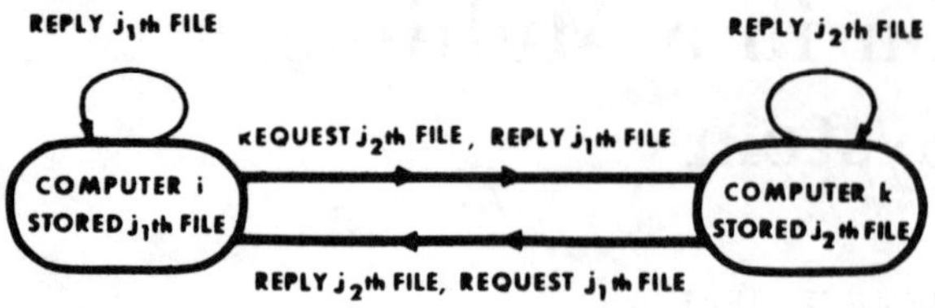

REPLY j_1th FILE

REPLY j_2th FILE

REQUEST j_2th FILE, REPLY j_1th FILE

COMPUTER i STORED j_1th FILE

COMPUTER k STORED j_2th FILE

REPLY j_2th FILE, REQUEST j_1th FILE

Fig. 1. Transmission paths between each pair of computers.

Next we will discuss the mechanism involved in the queuing delay. Each pair of computers is assumed to be able to transmit information in both directions simultaneously. This is known as single-channel full-duplex operation. Further, the files can be accessed by the local and remote computers at the same time. One pair of transmission paths links each pair of computers; one of these paths carries *requests* for the files from the ith computer to the kth computer, and *reply* messages (files) from the ith computer to the kth computer, whereas the other path carries *requests* for files from the kth computer to the ith computer, and *reply* messages from kth to the ith computer (Fig. 1). In most cases, the request message is much shorter than the reply message. Therefore, we shall assign a higher priority to request messages than to reply messages. Messages of the same priority are served in the order of their arrival. Assume, for example, a reply message is being transmitted on a particular transmission path at the time a new request is initiated. The request will interrupt the current reply and the computer will transmit the request first. After finishing transmission of that new request, the computer resumes transmitting the previous reply. Such preemptive-resume priority servicing faciltates optimization, since the queuing delay will be minimum if the shortest messages are serviced first [1], [2]. Recalling that the requested message length is much shorter than that of the reply message, the delay due to the request message can be neglected.[2] Under these conditions, the queuing system can be viewed as a single server queue with constant service time.

In many cases, it is reasonable to model the file accessing process as a Poisson process. Then the rate of requests from the ith computer to the kth computer (arrival rate) λ_{ik} is the sum of the rates of request of those files not stored in the ith computer but stored in the kth computer. The requested file length may be less than the entire storage file length and is defined as the length of each transaction; that is, the length of each transaction of the jth file l_j should be less or equal to the entire jth file length L_j. The average time required to transmit the reply from the kth computer to the jth computer $1/\mu_{ik}$ (i.e., service time) is dependent on l_j and λ_{ik}. Clearly, both λ_{ik} and $1/\mu_{ik}$ depend on the file allocation, yet the allocation is unknown in advance. Hence, we shall express λ_{ik} and $1/\mu_{ik}$ in terms of the X_{ij}'s:

$$\lambda_{ik} = \sum_j u_{ij}(1 - X_{ij})X_{kj} \tag{7}$$

where

u_{ij} = the request rate[3] of the entire or part of the jth file at the ith computer per unit time.

The average time required to transmit a reply message from the kth to the ith computer via a line with transmission rate R is

$$1/\mu_{ik} = \frac{1}{\lambda_{ik}} \sum \frac{1}{\mu_j} u_{ij}(1 - X_{ij})X_{kj} \tag{8}$$

where

$1/\mu_j = l_j/R$ = required time to transmit each transaction of the jth file.

Equation (8) states that $1/\mu_{ik}$ is equal to the time required for the kth computer to reply all the messages requested from the ith computer divided by the total number of requests initiated from the ith computer to the kth computer. Since the l_j's and R are constants, μ_j and μ_{ik} are also constants.

The traffic intensity from the kth to the ith computer ρ_{ik} measures the degree of congestion of the line that provides the transmission path between the kth and ith computer, or the fraction of time that the line is busy. It is defined as

$$\rho_{ik} = \lambda_{ik}/\mu_{ik} = \sum_j \frac{1}{\mu_j} u_{ij}(1 - X_{ij})X_{kj}. \tag{9}$$

Since physically it is impossible for the transmission line to be 100 percent busy, the traffic intensity is less than unity, i.e., $\rho_{ik} < 1$.

When only a single copy of the file is stored in the information system, then $X_{ij}X_{kj} = 0$ for $i \neq k$. Hence

$$\lambda_{ik} = \sum_j u_{ij}X_{kj} \qquad \text{for } i \neq k \tag{10}$$

and

$$1/\mu_{ik} = \frac{1}{\lambda_{ik}} \sum_j u_{ij} \frac{1}{\mu_j} X_{kj} \qquad \text{for } i \neq k \tag{11}$$

when all the $\mu_j = \mu$; then (11) reduces to

$$1/\mu_{ik} = 1/\mu. \tag{12}$$

The average waiting time [1], [2] from the initiation of a request at the ith computer to the receipt of the requested message from the kth computer, with the above assumptions (single server queue with Poisson arrivals and constant service time), is

[2] Preemptive priority servicing permits the assumption that $w_{ik} \doteq w_{ki}^{(2)}$. Note that the file retrieval time constraint as shown in (4) also applies to the nonpremptive priority case, but a more complex expression would be required for w_{ik} since $w_{ik}^{(1)}$ can no longer be neglected.

[3] In general, the request rate may be time dependent. In the analysis here, we are concerned with the request rate of the busy period.

$$w_{ik} \doteq w_{ki}^{(2)} = \frac{1}{\mu_{ik}} \frac{\rho_{ik}}{2(1-\rho_{ik})} \qquad \text{for } i \neq k \tag{13}$$

where $1/\mu_{ik}$ and ρ_{ik} are functions of X_{ij}'s as given by (8) and (9). The variance and probability distribution of w_{ik} for a specific allocation can be computed from its ρ_{ik} and μ_{ik} [1], [2].

Substituting (13) into (6) and (4), we have

$$(1 - X_{ij})X_{kj}\frac{1}{\mu_{ik}}\frac{\rho_{ik}}{2(1-\rho_{ik})} \leq T_{ij},$$

which can be rearranged into the form

$$(1 - X_{ij})X_{kj}\lambda_{ik} - 2\mu_{ik}(\mu_{ik} - \lambda_{ik})T_{ij} \leq 0. \tag{14}$$

For the special case that $\mu_{ik} = \mu$ and $r_j = 1$, (14) reduces to

$$\sum_{\substack{j_1 \\ j \neq j_1}} u_{ij}X_{kj_1}X_{kj} + 2T_{ij}\mu \sum_{j_1} u_{ij_1}X_{kj_1} + u_{ij}X_{kj} - 2\mu^2 T_{ij} \leq 0. \tag{15}$$

Finally, we shall express the operating cost (objective function) in terms of the allocation (X_{ij}'s). Suppose we know the storage cost of the jth file per unit length and unit time at the ith computer C_{ij}, the transmission cost from the kth computer to the ith computer per unit time C_{ik}', the request rate for the entire or part of the jth file at the ith computer per unit time u_{ij}, the frequency of modification of the jth file at the ith computer after each transaction P_{ij}, the length of each transaction for the jth file l_j, and the number of redundant copies of the jth file stored in the system r_j. Then the overall operating cost per unit time C for processing m distinct files required in common by n computers is

$$C = \underbrace{\sum_{i,j} C_{ij}L_jX_{ij}}_{\text{storage cost}} + \underbrace{\sum_{i,j,k} \frac{1}{r_j} C_{ik}'l_ju_{ij}X_{kj}(1 - X_{ij}) + \sum_{i,j,k} C_{ik}'l_ju_{ij}X_{kj}P_{ij}}_{\text{transmission cost}},$$

which can be rearranged into the form

$$= \sum_{i,j} D_{ij}X_{ij} - \sum_{i,j,k} E_{ijk}X_{kj}X_{ij} \quad \text{where} \quad D_{ij} > 0, \qquad E_{ijk} > 0 \tag{16}$$

when $r_j = 1$, $1 \leq j \leq m$; then $X_{kj}X_{ij} = 0$ for $k \neq i$, and $C_{ii}' = 0$. Under this case, (16) reduces to

$$C = \sum_{i,j} D_{ij}X_{ij}. \tag{17}$$

We want to minimize (16) subject to storage and access time requirements constraints given in (1), (2), (3), and (14). As X_{ij}'s take on value zero or one, the allocation problem becomes solving a nonlinear zero-one programming problem. In the next section, we shall introduce a technique to reduce the nonlinear zero-one equations to the linear zero-one equations. With this technique, the allocation problem can be then solved by standard linear zero-one programming techniques [3], [4].

Reduction of Zero-One Nonlinear Programming Problems to Zero-One Linear Programming Problems[4]

Because nonlinear programming problems are so complex, we are able to obtain a global optimal solution only for special cases (e.g., convexity). Therefore, it is desirable to reduce the nonlinear zero-one programming problems to the linear zero-one programming problems. We shall now show such a reduction, which is derived from the integer (0 or 1) property.

Suppose we want to minimize an arbitrary cost function (which need not be convex)

$$C = \min_X F(X_1, X_2, \cdots, X_k) \tag{18}$$

subject to a set of nonconvex constraint equations

$$G_i(X_1, X_2, \cdots, X_k) \leq B_i \qquad i = 1, 2, \cdots, N \tag{19}$$

where the X_i's are zero-one variables, F and G_i are polynomials of the X_i's with constant coefficients, and B_i is a constant. Clearly, $X_i^q = X_i$ (q = positive integer). Let the coefficient of the product terms in (18) or (19), $X_iX_j, \cdots, X_uX_v$, be denoted as $C_{ij\cdots uv}$.

To reduce the above nonlinear zero-one problem to a linear zero-one problem, first we consider the objective function (18). Let us define

$$X_{ij\cdots uv} = \underbrace{X_iX_j \cdots X_uX_v}_{q} \qquad q = 2, \cdots, Q \tag{20}$$

which takes value zero or one where Q is the highest degree of nonlinearity. We then represent each nonlinear term in (18) by terms of the form (20) and then examine its coefficient. If the coefficient of the nonlinear term is positive, we introduce the following constraint equation:

$$\underbrace{X_i + X_j \cdots + X_u + X_v}_{q} - q + 1 \leq X_{ij\cdots uv}. \tag{21}$$

[4] A similar but less general result has also been obtained independently by Watters [5].

If the coefficient of the nonlinear term is negative, we introduce the following constraint equation:

$$\underbrace{X_i + X_j + \cdots + X_u + X_v}_{q} \geq qX_{ij\ldots uv}. \tag{22}$$

If all the X's in left side of (21) have value one, then $X_{ij\ldots uv}=1$. If one or more of the X's have value zero, then $X_{ij\ldots uv}$ may be either zero or one, but the coefficient of $X_{ij\ldots uv}$ in (18), $C_{ij\ldots uv}$, is positive. Thus minimizing (18) under X assures that $X_{ij\ldots uv}=0$. If we substitute (20) for each nonlinear term in (18) that has positive coefficient and introduce the additional constraint (21), then the X's in the transformed linear equations take on the same values as the original ones. Similarly, if one or more of the X's in (20) have value zero, then $X_{ij\ldots uv}=0$. If all the X's have value one, then $X_{ij\ldots uv}$ may either be zero or one, but the coefficient of $X_{ij\ldots uv}$ in (18), $C_{ij\ldots uv}$, is negative. Thus minimizing (18) under X assures that $X_{ijkl\ldots uv}=1$. If we substitute (20) for each nonlinear term in (18) that has negative coefficient and introduce the additional constraint (22), then the X's in the transformed linear equations take on the same values as the original ones. Thus, we have linearized the objective function (18).

To linearize the constraint equations, we represent the nonlinear terms in (19) by (20) and introduce its corresponding *two* additional constraint equations (21) and (22). If one or more of the X's in (20) have value zero, then $X_{ij\ldots uv}=0$; this condition is also satisfied by (21) and (22). If all the X_{ij}'s have value one in (20), then $X_{ij\ldots uv}$ is one. Similarly, from (21) $X_{ij\ldots uv}$ may be either zero or one, but from (22) $X_{ij\ldots uv}$ is one. Thus (21) and (22) assure that $X_{ij\ldots uv}=1$. Substituting (20) and introducing the additional constraint (21) and (22) for each nonlinear term in (19) satisfy all the relationships of X's. Thus, we have also linearized the nonlinear constraints equations.

With this reduction technique,[5] nonlinear zero-one programming problems may be transformed into solution of linear zero-one programming problems. Using available linear integer programming techniques [3], [4], we can obtain the global optimal solutions.

Linearization of the Objective Function and Access Time Constants

To apply the above technique to linearize the objective function (16), we let $X_{ij}X_{kj}=X_{ijkj}$. Since the coefficients of X_{ijkj} in (16) are negative, for each X_{ijkj}, we introduce the additional constraint equation

$$X_{ij} + X_{kj} \geq 2X_{ijkj}. \tag{23}$$

Next, we shall linearize the constraint equation (15). We let $X_{kj_1}X_{kj}=X_{kj_1kj}$. For each X_{kj_1kj}, we introduce two additional constraint equations

$$\begin{cases} X_{kj_1} + X_{kj} \geq 2X_{kj_1kj} \\ X_{kj_1} + X_{kj} - 1 \leq X_{kj_1kj} \end{cases} \quad \text{for } j \neq j_1. \tag{24}$$

In the same manner, we can linearize (14). Hence, solution to the optimal file allocation problem is reduced to: minimize (16) subject to (1), (2), (3), (14) or (15), (20), (23), and (24) which is a linear zero–one programming problem.

File Allocation in a Multiprocessor

Let us consider a multiprocessor with virtual memory system that operates in a paging environment. One of the important problems in such a system is how to allocate files to various types of available storage systems such as thin films, cores, disks, drums, data cells, tapes, etc., so that the operating cost is minimum yet the access time requirements are satisfied for each file, and the storage limitation of each storage system is not exceeded. The model developed in this paper can be directly applied to this problem by letting the distances between computers equal to zero. Clearly, under this condition, a multiple computer system becomes a multiprocessor.

Example

Consider a specific computer communication system consisting of three computers that process five information files in common, as shown in Fig. 2. These computers are located about 20 miles from each other. The transmission facility between each pair of computers has a rate of $R=5\times10^3$ char/second. The cost of each such facility is \$1050 per month or $\$1.4\times10^{-7}$/char (based on 100 hours per week and 4.2 weeks per month). The first cost of storage is 35 cents per character or $\$5.8\times10^{-7}$/char second.[6] Table I gives the lengths of each file, file length for each transactions, the request rate of these files at each computer, the rate of modification of these files at each computer after each transaction, the available storage capacity of each computer, and the maximum allowable retrieval time of each file. Using the linearized model developed above and the Gomory cutting technique [3], [4] for solving the integer linear programming problem, the example was solved on the IBM 360/65. Table II lists the optimal allocation for the case of no redundant files. The computation time required for this example is about 25 seconds.

Some characteristics of the optimum allocation are worthy of note. File 4 is stored in computer 2 as it is only used by that computer. File 1 has highest request

[5] This reduction technique can be easily extended to the case when the X_i's in (18) or (19) are real numbers. In this case, we shall express each X_i in terms of binary variables X_{il}'s as follows:

$$X_i = \sum_{l=1}^{\alpha_i+\beta_i} (X_{il})2^{\alpha_i-l}$$

where α_i is chosen large enough for 2^{α_i-1} to be an upper bound on the value of X_i, while β_i is chosen large enough for $2^{-\beta_i}$ to be the maximum allowable accuracy tolerance on the value of X_i. Thus (18) or (19) is reduced from a nonlinear equation to a nonlinear zero–one equation.

[6] The calculation is based on 40 months of machine life operating at 100 hours per week and 4.2 weeks per month.

TABLE I

DATA OF EXAMPLE FOR FILE ALLOCATION

File j	L_j	l_j	P_j	Computer 1		Computer 2		Computer 3	
				u_{1j}	T_{1j}	u_{2j}	T_{2j}	u_{3j}	T_{3j}
1	100×10^3	500	0.5	5	30	2	10	0	0
2	10×10^3	500	0.5	0	0	2	30	5	1
3	10×10^3	500	0.5	3	10	0	0	4	1
4	10×10^3	500	0.5	0	0	4	0.1	0	0
5	100×10^3	500	0.5	1	1	1	1	5	1

P_j = the frequency of modification of the jth file after each transaction.
L_j = length of the jth file in characters.
l_j = file length (in characters) of each transaction for the jth file.
u_i = average hourly request rate of the entire or part of the jth file at the ith computer. Request arrivals are assumed to be Poisson distributed.
T_{ij} = maximum allowable average retrieval time in seconds for the jth file to the ith computer.
C_{ij} = (storage cost) = \$0.58 $\times 10^{-8}$/char second.
C_{ik}' = (transmission cost) = \$1.4 $\times 10^{-7}$/char.
b_i = (available storage capacity of the ith computer) = 110×10^3 char for $i = 1, 2, 3$.
$1/\mu = l/R$ (the time required to transmit the reply message) = 0.1 second.

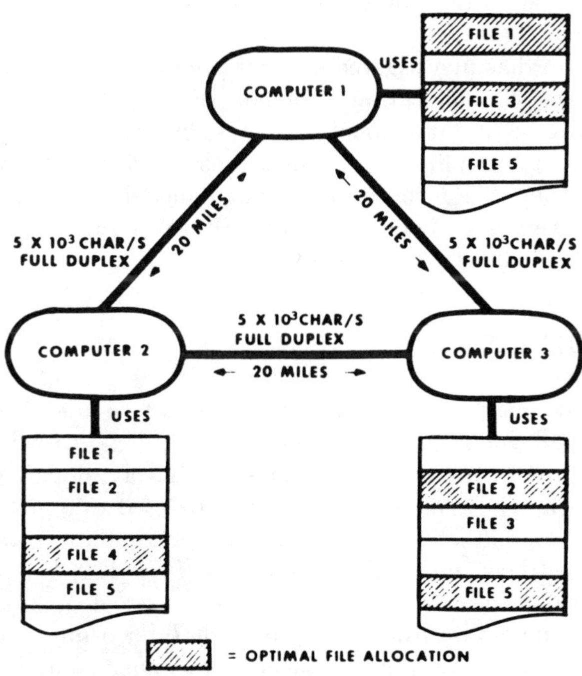

Fig. 2. A specific multiple computer system.

rate at computer 1; to minimize the transmission cost, it is stored in computer 1. For the same reason, Files 2 and 5 are stored in computer 3. Although File 3 has a high request rate at computer 3, the available storage size of computer 3 (110×10^3 char) forced File 3 to be stored in computer 1. The overall operation cost under the optimal allocation is \$3620 per month. If each file is stored at the computer where it is used, the total operating cost under such arrangement is \$6670 per month. The higher operating cost is due to the extra storage cost and the file updating cost.

CONCLUSION

The file allocation problem can be formulated into a nonlinear zero–one programming problem. By adding additional constraint equations, these nonlinear terms

TABLE II

OPTIMAL FILE ALLOCATION FOR EXAMPLE

File j	X_{ij} Computer 1	Computer 2	Computer 3
1	1	0	0
2	0	0	1
3	1	0	0
4	0	1	0
5	0	0	1

in the objective and constraint equations can be reduced to linear equations. Thus, solution of the optimal allocation requires solving a linear zero–one programming problem. The model introduced in this paper provides a common denominator for analysis and comparison of various proposed information system configurations, a tool to study the sensitivity of various parameters and constraints to the operating cost, and a method for evaluating the growth potential of information systems. However, some related problems still require further studies, such as file reliability, privacy, file partition, etc. All these problems are important considerations for optimal file allocation in multicomputer information systems.

ACKNOWLEDGMENT

The author would like to thank E. Fuchs of Bell Telephone Laboratories for his stimulating discussions.

REFERENCES

[1] D. R. Cox and W. L. Smith, *Queues, Methnen's Statistical Monographs.* London, England: Spottiswoode, Ballantyne, and Co., 1961, pp. 50–59.
[2] T. L. Saaty, *Elements of Queuing Theory.* New York: McGraw-Hill, 1961, pp. 153–161.
[3] R. Gomory, "All-integer integer programming algorithm," *Industrial Scheduling,* Muth and Thompson, Eds. Englewood Cliffs, N. J.: Prentice-Hall, 1963, pp. 195–206.
[4] J. Haldi and L. M. Isaacson, "Linear integer programming," Graduate School of Business, Stanford University, Stanford, Calif., working paper 45, December 1964.
[5] L. J. Watters, "Reduction of integer polynomial programming problems to zero–one linear programming problems," *Operations Res.,* vol. 15, pp. 1171–1174, November–December 1967.

Allocation of copies of a file in an information network

by R. G. CASEY

IBM Research Laboratory
San Jose, California

INTRODUCTION

We consider a mathematical model of an information network of n nodes, some of which contain copies of a given data file. Within this network, every node is able to communicate with every other node over communication links (a process which may entail routing through intermediate nodes). In particular, we are concerned with transactions with the multiply-located file. Such transactions fall into one of two classes: (1) query traffic between a node and the file, and (2) update traffic. An update message is assumed to be transmitted to every copy of the file, whereas a query is communicated only to a single copy.

We proceed to demonstrate, within a simple linear cost model for the network, several properties of the optimal assignment of files to nodes. One set of results expresses bounds on the number of copies of the file that should be included in the network, as a function of the relative volume of query and update traffic. Secondly, a test useful in determining the optimum configuration is derived.

The problem of allocating resources in a network first arose within the context of determining the most economical location for manufacturing plants and warehouses.[1,2,3] In some studies, the model of the network is made in such a way that an efficient algorithm yielding the optimal allocation is not readily obtainable, and heuristic or approximate techniques are tried instead. Frazer,[4] for example, has developed a method for allocating production facilities when the cost of deploying a resource at a given node consists of a fixed overhead expenditure plus an amount proportional to the total demand on the facility.

These manufacturing models are conceptually different from the file allocation problem, when updating traffic is considered in the latter. Since all copies of a file are modified by each update message, the total volume of data transmitted in the network is not independent of the allocation policy, as is the total volume of goods shipped in a manufacturing environment, but rather increases with the number of file copies allocated. Yet, as will be shown, the models are mathematically equivalent to the file model analyzed here.

Chu[5] has investigated a linear programming solution to the file allocation problem. His model includes storage costs and queuing delays, but the number of copies of each file in the system is assumed to be known. Whitney[6] has formulated a similar model, and applied it to the task of designing network topology, as well as that of allocating copies of the file.

THE MODEL

The fixed cost (mainly for storage) of locating a copy of the file at the kth node ($k=1, 2, \ldots, n$) will be denoted by an amount σ_k, measured in, say, dollars per month. The symbols λ_j and ψ_j will be used to represent the volume of query traffic and of update traffic, respectively, emanating from node j ($j=1, 2, \ldots, n$). The quantities d_{jk} and d_{jk}' are the costs of a unit of communication from node j to node k for a query and an update transaction, respectively. Thus, d_{jk} and d_{jk}' might be measured in dollars per megabit transmitted, and λ_j and ψ_j expressed in megabits per month. The possibility of a difference in cost rates is included in the model on the premise that in many applications updates can be accumulated and transmitted either via a cheaper medium (e.g., by mailing magnetic tapes), or at a time when communications rates are lower (e.g., at night using switched lines).* Queries are assumed to be entered on-line, at a higher communication rate. If the kth node contains a copy of the file, then communications from the jth node produce a cost term of $\lambda_j d_{jk}$ for query transactions and an amount $\psi_j d_{jk}'$ for update

* The author is indebted to Dr. W. D. Frazer of IBM Research for pointing out this generalization.

Reprinted with permission from *AFIPS Conf. Proc., 1972 Spring Joint Comput. Conf.*, vol. 40, pp. 617–625.

transactions. Actually, in much of the discussion that follows, and in the experiments carried out, we assume equal cost rates for inquiry and update.

In practice, the cost of shipping information may not be linear with the amount sent; the assumption is nonetheless of theoretical interest in order to obtain a first-order approximation to a rather complex monotonically increasing function.

We are concerned with the problem of determining at which nodes of the network copies of the file shall reside. We shall assume that this allocation is to be done in such a way as to minimize the total cost of communication between users and files. In general, the cost of querying is reduced as we increase the number of file nodes in the network (users near a new file node find their querying more economical; the other users are no worse off). On the other hand, storage costs and the cost of updating go up as new copies of the file are introduced, since every copy must be updated. In the limiting cases, if no updating is done, and if storage costs are low, a copy of the file should be kept at every node (and network communication not used), whereas if only updating is done, and no querying, a single copy of the file should be maintained at some optimal node of the network.

By an assignment of the file we shall mean a choice of nodes at which to locate the file. Let I denote a set of node indexes representing a given assignment. The total communication cost resulting from this choice of file locations is a sum over individual user nodes. In the case of query traffic, we assume that the user accesses that copy of the file which minimizes his communication cost. His updates, of course, must be transmitted to all the file nodes. The general expression for total cost is therefore:

$$C(I)=\sum_{j=1}^{n}\left[\sum_{k\epsilon I}\psi_j d_{jk}'+\lambda_j \min_{k\epsilon I} d_{jk}\right]+\sum_{k\epsilon I}\sigma_k$$

The problem of file allocation in this context is to choose the index set, I, so as to minimize $C(I)$.

This cost function can be written in the form

$$C(I)=\sum_{k\epsilon I} U_k+\sum_{j=1}^{n} G_j(I)$$

where

$$U_k=\sigma_k+\sum_{j=1}^{n}\psi_j d_{jk}'$$

$$G_j(I)=\lambda_j \min_{k\epsilon I} d_{jk}$$

With $C(I)$ expressed in this form the problem of minimizing cost is seen to be exactly the problem investigated by Efroymson and Ray,[1] Feldman, et al.,[2] Frazer,[4] and others. The update costs of the file model are analogous to the fixed costs of the plant location model, while query costs are analogous to the transportation costs. Previous researchers tried mixed integer-linear programming techniques for obtaining solutions to the minimization problem. Generally, the true minimum of $C(I)$ is computationally very expensive to obtain by such methods, and heuristics are developed that sacrifice optimality in order to arrive at "good" solutions quickly.

Here, we take an alternative approach. We shall first exhibit several mathematical properties of the cost function. We shall use these to construct a search procedure which is guaranteed to produce the minimum of $C(I)$. Finally, we suggest heuristic modifications to the general agorithm for use in cases where it is too expensive to be applied. Thus, both attempts to solve the problem, by means of integer programming and by exploiting the properties of the cost function, turn to *ad hoc* adjustments in order to obtain relief from the expense of guaranteeing an optimum solution. It would be of interest to compare the performance of the two approaches on the same problems.

The initial examination of the properties of $C(I)$ yields bounds on the number of elements in the optimal file node set I, when storage costs do not vary. This will be shown by means of the following theorem.

Let the cost of update communication be equal to the cost of query communication ($d_{jk}=d_{jk}'$).

Theorem 1:

If for some integer $r\leq n$ $\psi_j>\lambda_j/(r-1)$ for each $j=1,2,\ldots,n$ then any r-node file assignment is more costly than the optimal one-node assignment.

We prove the theorem by means of the following lemma:

Lemma:

If $\psi_j=\rho\lambda_j$ for $j=1,2,\ldots,n$ then, an r-node assignment cannot be less costly than the optimal one-node assignment if $\rho\geq 1/(r-1)$.

Proof of Lemma:

Consider an arbitrary assignment $I=\{1,2,\ldots,r\}$. Let the elements of I be ordered such that node 1 is the lowest cost single-node assignment.

We have

$$C(I)=\rho\sum_{k=1}^{r}\sum_{j=1}^{n}\lambda_j d_{jk}+\sum_{j=1}^{n}\min_{k\epsilon I}\lambda_j d_{jk}+\sum_{k=1}^{r}\sigma_k$$

and

$$C(\{k\})=(1+\rho)\sum_{j=1}^{n}\lambda_j d_{jk}+\sigma_k \qquad k=1,2,\ldots,r$$

By the optimality of node 1 there are nonnegative numbers $\alpha_2,\ldots,\alpha_r$ such that

$$\sum_{j=1}^{n}\lambda_j d_{jk}=\sum_{j=1}^{n}\lambda_j d_{j1}+\alpha_k+\frac{\sigma_1-\sigma_k}{1+\rho} \qquad k=2,3,\ldots,r.$$

Substituting the above, we can write

$$C(I)-C(\{1\})=[\rho r-\rho-1]\sum_{j=1}^{n}\lambda_j d_{j1}+\sum_{k=2}^{r}\rho\alpha_k$$
$$+\sum_{j=1}^{n}\min_k \lambda_j d_{jk}+\frac{\rho(r-1)\sigma_1}{1+\rho}$$
$$+\frac{1}{1+\rho}\sum_{k=2}^{r}\sigma_k$$

which is certainly nonnegative if $(\rho r-\rho-1)$ is nonnegative. That is, $\rho\geq 1/(r-1)$ implies that $C(I)\geq C(\{1\})$.

If the optimal single node assignment is in I, then it is node 1 and the lemma is proved. If the optimal node, say k', is not in I, then we have $\rho\geq 1/(r-1)$ implies $C(I)\geq C(\{1\})>C(\{k'\})$ and so the lemma is true in this case as well.

Proof of Theorem 1

The lemma concerns the case where each user generates the same proportion of update traffic to query traffic. Suppose now that the proportions vary from node to node, but always exceed a given amount ρ. Then, there are nonnegative quantities ϵ_j such that

$$\psi_j=(\rho+\epsilon_j)\lambda_j \qquad j=1,2,\ldots,n$$

The cost functions can now be written:

$$C'(\{1\})=\sum_{j=1}^{n}(1+\rho+\epsilon_j)\lambda_j d_{j1}+\sigma=C(\{1\})+\sum_{j=1}^{n}\epsilon_j\lambda_j d_{j1}$$

$$C'(I)=\sum_{j=1}^{n}(\rho+\epsilon_j)\lambda_j\sum_{k=1}^{r}d_{jk}$$
$$+\sum_{j=1}^{n}\min_k(\rho+\epsilon_j)\,d_{jk}+r\cdot\sigma$$
$$=C(I)+\sum_{j=1}^{n}\epsilon_j\lambda_j\sum_{k=1}^{r}d_{jk}+\sum_{j=1}^{n}\epsilon_j\min_k d_{jk}$$

where the unprimed costs are those given in the lemma.

But clearly $C'(I)\geq C'(\{1\})$ whenever $C(I)\geq C(\{1\})$. Then applying the lemma, the condition $\rho\geq 1/(r-1)$ is sufficient to ensure that the r-node assignment is not optimal. In addition, if at least one of the ϵ_j's is greater than zero, we must have the strict inequality $C(I)>C(\{1\})$.

Corollary 1

If the update/query traffic ratio satisfies $\rho\geq 1/(r-1)$ (r an integer) then the optimal allocation consists of no more than r nodes.

Proof

If $\psi_j\geq\lambda_j/(r-1)$ for each j then certainly for any integer l

$$\psi_j>\lambda_j/(r+l-1)$$

and so theorem 1 rules out the optimality of an $(r+l)$-node assignment.

Corollary 2

If each user generates at least 50 percent of his traffic in the form of updates, then the optimal assignment policy is to locate only a single copy of the file in the network.

The corollary follows directly from the theorem by setting $r=2$, but is worth stating separately since it sets a bound beyond which multiple copies of the file should not be considered. Furthermore, it is easy to show that for equal proportions of update and query traffic the two-node assignment is no more costly than a one-node assignment of the file only if storage costs are neglected, and the rows and columns of the cost matrix can be permuted to yield the form:

$$\begin{bmatrix} 0 & 0\ldots 0 & a_1 & a_2\ldots a_m & 0 & 0\ldots 0\\ b_1 & b_2\ldots b_l & 0 & 0\ldots 0 & 0 & 0\ldots 0\\ & & & \text{(rest of matrix)} & & \end{bmatrix}$$

where

$$\sum_{i=1}^{m}a_i\lambda_a=\sum_{i=1}^{m}b_i\lambda_b,$$

λ_a and λ_b being the respective traffic volumes for the first two rows (query or update).

A PROPERTY OF THE OPTIMAL FILE ALLOCATION

In this section, we examine the behavior of the cost function as additional file nodes are added. In particular, we consider a graph such as Figure 1, where each vertex is identified with a file assignment (denoted by a binary vector having 1's in those positions corresponding to file nodes, 0's elsewhere). Associated with each vertex is the corresponding value of the cost function (not shown in Figure 1). For mathematical convenience the null vertex is assigned infinite cost. The edges of the graph are directed paths corresponding to the addition of a single file node to the previous assignment. The graph is conveniently arranged in levels where the vertices at the kth level represent all k-node file assignments.

We demonstrate the significant property of this graph (which we shall call the "cost" graph) that if a given vertex has a cost less than the cost of any vertex along the paths leading to it, then the sequence of costs encountered along any one of these paths decreases monotonically. Thus, in order to find the optimal allocation policy, it is sufficient to follow every path of the cost graph until the cost increases, and no further. Because of this property, only a small subset of the possible assignments need be tested, compared with the exhaustive search procedure in which 2^n different file allocations must be evaluated.

The monotonicity will be exhibited in two stages: first, for the case of two steps through the graph, and then for the general case.

Let $I \sim X$, where $X \subset I$, denote the index set I with the elements of set X removed.

Consider an arbitrary file assignment corresponding to index set I, and assume the nodes are so numbered that $I = [1, 2, \ldots, r]$. We proceed to show:

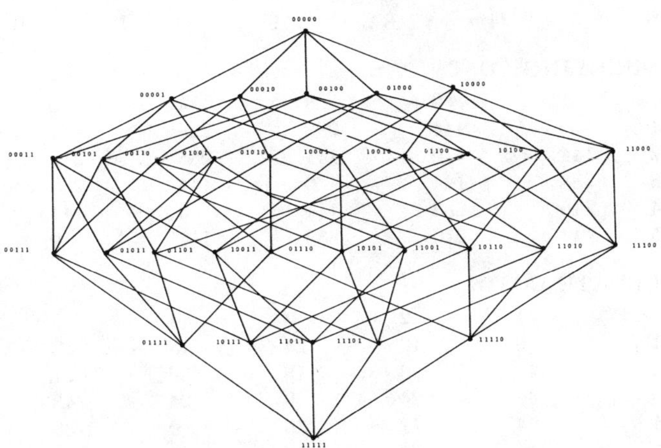

Figure 1—Graph of the allocation process

Lemma:

If $C(I) \leq C(I \sim \{k\})$ for $k = 1, 2$, then $C(I \sim \{k\} \leq C(I \sim \{1, 2\})$ for $k = 1, 2$.

Proof of Lemma:

The cost function can be written, in general,

$$C(I \sim X) = \sum_{k \epsilon I \sim X} U_k + \sum_{j=1}^{n} \lambda_j \min_{k \epsilon I \sim X} d_{jk}$$

Thus

$$C(I) - C(I \sim \{1\}) = U_1 - \sum_{j=1}^{n} \lambda_j \Delta_j$$

where

$$\Delta_j = \min_{k \epsilon I \sim \{1\}} d_{jk} - \min_{k \epsilon I} d_{jk}$$

Also

$$C(I \sim \{2\}) - C(I \sim \{1, 2\}) = U_1 - \sum_{j=1}^{n} \lambda_j \Delta_j'$$

where

$$\Delta_j' = \min_{k \epsilon I \sim \{1,2\}} d_{jk} - \min_{k \epsilon I \sim \{2\}} d_{jk}$$

Consider the difference

$$\Delta_j' - \Delta_j = \min_{k \epsilon I \sim \{1,2\}} d_{jk} + \min_{k \epsilon I} d_{jk} - \min_{k \epsilon I \sim \{2\}} d_{jk} - \min_{k \epsilon I \sim \{1\}} d_{jk}$$

We have

$$\min_{k \epsilon I} d_{jk} = \min(\min_{k \epsilon I \sim \{1\}} d_{jk}, \min_{k \epsilon I \sim \{2\}} d_{jk})$$

$$\min_{k \epsilon I \sim \{1,2\}} d_{jk} \geq \max(\min_{k \epsilon I \sim \{1\}} d_{jk}, \min_{k \epsilon I \sim \{2\}} d_{jk})$$

Therefore

$$\Delta_j' - \Delta_j \geq 0, \text{ that is } \Delta_j' \geq \Delta_j,$$

and so

$$C(I \sim \{2\}) - C(I \sim \{1, 2\}) \leq C(I) - C(I \sim \{1\})$$

thus,

$$C(I) \leq C(I \sim \{1\})$$

implies that

$$C(I \sim \{2\}) \leq C(I \sim \{1, 2\})$$

By a mere permutation of indexes we may likewise prove that

$$C(I) \leq C(I \sim \{2\})$$

implies that

$$C(I\sim\{1\})\leq C(I\sim\{1,2\})$$

and so the lemma is true.

By means of this lemma, we can now prove the general theorem:

Theorem 2:

Given an index set $X\subseteq I$ containing r elements, and having the property

$$C(I)\leq C(I\sim\{x\}) \text{ for each } x\epsilon X$$

then for every sequence $R^{(1)}, R^{(2)}, \ldots, R^{(r)}$ of subsets of X such that $R^{(k)}$ has k elements, and $R^{(k)}\subset R^{(k+1)}$ it is true that

$$C(I)\leq C(I\sim R^{(1)})\leq C(I\sim R^{(2)})$$
$$\leq C(I\sim R^{(3)})\leq\cdots\leq C(I\sim R^{(r)})$$

Proof: (by induction)

The first inequality above is given in the hypothesis. Since $R^{(2)}$ has two elements the second inequality follows from the lemma. It may thus be taken as hypothesis to prove the third, and so on. Each inequality proved can be used together with the lemma to prove the inequality to its right.

Observations:

If we take $X=I$ in the theorem, then it states that along any path in the cost graph from the null vertex (which we have assigned infinite cost) to the vertex corresponding to I, cost decreases monotonically from one vertex to the next, providing of course that index set I satisfies the hypothesis of the theorem. The monotonic decreasing property can also be shown to hold in the reverse direction; i.e., for paths from the vertex $\{1, 2, \ldots, n\}$ to the optimum.*

APPLICATION TO FILE ALLOCATION

The theorem just proved provides a test that is useful in determining the minimum cost allocation of file copies to nodes of the network. Referring to the cost graph (Figure 1), let us define an "antecedent" of an arbitrary vertex v as a vertex which has a connection to v from the next lower level, and a "successor" of v as a vertex connected to v at the next higher level. An antecedent contains the file nodes of v less one node, while each successor contains the nodes of v plus one additional node. A vertex at the rth level of the graph has r antecedents, and $(n-r)$ successors, where n is the number of nodes in the network. (Note that, for clarity, we use the term "node" in referring to the computer network, and the term "vertex" with respect to the cost graph.)

We shall also define a "local optimum" of the cost graph as a vertex which is less costly than all of its antecedents and successors. Clearly, the global optimum we seek belongs to the set of local optima of the graph.

The theorem permits us to discover all the local optima without computing the cost of every vertex, for each path leading from the 0 level to a local optimum must give rise to a monotonically decreasing sequence of costs. Whenever an increase is encountered in a step forward through the graph, that path can be abandoned since it cannot lead to a local (or global) optimum. A "path-tracing" routine which evaluates each possible sequence of node additions in this way is certain to produce the minimum value of $C(I)$. The amount of computation needed to extract the minimum will increase with the number of local optima, and with the number of nodes in the optimal configuration.

A computer algorithm can be implemented in several different ways to select file nodes one at a time up to the optimum configuration. One approach is to follow all paths in parallel through the cost graph, stepping

INPUT PARAMETERS — COST PER MEGABYTE SHIPPED

		QUERY TRAFFIC	UPDATE TRAFFIC	FILE NODES 1	2	3	4	5
U	1	24	2	0	6	12	9	6
S	2	24	3	6	0	6	12	9
E	3	24	4	12	6	0	6	12
R	4	24	6	9	12	6	0	6
S	5	24	8	6	9	12	6	0

QUERYING COSTS

	1	2	3	4	5
1	0	144	288	216	144
2	144	0	144	288	216
3	288	144	0	144	288
4	216	288	144	0	144
5	144	216	288	144	0

UPDATE COSTS

	1	2	3	4	5
1	0	12	24	18	12
2	18	0	18	36	27
3	48	24	0	24	48
4	54	72	36	0	36
5	48	72	96	48	0

Figure 2—A five-node example

* A reviewer pointed out this generalization.

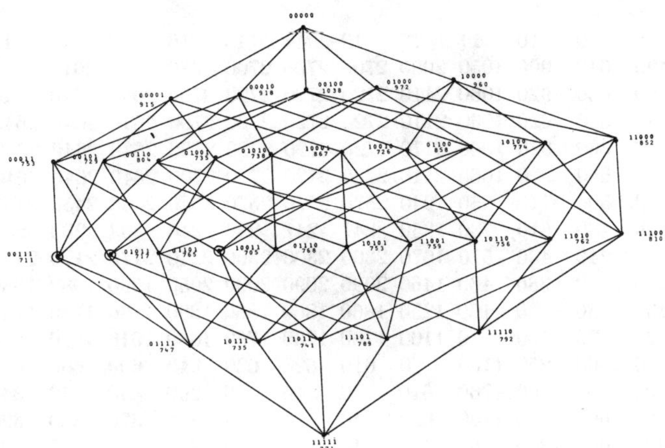

Figure 3—The cost graph for the example.
Local optima are circled

one level per iteration. This method is computationally efficient, but may require a great deal of storage in a large problem. Alternatively, a program can be written to trace systematically one path at a time. Such a technique uses less storage, but may require redundant calculations since many different paths intersect each vertex.

EXAMPLES

We consider a five-node network with query and update parameters, and cost matrix as in Figure 2. Figure 3 shows the file node cost graph, and indicates the optimal allocations. This small-scale example illustrates the monotonicity of the cost function along paths leading to a local optimum.

Note that the matrix $\{d_{jk}\}$ is symmetric and has zero elements along the main diagonal. This is a plausible condition in a practical case, but is not required in any way by the theorems proven here.

As a second example, we postulate the ARPA computer network and its traffic matrix as given by Kleinrock.[7] In order to treat this case, which is not initially posed as a centralized data base configuration, we make the following rather arbitrary assumptions:

(1) All the resources of the network represented in the traffic matrix are gathered into one large file, copies of which are to be allocated to a subset of the nodes.

(2) The query traffic (Figure 4) from each user to the file is as given under the "node output" column in Kleinrock's table. If the user is accessing a program, we may think of this "query" traffic as comprising the command messages he must send in order to run the program, plus the program output sent back to him. (Note: Kleinrock does not give figures for each node's use of its own facilities.)

(3) "Update" traffic, which causes modification of programs and data in all copies of the file, is a fixed percentage of the query traffic defined in (2). The update/query ratio is the same for each user, and is varied as a parameter in the computer runs described below.

(4) The "cost" of communicating between two network nodes is as shown in Figure 4. The quantities given here are roughly the straight-line distances between nodes. Thus, the cost function to be minimized is the total amount of "flow" in the network, i.e., the product of message length in bits, multiplied by the distance through which the message must travel on a direct path to its destination, summed over all messages. In this view an update message is assumed to be sent separately to each file location, rather than relayed.

Assumptions (1)-(4) ignore the network communication links as configured by Kleinrock. Ordinarily these would determine the cost matrix. Substituting "distance" for "cost," as done here, might be expedient in a preliminary analysis to allocate resources prior to a topological design of the network. We employ the ARPA data primarily because it tests our model on a problem involving many nodes. In addition, we should like to encourage speculation on the concept of multiple copies of a resource (data or programs), and whether such a facility is attractive in future ARPA-like networks.

Figure 5 summarizes the file allocation experiments conducted using this data, in which the proportion of update traffic to query traffic was varied from 100 percent to 10 percent in steps. As expected, only single node allocations are indicated when the two types of traffic are equal. As a smaller volume of update traffic is generated, multiple node solutions begin to appear. The copies of the file are widely distributed geographically, and the single node solution is centrally located. However, such features result from the particular traffic distribution assumed, and are not generalizations valid for every case.

It is interesting to note the large number of local optima generated (see Figure 5). Because certain ARPA sites, e.g., MIT, BBN, Harvard, and Lincoln Laboratories, are very near one another, if one occurs in a local optimum one of its neighbors may be substituted for it to produce a second configuration that

COST PER MEGABYTE SHIPPED

		QUERY TRAFFIC	FILE NODES 1	2	3	4	5	6	7	8	9	10	11	12	13	14	15	16	17	18	19
U	1	8	0	75	75	75	75	350	450	490	640	900	1050	2080	2700	2700	2700	2670	2610	2610	2610
S	2	21	75	0	5	5	5	300	400	480	660	920	1060	2110	2720	2720	2720	2700	2640	2640	2640
E	3	7	75	5	0	5	5	300	400	480	660	920	1060	2110	2720	2720	2720	2700	2640	2640	2640
R	4	6	75	5	5	0	5	300	400	480	660	920	1060	2110	2720	2720	2720	2700	2640	2640	2640
S	5	10	75	5	5	5	0	300	400	480	660	920	1060	2110	2720	2720	2720	2700	2640	2640	2640
	6	4	350	300	300	300	300	0	160	280	500	710	850	1940	2570	2570	2570	2520	2450	2450	2450
	7	3	450	400	400	400	400	160	0	190	430	610	730	1850	247	247	247	240	233	233	233
	8	10	490	480	480	480	480	280	190	0	240	430	570	1670	2300	2300	2300	2240	2170	2170	2170
	9	9	640	660	660	660	660	500	430	240	0	280	430	1460	2090	2090	2090	2050	1980	1980	1980
	10	50	900	920	920	920	920	710	610	430	280	0	160	1250	1860	1860	1860	1800	1730	1730	1730
	11	3	1050	1060	1060	1060	1060	850	730	570	430	160	0	1160	1760	1760	1760	1680	1610	1610	1610
	12	26	2080	2110	2110	2110	2110	1940	1850	1670	1460	1250	1160	0	610	620	620	640	600	600	600
	13	20	2700	2720	2720	2720	2720	2570	2470	2300	2090	1860	1760	610	0	40	40	290	340	340	340
	14	21	2700	2720	2720	2720	2720	2570	2470	2300	2090	1860	1760	620	40	0	5	250	320	320	320
	15	3	2700	2720	2720	2720	2720	2570	2470	2300	2090	1860	1760	620	40	5	0	250	320	320	320
	16	5	2670	2700	2700	2700	2700	2520	2400	2240	2050	1800	1680	640	290	250	250	0	80	80	80
	17	4	2610	2640	2640	2640	2640	2450	2330	2170	1980	1730	1610	600	340	320	320	80	0	10	10
	18	8	2610	2640	2640	2640	2640	2450	2330	2170	1980	1730	1610	600	340	320	320	80	10	0	5
	19	7	2610	2640	2640	2640	2640	2450	2330	2170	1980	1730	1610	600	340	320	320	80	10	5	0

Figure 4—The ARPA example. The locations of the nodes (from Kleinrock[7]) are: (1) Hanover, N.H., (2)-(5) Boston Area, (6) Murray Hill, N.J., (7) Washington, D.C., (8) Pittsburgh, Pa., (9) Ann Arbor, Michigan, (10) Urbana, Illinois, (11) St. Louis, Mo., (12) Salt Lake City, Utah, (13)-(15) San Francisco Bay Area, (16) Santa Barbara, California, (17)-(19) Los Angeles Area

is also locally optimum. Most of the local optima are due to this phenomenom, suggesting that greater computational efficiency would have resulted from lumping neighboring sites into a single network node for an initial application of the algorithm, followed by a stage of finer calculations. Such artifices are hardly necessary in problems of this size, however. The sequence of six runs depicted in Figure 5 was carried out on an IBM 360/91 in less than ten seconds, including Fortran compilation.

EXTENSIONS

Path tracing on a related problem

One feature of the path-tracing technique is its versatility. It can be applied to problems that do not fit the linear programming framework. As one example consider the following modification of the file allocation model. The cost function as defined in the text assumes that the expense of transmitting an update message to all copies of the file is the sum of the costs of communicating with each copy separately, as if a distinct message had to be sent from the updater to every file node.

Actually, the preferred mode of operation would be to relay the message through the network in the most economical manner. The resulting cost is less than that incurred by sending duplicate messages. It is the cost associated with the most economical subtree of the network that contains the originating node and the file nodes (see Figure 6). This new cost function defined when update costs are calculated in this way is nonlinear in a very complex way. Yet the path-tracing algorithm can still be applied to the allocation problem. We no longer have the assurance provided by Theorem 2, which guarantees that the method will generate the optimal allocation. However, the cost function behaves in much the same manner as before. It still consists of two parts: an update (and fixed cost) term that increases as additional file copies are allocated, and a query term that decreases with additional copies. The algorithm may be heuristic in the new framework, but with only slight modification it can be programmed to determine at least allocations of the type we have called "local optima," of which the true optimum is one.

Update/Query Percent	Optimal Allocation	Cost	#Local Minima
10	2, 10, 14	117, 544	140
20	9, 14	188, 738	88
30	10, 14	242, 546	88
40	10, 12	291, 754	77
100	10	427, 460	19

Figure 5—Results for the ARPA example

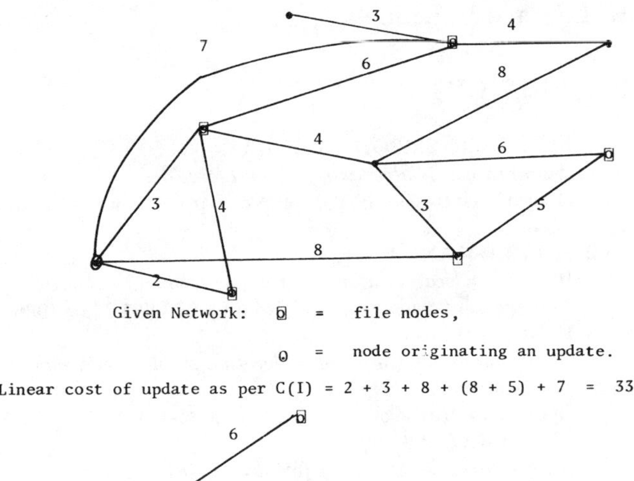

Figure 6—Most economical subtree for relaying an update message

Heuristic modification of the path-tracing routine

If the optimal solution to the allocation problem consists of many network nodes then the general rule of following every monotonically decreasing path in the cost graph may be computationally too expensive. For example, if the optimum contains 40 nodes then at least $2^{40} \doteq 10^{12}$ values of the cost function must be evaluated. In order to decrease the amount of computation, it is necessary to sacrifice optimality for speed. We suggest several methods by which this may be done in a reasonable manner.

Assume that the cost graph is being searched level-by-level (i.e., in parallel). At each level, the vertices which are lower in cost than their antecedents are recorded. We call these vertices "admissible" and denote them by the set A_k at the kth level. We wish to carry only a limited number of the members of A_k into the $(k+1)$th stage. One plausible selection rule is to keep the vertices having the lowest cost. Alternatively, we may reason that if two assignments are similar (i.e., differ in only a few file nodes) then probably their union will also lie on a monotonic cost path, and it would be redundant to trace paths through both. In this view, we want to select the most "dissimilar" vertices from A_k. Several techniques are available to do this selection. One method, previously used in pattern recognition, is the following. Order the members of A_k arbitrarily, specify a threshold τ (a parameter), and examine the members of A_k in order. Denote by A_k' the subset being formed. The first member of A_k' is the first member of A_k, say a_1. The next member of A_k' (denoted a_2) is the first member of A_k which differs from a_1 by at least τ units. Next, test for an a_3 which differs from both a_1 and a_2 by at least τ and so on. If A_k' has too many members, or too few, the routine may be repeated with τ larger, or smaller, respectively. The set A_k' is used to generate A_{k+1}, which is in turn thinned down to A_{k+1}'.

A third method has actually been programmed and compared with the general search technique. The procedure is to do complete path-tracing (applying Theorem 2) up to a level of the cost graph at which set A_k begins to get too large. From this level on, only the most "promising" paths are followed. For example, as programmed the cost graph is completely evaluated through the second level (2-file nodes per vertex). From each admissible second level vertex only a single path is followed; namely, that path which gives minimal cost at each succeeding level. Since this program only has one-step look ahead, the optimum may be missed. In sample runs on the ARPA problem, the optimum was always found (for each value of the update/query parameter), although local optima were sometimes overlooked.

This heuristic program was also tested on the ARPA configuration using the revised cost function described above, i.e., a function which assumes that updates are relayed between file notes in the most economical manner. Use of a simplified program is called for in this case; the heuristic program required 12 minutes to repeat the five runs of Figure 5, which were performed in under ten seconds using the linear cost relationship. Figure 7 shows the allocations produced by this experiment. These assignments may not be global optima. They do satisfy our definition of a local optimum. Note that, as expected, for the same traffic more copies of the

Update/Query Percent	Optimal Allocation (Nodes)	Cost
10	2, 6, 8, 9, 10, 12, 13, 14, 16, 18	38, 285
20	2, 8, 10, 12, 14	105, 800
30	2, 8, 10, 12, 14	171, 225
40	8, 10, 12	227, 340
100	10	427, 460

Figure 7—Allocation results using the nonlinear cost model (ARPA network)

file are assigned if updates are relayed. In addition, total cost is reduced markedly under conditions of low update traffic, indicating the importance of including the more complex cost relations in the model.

CONCLUSION

The analytical properties of a linear-cost model of an information network have been investigated. The proportions of update traffic to query traffic generated by the users of a given file in the network were shown to determine an upper bound on the number of copies of the file present in the least-cost network. In addition, a basic property of the cost function was demonstrated and shown to justify a path-tracing procedure for determining the optimal assignment of copies of the file to nodes of the network.

The model, while simple, expresses relevant features of the tradeoff between the costs of querying and updating in the network. Presumably, the general properties derived apply at least approximately when more complex models are considered.

ACKNOWLEDGMENT

Dr. M. E. Senko first pointed out to the author the need for an allocation model which would distinguish between the query and update activity in a network. The work reported here owes additional debts to the encouragement and commentary of Drs. C. P. Wang, H. Ling and V. Lum.

REFERENCES

1 M A EFROYMSON T L RAY
A branch-bound algorithm for plant location
Operations Research Vol 14 No 3 pp 361-368 May-June 1966

2 E FELDMAN et al
Warehouse location under continuous economies of scale
Management Science Vol 12 No 9 pp 670-684 May 1966

3 K SPIELBERG
Algorithm for the simple plant-location problem with some side conditions
Operations Research Vol 17 1969 pp 85-111

4 W D FRAZER
An approximate algorithm for plant location under piecewise linear concave costs
IBM Research Report RC 1875 IBM Watson Research Center Yorktown Heights N Y July 25 1967

5 W W CHU
Optimal file allocation in a multiple computer system
IEEE Trans on Computers Vol C-18 No 10 October 1969

6 V K M WHITNEY
A study of optimal file assignment and communication network configuration in remote-access computer message processing and communication systems
SEL Technical Report No 48 Systems Engrg La
Dept of Elect Engrg University of Michigan September 1970 (PhD Dissertation)

7 L KLEINROCK
Models for computer networks
Proc International Conference on Comm Boulder Colorado pp 2.9-2.16 June 1969

Management Science D.F. Shanno
Operations Research Editor

Some Theorems to Aid in Solving the File Allocation Problem

Enrique Grapa and Geneva G. Belford
University of Illinois at Urbana-Champaign

The file allocation problem – i.e. the problem of finding the optimal set of network sites at which to locate copies of a file – is known to be, in general, polynomial complete. Heuristics and other aids to finding optimal, or near-optimal, solutions are therefore much needed. In this paper we present three theorems which can be applied a priori to indicate that certain sites should (or should not) be included in an optimal allocation.

Key Words and Phrases: File allocation, computer networks, distributed data management
CR Categories: 4.33

This work was performed as part of Contract DCA100-75-C-0021 with the Command and Control Technical Center – WWMCCS ADP Directorate of the Defense Communications Agency.

Authors' address: Center for Advanced Computation, University of Illinois at Urbana-Champaign, Urbana, IL 61801.

Introduction

As computer networks come into common use, the concept of the distributed database – i.e. distributing the files among the various sites – becomes increasingly attractive. A problem which immediately arises is how to best allocate the files among the sites. A number of researchers have studied this problem over the last several years, but there are still questions of a pragmatic nature to be answered.

The earliest work on the problem seems to be that of Chu [3, 4]. He formulated a simple model and defined the problem in terms of minimizing total cost, with constraints on availability and response. Chu showed that his optimization problem may be solved as a standard zero-one integer programming problem. Although this technique is straightforward, it is computationally expensive. Casey [1], in the context of a somewhat different model, suggests a search procedure for finding a minimum. Although Casey presents some theorems for truncating the search, the computation still generally grows exponentially with the number of sites. (Indeed, the general problem has been shown [5] to be polynomial complete.)

Exponential growth of the computation means that the problem becomes impossible to solve for even moderate-sized networks. Casey notes that a program run in the 360/91 took less than 10 seconds to solve six different optimal allocation problems for a network of 19 sites. (This time included the Fortran compilation.) Each additional site multiplies the computation time by a factor of 2. Thus, if we assume that it takes about 2 seconds to optimally allocate a file in a 19-site network, it will take over an hour in a 30-site network, about 48 days in a 40-site network, and about 136 years in a 50-site network.

In an attempt to decrease the size of the problem, Urano et al. [8] have shown that the sites may be partitioned into sets of neighboring sites in such a way that at most one member of each set should be included in an optimal allocation. More recently, Chandy and Hewes [2] have reformulated what is essentially Casey's model as a simple linear integer programming problem. They find that solving the problem by a standard linear programming algorithm (*without* the integrality constraints) leads in many cases to correct integer solutions. (The same phenomenon has been noted in similar optimization problems [7] and hence appears to be more than just an artifact of the particular examples tried.)

We have attempted to decrease the size of the problem by a different approach, namely, by deriving rules for determining a priori that certain sites will (or will not) be included in an optimal allocation. Three theorems providing rules of this sort are presented in this note. In the next section, we state and prove these theorems. The last section includes some examples and further discussion.

The Theorems

We use Casey's notation and formulation of the problem [1]. Let

I = index set of sites with a copy of the file
n = number of sites in the network
Ψ_j = update load originating at site j
λ_j = query load originating at site j

d_{jk} = cost of communication of one query unit from site j to site k

d'_{jk} = cost of communication of one update unit from site j to site k

σ_k = storage cost of file at site k.

An optimal allocation for a given file is then defined as an index set I which minimizes the cost function

$$C(I) = \sum_{j=1}^{n} \left[\sum_{k \in I} \Psi_j d'_{jk} + \lambda_j \min_{k \in I} d_{jk} \right] + \sum_{k \in I} \sigma_k.$$

For simplicity we assume that $d'_{jj} = d_{jj} = 0$ for all j. Thus we neglect the costs of queries and updates applied locally. Relaxing this assumption, however, as well as making other minor alterations in the formulation, requires only small compensating alterations in our theorems.

Our first theorem essentially states that if the cost of having a local file copy is smaller than the smallest possible cost of sending the locally generated queries elsewhere, then a local copy should unquestionably be included in the optimal allocation. The cost of storing and updating a copy at site i is an important quantity; we denote it by Z_i. That is, we let

$$Z_i = \sigma_i + \sum_{j=1}^{n} \Psi_j d'_{ji}.$$

THEOREM 1. *All optimal allocations will include site i if*

$$\lambda_i \min_{j \neq i} d_{ij} > Z_i. \tag{1}$$

PROOF. Assume that site i satisfies (1) and that there is an optimal allocation I which does not include i. Let $I' = I \cup \{i\}$. By straightforward computation, $C(I') = C(I) + Z_i + S$, where $S = \sum_{j=1}^{n} \lambda_j(\min_{k \in I'} d_{jk} - \min_{k \in I} d_{jk})$. Clearly each term in S is nonpositive, since taking a minimum over a larger set cannot increase that minimum. Furthermore, since for $j = i$ the contribution to S is $-\lambda_i \min_{k \in I} d_{ik}$, it follows that $S \leq -\lambda_i \min_{k \in I} d_{ik} \leq -\lambda_i \min_{j \neq i} d_{ij}$. Therefore (from (1)), $S + Z_i < 0$, and hence $C(I') < C(I)$. This contradicts the assumed optimality of I and proves the theorem. □

Our second theorem gives the other side of the coin. If it costs more to maintain a local copy than we can possibly save by having one, then we do not want one.

THEOREM 2. *No optimal allocation including more than one site will include site i if*

$$Z_i > \sum_{j=1}^{n} \lambda_j \left(\max_k d_{jk} - d_{ji} \right). \tag{2}$$

PROOF. Given an allocation $I \neq \varnothing$, let $I' = I \cup \{i\}$. Just as in the proof of Theorem 1, $C(I') = C(I) + Z_i + S$. Making a term by term comparison, we see that the right side of inequality (2) is greater than or equal to $-S$ provided that

$$\max_k d_{jk} - d_{ji} + \min_{k \in I'} d_{jk} - \min_{k \in I} d_{jk} \geq 0 \tag{3}$$

for all j. Examining (3), we see that if $\min_{k \in I'} d_{jk} = d_{ji}$, then the second and third terms cancel and (3) is clearly satisfied. Otherwise, the last two terms cancel and (3) is again satisfied. It then follows from (2) that $Z_i + S > 0$. Hence $C(I') > C(I)$, and the theorem is proved. □

Theorems 1 and 2 can be summarized as follows. Let

$$m_i = \lambda_i \min_{j \neq i} d_{ij} \text{ and } M_i = \sum_{j=1}^{n} \lambda_j \left(\max_k d_{jk} - d_{ji} \right).$$

Then for each i the real line is partitioned by m_i and M_i into three regions, as shown in Figure 1. If Z_i falls in region 1, then it should unquestionably be included in any optimal allocation. If it falls in region 3, it will generally be excluded. An exceptional case is when all sites fall in region 3, i.e. satisfy inequality (2). In this case, all optimal allocations will be single-copy ones, and we need only choose the best of these. Sites whose costs Z_i fall in region 2 (including the boundary points) must be considered further.

Fig. 1. Partitioning of the real line into three regions by inequalities (1) and (2).

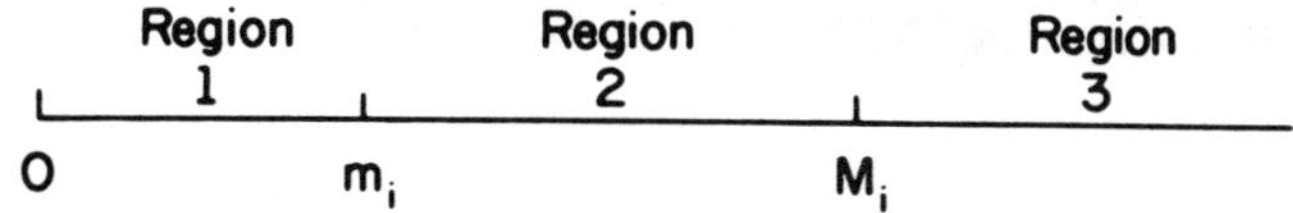

One other comment should be made. If network transmission costs are independent of distance, so that $d_{ij} = d$ for all $i \neq j$, then $m_i = M_i = \lambda_i d$, and region 2 collapses to a single boundary point. Unless the cost Z_i of some site lies on the boundary, every site is a priori either included or excluded. Immediately we see that the set of sites in region 1 forms the optimal allocation unless the exceptional case noted above obtains. Computation is therefore reduced to a minimum (essentially n cost evaluations) for many real network environments, including that of the ARPA network. There are, of course, real cost differentials incurred in the longer lines between sites, but from the user's point of view it is the network charging policy that matters.

Our third theorem is somewhat in the spirit of the approach to simplification taken by Urano et al. [8]. However, Urano's results depend on a more complex model, involving "relay costs" at network nodes and restrictive hypotheses on the d_{ij}. Also, instead of determining that no more than one of some group of geographically close sites can be included in an optimal allocation, we show that certain sites may a priori be precluded from being in an optimal allocation by the existence of a "better" site nearby. Thus again we have a theorem which allows us to eliminate initially certain sites from any further consideration in the search for the optimum.

THEOREM 3. *A site i cannot be included in any optimal allocation if there exists another site k in the network such that*

$$Z_i - Z_k > \sum_{j=1}^{n} \lambda_j(d_{jk} - d_{ji})_+, \quad (4)$$

$$\text{where } (f)_+ = \begin{cases} f & \text{if } f \geq 0, \\ 0 & \text{if } f < 0. \end{cases}$$

This theorem is most readily proved in two parts. We give these parts as two preliminary lemmas. As in the previous theorems, let I be an arbitrary allocation (but not including i or k). Let $I' = I \cup \{k\}$ and $I'' = I' \cup \{i\}$. The first lemma states that, if site i is sufficiently costly, then adding site i to an allocation which already includes k increases the total cost.

LEMMA 1. *If site i satisfies* $Z_i > \sum_{j=1}^{n} \lambda_j(d_{jk} - d_{ji})_+$ *for some site k in the network, then* $C(I'') > C(I')$.

PROOF. By straightforward computation,

$$C(I'') - C(I') = Z_i + \sum_{j=1}^{n} \lambda_j \left(\min_{m \in I''} d_{jm} - \min_{m \in I'} d_{jm} \right).$$

As in the proof of Theorem 2, the lemma is proved if, for all j,

$$(d_{jk} - d_{ji})_+ + \min_{m \in I''} d_{jm} - \min_{m \in I'} d_{jm} \geq 0. \quad (5)$$

The inequality (5) follows easily from consideration of two cases. (i) If $\min_{m \in I''} d_{jm} \neq d_{ji}$, then the last two terms cancel and clearly the left side is positive. (ii) If $\min_{m \in I''} d_{jm} = d_{ji}$, then (5) reads

$$d_{jk} - d_{ji} + d_{ji} - \min_{m \in I'} d_{jm} \geq 0,$$

which again is clearly satisfied. □

Our second lemma says that, if (4) is satisfied, replacing site k by site i in an allocation also increases the cost.

LEMMA 2. *Let* $I''' = I \cup \{i\}$. *If sites i and k satisfy inequality* (4), *then* $C(I''') > C(I')$.

PROOF. By straightforward computation,

$$C(I''') - C(I') = Z_i - Z_k + \sum_{j=1}^{n} \lambda_j \left(\min_{m \in I'''} d_{jm} - \min_{m \in I'} d_{jm} \right).$$

As in the preceding lemma, the proof follows from showing that

$$\sum_j \lambda_j(d_{jk} - d_{ji})_+ \geq \sum_j \lambda_j \left(\min_{m \in I'} d_{jm} - \min_{m \in I'''} d_{jm} \right).$$

And this inequality holds if, for all j, we have

$$(d_{jk} - d_{ji})_+ - \min_{m \in I'} d_{jm} + \min_{m \in I'''} d_{jm} \geq 0. \quad (6)$$

Inequality (6) can be verified by checking cases. (i) If $\min_{m \in I''} d_{jm} \neq d_{ji}$ or d_{jk}, then the last two terms cancel and (6) obviously holds. (Recall that $I'' = I \cup \{i, k\}$.) (ii) If $\min_{m \in I''} d_{jm} = d_{ji}$, then (6) becomes $d_{jk} - d_{ji} - \min_{m \in I'} d_{jm} + d_{ji} \geq 0$. (iii) If $\min_{m \in I''} d_{jm} = d_{jk}$, then the left side of (6) becomes $0 - d_{jk} + \min_{m \in I'''} d_{jm}$, which must be nonnegative by the assumption defining this case. □

PROOF OF THEOREM 3. If inequality (4) holds, then Lemmas 1 and 2 both apply. Since Lemma 2 says that an allocation containing i is always improved by replacing i by k, and Lemma 1 eliminates any allocation containing both i and k from being optimal, nothing more is needed. □

Theorem 3 looks particularly simple if all transmission costs are equal. In this case, inequality (4) becomes

$$Z_i > Z_k + \lambda_i d. \quad (4')$$

The interpretation of Theorem 3 is transparent in this form. We do not want a copy at site i if it is cheaper to maintain a copy at site k and ship i's queries there. (An analogous, only slightly more complicated statement, can be read from (4). The summation includes all savings obtainable if queries can be sent to site i instead of to site k.) In the case of equal transmission costs, however, any site i which satisfies (4′) also satisfies the condition for Theorem 2. Thus it is already excluded, except in the singular case that (2) is satisfied by all sites. In this latter case, (4′) may still be useful in the determination of the best single-site allocation.

In view of the simple interpretation given above, it might be asked in what sense the theorem eliminates neighboring sites, as claimed. Suppose sites 1, 2, . . . , p are close together and the remaining n-p sites are scattered and relatively distant from the first group. The largest d_{jk} (or d_{ji}) will then be those with $j = p + 1, \ldots, n$, for $i, k = 1, 2, \ldots, p$. But the *differences* $(d_{jk} - d_{ji})$ will be small in magnitude. Thus the right side of (4) will tend also to be small. Suppose that Z_1 is much less than Z_i for $i = 2, \ldots, p$. Then (4) is likely to be satisfied for one or more members of the group $i = 2, \ldots, p$, and such sites will therefore be eliminated from any optimal allocation by the nearby site 1.

Examples and Further Discussion

In order to assess their value, we have applied our theorems to several of the examples in Casey's paper [1]. Casey assumes throughout that it costs the same to transmit a query as an update ($d'_{ij} = d_{ij}$), that transmission costs are symmetric ($d_{ij} = d_{ji}$), and that storage costs are zero. In Casey's 5-site example, the data are as follows. The matrix of transmission costs d_{ij} is

0	6	12	9	6
6	0	6	12	9
12	6	0	6	12
9	12	6	0	6
6	9	12	6	0

All λ_j are 24, and the vector of Ψ_j is (2, 3, 4, 6, 8). In order to apply Theorems 1 and 2, we tabulate Z_i, m_i, and M_i for all sites i.

Site	1	2	3	4	5
Z_i	168	180	174	126	123
m_i	144	144	144	144	144
M_i	648	648	576	648	648

Theorem 1 then states that both sites 4 and 5 should be included in any optimal allocation. Theorem 2 does not eliminate any sites, so the effect of adding sites 1, 2, 3 would have to be checked. However, the problem has been reduced from an optimization among 32 ($=2^5$) choices to one among 8 ($=2^3$). (The optimal allocation I is {1, 4, 5}.) It is virtually obvious by inspection that costs (Z_i) are sufficiently similar and query loads and distances sufficiently large that Theorem 3 will not be useful. More will be said about this later.

As another example of the usefulness of Theorem 1, consider Casey's 5-site example reduced to four sites by the elimination of site 5. The table of Z_i, m_i, and M_i is then

Site	1	2	3	4
Z_i	120	108	78	78
m_i	144	144	144	144
M_i	504	576	576	504

Since for all i, $Z_i < m_i$, Theorem 1 says that the optimal allocation consists of all four sites, and no further computation is necessary.

In another of Casey's examples—the 19-site ARPA network example with d_{ij} equal to distance—Theorem 3 does turn out to be useful. This is what is to be expected in a geographically widespread network in which there are groups of sites that are very close together (e.g. in the Boston and Los Angeles areas). We do not give the details (the interested reader may consult the data and notation in Casey's paper), but we find that Theorem 3 eliminates six sites. Specifically, sites 3, 4, and 5 are excluded by site 2, site 15 by site 14, and sites 17 and 19 by site 18. This reduces by a factor of 64 the maximum size of the search required to find the optimum.

The reader might question whether it is worthwhile, in general, to carry out the computations needed to check the conditions for our theorems. In this connection, we point out that the costs Z_i are needed in any cost optimization algorithm, and it only increases efficiency to precompute them. Computation of m_i for $i = 1, \ldots, n$ is easy, requiring $O(n^2)$ operations altogether (n to find the minimum d_{ij} for each i). Application of Theorem 1 is therefore highly advisable since for each site successfully identified as satisfying inequality (1) the optimal search is reduced by a factor of $\frac{1}{2}$. Furthermore, it may happen that the set of sites satisfying (1) forms an acceptible suboptimal allocation, and so no further search is necessary.

Computation of M_i is more time-consuming, requiring $O(n^2)$ operations for *each* i. It may be that one would only want to try Theorem 2 selectively, say when Z_i (or Z_i/λ_i) is "big." Testing for Theorem 3 is even more time-consuming because of the dependence on k. However, the quantities involved in the test (the right sides of inequality (4)) are sufficiently similar to M_i that it is not difficult to work out an efficient scheme for carrying out the computations needed for Theorems 2 and 3 together. Again, to save time one can readily eliminate from the process many cases where checking inequality (4) is (or is likely to be) useless. For example, when $Z_i < Z_k + \lambda_i d_{ik}$, (4) clearly cannot be satisfied. This simple condition suffices to show conclusively that Theorem 3 is of no help in the 5-site example discussed above.

Our intuitive idea of Theorem 3—the elimination of more expensive neighboring sites by the existence of a given site—can be used to identify situations when Theorem 3 is likely to be useful. Thus, if a number of network sites are clumped together (in the sense of small d_{ij}), then the "cheapest" of these (small Z_i/λ_i) may serve to eliminate others of the clump. Notice also that the minimization carried out in the test for Theorem 1 identifies the "closest" site to site i in the sense of smallest d_{ij}. This information can be saved and used to identify promising pairs for the Theorem 3 test.

The quantity Z_i/λ_i appeared above as a measure of the cheapness of site i. Since an optimal allocation is likely to include the cheaper sites, this quantity is also a rough measure of the probability that site i will be included in an optimal allocation. We have successfully used Z_i/λ_i as a heuristic "search factor" to expedite search procedures for optimal or near-optimal allocations. This work will be reported elsewhere.

If constraints are imposed on the problem, then our theorems may not be immediately applicable. For example, Chu [4] imposes an availability constraint which sets a minimum number of copies. In his work on file allocation, Levin [6] provides for other restrictions (such as those imposed by security requirements) on which sites may have a copy of a given file. If there are constraints of these kinds, our theorems are still useful as long as they are not applied mindlessly. Thus one must make adjustments if Theorem 1 would include some of the wrong sites—or too many sites—or if Theorem 2 excludes too many sites. In some cases, one might want to consider the proofs of the theorems in determining how they might be applied, since the proofs provide the basic cost comparisons which follow from the theorem hypotheses.

For example, suppose we wish to find the best 2-site allocation, and one copy is required to be at site 1. Then it may be possible to exclude a number of sites from consideration as the second site by applying Lemma 1 with $k = 1$. If *all* sites are "excluded" by this lemma, one is reduced to brute-force comparisons of the possibilities. On the other hand, Theorem 1 may show that some site – say site 2 – should appear in any globally optimal allocation. Then $I = \{1, 2\}$ is certainly a "good" allocation, and application of Lemma 2 with $k = 2, i = 3, \ldots, n$, may in fact serve to prove that $\{1, 2\}$ is the best 2-site allocation containing site 1.

The example above is, of course, very simplistic. Application of the theorems in this case is likely to save little over the brute-force cost computations and comparisons. The example is only designed to show the reader the kinds of variations on our results which are obtainable for application in some nonstandard situations.

Constraints may take on many forms, and for some forms it may not be clear that anything like our theorems can be derived. We believe, however, that for any file allocation problem it is worth investigating the possibility of deriving as much a priori information on the optimum as possible. The savings may well be enough to turn an impractically large computing problem into one that is of acceptable size.

Received May 1976; revised December 1976

References

1. Casey, R.G. Allocation of copies of a file in an information network. Proc. AFIPS 1972 SJCC, Vol. 40, AFIPS Press, Montvale, N.J., pp. 617–625.
2. Chandy, K.M., and Hewes, J.E. File allocation in distributed systems. Proc. Int. Symp. on Comptr. Performance Modeling, Measurement and Evaluation, March 1976, pp. 10–13.
3. Chu, W.W. Optimal file allocation in a multi-computer information system. *IEEE Trans. Comptrs. C-18* (1969), pp. 885–889.
4. Chu, W.W. Optimal file allocation in a computer network. In *Computer-Communications Networks*, N. Abramson and F. Kuo, Eds., Prentice-Hall, Englewood Cliffs, N.J., 1973.
5. Eswaran, K.P. Placement of records in a file and file allocation in a computer network. Information Processing 74, North-Holland Pub. Co., Amsterdam, 1974, pp. 304–307.
6. Levin, K.D. Organizing distributed data bases in computer networks. Ph.D. Diss., U. of Pennsylvania, Philadelphia, Pa., 1974.
7. Spinetto, R.D. A facility location problem. *SIAM Review 18* (1976), 294–295.
8. Urano, Y., Ono, K., and Inoue, S. Optimal design of distributed networks. Second Int. Conf. on Comptr. Comm., 1974, pp. 413–420.

Dynamic File Assignment in a Computer Network

ADRIAN SEGALL, MEMBER, IEEE

***Abstract*—We present the models describing a problem of dynamic file allocation in a network of interacting computers and use dynamic programming to solve for the optimal strategies. The problem is treated for the case when the rates of the file requests are known in advance, as well as when only prior statistics is available for these rates. A separation theorem between estimation of the rates and the optimal control is proven, similar to Wonham's separation theorem for linear Gaussian models.**

I. Introduction

IN THE LAST few years, there has been an increasingly growing interest in problems of modeling, analysis, and design of networks of interacting computers. A major function of a computer network is to provide the facility for common use of data bases and information files by all computers in the system. When a file is used by several computers in the network, it can be stored in the memory of (at least) one of them and be accessed by the other computers via the communication channels. Because of updating and memory limitations, it is desirable to have in the system as few copies of any single file as possible. On the other hand, high transmission costs might dictate keeping a large number of copies. In this paper, we shall assume that the decisive factor is the updating of the files and therefore *only one copy of each file is allowed to exist in the system at any given time*. The extension of the present work to problems where multiple copies of the file exist in the system is being studied presently in the work for a master's thesis [20].

In a static analysis, considered in [1]–[6], it is assumed that all parameters of the system (demand rates, costs of storage and transmission, etc.) are known *a priori* and that the design is based on their average value over the period of operation of the system. The goal is to find the best location for the files, under the assumption that this location will remain fixed for the entire operating period.

On the other hand, if the parameters of the system—for instance the demand rates—vary with time, a dynamic allocation might give a substantial improvement in performance. Dynamic file assignment might also be necessary when there is the possibility of node or link failures, in which case the files may have to be reallocated according to the changing topology of the network. In addition, it is usually the case that the pattern of the demand rates as a function of time is not perfectly known in advance. In this case, it will be necessary to estimate these parameters from the observed requests and investigate how to incorporate these estimates in the allocation design.

The purpose of this paper is to find optimal policies for dynamical allocation of files in a computer network which works under time-varying operating conditions. The proposed procedure is as follows. Suppose the file is stored at time t in the memory of computer i. If at time t, it is requested only by computer i, then no transmission cost is incurred and there is no decision to be made. If it is requested by another computer, j say, the file is transmitted for use to computer j (where it is kept temporarily in a buffer) and now a decision is to be made, whether the file is to be left in memory i or erased from memory i and written in memory j. A similar decision is to be made if the file is requested by more than one computer at time t. The restriction of reallocating the file only in conjunction with a regular transmission is reasonable for this model, because if a change of location is decided upon, one might as well wait until the file is requested for the next time by the appropriate computer. Otherwise it is conceivable that the file might be transferred back and forth, without anybody actually using it.

Of course, there are various levels at which the problem can be treated. In this first work, a relatively simple model is considered to present the main methods and ideas for solving such problems. In Section VIII we indicate some other issues of importance to the design of file assignment in computer networks, and generalizations of the present model to incorporate these issues.

In addition to the application-oriented contribution in modeling and analysis of problem of file assignment in a computer network, this paper also contains a theoretical contribution in the theory of optimal control. It appears mainly in Section V, where it is shown that for the controlled continuous-time finite state Markov process describing the location of the file and for random request rates, a *separation property* holds in the sense that the estimates of the state of the rates are sufficient statistics for the optimal controls. The method used in the proof is similar to Wonham's approach [19] in proving separation for linear Gaussian models.

Section II presents the basic model used in the rest of the paper and the basic assumptions on the request statistics. Sections III and IV solve the problem of file assignment under the assumption of perfectly known request rates, and Sections V and VI treat the usually more

Manuscript received February 24, 1975; revised December 2, 1975. Paper recommended by E. Tse, Chairman of the IEEE S-CS Stochastic Control Committee. This work was supported by a Hayes Vinton Research Fellowship, by the NSF under Grant GK-41647, and by the Advanced Research Project Agency of the Department of Defense, and was monitored by the ONR under Contract Nr. N00014-75-C-1183.

The author is with the Electronic Systems Laboratory, Research Laboratory of Electronics and Department of Electrical Engineering and Computer Science, Massachusetts Institute of Technology, Cambridge, MA 02139.

Reprinted from *IEEE Trans. Automat. Contr.*, vol. AC-21, pp. 161–173, Apr. 1976.

realistic situation when only *a priori* statistics are available for the rate patterns. An illustrative example is briefly presented in Section VII, and Section VIII gives several concluding remarks and indications for further research.

II. The Model and Basic Assumptions

This being the first analysis of the problem of dynamic file allocation, we shall make here several simplifying assumptions, that are still consistent, however, to the models appearing in real networks. We shall assume that the files are requested by the computers according to mutually independent processes (with statistics to be specified presently) and also that the files are sufficiently short. Moreover the communication lines are taken to have sufficient capacity and the computers sufficient memory, so that the transmission of the file takes a very short time and there is no restriction on how many files a computer can carry. Under these assumptions, it is clear that in fact the files do not interfere with each other, and we can therefore treat each file *separately*.

The analysis can and will be carried out both in continuous time, and, if one assumes that the system has a central synchronizing clock, in discrete time.

Consider a completely connected system of M computers. Let $Y_i(t)$ be defined as

$$Y_i(t)=\begin{cases}1, & \text{if the file in consideration is stored at computer } i \text{ at time } t\\ 0, & \text{otherwise,} \quad i=1,2,\cdots,M\end{cases} \tag{1}$$

where $t=1, 2,\cdots$ for the discrete time analysis and $t \geqslant 0$ for continuous time. Clearly, at any given time only one of the variables $\{Y_i(t), i=1,\cdots,M\}$ can be one and all others will be zero.

We now model the requests of the file of interest by the various computers.

Discrete Time (Synchronized System)

Let $\{n_i(t), t=1, 2,\cdots\}$ be M independent binary sequences describing the requests of the file by computers $i=1,\cdots,M$ where $n_i(t)=1$ if there is a request at time t from computer i and $n_i(t)=0$, otherwise. Binary sequences are sometimes called discrete-time point processes. Let $a_i(t)$ be the random rate of $n_i(t)$, namely the conditional probability that a request from i will occur at time t. We write this [14, formula (1.4)]

$$P\{n_i(t)=1|\mathcal{B}(t-1)\}=a_i(t) \tag{2a}$$

or equivalently,

$$w_i(t)=n_i(t)-a_i(t) \tag{2b}$$

is a martingale difference (MD) sequence (see [9])[1] with respect to $\{\mathcal{B}\}$ where $\mathcal{B}(\cdot)$ contains all the past information relevant to the evolution of $n(\cdot)$. If for some i, $a_i(\cdot)$ is deterministic—and this implicity says that it is known to the designer—then $n_i(\cdot)$, the request pattern from computer i, is a Bernoulli process. The case with perfectly known rates will be discussed in Section III. If for some i, $a_i(\cdot)$ is not perfectly known in advance and only a prior statistics is available, then it will be modeled as a stochastic process.

[1]Throughout the paper, we refer the reader to [9], where a tutorial presentation of these properties is given, along with references to the rigorous proofs.

Continuous Time

Let $\{N_i(t), t>0\}$ be M independent counting processes (i.e., unity-jump processes) describing the request of the file by computers $i=1,\cdots,M$, namely, the process N_i has jumps (of size $+1$) at the times when the file is requested by the ith computer. We denote by $\lambda_i(t)$ the random rate (see [17], [13]) of $N_i(t)$, i.e.,

$$W_i(t)\equiv N_i(t)-\int_0^t \lambda_i(\tau)\,d\tau \tag{3}$$

is a $\{\mathcal{B}\}$ martingale, where $\mathcal{B}(\cdot)$ includes all the past relevant information related to the evolution of $N(\cdot)$. If for some i, $\lambda_i(\cdot)$ is deterministic (and known), then $N_i(\cdot)$ is a (nonhomogeneous) Poisson process. Otherwise $\lambda_i(\cdot)$ will be modeled as a stochastic process.

The operation costs are

C_i Storage cost per unit time per file at memory i,

$$i=1,\cdots,M.$$

C_{ij} Communication cost per transmission from computer i to computer j

$$i,j=i,\cdots,M, \qquad i\neq j. \tag{4}$$

It is assumed that these costs are time-invariant; the case with time-varying costs can be handled by simply writing $C_i(t)$ and $C_{ij}(t)$ throughout the paper. The total expected cost over the period $[0,T]$ is therefore, for example, in continuous time

$$C=E\left\{\int_0^T\left[\sum_{i=1}^M C_iY_i(t)\,dt+\sum_{i=1}^M\sum_{j\neq i}C_{ij}Y_i(t-)\,dN_j(t)\right]\right\}. \tag{5}$$

The first term shows that we pay $\$C_i$ per unit time if the file is in memory i at time t, i.e., if $Y_i(t)=1$. The second term shows that if the file is in memory i just before a request is made by computer $j\neq i$, then one pays $\$C_{ij}$ for the transmission from i to j. The goal is to design a closed-loop control that will dynamically assign the location of the file and will minimize the expected cost (5).

We shall start in Section III by finding the optimal control in the (analytically) simplest context and then build our way up to more complicated cases in the following sections.

III. Discrete-Time File Allocation in a Two-Computer Network with Perfectly Known Rates

As a motivation to the analysis in this section, consider the file containing at any given time the information about the availability of seats on various flights from New York to Los Angeles. This information might be requested at any time by travel agencies on both coasts (in Los Angeles to make return reservations), but since the file is updated very often one would prefer to keep only one copy of the file at any given time. The question is where to keep the file at what time.

We shall do here a discrete time analysis of a two-computer network. In the notation in Section II, there are $M=2$ memories, and the variables $\{Y_i(t), t=1, 2, \cdots\}$, $i=1, 2$ take value 1 or 0 according to whether the file is located in memory i or not at time t. Observe that in this case

$$Y_2(t)=1-Y_1(t) \tag{6}$$

so that the system dynamics is completely described by the evolution of $Y_1(t)$. The expected total cost over the period $t=1, 2, \cdots, T$ is [analogously to (5)]

$$C=E\sum_{t=1}^{T}\big[C_1Y_1(t)+C_2Y_2(t)$$
$$+C_{12}Y_1(t)n_2(t)+C_{21}Y_2(t)n_1(t)\big] \tag{7}$$

where $n_1(t)$, $n_2(t)$ are the request processes at location 1, 2, respectively. We assume in this section that $n_1(\cdot)$ and $n_2(\cdot)$ are independent Bernoulli sequences with (perfectly *known*) rates $a_1(t)$, $a_2(t)$, respectively. The control variables are defined by

$$u_1(t)=\begin{cases}1, & \text{if the decision is to transfer the file to memory 1 at time } t+, \text{ provided it was not there at time } t.\\ 0, & \text{otherwise}\end{cases} \tag{8}$$

and similarly for $u_2(t)$. The evolution of the state $Y_1(t)$ is given then by

$$Y_1(t+1)=Y_1(t)[1-u_2(t)]+Y_2(t)u_1(t), \qquad t=1, 2, \cdots. \tag{9}$$

As stated in Section I, transfer of the file from memory i to memory j is not allowed except in response to a request for use from computer j and therefore the controls $u_1(t)$, $u_2(t)$ are restricted to be of the form

$$\begin{aligned} u_1(t)&=\alpha_{21}(t)Y_2(t)n_1(t)\\ u_2(t)&=\alpha_{12}(t)Y_1(t)n_2(t).\end{aligned} \tag{10}$$

The control variables $\alpha_{21}(t)$, $\alpha_{12}(t)$ (taking values 0 or 1) can be functionals of all the past observations

$$\alpha(t)=\alpha(t, Y_1(s), Y_2(s), n_1(s), n_2(s), \quad s\leqslant t-1). \tag{11}$$

The Optimization Problem

Find optimal control laws $\{\alpha_{12}^*(t), \alpha_{21}^*(t), t=1, 2, \cdots, T\}$ of the form (11) and find the initial location $Y_1(1)$ to minimize the expected cost (7).

Before we present the solution, we may note that if we let

$$\mathcal{F}_t=\sigma\{Y_1(s), Y_2(s), n_1(s), n_2(s), \quad s=1,2,\cdots,t\}, \tag{12}$$[2]

then it is clear from (9), (10), and (6) that $Y_1(t)$, $Y_2(t)$ are completely determined by the values of the processes in (12) up to (and including) time $t-1$, and, therefore, are $\mathcal{F}_{t-1}$ measurable. In other words, in the terminology of [9], the sequences $\{Y_1(\cdot), Y_2(\cdot)\}$ are $\{\mathcal{F}\}$ predictable. We denote this by

$$Y_1(t), Y_2(t)\in\mathcal{F}_{t-1}, \tag{13}$$

which in particular implies that

$$\begin{aligned} EY_1(t)n_2(t)&=EE^{\mathcal{F}_{t-1}}Y_1(t)n_2(t)\\ &=\{EY_1(t)E^{\mathcal{F}_{t-1}}n_2(t)\}=EY_1(t)a_2(t)\end{aligned} \tag{14}$$

from (2). Here $E^{\mathcal{F}}x$ denotes conditional expectation of x with respect to $\mathcal{F}$. We have a similar relation for $EY_2(t)$ $n_1(t)$ and therefore (7), also using (6), becomes

$$\begin{aligned} C&=E\sum_{t=1}^{T}\big[C_1Y_1(t)+C_2Y_2(t)\\ &\quad+C_{12}Y_1(t)a_2(t)+C_{21}Y_2(t)a_1(t)\big]\\ &=E\sum_{t=1}^{T}\{[C_1+C_{12}a_2(t)]Y_1(t)\\ &\quad+[C_2+C_{21}a_1(t)](1-Y_1(t))\}\\ &\equiv E\sum_{t=1}^{T}L(t, Y_1(t)).\end{aligned} \tag{15}$$

We have not included $a_1(t)$, $a_2(t)$ as variables in $L(\cdots)$, since they are assumed here to be perfectly known.

Under this formulation, the process $Y_1(t)$ is a controlled finite-state Markov process. Using dynamic programming [10] one can show that the optimal controls satisfy (16). The proof is easy and therefore omitted.

Theorem 1: The optimal controls $\alpha_{12}^*(t)$, $\alpha_{21}^*(t)$ for the dynamic file allocation problem are found from the following backward *deterministic* equations:

$$\begin{bmatrix}V_1^*(t)\\ V_2^*(t)\end{bmatrix}=\begin{bmatrix}C_1+a_2(t)C_{12}\\ C_2+a_1(t)C_{21}\end{bmatrix}+\begin{bmatrix}1-\alpha_{12}^*(t)a_2(t) & \alpha_{12}^*(t)a_2(t)\\ \alpha_{21}^*(t)a_1(t) & 1-\alpha_{21}^*(t)a_1(t)\end{bmatrix}\begin{bmatrix}V_1^*(t+1)\\ V_2^*(t+1)\end{bmatrix} \tag{16a}$$

[2] $\sigma\{x\}$ denotes σ-algebra generated by x.

with

$$1-\alpha_{12}^*(t)=\alpha_{21}^*(t)=\begin{cases}1, & \text{if } V_1^*(t+1)\leqslant V_2^*(t+1)\\ 0, & \text{if } V_1^*(t+1)>V_2^*(t+1)\end{cases} \quad (16b)$$

and with terminal conditions

$$\begin{aligned}V_1^*(T)&=C_1+a_2(T)C_{12}\\ V_2^*(T)&=C_2+a_1(T)C_{21}.\end{aligned} \quad (16c)$$

Here $V_i^*(t)$, $i=1$, 2 denotes the optimal cost-to-go given that the file is in memory i at time t, namely given that $Y_i(t)=1$.

The optimal initial location is

$$1-Y_2(1)=Y_1(1)=\begin{cases}1, & \text{if } V_1^*(1)\leqslant V_2^*(1)\\ 0, & \text{if } V_1^*(1)>V_2^*(1).\end{cases} \quad (17)$$

For simplicity, we have presented here explicitly only the two computer network. The analysis (in discrete-time) for a network with an arbitrary number of computers is a straightforward extension of the above. The only difference is that the file may be requested at any given time by two or more computers (k say), in which case the number of possible decisions is $(k+1)$: keep the file in the computer where it was stored before or transfer it to one of the k requesting computers. The dynamics of the file is still represented by a finite-state Markov process, so that the Markovian decision theory [10] can be used as before to find the optimal controls.

IV. Continuous-Time File Allocation in a Multicomputer Network: Known Request Rates

In a network with more than two computers, the analysis in continuous time is somewhat easier than in discrete time. The reason is that in the continuous-time case, we modeled the requests of the file by the M computers as M independent Poisson processes, and it is easy to see then that there is zero probability that any two (or more) processes will jump at the same time, i.e., that two or more computers request the file at the same time. If the average time between requests is relatively large compared to the time it takes to transmit the file, this is a reasonable assumption. We keep the notation introduced in Section II, and also introduce the control variables

$$\{\alpha_{ij}(t), \quad i=1,\cdots M; \quad j=1,\cdots M; \quad i\neq j\}. \quad (18)$$

The variable $\alpha_{ij}(t)$ is defined to take value 1 at time t if, given that the file was stored at t- in memory i and was requested at time t by computer $j\neq i$, the controller decides at time t to erase it from memory i and write it in memory j. The variable $\alpha_{ij}(t)$ takes value 0 at time t, if given the same situation, the controller decides to keep it in memory i. Observe that we do not have to worry about the case where the file is requested at time t by two (or more) computers, since this happens with zero probability. The dynamics of the file is therefore described by the equations

$$dY_i(t)=-Y_i(t-)\sum_{j\neq i}\alpha_{ij}(t)\,dN_j(t) + \sum_{j\neq i}\alpha_{ji}(t)Y_j(t-)\,dN_i(t). \quad (19)$$

We take here $Y(t)$ to be right continuous and denote by $Y(t-)$ the value of Y just before it jumps. The first term in the right-hand side of (19) reflects the fact that if the file as in memory i at time $t-$, and is transferred to memory j at time t, then $Y_i(t)$ changes from $Y_i(t-)=1$ to $Y_i(t)=0$. The second term reflects an opposite transfer and if there is no transfer from or into memory i, then $dY_i(t)=0$. The controls $\alpha_{ij}(t)$ can, in general, depend on the past history of the processes, but as in Section III the optimal ones will prove to be independent of $Y(\cdot)$.

We look next at the expression for the total cost (5). Analogously to (14) one can see that if $N_j(t)$ has rate $\lambda_j(t)$ (assumed in this section to be perfectly known), then

$$dN_j(t)-\lambda_j(t)\,dt$$

is independent from the past and has zero mean; hence,

$$E\int_0^T Y_i(t-)\left[dN_j(t)-\lambda_j(t)\,dt\right]=0. \quad (20)$$

(This can be proven rigorously [9], (see also [11]), since $Y_i(t-)$ is predictable and $N_j(t)-\int_0^t\lambda_j(\tau)\,d\tau$ is a zero-mean martingale, (since it has independent increments) which imply that the expression under the expectation sign in (20) is also a zero-mean martingale.) We also observe that integration with respect to t does not distinguish between left- or right-continuous versions of the same function, so that

$$\int_0^T Y_i(t-)\lambda_i(t)\,dt=\int_0^T Y_i(t)\lambda_i(t)\,dt$$

and therefore the cost (5) becomes

$$C\equiv E\int_0^T L(t,Y(t))\,dt$$

$$\equiv E\int_0^T\left\{\sum_{i=1}^M\left[C_i+\sum_{j\neq i}C_{ij}\lambda_j(t)\right]Y_i(t)\right\}dt. \quad (21)$$

Again we have not included $\lambda_i(\cdot)$ as parameters of $L(\cdot,\cdot)$ since the rates are assumed in this section to be *perfectly known*.

We are now ready to display the equations for the optimal controls of the form

$$\alpha_{ij}(t)=\alpha_{ij}(t,Y_i(s),\ \ s<t,\ \ i=1,\cdots,M). \quad (22)$$

Theorem 2: The optimal control variables $\alpha_{ij}^*(t)$ in the class (22) for the file allocation problem described by (19) with cost (21) are given by

$$\alpha_{ij}^*(t)=\begin{cases}0, & V(t,j)\geqslant V(t,i)\\ 1, & V(t,j)<V(t,i)\end{cases}\triangleq I_{\{V(t,j)<V(t,i)\}},$$

$$i=1,\cdots,M;\, j=1,\cdots,M;\, i\neq j \quad \text{(23a)}$$

where $V(t,i)$ is given by the set of backward differential equations

$$-\frac{dV(t,i)}{dt}=\Big[C_i+\sum_{j\neq i} C_{ij}\lambda_j(t)\Big]$$

$$+\sum_{j\neq i}\lambda_j(t)\big[V(t,j)-V(t,i)\big]I_{\{V(t,j)<V(t,i)\}} \quad \text{(23b)}$$

with terminal condition

$$V(T,i)=0, \qquad \text{for all } i, \qquad i=1,\cdots,M. \quad \text{(23c)}$$

Proof: Since $Y(t)$ is a Markov process, we can follow Wonham [12] by first developing the backward Kolmogorov equation for

$$P(t,i)=\Pr\{Y(T)\in\Gamma \mid Y_i(t)=1\} \quad \text{(24)}$$

where Γ is an arbitrary set, and then obtain the stochastic Hamilton–Jacobi–Bellman equation. One can easily see that the backward Kolmogorov equation for the Markov process $Y(\cdot)$ of (19) is

$$-\frac{dP(t,i)}{dt}=\sum_{j\neq i}\alpha_{ij}(t)\lambda_j(t)\big[P(t,j)-P(t,i)\big],$$

$$i=1,\cdots,M \quad \text{(25a)}$$

with terminal condition

$$P(T,i)=\begin{cases}1, & \text{if } i\in\Gamma\\ 0, & \text{if } i\not\in\Gamma.\end{cases} \quad \text{(25b)}$$

With the cost function (21), the stochastic Hamilton–Jacobi–Bellman equation for the *optimal* cost-to-go

$$V(t,i)=E\Big\{\int_t^T L(\tau,Y(\tau))\,d\tau \mid Y_i(t)=1\Big\}, \qquad i=1,\cdots,M \quad \text{(26)}$$

(where the optimal control is used) is [12]

$$-\frac{dV(t,i)}{dt}=\min_{\alpha}\Big\{\Big[C_i+\sum_{j\neq i}C_{ij}\lambda_j(t)\Big]$$

$$+\sum_{j\neq i}\alpha_{ij}(t)\lambda_j(t)\big[V(t,j)-V(t,i)\big]\Big\} \quad \text{(27a)}$$

with terminal condition

$$V(T,i)=0. \quad \text{(27b)}$$

The solution of (27) is obviously (23).

This completes the proof. The value of the optimal cost-to-go $V(t,i)$ at time $t=0$ gives the minimal value C^* of the cost given that the file is in memory i at time 0.

$$V(0,i)=\min E\Big\{\int_0^T L(t,Y(t))\,dt \mid Y_i(0)=1\Big\}. \quad \text{(28)}$$

This also provides the best choice for the initial location (at time $t=0$) as being the one with minimal $V(0,i)$.

One may also note that the solution of equations (23) is very simple, since (23b) is a set of *linear* equations except for some coefficients $I_{\{V(t,j)<V(t,i)\}}$ taking values 0 or 1 depending if $V(t,j)$ is larger or smaller than $V(t,i)$.

V. Continuous-Time Analysis with Random Rates of Demand

In previous sections, we have shown how to use dynamic programming to obtain the optimal file allocation strategy under the assumption that the evolution of system parameters is perfectly known to the designer. Although this assumption is often made in the data communication networks literature, it is hardly realistic; in any practical system, only some prior distribution on the request rates of the data bases will be available in advance. As the system evolves, the information gathered from the current file requests should be used to update the estimates of the rates. In turn these estimates are to be used in the allocation strategy.

Methods for estimating the rates of a point process have been presented in [13]–[15], and are directly applicable in this paper, where the "points" of the point processes will represent the requests of the files by the users. It only remains to investigate how should these estimates be incorporated in the allocation strategy, and this is the subject of this and the following sections.

One possible ad hoc method is to use the certainty equivalence control [16], namely to use the optimal strategy designed for the case when the rates are perfectly known, with the estimates replacing the deterministic rates. However, since the estimates are never perfect, it is only in very special cases, like the linear-quadratic-Gaussian model, that the certainty-equivalence control is optimal, and in fact there are cases when it performs very badly. In fact it happens very often that the optimal control at every time t is not a function of the estimates only, but rather is a more general functional of the entire past data. In these cases, one usually has to use various suboptimal schemes.

It has been shown in [14]–[15], that if the rate process is modeled as a finite-state Markov process, one can find an explicit finite-dimensional recursive filter for estimating the rate. For these models of the request processes, it will be shown that the problem of dynamic file allocation has a separation property [18], i.e., the optimal assignment strategy will be shown to depend on the data only through the estimates of the demand rates. Explicit methods for finding the optimal strategy will also be given. The fact that the separation property holds for this problem is quite surprising, since it is quite far from the linear-Gaussian model. On the other hand, it is quite easy to see that the three basic ingredients for the separation property to hold are there:

Remark 1: The control does not affect the observation pattern (i.e., the observations σ-algebras).

Remark 2: The control does not affect the estimation.

Remark 3: The posterior distribution of the rates is completely characterized by the solution of the recursive filter, which moreover is an explicit finite-dimensional (nonlinear) filter.

To see this, note first that the observation field at time t is

$$\mathcal{F}_t = \sigma\{N_i(s), Y_i(s), \quad s \leqslant t, \quad i=1,\cdots,M\}. \tag{29}$$

At a first glance, it seems that these σ-algebras are dependent on the control law, since $Y_i(\cdot)$ is affected by the control. It is clear, however, both from (19) and the model itself that for any given causal control law $\alpha(\cdot)$, the processes $\{Y_i(s), s \leqslant t\}$ are completely determined by the request patterns $\{N_i(s), s \leqslant t\}$. This says that the observation fields are in fact

$$\mathcal{F}_t = \sigma\{N_i(s), \quad s \leqslant t, \quad i=1,\cdots,M\} \tag{30}$$

and since these are not affected by the control law, Remark 1 follows.

The discussion above also shows that since the request processes are mutually independent and are not influenced by the control, the best estimate $\hat{\lambda}_i(t)$ of $\lambda_i(t)$ given $\mathcal{F}_t$ is the same as the best estimate of $\lambda_i(t)$ given $\{N_i(s), s \leqslant t\}$ alone and can be found by the methods of [13], [14]. In particular this says that neither the control, nor the other request processes, affect the estimation procedure of any particular rate. This is remark 2. Of course a similar statement is true for the estimate $\hat{a}_i(t|t-1)$ in the discrete-time case and methods for recursively obtaining these estimates were given in [14], [15].

If we model now the stochastic evolution of the rate $\{a_i(t), t=1,2,\cdots\}$ or $\{\lambda_i(t), t \geqslant 0\}$ as a (possibly nonhomogeneous) finite-state Markov process, it has been shown in [14, sec. IV, VI] that the best estimates as well as the entire posterior distribution of the rates can be found in terms of a solution of a finite-dimensional recursive equation. This is Remark 3.

In view of the previous remarks, it is expected that the separation property will hold for this problem, namely the optimal control for dynamically assigning the file location will be dependent on the data only through the state estimates. We next derive the optimal control scheme for the continuous-time model with unknown rates.

The dynamics of the system is represented by (19) and the problem is to determine the optimal controls $\alpha_{ij}^*(t)$ of the form

$$\alpha_{ij}^*(t) = \alpha_{ij}^*(t, N_i(s), Y_i(s), \quad s < t, \quad i=1,\cdots,M) \tag{31}$$

that will minimize the cost (5). The first step here is to recognize that under the model we can replace in the cost function $dN_j(t)$ by $\hat{\lambda}(t)dt$; this is because with model (3), the innovations process

$$\nu_j(t) = N_j(t) - \int_0^t \hat{\lambda}_j(\tau)\,d\tau \tag{32}$$

is a zero-mean $\{\mathcal{F}\}$ martingale (see [9], [17]) and from (29), the process $Y(\cdot)$ is $\{\mathcal{F}\}$ adapted and hence $\{Y(t-)\}$ is $\{\mathcal{F}\}$ predictable, which imply that

$$\int_0^t Y_i(s-)\left[dN_j(s) - \hat{\lambda}_j(s)\,ds\right] \tag{33}$$

is a stochastic integral of a predictable process with respect to a zero-mean martingale, and therefore is itself a zero-mean martingale [9, formula (75)]. Hence, the cost function (5) is now

$$C = E\left\{\int_0^T \sum_{i=1}^M C_i Y_i(t)\,dt + \sum_{i=1}^M \sum_{j \neq i} C_{ij} Y_i(t)\hat{\lambda}_j(t)\,dt\right\}. \tag{34}$$

Now to avoid complicated notational technicalities, we shall treat explicitly only the case in which only $\lambda_1(t)$ is random and all the other request rates $\lambda_2(\cdot),\cdots,\lambda_m(\cdot)$ are deterministic. The extention to the case when all rates are random will be clear from the presentation. It is also convenient to define here a function of time $J(t)$ taking values $1, 2, \cdots, M$, as

$$J(t) = i \quad \text{if} \quad Y_i(t) = 1, \qquad i=1,\cdots,M, \tag{35}$$

i.e., if the file is in the memory of computer i at time t. Clearly there is a one to one correspondence between $J(\cdot)$ and $\boldsymbol{Y}(\cdot)$, so that cost (34) can be written compactly as

$$C = E\int_0^T L'(t, J(t), \hat{\lambda}_1(t))\,dt. \tag{36}$$

We do not explicity include in L' the rates $\lambda_2,\cdots,\lambda_M$, since they are assumed to be deterministic and perfectly known.

We model the random rate $\lambda_1(\cdot)$ as a finite-state Markov process with states

$$\rho' < \rho'' < \cdots \rho^{(m)}, \tag{37a}$$

transition probabilities

$$\Pr\{\lambda_1(t+dt) = \rho^{(j)} | \lambda_1(t) = \rho^{(k)}\} = q_{kj}(t)\,dt + o(dt), \qquad k \neq i$$
$$\Pr\{\lambda_1(t+dt) = \rho^{(k)} | \lambda_1(t) = \rho^{(k)}\} = 1 + q_{kk}(t)\,dt + o(dt) \tag{37b}$$

where

$$q_{kk}(t) = -\sum_{j \neq k} q_{kj}(t) \tag{37c}$$

and initial distribution

$$\Pr\{\lambda_1(0) = \rho^{(k)}\} = \pi_k, \qquad k=1,\cdots,m. \tag{37d}$$

If we define

$$x_k(t)=\begin{cases}1, & \text{if } \lambda_1(t)=\rho^{(k)}\\ 0, & \text{otherwise}\end{cases} \tag{38}$$

and write

$$\begin{aligned} x(t)&=[x_1(t),\cdots,x_m(t)]^T\\ \rho&=[\rho',\cdots,\rho^{(m)}]^T\\ \pi&=[\pi_1,\cdots,\pi_m]^T\\ Q(t)&=\{Q_{kj}(t)\}, \qquad k,j=1,\cdots,m \end{aligned} \tag{39}$$

it has been shown in [14, sec. VI] that the posterior distribution of $\lambda_1(t)$ given $\{N_1(s),\ s\leqslant t\}$ is completely characterized by the least-squares estimate $\hat{x}(t)$ of $x(t)$ given $\{N_1(s),\ s\leqslant t\}$. This can be found from the explicit m-dimensional recursive equation

$$d\hat{x}(t)=[Q^T(t)\hat{x}(t)-P(\hat{x}(t))\rho]\,dt+\frac{P(\hat{x}(t-))\rho}{\rho^T\hat{x}(t-)}dN_1(t). \tag{40a}$$

Here

$$P(\hat{x}(t))=E^{\mathcal{F}_t}[\hat{x}(t)\hat{x}^T(t)] \tag{40b}$$

is an $m\times m$ matrix with elements

$$P_{kj}(\hat{x}(t))=\begin{cases}-\hat{x}_k(t)\ \hat{x}_j(t), & \text{if } k\neq j\\ \hat{x}_k(t)\ -[\hat{x}_k(t)]^2, & \text{if } k=j\end{cases} \tag{40c}$$

and $\hat{x}(t-)$ denotes that in the integration one has to use $\hat{x}(t)$ evaluated just before the jump occurs. We write (40a) in the compact form

$$d\hat{x}(t)=a(t,\hat{x}(t))\,dt+b(\hat{x}(t-))\,dN_1(t). \tag{41}$$

In particular, the best estimate $\hat{\lambda}_1(t)$ of $\lambda_1(t)$ given $\{N_1(s),\ s\leqslant t\}$ is

$$\hat{\lambda}_1(t)=\rho^T\hat{x}(t) \tag{42}$$

so that (36) can be rewritten

$$C=E\int_0^T L(t,J(t),\hat{x}(t))\,dt. \tag{43}$$

In preparation for the statement and proof of the separation theorem, consider an arbitrary twice differentiable function of $(m+2)$ variables $V(t,J,x)$, where x is m dimensional. Later we shall be interpreting V as the conditional cost-to-go. We have from the Itô–Doleans Dade–Meyer differential rule [9, formula (101)]

$$\begin{aligned} dV(t,J(t),\hat{x}(t))&=\frac{\partial V}{\partial t}dt+\left(\frac{\partial V}{\partial x}\right)d\hat{x}^c(t)\\ &\quad+V(t,J(t),\hat{x}(t))-V(t,J(t-),\hat{x}(t-)) \end{aligned} \tag{44}$$

since $J(t)$ changes only by jumps and hence has no continuous part and neither $J(\cdot)$ nor $\hat{x}(\cdot)$ have continuous martingale parts. Here $\hat{x}^c(t)$ is the continuous part of $\hat{x}(t)$, which is from (41)

$$d\hat{x}^c(t)=a(t,\hat{x}(t))\,dt \tag{45}$$

and $(\partial V/\partial x)\ d\hat{x}^c$ denotes scalar product of the gradient of V and $d\hat{x}^c$. Now, (41) shows that $\hat{x}(t)$ jumps only when $N_1(t)$ does, so that

$$\hat{x}(t)=\hat{x}(t-)+b(\hat{x}(t-))\,dN_1(t). \tag{46}$$

Moreover $J(t)$ can jump only when one of the request processes $\{N_i(t),\ i=1,\cdots,M\}$ jumps, and therefore we have for the last part of (44)

$$\begin{aligned} &V(t,J(t),\hat{x}(t))-V(t,J(t-),\hat{x}(t-))\\ &=\sum_{j\neq 1}[V(t,1,\hat{x}(t-)+b(\hat{x}(t-)))-V(t,j,\hat{x}(t-))]\\ &\quad\cdot Y_j(t-)\alpha_{j1}(t)\,dN_1(t)\\ &\quad+\sum_{j\neq 1}[V(t,j,\hat{x}(t-)+b(\hat{x}(t-)))-V(t,j,\hat{x}(t-))]\\ &\quad\cdot Y_j(t-)[1-\alpha_{j1}(t)]\,dN_1(t)\\ &\quad+[V(t,1,\hat{x}(t-)+b(\hat{x}(t-)))-V(t,1,\hat{x}(t-))]\\ &\quad\cdot Y_1(t-)\,dN_1(t)\\ &\quad+\sum_{i=2}^{M}\sum_{j\neq i}[V(t,i,\hat{x}(t-))-V(t,j,\hat{x}(t-))]\\ &\quad\cdot Y_j(t-)\alpha_{ji}(t)\,dN_i(t). \end{aligned} \tag{47}$$

For example, the first term in the right-hand side of (47) shows that if the file is at time $t-$ in memory $j\neq 1$ and is requested by computer 1 at time t and the control decides to transfer it to memory 1, then $J(\cdot)$ changes from $J(t-)=j$ to $J(t)=1$ and $\hat{x}(\cdot)$ changes from $\hat{x}(t-)=\hat{x}(t-)$ to $\hat{x}(t)=\hat{x}(t-)+b(\hat{x}(t-))$. The other terms have similar interpretations.

We need the following notations:

$$\phi_i^{(\alpha)}(V(t,J(t-),x(t-)))=\text{coefficient of } dN_i(t) \text{ in (47) with } Y_j(t-) \text{ replaced by } I_{\{J(t-)=j\}}. \tag{48}$$

Observe that these are $\{\mathcal{F}\}$ predictable processes, since they are all $\{\mathcal{F}\}$ adapted and left continuous. Therefore, from (32), (42) and similarly to (33)

$$\begin{aligned} &\int_0^t \phi_1^{(\alpha)}(V(s,J(s-),x(s-)))[dN_1(s)-\hat{\lambda}_1(s)\,ds]\\ &\quad=\int_0^t \phi_1^{(\alpha)}(V(s,J(s-),\hat{x}(s-)))[dN_1(s)-\rho^T\hat{x}(s)\,ds] \end{aligned} \tag{49}$$

and

$$\int_0^t \phi_j^{(\alpha)}(V(s,J(s-),\hat{x}(s-)))[dN_j(s)-\lambda_j(s)ds],\qquad j=2,\cdots,M \quad (50)$$

are all zero-mean $\{\mathcal{F}\}$ martingales (recall that $\lambda_2,\cdots,\lambda_m$ are all assumed for this analysis to be deterministic). We also consider the operator

$$\mathcal{L}^{(\alpha)}V(t,J,x)=a(t,x)\frac{\partial V}{\partial x}(t,J,x)+\phi_1^{(\alpha)}(V(t,J,x))\rho^T x + \sum_{i=2}^{M}\phi_i^{(\alpha)}(V(t,J,x))\lambda_i(t). \quad (51)$$

Observe the similarity between (51) and the Kolmogorov backward operator for signals in white Gaussian noise.

We are now ready to state the optimality criterion for this problem. Both the statement and the proof are similar to Wonham's separation theorem for linear Gaussian models [19, p. 321].

Theorem 3 (separation criterion): Suppose there exist functions $\alpha_{ij}^*(t,x)$ and $V(t,J,x)$ such that for all $t\in[0,T]$, $\{J=1,\ 2,\cdots,M\}$, $\{0\leqslant x_i\leqslant 1,$ all $i=1,\cdots,m\}$ and all admissible controls α the following holds:

$$0=\frac{\partial}{\partial t}V(t,J,x)+\mathcal{L}^{(\alpha^*(t,x))}V(t,J,x)+L(t,J,x) \leqslant \frac{\partial}{\partial t}V(t,J,x)+\mathcal{L}^{(\alpha)}V(t,J,x)+L(t,J,x) \quad (52a)$$

with terminal condition

$$V(T,J,x)=0, \qquad \text{for all } J,x. \quad (52b)$$

Then the controls

$$\alpha_{ij}^*(t,\hat{x}(t-)) \quad (53)$$

are optimal in the sense that they minimize (36) in the class of admissible controls (31), and the minimum cost is

$$\min_{\alpha} C=V(0,J(0),\hat{x}(0)). \quad (54)$$

The proof will be defered to Appendix A. It remains to show that α^* and V as in Theorem 3 exist. We shall do this by solving (52), which can be rewritten as

$$-\frac{\partial}{\partial t}V(t,J,x)=L(t,J,x)+\min_{\alpha}\mathcal{L}^{(\alpha)}V(t,J,x). \quad (55)$$

Substituting from (34)–(36), (40)–(43), (47)–(51), (55) without the minimization in the right-hand side reads

$$\begin{aligned}-\frac{\partial}{\partial t}V(t,1,x)&=C_1+\sum_{i=2}^{M}C_{1i}\lambda_i(t)\\&+[Q^T(t)x-P(x)\rho]\frac{\partial}{\partial x}V(t,1,x)\\&+\left[V\left(t,1,x+\frac{1}{\rho^T x}P(x)\rho\right)-V(t,1,x)\right]\rho^T x\\&+\sum_{i=2}^{M}[V(t,i,x)-V(t,1,x)]\alpha_{1i}(t)\lambda_i(t)\end{aligned} \quad (56a)$$

and for $j\geqslant 2$

$$\begin{aligned}-\frac{\partial}{\partial t}V(t,j,x)&=C_j+C_{j1}\rho^T x+\sum_{\substack{i=2\\i\neq j}}^{M}C_{ji}\lambda_i(t)\\&+[Q^T(t)x-P(x)\rho]\frac{\partial}{\partial x}V(t,j,x)\\&+\left[V\left(t,1,x+\frac{1}{\rho^T x}P(x)\rho\right)-V(t,j,x)\right]\alpha_{j1}(t)\rho^T x\\&+\left[V\left(t,j,x+\frac{1}{\rho^T x}P(x)\rho\right)-V(t,j,x)\right](1-\alpha_{j1}(t))\rho^T x\\&+\sum_{i=2}^{M}[V(t,i,x)-V(t,j,x)]\alpha_{ji}(t)\lambda_i(t).\end{aligned} \quad (56b)$$

Now since $\lambda_i(t)\geqslant 0$ and $\rho^T x\geqslant 0$, the controls α^* that minimize the right-hand side of (56) are

$$\alpha_{1i}^*(t,x)=\begin{cases}1, & \text{if } V(t,i,x)\leqslant V(t,1,x)\\ 0, & \text{otherwise}\end{cases}$$

$$\equiv I_{\{V(t,i,x)\leqslant V(t,1,x)\}}, \qquad i=2,3,\cdots,M \quad (57a)$$

$$\alpha_{j1}^*(t,x)=I\left\{V\left(t,1,x+\frac{1}{\rho^T x}P(x)\rho\right)\leqslant V\left(t,j,x+\frac{1}{\rho^T x}P(x)\rho\right)\right\},\qquad j=2,3,\cdots,M \quad (57b)$$

$$\alpha_{ji}^*(t,x)=I_{\{V(t,i,x)\leqslant V(t,j,x)\}},\qquad i,j=2,\cdots,M \ i\neq j. \quad (57c)$$

It is clear that these controls are of the form as required by Theorem 3 and therefore we have shown Theorem 4.

Theorem 4: (Theorem and expression for optimal control). The optimal controls α_{ji}^* are given by

$$\alpha_{ji}^*(t)=\alpha_{ji}^*(t,\hat{x}(t-))$$

where α_{ji}^* are the solutions of (57) and (56). The minimum expected cost given that the file is in computer i at time 0 is

$$V(0,i,\hat{x}(0))=V(0,i,Ex(0)).$$

Remarks:

1) The set of M partial differential equations that gives the optimal control can be solved off-line before the system starts operating. Moreover, the solution of the equations can be used repeatedly as long as the pattern of the parameter variation and the costs remains the same. Also note that the range of the independent variables $\hat{x}$ is only $0\leqslant\hat{x}_k\leqslant 1$ $k=1,\cdots,m$, since each one is a (conditional) probability, and therefore the number of grid points necessary to discretize the space may not be too large. Finally observe that even if one does not want to actually solve the partial differential equations, knowledge of the fact that the optimal control satisfies the separation principle is of major importance in designing suboptimal schemes. It tells us that all the past necessary information for the purpose of designing the optimal control can be summarized in the current state estimate, which moreover can be calculated recursively via (40).

2) The problem of existence of solutions with the ap-

propriate properties to the partial differential-difference equations (56) and (57) is still an open question (remark of Davis). For the Gaussian noise problem, Wonham [19] uses rather heavily the theory of parabolic differential equations to show existence of the equation for the minimum cost-to-go. It is not clear at this time if similar methods can be used for solutions of equations of the form (56) and (57). Another interesting question is whether there exist special cases when (56) will have a relatively simple solution, analogously to the linear quadratic Gaussian case.

VI. Syncronized Computer Networks: Random Rates of Demand

For a syncronized network we shall treat here as before only the simplest case, when the system consist of only two computers and only one of the time-varying rates is random. The extension to a general network with possibly all rates unknown in advance will be along the lines indicated at the end of Section III and involves only notational complications without providing any additional insight.

As in the continuous-time case, we shall model the unknown rates as finite-state Markov processes and then the problem of finding optimal controls reduces to a finite-state Markovian decision problem with partial observations. Such problems have been treated in [15], but we feel that some elaboration on the problem using the control approach would be valuable, especially to emphasize the similarity between the discrete-time and the (theoretically somewhat harder) continuous-time treatments and to provide the notational background to various extensions that are indicated in Section VIII. On the other hand, to limit the length of this paper, we shall only outline the proofs of the results and refer the reader either to [15] or to similar proofs in Section V.

The system dynamics is as in (9), (10) where here we assume that $n_2(t)$ is Bernoulli with *known* rate $a_2(t)$, and $n_1(t)$ has a *random* rate $a_1(\cdot)$. The random rate $a_1(\cdot)$ will be modeled as a finite-state Markov process with states

$$\rho' < \rho'' < \cdots < \rho^{(m)}, \tag{58}$$

transition probabilities

$$\Pr\{a_1(t+1)=\rho^{(j)} | a_1(t)=\rho^{(i)}\} = q_{ij}(t), \tag{59}$$

and initial distribution

$$\Pr\{a_1(1)=\rho^{(k)}\} = \pi_k, \qquad k=1,\cdots,m. \tag{60}$$

Defining

$$x_k(t)=\begin{cases} 1, & \text{if } a_1(t)=\rho^{(k)} \\ 0, & \text{otherwise}\end{cases} \tag{61}$$

and with the same notations as in (14), it has been shown in [14, sec. IV], that the posterior distribution of $a_1(t)$ given $\{n_1(1),\cdots,n_1(t-1)\}$ is completely characterized by the least squares estimate $\hat{\boldsymbol{x}}(t|t-1)$ of $\boldsymbol{x}(t)$ given $\{n_1(t),\cdots,n_1(t-1)\}$. This can be found recursively via

$$\hat{\boldsymbol{x}}(t+1|t) = Q^T(t)\left[\hat{\boldsymbol{x}}(t|t-1) - \frac{P(\hat{\boldsymbol{x}}(t|t-1))\boldsymbol{\rho}}{1-\boldsymbol{\rho}^T\hat{\boldsymbol{x}}(t|t-1)}\right] + \frac{Q^T(t)P(\hat{\boldsymbol{x}}(t|t-1))\boldsymbol{\rho}}{\boldsymbol{\rho}^T\hat{\boldsymbol{x}}(t|t-1) - \left[\boldsymbol{\rho}^T\hat{\boldsymbol{x}}(t|t-1)\right]^2}\cdot n_1(t) \tag{62a}$$

with initial condition

$$\hat{\boldsymbol{x}}(1|0) = \boldsymbol{\pi} \tag{62b}$$

where $P(\hat{x}(t|t-1))$ is an $m\times m$ matrix with entries

$$P_{kj}(\hat{\boldsymbol{x}}(t|t-1)) = \begin{cases} -\hat{x}_k(t|t-1)\hat{x}_j(t|t-1), & k\neq j \\ \hat{x}_k(t|t-1) - [\hat{x}_k(t|t-1)]^2, & k=j. \end{cases} \tag{63}$$

An equivalent expression to (62a) for the best estimate $\hat{x}(t|t-1)$ can be derived using Bayes rule (see, e.g., [15]), but we have preferred to display it in the form (62) to emphasize the similarity with the continuous-time formula (40a).

We write (62) in compact form

$$\hat{\boldsymbol{x}}(t+1) = c(t,\hat{\boldsymbol{x}}(t|t-1)) + b(\hat{\boldsymbol{x}}(t|t-1))\cdot n_1(t). \tag{64}$$

In particular the best estimate of $a_1(t)$ given $\{n_1(1),\cdots, n_1(t-1)\}$ is

$$\hat{a}_1(t|t-1) = \boldsymbol{\rho}^T\hat{\boldsymbol{x}}(t|t-1). \tag{65}$$

As in Section V, the problem is to find the optimal controls α_{12}^*, α_{21}^* of the form (11) to minimize the criterion

$$C = E\sum_{t=1}^{T}\{[C_1 + C_{12}a_2(t)]Y_1(t) + [C_2 + C_{21}\hat{a}_1(t|t-1)](1-Y_1(t))\} \triangleq$$

$$\triangleq E\sum_{t=1}^{T} L(t, Y_1(t), \hat{\boldsymbol{x}}(t|t-1)). \tag{66}$$

The first equality follows from (7) similarly to (33), since with

$$\mathcal{F}_t \triangleq \sigma\{n_1(s), n_2(s), \qquad s=1,2,\cdots,t\} \tag{67}$$

the variable $Y_1(t)$ is $\mathcal{F}_{t-1}$ measurable and

$$\nu(t) = n_1(t) - \hat{a}_1(t|t-1) \tag{68}$$

is an $\{\mathcal{F}\}-$ MD sequence and therefore

$$EY_1(t)\nu(t) = EE^{\mathcal{F}_{t-1}}Y_1(t)\nu(t) = EY_1(t)E^{\mathcal{F}_{t-1}}\nu(t) = 0 \tag{69}$$

(see [9] for a detailed discussion of these properties). Finally, it will be convenient for notational purposes to define as in Section III a function

$$J(t) = i, \qquad \text{if } Y_i(t) = 1, \tag{70}$$

namely, if the file is in the memory of computer i at time t.

We now proceed to find expressions for the optimal control using dynamic programming: The optimal cost to go defined as

$$V^*(t)=\min_{\alpha} E\sum_{\tau=t}^{T}\{L(\tau,Y_1(\tau),\hat{x}(\tau|\tau-1))|\mathcal{F}_{t-1}\} \quad (71)$$

satisfies the Bellman equation

$$V^*(t)=\min_{\alpha(t)} E\{L(t,Y_1(t),\hat{x}(t|t-1))+V'(t+1)|\mathcal{F}_{t-1}\}$$
$$V^*(T+1)=0. \quad (72)$$

Theorem 5: (Separation theorem and optimal controls.) For

$$t=1,2,\cdots,T$$
$$J=1,2$$

x an m-dimensional vector with components $0\leqslant x_k\leqslant 1$ (73)

consider the solution $V(t,J,x)$ of the backward equations

$$\begin{aligned}V(t,1,x)=&[C_1+C_{12}a_2(t)]\\&+V(t+1,1,c(t,x)+b(x))\cdot\rho^Tx\\&+V(t+1,1,c(t,x))(1-\rho^Tx)\\&+\alpha_{12}(t,x)\cdot a_2(t)\{[V(t+1,2,c(t,x)+b(x))\\&-V(t+1,1,c(t,x)+b(x))]\rho^Tx\\&+[V(t+1,2,c(t,x))\\&-V(t+1,1,c(t,x))](1-\rho^Tx)\}\end{aligned}$$

$$\begin{aligned}V(t,2,x)=&[C_2+C_{21}\rho^Tx]+V(t+1,2,c(t,x)+b(x))\cdot\rho^Tx\\&+V(t+1,2,c(t,x))\cdot(1-\rho^Tx)\\&+\alpha_{21}(t,x)\cdot\rho^Tx\cdot[V(t+1,1,c(t,x)+b(x))\\&-V(t+1,2,c(t,x)+b(x))]\end{aligned} \quad (74a)$$

with

$$\alpha_{12}(t,x)=\begin{cases}1, & \text{if } \rho^Tx\cdot V(t+1,2,c(t,x)+b(x))\\ & \quad +(1-\rho^Tx)V(t+1,2,c(t,x))\\ & \quad <\rho^Tx\cdot V(t+1,1,c(t,x)+b(x))\\ & \quad +(1-\rho^Tx)V(t+1,1,c(t,x))\\ 0, & \text{otherwise}\end{cases}$$

$$\alpha_{21}(t,x)=\begin{cases}1, & \text{if } V(t+1,1,c(t,x)+b(x))\\ & \quad <V(t+1,2,c(t,x)+b(x))\\ 0, & \text{otherwise}\end{cases} \quad (74b)$$

with terminal conditions

$$V(T+1,J,x)=0 \quad (74c)$$

and where the functions $c(t,x)$, $b(x)$ are defined in (64). Then the optimal controls $\alpha_{12}^*(t)$, $\alpha_{21}^*(t)$ in the class (11) are given by

$$\begin{aligned}\alpha_{12}^*(t)&=\alpha_{12}^*(t,\hat{x}(t|t-1))\\ \alpha_{21}^*(t)&=\alpha_{21}^*(t,\hat{x}(t|t-1))\end{aligned} \quad (75a)$$

and

$$V^*(t)=V(t,J(t),\hat{x}(t|t-1)) \quad (75b)$$

is the optimal cost-to-go (71) given that the file is at time t in memory J and that the state estimate is $\hat{x}(t|t-1)$. In particular, the minimal cost C is

$$V(0,J(0),\pi). \quad (75c)$$

Proof: We shall only outline the proof, since it is quite similar to the proof of Theorem 3 and also appears in a different form in [15]. From (71), it is clear that the optimal cost-to-go $V^*(t)$ depends on the pattern of the previous requests

$$\mathcal{F}_{t-1}=\sigma\{n_1(s),n_2(s),\quad s\leqslant t-1\}. \quad (76)$$

It will be shown by induction that in fact $V^*(t)$ depends on $\mathcal{F}_{t-1}$ only through the position $J(t)$ of the file at time t and the state estimate $\hat{x}(t|t-1)$. This statement is clear for $t=T$. Suppose it is true for $t=t+1$. We have by substituting from (66) into (72)

$$\begin{aligned}V^*(t)=\min_{\alpha(t)} E\{&[C_1+C_{12}a_2(t)]Y_1(t)\\&+[C_2+C_{21}\hat{a}_1(t|t-1)]Y_2(t)\\&+V(t+1,J(t+1),\hat{x}(t+1|t))|\mathcal{F}_{t-1}\}.\end{aligned} \quad (77)$$

From (9) and (10) and (64) we have

$$\begin{aligned}&V(t+1,J(t+1),\hat{x}(t+1|t))\\&=V(t+1,1,c(t,\hat{x}(t|t-1))\\&\quad+b(\hat{x}(t|t-1)))\alpha_{21}(t)Y_2(t)n_1(t)\\&\quad+V(t+1,2,c(t,\hat{x}(t|t-1))\\&\quad+b(\hat{x}(t|t-1)))\alpha_{12}(t)Y_1(t)n_2(t)n_1(t)\\&\quad+V(t+1,2,c(t,\hat{x}(t|t-1)))\alpha_{12}(t)Y_1(t)n_2(t)(1-n_1(t))\\&\quad+V(t+1,J(t),c(t,\hat{x}(t|t-1))+b(\hat{x}(t|t-1)))\\&\quad\cdot[1-\alpha_{21}(t)Y_2(t)-\alpha_{12}(t)Y_1(t)n_2(t)]n_1(t)\\&\quad+V(t+1,J(t),c(t,\hat{x}(t|t-1)))\\&\quad\cdot[1-\alpha_{12}(t)Y_1(t)n_2(t)](1-n_1(t)).\end{aligned} \quad (78)$$

Observe now that all variables in (77) and (78) are $\mathcal{F}_{t-1}$ measurable, except for $n_1(t)$ and $n_2(t)$ which are independent and

$$E^{\mathcal{F}_{t-1}} n_1(t) = \hat{a}_1(t|t-1) = \rho^T \hat{x}(t|t-1)$$
$$E^{\mathcal{F}_{t-1}} n_2(t) = a_2(t). \tag{79}$$

Substituting this together with (78) into (77) and minimizing with respect to $\alpha_{12}(t)$, $\alpha_{21}(t)$, we observe that the optimal controls $\alpha_{12}^*(t)$, $\alpha_{21}^*(t)$ are functions of $\hat{x}(t|t-1)$ only and $V^*(t)$ is a function of $Y_1(t)$ and $\hat{x}(t|t-1)$ as stated before. Moreover, the substitution and minimization leads exactly to (74).

Discussion: There are two ways to find the optimal controls from (74) and (75). One possibility is to solve the equations *a priori* before the system runs and to find the values of $V(t,J,x)$ and $\alpha(t,x)$ for all x (with components $0 \leqslant x_k \leqslant 1$). Then during the operation of the system one recursively calculates on line $\hat{x}(t|t-1)$ and one evaluates $\alpha(t,\hat{x}(t|t-1))$. The second possibility may somewhat reduce the amount of computation, which, however, has to be done on line. For example at time $t=2$, one calculates the value of $\hat{x}(2|1)$. Now to compute the control $\alpha(2,\hat{x}(2|1))$ one has to calculate

$$V(3,J,c(2,\hat{x}(2|1))) \text{ and } V(3,J,c(2,\hat{x}(2|1))) + b(\hat{x}(2|1)). \tag{80}$$

Then we can find out from (74a) for what values of x_4 one has to calculate $V(4,J,x_4)$ to be able to compute (80). Then for what values of x_5 one has to compute $V(5,J,x_5)$ so that we can compute the appropriate $V(4,J,x_4)$ and keep going until we get to $V(T,J,x_T)$.

VII. Examples

When the request rates of the file vary with time, it is clear that a dynamic file assignment is much more preferable than a static one. This is further illustrated in the following simple examples of allocation in a two-computer network. Figs. 1 and 2 give examples of hourly request rates patterns over 24 h and the appropriate optimal allocation pattern. The optimal control variable $\alpha_{12}^*(t)$ is defined after (18) and in our case is

$\alpha_{12}^*(t) = 1$, if the file is to be transferred to memory 2 (if it is not there already), as soon as it is requested by computer 2.

0, if the file is to be transferred to memory 1 (if it is not there already), as soon as it is requested by computer 1.

The storage cost in each computer is $\$C_s$/h-file, and the transmission cost in every direction is $\$C_t$/transmission.

It is seen that in the case of Fig. 1, an optimal dynamic

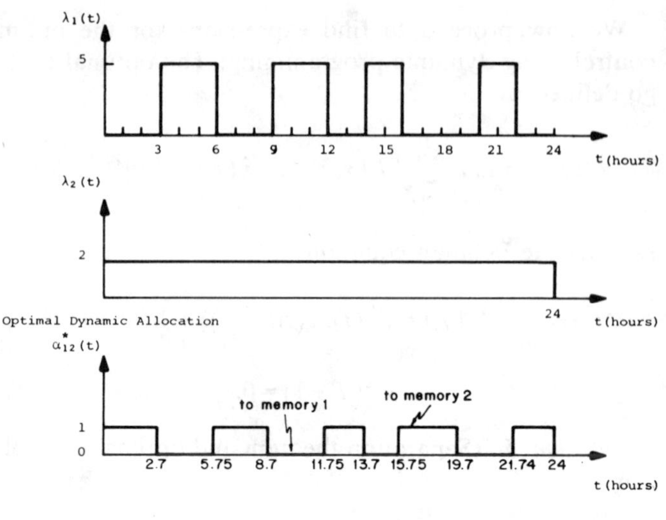

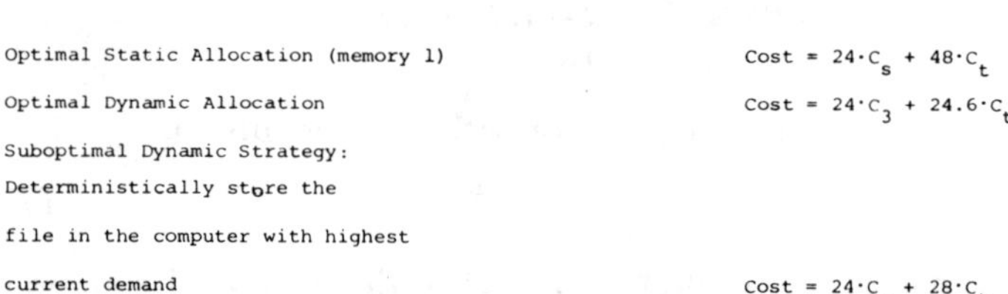

Fig. 1. An example of dynamic file assignment.

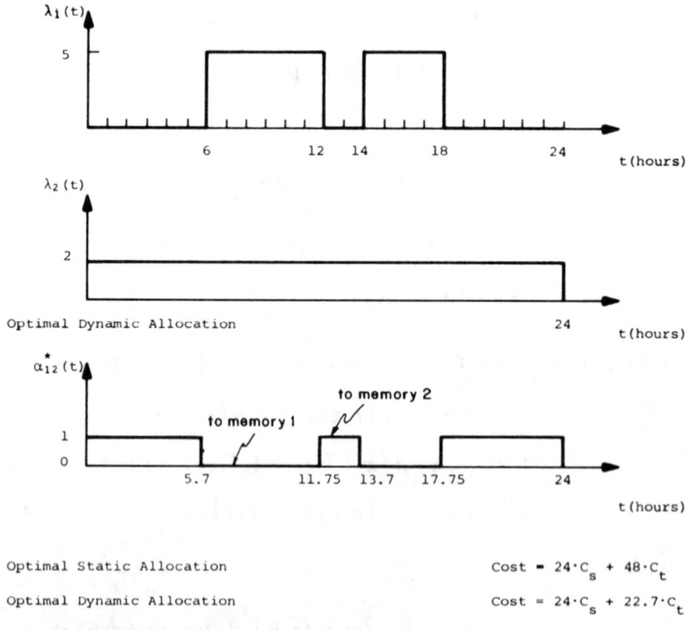

Fig. 2. A second example of dynamic file assignment.

strategy saves 50 percent of the transmission cost compared to a static strategy and is 15 percent cheaper in transmission cost than the obvious suboptimal dynamic strategy (which in fact is the best open-loop control.) We may also mention that the solution of (23) requires very little computation time, since they are linear equations except for some coefficients that are 0 or 1.

In the case of Fig. 2, the transmission cost of the dynamic strategies is lower, because there are less changes in the demand rates. The savings of the optimal dynamic strategy compared to the static strategy are higher, but compared to the best open-loop strategy the savings are lower.

VIII. Concluding Remarks

We have presented in this paper the models describing the dynamics of files whose location in a computer network is controlled by a central controller. Assuming that the pattern of the rates of demands in all computers is known to the controller, we have found the optimal strategy for the dynamic location assignment of the file. We then extended the model to include unknown rates of demand and we have shown that the separation property holds for this problem, in the sense that the only information needed by the controller is the current estimate of the state in which the rate is. This estimate can be calculated recursively using a finite-dimensional filter.

There are various directions in which the results of this paper have to be extended. We are currently investigating [20] problems of file assignment in which multiple copies and updating traffic are being considered, as well as the possibility of computer and memory failures. Moreover, the effects on the results of finite storage, finite file length, and finite channel capacity will have to be studied. Another problem of interest is that in a large computer network it will be very difficult to control the entire operation from a central site, so that schemes of decentralized control and control with delays will have to be examined.

Finally, we may mention that dynamic file assignment is only one of the aspects in computer networks that can and should be attacked via methods in optimal control. There are many other problems awaiting solution, like dynamic routing [21], [22], load sharing, processor allocation, reliability, and connectivity to which optimal control and estimation theories can make a considerable contribution.

Appendix A
Proof of Theorem 5.1

The proof will be similar to Wonham's proof of the separation theorem for linear signals in additive white Gaussian noise [19]. Let $L(\cdot,\cdot,\cdot)$ be defined as in (43), $\mathfrak{F}_t$ as in (29), (30) and let $J^{(\alpha)}(t)$ be as in (35) the function describing where the file is at time t when control law α is used. For an arbitrary admissible control law α, we use consecutively (51), (49) and (50), (47) and (44), and (52b) to obtain

$$
\begin{aligned}
&-E^{\mathfrak{F}_t}\int_t^T\left[\frac{\partial}{\partial s}V(s,J^{(\alpha)}(s),\hat{\boldsymbol{x}}(s))+\mathfrak{L}^{(\alpha)}V(s,J^{(\alpha)}(s),\hat{\boldsymbol{x}}(s))\right]ds\\
&=-E^{\mathfrak{F}_t}\int_t^T\Bigg[\frac{\partial}{\partial s}V(s,J^{(\alpha)}(s),\hat{\boldsymbol{x}}(s))\\
&\quad+\boldsymbol{a}(s,\hat{\boldsymbol{x}}(s))\frac{\partial}{\partial \boldsymbol{x}}V(s,J^{(\alpha)}(s),\hat{\boldsymbol{x}}(s))\\
&\quad+\phi_1^{(\alpha)}\big(V(s,J^{(\alpha)}(s),\hat{\boldsymbol{x}}(s))\big)\cdot\boldsymbol{\rho}^T\hat{\boldsymbol{x}}(s)\\
&\quad+\sum_{i=2}^{M}\phi_i^{(\alpha)}\big(V(s,J^{(\alpha)}(s),\hat{\boldsymbol{x}}(s))\big)\lambda_i(s)\Bigg]ds\\
&=-E^{\mathfrak{F}_t}\int_t^T\Bigg[\frac{\partial}{\partial s}V(s,J^{(\alpha)}(s),\hat{\boldsymbol{x}}(s))\\
&\quad+\boldsymbol{a}(s,\hat{\boldsymbol{x}}(s))\frac{\partial}{\partial \boldsymbol{x}}V(s,J^{(\alpha)}(s),\hat{\boldsymbol{x}}(s))\\
&\quad+\phi_1^{(\alpha)}\big(V(s-,J^{(\alpha)}(s-),\hat{\boldsymbol{x}}(s-))\big)\,dN_1(s)\\
&\quad+\sum_{i=2}^{M}\phi_i^{(\alpha)}\big(V(s-,J^{(\alpha)}(s-),\hat{\boldsymbol{x}}(s-))\big)\,dN_i(s)\Bigg]\\
&=-E^{\mathfrak{F}_t}\int_t^T dV(s,J^{(\alpha)}(s),\hat{\boldsymbol{x}}(s))\\
&=-E^{\mathfrak{F}_t}\big[V(T,J^{(\alpha)}(T),\hat{\boldsymbol{x}}(T))-V(t,J^{(\alpha)}(t),\hat{\boldsymbol{x}}(t))\big]\\
&=V(t,J^{(\alpha)}(t),\hat{\boldsymbol{x}}(t)).
\end{aligned}
\tag{A1}
$$

Now observe first that from the first part of (52a) we have

$$
\begin{aligned}
E^{\mathfrak{F}_t}&\int_t^T L(s,J^{(\alpha^*)}(s),\hat{\boldsymbol{x}}(s))\,ds\\
&=-E^{\mathfrak{F}_t}\int_t^T\left[\frac{\partial}{\partial s}V(s,J^{(\alpha)}(s),\hat{\boldsymbol{x}}(s))+\mathfrak{L}^{(\alpha^*)}V(s,J^{(\alpha^*)}(s),\hat{\boldsymbol{x}}(s))\right]ds\\
&=V(t,J^{(\alpha^*)}(t),\hat{\boldsymbol{x}}(t))
\end{aligned}
\tag{A2}
$$

where the second equality follows from (A1). Similarly for any admissible control α, (A1) and the second part of (52a) gives

$$
\begin{aligned}
V(t,J^{(\alpha)}(t),\hat{\boldsymbol{x}}(t))&=-E^{\mathfrak{F}_t}\int_t^T\left[\frac{\partial}{\partial s}V(s,J^{(\alpha)}(s),\hat{\boldsymbol{x}}(s))+\mathfrak{L}^{(\alpha)}V(s,J^{(\alpha)}(s),\hat{\boldsymbol{x}}(s))\right]ds\\
&\leqslant E^{\mathfrak{F}_t}\int_t^T L(s,J^{(\alpha)}(s),\hat{\boldsymbol{x}}(s))\,ds.
\end{aligned}
\tag{A3}
$$

Now comparing (A2) and (A3) evaluated at $t=0$ and observing that $J^{(\alpha)}(0)$ is the same for any admissible control α, since a causal control does not affect the initial condition, it follows that

$$E\int_0^T L\left(s,J^{(\alpha^*)}(s),\hat{x}(s)\right)ds = V\left(0,J^{(\alpha)}(0),\hat{x}(0)\right)$$

$$\leq E\int_0^T L\left(s,J^{(\alpha)}(s),\hat{x}(s)\right)ds \quad \text{(A4)}$$

which proves simultaneously (53) and (54).

References

[1] S. L. Hakimi, "Optimum locations of switching centers and the absolute centers and medians of a graph," *Oper. Res.*, vol. 12, pp. 450–459, 1964.

[2] ——, "Optimum distribution of switching centers in a communication network and some related problems," *Oper. Res.*, vol. 13, pp. 462–475, 1965.

[3] H. Frank, "Optimum locations on a graph with probabilistic demands," *Oper. Res.*, vol. 14, pp. 409–421, 1966

[4] V. K. Whitney, "A study of optimal file assignment and communication network configuration in remote-access computer message processing and communication systems," Univ. Michigan, EE-Rep. 02641-2, Sept. 1970.

[5] W. W. Chu, "Optimal file allocation in a multiple computer system, *IEEE Trans. Comput.* (Short Papers), vol. C-18, pp. 885–889, Oct. 1969.

[6] ——, "Optimal file allocation in a computer network," in *Computer Communication Networks*, N. Abramson and F. F. Kuo, Eds. Englewood Cliffs, NJ: Prentice-Hall, 1973.

[7] R. Boel and P. Varaiya, "Optimal control of jump processes," *SIAM J. Contr.*, to be published.

[8] R. Rishel, "Control of systems with jump Markov disturbances," *IEEE Trans. Automat. Contr.* (Short Papers), vol. AC-20, pp. 241–244, Apr. 1975.

[9] A. Segall, "Stochastic processes in estimation theory," *IEEE Trans. Inform. Theory*, vol. IT-22, May 1976, to be published.

[10] R. A. Howard. *Dynamic Programming and Markov Processes*. New York: Wiley, 1960.

[11] P. A. Meyer, *Integrales Stochastiques, Lecture Notes in Mathematics*. New York: Springer, 1967, pp. 72–162.

[12] W. M. Wonham, "Stochastic problems in optimal control," *IEEE Int. Conv. Rec.*, vol. 11, pt 2, 1963, pp. 114–124.

[13] A. Segall, M. H. A. Davis, and T. Kailath, "Filtering of signals in counting processes," *IEEE Trans. Inform. Theory*, vol. IT-21, pp. 53–58, Mar. 1975

[14] A. Segall, "Recursive estimation from discrete-time point process," *IEEE Trans. Inform. Theory*, vol. IT-22, July 1976, to be published.

[15] R. D. Smallwood and E. J. Sondik, "The optimal control of partially observable Markov processes over a finite horizon," *Oper. Res.*, vol. 21, no. 5, pp. 1071–1088, 1973.

[16] M. Aoki, *Optimization of Stochastic Systems*. New York: Academic, 1967.

[17] A. Segall and T. Kailath, "The modeling of randomly modulated jump processes", *IEEE Trans. Inform. Theory*, vol. IT-21, pp. 64–71, Mar. 1975.

[18] Y. Bar Shalom and E. Tse, "Dual effect, certainty equivalence and separation in stochastic control," *IEEE Trans. Automat. Contr.*, vol. AC-19, pp. 494–501, Oct. 1974.

[19] W. M. Wonham, "On the separation theorem of stochastic control," *SIAM J. Contr.*, vol. 6, no. 2, pp. 312–326, 1968.

[20] F. Ros, S. M. thesis, Massachusetts Inst. Technol., Cambridge, MA, 1976.

[21] A. Segall, "New analytical models for dynamic routing in computer networks," in *Proc. Nat. Telecommunication Conf.*, 1975.

[22] N. R. Sandell, Jr., and M. Athans, "Relativistic control theory and the dynamic control of communication networks," in *Proc. Decision and Control Conf.*, 1975.

Section IV-B
Query Processing

EXECUTING a database query in an optimal manner is a difficult problem even when the database is centralized. For example, in a relational system [5], a query may be decomposed into a series of restriction, projection, and join operations. However, even for straightforward queries, the number of different ways those operations can be executed is extremely large. Hence, an integral part of most such systems is an optimizer which serves to search through the state space to find either an excellent or an optimal order of execution. The topic of "optimizer" algorithms has been a fairly active area for database researchers [6].

The case of optimization becomes even more difficult when the database is distributed. Here, data transmission costs play a role that is potentially devastating to the operation of the system. Consider the straightforward query requesting, in effect, that two relations R_1 and R_2 be joined. In relational algebra this is written

$$R_1 * R_2.$$

Furthermore, assume that the query is issued at the node where R_1 resides and that R_2 resides at a different node. Without attempting to be exhaustive, there are two obvious ways of performing this query:

1) The contents of R_2 can be sent to the requesting node and the join performed there.

2) The contents of R_1 can be sent to R_2's node and the join performed there with the results being sent back to the requesting node.

Clearly, if R_1 and R_2 contain 10 and 10^{10} records respectively, selecting method 1) could devastate network operations; an incredible amount of data would have to be transferred from one node to the other. In this trivial example, method 2) appears to be superior since it would lead to less data being transferred.

The general problem of query optimization for a distributed system is discussed in the two papers contained in this section, "Query Processing in Distributed Database Systems," by A.R. Hevner and S.B. Yao, and "A Model for Optimal Query Processing for Distributed Data Bases," by W.W. Chu and P. Hurley. In the former paper, the authors specifically discuss query processing within the realm of the relational data model. They base their analysis upon the minimization of time related costs for a certain category of queries called "simple queries."

In the latter paper, the authors develop "data reduction functions" for estimating the output data volume relative to the input data volume. The functions are then utilized to compute the cost of various queries. The authors also develop a set of theorems for determining the optimal processing site for a given query.

Both papers reprinted here provide very good overviews of the distributed query optimization problem. Other related papers are listed in the Bibliography to this volume. Some of these are excellent and, had it not been for page limitations, would have been included here.

Query Processing in Distributed Database Systems

ALAN R. HEVNER AND S. BING YAO

Abstract—Query processing in a distributed system requires the transmission of data between computers in a network. The arrangement of data transmissions and local data processing is known as a distribution strategy for a query. Two cost measures, response time and total time are used to judge the quality of a distribution strategy. Simple algorithms are presented that derive distribution strategies which have minimal response time and minimal total time, for a special class of queries. These optimal algorithms are used as a basis to develop a general query processing algorithm. Distributed query examples are presented and the complexity of the general algorithm is analyzed. The integration of a query processing subsystem into a distributed database management system is discussed.

Index Terms—Computer network, database, distributed database systems, distributed processing, distribution strategy, heuristic algorithms, query processing, redundant data, relational data model, system modeling.

I. Introduction

THE distribution of data in a network or decentralized computer system offers several attractive advantages over the centralization of data at a single computer. These advantages include increased data reliability; faster, localized access to data; and the potential for upward scaling of data capacity [6]. One of the important problems is the efficient processing of queries in a distributed system. Accessing data that are stored at separate computers differs in two important ways from accessing data from a centralized computer. The necessary transmission of data over communication lines introduces substantial time delays. An advantage of the distributed system is the ability to process and transmit data in parallel at separate points in the network. The database management system must consider these facts and derive an effective arrangement of local data processing and data transmissions in order to process distributed queries. This arrangement of data processing and data transmissions is known as a *distribution strategy* for a query [8]. Among feasible distribution strategies for a given query, great variations in time cost exist [6], [4]. The importance of using efficient query processing methods on distributed systems is thus emphasized.

Previous research in this area has utilized classical optimization search techniques to find efficient distribution strategies. Wong has proposed an algorithm that is currently being implemented in the SDD-1 system [8], [2]. An initial feasible strategy is selected. Then a standard "hill-climbing" optimization technique recursively finds lower cost strategies until no further cost improvements can be discovered. The resultant distribution strategy is a local minimum cost solution in the search space.

Other data access methods extend centralized query tactics [10], [11] to a distributed environment in order to find feasible distribution strategies on the network [7], [3].

For a class of simple queries, it is possible to design optimization algorithms that will derive optimal distribution strategies in the sense that some cost measure is minimized [4]. In this paper an optimization algorithm for general queries in a distributed system is developed. The general algorithm is shown to be computationally efficient. The derived distribution strategy is shown to compare favorably with other feasible distribution strategies. The ability to integrate the query optimization algorithm into the design of a distributed database management system is discussed.

II. Distributed Query Processing

We consider a network of interconnected computers. Each computer, known as a node in the network, contains a distributed database management system (DDBMS) and a possibly redundant portion of the database. Data are logically viewed in the relational data model [1]. The unit of data distribution is a relation. The DDBMS will maintain system directories so that each query will receive a nonredundant consistent mapping of its required data. The distributed system can be characterized by the parameters defined in Table I.

Data transmission in the network is via communication links. The data transmission cost between any two nodes is defined as a linear function $C(X) = c_0 + c_1 X$, where X is the amount of data transmitted. We define our cost measure in units of time. The constant c_0 represents an initial start-up time for each separate transmission. An important property of $C(X)$ is that if $X \leqslant Y$, then $C(X) \leqslant C(Y)$. It is further assumed that the cost of data transmissions between nodes is significantly greater than the cost of local processing and intranodal data transfers between local storage devices.

A relational query performs the operations RESTRICTION, PROJECTION, and JOIN in order to retrieve data [1]. PROJECT eliminates unneeded domains from relations. RESTRICT selects rows of a relation that satisfy specified data conditions. JOIN

Manuscript received February 6, 1978; revised November 1, 1978. This research was supported by the National Science Foundation under Grant MCS76-16604. This is an expanded version of a paper presented at the Third Berkeley Workshop on Distributed Databases.

A. R. Hevner is with the Department of Computer Science, Purdue University, West Lafayette, IN 47907.

S. B. Yao is with the Department of Computer Science, Purdue University, West Lafayette, IN 47907.

Reprinted from *IEEE Trans. Software Eng.*, vol. SE-5, pp. 177–187, May 1979.

TABLE I
SYSTEM PARAMETERS

For the distributed system:

- N Number of nodes.
- M Number of unique relations.

For each relation $R_i, i = 1, \cdots, M$:

- n_i Number of records.
- a_i Number of domains.
- s_i Size. $s_i = n_i \cdot \sum_{j=1}^{a_i} w_{ij}$.

For each domain $d_{ij}, j = 1, \cdots, a_i$, of relation R_i:

- v_{ij} Number of possible domain values.
- u_{ij} Number of values domain currently holds.
- p_{ij} Selectivity. $p_{ij} = u_{ij}/v_{ij}$. $(0 < p_{ij} \leq 1)$.
- w_{ij} Size of data item in domain.
- b_{ij} Projected size of domain (no duplicate values). $b_{ij} = u_{ij} \cdot w_{ij}$.

combines relations and in the process eliminates rows whose domain values do not match between relations. This operation is also known as a JOIN RESTRICTION since, in essence, each relation is being restricted by the other. Assume a query has a selectivity of q on domain d_{kl}. After the RESTRICTION is performed the parameters of R_k are changed as follows:

1) $s_k \leftarrow s_k \cdot q$,
2) $p_{kl} \leftarrow p_{kl} \cdot q$.

A JOIN between domains d_{ij} and d_{kl} produces a pair of JOIN RESTRICTIONS. These restrictions result in the same parameter changes on both relations where the selectivity parameter q becomes p_{ij} for the restriction on relation R_K and p_{kl} for the restriction on R_i.

Query processing involving data at a single node is termed *local processing*. The effect of local processing is to reduce the amount of data that needs further processing. In a distribution strategy, all possible initial local processing should be done first. This processing results in the following parameters being defined.

- m Number of relations in the remaining query.
- α_i Number of domains in relation R_i.
- β_i Number of internodal joining domains in relation R_i.

The reduced size of each relation is $s_i = n_i \cdot \sum_{j=1}^{\alpha_i} w_{ij}$, where the projected domains can be renumbered to be the first α_i domains. Between the initial local processing and the final local processing at the result node the distribution strategy (the intermediate sequence of data transmission and local processing) is optimized by minimizing an appropriate cost function.

In order to visualize clearly the structure and interaction within a strategy we introduce a graphic notation. The data transmission pattern containing the transmission of relation R_i to the result node is called the *schedule for* R_i. Consider the cost graph of a distribution strategy in Fig. 1. Assume that each relation is at a separate node and the R_3 is at the result node. Consider the schedule for R_2 in the cost graph. Joining domains d_{11} and d_{32} are transmitted in parallel to relation R_4. The size of R_4 is reduced and domain d_{41} is transmitted to relation R_2. The size of R_2 is reduced and R_2 is transmitted to the result node.

Node 1: $R_1(d_{11}, d_{12})$
Node 2: $R_2(d_{21}, d_{22})$
Node 3 (result): $R_3(d_{31}, d_{32})$
Node 4: $R_4(d_{41})$
Node 5: $R_5(d_{51}, d_{52})$

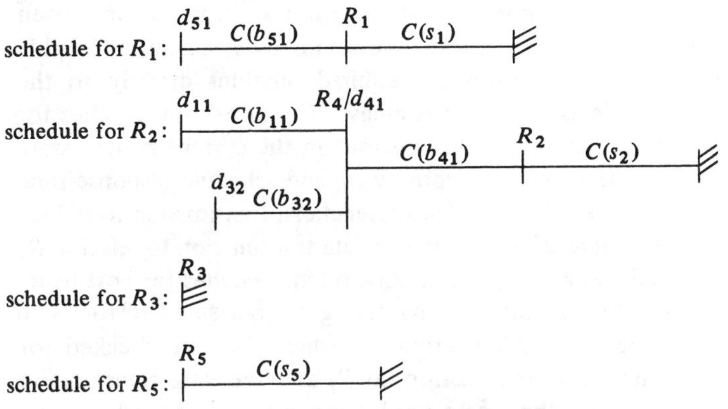

schedule for R_1: d_{51} $C(b_{51})$ R_1 $C(s_1)$
schedule for R_2: d_{11} $C(b_{11})$ R_4/d_{41} $C(b_{41})$ R_2 $C(s_2)$; d_{32} $C(b_{32})$
schedule for R_3: R_3
schedule for R_5: R_5 $C(s_5)$

Fig. 1. Cost graph of a distribution strategy.

In a distribution strategy it is possible to combine two schedules. This occurs when the entire data of one relation is transmitted to another relation for a join. In Fig. 1 relation R_4 consists of only domain d_{41}. Its schedule can be eliminated since the domain d_{41} is already included in the schedule of R_2.

We define the *schedule response time* r_i for relation R_i as the time from the start of the schedule until relation R_i is received at the result node. We define *schedule delay time* γ_i as the time from the start of the schedule until the start of relation R_i's data transmission to the result node. Thus, $r_i = \gamma_i + C(s_i)$. For the R_2 schedule in Fig. 1, $r_2 = C(b_{11}) + C(b_{41}) + C(s_2)$ and $\gamma_2 = C(b_{11}) + C(b_{41})$, where b_{ij} is the projected size (no duplicate values) of the domain d_{ij}. The time $C(b_{32})$ is not included because it occurs in parallel with time $C(b_{11})$. We define *schedule total time* t_i as the sum of all times in the schedule. For relation R_2, $t_2 = C(b_{11}) + C(b_{32}) + C(b_{41}) + C(s_2)$. We define the *minimal response time of a schedule* as $\hat{r}_i = \min(r_i)$ where the minimization ranges over all possible schedules. The *response time* of the distribution strategy is defined as $r = \max_{1 \leq i \leq m}(r_i)$ and the *total time* of the distribution strategy is defined as $t = \sum_{i=1}^{m} t_i$.

In this paper the optimization of distribution strategies under two cost objectives are analyzed: the minimization of response time r and the minimization of total time t.

III. OPTIMAL DISTRIBUTION STRATEGIES FOR SIMPLE QUERIES

A query optimization algorithm is an algorithm that derives a distribution strategy for a given query. We have introduced query optimization algorithms that derive optimal distribution strategies for a class of distributed queries called *simple queries* [4]. A simple query is defined such that after initial local processing each relation in the query contains only one domain—the common joining domain. Thus $\alpha_i = \beta_i = 1$ for all $R_i, i = 1, \cdots, m$. In what follows, we will review the query optimization algorithms for simple queries. An outline of the optimality proof is given in the Appendix. These algorithms will be used as a basis for the development of a general optimization algorithm in the next section.

A. Minimizing Response Time

The optimization algorithm PARALLEL was shown to derive a minimal response time distribution strategy for any given simple query. Algorithm PARALLEL uses the initial feasible solution which moves all required relations directly to the result node as a starting strategy. The algorithm searches for cost beneficial data transmissions in the current system state given by the size s_i, selectivity p_i, and schedule response time r_i of each relation R_i. A cost beneficial transmission to reduce response time is defined as any data transmission to relation R_i that reduces r_i. Algorithm PARALLEL searches for cost beneficial data transmissions by trying to join small relations to large relations. All relations R_j where $j < i$ are checked for potential data transmission to R_i and the data transmission that produces the greatest reduction in r_i is integrated into the distribution strategy. For the data transmission from R_j to R_i, the accumulated selectivity of R_j is $\pi_{k=1}^{j} p_k$ since all relations R_k can be transmitted to R_i in parallel with R_j for no additional response time.

Briefly, Algorithm PARALLEL can be described as follows.

Algorithm PARALLEL

1) Order relations R_i so that $s_1 \leqslant s_2 \leqslant \cdots \leqslant s_m$.

2) Initialize the parameters of the system state s_i, p_i, and $r_i = C(s_i)$ for all R_i.

3) Repeat Steps 4-6 for $i = 1$ to $i = m$.

4) (Find $\hat{r}_i$.) For each relation R_j, $j < i$, calculate the value $r'_i = \hat{r}_j + C(s_i \cdot \pi_{k=1}^{j} p_k)$. Find the j which produces the minimal such r'_i value.

5) Integrate the R_j to R_i data transmission into the distribution strategy along with the required parallel data transmissions.

6) Update s_i, p_i, and r_i values. ■

It is easy to see that the complexity of Algorithm PARALLEL is of order $O(m^2)$ where m is the number of required relations in the query [4].

B. Minimizing Total Time

Given an ordering on the required relations of a simple query, the SERIAL strategy consists of transmitting each relation, starting with R_1, to the next relation in a serial order. The strategy is represented by $R_1 \to R_2 \to \cdots \to R_m \to R_r$, where R_r is the relation at the result node. There are two cases of the SERIAL strategy. In Case 1 R_r is included in its proper order in the transmission pattern, $R_1 \to R_2 \to \cdots \to R_r \to \cdots \to R_m \to R_r$. In Case 2 R_r is not included in its proper order, $R_1 \to \cdots \to R_{r-1} \to R_{r+1} \to \cdots \to R_m \to R_r$. It was shown in [4] that for a given simple query one of the cases of the SERIAL strategy has minimal total time when the required relations are ordered so that $s_1 \leqslant s_2 \leqslant \cdots \leqslant s_m$.

C. A Simple Query Example

A simple query example is presented to illustrate the use of Algorithm PARALLEL and the SERIAL strategy. Response times and total times will be compared for the initial feasible solution, the Algorithm PARALLEL strategy, and the optimal SERIAL strategy.

Example 1: Assume a simple query requires data from four relations at four separate nodes. After initial processing, the size and selectivity values are:

	Size (s_i)	Selectivity (p_i)
R_1:	200	0.2
R_2:	400	0.4
R_3:	600	0.6
R_4:	1000	1.0

Assume that the result node is separate from the nodes containing the required relations. Let the transmission time cost be $C(X) = 20 + X$.

Initial Feasible Solution

The cost graph of the initial feasible solution is:

R_1: R_1 220

R_2: R_2 420

R_3: R_3 620

R_4: R_4 1020

Response time = r = 1020.
Total time = t = 2280.

Algorithm PARALLEL

Algorithm PARALLEL finds $\hat{r}_i$, the minimum data transmission response time for R_i, in the relation order R_1, R_2, R_3, and R_4.

R_1 response time reduction:

No transmissions to R_1 are considered.

Let $\hat{r}_1 = 220$.

R_2 response time reduction:

Transmit R_1 to R_2: $r'_2 = 220 + C(0.2 \cdot 400) = 220 + 100 = 320$.

Since $320 < 420 = r_2$, the transmission from R_1 to R_2 is integrated into the strategy. Let $\hat{r}_2 = 320$.

R_3 response time reduction:

Transmit R_2 to R_3: $r'_3 = 320 + C(0.08 \cdot 600) = 320 + 68 = 388$.

Transmit R_1 to R_3: $r'_3 = 220 + C(0.2 \cdot 600) = 220 + 140 = 360$.

Since $360 < 388 < 620 = r_3$, the data transmission from R_1 to R_3 is integrated into the strategy. Let $\hat{r}_3 = 360$.

R_4 response time reduction:

Transmit R_3 to R_4: $r'_4 = 360 + C(0.048 \cdot 1000) = 360 + 68 = 428$.

Transmit R_2 to R_4: $r'_4 = 320 + C(0.08 \cdot 1000) = 320 + 100 = 420$.

Transmit R_1 to R_4: $r'_4 = 220 + C(0.2 \cdot 1000) = 220 + 220 = 440$.

TABLE II
EXAMPLE 1: STRATEGY TIMES

	Response Time	Total Time
Initial Feasible Solution	1020	2280
Algorithm Parallel Strategy	420	780
Serial Strategy	456	456

Since $420 < 428 < 440 < 1020 = r_4$, the data transmission from R_2 to R_4 is integrated into the strategy.

The final cost graph is:

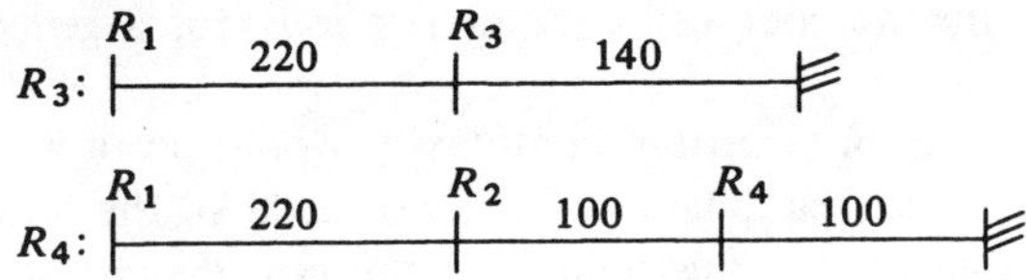

Response time $= r = 420$.
Total time $= t = 780$.

SERIAL Strategy

Since there is no required relation at the result node, both cases of the SERIAL strategy are identical. The final cost graph is:

R_4: R_1 — 220 — R_2 — 100 — R_3 — 68 — R_4 — 68

Response time $= r = 456$.
Total time $= t = 456$.

Table II shows the times for the three distribution strategies of this query. ∎

IV. A GENERALIZED ALGORITHM

While the optimization algorithms presented in the previous section work for special situations, they do not necessarily derive efficient distribution strategies for general queries. The basic distribution tactics of Algorithm PARALLEL and the ordered SERIAL strategy can, however, be extended to a general query environment. In this general environment the assumptions that have been made on the distributed system still hold but the restriction that only simple queries be considered is removed.

In a general query, each required relation may have any number of joining domains and output domains. Thus, after initial processing, $\alpha_i \geqslant \beta_i \geqslant 1$ for all $i = 1, \cdots, m$. Each node may contain any number of required relations. We define the parameter δ to represent the number of internodal joining domains in the query. For each common joining domain, we shall assume transitivity of joining paths. In other words, if a common joining domain exists on n relations at separate nodes, then data may be transmitted between any two of these relations for a JOIN RESTRICTION. For simplicity in analysis, joining domains within each relation are assumed to be independent. Thus a selectivity reduction on one domain does not affect the selectivity of the other joining domains.

The general algorithm is a heuristic that uses an improved exhaustive search to find efficient distribution strategies. Each relation R_i is examined in a small to large order to find a schedule that has a minimal response time value $\hat{r}_i$ or a minimal total time value $\hat{t}_i$, depending upon the declared cost objective. Each joining domain in the relation R_i is handled separately because of the assumption of domain independence. When the minimal time schedules are found for each joining domain, the algorithm integrates these schedules into the overall schedule for relation R_i. The distribution strategy is then constructed by synchronizing the schedules of all required relations in the query. To construct the schedules of the distribution strategy, the algorithm considers only the transmission of join domains between nodes that reduce the size and further transmission cost of the receiving relation by JOIN RESTRICTIONS. The minimal cost schedule for each joining domain is marked with an asterisk (*). However, the algorithm must maintain other candidate schedules containing cost beneficial data transmissions since these schedules may lead to more beneficial cost reductions on the other relation schedules. In fact, this can be viewed as a type of "active backtracking."

We define the following system parameters of the query after initial processing. There are m required relations. Each relation R_i has size s_i and β_i joining domains. Each joining domain d_{ij} of R_i has u_{ij} distinct values and a selectivity of p_{ij}. The algorithm uses a connectivity matrix to represent the joining paths between joining domains. Each candidate schedule for joining domain d_{ij} has the following parameters:

- s'_{ij} reduced size of relation R_i,
- b'_{ij} reduced size of distinct values in domain d_{ij},
- p'_{ij} accumulated incoming selectivity to domain d_{ij},
- γ'_{ij} schedule delay time,
- sch'_{ij} schedule representation consisting of the pattern of data transmissions to relation R_i.

Recall that when the joining domain d_{kl} is transmitted on a joining path to domain d_{ij} the accumulated selectivity p'_{kl} (Πp_{uv} such that d_{uv} is in the d_{kl} schedule) of d_{kl} is used to reduce the size of relation R_i. However, the selectivity value p_{ij} cannot be used to reduce the size of R_i by definition. Thus, we define the notation

$$p'_{kl\backslash ij} = \begin{cases} p'_{kl} \text{ if } d_{ij} \text{ is not in } d_{kl} \text{ schedule} \\ p'_{kl}/p_{ij} \text{ if } d_{ij} \text{ is in } d_{kl} \text{ schedule.} \end{cases}$$

The general algorithm is now presented. For response time minimization parallel data transmissions on a common joining domain will be considered, as was done in Algorithm PARALLEL. For total time minimization no parallel data transmission will be considered in candidate schedules.

Algorithm G

1) (Initialization.) After initial local processing, order the relations so that $s_1 \leqslant s_2 \leqslant \cdots \leqslant s_n$. For each joining domain d_{ij} of each relation R_i, initialize the parameters of the first marked schedule as:

$$s^*_{ij} \leftarrow s_i,$$
$$b^*_{ij} \leftarrow b_{ij},$$
$$p^*_{ij} \leftarrow 1,$$

$\gamma_{ij}^* \leftarrow 0$,
$sch_{ij}^* \leftarrow \Lambda$.

2) Repeat Step 3) for each R_i, $i = 1, \cdots, m$, then GO TO Step 4).

3) (Build candidate schedules for R_i.) For relation R_i repeat the following for each joining domain d_{ij}:

For each incoming domain d_{kl}, examine each candidate schedule of d_{kl} that has not been considered previously for a cost beneficial data transmission to d_{ij}.

If $((C(b_{kl}') + \gamma_{kl}') < \gamma_{ij}^*)$ or $((p_{kl} \cdot p_{kl\backslash ij}') < p_{ij}^*)$ then build a new candidate schedule for d_{ij} if $(C(b_{kl}') + \gamma_{kl}') < (C(s_{ij}^*) + \gamma_{ij}^*)$.

The parameters of the new candidate schedule are:

$$s_{ij}' \leftarrow p_{kl} \cdot p_{kl\backslash ij}' \cdot s_{ij},$$
$$b_{ij}' \leftarrow p_{kl} \cdot p_{kl\backslash ij}' \cdot b_{ij},$$
$$p_{ij}' \leftarrow p_{kl} \cdot p_{kl\backslash ij}',$$
$$\gamma_{ij}' \leftarrow C(b_{kl}') + \gamma_{kl}',$$
$$sch_{ij}' \leftarrow sch_{kl} | d_{kl}.$$

For the new candidate schedule, if $(C(s_{ij}') + \gamma_{ij}') < (C(s_{ij}^*) + \gamma_{ij}^*)$, then mark the new candidate schedule and remove the asterisk from the previously marked candidate schedule.

After all d_{ij} candidates have been constructed, eliminate all candidates for which $(C(b_{ij}') + \gamma_{ij}') \geq (C(b_{ij}^*) + \gamma_{ij}^*)$ and $(p_{ij}' \geq p_{ij}^*)$.

4) (Integrate schedules.) Eliminate all unmarked candidate schedules for all joining domains. For each relation R_i, $i = 1, \cdots, m$, integrate its schedules over all joining domains by considering the best parallel data transmissions to reduce the required cost objective, response time or total time.

5) (Build strategy.) Eliminate the schedules for relations with no output domains and all of whose joining domains have been transmitted to another relation in the distribution strategy. ∎

The feature of Algorithm G that makes the optimization computationally efficient is that data transmissions are quickly eliminated from consideration if they cannot possibly be part of a minimal time schedule. Thus only the potentially cost beneficial data transmissions are examined. In almost all cases the number of these transmissions is considerably smaller than the number of all possible data transmissions.

Algorithm G can be implemented using either the minimization of schedule response time or schedule total time as its cost objective. The difference in implementation would be found in Step 3) of the algorithm when each schedule candidate is examined as a potentially beneficial transmission. For response time all possible parallel data transmissions for that common joining domain are included and contribute to the selectivity of the considered transmission. For total time these parallel transmissions are not included. In almost all cases, considering parallel transmissions to minimize the response of a schedule increases the complexity of Algorithm G by a significant amount while the decrease in schedule response time is limited. The point will be illustrated in Section V. For this reason, the analysis of Algorithm G is carried out only for total time minimization.

The complexity of Algorithm G while minimizing total time can be measured by the number of candidate schedules that must be constructed for a given query. Since the algorithm uses an improved exhaustive search, in the worst case we can find an upper bound on algorithm complexity by considering a query with the following characteristics. Assume that all m relations are joined on all δ joining domains in a given query. In Algorithm G there are four embedded loops in Steps 2) and 3). Thus for a worst case situation the algorithm would construct one new candidate for each relation (m), for each joining domain (δ), for each incoming domain (m), and for each possible domain candidate (m). That is, the algorithm requires δm^3 schedule constructions in this situation. Therefore, Algorithm G has an upper complexity bound of $O(\delta m^3)$ where m is the number of required relations for a general query.

A lower bound on algorithm complexity would occur when a query requires no candidate schedules other than the initial feasible schedules to be constructed. In this case the complexity is $O(m)$, since one schedule must be constructed for each required relation (m).

Consider now an "average" situation. Even for a worst case type query in which all m relations are joined on all δ joining domains, Algorithm G would eliminate most nonbeneficial candidate schedule data transmissions. Assume that, on average, for each incoming joining domain a constant c number of candidates were found to require a new schedule to be constructed. The algorithm would then require δcm^2 schedule constructions to derive a distribution strategy. Thus for a general query, Algorithm G is, on average, of order $O(\delta m^2)$.

For schedule response time minimization, Algorithm G derives the identical distribution strategies for simple queries as does Algorithm PARALLEL. Algorithm PARALLEL can be seen to be a degenerate case of Algorithm G in which simple query features allow a provably minimal response time distribution strategy to be found. Only a restricted set of data transmissions are potentially cost beneficial for simple queries. Thus, the extensive looping required in Steps 2) and 3) of Algorithm G can be reduced to the simple looping of Steps 3) and 4) in Algorithm PARALLEL. The backtracking feature of Algorithm G is not required for simple queries. Also, since each relation has only one domain in a simple query, Algorithm PARALLEL implicitly eliminates relation schedules whenever the data of that relation are transmitted in the distribution strategy. These simplifications reduce Algorithm G to Algorithm PARALLEL. Therefore, for simple queries, Algorithm G derives minimal response time distribution strategies.

V. An Illustrative Example

In order to illustrate Algorithm G, let us consider a distributed database with four relations at separate network nodes.

Relation	Variable
EMPLOYEE (*E#*,ENAME,SEX)	*E*
COURSE (*C#*,CNAME,LEVEL)	*C*
STUDENT-COURSE (*E#*,*C#*)	*SC*
TEACHER-COURSE (*E#*,*C#*,ROOM)	*TC*

The multivariable query illustrated in Fig. 2 is entered into

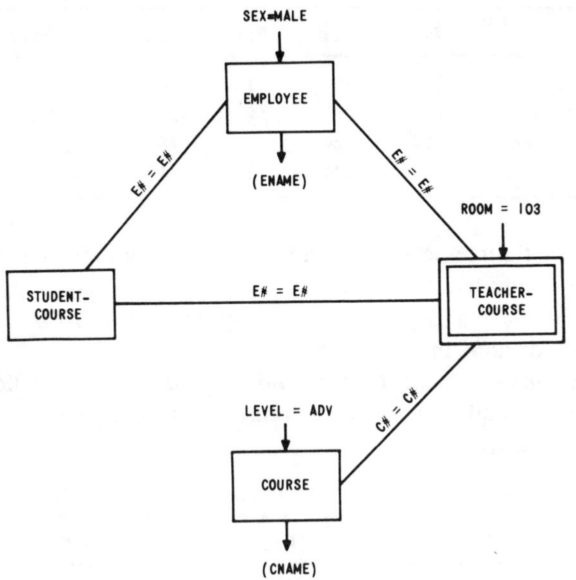

Fig. 2. Query for Example 2.

the system. Assume that the node containing the TEACHER-COURSE relation is at the result node (indicated by the double box in Fig. 2). The query can be stated as follows: for all male employees who are teaching advanced courses in Room 103 and are students in at least one course, list the employees' names and the courses they are teaching.

The first step of all distribution strategies is to do local processing. The local restrictions on *E*.SEX, *C*.LEVEL, and *TC*.ROOM are performed and the required joining domains and output domains *E*.ENAME and *C*.CNAME are projected. For convenience, number the relations in order of size s_i and let domain d_{i1} represent *E#* and domain d_{i2} represent *C#*. Assume the sizes and selectivities are:

		$d_{i1}(E\#)$		$d_{i2}(C\#)$	
Relation	s_i	b_{i1}	p_{i1}	b_{i2}	p_{i2}
R_1 - *TC:*	600	200	$\frac{1}{5}$	200	$\frac{1}{2}$
R_2 - *SC:*	600	600	$\frac{3}{5}$		
R_3 - *C:*	1200			100	$\frac{1}{4}$
R_4 - *E:*	2000	200	$\frac{1}{5}$		

Let $C(X) = 10 + X$.

Initial Feasible Solution

The cost graph of the initial feasible solution is:

TC:

SC: 610

C: 1210

E: 2010

Response time = 2010.
Total time = 3830.

Algorithm G for Response Time

Algorithm G examines all incoming joining domain candidate schedules for each relation from small to large values of s_i. In the schedule representation sch_{ij}, the notation $d_{ij} + d_{kl}$ indicates a parallel data transmission from d_{ij} and d_{kl}.

1) Examine relation TC: On joining domain d_{11}, the initial candidate schedule is built as described in Step 1) of the algorithm.

	s^*_{11}	b^*_{11}	p^*_{11}	γ^*_{11}	sch^*_{11}
*	600	200	1	0	Λ

Each incoming candidate schedule on the *E#* joining domain is tested for cost benefit. The transmission of domain d_{21} is not potentially beneficial since the test $C(b_{21}) + \gamma_{21} < C(s_{11}) + \gamma_{11}$ or $600 < 600$ is not satisfied. The transmission of domain d_{41} is potentially beneficial since all the tests of Step 3) of the algorithm are satisfied. Thus, a new candidate schedule for d_{11} is built. The parameters of this schedule are:

$$s'_{11} \leftarrow \tfrac{1}{5} \cdot 600 = 120.$$
$$b'_{11} \leftarrow \tfrac{1}{5} \cdot 200 = 40.$$
$$p'_{11} \leftarrow \tfrac{1}{5} \cdot 1 = \tfrac{1}{5}.$$
$$\gamma'_{11} \leftarrow C(200) = 210.$$
$$sch'_{11} \leftarrow d_{41}.$$

The new candidate is compared with the marked candidate for the most cost benefit. In this case the new candidate is more beneficial since

$$(C(s'_{11}) + \gamma'_{11}) < (C(s^*_{11}) + \gamma^*_{11}) \quad \text{or} \quad 130 + 210 < 610.$$

Therefore, the new schedule becomes the marked candidate.

In summary, the candidate schedules for domain d_{11} are:

	s_{11}	b_{11}	p_{11}	γ_{11}	sch_{11}
	600	200	1	0	Λ
*	120	40	$\frac{1}{5}$	210	d_{41}

On joining domain d_{12}, only one potential data transmission exists from d_{32}. This transmission is potentially beneficial since the tests of Step 3) of the algorithm are passed. The parameters of the new candidate schedule are:

$$s'_{12} \leftarrow \tfrac{1}{4} \cdot 600 = 150.$$
$$b'_{12} \leftarrow \tfrac{1}{4} \cdot 200 = 50.$$
$$p'_{12} \leftarrow \tfrac{1}{4} \cdot 1 = \tfrac{1}{4}.$$
$$\gamma'_{12} \leftarrow C(100) = 110.$$
$$sch'_{12} \leftarrow d_{32}.$$

This new candidate is more beneficial than the initial marked candidate since $(C(s'_{12}) + \gamma'_{12}) < (C(s^*_{12}) + \gamma^*_{12})$ or $160 + 110 < 610$.

In summary, the candidate schedules for domain d_{12} are:

	s_{12}	b_{12}	p_{12}	γ_{12}	sch_{12}
(deleted)	600	200	1	0	Λ
*	150	50	$\frac{1}{4}$	110	d_{32}

The first candidate schedule can be eliminated from further consideration since $(C(b'_{12}) + \gamma'_{12}) > (C(b^*_{12}) + \gamma^*_{12})$ and $p'_{12} > p^*_{12}$. Only the marked candidate remains for domain d_{12}.

2) Examine relation SC: On joining domain d_{21}, the initial candidate schedule is:

	s^*_{21}	b^*_{21}	p^*_{21}	γ^*_{21}	sch^*_{21}
*	600	600	1	0	Λ

Four potential data transmissions to relation *SC* are tested. The two candidate schedules from domain d_{11} are considered for transmission. Candidate schedules are built for both.

For the data transmission of d_{11} to d_{21}, the parameters are:

$$s'_{21} \leftarrow \tfrac{1}{5} \cdot 600 = 120.$$
$$b'_{21} \leftarrow \tfrac{1}{5} \cdot 600 = 120.$$
$$p'_{21} \leftarrow \tfrac{1}{5} \cdot 1 = \tfrac{1}{5}.$$
$$\gamma'_{21} \leftarrow C(200) = 210.$$
$$sch'_{21} \leftarrow d_{11}.$$

For the data transmission of the marked candidate schedule (d_{41}, d_{11}) to d_{21}, the selectivity becomes $\frac{1}{5} \cdot \frac{1}{5} = \frac{1}{25}$. The parameters of the new candidate are:

$$s'_{21} \leftarrow \tfrac{1}{25} \cdot 600 = 24.$$
$$b'_{21} \leftarrow \tfrac{1}{25} \cdot 600 = 24.$$
$$p'_{21} \leftarrow \tfrac{1}{25} \cdot 1 = \tfrac{1}{25}.$$
$$\gamma'_{21} \leftarrow C(40) + 210 = 260.$$
$$sch'_{21} \leftarrow d_{41} \,|\, d_{11} = d_{41}, d_{11}.$$

The candidate schedules are compared. The candidate schedule $sch'_{21} = (d_{41}, d_{11})$ is the most beneficial and is marked.

The data transmission from d_{41} to d_{21} is tested. A new candidate is not built. In order to minimize schedule response time, Algorithm G will also test parallel data transmissions. The parallel transmission of d_{11} and d_{41} to d_{21} is tested and a new schedule candidate is built. The parameters are:

$$s'_{21} \leftarrow \tfrac{1}{25} \cdot 600 = 24.$$
$$b'_{21} \leftarrow \tfrac{1}{25} \cdot 600 = 24.$$
$$p'_{21} \leftarrow \tfrac{1}{25} \cdot 1 = \tfrac{1}{25}.$$
$$\gamma'_{21} \leftarrow C(200) = 210.$$
$$sch'_{21} \leftarrow d_{11} + d_{41}.$$

After testing, this parallel schedule is found to be the most beneficial and marked.

In summary, the candidate schedules for domain d_{21} are:

	s_{21}	b_{21}	p_{21}	γ_{21}	sch_{21}
(deleted)	600	600	1	0	Λ
(deleted)	120	120	$\frac{1}{5}$	210	d_{11}
(deleted)	24	24	$\frac{1}{25}$	260	d_{41}, d_{11}
*	24	24	$\frac{1}{25}$	210	$d_{11} + d_{41}$

The first three schedule candidates can be eliminated from further consideration since in each case $(C(b'_{21}) + \gamma'_{21}) > (C(b^*_{21}) + \gamma^*_{21})$ and $p'_{21} \geqslant p^*_{21}$. Only the marked candidate remains for domain d_{21}.

3) Examine relation C: On joining domain d_{32}, a candidate schedule is built for the data transmission from the marked schedule of d_{12}.

	s_{32}	b_{32}	p_{32}	γ_{32}	sch_{32}
	1200	100	1	0	Λ
*	600	50	$\frac{1}{2}$	170	d_{32}, d_{12}

4) Examine relation E: On joining domain d_{41}, four candidate schedules are built.

	s_{41}	b_{41}	p_{41}	γ_{41}	sch_{41}
	2000	200	1	0	Λ
	400	40	$\frac{1}{5}$	210	d_{11}
(deleted)	240	24	$\frac{3}{25}$	610	$d_{11} + d_{21}$
*	240	24	$\frac{3}{25}$	252	$(d_{11} + d_{41}), d_{21}$

The third candidate schedule is eliminated from further consideration.

A second loop through the relations finds no further new candidate schedules. Therefore, the algorithm integrates the marked schedules into a distribution strategy. No schedule is needed for relation *TC* since it is at the result node. Since relation *SC* consists of only one joining domain that is transmitted to relation *E* in the strategy, its schedule can be eliminated.

The final distribution strategy is

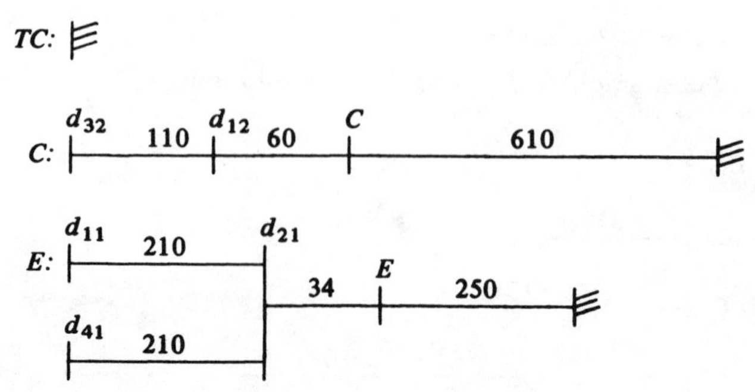

Response time = 780.
Total time = 1484.

Algorithm G for Total Time

For total time schedule minimization, Algorithm G does not consider parallel data transmission of candidate schedules. Thus, the processing steps are similar to Algorithm G for response time except fewer candidates are built. The candidate schedules built for each relation joining domain are:

1) Relation TC:

Domain d_{11}.

	s_{11}	b_{11}	p_{11}	γ_{11}	sch_{11}
	600	200	1	0	Λ
*	120	40	$\frac{1}{5}$	210	d_{41}

Domain d_{12}.

	s_{12}	b_{12}	p_{12}	γ_{12}	sch_{12}
(deleted)	600	200	1	0	Λ
*	150	50	$\frac{1}{4}$	110	d_{32}

2) Relation SC:

Domain d_{21}.

	s_{21}	b_{21}	p_{21}	γ_{21}	sch_{21}
(deleted)	600	600	1	0	Λ
(deleted)	120	120	$\frac{1}{5}$	210	d_{11}
*	24	24	$\frac{1}{25}$	260	d_{41}, d_{11}

3) Relation C:

Domain d_{32}.

	s_{32}	b_{32}	p_{32}	γ_{32}	sch_{32}
	1200	100	1	0	Λ
*	600	50	$\frac{1}{2}$	170	d_{32}, d_{12}

4) Relation E:

Domain d_{41}.

	s_{41}	b_{41}	p_{41}	γ_{41}	sch_{41}
	2000	200	1	0	Λ
	400	40	$\frac{1}{5}$	210	d_{11}
*	240	24	$\frac{3}{25}$	302	d_{41}, d_{11}, d_{21}

A second loop finds no new candidate schedules. The algorithm integrates the marked schedules into a distribution strategy, eliminating the schedule for relation *SC* as before. The final distribution strategy is:

TABLE III
PROCESSING TIMES FOR THE DISTRIBUTION STRATEGIES

	Response Time	Total Time
Initial Feasible Solution	2010	3830
Algorithm G (Response Time)	780	1484
Algorithm G (Total Time)	780	1324

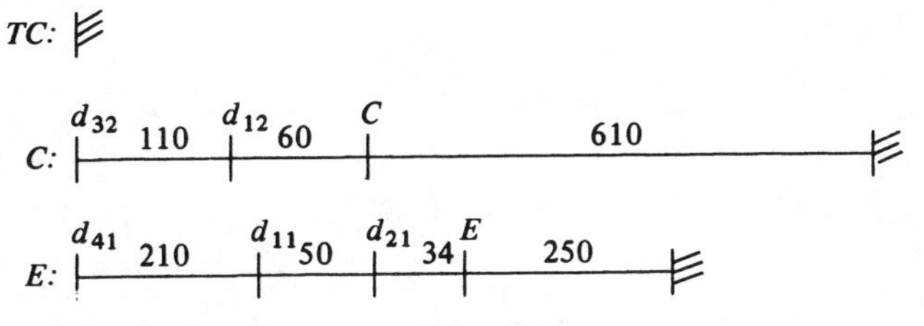

TC:

C: d_{32} 110 d_{12} 60 *C* 610

E: d_{41} 210 d_{11} 50 d_{21} 34 *E* 250

Response time = 780.
Total time = 1324.

We note in this example that the response time case required 14 candidate schedules while the total time case required 12 candidate schedules. Fewer candidate schedule constructions allow more efficient processing. Another advantage of the total time algorithm is that in most cases implementing a total time strategy on a network requires less synchronization and message passing between nodes.

Table III shows the times for the three distribution strategies of this example.

The most striking observation in Table III is the large time differences between the initial feasible solution and the other two distribution strategies. The use of an optimization algorithm can be concluded to be an important part of a distributed database management system. For this example, the total time strategy of Algorithm G performs best in both cost measures.

VI. IMPLEMENTATION

A distributed database system contains four major subsystems: the query processing subsystem, the integrity subsystem, the scheduler subsystem, and the reliability subsystem.

The query processing subsystem which implements the query optimization algorithm is highly interdependent with other subsystems in the DDBMS. This interdependence is illustrated in Fig. 3. In this section the interactions between distributed query processing using an optimization algorithm such as Algorithm G and other distributed system functions are discussed.

Consider a query submitted to the query processing subsystems. Before the query can be processed by an optimization algorithm the subset of the database required to satisfy the query must be determined. Once the data needs (i.e., the required relations) of the query are recognized by query analysis, the location of the data in the network must be found by using a data directory. Since data may be stored redundantly at network nodes, a specific nonredundant materialization [5] of the required data must be assigned to each query for its processing. The optimization algorithm uses a specific data

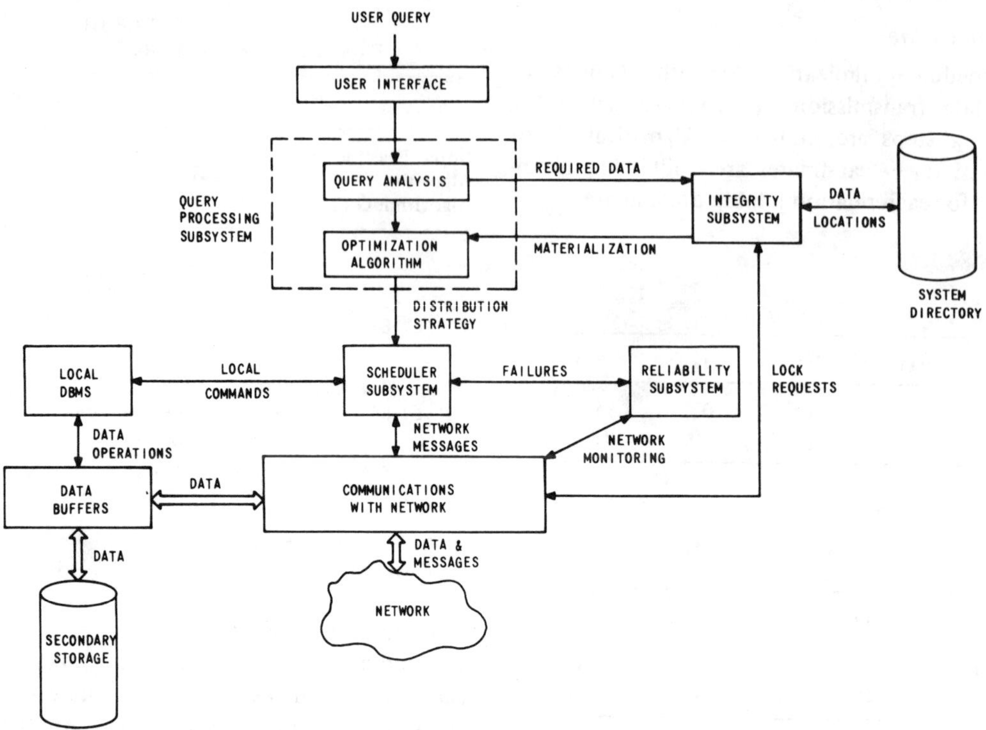

Fig. 3. Query processing in a distributed database system.

materialization to design an efficient distribution strategy for each query.

The subsystem that is responsible for assigning materializations to queries is the *integrity subsystem.* This subsystem uses the system data directory to find the most cost beneficial copies of data to include in a query's materialization. At the same time, however, this subsystem is responsible for maintaining database integrity and consistency.

Queries on a distributed system may update data in the database. The integrity subsystem must handle the problem of synchronizing update queries on the redundant data in the network. All redundant copies of data must be updated correctly and consistently by update queries; and retrieval queries should be guaranteed correct, up-to-date data at the time a materialization is assigned.

Update synchronization is controlled in nondistributed systems by data locking rules. For consistency, most update queries require exclusive locking on all copies of the data to be modified while retrieval queries require a share lock on just the copy of data it is using [9]. However, in a distributed database environment the time delays introduced by transmitting this locking information throughout the network is often substantial and unmanageable. The integrity subsystem must solve the problem of controlling concurrent queries so that database integrity and consistency is maintained while the communication overhead of transmitting control information among network nodes is minimized.

Once the query processing subsystem receives a materialization for each query, the optimization algorithm (such as Algorithm G) is called upon to derive a distribution strategy for the query. The distribution strategy is passed to a subsystem that schedules the local processing and data transmissions of the strategy.

One function of the *scheduler subsystem* is to send commands to the local DBMS's in the network in order to do local data processing. In addition, the scheduler must interact with the network communication facilities at each node in order to transmit data between nodes as determined by the distribution strategy. The scheduler coordinates the various schedules in the strategy so that the query response is presented at the result node. It is easily recognized that a complex distribution strategy will require considerable network coordination of transmissions and local processing. This, in turn, requires increased message passing by the scheduler. Often simple distribution strategies are beneficial in a distributed system because the scheduler is required to transmit fewer messages on the network. This consideration must be kept in mind when optimization algorithms are designed. Complex, optimal distribution strategies may be suboptimal when the coordination requirements (i.e., message passing) of implementing the complex strategy are considered. This is a major part of the rationale behind constructing Algorithm G to minimize the total time of relation schedules as its cost objective. Parallel data transmissions in a schedule often require considerable coordination in return for little reduction in schedule response time.

One of the primary advantages of a distributed database system is system reliability. With the storage of redundant data at separate nodes, even though single system components such as nodes and communication lines may fail, specific data items will still be available at other nodes. The *reliability subsystem* of a DDBMS continuously monitors system components for failures. In the event of failures, control information is distributed in the network so that normal operations may continue while the failed component is being repaired. The reliability subsystem then attempts to integrate the repaired component back into the system in a state of database consistency.

A component failure affects query processing when the failed node contains data that are part of a query's materialization. Since the distribution strategy was derived on that specific materialization, the strategy may no longer be valid. Two alternatives exist: to wait for the failed node to be repaired and continue the original distribution strategy; or to back out the query and restart it for a new materialization and new distribution strategy. The latter alternative would seem to be preferable in most cases.

The complete design of a distributed database system requires a thorough understanding of interactions among its subsystems. The implementation of a distribution algorithm such as Algorithm G for query processing is an integral part of the DDBMS development. The efficiency of the query processing subsystem has a strong influence on the overall DDBMS efficiency.

VII. Conclusion

Efficient query processing is an essential function of a distributed database system. In this paper a general algorithm (Algorithm G) is developed that will derive a distribution strategy for a general distributed query. Algorithm G is developed in a two-step approach. In a previous paper [4], two simple algorithms (Algorithm PARALLEL for response time and the ordered SERIAL strategy for total time) were proven to produce minimal time distribution strategies for a special class of queries.

Algorithm G is shown to be a straightforward extension of these simple algorithms to a general query environment. It is computationally efficient for average distributed queries. An example illustrated that the distribution strategies derived from Algorithm G are much more cost effective than an initial feasible distribution strategy in which no data access optimization is done.

It is clear that the query processing subsystem embodying the optimization algorithm cannot function alone in a distributed database system. The interdependency of the query processing subsystem with other subsystems is discussed. An especially critical phase of query processing is the actual implementation of the derived distribution strategy on the network by the scheduler subsystem. A distribution strategy that requires extensive message passing on the network will adversely affect the performance of the entire system. In a distributed database system, the need for data access optimization is evident, however, at the same time, distribution strategies should be kept as simple as possible for efficient implementation.

Algorithm G is developed in such a way that its use in the query processing subsystem is efficient. In addition, the derived distribution strategies of Algorithm G are simple enough that they can be executed efficiently on the distributed system.

Appendix

The formal proofs that 1) Algorithm PARALLEL minimizes the response time for a simple query and 2) the SERIAL strategy minimizes the total time for a simple query are detailed in [4]. A brief outline of these proofs will be given here.

A. Minimizing Response Time

We prove that Algorithm PARALLEL finds a distribution strategy for a simple query that is optimal in the sense of having a minimal response time. The basis of the proof is found in the following Lemma. Recall that $\hat{r}_i$ is the minimal response time for the schedule of relation R_i.

Lemma 1: For a simple query if, after initial processing, the required relations $R_1, \cdots, R_m$ are ordered so that $s_1 \leqslant s_2 \leqslant \cdots \leqslant s_m$ then $\hat{r}_1 \leqslant \hat{r}_2 \leqslant \cdots \leqslant \hat{r}_m$. ∎

This lemma is proved by induction on relation order $i = 1$ to $i = m$. From the data transmission cost assumption, if $s_i \leqslant s_j$ then $C(s_i) \leqslant C(s_j)$. Initially $r_i = C(s_i)$ for all i. Therefore it is clear that $\hat{r}_1 = C(s_1)$ and $\hat{r}_1 \leqslant \hat{r}_j$ for all $j = 1, \cdots, m$. For an arbitrary i the minimum response time schedule of R_i is studied. Two cases are considered depending upon whether the schedule of R_{i-1} is part of the schedule of R_i or not. For both cases it is shown that $\hat{r}_{i-1} \leqslant \hat{r}_i$.

Theorem 1: For a simple query, if, after initial processing, the required relations $R_1, \cdots, R_m$ are ordered so that $s_1 \leqslant s_2 \leqslant \cdots \leqslant s_m$ then Algorithm PARALLEL will derive a minimum response time distribution strategy. ∎

The proof shows inductively that Algorithm PARALLEL correctly derives minimum response time schedules for each R_i, $i = 1, \cdots, m$. The result of Lemma 1 limits the search space for cost beneficial data transmissions so that to reduce the response time of the R_i schedule, only transmissions from relations R_j, $j < i$, when $r_j = \hat{r}_j$, need be considered. Algorithm PARALLEL is shown to implement a strategy that finds $\hat{r}_i$ from $i = 1$ to $i = m$. Then from Lemma 1 the response time for a simple query $r = \max_i(r_i) = \max_i(\hat{r}_i) = \hat{r}_m$. Since the response time of any distribution strategy must be at least $\hat{r}_m$, $r = \hat{r}$ as required.

B. Minimizing Total Time

We prove that the SERIAL strategy for simple queries is optimal in the sense of having a minimal total time. We define a serial schedule for a relation to be a schedule in which there are no parallel data transmissions. Two schedules for a relation R_i are *equivalent* if the relations transmitted in one schedule are a subset of the relations transmitted in the other schedule and the size and selectivity reductions at relation R_i are identical. Three lemmas are used to prove that the ordered serial strategy finds the minimal total time for a simple query.

Lemma 2: Given a serial schedule $\overline{Q} = R_{i_1}, \cdots, R_{i_l}$, if $i_j = i_k$ for some $j < k$ then the schedules $\overline{Q}$ and $\overline{Q}' = R_{i_1}, \cdots, R_{i_j}, \cdots, R_{i_{k-1}}, R_{i_{k+1}}, \cdots, R_{i_l}$ are equivalent and $\text{COST}(\overline{Q}') < \text{COST}(\overline{Q})$. ∎

This lemma follows directly from the definition of relation selectivity and size reduction. Once a relation's selectivity is included in the accumulated selectivity of a serial schedule, another transmission on the same relation can cause no further selectivity or size reduction.

Lemma 3: Given a nonserial schedule containing at least one instance of parallel data transmission, an equivalent serial schedule $\overline{Q}$ exists such that $\text{COST}(\overline{Q})$ is less than or equal to the total time cost of the nonserial schedule. ■

It is proved in a straightforward manner that any instance of data transmissions occurring in parallel can be transformed into a sequence of serial transmissions which has a total time less than or equal to the parallel transmissions.

The application of Lemmas 2 and 3 to any feasible distribution strategy would transform it into a serial schedule in which each required relation is transmitted exactly once (except, perhaps, the relation at the result node). Lemma 4 shows that performing the serial data transmissions in a specified order has the least total time.

Lemma 4: For a simple query if, after initial processing, the required relations $R_1, \cdots, R_m$ are ordered so that $s_1 \leqslant s_2 \leqslant \cdots \leqslant s_m$ then the serial schedule $\overline{Q} = R_{i1}, \cdots, R_{i_l}$, where $i_j < i_{j+1}$ for all $j = 1, \cdots, l-1$, has the minimum total cost among all equivalent schedules. ■

Theorem 2 can now be proved by the use of Lemmas 2-4.

Theorem 2: For a simple query if, after initial processing, the required relations $R_1, \cdots, R_m$ are ordered so that $s_1 \leqslant s_2 \leqslant \cdots \leqslant s_m$ then the SERIAL strategy has the minimum total time. Case 1 of the SERIAL strategy is optimal if

$$(1 - p_r) > \frac{\dfrac{c_0}{c_1} + s_r \prod_{j=1}^{r=1} p_j}{\sum_{i=r+1}^{m} s_i \prod_{\substack{j=1 \\ j \neq r}}^{i-1} p_j}.$$

Otherwise Case 2 of the SERIAL strategy is optimal. ■

Any feasible distribution strategy must include the transmission of all required relations to the result node. Among all feasible distribution strategies there must exist at least one strategy with minimal total time. By the use of Lemmas 2-4 any such optimal distribution strategy has an equivalent SERIAL strategy with less or equal total time. Thus the SERIAL strategy must have minimal total time.

There are two possible cases of the SERIAL strategy. Which case has the minimum total time must be tested. From the definition of the SERIAL strategy, the total time for Case 1, where R_r is included in the ordered SERIAL strategy, is

$$\sum_{i=1}^{m} C\left(s_i \cdot \prod_{j=1}^{i-1} p_j\right).$$

For Case 2, where R_r is not included in the SERIAL strategy, the total time is

$$\sum_{\substack{i=1 \\ i \neq r}}^{m} C\left(s_i \cdot \prod_{\substack{j=1 \\ j \neq r}}^{i-1} p_j\right).$$

Case 1 of the SERIAL strategy is optimal if:

$$\sum_{i=1}^{m} C\left(s_i \cdot \prod_{j=1}^{i-1} p_j\right) < \sum_{\substack{i=1 \\ i \neq r}}^{m} C\left(s_i \cdot \prod_{\substack{j=1 \\ j \neq r}}^{i-1} p_j\right).$$

Algebraic manipulation of this equation results in the formula given in Theorem 2.

REFERENCES

[1] E. F. Codd, "A relational model of data for large shared data banks," *Commun. Ass. Comput. Mach.*, vol. 13, pp. 377-387, June 1970.

[2] Computer Corporation of America, "A distributed database management system for command and control applications: Semi-annual technical report 2," Tech Rep. CCA-78-03, Jan. 30, 1978.

[3] R. Epstein, M. Stonebraker and E. Wong, "Distributed query processing in a relational data base system," in *Proc. ACM 1978 SIGMOID Conf.*, Austine, TX, June 1978, pp. 169-180.

[4] A. R. Hevner and S. B. Yao, "Optimization of data access in distributed systems," Comput. Sci. Dep. Purdue Univ., Tech. Rep. TR281, July 1978.

[5] J. B. Rothnie and N. Goodman, "An overview of the preliminary design of SDD-1: A system for distributed databases," in *Proc. 1977 Berkeley Workshop on Distributed Data Management and Computer Networks*, Lawrence Berkeley Lab., Univ. California, Berkeley, May 1977, pp. 39-57.

[6] —, "A survey of research and development in distributed database management," in *1977 Proc. Very Large Data Bases*, Tokyo, Japan, Oct. 1977, pp. 48-62.

[7] M. Stonebraker and E. Neuhold, "A distributed database version of INGRES," in *Proc. 1977 Berkeley Workshop on Distributed Data Management and Computer Networks*, Lawrence Berkeley Lab., Univ. California, Berkeley, May 1977, pp. 19-36.

[8] E. Wong, "Retrieving dispersed data from SDD-1: A system for distributed databases," in *Proc. 1977 Berkeley Workshop on Distributed Data Management and Computer Networks*, Lawrence Berkeley Lab., Univ. California, Berkeley, May 1977, pp. 217-235.

[9] K. P. Eswaran, J. N. Gray, R. A. Lorie, and I. L. Traiger, "The notion of consistency and predicate locks in a database system," *Commun. Ass. Comput. Mach.*, vol. 19, pp. 624-633, Nov. 1976.

[10] E. Wong and K. Youssefi, "Decomposition–A strategy for query processing," *ACM Trans. on Database Systems*, vol. 1, pp. 223-241, Sept. 1976.

[11] S. B. Yao, "Optimization of query evaluation algorithms," *ACM Trans. on Database Systems*, vol. 4, June 1979, to be published.

A MODEL FOR OPTIMAL QUERY PROCESSING FOR DISTRIBUTED DATA BASES *

Wesley W. Chu and Paul Hurley

University of California
Los Angeles, California 90024

Abstract

A model is developed in this paper for an optimal query processing policy which is based on processing cost, communication cost and data reduction functions. Data reduction functions describe the relationship between input data traffic volume and output data traffic volume of an operation and are useful in determining query processing cost. A set of graphs, called query operation graphs, can be generated for a given query. Theorems are developed for determining the optimal sites for processing for a given query operation graph and for selecting local optimal query processing policies. Use of these theorems greatly reduces the computation requirements in determining the optimal query processing policy. An example is given to illustrate the model.

Introduction

Optimal query processing is an important concern in the field of distributed data bases. The main problem is: If a query can be decomposed into subqueries that require operations at geographically separated data bases, determine the sequence and the sites for performing this set of operations such that the operating cost (communication cost and processing cost) for processing this query is minimized. The problem is complicated by the fact that query processing not only depends on the structure of the query, but also on the operational parameters associated with the query.

Prior works in query processing [1,2,3] were either limited to the relational model or were of narrow scope in treatment. In this paper we will present a general and systematic approach to treatment of this problem. A parameter called the data reduction function is introduced which describes the volume of output data in relation to the volume of input data for performing a specific operation. This function enables us to estimate the output file length of an operation, thus allowing us to compute the operating cost of a given query processing policy.

In this paper, we will first define the query operation graph and its relationship to the query processing policy. Next, theorems are derived for optimal site selection for performing the operations and for locating local optimal query processing policies. Then a mathematical model is developed to compute the operating cost for a given query processing policy. An example is also given to illustrate the procedure in determining the optimal policy for processing a given query.

2. Query Operation Graph

We assume that a given query can be decomposed into a set of operations $\{\beta_0^1,\ldots,\beta_0^r, \beta_1, \ldots, \beta_n, \beta_e\}$ which will provide the answer to the query. $\{\beta_0^i, i=1, \ldots, r\}$ is the set of initial query processing operations, where r is the number of files initially referenced by the query. The operation β_0^i performed at the site of file F_i selects the subset of F_i for processing the query. The end query processing operation, β_e, is performed at the site which originated the query and represents transmission of the query results to the originating site.

The operations $\{\beta_1, \ldots, \beta_n\}$ are data manipulation operations that involve multiple files. Such an operation may bring files from remote locations to a single site for processing.

In general, the operations $\{\beta_1, \ldots, \beta_n\}$ can be executed in many different sequences. Given such a sequence, we partition it into one or more subsets of operations such that each subset is to be performed at a single site, while preserving the operation sequence. In addition, we specify that two sets of operations that are adjacent in the sequence must be executed at different sites. Given such a partitioned sequence, we construct a graph called a query operation graph. In this graph, each subset of the sequence of operations is represented by one node, called an operation node. All the operations of a given operation node must be executed at the same site. The output temporary file(s) generated by the operations of such a node are indicated by arcs which originate at that node and lead to other operation nodes. Since the operations of adjacent operation nodes are performed at different sites, these arcs represent data transmissions between sites.

The operation nodes also receive data from the β_0^i, i=1,...,r, operations which are represented by another type of node--the file node, which has no input arcs. Output arcs originating in the file nodes represent the transfer of temporary files from file nodes to operation nodes.

*This research is supported by the U.S. Office of Naval Research, Contract no. N00014-75-C-0650.

Reprinted from *Proc. 18th IEEE COMPCON,* Feb. 26–Mar. 1, 1979, pp. 116–122.

An example of a query operation graph is shown in Figure 1. It consists of four file nodes which are labelled F_1, F_2, F_3, and F_4, and three operation nodes which are labelled β_2, $\beta_1\beta_3$, and β_e. Files f_1, ..., f_6 are temporary files that are transferred from one operation to another. This graph represents the operation sequence $\beta_2\beta_1\beta_3\beta_e$ such that β_2 is executed at one site, followed by β_1 and β_3 at a second site, followed by β_e which transmits the final result file f_6 to the originating site.

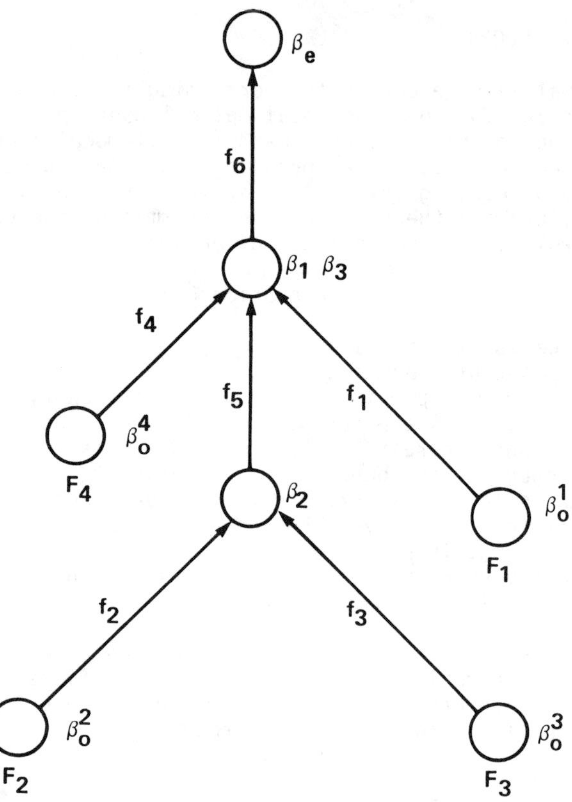

Figure 1 A Query Operation Graph

The query operation graph displays two properties of a query processing policy: (1) the sequence of operations, and (2) the separation between operations which are performed at different sites. To determine a query processing policy, we further need to select a site for performing the operations represented by each operation node in the graph. If the site selection method selects the same site for two adjacent operation nodes of a graph, we call that selection an inconsistent site selection.

Given a query, we construct the set of query operation graphs which represent the query processing policies. We are particularly interested in sets of graphs which have the same sequence of operations. We call these sets of graphs sequence groups.

When a query can be decomposed into independent subsets of operations, these sets of operations can be used to construct independent subgraphs. The query operation graph that consists of these independent subgraphs allows processing these sets of operations in parallel, and yields lower response time.

3. Properties of Query Operation Graphs

The operating cost for processing a query with a given policy consists of communication cost and processing cost. To apply a query operation graph to a given distributed data base, we assume that the communication cost between each pair of computers is proportional to the volume of data, and that the processing cost for all computers depends on the operation performed and on the volume of data. We study the properties of query operation graphs under these conditions.

Theorem 1

For a given query operation graph, if the unit communication costs among different pairs of computers are the same, and the processing costs for a given operation are the same for all the computers, then for each operation node of the graph, selecting the file node site that sends the largest amount of data to that operation node as the site for performing its operations yields minimum operating cost for that graph.

Proof

The operating cost consists of communication cost and processing cost. For a given graph, the sequence of operations is fixed, which implies that the input volume to each operation is fixed. Since the unit processing cost for a given operation is the same for all sites in the network, the total processing cost is constant. Therefore, to minimize operating cost, we need only minimize communication cost.

The communication cost of the given graph consists of two parts: (1) the communication cost of transmission between the operation node sites, and (2) the communication cost of transmission from file node sites to operation node sites. Since all unit communication costs are the same, and since the operations of adjacent operation nodes must be executed at different sites, cost (1) is constant for a given graph. Therefore, minimizing cost (2) minimizes communication cost.

For a given operation node, we select the file node site that sends the largest volume of data to the site of that operation node as the site for performing its operations. This site selection minimizes the volume of data transmitted from file node sites to the site of that operation node, and since unit communication costs are the same between any pair of computers, such a selection minimizes communication cost (2) for that operation node. Since site selection does not affect the volume of output data generated by the operation node, the site selections of the remaining operation nodes are independent of the site selection of the said node, and the sites of the remaining operation nodes in the graph can be selected one at a time in the same manner. Since the set of operation nodes is fixed for the graph, using this theorem for site selection minimizes communication cost (2), thus minimizing operating cost.♦

If this site selection method generates an inconsistent site selection, then the graph can be reduced to a simpler graph (one that has a lesser number of operation nodes) that yields a lower operating cost than that of the original graph as will be shown in Theorem 2.

Theorem 2

If the unit communication costs among different pairs of computers in the distributed data base are the same, and the processing cost for a given operation is the same for all the computers, if the site selection for a given query operation graph based on Theorem 1 is inconsistent, then that graph can be reduced to a simpler graph (one with a lesser number of operation nodes) which is contained in the same sequence group. Further, the reduced graph yields lower operating cost than that of the original graph.

Proof

If the site selection based on Theorem 1 is inconsistent, we combine the two adjacent operation nodes causing the inconsistency into one node. The resultant graph performs the same set of operations in the same sequence. Thus, it is a member of the same sequence group as the original graph.

Since the sequence of operations of the reduced graph is the same as that of the original graph, the processing cost of the two graphs is the same. Therefore, it will suffice to show that the communication cost of the reduced graph is lower than that of the original graph.

Let the two operation nodes that caused the inconsistency be denoted as node N_a and node N_b. The difference in communication cost between the original graph and the reduced graph is: (1) the communication cost of data transferred between the sites of nodes N_a and N_b, and (2) the communication cost of data transferred from file node sites to the sites of N_a and N_b. Communication cost (1) is eliminated in the reduced graph because nodes N_a and N_b are combined into one node and thus their operations are executed at the same site. As shown in the proof of Theorem 1, communication cost (2) for an operation node is minimized by executing the operation(s) at the file node site S_k that sends the largest amount of data to the site of that operation node. In this case, because of the inconsistent site selection, that file node site S_k is the site selected for performing the operations of both nodes N_a and N_b. Since S_k is the site that sends the largest amount of data both to the site of node N_a and to the site of node N_b, site S_k sends the largest amount of data to the site of the combined node (N_a, N_b). Therefore, file node site S_k is selected for performing the operations of the combined node (N_a, N_b) in the reduced graph. Thus, the communication cost (2) of the reduced graph and of the original graph (when site selection is based on Theorem 1) are identical. This implies that total communication cost of the reduced graph is lower than that of the original graph.♦

If an operation node consists of more than one operation, we call it a multi-operation node. Theorem 3 deals with graphs containing such operation nodes.

Theorem 3

For a given query operation graph that contains a multiple operation node consisting of a set of operations $\{\beta_i \ldots \beta_j\}$, the sequence of operations from this set which has least processing cost is used by the policy that has least operating cost for this graph.

Proof

The set of operations $\{\beta_i \ldots \beta_j\}$ is performed at a single site and its output volume is independent of its sequence. Therefore, for any two policies for this graph, if their only difference is in the sequence of the set of operations $\{\beta_i \ldots \beta_j\}$, then their communication costs will be the same. Therefore the sequence of the set $\{\beta_i \ldots \beta_j\}$ that has least processing cost is used by the policy that has least operating cost for the graph.♦

Corollary

Theorem 3 is true for a query operation graph with more than one multiple operation node.

Proof

Since the output volume of each multi-operation node is fixed regardless of the sequence of the operations of that node, the sequences of operations of each multi-operation node can be optimized independently. Therefore, we can apply Theorem 3 to each of the multi-operation nodes.♦

Theorem 4

If the processing cost for a given operation is the same for all the computers in the distributed data base and, further, if the sequence of operations for processing a given query is fixed, then the query processing policy that minimizes the communication cost (total volume of traffic for the case of the communication cost among each pair of computers being equal) yields the lowest operating cost among the set of policies that uses this fixed sequence of operations.

Proof

For a given query, if the sequence of operations is fixed, the output volume of each individual operation will be the same for all the policies that use this sequence of operations. Since the unit processing cost for each operation is the same for all the computers, the total processing cost for all policies using this fixed sequence of operations is the same. This implies that the policy that requires the lowest communication cost (total volume of traffic for the case of identical unit communication cost) yields lowest operating cost.♦

Theorems 1 and 2 together with the known file allocation information provide guidelines in site selection for performing operations. Theorem 3 can be used to reduce the number of graphs in some sequence groups and Theorem 4 provides a way of locating local optimal query processing policies (optimal among the set of policies that perform the given fixed sequence of operations). Using these theorems greatly reduces the computation requirements for determining the optimal query processing policy.

4. Query Operating Cost Model

The operating cost for processing a query consists of communication cost and processing cost. The communication cost depends partially on the sites selected for the file operations. Both the communication and processing costs depend on the data reduction functions, sequence of operations, and on the data volumes of the files involved. The data reduction function, $\alpha(\beta_j,\overline{F},\overline{\gamma})$, is the ratio of the output data volume to the input data volume for the operation β_j, input files $\overline{F}$, and the query operation parameter $\overline{\gamma}$. The data reduction function further depends on the previous operations. The data reduction function of operation β_i preceded by operations $\overline{\beta}$ with input files $\overline{F}$ and query operation parameter $\overline{\gamma}$ is denoted as $\alpha(\beta_i|\overline{\beta}, \overline{F}, \overline{\gamma})$. $\alpha(\beta_j, \overline{F}, \overline{\gamma})$ permits us to estimate the output temporary file length $\ell(f_i)$ for operation β_j from its input file size. Such data reduction functions may be estimated by simulation or measurement on the actual data base system [4] and their values are stored in the directory system [5].

Let C_o^i be the processing cost for operation β_o^i, and C_j be the processing cost for operation β_j per unit input file data (byte). Further, let C'_{ij} be the communication cost for transmitting a unit of data (byte) from the site that generates file f_i to the site of operation β_j. We will further define two indicating functions, X_{ij} and D_{ij}. We use X_{ij} for indicating whether temporary file f_i is an input to operation β_j; that is,

$$X_{ij} = \begin{cases} 1 & \text{if } f_i \text{ is an input to operation } \beta_j \\ 0 & \text{otherwise.} \end{cases}$$

We use D_{ij} for indicating whether f_i is available for processing at the site for performing β_j; that is,

$$D_{ij} = \begin{cases} 1 & \text{if file } f_i \text{ is needed but is not available for processing at the site for performing } \beta_j \\ 0 & \text{otherwise.} \end{cases}$$

Thus if $D_{ij} = 1$, it is required to transmit file f_i to the site for performing β_j, $s(\beta_j)$. D_{ij} is determined from the file allocation and the query processing policy. The operating cost for processing a query with policy π equals

$$C(\pi) = \sum_{i=1}^{r} C_o^i \,\ell(F_i) + \sum_{j=1}^{m} C_j \sum_{i=1}^{n} \ell(f_i) X_{ij} + \sum_{j=1}^{m} C'_{ij} \sum_{i=1}^{n} \ell(f_i)\, D_{ij} + \delta_{em} \cdot C'_{ne} \cdot \ell(f_n) \qquad (1)$$

where $\ell(F_i)$ = file length of F_i.

$\ell(f_i)$ = file length of temporary file f_i.

n = total number of temporary files required for processing of a given query.

m = total number of operations β_i, $i>0$, required for completing processing of a given query.

$$\delta_{em} = \begin{cases} 1 & \text{if } \beta_e \text{ is not at the same site as } \beta_m \\ 0 & \text{otherwise} \end{cases}$$

f_n = the result of the query.

The first term of Eq.(1) is for the cost of the set of initial operations $\{\beta_o^i, i = 1, \ldots, r\}$ on the files F_i, $i = 1, \ldots, r$. The second term represents the total processing cost for performing operations β_j, $j = 1, \ldots, m$, the third term represents the total communication cost for transmitting temporary files f_i, $i = 1, \ldots, n$, to the sites of operations β_j, $j = 1, \ldots, m$, and the last term represents the cost of transferring the final query result file to the originating site. The δ_{em} function indicates whether this transfer is necessary.

Different query processing policies yield different sequences of query operations, as well as different locations for processing these operations. As a result, different policies yield different operating costs for processing a given query on a distributed data base, using Eq.(1) to compute the operating cost for the given query processing policy. With the aid of the theorems developed in the last section and the use of Eq.(1), we can determine the optimal policy that yields minimum operating cost for processing a given query.

5. Example

Consider a four node computer network(Figure 2) which contains an inventory relational data base consisting of three relations stored as files. The allocation and the descriptions of the files are given in Table 1.

Table 1. File Characteristics of a Distributed Data Base

File	Location	Contents	Length(in bytes)
F_1	1	(Part#,Part Name)	10^5
F_2	2	(Supplier#,Part#, Quantity)	10^5
F_3	3	(Supplier#,Supplier Name,City)	10^4

The following query is initiated at node 4: "Generate a listing of <part number, supplier name, quantity> for all "wheels" produced in Los Angeles in a quantity greater than 1,000 by any one supplier." For processing this query, the following four operations are required.

- β_o^i Initial restriction and projection operations on files F_i for i = 1, 2, 3.
- β_1 Join operation on part number.
- β_2 Join operation on supplier number.
- β_e Transmission of the query result from the last operating site to the query originating site.

The operations β_o^i, i = 1, 2, 3, reduce the files F_1, F_2, and F_3 to f_1, f_2, and f_3 respectively. The temporary file sizes $\ell(f_i) = \alpha(\beta_o^i,F_i,\overline{\gamma}) \cdot \ell(F_i)$ for i = 1, 2, 3. These temporary files have the characteristics summarized below:

Table 2 Temporary File Characteristics

f_i	Contents	$\overline{\gamma}$ for β_o^i	$\alpha(\beta_o^i, F_i, \overline{\gamma})$	$\ell(f_i)$ in bytes
f_1	Part#	Part Name is "wheel"	0.05	0.5×10^4
f_2	Supplier#, Part#, Quantity	Quantity>1000	0.1	1×10^4
f_3	Supplier#, Supplier Name, City	City is Los Angeles	0.3	0.3×10^4

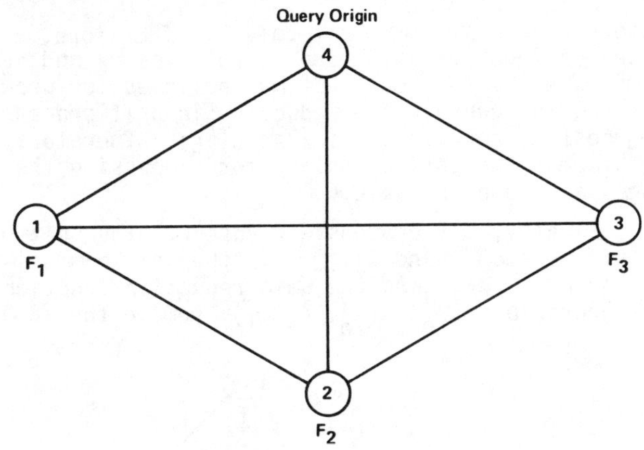

Figure 2 Computer Network for Example

The set of operations for processing this query is $\{\beta_o^1, \beta_o^2, \beta_o^3, \beta_1, \beta_2, \beta_e\}$. Let us briefly describe the set of query operation graphs for this query. Figure 3a corresponds to the policy that transmits the files f_1, f_2, f_3 resulting from the initial operations $\beta_o^1, \beta_o^2, \beta_o^3$ to site 4 and processes them there. Figure 3b represents performing operations β_1 and β_2 at either site 1, 2 or 3 and then transmitting the query result to site 4. Figures 3c and 3d correspond to performing one of the operations (either β_1 or β_2) at either site 1, 2 or 3 and then performing the remaining operation at site 4. Figures 3e and 3f correspond to performing operations β_1 and β_2 separately at two of the sites 1, 2 and 3 and then transmitting the result to site 4.

We will study the example under three different cases by varying the parameter values. In all three cases, we assume that the unit communication cost is the same for all pairs of sites i and j and that the unit processing cost for each operation is the same for all the computers. Since file f_2 is an input to both operations, for simplicity we express the data reduction functions for operations β_1 and β_2 in terms of the length of file f_2.

We will first consider case A. The data reduction function values are $\alpha(\beta_o^i, F_i, \overline{\gamma})$ for i=1,2,3 as given in Table 2, $\alpha(\beta_1, f_2, \overline{\gamma}) = 10^{-1}$, $\alpha(\beta_2, f_2, \overline{\gamma}) = 2 \times 10^{-1}$, and $\alpha(\beta_2|\overline{\beta}, f_2, \overline{\gamma}) = \alpha(\beta_1|\overline{\beta}, f_2, \overline{\gamma}) = 5\times10^{-2}$. The unit communication cost value is $C'_{ij} = C' = \$10^{-3}$/byte and the unit processing cost values are $C_o^i = C_o = \$10^{-6}$/byte for i = 1,2,3, and $C_1 = C_2 = \$0.5 \times 10^{-3}$/byte.

The graph shown in Figure 3b has a multiple operation node that consists of a set of operations, $\{\beta_1, \beta_2\}$, such that this set of operations can be executed in either of the sequences $\beta_1\beta_2$ or $\beta_2\beta_1$. It can be shown that the processing cost of the sequence of operations $\beta_1\beta_2$ is lower than that of the sequence $\beta_2\beta_1$. Therefore, based on Theorem 3, we use the sequence $\beta_1\beta_2$ for the multi-operation node of this graph. Likewise, we use the sequence $\beta_1\beta_2\beta_e$ for the corresponding multi-operation node of the graph shown in Figure 3a.

Next, we use Theorem 1 to select the sites of all the operation nodes in a given graph. This determines the optimal query processing policy π for that graph. Table 3 displays the optimal sites selected for operations for all the query operation graphs.

Table 3 Optimal Sites for Operations

Policy	Site for β_1	Site for β_2	Site for β_e
π_o	4	4	4
π_1	2	2	4
π_2	2	4	4
π_3	4	2	4
π_4	2	3	4
π_5	1	2	4

All the policies in the set $\{\pi_o, \pi_1, \pi_2, \pi_4\}$ have the sequence of operations $\beta_o^1\beta_o^2\beta_o^3\beta_1\beta_2\beta_e$. Both of the policies in the set $\{\pi_3, \pi_5\}$ have the sequence of operations $\beta_o^1\beta_o^2\beta_o^3\beta_2\beta_1\beta_e$. In order to find the best policy within each of these sets, we need to compute the total communication cost $C'(\pi)$ for each policy in the set as follows.

$$C'(\pi_o) = C' \cdot [\ell(f_1)+\ell(f_2)+\ell(f_3)] = 18$$

$$\begin{aligned} C'(\pi_1) &= C' \cdot [\ell(f_1)+\ell(f_3)+\ell(f_6)] \\ &= C' \cdot [\ell(f_1)+\ell(f_3)+\alpha(\beta_2|\overline{\beta}, f_2, \overline{\gamma}) \cdot \ell(f_2)] \\ &= 8.5 \end{aligned}$$

$$\begin{aligned} C'(\pi_2) &= C' \cdot [\ell(f_1)+\ell(f_3)+\ell(f_4)] \\ &= C' \cdot [\ell(f_1)+\ell(f_3)+\alpha(\beta_1, f_2, \overline{\gamma}) \cdot \ell(f_2)] = 9 \end{aligned}$$

$$\begin{aligned} C'(\pi_3) &= C' \cdot [\ell(f_1)+\ell(f_3)+\ell(f_5)] \\ &= C' \cdot [\ell(f_1)+\ell(f_3)+\alpha(\beta_2, f_2, \overline{\gamma}) \cdot \ell(f_2)] = 10 \end{aligned}$$

$$\begin{aligned} C'(\pi_4) &= C' \cdot [\ell(f_1)+\ell(f_4)+\ell(f_6)] \\ &= C' \cdot [\ell(f_1)+\alpha(\beta_1, f_2, \overline{\gamma}) \cdot \ell(f_2) \\ &\quad + \alpha(\beta_2|\overline{\beta}, f_2, \overline{\gamma}) \cdot \ell(f_2)] = 6.5 \end{aligned}$$

$$\begin{aligned} C'(\pi_5) &= C' \cdot [\ell(f_3)+\ell(f_5)+\ell(f_6)] \\ &= C' \cdot [\ell(f_3)+\alpha(\beta_2, f_2, \overline{\gamma}) \cdot \ell(f_2) \\ &\quad + \alpha(\beta_1|\overline{\beta}, f_2, \overline{\gamma}) \cdot \ell(f_2)] = 5.5 \end{aligned}$$

Since $C'(\pi_4) < C'(\pi_1) < C'(\pi_2) < C'(\pi_o)$, based on Theorem 4, π_4 is the optimal policy among the set of policies $\{\pi_o, \pi_1, \pi_2, \pi_4\}$. Likewise, π_5 is the optimal policy among the set of policies $\{\pi_3, \pi_5\}$.

Finally, we use Eq.(1) to compute the operating cost of policies π_4 and π_5. Based on policy π_4 and the file allocation information in Table 1, we construct the following indicating functions:

$$X(\pi_4) = \begin{vmatrix} 1 & 0 \\ 1 & 0 \\ 0 & 1 \\ 0 & 1 \\ 0 & 0 \\ 0 & 0 \end{vmatrix} \qquad D(\pi_4) = \begin{vmatrix} 1 & 0 \\ 0 & 0 \\ 0 & 0 \\ 0 & 1 \\ 0 & 0 \\ 0 & 0 \end{vmatrix}$$

Substituting the parameter values into Eq.(1), we have

$$\begin{aligned} C(\pi_4) &= C_o \cdot [\ell(F_1)+\ell(F_2)+\ell(F_3)]+C_1 \cdot [\ell(f_1)+\ell(f_2)] \\ &\quad + C_2 \cdot [\ell(f_3) + \ell(f_4)]+C'(\pi_4) \\ &= 9.71 + 6.5 = 16.21 \end{aligned}$$

Likewise, for policy π_5 we have

$$X(\pi_5) = \begin{vmatrix} 1 & 0 \\ 0 & 1 \\ 0 & 1 \\ 0 & 0 \\ 1 & 0 \\ 0 & 0 \end{vmatrix} \qquad D(\pi_5) = \begin{vmatrix} 0 & 0 \\ 0 & 0 \\ 0 & 1 \\ 0 & 0 \\ 1 & 0 \\ 0 & 0 \end{vmatrix}$$

In the same manner, the operating cost of π_5 equals

$$\begin{aligned} C(\pi_5) &= C_o \cdot [\ell(F_1)+\ell(F_2)+\ell(F_3)]+C_1 \cdot [\ell(f_1)+\ell(f_5)] \\ &\quad +C_2 \cdot [\ell(f_2)+\ell(f_3)]+C'(\pi_5) \\ &= 10.21 + 5.5 = 15.71 \end{aligned}$$

We note that $C(\pi_5) < C(\pi_4)$; therefore, π_5 is the optimal query processing policy for case A as shown in Table 4.

Let us now consider case B. All the parameter values remain the same as for case A except that the unit processing cost for operation β_1, C_1, has been reduced from \$0.5x10^{-3}/byte to \$0.25x10^{-3}/byte. The communication costs $C'(\pi_i)$ for i = 0,1,...,5 of case A remain the same for case B. Therefore, based on Theorems 1, 3, and 4, policies π_4 and π_5 remain as the two local optimal policies for processing the query. The reduction in unit processing cost C_1 results in $C(\pi_4) < C(\pi_5)$. Therefore, π_4 becomes the optimal policy for processing the query as shown in Table 4.

Finally, let us consider case C. The unit processing costs C_o^i and C_j, j=1,2, the unit communication costs C_{ij}^i, and the data reduction functions for operations β_o^i, $\alpha(\beta_o^i, F_i, \overline{\gamma})$, remain the same

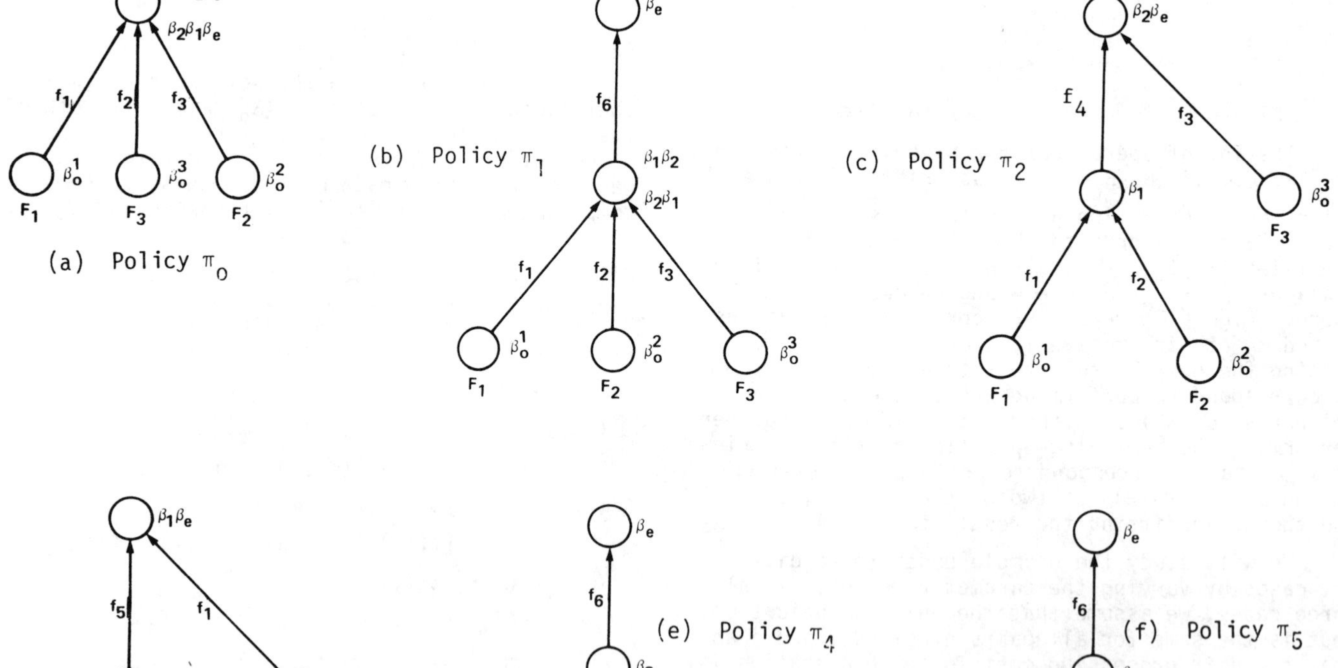

Figure 3 Query Operation Graphs for Example

as for case B. However, the data reduction functions for operations β_1 and β_2 have been increased. Their new values are: $\alpha(\beta_1,f_2,\bar{\gamma}) = 0.3$, $\alpha(\beta_2,f_2,\bar{\gamma}) = 0.45$, and $\alpha(\beta_2|\bar{\beta},f_2,\bar{\gamma}) = \alpha(\beta_1|\bar{\beta},f_2,\bar{\gamma}) = 0.4$. From Theorem 1, we know that site selections for the query operation graphs are independent of the data reduction functions for operations β_1 and β_2. Therefore, the sites for performing β_1 and β_2 remaing the same as in cases A and B.

Due to the increase in the data reduction functions for operations β_1 and β_2, the output data volumes from these operations have increased. As a result, policy π_2 yields the lowest total communication cost among the set of policies $\{\pi_0,\pi_1,\pi_2,\pi_4\}$. Therefore, by Theorem 4, π_2 is the optimal policy among that set of policies. Likewise, policy π_5 is the optimal policy among the set of policies $\{\pi_3,\pi_5\}$. Comparing π_2 and π_5, we note that $C(\pi_2)<C(\pi_5)$. Thus the policy π_2 is the optimal policy for case C.

Table 4 Operating Costs of the Three Cases for the Example

Case	Policy	Communications Cost	Processing Cost	Operating Cost
A	π_4	6.5	9.71	16.21
	(π_5)	5.5	10.21	15.71
B	(π_4)	6.5	5.96	12.46
	π_5	5.5	8.46	13.96
C	(π_2)	11.0	6.96	17.96
	π_5	11.5	9.08	20.58

The optimal policy is shown circled.

6. Conclusion

The query processing policy depends on the sequence of logical operations and on the sites for performing such operations. In this paper, we have developed an operating cost model based on communication cost, processing cost, and data reduction functions for processing a query for a given environment. Data reduction functions provide an estimate of the volume of output from a given operation which enables us to estimate output file length(s), and this allows us to compute the operating cost of a query processing policy. Query operation graphs are used to represent sets of policies having a common sequence of operations and having the same subsets of operations performed at a single site. Theorems are developed to find the best sites for performing the operations of a given graph and to locate graphs representing local optimal policies. Such theorems greatly reduce computation requirements for determining the optimal query processing policy.

References

[1] Wong, E., "Retrieving Dispersed Data from SSD-1: A System for Distributed Databases," Proceedings of the Second Berkeley Workshop on Distributed Data Management and Computer Networks, May 1977, pp. 217-235.

[2] Epstein, R., M. Stonebraker and E. Wong, "Distributed Query Processing in a Relational Data Base System," SIGMOD Proceedings, May 1978, pp. 169-180.

[3] Hevner, A. R. and S. B. Yao, "Query Processing on a Distributed Database," Proceedings of the Third Berkeley Workshop on Distributed Data Management and Computer Networks, August 1978, pp. 91-107.

[4] Small, D. and W. W. Chu, A Distributed Data Base Architecture for Data Processing in a Dynamic Environment," Proceedings of COMPCON, this issue, March 1979.

[5] Chu, W. W., "Performance of File Directory Systems for Data Bases in Star and Distributed Networks," AFIPS Proceedings, pp. 577-587, 1976.

Section IV-C
Data Security

COMPUTER system security has been a fertile area for both research and debate over the last ten years. Novel techniques of data encryption, for example, have been developed and applied to large distributed systems. Additionally, a myriad of methods to protect data from unauthorized disclosure, modification, restriction, and destruction have been implemented.

Three papers have been selected for reprinting: "The Total Computer Security Problem: An Overview" by K.S. Shanker, "Network Security in Distributed Data Processing" by H.B. Becker, and "A Distributed Secure System" by J. Rushby and B. Randell. By no means is it intended for these papers, either individually or together, to represent an all-inclusive summary of the state-of-the-art in distributed computer system security; such a topic is far too expansive and complex for any two papers to consider. Rather, for this topic—more than any other topic covered in this book—these papers are intended to comprise a high-level starting point for further reading and research.

The Total Computer Security Problem: An Overview

K. S. Shankar
IBM*

Introduction

As society becomes more dependent on computers, computer crime is becoming not only more disastrous in its potential impact, but also more attractive to the criminal.[1-3] However, with adequate protection techniques, data theft can be prevented. This paper analyzes the total computer system security problem, using six major factors to sort out the issues involved. The entire problem is visualized in Figure 1, with the six factors listed along the left-hand side.

The first issue is the kind of environment in which the information is to be stored and in which the computer system is to operate, characterized as the external or "real" environment. From this user environment is obtained a set of security requirements. If the requirements include certification, a formal model of the proposed system of security has to be built. Even if certification is not explicitly required, building a model will lead to better understanding and improved reliability, as implied by the dotted line in Figure 1.

The second factor refers to protection mechanisms outside of the computer system itself. These mechanisms, which may be broadly labeled administrative controls and physical security, have as their purpose preventing unauthorized access to the system. In the case of networks and remote terminals, principal reliance must be placed on nonphysical means of entry control.

After the external protection mechanisms have been passed or bypassed, the next line of defense is mechanisms within the computer system. These internal protection mechanisms consist of communications security, authentication, access control, and surveillance. There may be a tradeoff between external and internal protection mechanisms in terms of authentication and access control.

The problem of organizing and arranging the information to be protected comes next. Since this information is stored in a computer, the characteristics of the hardware and the operating system have to be considered. Finally, the reliability of the hardware and software systems is a factor in the security problem.

Attention is then directed to internal protection mechanism requirements. For a computer system to be secure, these mechanisms must be complete, tamperproof, and certified. Certification, when required, strongly impacts all the steps in system development and verification.

Another issue closely related to the problem of computer security is the notion of integrity. In concluding, this paper analyzes the system integrity concept along with its relation to system security.

User environment

For security purposes, the environment within which a user operates a computer system may be factored into four areas. One is threats to the system that will cause a breech of security. The second is the uneasy balance between protection and sharing among users. The third is the increasing complexity of the organization of computer services. And fourth is the security value of the information being processed.

Threats to computer services. Security threats can originate from both malicious and non-malicious sources. In other words, a threat may be deliberate, in which case a person must be involved, or it may be accidental, in which case either a person or a malfunction may be responsible.

The first step in the provision of appropriate security is to identify the potential threats. Complete security, in theory, consists of safeguarding the computer system from all threats, not only those identified, but those not

*This paper is an outgrowth of earlier work done by the author while he was with the Burroughs Corporation.

Reprinted from *Computer*, vol. 10, pp. 50–62 and 71–73, June 1977.

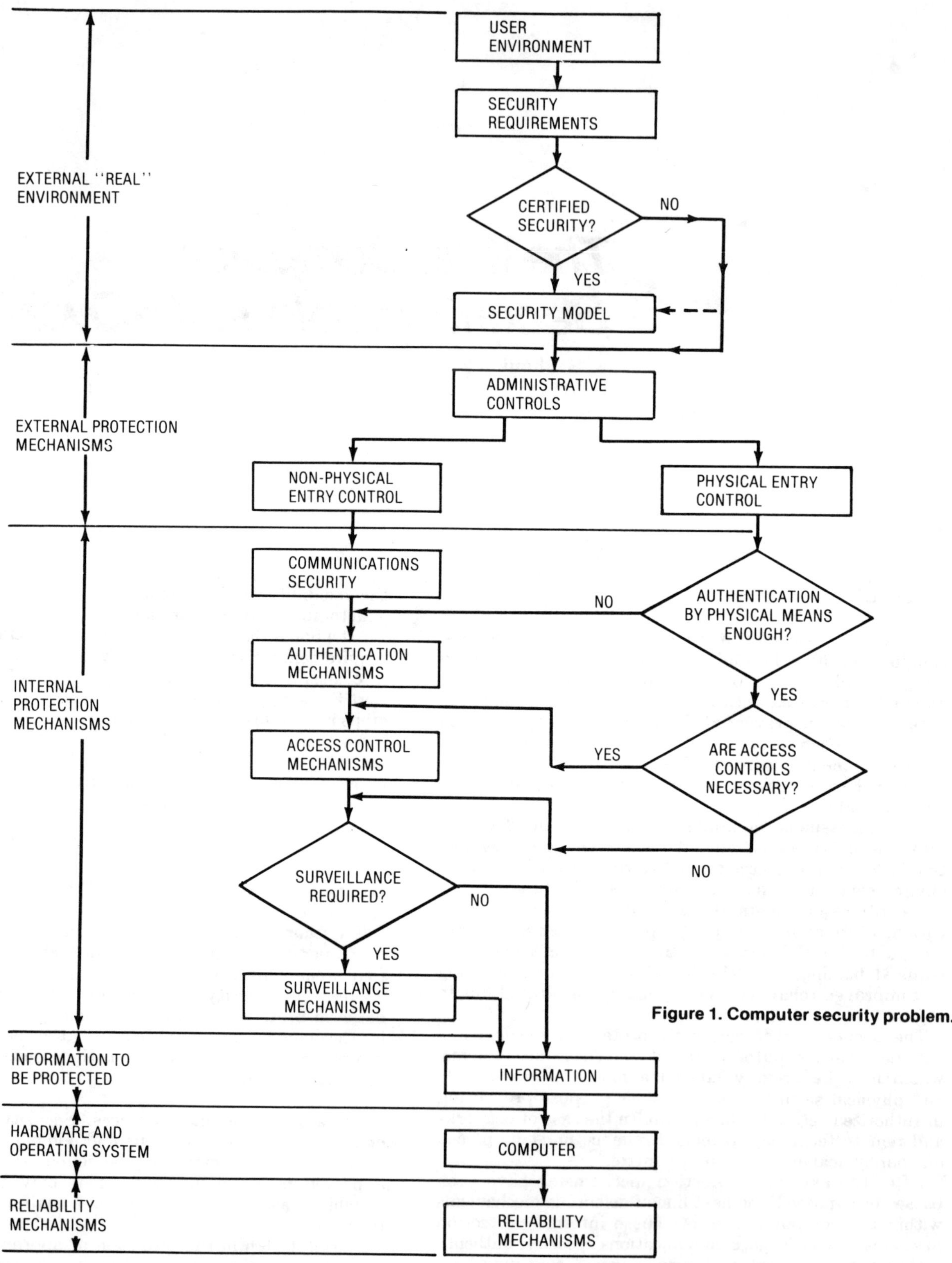

Figure 1. Computer security problem.

yet known, In practice, of course, such 100-percent security is unattainable.

Still, if it is not possible to be certain that all security threats have been identified, it has been found useful[4,5] to classify security violations into unauthorized release or modification of information or denial of service, as shown in Table 1.

Protection vs sharing. Protection of information in a computer system and sharing it are contradictory goals. At the one extreme, programs are completely isolated from each other by being executed on separate machines. At the other extreme, programs executing on the same system have shared access and cooperate with each other. Within this range security policies depend on the users

Table 1. Nature and sources of threats.

NATURE	*SOURCE*	*EXAMPLES*
UNAUTHORIZED RELEASE OF INFORMATION	MALICIOUS	1. DELIBERATELY ADDING AN UNAUTHORIZED USER OR GIVING ACCESS 2. GIVING AWAY PASSWORDS 3. BRIBING A GUARD 4. UNAUTHORIZED EXECUTION OF A PROPRIETARY PROGRAM
	NON-MALICIOUS	1. HARDWARE ERRORS 2. SOFTWARE BUGS 3. USER ERRORS 4. GUARDS INCOMPLETENESS 5. EMANATIONS 6. CARELESS DISPOSAL
UNAUTHORIZED MODIFICATION OF INFORMATION	MALICIOUS	1. CHANGING A CREDIT RATING 2. DELIBERATE TRANSFER OF MONIES 3. CHANGING SOMEBODY'S VD STATUS 4. INTERFERING WITH COMMUNICATIONS
	NON-MALICIOUS	1. MISTAKENLY DEMAGNETIZING TAPES (COULD BE DELIBERATE) 2. DATA INPUT ERROR 3. PROGRAM ERROR 4. OPERATOR ERROR (E.G., MOUNTING WRONG TAPE)
UNAUTHORIZED DENIAL OF USE	MALICIOUS	1. CRASH THE SYSTEM 2. CLOG THE SYSTEM AND DEGRADE PERFORMANCE 3. CREATE DEADLOCKS 4. MALICIOUS DESTRUCTION 5. FIRE A BULLET INTO THE SYSTEM
	NON-MALICIOUS	1. FIRE 2. HEAT 3. POWER FAILURE 4. FLOODS

and applications. Security policy may be defined as a finite set of rules which delimits access to information during the progress of a computation. To be satisfactory, a security policy should state precisely what is accessible (and not accessible) to a program at every point in time. Some examples of existing security policies are summarized in Table 2.

Complexity of services. Third-generation computers have introduced complex new capabilities that involve the concurrent processing of many jobs, extensive sharing of resources, and the use of remote terminals. While these new capabilities bring benefits of substantially lower cost, sharing of large data bases, and remote access to computers, they also introduce a difficult security problem. This problem arises because the complex systems afford opportunities for accidental or deliberate acquisition of information by users who have no right to it. In general, the more facilities and services a system offers, the more doors it opens for penetration.

Despite the diversity of system types—and the views about them—these new systems exhibit many common properties. Many systems are capable of batch processing and multiprocessing, for instance. Data base systems, distributed data bases, and computer networks are related. Other properties might be listed, but the point is that

Table 2. Security policies.

POLICY	*COMMENTS*
NO SHARING[6,77]	Users are separated into groups between which no flow of information or control is possible. If a group consists of only one user, there is no sharing between him and other groups. Sometimes the no-sharing policy is moderated by sharing such information as the program library.[82] Most of the commercial timesharing systems, including the Dartmouth Time Sharing System and the IBM VM/370, fall into this latter category.
SIMULTANEOUS USE[7]	Users are permitted the simultaneous use of stored information, as in airline reservation systems and time sharing bureaus. However, for applications in which all users should not have identical authority, some scheme is needed to assure that the computer system implements the desired authority structure.
MUTUALLY SUSPICIOUS SUBSYSTEMS[94]	Each cooperating subsystem has local data which must be safeguarded from the other, but still must pass some parameters in a dynamic and efficient way.
CONFINEMENT[8,9,10,11]	A borrowed program is allowed access to data, but is prevented from releasing the information.
FILTERING[12,13,14]	Sometimes it is necessary to have a gatekeeper which decides what portion of an information object (e.g., a file) a user can actually access. Such a filter is useful in data base applications where a decision procedure capable of an arbitrary computation is interposed between a user and the object. This filter could be used to support statistical access, e.g., census data.
DATA AGGREGATION[5,34]	Individual data elements which are not by themselves sensitive may be capable of being aggregated into security sensitive information. Sound policies that would prevent improper data aggregation are difficult to formulate.
DATA INFERENCE[5,34]	Certain functions of the aggregation of elements are not sensitive, but the elements themselves are sensitive. For example, individual salaries may be sensitive, but total salaries or average salary may not be. As another example, elaborate forms of "traffic analysis" may be employed to derive information content from patterns of information use.
MILITARY SECURITY[15,16,83]	Users are cleared to different levels for access to information at different levels of sensitivity.
PRIVACY[17]	Privacy policies must be specified by legal or regulatory means, but technology is required to help enforce these means. Privacy is not basically a technological problem.
REVOCATION[7,76]	What happens when the owner revokes a user's access to a file while that file is being used? When it is not being used, this problem is easier to solve. In any case, policies must be formulated for both static and dynamic revocation.
PROGRAMMABLE PROTECTION[7,94]	A user may want to restrict access to a file in a way not provided in the standard facilities for controlled sharing. This restriction is similar to content-based protection, except that the protection may not be based on information content.
CERTIFIED SECURITY[18,88,103]	Correctness of the subsystem has been completely validated and is guaranteed a priori.

the nature of the security measures to be provided for one system may differ greatly from those required by another.

Value of information. Differences in the nature of the information being processed—and in the value attached to it by users—give rise to different security goals.[19]

In the financial environment,[20] for example, the value of the information is rated very high, because of the substantial monetary gain that could result from penetrating the system. In this industry the primary security concern is to prevent losses, especially through embezzlement or fraud.

In medical information processing,[21] on the other hand, while the financial value of the information is lower, the "life and death" value is much higher. In this community the intent is to prevent catastrophes, the impairment of health, and even embarrassment, as well as to maintain the viability of the institution.

In the educational field,[22] the awareness of the need for security is quite high. Every type of threat is possible in the university, because the internal users are probably the most ingenious of all users. In educational institutions a primary objective of a security system is to prevent mischief. In primary and secondary schools it is important to protect sensitive student files.

Service bureaus[23] are somewhat similar to educational institutions because they too operate in a high concentration of technical expertise. However, they differ from educational institutions because the atmosphere is much more competitive. Prevention of financial losses as a result of breakdown of the system, manipulation of the accounting mechanism, or theft of proprietary data[95] has thus been the objective of the security systems in this area.

In the military environment,[15,16,24] the principal technical problem is to make multilevel resource and information-sharing systems secure against threats from malicious users. It has been concluded[5] that this problem cannot be resolved very effectively by patching the penetration holes known to exist in present systems. The fundamental need here is for completeness, and this necessitates that security be designed into the systems at their inception.

In systems where privacy of information must be safeguarded by law,[17] failure of the protection mechanisms may expose the operator to legal penalties.

Security requirements

After a particular user environment has been analyzed, as discussed in the preceding section, the next step is to formulate a set of security requirements. Unfortunately, there are really no standard techniques for formulating these requirements. It would be helpful if each requirement expressed the necessity for one or more protection features. A Mitre study[86] of the correlation between requirements and protection features showed the architectural features for a computer system that would correspond to the military multilevel security policy.

In any event, the security requirements for a system should be formulated with great care since they will later be the basis for evaluating the security of the system. In fact, a good set of security requirements can serve as one of the bases for the design of new computer systems. Of major importance is the set's completeness—i.e., the extent to which the security requirements, if complied with, provide assurance that the system is not vulnerable to penetration. Naturally, it would be beneficial to have techniques to establish the completeness of a set, but such means do not currently exist and may never exist. At present, the best way to judge the degree of completeness is to evaluate how the requirements have been put together.

There has been some work in formulating security requirements for user environments. Notable among them are the following:

DOD Directive 5200.28.[15] This is a statement of policies and regulations to be followed by Department of Defense agencies for protecting classified information stored, processed, communicated, and displayed by data processing systems.

DOD Directive 5200.28-M.[16] This document provides uniform guidelines for techniques to be used in implementing, deactivating, testing, and evaluating secure resource-sharing computer systems.

Computer Security Technology Reference Manual.[25] This manual provides a basis for evaluating and improving the security of existing Air Force computer systems with emphasis on hardware and software components.

AFR 205-1.[24] This Air Force security regulation delineates the necessity to keep distinct and separate information classified as confidential, secret, and top secret. Orthogonal to each of these classifications are formal categories. The combination of these two descriptors is defined as a security level. Thus, this regulation leads to multilevel security in Air Force systems.

The Privacy Act of 1974.[26,27] This act imposes numerous requirements upon federal agencies to prevent the misuse of information about individuals and assure its integrity and security. Although this act applies only to personal data systems operated by federal agencies, it may indicate the type of regulation likely to be imposed on the private sector as well.

Security models

The development of security models involves the formalization of security requirements. This step poses the difficult problem of creating a mathematical model of a secure system.

A mathematical model is a prerequisite to a convincing argument that a system is truly secure. Such a model must demonstrate by its consistency that it can be translated into the design of a secure computer system. This connection between the model and the design provides the groundwork for arguing that the system correctly meets the requirements. Despite the importance of modelling in the development of secure computer systems, not much has been reported on the subject. However, significant contributions have been reported by Mitre,[83,84] CWRU,[39] and SRI.[103,104]

Mitre model. The Mitre model describes an abstract directory machine in terms of state transitions. Subjects may be thought of as processes which access objects (or directory elements) in the machine. Each request for an action by a subject moves the machine from one state to another. A secure state is defined, and then certain actions or rules are defined governing how each state may change. The model formalizes local and global security conditions. The local condition applies between each subject and object, whereas the global condition states the terms under which a subject may access objects concurrently.

In brief, this mathematical model identifies in abstract form a data base that describes the security state of a computer system. It defines security in terms of relations (labeled) among elements of the data base, and it provides rules for dynamic alteration of the data base in a manner that preserves security.

SRI effort. The goal of this work was the design and certification of a secure computer system. Certification implied that the security requrements had to be formalized. A precise definition of what it means for a computer system to be secure was developed. This definition involves the establishment of two types of global assertions—namely, the invariant assertions, which specify how the system state must not change, and the variant assertions, which specify how the system state must change. Proof involves showing the consistency of these assertions with the specifications.

The invariant assertions are stated as a set of four principles.

(1) *Alteration principle:* There shall be no unauthorized alteration of information.
(2) *Detection principle:* There shall be no unauthorized acquisition of information.
(3) *Guaranteed service principle:* There shall be no unauthorized denial of service.
(4) *Confinement principle:* There shall be no unauthorized leakage of information.

The word "authorization" has meaning only with respect to a mapping from capabilities[103] to the information in the system. Then the authorization to access a particular piece of information implies having access to an appropriate capability (itself obtained in an authorized way). These four invariant principles are intended to exclude erroneous behavior on the part of inter-user interactions or user-system interactions. As stated above, they are intuitively obvious, although their formalizations are hard.

External protection mechanisms

Administrative controls. An effective administrative framework—a prerequisite to security—includes all the administrative techniques utilized to protect the information within an organization, including the computer installation. Of particular interest here are those controls related to security.

As mentioned earlier, absolute security is unattainable. Some risks, such as malicious destruction, are administratively uncontrollable; others, such as natural disaster or power failure, are humanly uncontrollable as well. Hence, the basic goal must be to minimize vulnerability to such hazards, rather than to eliminate them.

For each type of exposure to a security hazard, a three-level attack[28] should be considered: (1) minimizing the probability of it happening at all, (2) minimizing the damage if it does happen, and (3) furnishing a method of recovering from the damage.

Administrative controls can be broadly categorized into the following areas:

High-level management decisions. These include decisions pertaining to safeguard selection and evaluation. Each installation should consider the cost of each safeguard when selecting from among the several options available. Costs fall into two major areas: initial and operating costs. Initial costs include the purchase of new system elements, modification of existing systems to accept the new element, one-time administrative measures to support the new elements, and initial testing of effectiveness. Operating costs include the increased day-to-day costs of running the enhanced system, including such cost components as personnel, computer processing, storage, and system monitoring.

Security risk assessment studies. The first step toward improving a system's security is to determine its security risks. The goal of a risk assessment study is to identify and rank the events that would compromise the security of the computer installation and the information stored in it. The seriousness of a risk depends both on the potential impact of the event and its probability of occurrence.

Personnel management. This area pertains to employee hiring and firing procedures, employee rules of conduct, enforcement of rules, etc.

Data handling techniques. A well-defined set of rules should be put down in a procedures handbook describing the precautions to be used and the obligations of computer facility personnel during the handling of all data.

Data processing practices. These practices include, but are not limited to, such items as

(1) use of methods to control numbers to account for personal data upon receipt and during input, storage, and processing;
(2) verification of the accuracy of personal data acquisition and entry methods; and
(3) regular and unscheduled inventories of tape and disk storage media.

Programming practices. These pertain to the discipline employed in the specification, design, implementation, programming, coding, and debugging of the system. Mention should be made here of the systematic and disciplined approach taken by SRI[103,104] toward the design of a provably secure operating system.

Assignment of responsibilities. Assign each individual a specific set of responsibilities toward carrying out certain functions (for which he is held accountable). It is then easier to pinpoint an individual in case of a security violation.

Procedural auditing. Whenever appropriate, an independent examination of established procedures should be conducted.

Physical security. Physical security in connection with the protection of data does not differ from physical security for protecting other assets. It is probably the best known type of security, because it is employed when dealing with banks, stores, museums, etc. The concepts of guards, alarms, locks, vaults, fire protection, etc., are common to all of them.

Physical security should be reviewed first and improved where necessary. For most installations, the application of physical security measures provides sufficient protection against intentional external acts against data. However, it provides little protection against accidental or malicious damage to files or against overt internal acts.

Unauthorized entry into a facility can be prevented by the following techniques:

(1) establishing a guard force;
(2) controlling all other means of access (air conditioning vents, etc.);
(3) sign-in procedures;
(4) badges;
(5) special locks;
(6) exterior lighting;
(7) tv cameras;
(8) barriers (fences); and
(9) intrusion detection devices.

Physical security measures are the first line of defense against risks which stem from the uncertainties in the environment as well as from the unpredictability of human behavior. Frequently, they are the simplest safeguards to implement and can be put into practice with the least delay. Since physical security is so important in so many other fields, there is a large body of good work available to draw on.

Internal protection mechanisms

Authentication. An authentication mechanism prohibits the use of the system by unauthorized users by verifying the identity of a user making a request. User identification and authentication have already been performed to some degree at the physical security level. However, in most cases that alone is not enough.

Determination of identity can range from the personal recognition by a system employee of a user submitting a batch job to a fully automated system log-on procedure from a remote terminal. The chance for misidentification is much greater when jobs are submitted directly into a data processing facility from a remote site.

There are three categories[27] of methods by which a person's identity may be established for the purpose of allowing access to an information system. The methods, which can be applied singly or in a combination, are based on

(1) *something the person knows:* (e.g., passwords, combinations to locks, or series of facts about the individual's personal background);
(2) *something the person has:* (e.g., badges, cards with machine reading information, and keys to locks); and
(3) *something the person is:* (e.g., the person's appearance, fingerprints, hand geometry, voice, and signature). This category includes recognition by guards, which is frequently the best defense against unauthorized access.

Passwords are perhaps today's most widely used identification technique for granting system access. They can be used to relate system users with specific system resources to which they are authorized access. However, passwords as a general technique have some notorious defects, if not properly taken care of:

(1) *Password choice.* If a user is allowed to choose his own password, he may choose something easily guessed by someone else who knows his habits. For this reason, some systems have programs that generate random sequences of letters for use as passwords.

(2) *Password length.* The length of the password is important, since it determines the ease with which a password can be found by exhaustion. For example, the number of experiments needed to try all possible three-letter alphabetic passwords is $26^3 = 17,576$. The work factor can be increased by increasing the length of the password.

(3) *Frequent changes.* One way of making password guessing difficult is by changing it frequently to make the old one useless. But frequently changed passwords become difficult to memorize. Such systems tend to cause users to make written copies of their passwords, inviting compromise.

(4) *Password guarding.* It is important that all the passwords currently in use by the system be protected. If they can be observed or tampered with, there will be no password protection. In some systems, all passwords are passed through a hard-to-invert[29,30] transformation before being stored. Since the transform is supposed to be hard to invert, the original password is very difficult to determine from the transformed version.

(5) *Password exposure.* A significant defect with using passwords is that they must be exposed to be used. In systems where the terminal is distant from the computer, the password must be sent through some communication system, during which passage a wiretapper may be able to intercept it.

(6) *One-way authentication.* This problem concerns the password approach as a "one-way" authentication scheme. It authenticates the user to the computer system, but not vice versa. Solutions to this problem utilize[31] encryption and secret transformation keys.

Access control. These mechanisms control the accessing of information by programs in execution. Controlled access is necessary to ensure authorized access of the information managed by a computer system.

The first step in designing an access control mechanism is to specify the main parties and their interactions. This is done by identifying the entities to be protected and the entities to be protected against. Then the access rules are formulated.

Developing the concept of an entity to be protected requires a more explicit notion of "information" as recorded within a computer system. Today's computers manipulate information, not in terms of its content, but in terms of the information-containing structures used to hold encoded information. *Objects* are defined to be these information-holding entities. An object may be abstract (created by software), such as a tree or a process object, or it may correspond to physical hardware—e.g., a tape, a processor, or a memory word. To distinguish between the use made of two items of information (for purposes of control), they are encoded within separate objects.

To develop the concept of an active entity against which the objects are to be protected, an abstraction for accountability is introduced. This abstraction is to be an entity accountable for the activities inside the computer system. It will be referred to as a *subject* and is the entity in the computer system to which authorizations are granted. Examples of subjects are programs, processes, domains, and users.

After defining subjects and objects, the ways in which they interact are specified. This is done by formalizing the notion of an access. For every type of object there exists a finite set of distinct ways in which objects of that type can be manipulated; each type of manipulation is called an *access.* Note that access may be conceptually simple, e.g., reading of a value; or more complex, e.g., sorting a set of values, augmenting the size of an object, or even erasing the object. Every access to an object is made on behalf of some subject. The access

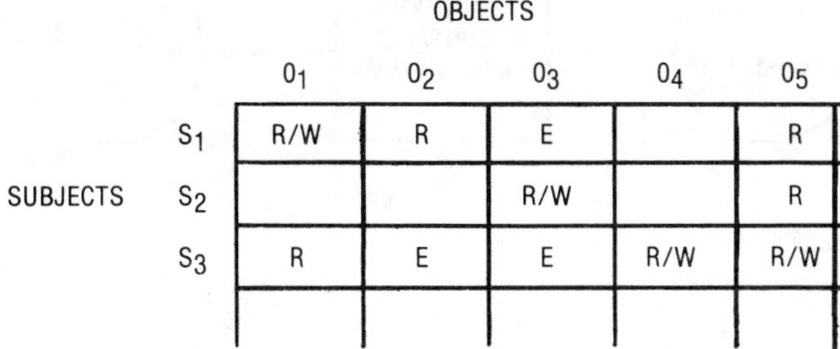

Figure 2. Portion of an access control matrix.

relations or the access rules are best abstracted by means of an access matrix.[32,33,34] Before granting an access to a subject, a check must be performed using the access control matrix (example shown in Figure 2).

After the notions of subjects, objects, and their interactions have been specified, the following problems still remain:

(1) implementation of objects,
(2) implementation of subjects,
(3) implementation of access control matrix,
(4) filling the access control matrix, and
(5) dynamic updating of access control matrix.

There are a variety of ways by which the first three issues can be addressed (see Case Studies, p. 71).

The fourth issue is concerned with the contents of the access control matrix. A formal security policy is a fundamental aspect of the access control mechanism definition. It should state precisely the contents of the matrix at all times. A good example of this is the Mitre[83,84] model in which the military multi-level security policy has been modeled using an access control matrix.

The dynamic updating of the access control matrix has to do with how one establishes and changes the specification of who may access what. It is relatively easy to envision and design systems that express a particular protection content. But the need to change access authorizations dynamically and the need for such changes to be requested by executing programs introduce much complexity in access control mechanisms.

Surveillance mechanisms. Some protection measures are either incompletely defined or made incomplete as the result of hardware or software failures. Consequently, there is a need for additional deterrents to attacks. A user's knowledge that his activities are being monitored may be sufficient to deter him from conducting attacks. Surveillance provides such a deterrent and involves two major types of activities—threat monitoring and security auditing.

Threat monitoring is the real-time or active monitoring, detection, and modification of attempted or successful penetrations. The set of events to be monitored during the system's operational phase should be specified. The threat-monitoring activity involves notifying a security administrator of an attack immediately upon detection and in a manner sufficient to ensure an immediate response.

Security auditing concerns the logging, reduction, ex post facto analysis, and reporting of security-related events indicating system penetration activities. The logging activity involves collecting system operational data which is indicative of system attacks, but which cannot be analyzed and responded to until sometime after the attack has occured. Thus, the amount and type of information required for security auditing differs from that needed for threat monitoring. It typically involves information which is indirectly indicative of attacks and must be obtained from extensive analysis of a system's operational states, data inputs, and processing results.

Communications security. The communications aspect of the security problem involves the protection of information transmitted over computer networks[35] and between remote terminals. As depicted in Figure 3, not only must the two hosts be protected; the communication path as a whole must be made secure as well. One approach is to provide physical security in much the same way as one protects a computer installation. For example, guards could stand every 100 yards along the communication line, or electronic devices could be used like TV cameras, radar, or other sophisticated intrusion detection devices. The costs involved in these methods are usually prohibitive. They could, however, be used for short distances.

The second approach involves the use of data encryption[36,37] and decryption techniques. The government has been using cryptographic techniques for many years for transmitting sensitive information. Now computer scientists are starting to look at encryption methods to protect important information in data processing equipment (data at rest) and over communication lines (data in motion). The encryption process consists of transforming the sensitive information into another form and using that for transmission purposes. The intruder would be unable to determine the sensitive information unless he knows (or can find) the transformation.

The secrecy of transformation is maintained by making the encryption process or key secret. In the latter case the encryption process is specified in a generally known algorithm, and the secret parameter supplied to the algorithm is called the key. To allow encryption processes to be compatible with the typical variety of network components, the key method is preferred.

Decryption is just the inverse process of encryption. With data encryption/decryption techniques, a thief could still obtain garbled information but would be unable to read it without risking more money to break the cipher than he may be willing to spend.

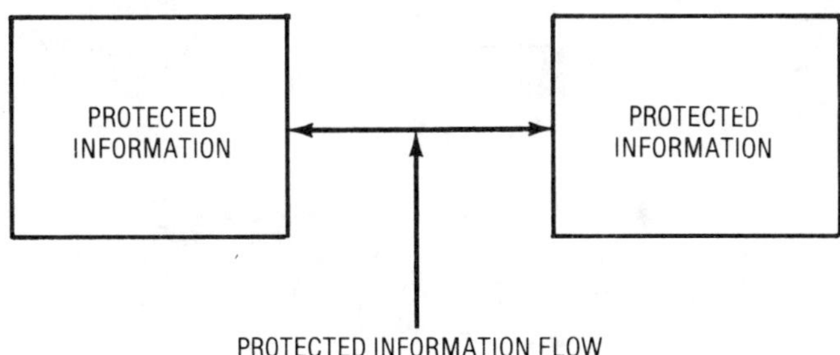

Figure 3. Communication security.

Reliability mechanisms

Failure results from errors in either hardware or operating system components of a computer system.[81] A prerequisite for a secure system, therefore, is the absence of software errors and a minimum of hardware errors. Note that there is a fundamental difference between hardware and software reliability in the sense that because of its physical and operating characteristics a hardware component can never be completely error-free.

The hardware and software components of a computer system are susceptible to algorithmic errors, whereas hardware components are also susceptible to probabilistic errors. These are the unpredictable failures of physical elements; protection against such failures is usually accomplished through redundancy (static & dynamic), fault detection and location, fault tolerance, and dynamic reconfiguration/recovery.

Algorithmic errors are design or implementation defects that can occur in either the hardware or software components. Protection against such failures is achieved through software redundancy[38] and certification.[88,103,104]

Internal protection mechanism requirements

For a computer system to be secure, its internal protection mechanisms must be complete, tamperproof, and certified.

Completeness. Completeness in the general sense implies that all requests which are security sensitive must pass through the internal protection mechanisms before being honored. As shown in Figure 4, under no circumstances should the internal protection mechanisms be circumvented.

The notion of completeness actually solves a fundamental problem in the field of computer security. Suppose, for example, every hole that allowed a known penetration approach to work were repaired. One could still not consider the resulting operating system to be secure, because a given collection of penetration programs exposes only the holes that these programs exploit. It is instructive to examine the completeness property for each of the four divisions of the internal protection mechanism: access control completeness, authentication completeness, surveillance completeness, and encryption completeness.

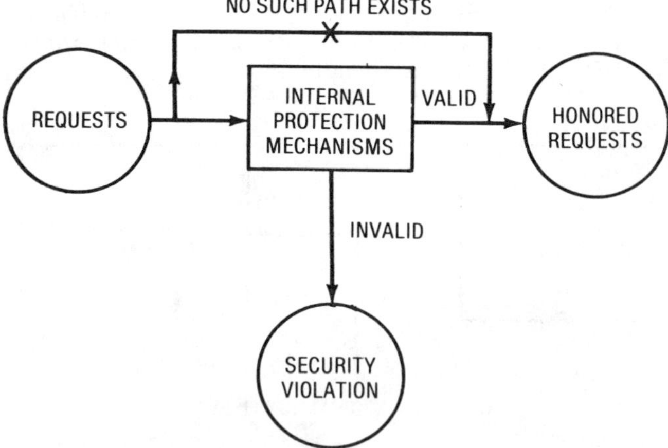

Figure 4. Completeness.

Access control completeness. An access control mechanism is said to be complete when every attempt to access information during the progress of a computation is validated. In other words, as shown in Figure 5, every access to every object must be validated. In this case, what is requested is information; the outcome is either the requested information (if valid), or a security violation

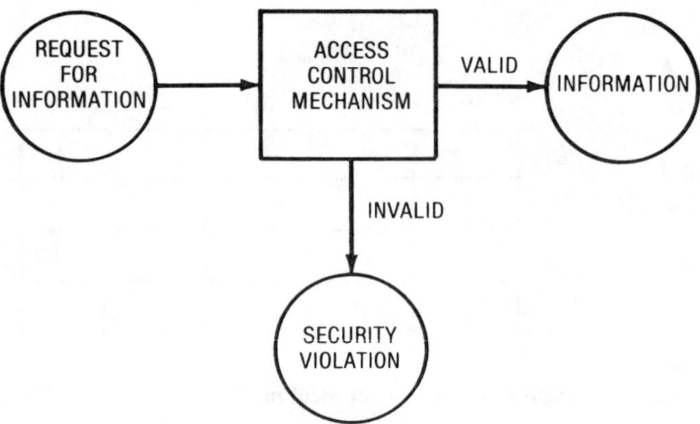

Figure 5. Access control completeness.

(if invalid). A good example of an access control mechanism is the Mitre Security Kernel,[85] wherein the access rules are specified by the military multilevel security policy.

As explained before, information in a computer system is protected by dividing it into mutually exclusive partitions called objects,[7] and then protecting the objects. Conceptually, it's like building an impenetrable wall around each distinct object, constructing a door in the wall through which accesses can be obtained, and posting a guard at the door to control its use. Of course, this means that the guard has some way of knowing which users are authorized to have accesses, and that each user has some reliable way of identifying himself to the guard. This authority check is usually implemented by having the guard demand a match between something he knows and something the prospective user possesses. Completeness is achieved when every attempt to access an object is validated by the guard.

As implemented, the guard concept will either be *list oriented,* in which case the guard holds a list of identifiers of authorized users and the users carry a unique, unforgeable identifier; or *ticket oriented,* in which case the guard holds the description of a single identifier and each user has a collection of unforgeable identifiers (tickets).

In a secure computer system, access control completeness is usually enforced by means of descriptor-driven processors. A descriptor-driven processor[39,40,41] is one whose hardware interprets each virtual address issued by a program in terms of a set of descriptors specifying the real physical address and the permitted access modes (e.g., read, write, execute) to be associated with every possible "virtual" address. The descriptors are of concern here to protect information, although they are also used in some systems to modularize addressing and storage allocation.

Access control systems can be broadly categorized* into cabability systems and access control list systems.

A capability serves both as the name of an object and as a set of privileges to access that object.[7] As explained earlier, a capability is actually a ticket. The chief virtues of the capability system are its inherent efficiency, simplicity, and flexibility. Efficiency comes from the ease of testing the validity of a proposed access: if the accessor can present a capability, the request is valid. Simplicity comes from the natural correspondence between the mechanical properties of

*For more details on this topic, see the paper by Saltzer & Schroeder,[7] which contains a thorough analysis of capability and access control list systems.

capabilities and the semantic property of address variables. Flexibility comes from allowing the user to decide which of his addresses contain capabilities and to develop a data structure with an arbitrary pattern of access authorizations to his liking.

In spite of the above advantages, there are several potential problems with capability-based systems: revocation,[113,114] propagation,[112,113,114] review of access,[66,73,112] and the lost object problem.[103]

Where the capability system is basically a ticket-oriented strategy, the access control list system is a list-oriented strategy. The basic idea is the association of an access controller with each object. Access to the object is granted if the principal name appears in the access controller. This mechanism can be implemented in hardware, although access control list systems have historically been implemented partly with interpretive software. For example, the MULTICS system uses software-interpreted access control lists together with hardware-interpreted tables of descriptors. Similarly, the guard file of the B6700 MCP is an example of an access controller implemented interpretively.

The access control list organization brings one issue into focus: control of who may modify the access control information. In the capability system, the corresponding consideration is diffuse. Any program having a capability may make a copy and put that copy in a place where other programs can make use of it. Two different policies for changing the access control lists can be envisioned: self-control and hierarchical control. In the self-control approach, permission to change the access control list is part of the access controller itself, whereas in hierarchical control the creator of an object must specify some previously existing access controller to regulate future changes to the access control list.

REQUESTS FOR COMPUTER SYSTEM USE
AUTHENTICATION MECHANISM
VALID
COMPUTER
INVALID
SECURITY VIOLATION

Figure 6. Authentication completeness.

Authentication completeness. An authentication mechanism is said to be complete when every attempt to use the computer is validated. This notion is similar to that of access control completeness except that instead of the information being accessed, it is the computer itself. The guard model is still valid where the protected object is the computer itself and the requestor is a computer system user rather than the executing program. As shown in Figure 6, what is requested is the use of the computer itself; the outcome is either yes or no.

Surveillance completeness. A surveillance mechanism is said to be complete when every attempt to access information during the progress of a computation is monitored, detected, and recorded. This would, of course, be true only for information for which auditing was required. For example, user A might want a particular file X audited whenever it is accessed. A malicious user should not be able to circumvent the auditing mechanism. As shown in Figure 7, if surveillance of a certain object is required, access can only be granted after proper auditing has been done.

Encryption completeness. An encryption mechanism is said to be complete when every attempt to transmit information is first encrypted. This would be true only for information for which encryption was required. This aim is accomplished in current systems by physically securing the encryption device between the computer (or terminal) and the communication lines. In other words, completeness is achieved by ensuring that the computer (or terminal), the encryption device, and the communication line are in series, as shown in Figure 8.

Tamperproofness. A protection mechanism is said to be tamperproof when it is protected from unauthorized alteration.

In the case of descriptor-based protection, the key issue is who loads the descriptor registers. If any running program could load it with any arbitrary value, there would be no protection. The instruction that loads the descriptor register with a new descriptor must have some special controls—either on the values it will load or who may use it.

It is easier to control who may use the descriptor, and a common scheme is to introduce an additional bit

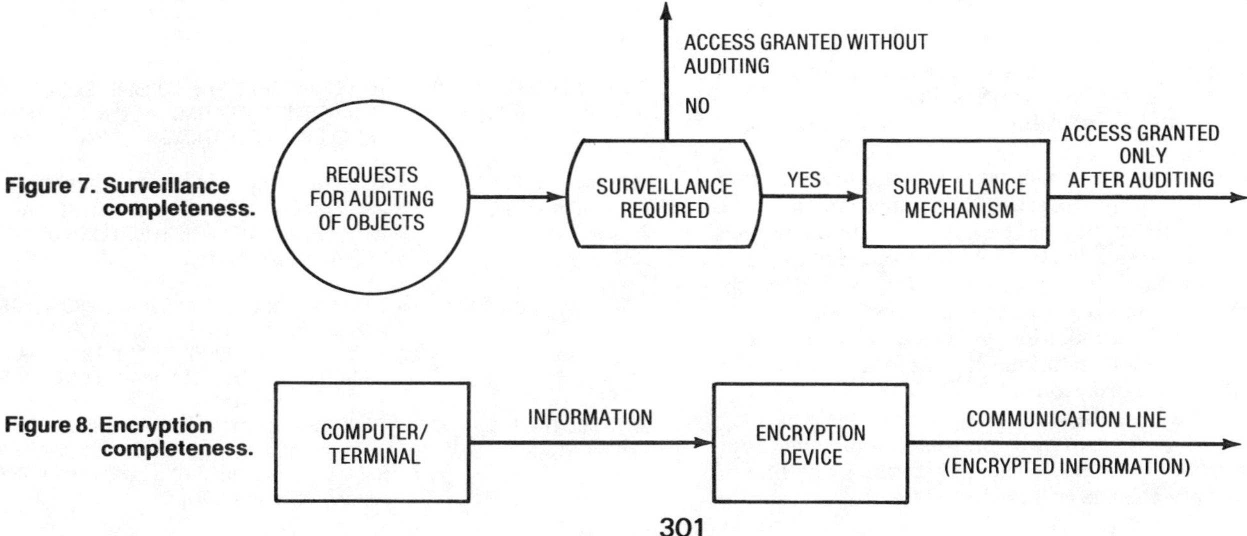

Figure 7. Surveillance completeness.

Figure 8. Encryption completeness.

in the processor state called the "privileged-state bit." All attempts to load the descriptor register are checked against the value of the privileged-state bit; the privileged-state bit must be ON for the register to be changed. What is needed to make the scheme complete is to ensure that the privileged-state bit cannot be changed by the user programs except, perhaps, by an instruction that simultaneously transfers control to the supervisor program at a planned entry location.

The second method of maintaining the integrity of these registers would be to allow any program to load the descriptor registers, but only from locations in memory that previously have been certified to contain acceptable descriptor values. Two schemes have been proposed for this method: partitioned memory and tagged memory.

Partitioned memory. As its name suggests, this scheme involves partitioning the segments in the system into two classes: capability segments which contain capabilities, and data segments which never contain capabilities. In addition, one set of processor registers is used for data and one for capabilities. The processor instruction set satisfies rules analogous to these above: data can be copied only into data segments and registers; capabilities can be copied only into capability segments and registers, and so on. This scheme is used on MAGNUM[42] and PLESSEY 250.[110,111,112]

Tagged memory. The tagged memory approach adds one or more tag bits to each word in a segment and to each processor register. The tag is used to specify whether the contents of the word or register are a capability or not. Tag bits are tested and set by the processor each time an access is made, and certain simple rules are used. When a word is copied, the copy is given the same tag as the original; arithmetic or logical instructions must be applied to words tagged as data and always produce a data tag on result; addressing always verifies that the segment addresses are tagged as a capability; and so on. This scheme is used on the B6700,[40,41] Rice Computer,[43] and NCS.[113,114]

A principal disadvantage[44] of the partitioned memory approach is that most objects require both data and capabilities and that this requires two segments. The artificial division of user memory into two parts is inconvenient. An advantage of the partitioned approach is that it is simple for capabilities and data words to be different lengths. This may be important, since capabilities tend to be big—at least 64 bits or longer. This approach also allows the operating system to locate capabilities more easily since they are in known places.

Certifiability. Certification is the process of checking for the completeness and correctness of a protection mechanism. Given current verification techniques, the mechanism should preferably be small, simple, and understandable.

If the secure system must be certified, the designer gets into a completely different ball game. In fact, the certification requirements have such a profound impact that they affect the system specification, design, and implementation. Such a combination of system development and verification gives rise to a new methodology[103,104] to facilitate specification, design, implementation, and proof. A similar proof technique has been applied to the verification[88] of a security kernel.

The design and verification stages are illustrated by Tables 3 and 4. These two phases should be kept separate from one another, although at times the line of demarcation between the two tends to blur.

Table 3. System development.

SYSTEM DEVELOPMENT PHASE	*PURPOSE*
SYSTEM DECOMPOSITION	TO CREATE THE HIERARCHY OF ABSTRACT MACHINES (M_0, M_1, . . . M_n)
FEATURE SELECTION	SELECTING THE FEATURES TO BE PRO— VIDED BY THE OPERATING SYSTEM
FUNCTION SELECTION	SELECTING THE FUNCTIONS TO BE IN— CLUDED IN EACH OF THE ABOVE MACHINES
FORMAL SPECIFICATION OF FUNCTIONS	FORMAL DESCRIPTION OF EACH OF THE ABSTRACT M/CS
FORMAL SPECIFICATION MEDIUM	FRAMEWORK FOR FORMALLY DESCRIBING EACH ABSTRACT MACHINE
MAPPING FUNCTION SELECTION	SELECTING THE FUNCTIONS FOR REPRE-SENTING THE DATA STRUCTURES OF LEVEL i IN TERMS OF DATA STRUCTURE OF LOWER LEVELS
FORMAL SPECIFICATION OF MAPPING FUNCTIONS	FORMAL DESCRIPTION OF THE MAPPED SPECIFICATIONS
MAPPING FUNCTION SPECIFICATION MEDIUM	FRAMEWORK FOR FORMALLY DESCRIBING MAPPING SPECIFICATIONS
ABSTRACT IMPLEMENTATION	FUNCTIONS OF EACH M_i, i 0 TO BE IMPLEMENTED AS AN ABSTRACT PROGRAM USING FUNCTIONS OF M_{i-1}
IMPLEMENTATION LANGUAGE	LANGUAGE IN WHICH TO WRITE THE ABSTRACT PROGRAMS
ACTUAL HARDWARE IMPLEMENTATION	REALIZATION IN TERMS OF THE HARD-WARE

Table 4. System verification.

SYSTEM VERIFICATION PHASE	*PURPOSE*
GLOBAL ASSERTIONS	TO DEFINE THE DESIRED SYSTEM BEHAVIOR TO BE PROVEN
FORMAL DEFINITION OF ASSERTIONS	FORMAL DESCRIPTION FOR EACH OF THE ABOVE GLOBAL ASSERTIONS
INTERNAL CONSISTENCY OF FORMAL SPECIFICA-TION	TO VERIFY THAT THE SPECIFICATIONS ARE INTERNALLY CONSISTENT FOR EVERY LEVEL
SATISFACTION OF GLOBAL ASSERTIONS	TO VERIFY THAT THE FORMAL SPECIFICA-TION OF THE OPERATING SYSTEM SATISFIES THE GLOBAL ASSERTIONS
INTERNAL CONSISTENCY OF MAPPING SPECIFICA-TION	TO VERIFY THAT THE MAPPING FUNCTIONS ARE CONSISTENT WITH EACH OTHER AND WITH THE FORMAL SPECIFICATIONS OF THE OPERATING SYSTEM
ABSTRACT PROGRAM VERIFICATION	TO VERIFY THAT THE ABSTRACT PROGRAMS ARE CORRECT WITH RESPECT TO THE FOR-MAL SPECIFICATIONS OF ABSTRACT MA-CHINES AND THE MAPPING FUNCTIONS
IMPLEMENTATION VERIFICATION	TO VERIFY THAT THE ABSTRACT PROGRAMS ARE CORRECTLY IMPLEMENTED IN THE HARDWARE INSTRUCTIONS, AND VERIFY THE HARDWARE CORRECTNESS

System development. The system decomposition step involves decomposing the system into a hierarchy of abstract machines. In the SRI effort, the operating system has been represented by 11 levels (level 0 to level 10). Levels 11 and 12 are the user environment level and the command interpreter level. Such a decomposition methodology has been applied recently to the design of a communication switch.[45,46]

Considerable work has been done on such a design methodology. Especially noteworthy are the works of Simon,[47] Dijkstra,[48,49,50] Hoare,[51,52] Parnas, [53] and Liskov.[54] Two current hierarchical operating systems—THE[48] and VENUS[54]—are fully implemented.

The feature selection step consists of selecting those features that the system is to provide. The features included in the SRI effort are capabilities, selective revocation, lost object handling, virtual memory, extended types, directories, process management, and dynamic linking.

The function selection step involves the selection of functions to be included in each abstract machine, and the determination of which functions are available at which levels in the hierarchy. The selection of functions is based on the features chosen to be included in the operating system.

After the features are selected, the approximate relationship of these features among the machines in the hierarchy is determined. This is done on the basis of judgment and experience. Some examples of difficult design decisions in the SRI[103] effort have been the placement of revocation at the same level as segment management, the placement of extended types immediately above segments, and the creation of a separate level to solve the lost object problem. After this, the various functions are selected for the various features in the abstract machines.

The formal specification step consists of formally describing the various functions for each of the abstract machines.

The formal specification medium consists of designing a framework for formally describing each abstract machine. The framework chosen is based on Parnas'[55,56] method of "module specifications," for both the SRI[103] and the security kernel[85] approaches.

The mapping function selection step involves the selection of functions for representing the data structures of level i in terms of data structures of lower levels.

The formal specifications for mapping functions consist of formal descriptions of those functions. The medium or framework for describing the mapping specifications could be similar to Hoare's[34] technique of data representation.

The abstract implementation step involves the implementation of each of the functions of each machine M_i $(i > 0)$ as a program using the functions of M_{i-1} and possibly lower levels. In the SRI approach these implementations are referred to as "abstract programs."

The implementation language step consists of choosing a language—either existing or custom designed—in which to write the abstract programs. Such a language has not yet been defined in the SRI[103] approach.

In the implementation of the security kernel,[85] the choice was the SUE[57] systems language. There were two main reasons for this selection. First SUE is a structured systems programming language in which the O&V (operational and value returning) functions[55,56] can be implemented with ease. Second, a cross compiler is available on an IBM system to produce PDP 11/45 code from the SUE systems language.

The actual hardware implementation step involves the realization of primitive functions in terms of hardware. One could specify a hardware architecture from scratch, or else choose an existing hardware configuration with possible modifications to it.

The SRI design is based on capabilities. There are a number of machine designs based on capabilities; however, Plessy 250[111,112] is the only machine which implements capabilities directly in hardware and which is available commercially. Redell[114] has discussed in a fairly detailed fashion the implementation considerations for capabilities design.

The most obvious necessity in implementing a capability system is some mechanism to protect the representation of capabilities themselves from unauthorized alteration. All existing capability systems use partitioned memory[42,62,63,66,71,111,112] except the one proposed by Redell,[114] which uses a tagged[43] approach. Such an approach has been recommended for the SRI design, although a processor to interpret these tags has to be completely specified.

The security kernel has been implemented on the PDP 11/45, a descriptor-based machine that provides three states in hardware for the kernel, operating system, and user.

System verification. The verification phase is closely associated with the system development phase. After each step of system development, there is some kind of correctness proof associated with it to determine whether that particular step was carried out correctly. Table 4 defines the verification steps.

The global assertions phase formalizes the desired system behavior as a set of assertions to be proven. If the interest is security, global assertions relating to security are considered. As stated earlier, there are two types of assertions: invariant assertions, which specify how the system state must not change; and the variant assertions, which specify how the system state must change. The invariant assertions in the SRI approach are stated as a set of four principles: alteration, detection, guaranteed service, and confinement. The formal description of desired system behavior involves the description of these properties as sets of assertions. At this point, the first two principles have been more or less formalized.[103,104] In the security kernel[88] approach, the simple security property and the star property have been formalized.

The internal consistency check consists of verifying that the specifications are internally consistent for every level.

The security verification step consists of proving that the global assertions are satisfied by the formal specification. This step is the most critical part, since the desired security behavior of the system is guaranteed here by carrying out the proofs. The proof involves showing that the global assertions (formalized before) are satisfied by the formal specifications.

The proof structures here would be similar to the one developed by Price,[58] who proved the correctness of a virtual memory by establishing global assertions and proving that they are satisfied. It is more complex in the SRI[103] case, since they are dealing with the whole operating system.

The internal consistency check of mapped specifications consists of verifying that the mapping functions are consistent with each other and with the formal specifications of the operating system. It seems likely that Hoare's[59] proof technique will be used for this purpose.

The abstract program verification consists of verifying that the abstract programs are correct with respect to the formal and mapping specifications. The input and output assertions are derived from these specifications, and the correctness of abstract programs would be shown by using an extension of Floyd's[60] technique. Floyd's

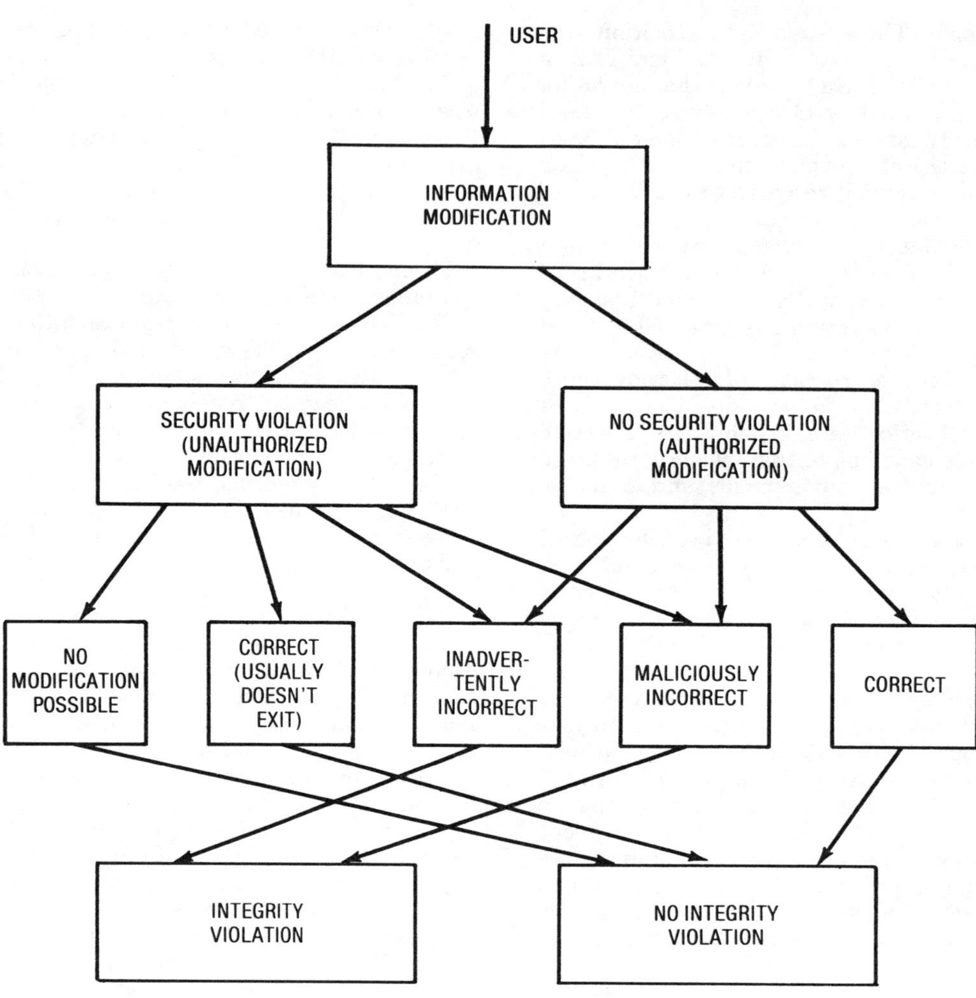

Figure 9. System integrity concept.

method, which is used in most automated verification systems, is described nicely by Elspas.[61]

The implementation verification check consists of verifying that the abstract programs are correctly implemented in hardware instructions, and show the correctness of hardware.

On the whole, such an effort and approach seem to be very promising, although additional work still remains to be done in the areas of implementation and proof structures.

Integrity

Another problem closely related to the concept of security is that of system integrity.[81] There appears to be no current universally accepted definition of integrity, but it seems safe to say that integrity is closely related to the alteration principle[103]—*viz.*, there shall be no unauthorized alteration of information. However, this definition alone does not cover all the possible causes of an integrity violation, as shown in Figure 9. The figure clearly distinguishes between security and integrity violations and shows that an integrity violation may occur with or without a security violation. Unauthorized modification of information is one case of a potential security violation.[4] The possibility of correct information modification after a security violation has taken place usually does not occur in practice. If one could design a system so that no modification of information would be possible after a security violation has been detected, this would prevent two possible cases of integrity violation. The other two possible cases of integrity violation occur when one is authorized to modify, but does it incorrectly, either maliciously or inadventently.

An *integrity policy* can be defined as a finite set of rules which specifies the modification of information during the progress of a computation. Any sound integrity policy has to make sure that the paths taken always lead to the box showing NO INTEGRITY VIOLATION in Figure 9. Note the use of the word *policy*. In this case (as for security), one would have to face the hard task of providing the mechanisms (maybe as part of the protection mechanisms) to support and enforce the desired integrity policies. ■

Acknowledgments

The author would like to give special thanks to J. T. Lynch, director, Advanced Development Organization, Federal and Special Systems Group, for his continuous support and encouragement while he was with the Burroughs Corporation. In addition, it is a pleasure to thank C. S. Chandersekaran and J. P. Anderson for carefully reviewing drafts of the manuscript and offering many suggestions.

References and bibliography

References 1-61 are general ones in the area of computer security and are numbered in the order of their citation in the text. References 62-120, most of which are cited in the text, are intended as a bibliography on case studies of existing systems and are listed alphabetically within each system area.

1. D. B. Parker, "Computer Related Crime and Data Security," Stanford Research Institute, Palo Alto, 1972.

2. D. B. Parker et al., "Computer Abuse," Stanford Research Institute, Palo Alto, November 1973.

3. D. B. Parker, *Crime by Computer,* Charles Scribner & Sons, New York, 1976.

4. J. Anderson, "Information Security in a Multi-user Computer Environment," *Advances in Computers,* Morris Rubinoff, ed., Academic Press, New York, 1972, pp. 1-35.

5. J. P. Anderson, "Computer Security Technology Planning Study," ESD-TR-73-51, Vol. 1, October 1972.

6. R. Hargraves and A. Stephenson, "Design Considerations for an Educational Time Sharing System," *AFIPS Conf. Proc., Vol. 34, 1969 SJCC,* pp. 657-664.

7. J. H. Saltzer and M. D. Schroeder, "The Protection of Information in Computer Systems," *Proc. of the IEEE,* Vol. 63, No. 9, September 1975, pp. 1278-1308.

8. B. W. Lampson, "A Note on the Confinement problem," *CACM,* Vol. 16, October 1973, pp. 613-614.

9. A. K. Jones, "Protection in Programmed Systems," PhD dissertation, Carnegie-Mellon University, 1973.

10. D. Denning, "Secure Information Flow in Computer Systems," PhD dissertation, Purdue University, 1975.

11. J. S. Fenton, "Memoryless Subsystems," *The Computer Journal,* Vol. 17, No. 2, May 1974.

12. R. Conway, W. Maxwell, and H. Morgan, "On the Implementation of Security Measures in Information Systems," *CACM,* Vol. 15, April 1972, pp. 211-220.

13. D. Hsaio, D. Kerr, and F. Stahl, "Research on Data Secure Systems," *AFIPS Conf. Proc., Vol. 43, 1974 NCC,* pp. 994-996.

14. L. Hoffman and W. Miller, "Getting a Personal Dossier from a Statistical Data Bank," *Datamation,* Vol. 16, May 1970, pp. 74-75.

15. DOD Directive 5200.28, "Security Requirements for Automatic Data Processing Systems."

16. DOD Directive 5200.28-M, "Techniques and Procedures for Implementing, Deactivating, Testing, and Evaluating Secure Resource Sharing ADP Systems."

17. "Privacy, Security, and the Information Processing Industry," prepared by The Ombudsman Committee on Privacy, Los Angeles Chapter, ACM, 1976.

18. S. Lipner, "A Panel Session—Security Kernels," *AFIPS Conf. Proc., Vol. 43, 1974 NCC,* pp. 973-980.

19. T. Groning et al., "Data Security and Data Processing, Part I: User Requirements Survey," CISR-8, MIT, Cambridge, March 1975.

20. T. Groning, "Data Security and Data Processing, Part V: Data Security and the Financial Community," CISR-8, MIT, Cambridge, September 1975.

21. B. E. Stangle, "Data Security and Data Processing, Part IV: Data Security in the Medical Community," CISR-8, MIT, Cambridge, September 1975.

22. D. O. Hewitt and P. F. Hollings, "Data Security in University Environments, Part II," CISR-8, MIT, March 1975.

23. G. N. Smith, "Data Security in the Service Bureau Industry," CISR-8, Sloan WP-771-75, MIT, Cambridge, March 1975.

24. Air Force Regulation AFR 205-1.

25. Computer Security Technology Reference Manual, RADC, Griffiss Air Force Base, New York.

26. The Privacy Act of 1974, *5 U. S. C.,* Section 552a.

27. "Computer Security Guidelines for Implementing the Privacy Act of 1974," NBS, FIPS Pub 41, May 30, 1975.

28. J. Martin, *Security, Accuracy, and Privacy in Computer Systems,* Prentice-Hall, Inc., Englewood Cliffs, N.J., 1973.

29. G. Purdy, "A High Security Log-in Procedure," *CACM,* Vol. 17, August 1974, pp. 442-445.

30. A. Evans, W. Kantrowitz, and E. Weiss, "A User Authentication Scheme Not Requiring Secrecy in the Computer," *CACM,* Vol. 17, August 1974, pp. 437-442.

31. H. Feistel, "Cryptographic Coding for Data Bank Privacy," IBM Res. Rep., RC 2827, March 1970.

32. B. W. Lampson, "Protection," *Proc. Fifth Princeton Symposium on Information Sciences and Systems,* Princeton University, March 1971, pp. 437-443.

33. G. S. Graham and P. J. Denning, "Protection—Principles and Practice," *AFIPS Conf. Proc., Vol. 40, 1972 SJCC,* pp. 417-429.

34. G. J. Popek, "Protection Structures," *Computer,* June 1974, pp. 22-33.

35. D. Branstad, "Security Aspects of Computer Networks," *Proc., AIAA Computer Network Systems Conf.,* April 1973, Paper 73-427.

36. D. J. Bartek, "Encryption for Data Security," *Honeywell Computer Journal,* Vol. 8, No. 2 March 1974, pp. 86-89.

37. R. R. Keys and E. H. Clamons, "File Encryption as a Security Tool," *Honeywell Computer Journal,* Vol. 8, No. 2, March 1974, pp. 90-93.

38. B. Randell, "System Structure for Software Fault Tolerance," *IEEE Trans. Software Engineering,* Vol. SE-1, No. 2, June 1975.

39. K. G. Walter et al., "Modelling the Security Interface," Jennings Computer Center, Case Western Reserve University, Report No. 1158, August 1974.

40. E. Organick, *Computer Systems Organization: The B5700/B6700 Series,* Academic Press, New York, 1973.

41. K. S. Shankar, "Protection Implications of the B6700 Architecture," TR 76-1, Burroughs Corp., Paoli, Pa. 19301, February 1976.

42. R. S Fabry, "Preliminary Description of a Supervisor for a Machine Oriented Around Capabilities," *ICR Quarterly Report* 18, August 1968, ICR, University of Chicago.

43. E. Feustal, "On the Advantages of Tagged Architecture,"

IEEE Trans. on Comp., Vol. C-22, No. 7, pp. 644-656, July 1973.

44. R. S. Fabry, "Capability Based Addressing," *CACM,* Vol. 17, No. 7, July 1974.

45. K. S. Shankar and C. S. Chandersekaran, "Data Flow, Abstraction Levels, and Specifications for Communications Switching Systems," *2nd International Conference on Software Engineering,* Oct. 1976, pp. 585-591.

46. C. S. Chandersekaran and K. S. Shankar, "Towards Formally Specifying Communication Switches," *Proc., Computer Networks: Trends and Applications,* Nov. 1976, pp. 104-112.

47. H. A. Simon, "The Architecture of Complexity," *Proc. Am. Phil. Soc.,* Vol. 106, December 1962, pp. 467-482.

48. E. W. Dijkstra, "The Structure of THE Multiprogramming System," *CACM,* Vol. II., No. 5, May 1968, pp. 341-346.

49. ______________, "Co-operating Sequential Processes," in *Programming Languages,* F. Genuys (ed.), Academic Press, 1968, pp. 43-112.

50. ______________, "Complexity Controlled by Hierarchical Ordering of Function and Variability," in *Report on a Conference on Software Engineering,* NATO 1968, pp. 181-185.

51. C. A. R. Hoare, "Procedures and Parameters: An Axiomatic Approach," in *Symposium on Semantics of Algorithmic Languages,* E. Engeler (ed.), Springer-Verlag, 1971, pp. 102-116.

52. ______________, "Monitors: An Operating System Structuring Concept," *CACM,* Vol. 17, October 1974, pp. 549-557.

53. D. L. Parnas, "On a Buzzword: Hierarchical Structure," *Information Processing 74,* Vol. 2, North-Holland Publishing, 1974, pp. 336-339.

54. B. H. Liskov, "The Design of the Venus Operating System," *CACM,* Vol. 15, No. 3, March 1972, pp. 144-149.

55. D. L. Parnas, "A Technique for Software Module Specifications with Examples," *CACM,* Vol. 15, May 1972, pp. 330-336.

56. ______________, "On the Criteria to be used in Decomposing Systems into Modules," *CACM,* Vol. 15, December 1972, pp. 1053-1058.

57. K. C. Sevcik, "Project SUE as a Learning Experience," *AFIPS Conf. Proc., Vol. 41, 1972 FJCC,* pp. 331-337.

58. W. R. Price, "Implications of a Virtual Memory Mechanism for Implementing Protection in a Family of Operating Systems," PhD dissertation, Carnegie-Mellon University, Dept. of Computer Science, 1973.

59. C. A. R. Hoare, "Proof of Correctness of Data Representations," *ACTA Informatica 1,* 1972, pp. 271-281.

60. R. W. Floyd, "Assigning Meaning to Programs," in *Mathematical Aspects of Computer Science,* Vol. 19, J. T. Schwartz (ed.), American Mathematics Society, Providence, R. I. 1967, pp. 19-32.

61. B. Elspas et al., "An Assessment of Techniques for Proving Program Correctness," *Computing Surveys,* Vol. 4, No. 2, June 1972, pp. 97-147.

Case Studies

CAL-TSS

62. B. W. Lampson, "Dynamic Protection Structures," *AFIPS Conf. Proc. Vol. 35, 1969 FJCC,* pp. 27-38.

63. H. Sturgis, "A Post-Mortem for a Time Sharing System," Xerox Palo Alto Research Center, Tech. Report CSL 74-1.

64. B. W. Lampson, "Dynamic Protection Structures," *AFIPS Conf. Proc., Vol. 35, 1969 FJCC,* pp. 27-38.

65. ______________, and H. Sturgis, "Reflections on an Operating System Design," *CACM,* Vol. 19, No. 5, May 1976, pp. 251-265.

CAP

66. R. M. Needham, "Protection Systems and Protection Implementations," *AFIPS Conf. Proc., Vol. 41, 1972, FJCC,* pp. 271-278.

67. R. M. Needham and M. V. Wilkes, "Domains of Protection and the Management of Processes," *The Computer Journal,* Vol. 17, No. 2, pp. 117-120.

68. R. M. Needham and R. D. H. Walker, "Protection and Process Management in the 'CAP' Computer," *Proc., Workshop on Protection in Operating Systems,* IRIA, Rocquencourt, France, August 1974, pp. 35-53.

HYDRA

69. W. A. Wulf et al., "HYDRA: The Kernel of a Multiprocessor Operating System," *CACM,* Vol. 17, July 1974, pp. 337-345.

70. A. K. Jones, "Protection in Programmed Systems," PhD disseration, Carnegie-Mellon University, June 1973.

71. W. A. Wulf et al., "Overview of the Hydra Operating System Development," *Proc., Fifth Symposium on Operating System Principles,* University of Texas at Austin, Nov. 19-21, 1975, pp. 122-131.

72. R. Levin et al., "Policy/Mechanism Separation in HYDRA," *op. cit.,* pp. 131-140.

73. E. Cohen et al., "Protection in the Hydra Operating System," *op. cit.,* pp. 141-160.

74. W. Wulf et al., "Bliss: A Language for systems programming," *CACM,* Vol. 14, No. 12, December 1971, pp. 780-790.

75. W. Wulf, "Alphard: Toward a Language to Support Structured Programs," Carnegie-Mellon University, Tech. Report, 1974.

76. A. K. Jones and W. A. Wulf, "Towards the Design of Secure Systems," *Software—Practice and Experience,* Vol. 5, Month, 1975, pp. 321-336.

IBM VM/370

77. R. Meyer and L. Seawright, "A Virtual Machine Time Sharing System," *IBM Sys. Journal,* Vol. 9, No. X, Month 1970, pp. 199-218.

78. C. R. Attanassio et al., "Penetrating an Operating System: a Study of VM/370 Integrity," *IBM Sys. Journal,* Vol. 15, No. 1, January 1976, pp. 102-116.

79. L. A. Belady and C. Weissman, "Experiments with Secure Resource Sharing for Virtual Machines," *Proc. Workshop on Protection in Operating Systems,* IRIA, Rocquencourt, France, August 1974, pp. 27-33.

80. J. J. Donovan and S. E. Madnick, "Hierarchical Approach to Computer System Integrity," *IBM Sys. Journal,* Vol. 14, No. 2, March 1975, pp. 188-202.

81. C. S. Chandersekaran and K. S. Shankar, "On Virtual Machine Integrity," *IBM Sys. Journal,* Vol. 15, No. 3, Aug. 1976, pp. 264-269.

82. J. D. Bagley et al., "Sharing Data and Services in a Virtual Machine System," *Proc., Fifth Symposium on Operating System Principles,* University of Texas at Austin, Nov. 19-21, 1975, pp. 82-88.

MITRE Security Kernel

83. L. J. Lapadula and D. E. Bell, "Secure Computer Systems: A Mathematical Model," MTR-2547, Vol. II, MITRE, May 1973.

84. D. E. Bell, "Secure Computer Systems: A Refinement of the Mathematical Model," MTR-2547, Vol. III, MITRE December 1973.

85. W. Schiller, "Design of a Security Kernel for the PDP 11/45," Air Force Elec, Syst. Div., MTR-2934, MITRE, March 1975.

86. L. Smith, "Architectures for Secure Computing Systems," MTR-2722, MITRE, June 1974.

87. D. F. Stork, "Downgrading in a Secure Multilevel Computer System: the Formulary Concept," NTIS, AD-A011696, U.S. Dept. of Commerce, May 1975.

88. J. K. Millen, "Security Kernel Validation in Practice," *CACM,* Vol. 19, No. 5, May 1976.

89. D. E. Bell and E. L. Burke, "A Software Validation Technique for Certification: the Methodology," ESD-TR-75-54, Vol. I, MITRE, November 1974.

Multics

90. E. Organick, "The Multics System: An Examination of its Structure," MIT Press, Cambridge, Mass., 1971.

91. J. Saltzer, "Protection and the Control of Information Sharing in Multics," *CACM,* Vol. 17, No. 7, July 1974, pp. 388-402.

92. A. Bensoussan et al., "The Multics Virtual Memory: Concepts and Design," *CACM,* Vol. 15, No. 5, May 1972, pp. 308-318.

93. M. Schroeder and J. Saltzer, "A Hardware Architecture for Implementing Protection Rings," *CACM,* Vol. 15, No. 3, March 1972, pp. 157-170.

94. M. Schroeder, "Cooperation of Mutually Suspicious Subsystems on a Computer Utility," MIT Project MAC Tech. Rep. TR-104.

95. L. Rotenberg, "Making Computers Keep Secrets," MIT Project MAC Tech. Rep. TR-115.

96. F. Corbato et al., "Multics—The First Seven Years," *AFIPS Conf. Proc., Vol. 40, 1972 SJCC,* pp. 571-583.

97. R. Daley and J. Dennis, "Virtual Memory, Processes and Sharing in Multics," *CACM,* Vol. 11, No. 5, May 1968, pp. 306-312.

98. P. A. Janson, "Removing the Dynamic Linker from the Security Kernel of a Computing Utility," MAC TR-132, MIT, June 1974.

99. R. G. Bratt, "Minimizing the Naming Facilities Requiring Protection in a Computing Utility," MS thesis, EE Dept., MIT, Sept. 1975.

100. M. D. Schroeder, "Engineering a Security Kernel for Multics," *Proc., Fifth Symposium on Operating System Principles,* University of Texas at Austin, November 19-21, 1975, pp. 25-32.

101. P. A. Janson, "Dynamic Linking and Environment Initialization in a Multi-Domain Process," *op. cit.,* pp. 43-50.

102. D. P. Reed, "Processor Multiplexing in a Layered Operating System," MIT/LCS/TR-164, 1976.

SRI's Provable Security

103. P. G. Neuman et al., "A Provably Secure Operating System," SRI Project 2581, Stanford Research Institute, 1975.

104. K. S. Shankar and C. S. Chandersekaran, "On Certifiably Secure Systems," working paper, ADO, FSSG, Burroughs Corp., October 1975.

105. O. Roubine et al., "SPECIAL Reference Manual," SRI Report, CSG-45, SRI, 1976.

106. L. Robinson et al., "Proof Techniques for Hierarchically Structured Programs," *CACM,* Vol. 20, No. 4, April 1977, pp. 271-283.

107. A. R. Saxena and T. Bredt, "A Structural Specification of a Hierarchical Operating System," *Proc., 1975 International Conf. on Reliable Software,* pp. 310-318.

108. J. M. Spitzen, "An example of Hierarchical Design and Proof," CSG, SRI, October 1975.

109. P. G. Neumann et al., "On the Design and Verification of a Secure Operating System," *AFIPS Conf. Proc., Vol. 43, 1974 NCC,* pp. 978-979.

PLESSY 250

110. D. C. Cosserat, "A Capability Oriented Multiprocessor System for Real Time Applications," *Proc., I. C. C. Conference,* Washington, D. C., Oct. 1972, pp. 282-289.

111. ______________, "A Data Model Based on the Capability Protection Mechanism," *Proc., Workshop on Protection in Operating Systems,* IRIA, Rocquencourt, France, August 1974, pp. 35-53,

112. D. M. England, "Capability Concept Mechanisms and Structure in System 250," *op. cit.,* pp. 241-260.

Redell's NCS

113. D. D. Redell and R. S. Fabry, "Selective Revocation of Capabilities," *op. cit.,* pp. 197-209.

114. D. Redell, "Naming and Protection in Extendible Operating Systems," MIT, MAC TR-140, November 1974.

UCLA Security Kernel

115. G. J. Popek and C. S. Kline, "Verifiably Secure Operating System Software," *AFIPS Conf. Proc., Vol. 43, 1974 NCC,* pp. 145-152.

116. E. J. Walton, "The UCLA Security Kernel," Master's thesis, UCLA Computer Science Dept., 1975.

117. C. Weissman, "Secure Computer Operating with Virtual Machine Partitioning," *AFIPS Conf. Proc., Vol. 44, 1975 NCC,* pp. 929-934.

118. G. J. Popek and C. S. Kline, "The PDP-11 Virtual Machine Architecture: A Case Study," *Proc., Fifth Symposium on Operating System Principles,* The University of Texas at Austin, November 19-21, 1975, pp. 97-105.

119. ______________, "The Design of a Verified Protection System," *Proc., Workshop on Protection in Operating Systems,* IRIA, Rocquencourt, France, August 1974, pp. 183-196.

120. P. Fiorani, "The UCLA Virtual Machine Monitor," Master's thesis, UCLA Computer Science Dept., 1975.

Foiling data thieves

Network security in distributed data processing

Hal B. Becker, Honeywell Information Systems, Phoenix, Ariz.

Overview of the various network elements, defined in terms of their security implications, gives users a framework for action

Computer crime, although relatively new in the annals of lawmen, poses a greater problem for operators of the far flung equipment and lines of distributed data processing networks than it did for managers of centralized networks. Security of the systems has become of prime importance as the distribution of the operations has opened up links and increased the difficulty of guarding the many computer and terminal sites.

The untold treasures of data locked in computer memories and the blind (to those who know the key) obedience to orders have proved to be an attractive goal for some unlawful citizens. Consider a typical case: an enterprising young thief managed to gain access to a utility company's computer by buying used telephone equipment, and by retrieving computer listings and operational documents from trash bins. Armed with this simple equipment, he caused several hundred thousand dollars worth of the utility company's equipment to be delivered to him at various addresses. When the delivery arrived, he simply reloaded the equipment onto a legally purchased second-hand company van and drove off. He then sold the equipment—sometimes back to the company from which it was stolen—at an enormous profit.

It was not necessary to gain physical access to either the computer or even to a terminal belonging to the company. The company had sold him the proper access device as scrap and the entry codes and procedures were made available to him through the company's own refuse system.

The ease of access that this young thief enjoyed is not exaggerated and points up the need for security. As data links become more numerous, as in distributed processing networks, and different processing functions are assigned to distant nodes, the security problems intensify. Further examples are cited in the panel: "Security Breaches." However, measures—some easy, some difficult—do exist for providing security to all processors and links in the distributed data processing network.

In centralized configurations and early network implementations, information-, networking-, and database-processing functions were resident in the same computer, usually an information processor. The increasing interference due to competition for a finite set of resources (processor time, memory, etc.), led to an initial separation of function in the middle of the 1960's.

This separation resulted in leaving the information-processing and database-processing functions in the information processor and putting the network processing or data communications function in a separate

Reprinted from *Data Commun.*, vol. 6, pp. 33–39, Aug. 1977.

1 Separation of functions

Separate processors. *In a distributed data processing network, three basic functions reside in three separate machines. The information processor manipulates data to produce the desired output. The network processor makes sure that the data reaches the proper destination. The database processor stores data for subsequent use.*

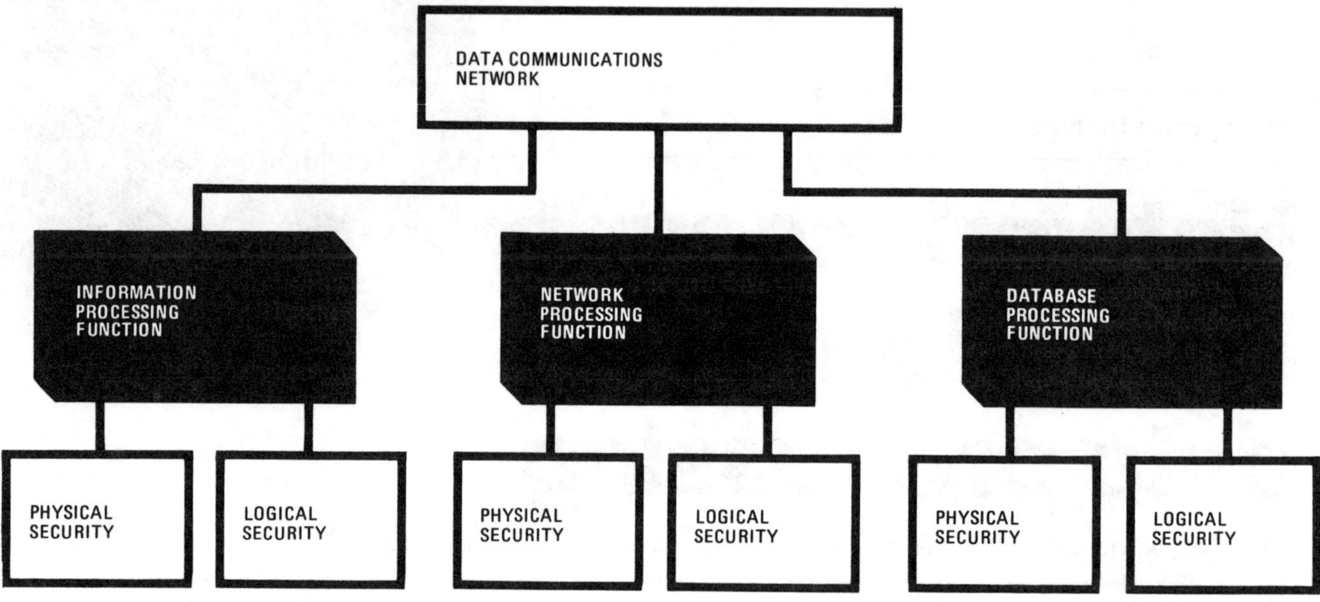

front-end processor. The efficiencies inherent in this approach are attested to by the industry's almost universal adoption of the front-end processor approach to data communications. The separation, also however, changed the security considerations. An additional link was provided which did not previously exist.

The continuing evolution of on-line applications, transaction processing, and other interactive areas has resulted in a greater emphasis and reliance on databases accessible by the data communications network and its users. Predictably, this trend is resulting in increased levels of interference between the information-processing and the database-processing functions which still reside in the information processor.

A second separation of function is about to occur. The database function will be moved from the information processor into a separate database processor. All three of the basic functions—information processing, network processing and database processing—will then reside in separate machines, each optimized for one function. Greatly improved performance will result due to the reduced interference. Security problems, too, can be expected to increase.

The three functions can be defined in terms of their physical and logical function subsets. Physical function subsets consist of the various hardware devices and facilities available to the designers of the network. Logical function subsets consist of software or other stored program logic executed in the various processors. Logical functions control the physical devices of the configuration, and the flow of information within and between the various devices of the network. Figure 1 illustrates the first three levels of a structure that defines data communications networks in terms of the three basic functions and their physical and logical subsets.

The three basic functions shown in Figure 1 thus become the building blocks for all types of data communications networks, ranging from totally centralized to totally distributed configurations, with many intermediate combinations possible.

In a totally centralized configuration, all three functions—information processing, network processing, and database processing—exist at a single site. This site provides all of the resources required by the terminal users in the surrounding network. In a totally distributed configuration, each of the three functions exists in more than one location.

Intermediate configurations include centralized information processing and database processing with distributed network processing, and centralized database processing with distributed information processing and network processing.

Network relationships

Figure 2 includes the three basic types of nodes which make up all networks.

Source nodes are points at which information enters the network. Source nodes can be such devices as teleprinters and visual display terminals, as well as information processors and network processors.

Destination nodes are points to which information is delivered and leaves the network. Terminals, information processors, and network processors can all act as destination nodes.

Information being routed from its source to its destination can pass through one or more relay nodes. Relay nodes perform two basic functions: to save on line costs and to provide alternate access and/or routing capabilities in networks with high availability requirements. Network processors are active relay nodes. They are program-controlled devices capable of exerting logical control over information passing through them. Passive relay nodes (such as multiplexers and switches) are devices that are not program-controlled and, therefore, can exert little or no logical control over information passing through them.

Figure 3 illustrates a portion of a distributed network. The information processors can come from one or many vendors as long as they work together and can act as both information sources and destinations. Similarly, the terminals clustered around the network processors can be both sources and destinations.

Both the front-end network processors (FNP) and the remote network processors (RNP) can act as information sources, destinations, and relay nodes in the configuration. Since they are program controlled, they are active relay nodes. The frequency-division multiplexer (FDM) is a passive relay node and cannot exert logical control over information flowing through it. The controlling logic for the terminals clustered around the FDM is executed in the remote network processor near the center of the illustration.

As the network becomes more and more distributed security problems change in nature and in difficulty of solution. The remainder of this article discusses distributed-data-processing network security within the framework presented in the first three figures.

Physical and logical security

Network security considerations can be divided into two distinct categories: physical security and logical security. These categories can then be applied to the information processing, network processing, and database processing functions.

Figure 4 indicates the application of physical and logical security to the information and database processing functions. If the entire information processing site is under constant physical surveillance, a first level of security is provided. By limiting physical access through personal recognition and badge or identification card checks, an extra level of security is added. Still greater levels are added by inspecting all personnel for cameras, recording devices, transmitters, receivers, documents carried in and out, and similar measures.

In situations where the processing site is not isolated and where close proximity is easily attained, additional measures may be required. The entire facility, for example, can be placed in a radio-frequency shielded room. This shielding holds in the electrical signals that radiate from operating hardware.

One element of physical security that appears to defy an absolute solution is that of the information that can be carried out of the facility in an employee's head. Stopping someone from memorizing portions of sensitive information can only be achieved by controlling access to the information itself. This leads to a discussion of logical security measures employed within a physically secure processing site.

Logical security measures are those employed to control access to data maintained by the network's information processors. Personnel attempting access can include those authorized for admission to the information processing site and others whose authorization is gained at some remote terminal. Those thus authorized may be further authorized to access either none of the information, or portions of the information, or all of the information. A final class of people includes those who are neither authorized to enter the physically secure facility nor initiate access from a terminal.

Levels of logical security

Several levels of logical security can be used to prevent unauthorized access to information once physical access to the network has been gained. Password sequences of one or more levels can grant or deny further access to the network following the initial connection.

The first level of logical security can simply establish that the user is valid and authorized to connect to the network. A second level can be applied to grant access to such specified dimensions of the network as time-sharing and transaction processing.

Still further levels of clearance can be required for controlling access to the databases maintained by the information processors of the network. Clearance can be assigned on a need-to-know basis.

Additional levels of security within the information processor are attainable through various cryptographic or coding techniques, and secure or privileged software methods.

Figure 4 can also be used to illustrate the application of physical and logical security when dealing with the network processing function. The previous definition of network processing is repeated here to emphasize the separation between the information and network processing functions: network processing is that set of functions necessary for moving the information from the source to the processing site, and on to the intended destination.

The distinction between physical and logical security still exists, but takes a somewhat different form due to the geographic distances between network elements.

In general, maintaining physical surveillance over the entire network is impractical, if not impossible. Exceptions to this include government, military, and other high-security installations.

The next level of organization under the heading of physical security involves the terminals and the communications links. Physical surveillance can usually be maintained over the terminals. This reduces unauthorized access to them and affords some security.

Link surveillance

Physical surveillance of the communications links is the area that presents the greatest difficulty. If the links are contained within the boundaries of the user's property, physical surveillance may be practical. Additional security is provided for such links by burying them in metal conduits in concrete-filled trenches. By doing this, manual access to, and hence tapping, the link is difficult. Additionally, the use of a radio receiver capa-

2 Relationship of network nodes

Nodal composition. *Data entering the network at a source node may originate at any one of three basic devices. When the data is passed to a relay node, it may be manipulated by an active network processor or simply switched by a multiplexer. Destination node devices are the same as source node devices, acting as receptors.*

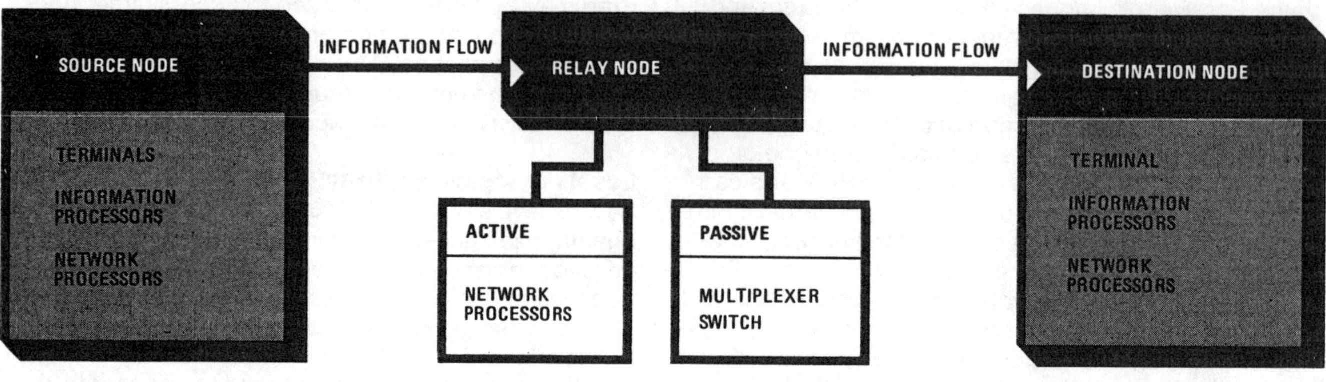

ble of detecting the link's radiated signal becomes difficult, if not impossible.

Commercial network users rely heavily on common carriers for the links that are not contained on their property and, thus, surveillance is usually impossible. For these situations, one or more forms of logical security must be employed.

Security measures applied to the links can vary, depending on a number of factors including: the speed of the link, the coupling and modulation technique used, and whether the link is dedicated or switched.

The logical security techniques for the network processing function are a combination of encryption and access-control procedures at the terminals. Much of the logical security can exist in software modules in network processors. The modules can apply initial tests to requests for access originating from terminals under their control.

While complete clearance for all database activities following access may not be possible at this level, it is possible to screen initial access requests. The security of the software in the network processor itself presents additional problems. Steps must be taken to assure that the software granting or refusing access to terminals cannot be altered.

The security measures provided by the software modules can be static; i.e., they do not change, but remain constant. Other, more complicated, measures involve randomly occurring changes in the procedures that make unauthorized access more difficult.

Network physical security

Figure 5 illustrates the physical functions contained in the network processing hierarchy. These functions form the superset from which the physical configuration for any network is derived. The following paragraphs briefly describe the physical security considerations associated with these functions.

The relay nodes are usually located in places where surveillance and/or controlled access to the site can be maintained. The passive devices (multiplexers) do not have the secure software problems faced by the active relay nodes (network processors). The growing use of radio links (orbiting satellites and others) presents additional problems, even though physical security can be maintained over the relay node itself. Encryption, scrambling, and other forms of logical security must be applied for these relay nodes.

Coupling devices are those hardware elements used to connect the source/destination devices to the communications lines and trunks of the network. As such, they are usually attached to, or are in close proximity to, the source/destination device itself. The physical security maintained over the source/destination device itself usually can be applied to the coupler.

The distribution function consists of the set of lines and trunks that interconnect the various nodes of the information network. Physical surveillance of the entire configuration is practically impossible for all but the in-plant networks. In-plant is defined as those links that are bounded by public highways and throughfares. This usually places the links on the user's property, where surveillance can be maintained.

Dial or switched links make it impossible to totally prevent unauthorized access attempts. The use of unlisted telephone numbers or private switched facilities provides little security. Eventually, telephone numbers can be determined and methods can be identified that will give access to private switched networks. Various forms of logical security (scrambling, encryption, etc.) are essentially the only security measures available.

Dedicated links provide a slightly higher level of security in that they cannot normally be accessed from a switched link. However, access to utility poles, cables in an underground conduit, and carrier facilities in general is not a difficult task. Higher levels of security for dedicated links must also be obtained through the use of encryption and scrambling techniques.

Reconfiguration switches are frequently used in data communications networks. They can be manual switches requiring an operator to activate them, or they can be under control of an adjacent or distant network processor. Switches are not normally capable of exerting logical control over information flowing through them, and thus do not require any secure software measures. If the switches are configured in locations that are under surveillance, an initial level of security is provided. If links interfaced to the switch are not under surveillance, one or more logical security measures must be employed.

Source/destination devices are those hardware elements capable of initiating and executing access to the network. Information processors are among the source/destination devices discussed earlier and are not covered here. Source/destination terminals occur in three basic categories: fixed, portable, and mobile. Varying degrees of difficulty are associated with their physical security.

Fixed terminals are those interfaced to the network through dedicated lines or trunks. Once in place, they usually remain in that location for relatively long time periods. Surveillance over these fixed terminals is the easiest aspect of physical security to maintain.

Portable terminals are those that access the network through a switched or dial-up interface. Mobile terminals are those that access the network through a radio frequency coupler and link (hard copy teleprinters in vehicles). Physical security and/or surveillance over these types of source/destination devices is obviously more difficult than for fixed devices. Logical security techniques ranging from passwords to cryptography must be applied for these types of terminals.

Network logical security

The logical network functions are the next security consideration. These functions, in various subsets dependent on the individual network, accomplish two things: control of the physical network (Fig. 5); and control of the information flowing through the network. These functions are achieved through the execution of software routines in the network processors of the configuration.

The concept of secure software remains a moving target, and is dependent on a number of considerations. If the network processors are physically secure, one level of security is provided. Access to the operating software modules by way of control panels, supervisory control stations, or remote terminal devices present additional considerations. A network processor capable of software execution with one or more privileged levels provides an additional level of security.

The tables and control fields that are utilized by the protected or privileged software modules must also be

Security breaches

These are examples of four basic ways in which the security of data communications networks has been violated in the past.

1. *False disconnect.* A remote terminal user establishes a connection to a central computer port and requests that a particular file be printed out at his location. During the brief period it takes the central processor to retrieve the file, a second terminal is connected to the same port. Then, the port side of the link to the first terminal is disconnected to make room at the port for the link with the other terminal. The first user—unaware of the disconnection—waits for the file to print out while the information is actually being delivered to the second terminal site.

2. *Exploitation.* A remote terminal or computer can use a weakness in the architecture of an operating system to gain unauthorized access to a file's contents. In 1973, a staff group at the Washington, D.C., Naval Research Laboratory used a structural weakness in the operating system of a distant Univac 1107 to gain access to its classified files.

3. *Link failure.* It is possible for critical links in the common carrier network to fail completely. This was the practical result, for example, of the February 1975 fire that destroyed a New York City switching center. Loss of local links to the central office switch frame made network security measures impossible to implement.

4. *Masquerading.* The intruder makes himself and the transactions that he originates appear legitimate to the computer—or the terminals involved. In one instance, an automatic teller machine was ordered from a remote site to discharge several thousand dollars in cash onto the sidewalk, and it did.

Belden Menkus
Consultant and Editor, Computer Security
Bergenfield, N.J.

3 Portion of a distributed network

Network interaction. *Network processors and multiplexers can come from several different vendors. Their only network requirement is the ability to exchange data.*

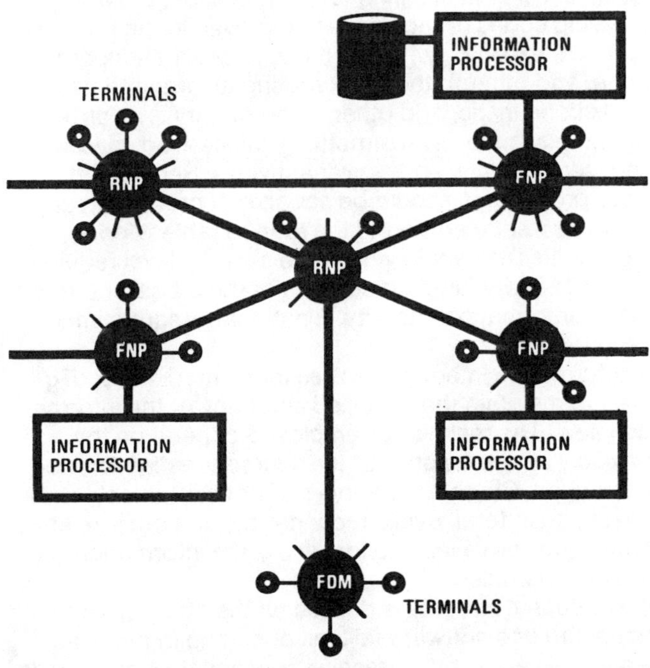

4 Physical and logical security

Security considerations. *Processors must be protected by brains as well as brawn. Allowing the processor to determine if the user is valid is a necessary part of security.*

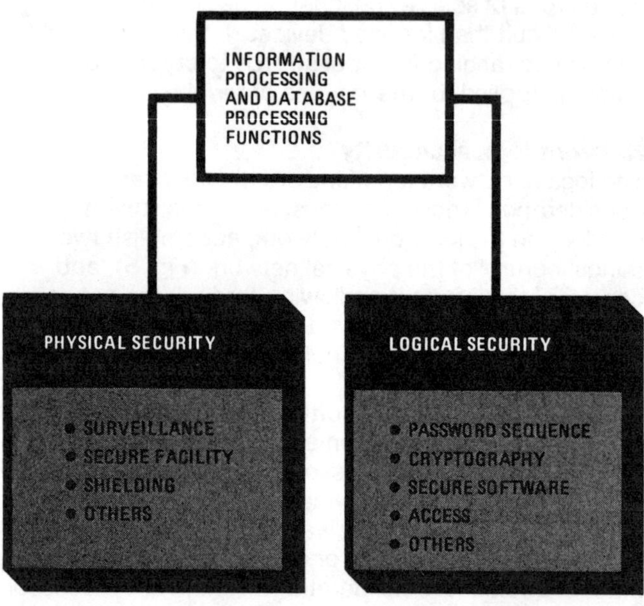

protected. This protection should also include tables in memory and various auxiliary storage media.

The six functions relating to logical security are described briefly in following paragraphs. Those with particular security implications are identified.

The routing function includes those modules required to move incoming information from the source devices through the network to the intended destinations. The lower levels of the routing function include: the addressing codes or techniques employed in the network (implicit, explicit, symbolic, multiple destination, group code, and others), the trunk routing algorithm (implicit, explicit, heuristic, and others), the priority level structure, the security level structure (unclassified, classified, secret, etc.), and similar activities. Secure software procedures should be capable of preventing any unauthorized alteration of the routing tables and/or algorithms that would violate the security level required.

The integrity function consists of three basic components: information integrity, functional integrity, and security itself.

■ Information integrity involves those modules configured to maintain the specified accuracy of the information flow. The techniques employed depend on the physical characteristics of the source/destination devices used. Character parity (odd or even), block check, hash total, cyclic redundancy, and other related techniques are available for use by the information integrity modules.

■ Functional integrity is defined as the ability to detect hardware and software failures occurring in the network. This area should receive appropriately high levels of attention during the design of software for networks with high security requirements. Any restart/recovery procedures implemented to handle such failures should not be allowed to compromise other security measures.

■ The security within the context of the network structure described above is a relative concept. Security for some classes of networks is limited to establishing the identity of the terminal attempting to access the network. Other networks can require both the identification of the terminal and the human operator, perhaps with a correlation of matching algorithms included. Still others can require the above, and, in addition, extensively structured database access clearance techniques. Several other relative levels exist, up to those military and governmental installations with extremely high security requirements.

The journaling function is the ability to retain, in one or more storage media, copies of information that has passed through the network and was delivered to the intended destinations. The volume of information retained and the time required for retrieval can vary, depending on specific network requirements. Small networks can retain a single, centrally located journal facility, while larger networks can include the journal capability at several locations.

The maintenance of a journal can provide two significant capabilities: the ability to retransmit one or more copies of information previously delivered, and the ability (through analysis of the journal file) to restart and recover from hardware or software failures more efficiently.

This restart/recovery capability is frequently more desirable than having every operator in the network resubmit the entire day's traffic, because it is impossible to determine what was and was not delivered.

The maintenance of such journals presents obvious physical and logical security problems. If the journal media are configured at physically secure locations, logical security measures must be provided to prevent unauthorized access to, and possible alteration of, the journals themselves.

The statistical function involves the collection of a wide variety of statistics concerning the operation of the network itself. These statistics, when compiled into hourly and/or daily reports, are a very valuable technique establishing the performance of a network. In addition to recording the normal traffic flow statistics, it is quite an easy task to record the number of operator errors, unauthorized access attempts, authorized access attempts, authorized accesses at various priority and/or security levels, and other similar security-related statistics.

The hourly and summary statistics and reports can, themselves, require that security measures be applied. It is then necessary to secure the software involved in the statistical modules, and also, to assure that hourly or periodic reports are not routed to unsecure locations or devices.

The utility function is a collection of activities that are not directly related to the main routing, integrity, journaling, and other activities that fall under logical control, but act rather in a supporting role. Code translations, basic format checking (mandatory fields, se-

5 Physical security functions

Weak link. *Providing physical security over the entire data communications network presents the most difficult protection problem for the network planner. While relay nodes and source/destination devices can be kept under lock and key, reliance on common carriers for data transfer makes total surveillance of the link impossible.*

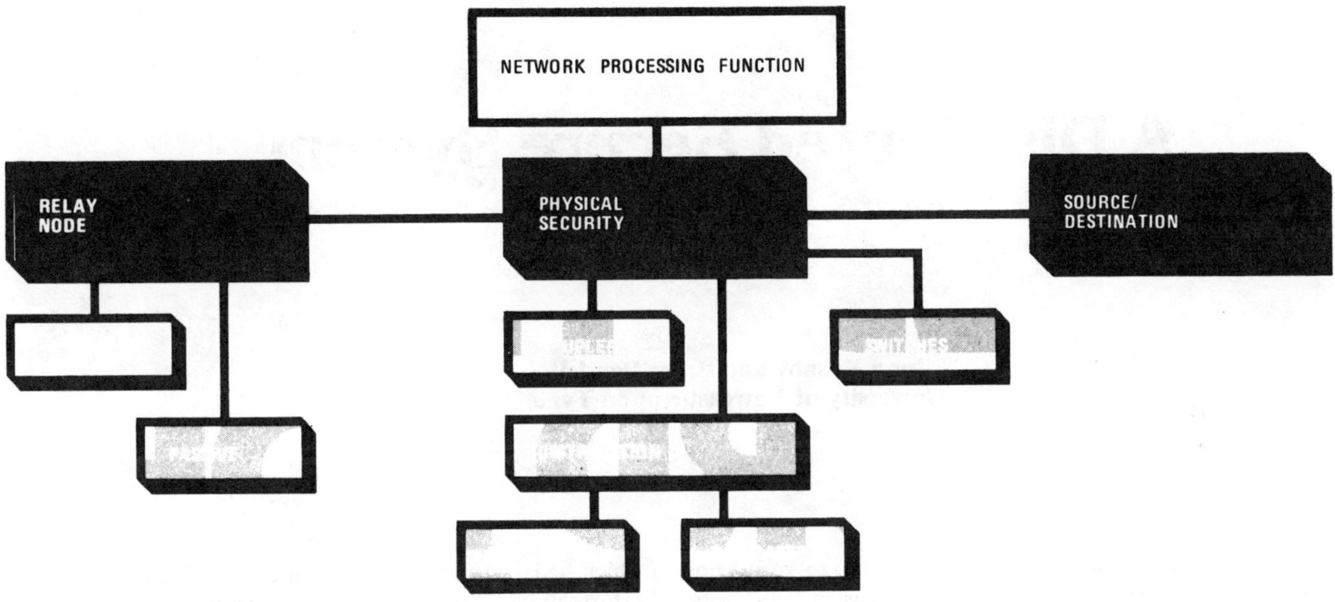

quence numbers, etc.), and destination code validation are examples of utility functions.

Utility functions do not normally fall under the privileged or secure software category. Should any security-sensitive module be required in the utility function, that module—or perhaps all utility modules—can be given appropriate security measures.

The supervisory control function represents perhaps the most security-sensitive aspect of software protection. This is due primarily to the interaction between the network and the personnel designated as supervisory operators.

Small-to-medium scale networks may only require a single supervisory control location, perhaps a single teleprinter. Larger networks can require several supevisory stations, possibly arranged in some hierarchical structure. These structures generally will involve three levels of management.

The first, or master, supervisory level is a single station whose privilege mapping permits it to initiate and execute any supervisory function the network is capable of performing. The intermediate level consists of several supervisory stations—each capable of an individual, possibly unique, subset of the master, supervisory, level functions.

The lowest level is represented by the even smaller subsets that individual terminal privilege mappings permit.

Physical surveillance of all terminals capable of supervisory functions provides an initial level of security. Multiple levels of logical security are needed to assure that only authorized operators are allowed to initiate and execute supervisory functions.

The use of secure software and privileged execution modes within the network processors appears to be mandatory for relatively secure supervisory control.

Proceed with caution

The evolution into the distributed environment creates a question for the user of a centralized network—"Should I convert to a distributed configuration?"

There is no single answer to this question. It can be shown that some users will be best served by a centralized data network. Others, for a variety of reasons, will find centralization difficult, it not impossible, and therefore, must pursue the distributed environment.

Those users following the latter course must do so with an appropriate element of caution. The computer industry, from its inception up until very recently, has pursued a philosophy of centralization. Most, if not all, current hardware and software architectures reflect this trend.

The shift to, or addition of, the distributed philosophy will be a gradual, step-by-step, activity, proceeding only as fast as the exploration of new concepts and technologies will permit. The distributed environment philosophies are not simply a rewrite of the classical centralized concepts.

The security-conscious user is thus provided with an added incentive to explore the security levels provided by the evolving technologies. This article has presented a product-independent frame of reference within which users can: define data networks in terms of basic functions; explore various centralized and/or distributed configurations; and identify the levels of physical and logical security measures required. ■

A distributed general-purpose computing system that enforces a multilevel security policy can be created by properly linking standard Unix systems and small trustworthy security mechanisms.

A Distributed Secure System

John Rushby and Brian Randell
University of Newcastle upon Tyne

A secure system is one that can be trusted to keep secrets, and the important word here is "trusted." Individuals, governments, and institutions such as banks, hospitals, and other commercial enterprises will only consign their secrets to a computer system if they can be absolutely certain of confidentiality.

The problems of maintaining security are compounded because the sharing of secrets is generally desired—but only in a tightly controlled manner. In the simplest case, an individual can choose other individuals or groups with whom he wishes to share his private information. This type of controlled sharing is called discretionary security because it is permitted at the discretion of the individual.

When the individuals concerned are members of an organization, however, that organization may circumscribe their discretionary power to grant access to information by imposing a mandatory security policy to safeguard the interests of the organization as a whole. The most widely used scheme of this type is the multilevel security, or MLS, policy employed in military and government environments.[1] Here, each individual is assigned a clearance chosen from the four hierarchically ordered levels, Unclassified, Confidential, Secret, and Top Secret, and each item of information is assigned a classification chosen from the same four levels. The fundamental requirement is that no individual should see information classified above his clearance.

The fewer the people who share a secret, the less the risk of its disclosure through accident or betrayal to unauthorized persons. Consequently, the basic MLS policy is enhanced by the use of compartments or categories designed to enforce "need-to-know" controls on the sharing of sensitive information. Each individual's clearance includes the set of compartments of information to which he is permitted access, and the classification of information is similarly extended to include the set of compartments to which it belongs. The combination of a set of compartments and a clearance or classification is called a security partition. An individual is permitted access to information only if his clearance level equals or exceeds the classification of the information *and* if his set of compartments includes that of the information. Thus an individual with a Secret-level clearance for the NATO and Atomic compartments, abbreviated as a Secret(NATO, Atomic) clearance, may see information classified as Secret(NATO) or Confidential(NATO, Atomic), but not that classified as Top Secret(NATO) or Confidential(NATO, Crypto).

A multilevel secure system should enforce the policy outlined above; unfortunately, conventional computer systems are quite incapable of doing so. In the first place, they generally have no cognizance of the policy and therefore make no provision for enforcing it; there is usually no way of marking the security classification to which a file, for example, belongs. In the second place, experience shows that conventional systems are vulnerable to outside penetration. Their protection mechanisms can always be broken by sufficiently skilled and determined adversaries. Finally, and most worrisome of all, there is no assurance that the system itself cannot be subverted by the insertion of "trap doors" into its own code or by the infiltration of "Trojan horse" programs. In these cases, the enemy is located "inside the walls" and the system's protection mechanisms may be rendered worthless. This type of attack is particularly insidious and hard to detect or counter because it can compromise security without doing anything so flagrant as directly copying a Top Secret file into an Unclassified one. A Trojan horse program with legitimate access to a

Reprinted from *Computer*, vol. 16, pp. 55-67, July 1983.

Top Secret file can convey the information therein to an Unclassified collaborator by "tapping it out" over clandestine communication channels that depend on the modulation of some apparently innocuous but visible component of the system state, such as the amount of disk space available.

Drastic measures have been adopted to overcome these deficiencies in the security mechanisms of conventional systems. One approach is to dedicate the entire system to a single security partition. Thus a system dedicated to Secret(NATO) operations would support only information and users belonging to that single security partition. The principal objection to this method of operation is that it fails to provide one of the main functions required of a secure system—the controlled sharing of information between different security partitions. Another drawback is the cost of providing separate systems for each security partition. This problem can be mitigated to some extent by employing *periods processing* in which a single system is dedicated to different security partitions at different times and is cleared of all information belonging to one partition before it is reallocated to a different one.

Another crude method for coping with the security problems of ordinary systems is to require all users to be cleared to the level of the most highly classified information that the system contains. This is called "system high" operation. The rationale is that even if the system has been subverted, it can reveal information only to those who can be trusted with it. The disadvantage to this scheme is that it is very expensive (and counter to normal security doctrines) to clear large numbers of people for highly classified information that they have no real need to know. Furthermore, many excellent people may be unable or unwilling to obtain the necessary clearances. This approach can also lead to the overclassification of information, thereby reducing its availability unnecessarily.

Several attempts have been made to construct truly secure systems for use in classified and other sensitive environments. However, the builders of such systems face a new problem: They must not only *make* their systems secure, but also convince those who will rely on them that they *are* secure. A full general-purpose operating system is far too complex for anyone to be able to guarantee this security. Accordingly, most efforts have focused on partitioning the system into a small and simple *trusted* portion and a much larger and more complex *untrusted* one. The system should be structured so that all security-relevant decisions and operations are performed by the trusted portion in a way that makes the untrusted portion irrelevant to the security of the overall system. It is then necessary to rigorously establish the properties required of the trusted portion and prove that it does indeed possess them. Such proofs constitute security verification; they use the techniques of formal program verification to show that the system implementation (usually its formal specification) is consistent with a mathematical model of the security properties required.[1,2]

The trusted portion of a secure system is generally identified with a small operating system nucleus known as a security kernel; the rest of the operating system and all applications and user programs belong to the untrusted component. Certain difficulties attend the use of such kernelized systems, however.

Because it provides an additional level of interpretation beneath the main operating system, a security kernel necessarily imposes some performance degradation. This can be minor when specialized applications are concerned, since the kernel can be tuned to the application, but general-purpose kernelized operating systems are three to ten times slower than their unsecure counterparts. Also, the division of a conventional operating system into trusted and untrusted components is a complex and expensive task that cannot easily accommodate changes and enhancements to its base operating system. Consequently, kernelized systems often lag many versions behind the conventional operating systems from which they are derived.

Finally, and as we have argued elsewhere,[3] security kernels for general-purpose operating systems tend to be complex, and their interactions with nonkernel trusted processes are also complex. The result is that the verification of their security properties is neither as complete nor as convincing as might be desired. None of these problems are arguments against security kernels per se, which have proved very successful for certain limited and specialized applications such as cryptographic processors and message systems[4]; but they do indicate that security kernels are unlikely to prove satisfactory as the primary security mechanism for general-purpose systems.[5]

Our approach is to finesse the problems that have caused difficulty in the past by constructing a distributed secure *system* instead of a secure *operating system.* Our system combines a number of different security mechanisms to provide a general-purpose distributed computing system that is not only demonstrably secure but also highly efficient, cost-effective, and convenient to use. The approach involves interconnecting small, specialized, provably trustworthy systems and a number of larger, untrusted host machines. The latter each provide services to a single security partition and continue to run at full speed. The trusted components mediate access to

Acronym definitions

- CBC: Cipher block chaining
- DES: Data Encryption Standard
- FARM: File access reference monitor
- FIG: File integrity guarantor
- IFS: Isolated file store
- LAN: Local area network
- MARI: Microelectronics Applications Research Institute
- MLS: Multilevel security
- RPC: Remote procedure call
- RSRE: Royal Signals and Radar Establishment
- SFM: Secure file manager
- SFS: Secure file store
- TNIU: Trustworthy network interface unit
- TTIU: Trustworthy terminal interface unit

and communications between the untrusted hosts; they also provide specialized services such as a multilevel secure file store and a means for changing the security partition to which a given host belongs.

The most significant benefits of our approach to secure computing are that it requires no modifications to the untrusted host machines and it allows them to provide their full functionality and performance. Another benefit is that it enables the mechanisms of security enforcement to be isolated, single purpose, and simple. We therefore believe that this approach makes it possible to construct secure systems whose verification is more compelling and whose performance, cost, and functionality are more attractive than in previous approaches.

Principles and mechanisms for secure and distributed systems

The structure of all secure systems constructed or designed recently has been influenced by the concept of a reference monitor. A reference monitor is a small, isolated, trustworthy mechanism that controls the behavior of untrusted system components by mediating their references to such external entities as data and other untrusted components. Each proposed access is checked against a record of the accesses that the security policy authorizes for that component.

It is implicit in the idea of a reference monitor, and utterly fundamental to its appreciation and application, that information, programs in execution, users, and all other entities belonging to different security classifications be kept totally separate from one another. All channels for the flow of information between or among users and data of different security classifications must be mediated by reference monitors. For their own protection, reference monitors must also be kept separate from untrusted system components.

Our approach to the design of secure systems is based on these key notions of *separation* and *mediation*. These are distinct logical concerns, and for ease of development and verification, the mechanisms that realize them are best kept distinct also. We consider it a weakness that many previous secure system designs confused these two issues and used a single mechanism—a security kernel—to provide both. Once we recognize that separation is distinct from mediation, we can consider a number of different mechanisms for providing it and use each wherever it is most appropriate. In fact, our system uses four different separation mechanisms: physical, temporal, logical, and cryptographical.

Physical separation is achieved by allocating physically different resources to each security partition and function. Unfortunately, the structure of conventional centralized systems is antithetical to this approach; centralized systems constitute a single resource that must be shared by a number of users and functions. For secure operation, a security kernel is needed to synthesize separate virtual resources from the shared resources actually available. This is not only inimical to the efficiency of the system, but it requires complex mechanisms whose own correctness is difficult to guarantee.

In contrast with traditional centralized systems, modern distributed systems are well suited to the provision of physical separation. They necessarily comprise a number of physically separated components, each with the potential for dedication to a single security level or a single function. To achieve security, then, we must provide trustworthy reference monitors to control communications between the distributed components and to perform other security-critical operations. The real challenge is to find ways of structuring the system so that the separation provided by physical distribution is fully exploited to simplify the mechanisms of security enforcement without destroying the coherence of the overall system.

Because it is costly to provide physically separate systems for each security partition and reference monitor, we use physical separation only for the untrusted computing resources (hosts) of our system and for the security processors that house its trusted components. *Temporal* separation allows the untrusted host machines to be used for activities in different security partitions by separating those activities in time. The system state is reinitialized between activities belonging to different security partitions.

The real challenge is to find ways of structuring the system so that the separation provided by physical distribution is fully exploited to simplify the mechanisms of security enforcement without destroying the coherence of the overall system.

The security processors can each support a number of different separation and reference monitor functions, and also some untrusted support functions, by using a *separation kernel* to provide *logical* separation between those functions. Experience indicates that separation kernels (simple security kernels whose only function is to provide separation) can be relatively small, uncomplicated, and fast, and verification seems simpler and potentially more complete for them than it does for general-purpose security kernels.[3]

Our fourth technique, *cryptographic* separation, uses encryption and related (checksum) techniques to separate different uses of shared communications and storage media.

The four separation techniques provide the basis for our distributed secure system. This is a heterogeneous system comprising both untrusted general-purpose systems and trusted specialized components, and to be useful it must operate as a coherent whole. To this end, our mechanisms for providing security are built on a distributed system called Unix United, developed in the Computing Laboratory at the University of Newcastle upon Tyne.[6] A Unix United system is composed of a (possibly large) set of interlinked standard Unix systems, or systems that can masquerade as Unix at the kernel interface level, each with its own storage and peripheral devices, accredited set of users, and system administrator. The naming structures (for files, devices, commands, and directories) of each component Unix system are joined into a single naming structure in which each Unix system is, to all intents and purposes, just a directory. The result is that, subject to proper accreditation and appropriate access control, each user on each Unix system can read or write any file, use any device, execute any command, or inspect any directory regardless of which system it belongs to. The directory naming structure of a Unix United system is set up to reflect the desired logical relationships between its various machines and is quite independent of the routing of their physical interconnections.

The simplest possible case of such a structure, incorporating just two Unix systems, named unix1 and unix2, is shown in Figure 1. From unix1, and with the root ("/") and current working directory (".") as shown, one could copy the file "a" into the corresponding directory on the other machine with the Unix shell command

```
cp a /../unix2/user/brian/a
```

(For those unfamiliar with Unix, the initial "/" symbol indicates that a path name starts at the root directory rather than at the current working directory, and the ".." symbol is used to indicate a parent directory.)

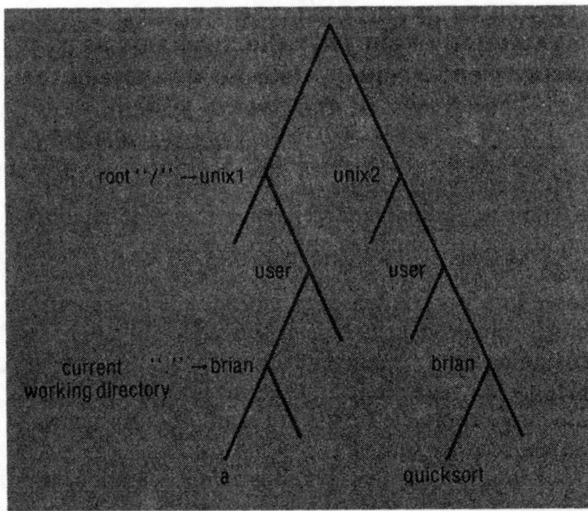

Figure 1. The naming structure of a simple Unix United system.

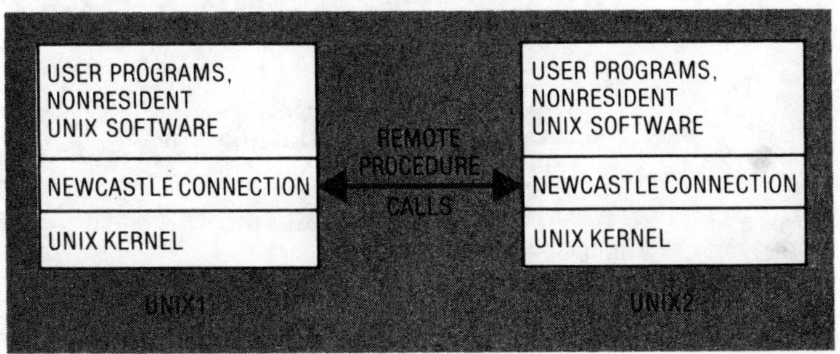

Figure 2. The Newcastle Connection.

This command is in fact a perfectly conventional use of the standard Unix shell command interpreter and would have exactly the same effect if the naming structure shown had been set up on a single machine and unix1 and unix2 had been conventional directories.

All the standard Unix facilities, whether invoked by shell commands or by system calls within user programs, apply unchanged to Unix United, causing intermachine communication as necessary. A user can therefore specify a directory on a remote machine as his current working directory, request execution of a program held in a file on a remote machine, redirect input and/or output, use files and peripheral devices on a remote machine, and set up pipelines that cause parallel execution of communicating processes on different machines. Since these are completely standard Unix facilities, a user need not be concerned that several machines are involved.

Unix United conforms to a design principle for distributed systems that we call the "recursive structuring principle." This requires that each component of a distributed system be functionally equivalent to the entire system. Applying this principle results in a system that automatically provides network transparency and can be extended (or contracted) without requiring any change to its user interface or to its external or internal program interfaces. The principle may seem to preclude systems containing specialized components such as servers, but this is not so. Any system interface must contain provisions for exception conditions to be returned when a requested operation cannot be carried out. Just as the operating system of an ordinary host machine can return an exception when asked to operate on a nonexistent file, so a specialized server that provides no file storage can always return exceptions when asked to perform file operations.

Unix United has been implemented without changing the standard Unix software in any way; neither the Unix kernel nor any of its utility programs—not even the shell command interpreter—have been reprogrammed. This has been accomplished by incorporating an additional layer of software called the Newcastle Connection in each of the component Unix systems. This layer of software sits on top of the resident Unix kernel; from above it is functionally indistinguishable from the kernel, while from below it looks like a normal user process. Its role is to filter out system calls that have to be redirected to another Unix system and to accept system calls that have been directed to it from other systems. Communication between the Newcastle Connection layers on the various systems is based on the use of a remote procedure call protocol[7] and is shown schematically in Figure 2.

All requests for system-supported objects such as files ultimately result in procedure calls on the Unix kernel interface. If the service or object required is remote rather than local, the local procedure call is simply intercepted by the Newcastle Connection and replaced with a remote one. This substitution is completely invisible at the user or program level, providing a powerful yet simple way of putting systems together. Equally important, it provides a means of partitioning what appears to be a single system into a number of distributed components.

From our perspective, this partitioning is the crucial property of Unix United, since it enables a large, insecure Unix system to be broken into a number of physically separate components with no visible change at the user level. The following sections will explain how we exploit this physical separation to construct a secure system. We begin with a very simple system that merely isolates different security partitions from one another.

A securely partitioned distributed system

We will describe a secure Unix United system composed of standard Unix systems (and possibly some specialized servers that can masquerade as Unix) interconnected by a local area network, or LAN. We assume that all the component Unix systems are untrustworthy and that the security of the overall system must not depend on assumptions concerning their behavior—except that the LAN provides their only means of intercommunication.

The consequence of not trusting the individual systems is that the unit of protection must be those systems themselves; thus, we will dedicate each to a fixed security partition. We might allocate two systems to the Secret level, one to the Top Secret level, and the rest to Unclassified use. Limited need-to-know controls can be provided by dedicating individual machines to different compartments within a single security level; thus, one of the Secret systems could be dedicated to the Atomic compartment and another to NATO. In a commercial environment, some systems could be dedicated to Finance and others to Personnel and Management. Users are assigned to hosts with the knowledge that no security is guaranteed within those individual systems. Note also that since the hosts are not trusted, they cannot be relied upon to authenticate their users correctly. Therefore, access to each system must be controlled by physical or other external mechanisms.

Although there is no security *within* an individual Unix system, the key to our proposal is to enforce security on the communication of information *between* systems. To this end, we place a trustworthy mediation device between each system and its network connection; we call it a trustworthy network interface unit, or TNIU (see Figure 3).

The initial and very restrictive purpose of TNIUs is to permit communication only between machines belonging to the same security partition. The single Unix United system is therefore divided into a number of disjoint subsystems. We will describe later how our system can be extended to move information between partitions securely, thereby providing true multilevel security.

Controlling which hosts can communicate with one another is a reference monitor function, but because the LAN can be subverted or tapped, the TNIUs must also provide a separation function to isolate and protect the legitimate host-to-host communications channels. This separation function is provided cryptographically, with TNIUs encrypting all communications sent over the LAN. Encryption is traditionally used to protect communications between parties who share a common interest in preserving the secrecy of that communication, but this is not the case here. Host machines are untrusted and may attempt to thwart the cryptographic protection provided by their TNIUs. For this reason, the encryption must be managed very carefully to prevent clandestine communication between host machines, or between a host machine and a wiretapping accomplice.

Although the basic principles of encryption management are well established,[8] a tutorial outline of the issues and techniques as they affect our system may benefit readers to whom this material is new.

Encryption and the protection of communications. Trustworthy network interface units use the Data Encryption Standard, or DES,[8] to protect information sent over the LAN. However, since host machines are untrusted and the LAN can be tapped, the simplest form of DES encryption—the so-called electronic code book mode—is ruled out. In this mode, each 64-bit block of data is encrypted as a separate unit, and even a very powerful encryption algorithm such as the DES cannot prevent the leakage of information from a corrupt host machine under these circumstances. For example, suppose that a corrupt host wishes to communicate the bit pattern 01101 to a wiretapping accomplice. The host constructs a message *XYYXY*, where *X* and *Y* are arbitrary but distinct bit patterns of the same length and alignment as the units of block encryption, and sends it to its TNIU for transmission. The TNIU will encrypt the message to yield, say, *PQQPQ* before transmitting it over the LAN, but the bit pattern 01101 remains visible in this encrypted message and can easily be extracted by a wiretapper. Notice that the threat here is not due to any weakness in the encryption algorithm employed, but to the way in which it is used; one need not be able to decrypt messages to extract information planted by a corrupt machine.

Clandestine communications channels based on plaintext patterns that persist into the ciphertext can be thwarted by employing a more elaborate mode of encryption called cipher block chaining, or CBC, which uses a feedback technique to mask such patterns by causing the encrypted value of each block to be a complex function of all previous blocks.[8] Of course, identical

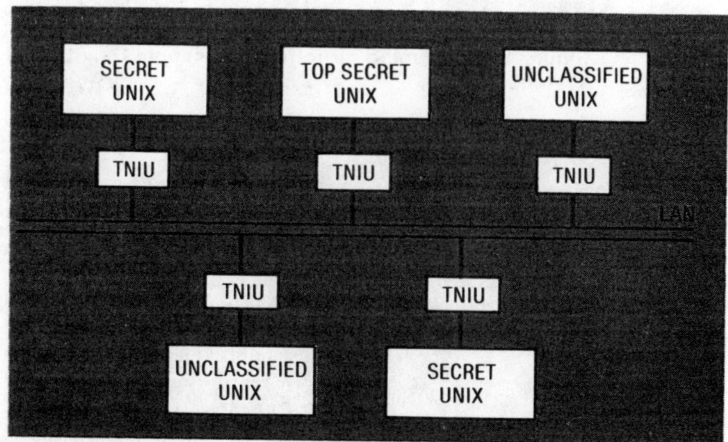

Figure 3. A securely partitioned system.

messages will yield identical ciphertexts, even when CBC-mode encryption is used. More importantly, messages that begin with the same prefix will yield ciphertexts that also share a common prefix. A corrupt host can therefore signal to a wiretapping accomplice by modulating the length of the prefix that successive messages have in common. This channel for clandestine information flow must be closed, and this will be achieved if TNIUs attach a random block of data, different in each case, to the front of each message before encrypting it.

The careful use of CBC-mode encryption prevents information from leaking through channels that modulate message *contents,* but significant channels for information leakage still remain. These are pattern-of-use channels whereby a corrupt host modulates the visible parameters of messages in a way that can be decoded by a wiretapping accomplice. The properties that can be modulated are the lengths of individual messages, their time and frequency of transmission, and their destination.

All techniques for introducing noise inevitably reduce the bandwidth available for legitimate communications and may increase the latency of message delivery.

(Presumably the source is fixed at the location of the corrupt host.) These properties, of which length and destination are by far the most important, can be modulated to yield clandestine communication channels of surprisingly high bandwidth. Unless link encryption is used to reinforce the end-to-end encryption described here, it will not be possible to completely sever these channels. Since link encryption is infeasible with most LAN technologies, the best approach is to reduce the bandwidth of these pattern-of-use channels to a tolerable level, either directly or through the introduction of noise.

The length channel is the easiest to deal with. TNIUs process message units of a fairly large, fixed size—say 1024 bytes. Long messages must be broken into a number of separate message units; short ones, and the residue of long ones, must be padded to fill a whole unit. (If this technique causes great numbers of largely empty message units to be generated, some of the legitimate bandwidth of the LAN will be wasted; but this is not usually a scarce resource and some tuning of the choice of the unit size is possible in any case.) When this is done, a wiretapper cannot observe the exact length of a message but can only estimate the number of message units that it occupies. This information will be difficult to extract, and the corrupt host will also have to modulate a second parameter (e.g., destination) so that the wiretapper can identify the message units constituting each message.

The bandwidth of the channel that modulates message destinations can only be reduced by introducing noise, thereby complicating traffic patterns so that the wiretapper finds it hard to detect and extract any deliberate modulation. The obvious way to do this is for each TNIU to generate a steady stream of spurious messages to all other TNIUs in its own security partition. Spurious messages are marked as such (under encryption, of course) and are discarded by TNIUs that receive them. More refined strategies, such as routing messages indirectly through a number of intermediate TNIUs before delivering them to their final destination, are clearly possible, but all techniques for introducing noise inevitably reduce the bandwidth available for legitimate communications and may increase the latency of message delivery. Each installation must choose its priorities in such a trade-off.

The techniques described so far enforce separation between the outside world and communications internal to the distributed secure system. They do not, however, provide separation between the different *internal* communications channels of the system. Thus, the reference monitor component of a Secret-level TNIU can determine that its host is attempting to communicate with another Secret-level host and that this communication accords with the security policy and may therefore proceed; however, it cannot prevent the LAN messages that constitute the communication from being delivered, either through error or malice, to the TNIU of, say, an Unclassified host. Furthermore, unless additional mechanisms are introduced, the receiving TNIU will not necessarily be able to detect that the messages have been sent to it in error.

Incorrect delivery can occur because the LAN hardware, by accident or intent, misinterprets message destination fields, or because those fields are modified by an active wiretapper. (Remember that these fields must be in the clear so that the LAN hardware can interpret them.) TNIUs may attempt to overcome this threat by embedding the true source, destination, and security partition of each message unit inside the data portion of the message unit itself, where it will be protected by encryption. However, this technique can be defeated by an active wiretapper who splices the identification portion of a genuinely Unclassified message onto the body of a Secret one.

It might appear that CBC-mode encryption automatically protects against this type of attack and that because the encrypted value of each block within a message unit is a complex function of all previous blocks, messages formed by splicing parts of different messages together will decrypt unintelligibly. In fact, this is not so. Although the encrypted value of each block produced by CBC-mode encryption depends *implicitly* on all prior plaintext blocks, it depends *explicitly* on only the *immediately preceding* ciphertext block.[8] Thus, damage to the contents or sequencing of ciphertext blocks affects only the decryption of the block immediately following the damaged or misplaced block; in other words, CBC-mode decryption is "self-healing."

Two methods are available for securely separating the communications channels belonging to different security partitions. The first uses a high-quality checksum to guarantee the integrity of each message unit, including its identification fields. TNIUs must calculate the checksum of each message unit before they encrypt it, and they must encrypt the message unit and its checksum as a single unit so that the checksum will be protected by encryption. Whenever a TNIU receives a message unit, it must first decrypt it and recompute its checksum. Only if the recomputed checksum matches the one sent with the message unit should the unit be accepted by the TNIU for further processing. The integrity of all message units accepted is thereby guaranteed because they cannot be forged, modified, or formed by splicing parts of different units together during transmission over the LAN. Consequently, TNIUs can trust the value of the security partition identifier embedded in each message unit; then they can (and must) reject those bearing a different identifier.

The second method for distinguishing the communications belonging to different security partitions is to use a different encryption key for each partition. (Until now, we have implicitly assumed that the same key is used for all communications.) Each TNIU will be provided with only the single key associated with its own security partition and will therefore have no way of communicating with TNIUs belonging to different partitions. If a message unit is delivered to a TNIU belonging to a different security partition from its sender, it will be encrypted using one key and decrypted using another, making it unintelligible to the host attached to the receiving TNIU. It is unwise, however, to allow the untrusted host machines to see even such unintelligible transmissions from another security partition, so we propose to combine the use of different encryption keys with the checksum technique described earlier. A message delivered to a TNIU in a different security partition from its sender, and therefore encrypted and decrypted with different keys, will certainly fail to checksum correctly.

The use of both checksums and different encryption keys is not strictly necessary, since either technique is sufficient to separate the communications channels belonging to different security partitions. The two techniques are complementary, however, and provide worthwhile redundancy. Checksums guarantee the integrity of message contents, a very desirable property in its own right, while the use of different encryption keys provides fail-safe separation.

Any system using encryption must contain mechanisms for generating and distributing keys securely. But unlike connection-oriented (virtual circuit) schemes in which a unique key must be manufactured and distributed every time a new circuit is opened, our system imposes no requirement for frequent or rapid key distribution. The key allocated to a TNIU is a function of the (fixed) security partition to which its host belongs. This, combined with the presumption that a LAN-based system is geographically compact, makes manual key distribution perfectly viable. Because of its evident simplicity and security, this is the mechanism we employ. If the fear of cryptanalysis calls for more frequent key changes than is convenient for manual distribution, a *set* of keys can be installed on each occasion or a single *master key* can be installed from which the TNIU can manufacture a whole set of communications keys. In either case, the TNIUs must contain mechanisms for synchronizing their current encryption keys.

Although not strictly necessary, it is highly desirable to be able to detect and counter the activity of an active wiretapper who attempts to "spoof" the system by replaying recordings of genuine LAN messages. (Consider, for example, a banking system that carries messages such as "move $100 from account A to account B.") Spoofs can be detected if sequence numbers or time stamps are embedded in each message unit. Of course, it is perfectly feasible for hosts to do this themselves, but it seems more appropriate for TNIUs to provide this function. The sequence number or time stamp of each message unit can constitute the unique material that should be attached to the front of each message prior to encryption to mask the similarity between messages that share a common prefix. Synchronizing the sequence numbers or time stamps used between each pair of TNIUs requires a special TNIU-to-TNIU protocol. This protocol must be resistant to spoofs, but it obviously cannot use sequence numbers or time stamps itself for this purpose. A challenge-response technique first proposed by Needham and Schroeder[9] can be used instead.

The integration and construction of TNIUs. The interposition of a TNIU between a host and its LAN station raises interesting questions concerning the location of various protocol functions. The whole issue of assigning function to layers in a protocol hierarchy can become quite complex in the presence of encryption because standard functions such as checksums and sequence numbering, for example, are duplicated—though in a different and more sophisticated way—by the protection and security mechanisms. For this reason, TNIUs should not operate below the normal protocol layering hierarchy but must be integrated with it. In fact, we propose that TNIUs take over *all* protocol functions, except those at the highest level. The benefit of this approach is that the TNIUs act as network front ends, relieving their hosts of the low-level network load and thereby boosting overall performance.

The top-level protocol of the Newcastle Connection provides a remote procedure call, or RPC, service and requires a fairly reliable datagram service[7] from the lower levels of its protocol hierarchy. We use this datagram service as the interface between host machines and their TNIUs; individual datagrams form the message units that are encrypted and protected by the TNIUs. Most RPCs and their results can be encoded into a single datagram, but those concerned with file reads and writes, which can transfer arbitrarily large amounts of data, are broken into as many separate datagrams as necessary by a subprotocol of the host machines' RPC protocol.

The cryptographic techniques employed by TNIUs counter the threat of information disclosure. The remaining danger is denial of service caused by the destruction of genuine LAN traffic or the injection of large quantities of garbage. Although they can do nothing to prevent or defeat such attacks, TNIUs must, as a correctness requirement, continue to provide reliable (though necessarily degraded) service in spite of such occurrences. It is also a correctness requirement of TNIUs that they recover from crashes safely. (Of course, verified software does not crash, but we must allow for the possibility of a power failure.)

TNIUs that perform all the functions described certainly present a challenge in both construction and verification. We argue, however, that they are very similar to the cryptographic front ends of wide-area networks, and examples of these have already been built and, in some cases, verified.[4] Modern 16-bit microprocessors provide a suitable hardware base for the construction of TNIUs, and single-chip implementations of the DES algorithm are available that can perform CBC-mode encryption at LAN speeds. A separation kernel must be used to enforce cleartext/ciphertext (so-called red/black) separation within each TNIU, with the basic physical protection provided by the memory management chips appropriate to the chosen processor. Since no disks are needed (the software can be held in ROM), a complete TNIU should fit on a single board and cost less than a thousand dollars.

Unclassified hosts can generally be considered to belong to the same security partition as the outside world. They need not be separated from it, and therefore their TNIUs need not use encryption to protect their communications. In this case, there is no need to provide TNIUs to Unclassified hosts, and this provides a worthwhile economy in systems where the majority of hosts are Unclassified. It also permits a standard, unpartitioned Unix United system to be smoothly upgraded to a securely partitioned one by the addition of a limited number of TNIUs.

A multilevel secure file store

The design introduced so far imposes a very restrictive security policy. The security partitions are isolated from one another with no flow of information possible across different levels or compartments. We will now explain how to extend this design to permit information to cross security partitions in a multilevel secure manner. This will allow information to flow from the Secret to the Top Secret levels, for example, but not vice versa.

It might seem that multilevel secure information flow could be provided by simply modifying the policy enforced at the TNIUs so that, for example, Top Secret machines could receive communications from Secret machines as well as Top Secret ones. Top Secret TNIUs would be provided with the Secret as well as the Top Secret encryption keys and would permit incoming but not outgoing communications with Secret-level machines. The flaw in this scheme is that the communication could not be truly one way; a Secret machine cannot reliably send information to a Top Secret one without first obtaining confirmation that the Top Secret machine is able to accept it and, later, that it has received it correctly. The Secret machine must therefore be able to receive information from the Top Secret machine as well as send to it. This conflicts with the multilevel security policy.

Certainly the trustworthy TNIUs in the system could be enhanced to undertake reliable delivery of data across security partitions, but this misses the point. If one host sends a file to another, the sender needs to know that the receiver has been able to store the file correctly, not merely that its TNIU received it correctly. Notice, too, that this scheme would only provide for unsolicited communications; a Secret machine could send information to a Top Secret machine of its own volition, but the Top Secret machine could not request that the information be sent because its request would constitute an insecure information flow.

The best way to provide secure information flow across security boundaries is through a trustworthy intermediary that provides an independent and useful service. The complexity of such an intermediary will depend on the generality of that service. Combining simplicity with the most useful function, we have selected files as the only objects allowed to cross security boundaries, and we have chosen the multilevel secure storage and retrieval of files as the service provided by the trustworthy intermediary. This is achieved by adding to the system a secure file store with the ability to communicate with hosts of all security classifications. The idea is that when a Secret-level host wishes to make one of its files available to higher levels, it "publishes" it by sending it to the secure file store. A Top Secret host can subsequently acquire a copy of this file from the secure file store.

Before describing the mechanism of the secure file store, we need to outline its logical position and role within the overall Unix United system. Conceptually, the secure file store is just an ordinary Unix system that returns exceptions to all system calls except certain ones concerned with files. As with any other component, it will be associated with a directory, say SFS, in the Unix United directory structure. The SFS directory will contain subdirectories for each security partition in the overall system. A simple Unix United directory structure containing just the secure file store and two ordinary hosts is shown in Figure 4.

The ordinary hosts are associated with the directories TSUnix and SUnix and are allocated to the Top Secret and Secret security partitions, respectively. Of course, from within SUnix, the TSUnix branch of the directory tree is invisible, and vice versa. Even if the Newcastle Connections within TSUnix and SUnix are aware of each other's existence, any attempted intercommunication will be stopped by their TNIUs.

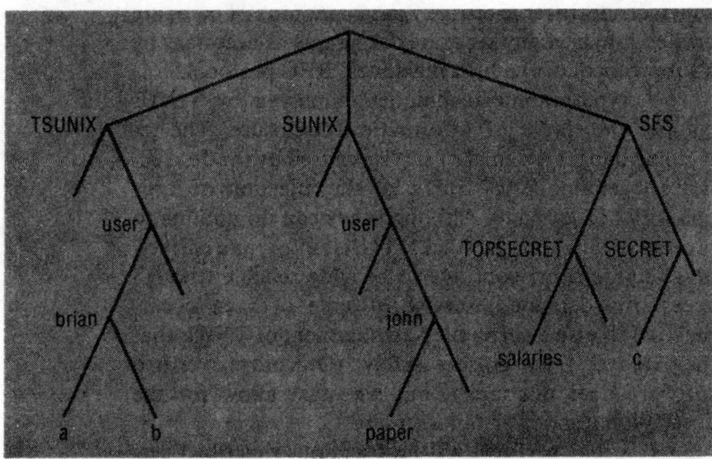

Figure 4. The naming structure of a simple Unix United system incorporating a secure file store.

If the Secret-level user John of SUnix wishes to make his "paper" file available to the Top Secret user Brian, he does so by simply copying it into a directory that is subordinate to the SFS directory. For example:

publish <paper / ../SFS/SECRET/john/paper.

(We explain later why this command uses "publish" and a later one uses "acquire" instead of the standard Unix command "cp.") This command will cause the secure file store machine to receive a remote procedure call from SUnix requesting it to create and write a file called paper located as a sibling of the file "c." The secure file store will consult its record of the security policy to determine whether such a machine is allowed to create Secret-level files. Assuming that it is, the requested file operation will be allowed to proceed and the copy of the file will be created. Similarly, when the Top Secret user Brian attempts to print a copy of the paper by issuing the command

acquire /../SFS/SECRET/john/paper | lpr

the secure file store will receive a remote procedure call from the machine TSUnix requesting a copy of the file. Once again, it can consult the security policy, where it will see that the request should be allowed to proceed. The secure file store will, however, refuse requests from TSUnix to write into this "paper" file, or to delete it, since these contravene the requirements of multilevel security. Similarly, John will not be allowed to read the "salaries" file held under the TOPSECRET directory.

We now move from the services provided by the secure file store to its construction. A multilevel secure Unix file system might seem to demand a substantial number of provably trustworthy mechanisms—virtually a secure Unix. With careful design, however, we can reduce the number of trusted mechanisms considerably.

The basic idea is to partition the secure file store into trusted and untrusted components housed in physically separate machines. The trusted component, called the secure file manager, or SFM, is a reference monitor concerned with enforcing the security policy; its file storage is provided by the untrusted components. These untrusted components can be thought of as separate, standard Unix systems connected directly to the SFM. Each untrusted file storage machine is dedicated to a single security partition and is identified with one of the subdirectories of the SFS directory (see Figure 5).

Communicating with hosts in different security partitions requires an enhanced TNIU for the SFM, one that contains the encryption keys of all security partitions. The internal structure of a TNIU with multiple encryption keys will be slightly more complex than that of one with just a single key, particularly if communications using different keys can be in progress simultaneously. Cleartext belonging to logically separate channels should be managed by separate virtual machines, and temporal separation must be provided for different uses of its single DES chip. These are not significant complications, however, and the responsibility for correctly managing more than one encryption key is a small additional burden for the trusted mechanism of a TNIU.

Host machines requiring access to secure files send remote procedure calls, or RPCs, to the SFM. The TNIU of the SFM determines the sender's security partition and passes this information to the SFM along with the decrypted RPC. The SFM can then inspect the RPC to check if the requested operation complies with its security policy. If it does, the SFM simply forwards the RPC to the appropriate file storage machine for processing and relays the results (suitably encrypted) back to the original caller.

There is an obvious flaw in this scheme, however. Because the Unix file storage machines cannot be trusted, they constitute a security weakness—even though each holds files belonging to only a single security partition. A host machine in the Top Secret partition could modulate its legitimate requests for reading secure files belonging to the Secret partition to convey Top Secret information to the Secret-level file storage machine. For example, suppose the secret file storage machine contains a group of 26 files, each a different length. If a corrupt Top Secret host requests, as it may legitimately do, copies of the fifth, fourteenth, ninth, seventh, thirteenth, and first shortest files in that order, then the Top Secret string E-N-I-G-M-A will have been communicated to the Secret file storage machine. This machine could then encode the information received into a file that could subsequently and legitimately be retrieved by a Secret-level host.

Although we cannot prevent Top Secret information from getting *into* the Secret-level file store, we *can* prevent it from getting back *out* again. Once we recognize this, the solution to the above problem is at hand.

The only objects that leave file storage machines are files retrieved in response to external requests. Consequently, any clandestine information that is to reach the outside world must be encoded into those files. Since all movement of files into and out of the file storage machines is mediated by the SFM, security will be maintained if the SFM prevents the file storage machines from encoding information into (i.e., modifying) outgoing files. In other words, security depends on the SFM being able to guarantee the integrity of files retrieved from the file storge machines.

This can be achieved if a checksum is added to each file by the SFM before it is stored in one of the untrusted file storage machines. Any attempt by a file storage machine

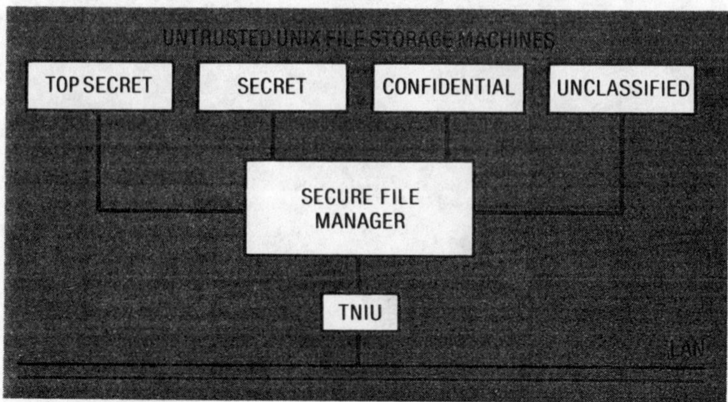

Figure 5. Conceptual structure of the secure file store.

to modify a file will be detected on its subsequent retrieval by the SFM when the recomputed checksum fails to match the one stored with the file. Of course, this only works so long as the file storage machines are unable to forge the checksums. This can be ensured in two ways (other than by keeping the checksums in the SFM). The first is to use a conventional checksum (i.e., one computed by an algorithm that may be known to the file storage machines) but to protect it by encrypting the file and the checksum as a single unit. The second technique is to use a crypto-checksum that depends on a secret key for its computation. An example of a crypto-checksum is the final block of ciphertext produced during CBC-mode encryption; an alternative is to simply encrypt a conventional checksum. The advantage of crypto-checksums is that they cannot be forged by those who do not possess the key; they can therefore be used with information stored in the clear.

Either technique can be used to guarantee the integrity of files retrieved from the untrusted file storage machines. We prefer the crypto-checksum approach because it requires only a single operation. Intermediate checksums can be included at intervals within the file if the SFM has insufficient space to buffer an entire file. If part of a file has already been delivered to a host when modification to a later part is detected by the SFM, then some clandestine information may have been conveyed to the host through the position at which the modification began and file transfer was aborted by the SFM. This channel has very limited bandwidth, and as long as all checksum failures raise a security alarm and are logged by the SFM, it is not considered a serious security risk.

Checksums prevent the untrusted file storage machines from modifying the files consigned to them and from manufacturing forgeries, but they do not prevent them from signaling to a collaborator by choosing *which* legitimate files they return in response to requests. For example, a Secret host could send a steady stream of requests for file X, but the files actually returned by the Secret file storage machine could be quite different. In particular, they could be files selected on the basis of length, say, to convey information in the manner of the E-N-I-G-M-A example given earlier. To close this channel, the SFM must be able to verify that the correct file is returned in response to each request. This is easily accomplished by including the name of each file in the checksum calculation.

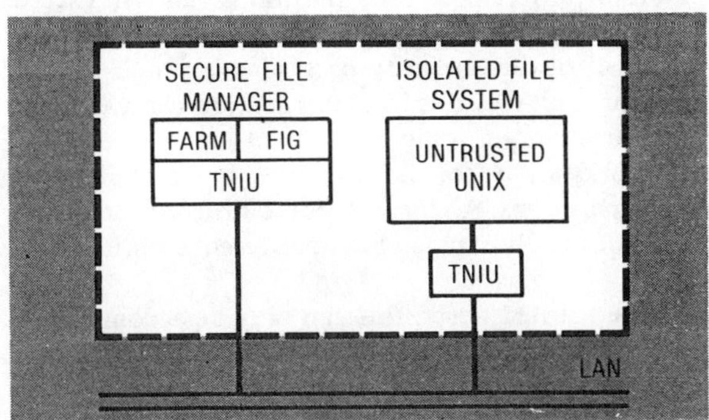

Figure 6. Actual structure of the secure file store.

A variation on this method of covert communication is not so easily countered, however. A file storage machine can keep several old copies of a legitimate file and signal to an outside collaborator by choosing which version of the file to return in response to each request. This type of attack can be countered by recording a time stamp with each file and keeping a separate record of the time stamp that identifies the current version of the file. The problem here is to find a safe place to keep the record of each file's current time stamp. It cannot be entrusted to the file storage machines without additional mechanisms for safeguarding its own integrity, and keeping it in the SFM will impose a substantial storage requirement on a machine that is intended to have no disks of its own.

To keep the trusted mechanism of the SFM simple, we prefer to reduce the bandwidth of this channel rather than attempt to close it completely. The SFM embeds a time stamp into each file before calculating its checksum and consigning it to an untrusted file storage machine. In addition, the SFM maintains, in its own private storage, a cache of the names and time stamps of all files read from or written to an untrusted file storage machine during, say, the last five minutes. Any attempt to return different versions of the same file within a shorter period will be detected by the SFM and will raise a security alarm. Attacks that operate over a longer period will go undetected, but their bandwidth will then be so low that they can be discounted as serious threats.

Once clandestine information has been prevented from leaving a file storage machine, there is no longer any need to provide separate file storage machines for each security partition; the integrity checks performed by the SFM constitute the required separation mechanism. Accordingly, the file storage machines can all be replaced by a single Unix system called the isolated file store, or IFS. Rather than connect the IFS directly to the SFM, we prefer to connect it to the LAN via a TNIU in the standard way. For it to be truly isolated from the rest of the system, however, the TNIU of the IFS must be loaded with a special encryption key that is shared only with the TNIU of the SFM (see Figure 6).

The revised SFM is required to perform two security-critical tasks and is therefore split into two logically separate components: the file access reference monitor, or FARM, and the file integrity guarantor, or FIG. The task of the FARM is to ensure that all file access requests comply with the security policy; the FIG is responsible for computing and checking the checksums and time stamps on files sent to or received from the IFS.

The FIG achieves its purpose by employing checksum techniques very similar to those used for LAN messages by the TNIUs. We therefore suggest constructing the FIG by making minor modifications and extensions to an ordinary TNIU. The FARM function of the SFM is also straightforward, requiring only the imposition of simple access control rules determined by a security policy. This function can be performed inside a separate virtual machine provided by the separation kernel of the machine that supports the TNIU/SFM functions.

We therefore conclude that all the functions of a complete SFM can be easily integrated into the TNIU that connects it to the LAN. The development and verification costs of an integrated TNIU/SFM should be little more than those for a TNIU alone, and production costs should be about the same—approximately a thousand dollars.

The FIG checksum mechanism allows files to be read or written only in their entirety. This is different from the standard Unix file system interface, which permits incremental reading and writing, and the repositioning of the file pointer. For this reason, secure files cannot be accessed through the normal Unix file system interface but must use a special extension to that interface provided by the Newcastle Connection. This extension adds new system calls to publish, acquire, and delete secure files, and to list the names of the secure files belonging to a given security partition. (The list operation must be implemented very carefully so as not to provide the IFS with a clandestine information channel.) The minor inconvenience caused for users by this nonstandard interface is certainly no worse than that imposed by the file transfer programs used in conventional network architectures and is more than outweighed by the simplicity of the trusted mechanisms needed to implement it. Extensions to this scheme that do provide the full, standard Unix file system interface are described in a technical report,[10] but the difficulties of providing secure access to Unix i-node information and to directories tend to compromise the attractive simplicity of the basic scheme. Completely different mechanisms are known and are probably preferable in this case.

The accessing and allocation of security partitions

A system in which terminals are attached to machines of fixed security level can be somewhat inconvenient to use. A Secret-level user can send mail to a Top Secret user via the secure file system, but the recipient can only reply by leaving his Top Secret machine and logging in to one at the Secret level, or lower. We can avoid this inconvenience and make additional services possible by connecting terminals to trustworthy terminal interface units, or TTIUs, rather than to hosts directly. Moreover, we can then include provisions for dynamically changing the allocation of machines to security partitions.

Accessing different security partitions. What we term a trustworthy terminal interface unit is basically a TNIU enhanced with some additional trusted functions, including a terminal driver, some very limited Newcastle Connection software, and an authentication mechanism. Each of these logically separate mechanisms runs in an individual virtual machine provided by the separation kernel supporting the TTIU.

A TTIU in the "idle" state simply ignores all characters reaching it from the LAN or from its terminal until a special character sequence is typed at the keyboard. This will cause the TTIU to connect the terminal to its authentication mechanism, which will then interrogate the user to determine his identity. Once the user has been authenticated, he can be asked for the security partition to which he wishes to be connected. If the requested partition is within his clearance and all other requirements of the security policy are satisfied (for example, a terminal located in a public place is not permitted a Top Secret connection even if its user is authorized to that level), then the TTIU will load the encryption key of the partition concerned into its DES chip. The Newcastle Connection software in the TTIU will then be able to contact its counterpart in a host machine belonging to the appropriate security partition, and the user will thereafter interact with that remote machine exactly as if he were connected to it directly.

The Newcastle Connection component in the TTIU must be able to respond to remote procedure calls directed to it by the Newcastle Connection of the remote machine. The only calls that require a nonerror response are those appropriate to terminals, namely "read from the keyboard," "write to the screen," and a couple of others concerned with status information. Thus, only a fraction of the full Newcastle Connection software is required for a TTIU, and just like the similar software in a conventional host, it need not be trusted.

A system in which terminals are attached to machines of fixed security level can be somewhat inconvenient to use.

None of the additional trusted mechanisms required to upgrade a TNIU to a TTIU should present an undue challenge in either construction or verification. Nor should the presence of these additional mechanisms affect the construction or verification of the TNIU components themselves, since TNIUs are constructed on top of a separation kernel. In fact, the presence of a separation kernel makes it perfectly feasible to support multiple terminals, each with a separate set of TTIU and TNIU components, on a single processor.

Changing security partitions dynamically. TTIUs enable users to connect to machines in different security partitions, thereby allowing them to perform each of their activities at the most appropriate level within their clearance. If a security policy with a large number of need-to-know compartments is supported, however, the number of different security partitions can well exceed the number of physical hosts available. Even when the number of distinct security partitions is small, the demand for resources within each partition can vary with time. Furthermore, some users might prefer to use personal workstations for their activities in many different security partitions. All these cases require some provision for reallocating host machines to different security partitions.

With untrusted hosts, this can only be accomplished by temporal separation, which in its simplest form is periods processing. This requires manual intervention to exchange all demountable storage and the reinitialization of all fixed storage to remove every trace of information from the old security partition before the machine can be brought up again at its new level, either "clean" or reloaded with the suspended state of some previous activation at that level.

Manual periods processing requires very rigid administrative controls, and it is slow and expensive. We therefore propose mechanisms for automating the process, making it both rapid and secure. The mechanisms required include one that causes a host's TNIU to load the encryption key of a new security partition, and another that provides temporal separation for different uses of the host machine.

The system state of a host machine is contained in its writable storage: CPU registers, RAM, and disks. The disks of a Unix system provide swap space and contain the local file system. With the exception of the file system, the local storage available to a host is all used for strictly temporary purposes and can simply be erased and reinitialized when the host changes security partitions. This is achieved by causing the host to boot-load a trusted stand-alone purge program from ROM on power-up, or on command from its TNIU. This program systematically clears and reinitializes all temporary storage available to its host processor.

A project to develop an implementation of the system described here has a sponsor and is being carried out.

Unlike temporary storage, the local file system cannot just be erased when the host changes security partitions; it must be retained (inaccessibly) for later activations of the host in the same partition. Since Unix United provides convenient access to remote files, this requirement can be satisfied by holding files remotely, either in file servers dedicated to particular security partitions, or in the secure file store.

Operating host machines without local file store is inefficient. Accordingly, the purge program creates a local file system on its host's disk and initializes it to contain the standard utility programs. (These can be obtained from a local read-only floppy disk, or from a "boot server" accessed over the LAN.) Each reference to an apparently local file is intercepted by a local file relocation process added to the Newcastle Connection. This process checks to see if the requested file is already present in the local file system. If it is, the access is allowed to proceed normally. If it is not, the relocation process first obtains a local copy of the file from the machine that maintains the permanent version of the host's file system for the security partition concerned. For example, if the host is known as PW5 (personal workstation number 5) and is currently operating in the Secret(NATO) partition, then a reference to the local file /user/john/paper might cause the local file relocation process to obtain a copy of the file /../SNSERVER/ PW5/user/john/paper, where SNSERVER is the name of the machine that maintains the Secret(NATO) file system. This process is perfectly straightforward and need not be trusted, since an attempt to name a machine in the wrong security partition will be caught by the standard TNIU mechanisms (the local and remote machines will have incompatible encryption keys). Files modified or created during a session must, of course, be written back to their permanent file system by the local file relocation process at or before the end of the session.

In outline, the complete scenario for automatically changing the security partition in which a host operates is as follows. A user at a terminal attached to a TTIU is authenticated and asked for the security partition in which he wishes to work. If this partition is within his clearance, a signal is sent to the TNIU of a vacant host machine (or to the user's personal workstation) instructing it to switch to the indicated security partition. This signal is protected against forgery or spoofing by the standard encryption techniques employed between TNIUs. Upon receipt of the signal, the host's TNIU loads the encryption key appropriate to the new security partition, initiates the purging and reinitialization of its host machine, and informs the host's local file relocation process of the identity of its new security partition.

We have described a distributed system that provides a limited but useful form of multilevel secure operation. Four distinct methods for achieving separation (physical, temporal, cryptographical, and logical) have been illustrated. When used judiciously, they can provide security without inefficiency and with only a limited number of trusted mechanisms. Moreover, our trusted mechanisms are relatively simple and within the current state of the art. Indeed, a number of them have previously been proposed (and some implemented) by others, though usually as stand-alone systems. A more extensive treatment of the topics covered in this article is available as a technical report.[10] It describes our mechanisms in more detail, relates them to their precursors, and discusses some enhancements to the basic system (the inclusion of downgraders or guards, and support for multilevel objects, for instance). Readers who wish to learn more about issues and techniques relating to computer security should consult the excellent book by D. E. Denning.[8]

A project to develop an implementation of the system described here is being sponsored by the Royal Signals and Radar Establishment, or RSRE, of the UK Ministry of Defence, and is being carried out by System Designers Ltd. of Camberley in conjunction with the Microelectronics Applications Research Institute, or MARI, and the Computing Laboratory of the University of Newcastle upon Tyne. The first stage of this project will result in the delivery of a prototype to RSRE in mid-1983. The security mechanisms of the prototype will be provided by ordinary user processes in a standard Unix United system. This will not, of course, be secure, but it will allow the operation of the various mechanisms to be studied in practice, enable the overall performance of the system to be evaluated, and most importantly, permit the impact of a mechanically enforced security policy to be observed in a realistic environment. If this stage is judged a success, a prototype implementation of the real system will follow. We hope that before long we will be able to report on the progress of this project and, in due course, on how well it achieves its security, usability, and performance goals. ■

Acknowledgments

This research was sponsored by the Royal Signals and Radar Establishment, Malvern, England. We very much appreciate the enthusiastic encouragement of Derek Barnes of RSRE and the stimulation of our many colleagues at Newcastle, particularly those involved with Unix United. The Newcastle Connection, a commercial product licensed by MARI, is the creation of Lindsay Marshall and Dave Brownbridge, while the remote procedure call mechanism is the work of Fabio Panzieri and Santosh Shrivastava.

Two anonymous referees directed our attention to a number of vexatious technical problems with some of our mechanisms and led us to make several improvements. The final form of this article benefited considerably from the careful reading, criticism, and advice of Pete Tasker of the Mitre Corporation. Sarah Rolph, also of the Mitre Corporation, suggested many improvements in the presentation of this material.

References

1. C. E. Landwehr, "A Survey of Formal Models for Computer Security," *Computing Surveys,* Vol. 13, No. 3, Sept. 1981, pp. 247-278.
2. M. H. Cheheyl et al., "Verifying Security," *Computing Surveys*, Vol. 13, No. 3, Sept. 1981, pp. 279-339.
3. J. M. Rushby, "The Design and Verification of Secure Systems," *Proc. Eighth ACM Symp. Operating System Principles*, Dec. 1981, pp. 12-21, (*ACM Operating Systems Review*, Vol. 15, No. 5).
4. G. Grossman, "A Practical Executive for Secure Communications," *Proc. 1982 Symp. Security and Privacy*, IEEE Computer Society, Apr. 1982, pp. 144-155.
5. D. Lomet et al., "A Study of Provably Secure Operating Systems," research report RC9239, IBM T. J. Watson Research Center, Feb. 1982.
6. D. R. Brownbridge, L. F. Marshall, and B. Randell, "The Newcastle Connection, or UNIXes of the World Unite!" *Software—Practice and Experience*, Vol. 12, Wiley Interscience, Dec. 1982, pp. 1147-1162.
7. S. K. Shrivastava and F. Panzieri, "The Design of a Reliable Remote Procedure Call Mechanism," *IEEE Trans. Computers*, Vol. C-31, No. 7, July 1982, pp. 692-697.
8. D. E. Denning, *Cryptography and Data Security*, Addison-Wesley, Reading, Mass., 1982.
9. R. M. Needham and M. Schroeder, "Using Encryption for Authentication in Large Networks of Computers," *Comm. ACM,* Vol. 21, No. 12, Dec. 1978, pp. 993-999.
10. J. M. Rushby and B. Randell, "A Distributed Secure System," tech. report 182, Computing Laboratory, University of Newcastle upon Tyne, England, Feb. 1983. (Also available from first author at SRI International.)

Section IV-D
Languages for Distributed Computing

THE centerpiece of this section is P. B. Hansen's relatively recent, but near classic paper "Distributed Processes—A Concurrent Programming Concept." This work stands by itself and should be read thoroughly.

Following Hansen's paper are "High Level Programming and Distributed Computing" by J. A. Feldman and "*MOD—A Language for Distributed Programming" by R.P. Cook. These two papers present excellent summaries of the advantages and problems of language development for a distributed computer system. Both authors speak from experience, having played integral roles in the design and development of such languages.

Programming Languages

J.J. Horning Editor

Distributed Processes: A Concurrent Programming Concept

Per Brinch Hansen
University of Southern California

A language concept for concurrent processes without common variables is introduced. These processes communicate and synchronize by means of procedure calls and guarded regions. This concept is proposed for real-time applications controlled by microcomputer networks with distributed storage. The paper gives several examples of distributed processes and shows that they include procedures, coroutines, classes, monitors, processes, semaphores, buffers, path expressions, and input/output as special cases.

Key Words and Phrases: concurrent programming, distributed processes, microprocessor networks, nondeterminism, guarded regions, programming languages, process communication and scheduling, sorting arrays, coroutines, classes, monitors, processes, semaphores, buffers, path expressions, input/output

CR Categories: 3.8, 4.2, 4.22, 4.32, 5.24

1. Introduction

This paper introduces *distributed processes*—a new language concept for concurrent programming. It is proposed for real-time applications controlled by microcomputer networks with distributed storage. The paper gives several examples of distributed processes and shows that they include procedures, coroutines, classes, monitors, processes, semaphores, buffers, path expressions and input/output as special cases.

Real-time applications push computer and programming technology to its limits (and sometimes beyond). A real-time system is expected to monitor simultaneous activities with critical timing constraints continuously and reliably. The consequences of system failure can be serious.

Real-time programs must achieve the ultimate in simplicity, reliability, and efficiency. Otherwise one can neither understand them, depend on them, nor expect them to keep pace with their environments. To make real-time programs manageable it is essential to write them in an abstract programming language that hides irrelevant machine detail and makes extensive compilation checks possible. To make real-time programs efficient at the same time will probably require the design of computer architectures tailored to abstract languages (or even to particular applications).

From a language designer's point of view, real-time programs have these characteristics:

(1) A real-time program interacts with an environment in which many things happen simultaneously at high speeds.

(2) A real-time program must respond to a variety of *nondeterministic requests* from its environment. The program cannot predict the order in which these requests will be made but must respond to them within certain time limits. Otherwise, input data may be lost or output data may lose their significance.

(3) A real-time program controls a computer with a fixed configuration of processors and peripherals and performs (in most cases) a fixed number of concurrent tasks in its environment.

(4) A real-time program never terminates but continues to serve its environment as long as the computer works. (The occasional need to stop a real-time program, say at the end of an experiment, can be handled by ad hoc mechanisms, such as turning the machine off or loading another program into it.)

What is needed then for real-time applications is the ability to specify a fixed number of concurrent tasks that can respond fast to nondeterministic requests. The programming languages *Concurrent Pascal* and *Modula* come close to satisfying the requirements for abstract concurrent programming [1, 2, 10]. Both of them are based on the *monitor* concept [3, 7]. Modula, however, is primarily oriented towards multiprogramming on a single processor. And a straightforward implementation of Concurrent Pascal requires a single processor or a multiprocessor with a common store. In their present form, these languages are not ideal for a microcomputer network with distributed storage only.

It may well be possible to modify Concurrent Pascal to satisfy the constraints of distributed storage. The ideas proposed here are more attractive, however, because they unify the monitor and process concepts and result in more elegant programs. The new language concepts for real-time applications have the following properties:

(1) A real-time program consists of a fixed number of concurrent processes that are started simultaneously

This work was partially supported by the Office of Naval Research under Contract NR049-415.

Author's address: Computer Science Department, University of Southern California, Los Angeles, CA 90007.

Reprinted with permission from *Commun. Ass. Comput. Mach.*, vol. 21, pp. 934–941, Nov. 1978.

and exist forever. Each process can access its *own variables* only. There are no common variables.

(2) A process can call *common procedures* defined within other processes. These procedures are executed when the other processes are waiting for some conditions to become true. This is the only form of process communication.

(3) Processes are synchronized by means of nondeterministic statements called *guarded regions* [4, 8].

These processes can be used as program modules in a multiprocessor system with common or distributed storage. To satisfy the real-time constraints each processor will be dedicated to a single process. When a process is waiting for some condition to become true then its processor is also waiting until an external procedure call makes the condition true. This does not represent a waste of resources but rather a temporary lack of useful work for that processor. Parameter passing between processes can be implemented either by copying within a common store or by input/output between separate stores.

The problems of designing verification rules and computer architectures for distributed processes are currently being studied and are not discussed. This paper also ignores the serious problems of performance evaluation and fault tolerance.

2. Language Concepts

A concurrent program consists of a fixed number of sequential processes that are executed simultaneously. A *process* defines its own variables, some common procedures, and an initial statement

process name
own variables
common procedures
initial statement

A process may only access its *own variables*. There are no common variables. But a process may call *common procedures* defined either within itself or within other processes. A procedure call from one process to another is called an *external request*.

A process performs two kinds of *operations* then: the *initial statement* and the *external requests* made by other processes. These operations are executed one at a time by *interleaving*. A process begins by executing its initial statement. This continues until the statement either terminates or waits for a condition to become true. Then another operation is started (as the result of an external request). When this operation in turn terminates or waits the process will either begin yet another operation (requested by another process) or it will resume an earlier operation (as the result of a condition becoming true). This interleaving of the initial statement and the external requests continues forever. If the initial statement terminates, the process continues to exist and will still accept external requests.

So the interleaving is controlled by the program (and *not* by clock signals at the machine level). A process switches from one operation to another only when an operation terminates or waits for a condition within a guarded region (introduced later).

A process continues to execute operations except when all its current operations are delayed within guarded regions or when it makes a request to another process. In the first case, the process is idle until another process calls it. In the second case, the process is idle until the other process has completed the operation requested by it. Apart from this nothing is assumed about the order in which a process performs its operations.

A process guarantees only that it will perform *some* operations as long as there are any unfinished operations that can proceed. But only the programmer can ensure that *every* operation is performed within a finite time.

A *procedure* defines its input and output parameters, some local variables perhaps, and a statement that is executed when it is called.

proc name (input param#output param)
local variables
statement

A process P can call a procedure R defined within another process Q as follows:

call $Q.R$ (expressions, variables)

Before the operation R is performed the expression values of the call are assigned to the *input* parameters. When the operation is finished the values of the *output* parameters are assigned to the variables of the call. Parameter passing between processes can therefore be implemented either by copying within a common store or by input/output between processors that have no common store.

In this paper processes can call procedures within one another without any restrictions. In a complete programming language additional notation would be added to limit the access rights of individual processes. It may also be necessary to eliminate recursion to simplify verification and implementation. But these are issues that will not concern us here.

Nondeterminism will be controlled by two kinds of statements called *guarded commands* and *guarded regions*. A guarded region can delay an operation, but a guarded command cannot.

A guarded command [6] enables a process to make an arbitrary choice among several statements by inspecting the current state of its variables. If none of the alternatives are possible in the current state the guarded command cannot be executed and will either be skipped or cause a program exception.

The guarded commands have the following syntax and meaning:

if $B1: S1 \mid B2: S2 \mid$ ... **end**
do $B1: S1 \mid B2: S2 \mid$ ... **end**

If statement: If some of the conditions $B1$, $B2$, ..., are true then select one of the true conditions Bi and execute the statement Si that follows it; otherwise, stop the program.

(If the language includes a mechanism whereby one process can detect the failure of another process, it is reasonable to let an exception in a process stop that process only. But, if recovery from programming errors is not possible then it is more consistent to stop the whole program. This paper does not address this important issue.)

Do statement: While some of the conditions are true select one of them arbitrarily and execute the corresponding statement.

A guarded region [4, 8] enables a process to wait until the state of its variables makes it possible to make an arbitrary choice among several statements. If none of the alternatives are possible in the current state the process postpones the execution of the guarded region.

The guarded regions have the following syntax and meaning:

```
when B1:S1|B2:S2| ... end
cycle B1:S1|B2:S2| ... end
```

When statement: Wait until one of the conditions is true and execute the corresponding statement.

Cycle statement: Endless repetition of a when statement.

If several conditions are true within a guarded command or region it is unpredictable which one of the corresponding statements the machine will select. This uncertainty reflects the nondeterministic nature of real-time applications.

The *data types* used are either integers, Booleans, or characters, or they are finite sets, sequences, and arrays with at most *n* elements of some type *T*:

```
int        bool       char
set[n]T    seq[n]T    array[n]T
```

The following statement enumerates all the elements in a data structure:

```
for x in y:S end
```

For statement: For each element *x* in the set or array *y* execute the statement *S*. A **for** statement can access and change the values of array elements but can only read the values of set elements.

Finally, it should be mentioned that the empty statement is denoted *skip* and the use of semicolons is optional.

3. Process Communication

The following presents several examples of the use of these language concepts in concurrent programming. We will first consider communication between processes by means of procedure calls.

Example: *Semaphore*

A general semaphore initialized to zero can be implemented as a process *sem* that defines *wait* and *signal* operations.

```
process sem; s: int
proc wait when s > 0: s := s - 1 end
proc signal; s := s + 1
s := 0
```

The initial statement assigns the value zero to the semaphore and terminates. The process, however, continues to exist and can now be called by other processes

```
call sem.wait     call sem.signal
```

Example: *Message Buffer*

A buffer process stores a sequence of characters transmitted between processes by means of *send* and *receive* operations.

```
process buffer; s: seq[n]char
proc send(c: char) when not s.full: s.put(c) end
proc rec(#v: char) when not s.empty: s.get(v) end
s := [ ]
```

The initial statement makes the buffer empty to begin with. The buffer operations are called as follows:

```
call buffer.send(x)     call buffer.rec(y)
```

The semaphore and buffer processes are similar to *monitors*: They define the representation of a shared data structure and the meaningful operations on it. These operations take place one at a time. After initialization, a monitor is idle between external calls.

Example: *Character Stream*

A process inputs punched cards from a card reader and outputs them as a sequence of characters through a buffer process. The process deletes *spaces* at the end of each card and terminates it by a *newline* character.

```
process stream
b: array[80]char; n, i: int
do true:
  call cardreader.input(b)
  if b = blankline: skip|
    b ≠ blankline: i := 1; n := 80
      do b[n] = space: n := n - 1 end
      do i ≤ n: call buffer.send(b[i]); i := i + 1 end
  end
  call buffer.send(newline)
end
```

This use of a process is similar to the traditional *process* concept: the process executes an initial statement only. It calls common procedures within other processes, but does not define any within itself. Such a process does not contain guarded regions because other processes are unable to call it and make the conditions within it true.

The example also illustrates how *peripheral devices* can be controlled by distributed processes. A device (such as the card reader) is associated with a single process. Other processes can access the device only through common procedures. So a peripheral device is just another process.

While a process is waiting for input/output, no other operations take place within it. This is a special case of a more general rule: When a process *P* calls a procedure *R* within another process *Q* then *R* is considered an indivisible operation within process *P*, and *P* will not execute any other operation until *R* is finished (see Section 2).

Notice, that there is no need for *interrupts* even in a real-time language. Fast response to external requests is achieved by dedicating a processor to each critical event in the environment and by making sure that these processors interact with a small number of neighboring processors only (to prevent them from being overloaded with too many requests at a time).

Exercise: Write a process that receives a sequence of characters from a buffer process and outputs them line by line to a printer. The process should output a *formfeed* after every 60 lines.

4. Resource Scheduling

We will now look at a variety of scheduling problems solved by means of guarded regions. It should perhaps be mentioned that resource schedulers are by nature *bottlenecks*. It would therefore be wise in a real-time program to make sure that each resource either is used frequently by a small number of processes or very infrequently by a larger number of processes. In many applications it is possible to avoid resource scheduling altogether and dedicate a resource to a single process (as in the card reader and line printer examples).

Example: *Resource Scheduler*

A set of user processes can obtain exclusive access to an abstract resource by calling request and release operations within a scheduling process.

```
process resource; free: bool
proc request when free: free := false end
proc release if not free: free := true end
free := true

call resource.request ... call resource.release
```

The use of the Boolean *free* forces a strict alternation of request and release operations. The program stops if an attempt is made to release a resource that already is free.

In this example, the scheduler does not know the identity of individual user processes. This is ideal when it does not matter in which order the users are served. But, if a scheduler must enforce a particular scheduling policy (such as *shortest job next*) then it must know the identity of its users to be able to grant the resource to a specific user. The following example shows how this can be done.

Example: *Shortest Job Next Scheduler*

A scheduler allocates a resource among *n* user processes in shortest-job-next order. A request enters the identity and service time of a user process in a queue and waits until that user is selected by the scheduler. A release makes the resource available again.

The scheduler waits until one of two situations arise:

(1) A process enters or leaves the queue: the scheduler will scan the queue and select the next user (but will not grant the resource to it yet).

(2) The resource is not being used and the next user has been selected: the scheduler will grant the resource to that user and remove it from the queue.

User processes identify themselves by unique indices 1, 2, ... , *n*. The constant *nil* denotes an undefined process index.

The scheduler uses the following variables:

queue	the indices of waiting processes
rank	the service times of waiting processes
user	the index of the current user (if any)
next	the index of the next user (if any)

```
process sjn
queue: set[n] int; rank: array[n]int
user, next, min: int
proc request(who, time: int)
begin queue.include(who); rank[who] := time
  next := nil; when user = who: next := nil end
end
proc release; user := nil

begin queue := [ ]; user := nil; next := nil
  cycle
    not queue.empty & (next=nil):
      min := maxinteger
      for i in queue:
        if rank[i] > min: skip|
          rank[i] ≤ min: next := i; min := rank[i]
        end
      end|
    (user=nil) & (next≠nil):
      user := next; queue.exclude(user)
  end
end
```

In a microprocessor network where each processor is dedicated to a single process it is an attractive possibility to let a process carry out computations *between* external calls of its procedures. The above scheduler takes advantage of this capability by selecting the next user while the resource is still being used by the present user. It would be simpler (but less efficient) to delay the selection of the next user until the previous one has released the resource.

The scheduling of individual processes is handled completely by means of guarded regions without the use of synchronizing variables, such as semaphores or event queues.

The periodic evaluation of a synchronizing condition, such as "user = who," might be a serious load on a *common* store shared by other processors. But it is quite acceptable when it only involves the *local* store of a single processor that has nothing else to do. This is a good example of the influence of hardware technology on abstract algorithms.

Exercise: Write a first-come, first-served scheduler.

Example: *Readers and Writers*

Two kinds of processes, called readers and writers, share a single resource. The readers can use the resource simultaneously, but each writer must have exclusive access to it. The readers and writers behave as follows:

```
call resource.startread        call resource.startwrite
read                           write
call resource.endread          call resource.endwrite
```

A variable *s* defines the current resource *state* as one of the following:

```
s = 0     1 writer uses the resource
s = 1     0 processes use the resource
s = 2     1 reader uses the resource
s = 3     2 readers use the resource
 ...       ...
```

This leads to the following solution [4]:

```
process resource; s: int
proc startread when s ≥ 1: s := s + 1 end
proc endread if s > 1: s := s − 1 end
proc startwrite when s = 1: s := 0 end
proc endwrite if s = 0: s := 1 end
s := 1
```

Exercise: Solve the same problem with the additional constraint that further reader requests should be delayed as long as some writers are either waiting for or are using the resource.

Example: *Alarm Clock*

An alarm clock process enables user processes to wait for different time intervals. The alarm clock receives a signal from a timer process after each time unit. (The problems of representing a clock with a finite integer are ignored here.)

```
process alarm; time: int
proc wait(interval: int)
due: int
begin due := time + interval
  when time = due: skip end
end
proc tick; time := time + 1
time := 0
```

5. Process Arrays

So far we have only used one instance of each process. The next example uses an array of *n* identical processes [9]

```
process name[n]
```

A standard function *this* defines the identity of an individual process within the array ($1 \leq \text{this} \leq n$).

Example: *Dining Philosophers*

Five philosophers alternate between thinking and eating. When a philosopher gets hungry, he joins a round table and picks up two forks next to his plate and starts eating. There are, however, only five forks on the table. So a philosopher can eat only when none of his neighbors are eating. When a philosopher has finished eating he puts down his two forks and leaves the table again.

```
process philosopher[5]
do true: think
  call table.join(this); eat; call table.leave(this)
end
```

```
process table; eating: set[5]int
proc join(i: int)
when ([i⊖1, i⊕1] & eating) = [ ]: eating.include(i) end
proc leave(i: int); eating.exclude(i)
eating := [ ]
```

This solution does not prevent two philosophers from starving a philosopher between them to death by eating alternately.

Exercise: Solve the same problem without starvation.

Example: *Sorting Array*

A process array sorts *m* data items in time $O(m)$. The items are input through sort process 1 that stores the smallest item input so far and passes the rest to its successor sort process 2. The latter keeps the second smallest item and passes the rest to its successor sort process 3, and so on. When the *m* items have been input they will be stored in their natural order in sort processes 1, 2, ... , *m*. They can now be output in increasing order through sort process 1. After each output the processes receive the remaining items from their successors.

A user process behaves as follows:

```
A: array[m] int
for x in A: call sort[1].put(x) end
for x in A: call sort[1].get(x) end
```

The sorting array can sort *n* elements or less ($m \leq n$). A sorting process is in equilibrium when it holds one item only. When the equilibrium is disturbed by its predecessor, a process takes the following action:

(1) If the process holds two items, it will keep the smallest one and pass the largest one to its successor.

(2) If the process holds no items, but its successor does, then the process will fetch the smallest item from its successor.

A sorting process uses the following variables:

```
here   the items stored in this process (0 ≤ here.length ≤ 2)
rest   the number of items stored in its successors
```

A standard function *succ* defines the index of the successor process (succ = this + 1).

```
process sort[n]
here: seq[2]int; rest, temp: int
proc put(c: int) when here.length < 2: here.put(c) end
proc get(#v: int) when here.length = 1: here.get(v) end
```

```
begin here := [ ]; rest := 0
  cycle
    here.length = 2:
      if here[1] ≤ here[2]: temp := here[2]; here := [here[1]] |
        here[1] > here[2]: temp := here[1]; here := [here[2]]
      end
      call sort[succ].put(temp); rest := rest + 1 |
    (here.length = 0) & (rest > 0):
      call sort[succ].get(temp); rest := rest − 1
      here := [temp]
  end
end
```

A hardware implementation of such a sorting array could be used as a very efficient form of a priority scheduling queue.

Exercise: Program a process array that contains $N = 2^n$ numbers to begin with and which will add them in time $O(\log_2 N)$.

Since a process can define a common procedure it obviously includes the *procedure* case as a special case. In [9] Hoare shows that a process array also can simulate a *recursive* procedure with a fixed maximum depth of recursion.

Exercise: Write a process array that computes a Fibonacci number by recursion.

6. Abstract Data Types

A process combines a data structure and all the possible operations on it into a single program module. Since other processes can perform these operations only on the data structure, but do not have direct access to it, it is called an *abstract* data structure.

We have already seen that a process can function as a *monitor*—an abstract data type that is shared by several processes. The next example shows that a process also can simulate a *class* - an abstract data type that is used by a single process only.

Example: Vending Machine

A vending machine accepts one coin at a time. When a button is pushed the machine returns an item with change provided there is at least one item left and the coins cover the cost of it; otherwise, all the coins are returned.

```
process vending_machine
items, paid, cash: int
proc insert(coin: int) paid := paid + coin
proc push(#change, goods: int)
if (items > 0) & (paid ≥ price):
    change := paid − price; cash := cash + price
    goods := 1; items := items − 1; paid := 0 |
  (items = 0) or (paid < price):
    change := paid; goods := 0; paid := 0
end
begin items := 50; paid := 0; cash := 0 end
```

7. Coroutines

Distributed processes can also function as coroutines. In a coroutine relationship between two processes P and Q only one of them is running at a time. A resume operation transfers control from one process to the other. When a process is resumed it continues at the point where it has transferred control to another process.

```
process P; go: bool
proc resume; go := true

begin go := false
  ...
  call Q.resume
  when go: go := false end
  ...
end
```

Process Q is very similar.

8. Path Expressions

Path expressions define meaningful *sequences* of operations $P, Q, \ldots$, [5]. A path expression can be implemented by a scheduling process that defines the operations $P, Q, \ldots$, as procedures and uses a state variable s to enforce the sequence in which other processes may invoke these procedures.

Suppose, for example, that the operation P only can be followed by the operation Q as shown by the graph below:

$\rightarrow P \rightarrow Q \rightarrow$

To implement this path expression one associates a distinct state a, b, and c with each arrow in the graph and programs the operations as follows:

```
proc P if s = a: ... s := b end
proc Q if s = b: ... s := c end
```

If P is called in the state $s = a$ it will change the state to $s = b$ and make Q possible. Q, in turn, changes the state from b to c. An attempt to perform P or Q in a state where they are illegal will cause a program exception (or a delay if a *when* statement is used within the operation).

The next path expression specifies that either P or Q can be performed. This is enforced by means of two states a and b.

P

Q

```
proc P if s = a: ... s := b end

proc Q if s = a: ... s := b end
```

If an operation P can be performed zero or more times then the execution of P leaves the state $s = a$ unchanged as shown below.

P

```
proc P if s = a: ... end
```

The simple resource scheduler in Section 4 implements a composite path expression in which the sequence *request* ... *release* is repeated zero or more times.

The readers and writers problem illustrates the use of a state variable to permit some operations to take place *simultaneously* while other operations are temporarily *excluded* (in this case, simultaneous reading by several processes excludes writing). Each simultaneous operation *P* is surrounded by a pair of scheduling operations, *startP* and *endP*. The state variable counts the number of *P* operations in progress.

9. Implementation Hints

The following outlines the general nature of an implementation of distributed processes but ignores the details which are currently being studied.

In a well-designed concurrent program one may assume that each process communicates with a small number of neighboring processes only. For if the interactions are not strongly localized one cannot expect to gain much from concurrency. (A few resource schedulers may be an exception to this rule.)

Each processor will contain a distributed process *P* and a small, fixed number of anonymous processes which are the *representatives* of those distributed processes that can call process *P*. Additional notation in the language should make it possible for a compiler to determine the number of processes which call a particular process.

Whenever a processor is idle it activates a local representative which then waits until it receives a request with input data from another processor. The representative now calls the local procedure requested with the available input. When the procedure terminates, its output data are returned to the other processor and the representative becomes passive again. The switching from one *quasiconcurrent* process to another within a processor takes place as described in Section 2.

Since processes are permanent and procedures are nonrecursive, a compiler can determine the maximum storage required by a distributed process and the local representatives of its environment. So the storage allocation is *static* within each processor.

The parameter passing between two processors requires a single *input* operation before a procedure is executed and a single *output* operation when it terminates.

The speed of process switching within a single processor will probably be crucial for its real-time response.

The technique of representing the environment of a processor by local processes synchronized with external processes seems conceptually attractive. Although these processes are anonymous in this proposal one could design a language in which the store of a single processor is shared by local quasiconcurrent processes which communicate with nonlocal processes by input/output only.

10. Final Remarks

It would certainly be feasible to adapt the processes and monitors of Concurrent Pascal to multiprocessor networks with distributed storage by restricting the parameter passing mechanism as proposed here. All the examples discussed here could then be programmed in that language—but not nearly as elegantly!

What then are the merits of distributed processes? Primarily, that they are a combination of *well-known* programming concepts (processes, procedures, and conditional critical regions) which *unify* the class, monitor, and process concepts. They include a surprising number of basic programming concepts as special cases:

procedures
coroutines
classes
monitors
processes
semaphores
buffers
path expressions
input/output

Since there is a common denominator for all these concepts, it may well be possible to develop common proof rules for them. The use of a single concept will certainly simplify the language implementation considerably.

The Concurrent Pascal machine distinguishes between 15 virtual instructions for classes, monitors, and processes. This number would be reduced by a factor of three for distributed processes. In addition, numerous special cases would disappear in the compiler.

It is also encouraging that distributed processes can be used to write elegant algorithms both for the more well-known concurrent problems and for some new ones that are non-trivial.

A recent proposal by Hoare has the same pleasant properties [9]. Both proposals attack the problem of concurrency without shared variables and recognize the need for nondeterminacy within a single process.

Hoare's *communicating sequential processes* can be created and terminated dynamically. A single data transfer from one process to another is the communication mechanism. A process synchronizes itself with its environment by guarded input commands which are executed when a Boolean expression is true *and* input is available from another process. The relationship between two communicating processes is symmetrical and requires both of them to name the other. The brief and nonredundant notation does not require declarations of communication channels but depends (conceptually) on dynamic type checking to recognize matching input and output commands in two processes.

In their present form communicating sequential processes seem well-suited to a theoretical investigation of concurrency and as a concise specification language that suppresses minor details. However, as Hoare points out, the language concepts and the notation would have to be modified to make them practical for program implementation.

The proposal for *distributed processes* is intended as a first step toward a practical language for networks. The proposal recognizes that the exchange of input and output in one operation is a frequent case, particularly for peripheral devices which return a result after each operation. The notation is redundant and enables a compiler to determine the number of processes and their storage requirements. The relationship between two communicating processes is asymmetrical and requires only that the caller of an operation name the process that performs it. This asymmetry is useful in hierarchical systems in which servants should be unaware of the identities of their masters.

Distributed processes derive much of their power from the ability to delay process interactions by means of Boolean expressions which may involve both the global variables of a process *and* the input parameters from other processes (as illustrated by the *sjn* scheduler and the alarm clock). The price for this flexibility is the need for quasiconcurrent processes in the implementation. A more restricted form of Hoare's proposal might be able to implement process synchronization by the simpler method of polling a number of data channels until one of them transmits data.

But more work remains to be done on verification rules and network architectures for these new concepts. And then the ideas must be tested in *practice* before a final judgment can be made.

Acknowledgments. I am grateful to Nissim Francez, Wolfgang Franzen, Susan Gerhart, Charles Hayden, John Hennessy, Tony Hoare, David Lomet, David MacQueen, Johannes Madsen, David Musser, Michel Sintzoff, Jørgen Staunstrup and the referees for their constructive comments.

Received September 1977; revised December 1977

References

1. Brinch Hansen, P. The programming language Concurrent Pascal. *IEEE Trans. Software Eng. 1*, 2 (June 1975), 199–207.
2. Brinch Hansen, P. *The Architecture of Concurrent Programs.* Prentice-Hall, Englewood Cliffs, N.J., 1977.
3. Brinch Hansen, P. *Operating System Principles.* Prentice-Hall, Englewood Cliffs, N.J., 1973.
4. Brinch Hansen, P., and Staunstrup, J. Specification and implementation of mutual exclusion. Comptr. Sci. Dept., U. of Southern California, Los Angeles, Sept. 1977.
5. Campbell, R.H., and Habermann, A.N. The specification of process synchronization by path expressions. *Lecture Notes in Computer Science 16*, Springer-Verlag, 1974, pp. 89–102.
6. Dijkstra, E.W. Guarded commands, nondeterminacy, and formal derivation of programs. *Comm. ACM 18*, 8 (Aug. 1975), 453–57.
7. Hoare, C.A.R. Monitors: an operating system structuring concept. *Comm. ACM 17*, 10 (Oct. 1974), 549–57.
8. Hoare, C.A.R. Towards a theory of parallel programming. In *Operating Systems Techniques*, Academic Press, New York, 1972.
9. Hoare, C.A.R. Communicating sequential processes. Comptr. Sci. Dept., Queen's U., Belfast, N. Ireland, March 1977.
10. Wirth, N. Modula: A programming language for modular multiprogramming. *Software—Practice & Experience 7*, 1 (Jan. 1977), 3–35.

Programming Languages

J.J. Horning Editor

High Level Programming for Distributed Computing

Jerome A. Feldman
University of Rochester

Programming for distributed and other loosely coupled systems is a problem of growing interest. This paper describes an approach to distributed computing at the level of general purpose programming languages. Based on primitive notions of module, message, and transaction key, the methodology is shown to be independent of particular languages and machines. It appears to be useful for programming a wide range of tasks. This is part of an ambitious program of development in advanced programming languages, and relations with other aspects of the project are also discussed.

Key Words and Phrases: distributed computing, modules, messages, assertions

CR Categories: 4.22, 4.32

1. Introduction and Overview

When the University of Rochester Computer Science Department was started in 1974, our initial research goals included taking a really serious look at programming languages. There were two underlying assumptions: (1) that programming languages had changed little in the previous decade despite advances in many related areas and (2) that one could envision compilers as sophisticated as the best current artificial intelligence programs. We began by trying to isolate the most important concepts available in programming systems to see how they interacted with each other. The project was called PLITS (Programming Language in the Sky) and, although it has come down a little closer to the ground, the name has stuck. The study is far from complete, but we claim to have an interesting preliminary result, namely that a judicious incorporation of three constructs: modules, messages, and assertions, can lead to programming language systems of considerable power and elegance.

This paper concentrates on the implications of the continuing advance of distributed computing on the design for high-level programming languages. Many problems of distributed computing (DC) do not arise in conventional programming. Solutions of these problems lead in a natural way to new programming language constructs. A distributed computation is spread among several computers which are assumed to be connected by some communication paths. For the foreseeable future these communication paths will be less reliable and have lower bandwidth than is available in the processors themselves. This leads us to expect that DC programs will be made up of largely self-contained *modules* which will share very little information directly. One would also want to have the communication between modules be some asynchronous *message* protocol, rather than subroutine or coroutine calls where one module would always have to wait for a response from the other. It appears to us that the module-message paradigm is inherently well suited to DC and is likely to appear in some form in any proposed high level language for DC. Even if we restrict consideration to a single machine, modules and messages seem to provide important advantages over existing languages and abstraction proposals such as Alphard [29], CLU [27] and Euclid [24].

The choice of the primitive high level language constructs for PLITS was not made a priori. Starting from a survey of the "powerful ideas" of programming systems, we attempted to see if there were inherent incompatibilities among them. There were only a few such situations, such as the incompatibility between separately compilable procedures and code optimization through procedure integration. A significant conclusion was that parallelism and data sharing are inherently difficult to combine effectively. Our interest in networking and our work on a message-based operating system [2] strongly suggested the idea of messages, but did not totally solve the problem of how to communicate without data sharing.

The decision to have symbolic names as the basis of communication seems obvious in retrospect, but was difficult to arrive at. By using *names* of message slots as the shared notion and having no name-valued constructs, we are able to have flexible communication among modules with no sharing of storage. It was clear from work in automatic programming and verification that more declarative information was needed—hence the general notion of assertions was included. Transaction keys were added later as a solution to several problems in selective reception, protection, flow control, and multiplexed servers. The bulk of the paper is concerned with

Author's address: Dept. of Computer Science, Mathematical Sciences Building, University of Rochester, Rochester, N.Y. 14627.

Fig. 1.

```
Const George = mod
  Begin
  Public Recipient: module
         Object: integer
  var I, J, Next_Fib: integer
      Mess1, Mess2: message
      .
      .
      .
  Send message (Recipient ~ Me) To
                Fibonacci
  Receive Mess2 From Fibonacci
  Next_Fib := Mess2·Object
      .
      .
      .
  End
```

```
Const Fibonacci = mod
  Begin
  Public Recipient: module
         Object: integer
  var This, Last, Previous: integer
      Request: message
  Last := 0
  This := 1
  While True Do
    Begin
      Receive Request
      Previous := Last
      Last := This
      This := Last + Previous
      Send message (Object ~ This) To
                         Request·Recipient
    End
  End
```

the important questions that arose from attempting to implement this set of ideas and use them to solve hard problems. Although many difficult questions remain, enough clean solutions have been found to convince us that there is something fundamentally sound in the PLITS world view.

The use of the modules and messages can be illustrated by some simple examples. A module is a self-contained entity, like a Simula or Smalltalk *class*, a SAIL *process*, or a CLU *cluster*. It is not important which programming language is used to encode the body of a module; we will explicitly have to account for the case in which various modules are coded in different languages on a variety of machines. The presentation here is based on a specific choice of body language: PASCAL as defined in [22]. This should be easier to understand than definitions based on abstract syntax.

Modules communicate with one another solely through *messages*. In order to have communication, there must be something that is understood by both communicating modules. The shared element in PLITS is a *name* which may be thought of as an uninterpreted string of characters. A message is a *set* of (name ~ value) pairs called *slots*. The value portion of a slot will be an element of some primitive domain (e.g. integers) whose representation is also generally understood.

The modules of any PLITS system must compose, send, receive, and decompose messages. For this purpose, we add some data types and operations to PASCAL or any other body language. In the PASCAL case, the primitive data types are extended to include module and message. Each module explicitly declares (**public**) every slot name that it deals with along with the data type of that slot. As we will see later, there is a process analogous to linkage-editing that ensures that public slot names are used consistently. The word "public" refers to sharing within a job but not across jobs; the notion of job is extended to distributed job (DJOB) in Section 3.

PASCAL has four primitive types: integer, Boolean, char, and real, and three structure types: arrays, records, and sets. We will ignore sets and subrange types, but will use enumeration types. The PLITS constructs do not have a particular obvious encoding in PASCAL (if they did, we might not need them). We have chosen to represent modules as additional **type** constructors analogous to **array** or **record**. In keeping with PASCAL's fairly strong typing, each kind of module class will be a different type. Part of PLITS is deeply incompatible with strong typing (much more will be said about this below). In particular, we want to allow some slots to have as the

Fig. 2.

```
Const Fibonacci = mod
Begin
  Public Object: integer
  Public Recipient, Complaint_Dept, Complainer: module
  Public Problem: problem_type
  var Request, My_Complaint: message
      Complainee: module
      This, Last, Previous, Biggest: integer
  Last := 0; This := 1; Biggest := 2 ↑ 35 − 1
    My_Complaint := message (Problem ~ Overflow,
                             Complainer ~ Me
                             )
  While True do
    Begin
      Receive Request
      Previous := Last;
      Last := This;
      If Biggest − Last > Previous
      Then Begin This := Last + Previous;
             Send message (Object ~ This) To
              Request·Recipient About Request·About
           End
      Else Begin
             Put (Recipient ~ Request ·Recipient)
               In My_Complaint;
             Complainee :=
               If Present Request·Complaint_Dept
               Then Request·Complaint_Dept
               Else City_Hall;
             Send My_Complaint To Complainee About
               Request·About
           End
    End While Loop
End
```

data type the union of all module types, which we denote **module**. It is crucial that any module (written in PASCAL-PLITS or some other X-PLITS) be able to send a message to any other.

We also add a type **message** which is like the PASCAL type **record** except that it has all the **public** slot names of the module as potential field names. The global constructs in PASCAL-PLITS will be the public slot names, module type declarations (including **constant** modules) and some enumeration types. There are to be no global variables of any type.

For a first example (Figure 1), suppose there were a module, Fibonacci, which provided the service of supplying consecutive positive Fibonacci numbers, and a module, George, which wanted to make use of this service. (George and Fibonacci are actual module names, not module prototypes or class definitions.)

George is declared to be a constant of type **module** (using the **mod** construct) and to have two **public** slot names: "Recipient" of type **module** and "Object" of type **integer.** The type constructor **mod** is analogous to the PASCAL constructor **record**. The primitive type **module** denotes the union of all types declared with a **mod** constructor; PASCAL does not have an analogous union of all records. We will refer to types declared using **mod** as "module types." The variables Mess1 and Mess2 are declared to be of type **message**. The **Send** statement in line 7 uses the PASCAL constructor syntax to build a message and send it. After sending the message to Fibonacci, George is automatically suspended until a message from Fibonacci is received (line 8). This particularly simple control regime is equivalent to a subroutine call. Since Fibonacci has the same two public slot names as George, they can communicate. Fibonacci is a server module that waits for a request, computes the next value, and sends an answer message to the module named in the request. Although this is George in the example, it could be a general continuation.

One of the major goals of the PLITS effort is the development of techniques for programming reliable systems. Since each PLITS module has complete control over its internal state and the messages it accepts, one can program any module so that it never reaches an undesirable internal state. Of course, a module which contains internal protection against a wide variety of external errors can become quite bulky. There is a fundamental design tradeoff between hardening individual modules and guaranteeing at the system level that certain global conditions cannot arise. A detailed discussion of these issues is beyond the scope of this paper (cf. [16]). However, in Figure 2, we present a somewhat more protected Fibonacci module which will not be subject to integer overflow. Figure 2 also includes instances of several additional PLITS constructs.

The first new notion occurs on line 4 where a public slot name of type "*problem_type*" is declared. The type *problem_type* is a fixed collection of uninterpreted symbols exactly like the PASCAL "enumeration" type. There will be several public enumeration types in a PLITS system. In lines 9–11, a prepackaged message is assembled and stored in the message variable, *My_Complaint.* In lines 19 and 24, the **Send** statements contain an extra component **"About"**; this specifies a particular **transaction** key in a way which is described below. The other new code is in lines 21–27; the Recipient slot of *My_Complaint* is filled in from the Request. If there is a *Complaint_Dept* (cf. [20]) slot in this request, the module which is its value will be sent the complaint. Otherwise some default complaint handler, *City_Hall,* will hear about it. The name of the Recipient module (which may have been awaiting an answer) is passed along to the *Complaint_Dept*, because there might be some appropriate response to the problem. For example, there could be some double precision Fibonacci module which would be able to return an appropriate value if George were prepared to accept it. This could require that George handle the double size integers; that is not very hard to arrange, for example, by an extra slot for the high order part.

There is a more interesting problem in the control discipline used in the coding of the module George given in Figure 1. The statement on line 8 is:

```
Receive Mess2 from Fibonacci
```

But we saw in the expanded Fibonacci module of Figure 2 that there might be an error recovery module that would supply the answer if Fibonacci could not. The coding style of line 8 requires that the answer be conveyed back to Fibonacci and then to George, but there is nothing to be gained by retracing our steps. To solve this and a number of other control problems, we will add one more construct, **transaction**, to PLITS. Intuitively, a transaction is a unique key which can be used in the regulation of message traffic. A transaction is required in the **About** slots of the **Send** statements of lines 19 and 24 of Figure 2. In this case, the outgoing transaction key is just the one accompanying the request message. If some *Complaint_Dept* were able to rectify the overflow problem, it could forward the correct answer to a slightly modified George. Our third example (Figure 3) shows a recoding of the module George which does selective reception on the transaction, Fibkey, which it originally provided. Figure 3 is an overview of a complete PASCAL-PLITS program containing the expanded version of Fibonacci, etc.

These introductory examples are intended to provide an intuitive notion of what is being proposed. In the next section a precise definition of PASCAL-PLITS is given, roughly following the style of [22]; this will be used for examples throughout the paper. Section 2 also shows how we capture key notions from several areas of computer science in a PLITS system. Section 3 considers the implementation problems arising in extending these ideas to distributed computing systems. In Section 4, we return to the consideration of a one-language PLITS system, more or less assumed to run on a single machine. Properties are introduced as a special kind of assertion which are an improvement on strong typing. Assertions are shown to be the key to verification and optimization of PLITS programs. Finally, we present a brief overview of debugging and exception handling in a PLITS environment. The material of Sections 3 and 4 summarizes a number of ongoing research efforts, for which references are provided.

A word about the current state of PLITS implementation seems to be called for. The basic concepts of PLITS were crystalized early in 1976 and some students attempted to carry out toy implementations. A serviceable SAIL-PLITS was implemented that summer by Jim Low using the SAIL macro facility; it has been used for running examples like those in this paper and for course problems and term projects. This version incorporates essentially the constructs described in Section 2. The underlying support system described in Section 3 has been implemented on our local network [2] under the direction of Paul Rovner, and is being used in current distributed systems [10] and artificial intelligence research [40]. Most of the ideas of Section 4 are being incorporated into Zeno [3], the base language for the Advanced Compiler project in our laboratory. A complete high level multilanguage multimachine PLITS system is under development, but has lower priority than the more basic efforts.

Fig. 3.

```
Program Everything
        Problem_type = (Overflow, Time Out,
                        Absent Slot, Illegal Module, ...)
  public Recipient, Complaint_Dept, Complainer: module
        Object: integer
        Problem: problem_type
        :
  const George = mod
        Begin
          Public Recipient: module
                 Object: integer
          var I, J, Next_Fib: integer
              Mess1, Mess2: message
              Fibkey: transaction
          Fibkey := New Transaction
          Send message (Recipient ~ Me)
            To Fibonacci About Fibkey
          Receive Mess2 About Fibkey
          Next_Fib := Mess2·Object
          :
        End
        :
  const Fibonacci = mod
                    :  [cf. Figure 2]
                    End
  const City_Hall = mod
                    :
                    End
  :
  End
```

2. Definitions

2.1 A Precise Definition of Minimal PLITS

We now state more precisely what is proposed to be included in a PLITS system. The language described is somewhat more restrictive than one would want to use for the construction of large systems (cf. [2]), and the definition is being kept minimal so that the fundamental issues can be more easily addressed. For example, the current definition allows no block structure or other partitioning of the space of public slot names. A number of other straightforward extensions are mentioned in passing. Even so, we will omit all consideration of three important issues to be covered in Sections 3 and 4: computer networking, assertions and program transformation, errors, and other system issues.

We now proceed to a fairly precise definition of a PASCAL-PLITS. The purpose is to provide a fixed language in which to present subsequent PLITS examples, not to propose an extension to PASCAL. We will define the syntax of the additions locally rather than present modified syntax graphs. We will also (for now) be even less formal than [22].

Recall that a message is a set of name ~ value pairs, where the names and their associated types are publicly known. The first new construct is the public slot name definition, which is of the form:

Public $S_1{:}T_1,\ S_2{:}T_2,\ \ldots\ S_m{:}T_m;$

where the S_i are all public slot names and the T_i are their associated elementary types. An elementary type is either a PASCAL primitive type or **transaction** or a **module** type. We also add a type **message** which is similar to the PASCAL **record** type. The legal message constructors in module P are all of the form:

message $(S_j \sim X_j,\ S_k \sim X_k,\ \ldots)$

where each X_j is an element of type T_j and the slot name $S_j{:}T_j$ has been declared **public** in P. This differs from the **record** constructor in that the field names are given explicitly in any order and need not all be present. Every message implicitly includes two extra slots: **Source** of type **module** and **About** of type **transaction.**

In analogy with PASCAL record field extractors, we define for a message M

$M \cdot S_i = X_i$

to hold, providing that the pair $S_i \sim X_i$ is an element of M. If there is no $S_i \sim X_i$ pair in M, an exception condition occurs; exceptions will be discussed in Section 4. We also extend the PASCAL **with** construct from implicitly naming the record to implicitly naming the message in the obvious way. This definition of **message** allows a module P to send and receive messages with slots not known to P but not to examine or alter these slots. There are some additional operations on a message:

Put $S_i \sim X_i$ **In** M
Remove S_i **From** M
$M \cdot S := X_i$

All of these require that X_i be of type T_i and that the slot S_i:T_i has been declared **public** in module P. The **put** statement adds the slot $S_i \sim X_i$ or replaces the existing value of S_i. The **remove** statement totally removes an $S_i \sim X_i$ if it is present; no error results if the slot is absent. The assignment statement updates the value of the slot S if it is present; otherwise an exception condition (see Section 4) is generated.

If M is a message, V is of a module type, and K is a transaction identifier, then there are valid statements of the form:

```
Sand M To V {About K}
```

In any PLITS messages are always sent by value (copied). There are also two predicates on message slots:

```
Absent S, In M
Present S, In M
```

The **Present (Absent)** predicate returns **True** if there is (is not) an $S_i \sim X_i$ pair present in M. The predicates of equality and inequality are extended to objects of **transaction**, **message**, and **module** type. This completes the discussion of message types from the internal PASCAL point of view. In addition to its importance for messages, the data structure consisting of a set of name ~ value pairs has many other good uses. We are currently calling this data structure an *A*-set (analogous to the LISP notion of *A*-list) and are exploring their use in a number of contexts.

An alternative PASCAL-PLITS syntax for the slots known to a module P would be achieved by declaring, in P, a local instance *Pmessage* of the type constructor **message**

```
type Pmessage = messageS1:T1
                       S2:T2
                        .
                        .
                        .
                end;
```

where the $\{S_i:T_i\}$ are exactly the pairs that appeared in the **public** declaration in the definition used above. This definition of message is more PASCAL-like, allowing the compiler to carefully control what kind of messages a module could receive. What this definition gives up is the ability for a module to handle messages some of whose slots it knows nothing about. An important claim of this paper is that very strong typing is ineffective as a way to promote careful programming and that the PLITS methodology offers a way of saying more precisely what conditions a message must satisfy in order to be acceptable to a module. Similarly, one might want to have stronger restrictions on variables of type **module**. For example, a strongly typed language would have constructs like "fixed-length queue of real module." The proposed way of treating such issues with **properties** is discussed briefly in Section 4 and in detail in [16]. In general, PLITS does not currently support structured types in public slots (but see Section 3). In particular, there can be no message slot of type **message**. If K is of type **transaction** and V is of **module** type, then

```
Receive <message exp.> {From V} {About K}
```

is the pattern for the four types of **Receive** statements. The internal axiomatic semantics of **Send** and **Receive** can be treated simply. A **Send** statement has no direct effect on the sending module. A **Receive** statement has the internal semantics of an assignment to a **message** variable. In many implementations, the failure of a message to arrive in a specified (perhaps by default) amount of time will result in an exception condition. The use of the axiomatic semantics for verification and the discussion of exception handling is presented in Section 4.

The sending and receiving of messages are central to any PLITS implementation and must be considered with some care; most of Section 3 is concerned with some issues arising in message-based systems. For our definition of PASCAL-PLITS, we need two semantic rules on message transfer. The first is that message queues are assumed to be unbounded, in the sense that the stack and the heap are considered unbounded in PASCAL and similar languages. Queue management, error detection, etc., are important system considerations but can be omitted at this stage of definition.

The second semantic rule concerns the preservation of order among messages. The rule is: for each triple (Sender, Transaction, Receiver) messages are guaranteed to arrive at the receiver in the same time order as they were sent from the sender. No other order properties can be relied upon. For all communication between a particular sender and receiver which does not have an ⟨**About** transaction⟩ clause, the system will assign a single fixed transaction identifier. Thus if no transactions at all are used between a sender and receiver, messages will all arrive in sequence.

A module type in PASCAL-PLITS is given by a declaration of the form:

```
type T = mod L; Begin S End
```

The module type notion does not have a direct counterpart in PASCAL. A module has some of the properties of a procedure and some of the properties of a record (like Simula classes, etc.). We have chosen to define it as a **type** constructor so we could easily have module classes and instances. The parameter list L is the same as that of a PASCAL procedure and is used to initialize new modules of the given type. All parameters are passed by value. The special case of a **constant** of module type was shown in Figure 3.

Module instances come into being in the standard PASCAL way. If T is a module type and V is of type T, we can write:

```
V := T(L)
```

where L is an actual parameter list. This creates a new instance of a module of type T and assigns a reference to this module to V. The next example (Figure 4) presents

Fig. 4.

```
1  Program Everything
2    type qactions = (Clear, Empty?, Size?, Remove, Append,
                      Generate, Next, Print)
3    :
4    type qmod = mod Length: integer
5      Begin
6        public Recipient:  module
7               Command:    qactions
8               Datum:      real
9               Flag:       Boolean
10       var First, Next: integer
11           Mess1:       message
12       const Q = array [0: Length] Of real
13       First := 1; Next := 1
14       While True Do
15       Begin
16         Mess1 := Receive
17         With Mess1 Do
18           Case Command Of
19           Clear: Begin
20                    First := 1; Next := 1
21                    Send message (Flag ~ True) To Recipient
22                  End;
23           Empty?: Begin var Ans: Boolean
24                         Ans := (First = Next)
25                     Send message (Flag ~ Ans) To Recipient
26                   End
                     :
27       End of while loop
28     End of qmod definition
29     Const Fred = mod
30       Begin
31         public Recipient: module
                 :
32         var Diskq: module
                 :
33         Diskq := qmod (14)
34         Send {Recipient ~ Fred, Command ~ Append,
                 Datum ~ 3.14} To Diskq
           :
35       End of Fred
```

a fragment of the code for a fixed-length queue of **real** values. The style of coding of Figure 4 follows the Smalltalk [19] idea of having a data structure interpret messages with a command slot. The enumeration type *qactions* on line 2 defines the commands which are meaningful to qmod modules. The command *Generate* is intended to start the sequencing; the remaining qactions are obvious. The definition starting in line 4 of the prototype *qmod* has one formal parameter, *Length*, which is used in line 12 to fix the size of the array used for the queue instance. The **public** slot names, **vars**, and the **const** array are the minimal constructs needed for a simple queue module. Lines 14–18 lay out the standard PLITS style for a server module which waits for any message and then branches on the value of some action or command slot. In line 17, the PASCAL **With** construct is used to implicitly prefix all slot names within its scope with the message variable, *Mess*1. For example, line 18 is equivalent to:

Case Mess1·Command **Of**

Starting in line 29, we have a constant module, *Fred*, which makes use of a private instance of qmod which it refers to through its local **module** variable *Diskq*. Line 33 gives the code for establishing an instance of *qmod* with the *Length* of the queue equal to 14. Line 34 shows how Fred would put an element on the queue, providing its own name as the *Recipient* for error messages.

In keeping with the general PLITS philosophy, a module cannot be killed from outside. There is a single statement:

Self destruct

which will allow a module to eliminate itself. The problem of messages to and from a destroyed module is a standard one in operating systems and in networking and is discussed in Sections 3 and 4.

There are five additional constructs which return Boolean values:

Pending {**From** P} {**About** K}
Extant P

where *P* is of **module** type and *K* is a **transaction**. The first four test if there is a message ready for the module executing them, and the fifth, if a given module instance is still active.

The final new construct to be defined is an additional simple type, **transaction**. An object of type **transaction** is specified to be unique across all "sites" in a PLITS environment. (The definition of a site and the implementation of **transaction** type objects is discussed in Section 3.) In PASCAL-PLITS, we declare **transaction** variables in the usual way:

T1, Key:**transaction**.

In addition to **transaction** variables and slots, there is one expression of type transaction, **New-transaction**; it is used in statements of the form:

Key := **New-transaction**.

As we discussed above, any **Send**, **Receive**, or **Pending** command can have an optional part

About K

where *K* is a transaction expression. Transaction objects are used in a variety of ways in the coordination of modules. For example, a *Fibonacci* module could assign separate transaction objects to each of a number of Fibonacci sequences which could be pulsed asynchronously.

Interesting design issues arise in the choice of the **receive** and **pending** constructs. One would like a module to be able to do quite selective **receive**'s and not be bothered with messages that it was not ready to process. For example, one could allow **receive** to take an arbitrary predicate on the values of slots in the message. There are several difficulties. One cannot build into the system all the generality that might ever be required—for example, a module might want to receive that message which has the greatest value for some slot. Another problem is that having very selective **receive**'s puts a great burden on the system for storing, checking, and keeping track of messages. Finally, there are problems of defining the correct sequencing for messages which are being controlled by complex predicates. The definition we have chosen is a compromise. Clearly, having **receive** only specify the source is too restrictive. Many different kinds of selective **receive**'s can be coded into **transaction** keys. The proposed way of handling more complex **receive** specifications is through the use of a "front-end" module. The sender-transaction encoding has proved to be a convenient basis for the low level communication protocols required for reliable transmission and flow control (cf. Section 3 and [39]). A PLITS system should provide primitives, data structures, etc., which make this relatively easy. It probably is worth adding negation and sets of senders and transactions to the primitive **receive** and **pending**.

2.2 Discussion

One important feature of PLITS systems is the use of messages as the basic control primitive. Although there have been many proposals for synchronization and control disciplines, all of these are easily captured by the **message** construct often leading to clearer solutions to classic control problems. We also can deal with hardware or software interrupts and with timing signals as messages. All of this is well known, and has been incorporated in several systems, but has not been enunciated in high level constructs or languages ([20, 22] are partial exceptions). The notion of module-valued slots seems to provide easily a very flexible, but safe discipline for control transfers, incorporating continuations, complaint departments, etc.

The use of messages is also valuable in solving the problems of shared resources, particularly data structures. The general idea that a resource always be allocated by a single controlling module greatly simplifies all the common exclusion problems. The currently fashionable way [28] of manipulating data in an external module (class, form, etc.) is to execute a procedure in that module. The message paradigm has several advantages over subroutine calls. If the modules were in different languages, the subroutine call mechanisms would have to be made compatible. Any sophisticated lockout procedure would require the internal coding of queues equivalent to what the message switcher provides. In the subroutine discipline, a module which tries to execute a locked subroutine is unable to proceed with other computation. The total picture on the relative value of messages and calls is much more complex; Section 4 contains some additional discussion.

Another view of PLITS messages (*A*-sets) is as a generalization of parameter lists in subroutine or coroutine calls. The idea of explicitly naming parameters is common in assembly languages where the total number of parameters to a routine may be very large. More importantly, the set of slots presents a collection of suggested parameters rather than filling in the values of parameters. This leads naturally to the use of semantic checks on the consistency of parameters and to the use of default values for unspecified ones. This is already stronger than strong typing and can be further strengthened by using *Assertions* (cf. Section 4). Three other advantages also fall out. The use of return messages frees us from the constraint of single-valued functions—there is no reason why an answer message should have only one slot. The use of *A*-sets of name~value pairs as the input and output of all modules provides the cleanest form we have seen for the composition of multiple-valued functions. For intermodule communication, we also solve the so-called "uniform reference problem"—one need not be concerned with whether an answer (say an array element) is computed by a procedure or a table. Mesa [18] also attempts to achieve these goals by a quite different method.

There is yet another useful view of messages. One can view a message as a partially specified relation (or pattern), with some slot values filled in and some unbound. This is common in relational databases [1] and artificial intelligence languages [5]. In this view, a message is a task specification with some Recipient and some Complaint Departments to talk to about it. Various modules can attempt to satisfy or contract out parts of the task of filling in the remaining slots. One nice feature of the current design is the ability for a module to handle messages containing slots unknown to it. This allows for several modules working together on a task while maintaining locality. For example, an executive module could route messages (on the basis of a few slots that it understood) to modules which deal with totally different public slot names. We can also view a message *A*-set (set of name~value pairs) as a collection of bindings of variables. This shares many of the properties of LISP *A*-lists and SAIL contexts and seems to be an excellent way to handle the problem of evaluation relative to an environment.

There is no apparent conflict among these alternative views of PLITS messages. It is too early in the development to be sure, but the combined power of these paradigms seems to provide a qualitative improvement in our ability to develop programs.

There are other interesting features that arise when messages are combined with the idea of modules. The most obvious feature of PLITS programming is the high degree of locality and protection it provides. Each PLITS module is totally self-contained and communicates solely through messages. This means that no local variables can even be examined from the outside, no procedures invoked, etc. A module can be asked to return or update a value, execute a function, etc. It now becomes quite natural to screen requests for validity (much more than type checking), to guard against conflicting demands on a data structure, etc. This does not solve all the problems attacked by structured programming strictures, but does make it clear what has to be done and where. For

Fig. 5.

```
const Alphonse = mod
 1  Begin
 2    public A, B: integer
 3          Action: actions
 4          Recipient: module
 5    var In_Mess, Out_Mess: message
 6          Key: transaction
 7    Key := New_Transaction
 8    Send message (Action ~ Lock, A ~ 0, B ~ 0) To Gaston
        About Key
 9    Send message (Action ~ Fetch, A ~ 0, B ~ 0,
        Recipient ~ Me)
10      To Gaston About Key
11    Receive In_Mess from Gaston About Key
12    Out_Mess := message (A ~ - In_Mess·B,
        B ~ - In_Mess·A, Action ~ Update,
13      Recipient ~ Me)
14    Send Out_Mess To Gaston About Key
15    Receive In_Mess from Gaston About Key
16    If In_Mess·Action ≠ Reject
17      Then Send message (Action ~ Unlock, A ~ 0, B ~ 0) To
          Gaston About Key
18      Else Comment whatever;
19  End
```

example, consider the problem of maintaining consistency in a multiply-accessed database.

First let us consider a simple exclusion problem: Suppose a module *Alphonse* wants to swap and negate two integers *A* and *B* in another module *Gaston*, which we can think of as a global data structure. *Alphonse* must get the values of *A* and *B*, swap and negate them, and put them back. The problem is to do this without unduly locking Gaston and in such a way that no inconsistencies can arise. One rather elaborate PASCAL-PLITS solution to this problem is shown in the next example (Figure 5). The module *Alphonse* first sends a message to *Gaston* to lock *A* and *B* except for messages using transaction *Key*. It then fetches the two values, swaps and negates them, sends them back and waits for a response. When *Gaston* has completed the internal update, a message is returned to *Alphonse*. If all went well, *Alphonse* will send an unlock message to *Gaston* to complete the transaction. There are simpler ways to accomplish this, but this program above makes much of the discipline explicit.

The module *Gaston*, which we are viewing as a global data structure, must have a way of locking *A* and *B* during the critical period when their values are not stable. The easiest way is to delay response to any message involving *A* or *B* which does not have the magic key. Notice here that we are assuming that the public slot names *A* and *B* each correspond to a single "global variable" which we wish to regulate. This is a specialized use of public slot names, but an important one and one which naturally gives rise to exclusion problems.

As before, the key for this transaction can be passed from module to module. The pair of **send**'s on lines 8 and 9 could be made into a single fetch and lock statement, either by adding such a primitive action or adding a **postaction** slot to the message. Similarly, one could simplify lines 14–17 by using an update and unlock construct. There is no difficulty making these constructs indivisible, because a module (e.g. *Gaston*) is never interrupted. There can be no deadlock (in this simple case) because *Alphonse* locks all the resources that it needs (*A* and *B*) before starting. The module *Gaston* can receive and process other messages while waiting for *Alphonse*—the entire module is not locked.

There is a potential problem of code in *Gaston* using the local variables associated with *A* and *B* but not mentioning them in messages. If one really wants a variable to be totally protected in PLITS, one must make it a module. A more plausible solution is that any module which allows locking of particular variables must maintain internal consistency by not modifying these variables itself while they are locked. The potential deadlock situations are internal to the module and should be easily avoidable.

More commonly, one is concerned with the exclusion problem in large complex data structures. One very clean analysis of this problem can be found in [9]. They develop a notion of a sufficient discipline for locking and extend it to "predicate" locks which are logical conditions set up by one module to guarantee the integrity of its modifications. The PLITS implementation of this algorithm is a straightforward extension of the ideas developed above [32].

The coding of the structure-monitoring module *Gaston* could be done in a number of different ways. We have suggested that *Gaston* could simply ignore messages that involve *A* or *B*. This could be done using a *Smart_Receive* function call of the form

```
Mess3 := Smart_Receive (Transaction = Key ∨
                        (Absent(A) ∧ Absent(B)))
```

We have already discussed some of the alternative ways of coding a *Smart_Receive*, for example, using a filtering front end module. It is almost equivalent to have *Gaston* accept all messages and only process the appropriate ones, but there are advantages and disadvantages to each method. If *Gaston* deals with all messages, it must have an internal data structure which duplicates much of the system function of queuing messages. On the other hand, by looking at all messages, *Gaston* has the opportunity to detect high priority messages, time-critical situations, contradictions, etc. This discussion suggests the kind of issue that arises in the design of a system that is based on PLITS. We are attempting to provide a set of primitives that will support a variety of solutions to problems like the monitoring of global variables.

3. Implementation Considerations

The implementation of PLITS ideas has proceeded in parallel with the formulation of the general concepts described above. The development of an operating system for RIG (Rochester's Intelligent Gateway) [2] used the message-module paradigm, but no higher level language forms. A serviceable SAIL-PLITS with essentially the features described in Section 2 was written by Jim Low in the summer of 1976 and has been used for experimental and student work. One outgrowth of this effort is an "advanced compiler" project, which is discussed briefly in Section 4. The other major current effort is the implementation of a uniform framework for multimachine, multilanguage distributed user jobs ("DJOBs") in the PLITS style. This is being carried out in the context of our local network which currently contains four Altos, two Eclipses, and a DEC KL10 and is described in [12]. The discussion here is intended to point out the issues arising in the implementation of PLITS or any similar high level language for distributed computing. Once arrangements for starting a DJOB are made, the underlying system should be invisible to a PLITS user who will program as described in Section 2.

We first look more carefully at the process of sending and receiving messages. Even on a single machine, there will have to be some underlying programs which handle messages and schedule modules for execution. We will call such a collection of programs a *Kernel.* A Kernel is a conventional multiprogramming monitor which sequences through the modules on its "ready" queue. A Kernel also maintains data structures describing modules which are "suspended" waiting to **Receive** a message of a specified sort. These data structures, together with analogous ones for messages which result from **Send** statements, suffice to implement the PLITS message primitives.

With an underlying operating system like TOPS/10 or TENEX, it may be convenient to group modules into a single job if they communicate mainly with one another, or comprise a package, or share code. Such a group is called a *Site.* In general, each site will have its own kernel. A problem arises if the modules of a DJOB are written in different body languages. It may be the case that languages differ in their representation of primitive data types (e.g. **real**). We require that the representation of primitive data types be uniform within a site. This, as well as other considerations, may give rise to the situation where there is more than one site on a given machine involved in an individual distributed job.

A DJOB might consist of modules on several computers. For example, a distributed vision application might consist of an image processing site on the PDP-10, an interactive site on an Alto, a site on an Eclipse for managing a color display, and file servers on both the PDP-10 and on the Eclipse. One of the modules in each DJOB is designated the "controlling module" for the DJOB. In this example, the controlling module might be one on the Alto. The controlling module for a DJOB is responsible for initializing and terminating the DJOB and for taking appropriate action when one of the other modules of the DJOB fails.

Figure 6 is a graphic representation of the breakdown of functions and terminology which we have adopted. It is convenient to divide the PLITS support functions into

Fig. 6.

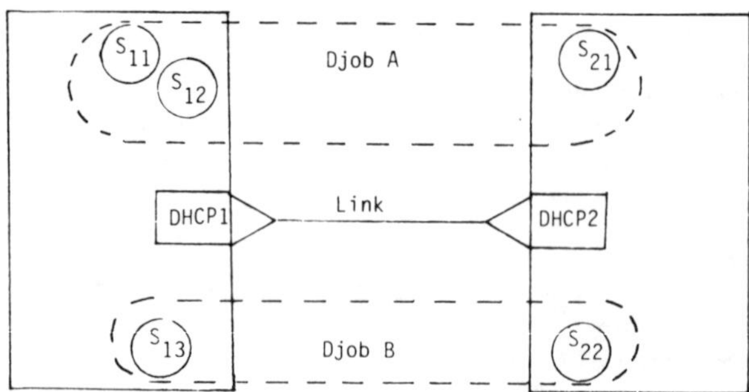

two subsets carried out by the site Kernel and by the *Host Control Program* (HCP) respectively. In Figure 6, there are two DJOBS, *A* and *B*, which have no connection but happen to be both distributed over Machines 1 and 2. DJOB A consists of three sites: *S*11 and *S*12 on Machine 1 and *S*21 on Machine 2. Each site has a Kernel assigned to it as described above. The Kernel performs the following functions:

(1) distributes messages to and from modules within the site;
(2) forwards messages to and from other sites;
(3) carries out needed representation shifts for intersite messages;
(4) allocates resources within the site;
(5) generates unique (world-wide) module and transaction identifiers;
(6) checks for errors and assertion violations.

We have discussed the first three functions briefly and will give more details on them below. The fourth function, resource allocation within the site, is concerned with storage allocation and reclamation, scheduling of ready modules, etc. The fifth function is discussed later in this section. Error and assertion checking are discussed in Section 4.

Each HCP is an extension of its machine's operating system. It performs four main functions:

(1) distributes messages among sites local to this machine;
(2) forwards messages to and from other machines;
(3) starts and stops DJOBS, and provides access to other operating system services;
(4) checks for intersite errors and assertion violations.

When a PLITS message is sent by a module, its destination is checked. If it is within the sender's site, the site Kernel handles it; if not, it is given to the local HCP. If the destination is within another site on the same machine, it is given to the Kernel for that site; if not, the HCP has it forwarded to the appropriate machine—the job of HCP functions 1 and 2 above. To do this effectively requires quite a lot of mechanism beneath the surface. Problems faced include reliable transmission, flow control, error handling, and providing user services for distributed computations. This has led us to view the underlying support facilities as a distributed operating system (DSYS).

Each machine HCP has two parts: a "DSYS Job Manager" (for distributed jobs) and a "DSYS Communications Manager." This organization reflects the two separate facilities of DSYS: operating system support and services for PLITS DJOBS, and basic message communication in the PLITS style.

Each Job Manager:

(1) provides services for DJOBS (i.e. start, stop, access to services of the local operating system);
(2) remembers which local services are allocated to which DJOBs, and which module is the controlling module for each DJOB;
(3) arranges to recover resources used by such services when a DJOB finishes.

In addition, each Job Manager keeps track (for each DJOB whose controlling module is local) of the other computers that are involved in the DJOB. The Job Manager for the controlling module of a DJOB knows which other HCP's to notify when the DJOB finishes (or dies).

Consider the problem of setting up a DJOB. If there are two sites on the same machine with the same primitive data representations, the HCP must check that the use of public slot names is compatible—essentially the same process as binding the externals of two load modules. If two sites have incompatibility in representation of a primitive data type, then some conversion routines will be automatically invoked for inter-site messages when they are sent. The ARPA network voice protocol [7] presents a good model of a scheme in which a dialogue between machines is used to reconcile representation differences before messages containing data are sent. All of this is fairly messy, but should only be necessary when a new PLITS language processor is brought up on a machine. In the usual case, the standard conversions between sites will have been established and the negotiations between machines will be simple.

The DSYS Communications Manager (DCM) on each computer is responsible for forwarding messages to and from modules on other local sites and on other computers. The DCM accepts messages to be forwarded to remote modules from local ones, and passes messages to local modules that arrive from remote ones. In addition to dealing with communications I/O devices, the DCM controls the flow of messages from local senders based on the rate of acceptance by intended receivers and the availability of buffer space. The DCM also provides a "reliable transmission" service.

The DCM allocates buffer space for messages on a "destination" basis. Each (receiving module, transaction) pair is considered a "destination" for messages. A descriptor which includes a "destination queue" exists for each destination. Each such queue has its own allotment of buffer space for messages. This space is not committed a priori, but is rather a (changeable) estimate of how much of a backlog of messages should be allowed for the destination. The basic flow control mechanism is simple: a sending module is kept suspended until space on the destination queue becomes available. If the destination is in the same site as the sender, the site Kernel controls message flow. If the destination is at a different site, the message is passed to the DCM, which arranges to forward it.

A destination descriptor is a distributed data structure. The destination's site Kernel has a portion, and each computer upon which there is at least one module sending messages to the destination has a portion (maintained by the sender's DCM). One can view the portions on remote computers as queue extensions. The primary job of each DCM is to maintain its part of this distributed data structure to support module-to-module communication across computer boundaries. The system is designed in such a way that a DCM can "forget" about its part of a remote destination descriptor if there is no message activity for a while. A scheme for "implicit connections" is the basis for this design: local knowledge about remote destinations is acquired when needed, automatically. There is purposely no requirement that state information about a remote module be maintained arbitrarily long.

There is a question of how to identify modules in a distributed system. If there were a central source of identifiers, it might take a long time to get one and the central source might be sometimes inaccessible. If each module created its own, there would either have to be a lot of handshaking or there would be a danger of duplications. Our solution is simple and quite general: an identifier (in the present design) is a 32-bit number composed of four fields: a computer number, an "incarnation number," a site number, and a "local module number." Such an identifier is a network "address" [33]. The computer number uniquely identifies one of the computers in our network. The incarnation number is used to distinguish old incarnations of the operating system on the indicated computer from the most recent one. DSYS uses this information to trap references to defunct operating system incarnations. The site number identifies a site on the indicated computer, and the local module number identifies a module at the site. Thus a module address uniquely identifies a module in the distributed system.

One consequence of this definition is that a given module always resides on the same machine, somewhat contrary to current fantasies about distributed computing. In our view, a module will be compiled to take full advantage of the hardware and software resources of its machine. There may be *equivalent* modules on various machines, and programs will be able to choose between them, but each will have a distinct unique address, hence machine of residence.

There is one additional question that should be ad-

Fig. 7.

12
2
real
Re1
Im1
2
real
Re2
IM2
1
action
Update

dressed at this time—sending structured data objects in messages. As defined, PLITS allows only single elements to be the value of a message slot. This is defensible in a one-site system where one can assume that access to arrays, for example, can be by message, with an advanced compiler (Section 4) making the simple cases efficient. This model simply breaks down in the case of remote sites and we are forced to consider sending blocks of information in messages. This also means that a PLITS user cannot, in practice, totally ignore the location of his modules, but one would hardly expect it to be otherwise.

There are several possible ways to add structured types to PLITS messages. The most general would be to allow for constructed modes (as in Algol 68) and the use of these modes as data types for public slot names. In this case, the initial connection dialogues would also have to come to agreement about all the publicly defined modes, but there does not seem to be any inherent difficulty about this (we already require checking enumeration types). One would not, of course, allow the use of references or pointers in the defined modes. General structured types are omitted from this version of PLITS for simplicity and because our ideas on a universal structure mechanism are just beginning to take shape [16].

We are using a somewhat simpler extension—a single additional public type: **bundle**. A **bundle** object is a self-describing collection of objects of primitive type. We will first present the syntax of **bundle** and then discuss its use.

⟨group⟩ ::= ⟨repetition⟩ ⟨elementary type⟩ ⟨repetition values of type⟩
⟨bundle⟩ ::= ⟨total length⟩ ⟨group⟩|⟨bundle⟩ ⟨group⟩

Thus a bundle is a collection of one level structures. For example, a bundle of two complex numbers followed by an **action** update would be of the form given in Figure 7 (where **action** is a public enumeration type). The idea is that bundles are relatively simple and are handled by relatively few modules at each site. If two sites wanted explicitly to include the information that a pair of reals was a complex number rather than a 2-vector, they would use another enumeration type to provide descriptors in bundles. Similarly, one could have bundle descriptors either in the bundle or in accompanying slots. Our current interest in bundles is primarily for passing very large collections of data such as images [40] and, to a lesser extent, for buffer management within a site. In connection with this, one probably wants to add a **Sendoff** construct which asserts that the sending module has no further need for the data in this message. It is too early to tell how much elaboration of the bundle mechanism will prove worthwhile.

4. Related Issues

The overall aims of the PLITS project go well beyond the distributed computing proposals presented above. The project originated as an attempt to look very carefully at programming languages and their use in a very broad context. There is a great deal that we do not yet understand, but a surprising number of questions do seem to yield to mutually compatible solutions, such as the module-message paradigm. The first technical report [10] on the PLITS project contains a loose overview of our ideas on a variety of topics. Some of these are being treated in detail in current reports [11, 16, 39], and others will follow. We include here just enough discussion of these issues to show how the material of the first three sections fits into the overall project.

A major focus of effort in PLITS is the use of declarative information in programming languages. Our concerns cover a broad range of issues, ranging from a careful study of type mechanisms [16] to general nonprocedural programming. We are attempting to develop a uniform solution, involving a general notion of *assertions* and very sophisticated compilers that will encompass conventional optimizations, language extension, verification and automatic programming within a single framework. We will outline the issues most closely related to distributed computing, starting with the issue of primitive data types.

In current programming languages, data types and the associated type machinery are used for a variety of purposes. In some cases alternatives to ordinary data types may serve better, providing language facilities which are more expressive and more extensible. At the simplest level, data types are used to indicate a particular hardware representation for variables. The compiler must have this information in order to generate correct code. **Real** and **integer** are common examples, directly related to the difference in code generated for real and integer variables. In a tagged architecture where the reals and integers were not distinguished, there might be a single type **number**, which combined both.

Given that the number of types which have a distinct, direct hardware representation is small and fixed, it seems appropriate to regard them as primitive. The present data type machinery is perfectly adequate for this purpose, if we accept that for a given site, each simple variable has a single particular hardware representation which we wish to specify. The compiler will ensure that we do not mix different representations in a meaningless way. It is central to the present conception of data type that the compiler checks type correctness.

This has led to the unfortunate notion that if the compiler is to check something, then it must be a data type. Data types are now being used to encode all those properties of a variable which the compiler checks. Strong typing (e.g. PASCAL) attempts to provide for assertional information and consistency checking, but uses much too weak an expressive mechanism. A strong type is essentially the logical AND of a set of properties, with the OR of these conjunctions expressible as a union type. This does not allow the programmer a convenient way of asserting the desired consistency checks. The use of union types also gives rise to some subtle aliasing effects [38].

As a simple case of the difficulty, suppose that a programmer would like to have three independent properties, such as

small(x) ≡ |x| < 15; **odd**(x) ≡ mod 2 = 1; **positive**(x) ≡ x > 0

In a strongly typed language, he can do this only by defining composite properties like **small odd** or **odd positive.** Unless a coercion is defined, one cannot, for example, use a **small odd** variable in a procedural call which requires a **small** argument. Composite types can be combined using the **union** construct, which has the effect of **or**ing properties together.

Even with three basic properties over a hundred different plausible types can be produced. For example:

union (**small**, **odd**)
union (**small positive**, **odd**)
union (**small positive**, **small odd**)

where presumably any property may also be negated.

This creates even greater problems with generic operators, which are operators associated with different function procedures for arguments of different type. For example:

small + **small**
odd + **odd**
positive + **positive**

might each invoke a different procedure. This might be adequate if three procedures were all that are needed, but what about:

small + **small odd**
small + **odd**

Perhaps the first can use the same procedure as

small + **small**

by invoking the coercion of **small odd** to **small**, but what about the second? The variable of type **small** might be odd, so that the **odd** + **odd** would be correct, or perhaps the variable of type **odd** is small, or perhaps they are both positive! A profusion of composite and union types could not possibly help; it would multiply the number of cases to be considered alarmingly.

The problem rests on two fundamental assumptions of the type mechanism: that a variable has just one type; and that types match only if they are identical or can be coerced to be so. But neither assumption is necessary to do the job that property types are here being required to do. If a programmer wants to declare that a variable always satisfies some predicate P, or that the actual argument to a procedure must satisfy another, then it should be possible to say just that.

The solution to this and a number of related problems is to add a simple *property* mechanism to the primitive type facilities of a language. For problems involving only simple variables such as that described above, the use of separate properties for **small**, **odd**, and **positive** make it quite easy to specify the "type" requirements for variables and functions. For composite data structures, such as arrays or records, the property mechanism becomes more complex. Our current ideas on this are given in [16].

Even with the property mechanism, we are restricted to specifying only conditions involving one variable or argument. There is no way, for example, to specify that the arguments to a procedure sum to one (or approximately one). For this and a number of other reasons we propose to include a more general *assertion* facility in PLITS.

An assertion is a predicate which the compiler will guarantee to be true at run time. It will either prove it true (at compile time), or generate code to check the assertion. Assertions may be used to describe important properties of variables and data structures. A property is a special kind of assertion that applies to only one variable and holds throughout the lifetime of that variable. They help the programmer to write provably correct code, and can be used for error checking. Assertions may be used by the compiler to generate more efficient code. Since they have to be proved or checked, they function as "hints" as to what program properties the optimizer might use. There is no attempt, however, to coerce the programmer into providing enough assertions to allow formal verification of all programs.

We will present assertions and their uses more concretely, continuing the use of PASCAL-PLITS as a basis. Certainly the notion of ⟨assertion⟩ will include the existing ⟨Boolean⟩ expressions, but may be more extensive. As a first example, consider the reception of messages by a module. One would like to be able to **Assert** that a given **Receive** will acquire only certain kinds of messages. With our definitions, the obvious thing is to accompany the **Receive** statement with

Assert Slots Must Be (set of **Public** slot names)

This assertion allows the compiler to assume that no other public slot names known to this module will appear in any message picked up at this point. One could also assert, e.g. that the *action* slot of incoming messages at this point could not have the value *Update*; the compiler should then be able to generate much better code for this read-only access. A well-written PLITS program will have every **Receive** statement accompanied by one or more assertions. Since modules are otherwise totally self-contained, the compiler can then analyze the receiving module for consistency, code-optimization, etc. The execution-time truth of an assertion might be provable at compile time, but otherwise it will require a compiled-in check. The idea here is that we can develop proofs of conditional correctness of individual modules given their assertions with errors being detected as run-time violation of specific assertions. The problem of verifying the correctness of a collection of modules is more complex and is addressed in [11]. The method proposed there is to characterize each module as a finite-state machine and to establish the properties of the system by reachability theorems in the vector space of states of the modules. The propagation of information among modules which communicate only by messages is addressed in [37].

The specifications of a module in PLITS should include the assertions on its incoming and outgoing messages. Assertions will enable us to capture easily constructs like the pre, post, invariants, and requires of Alphard [29]. For automatic programming, the specification of a module must also include other information, like the resource utilization [31] of the module.

More formally, there are two ⟨statement⟩ constructs involving assertions proposed for PASCAL-PLITS.

(a) **Assert** ⟨assertion⟩
(b) **Under** ⟨assertion⟩ **Do** ⟨statement⟩

The first of these is the basic form which generates an exception condition if the assertion fails to hold. Construct (b) specifies that the ⟨assertion⟩ is to hold throughout the ⟨statement⟩. This idea has also been called "invariants" or "continuously evaluating expressions" and is extremely powerful. Unfortunately, it is not easy to specify or to implement in a general and useful way. There are two difficulties: efficiency and the grain of evaluation. The efficiency question is easy to understand—how can we implement invariants without unduly slowing down the computation. It is our claim that standard flow analysis and value propagation techniques can make this feasible in the usual cases. This is a good example of what we would like from an advanced compiler.

The grain problem for invariants is much deeper. Should the semantics of **Under** specify that the ⟨assertion⟩ must hold at every individual machine cycle or at some coarser grain? Our current definition is that the ⟨assertion⟩ must hold at the end of each first level substatement of the ⟨statement⟩ which is the body of the **Under**.

In addition to their use in verification, assertions play a central role in our work on code optimization. One of the key problems in bringing PLITS-style programming into widespread use is the development of techniques for producing efficient code from the decoupled and protected constructs of PLITS. The idea here is to have the compiler understand those cases where certain checks are not needed at execution time.

One can get a feeling for this problem by considering the implementation of standard variables and arrays in PLITS. It is certainly true that we could have **array** (even individual variable: cf. [20]) modules which took messages and returned values. Doing this in the obvious way would cause an unacceptable slowdown of about a hundred in the execution of simple programs. One solution to this "grain" problem is to make modules be rather large subsystems, coded in the usual way. The better solution is to use a more sophisticated compiler. In general, there are times when one would want the full PLITS paraphernalia for accessing a global array. For example, one might want to have critical sections or check the range of values or trace the updates or change the internal representation of the array or lots of other things. What we would like is to be able to **close** [45] a collection of PLITS modules and get very good code for the simple cases.

This module integration problem is the direct extension of the standard procedure integration task which is an important aspect of current optimization efforts. One encouraging initial result is that the narrow message-based interface among modules makes global flow analysis much less costly than in other proposed schemes for parallelism [37]. Similar module integration problems would arise in any of the proposed data abstraction languages like Alphard [29] or CLU [27] or EUCLID [24].

Debugging calls for some new techniques in a PLITS (or any Distributed Computing) environment. A direct ancestor of PLITS was the Stanford Hand-Eye System [15] in which some of these problems were addressed. The major additional debugging tools there were time-labeled selective message tracing and the ability to interact separately with individual modules. A major difficulty was that the user console handled everything sequentially, merging all communication streams. The use of multiple streams was developed by Swinehart [43] and is a central feature of the Rochester RIG system [2] which has a PLITS-like message basis.

Another important set of issues arises from the fact that message switching systems manifest errors in characteristic ways. Since modules are self-contained, careful coding can guarantee that a module never process a message that would force it into a bad state. Messages that violate assertions can be found and reported. The difficult error conditions come from situations like deadlock, flooding, starvation, etc.

A *deadlock* in PLITS arises when two (or more) modules are in a situation where each is attempting to receive a message which must be sent by another. *Flooding* occurs when a module generates too many messages and *starvation* where a module does not receive messages intended for it. There are a variety of other error conditions that can arise in a multiprocessing environment involving critical race conditions, inconsistent shared data, etc., but these will not normally be detectable as problems in queue management. The hope is that the message discipline and the use of assertions will make it easier and more natural to write correct programs and find errors.

We have developed two kinds of solutions to error conditions arising in queue management. The first kind of solution involves having the PLITS kernel use more sophistication in its management of message queues in order to minimize the number of avoidable deadlocks, etc. These techniques were described briefly in Section 3 and are treated more thoroughly in [39].

The second class of solution to error conditions involves the use of system-generated exception conditions. The system (DSYS) underlying a PLITS implementation will have a great deal of information about the message state of the various modules. It is straightforward to have the system detect a variety of illegal and dangerous situations. It is also possible (cf. [10]) to provide for the checking of user-provided assertions on message behavior. Errors or assertion violations can be treated as types of exception conditions.

In PLITS, exception conditions can be clearly divided into two classes: those that arise within a module and those that are external to the module. Since much PLITS programming is event driven, exception conditions will cover much more than the usual error conditions. Typical internal conditions include overflow, type violations, message arrival, and absent slots. External exception conditions include invalid messages, time-out notifications and the availability or demise of other modules. In the PLITS environment, the notification for an external exception condition will be through messages. Although it is not strictly necessary, it is preferable to have the notion of *priority* message for exception conditions (among other things). In our proposal, a priority message will be received (if present) immediately before the next **Send** or **Receive** statement executed by the module. This is equivalent to having a statement of the form:

```
1  While Pending About ⟨priority transaction⟩ Do
2     Begin Message M1;
3           Receive M1 About ⟨priority transaction⟩
4           Cause (priority_message, M1)
5     End
```

before each **Send** and **Receive** statement. The **Cause** statement in line 4 triggers an internal exception condition within the module. Thus, an external exception condition is announced as a priority message to the module; this could be explicitly checked for at any time, but will normally be converted to an internal exception condition of type *priority_message*.

The treatment of internal exception conditions will, of course, be different in different body languages. The following proposal for PASCAL-PLITS is a simplification of ideas of [26] made possible by the elimination of data sharing across modules. A PASCAL-PLITS program has a fixed set of named exception conditions and a (generally larger) set of procedures, called handlers. Following Levin, we assume that the handler to be invoked for a given condition can be *declared* as part of the declaration of a block by a statement of the form:

```
On ⟨condition⟩ Invoke ⟨handler⟩
```

The record of which handler is currently appropriate for each condition follows the PASCAL dynamic nesting structure. When invoked, a handler runs as a normal procedure called in the block where its condition was caused. This is all straightforward—the difficult problems are how to pass information to the handler and how the handler should complete. We expect the following simple solutions to suffice for PASCAL-PLITS.

There are two basic completion paths commonly needed for exception handlers—either the handler returns to the point of invocation or it must exit to some higher level. It might also need to pass on the situation to another handler. The following four statements:

```
Return {Causing (⟨condition⟩, ⟨arg⟩)}
Exit {Causing (⟨condition⟩, ⟨arg⟩)}
```

cover the possibilities. A handler might call other routines, change global data within its module, send messages, etc. while operating. When it is finished, it must either Return to the point of invocation or Exit from the block in which it was **declared**. Optionally, it can also cause another condition after it completes.

A thorough discussion of exception handling and the advantages of this design are beyond the scope of this paper. The astute reader will have observed that the ⟨arg⟩ accompanying a Cause was a ⟨message⟩ (*A*-set) in the previous example. The use of sets of name ~ value pairs as arguments to condition handlers seems particularly appropriate, because various handlers might deal with different slots. As was mentioned in Section 2, we are currently exploring the use of *A*-sets in a number of programming contexts.

Acknowledgments. The ideas presented here owe their present form to continual discussions and interactions. I would especially like to acknowledge the help of J. Low and P. Rovner, the students of CSC 400 and 520, and the former friends and captive seminar audiences who had to listen to various partial formulations.

We have had enough experience with PLITS to understand that it behaves as a mirror in which each observer sees a reflection of something different—this indicates the presence of many unacknowledged intellectual debts. The most direct ancestor of PLITS is the message procedure facility [15] which was put into SAIL for robotics work and which no one remembers.

Received March 1977; revised December 1978

References

(Note. References [4, 6, 8, 13, 14, 17, 21, 23, 25, 30, 34–36, 41, 42, and 44] are not cited in the text.)

1. Astrahan, M.M., et al. System R.: A relational approach to data base management. IBM Res. Lab., Feb. 1976.

2. Ball, E., Feldman, J., Low, J., Rashid, R., and Rovner, P. RIG, Rochester's intelligent gateway: System overview. *IEEE Trans. Software Eng. SE-2*, 4 (Dec. 1976), 321–328.

3. Ball, J., Williams, G., and Low, J. Preliminary ZENO language description. TR41, Comptr. Sci. Dept., U. of Rochester, Rochester, N.Y., Dec. 1978.

4. Birtwistle, G., et al. *Simula Begin.* Auerbach, Philadelphia, Pa., 1973.

5. Bobrow, D.G., and Raphael, B. New programming languages for artificial intelligence. *Computing Surv. 6*, 3 (Sept. 1974), 155–174.

6. Bolt, Beranek and Newman, Inc. Interface message processor: Specifications for the interconnection of a host and an IMP. Rep. 1822, BBN, Cambridge, Mass., 1978 (revised).

7. Cohen, D. Specifications for the network voice protocol. ISI/RR-75-39, Inform. Sci. Inst., U. of S. Calif., Los Angeles, March 1976.

8. Demers, A., Donahue, J., and Skinner, A. Data types as values: Polymorphism, type checking, encapsulation. Conf. Record Fifth Annual ACM Symp. on Principles of Programming Languages, 1978, pp. 23–30.

9 Eswaran, K.P., et al. The notions of consistency and predicate locks in a database system. *Comm. ACM 19*, 11 (Nov. 1976), 624–633.

10. Feldman, J.A. A programming methodology for distributed computing (among other things). TR9, Comptr. Sci. Dept., U. of Rochester, Rochester, N.Y., Jan. 1977.

11. Feldman, J.A. Synchronizing distant cooperating processes. TR26, Comptr. Sci. Dept., U. of Rochester, Rochester, N.Y., 1977.

12. Feldman, J.A., Low, J.R., and Rovner, P.D. Programming distributed systems. Proc. 1978 Annual ACM Conf., Washington, D.C., Dec. 1978, Vol. 1, pp. 310–316.

13. Feldman, J.A., Low, J.R., Swinehart, D., and Taylor, R. Recent developments in SAIL, an Algol-based language for artificial intelligence. Proc. AFIPS 1972 FJCC, AFIPS Press, Montvale, N.J., pp. 1193–1202.

14. Feldman, J.A., and Rovner, P.D. An Algol-based associative language. *Comm. ACM 12*, 8 (Aug. 1969), 439–449.

15. Feldman, J.A., and Sproull, R.F. System support for the Stanford hand-eye system. Proc. Second Int. Joint Conf. on Artif. Intell., London, Sept. 1971.

16. Feldman, J.A., and Williams, G.J. Some comments on data types. TR28, Comptr. Sci. Dept., University of Rochester, Rochester, N.Y., 1977.

17. Floyd, R.W. Assigning meanings to programs. Proc. Symp. Appl. Math., Vol. 19, 1967, pp. 19–32.

18. Geschke, C.M., and Mitchell, J.G. On the problem of uniform references to data structures. *IEEE Trans. on Software Eng. SE-3* (June 1975), 207–219.

19. Goldberg, A., and Kay, A., Eds. SMALLTALK-72 Instruction Manual. SSL 76-6, Xerox PARC, Palo Alto, Calif., 1976.

20. Hewitt, C.E., and Smith, B. Towards a programming apprentice. *IEEE Trans. Software Eng. SE-1*, 1 (March 1975), 26–45.

21. Hoare, C.A.R. Communicating sequential processes. *Comm. ACM 21*, 8 (Aug. 1978), 666–677.

22. Hoare, C.A.R., and Wirth, N. An axiomatic definition of the programming language Pascal. *Acta Informatica 2* (1973), 335–355.

23. Jones, A.K., and Liskov, B.H. A language extension for controlling access to shared data. *IEEE Trans. Software Eng. SE-2*, 4 (December 1976).

24. Lampson, B.W., et al. Report on the programming language Euclid. SIGPLAN Notices (ACM) *12*, 2 (Feb. 1977).

25. Lampson, B.W., and Sturgis, H. Crash recovery in a distributed data storage system. Unpublished paper, Xerox PARC, submitted to *Comm. ACM*.

26. Levin, R. Program structures for exceptional condition handling. Ph.D. Th., Carnegie-Mellon U., Pittsburgh, Pa., 1977.

27. Liskov, B., et al. Abstraction mechanisms in CLU. *Comm. ACM 20*, 8 (Aug. 1977), 564–576.

28. Liskov, B., and Zilles, S. Programming with abstract data types. Proc. Symp. Very High Level Languages, SIGPLAN Notices (ACM) *9*, 4 (April 1974), 50–59.

29. London, R.L., Shaw, M., and Wulf, W.A. An introduction to the construction and verification of Alphard programs. *IEEE Trans. Software Eng. SE-2*, 4 (Dec. 1976), 253–264.

30. Low, J.R. *Automatic Coding: Choice of Data Structures.* Birkhauser-Verlag, Basel und Stuttgart, 1976.

31. Low, J.R., and Rovner, P.D. Techniques for the automatic selection of data structures. Conf. Rec. Third ACM Symp. on Principles of Programming Languages, Atlanta, Ga., Jan. 1976, 58–67.

32. Mitchell, J.A., and Wegbreit, B. Schemes: A high level data structuring concept. CSL-77-1, Xerox PARC, Palo Alto, Calif., Jan. 1977.

33. McQuillan, J.M., and Walden, D.C. The ARPA network design decisions. *Computer Networks 1*, 5 (Aug. 1977), 243–290.

34. Owicki, S.S., and Gries, D. Verifying properties of parallel programs: An axiomatic approach. *Comm. ACM 19*, 5 (May 1976), 279–285.

35. Parnas, D.L., Shore, J.E., and Weiss, D.M. Abstract types defined as classes of variables. SIGPLAN Notices (ACM) *8*, 2 (1976), 149–154 (Vol. II, 1976 Special Issue).

36. Peterson, G.L., and Fischer, M.J. Economical solutions for the critical section problem in a distributed system. Proc. Ninth Annual ACM Symp. on Theory of Comptng., Boulder, Colo., May 1977, pp. 91–97.

37. Reif, J. Data flow analysis for communicating Modules. TR30, Comptr. Sci. Dept., U. of Rochester, Rochester, N.Y., 1978; also available as Data flow analysis of communicating processes, Conf. Rec. Sixth Annual ACM Symp. on Principles of Programming Languages, Jan. 1979, pp. 257–268.

38. Reynolds, J. On the syntactic control of interference. Conf. Rec. Fifth Annual ACM Symp. on Principles of Programming Languages, Jan. 1978, pp. 39–46.

39. Rovner, P.D. Message flow control in a local network. Comptr. Sci. Dept., U. of Rochester, Rochester, N.Y., 1978.

40. Selfridge, P.G. A flexible data structure for accessory image information. TR45, Comptr. Sci. Dept., U. of Rochester, Rochester, N.Y., Nov. 1978.

41. Sproull, R.F., and Thomas, E.L. A network graphics protocol. SIGGRAPH *8*, 3 (Aug. 1974).

42. Sturgis, H.E. A postmortem for a time-sharing system. Ph.D. Diss., U. of California, Berkeley, 1974.

43. Swinehart, D.C. Copilot: A multiple process approach to interactive programming systems. Ph.D. Diss., Stanford U., Stanford, Calif., 1974.

44. Thomas, R.H. A solution to the update problem for multiple copy data bases which uses distributed control. Rep. No. 3340, Bolt, Beranek and Newman, Cambridge, Mass., July 1976.

45. Wegbreit, B., and Spitzen, J.M. Proving properties of complex data structures. *J. ACM 23*, 2 (April 1976), 389–396.

*MOD—A Language for Distributed Programming

ROBERT P. COOK, MEMBER, IEEE

Abstract—Distributed programming is characterized by high communications costs and the inability to use shared variables and procedures for interprocessor synchronization and communication. *MOD is a high-level language system which attempts to address these problems by creating an environment conducive to efficient and reliable network software construction. Several of the *MOD distributed programming constructs are discussed as well as an interprocessor communication methodology. Examples illustrating these concepts are drawn from the areas of network communication and distributed process synchronization.

Index Terms—Computer networks, distributed programming, Modula, processor module, programming languages.

I. Introduction

*MOD (starmod), a language derived from Modula [35]–[37], is intended for systems or application programming in a network environment. The *MOD design is based on experience with our PDP-11/VAX Modula compiler [7] and was inspired by Brinch Hansen's "distributed processes" concepts [3]. A *distributed program* can be characterized as an algorithm which requires multiple processors for its implementation, whereas a *concurrent program* requires multiple processes for its implementation. A *sequential program* is an algorithm which is implemented using only procedural constructs.

It is interesting to observe that after 25 years of experience with sequential programming, there is still no consensus on language features. The current discussions involving Ada [19], [20] provide a case in point. Since even less is known about the requirements for distributed and concurrent programs, *MOD was developed as an experimentation media and is not presented here as the ultimate solution. The primary design criteria were transparency, extensibility, and program adaptability.

Following Parnas' definition [29], a language is *transparent* with respect to a given computer system if any system state and any sequence of system states which could be obtained by programming the component machines could also be obtained by using the high-level language. For instance, experimentation would be severely hampered if the language were inflexible with respect to process definition and scheduling. Therefore, *MOD provides low-level operations which can be extended by the programmer to define high-level abstractions appropriate to a particular machine environment. *MOD programs can also adapt to changes in workload or response time requirements. The language is designed so that a library module could be upgraded from a collection of procedures to a collection of processes without changing any of its users' programs. Finally, *MOD permits the user to organize his/her program to reflect the structure of the physical processors and the connectivity of the network.

This paper discusses the rationale behind the design of the *MOD system and contrasts the language features chosen with those of the Department of Defense (DoD) Ada language [19], Hoare's communicating sequential processes (CSP) [18], Feldman's PLITS [1], [13], and Brinch Hansen's "distributed processes" [3]. In particular, we address the distributed programming problem areas of interprocessor communication, software testing, and kernel efficiency. The *MOD design decisions in other areas such as data abstraction [8] and synchronization [9] are described elsewhere.

II. Program Organization

Before proceeding further with a more detailed discussion of the *MOD distributed programming mechanisms, the *module* concept of Modula [35] will be considered as a focal point for network software development. A module usually corresponds to a program abstraction and consists of an external

Manuscript received October 1, 1979; revised March 18, 1980. This work was supported in part by the U.S. Army under Contract DAAG29-75-C-0024 and in part by the National Science Foundation under Grant MCS-7903947.

The author is with the Department of Computer Sciences, University of Wisconsin, Madison, WI 53706.

Reprinted from *IEEE Trans. Software Eng.*, vol. SE-6, pp. 563–571, Nov. 1980.

interface specification, data structure definitions, procedures, processes, and an optional initialization part. In *MOD, a module can be used as a type definition or to delineate a lexical scope as in Modula; therefore, both the information-hiding properties proposed by Parnas [28] and the flexibility of the Simula [10] "class" mechanism are maintained.

In Modula, if the prefix "device" or "interface" is used before the "module" keyword, the semantics of the module change. For instance, "interface" denotes a module which semantically is similar to a monitor [17]. *MOD extends the Modula prefix notation to provide the user with the following module types:

```
PROGRAM ::= network module IDENTIFIER [= LINKLIST];
                [MODULEBODY]
                end IDENTIFIER.
PROCESSORDECLARATION ::= processor module IDENTIFIER
                [REPLICATIONCOUNT];
                [MODULEBODY]
                [begin STATEMENTLIST]
                end IDENTIFIER
MODULETYPEDECLARATION ::=
        type IDENTIFIER = [MODULETYPE] module;
        [MODULEBODY]
        [begin STATEMENTLIST]
        end IDENTIFIER
MODULEDECLARATION ::=
        [MODULETYPE] module IDENTIFIER;
        [[MODULEBODY]
         [begin STATEMENTLIST]
         end IDENTIFIER]
MODULETYPE ::= MODULETYPEID
LINKLIST ::= LINK [,LINK] . . .
LINK ::= (PROCESSORVAR [,PROCESSORVAR] . . .)
REPLICATIONCOUNT ::= '[' EXPRESSION ']'
```

A network module is required to define processor connectivity and to declare any types, constants, procedures, or processes which are global to the processor modules. The LINKLIST details the communication paths among processor modules in terms of a source specification and a list of destinations. Variable declarations and the initialization STATEMENTLIST are prohibited at the network level since there is no instruction or data storage outside of a physical processor. Procedures and processes are allowed within network modules for global standardization but are copied automatically by the compiler into each processor module. Fig. 1 gives an example of a five processor module "star" system.

Processor modules were introduced as part of the *MOD design to allow the programmer to partition a computation into collections of processes. All procedures and processes within a processor module can directly access shared variables, whereas interprocessor references must be in the form of messages. By using combinations of processes and the ability to specify processor modules, a *MOD user can take full advantage of the physical hardware available in order to exploit the inherent parallelism in his/her algorithm. In some situations, an algorithm may contain more processor modules than the number of physical processors available. In this case, a mechanism such as Jones' "task force" language [21] must be used to *map* the *MOD virtual processor set onto the physical network. It may also be advantageous to use a mapping specification for networks with nonuniform communication costs. In addition, the performance of processes within a processor module can be improved by mapping the module to a multiprocessor. We should also point out that the availability of a hardware multiprocessor to implement a particular processor module should be regarded as a fortuitous circumstance and should not be counted on by the programmer.

The MODULETYPEDECLARATION can be used to define a module as an extended type, such as "complex" or "stack." The variables in the module represent the type's data structures and the exported procedures define the operators for the new type. If a MODULETYPE name is used as a prefix in a MODULEDECLARATION, the module body declared with the MODULETYPE is replicated as the body for the new module. The first option, which is similar to the Simula [10] "class" notation, duplicates data while sharing the type module's procedures. The second option duplicates both data and code. For instance, a communications module might be declared as a "type" which could then be replicated for each use. Next, the syntax of a MODULEBODY will be illustrated:

```
MODULEBODY ::= EXTERNALINTERFACE
               BLOCKHEADING
EXTERNALINTERFACE ::=
               [define ELEMENT [,ELEMENT] . . . ;]
               [export ELEMENT [,ELEMENT] . . . ;]
               [pervasive ELEMENT [,ELEMENT] . . . ;]
BLOCKHEADING ::=
               [import IDENTIFIER [,IDENTIFIER] . . . ;]
               [DECLARATIONLIST]
ELEMENT ::= IDENTIFIER [(readonly|protected)]
```

A module boundary delineates a closed lexical scope which can only be superseded by the explicit specification of "define," "export," "import," or "pervasive." The external interface for a processor module usually lists any message types and process names which are used for communication.

An IDENTIFIER specified in an "import" list causes a declaration from a global lexical scope to be made accessible within the module. The "export" attribute allows a local declaration to be visible at the enclosing lexical level, while "pervasive" makes the IDENTIFIER known at the enclosing and all nested levels where the same name is not already declared. The latter option is most useful for making functions appear to their users as "builtin" to the language. For instance, the "sine" and "cosine" functions are declared as "pervasive" in the math library module; therefore, any use of that library automatically imports the math routines into the enclosed scopes.

The "define" statement is provided as an alternative to "export." It gives the user the ability to list those IDENTIFIERS which can be referenced externally, but only by prefixing the

```
network module star = (center,pr),(pr,center);
    const NOPROCESSORS = 4;
    processor module center;
        define communicator;
        process communicator(...);
                 .
                 .
                 .
          pr[i].communicator(...); (*call processor i*)
                 .
                 .
                 .
         end communicator;
       begin (*initialization*)
       end center;
    processor module pr[NOPROCESSORS]; (*four peripheral processors*)
        define communicator;
        import center;
        process communicator(...);
                .
                .
                .
          center.communicator(...); (*call center*)
                .
                .
                .
          end communicator;
        begin (*initialization*)
        end pr
    end star.
```

Fig. 1.

reference with the module name as in the Simula [10] "class" notation. "define" is used to reduce the size of "import" lists since "importing"ing a module name permits references to any of its "define"d symbols. Secondly, a qualified reference to a "define"d name serves a useful documentation function. The ability to specify the external interface for each module is becoming a standard feature of modern programming as is demonstrated by its use in Mesa [14], Euclid [23], Alphard [32], Ada [19], etc.

The *MOD user can also restrict variables and types to read-only access or to no access. These restrictions are not applied within the exporting module. Since the access checking is enforced by the compiler, it can be maintained even across distributed processors. The only exception is that any restricted variable or instance of a restricted type can be passed as an argument to a procedure exported from the defining module.

III. Language Concepts

From the *MOD viewpoint, a computer network can be characterized as an arbitrary collection of processors with fixed communication paths for interprocessor message transfer. We have adopted the traditional [33] definitions that a processor executes commands or instructions, a procedure is a sequence of instructions for a processor, and a process is one or more procedures together with the state vector which controls and defines the virtual processor on which the process runs. It should be noted that a procedure cannot execute except as part of a process. Since *MOD programs are intended to run on a bare machine, a *MOD process is a *much simpler* entity than the processes found in most operating systems. For instance, the state vector for a UNIX [30] process on a PDP-11 contains over 1000 bytes of information while the *MOD kernel for the same computer uses 32 bytes for a process' state vector. Processes in the same processor module can communicate using shared variables or messages; however, interprocessor communication can only consist of messages.

Messages are assumed to range from no content (signal or interrupt) to arbitrary data structures. We will refer to the recipient of a message as the *message handler*, or handler. Furthermore, *MOD enforces strong type checking on messages both within and across processors to maintain system consistency. Finally, any communication mechanisms presented should be efficient and should not constrain the options of the programmer. In the next sections, the *MOD design will be discussed along with a detailed analysis of the alternatives, advantages, and disadvantages.

A. Message Handlers

A procedure is a simple example of an intraprocessor message handler. Since a message can be an arbitrary data structure composed of many subfields, the syntax for the argument list and returned value was expanded to permit record and array types. Thus, the familiar argument list notation is used to represent the component fields of a message:

```
PROCEDUREDECLARATION ::=
        procedure IDENTIFIER [(FORMALS)] [:TYPEID];
                  BLOCKHEADING
                  [begin STATEMENTLIST]
                  end IDENTIFIER
PROCEDUREREFERENCE ::= PROCEDUREID [(ARGUMENTS)]
```

A procedure is an example of a *dependent* service in that the procedure's activation record must be attached to the activation record stack of an existing process, usually the caller, in order to execute. *MOD does not permit procedures as interprocessor message handlers. As an alternative, *MOD uses a process-oriented communication methodology.

1) Processes: Each "processor module" consists of one or more concurrent processes declared as follows:

```
PROCESSDECLARATION ::=
    process IDENTIFIER [(FORMALS)] ['['PRIORITY']']:TYPEID;
        BLOCKHEADING
        [begin STATEMENTLIST]
        end IDENTIFIER
PROCESSREFERENCE ::= PROCESSID [(ARGUMENTS)]
```

Except for the keyword "process" and the optional PRIORITY expression, the declaration is identical to that of a procedure. This correspondence was made intentionally to make it easier for a programmer to convert a sequential program to a concurrent or distributed program. A PROCESSREFERENCE must specify a list of arguments corresponding exactly in type and number to the FORMALS. Every procedure call creates a new activation record; however, a PROCESSREFERENCE creates a new activation record stack and state vector. Thus, each process can have multiple activations all executing in parallel.

The returned value for a functional process is set by assignment to the process identifier and must match the specified TYPEID. A reference to a functional process within the same processor is the same as a procedure reference. However, an interprocessor functional reference implies independent execution for the called process; the caller must wait. Also, the compiler will flag a process reference as an error if there are no direct communication links between the caller and handler processes.

The optional PRIORITY must evaluate to a compile-time constant which specifies the initial (default zero) priority of the process. The initial priority can be modified by altering the value of the pseudovariable "priority." Priority can be used to improve the performance or response time of an algorithm by establishing precedence relationships among its processes.

Consider the following execution options for a process as a message handler:

1) execute in parallel with caller	no reply message
2) execute in parallel with caller	reply message
3) caller waits for completion	no reply message
4) caller waits for completion	reply message.

Option 1 is implemented by a *MOD process which does not return a value while option 4 is represented by a functional process. The reply message is the returned value which can range from a simple variable to an arbitrary record. Option 3 is easily programmed by using option 4 to return a completion indication. Option 2, which corresponds to Conway's [5] "fork" and "join" methodology, is available using the "port" mechanism described in Section III-A2.

The example in Fig. 2 illustrates these concepts with a ring network version of Dijkstra's Dining Philosophers [11] problem. As in the original version, five philosophers are each trying to eat from a plate of special spaghetti which has been placed in the middle of a round table. The spaghetti is special since each philosopher requires two forks to eat it. In our example, each philosopher can directly control only the right-hand fork; to get the left fork, the philosopher to the left must be consulted. However, each philosopher is also restricted to cónversation with the right neighbor only; therefore, messages must be sent around the ring (table) to get permission to use the left-hand fork and to give it back. The algorithm is based on an ordered resource allocation strategy developed by Havender [16] which prevents deadlock and starvation.

Each philosopher is required to call "getforks" to start eating and "putforks" to stop. The lower level protocol as well as the problem restrictions and network topology are completely hidden from the user. The "get" process accepts fork requests and either passes the request to the right in the ring or else gets control of its own fork and sends an acknowledgment to the "who" philosopher. "pid" is a built-in function which identifies each processor by its index value. "got" acknowledges fork allocations and "put" frees forks. The algorithm works correctly without process priority but we have specified a higher priority for the "got" process to illustrate how performance can be "tuned" by such assignments. Note that every message in the ring activates a parallel process; thus, the performance of the algorithm can also be improved by using multiprocessors for the nodes of the ring.

2) Ports: In addition to the call/return form of message communication described in Section III-A1, it is often desirable to implement coroutine [6], rendezvous [19], or multiple handler protocols. We have integrated Balzer's [2] port mechanism into the *MOD design to provide these facilities:

```
PORTDECLARATION ::=
        port IDENTIFIER [(FORMALS)] [:TYPEID];
PORTREFERENCE ::= PORTID [(ARGUMENTS)]
```

A procedure provides a dependent message handler; a process is an independent message handler; and a port is a message queue which is independent of a handler. Thus, a port can be thought of as a queue of procedure or process messages (argument lists) waiting for execution. With a procedure or process, the caller initiates execution; with a port, only the handler can initiate execution as follows:

```
REGIONSTATEMENT ::= region PORTID [,PORTID] ...;
                        [PORTBODY]
                        end region
PORTBODY ::= STATEMENTLIST | PORTCASE [;PORTCASE] ...
PORTCASE ::= PORTID: begin STATEMENTLIST
                     end PORTID
```

If only a single PORTID is present, the PORTBODY must be a STATEMENTLIST; otherwise, a PORTCASE is required for each PORTID listed. The latter option permits a process to service requests with nondeterministic arrival times. The region statement copies the selected message into the current activation record and reserves a return value cell if the port is a function.

```
network module diningroom=(phil[1],phil[2]),(phil[2],phil[3]),
                          (phil[3],phil[4]),(phil[4],phil[5]),
                          (phil[5],phil[1]); (*ring network*)
  processor module phil[5];
      define get, put, got; (*communication processes*)
      module at_table;
          export get, put, got, getforks, putforks;
          import phil;
          var myfork, gotone: semaphore;
          process get(who, fork: integer); (*get "fork" for "who"*)
              begin
              if fork <> pid then phil[pid mod 5 + 1].get(who,fork)
                             else p(myfork);    got(who)
                             end if
              end get;
          process put(fork: integer);   (*give "fork" back*)
              begin
              if fork <> pid then phil[pid mod 5 + 1].put(fork)
                             else v(myfork)
                             end if
              end put;
          process got(who: integer) [1];   (*let "who" use fork*)
              begin
              if who <> pid then phil[pid mod 5 + 1].got(who)
                             else v(gotone)
                             end if
              end got;
          procedure getforks;   (*philosopher waits for both forks*)
              begin   get(if pid=1 then 1 else pid-1);  p(gotone);
                      get(if pid=1 then 5 else pid);    p(gotone)
              end getforks;
          procedure putforks;  (*give forks back and don't wait*)
              begin  put(pid);
                     put(if pid=1 then 5 else pid-1)
              end putforks
          end at_table;
      begin  loop
              (*think*)  getforks;
              (*eat  *)  putforks
             end loop
      end phil
  end diningroom.
```

Fig. 2.

When an "exit" from the region occurs, the returned value, if present, is transmitted to the PORTREFERENCE statement. As with processes, the caller only waits if the port returns a value. At compile-time, the scope of the argument list is opened on region entry and closed on region exit for a single port. For multiple ports, a scope is opened and closed for each PORTCASE. When the region statement is executed, the executing process will wait until a message is present at one of the listed ports. If multiple regions are waiting for the same port when a message arrives, the region to execute is chosen nondeterministically. If a region is waiting for several ports which simultaneously receive messages, the arrival order determines the processing order. Also, an "awaited" function is provided to test the status of a port.

Fig. 3 illustrates an implementation of the previous example using ports. The first example uses a process for every message which provides the maximum parallelism. In the port implementation, only one communication process is created for each processor and the messages are handled sequentially. However, multiple "communicator" processes could still be invoked to increase parallelism.

B. Processor Communication

In *MOD, processes, ports and procedures are all referenced with the same syntax; thus, the user of a module's services need never know how the service is provided. The advantage is that the implementation can be easily modified to adapt to changes in workload or response time requirements. The only restriction on such changes is that procedures cannot be used for interprocessor communication.

A procedure invocation implies the creation of an activation record which is added to the stack of the calling process. However, for an interprocessor call, the stack of the calling process is not available. The alternative is to attach the procedure's activation record to the stack of a randomly selected process in the called processor. We rejected this choice because the selected process could not continue execution until the procedure's activation record was removed. A more serious problem occurs if the process controls a resource needed by the procedure; in this case, deadlock could result. Therefore, *MOD provides only ports and processes for interprocessor communication.

A process provides parallel execution for each message handler but requires a storage allocation operation to create its stack. A port, or multiple ports, can be handled by a single process which remains permanently active; thus, a port communication involves only a context switch which can be performed very quickly with modern hardware. If the handler execution time is considerably longer than process creation time, a process is the appropriate implementation choice. Otherwise, a port will provide the fastest response time.

C. Comparison with Other Languages

*MOD integrates Brinch Hansen's [3] "distributed processes" (DP) concepts with the modular programming philosophy of Wirth [35]-[37]. Fig. 4 illustrates the compatability of a DP "process" with a *MOD "processor module." *MOD also provides the user with network and processor modules, ports, processes, and synchronization abstractions [9]. DP is oriented towards a single process per processor while *MOD

```
network module diningroom=(phil[1],phil[2]),(phil[2],phil[3]),
                          (phil[3],phil[4]),(phil[4],phil[5]),
                          (phil[5],phil[1]);   (*ring network*)
  processor module phil[5];
       define get, put, got;
       module at_table;
           export get, put, got, getforks, putforks;
           import phil;
           var myfork, gotone: semaphore;
           port get(who, fork: integer);    (*get "fork" for "who"*)
           port got(who: integer);          (*let "who" know*)
           port put(fork: integer);         (*give "fork" back*)
           process waitrep(who: integer);   (*local rep. for "who"*)
               begin  p(myfork);  got(who)
               end waitrep;
           process communicator;
               begin loop
                     region get, put, got;
       get:            begin
                       if fork<>pid then phil[pid mod 5+1].get(who,fork)
                                    else waitrep(who)
                                    end if
                       end get;
       put:            begin
                       if fork<>pid then phil[pid mod 5+1].put(fork)
                                    else v(myfork)
                                    end if
                       end put;
       got:            begin
                       if who<>pid then phil[pid mod 5+1].got(who)
                                   else v(gotone)
                                   end if
                       end got
                     end region
               end loop
           end communicator;
           procedure getforks;  (*philosopher waits for both forks*)
               begin    get(if pid=1 then 1 else pid-1);  p(gotone);
                        get(if pid=1 then 5 else pid);    p(gotone)
               end getforks;
           procedure putforks;  (*give forks back and don't wait*)
               begin   put(pid);
                       put(if pid=1 then 5 else pid-1)
               end putforks;
           begin   communicator
           end at_table;
      begin loop
           (*think*)   getforks;  (*eat *) putforks
           end loop
      end phil
   end diningroom.
```

Fig. 3.

is intended as a general-purpose language for distributed programming.

1) Ada: Ada [19], [20] is a language proposed by the Department of Defense for universal use; therefore, it should be instructive to compare an Ada "task" with a *MOD "process." In *MOD as in Modula, a process cannot be declared inside other processes or procedures. An Ada task "may be declared local to other task bodies, packages, subprograms, and blocks" and a "thread of control" is maintained between a task and its parent. In addition, "any subprogram, module, or block containing task declarations cannot be left until all local tasks have terminated." Furthermore, tasks can contain procedures which can be called by other tasks. Thus, tasks within blocks or procedures must be able to share activation record stacks and tasks which call procedures in other tasks must be able to share the procedure's global variable space. *MOD avoids these addressing and protection problems by allowing shared access only to global variables. *MOD also avoids maintenance of the "thread of control" information. All of these Ada conventions are even more difficult to implement across processors.

It is an error to initiate more than one instance of an Ada task; the user can declare vectors of tasks but each element must be individually addressed. Ada provides ports in the form of "entry" declarations which are restricted to a task body. Therefore, to communicate with a task, the user must name an entry point. If multiple instances of tasks with the same name were allowed, the entry point could not be named without ambiguity. *MOD avoids this restriction by requiring port declarations to occur outside of processes; thus, any port can be serviced by any process. This is not possible in Ada.

The Ada "accept" statement is equivalent to a *MOD "region" but always requires the caller to wait until the body of the "accept" completes execution. Thus, Ada does not have a direct equivalent to *MOD functional ports, functional processes, or multiple processes. Procedures, processes, and ports are referenced identically in *MOD; only procedure and entry references are similar in Ada.

2) Mesa: Mesa [27] includes both processes and ports in a format similar to *MOD. Mesa allows a procedure body to be called as a process by using the "fork/join" statements. The "join" statement allows the returned value to be retrieved after the call. We decided not to use this methodology because it would require changes to all user programs if a handler were changed from a procedure to a process. As pointed out in a recent paper [22], the "join" construct is infrequently

```
process distributed
      <own variables>
      proc name(input params#output params)
         <local variables>
         <statement>
      <initial statement>


processor module *MODdistributed;
      define name, nametype;
      <own variables>
      type nametype= record
                         output params
                         end record;
      process name(input params):nametype;
         <local variables>
         begin <statement>
         end name;
      begin <initial statement>
  end *MODdistributed;
```

Fig. 4.

used compared to the "detached" process option which is similar to the *MOD design. Ports in Mesa were designed to implement coroutines; procedures must have a special "start" phase, be "connect"ed to a port and then "restart"ed. The Mesa port mechanism is so complex because it was designed to set up a coroutine relationship between two or more procedures within the same process. The *MOD port is a more general mechanism which has a variety of uses including connecting processes as coroutines.

3) CSP and PLITS: Hoare's CSP [18] and Feldman's [1], [13] PLITS languages are oriented toward end-user programming on top of an operating system. PLITS, for instance, performs automatic routing and flow control of messages; these would be user-implemented services in *MOD. CSP is strongest in its exploration of nondeterministic programming features while PLITS is more completely specified with respect to distributed programming. Both languages are port oriented. Hoare's processes can be created dynamically as in *MOD; however, the relationship between two communicating processes is symmetrical and requires both of them to name the other. Communication is asymmetrical in *MOD so that in hierarchical systems, handlers can be created without knowing the identities of their callers.

4) CLU: Liskov [24] has recently proposed some distributed computing extensions to CLU [25]. A CLU "guardian" is similar to a *MOD "processor module" but is restricted to ports for communication. There is no equivalent to a "network module" for processor organization. Ports are global to processes as in *MOD and include timeout and error detection notation. The major difference between the two proposals arises because of the integrated definitions of procedures, processes, and ports in *MOD. All of the languages that we have examined, including CLU, have a special syntax for one or more of these constructs; thus, any change to a library program may require changes to all user programs.

IV. Software Testing

In order to test software in the distributed environment, it must be possible to experiment both with software algorithms and hardware organizations. The advent of high-level languages has greatly enhanced algorithm development but the same flexibility is not present for hardware. The virtual machine approach [15] was a step in the right direction but was primarily oriented towards the construction of multiprogrammed, single processor software. The VM environment has been suggested [34] as suitable for the development of network software but the user is still given a bare machine as a starting point.

Our proposal consists of a two-level approach: 1) a VHLN (virtual high-level language network) *MOD environment for network software development and testing on a single host computer (a PDP-11 or VAX in the current implementation effort); and 2) a compiler capable of producing code for a number of different machines. The VHLN system is a runtime package which executes all of the processor modules on a single processor. The package also provides debugging, simulation, and performance analysis aids. It is much more economical to develop software tools for one host development computer than for each target machine. Once a software system has been tested, it can be moved to the network for production use. We have used this methodology to construct operating systems for virtual processors, file systems, and simulations of the Ethernet [26] and DCS [12] networks.

The VHLN system also has some disadvantages. The simulated, multiple processor environment provided by the *MOD test system is unrealistic in the sense that events will not have a real-time correspondence to the performance of systems running on bare machines. However, even this problem can be solved by using the techniques proposed by Canon [4]. As we gain experience with the system, it will be possible to draw more definitive conclusions regarding the ease of moving from a simulated to a real network.

V. The *MOD Kernel

The code generated by the *MOD compiler is independent of its execution environment. For example, we have several bare machine kernels for different PDP-11's, a kernel for simulation, and a kernel which allows *MOD programs to run on UNIX [30]. The bare machine kernels are used for real-time testing, the simulation kernel for performance evaluation, and the UNIX kernel for system development and debugging. Except for simulation statements, the same *MOD program could be executed with any of the kernels. Next, the *MOD bare machine kernel will be described.

The *MOD kernel performs message transmission and synchronization functions only; any routing, scheduling, or flow control operations are the domain of the systems programmer. A process loses control of a hardware processor only by terminating, blocking, lowering its priority, or by receipt of a message for a higher priority process.

The compiler generates a list which details the processes and ports referenced by a processor module together with their processor addresses. In addition, a similar list is created for local ports or processes that have been "export"ed or "define"d. When an external process or port call occurs, the kernel constructs a message from the argument list as follows:

```
var message : record
              arg1  : TYPE1;
                    :
              argN  : TYPEN;
              end record
```

The processor address for the destination is available from the kernel tables to control message transmission. For a functional call, the originating kernel changes the process' status to indicate that it is waiting for a reply message from the target processor. When a reply arrives, its origin is verified against the saved value in the process' control block; the reply is appended to the process' activation record; and the process' status is changed to "ready." It will resume execution when it is the highest priority, "ready" process.

In *MOD, each interrupt or message is sent to either a port or a process. A message to a process creates a new process activation record stack. The new process' priority and start address are taken from the kernel control table. A process switch occurs only if the new process has a higher priority than any of the executing processes. A message to a port is logged if no process is waiting; otherwise, a process switch decision based on priority is made. Port communication only requires a process switch while a process call requires both the creation of an activation record and a process switch. The critical question is how quickly these operations can be performed. Table I lists the number of instructions executed for process/port communication on our PDP-11 standalone and UNIX kernels.

The UNIX kernel copies each process' stack segment from high core to a save area on every process switch. The standalone kernel has less work to do on context switches because there is no copying, although the state vector is more complicated. Also, the initial stack space for new processes is fixed in size which means that the allocate/free operations can be executed in constant time.

VI. SUMMARY

The *MOD system represents an exploration of the design decisions necessary to apply the modular programming philosophy of Wirth to the development of distributed software and to propose an environment conducive to the construction and testing of such systems. This paper would not have been written but for the impetus and inspiration of Brinch Hansen's article [3] on distributed processes.

The current design was developed by experimenting with extensions to our Modula compiler which is written in C [31] and runs on Version 7 UNIX. The compiler generates either PDP-11 or VAX11/780 machine code. A separate *MOD compiler is currently under development.

TABLE I

Operation	Standalone	Unix Kernel
process create(N arguments)	39+7N+A+S	31+2N+A+S
process delete	71+B+S	10+5E+B+S
port call(no arguments)	18+S	14+S
port call(N arguments)	24+7N+S	20+B+A+2N+S
(A) allocate memory	45	20+10C
(B) free memory	5	22+6D
(S) process switch	32	36+B+A+2F+2G

(C) number of free list cells of smaller size
(D) number of free list cells at a smaller address
(E) number of processes in scheduling list
(F) old process' stack size
(G) new process' stack size

REFERENCES

[1] J. E. Ball, G. J. Williams, and J. R. Low, "Preliminary ZENO language description," Univ. Rochester, Rep. TR41, Jan. 1979.

[2] R. M. Balzer, "PORTS–A method for dynamic interprogram communication and job control," in *Proc. AFIPS SJCC Comput. Conf.*, vol. 39, 1971, pp. 485–489.

[3] P. Brinch Hansen, "Distributed processes: A concurrent programming concept," *Commun. Ass. Comput. Mach.*, vol. 11, pp. 934-941, Nov. 1978.

[4] M. D. Canon *et al.*, "A virtual machine emulator for performance evaluation," *Commun. Ass. Comput. Mach.*, vol. 23, pp. 71–80, Feb. 1980.

[5] M. E. Conway, "A multiprocessor system design," in *Proc. AFIPS Fall Joint Comput. Conf.*, vol. 24, 1963, pp. 139–146.

[6] —, "Design of a separable transition-diagram compiler," *Commun. Ass. Comput. Mach.*, vol. 6, pp. 396–408, July 1963.

[7] R. P. Cook, "An introduction to modular programming for Pascal users," Univ. Wisconsin–Madison, Tech. Rep. 372, Nov. 1979.

[8] —, "Data abstraction in *MOD," in preparation.

[9] —, "Schedulers as abstractions–An operating system structuring concept," Univ. Wisconsin–Madison, Tech. Rep. 393, July 1980.

[10] O. J. Dahl *et al.*, "Simula 67 common base language," Norwegian Comput. Center, Oslo, May 1968.

[11] E. W. Dijkstra, "Cooperating sequential processes," in *Programming Languages*, F. Genuys, Ed. New York: Academic, 1968, pp. 43–112.

[12] D. Farber *et al.*, "The distributed computing system," in *Proc. COMPCON 73*, IEEE Comput. Soc., Feb. 1973, pp. 31–34.

[13] J. A. Feldman, "High level programming for distributed computing," *Commun. Ass. Comput. Mach.*, vol. 22, pp. 353–368, June 1979.

[14] C. M. Geschke, J. H. Morris, Jr. and E. H. Satterthwaite, "Early experience with mesa," *Commun. Ass. Comput. Mach.*, vol. 20, pp. 540–553, Aug. 1977.

[15] R. P. Goldberg, "Survey of virtual machine research," *Computer*, vol. 6, pp. 34–44, June 1974.

[16] J. W. Havender, "Avoiding deadlock in multitasking systems," *IBM Syst. J.*, vol. 7, pp. 74–84, 1968.

[17] C. A. R. Hoare, "Monitors: An operating system structuring concept," *Commun. Ass. Comput. Mach.*, vol. 17, pp. 549–557, Oct. 1974.

[18] —, "Communicating sequential processes," *Commun. Ass. Comput. Mach.*, vol. 21, pp. 666–677, Aug. 1978.

[19] Honeywell, Inc. and Cii Honeywell Bull, "Reference manual for the ADA programming language," *SIGPLAN Notices*, vol. 14, part A, June 1979.

[20] —, "Rationale for the design of the ADA programming language," *SIGPLAN Notices*, vol. 14, part B, June 1979.

[21] A. Jones and K. Schwans, "TASK Forces: Distributed software for solving problems of substantial size," in *Proc. 4th Int. Conf. Software Eng.*, SIGSOFT-ACM, Sept. 1979, pp. 315–330.

[22] B. W. Lampson and D. D. Redell, "Experience with processes and monitors in Mesa," *Commun. Ass. Comput. Mach.*, vol. 23, pp. 105–117, Feb. 1980.

[23] B. W. Lampson *et al.*, "Report on the programming language Euclid," *SIGPLAN Notices*, vol. 12, Feb. 1977.
[24] B. Liskov *et al.*, "CLU reference manual," Comput. Structures Group Memo 161, Lab. Comput. Sci., M.I.T., Cambridge, July 1978.
[25] B. Liskov, "Primitives for distributed computing," in *Proc. 7th Symp. Operating Syst. Principles*, Pacific Grove, CA, pp. 33–42, Dec. 1979.
[26] R. Metcalfe and D. Boggs, "Ethernet: Distributed packet switching for local computer networks," *Commun. Ass. Comput. Mach.*, vol. 19, pp. 395–404, July 1976.
[27] J. G. Mitchell, W. Maybury, and R. Sweet, "Mesa language manual," Xerox PARC Tech. Rep. CSL-79-3, Apr. 1979.
[28] D. L. Parnas, "A technique for software module specification with examples," *Commun. Ass. Comput. Mach.*, vol. 15, pp. 330–336, May 1972.
[29] D. L. Parnas and D. L. Siewiorek, "Use of the concept of transparency in the design of hierarchically structured systems," *Commun. Ass. Comput. Mach.*, vol. 18, pp. 401–408, July 1975.
[30] D. M. Ritchie and K. Thompson, "The UNIX time-sharing system," *Commun. Ass. Comput. Mach.*, vol. 17, pp. 365–375, July 1974.
[31] D. M. Ritchie, "C reference manual," Bell Labs., Jan. 1974.
[32] M. Shaw, W. A. Wulf, R. L. London, "Abstraction and verification in Alphard: Defining and specifying iteration and generators," *Commun. Ass. Comput. Mach.*, vol. 20, pp. 553–564, Aug. 1977.
[33] R. W. Watson, *Timesharing System Design Concepts.* New York: McGraw-Hill, 1970.
[34] J. M. Winett, "Virtual machines for developing systems software," in *Proc. IEEE Comput. Soc. Conf.*, Boston, MA, Sept. 1971.
[35] N. Wirth, "Modula: A language for modular multiprogramming," *Software–Practice and Experience*, vol. 7, pp. 3–35, 1977.
[36] —, "The use of modula," *Software–Practice and Experience*, vol. 7, pp. 37–65, 1977.
[37] —, "Design and implementation of modula," *Software–Practice and Experience*, vol. 7, pp. 67–84, 1977.

Part V
Distributed Computer Implementations

THERE is little question that distributed operating systems are in an embryonic state. A tremendous amount of research and experimentation remains to be done before such systems can be considered as completely developed. This part contains papers summarizing several distributed operating systems which have led the way toward such a state of complete development.

THE

Included as the first paper in this section is E.W. Dijkstra's "The Structure of 'THE'—Multiprogramming System." As the title states, the paper describes a multiprogramming, not a distributed, operating system. However, Dijkstra's summary of the system provides several particularly useful insights into general operating system development theory. Of special note are the summaries contained in the article's Appendix.

Carnegie-Mellon Research

Since the early 1970's, some of the premier work on distributed operating systems has been performed by a group of researchers at Carnegie-Mellon University. Mainly working with two distributed computer testbeds,[1] the group has gained a vast amount of experience developing the "StarOS" and "Medusa" distributed operating systems. Four of the group's papers have been reprinted here: "Hydra: The Kernel of Multiprocessor Operating System," "Software Management of Cm*—A Distributed Multiprocessor," "StarOS, a Multiprocessor Operating System for the Support of Task Forces," and "Medusa: An Experiment in Distributed Operating System Structure."

Stonybrook

A short paper summarizing recent research at SUNY, Stony Brook, has been included entitled "An Operating System Kernel for a Hierarchical Multicomputer." The system was developed based on an approach similar to Dijkstra's hierarchical kernel approach. Details are provided on both the features of each level in the hierarchy and the interface between levels.

Honeywell Experimental Distributed Processor (HXDP)

Reprinted here is "The Honeywell Experimental Distributed Processor—An Overview." The paper provides an excellent summary of HXDP and may be sufficient reading for those who do not want to delve into the intricate details of the system's operation. However, the references in the paper provide just those details for those who are interested.

University of Maryland Series/1

Recent research on the Series/1 distributed computer system is summarized in "Experiences with the Series/1 Distributed System."

d-RTOS

The last paper included in this section is "A Distributed Real Time Operating System." This paper describes the components of an operating system developed for a ballistic missile defense system application. The overall content of the paper is excellent, and references are provided for those readers who are interested in obtaining further details on the system.

As an aside, it should be noted that the work summarized in this paper was supported by the Data Processing Directorate of the U.S. Army Ballistic Missile Defense Advanced Technology Center (BMDATC). By funding this and similar excellent projects BMDATC has, over the past decade, been responsible for many of the developments in the areas of distributed computing and distributed operating systems.

[1] "Cm*" and "C.mmp"

The Structure of the "THE"-Multiprogramming System

Edsger W. Dijkstra
Technological University, Eindhoven, The Netherlands

A multiprogramming system is described in which all activities are divided over a number of sequential processes. These sequential processes are placed at various hierarchical levels, in each of which one or more independent abstractions have been implemented. The hierarchical structure proved to be vital for the verification of the logical soundness of the design and the correctness of its implementation.

KEY WORDS AND PHRASES: operating system, multiprogramming system, system hierarchy, system structure, real-time debugging, program verification, synchronizing primitives, cooperating sequential processes, system levels, input-output buffering, multiprogramming, processor sharing, multiprocessing
CR CATEGORIES: 4.30, 4.32

Introduction

In response to a call explicitly asking for papers "on timely research and development efforts," I present a progress report on the multiprogramming effort at the Department of Mathematics at the Technological University in Eindhoven.

Having very limited resources (viz. a group of six people of, on the average, half-time availability) and wishing to contribute to the art of system design—including all the stages of conception, construction, and verification, we were faced with the problem of how to get the necessary experience. To solve this problem we adopted the following three guiding principles:

(1) Select a project as advanced as you can conceive, as ambitious as you can justify, in the hope that routine work can be kept to a minimum; hold out against all pressure to incorporate such system expansions that would only result into a purely quantitative increase of the total amount of work to be done.

(2) Select a machine with sound basic characteristics (e.g. an interrupt system to fall in love with is certainly an inspiring feature); from then on try to keep the specific properties of the configuration for which you are preparing the system out of your considerations as long as possible.

(3) Be aware of the fact that experience does by no means automatically lead to wisdom and understanding; in other words, make a conscious effort to learn as much as possible from your previous experiences.

Presented at an ACM Symposium on Operating System Principles, Gatlinburg, Tennessee, October 1–4, 1967.

Accordingly, I shall try to go beyond just reporting what we have done and how, and I shall try to formulate as well what we have learned.

I should like to end the introduction with two short remarks on working conditions, which I make for the sake of completeness. I shall not stress these points any further.

One remark is that production speed is severely slowed down if one works with half-time people who have other obligations as well. This is at least a factor of four; probably it is worse. The people themselves lose time and energy in switching over; the group as a whole loses decision speed as discussions, when needed, have often to be postponed until all people concerned are available.

The other remark is that the members of the group (mostly mathematicians) have previously enjoyed as good students a university training of five to eight years and are of Master's or Ph.D. level. I mention this explicitly because at least in my country the intellectual level needed for system design is in general grossly underestimated. I am convinced more than ever that this type of work is very difficult, and that every effort to do it with other than the best people is doomed to either failure or moderate success at enormous expense.

The Tool and the Goal

The system has been designed for a Dutch machine, the EL X8 (N.V. Electrologica, Rijswijk (ZH)). Characteristics of our configuration are:

(1) core memory cycle time 2.5μsec, 27 bits; at present 32K;
(2) drum of 512K words, 1024 words per track, rev. time 40msec;
(3) an indirect addressing mechanism very well suited for stack implementation;
(4) a sound system for commanding peripherals and controlling of interrupts;
(5) a potentially great number of low capacity channels; ten of them are used (3 paper tape readers at 1000char/sec; 3 paper tape punches at 150char/sec; 2 teleprinters; a plotter; a line printer);
(6) absence of a number of not unusual, awkward features.

The primary goal of the system is to process smoothly a continuous flow of user programs as a service to the University. A multiprogramming system has been chosen with the following objectives in mind: (1) a reduction of turn-around time for programs of short duration, (2) economic use of peripheral devices, (3) automatic control of backing store to be combined with economic use of the central processor, and (4) the economic feasibility to use the machine for those applications for which only the flexibility of a general purpose computer is needed, but (as a rule) not the capacity nor the processing power.

The system is not intended as a multiaccess system. There is no common data base via which independent users can communicate with each other: they only share the configuration and a procedure library (that includes a translator for ALGOL 60 extended with complex numbers). The system does not cater for user programs written in machine language.

Compared with larger efforts one can state that quantitatively speaking the goals have been set as modest as the equipment and our other resources. Qualitatively speaking, I am afraid, we became more and more immodest as the work progressed.

A Progress Report

We have made some minor mistakes of the usual type (such as paying too much attention to eliminating what was not the real bottleneck) and two major ones.

Our first major mistake was that for too long a time we confined our attention to "a perfect installation"; by the time we considered how to make the best of it, one of the peripherals broke down, we were faced with nasty problems. Taking care of the "pathology" took more energy than we had expected, and some of our troubles were a direct consequence of our earlier ingenuity, i.e. the complexity of the situation into which the system could have maneuvered itself. Had we paid attention to the pathology at an earlier stage of the design, our management rules would certainly have been less refined.

The second major mistake has been that we conceived and programmed the major part of the system without giving more than scanty thought to the problem of debugging it. I must decline all credit for the fact that this mistake had no serious consequences—on the contrary! one might argue as an afterthought.

As captain of the crew I had had extensive experience (dating back to 1958) in making basic software dealing with real-time interrupts, and I knew by bitter experience that as a result of the irreproducibility of the interrupt moments a program error could present itself misleadingly like an occasional machine malfunctioning. As a result I was terribly afraid. Having fears regarding the possibility of debugging, we decided to be as careful as possible and, prevention being better than cure, to try to prevent nasty bugs from entering the construction.

This decision, inspired by fear, is at the bottom of what I regard as the group's main contribution to the art of system design. We have found that it is possible to design a refined multiprogramming system in such a way that its logical soundness can be proved a priori and its implementation can admit exhaustive testing. The only errors that showed up during testing were trivial coding errors (occurring with a density of one error per 500 instructions), each of them located within 10 minutes (classical) inspection by the machine and each of them correspondingly easy to remedy. At the time this was written the testing had not yet been completed, but the resulting system is guaranteed to be flawless. When the system is delivered we shall not live in the perpetual fear that a system derailment may still occur in an unlikely situation, such as might result from an unhappy "coincidence" of two or more critical occurrences, for we shall have proved the correctness of the system with a rigor and explicitness that is unusual for the great majority of mathematical proofs.

A Survey of the System Structure

Storage Allocation. In the classical von Neumann machine, information is identified by the address of the memory location containing the information. When we started to think about the automatic control of secondary storage we were familiar with a system (viz. GIER ALGOL) in which all information was identified by its drum address (as in the classical von Neumann machine) and in which the function of the core memory was nothing more than to make the information "page-wise" accessible.

We have followed another approach and, as it turned out, to great advantage. In our terminology we made a strict distinction between memory units (we called them "pages" and had "core pages" and "drum pages") and corresponding information units (for lack of a better word we called them "segments"), a segment just fitting in a page. For segments we created a completely independent identification mechanism in which the number of possible segment identifiers is much larger than the total number of pages in primary and secondary store. The segment identifier gives fast access to a so-called "segment variable" in core whose value denotes whether the segment is still empty or not, and if not empty, in which page (or pages) it can be found.

As a consequence of this approach, if a segment of information, residing in a core page, has to be dumped onto the drum in order to make the core page available for other use, there is no need to return the segment to the same drum page from which it originally came. In fact, this freedom is exploited: among the free drum pages the one with minimum latency time is selected.

A next consequence is the total absence of a drum allocation problem: there is not the slightest reason why, say, a program should occupy consecutive drum pages. In a multiprogramming environment this is very convenient.

Processor Allocation. We have given full recognition to the fact that in a single sequential process (such as can be performed by a sequential automaton) only the time succession of the various states has a logical meaning, but not the actual speed with which the sequential process is performed. Therefore we have arranged the whole system as a society of sequential processes, progressing with undefined speed ratios. To each user program accepted by the system corresponds a sequential process, to each input peripheral corresponds a sequential process (buffering input streams in synchronism with the execution of the input commands), to each output peripheral corresponds a sequential process (unbuffering output streams in synchronism with the execution of the output commands); furthermore, we have the "segment controller" associated with the drum and the "message interpreter" associated with the console keyboard.

This enabled us to design the whole system in terms of these abstract "sequential processes." Their harmonious cooperation is regulated by means of explicit mutual synchronization statements. On the one hand, this explicit mutual synchronization is necessary, as we do not make any assumption about speed ratios; on the other hand, this mutual synchronization is possible because "delaying the progress of a process temporarily" can never be harmful to the interior logic of the process delayed. The fundamental consequence of this approach—viz. the explicit mutual synchronization—is that the harmonious cooperation of a set of such sequential processes can be established by discrete reasoning; as a further consequence the whole harmonious society of cooperating sequential processes is independent of the actual number of processors available to carry out these processes, provided the processors available can switch from process to process.

System Hierarchy. The total system admits a strict hierarchical structure.

At level 0 we find the responsibility for processor allocation to one of the processes whose dynamic progress is logically permissible (i.e. in view of the explicit mutual synchronization). At this level the interrupt of the real-time clock is processed and introduced to prevent any process to monopolize processing power. At this level a priority rule is incorporated to achieve quick response of the system where this is needed. Our first abstraction has been achieved; above level 0 the number of processors actually shared is no longer relevant. At higher levels we find the activity of the different sequential processes, the actual processor that had lost its identity having disappeared from the picture.

At level 1 we have the so-called "segment controller," a sequential process synchronized with respect to the drum interrupt and the sequential processes on higher levels. At level 1 we find the responsibility to cater to the bookkeeping resulting from the automatic backing store. At this level our next abstraction has been achieved; at all higher levels identification of information takes place in terms of segments, the actual storage pages that had lost their identity having disappeared from the picture.

At level 2 we find the "message interpreter" taking care of the allocation of the console keyboard via which conversations between the operator and any of the higher level processes can be carried out. The message interpreter works in close synchronism with the operator. When the operator presses a key, a character is sent to the machine together with an interrupt signal to announce the next keyboard character, whereas the actual printing is done through an output command generated by the machine under control of the message interpreter. (As far as the hardware is concerned the console teleprinter is regarded as two independent peripherals: an input keyboard and an output printer.) If one of the processes opens a conversation, it identifies itself in the opening sentence of the conversation for the benefit of the operator. If, however, the operator opens a conversation, he must identify the process he is addressing, in the opening sentence of the conversation, i.e. this opening sentence must be interpreted before it is known to which of the processes the conversation is addressed! Here lies the logical reason for the introduction of a separate sequential process for the console teleprinter, a reason that is reflected in its name, "message interpreter."

Above level 2 it is as if each process had its private conversational console. The fact that they share the same physical console is translated into a resource restriction of the form "only one conversation at a time," a restriction that is satisfied via mutual synchronization. At this level the next abstraction has been implemented; at higher levels the actual console teleprinter loses its identity. (If the message interpreter had not been on a higher level than the segment controller, then the only way to implement it would have been to make a permanent reservation in core for it; as the conversational vocabulary might become large (as soon as our operators wish to be addressed in fancy messages), this would result in too heavy a permanent demand upon core storage. Therefore, the vocabulary in which the messages are expressed is stored on segments, i.e. as information units that can reside on the drum as well. For this reason the message interpreter is one level higher than the segment controller.)

At level 3 we find the sequential processes associated with buffering of input streams and unbuffering of output streams. At this level the next abstraction is effected, viz. the abstraction of the actual peripherals used that are allocated at this level to the "logical communication units" in terms of which are worked in the still higher levels. The sequential processes associated with the peripherals are of a level above the message interpreter, because they must be able to converse with the operator (e.g. in the case of detected malfunctioning). The limited number of peripherals again acts as a resource restriction for the processes at higher levels to be satisfied by mutual synchronization between them.

At level 4 we find the independent-user programs and at level 5 the operator (not implemented by us).

The system structure has been described at length in order to make the next section intelligible.

Design Experience

The conception stage took a long time. During that period of time the concepts have been born in terms of which we sketched the system in the previous section. Furthermore, we learned the art of reasoning by which we could deduce from our requirements the way in which the processes should influence each other by their mutual synchronization so that these requirements would be met. (The requirements being that no information can be used before it has been produced, that no peripheral can be set to two tasks simultaneously, etc.). Finally we learned the art of reasoning by which we could prove that the society composed of processes thus mutually synchronized by each other would indeed in its time behavior satisfy all requirements.

The construction stage has been rather traditional, perhaps even old-fashioned, that is, plain machine code. Reprogramming on account of a change of specifications has been rare, a circumstance that must have contributed greatly to the feasibility of the "steam method." That the first two stages took more time than planned was somewhat compensated by a delay in the delivery of the machine.

In the verification stage we had the machine, during short shots, completely at our disposal; these were shots during which we worked with a virgin machine without any software aids for debugging. Starting at level 0 the system was tested, each time adding (a portion of) the next level only after the previous level had been thoroughly tested. Each test shot itself contained, on top of the (partial) system to be tested, a number of testing processes with a double function. First, they had to force the system into all different relevant states; second, they had to verify that the system continued to react according to specification.

I shall not deny that the construction of these testing programs has been a major intellectual effort: to convince oneself that one has not overlooked "a relevant state" and to convince oneself that the testing programs generate them all is no simple matter. The encouraging thing is that (as far as we know!) it could be done.

This fact was one of the happy consequences of the hierarchical structure.

Testing level 0 (the real-time clock and processor allocation) implied a number of testing sequential processes on top of it, inspecting together that under all circumstances processor time was divided among them according to the rules. This being established, sequential processes as such were implemented.

Testing the segment controller at level 1 meant that all "relevant states" could be formulated in terms of sequential processes making (in various combinations) demands on core pages, situations that could be provoked by explicit synchronization among the testing programs. At this stage the existence of the real-time clock—although interrupting all the time—was so immaterial that one of the testers indeed forgot its existence!

By that time we had implemented the correct reaction upon the (mutually unsynchronized) interrupts from the real-time clock and the drum. If we had not introduced the separate levels 0 and 1, and if we had not created a terminology (viz. that of the rather abstract sequential processes) in which the existence of the clock interrupt could be discarded, but had instead tried in a nonhierarchical construction, to make the central processor react directly upon any weird time succession of these two interrupts, the number of "relevant states" would have exploded to such a height that exhaustive testing would have been an illusion. (Apart from that it is doubtful whether we would have had the means to generate them all, drum and clock speed being outside our control.)

For the sake of completeness I must mention a further happy consequence. As stated before, above level 1, core and drum pages have lost their identity, and buffering of input and output streams (at level 3) therefore occurs in terms of segments. While testing at level 2 or 3 the drum channel hardware broke down for some time, but testing proceeded by restricting the number of segments to the number that could be held in core. If building up the line printer output streams had been implemented as "dumping onto the drum" and the actual printing as "printing from the drum," this advantage would have been denied to us.

Conclusion

As far as program verification is concerned I present nothing essentially new. In testing a general purpose object (be it a piece of hardware, a program, a machine, or a system), one cannot subject it to all possible cases: for a computer this would imply that one feeds it with all possible programs! Therefore one must test it with a set of relevant test cases. What is, or is not, relevant cannot be decided as long as one regards the mechanism as a black box; in other words, the decision has to be based upon the internal structure of the mechanism to be tested. It seems to be the designer's responsibility to construct his mechanism in such a way—i.e. so effectively structured—that at each stage of the testing procedure the number of relevant test cases will be so small that he can try them all and that what is being tested will be so perspicuous that he will not have overlooked any situation. I have presented a survey of our system because I think it a nice example of the form that such a structure might take.

In my experience, I am sorry to say, industrial software makers tend to react to the system with mixed feelings. On the one hand, they are inclined to think that we have done a kind of model job; on the other hand, they express doubts whether the techniques used are applicable outside the sheltered atmosphere of a University and express the opinion that we were successful only because of the modest scope of the whole project. It is not my intention to underestimate the organizing ability needed to handle a much bigger job, with a lot more people, but I should like to venture the opinion that the larger the project, the more essential the structuring! A hierarchy of five logical levels might then very well turn out to be of modest depth, especially when one designs the system more consciously than we have done, with the aim that the software can be smoothly adapted to (perhaps drastic) configuration expansions.

Acknowledgments. I express my indebtedness to my five collaborators, C. Bron, A. N. Habermann, F. J. A. Hendriks, C. Ligtmans, and P. A. Voorhoeve. They have contributed to all stages of the design, and together we learned the art of reasoning needed. The construction and verification was entirely their effort; if my dreams have come true, it is due to their faith, their talents, and their persistent loyalty to the whole project.

Finally I should like to thank the members of the program committee, who asked for more information on the synchronizing primitives and some justification of my claim to be able to prove logical soundness a priori. In answer to this request an appendix has been added, which I hope will give the desired information and justification.

APPENDIX

Synchronizing Primitives

Explicit mutual synchronization of parallel sequential processes is implemented via so-called "semaphores." They are special purpose integer variables allocated in the universe in which the processes are embedded; they are initialized (with the value 0 or 1) before the parallel processes themselves are started. After this initialization the parallel processes will access the semaphores only via two very specific operations, the so-called synchronizing primitives. For historical reasons they are called the *P*-operation and the *V*-operation.

A process, "*Q*" say, that performs the operation "*P* (sem)" decreases the value of the semaphore called "sem" by 1. If the resulting value of the semaphore concerned is nonnegative, process *Q* can continue with the execution of its next statement; if, however, the resulting value is negative, process *Q* is stopped and booked on a waiting list associated with the semaphore concerned. Until further notice (i.e. a *V*-operation on this very same semaphore), dynamic progress of process *Q* is not logically permissible and no processor will be allocated to it (see above "System Hierarchy," at level 0).

A process, "*R*" say, that performs the operation "*V* (sem)" increases the value of the semaphore called "sem" by 1. If the resulting value of the semaphore concerned is positive, the *V*-operation in question has no further effect; if, however, the resulting value of the semaphore concerned is nonpositive, one of the processes booked on its waiting list is removed from this waiting list, i.e. its dynamic progress is again logically permissible and in due time a processor will be allocated to it (again, see above "System Hierarchy," at level 0).

Corollary 1. *If a semaphore value is nonpositive its absolute value equals the number of processes booked on its waiting list.*

Corollary 2. *The P-operation represents the potential delay, the complementary V-operation represents the removal of a barrier.*

Note 1. *P*- and *V*-operations are "indivisible actions"; i.e. if they occur "simultaneously" in parallel processes they are noninterfering in the sense that they can be regarded as being performed one after the other.

Note 2. If the semaphore value resulting from a *V*-operation is negative, its waiting list originally contained more than one process. It is undefined—i.e. logically immaterial—which of the waiting processes is then removed from the waiting list.

Note 3. A consequence of the mechanisms described above is that a process whose dynamic progress is permissible can only loose this status by actually progressing, i.e. by performance of a *P*-operation on a semaphore with a value that is initially nonpositive.

During system conception it transpired that we used the semaphores in two completely different ways. The difference is so marked that, looking back, one wonders whether it was really fair to present the two ways as uses of the very same primitives. On the one hand, we have the semaphores used for mutual exclusion, on the other hand, the private semaphores.

Mutual Exclusion

In the following program we indicate two parallel, cyclic processes (between the brackets **"parbegin"** and **"parend"**) that come into action after the surrounding universe has been introduced and initialized.

```
begin semaphore mutex; mutex := 1;
 parbegin
    begin L1: P(mutex); critical section 1; V (mutex);
      remainder of cycle 1; go to L1
    end;
    begin L2: P mutex); critical section 2; V (mutex);
      remainder of cycle 2; go to L2
    end
 parend
end
```

As a result of the *P*- and *V*-operations on "mutex" the actions, marked as "critical sections" exclude each other mutually in time; the scheme given allows straightforward extension to more than two parallel processes, the maximum value of mutex equals 1, the minimum value equals $-(n-1)$ if we have n parallel processes.

Critical sections are used always, and only for the purpose of unambiguous inspection and modification of the state variables (allocated in the surrounding universe) that describe the current state of the system (as far as needed for the regulation of the harmonious cooperation between the various processes).

Private Semaphores

Each sequential process has associated with it a number of private semaphores and no other process will ever perform a *P*-operation on them. The universe initializes them with the value equal to 0, their maximum value equals 1, and their minimum value equals -1.

Whenever a process reaches a stage where the permission for dynamic progress depends on current values of state variables, it follows the pattern:

P(mutex);
"inspection and modification of state variables including a conditional *V*(private semaphore)";
V(mutex);
P(private semaphore).

If the inspection learns that the process in question should continue, it performs the operation "*V* (private semaphore)"—the semaphore value then changes from 0 to 1—otherwise, this *V*-operation is skipped, leaving to the other processes the obligation to perform this *V*-operation at a suitable moment. The absence or presence of this obligation is reflected in the final values of the state variables upon leaving the critical section.

Whenever a process reaches a stage where as a result of its progress possibly one (or more) blocked processes should now get permission to continue, it follows the pattern:

P(mutex);
"modification and inspection of state variables including zero or more *V*-operations on private semaphores of other processes";
V(mutex).

By the introduction of suitable state variables and appropriate programming of the critical sections any strategy assigning peripherals, buffer areas, etc. can be implemented.

The amount of coding and reasoning can be greatly reduced by the observation that in the two complementary critical sections sketched above the same inspection can be performed by the introduction of the notion of "an unstable situation," such as a free reader and a process needing a reader. Whenever an unstable situation emerges it is removed (including one or more *V*-operations on private semaphores) in the very same critical section in which it has been created.

Proving the Harmonious Cooperation

The sequential processes in the system can all be regarded as cyclic processes in which a certain neutral point can be marked, the so-called "homing position," in which all processes are when the system is at rest.

When a cyclic process leaves its homing position "it accepts a task"; when the task has been performed and not earlier, the process returns to its homing position. Each cyclic process has a specific task processing power (e.g. the execution of a user program or unbuffering a portion of printer output, etc.).

The harmonious cooperation is mainly proved in roughly three stages.

(1) It is proved that although a process performing a task may in so doing generate a finite number of tasks for other processes, a single initial task cannot give rise to an infinite number of task generations. The proof is simple as processes can only generate tasks for processes at lower levels of the hierarchy so that circularity is excluded. (If a process needing a segment from the drum has generated a task for the segment controller, special precautions have been taken to ensure that the segment asked for remains in core at least until the requesting process has effectively accessed the segment concerned. Without this precaution finite tasks could be forced to generate an infinite number of tasks for the segment controller, and the system could get stuck in an unproductive page flutter.)

(2) It is proved that it is impossible that all processes have returned to their homing position while somewhere in the system there is still pending a generated but unaccepted task. (This is proved via instability of the situation just described.)

(3) It is proved that after the acceptance of an initial task all processes eventually will be (again) in their homing position. Each process blocked in the course of task execution relies on the other processes for removal of the barrier. Essentially, the proof in question is a demonstration of the absence of "circular waits": process *P* waiting for process *Q* waiting for process *R* waiting for process *P*. (Our usual term for the circular wait is "the Deadly Embrace.") In a more general society than our system this proof turned out to be a proof by induction (on the level of hierarchy, starting at the lowest level), as A. N. Habermann has shown in his doctoral thesis.

Operating Systems — C. Weissman, Editor

HYDRA: The Kernel of a Multiprocessor Operating System

W. Wulf, E. Cohen, W. Corwin, A. Jones, R. Levin, C. Pierson, and F. Pollack
Carnegie-Mellon University

This paper describes the design philosophy of HYDRA—the kernel of an operating system for C.mmp, the Carnegie-Mellon Multi-Mini-Processor. This philosophy is realized through the introduction of a generalized notion of "resource," both physical and virtual, called an "object." Mechanisms are presented for dealing with objects, including the creation of new types, specification of new operations applicable to a given type, sharing, and protection of any reference to a given object against improper application of any of the operations defined with respect to that type of object. The mechanisms provide a coherent basis for extension of the system in two directions: the introduction of new facilities, and the creation of highly secure systems.

Key Words and Phrases: operating system, kernel, nucleus, protection, security

CR Categories: 4.3, 6.2

This work was supported by the Advanced Research Projects Agency of the Office of the Secretary of Defense (F44620-70-C-0107) and is monitored by the Air Force Office of Scientific Research
Authors' address: Department of Computer Science, Carnegie-Mellon University, Schenley Park, Pittsburgh, PA 15213.

Introduction

The HYDRA system is the "kernel" base for a collection of operating systems designed to exploit and explore the potential inherent in a multiprocessor computer system. Since the field of parallel processing in general, and multiprocessing in particular, is not current art, the design of HYDRA has a dual goal imposed upon it: (1) to provide, as any operating system must, an environment for effective utilization of the hardware resources, and (2) to facilitate the construction of such environments. In the latter case the goal is to provide a meta-environment which can serve as the host for exploration of the space of user-visible operating environments.

The particular hardware on which HYDRA has been implemented is C.mmp, a multiprocessor constructed at Carnegie-Mellon University. Although the details of the design of C.mmp are not essential to an understanding of the material which follows, the following brief description has been included to help set the context (a more detailed description may be found in [9]). C.mmp permits the connection of 16 processors to 32 million bytes of shared primary memory through a cross-bar switch. The processors are any of the various models of PDP-11[1] minicomputers. Each processor is actually an independent computer system with a small amount of private memory, secondary memories, I/O devices, etc. Processors may interrupt each other at any of four priority levels; a central clock serves for unique-name generation (see below) and also broadcasts a central time base to all processors. Relocation hardware on each processor's bus provides mapping of virtual addresses on that bus to physical addresses in shared primary memory.

Design Philosophy

The design philosophy of HYDRA evolved from both the environment in which the system was to function and a set of principles held by its designers. The central goals of the system together with the attitudes expressed below suggest that, at the heart of the system, one should build a collection of facilities of "universal applicability" and "absolute reliability"—a set of mechanisms from which an arbitrary set of operating system facilities and policies can be conveniently, flexibly, efficiently, and reliably constructed. Moreover, lest the flexibility be constrained at any instant, it should be possible for an arbitrary number of systems created from these facilities to co-exist simultaneously. The collection of such basic facilities has been called the *kernel* or *nucleus* [1] of an operating system. The more specific considerations are listed below.

1. *Multiprocessor environment.* Although multiprocessors have been discussed for well over a decade and a

[1] Manufactured by Digital Equipment Corporation.

Reprinted with permission from *Commun. Ass. Comput. Mach.*, vol. 17, pp. 337–345, June 1974.

few have been built, both the potentials and problems of these systems are dimly perceived. The design of HYDRA was constrained to be sufficiently conservative to insure its construction and utility in a reasonable time frame, yet flexible enough to permit experimental exploration within the design space bounded by its hardware capabilities.

2. *Separation of mechanism and policy*. Among the major causes of our inability to experiment with, and adapt, existing operating systems is their failure to properly separate mechanisms from policies. (Hansen [1] has presented cogent arguments for this separation.) Such separation contributes to the flexibility of the system, for it leaves the complex decisions in the hands of the person who should make them—the higher-level system designer.

3. *Integration of the design with implementation methodology*. It has been observed that the structure of extant operating systems bears a remarkable resemblance to that of the organization which created them. This observation is one of a set which asserts the (practical) impossibility of separating the design from the methodology to be used in implementing the design. The authors' predisposition for implementation methodology is a hybrid of structured programming as advocated by Dijkstra and others [2] and the modularization philosophy of Parnas [8].

4. *Rejection of strict hierarchical layering*. The notion of a strict hierarchically layered system has become popular since first described by Dijkstra for the THE system [3]. While we believe that the system as viewed by any single user should be hierarchically structured, we reject the notion as a global design criterion. We believe that if the entire system is so structured, the design will severely limit the flexibility available to the high-level user and will strangle experimentation; in particular, there is no reason to believe that the same hierarchical relation should exist for control as for resource allocation, or as for protection, etc.

5. *Protection*. Flexibility and protection are closely related, but not inversely proportional. We believe that protection is not merely a restrictive device imposed by "the system" to insure the integrity of user operations, but is a key tool in the proper design of operating systems. It is essential for protection to exist in a uniform manner through the system, and not to be applied only to specific entities (e.g. files). The idea of capabilities (in the sense of Dennis [5]) is most important in the HYDRA design; the kernel provides a protection facility for all entities in the system. This protection includes not only the traditional read, write, execute capabilities, but arbitrary protection conditions whose meaning is determined by higher-level software.

6. *Reliability*. The existence of multiple copies of most critical hardware resources in C.mmp suggests the possibility of highly reliable operation. Our desire is to provide commensurate reliability in the software. Reliability not only requires that the system be correct, but that it be able to detect and recover from errors that do exist—as the result of hardware malfunction, for example.

Defining a kernel with all the attributes given above is difficult, and perhaps impractical at the current state of the art. It is, nevertheless, the approach taken in the HYDRA system. Although we make no claim either that the set of facilities provided by the HYDRA kernel is minimal (the most primitive "adequate" set) or that it is maximally desirable, we do believe the set provides primitives which are both necessary and adequate for the construction of a large and interesting class of operating environments. It is our view that the set of functions provided by HYDRA will enable the user of C.mmp to create his own operating environment without being confined to predetermined command and file systems, execution scenarios, resource allocation policies, etc.

Given the general decision to adopt the "kernel system" approach, the question remains as to what belongs in a kernel and, perhaps more important, what does not. Nonspecific answers to this question are implicit in the attitudes enumerated earlier; e.g. a set of mechanisms may be appropriate in a kernel, but policy decisions certainly are not. For other, more specific, answers we must step outside these attitudes alone and consider the nature of the entity to be built using the facilities of a kernel.

If a kernel is to provide facilities for building an operating system and we wish to know what these facilities should be, then it is relevant to ask what an operating system *is* or *does*. Two views are commonly held: (1) an operating system defines an "abstract machine" by providing facilities, or resources, which are more convenient than those provided by the "bare" hardware; and (2) an operating system allocates (hardware) resources in such a way as to most effectively utilize them. Of course these views are, respectively, the bird's-eye and worm's eye views of what is a single entity with multiple goals. Nevertheless, the important observation for our purposes is the emphasis placed, in both views, on the central role of *resources*—both physical and abstract.

The mechanisms provided by the HYDRA kernel are all intended to support the abstracted notion of a resource (incarnations of a resource are called *objects*). These mechanisms provide for the creation and representation of new *types* of resources, as well as operations defined on them, protected access to instances of one or more resources within controlled execution domains, and controlled passing of both control and resources between execution domains. The key aspects of these facilities are the generalized notion of resource, the definition of an execution domain, and the protection mechanism which allows or prevents access to resources within a domain. The remainder of this paper focuses on these issues, thus deemphasizing several of the other issues raised earlier.

Overview of the HYDRA Environment

Before proceeding to a detailed description of the mechanisms, it will be convenient to present a somewhat incomplete and simplistic view of the execution environment created by the HYDRA kernel. The material presented in this section will be elaborated further in the following sections; however, the overview will attempt to provide the context necessary to understand the more detailed information.

In order to understand the execution environment which the kernel provides, one must clearly understand the interrelationships of three object types: *procedure*, *LNS*, and *process*. These primitive objects are provided by the kernel specifically for the purpose of creating and manipulating an execution environment.

The procedure object is simply an abstraction of the intuitive notion of procedure or subroutine;[2] that is, a procedure has some "code" and some "data" associated with it, it may accept parameters, and it may return values. HYDRA procedures go beyond this simple model by including protection facilities, as we shall see shortly. The act of creating a procedure object is analogous to the task of writing an Algol procedure; one produces a body of code, associates the code with a name, declares the data which the code requires, and specifies the nature of the parameters and return values which are involved. In more abstract terms, one creates a sequence of instructions and describes the environment in which they will ultimately execute; in HYDRA this abstraction is made precise. Let us consider the environment description first.

A procedure object contains a list of references to other objects which must be accessed during the execution of the procedure's code. This is, in fact, a list of capabilities [7] and, therefore, defines not only which objects the procedure may reference, but also what actions it may perform on those objects. The capabilities which a procedure requires may be divided into two groups: those which are caller independent and those which are caller dependent. These groups naturally correspond to those objects which the procedure always accesses (at least potentially) and those objects which are considered parameters. Obviously, the former of these groups can be precisely specified at the time the procedure is created, while the latter can only be characterized since the actual objects passed as parameters are unknown until execution time. Thus, the environment defined by a procedure object contains some "holes" or "parameter positions" which are only partially specified at creation time. These holes are filled in for each execution of the procedure, using capabilities provided by the caller. We will return to a discussion of the mechanism by which a procedure characterizes its parameters, but first we must examine the LNS.

A *procedure* is a static entity; an LNS (local name space) is the record of the execution environment of a procedure when that procedure is invoked (called). There is a unique LNS for each invocation, which disappears after the procedure terminates. The LNS for a particular invocation is the result of combining the caller-independent capabilities (listed in the procedure object) with caller-dependent actual parameters (only characterized in the procedure object) to form a single list of capabilities. The LNS defines the totality of capabilities available to a procedure during the execution resulting from a particular invocation. Note that the LNS, while heavily dependent upon the corresponding procedure for its initialization, is a wholly independent object thereafter, and alterations of the LNS do not affect the procedure object; this implies, among other things, that procedures are reentrant and potentially recursive.

Up to this point the term "capability" has been used in a somewhat loose and intuitive sense; subsequently it will be used in a technical sense. A *capability* consists of a reference to an object together with a collection of "access rights" to that object. Possession of a capability is taken as prima facie evidence that the possessor may access the object in the ways, and in *only* the ways, described by the capability. Capabilities themselves are manipulated only by the kernel; hence it is impossible to "forge" a capability.

A procedure object may contain *templates* in addition to the usual collection of caller-independent capabilities. *Templates* characterize the actual parameters expected by the procedure. When the procedure is called, the slots in the LNS which correspond to parameter templates in the procedure object are filled with "normal" capabilities derived from the actual parameters supplied by the caller. This "derivation" is, in fact, the heart of the protection-checking mechanism, and the template defines the checking to be performed. If the caller's rights are adequate, a capability is constructed in the (new) LNS which references the object passed by the caller and which contains rights formed by merging the caller's rights with the rights specified in the template. This implies that a callee may have greater freedom to operate on an object than the caller who passed it as a parameter, but the caller can in no way obtain that freedom for himself. We shall see that this potential expansion of rights across environment domains is a key factor in achieving the flexibility goals of the kernel and in allowing us to reject enforced hierarchical structures without introducing chaos.

Before proceeding, let us review the major actions of the CALL mechanism. An executing body of code first notifies the kernel that it wishes to call a procedure. The kernel examines the actual parameter capabilities supplied by the caller and determines whether all pro-

[2] It should be noted however, that the cost of entering a HYDRA procedure is considerably greater than, say, a Fortran subroutine. We do not expect that simple subroutines, such as SIN, would use the HYDRA mechanism until better hardware is provided. The reader should visualize a procedure as replacing relatively large code units and/or at points where protection environments must change.

tection requirements are met. If so, the kernel creates a new LNS which defines the new environment; the caller's LNS is superceded by this new LNS for the duration of the called procedure's execution. The body of code associated with the callee receives control from the kernel and begins executing. When it completes its function, it will return control to its caller by way of the kernel. The kernel will delete the callee's LNS and restore that of the caller, thus returning to the previous environment.

Up to this point, nothing we have described suggests any exploitation of the parallel processing capabilities of C.mmp. The actions involved in calling and returning from procedures are strictly sequential in nature, being in essence formalizations of traditional subroutine behavior. We come now to the unit of asynchronous processing in HYDRA—the *process*. A process in the technical sense defined by HYDRA corresponds closely to one's intuitive notion of a process. Viewed from the outside, it is the smallest entity which can be independently scheduled for execution. Viewed from the inside, it constitutes a precise record of the changes of environment induced by a sequence of calls. In other words, a process is a stack of LNS's which represents the cumulative state of a single sequential task. HYDRA implements interprocess communication and synchronization by providing elementary message buffering primitives and Dijkstra-style semaphore operations. These facilities have been treated in [4] and elsewhere and will not be discussed here.

The Protection Mechanism

The protection mechanism is at the heart of the HYDRA design. In describing the mechanism it is important at the outset to distinguish between *protection* and *security* and to determine what is to be protected and against what.

In our view, protection is a mechanism; security is a policy. A system utilizing such a mechanism may be more or less secure depending upon policies governing the use of the mechanism (for example, passwords and the like are policy issues) and upon the reliability of the programs which manipulate the protected entities. Thus the design goal of the HYDRA protection mechanism is to provide a set of concepts and facilities on which a highly secure system may be built, but *not* to inherently provide that security. A particular consequence of this philosophy has been to discard the notion of "ownership." While ownership is a useful, perhaps even an important, concept for certain "security" strategies, to include the concept at the most primitive levels would be to exclude the construction of certain other classes of truly secure systems.

Our rejection of hierarchical system structures, and especially ones which employ a single hierarchical relation for all aspects of system interaction, is also, in part, a consequence of the distinction between protection and security. A failure to distinguish these issues coupled with a strict hierarchical structure leads inevitably to a succession of increasingly privileged system components, and ultimately to a "most privileged" one, which gain their privilege exclusively by virtue of their position in the hierarchy. Technologists like hierarchical structures—they are elegant; but experience from the real world shows they are not viable security structures. The problem, then, which HYDRA attempts to face squarely, is to maintain order in a nonhierarchical environment.

The obvious candidate for (the unit of) protection is the *object* since this is the abstracted notion of an arbitrary resource. Similarly, the HYDRA *procedure* is considered to be the abstraction of an operation. Thus HYDRA provides a protection mechanism for the application of operations (*procedures*) to instances of resources (*objects*). All of the familiar security for files (e.g. read, write, delete), memory (e.g. read, write, execute), etc., can be conveniently modeled in this way. In addition a large additional class of secure systems can be built.

Everything of interest in the HYDRA view is the abstracted notion of a resource, called an *object*, or a reference to an object, called a *capability*. Each object has a *unique name*, a *type part*, and a *representation* (consisting of a *capability part*, and a *data part*).

The unique name of an object distinguishes the object not only from all other extant objects, but from all objects which have existed or will exist. Knowledge of the unique name of an object does *not* grant access to the object since objects may only be referenced through capabilities (which are not manipulable except by the kernel).

The type part of an object serves to identify the object with that class of objects whose type parts have an identical value. The type part contains, in fact, the unique name of a distinguished object which serves as the representative of such a class. (By convention the type of these representatives is the name of a special distinguished object whose name is TYPE and which names itself in its type field.) Since there is a potentially infinite supply of unique names, there is a potentially infinite number of object types as well. A new class of objects may be created simply by creating a single object to serve as its distinguished representative.

Objects become inaccessible only when there are no references to them. It is possible to generate self-referential structures; and although a general garbage-collection deletion mechanism is required, these structures are rare. Hence a reference count is maintained in each object, and objects are deleted[3] when this count becomes zero.

The representation portion of an object contains whatever information is relevant to the representation of the resource which the object denotes. This information may be of two types: data (which is normally un-

[3] The deletion mechanism is not essential to an understanding of HYDRA, therefore this function of the kernel will not be discussed further.

interpreted by the kernel), and references to other objects. These two kinds of information are stored in the *data* and *capability* parts of the object respectively. Given the appropriate access rights, a program may manipulate the data part of an object freely. Even with the most liberal access rights, however, the capability part of an object may be manipulated only by invocation of kernel functions.

The fact that every object in HYDRA may contain capabilities referencing other objects is a significant departure from other capability-based systems [5, 7], and is a major factor in satisfying the flexibility goal of the design. It permits new object types to be represented wholly or partially in terms of existing types while preserving the protection philosophy through each level of representation. An understanding of the use of the capability-part of an object to represent new objects is essential to an understanding of the HYDRA philosophy; we will return to it after discussing capabilities, procedures, and the CALL mechanism further.

As mentioned several times previously, in addition to supporting objects, HYDRA supports *references to objects* (called *capabilities*). Capabilities are, however, more than simple pointers. Together with the actual/formal parameter "derivation" of the CALL mechanism (for crossing execution domains), capabilities are the key to the protection mechanism. As such, capabilities may only exist in the capability part of an object and may be directly manipulated only by the kernel.

Each capability includes information detailing the operations which may be performed on the object referenced by the capability. Whenever an operation is attempted on an object, the requestor supplies a capability referencing that object. The kernel examines the rights list and prevents the operation when a protection failure occurs (i.e. when the requestor does not have the appropriate rights). It is important to understand that the rights checking operation does not require *interpretation* of the list; the kernel can determine when a protection failure has occurred without assigning meaning to the individual rights bits.

Not all rights are type-dependent; there exist operations worthy of protection which are well-defined for any object. These are precisely the operations which the kernel provides for controlled manipulation of objects and capabilities. Accordingly, we partition the rights list of a capability into two mutually exclusive sets—the type-independent rights (called *kernel rights*), and the type-dependent rights (called *auxiliary rights*). A "right" in either set grants permission to pass the capability as a parameter to any procedure in a particular class. The kernel defines these classes for type-independent rights, and the creator of the type defines them for auxiliary rights.

The notions of *object* and *capability* now permit us to be more specific about one of the object types mentioned earlier—the LNS. At any instant, the execution environment (domain) of a program is defined by an LNS object associated with it. The capability part of the LNS contains references to objects which may be accessed by that program at that instant. (In addition, of course, the program may be able to access objects referenced by the objects referenced in its LNS, and so on.) The LNS provides a mapping function between local names in a program (i.e. small integers naming "slots" in the LNS) and globally unique objects. More than this, however, the rights lists in each capability define the permissible access rights of this program at this instant.

Thus far we have described two essential elements of the protection mechanism, *objects* and *capabilities*. The third and final element is the rule governing the passing from one execution domain to another and how protection changes at this interface. The execution domain is, at any instant, defined by the current LNS, and an LNS is uniquely associated with an invocation of a procedure; thus, execution domains change precisely when a procedure is entered or exited. The kernel provides two primitive functions, *CALL* and *RETURN* which allow a procedure to invoke a new procedure or to return to the current procedure's caller.

The essential function of the CALL mechanism is to instantiate a procedure: to create an LNS for its execution domain, and to transfer control to the code body. The essential aspect of the CALL mechanism for the present, however, is its parameter passing/checking mechanism, or "derivation" alluded to previously. Since a procedure is an object, it has a capability part; this capability part serves as the prototype for the procedure's LNS when it is instantiated (i.e. the procedure is CALLed). Thus the capability part of a procedure contains capabilities which reference the caller-independent capabilities of any invocation of the procedure.

In addition, the capability part of a procedure may contain parameter *templates* for capabilities which will be passed as actual parameters when the procedure is CALLed. The template contains a type attribute, which specifies the required type of the corresponding actual parameter. (One can also have a template which accepts any type.) If a type mismatch occurs, the call is not permitted and an error code is returned to the caller. If the types agree, the rights are then checked, using a special field present only in templates called the "check-rights field." The rights contained in the actual parameter capability must include the rights specified in the check-rights field of the template; otherwise, a protection failure occurs and the call is not permitted. If the caller's rights are adequate, a capability is constructed in the (new) LNS which references the object passed by the caller, but which contains a rights list specified by the template. (A template has a "regular" rights field distinct from the check-rights which specifies the rights which the callee (i.e. the procedure) will need to operate on the actual parameter.) This implies that a callee may have greater freedom to operate on an object than the caller who passed it as a parameter, but the caller can in no way obtain that freedom for himself (since the additional rights are present only in the callee's LNS—the caller's LNS is unchanged). Also, by appropriate use of the check-rights and type fields in a template, the creator of a procedure can implement rather general type-dependent protection checking. (This follows from the observation that the check-rights field is not interpreted by the kernel; the interpretation of the auxiliary rights is up to the user.)

Path Names and the Walk Right

We have avoided enumerating the specific primitives provided by HYDRA; this is intentional since we are more concerned with philosophy than with implementation. However, a few primitives must be discussed in order to fairly present the philosophy—one is *walk*. The *walk* primitive is a one-level coercion which, given a capability and a nonnegative integer, produces the capability which occupies the specified position in the capability part of the object named by the parameter capability. The *walk* primitive, like all kernel primitives, is an access right protected by the "kernel rights" bits in a capability.

Because of the *walk* primitive, the environment of a procedure does not consist of the objects named by capabilities in its LNS alone. Rather, it is the closure of the set of objects reachable along a path (originating in the LNS) such that every capability along the path (except possibly the last) grant the *walk* right. Recognizing this, all of the kernel primitives accept path names as parameters and the *walk* right is checked at each step along the path. The use of path names and walk rights effect a significant reduction in the number of capabilities needed in an LNS. Far more important, however, is that the *walk* right (or rather the lack of it) is used to prevent access to the representation of an object. The amplification *walk* rights is one of the most common when entering a procedure which implements operations on a particular object type.

Systems and Subsystems

The previous sections describe how the kernel supports the notion of an object, operations on objects, and protection. It is now time to question to what extent these mechanisms permit and facilitate the construction of operating systems; part of the response is implicit in what has already been described, and part is not.

An "operating system," in the sense of a monolithic entity which provides various facilities to the user, is not an appropriate image of a user environment in the HYDRA context. Rather, a user environment consists of a collection of resources (objects) of various types and procedures which operate on them. The environment in which one user operates may or may not be the same as that for another user, it may be totally different, or may partially overlap. It is entirely possible, for example, that at some point in the evolution of the HYDRA environment several different "file systems" will have been devised. Each such "system" will consist of a distinct object-type to denote the style of file supported by that system, and a collection of operations (procedures) for dealing with that style of file. The various styles of files, for example, may correspond to different access methods, different queueing strategies for dealing with disk, or different security policies. An individual user may use any one of the systems, or because the various systems are optimized along distinct dimensions, he may use more than one. Similar comments, of course, apply to every type of facility provided by an operating system, e.g. command interpreters, synchronization mechanisms, etc.

The flexibility necessary to obtain this form of extension results from both the representation of objects as both data and capabilities, and from the nature of the protection mechanism. Let us return, for a moment, to the issue raised earlier concerning the use of the capability-part of an object in the representation of new object types. First, an instance of an object may be created by invoking a kernel primitive *create* and passing to it a capability referencing the representative of type of object one wishes to create. In particular, then, invoking *create* with a capability referencing the distinguished object named TYPE will create the representative of a new type class. Subsequent calls on *create* passing capabilities referencing this new type representative will create instances of the new class of objects.

Suppose, for example, that at some instant at least the types[4] FILE, SEMAPHORE, and PROCEDURE exist. We wish to introduce the notion of a general directory object, which defines a mapping from print names to capabilities. One idea is to list the print names in the data part, and associate each such name with a capability in the capability part. (Clearly, a more sophisticated structure could be devised.) To support the mutual exclusion needed to permit shared access to directories, we also include a capability for a SEMAPHORE in the DIRECTORY's capability part. We may now create PROCEDURES which "understand" the representation just described and which provide typical directory functions. Notice that we have not restricted the capabilities contained in a DIRECTORY to be of the same type; indeed, the PROCEDURES which maintain directories may specifically allow directories of FILES, or PROCEDURES, or of arbitrarily mixed types. In fact, a directory may contain capabilities for other directories, which suggests the potential for general path names in a directory structure, and inherent search rules. Many variations are possible; the important idea is that the nature of the directory "subsystem" is completely user-specified.

[4] We have tried to use suggestive names for object and type names in the examples. In practice, of course, the unique names of objects have no visible representation; they are 64-bit values.

An Example

In this section we present an example which demonstrates the power of the protection mechanism described above to accomplish in a natural way a kind of protection which can be achieved in existing systems, if at all, only by rather artificial devices. While the specific example is itself somewhat artificial, it has very realistic counterparts.

Consider the case of a research worker who, being a diligent fellow, wishes to keep himself abreast of the relevant literature in his field. Also having access to a computer, this researcher has written some programs to maintain an annotated bibliography on that computer. The programs permit him to update the bibliography either by inserting new entries or changing existing ones; he may also print the bibliography in total, or selectively on any one of several criteria; he may also wish to completely erase an entire bibliography occasionally. In addition, our hero has organized both the programs and the bibliography structure to be very efficient. It's a nice system of programs, indeed!

Now, in the fullness of time, the researcher decides that it would be to his advantage to allow his colleagues, and perhaps his students, to use his programs and his bibliographies. In addition to creating their own independent bibliographies, the colleagues may be able to add new entries to the researcher's own or to add annotations which (may) provide the researcher with additional insights. He is concerned, however, about several aspects of the protection of both his programs and data.

1. No one, except himself, should be able to erase his bibliographies.
2. He worked hard on his system of programs, and he would not like anyone else to copy or modify them. In any case his supervisor has informed him that since the programs were developed on the employer's time, the employer is considering selling them as a proprietary package.
3. Some of the references cited in his own bibliography were written by his colleagues. His annotations are occasionally cryptic, and he would prefer that they were not read by everyone. He would like to choose selectively who may read the annotations.
4. The data structures used to contain the bibliography references are highly optimized and "delicate." He would like to insure that when an update is done, the data structures are correctly manipulated.
5. From time to time he changes the programs, either to correct errors or to add new features. For a period of time after the changes are made, he would like to allow only a small, sympathetic subset of his (growing) user community to use the new versions of his programs.
6. He suspects that after he has allowed others to use his programs and build their own bibliographies they will share some of his concerns, e.g. items (1), (3), and (5), above. In particular, they will not want *him* to be able to erase or examine their bibliographies, or to force a new version of the programs upon them.

Several of the concerns of our researchers can, of course, be handled by most "reasonable" protection systems; others, however, cannot. The most straightforward implementation of the bibliography would be to store the bibliographic information in a single file;[5] therefore, let us frame the discussion in that context.

Since most file systems only protect read access to an entire file, there is no way to enforce selective printing, i.e. to distinguish between the accessors who may print the entire file and those who may not print the annotations. Similarly, undifferentiated read access may permit an unscrupulous user to dump an entire bibliography file, determine its structure, and thus compromise the proprietary nature of the programs.

Undifferentiated write access implies analogous problems. Clearly, the operation of updating the file implies writing on it; in fact it may conceivably imply a massive reorganization in order to maintain the "optimal" data structure.

The concept of "ownership," and its corollary privileges, present in many extant systems may imply that the user of this system cannot protect himself (unless he takes special, explicit precautions) from examination of his bibliographies by the author of the system and/or from unexpected alteration of the system. In particular he may not be able to protect himself from alteration in ways which penetrate the security of his bibliographies.

Now let us consider the "natural" implementation of the bibliography system in HYDRA and how this implementation overcomes the problems mentioned above.

Clearly a bibliography is a new type of virtual resource. Therefore, we would create a new object type; call it BIBLIO. In fact, of course, we will want to use existing file mechanisms to represent bibliographies. In all likelihood an instance of a bibliography object will have an empty data part and its capability part will merely consist of a single capability which references an ordinary file object.

Even though the representation of a bibliography is a file, file operations are not applicable to bibliography objects; they are applicable only to file objects; we can create new operations (procedures), however, which are applicable to bibliography objects, for example:

$U(\beta,p_1,\ldots,p_n)$	Update
$P(\beta,p_1,\ldots,p_m)$	Print
$PWOA(\beta,p_1,\ldots,p_m)$	Print WithOut Annotations
$E(\beta)$	Erase

In each of these, β must be a capability which references a bibliography object and the p_i's further specify the nature of the update, print, etc., to be done. (Notice

[5] Some, but not all, of the problems raised can be solved by an esoteric multi-file structure for the bibliography; however, since these solutions violate the "naturalness" criterion, they will not be mentioned.

that even though P and PWOA are distinct procedures, in the sense of being distinct objects, they need not necessarily have distinct code bodies; that is, the capability part of each of these procedure objects, their prototype LNS's, may reference some or all of the same page objects.)

For simplicity, let us assume that each of the procedures above is uniquely associated with a single bit in the "auxiliary rights" field of a capability which references a bibliography object; denote these bits by the lowercase version of the procedure name, i.e. u, p, etc. Thus in order to validly execute "CALL U(β,...)" it is first necessary that β be a reference to a bibliography object, and second that the "u" bit of β be set.

Figure 1 illustrates (incompletely) a situation involving several "users" and several bibliographies which might exist at some instant. Rectangular boxes denote objects. Directed arrows illustrate capability references, and the lowercase letters along these arrows signify which of the auxiliary rights bits are set in these capabilities.

The following kinds of information may be gleaned by inspection of Figure 1.

1. User #1 may access all of the procedures U, P, PWOA, and E. He may also access bibliography objects B1 and B2. He may perform any of the operations U, P, PWOA, and E on B1, but he may only perform U and PWOA on B2.
2. User #2 may also access all of the procedures and, in addition, may access three bibliography objects: B2, B3, and B4. He may only perform PWOA on B2, but may perform U, P, or E on B3 and B4.
3. User #3 may only access three of the procedures; he does not have a reference to E. He may access three bibliography objects—B1, B4, and B5, and may, in principle, perform U or P on B4, and U, P, or E on B5, and P on B1. Notice, however, that the right, in principle, to perform E on B5 is useless to him since he does not have a reference to capability E.

It should now be clear that each of the protection concerns expressed by our friend the researcher is neatly handled by this scheme. For example,

1. Since the operation of printing is the protected "right" in the system rather than the act of reading, it is possible to distinguish between printing the entire bibliography and printing it without annotations. Moreover, since the concept of "read" is not defined with respect to bibliographies *at all*, it is simply impossible for someone to examine the representation of a bibliography object and determine its structure; the proprietary nature of the system is therefore insured.
2. Similarly, since the operation of updating a bibliography is distinct from that of writing the file which represents it, the internal integrity of the data structure is guaranteed (at least if the procedure U works correctly).

We would like to make two more points with respect to the example before leaving it. The conventional

Fig. 1. Bibliography example.

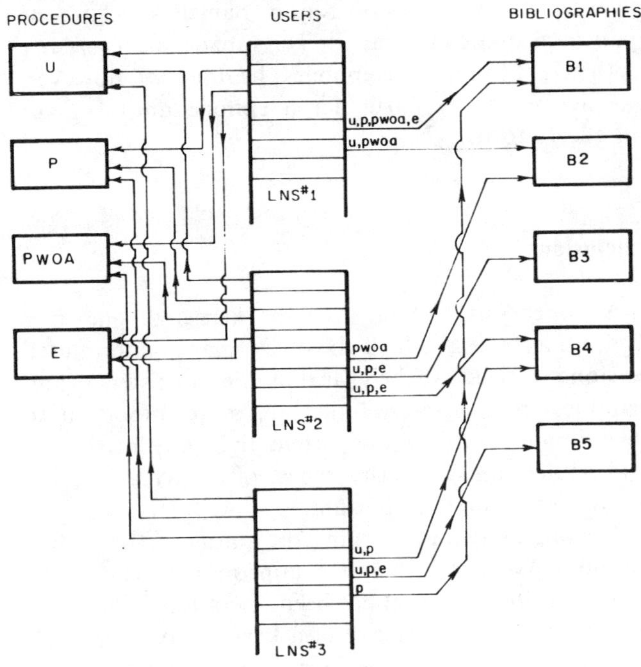

view with respect to sharing resources is that there are precisely two cases: (1) the shared resource is passed to another "user"—in which case the "rights" which may be passed must be a subset of those of the passer; or (2) the shared resource is owned by the "operating system"—in which case the set of "rights" expands drastically when an operating system function is invoked. We reject both of these cases as inadequate to serve as the basis of a truly secure system.

On several occasions we have referred to our rejection of "ownership" as a design concept. Consider the consequences of this statement in the context of the example; specifically, who "owns" object B1? We cannot tell from the static picture who originally created the object: indeed the creator may not be able to reference it any longer. We do know that user #1 has more rights to B1 than does user #2; however, even user #1 can only invoke BIBLIO-specific operations on B1—he cannot, for example, manipulate the representation of B1.

Nor does the BIBLIO subsystem "own" B1. As discussed in the previous section, the rights acquired by a procedure to a capability passed to it as an actual parameter are obtained from the template in that procedure's prototype LNS. These rights may be a subset, superset, or totally disjoint from those of the caller. The point is that a procedure is invested with those rights, and *only* those rights, which it needs to do its job. Note that the procedures comprised within the BIBLIO system do not have access to *any* BIBLIO objects except as parameters. (By way of analogy, I am not permitted to repair my telephone. I am permitted, however, to invoke an operation, namely a telephone repairman, that can repair it. The repairman *inherently* has the right to repair telephones; he does *not*, however, have access to my particular telephone until I grant him access to it.)

Conclusion

An operating system, even the kernel of one, is a large undertaking which involves many interrelated decisions. Indeed we believe that the consistency and cleanliness of this interrelation are more important to the ultimate utility of the system than any of the individual decisions. It is this aspect of the HYDRA design that we feel is most important.

A word or two concerning the status of the system and our experience with it seem appropriate. At the time of this writing the kernel has been operational for about nine months. The existence of a kernel, however, does not make a system usable, nor does it relieve the implementers from the responsibility of developing at least one version of the subsystems, e.g. a file system, which users require. We are currently developing these subsystems. The extent of our experience to date is that the facilities provided by the kernel do indeed significantly simplify the construction of these subsystems.

Acknowledgments. It is difficult to give proper credit to the sources of all the ideas presented above. Although we have felt free to change terminology, the works of Dennis [5], Dijkstra [4], Hansen [1], and especially Lampson [7] and Jones [6] have had significant impact. The ideas of these individuals will clearly show through to those who are familiar with them. The remaining ideas and the cement which holds the design together emerged in discussion between the authors.

Received June 1973; revised December 1973

References

1. Brinch-Hansen, P. The nucleus of a multiprogramming system. *Comm. ACM 13*, 4 (Apr. 1970), 238–241.
2. Dahl, O.J., Dijkstra, E.W., and Hoare, C.A.R. *Structured Programming*, Academic Press, New York, 1972.
3. Dijkstra, E.W. The structure of THE multiprogramming system. *Comm. ACM 11*, 5 (May 1968), 341–346.
4. Dijkstra, E.W., Cooperating sequential processes. In *Programming Languages*, F. Genuys, (Ed.), Academic Press, New York, 1968, pp. 43–112.
5. Dennis, J.B., and Van Horn, E.C. Programming semantics for multiprogrammed computations. *Comm. ACM 9*, 3 (Mar. 1966), 143–155.
6. Jones, A.K. Protection in programming systems. Ph.D. Th. Carnegie-Mellon U., 1973.
7. Lampson, B.W. Dynamic Protection Structures, Proc. AFIPS 1969 FJCC, Vol. 35, AFIPS Press, Montvale, N.J. pp. 27–38.
8. Parnas, D.L. On the criteria to be used in decomposing systems into modules. Comput. Sci. Dep. Rep., Carnegie-Mellon U., 1971.
9. Wulf, W.A., and Bell, C.G. C.mmp—a multi-mini-processor. Proc. AFIPS 1972, FJCC. Vol. 41, AFIPS Press, Montvale, N.J. pp. 765–777.

Software management of Cm*—A distributed multiprocessor†

by ANITA K. JONES, ROBERT J. CHANSLER, JR., IVOR DURHAM, PETER FEILER and KARSTEN SCHWANS

Carnegie-Mellon University
Pittsburgh, Pennsylvania

ABSTRACT

This paper describes the software system being developed for Cm*, a distributed multi-microprocessor. This software provides for flexible, yet controlled, sharing of code and data via a capability addressed virtual memory, creation and management of groups of processes known as task forces, and efficient interprocess communication. Both the software and hardware are currently under construction at Carnegie-Mellon University.

INTRODUCTION

Semiconductor technology advances are leading toward the inexpensive production of computer modules (i.e., a processor plus memory of a moderate size) on a single chip. Multiple computer modules interconnected to form a multiprocessor or a network offer a large number of processing cycles far more inexpensively than an equally fast uniprocessor. Yet, such a computer module system is useful only if a suitable fraction of the processing cycles can actually be used for applications.

The software designed to manage a computer module system can contribute substantially to making the system a cost effective environment in which to program applications. This paper discusses the software designed to manage a computer module system called Cm* which is currently under construction at Carnegie-Mellon University. We pay particular attention to the philosophy of software construction that influenced many of the design decisions.

For the purposes of this paper, we will only review some attributes of the architecture that are salient to the design of operating system software. Companion papers[1,2] describe and discuss the Cm* architecture in detail.

Cm* is a multiprocessor composed of computer modules, each consisting of a DEC LSI-11, a standard LSI-11 bus, memory and devices. We describe Cm* as a multiprocessor because the system's primary memory forms a single virtual address space; any processor can directly access memory anywhere in the system. To implement such a virtual memory, we introduced into each computer module a local switch, the Slocal‡ which routes locally generated references selectively to local memory or to the Map Bus (when the reference is to memory in another computer module). The Slocal likewise accepts references from distant sources to its local memory..

Connected to a single Map Bus may be up to fourteen computer modules that share a single address mapping and routing processor, called the Kmap. The computer modules, Kmap, and Map Bus together comprise a *cluster*. A Cm* configuration can be grown to arbitrary size by interconnecting clusters via Inter-cluster Busses (see Figure 1). (A cluster need not have a direct bus connection to every other cluster in a configuration.) Collectively, the Kmaps mediate each non-local reference made by a computer module, thus sustaining the appearance of a single virtual address space.

Because processors are numerous, applications of any size will tend not to be designed in the form of a single program executed by a sequential process. Instead we expect users to create *task forces*, i.e., groups of processes cooperating to achieve a goal. Because the number of processes in a task force may vary with the available resources and task parameters, and because processes tend to be small (due to the relatively slow processors or limitations on the amount of local memory), a user will often be unconcerned with individual processes, communicating only with the task force itself.

The Cm* architecture offers to a user the option of employing tightly or loosely coupled processes. Loosely coupled processes communicate rarely, usually in conventional ways via a message transmission mechanism. Tightly coupled processes communicate often, sometimes using the efficient unconstrained paths provided by shared memory. Cm* permits both types of communication since it provides a message transmission facility as well as direct addressing of shared memory. Effectively, a user is free to view Cm* as either a multiprocessor or a computer network.

† This work was supported by the Defense Advance Research Projects Agency under contract F44620-73-C-0074 which is monitored by the Air Force Office of Scientific Research.

‡ In several cases names of Cm* components are derived from the PMS notation described in Reference 3.

Reprinted with permission from *AFIPS Conf. Proc. 1977 Nat. Comput. Conf.*, vol. 46, pp. 657–663.

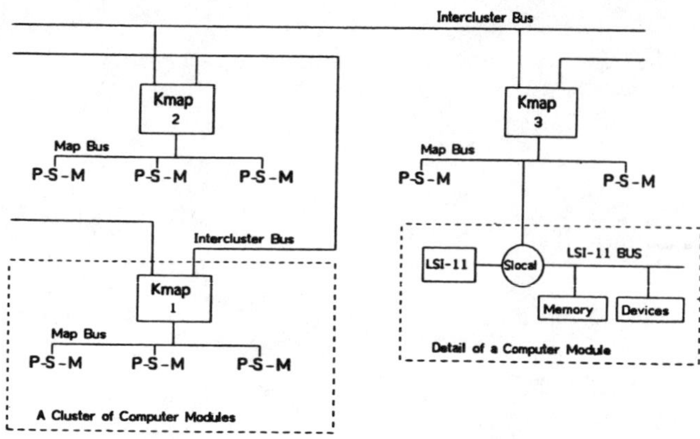

Figure 1—A three cluster Cm* configuration

SOFTWARE DESIGN METHODOLOGY

Cm* is a vehicle for experimentation, particularly in the area of parallel decomposition of algorithms and their efficient implementation on a computer module processing resource. We expect it to be rare that an experimenter (whom we will refer to as a user hereafter) is confident that all his code is debugged, since he will routinely alter parameters and even the code for his task forces in substantial ways. We also expect users to incrementally construct experiments. In addition we expect users to reconfigure modules (of software) combining them to form a new experiment.

Such a view of the user has led us to believe that it is as important for the kernel (or lowest level) software to support the user's software construction activities as it is to provide the primitive runtime facilities required for multiple users to share the computer resources in a disciplined cooperative fashion. Consequently, the software design reflects this concern. We view users as constructing their experiments by incrementally building *modules*.* Each module implements some abstraction useful to other modules that will come to depend upon it. A module then is a "unit of abstraction." It is implemented as

- code and data private to the module,
- a set of externally known functions that can be invoked by other modules making use of the abstractions, and
- a set of references to externally defined modules defining functions used in implementing the abstraction.

The kernel software supports the notion of a module by providing user facilities to create modules and to invoke functions of a module in a protected way. An invoked function is executed in an environment that gives it access to code and data that are part of the module, together with any actual parameters specified by the invoker. Thus the software enforces the boundaries of a module by providing a well defined transition between execution in one module and execution in another. Hopefully this will help contain the influence of errors and expedite debugging.

This notion of module is based on earlier work. In particular it is built on the ideas of modular decomposition discussed in Reference 4 and abstract data types[5] as used in language design.

Module boundaries are used for protection purposes at runtime. Each function is executed with access only to those objects which it requires. In designing the kernel software, we have found that some of its modules implement rather complex abstractions. Yet not all uses of a module require the entire abstraction; some uses rely only on part of the abstraction while others rely on a simplified abstraction. For design purposes a module may be partitioned into a strictly ordered set of *levels* as described in Reference 6. The purpose of dividing a module's design into levels is to permit either incremental introduction of the different parts of one abstraction or increasingly more complex (and powerful) versions of the entire abstraction. The introduction of complexity is postponed until it is truly required. Multiple levels of one module share data structures and even code.

The first level within a multi-level module may define only a subset of the functions of the complete abstraction, but that subset of functions is a useful self-contained, but limited version of the abstraction. Subsequent levels are introduced into the hierarchy as needed. Additional levels of a module may introduce entirely new data structures or extend existing ones. No protection boundaries exist between levels so that higher level code may manipulate data structures introduced in lower levels. Consequently, though module boundaries are translated into runtime protection boundaries, the boundaries between "levels of design" are not detectable in the runtime implementation structures. We will illustrate this difference between modules and levels later when we discuss the Cm* message transmission module.

Levels within a module are strictly ordered. We can define a level A to be "higher" than level B in another module in case A invokes a function defined in B. The set of all levels (of all modules) is partially ordered by dependency. In the design of operating system software, there is not necessarily a cleanly identifiable division of a hierarchy of levels into supervisory and user software. The operating system facilities required by one user differ from those required by another, particularly in an experimental setting. The partially ordered system structure is in a form such that it is readily possible to replace "upper" portions of the dependency hierarchy since level boundries are clear and the dependency relations between levels are known.

CM* SOFTWARE SYSTEM DESIGN

Before describing the kernel software design, we will define two notions that play an important part in that

* This paper always uses the words "computer module" to refer to the hardware structure, and will in the sequel use the (commonly accepted) single word "module" to refer to a programming abstraction. Context should also serve to eliminate any ambiguity.

design: objects and capability addressing of objects. The basic unit which can be named, shared and individually protected, and for which memory is allocated for representation purposes is the *object*. Each object has a unique name and a definitive description used by the software system. Every object has a type that determines the structure of its representation and the operations or accesses which can be performed on it. Current design specifies three types of objects: *data segments*, which are linear arrays of words that may be read and written; *capability lists*, which are structures containing capabilities (to be discussed below); and *mailboxes*, which are structures containing messages.

Objects are named (addressed) using *capabilities*.[7,8] A capability may only be created and manipulated in controlled ways (by kernel provided capability functions). Since users cannot create or forge capabilities, possession of a capability is evidence that the user can reference the object whose unique name appears within the capability. A capability not only identifies a unique object, it records a set of *rights* indicating which of the defined operation (accesses) are permitted to be performed on the object. Controlled use of objects is enforced because an object can be accessed only if a program presents a capability naming that object which contains a right for the desired access. Since possession of a capability endows the possessor with the ability to perform accesses, capabilities also record those rights which a possessor may exercise with respect to the capabilities themselves. (For example, copying a particular capability may not be permitted.)

Based on the above discussion, we next describe the Cm* kernel software. The purpose of the initial levels of software is to provide facilities required for shared usage of resources in an "enforceably cooperative" way. In addition we wish to assist users in programming and executing their experiments by providing convenient structures and functions for creating and executing modules. The operating system software itself is composed of a partially ordered set of levels. In several instances two modules are divided into a pair of levels. For convenient reference, levels are labeled with a tag in the format "module-level." Modules are given alphabetic names; levels are numbered in increasing order as they appear in the system construction hierarchy. The kernel levels to be discussed in this paper are:

CAP-1: Capability referencing
Performs mapping from a capability via a segment descriptor to physical representation of segment (including access control checking)

CAP-2: Capability addressing and memory allocation
Defines an object address space and interpretation of an address; performs memory allocation ensuring that the segments used to represent objects are pairwise exclusive

ME-1: Environments and Modules
Implements the creation and deletion of modules and execution environments

MSG-1: Conditional message transmission
Defines the structures message and mailbox; permits sending and receiving of messages when process suspension is not required

DSP: Dispatching
Defines hardware implemented data structures used to 'load' an environment onto the processor and commence execution

MPX: Multiplexing
Selects the next environment to execute on a processor

ME-2: Environment relations
Records the ancestry by which environments are related; provides for nested and parallel execution of environments

MSG-2: Unconditional message transmission
Provides for sending, receiving, and replying to messages even if environments involved are forced to wait for an indeterminate time to complete message transmission

TI: Trap and interrupt handling
Provides routing of control when either interrupts or traps occur

A diagram indicating the dependency relations among these levels appears as Figure 2. An arrow from level A to level B indicates that a function in level B is invoked in level A. In addition, it is possible that level A invokes functions in any of the levels 'below' B in the dependency graph.

Capability addressing

Module CAP provides capability addressing. Level CAP-1, which is implemented in Kmap microcode, interprets capability references to objects, i.e., it maps a capability to the physical representation of the object named by the capability. Because the state of an object may change and its physical representation may move, the system maintains a single definitive description of each object called a *descriptor* or *segment descriptor*. It records the type of the object, the physical description of its representation (including cluster, module, starting address, and size), state information (e.g., whether the representation is in core, dirty, or locked for Kmap usage), and the (reference) count of the number of outstanding capabilities for the object.

Every existing object has a unique name—the memory address of its descriptor. To perform a mapping from a capability to an object, the identity of the object's descriptor is determined from the capability. It, in turn, is referenced to determine the physical representation of the object. A capability reference fails if the right required to perform the operation desired by the addressing environment originating the reference is not in the capability.

Level CAP-2 extends level CAP-1 to provide for the generation of capability references (we refer to this as

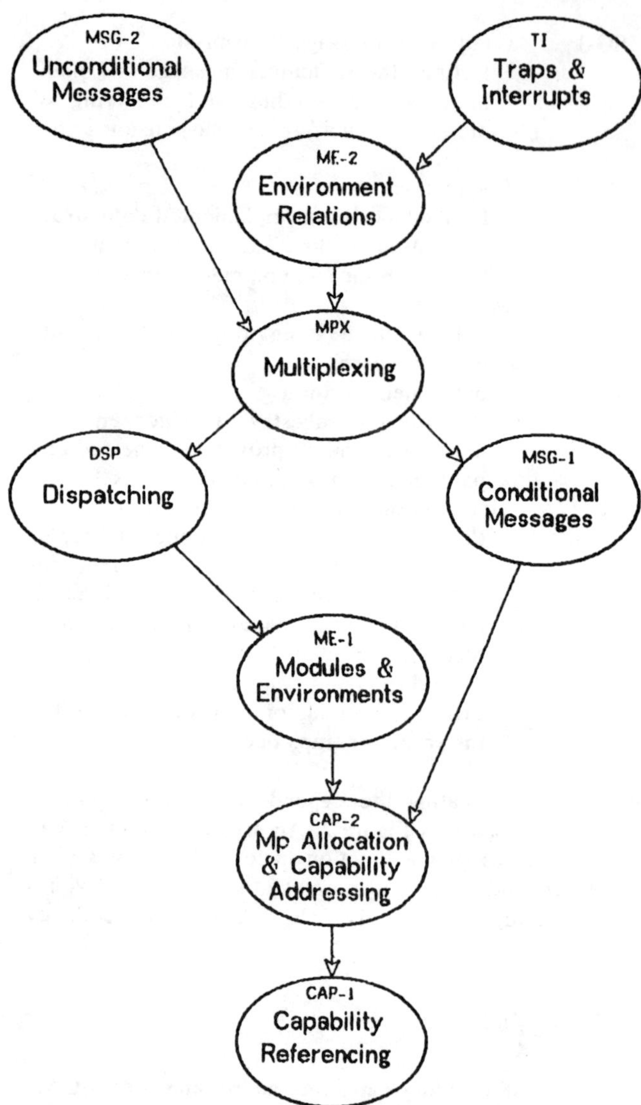

Figure 2—Levels and modules of Cm* software

capability addressing), and for capability manipulation. Capabilities used for addressing purposes are stored in capability array objects called *capability lists*. Given a capability list CL and an index X, one can determine the X-th capability in capability list CL. This may be a capability for an object of arbitrary type, including a capability list object. By repeated application of capability indexing, objects to any depth can be addressed. Because capability list indexing is performed in microcode as well as in software, the architecture restricts indexing to depth 2 in any single operation. This means that in a single addressing operation the path to a target object may "indirect through" at most two capability lists before arriving at the (third) target object. Whenever a processor is executing (i.e., generating capability addresses) one capability list is distinguished as the *primary capability list*. The first index of a capability address is an offset into this primary capability list.

CAP-2 also defines (microcoded) functions for creating, copying, moving, and deleting capabilities as well as for manipulating the rights encoded within a capability.

A Cm* processor (an LSI-11) has a word size of only 16 bits. To permit 16 bit addresses to be mapped to the arbitrarily sized Cm* memory, the notion of a *window* was introduced. It consists of 15 *window registers*, each of which can be thought of as holding a capability. (Actually, in the current design, each window register holds an index to a capability which can be indexed via the current primary capability list.) CAP-2 provides two (microcode implemented) functions *Segload* and *Unload* to associate and de-associate, a window register and a capability. To read or write a data segment, a capability for the segment must be *segloads* into a window register.

A 16 bit machine address is interpreted to select a window register (and thus a capability) and possibly to specify an offset into a segment of memory. For enhanced performance of capability referencing, the descriptors for the objects named in the capabilities associated with the window registers are cached in the Kmap. This mechanism provides virtual addressing and allows for conventional relocation of physical memory. It is sufficiently general to support the definition of Kmap microcoded operations on capability lists and mailboxes.

The last facility introduced in CAP-2 is that of memory allocation. Physical memory is allocated to hold segments so that no two segments overlap.

Modules and environments

Level ME-1 provides for the creation and deletion of modules (as discussed earlier) and for executing invoked functions. A module is implemented by a *module capability list* containing

- capabilities for the code and data segments required to perform the functions defined in this module,
- a data segment containing a vector of *function descriptors* which specify the code to be executed when a particular function is invoked (e.g., the index into the module capability list for the segment containing code for this function), the number of parameters expected and the size of stack required to perform the function,
- a list of other "known" modules containing functions that can be invoked by this module.

ME-1 also defines an *environment*, the structure created as a result of a function invocation. An environment is defined by several objects; one is the primary capability list which is private to a function invocation and acts as the root capability list for all addressing of objects during execution of the function.

The primary capability list contains capabilities for

- the execution stack (private to the environment)
- the module capability list which defines the module containing the invoked function,

- a *state vector* (private to the environment) which contains the processor and addressing state when the environment is not executing on a processor. (The state vector includes processor registers, processor status word, scheduling data, trap and error masks for communicating with the Kmap, and indices of the capabilities *Segload*ed into the window registers during the environments execution.)
- parameter objects specified by the invoker.

The module capability list contains capabilities for those objects shared by all who invoke a function in the module. The primary capability list contains capabilities which are local to a particular invocation of a function.

Level ME-1 provides functions for the creation, initialization and deletion of modules and environments. These, in turn, are used by level ME-2 in providing functions relating the execution of different environments. Functions *Call* and *Return* allow nested execution, i.e., the *Call*ing environment is suspended for the duration of the execution of the newly created *(Call*ed) environment which terminates when the *Called* environment *Returns*. The function *Fork* permits an environment to request that a function be invoked to execute in parallel with its invoker until the function *Join* is performed.

ME-2 initializes a newly created environment to record priority information for scheduling purposes and to record the existence of a newly created environment in the *lineage* (family tree) of its creator. It is this lineage which is used by still higher levels to keep track of a task force, the set of environments which are cooperating to achieve some goal.

Message transmission

The members of a task force need to be able to synchronize their actions and to communicate with one another. To this end module MSG defines an abstraction of a *mailbox* which can contain *messages*. A mailbox is capable of containing some fixed finite number of messages maintained in FIFO order. To permit users to communicate arbitrary objects to one another, rather than data only, messages are pairs of capabilities. (To transmit 16 bits of information, a user can create a *data capability* to contain this user specified information.)

Levels MSG-1 and MSG-2 differ in that MSG-1 provides only the functions *CondSend* and *CondReceive* to transmit messages when these functions can be completed without suspension of the invoker. *CondSend* succeeds in depositing a message into a mailbox only if the mailbox has room for it. *CondReceive* is a function which returns the oldest message in case the mailbox is not empty. Hence *CondReceive* can be used for polling. A received message is placed in the receiving environment's *message-pouch*, a designated pair of positions in the environment's primary capability list. *CondSend* and *CondReceive* will return an error code if the mailbox overflows (is full) or underflows (is empty), respectively.

The second level, MSG-2, extends the set of message transmission functions to provide a synchronization as well as a communication mechanism. MSG-2 relies on the hierarchy above the MPX level where the notion of blocked environments was introduced. MSG-2 provides the unconditional message functions: *Send, Receive,* and *Reply*. *Send* performs the same tasks as *CondSend*: except when the target mailbox is full, *Send* will cause the sending environment to be blocked awaiting an opportunity to deliver its message. Likewise, the *Receive* function causes the environment attempting to *Receive* a message from an empty mailbox to become blocked. *Send*ing a message to an empty mailbox on which an environment is waiting will cause that environment to *Receive* the message and become unblocked. Similarly, if *Receive* causes a full mailbox to no longer be full, it will awaken the oldest environment awaiting to deposit a message.

MSG-2 also defines a *Reply* function for mailboxes. This function differs from *Send* in that after executing the *Reply* function on a mailbox as permitted by a capability for that mailbox, the right to *Reply* to that mailbox is removed from the capability.

The two levels of the message transmission module provide an excellent example of a decomposition of a single module. MSG-1 defines both message and mailbox data structures, but provides functions which are of limited applicability; in some situations the functions fail returning an error code. Conditional functions are used to transmit messages in a well-defined fashion, but do not perform synchronization.

MSG-2 extends the definition of the mailbox data structure so that waiting environments can be recorded when necessary. It also provides new functions extending the usefulness of mailboxes, but not "covering up" or subsuming the conditional functions which are useful when polling is desired. The multiplexing module relies on the conditional message functions of MSG-1 and implements blocking and unblocking on which the second level of MSG depends.

Dispatching and multiplexing

Dispatching (DSP) and Multiplexing (MPX) are both levels and entire modules. DSP defines the hardware implemented state vector and its associated *Envload* function which loads an environment onto a computer module and begins execution. *Envload* is implemented in a combination of Kmap microcode and software. Software portions of *Envload* locate the process register values and the processor status word values in the state vector and load them into the physical processor registers. The software then stores the index of its capability for the environment in a special location which alerts the Kmap that an *Envload* is in progress. The Kmap portion of this function loads appropriate values found in the state vector into the window registers and various Slocal registers.

Functions in DSP are used exclusively by the multiplexing module (MPX) which is responsible for selecting the next environment to be *Envload*ed. Module MPX defines a set of *Runqueues*, each of which is a mailbox. If an environment is eligible for execution, i.e., it is not blocked nor already executing on some processor, then there is a message containing a capability for it in one of the runqueues.

Associated with each processor is an ordered list of at least some of the runqueues. The ordering selects the priority with which that processor services the mailboxes. The same Runqueue may appear in various positions in the ordered list of runqueues of different processors. The *Multiplex* function, invoked by the superior levels ME-2 and TI, cycles down the list of runqueues (private to the processor executing *Multiplex*) performing *CondReceives* on the runqueues. If the *CondReceive* is successful, then the result is a capability for the next environment to be *Envload*ed on the executing processor.

Trap and interrupt handling

Software traps and interrupts signal exceptional conditions caused by program action and external asynchronous events, respectively. With only a few exceptions (e.g., responding to a clock interrupt or to a high speed device interrupt), hardware traps and interrupts are translated into software traps and interrupts, so that modules can indicate what action is to be taken when they occur.

Defining a new trap (interrupt) means defining a new *trap (interrupt) vector entry* indicating what function in what module is to be invoked if the trap (interrupt) occurs. When a trap occurs, it was caused by the executing environment, so a *Call* is performed to suspend the current environment and cause the function named in the appropriate trap vector entry to be executed.

Interrupts are asynchronous and are not necessarily related to the current processor execution. TI offers two options. As a result of an interrupt a *Fork* can be performed to the function named in the associated interrupt vector. This will cause the interrupt to be serviced in parallel with execution of other environments. Alternatively, an interrupt vector or trap vector entry may direct that as a result of an interrupt, status information be sent as a message to a specified mailbox. Presumably some environment capable of handling the interrupt will *Receive* or *CondReceive* to get the message. Interrupts would then be processed sequentially by order of occurrence.

Two observations are appropriate here. One is that using the trap and interrupt mechanism, any level above TI can define vector entries so that code from higher levels can respond to exceptional conditions encountered when code from lower levels is executing. This effects "outward calls" so that lower levels can rely on higher levels when exceptional conditions arise. The second observation is that the trap and interrupt module is quite small, relying heavily on ME for *Fork* and *Call*, and on MSG for mailboxes.

The kernel system

The Cm* architecture provides alternative ways to implement functions. A function may be implemented in Kmap microcode, or it may be implemented in software to be executed by one or more of the computer modules. A computer module may execute a function in either of two address spaces (user or kernel space). The decision where to place a particular function of a particular level of a particular module is determined by considerations such as maximizing performance, providing for proper synchronization, and ease of implementation, as well as maintaining protection boundaries between modules. Because of this independence between the design and the physical realization, alternative implementations of a function are possible. This facility is expected to be valuable in a system designed for experimental use because it allows for function substitution and redesign.

The kernel software system described here is implemented in two parts: Kmap microcode and a set of programs which run in the kernel space of the computer module processors. It is intended that in the initial system all of the capability functions and message functions will be performed by Kmap microcode. The remaining functions will be implemented in software to be executed from the kernel space of the computer modules.

The kernel and user spaces have symmetric data structures because both are executing environments. Both the user and the kernel system have a primary capability list which acts as a "root" for capability addressing purposes. Both primary capability lists include a capability for a state vector and for a module capability list. It is the primary capability list and the state vector of the kernel space that maintain information particular to a processor. Shared data and code in the kernel are referenced via capabilities in the kernel's module capability list.

STATUS OF SOFTWARE DEVELOPMENT

As of December 1976, the microcode available provided only for simple relocation of physical addresses with no capability referencing. Development of microcode to support capability operations and the message facility will follow shortly.

Kernel space programs have been coded in BLISS-11,[9] a system implementation language. This set of programs is being tested using a simulator for the Cm* machine[10] which executes on C.mmp, another multiprocessor system developed at Carnegie-Mellon University.[11] The simulator models multiple computer modules as multiple processes, and is able to run at about half the speed of a Cm* processor by exploiting the writable control store features of the C.mmp multiprocessor. Since the kernel code is successfully executing on the simulator, it is expected that the software kernel will be available for use shortly after the completion of the Kmap microcoding.

Future software development

The kernel system modules as described constitute a very primitive system. A number of additional software levels and new modules are in various stages of design. It is expected that most of the levels in these modules will be implemented as programs in the user space. Modules under development include:

Secondary Store Management—Current design proposes adding some disk memory local to some clusters, with large file storage accessible via a high speed link to either the C.mmp or the DEC KL-10.

Linkediting—The creation and management of modules as Cm* modules will be performed by a linkeditor intended to simplify the construction and management of function tables, segments of code, and invocation sequences.

Command Interpreter—This module will provide on-line, interactive access to the Cm* machine. This will allow a programmer to dynamically manage a task force. Currently interactive terminal communication is provided by a PDP-11 connected to each computer module by a serial line unit.[12]

ALGOL 68 Runtime System—The first programming system to be available on the Cm* machine is expected to be ALGOL 68. (Until such a system is available, code will be cross-compiled on another machine). This version of ALGOL 68 will be designed to exploit the multiprocessing facilities of the Cm* machine.

Resource Policy Modules—A task force requires many runtime decisions concerning scheduling and resource allocation. It is the task of a policy module to provide for these decisions based up on the dynamic state of the task force and the Cm* machine as a whole.

SUMMARY

This paper represents a status report on the design of the firmware and software for management of a distributed multiprocessor called Cm* and the software construction philosophy which influenced its design. We have described the lowest levels of the kernel; some of the microcode and all of the software implementing what we have described now exists.

Besides continuing with the design and implementation of further levels of software, we intend to experiment with the placement and execution of kernel code within different Cm* configurations. Parameters of these experiments will include varying the physical location of the kernel code, the number of copies of that code as well as which computer modules can execute different portions of the code.

For example, one experiment is to limit the number of processors that can execute ME-2 code to (say) two processors in a cluster. If user programs executing on processors other than the designated two request ME-2 functions, their requests will be recorded so that the designated two processors can process these requests at some later time. The motivation for such an arrangement is that a processor is much more efficient if it executes code from its local memory.

In addition to such operating system experiments, we plan a number of experiments employing Cm* in the solution of different types of applications problems.

ACKNOWLEDGMENTS

The Cm* software design was strongly influenced by the ideas which emerged from the family of operating system project (reported in Reference 6) and the virtual memory project which predated the family of operating system effort (reported in Reference 4).

In addition we would like to thank three individuals, Richard Swan, Victor Lesser, and Lee Cooprider for their comments and suggestions.

REFERENCES

1. Swan, R. J., S. H. Fuller, and D. P. Siewiorek, "Cm*: a Modular, Multi-Microprocessor," AFIPS Conference Proceedings, Vol. 46, 1977 National Computer Conference.
2. Swan, R. J., A. Bechtolsheim, K. Lai, and J. Ousterhout, "The Implementation of the Cm* Multi-Microprocessor," AFIPS Conference Proceedings, Vol. 46, 1977 National Computer Conference.
3. Bell, C. Gordon and Allen Newell, *Computer Structures: Readings and Examples,* McGraw-Hill, 1971.
4. Parnas, D. L. and W. R. Price, "The Design of the Virtual Memory Aspects of a Virtual Machine," Proceedings ACM SIGARCH-SIGOPS Workshop on Virtual Computer Systems, 1973.
5. Liskov, B. and Steven Zilles, "Programming with Abstract Data types," *SIGPLAN Notices,* Vol. 9, No. 4, April 1974.
6. Habermann, A. N., Lawrence Flon, and Lee Cooprider, "Modularization and Hierarchy in a Family of Operating Systems," *Communications of the ACM,* Vol. 19, No. 4, April 1976.
7. Dennis, J. B. and E. C. Van Horn, "Programming Semantics for Multiprogrammed Computations," *Communications of the ACM,* Vol. 11, No. 3, March 1968.
8. Lampson, B. W., "Dynamic Protection Structures," *Proc. AFIPS 1969 FJCC 35,* AFIPS Press, Montvale, N.J., 1969.
9. Wulf, W., et al., "Bliss: A Language for Systems Programming," *Communications of the ACM,* Vol. 14, No. 12, December 1971.
10. Chansler, R. J., "Cm* Simulator Users' Manual," Department of Computer Science, Carnegie-Mellon University, 1976.
11. Wulf, W., et al., "HYDRA: the Kernel of a Multiprocessor Operating System," *Communications of the ACM,* Vol. 17, No. 6, June 1974.
12. Van Zoeren, H., "Cm* Host User's Manual," Department of Computer Science, Carnegie-Mellon University, December 1975.
13. Parnas, D. L., "On the Criteria to be used in Decomposing Systems into Modules," *Communications of the ACM,* Vol. 15, No. 12, December 1972.

StarOS, a Multiprocessor Operating System for the Support of Task Forces

Anita K. Jones, Robert J. Chansler Jr., Ivor Durham, Karsten Schwans and Steven R. Vegdahl
Department of Computer Science
Carnegie-Mellon University
Pittsburgh, PA 15213

StarOS is a message-based, object-oriented, multiprocessor operating system, specifically designed to support *task forces*, large collections of concurrently executing processes that cooperate to accomplish a single purpose. StarOS has been implemented at Carnegie-Mellon University for the 50 processor Cm* multi-microprocessor computer.

In this paper, we first discuss the attributes of task force software and of the Cm* architecture. We then discuss some of the facilities in StarOS that allow development and experimentation with task forces. StarOS itself is presented as an example task force.

1. Introduction

Technological advances have made it attractive to interconnect many less expensive processors and memories to construct a powerful, cost-effective computer. *Potential* benefits include increased cost-performance resulting from the exploitation of many cheap processors, enhanced reliability in the integrity of data and in the availability of useful processing cycles, and a physically adaptable computer whose capacity can be expanded or reduced by addition or removal of modular components.

Realizing these *potential* benefits requires software structures that make effective use of the hardware.

This work was sponsored by the Defense Advanced Research Projects Agency (DOD), ARPA Order No. 3597, monitored by the Air Force Avionics Laboratory Under Contract F33615-78-C-1551.

StarOS is an experimental operating system for Cm*, a multi-microprocessor with approximately 50 processors and 3M bytes of main memory (in 1979) [5]. StarOS is designed for the support of and experimentation with *task forces*, software composed of many cooperating, communicating "small" processes, together with supporting code and data. Collectively, the task force components accomplish a single task. Our objective is to determine whether task force software is conducive to achieving the potential benefits of multiprocessors, and to understand the design issues related to operating system facilities that support task forces. A limited version of StarOS has been running since 1977. An adapted and expanded version is now being completed.

It is appropriate to analyze task forces in detail. Processes of a task force are typically small in comparison to counterparts in a uniprocessor multiprogramming system, and there are more of them. The desirability of many small processes, rather than a few larger ones, derives directly from the three potential benefits listed above: To achieve cost-performance or even absolute performance, a computation is decomposed into small parts, each of which is performed by a separate process executing in parallel with the others. This strategy maximizes usage of the available parallelism. Enhanced reliability *may* result if the task is decomposed such that no one process performs an indispensable function. If an error can be contained so that it results in the destruction of no more than one process, the task might still be completed. In this case, a more reliable implementation results. The third potential benefit of hardware adaptability will be well served if the task force can grow (or shrink) with the addition (or removal) of processor and memory resources. This is particularly easy if data structures are separately locatable and addressable entities whose size or number can vary. Likewise, it is particularly easy to

Reprinted with permission from *Proc. 7th Symp. Oper. Syst. Princip.*, 1979, pp. 117–127.

do when the task force is composed, in part, of duplicated processes or data.

An individual process in a task force is specialized; it has only a small part of the overall work of the task force to accomplish. Hence, it needs to access relatively little data or code. As a result, the address domain of a process may be small. This suggests that each unit of code and each data structure should be separately addressable so that address domains can be tailored to the requirements of the individual process.

Processes of a task force rely more on other processes than is the case in the typical multiprogramming system. What is performed by a subroutine in the multiprogramming system may be performed by a separate process in the task force. Inter-process communication and synchronization are substantially more frequent. Hence, each process must be able to address some data objects, such as mailboxes and semaphores, for communication and synchronization.

Task forces vary along dimensions not even found in multiprogramming systems. For example, the number of processes in a single task force may vary not with the number of functions to be performed, but with available resources. Where several processors are available, input data may be partitioned and processes replicated so that each process performs the same function, but on a restricted portion of data.

In summary, the process in a task force is small--small because the function it executes is a small portion of the overall task, and small in the size of its addressing domain. A task force consists of potentially a large number of components, related in a complex structure. The structure and composition of a task force may vary to a considerable extent dynamically. The task force is the unit of responsibility for any functionality other than the most primitive. Hence, it is the unit of accountability and the unit for which major resource scheduling decisions are made.

We have defined task forces quite generally. For example, a sequence of three processes connected via Unix pipes would constitute a task force [14]. However, such a task force is exceedingly simple: neither its structure, nor its composition, change dynamically; it does not require any but straightforward synchronization based on data passing through the pipes; it exhibits no communication paths or organizational structure for handling errors so that they can be related to the task force as a whole, rather than a single process; and it provides no basis for coordinating the output that appears on the user terminal. While an extremely useful program organization, such structures are not sufficient to cope with the problems that arise in large applications designed to exploit the parallelism inherent in distributed systems--whether loosely or tightly coupled. It is our objective to explore facilities that do so.

2. Cm* Architecture

The design of an operating system is influenced by the hardware resources it manages. Hence, it is appropriate to sketch the salient aspects of the Cm* architecture. Additional descriptive detail can be found in papers by Fuller and Swan, et al. [5, 15]. Cm* was designed and a prototype implemented at Carnegie-Mellon University. The prototype began running in Spring, 1977. By Fall, 1979 it included 50 processors.

The Cm* multi-miniprocessor consists of interconnected *computer modules*, each an autonomous computing engine[1] In the existing system each computer module is implemented by a DEC LSI-11, a standard LSI-11 bus, memory, and devices. All primary memory in the system is potentially accessible to each processor. Each computer module includes a local switch, the Slocal, which selectively routes processor memory references either to the local memory of the computer module or else onto the *Map Bus*. The Slocal likewise accepts references to its local memory that emanate from distant processors. Up to fourteen computer modules may be connected to a Map Bus so that they share the use of a single *Kmap*, a processor responsible for routing memory requests and data between Slocals. Together, the Slocals and the Kmap implement a distributed switch.

The computer modules, Kmap, and Map Bus together comprise a *cluster*. Clusters are connected via *Intercluster Buses* running between the Kmaps. A Cm* configuration can have an arbitrary number of clusters, although clusters need not have direct Intercluster Bus connections to every other cluster in a configuration. The number of computer modules in a cluster and the number of clusters in a system may vary. Currently, our Cm* implementation consists of five clusters, 50 processors, and 3 megabytes of primary memory distributed relatively evenly across the clusters and across the computer modules. Synchronous Line Units are provided on several processors for connecting terminal devices or multiplexors. Each cluster is connected to to a DEC KL10 processor with high speed "DA Links." For on-line storage of data, each cluster is provided with one or more moving-head disk controllors. An example

---

[1]The name Cm* stands for an arbitrary number of Cm's, or Computer Modules. The * is derived from the notation introduced by Kleene for regular expressions.

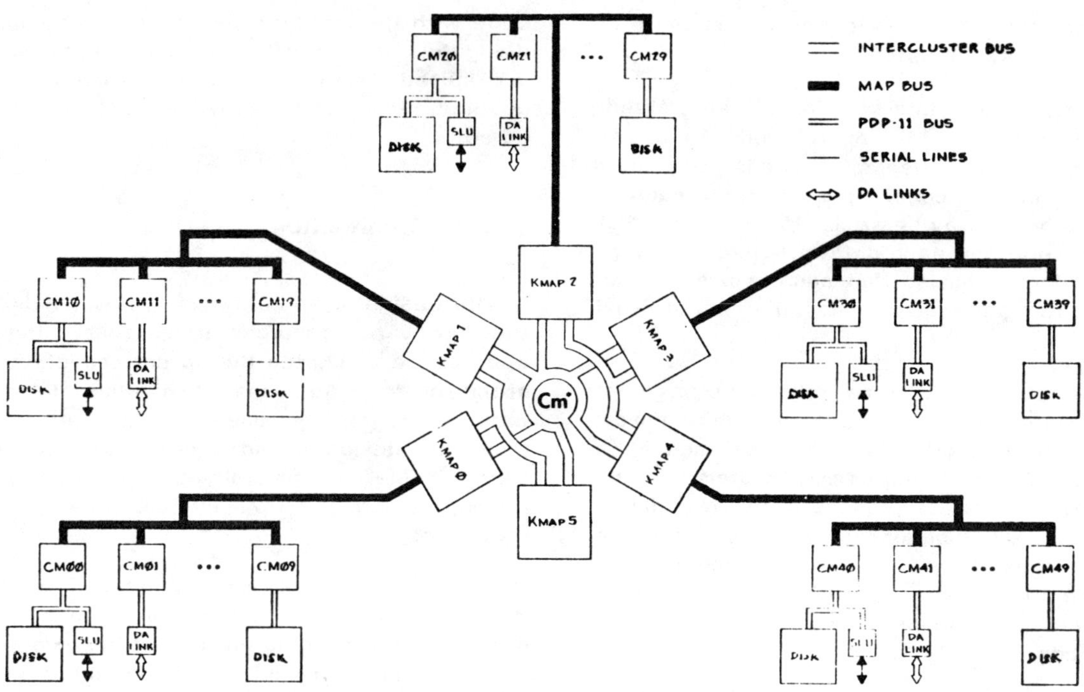

Figure 1: Five Cluster Cm* Configuration

configuration of Cm* is shown in Figure 1. It is quite similar to the current implementation.

Collectively, the Kmaps mediate each processor reference placed on the Map Bus; thus they can sustain the appearance of a single large memory. However, memory is organized in a *performance hierarchy*; approximate inter-reference times for local, intracluster, and intercluster references are 3, 9, and 26 μs, respectively, as measured in benchmark tests [4]. The distributed switch consisting of the Slocals, Kmaps and associated busses is message switched; references are interleaved.

Using the 4 kiloword writable control store of the Kmap, operating system functions beyond those for address mapping may be microprogrammed to increase system performance. The Kmap is multiprogrammed, and can retain sufficient context to manage up to eight active requests for memory references or microcoded operating system functions at once.

3. StarOS Architecture

The objectives of StarOS are to support the construction and execution of task forces and to exploit, and to allow the user to exploit, the facilities present in the Cm* architecture. An additional StarOS objective is to support experimentation and measurement with system behavior.

StarOS is an object-oriented system. In this regard it is similar to Plessey 250 [2], CAL time sharing system [10], CAP [12], and Hydra [16]. All information is encoded and stored in objects. Objects are *typed*; the type of an object determines that set of *functions*, which alone determine the behavior of the object. All objects are distinct and unique.

To access an object to extract information stored in it, or to alter the object, a process invokes some function defined on the object. To be successful in making such an access a process must possess a *capability* or "protected address" for the object [9, 3, 16]. A capability not only names a distinct, unique object; it also specifies authority to manipulate the object using some subset of the functions defined for that object. Permission to perform a specific function on an object is called a *right*.

The size of an object's representation in StarOS is between 2 and 4096 bytes. An object is comprised of two disjoint portions: the data portion, which contains a sequence of data words, and the capability list portion, which contains a sequence of capabilities. The symbolic names provided by the programming language can be used to mask the segregation of data from capabilities. StarOS differs from the Plessey

250 system in which objects contain either data or capabilities, but not both.

Each process has two name spaces, the capability name space and the immediate addressing space of 64 kilobytes, divided into 16 *windows*. The *Load* function will cause the 4 kilobytes of addresses of a specific window to address bytes of the data portion of an object. When this occurs, we refer to the object as *mapped*. In this manner, processor memory references have immediate access to the data portion of an object--that is, the data may be manipulated using the instructions of the LSI-11. This is in contrast to HYDRA where a kernel entry is required to read and write individual bytes in the data portion of all objects other then 8 kilobyte "page objects". The advantage of immediate addressing is that users are not penalized for using small objects tailored to the needs of the application.

The capability name space of a process is defined by the capability list portion of the process object (to be described later). A process may *directly* name all objects for which capabilities appear in this list together with the components of those objects. The microcoded capability functions can interpret these direct names for objects and perform the required function without software intervention. If an object is not directly nameable, some capability function must be performed to make it directly nameable. Only then may it be used as a parameter for some function.

The StarOS system defines several types of objects. In addition, users may freely define additional types together with the associated functions. Strong typing is uniformly enforced. To explain some of the ramifications of dynamic type creation by users, we first distinguish between *abstract* types and *representation* types. Representation types are defined by StarOS and are the basis for building all abstract types. Here we discuss the most useful two: basic and deque. The most general purpose type is called *basic*. It contains a vector of data words and a vector of capabilities. Individual words or capabilities may be named by index. The functions defined on data words include:

- *Read* the value,
- *Write* the value,
- *Increment* the value *indivisibly*, and
- *Decrement* the value *indivisibly* if it is not zero.

The *Increment* and *Decrement* functions are the basis for programming simple software locks. Cm* processors cannot otherwise perform an indivisible read-modify-write action. The basic type is defined so that if a basic object is mapped to the immediate address space of a process, the processor memory requests perform *Read* and *Write* functions on the data portion of the object. In this way the data portion behaves as a conventional memory segment. Program code is typically stored in basic objects that have no capability list.

A variety of functions are defined for the manipulation of capabilities:

- *Copy* a capability from a position in the capability list portion of an object into another position in the same or some different capability list,
- *Restrict* rights recorded in a capability, and
- *Transfer* a capability stored in one position to another position, perhaps in a different object. (Note that the original capability is erased.)

Another generally useful representation type is the deque, defined to buffer 16-bit words of data. Associated functions include:

- *PushFront*--to insert a data word at the front of the deque,
- *PushRear*--to insert a data word at the rear of the deque,
- *PopFront*--to remove a data word at the front of the deque, if any,
- *PopRear*--to remove a data word from the rear of the deque, if any.

Deques may be used to implement stacks by employing only the *PushFront* and *PopFront* functions, or queues by employing only the *PushRear* and *PopFront* functions, or deques, by using all the defined functions. When the deque is mapped onto the immediate address space of a process, memory references to the deque are interpreted by the Kmap as invocations on the deque functions; the specific function invoked depends on the specific address within the window.

3.1. Synchronization and Message Communication

StarOS is a message-based system. The motivation for this is to allow *concurrent*, and possible parallel, execution whenever feasible--that is, whenever not restricted by the logic of the algorithm. The scheduler and multiplexor are responsible for ensuring that concurrent processes execute in parallel whenever possible, consistent with the scheduling policy.

In this message-based system processes frequently send messages, which are requests for work to be done. A process may have multiple requests outstanding. Wherever possible, the StarOS design does not preempt the user's ability to program concurrent processes. Hence, a process does not ever suspend execution as a side-effect of a message send or receive. The process explicitly controls when execution is to be suspended to await the completion of actions taken by other processes.

StarOS supplies an *event* mechanism which processes may use to await the occurrence of specific events. A set of *events* is defined by each process. The process may *Block*, that is, suspend execution, awaiting any one of a subset of the defined events to occur. Routinely, a process associates an event with the receipt of a message from a specific mailbox.

To support rapid message communication among processes, StarOS implements a *mailbox* type of object. It is capable of buffering messages which are either single data words or single capabilities. When created, a mailbox is defined to buffer either data messages or capability messages, but not both. The type-specific functions are *Send* and *Receive*.

First consider the *Receive* function: it will remove, then return, a buffered message if the mailbox is not empty. If the mailbox is empty, the *Receive* function will act differently depending on whether *Receive* was invoked in *conditional* or *registration* mode. In conditional mode the *Receive* function merely returns with no message. If the invoker specified registration mode, then the name of the invoker together with an event name is written onto the *Registration* queue associated with the mailbox. The process must have defined the event to be associated with the receipt of a message from the particular mailbox. To define the event, the process specifies an event name, a capability for the mailbox, and a location within the address space of the process capable of storing a message delivered from the mailbox. The process may then select that event as a condition for the Block function.

Send will deliver a message to a registered receiver, if one is listed in the registration queue. Alternatively, *Send* will buffer the message if the registration queue is empty and the mailbox is not full. *Send* will fail if the mailbox is full. If the message is transmitted to a receiver, the receiver is removed from the registration queue, the transmitted message is stored in the location associated with the event. The event named in the registration queue is then *Signalled* to the receiving process. If the process is *Blocked* waiting on that event, execution of the process will be resumed.

Note that StarOS mailboxes are finite and that processes communicating via the mailboxes are not *Blocked* as side-effect of performing a message function on a mailbox. Note also that the mailbox functions complete before the invoker is permitted to continue operation. Mailbox functions are implemented partially in microcode and partially in software.

3.2. Program and Process Construction

Module objects are the basis for program construction and the dynamic creation of processes. From a behavioral point of view, a module defines and exports a set of functions for use by code in other modules. It may also define a new type of object. At any instant, each user or system process is executing a particular function of a particular module.

From an implementation point of view, a module is an object containing capabilities for those code and data objects shared by the processes executing the functions of the module. The *Invoke* function is defined on modules. Before *invoking* an asynchronously executed function, a process prepares a *carrier* to hold invocation parameters. A carrier is a small basic object; a capability for it will be sent to the process that is to execute the invoked function. One parameter always included in the carrier is a capability for a mailbox. The process executing the function will return the carrier to this mailbox when the function is completed. The requesting process can wait for the function completion by *Block*ing on an event associated with this mailbox.

Transmittal of the carrier may occur in several ways. In the simplest case, *Invoke* will cause the creation of a new process to execute the invoked function. That new process will be created with what is referred to as an "invocation" mailbox. Invocation is complete when the carrier is sent to the invocation mailbox of the new process. Such a process is said to be "transient" because it will terminate after the function execution is completed.

Alternatively, one or more processes may be pre-initialized to execute a particular function. Such processes are cyclic; they *Block* on a common invocation mailbox, awaiting arrival of a carrier that represents a function request. If one or more such processes exist executing the function, we refer to the function as being "present". Note that if multiple processes exist for the same present function, they share the module object, the invocation mailbox, and all objects for which there are capabilities in the module object.

It should be evident that the StarOS implementation of modules and processes provides support for programming according to the tenets of the "data abstraction" methodology [11, 13]. Recall that a module may define some new type of abstract object. The functions exported for invocation by code external to the module can implement the functions of the abstract type. Hence, only the code of the module can directly access the data words and capabilities that in the object of representation type that implements the representation of the object of abstract type.

The mechanism to support dynamic type creation is as follows. To create a new type, an initialization function of the module would dynamically request StarOS to create a new *type token*, which it would then place in the module object. To create an instance of the new abstract object, a function of the module would first create an object of the proper representation type. It would then manipulate the data and capability positions in that object to initialize the abstract object's representation. It would then mark the object as being of the abstract type by storing the name of the module in the descriptor of the object, maintained by StarOS. The type token is sufficient authority to mark an object. The type token also allows the *Conversion* of capabilities for the object into *abstract capabilities*. An abstract capability is a pointer to an abstract object; it authorizes no functions of the representation type of the object, but rather authorizes invocation of functions of the module that defines the abstract type.

Functions in a module defining some abstract type may, using the type token, *Amplify* an abstract capability to produce a capability for the representation object. Hence, *Amplify* returns a capability for the same object with rights so that the object can be manipulated using those functions defined as part of its representation type.

To maintain complete control over the behavior of all instances of the abstract type it defines, a module must observe the following:

- The type token must not be exercised by any process, other than those executing the functions of the module.

- All capabilities for objects defined by a module must be *Convert*ed to be abstract, before being transmitted to processes executing code that is outside the module.

If these rules are followed, no manipulation of the object can be accomplished except via the functions of the module.

3.3. Scheduling

The responsibility for scheduling is divided between processes, which are called *schedulers*, and a low level mechanism called the *multiplexor*, which is executed by each LSI-11 processor independently. The multiplexor makes short term decisions about which process to assign to execute on each processor. Each scheduler is designed to implement a specific policy. The StarOS multiplexor may be initialized to implement a variety of policies: round-robin, preemptive, first-come/first-serve, priority, and the scheduling of processes on prefered processors so that a process will execute in the same computer module where the objects containing the code and data are located. We intend to experiment with alternative scheduling policies, but have not yet done so.

At system load time, we associate--with each processor--a priority ordered set of mailboxes to serve as queues of processes. These sets of *run queues* may overlap arbitrarily, and the priority order is processor-specific. When it is appropriate for a processor to switch what process it is executing, the multiplexor determines the next process to execute by searching the queues in priority order. The selected process is assigned to execute on the processor for a prescribed maximum time quantum. If the sum total of time which the process executes ever exceeds a scheduler determined value, the multiplexor will *Send* the process back to the scheduler. It is assumed that only one scheduler is responsible for each process. Multiple schedulers may coexist. It is possible for a scheduler to alter the priority of a run queue for some processor or it may add or remove a queue from the set associated with a processor. It is assumed that if multiple schedulers exist, they do not act in conflict with one another.

3.4. StarOS Instructions

In a distributed system, parallelism is natural. Hence, for any function, its designer must decide if it is to be executed sequentially or concurrently with respect to further execution by its invoker. Where a function is to be performed sequentially, it can be viewed as an extension of the LSI-11 processor instruction set. Where we wish to state explicitly that a function is performed sequentially with respect to its invoker, we will refer to it as an *instruction*. All functions defined for representation types are instructions. All instructions are invoked, or triggered, by making a LSI-11 reference to a mapped object, or to special addresses reserved for communication between a process and its underlying machine. References to mapped objects are interpreted by the Kmap. If more than a single 16 bit parameter is required, the process first initializes a parameter block--typically on the process stack--and then then makes an appropriate mapped reference to transmit the address of the parameter block to the part of StarOS that implements instructions. The Kmap has "first refusal" of all StarOS instructions. Requests for instructions not in firmware are passed to software. An instruction may be implemented in software, firmware, or a mixture of the two.

We have given an overview of many StarOS functions. Those implemented as instructions, are in the following categories: accessing the representation types of objects, synchronization, message passing, invocation of a function, process switching, and trap and interrupt handling. The latter three categories are predominantly implemented in software. All other StarOS functions are asynchronous. That is, the invoking process may continue execution in parallel with the invoked function, which is executed by another process. The invoker may choose if and when it will await a reply from the invoked function. The important point to be made here is that only a modest portion of the operating system is defined to be synchronous.

4. Task Force Descriptions

To realize a task force in StarOS, we distinguish between the *executable task force*--that set of processes with supporting code and data objects that actually performs the desired computation--and the *static task force*--that code and perhaps initial input data from which the executable task force is instantiated. The difference between the two is analogous to the difference between an executing instance of a procedure and the procedure declaration in a programming language.

As an aid for the construction of task forces, StarOS supports the TASK language[8]. The author of a task force describes the components of his task force--code, input data, processes, and communication mailboxes. The TASK compiler generates a list of the sequence of functions calls that must be executed by the StarOS program loader. TASK provides three specialized services: initialization of the capability name space and the immediate address space of the task force processes; interface to the BLISS[1] programming language used to implement task forces to provide symbolic names for objects; and specification of the initial placement and assignment decisions for the objects and process of the task force to improve system performance.

In the following two sections we describe StarOS itself as an example task force. This will permit us simultaneously to show both a task force with interesting structure, and to explain some ramifications of its implementation. We do not intend to suggest that StarOS is a typical task force, or even an example of the style in which a large class of users might structure their applications.

4.1. The StarOS Static Task Force

Following the data abstraction methodology, we assume a static task force to be a set of modules, each exporting a set of functions, together with some input data. It is in this static form that the task force is originally constructed and updated. The StarOS loader creates module objects for each module in the static task force. Data may exist in the StarOS file system or in the DEC TOPS-10 system to which Cm* is directly connected via the high speed DA Link.

We have already discussed selected functions from some StarOS modules and the representation or abstract types which they define. StarOS includes modules for capability addressing of objects, defining basic objects and deque objects, message communication, dynamic type creation, object management (e.g. primary memory management), creation and maintenance of module objects and process objects, input/output transmission, the file system, loader, scheduler, clock, and reconfiguration.

Logically, the static StarOS task force is the collection of modules, each divided into levels. Each level is dependent only on lower levels of itself or levels of other modules. The levels form a hierarchy as defined by Habermann, et al. [6]. Detailed discussion of the structure of the original StarOS system are discussed in [7]. We do not discuss the static task force structure of the revised system in any further here, but turn to the executable task force.

4.2. The StarOS Executable Task Force

In this section we describe the components of the StarOS executable task force and their realization as StarOS objects. As discussed earlier, a subset of the StarOS functions, referred to as *instructions*, are defined to execute sequentially and synchronously with the process requesting the function; that is, the process is suspended for the duration of the function's execution. Collectively, the StarOS instructions are called the *nucleus* and they define the sequential portion of the abstract machine that StarOS provides to its users. The remaining functions are all performed by processes other than that of the requesting process, so that the two may execute concurrently.

The nucleus is implemented partly in Kmap microcode (about 2000 80-bit micro-instructions), and partly in software (roughly 4 kilobytes). The microcoded Kmap has "first refusal" of each request to execute a StarOS instruction. If it can perform the instruction, it does so while both the requesting process and its processor are suspended. If the instruction is not implemented in microcode, the Kmap arranges for the suspended processor to accept a trap into the "kernel addressing space" where the nucleus software commences execution. The Slocal and Kmap hardware allows StarOS to support two independent address spaces for each processor. These address spaces roughly correspond to the distinction between "kernel/supervisor/monitor" mode and "user" mode of a conventional processor. The kernel address space is reserved by StarOS for the nucleus. The multiplexor, part of the nucleus, chooses a process for the "user address space". Traps, interrupts and StarOS instruction invocations may cause a switch between spaces. As noted earlier, the nucleus software performs any StarOS instructions refused by the Kmap, or any instructions that could not be completed by the Kmap because of error or an unduely complicated situation.

For almost all purposes, the nucleus software that executes on each computer module appears to run as a standard StarOS process. In fact, it is implemented as a StarOS process object. It, like all other processes, is constrained to perform only those actions for which it has proper authority. In particular, it cannot access an object for which it does not possess a capability. However, by virtue of executing in the kernel space, the hardware permits the nucleus to execute the "privileged machine instructions" that change processor state such as the interrupt priority level. The nucleus is constrained more than other processes; it may not invoke any concurrent function, thus the nucleus is not dependent on the correct execution of other processes.

At any instant, the StarOS executable task force consists of a separate nucleus process for each physical computer module, together with a set of present and transitory processes that were created as a result of the invocation of asynchronous StarOS functions. The exact *configuration* of the executable task force will vary: transitory processes are created and terminate. Multiple present processes to perform the same function may exist. The assignment of specific processes to processors, or sets of processors, may change dynamically or with each system initialization.

System initialization is performed by functions of the reconfiguration module. The first program loaded includes the reconfiguration functions that measure the amount of available memory in the computer module; define the first few objects; provide the Kmap with the information required locate objects; and initialize the nucleus process. It is then possible for a reconfiguration function to execute as a StarOS process. This function locates and initializes the other computer modules in the cluster.

A nucleus process will be created and installed in each computer module successfully initialized. Subsequently, the reconfiguration process will attempt to configure additional clusters into the system if instructed to do so. Currently, the reconfiguration process expects to find the nucleus microcode already loaded, though we have plans to have microcode loaded automatically as part of system startup. Initialization is completed by creating the other modules of the StarOS task force and executing their initialization functions.

For both enhanced reliability and performance, the few thousand bytes of the nucleus code is typically duplicated in each computer module's memory; each nucleus process executes code from its local memory. Typically, but not necessarily, we configure StarOS so that each Cm* cluster is functionally complete: each StarOS function can be executed within the cluster. During system initialization the reconfiguration function determines the number of replicated, present processes to be created for each function, the placement of code for the function in specific physical memory, and the assignment of processes to run queues, and hence to individual processors or sets of processors. As part of nucleus initialization, each module which has some function implemented in the nucleus has the opportunity to execute initialization code. For example, it is this initialization code which creates the desired run queues and the priority ordered search list for each multiplexor.

Figure 2 depicts an example StarOS configuration on one cluster. A large rectangular box represents a physical computer module processor and its memory. Solid ovals represent present processes that are assigned to execute on the computer module; their code may be assumed to be local. Note that each computer module has a private nucleus process with local code. Dotted ovals represent transitory processes that exist only for the duration of the single invocation that they service.

Alternative configurations can be loaded. For example, it is possible to configure the task force so that two object manager processes share some or all of their code and that they execute on the same or different processors.

4.3. Variation in Configurations

As was mentioned above, StarOS is typically configured so that a cluster is functionally complete. Cluster autonomy, however, depends upon the behavior of resource managers as well as upon the

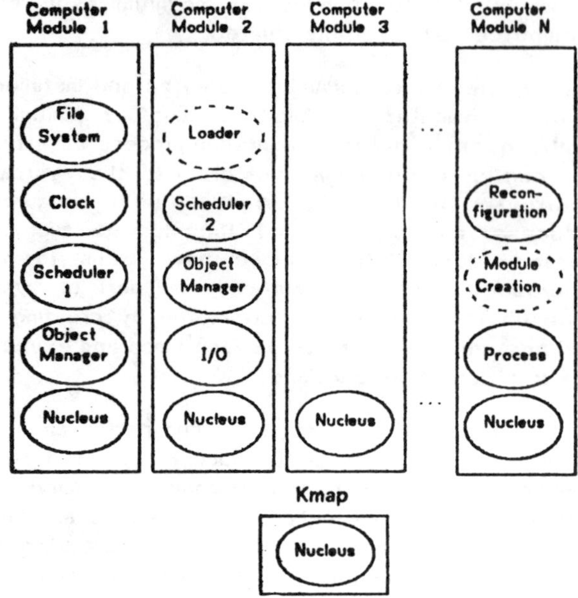

Figure 2: The StarOS Executable Task Force

configuration decisions. For example, the StarOS object manager partitions the physical memory into clusters. The object manager processes that execute in a cluster have jurisdiction over allocating physical memory in only that cluster. Any request to allocate space in a remote cluster is mailed to a companion object manager in the remote cluster. Object manager initialization provides the mailboxes for such communication.

Reliability is one of the potentials of a multiprocessor. To achieve this the software must be constructed so that single failures do not render an entire module useless. To cite one example, the object manager is designed so that a process responding to an allocation request will contain internal state about only a single request at a time. In addition, a separate data structure is used to record the allocation state of each computer module's memory. An object manager process may lock only one such structure at a time. In case of failure of a process, the module will continue to provide for object management, though in a possibly degraded fashion.

The configuration of StarOS may change from time to time for any of three reasons: performance enhancement, fault recovery, and accommodating environmental changes. Ideally, StarOS should respond to changing demands for its services. For instance, if demand for a particular function is high, more processes can be created to perform that function. Processes executing reconfiguration functions examine the environment and adjust the StarOS configuration to improve system performance. Note that the system does not spontaneously duplicate processes or physically move objects to enhance performance at the present time.

Dynamic reconfiguration can be exploited so that the system may recover from hardware or software failure. For instance, if an object manager process were to fail, a reconfiguration function could destroy that process, and then create another to assume its management responsibilities.

Similarly, if the physical environment changes--such as the addition of a new computer module or entire cluster, StarOS could be expanded to take advantage of this. Alternatively, if physical resources are removed, the task force configuration can be reduced. In this way an engineer might instruct the system to exclude a particular system resource from use so that it might be repaired.

4.4. Process Relations

The executable task force can be usefully envisioned as a graph of processes. For this purpose we ignore the module, code, data and mailbox objects which are also components of this task force. Such a graph can be constructed in different ways to reflect the different relations processes in a task force may have to one another. We will discuss two of the relations which StarOS supports.

The first relation is the *dependence* relation. Whenever a process is created as a result of an invocation, it is either *dependent* on the invoking process, or on a distinguished StarOS reconfiguration process. The choice is statically determined by a value recorded in the module of the function used to create the process--that is, it is determined by the author of the module of which the invoked function is a part.

The *dependence* relation defines forests of trees; it is used as the basis for process suspension and abnormal termination. For example, the function *Kill* will destroy all processes in the *dependence* tree rooted in the specified process. Note the following behavior based on the *dependence* relation. Suppose that a user process invoked a StarOS function which resulted in the creation of a new process *P* that is *not dependent* on the invoker. *Kill*ing the invoker process will not cause the destruction of the system process *P*, and *P* will be able to complete its work, restoring system data structures to a consistent state before terminating normally. Certainly, caution must be exercised to ensure that arbitrary users do not create such processes indiscriminately.

The *bailout* relation induces a second relation among processes. When a process is created, a *bailout mailbox* is associated with it. This mailbox is either specified by the invoker, or it is a system mailbox supplied by StarOS. When a process becomes incapable of further execution because of an internal error that it is unable to cope with, the process is suspended and a capability for the process is mailed to its *bailout* mailbox. Presumably, the receiver of a bailout message can respond to the process failure. Users are free to relate processes arbitrarily using the bailout relation.

The dependence relation among the StarOS processes establishes a shallow tree in each cluster. The roots are the reconfiguration processes for each cluster. All nucleus processes and any present processes are directly *dependent* on the reconfiguration processes of the cluster. Reconfiguration processes in different clusters are not dependent. Likewise, a mailbox serviced by the reconfiguration process is the bailout mailbox for all StarOS processes in a cluster, and for processes of user task forces that elect not to handle bailout processing.

5. Concluding Remarks

Because experience with the system is limited, it is uncertain how well StarOS facilities will support application task forces. However, a retrospective look at the StarOS design reveals some characteristics of the system are pervasive in the StarOS task force. It is likely that they would influence the design of any application task force.

The consistent use of typed objects and capability-based authorization. Except for the object manager, which creates capabilities and objects, and the nucleus which implements object addressing, no StarOS function can access an object without referencing it with a capability.[2] Two benefits accrue. First, processes are endowed with a limited sphere of influence derived from the corresponding module object. A process is granted authority commensurate with its responsibility, and thus the effects of process--both good and bad--are restricted to a limited domain. Second, the low level facilities of the system provide an attractive means of structuring the elements of computation. The system encourages the programmer to build multi-level structures in a natural way.

[2]Because the addresses generated by direct memory access I/O devices cannot be mapped by the Slocal or Kmap, functions controlling these devices must make use of the physical address of the objects used as buffers. We view this as a defficiency, and not an opportunity.

Interface Uniformity. From both within and without the StarOS system, functions are requested and executed in a uniform manner. For example, access to words or capabilities within representation types of objects is independent of the size or location of the object. This gives the user and system freedom to separate the issues of task force performance and task force correctness. At a higher level, the StarOS instruction *Invoke* provides a single uniform means of requesting functions of modules whether the modules belong to the StarOS task force or to a user task force. Because of the resulting uniformity of structures, StarOS processes can be distinguished from user processes only by examining the interprocess relations that define task forces.

Preservation of the multi-processor aspects of Cm.* The *Invoke* instruction results in the parallel execution of concurrent processes. The basic mechanisms for communication are built around the asynchronous transmission of messages. This type of process structure is well-suited to the asynchronous parallel execution of the Cm* processors. There is, of course, the constraint of processor scheduling. For the user who wishes to concern himself with the details of process assignment and scheduling, it is possible to obtain the proper capabilities for the user's processes and for a subset of the run queues. This is possible because StarOS distinguishes the basic mechanisms for the multiplexor from the management decisions made by system or user scheduler processes.

Allocation of overheads. For the most part, the use of simple features of the system does not incur overheads associated with the implementation of more complex features. For example, a reference to the data portion of a StarOS basic object requires about the same time as a similar memory reference in the most simple Cm* system. In general, the cost of referencing a StarOS object is directly proportional to the amount of data that must be transferred. For this reason, once processes have been created, an overhead directly related to the *Invoke* instruction, they may communicate rapidly using message communications. The cost of moving messages to and from mailbox objects is low.

6. Acknowledgments

No serious software is developed in a vacuum. StarOS was developed at CMU in an environment where there is a long history of interest in multiprocessing. A previous multiprocessor, C.mmp, its operating system Hydra, and the experiments performed on Hydra influenced us. Likewise, the FAMOS project, developed to investigate families of operating systems with differing versions of components, also influenced us [6]. We learned from the successes and the failures of these efforts as well as several other system efforts outside our immediate community. So we owe a debt to the people involved. Likewise, we would like to acknowledge Sam Fuller and Richard Swan, who were principals in the development of the Cm* hardware.

References

[1]
W. Wulf, et al.
Bliss Reference Manual.
DEC, 1970.

[2]
D. England.
Capability Concept Mechanisms and Structure in System 250.
In *Protection in Operating Systems*, pages 63-82. IRIA, 1974.

[3]
R. Fabry.
Capability Based Addressing.
Communications of the ACM 17(7):403-412, 1974.

[4]
S. Fuller, A. Jones, and I. Durham, eds.
Cm Review, June 1977.*
Technical Report, Carnegie-Mellon University Computer Science Department, 1977.

[5]
S. Fuller, J. Ousterhout, L. Raskin, P. Rubinfeld, P.Sindhu and R. Swan.
Multi-microprocessors: An Overview and Working Example.
Proceedings of the IEEE 66(2):216-228, Rebruary, 1978.

[6]
A. Habermann, L. Flon, and L. Cooprider.
Modularization and Hierarchy in a Family of Operating Systems.
Communications of the ACM 19:266-272, 1976.

[7]
A. Jones, R. Chansler Jr., I. Durham, P. Feiler and K. Schwans.
Software Management of Cm*--a Distributed Multiprocessor.
In *Proceedings National Computer Conference*, pages 657-663. AFIPS, 1977.

[8]
A. Jones and K. Schwans.
TASK Forces: Distributed Software for Solving Problems of Substantial Size.
In *Fourth International conference os Software Engineering*. SIGSOFT-ACM, 1979.

[9]
B. Lampson.
Protection.
In *Proc. Fifth Annual Princeton Conference on Information Sciences and Systems*, pages 437-443. Princeton University, 1971.

[10]
B. Lampson and H. Sturgis.
Refelctions on an Operating System Design.
Communications of the ACM 19:251-265, 1976.

[11]
B. Liskov and S. Zilles.
Programming with Abstract Data Types.
In *Proceedings of the ACM SIGPLAN Conference on Very High Level Languages*, pages 50-59. ACM, 1974.

[12]
R. Needham and R. Walker.
The Cambridge CAP Computer and Its Protection System.
In *Sixth Symposium on Operating Systems Principles*, pages 1-10. ACM, 1977.

[13]
D. Parnas.
On the Criteria to be Used in Decomposing Systems into Modules.
Communications of the ACM 15:1053-1058, 1972.

[14]
D. Ritchie and K. Thompson.
The UNIX Time-Sharing system.
Communications of the ACM 17(7), 1974.

[15]
R. Swan, S. Fuller and P. Siewiorek.
Cm*: a Modular, Multi-microprocessor.
In *Proceedings National Computer Conference*, pages 637-644. AFIPS, 1977.

[16]
Wulf, W., et al.
HYDRA: The Kernel of a Multiprocessor Operating System.
Communications of the ACM 17(6):337-345, 1974.

Operating Systems

R. Stockton Gaines Editor

Medusa: An Experiment in Distributed Operating System Structure

John K. Ousterhout, Donald A. Scelza, and Pradeep S. Sindhu
Carnegie-Mellon University

The design of Medusa, a distributed operating system for the Cm* multimicroprocessor, is discussed. The Cm* architecture combines distribution and sharing in a way that strongly impacts the organization of operating systems. Medusa is an attempt to capitalize on the architectural features to produce a system that is modular, robust, and efficient. To provide modularity and to make effective use of the distributed hardware, the operating system is partitioned into several disjoint *utilities* that communicate with each other via messages. To take advantage of the parallelism present in Cm* and to provide robustness, all programs, including the utilities, are *task forces* containing many concurrent, cooperating *activities*.

Key Words and Phrases: operating systems, distributed systems, message systems, task forces, deadlock, exception reporting

CR Categories: 4.32, 4.35

This research was supported by the Department of Defense Advanced Research Projects Agency, ARPA Order 3597, monitored by the Air Force Avionics Laboratory under Contract F33615-78-C-1551. The views and conclusions contained in this document are those of the authors and should not be interpreted as representing the official policies, either expressed or implied, of the Defense Advanced Research Projects Agency or the U.S. Government.

Authors' present addresses: J.K. Ousterhout and P.S. Sindhu, Department of Computer Science, Carnegie-Mellon University, Pittsburgh, PA 15213; D.A. Scelza, PRIME Computer, Inc., Old Connecticut Path, Framingham, MA 01701.

1. Introduction

Medusa is a multi-user operating system under development for Cm*, a multimicroprocessor system recently completed at Carnegie-Mellon University [7, 24, 25, 26]. The project is an attempt to understand the effect on operating system structure of the distributed Cm* hardware and to produce a system that capitalizes on and reflects the underlying architecture. The resulting system combines several structural features that make it unique among existing operating systems.

Medusa is the second operating system for Cm*. The first system, StarOS [10, 11, 12], has been concerned with making Cm* programmable at a high level by users. Thus the StarOS system embodies a general object addressing mechanism and a set of tools for manipulating parallel programs. For Medusa we have chosen to emphasize problems of structure, rather than facilities. The goal of the project has been to gain an understanding of how to build distributed operating systems and to exploit the hardware to produce a system organization with three attributes:

Modularity. The system should consist of a large number of small, cooperating subcomponents that may be built, modified, and measured independently. Such a structure complements the Cm* hardware, which consists of a large number of small processors.

Robustness. The system should be able to respond in a reasonable way to changes in its environment. These changes include an increase or decrease in workload and the failures of hardware, firmware, or software components. The multiplicity of processors should aid in achieving this goal.

Performance. Both the structure of the operating system and the abstractions it provides to user programs should reflect the underlying hardware. Application programs should be able to run with approximately the same efficiency using Medusa as they could on the bare hardware.

The software organization required to achieve the above goals has been strongly influenced by the Cm* architecture. Two general attributes of Cm* have been especially important. First, the physical arrangement of the hardware components is a distributed one. For each processor there is a small set of local resources that is accessible immediately and efficiently: the other facilities of the system are also accessible, but with greater overhead. The second fundamental attribute of the hardware is the power of the interprocessor communication facilities, which permits an efficient implementation of a variety of communication mechanisms ranging from shared memory to message systems. Section 2 discusses the Cm* hardware in more detail.

The combination of distribution and sharing in the hardware gives rise to two corresponding software issues: partitioning and communication. How should

Reprinted with permission from *Commun. Ass. Comput. Mach.*, vol. 23, pp. 92–105, Feb. 1980.

the operating system be partitioned in order to enhance its modularity and make use of the distributed hardware? How should the separate subunits communicate so as to function together in a robust way as a single logical entity? The remainder of this paper is a discussion of these issues and of the solutions embodied in Medusa.

Although the paper discusses the issues of partitioning and communication in a particular environment, that of Cm*, the issues have found relevance in many other areas of computer science. Research in structured programming has been concerned with reducing interactions within programs so that subportions of the programs can be designed and implemented separately [18]. Recent efforts in very large scale integrated (VLSI) circuit design are attempting to find ways to structure chip designs so as to reduce communication costs, since most of the area and complexity of the circuit stem from the interconnections [23]. Efforts to achieve fault tolerance must also be concerned with issues of partitioning and communication. For a system to be fault tolerant it must be subdivided into independent components with protected communication mechanisms so that (1) faults can be detected quickly, and (2) the occurrence of a fault in one portion of the system is not likely to destroy the other portions of the system [5].

The structure of Medusa resulted from the interaction of the three general goals (modularity, robustness, and performance) with the architecture of Cm*. The system has two significant characteristics:

(1) The control structure of the operating system is distributed. The functionality of Medusa is divided into disjoint *utilities*. Each utility executes in a private protected environment and implements a single abstraction for the rest of the system. Utilities communicate using messages.

(2) Parallelism is implicit and expected in Medusa. All programs are organized as *task forces*, each of which is a set of cooperating *activities*. By making the task force the central unit of control, Medusa makes it possible for very fine-grain interactions to occur within a task force. Each Medusa utility is a single task force.

Section 2 gives a brief discussion of the Cm* hardware and develops the distributed structure of Medusa. In Section 3 the task force notion is introduced. Section 4 gives an overview of the actual Medusa organization. Sections 5–7 discuss several topics in the implementation of the system: the use of pipes for utility communication (Section 5); the special privileges granted to utilities so that they can implement operating system functions (Section 6); deadlock in utility communication and the internal utility organization used to eliminate it (Section 7). Section 8 shows how the distribution and sharing in the system have impacted the exception reporting mechanism and discusses the benefits gained thereby. Section 9 concludes by comparing the Medusa structure with that of other systems.

2. The Distributed Structure

Figure 1 shows the organization of the Cm* hardware. It can be seen that the physical structure closely resembles that of a network. The system consists of a collection of 50 relatively autonomous processors called *computer modules* ("Cm"s in the PMS notation of Bell and Newell [2]), and five communication controllers (Kmaps). The Cm's are divided into *clusters*, with one Kmap presiding over each cluster. Each Kmap is respon-

Fig. 1. The 50-Processor Cm* System.

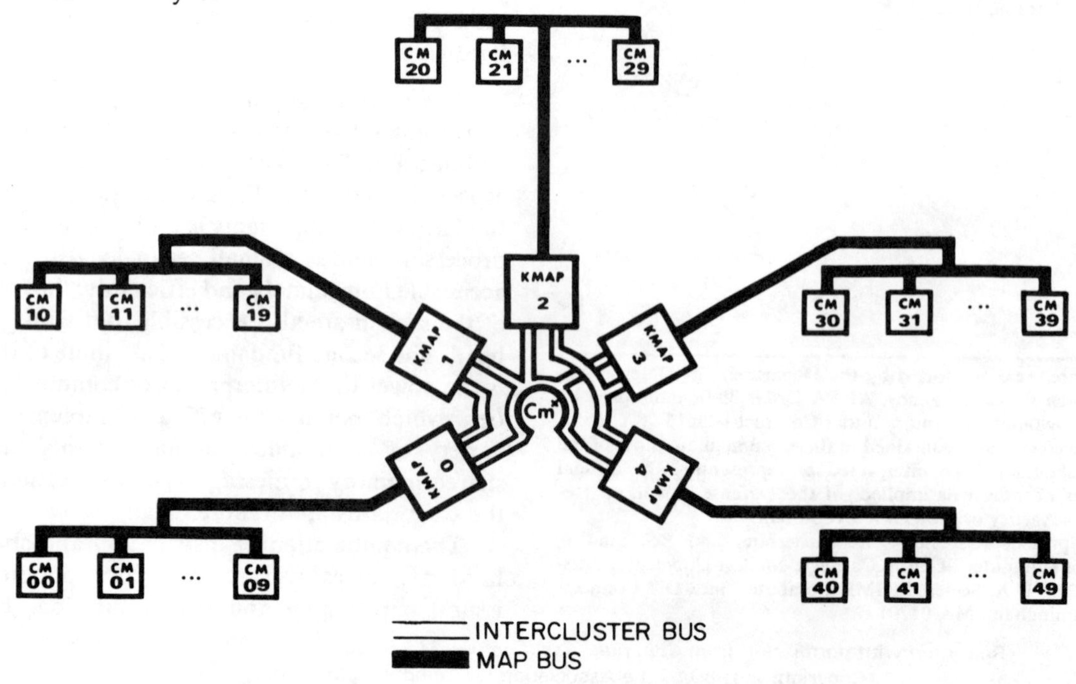

sible for the interprocessor communication to and from the Cm's in its cluster and must cooperate with the other Kmaps to handle intercluster transactions. All Kmaps are equal in stature; there is no central authority in the system.

Figure 2 gives a closer view of an individual computer module. Each Cm contains an LSI-11 processor, 64 or 128 kbytes of memory, and perhaps one or more I/O devices. A local switch, or Slocal, connects the computer module with the interprocessor communication structure. It is the presence of the Slocal as a switch in the computer module's addressing path (rather than as an I/O device on the Cm's bus) that distinguishes Cm* from networks. Tables in the Slocal allow it to decide on a reference-by-reference basis whether processor memory references are to proceed to local memory or be passed out to the Kmap of the cluster. Since Kmaps are general purpose processors with writable control stores, system designers have substantial freedom to choose their own methods of interprocessor communication. The Kmap microcode used by Medusa, which implements both shared memory and messages, is the third addressing structure to be implemented on Cm* (see [6] for a discussion of the others).

The ability to provide a variety of communication mechanisms efficiently, in spite of the distributed nature of the hardware, makes Cm* unique in the space of multicomputer systems and is fundamental to the development of Medusa.

Table I, taken from [19], shows the effect on program speed of making references to memory other than that of the processor executing the program. Although any processor may potentially access any memory location in the system, the cost of so doing varies by an order of magnitude, depending on the relative locations of processor and memory. The efficiency of a program running on Cm* is critically dependent on the "local hit ratio," or fraction of memory references that proceed from a processor directly to its local memory without involving a Kmap. A rule of thumb is that local hit ratios should generally be 90 percent or better in order to avoid serious performance degradation due to contention and/or the nonlocal access times.

Relatively high hit ratios can be achieved in a straightforward way by physically localizing information that need not be shared. Table II, also taken from [19], shows the dynamic distribution of memory references made by three multiprocess programs running on Cm*. Code references alone account for three-fourths of all memory references. Global information, that is, the information that must be accessible to all processes in a concurrent program, rarely accounts for more than a few percent of the references. Table II suggests that it makes relatively little difference where in the system global data is placed. On the other hand, code cannot be shared efficiently between concurrent processes; the primary problem facing system designers for Cm* is how to distribute the control structure.[1]

Fig. 2. Organization of a Cm.

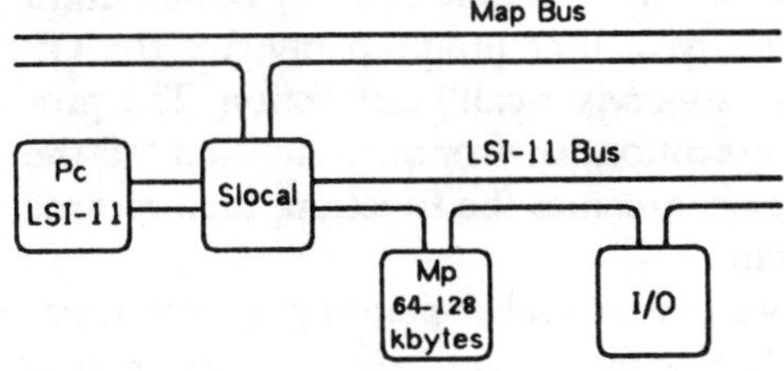

Table I. Average time per memory reference for a typical program making all code and data references to a single memory unit in a lightly loaded system

Memory position relative to Pc	Average reference time (microseconds)
Local	3.5
Nonlocal but within cluster	9.3
Cross-cluster	24

Fig. 3. One possible OS organization for Cm*: A single copy of the operating system code is shared by all processors.

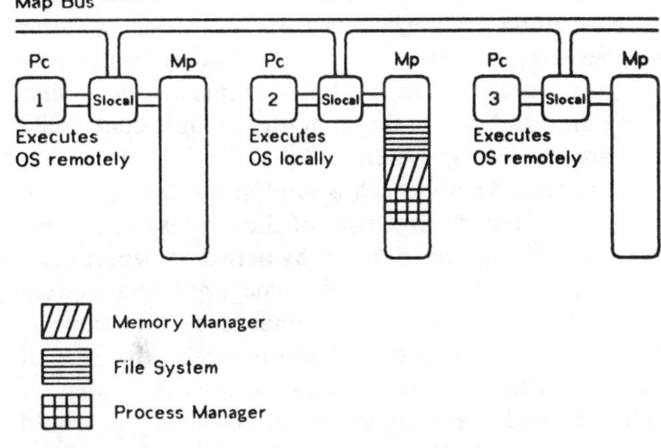

Table II. Dynamic distribution of memory references between four program components for three multiprocess programs

Program	Code (%)	Stack (%)	Owns (%)	Globals (%)
Partial differential equations	82	11.5	4	2.5
Quicksort	71	12.5	6	9.5
Set partitioning	71.5	23.5	4	1

2.1 Traditional Operating System Approaches

Using performance as a basis for judgment, this section shows why certain basic assumptions made by existing operating systems are inappropriate for Cm*.

Consider the application of a traditional operating system structure to Cm*. It is an assumption of virtually

[1] This is in contrast to most of the past work in distributed systems, which has been concerned with distributed data structures.

all existing operating systems that all of the functionality of the OS is immediately available at every point within the system. Typically, a user program invokes the OS using a "trap" or "supervisor call" instruction. The processor switches execution environment to that of the kernel or supervisor, executes the function, then returns to the user program.

Figure 3 shows one possible operating system organization for Cm*. For purposes of this discussion it is assumed that the operating system must provide three functions: memory management, a file system, and process management. These functions must be accessible to all programs running anywhere on the system. The approach of Figure 3 is much like that of a traditional uniprocessor or multiprocessor operating system. A single copy of the operating system resides in one of the memories of the system. One processor is capable of executing the code directly, and the other processors have their memory mapping tables set up so that they can execute the code remotely. Unfortunately, the processors executing the operating system remotely will run at only about one-third speed because of the nonlocal access times. Processors executing the code from other clusters will suffer even more than this. In systems of any size, contention for the shared communication facilities will also degrade performance. In addition to the performance problems, the reliability of this system is limited by the reliability of the computer module containing the shared operating system code.

An alternative approach is to replicate the operating system code in each processor of the Cm* system. This is similar to the approach taken by networks, where each processor contains a copy of basic operating system functions; sharing occurs at a higher level, for example, via a shared file structure. Unfortunately, the size of local memories in Cm* is only 64 or 128 kbytes. A moderate sized operating system of 40–60 kbytes would consume most of the primary memory of the system. The utilization of this memory would be very low, especially when compared with the utilization of the shared memory in Figure 3. (Of course, even in the replicated system some global data still has to be shared between processors; Table II indicates that references to this memory do not substantially affect system performance.)

A static form of caching could be used to combine the approaches of the preceding paragraphs. Frequently executed portions of the operating system code could be replicated in each processor, while infrequently used code could be centralized in a shared memory. This scheme was used by the first version of the StarOS system. Unfortunately, the determination of which portions of the operating system are frequently executed is relatively difficult to make and likely to be application dependent. We decided not to attempt to make such decisions statically. The availability of hardware caches would make this scheme rather more attractive; given that there are no caches on Cm* we have not pursued it any further.

Fig. 4. The organization of Medusa: The operating system is divided into utilities that are distributed around the system. A processor executes a particular utility only if it can do so locally.

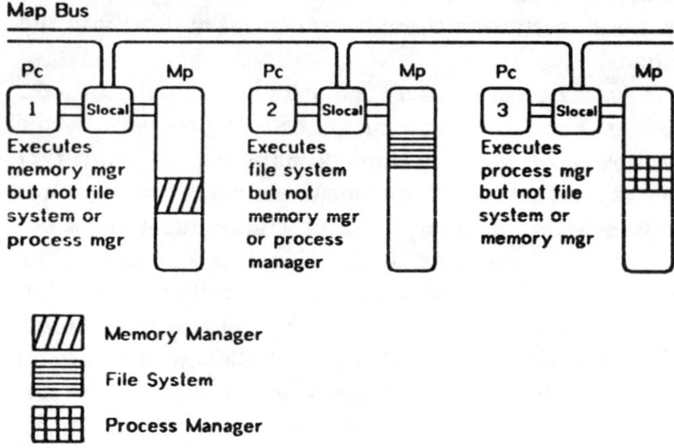

2.2 A Distributed Approach

The solution adopted for Medusa was to discard the assumption that all operating system code may be executed from any point in the system. A simplified example of this is depicted in Figure 4. The operating system is divided into disjoint *utilities.* Utilities are distributed among the available processors, with no guarantee that any particular processor contains a copy of the code for any particular utility. Furthermore, to avoid contention or memory access delays, a given processor is permitted to execute code for a particular utility only if it can do so locally.

Since no processor is guaranteed to be capable of executing any particular piece of utility code, it may be necessary for a program's flow of control to switch processors when it invokes utility functions. Trap or subroutine call instructions cannot be used for invocation because they are incapable of crossing processor boundaries. In Medusa, messages provide a simple mechanism for cross-processor function invocation. If one program wishes to invoke a function of another, it does so by sending a message to a particular *pipe* (see Section 5 for details of the pipe implementation). The invocation message contains parameters for the function invocation, as well as an indication of a *return pipe*; the return pipe is analogous to a return address for a subroutine call. The destination program receives the message, performs the requested operation, and sends a return message (containing result values) to the return pipe indicated in the invocation message. This message transaction is equivalent in power and effect to a call-by-value-result procedure invocation, with two major differences. First, the message crosses protection boundaries as well as processor boundaries, so that the invoker and server may exist in disjoint execution environments. Second, the invoker need not immediately suspend execution to await the requested service; if it has other functions to perform it may execute them concurrently with the execution of the server. Lauer and Needham discuss the duality between messages and procedure calls in more detail in [15].

There is an important difference of view between the Medusa system organization and the organizations presented in the previous sections. In the previous examples, a locus of control existed on a single processor. At the level of memory references, control and data information were transmitted to and from that processor by the Cm* hardware. In the Medusa paradigm, the control information (code) is fixed and is used by a single processor. As various loci of control (user programs and other utilities) need to access the control information, they must move to the processor containing the code. The message transaction is logically equivalent to a transfer of control from one processor to another.

2.3 Distribution for Modularity and Robustness

In the above development of Medusa's distributed structure, performance was used as the main motivation. However, the resulting structure is also desirable for other reasons; these may be even more compelling than the performance considerations. Given that the system must be partitioned into relatively autonomous subunits, the module scheme of Parnas [18] seems the most attractive. Each of the utilities encapsulates a single abstraction for the rest of the system. The use of messages for communication with utilities permits each utility to exist in its own protected execution environment. The boundaries between utilities are rigidly enforced and are crossed only by messages. Message communication is without side effects; that is, a message is received only when requested and the only effects it has on the receiver are those caused by the receiver. This is not true with shared writable memory, where either party may arbitrarily modify the memory without the other's knowledge. Although the utilities still depend on each other to perform certain services, Medusa has attempted to eliminate all interactions between utilities except those absolutely necessary for them to function. The strong separation between system components should simplify the tasks of building and maintaining the system.[2]

The distributed utility structure is also a first step toward robustness. Boundaries between utilities are firm enough that it is difficult for mishaps in one utility to contaminate the others. At the same time, message pipes do not restrict either the location or internal organization of the senders and receivers. Once the format of messages has been agreed upon and particular pipes have been selected for communication, utilities may migrate around the system without affecting their ability to communicate. A different pipe may be substituted for an existing one to change the handler for a particular class of requests. The use of pipes both limits damage and permits transparent system reconfiguration.

[2] The Family of Operating Systems project [9] has had favorable experiences with a system structure consisting of several isolated modules communicating only via a call-by-value-result mechanism.

System designers have traditionally resigned themselves to the "fact" that a performance penalty must be paid if a system is to have a manageable structure. Although the performance of Medusa has not yet been measured, it is encouraging to note that the same structure appears to be both efficient and modular. We speculate that the compatibility of good performance and good system structure is not just a statistical fluctuation in Medusa but a trend in large systems, where much of a system's cost stems from communication. For example, Sutherland and Mead suggest in [23] that the trend will hold for design in the domain of VLSI.

3. The Task Force Structure

LSI-11's are a relatively plentiful resource in Cm* but individually are not very powerful (16-bit virtual address space, 170,000 instructions per second). We have assumed in the design of Medusa that all interesting Cm* programs will be concurrent ones combining the computational power of several processors. This has led to the definition at the system's lowest level of a simple structure to support concurrency, called the *task force* after a similar structure of the same name used in the StarOS system [12, 13]. A task force is defined to be a collection of concurrent *activities* that cooperate closely in the execution of a single logical task. Activities are the entities that actually get scheduled for execution on processors. They are roughly analogous to processes or programs in other systems except that they exist only as part of a task force. A purely serial program is a degenerate task force with only one activity. All programs, including the operating system utilities, are task forces.

When a task force is created, its activities are allocated statically to individual processors (because of the importance of accessing code locally it makes little sense to execute an activity from any processor but the one containing its code). In general each of the activities of a task force will be allocated to a different processor. Individual processors may be multiplexed between several activities belonging to different task forces.

In addition to its activities a task force contains a collection of objects that may be manipulated by those activities. There are several types of objects in Medusa, each with its own set of type-specific operations. Access to objects is obtained through *descriptors* that are kept in protected objects called *descriptor lists*. The various types of objects may be divided into three general classes according to where the operations upon the objects are implemented. The simplest class consists of *page objects*; these may be associated with any of 16 portions of an activity's 64-kbyte virtual address space and may then be read or written using LSI-11 memory references. The second class of objects consists of *pipes* and *semaphores*, whose implementations are managed by Kmap microcode. Pipes and semaphores are protected so that LSI-11 programs cannot directly access their internal represen-

Fig. 5. The organization of the Medusa file system utility. All activities are identical; they serve different requests in parallel.

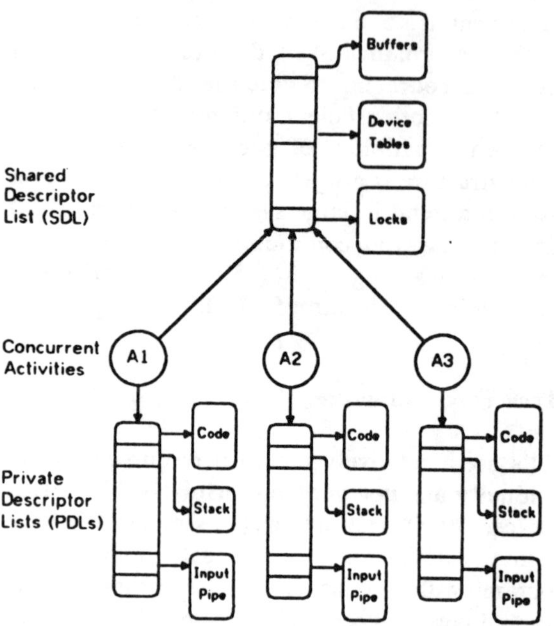

tations; requests must be made to a Kmap to manipulate them. The third class of objects, containing file control blocks, task forces, descriptor lists, and others, is implemented by the operating system utilities. User programs make requests to the utilities in order to perform operations upon these objects. Plans exist for a fourth class of objects, whose implementation would be managed by other user-level programs; the initial system will not provide for objects of this class.

The descriptors used by a task force to access objects are held in two kinds of descriptor lists. Each activity has exclusive access to a *private descriptor list* (PDL). A *shared descriptor list* (SDL) contains descriptors that may be used by all of the activities of the task force. The activities of a task force generally share a common abstract function; the SDL is the encapsulation of that shared task. In general, descriptors may be moved and/or copied, subject to the restriction that the total number of descriptors that may simultaneously exist for each object may not exceed a limit specified when the object was created. Page objects are special in that only a single descriptor may exist. Although a page may be shared within a task force by placing the descriptor in the SDL of the task force, it cannot be shared between task forces.[3]

As an example of a task force, the Medusa file system utility is shown in Figure 5. The several activities are identical. Each contains in its private descriptor list (PDL) a copy of the file system code and a stack page; both are allocated in the memory of the Cm executing the activity, so that access may be made locally. In addition, each PDL contains descriptors for one or more pipes over which service requests are made to that activity. The shared descriptor list contains information that must be accessed by all of the file server activities in order to use I/O devices in a consistent way. This includes the physical device registers, buffer space, device descriptors, and locks used to synchronize file access. The size of the file system task force varies dynamically to provide load-balancing and fault tolerance. If the existing activities become overloaded, they create new activities to assume some of the workload. When activities become underloaded, they give their work back to other activities and delete themselves. For reliability purposes, there will always be at least two activities in each utility task force. In this simple example, global data is centralized in the SDL while control information, particularly that associated with error handling, is replicated.

An alternative task force organization is shown in Figure 6. In this example we have speculated about the structure an optimizing compiler might take. The organization proposed here is a pipelined one. The program being compiled passes through every activity of the compiler, undergoing a transformation at each step. For example, the lexical scan activity reads the source code, generates symbol table entries, and outputs lexemes to the parser. The parser activity generates intermediate code from the lexemes and so on. The symbol table is the only piece of information needed by all of the activities; it is referenced through descriptors in the SDL and could probably be stored in any processor in the system without degrading the performance of the compiler (see Table II). The task force structure is used in different ways in these two examples. For the file system, the activities are used to serve multiple independent requests; the multiplicity of activities provides robustness and increased throughput. In the compiler the many activities serve to encapsulate subtasks of the compilation process and to speed up the processing of a single request.

The SDL/PDL task force organization has levels of locality that reflect the Cm* hardware organization. The PDLs are roughly analogous to individual computer modules, and the SDLs are roughly analogous to clusters. Of course, Medusa does not force all information in a PDL/SDL to be in the same Cm/cluster, but we hope that this structure will encourage programmers to organize their programs in ways that map cleanly onto Cm*. Each PDL is always allocated in the processor that will execute the corresponding activity, as is the *activity control block* that contains saved registers and other execution state of the activity. If an activity allocates its critical information in its own processor and keeps descriptors for that information in its PDL, then the activity is not likely to be destroyed by hardware failures in other processors in the system.

The Medusa structures are organized so as not to associate unrelated information arbitrarily. The strong

[3] We felt that activities that are not closely related in their abstract functions should not interact in uncontrolled ways. Since the task force is the unit of abstraction, we decided to restrict read/write memory sharing to within a single task force.

Fig. 6. A Concurrent Compiler. Each activity of the task force implements one stage of the compilation process.

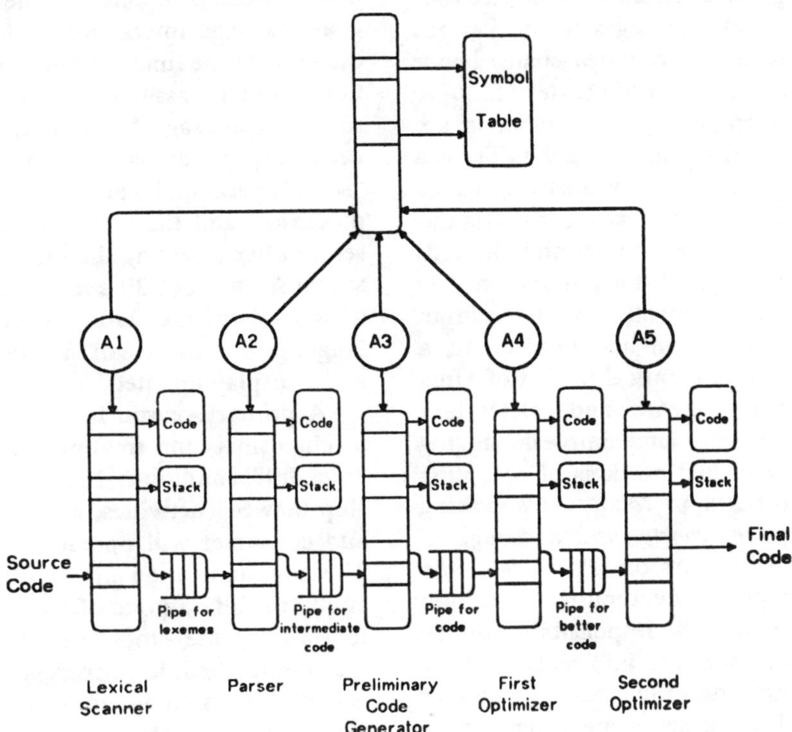

separation between the utilities is one example of this design goal. The descriptor organization is another. In many operating systems all of the descriptor information for all user programs is kept in one large array; a small failure in the array, or in a program that manipulates the array, may affect many otherwise unrelated portions of the system. In contrast, Medusa places descriptor information for each activity in a separate structure and places that structure in the processor that will execute the activity. The distribution and reliability of the system are roughly those of the user programs; the operating system imposes no hidden centralities.

There are two reasons for implementing the task force notion as a low-level system structure. First, most of the operating system functions are provided by task forces, hence the structure must exist at the operating system level. Second, for activities within a task force to interact on a fine grain, certain guarantees must be made to the task force. Foremost among these is the notion of *coscheduling* which, if not provided by the operating system, cannot be implemented using higher level protocols. A task force is said to be coscheduled if all of its runnable activities are simultaneously scheduled for execution on their respective processors. In large task forces whose activities interact frequently, it is often the case that the descheduling of a single activity can cause the whole task force to block on locks held by that activity. If the task force is not coscheduled, a form of thrashing occurs that is very similar to the thrashing in early demand paging systems. The set of activities that must execute together for a task force to make progress on its task is analogous to a process' working set in a paging system. If the operating system does not provide for coscheduling of this "activity working set," there is no way to simulate it at user level short of disabling time sharing. Simple algorithms have been developed for task force allocation and scheduling in Medusa to maximize coscheduling.

4. Overview of the Current System

The complete Medusa operating system consists of three parts:

The several Kmaps, each using about 4,000 80-bit words of microcode, cooperate to provide the basic interprocessor communication mechanisms. These include references to page objects, simple operations on descriptors that help to guarantee the consistency of descriptor space, block transfers, and operations upon message pipes and semaphore objects. A relatively powerful event system has been implemented, partially in Kmap microcode and partially by the utilities: it provides for events to be associated with many different kinds of objects in a similar way so that programs may signal and await events in a type-independent fashion.

A small *kernel* is replicated in each processor to respond to interrupts generated by that Cm. The kernels supply simple multiplexing and device handling code, currently amounting to about 400 words of basic kernel code and 250 additional words for each device type present on the processor's LSI-11 bus (most of the Cm's have no devices at all). The multiplexing code makes no policy decisions about which of the activities allocated to a processor should be executed; it merely provides a mechanism for switching execution contexts. Device routines translate interrupts into messages to the various utilities. In addition the device routines chain device commands to maximize throughput of the devices.

Almost all of the operating system functions are provided by a collection of five utilities. Each utility is a task force that implements one or a few abstractions for the rest of the system. The *memory manager* is responsible for the allocation of primary memory and also aids the Kmap microcode in descriptor list manipulation. The *file system* task force acts as a controller for all the input and output devices of the system and implements a hierarchical file system nearly identical to that of Unix [20]. The *task force manager* creates and deletes task forces and activities and provides some simple debugging functions. Two often overlooked portions of operating systems have been formalized in Medusa by making them utilities: the *exception reporter* and a *debugger/tracer*. When an exception occurs on a processor, the kernel of that processor reports the exceptional condition to the exception reporter. It is the responsibility of the exception reporter to communicate information about the exception to relevant parties. The debugger/tracer holds symbol tables and performance measurement information for all of the utilities. It provides facilities for on-line debugging of the system and for gathering performance data.

The activities of the utility task forces are spread among the available processors, typically with no more than one utility activity per processor. Although no memory is shared between utilities, central tables and synchronization locks for a given utility are shared between all the activities of that utility. The Kmaps route messages from user activities to utilities when the user activities request services from the utilities (see below); the same scheme is also used for service requests made by one utility of another.

5. Pipes and Utility Communication

5.1 The Implementation of Pipes

Pipes in Medusa are similar to those of Unix [20] in that they hold uninterpreted strings of bytes. The operation of Medusa pipes differs from that of Unix pipes in two important ways: (1) the integrity of messages in Medusa is insured by maintaining byte counts for each message and by permitting only whole messages to be read from pipes; (2) the identity of the sender of each message is made available to the receiver of the message. Descriptors may not be passed using the pipe mechanism; instead, descriptors are moved by the memory manager utility in response to requests issued via pipes.

In a system that uses message transactions as a procedure invocation mechanism, the overhead involved in such transactions is of fundamental importance. The degree to which the system can be partitioned is limited from an efficiency standpoint by the cost of an interaction between components. The time required for a 5–10 word message interaction in Medusa is approximately the same as the time used in executing 30 LSI-11 instructions; that is, assume that a server has attempted to receive a message from an empty pipe and hence has been suspended; the time between the initiation of a "send" operation by an invoker (executing on a different processor) and the fetch of the first instruction by the server after receiving the message is roughly 250 microseconds, or about 30 average LSI-11 instruction times. This is about the same time overhead as a high-level language procedure call in which registers must be saved and a display updated.

A primary reason for the efficiency of the message mechanism is the treatment of the "pipe empty" and "pipe full" conditions. In a producer–consumer relationship between activities, it is unlikely that the producer and consumer will operate at exactly the same speed. The communication pipe will almost always be either empty or full and one of the activities will usually have to wait for the other. Virtually all existing operating systems reschedule a processor as soon as the current activity blocks on an empty or full pipe; this means that when the pipe becomes nonempty or nonfull a second context swap must be executed to reactivate the now-runnable activity. Thus almost every interaction between activities results in processor context swaps. In uniprocessor systems the context swaps are necessary since only a single activity can execute at a time; however, in a multiprocessor system the context swaps may become the efficiency bottleneck in the interprocess communication mechanism.

For Medusa, we wished to provide a mechanism that would permit interactions to occur on a substantially finer grain than that of a context swap. When an activity attempts to send to a full pipe or receive from an empty pipe, its execution is suspended until the operation can proceed. However, the activity does not relinquish its processor immediately. For a small interval of time, called the *pause time* and specifiable by the activity, the activity's processor remains idle with the activity loaded. If the activity becomes runnable within the pause time it is reactivated without incurring any context swaps. If the pause time is exceeded, then the processor reschedules itself to another activity. Note that if the time for which the activity is blocked is less than two context swap times, then the lost processor time due to the pause is less than the time that would otherwise have been wasted in context swaps.

5.2 Utility Descriptor Lists

Communication between user activities and utilities, and also between utilities and other utilities, is accomplished via a set of message pipes using the message-passing mechanism described above. The collection of pipes used for utility communication is a critical system resource whose organization affects both the reliability and modularity of the system.

Every processor contains a special descriptor list, called a *utility descriptor list* (UDL), that is used by the activities of that processor to communicate with utilities. To invoke a utility operation a user activity specifies to its Kmap the index of a pipe descriptor in its processor's UDL and a message to be placed into the selected pipe. Each descriptor in a UDL corresponds to a set of operating system functions. The assignment of particular slots of utility descriptor lists was made at system design time, and is analogous to the assignment of trap numbers to particular functions in other operating systems. The descriptors in the UDLs are divided into two groups: the first group may be used by either user or utility activities; the second group is visible only to utility activities and is used to invoke functions that are privileged to utilities.

If there were only a single utility descriptor list, then both the reliability and performance of Medusa would be jeopardized. The assignment of UDL slots to functions is the same for all UDLs; however, having several UDLs makes it easier to share the implementation of a function between several activities. For example, consider the pipes used to invoke the OPEN operation provided by the file system. Normally, the file system task force contains two activities. Half of the UDLs in the system will contain descriptors for a pipe serviced by the first activity, and the other half will contain descriptors for a pipe serviced by the second. If one of the file system activities becomes overloaded, it will spawn a new activity in the file system task force and replace several of the OPEN descriptors in UDLs with descriptors for a new pipe served by the new activity. If at some later time the new activity becomes underloaded, it may overwrite its UDL descriptors with descriptors for the pipes serviced by the other file system activities and kill itself. Similarly, one activity may take over for another activity that has failed. Having one UDL per processor makes it relatively easy for workload to be exchanged between utility activities in a way that is transparent to the rest of the system. Note that it is also important that utility communication pipes are kept exclusively in the UDLs; if user activities were given private copies of these descriptors and allowed to move them around it would be extremely difficult for the utilities to find all the relevant descriptors during reconfiguration.

6. Utility Privileges

In order to guarantee the integrity of protected types such as descriptor lists, there must exist mechanisms to insure that the utility that implements each type may access its internal representation while other, less-trusted, programs may not. Thus, each utility activity executes with a status bit set to grant it several privileges not given to user activities. The privileges allow utilities to (1) share address space with other activities, and (2) perform certain special operations denied to user programs.

The sharing of address space is accomplished through an *external descriptor list* (XDL) accessible to each utility activity in addition to its PDL, the SDL of its task force, and the UDL of its processor. The XDL is not a distinct descriptor list, but just a mechanism to give a utility shared access to the PDL or SDL of another activity in the system. By presenting the absolute system name of a descriptor list to its Kmap, a utility activity maps its XDL onto that descriptor list such that references to the activity's XDL refer to the named descriptor list.

A simple form of *amplification* is provided to the utilities so that they can manipulate the representations of protected types of objects.[4] This is accomplished by allowing utilities to make special requests to the Kmaps, wherein an object is made readable and writable by the activity as if it were a page object, even though it is really of a protected type. The amplification affects only the utility activity that requested it: if other activities attempt to make read or write references to the object, then type violations will occur.

The combination of XDL usage and amplification provides a simple *seal* on objects. Thus objects can be stored with their owners yet be manipulated only by the utilities that implement them. Without this seal, each object would have to be stored with the utility that manipulated it and would consequently be more vulnerable to failures in the utility. Having some sort of seal mechanism is critical to our ability to distribute and reconfigure the system. Medusa's protection mechanism is a relatively simple one; readers are referred to [21] and the protection literature for a more detailed discussion of these issues.

The XDL and amplification privileges are used extensively by the utilities. For example, when a user activity requests that information be written into a file, the file system utility amplifies a *file control block* (accessible through the user's SDL or PDL) to determine where on disk to write the information. Upon completion of the write, the information in the file control block is updated. The file system uses its XDL to read information from the user activity's pages into the actual disk buffers. Task force creation also illustrates how the XDL and amplification privileges are used: the memory manager uses its utility privileges to access allocation tables and thereby create the descriptor lists for the new task force; the task force manager then amplifies the kernel areas of relevant processors to enter the new activities into scheduling tables.

During the design of Medusa a tradeoff was made between the number of special utility privileges and the degree of distribution of the system. The replicated por-

[4] Amplification is a mechanism that permits users to hold tokens for objects without being able to access their representations. When the token is passed to the subsystem responsible for the object's implementation, the subsystem *amplifies* the token to obtain access to the information that represents the object. Thus tokens for objects may be passed around the system at will, yet operations upon the object may be performed only by the subsystem with the ability to amplify the tokens [14].

tion of the system consists of 400 words of kernel code in each processor and 4,000 microinstructions in each Kmap. The kernel and Kmap code provide what we perceive to be the minimum functionality needed to tie together a distributed system in an efficient and protected way. The largest portion of the operating system (thirty to forty thousand words) is distributed among the utilities. It would have been desirable to provide a general enough object addressing mechanism that utilities could get all the privileges they needed via the object mechanism. For example, a mechanism like that of Hydra [4] would have provided a substantially finer grain of protection than we have with the single utility status bit, would have enabled a closer enforcement of the "need-to-know" principle, and would have eliminated the need for any special utility privileges. Unfortunately, the implementation of such a general mechanism would have enormously increased the complexity of the replicated kernel and Kmap code. This is not to say that such general mechanisms are undesirable. Rather, we contend that for a system to be distributed it must be *layered*; if all mechanisms are implemented at the system's lowest level, then they must be replicated everywhere. Since one of the principal design goals of Medusa was to distribute its functionality, we decided that the proper place to implement a general object mechanism would be *in* the utilities rather than underneath them.

7. The Internal Structure of Utilities

7.1 Deadlock

The potential for deadlock arises as a direct consequence of the low-level distribution of operating system functions among disjoint utilities. This section introduces the deadlock problem and the restrictions placed on utility interactions in order to eliminate it.

Consider the OPEN operation implemented by the file system utility. In order to open a file, storage must be allocated for the file control block that will be used during transfers to and from the file. Thus a file system activity executing the OPEN operation must invoke the memory manager utility to allocate the storage. It might turn out that the memory manager was unable to meet the allocation request without swapping information between primary and secondary memory, so it would have to request one or more I/O transfers from the file system. This circularity of requests between the file system and the memory manager could result in a deadlock situation with all the file system activities awaiting results from the memory manager and all of the memory manager activities awaiting I/O transfers from the file system; there would be no file system activities to service the I/O requests.

Another example of an operating system containing circular dependencies between system modules is described by Schroeder at al. in [22]. Habermann et al. [9] have argued that in general there is no correspondence between the notions of *module* and *invocation level*; even though the invocation dependencies of a system are hierarchical, the dependencies between modules may still be circular. Figure 7 depicts the example of the previous paragraph. There are three invocation levels, consisting of the OPEN, ALLOC, and I/O operations. There are two modules, the file system and memory manager, and two invocation dependencies, represented by arrows. Deadlock could occur if all of the service resources of the file system become allocated to OPEN requests, leaving none to service I/O requests.

The standard implementation used in operating systems has been to allocate service resources dynamically from a large central pool to each invocation level of an operation. For example, many uniprocessor systems allocate an independent kernel stack for each user process. When a kernel operation is invoked, frames on the user's kernel stack are allocated for each invocation of a procedure within the kernel. As long as the total depth of the stack is not exceeded, circularities may exist in the interactions between kernel modules.

The distribution of the Medusa utilities makes it impossible to share service resources between invocation levels. An invocation of one utility by another crosses execution environments such that a common call stack is infeasible. An alternative solution would be to pass all of the execution state of a transaction from each utility to the next one that it calls, thus freeing up the resources of the caller. Unfortunately this would be intolerably inefficient, and would make the execution state of each utility vulnerable to the whims of other utilities that it invokes. Another approach would be to allocate new resources at the time of each call, for example by creating a new utility activity to serve each request. In addition to being rather inefficient, the creation of a new activity, or even the allocation of memory, would itself require a utility call and hence could not be done as part of the calling sequence. The potential for deadlock is a result of the fact that even the low-level system functions are distributed among several disjoint environments.

Two conditions must be met for a distributed system like Medusa to be deadlock free. First, all of the functions provided by utilities must be divided up into *service classes* such that (1) a single utility provides all of the services in each class and (2) there are no circularities in the dependencies between service classes. A single utility may implement more than one service class. In the terminology of [9] each service class is the collection of functions provided by a single module at a single invocation level. In the example of Figure 7 the OPEN and CLOSE functions, as well as several others, are included in one service class while I/O functions are contained in another and memory allocation functions in a third. The second condition for deadlock avoidance is that each utility must contain separate (statically allocated) pools of resources so that it can provide independent service to each of its service classes. In the current Medusa system the utilities provide about five service classes apiece, and

Fig. 7. A hierarchical set of calls that leads to circular utility interactions.

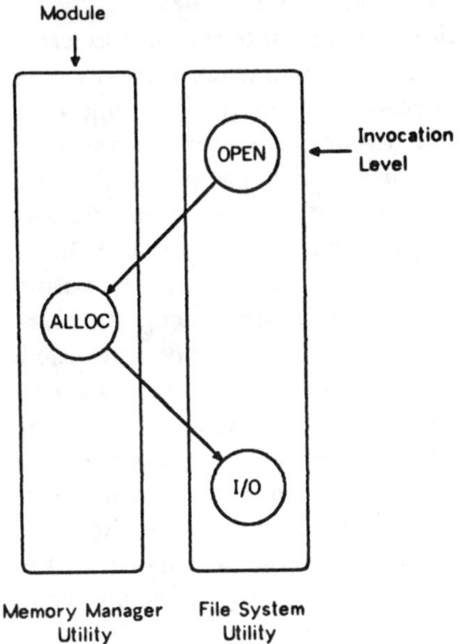

Fig. 8. The internal structure of a utility activity.

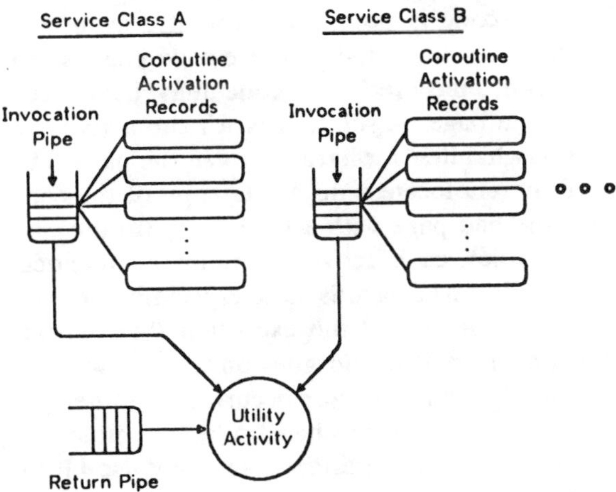

the invocation hierarchy of the system as a whole contains eight levels.

7.2 Coroutines and Multi-Eventing

One way to satisfy the requirement that independent facilities be provided for each class of utility service is to dedicate particular activities of a utility to provide each of the classes of service supported by the utility. This eliminates the possibility of deadlock, but makes relatively poor use of the utility activities since some service classes are rarely invoked. It also precludes load-sharing between utility activities that are responsible for different service classes.

The solution used in Medusa is to structure utility activities as collections of coroutines or processes, as shown in Figure 8. Every activity in a utility task force is capable of providing any and all of the classes of service implemented by the utility. For each class of service provided by the utility there is a separate invocation pipe and a pool of coroutines that serve requests received via the pipe. Descriptors with receive privilege for the invocation pipes are held in the PDL of the activity, and descriptors with send privilege are present in one or more UDLs around the system. Each coroutine has its own activation record containing a stack and other local information. The coroutines are allocated statically to the service of particular invocation pipes, so that the overloading of any one pipe cannot affect the activity's ability to service the others.

When a message arrives from an invocation pipe, one of that pipe's coroutines is allocated to serve the message. The coroutine remains allocated to the request until it completes, at which time the coroutine's activation record is returned to the free pool associated with the pipe. If the coroutine needs to request a service from another utility, then the activity executes other runnable coroutines while the remote service is being provided. When a reply is received for the coroutine it is reactivated and continues service. To the coroutine the remote service request appears like a procedure call. In addition to eliminating the deadlock problem, the use of coroutines increases the throughput of each utility activity by allowing it to process one transaction while another waits for remote service.

A single return pipe is shared by all of the coroutines of the activity to receive acknowledgments from other utilities. When an invocation message is sent from one utility to another, as in the case of the ALLOC request of Figure 7, a *transaction identifier* is sent in the message. The invoked utility must return the transaction identifier in the acknowledging message. The identifier indicates which coroutine is to be reactivated and provides a simple validity check on the acknowledging message.

At any given time a utility activity could potentially receive messages over any of several pipes. The Kmap microcode used by Medusa implements a *multi-event* system whereby an activity may wait for the first message to arrive from any of a set of pipes. For a utility this normally includes all of its invocation pipes and its return pipe. When the current coroutine of the activity cannot continue execution, either because it completed its current operation or because it invoked another utility, the *MultiEventWait* Kmap operation is invoked. This causes the activity to suspend until a message is received on one of the pipes in the set. When a message is received, the activity is reactivated with an indication of the pipe from which the message was received. If the pipe is an invocation pipe, then a coroutine is allocated to service the message and the activity begins executing the coroutine at a standard startup address. If the pipe is the return pipe, then the transaction identifier in the return message is verified and a return is made to the coroutine that invoked the transaction. If all the activation records for a particular invocation pipe become allocated, the pipe is removed from the activity's multi-event set so that requests via the pipe will be stored in the pipe until coroutines become available to service them.

The coroutine structure of the utilities is visible only to a few routines that are used to invoke other utilities and recycle coroutines after they have completed requests. The vast majority of utility code is completely unaffected by the internal multiplexing of each activity. Since the utilities already contain multiple concurrent activities, there are no additional synchronization constraints imposed by the internal multiplexing except that busy-waiting on locks cannot be permitted (busy-waiting prevents another coroutine of the same activity from executing code to release the lock).

8. Exception Reporting

The combination in Medusa of distribution and cooperation has had interesting effects on several portions of the system. Section 7 discussed some of the difficulties encountered in the design of the utilities because of their distribution. This section briefly describes two ways in which the distribution and sharing have impacted the exception reporting mechanism. The sharing of objects has led to two different views of exceptions, *internal* and *external*. The sharing of a control function within a task force, combined with the distribution of the activities of the task force, has resulted in the notion of a *buddy* that can handle exceptions remotely.

For a discussion of what constitutes an exception, readers are referred to [16]; our informal definition is that an exception is just an unusual occurrence, which may *or may not* be an error. Several exception classes are defined in Medusa, ranging from parity errors to the execution of unimplemented instructions. Each activity is allowed to specify for each class a *handler* to be invoked when an exception from that class is generated by the activity.

When an object is shared, it is reasonable for all the co-owners of that object to participate in the handling of exceptions that occur for the object. However, the exception may manifest itself in two ways to the different co-owners. For each detection of an exceptional condition there is exactly one activity whose explicit action uncovered the exception. To this activity the exception is manifested as an *internal condition*; the execution state of the activity is directly involved with the exception, and the handler may have to unwind operations in progress. The other co-owners, although interested in being notified of the exception, were not directly involved in its detection. The exception is seen by them as an *external condition* whose occurrence is not necessarily related to the current actions of the co-owners. The handler for an external condition is generally concerned with the state of the shared abstraction but not with the execution state of its activity. An exception may be reported internally without being reported externally if no shared abstraction is involved; however, all external conditions also have corresponding internal conditions.[5] The double view of exceptions arises only because it is possible to share objects between independent activities.

While the distinction between internal and external conditions arose because of data sharing, the notion of a buddy has arisen because of control sharing in a distributed environment. It is often easier to handle an exceptional condition at a point that is physically and logically distinct from the site of the exception's discovery (see the next paragraph for examples). Medusa allows an activity to present the name of a *buddy* activity within the same task force as handler for any exception class. When the exception occurs the buddy activity is notified. While handling the exception the buddy receives access to all the private information of the exception-generating activity, which is suspended. Buddies are only useful if the buddy is relatively distinct from the exception-generating activity, yet has enough knowledge of the other activity's function to take reasonable actions on its behalf; fortunately, this is almost exactly the relationship between the activities of a task force.

We believe the notion of a buddy to be an especially useful one: two examples follow. A failure in a code page is conceptually a simple one to recover, since virtually all modern-day code is pure. However, it may be extremely difficult for the activity whose code page is lost to recover itself, since recovery code may have been contained in the page. A solution is for the activity to specify a buddy handler for hard errors in the page. The buddy need merely locate a duplicate copy of the code and replace the bad page with a fresh copy (in the case of Medusa utilities, each activity contains an identical copy of the code, making this task especially simple). The activity that generated the exception then repeats the instruction that failed and goes on its way with no explicit knowledge that an error occurred. Another potential use of the buddy mechanism is in emulation. Programs written for an operating system that use TRAP instructions for invocation can be run as one activity of a task force, with TRAP instruction exceptions being handled by a buddy. The buddy activity uses Medusa calls to emulate the desired effects of the TRAP instruction and then allows the trapping activity to proceed. In this way programs written for other operating systems may be run on Medusa with no changes to their code.

9. Comparisons and Conclusions

Many similarities exist between Medusa and the StarOS system. Both systems are object oriented and both provide for task forces of cooperating activities. However, tradeoffs in StarOS generally were made in favor of providing an extremely flexible set of facilities to high-level users; tradeoffs in Medusa generally were made in favor of producing a highly distributed operating system structure that closely matched the hardware.

[5] This is just another way of saying that exceptional conditions do not arise spontaneously, but must be explicitly checked for.

For example, StarOS task forces are much more general than Medusa task forces. The precisely defined structure of Medusa task forces may occasionally constrain users, but allows us to support the structure with coscheduling and with buddy exception handling; these facilities would be much more difficult to support in the more general StarOS task force framework. The StarOS object mechanism provides a finer grain of protection than Medusa's mechanism, but has resulted in a more centralized structure.

Message communication in Medusa is similar to the usage of links in DEMOS to communicate with the operating system [1], while task forces are somewhat similar to teams of processes in Thoth [3]. A substantial difference between the systems is the presence of concurrency in Medusa. Thus issues not present in DEMOS arise concerning the sharing of work between the activities of a utility task force and the dynamic reconfiguration of the system. Memory sharing in Thoth is restricted to processes in the same team, just as it is restricted to activities of the same task force in Medusa. However, Thoth guarantees that only a single process of a team executes at any one time and that it is not interrupted by any other processes of the team; Medusa attempts to insure that ALL activities of a task force execute simultaneously.

Several designs for exception reporting mechanisms have been proposed in the literature, among them [8], [16], and [17]. All of these are based in programming languages; the reporting mechanism for Medusa is not intended to replace them. Rather it provides an entry mechanism into the reporting schemes of individual languages, leaving the languages to propagate exception information among the abstract levels of a program. Medusa's scheme also provides facilities for passing exception information between programs.

The design of Medusa was begun in the late fall of 1977, and coding started in the summer of 1978. The status of Medusa at the time of this writing (November 1979) is as follows: all of the Kmap microcode and utility code has been written and microcode testing is nearly complete. The Medusa system has been successfully loaded onto the machine and the debugger utility is operational. Testing of the remaining utilities has just begun, with roughly two-thirds of all the utility code yet to be tested. We expect preliminary utility testing to be complete by early 1980, with a Unix emulator running shortly thereafter.

In summary, Medusa has attempted to achieve modularity, robustness, and performance in a Cm* operating system using a structure that embodies at its lowest level both distribution and concurrency. No processor of the system is self-sufficient, yet no processor should be critical to the operation of the system. We intend to evaluate our success by measuring how well the system can deal with changes in its environment, including changes in user load as well as failures in hardware, firmware, and software.

Acknowledgments. The authors wish to thank Prof. Nico Habermann, whose comments concerning both the operating system and this paper have been extremely helpful.

Received June 1979; accepted September 1979; revised November 1979

References

1. Baskett, F., Howard, J.H., and Montague, J.T. Task communication in DEMOS. Proc. 6th Symp. Operating Systems Principles, SIGOPS, 1977, pp. 23–32.
2. Bell, G.C., and Newell A. *Computer Structures: Readings and Examples.* McGraw-Hill, New York, 1971.
3. Cheriton, D.R., Malcolm, M.A., Melen, L.S., and Sager, G.R. Thoth, a portable real-time operating system. *Comm. ACM 22,* 2 (Feb. 1979), 105–114.
4. Cohen, E., and Jefferson, D. Protection in the Hydra operating system. Proc. 5th Symp. Operating Systems Principles, SIGOPS, 1975, pp. 141–160.
5. Denning, P.J. Fault tolerant operating systems. *Comput. Surv. 8,* 4 (Dec. 1976), 359–389.
6. Fuller, S.H., Jones, A.K., Durham, I., Eds. Cm* Review, June 1977. Carnegie-Mellon Univ., June 1977.
7. Fuller, S.H., Ousterhout, J.K., Raskin, L., Rubinfeld, P., Sindhu, P.S., and Swan, R.J. Multi-microprocessors: An overview and working example. *Proc. IEEE 66,* 2 (1978), 216–228.
8. Goodenough, J.B. Exception handling: Issues and a proposed notation. *Comm. ACM 18,* 12 (Dec. 1975), 683–696.
9. Habermann, A.N., Flon, L., and Cooprider, L. Modularization and hierarchy in a family of operating systems. *Comm. ACM 19,* 5 (May 1976), 266–272.
10. Jones, A.K., Chansler, R.J. Jr., Durham, I., Feiler, P., and Schwans, K. Software management of Cm*—A distributed multiprocessor. Proc. AFIPS 1977 NCC, Vol. 46, AFIPS Press, Arlington, Va., 1977, pp. 657–663.
11. Jones, A.K., Chansler, R.J. Jr., Durham, I., Feiler, P., Scelza, D.A., Schwans, K., and Vegdahl, S.R. Programming issues raised by a multiprocessor. *Proc. IEEE 66,* 2 (1978), 229–237.
12. Jones, A.K., et al. StarOS, a multiprocessor operating system for the support of task forces. Proc. 7th Symp. Operating Systems Principles, SIGOPS, 1979, pp. 117–127.
13. Jones, A.K., and Schwans, K. TASK forces: Distributed software for solving problems of substantial size. 4th Int. Conf. Software Eng., SIGSOFT, 1979, pp. 315–330.
14. Jones, A.K. Protection in programmed systems. Ph.D. Th., Carnegie-Mellon Univ., Pittsburgh, Pa., 1973.
15. Lauer, H.C., and Needham, R.M. On the duality of operating system structures. Proc. 2nd Int. Symp. Operating Systems, IRIA, 1978; Reprinted in *Operating Syst. Rev. 13,* 2 (April 1979), 3–19.
16. Levin, R. Program structures for exceptional condition handling. Ph.D Th., Carnegie-Mellon Univ., Pittsburgh, Pa., June 1977.
17. Liskov, B., and Snyder, A. Structured exception handling. Lab. for Computer Science, M.I.T., Cambridge, Mass., March 1979.
18. Parnas, D.L. On the criteria to be used in decomposing systems into modules. *Comm. ACM 15,* 12 (Dec. 1972), 1053–1058.
19. Raskin, L. Performance evaluation of multiple processor systems. Ph.D. Th., Carnegie-Mellon Univ., Pittsburgh, Pa., Aug. 1978.
20. Ritchie, D.M., and Thompson, K. The UNIX time-sharing system. *Comm. ACM 17,* 7 (July 1974), 365–375.
21. Saltzer, J.H., and Schroeder, M.D. The protection of information in computer systems. *Proc. IEEE 63,* 9 (1975), 1278–1308.
22. Schroeder, M.D., Clark, D.D., and Saltzer, J.H. The Multics kernel design project. Proc. 6th Symp. Operating Systems Principles, SIGOPS, 1977, pp. 43–56.
23. Sutherland, I.E., and Mead, C.A. Microelectronics and computer science. *Sci. Amer. 237,* 3 (Sept. 1977), 210–229.
24. Swan, R.J. The switching structure and addressing architecture of an extensible multiprocessor: Cm*. Ph.D. Th., Carnegie-Mellon Univ., Pittsburgh, Pa., Aug. 1978.
25. Swan, R.J., Bechtolsheim, A., Lai, K., and Ousterhout, J.K. The implementation of the Cm* multi-microprocessor. Proc. AFIPS 1977 NCC, Vol. 46, AFIPS Press, Arlington, Va. 1977, pp. 645–655.
26. Swan, R.J., Fuller, S.H., and Siewiorek, D.P. Cm*—A modular, multi-microprocessor. Proc. AFIPS 1977 NCC, Vol. 46, AFIPS Press, Arlington Va., 1977, pp. 637–644.

AN OPERATING SYSTEM KERNEL FOR A HIERARCHICAL MULTICOMPUTER

by

Devesh Bhatt[1], P. Sadayappan[2],

Richard B. Kieburtz[3] and David R. Smith[3].

Abstract: The architecture of the Stony Brook Multicomputer is a "double-tree" - with a "control-tree" and a "communication-tree". The processors of the "control-tree" cooperate to solve a user task with file system support from the "communication-tree". This paper presents the design of an operating system kernel for the "control processors".

I. Introduction:

A wide variety of distributed computing architectures have recently been proposed ranging from tightly coupled multiprocessors to loosely coupled computer networks The potential benefits include modular and uniform extendability, increased performance/cost, continuous availability, management of complexity by replication of hardware and software modules and increased reliability. One such design, a hierarchical multicomputer, is currently being implemented at Stony Brook. The general principles behind the architecture and the details of the hardware design have been described in [HS79 BS79,Ki79]. The architecture is based on local rather than shared memory, with the processors operating quasi-independently and asynchronously, co-operating on the solution of a complex computational task. Therefore we refer to this system as a multicomputer.

Some of the initial attempts to design multiprocessor/multicomputer systems have resulted in great complexity of both hardware and software, such that the imagined potential benefits have remained rather illusory. One of the major goals of our multicomputer design is to demonstrate that considerable simplification can be achieved by proper organization of hardware and software subsystems.

This paper addresses the issues of the operating system structure for the multicomputer, especially the design of systems software responsible for the functions of communication and control, which has been referred to as the 'P-Kernel .

First, a brief description of the multicomputer hardware organization is included below for the sake of completeness.

I.1 Multicomputer Hardware Organization:

The typical "double tree" architecture being implemented is exemplified in fig.1, where the squares represent processors with local memory and the lines represent communication pathways of different kinds. The tree comprised of the P-modules, called the "control-hierarchy", is responsible for executing user application program(s). The "control link", shown by solid lines in fig.1 provides program controlled exchange of short messages. It is a full duplex parallel link which provides one word buffering in either direction. Besides message passing, the "control-link" provides asymmetric control features to enforce a superior-subordinate relationship in the P-hierarchy A P-processor can completely initialize, halt and restart/bootstrap a subordinate using these control mechanisms [BS79].

The tree consisting of G and T modules, called the "communications hierarchy", is dedicated to providing a distributed file system to the P-tree with two hierarchical levels of storage. The "data-links", shown as dotted lines in fig.1, are capable of supporting the exchange of short messages as well as transfer of large blocks of data by DMA from one local memory to another. G is the site for the operator's console, standard I/O peripherals, and is the ultimate repository for global files. A significant feature of the architecture is that it is uniformly expandable to a very large number of processors by iterating modules or levels.

One of the primary motivations behind the architecture is the philosophy of successively breaking down a computation into subtasks that can be executed concurrently and asynchronously [HS79,Ki79]. The simulation studies in [HS79] showed that a high degree of concurrency could be achieved for certain applications programmed in this manner. This and some other results of these simulation studies were used as guiding factors in

[1] Honeywell Inc., Systems & Research Center, Ridgway Parkway, MN55413.

[2] Department of Electrical Engineering, S.U.N.Y. at Stony Brook, NY11794.

[3] Department of Computer Science, S.U.N.Y. at Stony Brook, NY11794.

Reprinted from *Proc. 21st IEEE COMPCON,* Fall 1980, pp. 655–672.

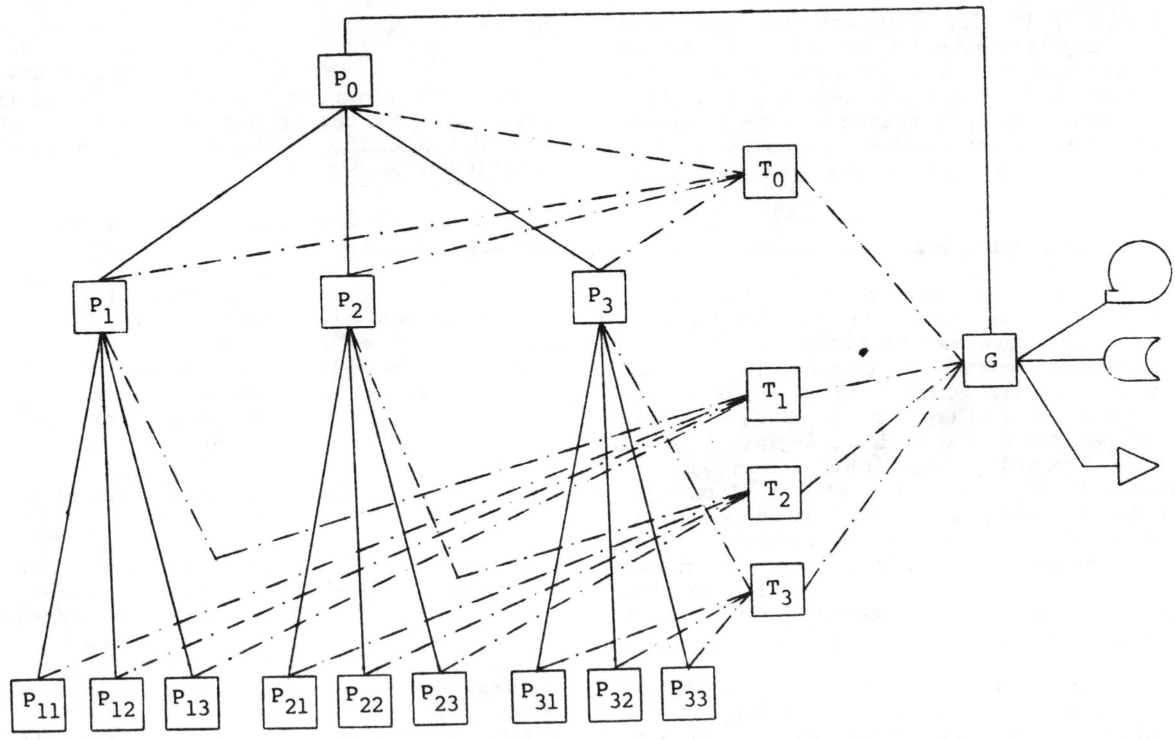

Fig.1 - An example of a "Double-Tree" Network

the design of the operating system and will be referred to in the following sections.

II. Overview of the Operating System Structure:

On this hardware, the file system functions have been physically separated and mapped onto processors (G and T) dedicated for this purpose. Besides relieving the P-processors of the functions of file system management and I/O handling, this structure provides every P processor with a uniform and efficient access to the mass storage, which does not deteriorate significantly with the expansion of the P-tree. Each T-processor provides an individual local file system, with capability based protection, to a father-son subset in the P-tree and acts in an analogous manner to a cache between the P-processors and the global file system at the G node. A detailed design of the file system can be found in [MK79] and in a companion paper [MK80].

The file system software is essentially passive servicing requests by software in the P-processors for file transfers. The active portion of the operating system resides in the P processors and in the G node. Among the functions it manages are - creation and scheduling of computational subtasks(processes), facilities for interprocess communication, detection and confinement of errors, reconfiguration and recovery, and reporting status of the local configuration to aid runtime monitoring at G. The system also provides facilities to add/remove, interactively debug, restart/bootstrap a P-node from the operator's console at G, concurrent with the execution of the user application program in the P-tree.

An identical copy of the systems software, called the P-kernel, resides in all the P processors which have identical address spaces. To provide adequate protection for the kernel, the hardware implements system/user modes of operation. The kernel-code resides in protected address space and executes in system-mode, which is the privileged mode of operation. A program can not modify the protected address space in the user-mode and therefore the kernel can be protected from inadvertant access from the user.

By virtue of the recursive nature of the hierarchy, the kernel at a node in the P-tree need only maintain a knowledge of the local configuration The software subsystem in G, called the 'control-process', runs on top of the UNIX operating system [RT75] and acts as the superior of P_0, utilizing the control-link from G to P_0. This control-process interfacing with the user via an operator's console, allows him to start up an application in the P tree and perform other control, debugging and diagnostic functions. It also monitors the run time status of the nodes in the P-tree. Clearly, in order to perform these functions, there is a need for communication between the control-process and the kernels in the various nodes of the P tree. This introduces another function in the P-kernel, namely, that of handling and forwarding of remote messages.

In the following sections, we will first discuss the objectives, specifications and design principles for the various functions of the P-Kernel. The design and the actual implementation of the P-kernel is then presented. The issues of fault tolerance and interactive control and their incorporation in the P-kernel are also addressed.

III. Specifications and Design Philosophy:

It is important to clarify at the outset that it is not our objective here to design a general purpose network operating system or to provide a general purpose environment in which the actual network structure is rendered transparent. Rather, our intention is to obtain simple solutions specific to the hardware organization of the multicomputer and the class(es) of applications it has been intended for. The major policy decisions were also guided by the performance results of previous simulation studies of typical applications and by certain performance principles that we believe are appropriate to this class of multicomputer architecture as well as to the emerging technology in general.

The primary objectives of the kernel design were that it should be simple and that it should allow for maximum concurrency possible in an application. Another important consideration was to make the design highly modular and structured so that it will be easy to understand and debug, and allow for the flexibility of experimenting with various policies regarding the different functions.

Keeping these goals in mind, let us now discuss some of the important functions implemented by the kernel:

III.1 Task Management and Scheduling :

Although efficient utilization of processors and memories is desirable, it is not necessary for this to be close to 100% because of recent advances in the LSI technology towards low cost processor and memory modules. Rather, it is more important that the average utilization does not decline as the network geometry is expanded. We have therefore adopted the policy of dedicating a processor for a given computational subtask from its creation till termination. This considerably simplifies the complexities and overhead associated with multiprogramming, such as process scheduling, dynamic memory management, relocation etc [Br73]. The results of previous simulation studies [HS79] lend support to this approach. With the processors co-operating on the solution of a single computational problem and one processor dedicated to one subtask at a time, the CPU utilization was found to vary between 25% and 98%, with heaviest use at the lower levels. Since most of the processors are located near the leaves of the tree, good utilization of these processors results in overall good utilization. Clearly, multiprogramming a processor would not make a significant improvement in these figures to justify the additional complexity and run time overhead.

The P-kernel provides the user task (process) running in this processor with primitives to create and delete subtasks, which are dynamically assigned to the available subordinate processors.

III.2 Interprocess Communication and Synchronization:

Since there is no shared memory in our system, interprocess communication is accomplished by explicit exchange of information. The user tasks (processes) in the P-tree can communicate basically in two different ways:

a) exchange of short messages over the control links between two processors in the P-tree.

b) transfer of large blocks of data between P and T processors over the data links.

Case 'b' above can be thought of as interprocess communication using a shared file in the file system. These issues are addressed in detail in [MK79]. Of primary concern here is the communication between user processes in the P-tree by explicit exchange of short messages. These messages will normally consist of control information and parameters and are expected to be quite frequent. It is also anticipated that for most applications, these communications will be localized, i.e., between father and son subtasks only, as shown in the simulations. Communication between remote tasks in the hierarchy is therefore not implemented directly in our initial P-Kernel. Two remote user tasks could still communicate by sharing a global file, although it may not be very efficient.

The P-kernel therefore implements strictly local communication. In this environment, synchronization among processes can be achieved by the exchange of messages. It is very important to understand the implications of the degree of synchronization imposed by the communications facility on the client processes and the closely related buffering issues. The communications facility may mandate more synchronization on the processes than required by an application, which would limit the degree of concurrency could be achieved. This is not very desirable since one of our major goals was to achieve maximum speedup possible in an application.

The user task (process) in a P-processor communicates and synchronizes its activity with the processes in neighboring processors by exchanging messages. For example, it may need inputs from other processes and may be forced to wait in situations where these inputs have not yet been provided. This has been called <u>causal</u> synchronization in [Ki79] because it arises due to lack of information needed to carry out further computations. On the other hand, a process waiting for another process to receive its message is an example of <u>non-causal</u> synchronization. A majority of protocols suggested for interprocess communication by message passing impose considerably more than causal synchronizâtion on the client processes. An example of such a scheme is that suggested by Hoare [Ho78]. In this scheme, the sending process is automatically delayed till the process named for receiving requests an input. Clearly this protocol imposes substantially more than causal synchronization. It was adopted in order to avoid implicit buffering of messages which was not thought to be realistic to implement on multiple, disjoint processors. Also, it is not very clear as to how many messages should be buffered on a channel.

We propose that automatic buffering may not be impractical in an environment where the communication is highly localized by the nature of the hierarchy and the types of applications it has been intended for. Furthermore, these messages are intended to be very short since the file system facility has been provided for communicating large blocks of data. Therefore, the buffering requirements for only local communication with short messages can be kept within reason. Regarding the question of the number of messages to be buffered, our previous simulation studies have indicated that buffering of one message was sufficient for typical applications without significant loss in the speedup. All these considerations have guided our design of the interprocess communication facility.

The basic constituent of this, called here a <u>logical-message-channel</u>, is implemented by the P-kernel,and provides buffering of one multiword message in each direction between the user tasks residing in connected P-processors. The message is buffered in the local memory of the processor on the receiving side. When a call is made by the user process to send a message, the systems software on the sending side goes into a tight polling loop trying to handshake one word at a time across the hardware link. Posting the first word of the message on the hardware link generates an interrupt to the processor on the receiving side. Upon interrupt, the systems software in the receiving processor disables all external interrupts and goes into a polling loop to handshake each word of the message across and buffer it. The use of interrupts provides efficient transmission of messages and negligible waiting time on the sending side. The interrupt, however, is totally transparent to the application tasks, which appear to the user to be sequential. The message flow control strategy adopted is that of preventing further transmission of messages to a processor till the previous message sent on that logical-channel has been received by the user task. The systems software on the sending side maintains a channel status flag for each logical channel. This is raised when a message is transmitted to the other processor, indicating that the channel is full. By querying the kernel, the sender can determine whether the message has been picked up by the user task on the other processor. The kernel on the receiving side of the logical channel sends a local acknowledgement, called 'Ack', to the sending side when the message is picked up by the user task. A second message cannot be sent by the sender to the same destination processor till the first message is received by the destined user task. An attempt to do so would result in an immediate return from the kernel with a return parameter indicating that the logical channel is still busy. The systems software on the sending processor interprets this message and clears the channel status flag on the designated logical-channel.

<u>III.3 Issues of Fault Tolerance</u>:

Some of the significant potential advantages of distributed computing systems are their high reliability, continuous availability and capability for graceful degradation [En78]. Because multiple, intelligent hardware modules (such as processors) are available, the system can be made tolerant to the failure of one or more modules. However, in order to realize these benefits, there are several problems in hardware and software organization which need to be addressed. Among these are - detection, localization and confinement of hardware and software faults, system reconfiguration, process recovery, the dynamic assignment of these responsibilities among the processors, and finally the provision of appropriate control mechanisms in the hardware to permit this [RLT78, Ec78].

Let us identify the goals for fault-tolerance and reliability which we believe are appropriate for the class of multicomputer architectures we are considering. The major goal is continuous availability and graceful degradation in performance (a "fail-soft" capability) in the event of one or more hardware faults. A very high reliability is desirable but not really necessary at this time since the system is intended to serve mainly as a testbed for further research. Among the functions to be performed to realize these objectives are - detection of hardware and software faults, isolation/deactivation of malfunctioning components, hardware and software reconfiguration, addition/removal of nodes while computational activity is going on, and software recovery.

An important and rather unique feature of our system is a powerful facility to interactively control and debug a processor either from the operator's console at G or from a dynamic debugging applications package in its superior, while computational activity is going on in the rest of the tree. Among the functions provided are - ability to completely initialize and "cold- or "warm-start" a processor, to halt a processor, examine/modify its entire state and start regular or single step program execution in it, and to load various interactive diagnostic programs in a processor. This is supported in the hardware by a hierarchical control structure, utilizing the "control-links" (solid lines in fig. 1). Achieving these objectives in a general network topology is a non-trivial problem and may lead to hardware and software complexity. However, by using a hierarchical control structure, we have achieved simple and efficient solutions to some of these problems. Each processor in the P-tree has the responsibility of monitoring the status of its subordinates, detect any malfunctions and take proper reconfiguration, recovery and diagnostic actions. To support this, appropriate control and status monitoring mechanisms have been implemented in the hardware [BS79, Bh80]. Using these, a processor can initialize, deactivate, restart, halt and examine/modify the state of a subordinate. These are features provided as part of the 'control-link' functions and therefore no additional control paths are required in the system.

The hierarchical control structure has the advantages that it is inherently simple and deadlock free. It simplifies the assignment of responsibilities for detection, localization and confinement of malfunctions. Hardware reconfiguration is accomplished by simply decommitting the malfunctioning subordinate(s). Since a node has to maintain knowledge only about its immediate local configuration, complexity of error handling software does not increase with the number of processors in the system. The designers of the X-TREE system [DP78, PFS79] have also advocated a similar philosophy.

One major disadvantage of a strictly hierarchical control structure is that the loss of a processor results in the loss of the subtree under it also. Furthermore, the system is vulnerable at the root from the reliability point of view. One possible way to overcome this in our system is to use redundant links and processors near the root of P-tree. We are planning to address these issues in our future research.

IV The Design of the P-kernel:

In the design of the P-kernel, we have adopted a level structured approach along the lines of Dijkstra [Di68]. The various functions of the kernel are arranged in a hierarchical manner in several levels as shown in figure 2. Each level provides an abstract machine to levels above, hiding some features of the levels below and adding some new features. There are well defined interfaces between the levels and absolutely no data is shared across the level boundaries. This type of organization greatly reduces the complexity of the system and makes it easy to understand, verify and debug. It also allows for the flexibility of experimenting with various

User	- Level 5
Task Handler (TH) & Exception Handler (EH)	- Level 4
File System Interface (FSI)	- Level 3
Message Forwarder (MF)	- Level 2
Message Handler (MH)	- Level 1
Hardware	- Level 0

Fig.2 - Level Structure of the P-kernel

schemes at different levels. Each level in figure 2 is defined as a set of procedures which may share data bases. There are two types of procedures - "regular" and "event-driven".

The regular procedures are those which can be called from the higher levels as standard procedure calls. They may in turn call other "regular" procedures at the lower levels. When execution of one of these procedures finishes, control returns to the calling environment.

The event-driven procedures are those which can be "triggered" by a particular event at a lower level. An event is defined as an occurrence of a special condition which can be recognized by a particular level. The simplest case of an event is a hardware level message interrupt which "triggers" the message-receiver procedure at level 1. In a similar manner, an event at a higher level can be regarded as a "virtual-interrupt" generated by the pseudo-machine defined by the current level. The "triggering" of a procedure is similar to a procedure call to some extent, and even parameter passing can be employed as a further classification of the event. However, a major difference is that unlike a procedure call, there is no concept of the control returning to the environment where the event occured. The execution of the procedure defining the occurrence of the event always finishes before the "event-driven" procedure is started. In general, the execution of any procedure, once started, can not be stopped or interrupted. These procedures handle very specific situations and are expected to give up control within a reasonably short period of time.

Triggering of "event-driven" procedures by "virtual interrupts" is done through a simple level switcher. The level switcher also handles the transfer from user mode to privileged mode when a user makes a kernel call. An "event-driven" procedure is coded just like a standard procedure which can be called by the level switcher. On completion, it returns control back to the level switcher with an indication (if any) of the next "event-driven" procedure to be triggered. Therefore a "virtual interrupt" always goes through the level switcher. A regular procedure cannot cause the triggering of an "event-driven" procedure; only "event driven" procedures can create "virtual interrupts".

In the following subsections we will briefly describe the functions performed at the various levels of the P-kernel.

IV.1 Level 1 - Message Handler:

This is the lowest level in the kernel, and the only level which interacts directly with the hardware. All the hardware interrupts and processor traps are handled at this level. This level also keeps track of the local hardware configuration, i.e. the number and types of the links connected and the hardware status of each subordinate processor. It also performs some elementary error detection functions. For example, watchdog timers are maintained in the communication protocols on the links, so as to detect possible hardware faults and latent bugs in the P-kernel code. Also, a software computed checksum is appended to all messages communicated on the links in order to detect any transmission errors. Whenever an error or a change in status is detected, or a message is received from the ODT monitor in a halted subordinate, an event-driven procedure is "triggered" at level 4 (TH-EH) to handle the situation.

This level also provides a facility for communicating multiword messages to the active neighbors (including the T-processors as well). However, no buffering of messages is done at level 1. It is the responsibility of the higher levels to buffer and maintain flow control over the messages used by it. Primitives to exercise the various control functions of the control-link and the DMA functions of the data-link are also provided at this level.

IV.2 Level 2 - Message Forwarder (MF):

At this level, a facility is provided to the higher levels for sending and receiving messages to/from the control process in G (ref. section II). The message forwarder (or MF in short) handles the complete routing and forwarding of these **"remote"** messages. For this purpose, MFs on adjacent processors communicate with each other using facilities provided at level 1 (MH).

The MFs employ a simple, packet switching type of strategy with only forwarding and no storing. Since the message length in our system is small, the whole message constitutes a single packet. The routing strategy is simplified considerably because of the tree structure and also because one point in every communication is always the G node. The entire routing and destination information is contained in a special header attached to the message, which is interpreted and modified (as required) by MF's along the path (see section V for details).

IV.3 Level 3 - File System Interface :

This level provides the interface to the file system software in the T-processors. A capability based protection mechanism is employed regarding access to files. The capabilties are handled at this level and are completely screened from the higher levels. A capability list is maintained for this purpose which can be referenced by indices used by the higher levels. Primitives are provided for manipulation of capabilities, and for performing basic operations on files like **read, write, open, create** etc, a detailed discussion of which can be found in [MK79, MK80].

IV.4 Level 4 - Task-Handler-Exception-Handler:

This Level provides the abstraction (to the user task) of having subtasks as progeny processes and defines primitives for their creation and termination and performs the mapping from logical subtasks to physical subordinates. It also implements **logical-message-channels**, as discussed in section II, for communicating with these subtasks and the father task.

This level is responsible for handling of all error situations. Detection of subordinate malfunction is done mainly by the MH level which interfaces directly with the hardware. Some possible error conditions which may be detected during a message transfer are: halted subordinate; timeout during transfer; invalidation of message protocols. Hardwrae diagnostics are also run in the subordinate everytime it is reset to load a new subtask. Whenever an error is detected by one of the lower levels, an event-driven procedure is activated at this level which takes further action which may include one or more of : sending an error message to G for status monitoring purposes and reconfiguration around malfunctioning hardware. Reconfiguration is accomplished simply by decommitting the malfunctioning components from further use.

This level also provides a facility for interactive control, debugging and diagnostics of a processor from the operator's console at the G node. Level 4 in the superior processor utilizes the ODT monitor facility of the LSI-11 [DEC78] to control and debug a subordinate and it communicates with the control-process in G using the message forwarding facility at level 2.

V Implementation Details

V.1 Level 1 - Message Handler:

Procedures:

SendMH - A "regular" procedure that transfers a message, word by word across the specified link.
RecvMH - A "regular" procedure that tests the specified link for an available message, and if available, reads in the message, word by word into the specified message buffer.
Sendword - A "regular" procedure that transfers a single word rather than a formatted message across the specified link. This procedure is used to communicate with the ODT microcode monitor of halted subordinate processors.
Recvword - A "regular" procedure that reads one word, if available, from the link. It is used in conjunction with Sendword to communicate with halted processors.
Control A "regular" procedure that can be used to test the status of a subordinate processor, and to halt or initialize the processor.
MHinit - An "event-driven" procedure that is triggered upon hardware interrupt from one of the links. It invokes RecvMH to read in the message, and interprets the header of the message. It then causes a virtual interrupt at the level where the message is destined and passes the received message as an argument.
DoDMA - A "regular" procedure that sets up the DMA registers on the P-T link specified and initiates DMA transfer. The direction of data transfer is supplied as a parameter of the call.
StatusDMA - A "regular" procedure that returns the status of the last DMA transfer initiated on

the specified link.

Timer - A "regular" procedure that returns a software computed time.

Timer-int - An "event-driven" procedure that is triggered by a line frequency clock. It updates the software computed time.

Message Format

The format of a message that is transferred across the link is shown in fig 3.

```
15          11          07                              00
----------------------------------------------------------
| 0|  Type  |  Subtype  |             Data              |
----------------------------------------------------------
```

Single-Word Message

```
15          11          07                              00
----------------------------------------------------------
| 1|  Type  |  Subtype  |            Length             |
|--------------------------------------------------------|
|                        Data                            |
|--------------------------------------------------------|
|                         .                              |
|--------------------------------------------------------|
|                         .                              |
|--------------------------------------------------------|
|                        Data                            |
|--------------------------------------------------------|
|                      Checksum1                         |
|--------------------------------------------------------|
|                      Checksum2                         |
----------------------------------------------------------
```

Multi-Word Message

Fig.3 Format of Message sent over Link

Multi-word messages contain a 1 word header. The header has a type field which signifies the level of the kernel where the message is destined, a subtype field and a length field. At the end of the message body, a pair of checksums are appended. The first checksum is obtained by exclusive-ORing the words of the message. The second checksum is the complement of the first checksum. The checksums are used to detect transmission errors. The length of the message body is limited to 16 words in order to limit buffer space required in the MF and TH levels which implement logical channels.

Single-word messages can only carry one byte of data. They are used for acknowledgement messages and also in communicating with the ODT microcode monitor of halted processors.

V.2 Level 2 - Message Forwarder:

Procedures:

SendMF - A "regular" procedure that is used by higher levels to send messages to the control process in G. It creates an MF type message which imbeds in it the message that was passed down as an argument. The created MF message is then forwarded by a call to the MH level.

MFint - An "event-driven" procedure that is triggered by the MH level when an MF-type message is received on the link. If the message is destined elsewhere, it is retransmitted using MH. If the message is destined to this processor, the imbedded message is extracted and passed to the appropriate level by triggering the receiving procedure at that level.

Message Format:

An MF message has a 2-word header. The first word of the header is identical to an MH message header. The second word is a routing header. It contains four 4-bit path fields which serve to identify the path used for message forwarding. The source is implicit in case of downward messages and the destination is implicit in upward messages; hence only one of them need be contained in the message. For downward messages, the path fields from right to left specify the physical index of the link to be used at successive levels of the tree to forward the message. A zero entry in the path field implies that the destination has been reached. At any node, the MF shifts the header right by 4 bits. The 4 bits shifted out give the physical index of thd link to be used, and the header is now correct for the next level to interpret. On upward bound messages, the destination is implicit - always to the superior. The path used is filled into the routing header as the message travels up the tree. At each node, the routing header is shifted left by 4 bits and the physical index of the link by which the message arrived is filled into the rightmost path field. This routing scheme can be used with trees with a maximum depth of 5 and maximum fanout of 15.

```
15          11          07                              00
----------------------------------------------------------
| 1|Type=MF |  Subtype  |            Length             |
|--------------------------------------------------------|
|  path3    |   path2   |    path1     |    path0       |
|--------------------------------------------------------|
|                       MFData                           |
|--------------------------------------------------------|
|                         .                              |
|--------------------------------------------------------|
|                         .                              |
|--------------------------------------------------------|
|                       MFData                           |
----------------------------------------------------------
```

Fig.4 - Format of MF-Message

V.3 Level 4 - Task and Exception Handler:

Procedures:

Createtask A "regular" procedure that is called by the user task to set up a subordinate task on an available subordinate processor. Through the use of the FSI and MH levels, the specified program file is loaded in a free subordinate and set executing.
Termtask - A "regular" procedure that causes the specified subordinate task to be aborted and its processor reset.

Send - A "regular" procedure used by the user task to send local messages to the subtask or to the superior task or send a remote message to the console process in G. Remote messages are sent through the MF level. Local messages are sent through the MH after a mapping from logical task id to a physical link index.
Recv - A "regular" procedure that returns a buffered message, if any, that had been earlier received by the kernel from the specified process.
Query - A "regular" procedure that returns the status of the last message sent on the specified logical channel. It can be called by the user task to determine whether the task at the other end of the logical channel has received the message.
THint - An "event-driven" procedure that is triggered when an MF or MH message is received by a lower level. The received message is buffered till the user task requests it through a Recv call.
Reset - A "regular" procedure that causes the subtree headed by the specified subordinate processor to be reset. This causes the subordinate processor to execute the Restart procedure, looping to receive parameters to set up a new user task on it.
Restart - An "event-driven" procedure triggered by the receipt of a Reset message from the superior. It invokes the Reset procedure repeatedly to reset all the subordinates and then loops continuously polling the superior link to receive parameters needed to set up a new user task on the processor.

EHint - An "event-driven" procedure that is triggered on the occurence of any exceptional condition - e.g. bad format on a received message, halted subordinate, timeout during message transfer, change in local configuration due to addition or removal of a subordinate processor. Malfunctioning subordinates are halted and diagnostic programs are run to attempt to locate the cause of malfunction. Status changes are reported to the console monitoring process. Communication between the console process and a halted subordinate is also done through this procedure.

V. Concluding Remarks:

We have presented here the design principles and the implementation of an operating system kernel for the hierarchical multicomputer being constructed at Stony Brook. The hardware implementation of the multicomputer is complete now with 17 modified LSI-11 processors for P and T nodes and a PDP-11/60 for the G node. The implementation of the file system and the P-kernel is in the final stages of completion utilizing C-language and PDP-11 assembly language.

References:

[Bh80] Bhatt, Devesh, Ph.D Thesis, Department of Electrical Engg., S.U.N.Y. at Stony Brook.

[Br73] Brinch Hansen, P., "Operating System Principles," Prentice Hall, Englewood Cliff, N.J., 1973.

[BS79] Bhatt, Devesh and Smith, David R., "Communications in a Hierarchical Multicomputer", proceedings of the IEEE Compcon, Fall 1979.

[DEC78] Digital Equipment Corporation, "Microcomputer Handbook," 1978.

[Di68] Dijkstra. E W., "The Structure of the THE-Multiprogramming System", Comm. ACM, 11, No. 5 May 1968.

[DP78] Despain, A.M. and Patterson, D.A., "X-TREE, a Tree Structured Multi-Processor Computer Architecture," proceedings of the 5th Annual Symp. on Computer Architecture, 1978.

[Ec78] Eckhouse, R.H. et. al, "Issues in Distributed Processing - an Overview of Two Workshops," Computer, vol. 11, no. 1, Jan. 1978.

[Ho78] Hoare, C.A.R., "Communicating Sequential Processes", Comm. ACM, August 1978.

[HS79] Harris, J. Archer and Smith, David R., "Simulation Experiments of a Tree Organized Multicomputer", Proceedings of the 6th Annual Symp. on Computer Architecture, 1979.

[Ki79] Kieburtz, R.B., "A Hierarchichal Multicomputer for Problem Solving by Decomposition", Proceedings of the 1st International Conf. on Distributed Computing Systems, Oct. 1979.

[MK79] Mukerji, Jishnu and Kieburtz, R.B., "A Distributed File System for a Hierarchical Multicomputer", Proceedings of the 1st International Cof. on Distributed Computing Systems, Oct. 1979.

[MK80] Mukerji, Jishnu and Kieburtz, R.B., "A Kernel for Supporting a Distributed File System," companion paper, submitted to

[RLT78] Randell, B., Lee, P.A., Treleaven, P.C., "Reliability Issues in Computing System Design," ACM Computing Surveys, vol. 10, no. 2, June 1978.

[RT75] Ritchie, D.M. and Thompson, K., "The UNIX Timesharing System: Programmer's Manual," 6th edition, Bell Laboratories, May 1975.

The Honeywell Experimental Distributed Processor - An Overview

E. Douglas Jensen
Honeywell Systems and Research Center

Introduction

The Honeywell Experimental Distributed Processor (HXDP) is a vehicle for research in the science and engineering of processor interconnection, executive control, and user software for a certain class of multiple-processor computers which we call "distributed computer" systems. Such systems are very unconventional in that they accomplish total system-wide executive control in the absence of any centralized procedure, data, or hardware. The primary benefits sought by this research are improvements over more conventional architectures (such as multiprocessors and computer networks) in extensibility, integrity, and performance. A fundamental thesis of the HXDP project is that the benefits and cost-effectiveness of distributed computer systems depend on the judicious use of hardware to control software costs.

In this paper we describe the class of computer systems of interest to the HXDP project, the motivations for our interest, our research approach, the initial application environment, the HXDP system philosophy, and the HXDP hardware facilities as seen by the executive programmer. The software portion of the executive will be described in a subsequent paper.

We begin by clarifying our use of the term "distributed computer." Like Enslow,[1] we view with dismay the current practice of labeling almost anything other than a uniprocessor as a "distributed processing" system. The various systems so labeled differ widely in kind, leaving the term "distributed processing" devoid of any substantive meaning. HXDP was named prior to our reaching this conclusion, but in this paper we abandon the term "distributed processing" as being beyond redemption; instead, we identify systems of interest to the HXDP project as "distributed computers."

We define a *fully distributed computer* to be a multiplicity of processors that are physically and logically interconnected to form a single system, in which overall executive control is exercised through the cooperation of decentralized system elements. It is not sufficient that the processors appear to the user as a *virtual* single system—they must constitute an *actual* single system at all levels of abstraction. Conceptually, a single executive manages all of the system's physical and logical resources in an integrated fashion, but its kernel logic (perhaps hardware as well as software) and data structures are replicated among a number of processors and memories. These executive kernel copies are individual entities that execute concurrently, asynchronously, synergistically, and without hierarchical or master/slave relationships, to form a single organism.

The extent of system-wide executive control and its degree of decentralization are independent, analog variables; thus, fully distributed computers are at one extreme in a two-dimensional space. Other, more familiar points in that space are multiprocessors with both full and centralized system control, and computer networks with little, although decentralized, system control.

Fully distributed computer systems are, in general, beyond the current state of the art. Most of the prevailing methods of executive control of computer systems are inherently centralized—they are based on the premise that all processes share a coherent and deterministic view of the entire system state. This premise is reasonable for a uniprocessor or a multiprocessor (which we consider to be a multiplicity

Reprinted from *Computer,* vol. 11, pp. 28-38, Jan. 1978.

of processors with intersecting primary memory address spaces). But in many loosely coupled multiple-processor systems (having disjoint primary memory address spaces), it is impractical or even impossible to make this premise true—the system state is fragmented into pieces that reside in different processors and memories, and that communicate among themselves subject to variable and unknown time delays. Such systems may not guarantee that different system elements will observe any given sequence of events identically, or that they will have the same perception of any given subset of the system state.[2] Under these conditions, the current executive concepts and techniques do not permit much control over the system as a whole—instead of a single system there is a multiplicity of individual systems that are interconnected but locally controlled. Complete and decentralized executive control over the entire system would appear to be advantageous in many applications, as we explain next. Therefore, the HXDP project was directed toward developing hardware and software technology for such distributed computer systems.

Motivations for distributed computers

We hypothesize that there is a positive correlation between the amount of decentralized system-wide executive control and the extent to which that system can achieve certain attributes. Foremost among those attributes are "extensibility," "integrity," and "performance."

Extensibility. *Extensibility*, sometimes referred to as modularity, expandability, flexibility, or adaptability, is the degree to which system functionality and performance can be changed without changing the system design.

The two major benefits of extensibility are ease of modification and ease of growth—the distinction between them has more to do with the purpose of a change than with the techniques. In the *modification* sense, extensibility refers to the simplicity of replacing a logical function or hardware element, despite the intimacy of its relationships with others. A high degree of extensibility in the *growth* sense permits (a) low cost configurations, (b) functionality and performance upgrades to an appropriate upper limit in small increments, and (c) correspondingly small cost increases.

The extensibility exhibited by conventional architectures, such as uniprocessors, multiprocessors, and computer networks, is limited in practice and (we surmise) in principle.

The software- and I/O interface-compatible family of computers provides the only extensibility available to uniprocessors. In such families, the capability and cost increments are usually too few and too large—an increase in performance and cost of 10 percent, for example, is usually not possible. Further, the various family members inevitably have different designs and components, and this causes support problems.

Conventional multiple-processor architectures, such as most multiprocessors and multicomputers (processors interconnected by coupled I/O channels), offer some improvements in extensibility over uniprocessors. However, their hardware and software for interconnection and control typically impose high-cost minimum configurations and a low limit on the maximum number of processors.

Some computer networks are quite extensible physically; for example, irregular polygrids such as Arpanet[3] and loops such as the Distributed Computer System at the University of California, Irvine.[4] But their need for effective extensibility is limited by the objective of resource sharing and the infrequency of adding or changing computers.

Distributed computer systems appear to offer extensibility improvements over these configurations, due to decentralization of the interconnection and control logic (both hardware and software). As the system is scaled up in size, nonlinearities and boundary conditions in performance are less likely than for centralized systems. Thus, it is feasible to specify minimum and maximum system sizes, together with the number and size of the increments between, to meet the application requirements. It is also more probable that the additional functionality and performance of each increment can be incorporated without hardware or software design changes.[5]

Integrity. *Integrity* is the degree to which a system tolerates faults (mechanical or algorithmic defects that may generate errors), errors (items of information that, when processed by the normal algorithms of the system, will produce failures), and failures (events at which a system violates its specifications).[6] Integrity involves confinement, detection and diagnosis, recovery (preventing further damage and restoring a stable, consistent system state), repair, restart, and reporting.[7] This attribute encompasses those referred to by the terms "fault-tolerance,"[2] "reliability," and others.

Numerous techniques are available for improving various aspects of a uniprocessor's integrity (almost all of which apply to the processors of multiple-processor systems as well), but voting either within the processor or among synchronized copies of the processor is the most effective. Even this expensive technique does not deal with certain integrity problems, such as detecting algorithm design flaws. Uniprocessors without voting can have only very limited integrity.

Centralized multiple-processor architectures can avoid having singular shared resources and can thus provide confinement and repair improvements over nonvoted uniprocessors. More often than not, however, these possible improvements are compromised by (sometimes implicit) tradeoffs in favor of other goals which result in processor multiplexing, memory interleaving, low integrity bus protocols, etc. Having a multiplicity of independent processors raises the opportunity for detection, diagnosis, and recovery through cooperation among the processors, but centralized procedure and data impair the effectiveness of this technique.

Less centralized architectures (such as multicomputers) notably suffer at this time from an inability to perform repair by dynamic reconfiguration.

Integrity considerations in most computer networks are primarily derived from the resource sharing objective of the network. That is, each host system is responsible for its own integrity as a uniprocessor or multiprocessor, while the communication subnet deals with data communication integrity. Arpanet proves that the nature of packet switching allows such data communication subnets to achieve a considerable degree of decentralized control, but much remains to be accomplished in the way of detection, diagnosis, recovery, and repair. Error confinement is enhanced by the very loose physical coupling in both the host network and the communication subnet, and by the loose logical coupling in the host network as well. Beyond this confinement there is little need or capability for integrity of the whole network in a single-system sense. Certain special-purpose (for example, military) networks do have such a need, but it is largely unfulfilled in the instances of which we are aware.

We believe that distributed computer systems will exhibit a high degree of integrity, for the following reasons. First, major improvements derive from reducing the number of bindings which exist between processes and individual hardware elements such as processors, memory banks, and communication paths; for this reduction to be extensive and effective, system control must be decentralized. Boebert* has observed that the first advantage of reduced bindings is fewer errors. A programmer constructs a *virtual* architecture from processes and interprocess communication paths. In so doing, he believes that the path designs limit the classes of phenomena which will occur among the processes. But if this virtual architecture is mapped through extra layers of software and multiplexing onto a substantially different *real* architecture, a variety of implicit relationships arises among the virtual architecture components which the programmer did not visualize. Interactions which he thought to be excluded by his design not only may occur, but may occur randomly. These side effects of virtual-to-real mappings are fundamentally yet subtly different from those caused by the mutual influence of multiple processors and other real resources, and they lead to obscure and intransigent errors.

Homomorphism and integrity

A structural correspondence, or "homomorphism," between the virtual and real architectures further benefits integrity by helping confine errors to a subset of system functionality and performance,[8] which also greatly enhances the prospects for all other aspects of integrity.[9] An additional advantage is that analytical verification of the system is more feasible.[10]

Decentralized executive control can also improve system integrity by causing much inter*process* communication to become inter*processor* communication. Externalizing this communication facilitates detection and diagnosis through the cooperation of multiple processors—even very difficult errors such as algorithm design flaws can become more visible.

The status of recovery in distributed computer systems is an open question: it is not yet clear whether the net effect of partitioned system state will be positive or negative; it is clear that processor cooperation and externalized interprocess communication will be valuable tools for accomplishing recovery.

The situation is similar for repair, where decentralized control appears to be an opportunity in some ways but an obstacle in others (at least with respect to current approaches). Maintaining a homomorphism between the virtual and real architectures implies limited repair, in that loss of a processor is accompanied by loss of the corresponding virtual element(s). Frequently this is a rational approach (at least in physically dispersed distributed computer systems), because if a processor fails, either there is a redundant one next to it, or no other processor is near enough to interface with the failed processor's I/O devices. The homomorphic structure is preserved in either case. Similarly, if an I/O device fails, its function is either taken up by another (attached to the same processor, or more commonly a different one), or dropped from the system, along with the corresponding processes. Processes that must be protected against processor failure should be replicated in separate processors. Even so, it may become necessary to combine processes from a failed processor with those in a functioning processor. In this situation, repair should be carried out on the basis that system survival takes precedence over subsidiary issues, such as homomorphism or even decentralization.

Performance. *Performance* is most frequently defined in terms of throughput or response time.

There are several bounds on the performance of uniprocessor computers. The first is the inherent ceiling imposed by a given hardware implementation technology—at any particular time, performance beyond a certain level can be achieved only with multiple-processor architectures.[11] Next, the necessary process multiplexing degrades response time, due to the context-switching overhead, and because rapid response to one event often requires preempting the response to a prior event (especially when events occur in bursts). A third bound on performance is the well-known exponential rise in software cost as the maximum performance of the processor is approached.

Multiple-processor architectures can potentially overcome these uniprocessor performance bounds—better so, we suspect, when executive control is decentralized. Response time can be decreased by

*See Acknowledgments, p. 426.

adding more processors, so that an event can immediately activate an idle processor without suspending other processing. The price for this fast response is throughput and/or processor inefficiency, and many applications are willing to pay it. Response time and throughput are both improved by a multiplicity of processors executing concurrently. Many multiple-processor architectures, as well as most computer networks, assign separate jobs to separate processors; even greater benefits can be obtained if multiple processors cooperate on a single job. Unfortunately, the concepts and techniques for partitioning a job[12] and assigning the pieces to processors[13,14] are very primitive, especially for systems other than multiprogrammed multiprocessors.[15] The effect of decentralized control on process assignment is the same as on repair, discussed earlier.

Another performance factor is the influence which the topology, latency, and bandwidth of any multiple-processor interconnection mechanism have on the suitability of an architecture for a given application. While in some environments (such as a university computing center) this effect could be a disadvantage of multiple-processor architectures, in many others it can be turned to an advantage. Selection of an interconnection mechanism which is oriented toward the nature of the application will lessen the need for virtualization, thus reducing run-time overhead (and software cost). This concept is an extension of the one which can increase error confinement in distributed computer systems, as described previously, and the value of decentralized control is the same.

There are also several cost-effectiveness arguments for using an aggregate of interconnected smaller processors instead of one larger processor of equivalent performance. First, the quantity and functionality of the smaller processor's logic is more amenable to higher levels of semiconductor integration than is that of the larger processor. Second, smaller processors can be designed and implemented more quickly, so they can make use of the latest, most cost-effective hardware technology. Finally, smaller processors are manufactured in greater quantities and thus benefit from production economies.

Research approach

The principles and practices of decentralized executive control are as yet too primitive to support fully distributed computers for general-purpose applications. We see three approaches for research to remedy this situation.

The first approach is to advance the state of the art through analysis and synthesis of paper designs. Such work should and does constitute the vast bulk of the research on distributed computing, in our group as in most others.

The second approach is an experimental one, initially restricting the application in such a way that the current state of the art permits implementing and meaningfully using a fully distributed computer in that environment. The restrictions must reduce the system control problem to feasible proportions. The valuable experience gained thereby can yield new concepts and techniques that expand the state of the art to encompass less restricted applications. The environment could be selected solely on the basis of its suitability for this research, in which case the second approach is oriented toward the development of distributed computer technology per se.

The third approach is also experimental and recognizes that some applications are of more interest than others to any particular individual or organization. An application can be selected on that basis, and a system implemented which incorporates as much decentralized executive control as is needed and now permitted by the state of the art. This approach is concerned with understanding the implications of extant distributed computer technology, and the requirements for improving it, in a specific context.

We wanted to augment the first approach with one of the remaining two, since experimentation is as important in computer science as in any other scientific discipline. Our choice of an application environment for HXDP was real-time control, because it is of interest to our corporate and government sponsors, and at the same time it appeared to be restricted in a manner that would permit a fully distributed computer system to be built. Thus, for this project, the only difference between the second and third research approaches is in the perspectives of the various individuals involved.

Application characteristics and requirements

Real-time control in an application sense refers to the computerized feedback control of physical processes such as those encountered in refineries, ships, and numerous other industrial and aerospace environments. (The distinction in this paper between the real-time control application and executive control of a computer should be clear from the context.)

HXDP is intended for that majority of real-time control applications which require the computer system to be physically dispersed up to 1000 meters between the extremes. These applications are also the most interesting from a research standpoint, in that their issues and tradeoffs are considerably less well developed than those of highly localized computers (such as multiprocessors) and highly diffuse computer networks. Furthermore, we had already examined the highly localized subset of real-time control systems in the Modular Computer System study.[16]

We narrowed the scope of HXDP further by concentrating on higher-performance applications, which gave us a more challenging problem as well as greater freedom in the economics of the solution. This was important because new high-technology solutions to problems tend to be initially expensive and affordable only by applications in which those problems are critical. Then as the technology matures, the solutions become economically feasible for a larger range of applications.

The final consideration was the application time frame, which we chose to be the 1980's.

While the potential distributed computer improvements in extensibility, integrity, and performance are desired to some extent by all computer systems, they are critical in many real-time control applications.

Both the modification and growth aspects of extensibility are very important in real-time control environments, because the computer is not a stand-alone entity but is deeply embedded within a larger application system.[17,18] The definition of the system interface to the computer is not ordinarily subject to influence by the computer designer, and is not tolerant of deviations by the computer. This interface, together with the processing requirements, will often continue to evolve, not just during the system design phase, but also throughout the entire system lifetime. Because of its programmability, the computer commonly becomes the final instrument of change, to which all of the unresolved problems in the remainder of the system seem to gravitate.[19]

And yet, modification and growth of the computer must have minimum side effects; otherwise they may precipitate expensive redesign and reverification of the computer, the interface, or the entire application system. It is not unusual today for the costs resulting from insufficient extensibility to considerably exceed those of the initial system design and implementation.

The importance of integrity in real-time control systems is clear—failures may have catastrophic consequences for property and human life. Approaches to repair must take into account the fact that the sensors and actuators are often much less reliable and more expensive than the computer, and that in physically dispersed systems they are interfaced only to the nearest processor(s).

Performance in real-time systems is measured more in terms of response time than throughput—violation of an application time constraint often constitutes a system failure. In addition, events tend to occur in bursts, requiring a large and immediate increase in processing over that needed under steady-state conditions.

Our studies and experience indicate that real-time control systems of interest to the HXDP project have typical processing characteristics, as outlined below. Some of these characteristics restrict the generality of the computer in such a way that research on fully decentralized executive control seemed to have a reasonable probability of success.

A real-time control computer performs specific functions, which are known at the time of system configuration. The ratio of cyclic to event-driven functions depends very much on the application, but the former always constitute a significant percentage. Many of the functions can be performed concurrently. The functions can be decomposed into a total of 10 to 100 "processes," where a process is most usefully thought of as a small virtual computer dedicated to one purpose. This decomposition is presently done a priori, manually, and heuristically. Criteria for decomposition include minimizing interprocess communication bandwidth[20]; permitting interprocess communication in the form of messages subject to reasonableness tests rather than data to be processed[21]; assigning physical or functional meaning to processes and interprocess communication messages[22]; and (for HXDP) Parnas' abstract interfaces.[18] Each process requires a modest 30K to 300K instructions to be executed per second. Most operands range in size from 1 to 16 bits. Process references to both code and operands tend to be highly localized both spatially and temporally. The code and local operands for each process are relatively compact, almost always fewer than 64K 16-bit words. Processes are loosely synchronized for the purposes of exchanging messages, accessing shared variables, and maintaining execution precedence constraints. Interprocess communication rates vary from hundreds of bits to tens of kilobits per second per process. Messages contain on the order of 1 to 100 data words. The physical inertia of the application makes interprocess communication latencies from hundreds of microseconds to tens of milliseconds tolerable. Processes frequently form clusters on the basis of interprocess communication—there is greater connectivity as well as more communication (by perhaps an order of magnitude) among processes within a given cluster than among processes in separate clusters. Each cluster communicates with nearly all other clusters.

The HXDP philosophy

The philosophy of the HXDP system is centered on exploring the role of unconventional hardware/software tradeoffs in attaining fully decentralized system control.

The major inhibition to the use of multiple-processor architectures in the past has been the high cost of processors. The need to utilize this expensive hardware efficiently led to expensive multiprogramming executive software, which added to the inhibiting effect of high hardware costs. However, the economic factors are changing and have now reached the point where processors are no longer the limiting resource—software activities such as configuring and programming are the dominant portions of system cost. This economic trend is widely expected to continue throughout the 1980's time frame of HXDP, and suggests that ways are needed to use the low cost of hardware to alleviate the high cost of software. Such ways fall into three classes—more and better functionality in processor hardware, more application processors, and new system control hardware.

The first of these three classes of hardware assistance, providing more (if not always better) functionality in the processor hardware, is the traditional one. It was rejected for HXDP because we wanted the system design to be independent of the processor design(s); then we could take advantage of standard low-cost minicomputers and microcomputers, while also allowing special-purpose application processors where necessary.

The second class of hardware assistance, providing more application processors, is employed less frequently than the first—historically, when processors were added to a system, it was not for the purpose of lowering software cost, and in fact quite often it had the opposite effect. Part of the HXDP philosophy is to be generous with processors and to de-emphasize individual processor efficiency. One way this lowers software cost is through minimization of contentious multiprogramming—that is, only processes that do not compete for activation or resources are allowed to share a processor. To avoid preemption, events should activate idle processors, messages arriving for active processes should be queued by the hardware, and routine error conditions that the hardware can handle should not interrupt the software. This approach relieves the high software cost of pursuing maximum performance on a processor (as opposed to a system) basis, and simplifies such executive functions as scheduling, resource management, and context-switching.

The third class of hardware assistance, providing system control hardware (in the form of processors and otherwise) external to the application processors, is quite rare—the Pluribus pseudo-interrupt device[23] and the HCCS network manager[24] (a paper design) are examples. We believe that one of the biggest limitations to the success of multiple-processor architectures has been that run-time management of the hardware has imposed too many requirements on both user and executive software. Such requirements are particularly difficult to meet, and distract the software from its primary objective of dealing with the system application. Decentralization of control could make this problem worse, due to the need for coordination among the executive instantiations. Therefore, one of the HXDP project goals is to study how the inclusion of external system control hardware mechanisms might free the software to concentrate on policies.

The most critical system control mechanisms in a distributed computer are clearly those involved with interprocess and interprocessor communication. The emphasis on monoprogrammed processors means that much application inter*process* communication will become inter*processor* communication; when taken together with the decentralization of executive control, this emphasis also implies that much resource management normally done *within* the processors will instead be done *among* the processors.

There are serious disadvantages to the conventional approach of implementing interprocess communication totally in software. Although uniform protocols improve the integrity and lower the cost of software, standardization calls for generality, even at the expense of efficiency. Interprocess communication mechanisms are frequently invoked; the amount of processor time that they consume when implemented in software may jeopardize the system performance goals, creating an incentive for programmers to circumvent the standard mechanisms. Software alone cannot prevent the resulting proliferation of private protocols, which obscure the system's structure, foster elusive malfunctions, and obstruct system development and maintenance.[25]

Another disadvantage of leaving interprocess communication entirely up to the software is that in real-time control systems many such executive functions are often largely the responsibility of the application programmers. At the other extreme, it is not unusual for the executive to be the single most complex (and most often executed) program in the system. If either of these is the case, then reducing system cost by reducing software cost requires reducing the executive cost.

Our philosophy of how best to provide hardware support mechanisms for system control functions such as interprocess communication is that of spreading the inherent complexity of a given function across the different system levels from user to hardware.[26] Various complexities should be assigned to levels in a manner ideal with respect to or at least consistent with) the global objectives of the system. For example, complexity extracts a cost every time it is encountered. This suggests that consideration should be given to handling more complexity at the lower system levels where the nonrecurring cost is paid once by the few designers and the recurring cost is inexpensive hardware, instead of at the higher system levels where the cost is paid repeatedly by many users in expensive software. However, these costs must also be weighed against others, including those of design and implementation modifications. The extensive ramifications of this complexity/level assignment make it one of the most important aspects of computer systems architecture design, and the difficulty of "correctly" perceiving the global system objectives and costs makes it one of the most creative.

In HXDP, we advocate an uncommonly synergistic relationship between the hardware and software: the hardware architecture should support and reflect contemporary software engineering principles, rather than impede them; the software should preserve and exploit the inherent advantages of distributed hardware, rather than virtualize them away. This philosophy implies that it is not sufficient to perform research only on decentralized virtual architectures implemented on centralized real architectures. Consequently, the HXDP project created new distributed computer hardware and software facilities in an integrated fashion. This was also done for Cm* but based on a somewhat different philosophy.[27,28]

HXDP hardware architecture

This section briefly outlines the HXDP hardware architectural facilities as seen by an executive programmer, and gives some insight into the reasons behind the most significant decisions. The detailed design and implementation is described elsewhere.[29] The concepts and facilities of the HXDP decentralized executive software kernel will be described in another paper.

Physical structure. The HXDP architecture comprises up to 64 loosely coupled processing elements, each of which is a processor/memory pair. These are connected to ("separated by"[30]) a bit-serial global bus through special-purpose communication processors called bus interface units (Figure 1). The number of processing elements is limited by complex tradeoffs between system functionality and bus analog design considerations.

The processor primary memory address spaces do not intersect because, as described earlier, the real-time control systems of interest to this project do not require extremely low latency or high bandwidth interprocess communication. Loosely coupled computer architectures are also intriguing from a research standpoint because they are less well understood than multiprocessors.

The "direct, shared bus" topology[31] was selected over the many alternatives because it more nearly fits our extensibility, integrity, and performance requirements. Unlike loops, for example, buses can employ passive interfaces in which failures are less likely to halt system operation, and which do not degrade response time with in-line buffer storage and repeater delays. Arguments that certain loop protocols more than compensate for their higher buffer delays by reducing queuing delays[32] may not be relevant for real-time applications, although we are currently investigating this issue. A two-level hierarchy of buses, such as that of the Distributed Processor/Memory system,[33] would more closely correspond to the process clusters, but a one-level (non-hierarchical) global bus structure allows all communication to be visible throughout the system, and thus probably simplifies the achievement of decentralized executive control.

The HXDP architectural and implementation tradeoffs were intended to reflect anticipated hardware costs of the 1980's. However, building such a system in 1974 occasionally necessitated that we compromise. One way we decided to save development time and money was to design and build HXDP with a single global bus. Without this constraint, we would have had a pool of autonomous buses, as in our earlier Modular Computer System.[16] The single bus somewhat limits our universe of experiments (particularly with regard to integrity), but so very much remains to be learned that there will be no shortage of valuable experiments.

The global bus is bit-serial because of the premium placed on small cable size and weight in many real-time control applications and the 1000-meter upper limit on physical dispersal. Furthermore, we had considerable experience with parallel buses and were anxious to discover the implications of bit-serial transmission on decentralized system control. Because real-time control computers are often subjected to extensive electrical noise, for better immunity our analog circuit designer chose shielded, balanced twisted pair over coaxial cable. The state of the art in data rates is much lower for twisted pair buses than for coax, on the order of one megabit per second per kilometer of length. Bus interface unit hardware considerations suggested a 1.25 Mb/sec rate, which appeared to be adequate for our small feasibility demonstration system.

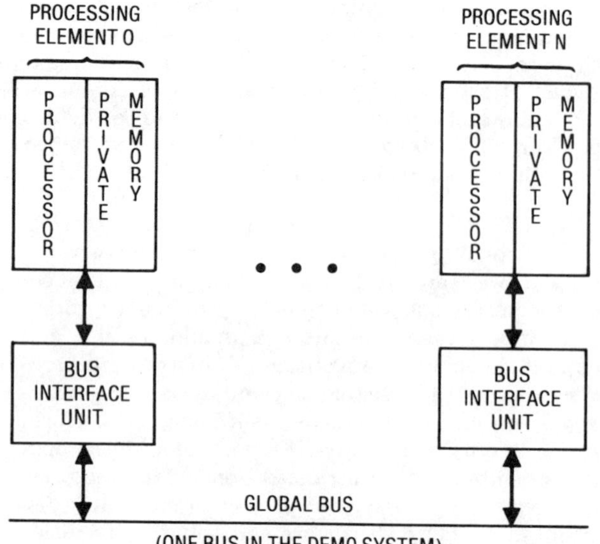

Figure 1. HXDP hardware architecture.

Logical structure. In HXDP, all interprocess communication is in the form of explicit messages, and access to shared data is obtained through an administrating process. Administration may include information (data type, format, etc.) hiding,[34] synchronization, and protection.[35]

All processes are considered to be equally remote from one another, even by the executive software. Consequently, all messages are transmitted on the global bus, including those between processes which (at the time) happen to reside in the same processing element. This requires higher bus bandwidth, but externalizes all interprocess communication and thus facilitates decentralized system control.

Messages to multiple destinations (broadcasts) are not currently supported by the bus interface units, because the most important case, that of an unknown number of destinations, lacks definitive acknowledgments, and thereby compromises integrity. A lesser broadcast facility (for example, to a multiplicity of known destinations), did not seem worthwhile at the hardware level. The executive software can provide any sort of virtual broadcast capability that may be desired. For decentralized system control purposes, the bus interface units "eavesdrop" on messages not addressed to their processes.

The bus interface unit hardware could have been oriented toward addressing messages by destination name or by message name. We felt that we could not afford both; since there were no broadcasts at the hardware level, destination name was the obvious choice. HXDP messages are addressed to software-defined names rather than to hardware processing elements. Each bus interface unit recognizes and receives messages for up to eight unique names; the software may elect for these names to be those of separate processes, aliases of one process, priority indicators, or function codes interpreted by one or more processes in the corresponding processing element.

Messages are transmitted and received through circular first-in-first-out queues. Each processing element has one output queue and up to eight input queues (one per destination name); lengths and locations of all queues in its memory are defined by the software. To send a message, the software merely places it in the output queue. (The decision to put messages rather than pointers to messages in the output queue was motivated by 1974 hardware costs.) Whenever the output queue is not empty, the bus interface unit waits for an opportunity to transmit on the bus, and sends the oldest message. The bus interface unit that recognizes the message destination name receives the message, adds it to the corresponding input queue, and makes available to the software a flag and a pointer to that queue (an interrupt is optional). The bus interface unit hardware and processing element software have simultaneous and asynchronous access to any input or output queue, without interference from each other. A physical message may contain up to 255 data words.

HXDP uses a unique global bus allocation scheme called Vector-Driven Proportional Access (VDPA), invented at Honeywell and previously used in the Distributed Processor/Memory[33] and Modular Computer System[16] designs (Figure 2). It allocates time on the bus nearly optimally for each bus interface unit in a decentralized fashion, without requiring bus control lines or significant extra time on the bus.

For the VDPA mechanism each bus interface includes a binary-valued circular vector of any length up to 256 bits and an index into the vector. The pattern of "1's" in the vectors is set at system configuration time according to the anticipated needs of each bus interface unit, depending on the application and the assignments of processes to processing elements. All indexes are initialized to vector bit position 0 at power-up and simultaneously incremented by a global bus signal at the end of each message. Exactly one bus interface unit will have a "1" in the indexed position of its vector, which

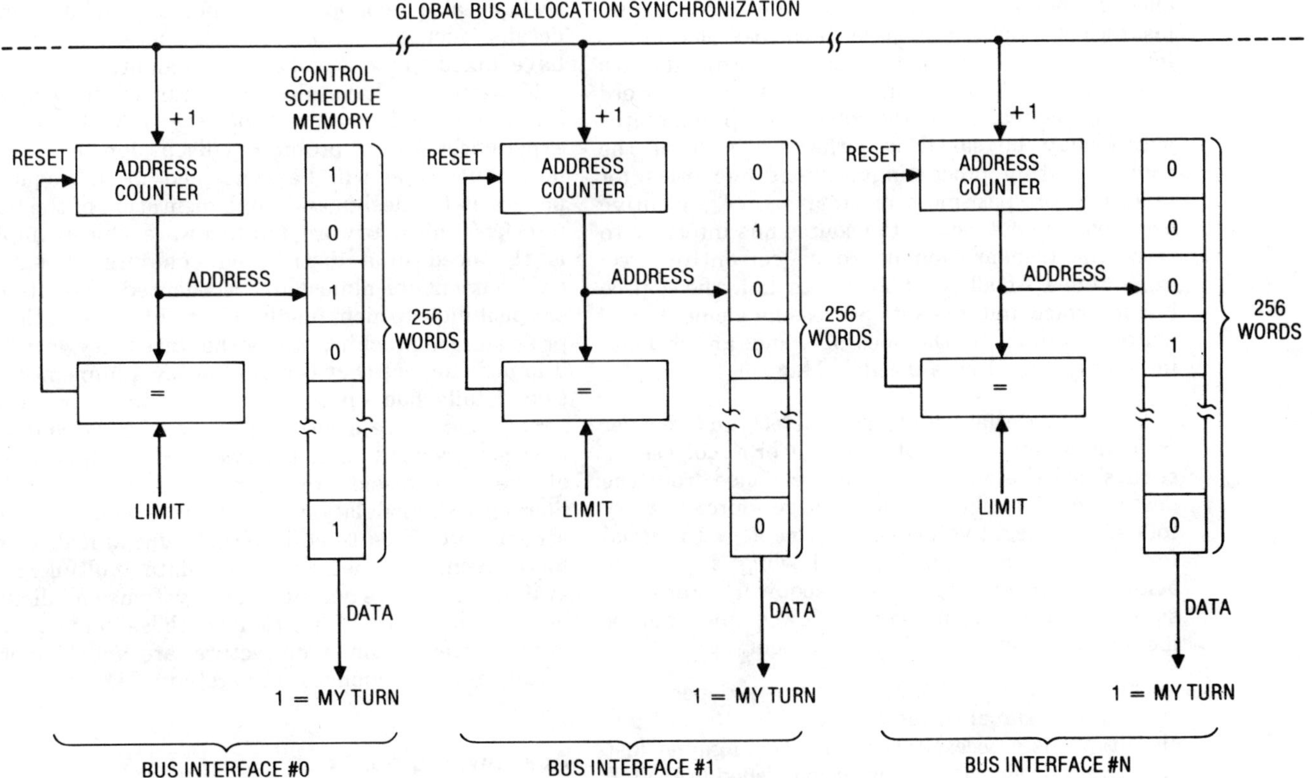

Figure 2. HXDP global bus control technique.

signifies its turn to transmit on the global bus. If a message is waiting in the output queue, it is transmitted; then the bus is released and all the indexes are incremented. However, if the output queue is empty, the bus interface immediately releases the bus with another reallocation (incrementing) signal as though it had completed sending a message.

The performance of VDPA depends on the degree to which the bus transmission requirements can be accurately established for each processor; reconfiguring the allocation pattern is time-consuming. For real-time control systems having bit-serial buses and in which response time is more important than dynamic reconfiguration, VDPA appears to provide performance superior to all other bus and loop control schemes we are aware of. (Analysis and simulation results will appear in a subsequent paper.)

Errors. To minimize interrupting the processing element software, a large percentage of the HXDP bus interface unit logic is associated with attempting to detect and recover from many (over 40) types of possible errors that can occur when messages are being passed across the bus. All bus interface units listen to every message (but only the named destination stores it), so that any error detected at the destination will likely also be deteced by all the others. This increases the probability that all bus interface units will maintain the same context, which is valuable for decentralized control.

One class of errors includes cyclic redundancy checks, modulation and word count errors, and insufficient input queue space. If the destination bus interface unit detects such an error, it responds with a negative acknowledgment and a status word detailing the reason. At the software's option, status words may be saved in either or both of the communicating processing element memories for real-time or post-mortem analysis. A negative acknowledgment causes the source bus interface to retry the transmission up to N (currently three) more times. If all $N+1$ attempts fail, the source bus interface unit gives its processing element software a pointer to the message and an optional interrupt, and releases the global bus.

The bus interface units also detect and recover from numerous types of message protocol errors, such as (a) the absence of any response from the destination; (b) failure of the message source to retry following a negative acknowledgment or to signal for reallocation of the bus following a positive acknowledgment; and (c) "non sequitur" transmissions, such as a message followed by another message instead of an acknowledgment.

The VDPA bus allocation scheme's dependence on a unique signal to increment all vector indexes simultaneously necessitates protection against lost or extraneous signals. This is accomplished in HXDP by including the current index value of the source bus interface unit in the message header; all other bus interface units receive, save, and use these values to maintain synchronization of their own indexes. Following a reallocation signal, if neither another such signal nor a message appears on the bus within a prescribed time interval, some bus interface will automatically issue the signal to reallocate.

Status and conclusion

The HXDP hardware was designed in 1974, and separate two-processor and three-processor feasibility demonstration systems were implemented in 1976. These have now been combined into a five-processor system, simply by connecting the two buses end-to-end. The size of our experimental system is constrained by the current cost of building LSI hardware of the future—each bus interface unit contains an order of magnitude more logic than the minicomputer which it supports. The decentralized executive software is currently being implemented and should be operational by the end of 1978.

Architecture and application type experiments have just begun, so we have as yet uncovered little significant evidence for or against our hypotheses regarding decentralized executive control and hardware/software tradeoffs.

In our experiments we will also be looking for indications of whether our budget-induced philosophical compromises (such as having messages rather than pointers in the output queues) were in reality false economies. Numerous architectural details (such as the broadcast issue) on which we have mixed opinions will also be evaluated.

However, we have already begun to draw some initial conclusions based on the HXDP design experience—space prohibits discussion of these here, but some will be contained in subsequent papers on the design and implementation of the bus interface unit hardware and firmware. One example is the need in a distributed computer research environment for almost unprecedented amounts of extensibility (which inspired our Modular Microprogrammed Machine[36]). Another discovery was the dramatic impact that certain low-level implementation details had on the system architecture. Bit-serial buses were a new experience for us, and we were not prepared for all the *system*-level implications of the transmission medium (coax, twisted pair, fiber optics), modulation format, bit synchronization scheme, etc. This topic is largely uncodified, even for conventional networks and data multiplexing systems. For more decentralized systems and distributed computers in particular, these impacts of implementation on architecture are much more significant and much less understood. ■

Acknowledgments

The HXDP hardware design and implementation project was administered initially by Terry Saxton and then by George Anderson. George Anderson also did most of the detailed logic design and contributed to all other phases of the effort. George Marshall implemented the bus interface unit microprogram and debugged the first two-processor configuration. Gene Salber was responsible for the analog aspects of the design.

Many of my other colleagues provided helpful advice during preparation of this paper, most notably Richard Kain, Andries van Dam, and Jack Stankovic.

Special credit is due to Earl Boebert, whose outstanding ability to extract and express the essence of any issue has greatly improved not only this paper but also my own perspective.

The HXDP hardware was funded in part by the U.S. Navy Ocean Sciences Center under contract N00123-74-C0891. We are also grateful for the moral and financial support of Honeywell's Systems and Research Center and Defense Electronics Division.

References

1. Philip H. Enslow, "What is a Distributed Processing System?" *Computer*, January 1978, pp. 13-21.

2. Gerard LeLann, "Distributed Systems—Toward a Formal Approach," *Proc. IFIP Information Processing Congress*, August 1977, pp. 155-160.

3. Peggy M. Karp, "Origin, Development, and Current Status of the ARPA Network," *Digest of Papers, Compcon 73*, February 1973, pp. 49-52.

4. David J. Farber and Kenneth C. Larson, "The System Architecture of the Distributed Computer System—The Communications Systems," *Proc. Symp. on Computer-Communications Networks and Teletraffic*, Polytechnic Press, 1972, pp. 21-28.

5. Jack B. Dennis, "Modularity," *Software Engineering —An Advanced Course*, Springer-Verlag, 1975, pp. 128-182.

6. P. M. Melliar-Smith, *A Project to Investigate Data-Base Reliability*, Computing Laboratory, University of Newcastle-upon-Tyne, England, 1975.

7. William A. Wulf, "Reliable Hardware/Software Architecture," *IEEE Trans. on Software Eng.*, June 1975, pp. 233-240.

8. W. Earl Boebert and William R. Franta, *Distributed Data Processing Technology, Vol. 2—DDP Rationale: The Program Planning Point of View*, Honeywell Systems and Research Center Report 77SRC76, September 1977.

9. Peter J. Denning, "Fault-Tolerant Operating Systems," *ACM Computing Surveys*, Vol. 8, No. 4, December 1976, pp. 359-390.

10. Niklaus Wirth, "Toward a Discipline of Real-Time Programming," *CACM*, Vol. 20, No. 8, August 1977, pp. 577-583.

11. F. R. Bailey, "Computational Aerodynamics—Illiac IV and Beyond," *Digest of Papers, Compcon 77 Spring*, February 1977, pp. 8-11.

12. C. V. Ramamoorthy and Mario J. Gonzales, "Survey of Techniques for Recognizing Parallel Processible Streams in Computer Programs," *AFIPS Conf. Proc., Vol. 35, 1969 FJCC*, November 1969, pp. 1-15.

13. Mario J. Gonzales and C. V. Ramamoorthy, "Parallel Task Execution in a Decentralized System," *IEEE Trans. on Computers*, Vol. 21, No. 12, December 1972, pp. 1310-1322.

14. Harold S. Stone, "Multiprocessor Scheduling with the Aid of Network Flow Algorithms," *IEEE Trans. on Soft. Eng.*, Vol. SE-3, No. 1, January 1977, pp. 85-93.

15. E. Douglas Jensen and W. Earl Boebert, "Partitioning and Assignment of Distributed Processing Software," *Digest of Papers, Compcon 76 Fall*, September 1976, pp. 348-352.

16. E. Douglas Jensen, "Distributed Processing in a Real-Time Environment," *Infotech State of the Art Report on Distributed Systems*, 1976, pp. 304-318.

17. E. C. Svenson and D. L. Ream, "What Is Different About the Hardware in Tactical Military Systems," *AFIPS Conf. Proc., Vol. 42, NCC 73*, June 1973, pp. 797-806.

18. David L. Parnas, *Use of Abstract Interfaces in the Development of Software for Embedded Computer Systems*, Naval Research Lab Report 8047.

19. Thomas O. Wolff, "Improvements in Real-Time Distributed Control," *Digest of Papers, Compcon 77 Fall*, September 1977, pp. 409a-409g.

20. Vidas B. Gylys and Judith A. Edwards, "Optimal Partitioning of Workload for Distributed Systems," *Digest of Papers, Compcon 76 Fall*, September 1976, pp. 353-357.

21. R. D. Smith, *System Partitioning Study, Final Report*, McDonnell-Douglas Astronautics Co.-West, Document MDC-66603, 1976.

22. Melvin D. Johnson et al., *All Semiconductor Distributed Aerospace Processor/Memory Study*, Vol. 2, USAF Report AFAL-TR-73-226, August 1973.

23. F. E. Heart, S. M. Ornstein, W. R. Crowther, and W. B. Barker, "A New Minicomputer/Multiprocessor for the ARPA Network," *AFIPS Conf. Proc., Vol. 42, 1973 NCC*, June 1973, pp. 529-537.

24. J. H. Rowan, D. A. Smith, and M. D. Swenson, "Toward the Design of a Network Manager for a Distributed Computer Network," *Proc. Sagamore Conf. on Parallel Proc.*, American Elsevier, August 1974, pp. 148-166.

25. Robert M. Metcalf, "Strategies for Interprocess Communication in a Distributed Computing System," *Proc. Symp. on Computer-Communications Networks and Teletraffic*, Polytechnic Press, April 1972, pp. 519-526.

26. Harold W. Lawson and Bengt Magnhagen, "Advantages of Structured Hardware," *Proc. Symp. on Computer Architecture*, December 1974, pp. 152-157.

EXPERIENCES WITH THE SERIES/1 DISTRIBUTED SYSTEM

Richard A. Hammond

Department of Electrical Engineering
University of Delaware, Newark, Delaware 19711

ABSTRACT

The Series/1 Distributed System (SODS), developed at the University of Delaware, is an experimental system for research in distributed computing. It consists of several IBM Series/1 computers, a local communications network, an operating system (SODS/OS), a file system (SODS/FS), and applications software. Experience in designing, implementing, and using the system has given insight into the basic strengths and weaknesses of its design.

INTRODUCTION

The Series/1 Distributed System (SODS) experiment has a long range goal of providing a distributed computing environment for automated office functions. Its short range goal is to test the feasibility of its design as a method for building a distributed system. The effort, thus far, has demonstrated feasibility, but also has exposed some areas for improvement.

This paper discusses our experiences with the SODS architecture. The system has been operational since January 1980. The current file system is a temporary one which will be used to support applications while a better one is being implemented. The applications running include an assembler, several passes of a C compiler, a text editor, and various utility programs. Experiences with the implementation and use of the applications have raised the issues discussed below.

The SODS operating system has been described elsewhere [1]. The operating system is based on an environment in which entities interact exclusively by sending messages. The distribution of the system is accomplished by not allowing the sending entity to know either its location or that of the receiver.

There are four major functions which should be provided for the user: interprocess communication, process management, data transfer (input and output), and data storage (file system). SODS/OS provides the first three functions while the file system is implemented as a cooperating set of user processes. The functions and the issues raised will be discussed in the order just given. A brief description of the entire system precedes the detailed discussion to provide a context for the discussion.

The operating system supports four types of objects: processes, messages, exchanges, and capabilities. SODS objects are indivisible; any instance of an object resides totally on one machine. A process is the combination of code and a context and is the only active object in SODS. A message is a variable length string of bytes. There are four types of messages, each having 8096 classes. The four types are normal, exception, interrupt, and control. An exchange is a FIFO queue of messages which exists outside the address space of any process. A capability consists of the name of an exchange and a set of permissions for operations on both the exchange and the capability. Capabilities are currently limited to naming exchanges.

INTER-PROCESS COMMUNICATION

The inter-process communication structure of SODS may be summarized as follows: any process may send a message to, or receive a message from, any exchange for which it holds a capability having the proper permissions. The inter-process communication structure raises many issues, involving the nature of exchanges, response handling, capabilities as messages, and reception from multiple exchanges. Each of these is discussed in more detail below.

The use of exchanges rather than direct process-to-process communication enables processes to avoid having to know the name(s) of receiving process(es). This has proven beneficial since it saves the sender from "over-specifying" the destination, permitting dynamic modifications which do not require changes to the sender's code. An analogy to a similar problem in the current postal system may be helpful. We have all had a fellow employee leave the company to move elsewhere. The problem is what to do with mail addressed to him after he has left. The problem arises because of our inability to determine for which of the former employee's roles the mail is intended. If it is for the business role it would be proper to give the mail to the person now handling his job, but if it were for the employee's personal role, then it should be forwarded to him. An exchange

Reprinted from *Proc. 21st IEEE COMPCON,* Fall 1980, pp. 585–589.

allows the role, rather than the process, to be specified.

Of course, if all that was desired was a mapping from one name to another, then exchanges might be unnecessarily costly, since simple table lookup could be used. Fortunately, there are other advantages to exchanges. They permit both a very dynamic mapping and multiple receivers. An exchange permits dynamic mapping since the receiver can be changed at will without interfering with the sender. Further, since the change merely requires the passing of the capability to the exchange to another process it can be done rapidly. Since the exchange is a queue, there is no problem with the former receiver having to forward messages, he merely lets them queue up until the new receiver starts accepting them. An example of the use of the dynamic mapping might be a server which could insert a filter process depending on the characteristics of the sender. For example, the first message to the server might specify that the data in following messages is either ASCII or EBCDIC characters. The server might insert a filter process to map one of the character sets into the other and then it would only process the one set, using the filter process as needed.

The ability to have more than one process receive from an exchange has several advantages. For example, a server process could spawn a duplicate of itself if the incoming message queue became too long. Since SODS is a distributed system, it is possible that the two servers could run in parallel, thus processing the input faster. Another example is the allocation of resources, such as line printers. If there were more than one line printer available, then an exchange which held the messages specifying the jobs to print could be accessed by all the line printer schedulers. An available printer would receive the next job at the exchange, thus keeping all the printers busy.

Since an exchange is a simplex communication device, there arises the problem of how to establish two-way communication between processes. Two-way communication may be used in two modes. One mode is the establishment of a "conversation" with many messages being exchanged between two or more processes. The other mode is similar to a question-and-answer exchange; a process sends a message and expects a message in response. SODS provides mechanisms for both modes.

To establish a conversation, each process must have capabilities to two common exchanges. The process starting the conversation makes use of the general ability to send a capability as a message to provide the other process with access to a second exchange. The ability to send a capability allows one process to permit others to send or receive messages at the exchange named by the capability. This permits dynamic rerouting of messages among processes, an important aspect of SODS.

A reply mode is provided by the ability to attach a capability to a message. The capability is called a response capability since it indicates where a response may be sent. A response capability is like any other capability, except that it may be used only once. It is then discarded automatically. The single-use restriction permits a process to be sure of receiving only one reply to a message. It is important to note that the right to that single use may be transferred to another process. If the response capability could not be transferred, a server which needed to invoke a subordinate would have to mediate the return of the response to the user. With the ability to transfer a capability, the server can pass the response capability on to the subordinate and start processing the next service request while the subordinate finishes the current request and returns the result directly to the user. This feature is heavily used in SODS.

All the operations which involve duplicating or transfering capabilities permit only a subset of the current permissions to be duplicated. This ensures that no capabilities gain permissions as they are passed along. Further, there is a "duplicate" permission, so that only capabilities with that permission set may be duplicated or transferred. This permits processes to restrict the propagation of capabilities.

One function which has turned out to be desirable, but which was not included in the original design, is the ability to receive the next message arriving at any of several exchanges. An example is having one server process for multiple users. If the server needed to know the identity of the users, it could accomplish that by giving each user a capability to a different exchange and then receive from all the exchanges. The user would be identified by which exchange the message was received from.

PROCESS MANAGEMENT

A major function of an operating system is to provide process management. In SODS, the process management is integrated into the inter-process communication structure by using messages to exchanges to control processes. The issues in process management involve process creation and control, and what to do when a process dies.

To create a new process the parent process first queues the instructions and initialized data of the new process at an exchange. It then asks the system to create a process using the messages. The parent process may pass any subset of its capabilities on to the child. The capabilities for the child are not required to be in the same order as those of the parent. The idea of capabilities being in an order arises because capabilities owned by a process are kept in a table in system space, rather than in the process's address space. What the process actually has is an index into the table called a capability descriptor. Thus, each process may have capability descriptors in the range from 0 to an implementation defined limit. The use of capability descriptors avoids giving the process too specific a name for an exchange. Since all the process gives the system is an index into the table, the parent process may fill the table with capabilities in the order it chooses. Then, for example, the child always reads from the exchange whose capability is at index one and writes to the capability at index two. The other advantage of the capability descriptor is that the process can't forge capabilities, since it can not touch them.

The process management of SODS/OS depends on the concept of setting a trap at an exchange. Setting a trap involves specifying a process, an exchange, and a message type and class. Once a trap is set any messages of the specified type and class arriving at the exchange cause action to be taken on the process. The action taken depends on the type of the message. Normal messages cannot be trapped. Exception and interrupt messages cause the trapping process to be interrupted and force a subroutine call to a routine which was specified when the trap was set. Interrupt messages take effect as soon as they arrive at an exchange, while exception messages take effect when they reach the head of the queue. Control messages are ones such as kill, suspend, and resume. They take effect when they arrive, the operation is performed by the system on the process. A process may set a trap at any exchange for which it has the permissions. Only one process may have a trap for a given type and class message at an exchange. Note that since processes do not have names they may only set traps for themselves.

The preceeding description indicates that processes may voluntarily set traps. To enable full control over the processes there must also be automatically set traps at some exchange. Whenever the system creates a new process it creates a corresponding exchange with control traps set for the new process. This exchange is called a control exchange. A capability to the control exchange is returned to the parent process. Other than the preset traps the control exchange is exactly like any other exchange, the parent process may discard it, pass it to another process, or keep it. An advantage of the use of control exchanges is the ability to pass control to some process other than an ancestor of the process to be controlled.

The final issue in process management is how to handle the death of a process. Often other processes need to be notified when a process has died. The method of notification is to send a message of a specific type and class. This message is called a death certificate. A process which wants to receive a death certificate sets a permission in the capability it gives to the client process. When that process dies, the system scans the capability table and sends a death certificate to each exchange whose capability had that permission set. One use of death certificates is for notifying server processes when their client is finished using their services. Death certificates notify a server even if the process did not die gracefully. Similarly to control traps, the system automatically sets the permission in the process's capability to its control exchange.

INPUT AND OUTPUT

The third function of an operating system is to support input/output. SODS provides device oriented input and output using four system calls: read, write, getstatus, and set-status. The calls are location dependent, since they affect the specified device on the local machine. I/O was implemented in this manner because it was not obvious how to implement it so as to be integrated with the message and exchange structure. The issues which I/O raises are resource location and management, error handling, inter-process communication conventions, and how to integrate I/O with the message and exchange structure.

One of the major problems in a distributed system is locating a desired resource. Specific device names should not be hard-wired into the user level programs. It is desirable to be able to assign an available device to a process which wishes to use a device of that type. To be able to assign the device it is necessary to locate it. This requires mapping from a generic name, i.e. "line printer", to the specific name of the device assigned to the user. The current implementation method is to have a process on each machine which is the resource allocation process. A capability to the resource process's input exchange is given to other processes as they are started. A process which desires a resource sends a request to the resource allocator. The resource allocator returns a capability to an exchange to which the process may send requests.

There is still the question of how the resource allocator finds the resource. It is the responsibility of each process which is a resource to send to the resource allocator the name(s) it wishes to be known by and a capability to its input exchange. Each I/O device has a user level process which makes the device available to the rest of the system and sends the name to the resource allocator. This makes I/O to the device location independent, since other processes may send to the input exchange of the process.

I/O processes make use of both the response capability and the death certificates. Since most devices require exclusive access, the device interface process gives the resource allocator a response capability. This permits the resource allocator to give it away once, thereby ensuring exclusive access. The device interface process also sets the permission requesting a death certificate, so that it knows when its client has died. It can then clean up as needed and make itself available again.

Error handling is an unresolved issue in the current implementation. It is quite obvious that for input errors the receiving process must be notified, since it is waiting for the data anyway. However, on output it is possible to have a number of different ways of handling errors. A process could wait until the output is completed, or it could assume that the output went properly and expect an interrupt if it didn't, or it could ignore errors. The choice depends on the application, and how much an error will matter. At the least, it should be a choice the user process makes, since only it knows what is important.

Another issue in I/O is inter-process communication conventions. The device interface routines make the device look like any other process so that a user process doesn't need to worry about whether it is communicating with a device or another process. This is only an issue because it has to be taken into account when the I/O is integrated into the inter-process communication structure.

Although the current implementation has special calls to perform I/O, it is possible to make devices appear as exchanges to the user processes, without having a user level interface process. To do so would require providing the ability to locate devices, set and get the status of the device, and making the device conform to the inter-process communication conventions. Location of devices could be accomplished by adding a system call which requests the exchange of a device of a particular type. To keep the system simple, the "locate" call would only provide local devices, it would be up to the resource allocator to find the device if it was not local. Exclusive access and client death could be handled as they are now. It would be necessary to provide for setting and reading the status. This could be accomplished either with separate exchange(s) or by using a particular type and class of message to the device exchange. Observing inter-process communication conventions mainly involves the stripping off of some data from the beginning of the message.

FILE SYSTEM

The file system is not part of the operating system proper. It is implemented as a collection of user processes. This has the advantage of allowing the file system to become as complex as desired without having to cram it into a limited amount of system space. It also allows the user to avoid the file system entirely if he so desires. The current file system is a temporary implementation until a more flexible file system design is implemented. Some issues of file system design are discussed in Crocker and Luckenbaugh's paper [2].

OTHER ISSUES

This section will cover briefly some issues that were not mentioned above. The issues are protection, location independence, the nature of a message, and performance. These problems deserve more attention, but were deliberately downgraded in importance during the design because this is an experimental system.

Protection involves restricting the access of users to objects. The intention of the operating system design was that protection could be accomplished through capabilities. If you do not have a capability to the object you can not get at it. While this is true, the result is that the number of processes tends to multiply, since a filter process must be put between the user process and any protected, common service or data. This is a reasonable way to do protection, except for performance problems, which are covered below.

Although SODS was designed with the intention of keeping a user ignorant of its location, a process sometimes needs to know its location. For example, if one wants reliability it might be desirable to have more than one process cooperating but located on different machines. If one machine went down then the other process would be able to recover. This suggests the need to be able to specify the location of the processes and that they should never be running on the same machine. A possible solution which avoids absolute location specification would be to permit a request that something else not reside on the same machine. This would provide the desired split without the need to specify exactly where to put the object. It would also be desirable to specify the same information for exchanges.

An observation about the use of messages raises an issue which deserves further consideration. Very often messages consist of two data parts: a header and a body. Since they are so often used this way, it might be desirable to add functions which treated messages as having multiple data parts. For example, one might want to be able to examine the header without having the body copied into your address space also. Another possible function would be to put a new header on the data, either making the old header part of the body, or discarding it. Functions such as these would be closer to what SODS processes actually do with messages. This is essentially the idea of "slots" proposed by Feldman [3].

A final issue is performance. The design of the system encourages proliferation of processes. Unfortunately, the associated context swapping is extremely expensive on a conventional machine. The solution is to build hardware which properly supports the system. The extra context swapping is due to the modularity required to allow distribution and not to the distribution itself.

CONCLUSIONS

The experiences with SODS have shown that the use of messages and exchanges to provide the inter-process communication, process management, and input and output is a viable method of building distributed systems. It is felt that with some modifications to the current design it will serve as a good experimental base for further research into distributed processing applications.

ACKNOWLEDGMENTS

This research has been sponsored by the General Systems Division of IBM and the University of Delaware. This paper has benefited from discussions with Chase Cotton, editoral comments from Dave Crocker and Dave Farber, and most of all from the existence of an implementation of SODS by Dave Sincoskie.

REFERENCES

[1] Sincoskie, W.D., Farber, D.J., "The Series/1 Distributed Operating System: Description and Comments", IEEE Compcon Proceedings, Fall 1980.

[2] Crocker, D., Luckenbaugh, G., "An Architecture to Support a Distributed File System", IEEE Micro-Delcon Proceedings, March 1980, pp 97-104.

[3] Feldman, J.A., "High Level Programming for Distributed Computing", CACM, Vol. 22, No. 6, June 1979, pp 353-360.

A DISTRIBUTED REAL TIME OPERATING SYSTEM

Michael L. Green, Edward Y.S. Lee, Samprakash Majumdar, Douglas C. Shannon

TRW Defense and Space Systems Group
Redondo Beach, Ca. 90278

Abstract

A distributed-Real Time Operating System (d-RTOS) is described which supported a distributed computer simulation with the following services: A Data Input Handler, Clock Manager, Conditional Enablement Handler, Reconfiguration Prescheduler, Scheduler, Task Completion Handler and Resource Manager. These services were tailored to a ballistic missile defense (BMD) application to achieve maximum performance at minimum overhead. The experiment proved that d-RTOS is efficient for BMD applications. The d-RTOS may be extended to other classes of distributed computer applications.

Introduction

A distributed computer simulation was conducted at the Advanced Research Center in Huntsville, Alabama, using a network of eight VAX 11/780 computers [1]. The simulation included a distributed-Real Time Operating System (d-RTOS) which employed a functioning distributed data base manager, distributed resource manager and process executive, and models of the target application software. This paper describes an overview of the d-RTOS. Companion papers describe the data base manager and resource manager [2, 3].

The d-RTOS was developed to both explicitly perform and functionally simulate the execution of several key d-RTOS tasks including the following:

(1) Dispatcher - cycles through six d-RTOS tasks.
(2) Initialization Routine - initializes variables and arrays.
(3) Data Input Handler - processes incoming task enablements and replicated file updates from other simulated computers.
(4) Clock Manager - monitors the real time clock for time enablements.
(5) Conditional Enablement Handler - checks for a matching pair of conditional enablements.
(6) Reconfiguration Prescheduler - generates a reconfiguration enablement when all requested resource management status reports have been received.
(7) Scheduler - selects, on a priority First-In First-Out (FIFO) basis, a task in the local task enablement queue and executes the selected task.
(8) Task Completion Handler - processes task enablements and outgoing replicated file updates generated by a local task completion.
(9) Resource Manager - detects one or more overloaded computers and redistributes their load.

Each computer in the simulated BMD defense unit contains a distributed-Real Time Operating System (d-RTOS), that is an operating system which acts independently but cooperatively with the other computers in the defense unit. A block diagram for the d-RTOS for a single computer is shown in Figure 1. This figure shows the control and data flow within a computer and the data flow to and from the other computers in the defense unit. The d-RTOS and application task models are presented as if they were in a true tactical environment.

Data is shared in a single computer (without overhead) between all d-RTOS and application tasks using FORTRAN named commons. Between computers, updates to replicated files and task enablements are formatted into a variable length message using a three-word tactical header and transmitted over a simulated shared bus or direct link.

The objectives of the d-RTOS are to simplify the design and to speed the execution of the application tasks for use in a distributed environment. The d-RTOS is not a general purpose operating system but is highly specialized to take advantage of every peculiarity of the BMD construct.

The d-RTOS model is transparent to the application tasks. Each application task is unaware that it is being executed on a distributed architecture. It need not know where the other application tasks are resident or where updates to its replicated files are sent. In addition, when an application task is enabled, all its files have already been updated by the d-RTOS data base manager and are waiting for it locally for immediate processing.

The d-RTOS uses a write-oriented design philosophy. When an application task updates a replicated file, these updates are transferred by the data base manager as soon as possible to all relevant computers. Thus an application task need never request data files since all data files are transferred as soon as they are updated. This design philosophy encourages parallelism between data flow and task execution, trading off message traffic for computation and reconfiguration speed.

Reprinted from *Proc. IEEE Distrib. Data Acquisit. Comput. Contr. Symp.*, 1980, pp. 175–184.

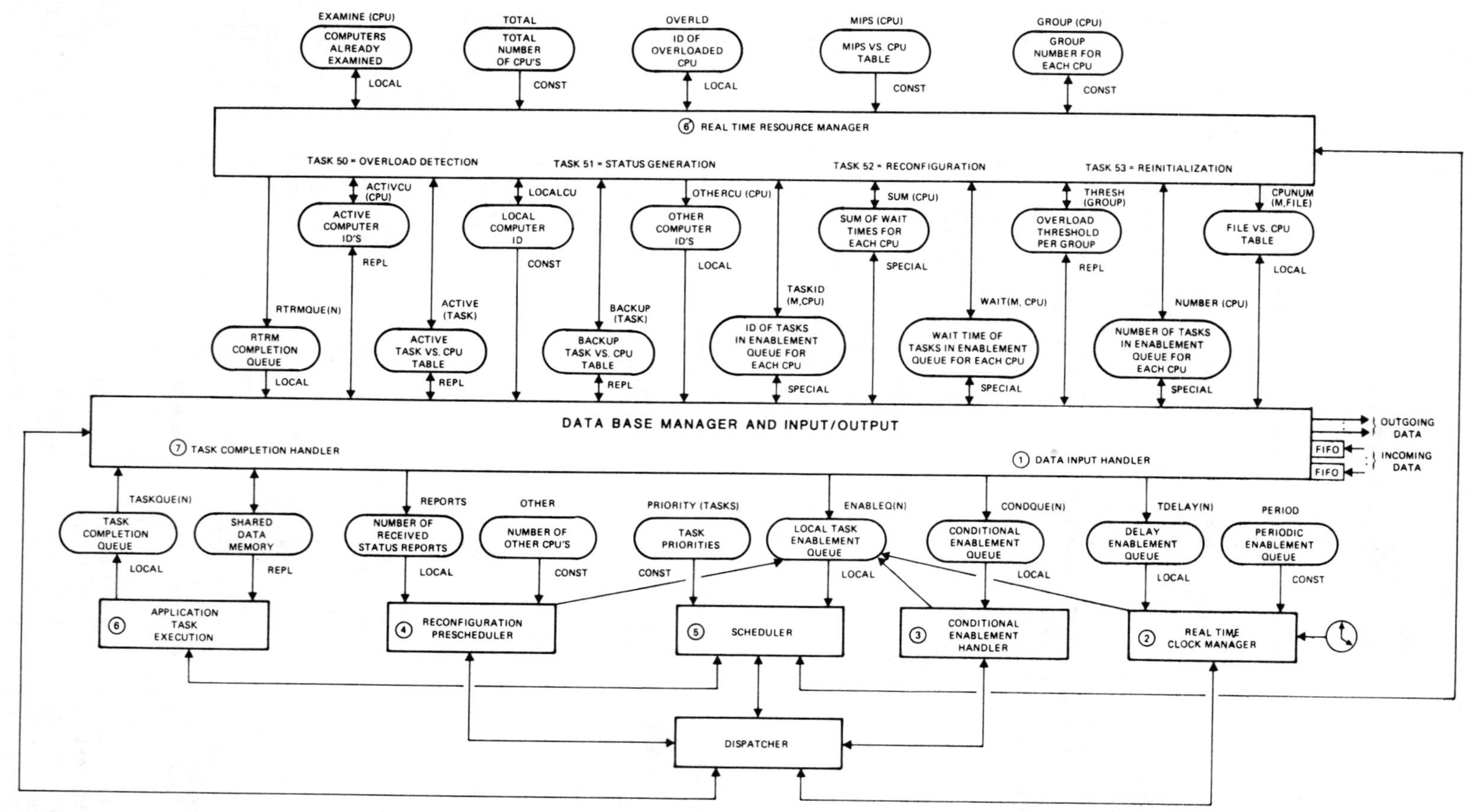

Figure 1. Distributed-Real Time Operating System (r-RTOS) for each Computer

The Real Time Resource Manager is used to balance the task load across all the computers in the defense unit. Load balancing is accomplished by locally detecting an overloaded condition, querying all other computers for their loading status and then dynamically changing the allocation of tasks to computers. The Resource Manager is fully distributed and consists of five tasks which reside on each computer in the defense unit.

Fundamental Assumptions

Several fundamental assumptions have been made in order to improve performance and to simplify the design of a tactical distributed RTOS for the Distributed Data Processing (DDP) Simulation Experiment [4, 5].

Assumption 1 - Files read by two or more computers in the DDP architecture will be replicated. These replicated files will be updated whenever a completing task updates its local files.

Assumption 2 - Updates for a file are only written into that part of the file corresponding to a unique ID.

Assumption 3 - A file may be written into by only one task in the DDP architecture. Several tasks may read a file.

Assumption 4 - Each computer has infinite main storage. Therefore, there is no limit as to the number of tasks and data files that can be stored within each computer. For this experiment, this memory will be assumed to be of a single high speed level. Thus a task can be enabled without dispatch and initialization overhead.

Assumption 5 - Computers are so closely spaced that communications between computers are error free. Thus error checking, acknowledgements, retransmissions, etc., will not be required nor modeled.

Assumption 6 - Computers are interconnected using point-to-point direct connections or shared buses, and FIFO buffers. FIFO buffers are assumed to be of infinite length, therefore overflow protection will not be required.

Assumption 7 - Within each computer all d-RTOS and application tasks can communicate with each other through FORTRAN common memory, i.e., local reads and writes are not required (zero overhead).

Detail of the Distributed Real Time Operating System

The Dispatcher

The simulated defense unit is dormant until the defense command authority transmits an initialization call to each computer. The dispatcher is the main program within each computer (see Figures 1 and 2). It initializes variables and arrays through a call to the Initialization Routine and then requests permission to start. When permission is received it begins cycling through six d-RTOS tasks: The Data Input Handler, Clock Manager, Conditional Enablement Handler, Reconfiguration Prescheduler, Scheduler, and Task Completion Handler. Through these six d-RTOS tasks, the Dispatcher executes either directly or indirectly all relevant d-RTOS and application tasks. If a d-RTOS task is called that has no entries in its input queue(s), it simply returns control to the Dispatcher. Otherwise, it performs its required function and, if necessary, calls other d-RTOS tasks and then returns to the Dispatcher.

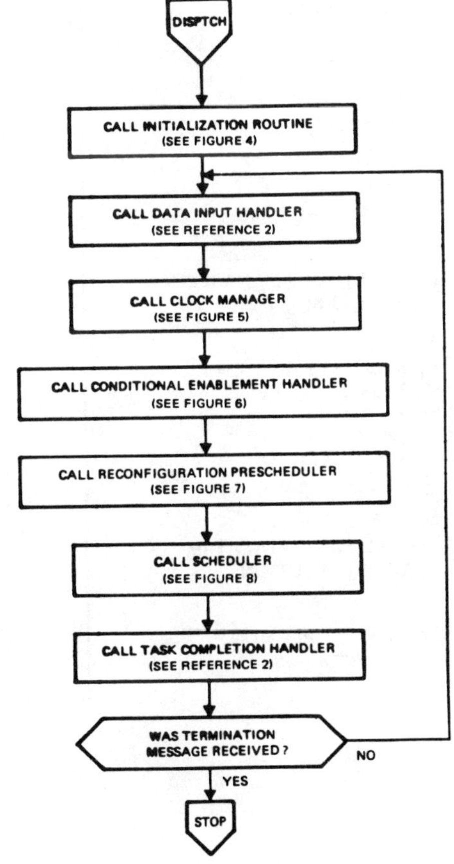

Figure 2. The Dispatcher

The cyclic nature of the execution sequence within each computer is graphically displayed in Figure 3. The execution time required by any d-RTOS task can range from negligible when its input queue(s) are empty, to the largest part of a cycle. The execution time of a cycle, being merely the sum of its composite parts, may also vary over a wide range.

The Initialization Routine

The initialization routine is used to initialize the variables and arrays used by d-RTOS and the application model within a computer (see Figures 2 and 4). It is called only once as the defense unit is readied for engagement. Since initialization occurs only during the preengagement period, its execution time is ignored.

The Clock Manager

An application task may write a task delay enablement into its task completion queue (see Figure 1). The Task Completion Handler (part of the data base manager) reads this task delay enablement and routes it to the computer which will eventually execute this task at the appropriate time. When the task delay enablement arrives at the destination computer, the Data Input Handler stores it in the local task delay enablement queue.

The Real Time Clock Manager is called once per cycle (see Figures 1, 3, and 5). It examines the real time clock and at the proper time places a task enablement in the local task enablement queue for task delay enablements (at a time specified by an application task) and for periodic enablements (every N milliseconds).

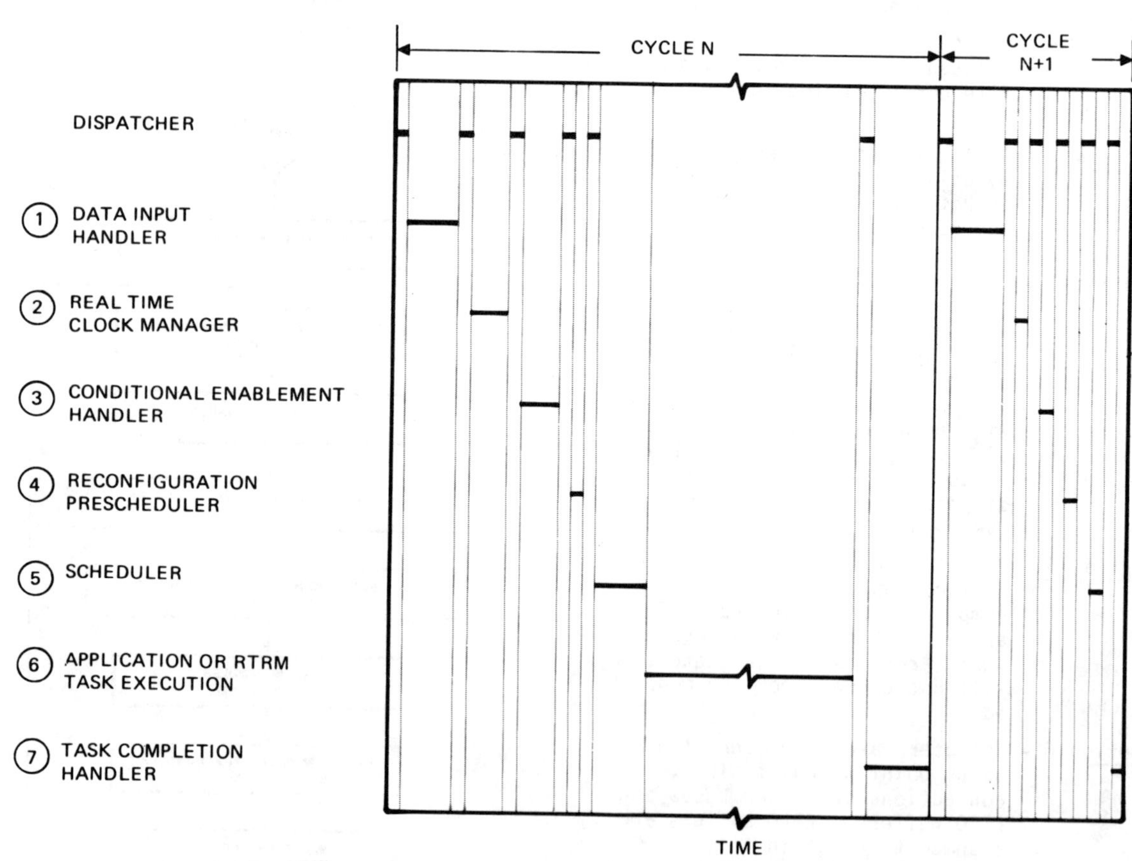

Figure 3. Execution Sequence Within Each Computer

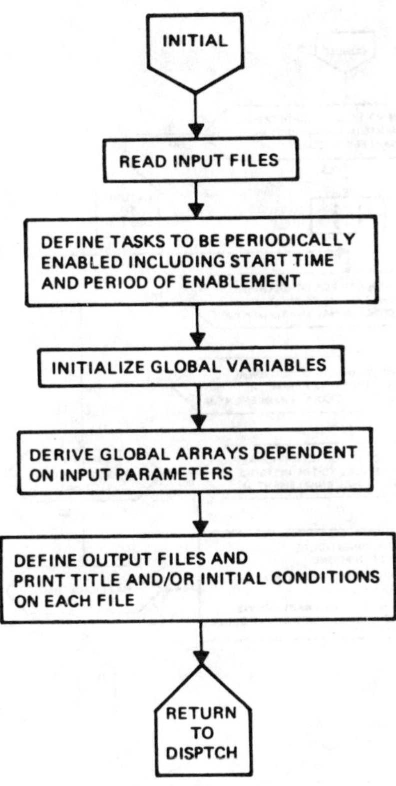

Figure 4. The Initialization Routine

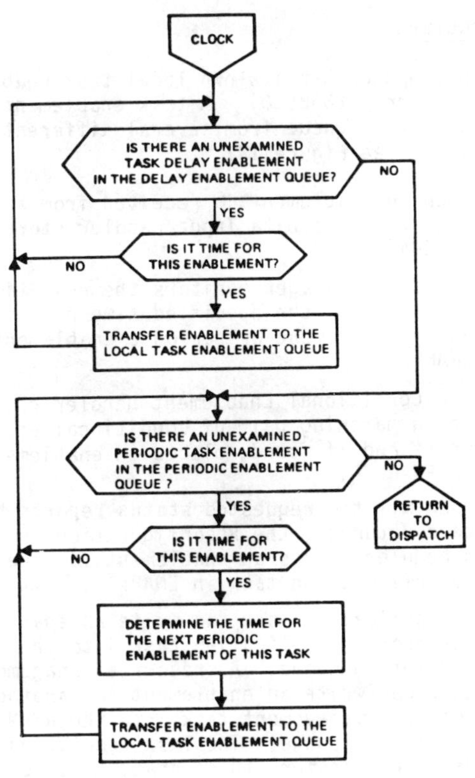

Figure 5. The Clock Manager

The Conditional Enablement Handler

A conditional enablement scheme is available in which two different application tasks operating on the same instance must both request the enablement of a third task before that task can be enabled. Each of the three tasks involved can be resident on different computers or can be reallocated to other computers by the resource manager without affecting the conditional enablement.

The scheme works as follows: Two application tasks independently write a conditional enablement into their respective task completion queues (see Figure 1). The Task Completion Handler of the local computer (part of the data base manager) reads each of these conditional enablements and routes them to the computer that will eventually execute this task. When each conditional enablement arrives at the destination computer, the Data Input Handler stores it in the conditional enablement queue.

The Conditional Enablement Handler is called once per cycle (see Figures 1, 3, and 6). It checks the conditional enablement queue for a matching pair of conditional enablements containing the same task number and the same instance ID but which are requested by different tasks. If such a pair of conditional enablements is found, it places an enablement in the local task enablement queue which will be processed by the Scheduler during a later part of the cycle.

The Reconfiguration Prescheduler

The Real Time Resource Manager (RTRM) consists of four d-RTOS tasks: Overload Detection, Status Report Generation, Reconfiguration and Reinitialization. The Overload Detection task (DETECT) is periodically enabled every 20 milliseconds via the Clock Manager. DETECT checks for an overloaded condition within the local task enablement queue. If an overload is detected, DETECT requests a status report from the other computers in the defense unit by writing an enablement for the Status Report Generation task in the RTRM Completion Queue. When all the status reports have been returned, the Reconfiguration Prescheduler places an enablement for the Reconfiguration task in the local task enablement queue. The Reconfiguration task attempts to redistribute the task load from one or more overloaded computers to one or more lightly loaded computers (see Figures 1, 3, and 7, and the companion paper entitled "A Distributed Real Time Resource Manager" [3].

The Scheduler

Each computer has its own local task enablement queue (array ENABLEQ). A task enablement can be placed in this queue from several different d-RTOS Tasks (see Figure 1):

- When an enablement is received from another computer, the Data Input Handler stores it in ENABLEQ.
- The Clock Manager monitors the real time clock and at the specified time places a delay enablement or periodic enablement in ENABLEQ.
- The Conditional Enablement Handler checks for a matching pair of conditional enablements and if found, places an enablement in ENABLEQ.
- When all the requested status reports have been returned, the Reconfiguration Prescheduler places an enablement for the Reconfiguration task in ENABLEQ.
- An application task can write an enablement for another application task into the task completion queue. A resource management task can write an enablement for another resource management task into the RTRM completion queue. The Task Completion Handler transfers these enablements either to ENABLEQ or to another computer after referring to the "Task vs. CPU" table.

The Scheduler examines the task enablement(s) placed in ENABLEQ by one or more of the above d-RTOS tasks. It selects on a priority first-in first-out basis one of these task enablements, it executes the selected task, and then returns control to the Dispatcher (see Figures1, 3, and 8).

Data Base Management

The Data Base Manager (DBM) of the distributed Real Time Operating System (d-RTOS) serves several very important functions in the overall d-RTOS design. It controls the flow of data and enablements among application tasks both within the local CPU and between the local CPU and other CPU's. It maintains all the replicated files and tables needed by the application tasks and the Real Time Resource Manager (RTRM), making sure all updates are performed correctly. It also services the four important queues related to task execution under the d-RTOS design. For more details, see the companion paper entitled "A Distributed Data Base Manager" [2].

Simulation Analysis Tools

This section presents a sample of the output listings available to analyze the performance of the simulation.

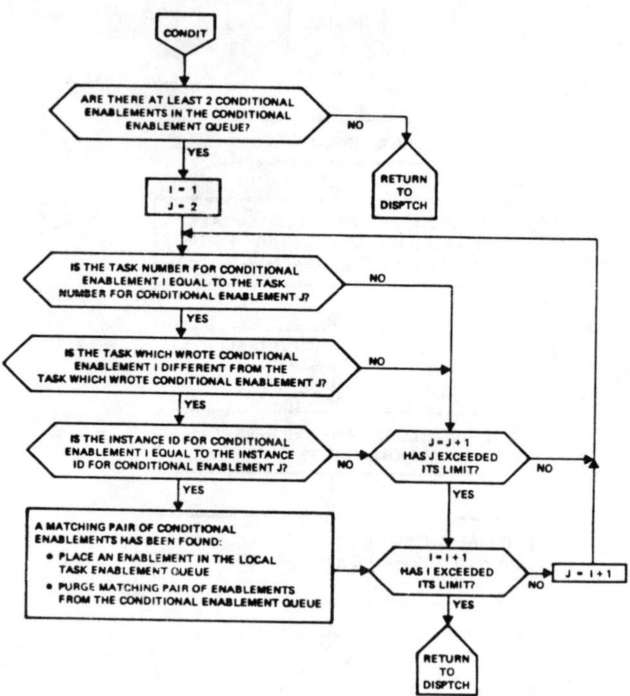

Figure 6. The Conditional Enablement Handler

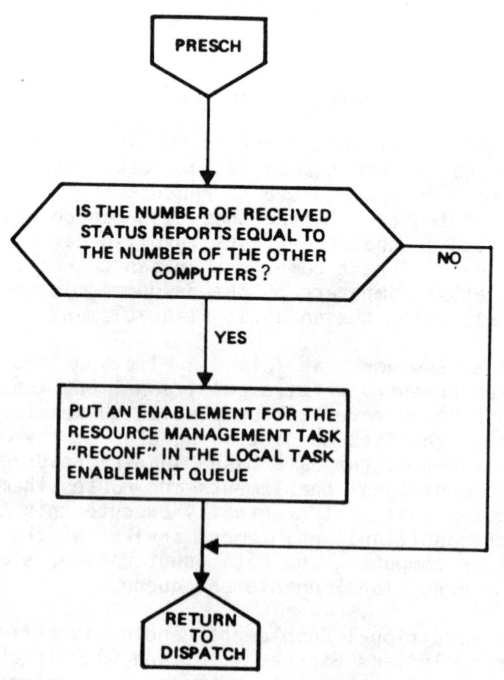

Figure 7. The Reconfiguration Prescheduler

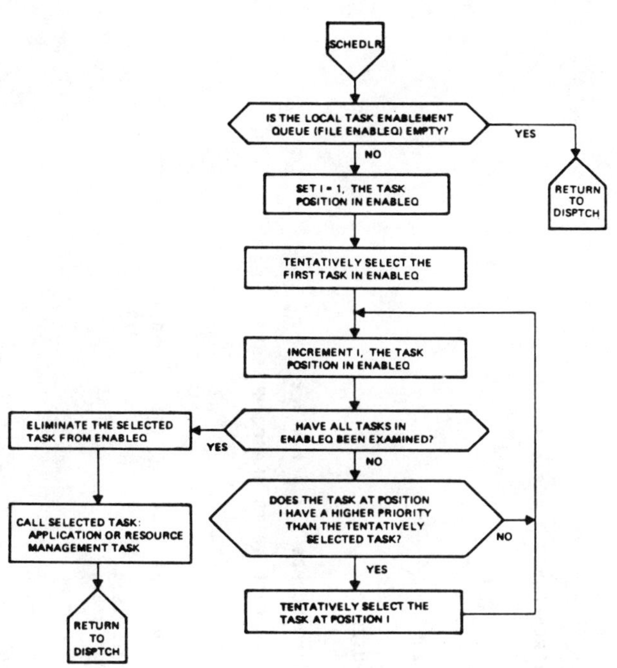

Figure 8. The Scheduler

Full Trace of the Run

A d-RTOS cycle may contain 6 d-RTOS tasks and 1 application or resource management task (see Figures 1 and 3). Application or resource management tasks are only selected and executed by the Scheduler if the relevant enablement is written into the local task enablement queue by another d-RTOS task. If a d-RTOS task executes in less than 15 machine language instructions (indicating that its input queue(s) are empty), it is defined as "idle" and it is not displayed in the full trace of the run.

As an example of the trace output, Figure 9 shows several d-RTOS cycles of tactical computer 2 in a six-computer architecture testcase. In cycle 1, 1 microsecond after BMD processing was initiated, the first non-idle d-RTOS task was executed, the Real-Time Clock Manager. The Clock Manager placed an enablement for tasks 13 and 14 into the local task enablement queue (ENABLEQ). The Scheduler then examined these enablements and selected the highest priority task, task 13. Task 13 ran and wrote into the task completion queue that it updated files 129, 128 and 131 (see Figure 1). The Task Completion Handler examined the task completion queue and with the aid of the File versus CPU table concluded that all 3 updated files were non-replicated.

In the second cycle, the scheduler selected the task enablement remaining in the local task enablement queue, task 14. Task 14 ran and wrote into the task completion queue that it updated files 147, 146 and 132 and that it requests the enablement of task 23. The Task Completion Handler examined this queue and concluded that only file 132 was replicated on another computer. The updated part of file 132 (6 actual words and 4 fictitious words making up a 10-word simulated tactical file update) were appended to a 3-word tactical header and transmitted to tactical computer 1. The Task Completion Handler next processed the task 23 enablement and with the aid of the Task versus CPU table concluded that this enablement should be placed in the local task enablement queue.

Note that no cycles are printed between cycles 3 and 74. These cycles are defined as "empty". An empty cycle does not contain an application task and all six d-RTOS tasks which are executed are "idle"; an idle task executes in less than 15 machine language instructions (see Figure 3).

Utilization Factors

The utilization factor is defined as the percentage of the time that a computer is utilized executing a specific type of code. Figure 10 shows the utilization factors for the following types of code:

TASKS	- all the application tasks
SCHED	- the d-RTOS Scheduler
RTOS	- the d-RTOS Clock Manager, Conditional Enablement Handler and Reconfiguration Prescheduler
RTRM	- the d-RTOS Resource Management tasks
DATAIN	- the d-RTOS Data Input Handler
INPUT	- the d-RTOS FIFO buffer to memory task
COMPL	- the d-RTOS Task Completion Handler
OUT	- the d-RTOS memory to output port task
TOTAL	- all of the above
IDLE	- 100% - TOTAL = utilization factor of all d-RTOS tasks executing in less than 15 machine language instructions

The column labeled INSTRUCTIONS shows the accumulated machine language instructions per approximately 10 millisecond interval. The four columns labeled CYCLES show the number and percentage of active and empty cycles. An empty cycle does not contain an application task and all six d-RTOS tasks which are executed are "idle". (An idle task executes in less than 15 machine language instructions.) An active cycle contains at least one non-idle d-RTOS or application task.

Other Tools

Several other output listings are also available to aid in the analysis of the simulation:

- Port-to-Port Times
- Incoming Messages from SETS (the threat)
- Maximum Number of Words in each FIFO
- Maximum Number of Words sent out per Cycle

```
*************************************************************************************************************************

BMD DATA PROCESSING WAS INITIATIATED BY THE DU COMMAND AUTHORITY  2982.000 SECONDS AFTER THE ENEMY MISSILES WERE LAUNCHED

*************************************************************************************************************************

2  * * * * *    CYCLE        1                ENABTOT  2                  1 MICROSECONDS    * * * * * *
D-RTOS TASK 62, CLOCK:  TIME ENABLEMENT(S) ARE WRITTEN IN ENABLEQ FOR TASK(S):  13  14
D-RTOS TASK 65, SCHEDLR:  EXAMINED ENABLEQ AND SELECTED TASK 13
         N     ENABLEQ(N,1)  ENABLEQ(N,2)  ENABLEQ(N,3)
         1         13            62            0
         2         14            62            0
TASK 13, TRPS RAN.  IT WAS ENABLED BY: 62 FOR IMAGE ID:        0
D-RTOS TASK 66, COMPLET:   TASK 13 UPDATED NON-REPLICATED FILE 129
D-RTOS TASK 66, COMPLET:   TASK 13 UPDATED NON-REPLICATED FILE 128
D-RTOS TASK 66, COMPLET:   TASK 13 UPDATED NON-REPLICATED FILE 131

5  * * * * *    CYCLE        2                ENABTOT  1                184 MICROSECONDS    * * * * * *
D-RTOS TASK 65, SCHEDLR:  EXAMINED ENABLEQ AND SELECTED TASK 14
         N     ENABLEQ(N,1)  ENABLEQ(N,2)  ENABLEQ(N,3)
         1         14            62            0
TASK 14, TRMS, SCHEDULED    1  RADAR COMMANDS FOR SETS
IT UPDATED FILES 132,146,147 AND PLACED AN ENABLEMENT FOR TASK 23 INTO TASKQUE
D-RTOS TASK 66, COMPLET:   TASK 14 UPDATED NON-REPLICATED FILE 147
D-RTOS TASK 66, COMPLET:   TASK 14 UPDATED NON-REPLICATED FILE 146
D-RTOS TASK 66, COMPLET:   6 +  4 WORD(S) OF REPLICATED FILE 132 SENT TO COMPUTER(S):   1
D-RTOS TASK 66, COMPLET:   PLACED AN ENABLEMENT FOR TASK 23 IN ENABLEQ

5  * * * * *    CYCLE        3                ENABTOT  1                277 MICROSECONDS    * * * * * *
D-RTOS TASK 65, SCHEDLR:  EXAMINED ENABLEQ AND SELECTED TASK 23
         N     ENABLEQ(N,1)  ENABLEQ(N,2)  ENABLEQ(N,3)
         1         23            14            1
TASK 23, THE RADAR COMPUTERS OUTPUT TASK, SENT  1 RADAR COMMANDS TO SETS.   IT UPDATED FILE 112 (&153) AND 145.   RDRSETS:
                1        SRCH        3689           1             0            0
D-RTOS TASK 66, COMPLET:   1 +  0 WORD(S) OF REPLICATED FILE 145 SENT TO COMPUTER(S):   1
D-RTOS TASK 66, COMPLET:   6 +  4 WORD(S) OF REPLICATED FILE 112 SENT TO COMPUTER(S):  10

2  * * * * *    CYCLE       74                ENABTOT  1               1000 MICROSECONDS    * * * * * *
D-RTOS TASK 62, CLOCK:  TIME ENABLEMENT(S) ARE WRITTEN IN ENABLEQ FOR TASK(S):  14
D-RTOS TASK 65, SCHEDLR:  EXAMINED ENABLEQ AND SELECTED TASK 14
         N     ENABLEQ(N,1)  ENABLEQ(N,2)  ENABLEQ(N,3)
         1         14            62            0
TASK 14, TRMS, SCHEDULED    1  RADAR COMMANDS FOR SETS
IT UPDATED FILES 132,146,147 AND PLACED AN ENABLEMENT FOR TASK 23 INTO TASKQUE
D-RTOS TASK 66, COMPLET:   TASK 14 UPDATED NON-REPLICATED FILE 147
D-RTOS TASK 66, COMPLET:   TASK 14 UPDATED NON-REPLICATED FILE 146
D-RTOS TASK 66, COMPLET:   6 +  4 WORD(S) OF REPLICATED FILE 132 SENT TO COMPUTER(S):   1
D-RTOS TASK 66, COMPLET:   PLACED AN ENABLEMENT FOR TASK 23 IN ENABLEQ

1  * * * * *    CYCLE       75                ENABTOT  1               1097 MICROSECONDS    * * * * * *
D-RTOS TASK 61, DATAIN:   PLACED AN ENABLEMENT FOR TASK 22 IN ENABLEQ
D-RTOS TASK 61, DATAIN:   8 + 24 WORD(S) OF REPLICATED FILE 111 TRANSFERRED FROM FIFO 10 TO SHARED MEMORY
D-RTOS TASK 65, SCHEDLR:  EXAMINED ENABLEQ AND SELECTED TASK 23
         N     ENABLEQ(N,1)  ENABLEQ(N,2)  ENABLEQ(N,3)
         1         23            14            1
         2         22            62            1
TASK 23, THE RADAR COMPUTERS OUTPUT TASK, SENT  1 RADAR COMMANDS TO SETS.   IT UPDATED FILE 112 (&153) AND 145.   RDRSETS:
                2        SRCH        4514          16             0            0
D-RTOS TASK 66, COMPLET:   1 +  0 WORD(S) OF REPLICATED FILE 145 SENT TO COMPUTER(S):   1
D-RTOS TASK 66, COMPLET:   6 +  4 WORD(S) OF REPLICATED FILE 112 SENT TO COMPUTER(S):  10
```

Figure 9. Example of Full Trace of the Run

			UTILIZATION FACTORS	(PERCENT)							INSTRUCTIONS	CYCLES			
TIME	TASKS	SCHED	RTOS	RTRM	DATAIN	INPUT	COMPL	OUT	TOTAL	IDLE	TOTAL	ACTIVE	%	EMPTY	%
10003	22.5	3.3	0.3	0.0	0.2	3.2	4.0	2.5	36.0	64.0	7597	25	5.9	396	94.1
20001	18.6	2.9	0.3	0.0	0.0	0.0	3.4	1.9	27.0	73.0	5674	22	4.6	452	95.4
30013	33.1	4.5	0.3	0.0	0.0	2.0	5.5	5.1	50.4	49.6	10762	33	9.8	303	90.2
40008	20.5	3.3	0.3	0.0	0.0	0.7	4.1	2.8	31.7	68.3	6674	25	5.6	422	94.4
50003	20.5	3.3	0.3	0.0	0.0	0.7	4.1	2.8	31.7	68.3	6674	25	5.6	422	94.4
60014	20.5	3.3	0.3	0.0	0.0	0.7	4.0	2.8	31.6	68.4	6674	25	5.6	423	94.4
70176	38.3	3.8	0.5	0.0	0.0	0.6	4.7	2.8	50.7	49.3	10982	29	8.6	308	91.4
80004	23.6	3.4	0.3	0.0	0.0	0.7	4.1	3.0	35.2	64.9	7294	26	6.2	393	93.8
90007	20.2	3.2	0.3	0.0	0.0	0.7	3.8	2.4	30.5	69.5	6421	24	5.3	430	94.7
100010	20.2	3.2	0.3	0.0	0.0	0.7	3.8	2.4	30.5	69.5	6421	24	5.3	430	94.7
AVERAGE UTILIZATION:			TASKS = 23.8%			D-RTOS = 11.7%			D-RTOS/TOTAL RATIO =		0.33				
110002	24.1	3.6	0.3	0.0	0.2	3.8	4.4	3.0	39.4	60.6	8344	28	7.0	372	93.0
120004	25.2	3.5	0.3	0.0	0.4	5.7	4.1	2.7	41.9	58.1	8878	26	6.8	359	93.2
130008	37.3	4.9	0.3	0.0	0.2	7.2	6.1	5.8	61.8	38.2	13280	37	14.0	228	86.0
140014	26.7	3.9	0.3	0.0	0.4	4.1	4.8	3.7	43.8	56.2	9305	30	8.0	345	92.0
150347	74.3	1.5	0.4	0.0	0.2	0.1	1.6	0.7	78.7	21.3	17651	11	7.3	139	92.7
160012	43.5	6.7	0.3	0.0	0.2	5.2	8.0	6.9	70.8	29.2	14800	47	22.8	159	77.2
170249	44.5	4.3	0.5	0.0	0.4	6.1	5.3	3.6	64.6	35.4	14236	33	13.1	218	86.9
180000	28.2	3.9	0.3	0.0	0.2	3.9	4.7	3.9	45.1	54.9	9351	30	8.4	327	91.6
190008	21.8	3.5	0.3	0.0	0.0	1.3	4.2	2.8	34.0	66.0	7168	26	6.0	408	94.0
202068	39.2	3.1	0.2	0.0	0.3	3.2	3.6	2.5	52.2	47.8	13434	28	7.3	357	92.7
AVERAGE UTILIZATION:			TASKS = 36.5%			D-RTOS = 16.7%			D-RTOS/TOTAL RATIO =		0.31				
210001	30.2	4.7	0.4	0.0	0.2	4.8	5.5	3.8	49.5	50.5	8375	28	10.4	242	89.6
220004	25.0	3.6	0.3	0.0	0.2	3.8	4.4	3.0	40.3	59.7	8545	28	7.1	367	92.9
230390	39.9	5.2	0.4	0.0	0.2	7.6	6.2	6.2	65.7	34.3	14686	40	16.0	210	84.0
240013	29.6	4.3	0.1	0.0	0.6	7.5	5.5	4.5	52.2	47.8	10718	32	10.3	280	89.7
250430	31.3	4.3	0.4	0.0	0.5	11.1	5.1	4.2	56.8	43.2	12673	35	11.4	271	88.6
264139	64.8	2.3	0.3	0.0	0.5	4.8	2.7	1.9	77.3	22.7	22968	23	10.6	193	89.4
270081	71.9	4.5	0.5	0.0	0.9	11.0	3.1	4.3	96.2	3.8	12572	13	100.0	0	0.0
280228	62.2	7.6	0.3	0.0	0.3	6.9	10.2	7.7	95.2	4.8	21240	62	100.0	0	0.0
290007	41.2	4.8	0.5	0.0	0.7	11.9	5.8	4.7	69.6	30.4	14709	38	18.3	170	81.7
302133	62.8	3.8	0.2	0.0	0.7	8.3	4.4	3.5	83.8	16.2	22132	34	23.6	110	76.4
AVERAGE UTILIZATION:			TASKS = 45.9%			D-RTOS = 22.8%			D-RTOS/TOTAL RATIO =		0.33				
310008	37.2	5.1	0.4	0.0	0.7	10.6	6.1	4.2	64.3	35.7	10896	32	16.4	163	83.6
320234	31.1	3.9	0.3	0.0	0.7	11.0	4.7	3.5	55.2	44.8	12070	31	10.0	279	90.0
330011	40.7	5.4	0.3	0.0	0.2	5.8	6.6	6.6	65.6	34.4	13806	39	16.5	198	83.5
340012	28.7	4.2	0.3	0.0	0.4	6.9	5.2	4.3	50.0	50.0	10651	31	9.2	306	90.8
350097	78.1	1.7	0.4	0.0	0.4	5.3	1.8	1.2	88.8	11.2	19574	12	15.0	68	85.0
360015	67.4	6.9	0.3	0.0	0.5	5.8	7.9	6.5	95.4	4.6	20788	49	100.0	0	0.0
370085	42.5	4.8	0.3	0.0	0.2	10.6	6.0	4.9	69.2	30.8	15051	41	18.9	176	81.1
380423	44.8	4.9	0.6	0.0	0.9	9.3	5.7	4.9	71.0	29.0	15857	38	17.9	174	82.1
390057	49.4	4.0	0.1	0.0	0.6	5.0	4.8	3.7	67.6	32.4	14033	29	13.4	187	86.6
400006	56.1	4.9	0.3	0.0	0.7	9.7	5.7	4.5	81.9	18.1	17738	36	27.3	96	72.7
AVERAGE UTILIZATION:			TASKS = 47.6%			D-RTOS = 23.3%			D-RTOS/TOTAL RATIO =		0.33				
410004	28.6	3.8	0.3	0.0	0.5	10.6	4.7	3.4	51.9	48.1	11083	35	10.9	287	89.1
423821	66.7	2.4	0.4	0.0	0.4	4.7	2.7	1.9	79.1	20.9	23717	24	11.9	177	88.1
430029	57.2	8.3	0.4	0.0	0.6	8.7	9.6	9.9	94.7	5.3	12920	35	100.0	0	0.0
440004	43.1	5.0	0.3	0.0	0.4	9.0	6.8	6.0	70.6	29.4	15232	45	21.4	165	78.6
451314	71.8	2.0	0.4	0.0	0.5	3.1	2.1	1.2	81.1	18.9	19924	15	10.1	133	89.9
460027	68.1	6.5	0.3	0.0	0.4	6.2	7.2	6.8	95.6	4.4	18314	39	100.0	0	0.0
470269	47.5	5.3	0.4	0.0	0.2	4.9	6.8	5.1	70.1	29.9	15511	43	19.7	175	80.3
480308	44.6	4.9	0.5	0.0	0.7	12.9	5.8	5.0	74.4	25.6	16185	37	20.2	146	79.8
490006	27.1	4.0	0.1	0.0	0.4	7.2	5.1	3.9	47.9	52.1	9884	31	9.1	308	90.9
500131	70.7	4.0	0.3	0.0	0.9	7.2	4.1	3.4	90.5	9.5	20042	29	38.2	47	61.8
AVERAGE UTILIZATION:			TASKS = 52.5%			D-RTOS = 23.1%			D-RTOS/TOTAL RATIO =		0.31				

Figure 10. Utilization Factors

- Number of Words sent out per 10 Milliseconds
- Radar Command Offset
- Resource Manager
  - Maximum Length and Wait Times of ENABLEQ
  - Resource Management Thread
  - Trace of the Reconfiguration Task

Summary and Conclusions

A distributed-Real Time Operating System (d-RTOS) was developed to support research in distributed computer system design. It is a highly specialized operating system designed to take full advantage of the peculiarities of a ballistic missile defense (BMD) application. It provides many special services to support the application software: Data Input Handler, Clock Manager, Conditional Enablement Handler, Reconfiguration Prescheduler, Scheduler, Task Completion Handler and Resource Manager. Since BMD applications are both demanding and time critical, the d-RTOS was designed to provide maximum performance at minimum overhead. It is believed those objectives were met. Analysis, refinement, and extension of the d-RTOS design are planned in the coming year.

Acknowledgement

The work described in this paper was performed as part of the research in Phase III of the Distributed Processing Architecture Design (DPAD) program sponsored by the U.S. Army Ballistic Missile Defense Advanced Technology Center (BMDATC) Data Processing Directorate under Contract DASG60-79-C-0039. The simulation experiment was performed with cooperation from personnel from TRW, General Research Corp. (GRC) and System Development Corp. (SDC). The authors wish to thank them for all the assistance provided.

References

[1] W. C. McDonald, J. R. Reynolds and H. D. Welch, "Distributed Simulation Host: A Distributed Testbed", 4th International Computer Software and Applications Conference (COMPSAC), Oct. 1980, Chicago.

[2] E.Y.S. Lee, M. L. Green and D. C. Shannon, "A Distributed Data Base Manager", a companion paper for this symposium.

[3] S. Majumdar and M. L. Green, "A Distributed Real Time Resource Manager", a companion paper for this symposium.

[4] R. H. Hoffman, R. W. Smith and J. T. Ellis, "Simulation Software Development", 4th International Computer Software and Applications Conference (COMPSAC), Oct. 1980, Chicago.

[5] M. L. Green, E.Y.S. Lee, S. Majumdar and D. C. Shannon, "Special Report Phase III of Distributed Processing Architecture Design (DPAD) Program - The DDP Underlay Simulation Experiment: Tactical Applications and d-RTOS Models", TRW Defense and Space Systems Group, 15 May 1980.

Bibliography

CONTAINED in this Bibliography are over 100 references for those readers interested in further pursuing the aspects of distributed computing systems. The outline used in the Bibliography is nearly identical to that used for the book itself.

Distributed Computing Systems: An Overview

J. W. Atwood, "Concurrency in operating systems," *Computer,* vol. 9, pp. 18–26, Oct. 1976.

J. Bacon, "An approach to distributed software systems," *Oper. Syst. Rev.,* pp. 62–73, Oct. 1981.

E. D. Carlson and M. C. Smyly, "Practical problems in a distributed application," *AFIPS,* vol. 47, pp. 823–828, 1978.

K. M. Chandy, "Models of distributed systems," in *Proc. Conf. Very Large Databases,* 1977, pp. 105–120.

R. desJardins, "Evolutionary distributed systems design," in *Proc. COMPSAC,* 1977, pp. 765–771.

H. S. Elovitz and C. L. Heitmeyer, "What is a computer network?" in *IEEE NTC Rec.,* 1974, pp. 1007–1014.

D. J. Farber *et al.,* "The distributed computing system," in *Proc. COMPCON,* 1973, pp. 31–34.

H. C. Forsdick *et al.,* "Operating systems for computer networks," *Computer,* vol. 11, Jan. 1978.

H. A. Freeman, "A distributed processing system control structure," in *Proc. Ass. Comput. Mach.,* 1977, pp. 28–32.

P. B. Hansen, "Distributed processes: A concurrent programming concept," *Commun. Ass. Comput. Mach.,* vol. 21, pp. 934–941, 1978.

——, "Multiprocessor architectures for concurrent processing," *Proc. Ass. Comput. Mach.,* pp. 317–323, 1978.

C. A. R. Hoare, "Monitors: An operating system structuring concept," *Commun. Ass. Comput. Mach.,* vol. 17, pp. 549–558, Oct. 1974.

W. Huen *et al.,* "A network computer for distributed processing," in *Proc. COMPCON,* 1977, pp. 326–330.

R. F. Kahn, "Resource-sharing computer communications networks," *Proc. IEEE,* Nov. 1972.

S. C. Kiely, "An operating system for distributed processing—DDPX," *IBM Syst. J.,* vol. 18, pp. 507–525, 1979.

S. R. Kimbleton, H. M. Wook, and M. L. Fitzgerald, "Network operating systems—An implementation approach," *AFIPS,* vol. 47, pp. 773–782, 1978.

S. R. Kimbleton and R. L. Mandell, "A perspective on network operating systems," *AFIPS,* vol. 45, pp. 551–559, 1976.

F. J. Maryanski, "A survey of developments in distributed data base management systems," *Computer,* vol. 11, pp. 28–38, Feb. 1978.

R. M. Metcalf, "Strategies for operating systems in computer networks," in *Proc. Ass. Comput. Mach.,* 1972, pp. 278–281.

C. Mohan, "Distributed data base management: Some thoughts and analyses," in *Proc. Ass. Comput. Mach.,* 1980, pp. 399–409.

R. Peebles and E. Manning, "System architecture for distributed data management," *Computer,* vol. 11, pp. 40–47, 1978.

D. A. Rennels, "Distributed fault tolerant computer systems," *Computer,* vol. 13, pp. 55–65, Mar. 1980.

C. Whitby-Strevens, "Software for distributed microcomputer systems," in *Proc. COMPCON,* 1977, pp. 404–409.

P. M. Whiting-O'Keefe, "Distributed processing: Some past advances and growing expectations," in *Proc. COMPCON,* 1978, pp. 345–347.

Process Management and Scheduling

V. Balachandran, J. W. McCredie, and O. I. Mikhail, "Models of the job allocation problem in computer networks," in *Proc. COMPCON,* 1973, pp. 211–214.

W. E. Boebert *et al.,* "Decentralized executive control in distributed computer systems," in *Proc. COMPSAC,* 1978, pp. 254–258.

S. H. Bokhari, "Dual processor scheduling with dynamic reassignment," *IEEE Trans. Software Eng.,* vol. SE-5, pp. 341–349, 1979.

E. K. Bowdon, "Priority assignment in a network of computers," *IEEE Trans. Comput.,* vol. C-18, pp. 1021–1026, 1969.

E. G. Coffman, Jr. and L. Kleinrock, "Computer scheduling methods and their countermeasures," *AFIPS,* vol. 32, pp. 11–21, 1968.

D. DeGroot, J. C. Droune, and M. Molek, "A resource scheduling problem for reconfigurable parallel processing systems," in *Proc. COMPCON,* 1981, pp. 218–224.

K. W. Doty, P. L. McEntire, and J. G. O'Reilly, "Task allocation in a distributed computer system," in *Proc. INFOCOM,* 1982.

M. J. Gonzales and C. V. Ramamoorthy, "Parallel task execution in a decentralized system," *IEEE Trans. Comput.,* vol. C-21, pp. 1310–1322, 1972.

E. D. Jensen and W. E. Boebert, "Partitioning and assignment of distributed processing software," in *Proc. COMPCON,* 1976, pp. 348–352.

G. Linsenmayer and P. Ligomenides, "Job allocation in a distributed computer network," in *Proc. COMPCON,* 1977, pp. 173–178.

J. E. Murphy, "Resource allocation with interlock detection in a multitask system," *AFIPS,* vol. 33, pp. 1169–1176, 1968.

C. C. Price, "The assignment of computational tasks among processors in a distributed system," *AFIPS,* vol. 50, pp. 291–296, 1981.

C. V. Ramamoorthy and M. J. Gonzales, Jr., "A survey of techniques for recognizing parallel processing streams in computer programs," *AFIPS,* vol. 35, 1969.

H. S. Stone, "Multiprocessor scheduling with the aid of network flow algorithms," *IEEE Trans. Software Eng.,* vol. SE-3, pp. 85–93, 1977.

K. Vairavan and V. Vairavan, "A model for the parallel representation and execution of programs," in *Proc. COMPSAC,* pp. 295–299, 1980.

Communication and Synchronization

E. Akkoyumlu, A. Bernstein, and R. Schantz, "Interprocess communication facilities for network operation," *Computer,* vol. 7, 1974.

P. A. Alsberg and J. D. Day, "A principle for resilient sharing of distributed resources," in *Proc. Int. Conf. Software Eng.,* 1976.

P. A. Bernstein *et al.,* "The concurrency control mechanism of SDD-1: A system for distributed databases, (the fully redundant case)," *IEEE Trans. Software Eng.,* vol. SE-4, pp. 516–530, 1978.

P. A. Bernstein, D. W. Shimpman, and W. S. Wong, "Formal aspects of serializability in database concurrency control," *IEEE Trans. Software Eng.,* vol. SE-5, pp. 203–216, 1979.

B. Bhargava and C. T. Hua, "The causal graph model for distributed database synchronization algorithms," in *Proc. COMPSAC,* 1980, pp. 444–452.

K. M. Chandy, C. V. Ramamoorthy, and A. E. Cowan, "A framework for hardware-software tradeoffs in the design of fault-tolerant computers," *AFIPS,* vol. 41, pp. 55–63, 1972.

K. M. Chandy *et al.,* "Analytical models for rollback and recovery strategies in data base systems," *IEEE Trans. Software Eng.,* vol. SE-1, pp. 100–110, 1975.

P. J. Courtois, F. Heymans, and D. L. Parnas, "Concurrent control with 'readers' and 'writers'," *Commun. Ass. Comput. Mach.,* vol. 14, pp. 667–669, 1971.

M. Courvoisier and R. Valette, "Description and realization of parallel control systems," in *Proc. COMPCON,* 1977, pp. 167–172.

D. J. Farber and K. C. Larson, "The system architecture of a distributed computer system—The communications system," in *Proc. Symp. Comput. Commun. Networks Teletraffic,* 1972, pp. 21–27.

E. Gelenbe and K. Sevcik, "Analysis of update synchronization for mulitple copy data-bases, in *Proc. 3rd Berkeley Workshop Distrib. Data Management Comput. Networks,* 1978.

J. N. Gray, R. A. Lorie, and G. R. Putzolu, "Granularity of locks in a shared data base," *Proc. Int. Conf. Very Large Data Bases,* 1975, pp. 428–451.

M. Hammer and D. Shipman, "An overview of reliability mechanisms for a distributed data base system," in *Proc. COMPCON,* 1978, pp. 63–65.

J. W. Havender, "Avoiding deadlock in multi-tasking systems," *IBM Syst., J.,* vol. 7, pp. 74–84, 1968.

E. D. Jensen, K. J. Thurber, and G. M. Schneider, "A review of systematic methods in distributed processor interconnection," *ICC,* pp. 7-17–7-22, 1976.

R. E. Kahn and W. R. Crowther, "Flow control in a resource-sharing computer network," *IEEE Trans. Commun. Technol.,* vol. COM-20, pp. 539–546, 1972.

S. R. Kimbleton and G. M. Schneider, "Computer communication networks: Approaches, objectives and performance considerations," *Comput. Surveys,* Sept. 1975.

P. F. King and A. J. Collmeyer, "Database sharing—An efficient mechanism for supporting concurrent processes," *AFIPS,* vol. 42, pp. 271–275, 1973.

S. Lauesen, "A large semaphore based operating system," *Commun. Ass. Comput. Mach.,* vol. 18, pp. 377–389, 1975.

C. H. Lee, R. Shastri, and R. Metzger, "Distributed control schemes for multiple-copied file access in a network," in *Proc. COMPSAC,* 1977, pp. 722–728.

F. J. Maryanski and K. A. Norsworthy, "A model of the performance of a rollback algorithm," in *Proc. Ass. Comput. Mach.,* 1979, pp. 54–61.

F. J. Maryanski and P. S. Fisher, "Rollback and recovery in distributed data base management systems," *AFIPS,* vol. 46, pp. 33–38, 1977.

J. E. Murphy, "Resource allocation with interlock detection in a multi-task system," *AFIPS,* vol. 33, pp. 1169–1176, 1968.

C. H. Papadimitrion, "The serializability of concurrent database updates," *J. Ass. Comput. Mach.,* vol. 26, Oct. 1979.

D. J. Rosenkrantz, R. E. Stearns, and P. M. Lewis, "System level concurrency control for distributed database systems," *Ass. Comput. Mach. Database Syst.,* vol. 3, 1978.

R. M. Shapiro and R. E. Millstein, "Failure recovery in distributed data base system," in *Proc. COMPCON,* 1978, pp. 66–70.

A. Shoshani and A. J. Bernstein, "Synchronization in a parallel-accessed database," *Commun. Ass. Comput. Mach.,* vol. 12, pp. 604–607, 1969.

M. Stonebraker, "Concurrency control and consistency of multiple copies of data in distributed INGRES," *IEEE Trans. Software Eng.,* vol. SE-5, pp. 188–194, 1979.

H. Sturgis, J. Mitchell, and J. Israel, "Issues in the design and use of a distributed file system," *Oper. Syst. Rev.,* pp. 55–69, July 1980.

H. Sturgis, "Crash recovery in a distributed data storage system," Xerox Palo Alto Res. Center, Palo Alto, CA, 1976.

C. Sunshine, "Factors in interprocess communication protocol efficiency for computer networks," *AFIPS,* vol. 45, pp. 571–576, 1976.

R. H. Thomas, "A solution to the concurrency control problem for multiple copy data bases," in *Proc. COMPCON,* 1978, pp. 56–62.

C. D. Walden, "A system for interprocess communication in a resource-sharing computer network," *Commun. Ass. Comput. Mach.,* vol. 15, pp. 221–230, 1972.

J. E. White, "A high-level framework for network-based resource sharing," *AFIPS,* vol. 45, pp. 561–570, 1976.

Database Allocation

R. S. Brice and J. C. Browne, "Feedback coupled resource allocation policies in the multiprogramming–multiprocessor computer system," *Commun. Ass. Comput. Mach.,* vol. 21, pp. 678–686, 1978.

P. P. S. Chen, "Optimal file allocation in multi-level storage systems," *AFIPS,* vol. 42, pp. 277–282, 1973.

W. W. Chu, "Performance of file directory systems for data bases in star and distributed networks," *AFIPS,* vol. 45, pp. 577–587, 1976.

K. P. Eswaran, "Placement of records in a file and file allocation in a computer network," in *Information Processing '74.* Amsterdam, the Netherlands: North-Holland, 1974, pp. 304–307.

D. V. Foster, L. W. Dowdy, and J. E. Ames, "File assignment in a computer network," *Comput. Net.,* vol. 5, pp. 341–349, 1981.

S. R. Kimbleton, "Network performance, user satisfaction, and data base access," in *Proc. Nat. Telecommun. Conf.,* vol. 2, 1975, pp. 44/12–44/17.

J. G. Kollias and M. Hatzopoulos, "Criteria to aid in solving the problem of allocating copies of a file in a computer system," *Comput. J.,* vol. 24, pp. 29–30, 1981.

S. Mahmoud and J. S. Riordan, "Optimal allocation of resources in distributed information networks," *Ass. Comput. Mach. Trans. Database Syst.,* vol. 1, pp. 66–78, 1976.

J. Mukerji and R. B. Kieburtz, "A kernel for supporting a distributed file system," in *Proc. COMPCON,* 1980, pp. 673–678.

H. C. Morgan and K. D. Levin, "Optimal program and data locations in computer networks," *Commun. Ass. Comput. Mach.,* vol. 20, pp. 315–321, 1977.

C. V. Ramamoorthy and B. W. Wah, "File placements of relations in a distributed relational data base," in *Proc. 1st Int. Conf. Distrib. Comput. Syst.*, 1979.

B. W. Wah, "An efficient heuristic for file placement on distributed database," in *Proc. COMPSAC*, 1980, pp. 462–468.

Query Processing

R. Epstein, M. Stonebraker, and E. Wong, "Distributed query processing in a relational data base system," in *Proc. SIGMOD Ass. Comput. Mach.*, 1978, pp. 169–180.

E. Wong and K. Youssefi, "Decomposition—A strategy for query processing," *Ass. Comput. Mach. Trans. Database Syst.*, vol. 1, pp. 223–241, 1976.

S. B. Yao, "Optimization of query evaluation algorithms," *Ass. Comput. Mach. Trans. Database Syst.*, vol. 4, pp. 133–135, June 1979.

Security

H. R. Burris, "Computer network cryptography engineering," *AFIPS*, vol. 45, pp. 91–96, 1976.

U. Bussolati and G. Martella, "On designing a security management system for distributed data bases," in *Proc. COMPSAC*, 1980, pp. 288–294.

J. G. Fletcher, "Octopus software security," in *Proc. COMPCON*, 1973, pp. 61–62.

K. J. Hamer-Hodges, "A comprehensive system for the on-line implementation of privacy and security measures," in *Proc. Int. Conf. Comput. Commun.*, 1976, pp. 416–420.

R. F. Heinrich and K. J. Kaufman, "A centralized approach to computer network security," *AFIPS*, vol. 45, pp. 85–90, 1976.

L. Lamport, "Time, clocks, and the ordering of events in a distributed system," *Commun. Ass. Comput. Mach.*, vol. 21, pp. 558–565, July 1978.

R. M. Needham and M. D. Schroeder, "using encryprtion for authentication in large networking computers,"*Commun. Ass. Comput. Mach.*, vol. 21, pp. 993–998, 1978.

J. Nelson, "Implementation of encryption in an 'open systems' architecture," in *Proc. Comput. Network. Symp.*, 1979, pp. 198–205.

R. Turn, "Privacy systems for telecommunication networks," in *Proc. IEEE Nat. Telecommun. Conf.*, 1974, pp. 151–156.

Languages

D. J. Farber and K. C. Larson, "The structure of a distributed computing system-software," in *Proc. Symp. Comput. Commun. Networks Teletraffic*, 1972, pp. 539–543.

J. A. Feldman, J. R. Low, and P. D. Rovner, "Programming distributed systems," in *Proc. Ass. Comput. Mach.*, 1978, pp. 310–316.

H. Z. Kriloff, "A high-level language for use with multi-computer networks," *AFIPS*, vol. 42, pp. 144–153, 1973.

C.-M. Li and M. T. Liu, "Communicating distributed processes—A language concept for distributed programming in distributed database systems," in *Proc. Distrib. Data Acquisit. Comput. Contr. Conf.*, 1980, pp. 47–60.

——, "Minimum-delay process communication: A language concept for highly parallel distributed programming," in *Proc. COMPCON*, 1981, pp. 225–228.

R. H. Thomas, "A resource sharing executive for the ARPANET," *AFIPS*, vol. 42, pp. 155–164, 1973.

Distributed Computer Implementations

P. J. Denning, "Fault tolerant operating systems," *Comput. Surveys*, vol. 8, pp. 361–486, 1976.

J. E. Donnelly, "Components of a network operating system," *Comput. Net.*, vol. 3, pp. 389–399, 1979.

A. K. Jones *et al.*, "Software management of Cm*—A distributed multiprocessor," *AFIPS*, vol. 46, pp. 657–663, 1977.

A. K. Jones and P. Schwarz, "Experience using multiprocessor systems—A status report," *Comput. Surveys*, vol. 12, pp. 121–165, 1980.

R. Kober, "The multiprocessor system SMS 201-combining 128 microprocessors into a powerful computer," in *Proc. COMPCON*, 1977, pp. 225–230.

E. Y. S. Lee, M. C. Green, and D. C. Shannon, "A distributed data base manager," in *Proc. IEEE Distrib. Data Acquisit. Comput. Contr. Conf.*, 1980, pp. 194–201.

S. Majundar and M. L. Green, "A distributed real time resource manager," in *Proc. IEEE Distrib. Data Acquisit. Comput. Contr. Conf.*, 1980, pp. 185–193.

S. Ornstein *et al.*, "Pluribus: A reliable multi-processor,' *AFIPS*, vol. 44, pp. 551–559, 1975.

W. D. Sincoskie and D. J. Farber, "SODS/OS: A distributed operating system for the IBM Series/1," *Oper. Syst. Rev.*, pp. 46–54, 1980.

M. H. Solomon and R. A. Finkel, "The Roscoe distributed operating system," in *Proc. Ass. Comput. Mach.*, Dec. 1979, pp. 108–114.

R. J. Swan, S. H. Fuller, and D. P. Siewiorek, "Cm*—A modular, multiprocessor," *AFIPS*, vol. 46, pp. 637–644, 1977.

R. J. Swan *et al.*, "The implementation of the Cm* multi-microprocessor," *AFIPS*, vol. 46, pp. 645–655, 1977.

R. W. Watson and J. G. Fletcher, "An architecture for support of network operating system services," *Comput. Net.*, vol. 4, pp. 33–59, 1980.

L. D. Wittie, "A distributed operating system for a reconfigurable network computer," in *Proc. 1st Int. Conf. Distrib. Comput. Syst.*, 1979, pp. 669–678.

W. A. Wulf and C. G. Bell, "C.mmp: A multi-miniprocessor," *AFIPS*, vol. 41, pp. 765–777, 1972.

Author Index

Subject Index

Editors' Biographies

Paul L. McEntire (S'59–S'80–A'80–M'81) received the B.S. in mathematics in 1965, the M.S. in engineering-economic systems (ESS) in 1981, and the Ph.D. in EES in 1982, all from Stanford University, Stanford, CA.

He is a founder and Vice President for Research and Development of Optimization Technology, Inc., in Cupertino, CA. He currently is directing activites in distributed computer system design, expert systems, and economic modeling. From 1965 to 1972 he was a Staff Engineer with TRW Systems Group, and from 1972 to 1982 he was a Senior Engineer and Department Manager for Systems Control, Inc. His fields of interest include distributed computing, optimization theory, and investment management. He has written three books, many articles, and has given seminars at Stanford University on these topics. His recent work applies modern optimization methods to the allocation of tasks and files in a distributed computer system.

Dr. McEntire is a member of the Mathematical Association of America, the Institute of Management Sciences, and Phi Beta Kappa.

John G. O'Reilly (M'82) was born in Waterbury, CT, on November 12, 1953. He did his undergraduate work at Worcester Polytechnic Institute, Worcester, MA, where he majored in physics. After his junior year, he began graduate studies at Case Western Reserve University, Cleveland, OH, from where he received the M.S. degree in physics in 1978. He received the Ph.D. degree in physics from Stanford University, Stanford, CA, in 1981. During graduate school he specialized in high-energy experimental quantum electrodynamics.

From 1979 to 1982 he was a Research Engineer at Systems Control Technology, Palo Alto, CA. While there he analyzed directed energy weapons systems, submarine communication techniques, and distributed computer systems. Following this, he served as Senior Engineer at Ford Aerospace and Communications Corporation, Palo Alto, CA, where he was responsible for the simulation and design of large special application local area networks. He is currently President of Network Design Associates, a company specializing in the design of local area networks, distributed computer systems, both centralized and distributed database management systems, and real-time computer systems. He is also a principal of Optimal Learning, Inc., a start-up company located in California's "Silicon Valley." He is the author of more than 50 journal and conference papers and a book, *Distributed Control* (Silver Spring, MD: IEEE Computer Society Press, 1982).

Robert E. Larson (S'58–M'66–F'73) received the S.B. degree from the Massachusetts Institute of Technology, Cambridge, in 1960, and the M.S. and Ph.D. degrees from Stanford University, Stanford, CA, in 1961 and 1964, respectively, all in electrical engineering.

In 1983 along with two colleagues, he founded Optimization Technology, Inc., in Cupertino, CA, where he is currently serving as Chairman of the Board and Chief Executive Officer. He previously worked at IBM, Hughes Aircraft, SRI International, and Systems Control, Inc. Since 1973 he has also been a Consulting Professor at Stanford University. His fields of specialization are dynamic programming, applications of control and estimation theory, and distributed data processing. He is the author of *State Increment Dynamic Programming* (1968), *Principles of Dynamic Programming,* vol. I (1977), *Principles of Dynamic Programming,* vol. II (1982), and *Distributed Control* (1979). He has also written over 140 technical papers.

Dr. Larson has received several awards for his work, including the IEEE Group on Automatic Control Best Paper Award in 1965 and the 1968 Donald P. Eckman Award for outstanding achievement in the field of automatic control from the American Automatic Control Council. He was named the Outstanding Young Electrical Engineer for 1969 by Eta Kappa Nu. He has been very active in the IEEE, having served as President in 1982 and as a member of the Board of Directors from 1983 to 1984. He also served as President of the Control Systems Society in 1975 and 1976. He was IEEE Division I Director in 1978 and 1979 and IEEE Vice President for Technical Activities in 1980 and 1981.